UNDERSTAND

SURVIVAL GUIDE

SPECIAL FEATURES

Welcome to Egypt

In spite of political, financial and social turmoil, Egyptians remain proud and defiant and are as welcoming as ever to visitors to their land.

Pyramids & More

With sand-covered tombs, austere pyramids and towering Pharaonic temples, Egypt brings out the explorer in all of us. Visit the Valley of the Kings in Luxor, where Tutankhamun's tomb was unearthed, and see the glittering finds in the Egyptian Museum in Cairo. Hop off a Nile boat to visit Dendara, Edfu or one of the other waterside temples, cross Lake Nasser to see Ramses II's masterpiece at Abu Simbel, or trek into the desert to find the traces of Roman trading outposts. You never know – your donkey might stumble across yet another find, for that is the way many previous discoveries were made.

Two Religions

Egypt once ruled an empire from Al-Qahira – Cairo, the 'city victorious'. The metropolis is packed with soaring minarets and medieval schools and mosques, some of the greatest architecture of medieval Islam. At the same time, Egypt's native Christians, the Copts, have carried on their traditions – such as the church's liturgical language and the traditional calendar – that in many respects link back to the time of the pharaohs. Tap into this history in remote desert monasteries and ancient churches.

Beaches & Beyond

An empty beach with nothing but a candle-lit cabin and a teeming coral reef offshore are waiting for you in Egypt. The coast along the Red Sea has a rugged desert beauty above the waterline and a psychedelic vibrancy below – explore it on a multiday outing to one of the globe's great dive sites or on an afternoon's snorkelling jaunt along a coral wall. There is just as much space and beauty in Egypt's vast deserts. Whether you're watching the sun rise between the beautiful shapes of the White Desert or the shimmering horizon from the comfort of a hot spring in Siwa Oasis, Egypt's landscapes are endlessly fascinating.

Going With the Flow

The old saying that Egypt is the gift of the Nile still rings true: without the river there would be no fertile land, no food, no electricity. And although people's lives are increasingly physically detached from the water, the Nile still exerts a uniquely powerful role. Luckily for visitors, the river is also the perfect place from which to see many of the most spectacular ancient monuments, which is one reason why a Nile cruise remains such a popular way to travel.

Why I Love Egypt

By Anthony Sattin, Author

Is it the way the glorious past casts long shadows over the present? Is it the way the lush Nile Valley gives way, from one footstep to another, to the harshness of the desert? Is it the light in the eyes of the person telling me a story in a cafe, who has just burst into laughter? The intensity of the light, the love of life, and the sense of family are just three reasons of many, many more.

For more about our authors, see page 512

Above: Luxor Temple (p193)

Egypt

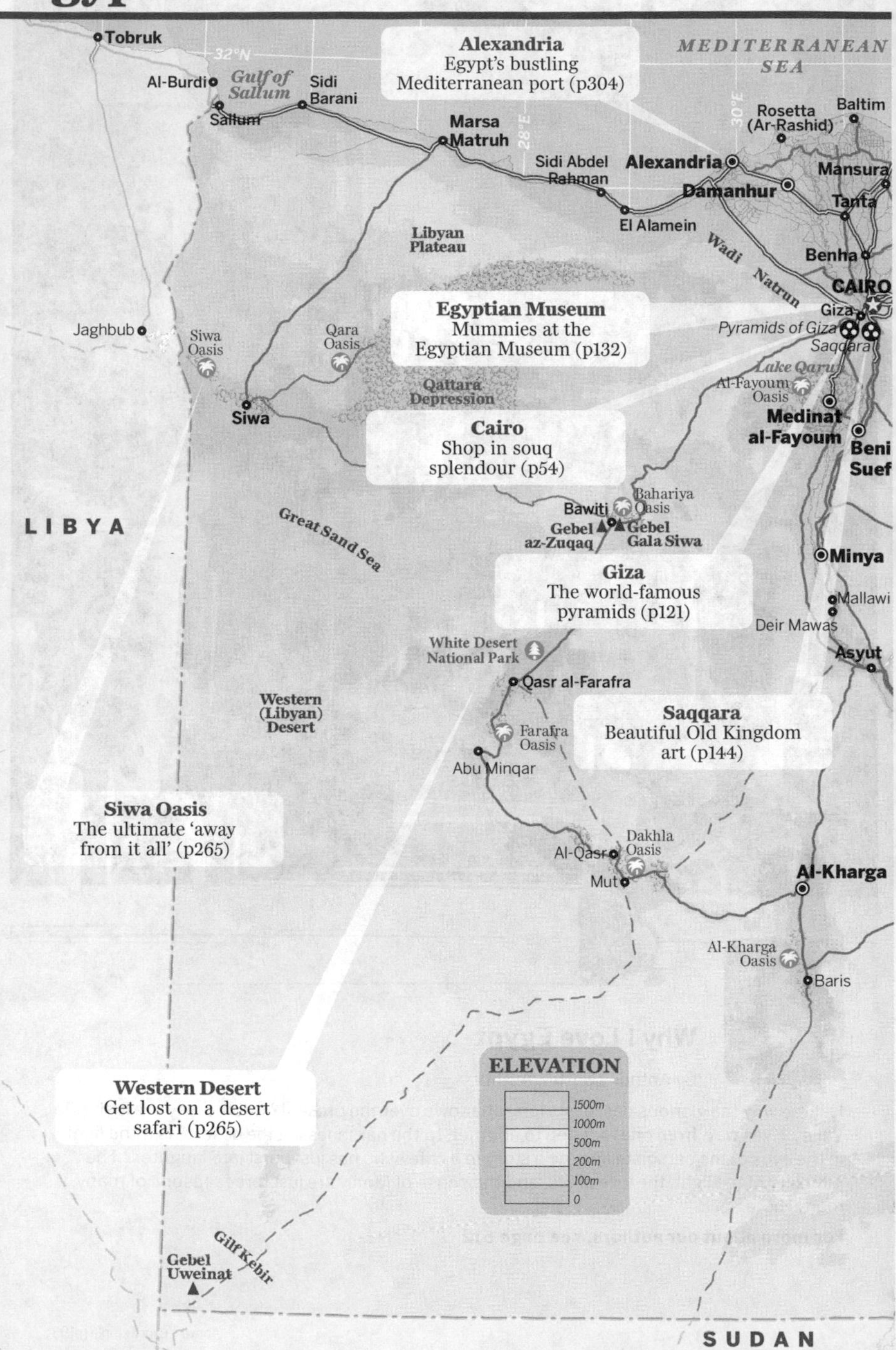

Alexandria
Egypt's bustling Mediterranean port (p304)
Egyptian Museum
Mummies at the Egyptian Museum (p132)
Cairo
Shop in souq splendour (p54)
Giza
The world-famous pyramids (p121)
Saqqara
Beautiful Old Kingdom art (p144)
Siwa Oasis
The ultimate 'away from it all' (p265)
Western Desert
Get lost on a desert safari (p265)
MEDITERRANEAN SEA
Tobruk
32°N
Al-Burdi
Gulf of Sallum
Sidi Barani
Sallum
Marsa Matruh
28°E
30°E
Sidi Abdel Rahman
El Alamein
Alexandria
Rosetta (Ar-Rashid)
Baltim
Mansura
Damanhur
Tanta
Wadi Natrun
Benha
CAIRO
Giza
Pyramids of Giza
Saqqara
Lake Qarun
Al-Fayoum Oasis
Medinat al-Fayoum
Beni Suef
Libyan Plateau
Jaghbub
Siwa Oasis
Qara Oasis
Qattara Depression
Siwa
LIBYA
Great Sand Sea
Bawiti
Bahariya Oasis
Gebel az-Zuqaq
Gebel Gala Siwa
Minya
Mallawi
Deir Mawas
Asyut
White Desert National Park
Qasr al-Farafra
Western (Libyan) Desert
Farafra Oasis
Abu Minqar
Al-Qasr
Dakhla Oasis
Mut
Al-Kharga
Al-Kharga Oasis
Baris
ELEVATION
1500m
1000m
500m
200m
100m
0
Gilf Kebir
Gebel Uweinat
SUDAN

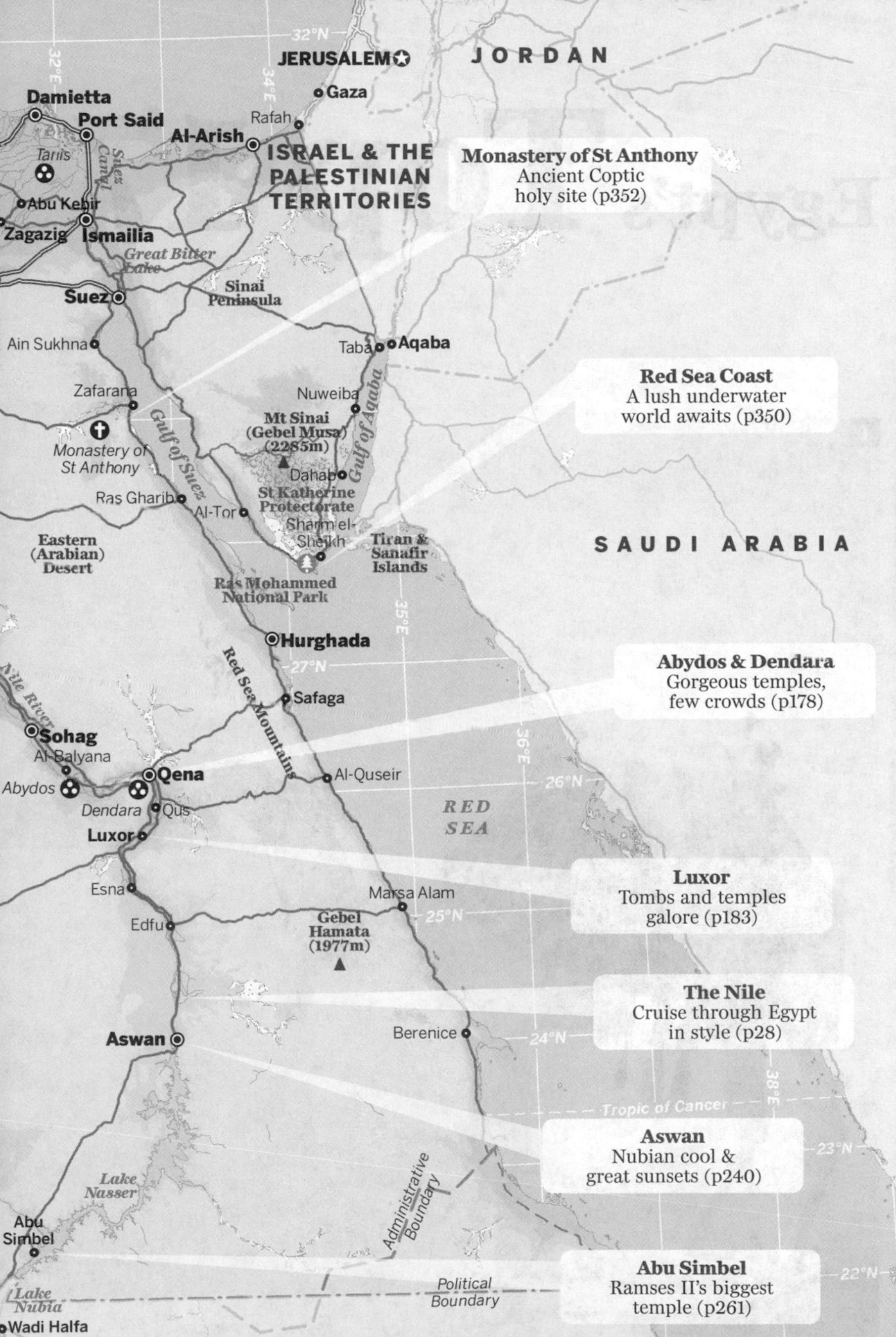
0 200 km
0 100 miles
JERUSALEM
JORDAN
Gaza
Damietta
Port Said
Rafah
Al-Arish
ISRAEL & THE PALESTINIAN TERRITORIES
Tanis
Suez Canal
Abu Kebir
Zagazig
Ismailia
Great Bitter Lake
Sinai Peninsula
Suez
Ain Sukhna
Taba
Aqaba
Zafarana
Nuweiba
Monastery of St Anthony
Mt Sinai (Gebel Musa) (2285m)
Gulf of Aqaba
Gulf of Suez
Dahab
Ras Gharib
Al-Tor
St Katherine Protectorate
Sharm el-Sheikh
Tiran & Sanafir Islands
Eastern (Arabian) Desert
Ras Mohammed National Park
SAUDI ARABIA
Hurghada
Red Sea Mountains
Nile River
Safaga
Sohag
Al-Balyana
Qena
Al-Quseir
Abydos
Dendara
Qus
RED SEA
Luxor
Esna
Marsa Alam
Edfu
Gebel Hamata (1977m)
Aswan
Berenice
Tropic of Cancer
Lake Nasser
Administrative Boundary
Abu Simbel
Political Boundary
Lake Nubia
Wadi Halfa
32°N
27°N
26°N
25°N
24°N
23°N
22°N
32°E
34°E
35°E
36°E
38°E
Monastery of St Anthony
Ancient Coptic holy site (p352)
Red Sea Coast
A lush underwater world awaits (p350)
Abydos & Dendara
Gorgeous temples, few crowds (p178)
Luxor
Tombs and temples galore (p183)
The Nile
Cruise through Egypt in style (p28)
Aswan
Nubian cool & great sunsets (p240)
Abu Simbel
Ramses II's biggest temple (p261)

Egypt's Top 17

Pyramids of Giza

1 Towering over the urban sprawl of Cairo and the desert plains beyond, the Pyramids of Giza (p121) and the Sphinx are at the top of almost every traveller's itinerary. Bring lots of water, an empty memory card and plenty of patience! You may have to fend off a few eager locals pushing horse rides and Bedouin head-dresses in order to enjoy this ancient funerary complex, but no trip to Egypt is complete without a photo of you in front of the last surviving ancient wonder of the world. For the best, and also the most clichéd, pic of all, head for the cliff beyond the third pyramid, with a panoramic view of the three pyramids with all of Cairo as a background.

Luxor

2 With the greatest concentration of ancient monuments of anywhere in Egypt, you can spend days, or weeks, visiting Luxor (p183). Walk through the columned halls of the great temple complexes of Luxor and Karnak on the east bank of the Nile, or climb into the tombs of pharaohs, their queens, courtiers and workmen, cut into the Theban hills on the west bank. Watching the sun rise over the Nile or set behind the Theban hills are some of Egypt's unforgettable moments.

SHANNA BAKER / GETTY IMAGES ©

2

ALBERTO CASSAN / GETTY IMAGES ©

Cruising the Nile

3 The Nile (p28) is Egypt's lifeline, the artery that runs through the entire country, from south to north. Only by being adrift on it can you appreciate its importance and beauty, and more practically, only by boat can you see some archaeological sites as they were meant to be seen. Sailing is by far the slowest and most relaxing way to go, but even from the deck of a multistorey floating hotel you're likely to glimpse the magic. Top: Nile River at Aswan

Old Kingdom Art

4 The walls of the tombs around the Step Pyramid of Zoser in Saqqara (p145) are adorned with some of the world's oldest art works. The exquisite painted reliefs in the Mastaba of Ti or tombs of Akhethotep and Ptahhotep give a subtle and very detailed account of daily life in 2500BC. The first rooms in the Egyptian Museum show the most brilliant Old Kingdom art. Looking at these masterpieces is essential to understanding what comes in the thousands of years that follow. Bottom: Step Pyramid of Zoser, Saqqara

3

J.D. DALLET / GETTY IMAGES ©

4

A. MARTIN UW PHOTOGRAPHY / GETTY IMAGES ©

DENIS-HUOT / HEMIS.FR / GETTY IMAGES ©

RICHARD I'ANSON / GETTY IMAGES ©

LUIS DAVILLA / GETTY IMAGES ©

Desert Safaris

5 Whether you travel by 4WD, camel or on foot, for a couple of hours or a couple of weeks, you'll be able to taste the simple beauty and sheer isolation of wildest Egypt. The highlights of an excursion in Egypt's Western Desert include camping under a star-studded sky among the surreal formations of the White Desert (p284), crossing the mesmerising dunes of the Great Sand Sea, and heading deep into the desert to live out *English Patient* fantasies at the remote Gilf Kebir. Above left: White Desert National Park

Souqs

6 The incessant salesmanship of Egyptians makes more sense when you see it at work in one of the country's many souqs. Here vendors are set up cheek by jowl, all hawking their wares in their set district, cajoling and haggling. Visit a centuries-old souq such as Khan al-Khalili (p70) first, and you'll see its pattern at work everywhere, even in ad hoc modern markets set up near the main tourist sights. Along the way, pick up rusty antiques, lovely Egyptian cotton, King Tut kitsch...or even a donkey. Top right: Khan al-Khalili

Oasis Trail

7 It's impossible not to relax in an oasis: this is, after all, what inspired the idea of paradise – here, with the endless desert shimmering on the horizon, you can float in hot springs or explore the remains of ancient Roman outposts and dusty villages. In Bahariya (p285), the most easily accessible oasis from Cairo, soak in hot or cold springs in the shade of a lush date palm. In Dakhla, the picturesque, restored mud-brick town of Al-Qasr gives a glimpse of centuries-old oasis living. Above right: Bahariya Oasis

GEORGETTE DOUWMA / GETTY IMAGES ©

NICO TONDINI / GETTY IMAGES ©

DAVID Q. CAVAGNARO / GETTY IMAGES ©

Red Sea Diving

8 Egypt's Red Sea (p36) coastlines are the doorstep to a wonderland that hides below the surface. Whether you're a seasoned diving pro or a first-timer, Egypt's underwater world of coral cliffs, colourful fish and spookily beautiful wrecks is just as staggeringly impressive as the sights above. Bring out your inner Jacques Cousteau by exploring the enigmatic wreck of WWII cargo ship the *Thistlegorm*, a fascinating museum spread across the sea bed. Even if diving isn't your thing, it's easy to snorkel and see this beautiful underwater world.

Abu Simbel

9 Ramses II built Abu Simbel (p262) a long way south of Aswan, along his furthest frontier and just beyond the Tropic of Cancer. But these two impressive temples are a marvel of modern engineering as well: in the 1960s they were relocated, block by block, to their current site to protect them from the flooding of Lake Nasser. To appreciate the isolation, spend the night at Abu Simbel, either on a boat on the lake or at Nubian cultural centre and ecolodge Eskaleh. Top right: Great Temple of Ramses II, Abu Simbel

Siwa Oasis

10 The grandest and most remote of Egypt's Western Desert oases, Siwa (p265), on the edge of the Great Sand Sea, offers the ultimate oasis experience. This is not only where Alexander the Great came to consult the gods, it is also the perfect place to hang out and relax after travelling along the Nile. Cycle through the palm groves, take a desert tour to the hot and cold water springs and lakes, or slide down a sand dune.

Abydos & Dendara

11 Time is short and everyone wants to see the Pyramids, Tutankhamun's gold and the Valley of the Kings. But some of the most rewarding moments are to be had away from the crowds in the less-visited monuments, where you can contemplate the ancients' legacy in peace. Nowhere is this truer than at Abydos (p178), an important place of pilgrimage for ancient Egyptians, and Dendara, one of the world's best-preserved ancient temples. They're north of Luxor – the opposite direction from the tour buses. Top: Abydos

Aswan Sunset

12 Watch the sun set over Aswan (p240), frontier of the ancient Egyptian empire and southernmost outpost for the Romans. It's still the gateway to Nubia, where cultures blend to create a laid-back place that values taking time to enjoy the view. There is something about the way the river is squeezed between rocks, the proximity of the desert, and the lonely burial places of the Aga Khan and forgotten ancient princes that makes the end of the day more poignant here than anywhere else along the Egyptian Nile.

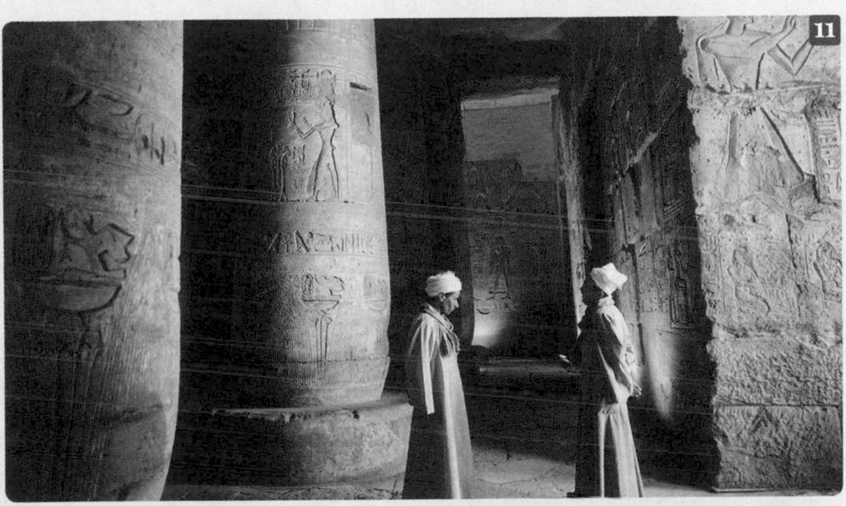

Coptic Sites

13 It was to the barren mountains and jagged cliffs of the sprawling desert that the first early ascetics came. Today Coptic monasteries such as those of St Anthony (p352) and St Paul, where the tradition of Christian monasticism began, still play an important role in the modern Coptic faith. Visit Wadi Natrun, or walk on the walls of St Anthony's monastery and ponder the impressive faith that took men away from the ease of the towns and into the wilderness. Top: Monastery of St Anthony

Ahwas

14 Though the ahwa gets its name from the Arabic word for coffee, *shai* (tea) is much more common at the traditional cafe that is a major centre of Egyptian social life. With your drink on a tiny tin-top table, a backgammon board in front of you and perhaps a bubbling sheesha (water pipe) to one side, you'll slip right into the local groove. These days, ahwas can be sawdust-strewn, men-only joints or a chic lounge with a mixed crowd and fruit-flavoured tobaccos. Bottom: Smoking a sheesha, Luxor

13

TONY MORAN / SHUTTERSTOCK ©

14

MASSIMO PIZZOTTI / ROBERT HARDING ©

DAVID CLAPP / GETTY IMAGES ©

NICO TONDINI / GETTY IMAGES ©

STUART WESTMORLAND / GETTY IMAGES ©

Relax in a Mosque

15 The quiet, shady arcades of a medieval mosque are the perfect place to take a break from modern Cairo. Far from being austere places of worship, many mosques also function as public break rooms – people drop in for a quiet chat or an afternoon nap. Al-Azhar Mosque bustles with theological students, the Mosque of Ibn Tulun (p83) is the oldest intact mosque in the city and oozes calm, and the Mosque of Al-Maridani is filled with trees. Kick your shoes off and stay a while. Above left: Al-Azhar Mosque (p75)

Alexandria

16 Flaunting the pedigree of Alexander the Great and powerful queen Cleopatra, Egypt's second-largest city (p304) is rich in history, both ancient and modern. Visit the Bibliotheca Alexandrina, the new incarnation of the ancient Great Library, or any number of great small museums around town. Explore the souqs of atmospheric Anfushi, the oldest part of the city, or hunt for dusty antiques in Attareen. Above all be sure to feast on fresh seafood with a Mediterranean view. Top right: Bibliotheca Alexandrina (p313)

Egyptian Museum

17 The scale of the Egyptian Museum (p132) is so overwhelming, it warrants at least two visits. The vast rooms are packed to the rafters with some of the world's most fascinating treasures: glittering gold jewellery, King Tut's socks and mummies of the greatest pharaohs, plus their favourite pets. After taking in the highlights, go back a second time and wander through the less-visited rooms on the 2nd floor.

Need to Know

For more information, see Survival Guide (p471)

Currency

Egyptian pound (E£)

Language

Arabic

Visas

Required for most visitors; usually possible to buy at airport on arrival. Typically valid for 30 days and can be extended.

Money

ATMs common in cities. Credit cards accepted at higher-end businesses. Shortage of small change so can be difficult to break large bills.

Mobile Phones

Egypt uses the same frequency as Europe and Australia. Local SIM cards can be used in all multiband phones.

Time

Egypt is two hours ahead of GMT/UTC.

When to Go

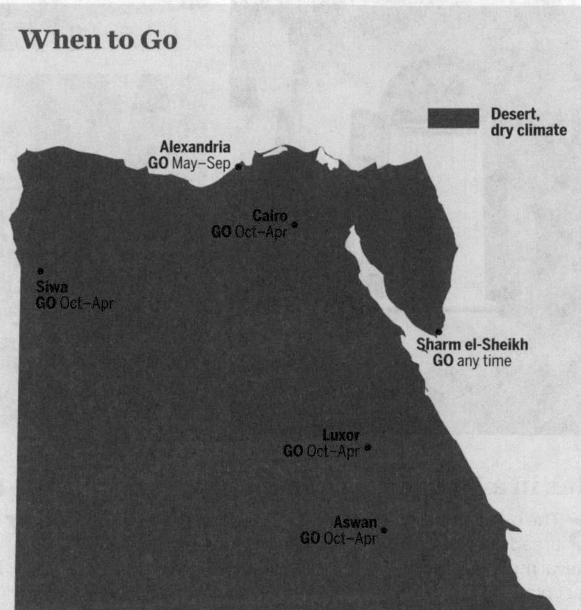

High Season (Oct–Feb)

➡ Egypt's 'winter' is largely sunny and warm, with very occasional rain (more frequent on the Mediterranean).

➡ Be prepared for real chill in unheated hotels, especially in damp Alexandria.

Shoulder (Mar–May, Sep–Oct)

➡ Spring brings occasional dust storms, disrupting flights.

➡ Heat can extend into October, when crowds are lighter.

➡ Warm seas and no crowds at Mediterranean spots in autumn.

Low Season (Jun–Aug)

➡ Scorching summer sun means only the hardiest sightseers visit Upper Egypt.

➡ Avoid the Western Desert.

➡ High season on the Mediterranean coast.

Useful Websites

Lonely Planet (www.lonelyplanet.com/egypt) Destination information, hotel bookings, traveller forum.

Egypt Tourism (www.egypt.travel) Official tourism site with trip-planning tools.

Daily News Egypt (www.thedailynewsegypt.com) Independent English newspaper.

Mada Masr (www.madamasr.com) Independent progressive online reporting in English.

Egypt Independent (www.egyptindependent.com) Respected online news.

Theban Mapping Project (www.thebanmappingproject.com) Archaeological database.

Important Numbers

Drop the 0 from the area code when dialling from abroad.

Ambulance	☎123
Country code	☎20
Fire	☎180
International access code	☎00
Tourist police	☎126

Exchange Rates

Australia	A$1	E£5.9
Canada	C$1	E£6.1
Europe	€1	E£8.6
Israel	1ISL	E£2
Japan	¥100	E£6.4
Jordan	JD1	E£10.8
New Zealand	NZ$1	E£5.6
UK	£1	E£11.6
USA	US$1	E£7.6

For current exchange rates see www.xe.com.

Daily Costs

Budget: Less than E£300

- Dorm bed: E£70–E£100
- *Fiteer* (Egyptian pizza): E£10–E£20
- Fresh produce for pennies
- Major sites are pricey

Midrange: E£300–E£1000

- Hotel with air-con: E£250
- Two sit-down meals: E£80
- Car and driver: E£350
- Sleeper to Luxor: E£100

Top End: More than E£1000

- Luxury hotel room: US$200
- Two meals: E£180
- Personal tour guide/driver: E£100 per hour
- Flight to Luxor: US$120

Opening Hours

The weekend is Friday and Saturday; some businesses close Sunday. During Ramadan, offices, museums and tourist sites keep shorter hours.

Banks 8.30am to 2.30pm Sunday to Thursday

Bars and clubs Early evening until 3am, often later (particularly in Cairo)

Cafes 7am to 1am

Government offices 8am to 2pm Sunday to Thursday. Tourist offices are generally open longer.

Post offices 8.30am to 2pm Saturday to Thursday

Private offices 10am to 2pm and 4pm to 9pm Saturday to Thursday

Restaurants Noon to midnight

Shops 9am to 1pm and 5pm to 10pm June to September, 10am to 6pm October to May

Arriving in Egypt

Cairo International Airport (p115) Prearrange taxi pickup (E£120 to E£150) or bargain on arrival (E£100); one hour to centre. Buses E£3; up to two hours to centre.

Sharm el-Sheikh Airport (p387) Bargaining required for taxi, ideally E£30 to E£40 to Sharm el-Sheikh or Na'ama Bay.

Burg al-Arab airport (Alexandria) (p328) Bargain for taxi on arrival (E£100 to E£150 to city centre). Bus E£7, plus E£1 per bag.

Getting Around

Transport in Egypt is fairly efficient and reasonably priced. Beware that for security reasons some areas are off limits, and some transport modes are not available to visitors.

Air Most domestic flights go through Cairo, and flight times may change at short notice. Prices are cheaper when combined with an international Egypt Air ticket.

Train Many trains are off limits for foreign visitors. The only train allowed between Cairo and Luxor is the Wagon Lit sleeper train.

Bus There are frequent buses between Egyptian cities. Buses are comfortable and reliable, but need to be booked in advance.

Car It is not advisable to drive in Cairo, but a car with driver is readily available and reasonably priced. *Servees* (communal taxis) are a fast way to travel between cities.

For much more on **getting around**, see p491

First Time Egypt

For more information, see Survival Guide (p471)

Checklist

➡ Ensure your passport is valid for a minimum of six months

➡ Check your country's foreign office advisory before booking your airline ticket. For UK: https://www.gov.uk/foreign-travel-advice/egypt. For USA: http://travel.state.gov/content/passports/english/alertswarnings/egypt-travel-alert.html

➡ Organise travel insurance that includes medical cover

➡ Inform your credit/debit card company before you leave home

➡ Check if you can use your mobile

➡ Book accommodation and domestic flights ahead of the trip

What to Pack

➡ Hat, sunglasses and a good sunscreen

➡ Electrical adaptor to recharge gadgets

➡ Good mosquito protection

➡ Patience to cope with a different concept of time

Top Tips for Your Trip

➡ Visit during the shoulder season (spring and autumn) when the weather is less extreme and there are fewer visitors around.

➡ Learn a few words in Arabic – greetings and thank you are the obvious ones – and you'll get a laugh or a smile. One of the highlights of the trip is often meeting good-humoured Egyptians.

➡ Keep small change to hand, as it is useful to give out as much-needed baksheesh (tips) just about everywhere.

➡ Start your visits early in the morning to avoid the midday heat.

➡ Avoid driving yourself; it's recommended to rent a car with a driver. Avoid travelling on roads outside cities and towns at night, as this is particularly dangerous. People and animals often sit or walk on the road in total darkness.

What to Wear

Egypt is a conservative country, so modest attire is recommended, especially when travelling as an individual. Women should wear loose clothes, covering arms and legs. In resort towns the dress code is more relaxed. Cotton or linen clothing is recommended for the heat, and a fleece or woolen sweater is needed for the cooler nights.

The dress code is fairly casual in most places, even at night, although Cairenes do dress up to go to the hip spots in town.

Sleeping

It's generally only necessary to book your accommodation in advance if you are planning to visit during the Christmas, Easter and half-term school holidays. See p476 for more accommodation info.

➡ **Hotels** Range from a dusty fleapit to deluxe accommodation in the larger cities and resorts. In smaller towns accommodation is mostly limited to basic.

➡ **B&Bs** Less common in Egypt, and places that call themselves that are often small family-run one- or two-star hotels.

➡ **Camping** Only recommended in Sinai, when the situation there calms down.

Safety

Although the situation in Egypt has been unstable since January 2011, most of the country is calm most of the time. Check government travel advisories before leaving home and make sure you are not going into any no-go areas. Avoid getting close to demonstrations as they can turn violent quite quickly. See p483 for more.

Bargaining

Bargaining is part of life when shopping in souqs and markets. It may seem an annoyance, but it pays to see it as a game. Just follow the basic rules:

➡ Shop around to get an idea of prices.

➡ Decide how much you want to pay, and then offer a lower price than that.

➡ Don't show any excitement.

➡ Walk away if you can't agree, and the vendor will follow you if your price was right.

Tipping

Always keep small change as baksheesh is expected everywhere. When in doubt, tip.

➡ **Cafes** Leave E£3 to E£5.

➡ **Restaurants** For good service leave 10%, in smart places leave 15%.

➡ **Mosque attendant** Leave E£5 to E£10 for shoe covers, more if you climb a minaret or have some guiding.

➡ **Metered taxis** Round off the fare or offer around 5% extra depending on the ride.

➡ **Guards on sites** £E5 to E£10.

MICHELE FALZONE / GETTY IMAGES ©

Islamic Quarter, Cairo (p54)

Etiquette

Egypt is a mostly conservative country, so the following will avoid any awkward moments:

➡ **Shoes** Take off your shoes before entering a mosque.

➡ **Touching** Don't touch someone from the opposite sex in public.

➡ **Feet** Don't show the soles of your feet: it's considered disrespectful.

➡ **Hands** Eat with your right hand; the left hand is used to wipe yourself in the toilet.

➡ **Ramadan** Don't eat or drink in public during the fasting month of Ramadan.

Eating

There is a great variety of restaurants in Cairo and the main resorts, but elsewhere eating options are more limited. See p460 for more information.

➡ **Restaurants** Range from very smart and expensive hotel dining to basic street food places at local prices. Booking ahead is essential in the more upmarket restaurants.

➡ **Cafes** Usually open for most of the day and night, and they only serve drinks and sheesha, no food.

➡ **Budget restaurants** Egyptian food in budget restaurants is usually well prepared and fresh, while Western-style dishes can be trial and error. Most budget restaurants do not serve alcohol.

If You Like...

Wildlife

Along the Nile, in the lush river delta and in sprawling salt lakes, bird life flourishes. Underwater coral reefs teem with color. Even Egypt's arid deserts host a surprising array of plants and critters.

Aswan Rise before dawn to spot squacco herons, hoopoes and more with expert birders. (p240)

Wadi Rayyan The brackish lake, not far from where the ancients worshipped crocodiles, is a lifeline for migrating birds – take your binoculars on a boat. (p154)

Shiatta Gazelles and flamingos frolic at this salt lake in the desert west of Siwa. (p296)

Lake Nasser Take a tour with African Angler to snare some fish for dinner – or just enjoy the view. (p259)

Marsa Alam Reefs off the coast here are home to mantas, spinner dolphins and even sharks. (p368)

Islamic Architecture

Most of the gems of Egypt's Islamic era, from the 8th century to late Ottoman times, are in Cairo, so aficionados should plan for extra time there. But other gorgeous examples of building craft can be found elsewhere in the country.

Bein al-Qasreen A string of the finest buildings from the Mamluk era, now restored as an open-air museum. (p73)

Mosque of Qaitbey Trek to Cairo's not-actually-that-spooky City of the Dead to admire the most beautiful stone dome in Cairo. (p84)

Al-Qasr This oasis town was built in the Ottoman era, starting in the 16th century – check the beautifully carved lintels over doorways. (p280)

Rosetta's Ottoman houses Try to find the secret staircase to the women's gallery in one restored residential compound, and admire the millworks at another. (p330)

Al-Quseir The old Hajj port is a tumble of Ottoman-era buildings that seem lost in time. (p365)

Deserts

Seeking blissful isolation? The desert landscape in Egypt is vast and surprisingly varied. And there's just as much variety in how you can explore it.

White Desert National Park For a truly mind-bending experience, schedule your overnight trip to this eerie landscape during the full moon. (p284)

Great Sand Sea These picture-perfect dunes extend hundreds of miles into Libya, but you can get a taste of the emptiness even on a short trip. (p303)

Monastery of St Simeon For desert beauty without the days-long trek, visit this Coptic site in Aswan. (p246)

Eastern Desert Once criss-crossed by ancient trade routes, with rock inscriptions, gold mines and great landscapes, now only accessible with a guide. (p369)

Souqs & Shopping

Whether you're just browsing or searching for gifts, Egypt's souqs are the perfect destination, with as much entertainment and offers of tea as actual products.

Khan al-Khalili Cairo's medieval trading zone is still a commercial hub for souvenirs such as a gold cartouche necklace – the perfect place to polish your haggling skills. (p129)

Souq al-Gomaa Get in the scrum at this weekly Cairo junk swap, and you might come out with new clothes...or old taxidermy. (p111)

Oum El Dounia One-stop shop in central Cairo for the best, most-stylish Egyptian crafts. (p110)

Attareen Antique Market Another Alexandria trove, where you can find some mid-20th-century gems. (p327)

Aswan Souq Nibble fresh peanuts and compare prices on Nubian talismans. (p241)

Adventure

Egypt isn't a high-adrenaline destination – the river and the desert heat have a way of slowing things down. But these more active outings can still inspire.

Hot-air ballooning Get a bird's-eye view of the tombs at Luxor. (p213)

Sandboarding Who needs snow? Try this dusty sport near Al-Fayoum, after spotting whale fossils. (p155)

Desert horse riding The most romantic way to see the desert around Siwa. (p297)

Hiking in the desert Whether it's the dunes around Dakhla Oasis or the hills behind Luxor, the desert is full of excitement and challenges. (p275)

Long-term desert safaris Pack up and head out for a week or more. (p267)

Ancient Traces

Given Egypt's Pharaonic riches, you could find something with a story thousands of years old in any destination. These are some of the more out-of-the-way sites to add to your itinerary.

Medinet Madi You need a 4WD to get here, but the sight of sphinxes half-buried in drifting sand is exactly what archaeology buffs come to Egypt for. (p156)

Red Pyramid At Dahshur, south of Cairo, you'll likely be the only visitor to this enormous monument, making the climb inside its tunnels all the more exciting. (p150)

Deir al-Muharraq In Egyptian terms, Christianity is relatively new history – but this Coptic monastery claims the world's oldest church, from 60 AD. (p173)

Dra Abu'l Naga Smaller than most, but hardly ever visited, these Luxor tombs reveal some finely executed paintings. (p211)

Traditional Arts

Traditional arts are harder to come by these days, but several organisations work towards their preservation or revival.

Fair Trade Egypt This shop in Cairo is a good starting point for finding traditional Egyptian crafts. (p111)

Makan This intimate space in Cairo hosts an intense Nubian musical ritual called a *zar*. (p107)

El Tanboura Hall Another traditional-music incubator in Cairo, this space sees regular shows by Suez Canal–area artists and others. (p108)

Eskaleh This Nubian cultural centre and hotel offers guests a chance to immerse themselves in local food and music. (p264)

Bedouin knowledge Wilderness Ventures Egypt teaches local star lore, as well as herbal medicine on nature walks. (p395)

Vintage Tourism

For those who long for the age of steamer trunks, pith helmets and softly scudding overhead fans, Egypt delivers. You may have to squint to see the sepia tone, but the country's long history of tourism means there's plenty of yesteryear left.

Dahabiyyas Cruise the Nile as 19th-century adventurer Amelia Edwards did, on one of these elegant sailboats. (p31)

Mena House Oberoi Splash out in the Pyramids-view suites, or just sip a beer amid the luxury enjoyed by Khedive Ismail. (p129)

Pension Roma A bargain way to live in the past, this Cairo hotel has antique furniture and original details like privacy screens. (p94)

Sofitel Old Cataract Hotel One of Agatha Christie's favourites, and a great place to watch the sun set. (p250)

Trains Egypt's trains have seen better days, but they can still be a relaxing way to see parts of the country, especially on the route to Aswan. (p227)

Cafe Culture

Sipping tea is a national pastime. The big cities, where this break is most needed, are best, but even in the hinterlands you'll find a convivial ahwa, as Egyptians call their coffeehouses.

Fishawi's The ahwa in Cairo's Khan al-Khalili has been open for centuries, and some regulars look like they've been smoking sheesha here almost as long. (p106)

Cafe next to Townhouse Gallery Hang out with a tea and a sheesha with downtown Cairo's young arty crowd. (p105)

Trianon Alexandria is known for its cafes where legendary writers have taken a breather. This one was Cavafy's favourite. (p325)

Month by Month

TOP EVENTS

D-Caf, March

Ramadan, June

Eid al-Adha, September

Siyaha, October

Cairo International Film Festival, November

January

Winter in most of Egypt means balmy days, perfect for sightseeing, but chilly nights, especially in unheated hotel rooms. Alexandria and the Mediterranean coast can be a bit rainy, but otherwise precipitation is still rare.

Cairo International Book Fair

Held in Heliopolis in the last week of January and the first of February, this is one of the city's major cultural events. But most of the lectures and other events (and the books themselves) are in Arabic only.

Moulid an-Nabi

Prophet Mohammed's birthday is a nationwide celebration with sweets and new clothes for kids. In Cairo, the week before is an intense Sufi scene at Midan al-Hussein.

Egyptian Marathon

Endurance runners take to the west bank of the Nile near Luxor. The race takes place in late January or early February, followed by a half-marathon in Sharm el-Sheikh in March. For dates, see www.egyptian-marathon.com.

February

The winter chill continues, though it's the perfect time of year in the south. Tourists think so too - Aswan and Luxor are packed, as are the beaches.

Ascension of Ramses II

Takes place on 22 February. One of the two dates each year when the sun penetrates the inner sanctuary of the temple at Abu Simbel, illuminating the statues of the gods within. Draws a big crowd.

International Fishing Tournament

Held at Hurghada on the Red Sea; attended by anglers from all over the world.

March

With warmer days come winds, especially the khamsin, a hot current that causes periodic, intense sandstorms lasting a few hours and often grounding flights. Bear this in mind when booking trips through to early May.

D-Caf

Downtown Cairo's Contemporary Arts Festival (http://d-caf.org/) is international, multi-disciplinary and great fun. Wonderful way too to see the often dilapidated venues in the city centre.

April

On days when the khamsin's not blowing, the air is pleasantly fresh. This is the shoulder season for tourism, and archaeological sites begin to empty out.

El-Limbo

Egypt's Suez Canal area has many distinct folk traditions, including this effigy-burning party held every year in Port Said, right before Shamm al-Nassim. Rooted in 19th-century protests against the British, the conflagration feels both pa-

WAYNE WALTON / GETTY IMAGES ©

PHILIP GAME / GETTY IMAGES ©

Top: Eid al-Fitr (p24) prayers ending Ramadan, Edfu
Bottom: Eid al-Adha (p24), Cairo

gan and modern, as today's effigies are contemporary celebrities and politicos.

Sham an-Nassim

The Monday after Coptic Easter (13 April 2015, 2 May 2016, 17 April 2017). Literally 'sniffing the breeze', this spring ritual came from Pharaonic tradition via the Copts. It's celebrated by all Egyptians, who picnic in parks, on riverbanks and even on traffic islands.

May

You won't meet a lot of 17-year-olds – they're all indoors studying for the nationwide final exam all secondary-school students take before graduation.

June

Egypt lets out a collective sigh of relief after exams, and summer ramps up. The heat is in full force by the end of the month, but this doesn't deter Muslims observing Ramadan. During the holy month of fasting, daytime activity slows down even more than usual in hot weather.

Moulid of Abu al-Haggag

In the third week of the Islamic month of Sha'aban (June 2015, June 2016, May 2017), this Sufi festival in Luxor offers a taste of rural religious tradition. Some villages have moulids around the same time.

Ramadan

The ninth month of the Islamic calendar is

dedicated to fasting by day and feasting by night. Foodies will love a visit during this time; ambitious sightseers may be frustrated.

July

 Eid al-Fitr

The feast that marks the end of Ramadan lasts three days and, if it's possible, involves even more food than the past month put together.

August

This is a major Egyptian vacation period. Expect beach zones, especially in the Mediterranean, to be thronged. Anywhere else is so hot you can feel your eyeballs burn. Life generally takes place after sundown.

September

The barest respite from the heat.

October

As the summer heat finally breaks, students head back to school and the cultural calendar revs up again, especially in Cairo. An ideal time for travelling, with manageable weather and few other visitors.

Birth of Ramses

On 22 October; the second date in the year when the sun's rays penetrate the temple at Abu Simbel.

International Festival for Experimental Theatre

A long-running event held at venues all over Cairo, from standard stages to antiques shops. Shows can be hit or miss, but many are very tourist-friendly as you don't have to speak Arabic to enjoy them. See www.cdf-eg.org for the line-up.

Siyaha

An oasis-wide celebration of the date harvest, Siwa's annual get-together takes place around the full moon this month. Much like a moulid, though not as raucous, there's Sufi chanting and plenty of food.

Moulid of Sayyed al-Badawi

In the last week of October, close to a million pilgrims throng the city of Tanta in the Nile Delta, where a 13th-century mystic founded an important Sufi order. Part family fun fair, part intense ritual, it's worth a trip if you don't mind crowds.

Eid al-Adha

For the Feast of the Sacrifice, a four-day Islamic (and national) holiday, families slaughter sheep and goats at home, even in densest Cairo. There's literally blood in the streets, and the air smells of roasting meat. In short, not for vegetarians.

November

With a light chill in the air, restaurants start serving up heartier stews, while visitors start trickling in to enjoy ruins and beaches at a moderate temperature.

Arab Music Festival

Early in the month, 10 days of classical, traditional and orchestral Arabic music held at the Cairo Opera House and other venues. See www.cairoopera.org for schedules, and buy tickets in person at the main hall.

Cairo International Film Festival

From the last weekend in November into December, this 10-day event shows recent films from all over the world, all without censorship. Anything that sounds like it might contain scenes of exposed flesh sells out immediately. Schedules at www.ciff.org.eg.

December

Not much is on the calendar in Egypt, but this is when winter tourism begins to peak, as visitors flood in for winter sun and sightseeing. There's a surprising amount of Santa Claus kitsch to be seen.

International Cairo Biennale

This fairly conservative government-sponsored show doesn't fully reflect the contemporary Egyptian art scene, but it's worth checking out if you're here. Go to www.cairobiennale.gov.eg for info and dates.

Itineraries

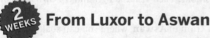

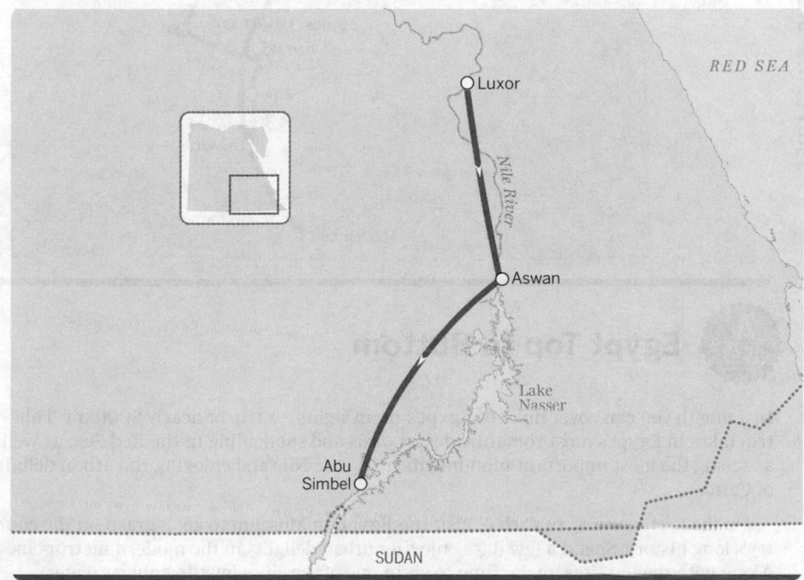

From Luxor to Aswan

Many visitors now prefer to avoid Cairo altogether and fly direct to Luxor. As the largest open air museum in the world, there's plenty to keep you busy here. Spent a few days cruising the Nile, definitely the most relaxed way to see Egypt.

In **Luxor** spend two days on the east bank visiting the temples of Luxor and Karnak and the brilliant Luxor Museum, as well as strolling through the souq. In the next few days, cycle around the west bank of the Nile where the major sights include the Valley of the Kings, the Ramesseum and the Memorial Temple of Hatshepsut. Try to save some energy for the less-visited sights such as Medinat Habu, the Tombs of the Nobles and Deir al-Medina, which can be just as rewarding.

In the second week arrange four days sailing up the Nile to **Aswan** on a budget-friendly felucca or a luxurious dahabiyya; the shorter version is to find a taxi who will take you there and stop at the temples on the way. From Aswan you can visit the temples at **Abu Simbel**, perched on the edge of Lake Nasser.

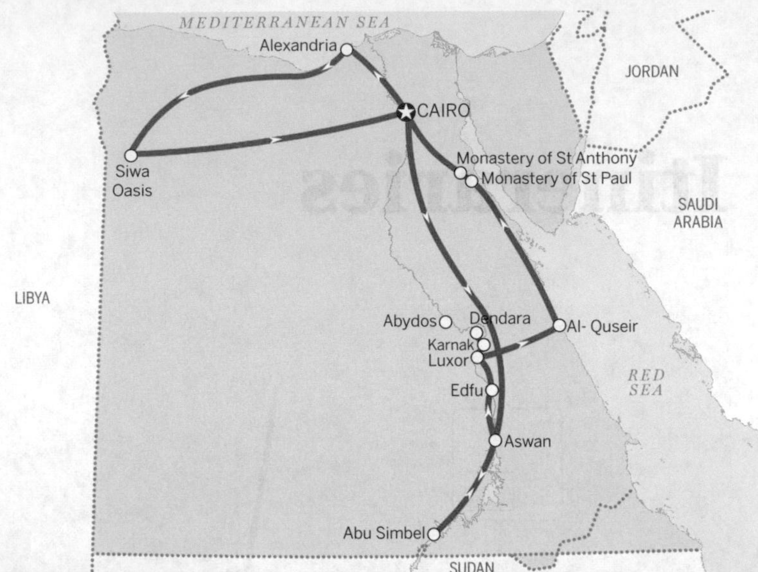

Egypt Top to Bottom

In a month you can cover most of Egypt's main sights – a trip of nearly 2000km. This trip takes in Egypt's most romantic desert oasis and snorkelling in the Red Sea, as well as seeing the most important monuments along the Nile and enjoying the urban delights of Cairo.

On the first morning in **Cairo**, visit the Egyptian Museum to get a grasp on the country's long history. Spend a few days enjoying urban delights in the modern metropolis. Along with the top sites, make time to sit in one of the city's bustling ahwas (cafes), wreathed in sweet sheesha (water pipe) smoke. Then visit the Pyramids of Giza and continue to the necropolis of Saqqara.

Head south from Cairo on the sleeper train to **Aswan**, where you can soak up Nubian culture and make the side trip for a day or two to the awesome temples of **Abu Simbel**. Sail back down the Nile from Aswan to **Edfu** on a felucca, or take a taxi stopping at various temples along the way. Visit the vast temple complex of **Karnak**, and the **Temple of Luxor** on the east bank of Luxor, and hang out on the west bank in Luxor for a few days – there is so much to see here. For a great day out of Luxor take a boat or drive to the sacred site of **Abydos**, visiting the Ptolemaic temple at **Dendara** on the way.

When you've had your fill of ancient ruins, take a servees from **Luxor** to **Al-Quseir** for some days of snorkelling and relaxing on the beach. Head back to Cairo, and on the way take in the **Monastery of St Paul** and **Monastery of St Anthony**.

Pass through Cairo, take the train to **Alexandria** and spend a couple of days in its wonderful cafes and museums. From there continue along the Mediterranean coast heading for **Siwa Oasis**, one of Egypt's most idyllic spots. This is the best spot for hanging out for a few days, cycling around the oasis and perhaps going on a desert safari before heading back to Cairo.

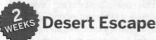

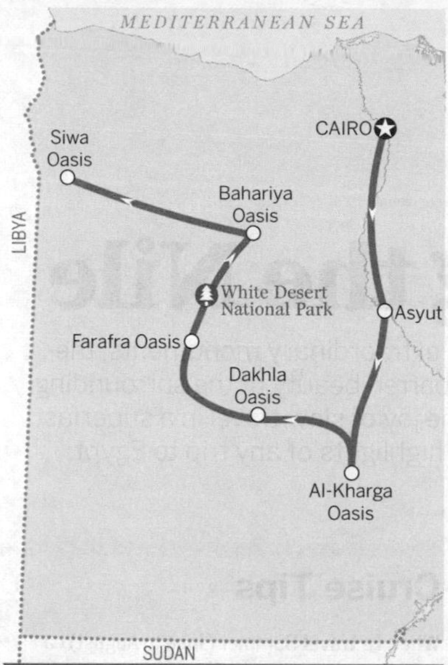

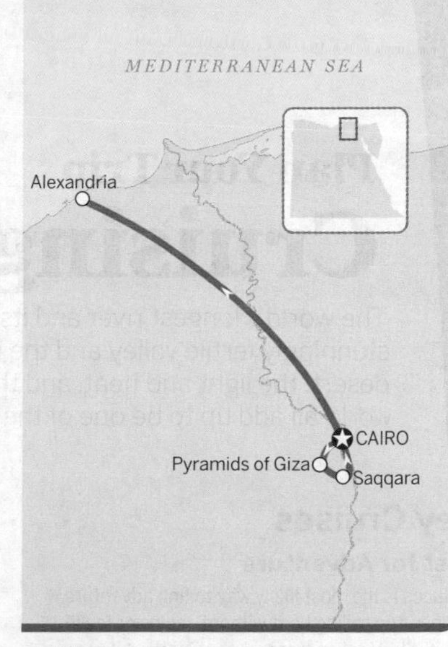

Desert Escape

The Western Desert offers a wonderful mix of lush desert oases gardens, a great variety of stunning desert landscapes, and some interesting ancient monuments.

Begin a trip to the amazing Western Desert with a bus from Cairo or Asyut to **Al-Kharga Oasis**, and explore the Al-Kharga Museum of Antiquities as well as the Graeco-Roman temples and tombs.

From Al-Kharga, go northwest to **Dakhla Oasis** to see the fascinating hive-like, mudbrick settlements of Balat and Al-Qasr. Next, hop north to the small but quaint **Farafra Oasis**. From there you can make a two- or three-day trip to camp in the stunning **White Desert National Park**, and then head for the closest oasis to Cairo, **Bahariya**.

From Bahariya you can strike west across several hundred kilometres of open sands to **Siwa Oasis** as part of an organised desert tour, hiring a 4WD to drive the remote desert highway. Perched on the edge of the Great Sand Sea, Siwa is renowned for its dates and for being the place of the oracle where Alexander the Great was declared son of the god Amon.

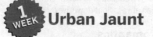

Urban Jaunt

Get a taste of contemporary urban life in Egypt's two largest cities. The heaving metropolis of Cairo allows you to wander through time in its different quarters. In Alexandria, soak up cafe culture and catch a glimpse of the Graeco-Roman achievement.

In **Cairo**, head to the Egyptian Museum to immerse yourself into Egypt's long history, and stroll through the faded elegance of downtown. The next day, visit the **Pyramids of Giza**, and continue to the necropolis of **Saqqara**. For contrast, on your third day, take the metro to Coptic Cairo and visit the excellent Coptic Museum. Take a taxi to Al-Azhar Park to enjoy lunch and great views over the city from the Citadel View Restaurant. Spend the rest of the afternoon wandering in Islamic Cairo. On your last day, cafe-hop in leafy Zamalek, take in some art galleries and ride the elevator up the Cairo Tower for a final view.

The next morning, take an express train to **Alexandria**. Visit the stunning Bibliotheca Alexandrina and the Alexandria National Museum. On your second day, indulge in Alexandrian nostalgia: ride the creaking streetcar and tour cafes where the city's literati once sipped coffee.

Plan Your Trip

Cruising the Nile

The world's longest river and its extraordinary monuments, the stunningly fertile valley and the barren beauty of the surrounding desert, the light and heat, and the joy of slow travel in a superfast world all add up to be one of the highlights of any trip to Egypt.

Key Cruises

Best for Adventure

A felucca is the most likely way to find adventure. An open-top sailing boat without cabins or facilities, it is best taken from south to north – if the wind fails, you can always float downriver.

Made for Romantics

Dahabiyyas – the name translates as 'the golden one' – will waft you back into the 19th century, when these large and luxurious sailing boats were the only viable form of transport for visitors.

Most Popular Route

Between Luxor and Aswan, although this is also the busiest part of the river and you might find yourself in a long line of boats.

Far from the Crowds

Lake Nasser is the place to go if you would rather see empty landscapes and the odd wild animal than crowds of tourists.

Cruise Tips

When to travel Summer (June to August) can be extremely hot (and is therefore the cheapest season to cruise). Christmas and Easter are usually the busiest (and most expensive) times. Spring and autumn are ideal, with the light being particularly good in October and November.

Where to start Most cruises starting from Luxor are a day longer than those starting from Aswan, partly because they are going against the Nile's strong current. If you want to spend longer in Luxor or are concerned about cost, start from Aswan and head north.

Cabin choice On cruisers, try to avoid the lowest deck. Many boats have decent views from all cabins, but the banks of the Nile are high (and get higher as the river level drops) and you want to see as much as possible. Ask for a deck plan when booking.

Sailing time Many passengers on Nile cruisers are surprised by how little time is spent cruising – the boats' large engines cover distances relatively quickly and cruise times are often only four hours per day.

Itineraries & Sites

Large cruisers stick to rigid itineraries on the busy Luxor–Aswan stretch of the Nile. On these trips, which generally last from three to six nights, days are spent visiting monuments, and relaxing by the pool or on deck. By night there is a variety of entertainment: cocktails, dancing and fancy-dress parties – usually called a *galabeya* (man's robe) party, as passengers are encouraged to 'dress like an Egyptian' – are all part of the fun. Actual sailing time is minimal on most of these trips – often as little as four hours each day, depending on the itinerary.

Feluccas and dahabiyyas determine their own schedules and do not need special mooring spots, so can stop at small islands or antiquities sites often skipped by the big cruisers. But even these boats usually have preferred mooring places. Because they use sail power instead of large engines, a far greater proportion of time is spent in motion. Night-time entertainment is more likely to be stargazing, listening to the sounds of the river, and occasionally riverbank fireside music from the crew or villagers.

The stretch of the Nile between Luxor and Aswan has the greatest concentration of well-preserved monuments in the country, which is why it also has the greatest number of boats and tourists (sailing in both directions). No boats have cruised between Cairo and Luxor since the 1990s, but this is now due to change.

Feluccas and dahabiyyas rarely sail between Luxor and Esna because police permits are difficult to get and because the big cruisers usually have priority using the busy Esna lock. Dahabiyya operators will bus passengers to Esna from Luxor. Felucca trips generally start in Aswan and end south of Esna; captains can arrange onward transport to Luxor, but this often costs extra.

Cairo to Luxor

This stretch of the river was removed from cruise itineraries after attacks on boats in the 1990s. The archaeological sites at Dendara and Abydos have been on some tour schedules for the past few years – it is also possible to take a day cruise to Dendara from Luxor. Cruises from Cairo to Luxor and Aswan resumed briefly in the 2012–13 season, but stopped again in the unrest following President Morsi's removal in summer 2013. It is hoped they will resume soon.

THE BEST OF THE NILE

Explore the Nile in luxury Enjoying a private cruise on a dahabiyya.

Economy cruise Taking a felucca trip from Aswan to Edfu.

Nubian adventure Safari to Abu Simbel on African Angler's *Ta Seti*.

Nostalgia trip Reliving Agatha Christie's Egypt on the Nile's last steamer, the *Sudan*.

Five-star plutocracy Style and luxury on Oberoi's award-winning *Philae*.

Family fun Combining luxury cruising and sightseeing with kid-friendly cooking on the *Sun Boat III*.

Luxor

The capital of Egypt's glorious New Kingdom pharaohs, home to Tutankhamun, Ramses II and many other famous names, Luxor is blessed with some of the world's most famous ancient monuments. Most cruises only cover the bare minimum, so if you are interested in seeing the sights, it pays to spend an extra day or two here away from the boat.

Highlights include the temples of Karnak (p186), Luxor Temple (p193), the Luxor Museum (p195), the Valley of the Kings (p199), the Tombs of the Nobles (p197), Deir al-Bahri and Medinat Habu (p208).

Luxor to Aswan

This most famous stretch of the river is studded with stunning architecture and varied scenes of great natural beauty. All

NILE FACTS

As the world's longest river, the Nile cuts through 11 countries and an incredible 6680km of Africa as it winds its way north towards the Mediterranean Sea. It has two main sources: Lake Victoria in Uganda, out of which flows the White Nile; and Lake Tana in the Ethiopian highlands, from which the Blue Nile emerges. The two rivers meet at Khartoum in Sudan. Some 320km further north, they are joined by a single tributary, the Atbara. From here, the river flows northwards to its end without any other tributary and almost no rain adding to its waters.

Cruising the Nile

0 50 km
0 25 miles

Sohag
Nile River
Eastern (Arabian) Desert
Al-Balyana
Abydos
Nag Hammadi Barrage
Qena
Dendara
Nile River
Valley of the Kings
Deir al-Bahri; Tombs of the Nobles
Karnak
Medinat Habu
Luxor
Luxor Temple
Esna Barrage
Esna
Nile River
Al-Kab
Edfu
Gebel Silsila
Western (Libyan) Desert
Kom Ombo
Daraw
Aswan Dam
Aswan
Philae
Kalabsha
High Dam
Lake Nasser
Amada
Wadi as-Subua
Temples of Abu Simbel
Qasr Ibrim
Abu Simbel

cruisers stop to visit the Ptolemaic temples of Esna, Edfu and Kom Ombo. On the shorter cruises, all three sites are visited in a single day. While none of the sites is so large that this is unrealistic, exploring three great temples is a lot to jam into one day and the rushed visit means that you will be moored longer at Luxor or Aswan.

Dahabiyyas and feluccas take longer to cover the distance between the three temples, usually seeing only one a day. Most dahabiyyas (and some feluccas) also stop at the rarely visited and highly recommended sites of Al-Kab and Gebel Silsila. Cruisers do not have moorings here, so visitors may be limited to your fellow passengers, giving a taste of how it might have been for 19th-century travellers.

Aswan

The Nile is squeezed between rocks and a series of islands at Aswan, which makes it particularly picturesque, especially with the desert crowding in on both sides of the river. If you embark here you will probably spend only one night in town, but some cruisers stay moored for two nights. Most itineraries include a visit to Philae, site of the Temple of Isis; the High Dam; and the Northern Quarries, site of the Unfinished Obelisk (p241). Occasionally cruisers offer a felucca ride around Elephantine Island as an excursion; if not, it is worth organising your own. Some also offer an optional half-day tour (usually by plane) to Abu Simbel.

Lake Nasser

The lake was created in the 1960s when the High Dam was built near Aswan, and now covers much of Egyptian Nubia, once home to hundreds of tombs, temples and churches. Some monuments were moved from their original sites prior to the building of the dam and are grouped together at four locations: Kalabsha, Wadi as-Subua (accessible only by boat), Amada (accessible only by boat) and, of course, **Abu Simbel**.

Because so few cruisers operate on Lake Nasser, moorings are never crowded and monuments – with the exception of the Temple of Ramses II at Abu Simbel – are not overrun. Itineraries are generally three nights/four days from Aswan to Abu Simbel, or four nights/five days from Abu Simbel to Aswan.

Sailing a Felucca

For many travellers, the only way to travel on the Nile is slowly, on board a traditional felucca (Egyptian sailing boat). Except for swimming, this is as close as you can get to the river. Read on to make sure that this is for you and that you avoid the pitfalls. Also see the boxed text on p32 for planning your felucca trip.

ANCIENT BARQUES

River travel was so central to the ancient Egyptian psyche that it seemed perfectly obvious that the sun god Ra travelled through the sky in a boat and that the dead would sail to the afterlife. The earliest boats are likely to have been simple skiffs made of papyrus bundles, best for hunting and travelling short distances. Ancient Egyptians then developed elaborate wooden boats powered by multiple sets of oars, a long narrow sail and a steering oar that later evolved into a rudder. The most elaborate surviving example of an ancient boat was among Pharaoh Khufu's funerary goods and can be seen at the Cheops Boat Museum at the Pyramids of Giza. Numerous models of simpler boats have been found in tombs.

A Slow Journey

Most felucca trips begin at Aswan; the strong northward current means that boats are not marooned if the wind dies. Trips go to Kom Ombo (two days/one night), Edfu (three days/two nights – the most popular option) or Esna (four days/three nights).

Feluccas are not allowed to sail after 8pm, so most stop at sunset and set up camp on the boat or on shore. Night-time entertainment ranges from stargazing and the crew singing to partying, depending on you and your fellow passengers.

Find the Captain

With so many feluccas (hundreds, thousands?), arranging a felucca trip can be daunting. Small hotels can be just as aggressive in trying to rope you in. To be sure of what you're getting, it's best to arrange things yourself.

Many of the better felucca captains can be found having a drink in Nileside restaurants such as the Aswan Moon; Emy, near the Panorama restaurant; or on Elephantine Island. Meet a few captains – and inspect their boats – before choosing one you get on well with. Women alone or in a group should try to team up with a few men if possible, as some women travellers have reported sailing with felucca captains who had groping hands. There have been some rare reports of assault.

Officially, feluccas can carry a minimum of six passengers and a maximum of eight. Fares are open to negotiation and dictated by demand. Expect to pay at least E£100 per person from Aswan to Kom Ombo, E£130 to Edfu and E£160 to Esna, including food. On top of this you need to add E£5 to E£10 per person for the captain to arrange the police registration. You can get boats for less, but take care; if it's much cheaper you'll either have a resentful captain and crew, or you'll be eating little more than bread and *fuul* (fava bean paste) for three days. Do not hand out the whole agreed amount until you get to your destination because there have been several reports of trips being stopped prematurely for a so-called breakdown.

If you do have problems, the tourist police or the tourist office should be the first port of call.

Dahabiyyas, the Golden Boats

> 'The choice between a dahabiyya and a steamer is like the choice between travelling with post-horses and travelling by rail. One is expensive, leisurely, delightful; the other is cheap, swift, and comparatively comfortless.'

When the 19th-century traveller Amelia Edwards wrote these lines in *A Thousand Miles Up the Nile,* package tours by steamer were already crowding dahabiyyas off the Nile. But they have made a comeback in the past few years and dozens of them are

PARKED UP

In Aswan and Luxor, the mooring scene can become very crowded, often with eight or 10 boats tied up together. For most people this means that the view from your cabin might be straight into the next boat. With the wide choice of hotels, particularly in Luxor, it makes sense to keep 'parked up' time to a minimum.

PLANNING YOUR FELUCCA TRIP

Toilet facilities There are no onboard toilet facilities, so you will need to go to the toilet overboard or find somewhere private when you stop on shore. Some dahabiyya captains now travel with basic toilet tents – really no more than a screen and a hole in the sand.

Ensure that your boat is riverworthy Check that the captain has what appears to be a decent, riverworthy boat, and the essential gear: blankets (it gets cold at night), cooking implements and a sunshade. If a different boat or captain is foisted on you at the last minute, be firm and refuse.

Establish whether the price includes food To be sure you're getting what you paid for, go with whoever does the shopping.

Agree on the number of passengers beforehand Ask to meet fellow passengers, because you are going to be sharing a small space.

Decide on the drop-off point before you set sail Many felucca captains stop 30km south of Edfu in Hammam, Faris or Ar-Ramady.

Don't hand over your passport Captains can use a photocopy to arrange the permit.

Bring comfort essentials It can get bitterly cold at night, so bring a sleeping bag. Insect repellent is a good idea. A hat, sunscreen and plenty of bottled water are essential.

Take your rubbish with you Wherever you stop, be sure to clean up after yourself.

now afloat. Meroe, La Flâneuse du Nil, Lazuli and The Orient are all companies with boats that are beautifully appointed, with an antique feel, tasteful decor and double lateen sails. With such small numbers of passengers, this is the most luxurious way to see the monuments without crowds. As most dahabiyyas have flexible itineraries and personalised service, it is also the best way to feel truly independent while still travelling in comfort, although often at considerably more expense than on feluccas or cruisers. Prices include all meals and usually also transfers to and from airports/train stations. Some include entrance to monuments and guide fees, but you should check when booking your trip. Trips are best arranged before you depart for Egypt.

Meroe (☎0100 657 8322; www.nourelnil.com; 5-night trip per person from €1700) A replica of a 19th-century dahabiyya indistinguishable from the original, the beautifully finished *Meroe* is the coolest dahabiyya currently on the Nile and is rare for being owner-operated. It has room for 20 passengers in 10 comfortable, stylish white cabins with private bathroom, and large windows overlooking the Nile. Because it is newly built, plumbing and water filtration are good, and there is plenty of storage for clothes and suitcases. During the day, when not visiting an ancient site or a local market, there is plenty of space on deck to read in your own corner, to watch the scenery or to dive off and swim in the strong current of the Nile. The chef buys from farmers and markets on the way, so the food is simple but fresh and delicious: plenty of fresh vegetables, farm-bred chicken, duck and fish. This tailor-made trip, with moorings at small islands and outside villages, is a unique way to see the Nile, reminiscent of another age. If there is no wind, the dahabiyya is towed by a motor boat. The same owners have three other boats, *Malouka*, *El Nil* and *Assouan*, whose cabins are significantly less expensive. All boats only run from Esna to Aswan (five nights).

La Flâneuse du Nil (☎in France 01 42 86 16 00; www.la-flaneuse-du-nil.com; 4-night trip per person in a double cabin from €875) *La Flâneuse* has been quickly picked up by several upmarket British tour operators and with good reason: the boat is well fitted and well run. Like original dahabiyyas, it relies on sails (or tugs) to move, but does have air-con in the seven cabins. Tours are shorter than some, taking four nights from Esna to Aswan and three nights from Aswan back to Esna.

Lazuli (☎0100 877 7115; www.lazulinil.com; 5-night trip per person from €990) There are now three *Lazulis* on the Nile, one with five cabins and two with six. The long, elegant boats have two lateen sails, a spacious deck with deck chairs, cushions and a long table at which most meals are served. The cabins are comfortable with compact but modern private bathrooms and solar-power energy.

MATT CHAMPLIN / GETTY IMAGES ©

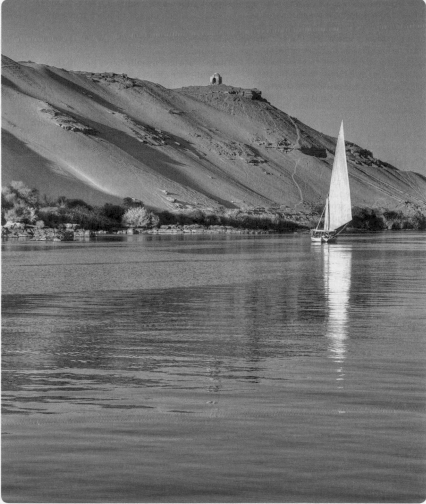

Top: The Nile River at Aswan

Bottom: A traditional felucca sailing boat

JD DALLET / GETTY IMAGES ©

The Orient (☎02-2395 9124; www.nile-dahabiya.com; 4-night trip per person s/d from €1100/700) With four double cabins and one suite, the *Orient* is smaller than many dahabiyyas but none the worse for that. Well turned out, run by Egyptians who also own one of our favourite restaurants in Luxor (Sofra), this and its sister ship *Zekrayaat* are good midrange choices. The *Orient* leaves Esna each Saturday, the *Zekrayaat* each Monday.

Cruisers

There are as many as 300 cruisers plying the waters between Aswan and Luxor. Like hotels, they range from slightly shabby to sumptuous, but almost all have some sort of pool, a large rooftop area for sunbathing and watching the scenery, a restaurant, a bar, air-con, TV, minibars and ensuite bathrooms.

A cruise remains the easiest way to see the Nile in comfort on a midrange budget and can be ideal for families with older children who want to splash in a pool between archaeological visits, or for people who want to combine sightseeing with relaxation. The downside is that monuments are almost always seen with large groups and the itineraries are generally inflexible. Boats are almost always moored together, and the sheer volume of traffic means that generators and air-con units overwhelm the peace of the river. The consensus from our research is that scrimping on cruises means substandard hygiene, no pool, cubby-hole cabins and lots of hidden extras, which makes a felucca trip a far better option.

The only way around this is to book an all-inclusive package to Egypt. Not only are the prices usually lower but, in the case of cut-price cruises, the agency guarantees the reliability of the boat. The best deals are from Europe. Avoid booking through small hotels in Egypt: the hotels are not licensed as travel agencies so you will have no recourse if there are problems. With the uncertain state of tourism at the time of writing, prices, which include all meals, entrance to monuments and guides, varied considerably; you should check prices with the company before you book.

Between Luxor & Aswan

M/S Sudan (☎in France 01 73 00 81 88; www.steam-ship-sudan.com) The *Sudan* was built as part of Thomas Cook's steamer fleet in 1885 and was once owned by King Fouad. It was also used as a set in the film *Death on the Nile*. It has been refurbished and offers 23 cabins, all with private bathroom, air-con and access to the deck. It's unusual in that it has no pool, but it's also unique because it has so much history and character, something sorely missing on most cruisers. Its configuration means it cannot moor to other cruisers, so night-time views are good. There is a choice of three- and four-night cruises. Note that the management does not accept children under seven.

M/S Sun Boat III (www.abercrombiekent.co.uk) Abercrombie & Kent's most intimate cruiser, the beautiful *Sun Boat III* has 14 cabins and

TRAVEL ACCOUNTS ON THE NILE

Sensual and spiritual *A Winter on the Nile* by Lonely Planet author Anthony Sattin – Sattin tells the parallel stories of Florence Nightingale and Gustave Flaubert, who both sailed up the Nile in 1849. While Nightingale was fascinated by the spirituality of ancient Egypt, Flaubert found his pleasures in the brothels.

Classical Egyptology *A Thousand Miles Up the Nile* by Amelia B Edwards – Edwards was so absorbed by the remains of ancient Egyptian civilisation she came across on her journey that she founded the London-based Egypt Exploration Fund, which still finances archaeological missions today.

Ancient encounter *The Histories* by Herodotus – Egyptian customs, curious manners, tall tales and a few facts from a curious Greek historian writing in the 5th century BC.

The long journey *Old Serpent Nile: A Journey to the Source* by Stanley Stewart – a view from the ground as Stewart travels from the Nile Delta to its source in the Mountains of the Moon, in Uganda, during the late 1980s.

four suites decorated in contemporary Egyptian style, straight out of a magazine. The seven-night itinerary includes visits to Dendara and Abydos. Dinner on board is à la carte or a set menu with two European choices and one Egyptian. There's also the option of in-room dining. The boat is impeccably run and operates a no-mobile-phone policy in public areas. Facilities include a pool and exercise machines. The company also operates the 40-cabin, deluxe M/S *Sun Boat IV* and the 32-cabin *Nile Adventurer,* back in service after a complete refit. All A&K boats have excellent Egyptologists as guides and private mooring docks in Luxor, Aswan and Kom Ombo.

M/S Philae (www.oberoihotels.com) Designed to resemble a Mississippi paddle boat, the award-winning *Philae* runs four- and six-night cruises. Its interior is filled with wood panelling and antiques, and all rooms have a balcony. The old-world feel is backed up by state-of-the-art water filtration, a library and all the comforts of a good five-star hotel. Prices more than double in high season around Christmas, Easter and the autumn/winter school holidays.

M/S Nile Goddess (www.sonesta.com/nilecruises) One of the top boats of the Sonesta's five cruisers, the *Nile Goddess* is a large, plush, five-star vessel with lots of marble and gilt. Sonesta's sister ship, the M/S *Sun Goddess*, is slightly cheaper; the M/S *Moon Goddess* and *Star Goddess* are even plusher and more expensive.

M/S Beau Soleil (www.msbeausoleil.com) The five-star *Beau Soleil* is more reasonably priced than many others and recommended for its good service and facilities. The smallest cabins are 15 sq m (large for such a boat) and many of the cabins have their own balcony from where you can watch the scenery go by.

M/S Darakum Not a boat you can book direct, but one that is offered by a number of international agencies. New, spacious and top-end, if not super-luxurious, the *Darakum* has 44 cabins and eight suites, plus a swimming pool. The decor is more 1970s than New Kingdom and you have to be quick to get a sunbed, but prices come right down out of the autumn/winter school holidays.

Lake Nasser

Of the handful of boats currently cruising on Lake Nasser, a few stand out above the rest.

Ta Seti (☎097-230 9748; www.african-angler.net) Something different: Tim Baily worked in safaris south of the Sahara before setting up African Angler, the first company to run Lake Nasser safaris. He has a staff of skilled guides, expert in the flora, fauna and fish life of the lake, and owns several styles of small boat. Two-cabin houseboats have toilet and shower, the two-bunk safari boats are more basic, while the mothership carries the kitchen and supplies. Cruises can be from one to seven nights and can start from Aswan or Abu Simbel.

Kasr Ibrim (☎02-2516 9653, 02-2516 9654, 02-2516 9656; www.kasribrim.com.eg) The *Kasr Ibrim* and its twin the *Eugénie* were the brainchild of Mustafa al-Guindi, a Cairene of Nubian origin who is almost single-handedly responsible for getting Lake Nasser opened to tourists. The boats are stunningly designed and each has a pool, a hammam (bathhouse) and French cuisine.

Nubiana (☎0122 104 0255; www.lakenasseradventure.com) The *Nubiana* is a small motorboat with three small cabins, a suite and a shared shower. Above is a lounge and sun deck. A speedboat can also be arranged for fishing trips or waterskiing. The same company also organises five-day boat trekking trips from Aswan to Abu Simbel.

Prince Abbas (☎02-2690 1797; www.moevenpick-hotels.com) A five-star deluxe ship operated by the Swiss chain Mövenpick, it has a library, a gym, a sun deck with a plunge pool and a Jacuzzi. The spacious cabins have TV, music system, minibar, picture windows and private bathroom.

WHY CRUISE THE NILE?

Rain seldom falls on this part of the Nile Valley, so without the river, the country would simply not exist. Ancient Egyptians recognised this fact when they likened their land to a lotus – the delta was the flower, the oasis of Al-Fayoum the bud, and the river and its valley the stem that supported them all.

But rather than the practical use of the waterway, the Nile's beauty strikes travellers most: the soft light of its mornings; the lushness of the plants and trees that grow along its banks; the thrill of flights of birds that shuttle up- or downriver on their migrations; the patience of fishermen, rowing out in the morning to cast their nets; the greatness of it all.

Plan Your Trip

Diving the Red Sea

The sights below Egypt's waters are just as magnificent as those above. Under the sea's surface lies a fantasia of coral mountains and shallow reefs swarming with brightly coloured fish. Submerge into this kaleidoscope world and you'll understand why the Red Sea boasts a legendary reputation among diving enthusiasts.

Best Diving Intro Experience

Gently submerging into Dahab's sloping Lighthouse Reef (p389), and discovering a colourful world of darting, curious fish only a few steps from the shore.

Best Famous-Dive-Site Experience

Plunging into the Blue Hole (p390).

Best Wreck-Diving Experience

Exploring the underwater museum of the *Thistlegorm* (p41), the WWII supply ship first discovered by Jacques Cousteau.

Best Marine-Life Experiences

Coming face to face with hammerheads and mantas, passing by large shoals of tuna and spotting emperor angelfish and turtles at world renowned Elphinstone Reef (p368).

Diving with the resident pod of dolphins at Sha'ab Samadai (p369).

Best Off-the-Beaten-Track Experience

Venturing to the far south near Marsa Alam (p368), where the pristine reefs of the Fury Shoals can be accessed as day trips.

When to Dive

The Red Sea can be dived year-round, though diving conditions are at their peak during the summer months of July to September. Despite this, if you're not great at dealing with heat you should try to avoid booking a dive holiday in August, when land temperatures regularly sky-rocket to over 40°C. If you're planning to dive in the Red Sea's southernmost sections (Marsa Alam and beyond), take into account that a plankton bloom reduces visibility for a few weeks during April and May and so is best avoided

Most Popular Period

➡ **July–September** The best time to dive the Red Sea is in Egypt's summer months, when calm sea conditions, sea temperatures averaging 26°C, and excellent visibility make for astonishingly good diving conditions.

Quietest Period

➡ **December–January** During winter, rough seas and strong winds can make access to some dive sites difficult and even impossible, though if you're happy to stick to shore dives you shouldn't have a problem. Visibility does take a hit during this period and sea temperatures also drop substantially. The plus side is that, unlike in summer, you'll be diving without the crowds.

Where to Dive

Diving tends to be concentrated at the northern end of the Egyptian Red Sea, although increasing numbers of advanced divers are pushing further south. The most popular sites are around the southern tip of the Sinai Peninsula where you'll find the jewels in the Red Sea's crown. The underwater spectacles of Ras Mohammed National Park and the Straits of Gubal led a panel of scientists and conservationists to choose the northern section of the Red Sea as one of the Seven Underwater Wonders of the World in 1989.

The thin strip of land jutting out into the sea forming **Ras Mohammed National Park** is home to the 'holy trinity' of Shark Reef, Eel Garden and the *Jolanda* wreck. Further off-shore, on the western side of the Sinai Peninsula, are the **Straits of Gubal**, a series of coral pinnacles just beneath the surface of the sea, famous for snagging ships trying to navigate north to the Suez Canal. This is where the majority of Egypt's shipwrecks lie, including the WWII wreck of the *Thistlegorm*, famously discovered in the 1950s by Jacques Cousteau.

Another major diving area is in the **Straits of Tiran**, which form the narrow entrance to the Gulf of Aqaba. The currents sweeping through the deep channel allow coral to grow prolifically, attracting abundant marine life.

Heading south, the best reefs are found around the many offshore islands. Although the reefs nearest to Hurghada have been damaged by tourist development, there is a plethora of pristine dive sites further south.

Where you base yourself for your Red Sea diving trip depends much on your own travelling style. Some travellers find themselves spending more time than they planned in the backpacker-friendly village of **Dahab**, while others enjoy the creature comforts of the resort towns of **Sharm el-Sheikh** and **El-Gouna**. For those who want to seriously maximise their underwater time, there's no better option than a week on a live-aboard.

RED SEA STATS

Depth 4m to 40m

Visibility 15m to 40m

Water Temperature Averages 21°C to 30°C, with January the coldest month and August the warmest.

Access Shore, boat and live-aboard

Taba & Nuweiba

Taba (p399) and Nuweiba (p394) attract significantly fewer divers than their more famous cousins in Sinai. However there are a handful of excellent dive sites in the area (although the diving here is not as rich and as varied as other spots in Sinai and the Red Sea) and are a suitable base for independent-minded divers looking for low-key ambience and minimal crowds. For an even more relaxed experience, some divers also base themselves at one of the beach camps on the Nuweiba–Taba coastal highway. Tourism has taken a significant hit in this area since the 2011 revolution and would-be divers should keep up-to-date with their government's travel advisories before planning a trip here.

Good For Escaping the crowds

Dahab

This laid-back village is surrounded by spectacular dive sites, and abounds with cheap guesthouses and chilled-out

CLIMBING & DIVING: A WORD OF CAUTION

Altitude can kill, particularly if your body is full of residual nitrogen. If you've been diving recently, be advised that Mt Sinai is high enough to induce decompression sickness. As a general rule, avoid climbing the mountain for 12 hours after one dive, or 18 hours if you've been on multiple dives. Although this may complicate your travel plans, trust us – you'll be delayed a lot longer if you end up confined in a hyperbaric chamber. And, of course, decompression sickness is anything but fun.

Diving the Red Sea

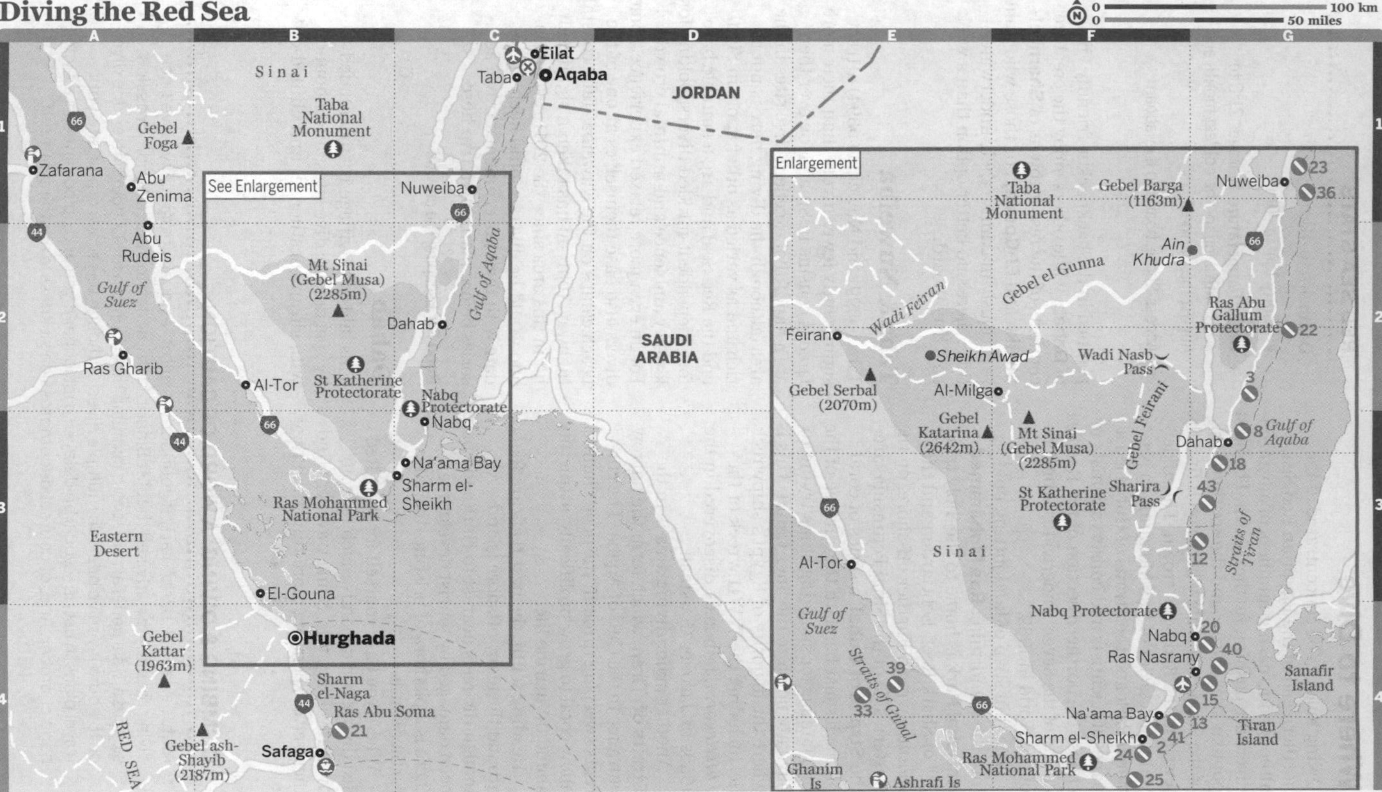

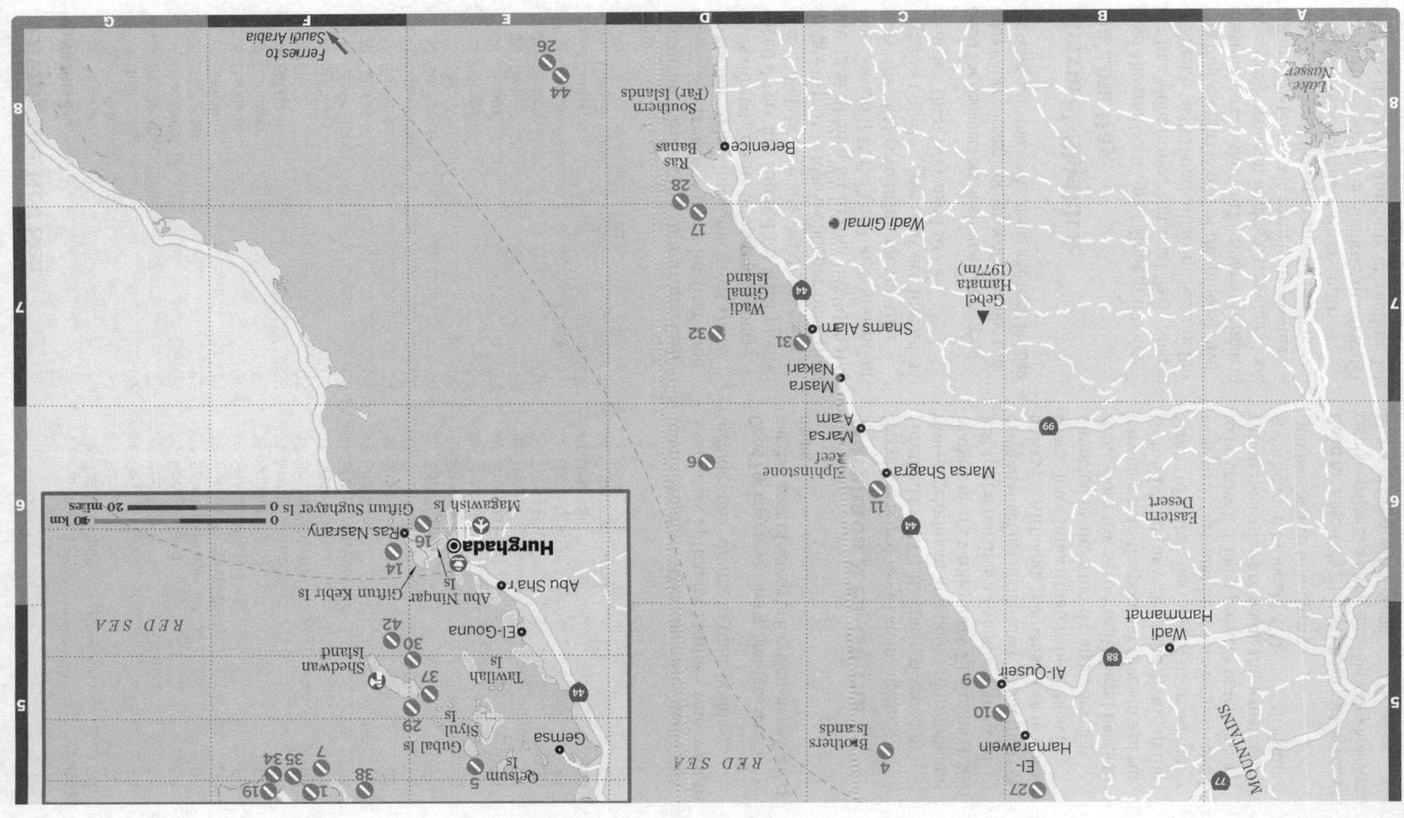
RED SEA
Brothers Islands
El-Hamarawein
Al-Quseir
Wadi Hammamat
MOUNTAINS
Eastern Desert
Marsa Shagra
Elphinstone Reef
Marsa Alam
Masra Nakari
Shams Alam
Gebel Hamata (1977m)
Wadi Gimal
Wadi Gimal Island
Berenice
Ras Banas
Southern (Far) Islands
Lake Nasser
Ferries to Saudi Arabia
RED SEA
Gemsa
Qeisum Is
Gubal Is
Siyul Is
Tawilah Is
Shedwan Island
El-Gouna
Abu Sha'r
Abu Ningar Is
Giftun Kebir Is
Hurghada
Ras Nasrany
Magawish Is
Giftun Sughayer Is
0 40 km
0 20 miles

Diving the Red Sea

Dive Sites

No.	Site	Grid
1	Alternatives	F5
2	Amphoras	F4
3	Bells	G2
4	Big Brother	C5
	Blue Hole	(see 3)
5	Bluff Point	E5
	Canyon	(see 8)
6	Daedalus	D6
7	Dunraven	F5
8	Eel Garden	G3
9	El Kaf	C5
10	El Qadim	C5
11	Elphinstone	C6
12	Gabr el-Bint	G3
13	Gardens	G4
14	Giftun Islands	F6
15	Gordon Reef	G4
16	Gota Abu Ramada	E6
17	Hamada	D7
18	Islands	G3
19	Jackfish Alley	F5
20	Jackson Reef	G4
	Jolanda Reef	(see 35)
	Kingston	(see 33)
	Little Brother	(see 4)
21	Panorama Reef	B4
22	Ras Mumlach	G2
23	Ras Shaitan	G1
24	Ras Um Sid	F4
25	Ras Za'atir	F4
26	Rocky Island	E8
27	Salem Express	B5
28	Sataya (Dolphin Reef)	D8
29	Sha'ab Abu Nuhas	E5
30	Sha'ab al-Erg	E5
31	Sha'ab Samadai	D7
32	Sha'ab Sharm	D7
33	Shag Rock	E4
34	Shark Observatory	F5
35	Shark Reef	F5
36	Sinker	G1
37	Siyul Kebira	E5
38	Small Crack	F5
	Stingray Station	(see 1)
39	Thistlegorm	E4
40	Thomas Reef	G4
41	Tower	F4
	Turtle Bay	(see 2)
42	Umm Qamar	F5
43	Umm Sid	G3
44	Zabargad Island	E8

restaurants lining the shorefront. Dahab (p387) is a fantastic place for first-time divers due to having some great shore dives directly on its doorstep. Experienced divers are catered for with plenty of world-class dive sites easily accessed from town. It is also a cheaper base than Sharm el-Sheikh for diving Ras Mohammed National Park. The tourism drop-off since the 2011 revolution means that Dahab's popular dive sites are much less crowded than they used to be.

Good For Backpackers; first-time divers; good value PADI courses; independently-minded families wanting to mix some diving into their holiday.

Sharm el-Sheikh & Na'ama Bay

Near the southern tip of Sinai and bordering Ras Mohammed National Park, Sharm el-Sheikh (p380) and adjacent Na'ama Bay together comprise one of the busiest dive destinations in the world. Sharm primarily caters to European package travellers looking for Western-style resorts brimming with four- and five-star amenities. There are also some excellent diver-centric resorts where Sharm el-Sheikh's underwater world is the main, and only, attraction. The town's Western-style amenities make this a very easy option for families who want to include some diving in their holiday.

Good For Easy resort living; first-time divers; families; ease of access to Ras Mohammed; wreck diving

Hurghada & El-Gouna

Egypt's original resort strip, ageing Hurghada (p357), has been plagued by over-development and poor environmental management, while glossy El-Gouna (p354) just to the north is a five-star tourist enclave that seems aeons apart from the rest of Egypt. Although the reefs close to both towns have unfortunately been heavily damaged by unfettered tourist development, both towns are well-placed bases for easy access to the popular dive sites of the Giftun Islands as well as the diving in the Straits of Gubal. Because of its mass tourism, dive trips (and hence dive sites) tend to be crowded. On a positive note, conservation measures are being implemented, spearheaded by local NGOs, and the situation has begun to improve.

Good for Resort-style living; cheap package deals; combined Red Sea diving and Nile Valley holidays; Straits of Gubal wreck diving

Safaga

For the most part, Safaga (p365) defies the tourist hordes, which is a good thing as there are some pristine reefs offshore from this rather unattractive port town. Unlike nearby Hurghada and El-Gouna, resorts here are extremely low-key, and cater almost exclusively to dedicated divers.

Good For Dive-centric holidays; technical diving training

Al-Quseir

A historic trade and export hub with a history stretching back centuries, the sleepy town of Al-Quseir (p365) has a charm absent from other Red Sea destinations. The comparative lack of tourist development means that the offshore dive sites here are generally empty, though you will have to contend with strong winds and rough seas.

Good For Escaping the crowds

Marsa Alam

The closest base to the south-coast dive sites, Marsa Alam (p368) still manages to hold on to its remote-outpost ambience despite the resort construction drive of recent years. It's great if you want to experience some of Egypt's most far-flung dives without the cost of a live-aboard. The reefs along this southernmost stretch of the coast lack the crowds further north, though be aware that high winds and strong currents make many of the dives more suitable for experienced divers. Veteran divers of these parts will tell you that once you've dived here nothing else will compare.

Good For Dive-centric holidays; intermediate and advanced divers; escaping the crowds

Live-Aboards

The vast majority of larger dive operators in Egypt organise dive safaris to sites

THISTLEGORM: THE RED SEA'S BEST WRECK DIVE

Built by the North East Marine Engineering Company, the 129m-long cargo ship christened the *Thistlegorm* was completed and launched in 1940 in Sunderland, England. Prior to setting out from Glasgow in 1941, she had previously made several successful trips to North America, the East Indies and Argentina. However, with a cargo full of vital supplies destined for North Africa, where British forces were preparing for Operation Crusader (the relief of Tobruk against the German 8th Army), the *Thistlegorm* met her end at 2am on 6 October 1941.

While the ship was waiting in the Straits of Gubal for a call sign to proceed up the Gulf of Suez, four German Heinkel He 111s that were flying out of Crete mounted an attack. The planes were returning from an armed reconnaissance mission up the Sinai coast, and targeted the ship to offload their unused bombs. One bomber scored a direct hit on the No 4 hold, which tore the ship in two and sent the two railway locomotives that the vessel was carrying hurtling through the air. Incredibly, they landed upright on the seabed, one on either side of the wreck. In less than 20 minutes, the ship sank to the ocean floor, taking with it nine sailors out of a crew of 49.

The *Thistlegorm* lay undisturbed until 1956 when legendary French diver Jacques Cousteau located the wreck, lying at a depth of 17m to 35m to the northwest of Ras Mohammed. Cousteau found a cache of WWII cargo packed in the hold, including a full consignment of armaments and supplies, such as Bedford trucks, Morris cars, BSA 350 motorbikes and Bren gun carriers. Although Cousteau took the ship's bell, the captain's safe and a motorbike, he left the wreck as he found it, and proceeded to keep its location secret. However, it was rediscovered in 1993 when some divers stumbled upon its location, and it has since become one of the world's premier wreck-dive sites.

The *Thistlegorm* (location: Sha'ab Ali; depth: 17m to 30m; rating: intermediate to advanced; access: boat) is best dived on an overnight trip since it takes 3½ hours each way from Sharm el-Sheikh by boat; dive operators throughout Sinai can easily help you arrange this. On your first dive, you will do a perimeter sweep of the boat, which is highlighted by a swim along the soldier walkways on the side of the vessel. On your second dive, you will penetrate the ship's interior, swimming through a living museum of WWII memorabilia.

MARINE PARK ISLANDS

For experienced divers the remote dive sites of Egypt's Marine Park Islands (Big Brother; Little Brother; Daedalus Reef; Zabargad; and Rocky Island) are home to some of the Red Sea's most pristine coral and abundant sealife. Accessing these dive sites is strictly regulated. Divers must have completed a minimum of 30 dives before entering; night diving or landing on the islands is prohibited; and fishing, spear fishing and the use of gloves are banned.

Due to these restrictions, permission must be given for each trip, and a park ranger will often accompany boats to ensure that the rules are being enforced. In order to carry divers, boats must have special safety equipment, which national park and Red Sea governorate officials inspect before each trip.

If you've been offered a trip to this area, check thoroughly that the boat is licensed. If you are caught on an unlicensed boat you could have your own equipment or belongings confiscated and find yourself in custody.

ranging from one night to two weeks' duration. The cost of these live-aboard dive safaris (also known as marine safaris) varies according to the boat and the destination, with the more remote sites in the far south generally the most expensive. While you won't see much of terrestrial Egypt, they allow you to access a greater range of dive sites, including many more distant areas that are too far to explore on day trips.

As a general rule, you should always ask to see the boat before agreeing to sail on it. Also, if a trip is very cheap, check whether the costs of diving and food are included. Furthermore, check that your live-aboard complies with the following two rules:

- There should be a diver-guide ratio of one guide to every 12 divers (or every eight divers in marine-park areas).
- Divers on live-aboards entering marine-park areas must be experienced, with a minimum of 30 logged dives, as well as insurance coverage.

While it's quite possible to book yourself a basic package on a live-aboard after arriving in Egypt, there are numerous agencies that specialise in Red Sea diving holidays. Here is a small sampling:

Emperor Divers (www.emperordivers.com) Emperor Divers offer live-aboard itineraries starting from Sharm el-Sheikh, Hurghada and Marsa Alam.

Blue O Two (www.blueotwo.com) This UK-based dive-holiday operator specialises in luxury live-aboards with its own fleet of ships based in Hurghada and Marsa Alam.

Crusader Travel (www.divers.co.uk) Live-aboard diving packages in the Red Sea, including diving for people with disabilities.

Oonasdivers (www.oonasdivers.com) Well-priced live-aboard trips from this dive centre based at Na'ama Bay in Sharm el-Sheikh.

What You'll See

The Red Sea is teeming with more than a thousand species of marine life, and is an amazing spectacle of colour and form. Fish, sharks, turtles, stingrays, dolphins, corals, sponges, sea cucumbers and molluscs all thrive in these waters. Around 20% of the fish species to be found in the Red Sea are endemic to the region.

Coral This is what makes a reef a reef – though thought for centuries to be some form of flowering plant, coral is in fact an animal. Both hard and soft corals exist, their common denominator being that they are made up of polyps, which are tiny cylinders ringed by waving tentacles that sting their prey and draw it into their stomach. During the day corals retract into their tube, only displaying their real colours at night.

Fish Most of the bewildering variety of fish species in the Red Sea – including many that are found nowhere else – are closely associated with the coral reef, and live and breed in the reefs or nearby seagrass beds. These include such commonly sighted species as the grouper, wrasse, parrotfish and snapper. Others, such as tuna and barracuda, live in open waters and usually only venture into the reefs to feed or breed.

Manta rays Spotting the graceful, frolicking form of a manta during a Red Sea dive is a major highlight for any diver lucky enough to have this experience. Mantas are easily recognisable for their pectoral 'wings' and huge bulk. They can grow to nearly 7m and can weigh up to 1400kg. They are usually sighted near the surface, where they feed on the plankton present there.

Sharks When diving, the sharks you're most likely to encounter include white- or black-tipped reef sharks. Tiger sharks, as well as the enormous, plankton-eating whale sharks, are generally found only in deeper waters. If you're skittish about these apex predators, you can take comfort in the fact that shark attacks in the Red Sea are rare (though not unheard of).

Turtles The most common type of turtle found in these waters is the green turtle, although the leatherback and hawksbill are occasionally sighted. Turtles are protected in Egypt, and although they're not deliberately hunted, they are sometimes caught in nets and end up on menus in restaurants in Cairo and along the coasts.

Marine life you're better off avoiding As intriguing as they may seem, there are some creatures that should be given a wide berth, especially moray eels, sea urchins, fire coral, blowfish, triggerfish, feathery lionfish, turkeyfish and stonefish. To help protect yourself, it's a good idea to familiarise yourself with pictures of all these creatures before snorkelling or diving – single-page colour guides to the Red Sea's common marine hazards can be bought in hotel bookshops around diving areas.

Responsible Diving

The Red Sea's natural wonders are just as magnificent as the splendours of Egypt's Pharaonic heritage, and appear all the more stunning when contrasted with their barren desert backdrop. However, care is needed if the delicate world of coral reefs and fish is not to be permanently damaged. Almost the entire Egyptian coastline in the Gulf of Aqaba is now a protectorate, as is the Red Sea coast from Hurghada south to Sudan. Divers and snorkellers should heed the requests of instructors *not* to touch or tread on coral – if you kill the coral, you'll eventually kill or chase away the fish, too.

Overall, the paramount guideline for preserving the ecology and beauty of reefs is to take nothing with you, leave nothing behind. Other considerations:

- Never use anchors on the reef, and take care not to ground boats on coral.
- Avoid touching or standing on living marine organisms or dragging equipment across the reef. Polyps can be damaged by even the gentlest contact. If you must hold on to the reef, only touch exposed rock or dead coral.
- Be conscious of your fins. Even without contact, the surge from fin strokes near the reef can damage delicate organisms. Take care not to kick up clouds of sand, which can smother organisms.
- Practise and maintain proper buoyancy control. Major damage can be done by divers descending too fast and colliding with the reef.

MARE ROSTRUM

Surrounded by desert on three sides, the Red Sea was formed some 40 million years ago when the Arabian Peninsula split from Africa, allowing the waters of the Indian Ocean to rush in. Bordered at its southern end by the 25km Bab al-Mandab Strait, the Red Sea is the only tropical sea that is almost entirely closed. No river flows into it and the influx of water from the Indian Ocean is slight. These unique geographical features, combined with the arid desert climate and high temperatures, make the sea extremely salty. It is also windy – on average the sea is flat for only 50 days a year.

In regard to the origins of its name (the Red Sea is in fact deep blue), there are two competing schools of thought. Some believe that the sea was named after the surrounding red-rock mountain ranges. Others insist it was named for the periodic algae blooms that tinge the water a reddish-brown. Whatever the spark, it inspired ancient mariners to dub these waters *Mare Rostrum* – the Red Sea.

THE RED SEA'S DUGONG

Little is known about the distribution and numbers of these enigmatic marine mammals in the Red Sea. Weighing up to 500kg, the dugong are easily recognisable for their fusiform shape and dolphin-like tail. These gentle herbivores' natural habitat is shallow coastal waters where they feed on seagrass and other plant forms. This makes them especially vulnerable to coastal degradation and pollution. Most dugong sightings in Egypt have occurred at sites along the coast south of Hurghada, with the Marsa Abu Dabab dive site (to the north of Marsa Alam) becoming famous for dugong-spotting. To help preserve the area and protect the resident dugong of the bay, zoning laws and access restrictions have now been put in place around this dive site.

- Take great care in underwater caves. Spend as little time within them as possible as your air bubbles may be caught within the roof and cause damage. Take turns to inspect the interior of a small cave.
- Resist the temptation to collect or buy corals or shells or to loot marine archaeological sites (mainly shipwrecks).
- Ensure that you take home all your rubbish and any litter you may find as well. Plastics in particular are a serious threat to marine life.
- Do not feed fish, and minimise your disturbance of marine animals.
- Report any violations of responsible diving practices by dive centres and diving groups to Hurghada Environmental Protection & Conservation Association (HEPCA; www.hepca.org).

Learning to Dive

Most dive clubs in Egypt offer **PADI** (www.padi.com) certification, though you'll occasionally find **NAUI** (www.naui.org), **SSI** (www.divessi.com), **CMAS** (www.cmas2000.org) and **BSAC** (www.bsac.com) as well.

PADI Scuba Diver (two days) and PADI Open Water (four intensive days) dive courses are offered by most dive centres in Egypt. PADI Scuba Diver usually costs between €190 and €240 and PADI Open Water courses cost between €275 and €350. When comparing prices, check to see whether the certification fee and books are included.

Beginner courses are designed to drum into you things that have to become second nature when you're underwater. They usually consist of classroom work, where you learn the principles and basic knowledge needed to dive, followed by training in a confined body of water, such as a pool, before heading out to the open sea. If you've never dived before and want to give it a try before you commit yourself, all dive clubs offer introductory Discover Scuba dives for between €45 and €95, including equipment.

In addition to basic certification, most of the well-established clubs on the coast offer a variety of more advanced courses as well as professional-level courses or training in technical diving.

Choosing a Dive Operator

Whether you choose to plunge into the Red Sea with a small local centre, an established resort or a live-aboard, you will have no problem finding a dive operator. Almost all of the large resorts and hotels along the Red Sea have attached dive centres, and there are a vast number of smaller, independent dive centres in the main coastal towns. Some centres and live-aboards are laid-back and informal, while others are slick and structured. Regardless of which diving style you choose, you're going to get wet – and love every minute of it.

As diving is a huge cash-cow in this area, there are invariably a few fly-by-night outfits. Avoid them by doing your research first. Look for a dive operator that has a high PADI rating or equivalent, and ask other divers for recommendations. When deciding which dive centre to use, among the considerations should be the operator's attention to safety and its sensitivity to environmental issues.

The **Chamber of Diving and Watersports** (CDWS; www.cdws.travel) is Egypt's only legal dive centre licensing agency. Since the 2011 Revolution the CDWS has been in disarray but it's still worthwhile to check the validity date of your dive centre's CDWS licence before choosing to dive with them.

Because of Egypt's tourism slowdown since the revolution, it is more important than ever to make sure your dive centre's equipment is in good condition. Due to a lack of business some dive centres are not replacing old, worn-out equipment.

Accidents still occasionally happen and are usually the result of neglect and negligence. Before making any choices, consider the following factors.

➡ Take your time when choosing clubs and dive sites, and don't let yourself be pressured into accepting something, or someone, you're not comfortable with.

➡ Don't choose a club based solely on cost. Safety should be the paramount concern; if a dive outfit cuts corners to keep prices low, you could be in danger.

➡ If you haven't dived for more than three months, take a check-out dive. This is for your own safety and all reputable operators will make this a requirement. The cost is usually applied towards later dives.

➡ If you're taking lessons, ensure that the instructor speaks your language well. If you can't understand them, you should request another.

➡ Check that all equipment is clean and stored away from the sun, and check all hoses, mouthpieces and valves for cuts and leakage.

➡ Confirm that wetsuits are in good condition. Some divers have reported getting hypothermia because of dry, cracked suits.

➡ Check that there is oxygen on the dive boat in case of accidents.

➡ If you're in Sinai, ask if the club donates US$1 per diver each day to the hyperbaric chamber; this is often a reflection of the club's safety consciousness. If you're diving in Hurghada, El-Gouna or Marsa Alam, check that the club is a HEPCA supporter. HEPCA lists all its supporting dive centres on its website (see boxed text below).

Safe Diving

The most important thing to remember when diving in the Red Sea is to use common sense. More often than not, most diving fatalities are caused by divers simply forgetting (or disregarding) some of the basic rules.

In Dahab, where the majority of accidents have occurred, drink and drugs have often played a starring role in these tragic and largely avoidable deaths. Many of those who lose their lives are experienced divers who should have known better than to go beyond safety limits or dive under the influence. Others are divers who were not experienced enough for the situations they found themselves in. The next time you complain about having to take a test dive, remember that dive clubs have a good reason to be cautious.

The following are some common-sense tips for safe diving:

RESEARCHING BEFORE YOU GO

The Chamber of Diving and Watersports (www.cdws.travel) Egyptian licensing body for dive operators. Its website provides a list of reputable dive centres in Egypt although it is unfortunately not kept up-to-date.

HEPCA (www.hepca.org) The Hurghada Environmental Protection & Conservation Association is a local NGO extremely active in promoting conservation issues throughout the Red Sea region. Their website is packed full of information on the Red Sea and a great resource for travellers.

Dive Site Directory (www.divesitedirectory.co.uk) Reviews of dive sites throughout the Red Sea.

Egypt Tourism Authority (www.egypt.travel) The official website of Egypt's Tourist board has some good basic information to get you started planning a Red Sea diving trip.

READING UP

Red Sea Diver's Guide from Sharm El Sheikh to Hurghada by Shlomo and Roni Cohen has excellent maps and descriptions of sites around Ras Mohammed, the Straits of Gubal and Hurghada. The book is unfortunately out of print but it's quite easy to find second-hand copies.

Sinai Dive Guide by Peter Harrison has detailed maps and explanations of the main Red Sea sites.

Sinai Diving Guide by Alberto Siliotti has maps and ratings of numerous sites around Sharm el-Sheikh and Ras Mohammed National Park. Although the book can be hard to source outside of Egypt, shops in Sharm el-Sheikh usually have it in-stock.

Red Sea Diving Guide by Andrea Ghisotti and Alessandro Carletti covers Egyptian sites, as well as others in Sudan, Israel and Eritrea.

The Red Sea: Underwater Paradise by Angelo Mojetta is one of the better glossy coffee-table books, with beautiful photos of the flora and fauna of Egypt's reefs.

The Official HEPCA Dive Guide produced by the Hurghada Environmental Protection & Conservation Association (HEPCA) details 46 sites with artists' drawings and a small fish index. Proceeds from the sale of this guide go towards maintaining mooring buoys on the Red Sea.

➡ Possess a current diving certification card from a recognised scuba-diving instructional agency.

➡ Be sure you are healthy and feel comfortable diving.

➡ Don't drink and dive. Alcohol dehydrates, especially in a dry climate such as Egypt's, and increases your susceptibility to decompression sickness.

➡ If you are taking prescription drugs, inform your medical examiner that you intend to go diving. Sometimes diving can affect your metabolism and your dosage might need to be changed.

➡ Dive within your scope of experience. The Red Sea's clear waters and high visibility often lull divers into going too deep. The depth limit for sports divers is 30m. Stick to it.

➡ Do not fly within 24 hours of diving. You also shouldn't climb above 300m, so don't plan a trip to St Katherine's Monastery or into the Eastern Desert mountains for the day after a dive.

➡ Be aware that underwater conditions vary tremendously from site to site, and that both daily and seasonal weather and current changes can significantly alter any site and dive conditions. These differences influence not only which sites you can dive on any particular day, but also the way you'll need to dress for a dive and the necessary dive techniques.

➡ Be aware of local laws, regulations and etiquette about marine life and the environment.

➡ Make sure you recognise your boat from the water. Some dive sites get crowded and boats can look similar from underneath. It's not unknown for divers to get left behind because they didn't realise their boat had left without them.

➡ Be insured. If something happens to you, treatment in the hyperbaric chamber can cost thousands. The most reputable clubs will make insurance a condition for diving with them. If you hadn't planned to dive before arriving in Egypt, many of the better clubs can provide insurance.

Plan Your Trip

Travel with Children

Visiting Egypt with children can be a delight. For them, seeing ancient monuments – or a camel for that matter – up close can be a fantasy made real. For you, the incredibly warm welcome towards young ones can smooth over many small practical hassles.

Best Regions for Kids

Cairo

Intensely crowded Cairo isn't obviously kid-scale, but kids may delight in finding exotic trinkets in the souq. In mosques, they're welcome to roam barefoot on carpets (but not yell). Kids love to ride horses, or a camel, around the pyramids, or enter the deep narrow corridor that leads to the heart of a pyramid.

Upper Egypt

All of Upper Egypt, from Luxor south, is straight out of picture books: temples, camels and old-time boats. Many of the family-friendly hotels have pools to recover in after the sightseeing and the heat.

Western Desert

The slow pace of the oases is well suited to children. Aside from in Bawiti, there's virtually no hassle, and out in the desert, kids can roll down sand dunes, find fossils and sleep in a tent.

Red Sea Coast

Plenty of beaches here, and plenty of entertainment for kids. Teens can learn to dive here, little ones can snorkel.

Egypt for Kids

Attitudes

What Egypt lacks in kiddie infrastructure such as playgrounds and nappy-changing tables, it more than makes up for in its loving attitude to little ones. In all but the finest restaurants, waiters are delighted to see kids – don't be surprised if your baby even gets passed around the place for everyone to hug and kiss, or your toddler is welcomed onto laps and fed sweets. (Yes, probably right before bedtime. Egyptians often have a different concept of 'bedtime'.)

Teenagers are less subject to this kind of attention, though their Egyptian counterparts will likely seem a bit younger and more sheltered. By adolescence, separation of the sexes is more typical, so teens should abide by grown-up etiquette when meeting Egyptians of their age.

Practicalities

Safety standards may make visitors nervous: don't expect car seats (or even seat belts, for that matter) in taxis or private cars, or child-size life preservers on boats.

Hygiene in food preparation can be inconsistent, so be prepared for diarrhoea or other stomach problems (and have a plan for when you're struck down and the kids are still raring to go). Rehydration salts, available very cheaply at all pharmacies

PLANNING

Before You Go

If they're not already, get kids reading about ancient Egypt. As a starter, Zilpha Keatley Snyder's classic fantasy *The Egypt Game* may get tweens hooked. For budding Egyptologists, the British Museum's website www.ancientegypt.co.uk is loaded with games and other material; www.greatscott.com introduces hieroglyphics.

For modern Egypt, look for *The Day of Ahmed's Secret* by Florence Parry Heide and Judith Heide Gilliland, a wonderful picture book set in one of Cairo's poor neighbourhoods. Teens may like *Aunt Safiyya and the Monastery* by Bahaa' Taher; *Life Is More Beautiful than Paradise* by Khaled al-Berry; or *I Want to Get Married!* by Ghada Abdel Aal.

Also make sure children are up-to-date with routine vaccinations, and discuss possible travel vaccinations with your doctor well before departure.

What to Pack

Stock up your first-aid kit, pack good sunhats and don't skimp on the sunscreen. For infants, you'll want a sling or back carrier – strollers will get you nowhere. Bring your own car seat if travelling by car.

(ask for Rehydran), can be a life-saver, as children can lose fluid rapidly in Egypt's hot, dry climate.

Keep kids away from stray animals, which can spread disease – street cats in particular are everywhere and liable to scratch if approached.

In resort towns formula is readily available, as are disposable nappies, but these can be hard to find in out-of-the-way places. High chairs are often available in better restaurants. Babysitting facilities are usually available in top-end hotels. Nutritious snacks such as peanuts, sesame-seed bars, dried fruit and dates are common; stock up for outings, though, as it's possible to wind up somewhere with no other services than someone selling Coke and potato chips.

If you need more enticements during your trip, stop by the bookshop in any five-star hotel – they're usually stocked with good Egypt-themed books and toys.

For more practical advice, pick up a copy of Lonely Planet's *Travel with Children,* written by a team of parent-authors.

Children's Highlights

There's plenty more to do in Egypt than look at pyramids and ride camels – though these are pretty fun too. Here are some tips for child-friendly fun in the desert, on the water and at some ancient sites.

Desert Life

- **White Desert** Bundle into a jeep for a Western Desert excursion, especially the otherworldly terrain of the White Desert. (p284)
- **Siwa** Siwa's mellow atmosphere is perfect for kids, though the bus ride is very long. Once there, they can dive-bomb into springs and graze on fresh dates. (p292)
- **Camel market** Getting to the Birqash camel market can be an adventure in itself. Once there, older kids will be awed, especially budding photographers, although the way the animals are treated can be upsetting. And little ones are likely to be a liability, given the camels' propensity to bolt in unexpected directions. (p160)
- **Wadi al-Hittan** How did a whale wind up in the desert? Find out in Wadi al-Hittan, where fossils are set in the sand. Trips here often include sandboarding on nearby dunes. (p155)

Ancient & Awesome

- **Giza** Older children will be astounded to enter the Great Pyramid of Khufu at Giza – though test for a tendency for claustrophobia beforehand. (p123)
- **Egyptian Museum** Devise a virtual treasure hunt for children at the Egyptian Museum. Can they find King Tut's wig box? How many miniature oarsmen does it take to row a miniature boat? Where are the baboon mummies? (p132)

➡ **Mummies** Children are fascinated by mummies, so visit the Royal mummy room at the Egyptian Museum in Cairo, or learn all about the processes at the Mummification Museum in Luxor. (p196)

➡ **Pharaohs** Let them feel like Tintin uncovering the mysteries of the pharaohs at the Tombs of the Nobles (p246) or the Valley of the Kings (p199).

➡ **Bibliotheca Alexandrina** At the Bibliotheca Alexandrina , bookworms can inspect antique manuscripts, while science fans can explore the science museum. And everyone loves the planetarium. (p313)

All Aboard!

➡ **Feluccas** Whether you go for an evening in Cairo or a multiday trip in Upper Egypt, a felucca ride is an excellent place to play pirate. (p30)

➡ **Trains** Egypt's trains are seldom crowded in 1st class, making a trip into the Delta region – perhaps to Tanta, famous for its sweets – a low-stress half-day out.

➡ **Boats** On a Friday, join Egyptian families on the boat to Qanater, the Nile Barrages just outside of Cairo.

➡ **Pick-up trucks** Travel in local pick-up trucks in the smaller towns: teens can hang onto the outside like locals do.

➡ **Bikes** Hop on a bike on Luxor's west bank – it's a great way to catch whatever breeze there is.

➡ **Trams** Ride the tram in Alexandria from end to end for a cheap, low-stress view of the city.

➡ **Horses** Ride a horse at sunset by the Pyramids of Giza, or on the west bank in Luxor. Many stables have helmets in all sizes.

On the Water

➡ **Snorkelling** Snorkelling in the Red Sea is a dazzling introduction to the underwater world. Seek out sites – in Sharm and el-Quseir for instance – where kids can drift along the side of a reef, rather than directly over it.

➡ **Shipyards** The Alexandria ship yards are where boats of all sizes get worked on. Ask aspiring captains which they'd like to helm. Round it out with a visit to the fish market, then dinner at one of many family-friendly restaurants.

➡ **Freighters** For shipping on an even larger scale, stop in Port Said and watch the massive freighters go through the Suez Canal.

Regions at a Glance

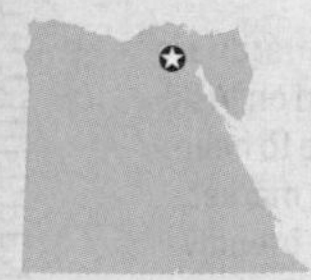

Cairo

Entertainment
History
Shopping

People Watching

Cairo, the very model of a modern megalopolis, is perfect for watching the human parade at night. Hit the town to see belly dancers in a dive such as Palmyra or a luxury-hotel cabaret, embark on a Downtown bar crawl or find some live music.

More than Pyramids

The Egyptian Museum is so crammed with thrilling artefacts that it's a destination in itself. Fast-forward through time to visit the early churches in Coptic Cairo, or stroll through picturesque Islamic Cairo, with its awesome mosques and palaces.

Souqs & Boutiques

Heaving with commerce for more than a millennium, the souq of Khan al-Khalili is a great browse. If nothing strikes your fancy there, try some of the city's many boutiques for stylish souvenirs, from vintage movie posters to leather-bound books.

p54

Cairo Outskirts & the Delta

Ancient History
Rural Life
Sufi Tradition

The Other Pyramids

The vast complex of Saqqara with Zoser's experimental step pyramid is a full-day outing from Cairo. Dedicated Egyptomaniacs can also visit Tanis, set between lush fields and desert.

Oases & Farms

Just an hour from Cairo is the semi-oasis of Al-Fayoum, where the arts colony of Tunis harbours ceramicists and other creative types. In the fertile Nile Delta, there are few tourist sites, but the countryside is lush.

Sufi Tradition

The birthday of 13th-century religious leader al-Sayyed Ahmed al-Badawi draws up to a million people each year to the town of Tanta.

p142

Nile Valley: Beni Suef to Qena

Ancient History
Coptic Heritage
Urban Charm

Temples & Tombs

A travel advisory currently warns against travelling to most of this part of Egypt, but when it changes the temples and tombs here – such as Beni Hasan and Tell al-Amarna – are well worth visiting. Abydos and Dendara are still accessible from Luxor.

Coptic Churches

At Deir al-Muharraq, in the oldest church of the world, monks conduct Mass in the Coptic language. At the Red Monastery, near Sohag, the walls still display 4th-century frescoes.

Minya

Minya, the official gateway to Upper Egypt, is a surprisingly elegant mid-size city with faded early-20th-century architecture.

p163

Nile Valley: Luxor

Ancient History
More History
Museums

Luxor & Karnak

Luxor has the highest concentration of ancient Egyptian monuments: the astonishing temples of Karnak, and Luxor Temple, open till late for atmospheric sightseeing.

Valley of the Kings

On the west bank, it just gets better: the Valley of the Kings, of King Tut fame; the Temple of Hatshepsut, cut out of the cliffs; and, oh, the 1000-tonne Colossi of Memnon just standing by.

Luxor Museum

Luxor Museum has an excellent and beautifully displayed collection of finds from nearby temples – including two royal mummies, displayed unwrapped. Follow up with a trip to the Mummification Museum, which explains the whole process.

p183

Nile Valley: Esna to Abu Simbel

Ancient History
Rural Landscapes
Nubian Heritage

Tremendous Temples

The Temple at Edfu is one of the best preserved in Egypt, and the quarries of Gebel Silsila is where so many monuments got their start. And in the southernmost spot is the grand Ramses II temple at Abu Simbel.

Lake Nasser & Aswan

A cruise along Lake Nasser's banks reveals crocodiles and gazelles, while around Aswanthe birdwatching is exceptional, especially in winter.

Nubian Heritage

Trancelike folk music, elegant mud-brick architecture and distinctive clothing are characteristics of the unique culture in this part of Egypt.

p229

Siwa Oasis & the Western Desert

Ancient History
Wilderness
Ecotourism

Graeco-Roman Traces

Ruined garrisons hint at the lively trade routes that criss-crossed the Western Desert in Roman times. Well before that, the Oracle of Amun foretold destruction in the 6th century BC.

Wild Deserts

'Desert' doesn't convey the full variety of wild land here: soak in hot springs or cold pools, and explore the White Desert gleaming like a snow field in full moon.

Ecotourism

Few trips are lower impact than a camel safari under the stars. Round out the adventure with a stay at one of several exceptional lodges designed to integrate seamlessly with the desert landscape.

p265

Alexandria & the Med Coast

Nostalgia
Ancient History
Fun in the Sun

Alexandria Cafes

Traces of Alexandria's cosmopolitan glamour can still be found in scores of old cafes where writers Lawrence Durrell, Constantine Cavafy and others once mused.

Port-City History

The Bibliotheca Alexandrina may have opened in 2002 but its model is the ancient library that once drew scholars from all over the Mediterranean. For a portrait of the city from Graeco-Roman times on, visit the excellent Alexandria National Museum.

Fun in the Sun

Seafront pleasures here include fresh fish dinners on Alexandria's corniche and beaches strung out to the west, mobbed in summer as Egyptians escape the heat.

p304

Suez Canal

Nostalgia
Ancient History
Industry

Ismailia & Port Said

Squint just right in downtown Ismailia and Port Said, and you can almost see the pashas and European dandies who built the canal, strolling in front of the decaying French-colonial buildings.

Ancient Waterways

Before the British and French opened up the shipping channel between Africa and Asia, the pharaohs and the Persians dug waterways here. See the archaeological traces at the Ismailia Museum.

Cruise the Canal

Watch global commerce in action as giant container ships transit through the canal. In Port Said hop a free ferry to get a glimpse of the action.

p340

Red Sea Coast

Fun in the Sun
Ancient History
Wilderness

Resorts & Beach Camps

The rather concrete resort towns of Hurghada and El-Gouna are offset by simpler pleasures such as the beach camps around Marsa Alam and, if you're a kitesurfer, the windy coast at Safaga.

Historic Outposts

The Coptic monasteries of St Anthony and St Paul, the first Christian hermitages, are adorned with 13th-century wall paintings. In the photogenically crumbling port of Al-Quseir, visit an Ottoman fortress.

Eastern Desert

Tourist infrastructure in the Eastern Desert is sparse but with a guide you can trek to abandoned Roman mines, spot migratory birds and even visit a remote camel market.

p350

Sinai

History
Fun in the Sun
Wilderness

Mt Sinai

God is said to have given Moses the law here at Mt Sinai, traditionally a popular hike for religious and secular travellers alike. St Katherine's Monastery, at the base of the peak, is home to early Byzantine icons.

Beach Camps & Resorts

The beach camps between Taba and Dahab are relaxed and low-key. At the other end of the scale, Sharm el-Sheikh serves up a glitzy, international holiday scene.

Desert & Reefs

The interior of the Sinai is the place for starlit treks with Bedouin guides, while Ras Mohammed National Park is a coral wonderland.

p373

On the Road

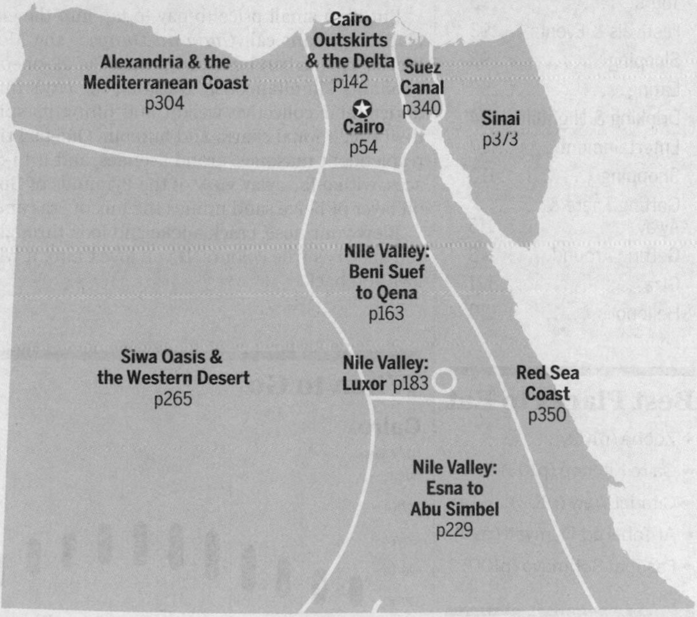

Cairo Outskirts & the Delta p142

Alexandria & the Mediterranean Coast p304

Suez Canal p340

Cairo p54

Sinai p373

Nile Valley: Beni Suef to Qena p163

Siwa Oasis & the Western Desert p265

Nile Valley: Luxor p183

Red Sea Coast p350

Nile Valley: Esna to Abu Simbel p229

Cairo

Includes ➜

Best Places to Eat

- ➜ Zööba (p102)
- ➜ Cairo Kitchen (p103)
- ➜ Citadel View (p102)
- ➜ At-Tabei ad-Dumyati (p99)
- ➜ Fasahat Soumaya (p100)

Best Places to Stay

- ➜ Hotel Longchamps (p98)
- ➜ Pension Roma (p94)
- ➜ Dina's Hostel (p94)
- ➜ Hotel Royal (p96)
- ➜ Sofitel El Gezirah (p98)

Why Go?

First, the drawbacks: Cairo's crowds make Manhattan look like a ghost town, papyrus sellers and would-be guides hound you at every turn, and your snot will run black from the smog.

But it's a small price to pay to tap into the energy of the place Egyptians call *Umm ad-Dunya* – the Mother of the World. This urban buzz is a product of 22-or-so million inhabitants simultaneously crushing the city's infrastructure under their collective weight and lifting its spirit up with their exceptional charm and humour. One taxi ride can pass resplendent mosques, grand avenues, and 19th-century palaces, with a far-away view of the Pyramids of Giza. A caked-on layer of beige sand unifies the mix of eras and styles.

Blow your nose, crack a joke and look through the dirt to see the city's true colours. If you love Cairo, it will definitely love you back.

When to Go

Cairo

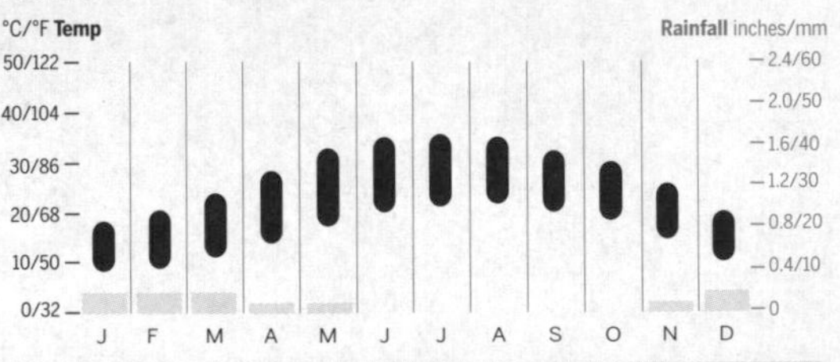

Mar-May In khamsin season the city gets choked with dust.

Jun-Aug Ramadan is a feast every night. Boiling in the daytime.

Oct-Jan Best time to visit: cooler days with sunhine, lots of cultural events.

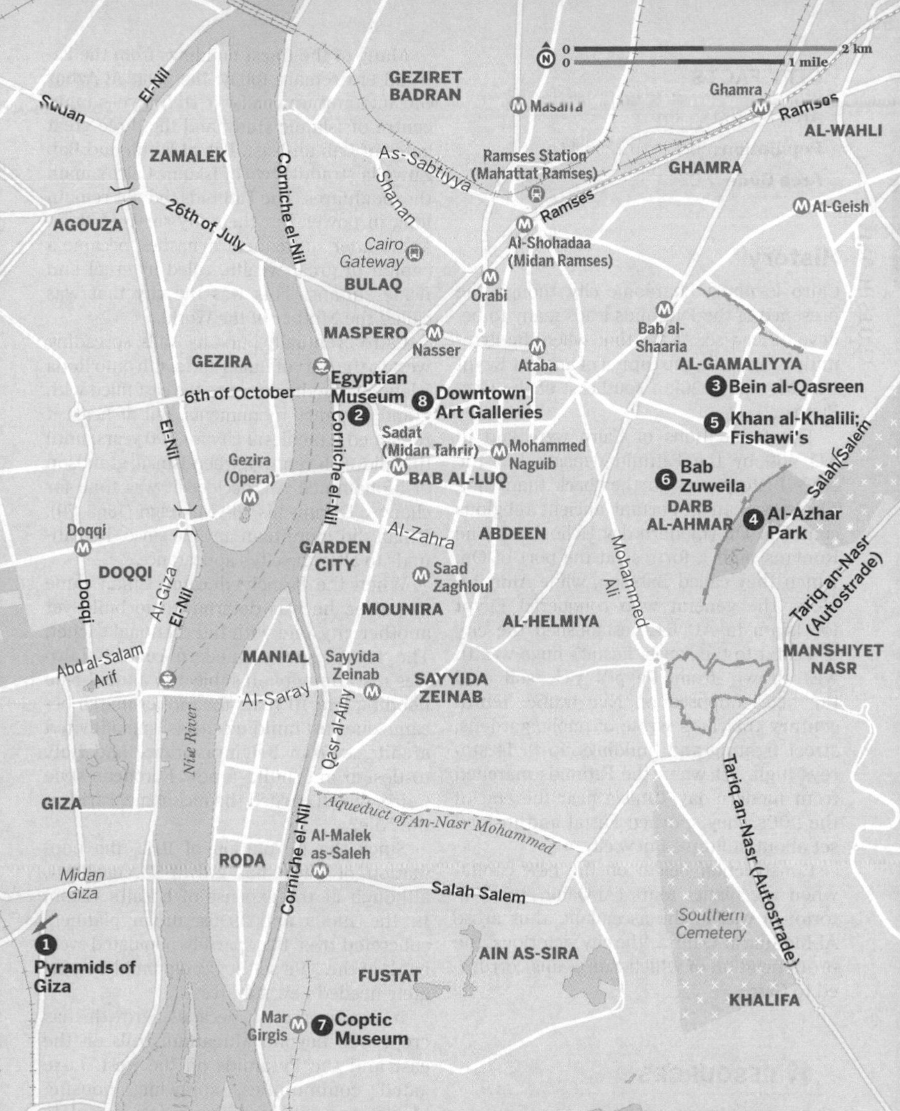

Cairo Highlights

❶ Tip your head back and gape at the **Pyramids of Giza** (p121).

❷ Give your regards to Tutankhamun and his cohorts in the **Egyptian Museum** (p132).

❸ Stroll the beautifully restored medieval street known as **Bein al-Qasreen** (p73).

❹ Escape the city noise in **Al-Azhar Park** (p80).

❺ Trawl **Khan al-Khalili** (p70) for deals, then recharge at the venerable ahwa **Fishawi's** (p106).

❻ Climb the minarets at **Bab Zuweila** (p78).

❼ Admire the beautiful syncretic artistic styles at the **Coptic Museum** (p66).

❽ Get with the beat in Downtown's **art galleries** (p67).

CITY FACTS

Area 86,369 sq km

Population more than 22 million

Area Code ☎02

History

Cairo is not a Pharaonic city, though the presence of the Pyramids leads many to believe otherwise. At the time when the Pyramids were built, the capital of ancient Egypt was Memphis, 20km southeast of the Giza Plateau.

The foundations of Cairo were laid in AD 969 by the Fatimid dynasty, but the city's history goes further back than that. There was an important ancient religious centre at On (modern-day Heliopolis). The Romans built a fortress at the port of On, which they called Babylon, while Amr ibn al-As, the general who conquered Egypt for Islam in AD 642, established the city of Fustat to the south. Fustat's huge wealth was drawn from Egypt's rich soil and the taxes imposed on Nile traffic. Tenth-century travellers wrote of public gardens, street lighting and buildings up to 14 storeys high. Yet when the Fatimids marched from modern-day Tunisia near the end of the 900s, they spurned Fustat and instead set about building a new city.

Construction began on the new capital when the planet Mars (Al-Qahir, 'the Victorious') was in the ascendant; thus arose Al-Madina al-Qahira, 'the city victorious', the pronunciation of which Europeans corrupted to Cairo.

RESOURCES

- Cairo 360 (www.cairo360.com) City listings and reviews
- Yallabina (www.yallabina.com) Movie and events listings
- Cairobserver (www.cairobserver.com) Smart articles on Cairo's urban fabric
- Egy.com (www.egy.com) 19th- and 20th-century Cairo history
- Cairo Scene (www.cairoscene.com) Contemporary lifestyle and culture

Many of the finest buildings from the Fatimid era remain today: the great Al-Azhar Mosque and university is still Egypt's main centre of Islamic study, and the three great gates of Bab an-Nasr, Bab al-Futuh and Bab Zuweila straddle two of Islamic Cairo's main thoroughfares. The Fatimids did not remain long in power, but their city survived them and, under subsequent dynasties, became a capital of great wealth, ruled by cruel and fickle sultans. This was the city that was called the Mother of the World.

Cairo eventually burst its walls, spreading west to the port of Bulaq and south onto Roda Island, while the desert to the east filled with grand funerary monuments. But at heart it remained a medieval city for 900 years, until the mid-19th century, when Ismail, grandson of Mohammed Ali, decided it was time for change. During his 16-year reign (1863–79), Ismail did more than anyone since the Fatimids to alter the city's appearance.

When the French-educated Ismail came to power, he was determined to build yet another city, one with international cachet. The future site of modern central Cairo was a swampy plain subject to annual Nile flooding. For 10 years the former marsh became one vast building site as Ismail invited architects from Belgium, France and Italy to design and build a new European-style Cairo, which earned the nickname 'Paris on the Nile'.

Since the Revolution of 1952, the population of Cairo has grown spectacularly, although at the expense of Ismail's vision. In the 1960s and 1970s, urban planners concreted over the sparsely populated west bank of the Nile so they could build desperately needed new suburbs.

In more recent decades, growth has crept well beyond Muqattam Hills on the east and the Pyramids on the west. Luxe gated communities, sprawling housing blocks and full satellite cities, complete with malls and megastores, spring up from the desert every year. Whether the desert and the economy can sustain them remains to be seen.

Cairo's slums have expanded as well. In 2011 Midan Tahrir in Downtown Cairo became the centre and the symbol of Egypt's revolution. The area has lots of graffiti, and the streets around the square have become a very energetic cultural hub.

Sights

Cairo's sights are spread all over the city, so it makes sense to do things in one area before moving on to the next – but don't try to cram too much into one day, or you'll soon be overwhelmed. The awe-inspiring but cluttered Egyptian Museum (see p130) requires at least half a day, and ideally two or three shorter visits. Khan al-Khalili and most of the medieval monuments are in Islamic Cairo, and you'll need a full day or several visits at different times of the day. Definitely allow a few hours of aimless wandering in this area (even if it comes at the expense of 'proper' sightseeing), as the back lanes give the truest sense of the city.

The Pyramids of Giza can be visited in four or five hours, but with the 10km trip to the edge of the city and back, it's inevitably a full-day outing. Coptic Cairo can be toured in a morning – made especially easy by metro access – and you'll likely soak up Downtown's atmosphere just by going to and from your hotel, or by hanging out there in the evenings.

Downtown Cairo

Though the Egyptian Museum is found here, the part of town between Midan Ramses and Midan Tahrir, which locals call Wust al-Balad, is better known for its practical offerings: budget hotels, eateries, cultural venues and a dazzling stream of window displays. (Don't rely on that shoe store/lingerie shop/prosthetic-limbs dealer as a landmark – there's another one just a block away.) Occasionally try to look away from the traffic and fluorescent-lit shops and up at the dust-caked but elegant Empire-style office and apartment buildings that drip faded glamour (or is that an air-conditioner leaking?). It's a wonderful part of town to explore – just be prepared for sensory overload and loads of perfume-shop touts.

Midan Tahrir SQUARE

(Map p62; P) Midan Tahrir (Liberation Sq) gained world renown in early 2011, when millions of Egyptians converged there to oust then-president Hosni Mubarak. On a regular day, it's just your average giant traffic circle, albeit one where half-a-dozen major arteries converge, and one that's still occasionally taken over by demonstrations. However the main reason for visiting this square is the lurid pink bulk of the Egyptian Museum.

One of the most distinctive orientation aids is the erstwhile Nile Hilton, currently being renovated as the Ritz-Carlton. The modernist slab, with its mod hieroglyphic facade, was built in 1959. Due north is the blackened shell of Mubarak's **National Democratic Party (NDP) headquarters**, torched during the revolution. Rumours have it that it will be bulldozed and turned into a garden for the neighbouring Egyptian Museum.

South of the hotel, the **Arab League Building** is the occasional gathering place of leaders from around the Middle East,

CAIRO IN...

Two Days

Start with the magnificent **Egyptian Museum** (p132), followed by a quick and delicious lunch at **Fasahat Soumaya** (p100) downtown. Make your way to the restored medieval Islamic **Bein al-Qasreen** area and browse in **Khan al-Khalili** (p70), then compare purchases over tea at **Fishawi's** (p106). Wander through the back alleys around **Darb al-Ahmar**, and finish with dinner of stuffed pigeons at **Farahat** (p102). On day two make an early start for the **Pyramids of Giza** (p121), followed by a relaxing late lunch at **Andrea** (p129). Just before sunset, stroll through **Garden City** (p64), then take a **felucca** ride. For dinner, head to a stylish restaurant in **Zamalek** (p102).

Four Days

With a couple more days, take the metro to **Coptic Cairo** (p65) to see the museum here, and save some shopping time for the tasteful **Souq al-Fustat** and the hip Egyptian boutiques of **Zamalek**. Plunge back into the maze of **Islamic Cairo** (p70) with a visit to the **Mosque of Ibn Tulun** and nearby monuments, and try to catch a Sufi dance performance at the **Wikala of al-Ghouri** (p77). Other nightlife musts: the chic weekend scene at **Vent** (p105), or the seedier one at Downtown bars and nightclubs such as **Shahrazad** (p109). Finally, treat yourself to the green respite of **Al-Azhar Park** (p80).

Cairo

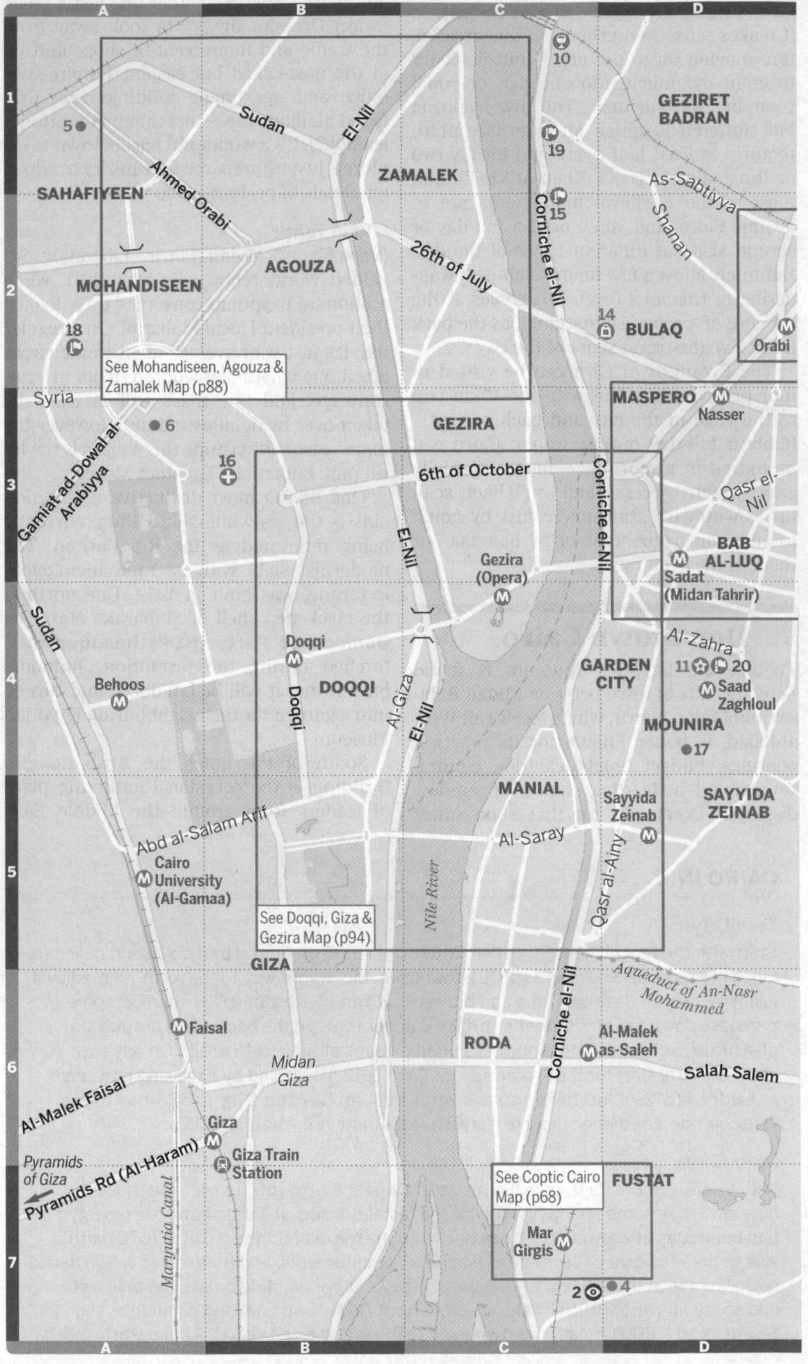

SAHAFIYEEN
MOHANDISEEN
AGOUZA
ZAMALEK
GEZIRET BADRAN
BULAQ
GEZIRA
MASPERO
BAB AL-LUQ
DOQQI
GARDEN CITY
MOUNIRA
MANIAL
SAYYIDA ZEINAB
GIZA
RODA
FUSTAT
Sudan
El-Nil
Ahmed Orabi
26th of July
Corniche el-Nil
As-Sabtiyya
Shanan
Syria
Gamiat ad-Dowal al-Arabiyya
6th of October
Qasr el-Nil
Al-Zahra
Al-Giza
Doqqi
Abd al-Salam Arif
Al-Saray
Qasr al-Ainy
Nile River
Aqueduct of An-Nasr Mohammed
Salah Salem
Midan Giza
Al-Malek Faisal
Pyramids Rd (Al-Haram)
Pyramids of Giza
Maryutia Canal
Orabi
Nasser
Sadat (Midan Tahrir)
Gezira (Opera)
Saad Zaghloul
Sayyida Zeinab
Behoos
Cairo University (Al-Gamaa)
Faisal
Al-Malek as-Saleh
Giza
Giza Train Station
Mar Girgis
See Mohandiseen, Agouza & Zamalek Map (p88)
See Doqqi, Giza & Gezira Map (p94)
See Coptic Cairo Map (p68)

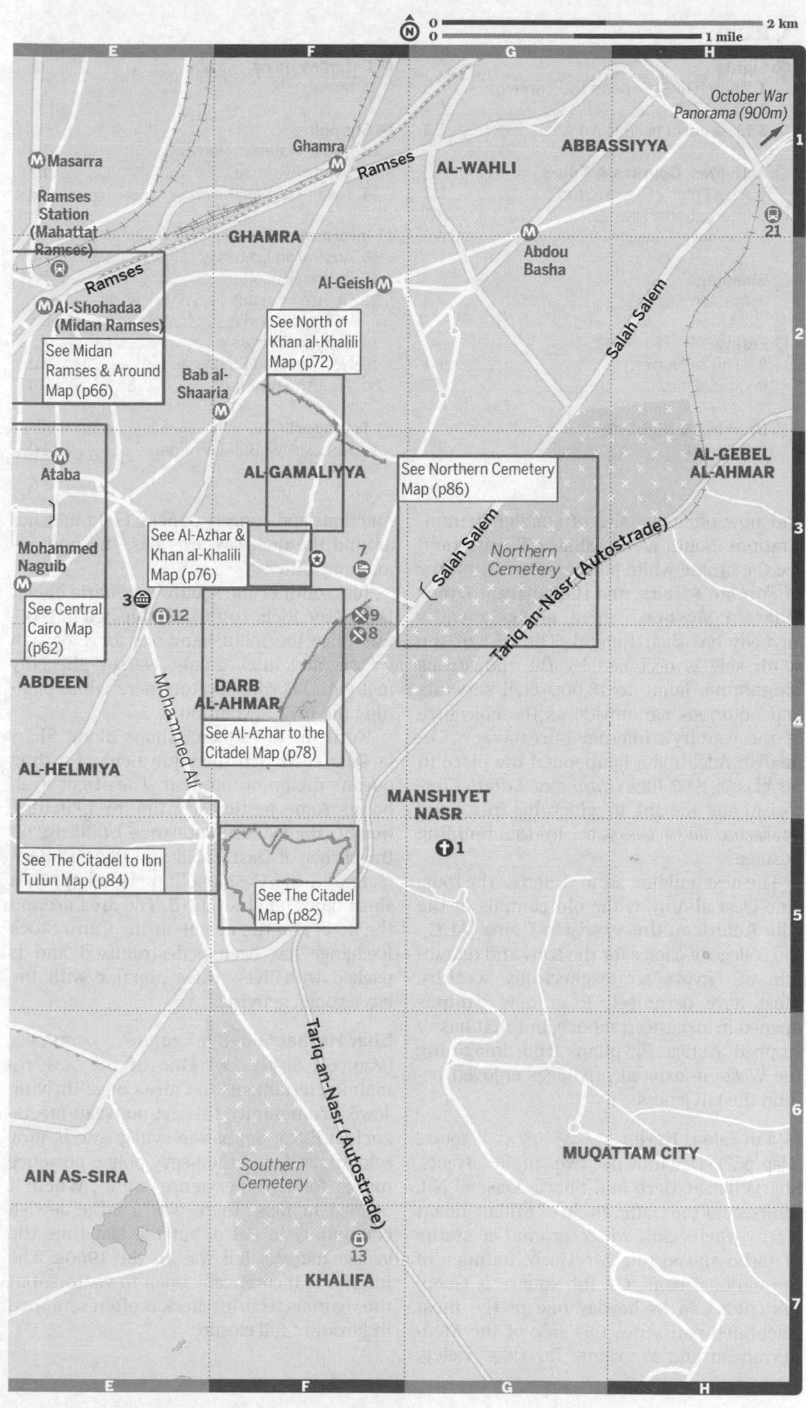
0
2 km
0
1 mile
E
F
G
H
October War Panorama (900m)
Masarra
Ramses Station (Mahattat Ramses)
Ghamra
Ramses
AL-WAHLI
ABBASSIYYA
GHAMRA
Abdou Basha
21
Ramses
Al-Geish
Al-Shohadaa (Midan Ramses)
Salah Salem
See Midan Ramses & Around Map (p66)
See North of Khan al-Khalili Map (p72)
Bab al-Shaaria
Ataba
AL-GAMALIYYA
See Northern Cemetery Map (p86)
AL-GEBEL AL-AHMAR
Mohammed Naguib
See Al-Azhar & Khan al-Khalili Map (p76)
7
Salah Salem
Northern Cemetery
Tariq an-Nasr (Autostrade)
3
12
9
8
See Central Cairo Map (p62)
ABDEEN
Mohammed Ali
DARB AL-AHMAR
See Al-Azhar to the Citadel Map (p78)
AL-HELMIYA
MANSHIYET NASR
1
See The Citadel to Ibn Tulun Map (p84)
See The Citadel Map (p82)
Tariq an-Nasr (Autostrade)
MUQATTAM CITY
AIN AS-SIRA
Southern Cemetery
13
KHALIFA
1
2
3
4
5
6
7

Cairo

Sights

1 Church of St Simeon the Tanner G5
2 Darb 1718 .... C7
3 Museum of Islamic Art E3

Activities, Courses & Tours

4 Azza Fahmy Design Studio D7
5 International House A1
6 Kalimat A3

Sleeping

7 Arabian Nights F3

Eating

8 Alain Le Nôtre F4
9 Citadel View F3

Drinking & Nightlife

10 Tamarai C1

Entertainment

11 Makan D4

Shopping

12 Abd al-Rahman Harraz E3
13 Souq al-Gomaa F7
14 Wikalat al-Balah D2

Information

15 Australian Embassy C2
16 Badran Hospital B3
17 Centre Français de Culture et de Coopération D4
18 Kenyan Embassy A2
19 New Zealand Embassy C1
20 Turkish Embassy D4

Transport

21 Abbassiyya Bus Terminal H1

and now often the site of smaller demonstrations. South across Sharia Tahrir you'll see the ornate white palace of the **Ministry of Foreign Affairs**, and the adjacent **Omar Makram Mosque**, where anybody who's anybody has their funeral. The rest of the south side is occupied by the monstrous **Mogamma**, home to 18,000 civil servants and notorious nationwide as the epicentre of the country's infernal bureaucracy. Comedian Adel Imam lampooned the place in his classic 1992 film *Irhab wal-Kabab* (Terrorism and Kabab), in which his frustrated character takes everyone in the building hostage.

The next building around, across the four-lane Qasr al-Ainy, is the old campus of the elite **American University in Cairo** (AUC), the college of choice for the sons and daughters of Egypt's stratospherically wealthy. Most have decamped to a new campus opened in an eastern suburb, but that hasn't stopped average Egyptians from imagining the Western-inspired privileges enjoyed behind the tall fences.

Midan Talaat Harb — SQUARE

(Map p62) Downtown's two main streets, Sharia Talaat Harb and Sharia Qasr el-Nil, intersect at the traffic circle of Midan Talaat Harb, where cars whizz around a statue of tarboosh-sporting Mr Harb, founder of the national bank. On the square is Groppi's (p106), in its heyday one of the most celebrated patisseries this side of the Mediterranean and *the* venue for ritzy society functions and concert dances. Gold mosaics around the doorway are, alas, the only remaining glitter.

Just south of the square on Sharia Talaat Harb, Café Riche (p100), established in 1908, was once the main hang-out for Egyptian writers and intellectuals. Nasser allegedly met with his collaborators here while planning the 1952 Revolution.

North of the square, shops along Sharia Qasr el-Nil sell the equivalent of a drag queen's dream of footwear. The street itself boasts some particularly fine architecture, notably the **Italian Insurance building**, on the corner of Qasr el-Nil and Sharia Sherifeen, and the Cosmopolitan Hotel (p97), a short block off Qasr el-Nil. The area around the hotel and the neighbouring Cairo Stock Exchange has been pedestrianised and is packed with lively cafes popular with the city's young activists.

Shar Hashamaim Synagogue — SYNAGOGUE

(Map p62; Sharia Adly) One of the few remaining testaments to Cairo's once-thriving Jewish community, this art-nouveau-meets-ancient-Egypt Sephardic synagogue is now seldom used, and the heavy police presence makes for a rather tense scene. When it opened in 1899, there was a large Jewish community in Cairo, but the last time the synagogue was full was in the 1960s. The interior is theoretically open to visitors, but the rigorous security check is often scrapped in favour of full closure.

Abdeen Palace MUSEUM

(Qasr Abdeen; Map p62; ☎2391 0042; www.abdeenmuseum.gov.eg/english/history.asp; Midan al-Gomhuriyya; adult/student E£20/10; ⏰9am-2pm Sat-Thu; P) Worth visiting if you're in the area, Abdeen Palace has a remarkable story. It is partially open to visitors as a military museum that also displays a rather tedious assortment of gifts to various Egyptian presidents. Enter the museum at the back (east) side.

Begun in 1863, the palace was a centrepiece of Khedive (Viceroy) Ismail's plan for a modern Cairo, inspired by Paris' then-recent makeover; the khedive even called in mastermind French planner Baron Haussmann as a consultant. He wanted the palace finished for the 1869 opening of the Suez Canal, to impress visiting dignitaries, but its 500 rooms weren't completed until 1874. It was the royal residence until the monarchy was abolished in 1952.

Midan Ataba SQUARE

(Map p62; P) This traffic-clogged area of park, markets and transit hub is the transition point from European-built Cairo, particularly its theatre and entertainment district, to the medieval Cairo of Saladin (Salah ad-Din), the Mamluks and the Ottomans. You'll likely find yourself at the Midan because it's a convenient walk from here to Islamic Cairo.

On the southwest side of Midan Ataba, past the flyovers, the domed **main post office** has a pretty courtyard. A window immediately on your right is where you buy tickets to the neighbouring **Postal Museum** (Map p62; ☎2391 0011; 2nd fl, Midan Ataba; admission E£2; ⏰8am-3pm Sun-Fri), a beautifully maintained collection of stamps, uniforms and even tiny scale models of great post offices throughout Egypt.

RAMSES' COLOSSUS

The eponymous Ramses, a multistorey Pharaonic colossus of red granite, stood on Midan Ramses, amid the traffic, until 2006, when he was removed, with much complex machinery, road closures and some emotion. He now stands swaddled in plastic wrap on the edge of the desert north of the city, waiting to stand sentry at the yet-to-be-opened Grand Egyptian Museum (p138), no doubt missing his old view over the action.

Just off Midan Ataba is Ezbekiyya. By night the crowded stalls of the Ezbekiyya Book Market (p110) are busy with browsers. By day **Ezbekiyya Gardens** (Map p62; admission E£2) are a dusty urban respite. The famous Shepheard's Hotel, the preferred accommodation of the British colonists, was once located opposite – it was destroyed by Black Saturday rioters in 1952. Next to the gardens, Midan Opera marks the site of the old opera house, which burnt down in 1971, and was rebuilt as a towering car park.

Midan Ramses

The northern gateway into central Cairo, Midan Ramses is a byword for bedlam. The city's main north–south access collides with overpasses and arterial roads to swamp the square with an unchoreographed slew of vehicles. Commuters swarming from the train station add to the melee.

Ramses Station NOTABLE BUILDING, MUSEUM

(Mahattat Ramses, Midan Ramses) Cairo's main train station, built in its current style in 1892, is an attractive marriage of Islamic

MIDAN TAHRIR

Its name translates as Liberation Sq and for more than a century it has been the heart of Cairo. Laid out in the 1860s, at the same time as the building of the Suez Canal, it was originally known as Ismailia Sq after the khedive or ruler of the time. The Egyptian army built a sizeable barracks between the square and the Nile, occupied by British troops after their 1882 invasion, the Egyptian Museum was opened in 1902 and the American University in Cairo (AUC) in 1920. The square had been renamed Tahrir by the time of the 1952 revolution, when the barracks were replaced by the Nile Hilton (now the Ritz-Carlton), ensuring that it remained one of the city's social hubs. The square took on political significance when it became the focus of massive protests against President Mubarak, famously those that started on 25 January 2011, and against President Morsi in June 2013, both of which ended in regime change.

Central Cairo

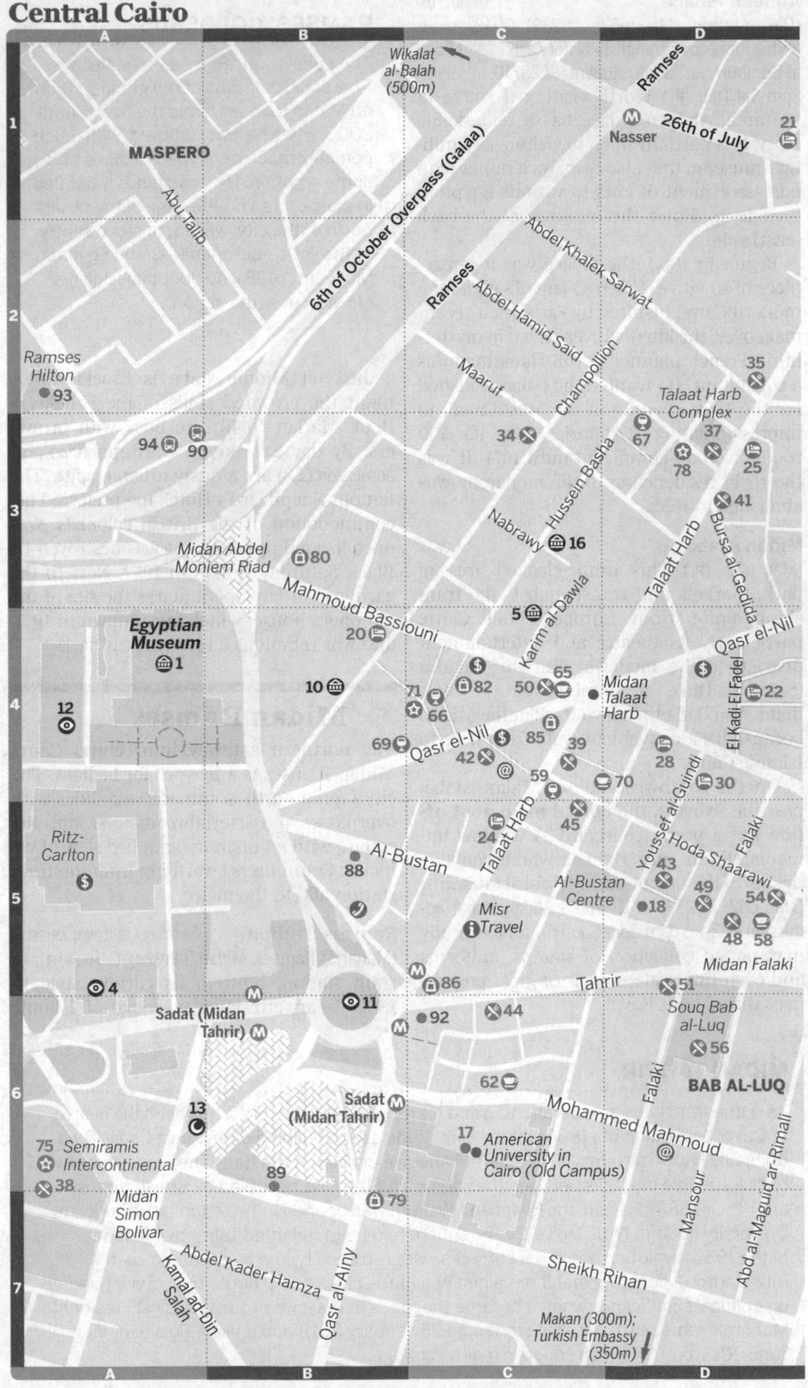

Wikalat al-Balah (500m)
Ramses
Nasser
26th of July
MASPERO
Abu Talib
6th of October Overpass (Galaa)
Abdel Khalek Sarwat
Ramses
Abdel Hamid Said
Champollion
Maaruf
Ramses Hilton
Talaat Harb Complex
Hussein Basha
Nabrawy
Talaat Harb
Bursa al-Gedida
Midan Abdel Moniem Riad
Mahmoud Bassiouni
Karim al-Dawla
Egyptian Museum
Qasr el-Nil
Midan Talaat Harb
El Kadi El Fadel
Qasr el-Nil
Talaat Harb
Youssef al-Guindi
Falaki
Hoda Shaarawi
Ritz-Carlton
Al-Bustan
Al-Bustan Centre
Misr Travel
Midan Falaki
Tahrir
Souq Bab al-Luq
Sadat (Midan Tahrir)
BAB AL-LUQ
Falaki
Sadat (Midan Tahrir)
Mohammed Mahmoud
American University in Cairo (Old Campus)
Semiramis Intercontinental
Mansour
Abd al-Maguid ar-Rimali
Midan Simon Bolivar
Abdel Kader Hamza
Kamal ad-Din Salah
Qasr al-Ainy
Sheikh Rihan
Makan (300m); Turkish Embassy (350m)

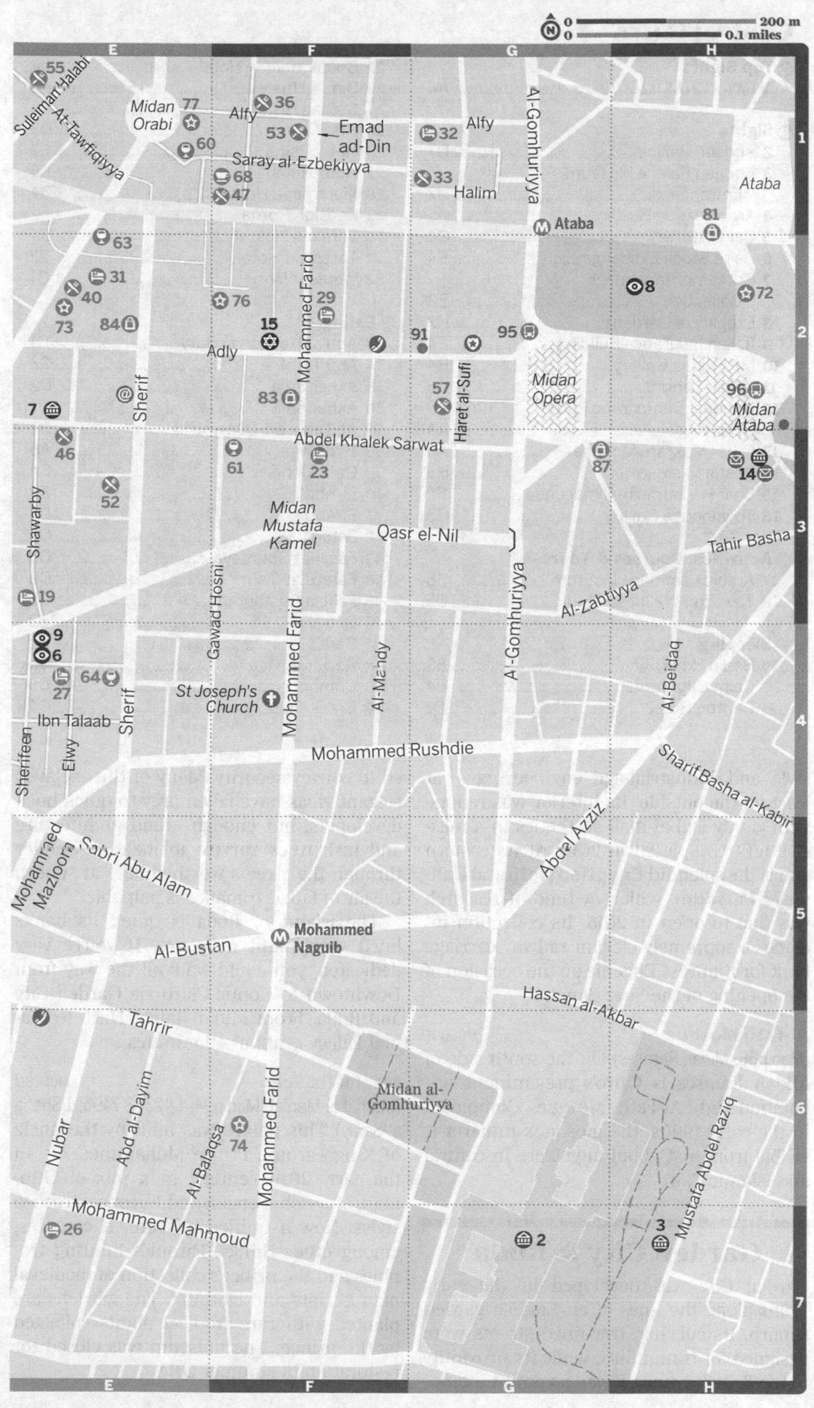

0 200 m
0 0.1 miles
Suleiman Halabi
At-Tawfiqiyya
Midan Orabi
Alfy
Emad ad-Din
Saray al-Ezbekiyya
Halim
Al-Gomhuriyya
Ataba
Adly
Mohammed Farid
Sherif
Midan Opera
Midan Ataba
Abdel Khalek Sarwat
Haret al-Sufi
Shawarby
Midan Mustafa Kamel
Qasr el-Nil
Tahir Basha
Al-Zabtiyya
Gawad Hosni
Al-Mahdy
Al-Beidaq
St Joseph's Church
Ibn Talaab
Sherifeen
Elwy
Mohammed Rushdie
Sharif Basha al-Kabir
Abdel Azziz
Mohammed Mazloom
Sabri Abu Alam
Al-Bustan
Mohammed Naguib
Hassan al-Akbar
Tahrir
Midan al-Gomhuriyya
Nubar
Abd al-Dayim
Al-Balaqsa
Mustafa Abdel Raziq
Mohammed Mahmoud
CAIRO

Central Cairo

Top Sights

1 Egyptian Museum A4

Sights

2 Abdeen Palace G7
3 Abdeen Palace Museum Entrance H7
4 Arab League Building A5
5 Cairo Atelier C4
6 Cairo Stock Exchange E4
7 Contemporary Image Collective E2
8 Ezbekiyya Gardens H2
9 Italian Insurance Building E4
10 Mashrabia Gallery B4
11 Midan Tahrir B6
12 National Democratic Party Building A4
13 Omar Makram Mosque A6
14 Postal Museum H3
15 Shar Hashamaim Synagogue F2
16 Townhouse Gallery C3

Activities, Courses & Tours

17 Arabic Language Institute C6
18 Tawazon Wellness Studio D5

Sleeping

19 Berlin Hotel E3
20 Cairo City Center B4
21 Carlton Hotel D1
22 Cosmopolitan Hotel D4
23 Dina's Hostel F3
24 Golden Hotel C5
25 Hotel Luna D3
26 Hotel Osiris E7
27 Hotel Royal E4
28 Meramees Hostel D4
29 Pension Roma F2
30 Sara Inn Hostel D4
31 Talisman Hotel E2
32 Windsor Hotel G1

Eating

33 Abu al-Hassan al-Haty G1
34 Abu Tarek C3
35 Akher Sa'a D2
36 Akher Sa'a F1
37 At-Tabei ad-Dumyati D3
38 Bird Cage A6
39 Café Riche C4
40 El-Abd E2
41 El-Abd D3
42 Estoril C4
43 Fasahat Soumaya D5
44 Fatatri at-Tahrir C6
45 Felfela Restaurant C5
46 Gad E3
47 Gad F1
48 Gad D5
49 Gomhouriya D5
50 Greek Club C4

style and industrial-age engineering – at least on the outside. Its interior was redone with gaudy Dubai-mall aesthetics in a massive refit completed in 2014. At its eastern end is the splendid **Egyptian National Railways Museum**, which at time of research was due to open in 2015. Its collection includes a supremely elegant railway carriage built for Empress Eugénie on the occasion of the opening of the Suez Canal.

Al-Fath Mosque MOSQUE

(Map p66; Midan Ramses) On the south side of Midan Ramses is Cairo's pre-eminent orientation aid, Al-Fath Mosque. Completed in the early 1990s, the mosque's minaret is visible from just about anywhere in central and Islamic Cairo.

Garden City & Roda

Garden City was developed in the early 1900s along the lines of an English garden suburb. Its curving, tree-lined streets were designed for tranquillity, while its proximity to the British embassy was no doubt intended to convey security. Many of the enclave's elegant villas have fallen prey to quick-buck developers, but enough grand architecture and lush trees survive to make a wander through the streets worthwhile – at sunset, the air of faded romance is palpable.

The island of Roda is quiet, its banks lined with plant nurseries. If you're very dedicated, you could walk all the way from Downtown to Coptic Cairo via Garden City and Roda. From Midan Talaat Harb to Manial Palace is about 40 minutes.

Manial Palace MUSEUM

(Mathaf al-Manial; Map p94; ☎ 2368 7495; 1 Sharia al-Saray) This palace was built by the uncle of King Farouk, Prince Mohammed Ali, in the early 20th century, in a mix of Ottoman, Moorish, Persian and European rococo styles. Now a quirky museum, it contains, among other things, Farouk's hunting trophies and the prince's collection of medieval manuscripts and clothing. The gardens are planted with rare tropical plants collected by the prince. The museum was closed for restoration in summer 2014.

Umm Kolthum Museum & Monastirli Palace MUSEUM

(Map p68; 2363 1467; Sharia al-Malek as-Salih, Roda; adult/student E£6/3; 9am-4pm) Set in a peaceful Nileside garden, Monastirli Palace was built in 1851 for an Ottoman pasha (provincial governor) whose family hailed from Monastir, in northern Greece. The *salamlik* (greeting area) that he built for public functions is an elegant venue for concerts, while the other part is the Umm Kolthum Museum, a shrinelike space dedicated to the most famous Arab diva.

The singer's signature rhinestone-trimmed glasses and glittery gowns are hung under spotlights, and you can listen to her music and watch a short biographical film, from the beginning when she performed disguised as a Bedouin boy, to her magnetic performances that brought Cairo to a standstill, to her funeral, when millions of mourners flooded the streets.

Nilometer NOTABLE BUILDING

(Map p68; Sharia al-Malek as-Salih, Roda; admission E£15; 9am-4pm) At the very southern tip of Roda, inside the Monastirli Palace compound, the Nilometer was constructed in AD 861. Like others built millennia before, it measured the rise and fall of the river, and thus predicted the fortunes of the annual harvest. The Turkish-style pencil-point dome is a Farouk-era reconstruction of an earlier one wrecked by Napoleon's troops.

If the water rose to 16 cubits (a cubit is about the length of a forearm) the harvest was likely to be good, inspiring one of the greatest celebrations of the medieval era. Any higher, though, and the flooding could be disastrous, while lower levels meant hunger. The measuring device, a graduated column, sits below the level of the Nile at the bottom of a flight of steep steps, which the guard will happily let you descend for a little baksheesh.

Coptic Cairo

A maze of ancient and modern churches and monasteries, set within the walls of the fortress of Babylon founded in 6th century BC and expanded by the Roman Emperor Trajan in AD 98, Coptic Cairo is a fascinating

Midan Ramses & Around

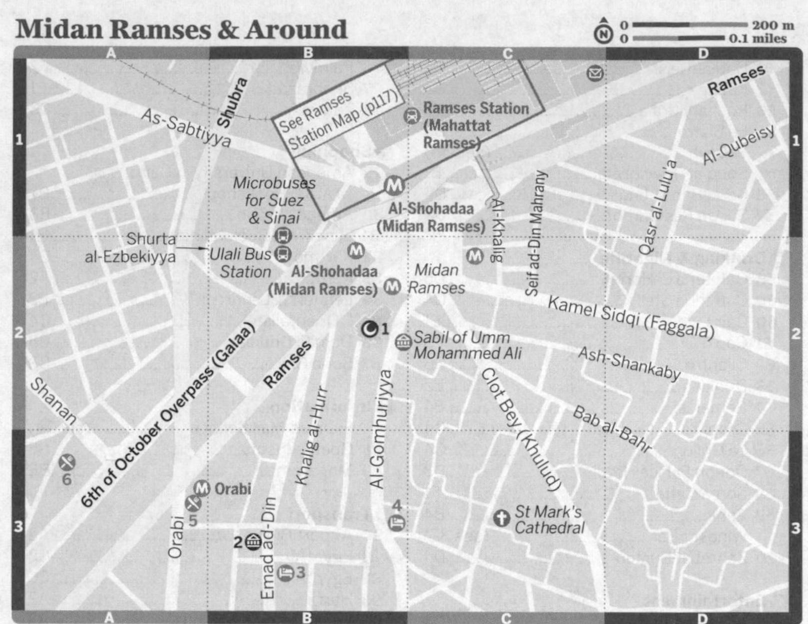

Midan Ramses & Around

counterpoint to the rest of the city, and holds a beautiful museum. You can visit the oldest church, the oldest mosque and the oldest synagogue in Cairo, as well as a dynamic contemporary arts centre and the quality shopping complex of Souq al-Fustat.

There are three entrances to the Coptic compound: a sunken staircase across from the footbridge over the metro gives access to a section of narrow cobbled alleyways, most churches and the synagogue; the main gate in the centre is for the Coptic Museum; and another doorway further south leads to the Hanging Church. At one time there were more than 20 churches clustered within less than 1 sq km.

★ Coptic Museum — MUSEUM

(Map p68; ☎2363 9742; www.coptic-cairo.com/museum; 3 Sharia Mar Girgis; adult/student E£60/30, audio guide E£10; 9am-4pm) This museum, founded in 1908, houses Coptic art from the earliest days of Christianity in Egypt up through early Islam. It is a beautiful place, as much for the elaborate woodcarving in all the galleries as for the treasures they contain. These include sculpture that shows obvious continuity from the Ptolemaic period, rich textiles and whole walls of monastery frescoes. Allow at least a couple of hours to explore the 1200 or so pieces on display.

The 2nd- to 5th-century funerary stelae from Kom Abou Billou clearly show the transition between Pharaonic and Coptic art, with the first crosses shaped like the *ankh*, key of life. The 4th- and 5th-century sculpture equally marks this transition, where Christian symbolism was influenced by Graeco-Roman mythology as well as older Pharaonic subjects. Rebirth through baptism of water is suggested through Aphrodite emerging from the waters on a seashell. Look out for the wonderful 7th- to 8th-century piece of three mice asking a cat for peace. In Egypt the depiction of animals behaving like humans dates back to 1500 BC.

Upstairs are two large rooms with exquisite 4th- to 7th-century Coptic textiles, woven and embroidered, and a room with the Nag Hammadi manuscripts, the primary source for Gnosticism, and the oldest book of psalms in the world, the Psalms of David, with two original wooden covers.

Hanging Church CHURCH

(Al-Kineesa al-Mu'allaqa; Map p68; www.coptic-cairo.com/oldcairo/church/mollaqa/mollaqa.html; Sharia Mar Girgis; ⏲ Coptic mass 8-11am Wed & Fri, 9-11am Sun) Just south of the Coptic Museum on Sharia Mar Girgis (the main road parallel with the metro), a stone facade inscribed with Coptic and Arabic marks the entrance to the 9th-century (some say 7th) Hanging Church, so named because it is suspended over the Water Gate of Roman Babylon. With its three barrel-vaulted, wood-roofed aisles, the interior of the church feels like an upturned ark, resting on 13 elegant pillars representing Christ and his apostles.

Steep stairs lead to a 19th-century facade topped by twin bell towers. In a small inner courtyard, vendors sell taped liturgies and videos of the Coptic pope, Shenouda III. The interior feels very similar to that of a mosque. The ebony and ivory inlaid screens hiding the altar show the same intricate geometric designs that are distinguishable from Islamic patterns only by the tiny crosses worked on them. One of the columns is darker than the rest; it is believed to represent Judas.

The church has 110 icons including a series of icons describing the life and torture of St George and the life of St John the Baptist, and a very sacred painting of Virgin Mary known as the Coptic 'Mona Lisa'. In the baptistry, off to the right, a panel has been cut out of the floor to reveal the Water Gate below. Still in use, it is equally crowded with tourists and parishioners who come to pray over a collection of saints' relics and an icon of Mary.

Church of St Sergius & Bacchus CHURCH

(Abu Sarga; Map p68; www.coptic-cairo.com/oldcairo/church/sarga/sarga.html; ⏲ 8am-4pm) This is the oldest church inside Coptic Cairo's walls, built in the 11th century with 4th-century pillars. It honours the Roman soldiers Sergius and Bacchus, who were martyred in Syria for their Christian faith in AD 296. It is built over a cave where Joseph, Mary and the infant Jesus are said to have taken shelter after fleeing to Egypt to escape persecution from King Herod of Judea, who had embarked upon a 'massacre of the first born'.

Abu Sarga is based on a basilican structure with a nave and two side aisles. The nave is defined by 12 columns, 11 in white marble and one in red granite, with some showing traces of images of saints. The church houses some great icons representing the life of Christ, various saints and

DOWNTOWN ARTS

Cairo's art scene is more active and diverse than ever, and much of the action is Downtown. In addition to these arts spaces, the city's cultural centres often mount interesting shows, and Darb 1718 (p69) is worth a trip.

Cairo Atelier (Atelier du Caire; Map p62; ☎ 2574 6730; www.facebook.com/groups/216621056906; 2 Sharia Karim al-Dawla; ⏲ 10am-1pm & 5-10pm Sat-Thu) FREE Off Sharia Mahmoud Bassiouni, as much a clubhouse as an exhibition space.

Contemporary Image Collective (Map p62; ☎ 2396 4272; www.ciccairo.com; 4th fl, 22 Abdel Khalek Sarwat; ⏲ noon-8pm Tue-Sat) FREE Excellent photo exhibits documenting Egyptian life, plus film and photo workshops.

Mashrabia Gallery (Map p62; ☎ 2578 4494; https://www.facebook.com/mashrabiagallery; 8 Sharia Champollion; ⏲ 11am-8pm Sat-Thu) FREE A bit cramped but represents the bigger names in painting and sculpture.

Studio Emad Eddin (SEE; Map p66; ☎ 2576 3850; www.seefoundation.org; 18 Sharia Emad al-Din) FREE Rehearsal and workshop space for performing artists; check the website for events.

Townhouse Gallery (Map p62; ☎ 2576 8086; www.thetownhousegallery.com; 10 Sharia Nabrawy; ⏲ noon-9pm Sat-Wed) FREE Set amid car-repair shops, Townhouse has launched many international Egyptian artists. Its workshop space, Rawabet, across the street, hosts performances.

Coptic Cairo

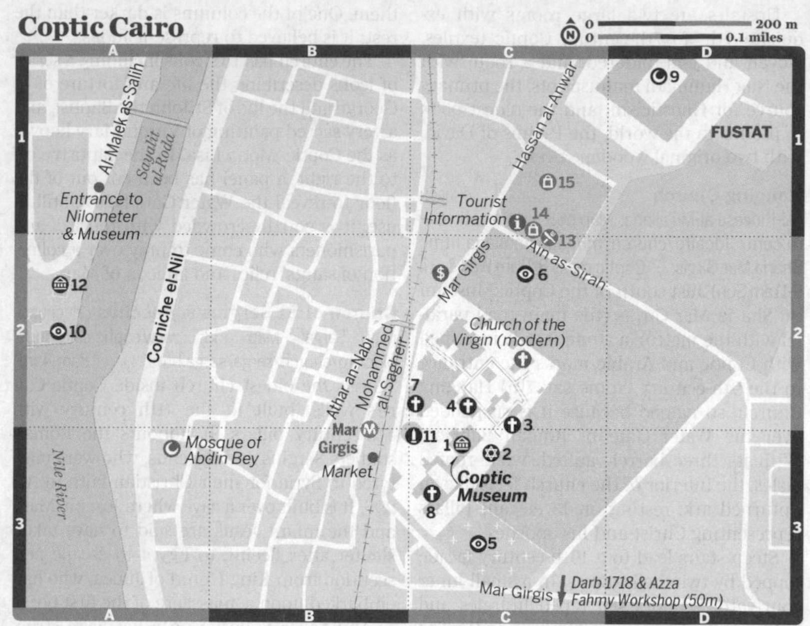

Coptic Cairo

Top Sights

1 Coptic Museum C3

Sights

2 Ben Ezra Synagogue C3
3 Church of St Barbara C2
4 Church of St Sergius & Bacchus C2
5 Coptic Cemetery C3
6 Greek Orthodox Cemetery C2
7 Greek Orthodox Monastery & Church of St George C2
8 Hanging Church C3
Monastirli Palace .... (see 12)
9 Mosque of Amr ibn al-As D1
10 Nilometer A2
11 Roman Towers C3
12 Umm Kolthum Museum & Monastirli Palace A2

Eating

13 Elfostat Tivoli C2

Shopping

14 Association for the Protection of the Environment C1
15 Souq al-Fustat C1

Virgin Mary. The cave of the Holy Family, now a crypt, is reached by descending steps in a chapel to the left of the altar (usually locked). Every year, on 1 June, a special Mass is held here to commemorate the event. To get here, walk down the central lane (Haret Al-Kidees Girgis), turning right at the T, then left as it turns; stairs lead down to the entrance, below street level.

Roman Towers MONUMENT

(Map p68; Sharia Mar Girgis) In AD 98 the Roman emperor Trajan enlarged an existing fortress here, called Babylon, likely a corruption of Per-hapi-en-on (Estate of the Nile God at On), a Pharaonic name for the area. What remains are two round towers of Babylon's western gate. These were part of riverfront fortifications and the Nile would have lapped right up against them. Emperor Trajan also reopened the canal that ran through this town connecting the Nile with the Red Sea.

Visitors can peer down around the southern tower, where excavations have revealed part of the ancient quay, several metres below street level. The Greek Orthodox Monastery and Church of St George sit on top of the northern tower.

Greek Orthodox Monastery & Church of St George CHURCH

(Map p68; Haret Al-Kidees Girgis; ⌚8am-4pm) The first doorway north of the museum gate leads to the Greek Orthodox Monastery and Church of St George. St George (Mar Girgis) is one of the region's most popular Christian saints. A Palestinian conscript in the Roman army, he was executed in AD 303 for resisting Emperor Diocletian's decree forbidding the practice of Christianity. There has been a church dedicated to him in Coptic Cairo since the 10th century; this one dates from 1909.

The neighbouring monastery is closed to visitors. The Coptic moulid (saints' festival) of Mar Girgis is held here on 23 April.

Church of St Barbara CHURCH

(Map p68; www.coptic-cairo.com/oldcairo/church/barbara/barbara.html) At the corner past Abu Sarga, the Church of St Barbara is dedicated to a martyr who was beaten to death by her father for trying to convert him to Christianity. Her supposed relics rest in a small chapel left of the altar, along with a few other saints' remains. The church houses some rare icons of St Barbara, Virgin Mary and Jesus Christ. Beyond the church an iron gate leads to the peaceful (if somewhat litter-strewn) **Coptic cemetery**.

Ben Ezra Synagogue SYNAGOGUE

(Map p68; donations welcome) FREE Just outside the walls of the Coptic enclave, the 9th-century Ben Ezra synagogue occupies the shell of a 4th-century Christian church. Tradition marks this as the spot where the prophet Jeremiah gathered the Jews in the 6th century after Nebuchadnezzar destroyed the Jerusalem temple. The adjacent spring is supposed to mark the place where the pharaoh's daughter found Moses in the reeds, and also where Mary drew water to wash Jesus.

In the 12th century the synagogue was restored by Abraham Ben Ezra, rabbi of Jerusalem. In 1890, a cache of more than 250,000 historic papers, known as the Geniza documents, was uncovered in the synagogue. From them, researchers have been able to piece together details of the life of the North African Jewish community from the 11th to 13th centuries.

Mosque of Amr ibn al-As MOSQUE

(Map p68; Sharia Sidi Hassan al-Anwar) FREE The first mosque built in Egypt, this structure was established in AD 642 by the general who conquered Egypt for Islam. On the site where Ibn al-As pitched his tent, the original structure was only palm trunks thatched with leaves. It expanded to its current size in AD 827, and has been continuously reworked since then – most recently, a wood roof was installed to mimic the original style more closely.

The oldest section is to the right of the sanctuary; the rest of the mosque is a forest of some 200 different columns, the majority taken from ancient sites. There's little else to see, but the vast space is a pleasant place to rest. To reach it, head north on Sharia Mar Girgis, beyond the Coptic compound and past Souq al-Fustat, a covered market with quality craft shops and a cafe.

Darb 1718 ARTS CENTRE

(Map p58; ☎2361 0511; www.darb1718.com; off Sharia Qasr al-Shama; ⌚10am-10pm Sat-Wed, 4-10pm Fri) This super-cool creative space aims to be a 'trampoline' for contemporary art, which gives an idea of the fun to be found here – there's usually an art show, as well as occasional movies and music performances at night. The centre also holds several workshops every week. Other organisations, among them the internationally renowned jeweller **Azza Fahmy Design Studio** (Map p58; ☎010 9012 7641; www.azzafahmydesign.com; Sharia Qasr al-Shama), have opened workshop-cum-gallery spaces here. A buzzing place in a quiet backwater of Cairo.

COPTIC CAIRO PRACTICALITIES

- Mar Girgis metro station is directly in front of the compound.
- Visitors must have shoulders and knees covered to enter churches or mosques.
- Churches celebrate Mass on Sunday, and some on Friday as well.
- Bring small money for church donation boxes.
- A few basic cafes, with restrooms, are scattered among the churches.
- For cheap street snacks, cross the metro tracks to the west side.
- Definitely check out the website of Darb 1718 for listings of events, and seek out Souq al-Fustat (p110) for excellent craft shopping.

VISITING ISLAMIC CAIRO

- Appropriate dress is not just polite but necessary if you want to enter mosques; legs and shoulders must be covered. Wear sturdy shoes that can be easily slipped off.
- Caretakers are usually around from 9am until early evening. Mosques are often closed to visitors during prayer times.
- Bring small change to tip caretakers at mosques – a bit of baksheesh for looking after shoes, pointing out details or climbing a minaret is typical. But be firm and don't pay more than you wish.
- With the exception of Sultan Hassan and Ar-Rifai, all mosques are free to enter, but some caretakers will claim an admission fee. If you're not sure, ask if there is a ticket ('fee taz-*kar*-a?') and politely refuse payment if there is none.
- In ticketed monuments, some guards will attempt to resell a previous visitor's ticket (cadged by another guard inside, assuring the visitor it's 'normal' to hand it over). If it is not torn out of the book in front of you, it's reused.

For listings check out their excellent website. To reach Darb, walk south on Sharia Mar Girgis and follow the road as it bears left. At the end of the street, turn left on Sharia Qasr al-Shama, then turn right two streets on – Darb 1718 is at the end.

Islamic Cairo

Despite the number of minarets on the skyline in this part of the city, 'Islamic' Cairo is a bit of a misnomer, as this area is not significantly more religious than other districts. But for many centuries it was one of the power centres of an Islamic empire, and its monuments are some of the most significant architecture inspired by Islam. Today it is still a more traditional part of town, the *galabeya* (men's full-length robes) still outnumber jeans; buildings and crowds press closer, and the din comes less from car traffic and more from the cries of street vendors and the clang of small workshops. Here the streets are a warren of blind alleys, and it's easy to lose not just a sense of direction but also a sense of time.

An ambitious restoration program is making over monuments as well as streets and everyday buildings, with fresh paint and turned-wood window screens. Return visitors may be shocked by the extent of change, although many projects came to a standstill with the downfall of President Mubarak. The changes that have survived have, for the most part, greatly benefited residents. Vast Al-Azhar Park, once an enormous rubbish heap, is hard to argue with as an improvement.

Midan al-Hussein & Around

Midan al-Hussein SQUARE

(Map p76) The square between the two venerated mosques of Al-Azhar and Sayyidna al-Hussein was one of the focal points of Mamluk Cairo and remains an important space at feast times, particularly on Ramadan evenings and during the moulids of Hussein and the Prophet Mohammed. The square is a popular meeting place, and the ahwas (coffeehouses) with outdoor seating at the entrance to the khan are often packed with equal parts locals and tourists.

Mosque of Sayyidna al-Hussein MOSQUE

(Map p76; Midan al-Hussein) One of the most sacred Islamic sites in Egypt, this mosque is the reputed burial place of the head of Hussein, the grandson of Prophet Mohammed. Most of the building dates from about 1870, except for the beautiful 14th-century stucco panels on the minaret. The modern metal sculptures in front are elegant Teflon canopies that expand to cover worshippers during Friday prayers. This is one of the few mosques where non-Muslims can't enter.

The death of Hussein in Karbala, Iraq, cemented the rift between the Sunni and Shia branches of Islam. It has to be said that the Umayyad Mosque in Damascus also claims this head, a Shiite relic, even though both mosques were established by Sunnis.

★Khan al-Khalili MARKET

(Map p76) Cairenes have plied their trades here since the khan was built in the 14th century, and parts of the market, such as the gold district, are still the first choice for thousands of locals. Open from early morning to sundown (except Friday morning and Sunday), although many shops are open as long as there are customers, even on Sunday.

The agglomeration of shops – many arranged around small courtyards, a sort of medieval 'minimall' – stock everything from soap powder to semiprecious stones, not to mention toy camels and alabaster pyramids. The khan used to be divided into fairly rigid districts, but the only distinct areas are now the gold sellers, the coppersmiths and the spice dealers. Apart from the clumsy 'Hey mister, look for free' touts, the merchants of Khan al-Khalili are some of the greatest smooth-talkers you will ever meet. Almost anything can be bought here and if one merchant doesn't have what you're looking for, he'll happily find somebody who does.

One of the few specific things to see in the khan, the historic ahwa Fishawi's (p106) is in an alley one block west of Midan al-Hussein. The other landmark, on the southwest side of the khan, is **Midaq Alley** (Zuqaq al-Midaq; Map p76), the setting for one of Naguib Mahfouz' best-known works. The tiny stepped alley may not be populated with the same colourful characters as the novel, but the way of life here is little changed from the author's 1940s depiction. Such is the alley's fame that the street sign is kept in the coffeehouse at the foot of the steps and produced only on payment of baksheesh.

Sharia al-Gamaliyya STREET

(Map p72) Sharia al-Gamaliyya was the heart of a trading district in medieval Cairo, and a major thoroughfare. Today it looks more like a back alley, with many of the Mamluk-era buildings obscured by webs of restorers' wooden scaffolding. One completed project: the 1408 **Mosque of Gamal ad-Din**, cleaned up to reveal a row of shops below, the rent from which contributed to the mosque's upkeep. To get there follow the street to the left of the Mosque of Midan al-Hussein.

Khanqah & Mausoleum of Sultan Beybars al-Gashankir MOSQUE, TOMB

(Sufi Monastery; Map p72; Sharia al-Gamaliyya; 9am-5pm) FREE Built in 1310, this *khanqah* is one of the city's first. It's distinguished by its stubby minaret, topped with a small ribbed dome. Thanks to a multipart 'baffled' entrance that orients the rooms away from the street, it is serene inside. Mamluk sultan Beybars al-Gashankir is entombed in a

ISLAMIC CAIRO: PLANNING A WALK

The district is quite large and packed with notable buildings, so we've subdivided it into several smaller areas:

Midan al-Hussein & Around Includes Khan al-Khalili, Bein al-Qasreen and the northern walls and gates.

Al-Azhar to the Citadel Monuments on the south side of Sharia al-Azhar, such as the Al-Ghouri buildings.

Darb al-Ahmar Between the street of the same name and Al-Azhar Park.

The Citadel to Ibn Tulun The hillside Ottoman military compound, plus the mosques of Sultan Hassan and Ibn Tulun.

Northern Cemetery East of the ring road, including the best Mamluk dome.

Each area is good for a half-day wander, and ideally you'll visit several times, perhaps once on a weekday to feel the throb of commerce and again on a Friday morning, when most shops are shut and it's easier to admire architectural details.

There are many more medieval buildings than we can identify here. For more detail, pick up the guide-maps published by the Society for Preservation of the Architectural Resources of Egypt (SPARE), on sale at the AUC Bookstore.

There are several good approaches. One is to come on foot from Downtown, so you can see the transition from the modern city; from Midan Ataba, bear east on the market street of Sharia al-Muski. (To bypass this and cut straight to the Khan al-Khalili, hail a taxi and ask for 'Al-Hussein' or hop on a microbus at Ataba.) The Bab al-Shaaria metro stop deposits you on the northwest edge of the medieval city – walk due east on Sharia Emir al-Guyush al-Gawani, and you'll reach the northern stretch of Sharia al-Muizz li-Din Allah.

Another strategy is to start at Al-Azhar Park, where you get a good view over the district, then exit through the downhill park gate and head north through Darb al-Ahmar.

North of Khan al-Khalili

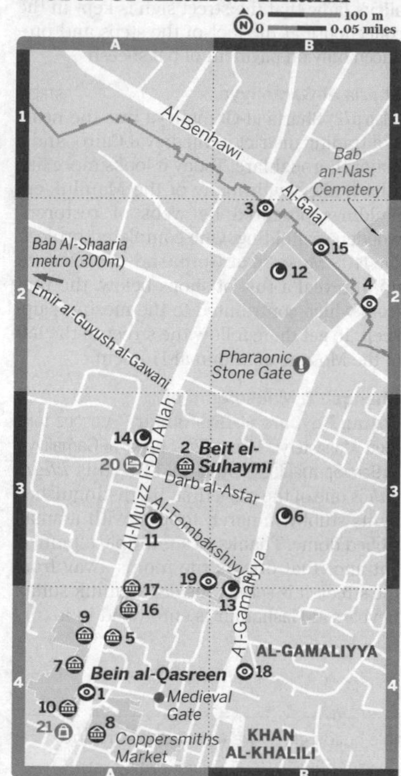

room that shimmers with black-and-white marble panelling and light from stained-glass windows. His name was excised from the building facade by order of his successor.

Wikala al-Bazara ARCHITECTURE

(Map p72; Sharia al-Tombakshiyya; adult/student E£20/10; 8am-5pm) This is one of about 20 remaining wikala (merchants' inn) in the medieval city, down from about 360 in the 17th century, when this one was built. All were built to the same plan: storerooms and stables surrounding a courtyard, with guestrooms for traders on the upper floors. Heavy front gates (check out the inlaid-wood door lock, and the anachronistic Lancashire fire badge) protected the merchandise at night. Climb up to the roof for the view.

Sharia al-Muski STREET

(Map p76) Congested and fabulous, the market street known as Sharia al-Muski begins in the khan (where it's formally called Sharia Gawhar al-Qaid) and runs parallel to Sharia al-Azhar to Midan Ataba. It's the 'real life' counterpoint to Khan al-Khalili's touristy maze, lined with carts selling cheap shoes, plastic toys, fireworks, bucket-sized bras and some truly shocking lingerie.

Sharia al-Muizz li-Din Allah STREET

(Map p76) Sharia al-Muizz, as it's usually called, named after the Fatimid caliph who conquered Cairo in AD 969, was Cairo's grand thoroughfare, once chock-a-block with storytellers, entertainers and food stalls. The part of Sharia al-Muizz just north

North of Khan al-Khalili

Top Sights
1 Bein al-Qasreen ... A4
2 Beit el-Suhaymi ... A3

Sights
3 Bab al-Futuh ... B2
4 Bab an-Nasr ... B2
5 Egyptian Textile Museum ... A4
6 Khanqah & Mausoleum of Sultan Beybars al-Gashankir ... B3
7 Madrassa & Mausoleum of An-Nasir Mohammed ... A4
8 Madrassa & Mausoleum of as-Salih Ayyub ... A4
9 Madrassa & Mausoleum of Barquq ... A4
10 Madrassa & Mausoleum of Qalaun ... A4
11 Mosque of al-Aqmar ... A3
12 Mosque of Al-Hakim ... B2
13 Mosque of Gamal ad-Din ... B4
14 Mosque of Suleiman Silahdar ... A3
15 Northern Walls & Gates ... B2
16 Qasr Beshtak ... A4
17 Sabil-Kuttab of Abdel Rahman Katkhuda ... A4
18 Sharia al-Gamaliyya ... B4
19 Wikala al-Bazara ... A3

Sleeping
20 Le Riad ... A3

Shopping
21 King Saleh Bazaar ... A4

GRAFFITI ART

The 2011 uprising against President Mubarak was referred to as the Facebook revolution, but it was also the graffiti revolution. Street art was known in Egypt, but it had not been used for social protest. One message painted in Tahrir in 2011 read 'don't be afraid – it's only street art,' but the authorities had reason to be afraid: graffiti became a key medium for expressing dissent, especially from the time of the so-called "Mad Graffiti Weekend" in May 2011. Among the most potent images was one, on a street blocked by the security forces, which showed the street as it looked before being blocked.

Graffiti is still a popular way to express dissent against the government, but the authorities are now quick to take action and most graffiti is quickly painted over. So it is impossible to point to any one location, but everywhere in Cairo, particularly in the downtown area and around Sharia Mohammed Mahmoud, you will see it. And if you miss it, you could look in Mia Grondahl's *Revolution Graffiti*, or Basma Hamdy's *Walls of Freedom*. Some of the best graffiti artists now show their work worldwide.

of Khan al-Khalili's gold district is known as **Bein al-Qasreen** (Palace Walk; Sharia al-Muizz li-Din Allah), a reminder of the great palace complexes that flanked the street during the Fatimid era. Great Mamluk complexes provide one of Cairo's most impressive assemblies of minarets, domes and striped-stone facades.

These days the street has been redone, from new pavement to the tips of the minarets of the monuments along its length. During daytime vehicle-free hours (9am-10pm), visitors may comfortably gawk at the sites without fear of being flattened by traffic. One stretch of the street is occupied by small places selling sheeshas, braziers and pear-shaped cooking pots for fuul (fava beans). Soon the stock expands to crescent-moon minaret tops, coffee ewers and other copper products, hence its more popular name, Sharia an-Nahaseen (Street of the Coppersmiths). Stroll along and admire the medieval architecture mixed with Cairo's hustle and bustle.

Madrassa & Mausoleum of as-Salih Ayyub — HISTORIC BUILDING

(Map p72; Sharia al-Muizz li-Din Allah; adult/student E£100/50, covers all the sights from Bein al-Qasreen to Bab al-Futuh; ⌚9am-5pm) This complex was built between 1242 and 1244 by the last Ayyubid sultan of Egypt, Al-Salih Najm al-Din Ayyub, who died defending Egypt against the Crusader attack that was led by Louis IX. His grandfather was the famous Salah ad-Din Al-Ayyubi, known in the West as Saladdin.

It is the first known example of a mausoleum attached to a madrassa, and it was in many ways a trendsetter for the Mamluk buildings that followed, and that can be visited further along the street. The madrassa was also the first to house all four of the Sunni legal schools. The adjoining tomb, where Sultan Ayyub resides, was built by his Turkic wife, Shagaret ad-Durr (Tree of Pearls), in 1250, well after the sultan's death, which she had concealed to keep the French crusader armies in Damietta from sensing weakness. Shagaret ad-Durr managed to defeat the crusaders, then ruled on as sultana and ushered in the Mamluk era, when the Turkic janissaries took power.

Madrassa & Mausoleum of Qalaun — HISTORIC BUILDING

(Map p72; Sharia al-Muizz li-Din Allah; adult/student E£100/50, covers all the sights from Bein al-Qasreen to Bab al-Futuh; ⌚9am-5pm) Built in just 13 months, the 1279 Madrassa & Mausoleum of Qalaun is both the earliest and the most splendid of the three buildings on this street. The mausoleum, on the right, is a particularly intricate assemblage of inlaid stone and stucco, patterned with stars and floral motifs and lit by stained-glass windows. The complex also includes a *maristan* (hospital), which Qalaun ordered built after he visited one in Damascus, where he was cured of colic.

The Arab traveller and historian Ibn Battuta, who visited Cairo in 1325, was impressed that Qalaun's hospital contained 'an innumerable quantity of appliances and medicaments'. He also described how the mausoleum was flanked by Quran reciters day and night chanting requiems for the dead within.

Madrassa & Mausoleum of An-Nasir Mohammed HISTORIC BUILDING
(Map p72; Sharia al-Muizz li-Din Allah; adult/student E£100/50, covers all the sights from Bein al-Qasreen to Bab al-Futuh; ⌚9am-5pm) Sultan an-Nasr ('the Victor'), was both despotic and exceedingly accomplished. His madrassa was built in 1304 in part with a Gothic doorway An-Nasir plundered from a church in Acre (now Akko, Israel) after he and his army ended Crusader domination there in 1290. Buried in the mausoleum (on the right as you enter but usually locked) is An-Nasr's mother and his favourite son; the sultan himself is next door in the mausoleum of his father, Qalaun.

Sabil-Kuttab of Abdel Rahman Katkhuda HISTORIC BUILDING
(Map p72; Sharia al-Muizz li-Din Allah; adult/student E£100/50, covers all the sights from Bein al-Qasreen to Bab al-Futuh) The Sabil-Kuttab of Abdel Rahman Katkhuda is one of the iconic structures of Islamic Cairo, depicted in scores of paintings and lithographs. Building this fountain-school combo was an atonement for sins, as it provided two things commended by the Prophet: water for the thirsty and enlightenment for the ignorant. This one was built in 1744 by an emir notorious for his debauchery. There's nice ceramic work inside.

Qasr Beshtak HISTORIC BUILDING
(Map p72; Sharia al-Muizz li-Din Allah; ⌚open periodically) At the Sabil-Kuttab of Kathkuda, take the little alleyway that leads to Qasr Beshtak (Palace of Amir Beshtak), a rare example of 14th-century domestic architecture, originally five floors high. It has been nicely restored and is open periodically as a concert venue. Inside is a small shop selling classical Arabic music and other items.

Egyptian Textile Museum MUSEUM
(Map p72; Sharia al-Muizz li-Din Allah; adult/student E£20/10 ; ⌚9am-4.30pm) The only one of its kind in the Middle East, this interesting museum features textiles from ancient Egypt and the Roman, Coptic and Islamic eras. The collection starts at the very beginning, with Pharaonic diapers, and moves on through beautifully embroidered Coptic tunics and great embroidered *qiswat* (the panels that adorn the Kaaba in Mecca). It's a small museum, but well worth a peek for anyone with an affinity for weaving and fabric.

Mosque of al-Aqmar MOSQUE
(Map p72; Sharia al-Muizz li-Din Allah) FREE This petite mosque, the oldest in Egypt with a stone facade, was built in 1125 by one of the last Fatimid caliphs. Several features appear here that became part of the mosque builders' essential vocabulary, including muqarnas vaulting (stalactite-like decorative stone) and the ribbing in the hooded arch. If you climb to the roof, you'll have a great view along Bein al-Qasreen.

Beit el-Suhaymi HISTORIC BUILDING
(Map p72; Darb al-Asfar; adult/student E£35/15; ⌚9am-5pm) With its new paving stones

LOCAL KNOWLEDGE

MOHAMED ELSHAHED, CAIROBSERVER.COM

Some of urban-planning expert Elshahed's favourite places in Cairo:

Green space Giza Zoo has a deservedly bad reputation for animal conditions, but it's a gem of 19th-century placemaking, with a wonderful lion's house, a Gustav Eiffel bridge and a Japanese pavilion.

Mosque Al-Hakim Mosque is one of the oldest in Cairo, but its pure form and all-white wash gives it a modern feel. One of the most calming spaces to relax or even read a book. It feels very secular, because of the mix of people.

Church St Joseph's Cathedral was built in 1909 in a Florentine style, as a little piece of Italy in Cairo for a large Italian congregation. Another peaceful space to sit for a few minutes.

Museum Mahmoud Mukhtar Museum is a beautiful little 1960s building. The famous sculptor is buried in the basement. While you're here visit the park next door and the opera grounds, built in 1936 by father of modern Egyptian architecture, Mustafa Fahmy.

View Southern tip of Roda Island, where you can get a sweeping view of the Nile and also visit the Nilometer and the Umm Kolthum museum, and peek at the Minasterli Palace.

and elaborate *mashrabiyya* (wooden lattice screens), Darb al-Asfar alley conjures up the Middle Ages – if the Middle Ages were clean. The first few buildings you pass are part of Beit el-Suhaymi, a family mansion and caravanserai built in the 17th and 18th centuries. After going through a narrow hall, you arrive at a peaceful courtyard surrounded by grand reception halls, bedrooms, storerooms and baths.

The house has been thoroughly restored, though barely furnished (the fire extinguishers, a precaution required by the extensive new woodwork, are the most prominent item on display). As a result it can feel a bit ghostly. The changes on Darb al-Asfar have been heavily debated, as they displaced at least 30 families in the name of restoration, but it has brought some peace to this crowded area, for the residents who were allowed to stay.

Mosque of Al-Hakim MOSQUE

(Map p72; Sharia al-Galal; 9am-5pm) FREE Completed in 1013, the vast Mosque of Al-Hakim, built into the northern walls, is one of Cairo's older mosques but it was rarely used for worship. Instead it functioned as a Crusaders' prison, a stable, a warehouse, a boys' school and, most appropriately considering its notorious founder, a madhouse. The real masterpieces are the two stone minarets, the earliest surviving in the city (thanks in part to a post-earthquake restoration in 1304 by Beybars al-Gashankir).

Sultan al-Hakim, the sixth Fatimid ruler of Egypt, took the throne at the age of 11 and his tutor nicknamed him 'Little Lizard' because of his frightening looks and behaviour. His 24-year reign was marked by violence and behaviour that went far beyond the usual court intrigues; modern historians speculate he may simply have been insane. Those nearest to him lived in constant fear for their lives. He had his nicknaming tutor killed, along with scores of others. Hakim reputedly often patrolled the streets in disguise, riding a donkey. Most notoriously, he punished dishonest merchants by having them dealt with by a well-endowed black servant. His death was as bizarre as his life. On one of his solitary nocturnal jaunts up onto the Muqattam Hills, Hakim simply disappeared; his body was never found. To one of his followers, a man called Al-Darizy, this was proof of Hakim's divine nature. From this seed Al-Darizy founded the sect of the Druze that continues to this day. An Ismaili Shiite group restored the mosque in the 1980s, but with its open-plan square and spare decoration, it's not nearly as interesting as the man behind it.

> **PLAYING CHICKEN**
>
> It may sound silly, but the greatest challenge most travellers face in Cairo is crossing the street. Traffic seldom stops, so you have to trust the cars will avoid you. Our advice: position yourself so that one or more locals forms a buffer between you and oncoming traffic, then cross when they do – they usually don't mind being used as human shields. Never, ever hesitate or turn back once you've stepped off the sidewalk, and cross as if you own the road. But do it fast!

Northern Walls & Gates GATE

(Map p72) **Bab an-Nasr** (Gate of Victory) and **Bab al-Futuh** (Gate of Conquests) were built in 1087 as the northern entrances to the walled Fatimid city. They never repelled a military attack, until the French adapted them to their cannons. Napoleon's commanders took the liberty of naming Bab an-Nasr's towers after themselves – and carved their names into it. Many stones were repurposed from Pharaonic sites, and the delicate carved stone arch at Bab al-Futuh was done by Syrian workers.

Al-Azhar to the Citadel

South of Sharia al-Azhar, Sharia al-Muizz li-Din Allah continues as a market street 400m down to the twin-minareted gate of Bab Zuweila. From here, you can carry on south through Sharia al-Khayamiyya another 30 minutes to Midan Salah ad-Din and the Mosque-Madrassa of Sultan Hassan.

★ **Al-Azhar Mosque** MOSQUE

(Gami' al-Azhar; Map p76; Sharia al-Azhar; 24hr) FREE Founded in AD 970 as the centrepiece of the newly created Fatimid city, Al-Azhar is one of Cairo's earlier mosques, and its sheikh is considered the highest theological authority for Egyptian Muslims. The building is a harmonious blend of architectural styles, the result of numerous enlargements over a thousand years. The tomb chamber, located through a doorway on the left just inside the entrance, has a beautiful mihrab (a niche indicating the direction of Mecca) and should not be missed.

Al-Azhar & Khan al-Khalili

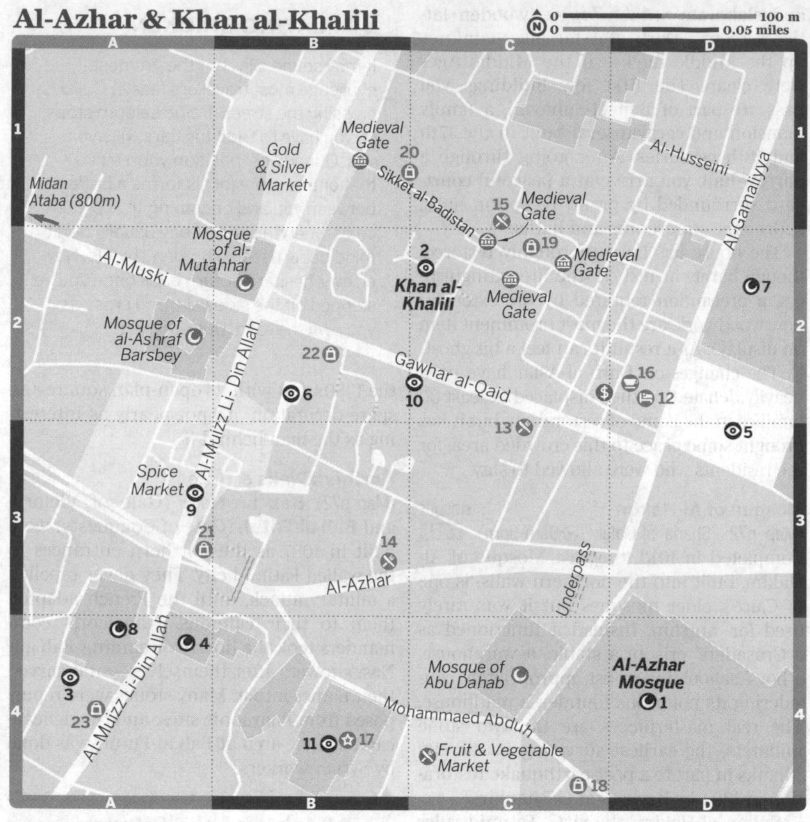

Al-Azhar & Khan al-Khalili

Top Sights
1 Al-Azhar Mosque D4
2 Khan al-Khalili C2

Sights
3 Carpet & Clothes Market A4
4 Mausoleum of Al-Ghouri A4
5 Midan al-Hussein D3
6 Midaq Alley B2
7 Mosque of Sayyidna al-Hussein D2
8 Mosque-Madrassa of Al-Ghouri A4
9 Sharia al-Muizz li-Din Allah A3
10 Sharia al-Muski C2
11 Wikala of Al-Ghouri B4

Sleeping
12 El Hussein D2

Eating
13 Al-Halwagy C3
14 Farahat B3
15 Khan el-Khalili Restaurant & Mahfouz Coffee Shop C1

Drinking & Nightlife
16 Fishawi's D2

Entertainment
17 Al-Tannoura Egyptian Heritage Dance Troupe B4

Shopping
18 Abd El Zaher C4
19 Ahmed El Dabba & Sons C2
20 Atlas B1
21 Karama A3
22 Mahmoud Abd El Ghaffar B2
23 Tarboosh (Fez) Maker A4

The central courtyard is the earliest part, while from south to north the three minarets date from the 14th, 15th and 16th centuries; the latter, with its double finial, was added by Sultan al-Ghouri, whose mosque and mausoleum stand nearby.

A madrassa was established here in AD 988, growing into a university that is the world's second-oldest educational institution (after the University of al-Kairaouine in Fez, Morocco). At one time the university was one of the world's pre-eminent centres of learning, drawing students from Europe and all over the Islamic empire. The large modern campus (due east) is still the most prestigious place to study Sunni theology.

Beit Zeinab al-Khatoun HOUSE

(House of Zeinab Khatoun; Map p78; ☎2735 7001; 3 Sharia Mohammed Abduh; admission E£20; ⊙9am-5pm) Beit Zeinab al-Khatoun is a small but interesting Ottoman-era house with a rooftop affording superb views of the surrounding minaret-studded skyline. The courtyard has a traditional ahwa or cafe, much frequented by young Cairenes. The house is on a little piazza at the end of a narrow street behind the Al-Azhar Mosque.

Across the plaza, **Beit al-Harrawi** is another fine 18th-century mansion, but its sparse interior isn't worth the entry fee. Both houses are often used as concert venues, and Beit al-Harrawi is home to the **Arabic Oud House**, a music school; at night it's often open and you can wander in for free.

Wikala of Al-Ghouri ARCHITECTURE

(Map p76; ☎2511 0472; Sharia Mohammed Abduh; adult/student E£25/15; ⊙9am-5pm Sat-Thu) Built in AD 1504 by the Mamluk Sultan al-Ghouri, this *wikala* was originally designed as an inn for traders following the caravan routes from the east and the west. The impressive stone facade has been beautifully restored. The upper rooms are artists' ateliers while the former stables were turned into craft shops. The courtyard serves as a theatre for the free Sufi dance performances by Al-Tannoura Egyptian Heritage Dance Troupe (p108).

Mausoleum of Al-Ghouri MOSQUE, TOMB

(Map p76; Sharia al-Muizz li-Din Allah; adult/student E£30/20; ⊙9am-5pm) The penultimate Mamluk sultan Al-Ghouri built his funerary complex in 1504, on both sides of Sharia al-Muizz. At the age of 78, Al-Ghouri was beheaded in Syria, and his body was never recovered. The elegant mausoleum actually contains the body of Tumanbey, his successor, hanged by the Turks in 1517. There is a weekly musical event on Sundays at 9pm, (not to be confused with the Sufi dancing at the Wikala of Al-Ghouri up the street).

Mosque-Madrassa of Al-Ghouri MOSQUE

(Map p76; Sharia al-Muizz li-Din Allah; ⊙9am-5pm) FREE On the western side of Sharia al-Muizz, opposite the mausoleum, is the second part of Al-Ghouri's funerary complex, the intimate and richly decorated mosque-madrassa. The interior reveals gilt and painted wood-panelling, panels of white and black marble, soaring ceilings and intricate geometric paving. Four *iwans* (vaulted halls) surround a small sunken courtyard. It's also possible to climb the four-storey, red-chequered minaret (for baksheesh; ignore claims of 'tickets').

Carpet & Clothes Market MARKET

(Map p76) The street between Al-Ghouri's mosque and the mausoleum, and the area around, was historically the city's silk market. While it isn't a particularly great place to buy anything, it's worth walking through the busy clothes market for its colourful atmosphere. Less than 50m south of the mosque is Cairo's last **tarboosh (fez) maker** (Map p76), who shapes the red felt hats on heavy brass presses. Once worn by every *effendi* (gentleman), the tarboosh is now mainly bought by tourists.

Sabil of Muhammed Ali Pasha ARCHITECTURE

(Map p78; Sharia al-Muizz li-Din Allah; admission E£10; ⊙8.30am-5pm) This elegant 1820 *sabil* (public fountain) was the first in Cairo to have gilded window grilles and calligraphic panels in Ottoman Turkish. It has been meticulously restored, with interesting displays about Muhammed Ali, who had the complex built to honor his son Tusun, who died of plague. Nifty details include access to the cistern below and desks in the *kuttab* (schoolroom) upstairs, which welcomed students until 1992.

Mosque of Al-Mu'ayyad Shaykh MOSQUE

(Map p78; Sharia al-Muizz li-Din Allah; ⊙9am-5pm) FREE Built into the Fatimid walls between 1415 and 1421, the red-and-white-striped Mosque of Al-Mu'ayyad Shaykh was laid out on the site of a prison where its patron Mamluk sultan had earlier languished. Its entrance portal, dripping with stalactite vaulting, is particularly grand. The enormous bronze door is thought to have been pilfered from the Mosque of Sultan Hassan.

Al-Azhar to the Citadel

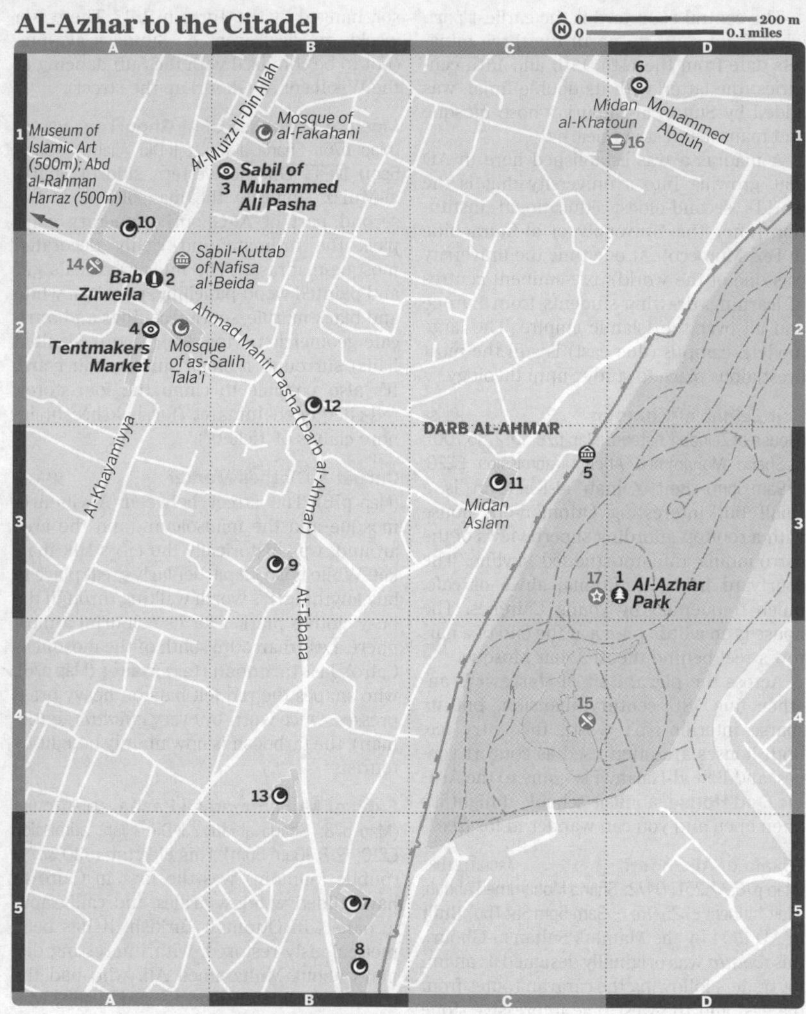

The elegant twin minarets soaring over the gate of Bab Zuweila have become one of the city's landmarks.

Bab Zuweila MONUMENT
(Map p78; Sharia al-Muizz li-Din Allah; adult/student E£20/10; ⌚9am-5pm) Built at the same time as the northern gates (11th century), beautiful Bab Zuweila is the only remaining southern gate of the medieval city of Al-Qahira. Visitors may climb the ramparts, where some intriguing exhibits about the gate's history are in place. The two minarets atop the gate offer one of the best available views of the area. In Mamluk times, the gate was the site of executions, a popular form of street theatre.

The spirit of a healing saint was (and still is) said to reside behind one towering wooden door, which supplicants have studded with nails and teeth as offerings over the centuries.

Museum of Islamic Art MUSEUM
(Map p58; ☎2390 1520; www.islamicmuseum.gov.eg/museum.html; Midan Bab al-Khalq; admission E£50/25; ⌚9am-5pm Sat-Thu, 9am-noon & 2-5pm Fri) This museum, on the edge of the

Al-Azhar to the Citadel

Top Sights

1 Al-Azhar Park D3
2 Bab Zuweila A2
3 Sabil of Muhammed Ali Pasha B1
4 Tentmakers Market A2

Sights

5 Bab al-Mahruq C3
6 Beit Zeinab al-Khatoun D1
7 Blue Mosque B5
8 Khayrbek Complex B5
9 Mosque of Al-Maridani B3
10 Mosque of Al-Mu'ayyad Shaykh A1
11 Mosque of Aslam al-Silahdar C3
12 Mosque of Qijmas al-Ishaqi B2
13 Mosque-Madrassa of Umm Sultan Sha'aban B4

Eating

14 Gad A2
15 Lakeside Cafe C4

Drinking & Nightlife

16 Coffeeshop Al-Khatoun D1

Entertainment

17 El Genaina C3

medieval city, holds one of the world's finest collections of Islamic applied art. What's on display is only a sliver of the 80,000 objects the museum owns, but the selected items are stunning, so you can easily spend a couple of hours here. Sadly the museum was heavily damaged in January 2014 in a car-bomb attack on nearby police headquarters. It was still closed for restoration at the time of research.

To the right as you enter are architectural details – frescoes, carved plaster so fine it looks like lace, an intricate inlaid-wood ceiling – and ceramics grouped by dynasty. A surprising amount of figurative work is on view, and not all of it strictly Islamic – a shard of an Ayyubid bowl shows Mary holding a crucified Christ. To the left, pieces are grouped by function and medium: medical tools, astrolabes, some breathtaking carpets, illuminated Qurans, even headstones.

The museum is 500m due west from Bab Zuweila. Coming from Midan Ataba, the museum is 700m southeast, straight down Sharia Mohammed Ali.

Tentmakers Market MARKET

(Map p78; Sharia al-Khayamiyya) The 'Street of the Tentmakers' is one of the remaining medieval speciality quarters – it takes its name from the artisans who produce the bright fabrics used for the ceremonial tents at wakes, weddings and feasts. They also hand-make intricate appliqué wall hangings, cushion covers and bedspreads, and print original patterns for tablecloths. The highest concentration of artisans is directly south after Bab Zuweila, in the covered tentmakers market.

Darb al-Ahmar

In its heyday in the 14th and 15th centuries, Darb al-Ahmar ('Red Road') and neighbouring alleys and cul-de-sacs had a population of about 250,000, and the district is still nearly as dense. It is also dense with historic monuments, most from the late Mamluk era, as the city expanded outside the Fatimid gates. As part of the Al-Azhar Park project, this neighbourhood has in parts been beautifully restored, along with various social programs to boost income in this long-poor area. It's a fascinating jumble and rewarding for an aimless wander. The historic street itself is now known as Ahmad Mahir Pasha on the north end and At-Tabana in its southern stretch.

Mosque of Qijmas al-Ishaqi MOSQUE

(Map p78; Sharia Ahmad Mahir Pasha; 9am-5pm) FREE This remarkable mosque, built in 1481 by Prince Sayf al-Din Qijmas, above a row of shops that occupy the street level, is one of the best examples of Mamluk architecture. Its plain but wonderful facade and minaret feature on the Egyptian £50 note. The craftmanship is exquisite. Note in particular the stunning multicoloured marble panel above the entrance, rich and well-preserved marble paving, beautiful stained-glass windows and a stunning decorated wooden ceiling.

Mosque of Al-Maridani MOSQUE

(Map p78; Sharia at-Tabana; 9am-5pm) FREE About 150m further on the right of the Mosque of Qijmas al-Ishaqi, this 1339 building incorporates architectural elements from several different periods: eight granite columns were taken from a Pharaonic monument; the arches contain Roman, Christian and Islamic designs; and the Ottomans added a fountain and wooden housing. Trees in the courtyard, attractive *mashrabiyya* and a lack of visitors make this a peaceful place to stop.

HOW TO BLEND IN

Even if your skin colouring allows it, it's next to impossible to 'pass' as a native Cairene. But you can look more like a resident expat, thus deflecting hustler attention onto the more obvious tourists walking behind you and leaving you free to enjoy the good things about Cairo. Here's how:

➡ Carry your stuff in a plastic shopping bag or a generic tote. Nothing screams 'tourist' like a multipocketed, zippered, heavy-duty-nylon backpack with visible water bottle.

➡ Wear impractical shoes. This is a city. Fashion counts.

➡ Cover your legs – this goes for men and women. Islamic rules aside, Egyptians have a high level of modesty, and it's clear you haven't been here long if you don't feel embarrassed to show your knees in public.

➡ Carry a copy of the *Al-Ahram Weekly* – or the Arabic *Al-Ahram*, if you want to go deep undercover.

Mosque-Madrassa of Umm Sultan Sha'aban MOSQUE

(Map p78; Sharia at-Tabana; ⌚9am-5pm) FREE With its towering red-and-white-striped facade and entrance trimmed with a triangular arrangement of muqarnas vaulting, this complex is more interesting on the outside than in. But it is worth entering briefly, through a long hallway, to see the interior of the building oriented away from the street, to align with Mecca. It was built in 1369 by Khawand Baraka, the mother of the reigning Mamluk, after completing the hajj. Ask at the Blue Mosque for the keys.

Blue Mosque MOSQUE

(Mosque of Aqsunqur; Map p78; Sharia at-Tabana; ⌚9am-5pm) Built in 1347, this building is highly touted by would-be guides, but it's nothing like its Istanbul namesake. It's classic Mamluk architecture throughout, except for one wall of flowery blue Ottoman tiles, looking a bit out of place, as they were installed 300 years later. The minaret affords an excellent view of the Citadel, though, as well as the remains of Saladin's city walls, to the east behind the mosque. It was closed for restoration at the time of research.

Khayrbek Complex MOSQUE, TOMB

(Map p78; Sharia at-Tabana; ⌚9am-5pm) FREE Emir Khayrbek, governor of Aleppo under Sultan al-Ghouri, defected to the Ottoman side in 1516, which effectively ended Mamluk rule. He then became the governor of Egypt under Selim I. Khayrbek's mausoleum and a mosque, built in 1521, are the anchors of this clutch of buildings, but what's interesting is how other structures – the 13th-century Alin Aq Palace, plus several later Ottoman houses – are all interconnected. The mosque's brick minaret sits on a Pharaonic stone block with hieroglyphs.

Mosque of Aslam al-Silahdar MOSQUE

(Map p78; Midan Aslam, off Darb al-Ahmar; ⌚9am-5pm) FREE As the closest monument to the Bab al-Mahruq entrance to Al-Azhar Park, this mosque makes a good landmark for finding your way there. The 14th-century structure is distinguished by beautiful stone-inlay floors, intricate carved-stucco medallions in the walls and a lovely tiled dome. Across the square is a gallery selling neighbourhood handicrafts. Coming from Bab Zuweila, to find the mosque (and Bab al-Mahruq) walk east behind the Mosque of Qijmas al-Ishaqi.

Al-Azhar Park PARK

(Map p78; ☎2510 3868; www.azharpark.com; Sharia Salah Salem; admission Mon-Wed/Thu-Sun E£5/7; ⌚9am-midnight) With funds from the Aga Khan Trust for Culture, what had been a mountain of garbage, amassed over centuries, was in 2005, almost miraculously, transformed into the city's first (and only) park of significant size. Cairenes stroll through a profusion of gardens, emerald grass and fountains, or sit beside the lake or on the terraces of one of the restaurants, admiring the superb views over Cairo. It's most fun on weekends, when families daytrip with picnics.

Depending on your outlook, the park is a gorgeous respite or a middle-class playground. This was offset slightly when the Bab al-Mahruq entrance, through a medieval gate in the old Ayyubid walls, finally opened in 2009. This granted easier access for residents of the lower-income Darb al-Ahmar district. You can enter here before 6pm, but after dark you can only exit through the main park gates on Sharia Salah Salem (taxis wait but overcharge; microbuses go to Ataba for E£2). If you enter from Darb al-Ahmar, check out the ongoing excavations of the Ayyubid walls – one major achievement was the rediscovery of Bab al-Barqiya gate, which had long ago been lost under the trash heap.

In addition to a couple of small cafes and the open-air theatre El Genaina (p108), there's an excellent restaurant here, Citadel View (p102), capitalising on the park's views across the medieval city and beyond. For a less substantial investment, **Alain Le Nôtre** (Map p58; ☎2510 9151, 19133; Al-Azhar Park, Sharia Salah Salem; pizza E£33-46, sandwiches E£36-48; ⏰11am-midnight) serves salads, wraps and ice cream, and the Lakeside Cafe (p102), on the other side of the park, serves more modest but good Egyptian mezzeh.

The Citadel to Ibn Tulun

South of Darb al-Ahmar, the late-Ottoman-era Citadel complex watches over the city. At its base, on Midan Salah ad-Din and along Sharia al-Saliba, is another important historic quarter, with two of Cairo's largest mosques, plus several other smaller monuments. Although works have started, in contrast with historic quarters further north this area has yet to see much revitalisation.

Citadel FORTRESS

(Al-Qala'a; Map p82; ☎2512 1735; Sharia Salah Salem; adult/student E£60/30; ⏰9am-4pm, mosques closed during prayers Fri) Sprawling over a limestone spur on the eastern edge of the city, the Citadel, started by Saladin in 1176 as a fortification against the Crusaders, was home to Egypt's rulers for 700 years. Their legacy is a collection of three very different mosques, several palaces (housing some underwhelming museums) and a couple of terraces with superb views over the city. This is one of the most popular tourist attractions in Cairo, although it's a hassle getting there.

Following their overthrow of Saladin's Ayyubid dynasty, the Mamluks enlarged the complex, adding sumptuous palaces and harems. Under the Ottomans (1517–1798) the fortress expanded westwards and a new main gate, the Bab al-Azab, was added, while the Mamluk palaces deteriorated. Even so, when Napoleon's French expedition took control in 1798, the emperor's savants regarded these buildings as some of the finest Islamic monuments in Cairo.

This didn't stop Mohammed Ali – who rose to power after the French – from drastically remodelling, and crowning the complex with the Turkish-style mosque that dominates Cairo's eastern skyline. After Mohammed Ali's grandson Ismail moved his residence to the Abdeen Palace, the Citadel became a military garrison. The British army was barracked here during WWII, and Egyptian soldiers still have a small foothold, although most of the Citadel has been given over to tourists.

Mosque of Mohammed Ali MOSQUE

(Map p82) Modelled on classic Turkish lines, with domes upon domes upon domes, this mosque took 18 years to build (1830-48) and its interior is all twinkling chandeliers and luridly striped stone, the main dome a rich emerald green. Mohammed Ali lies in the tomb on the right as you enter. In *The Levant Trilogy* Olivia Manning writes: 'Above them Mohammed Ali's alabaster mosque, uniquely white in this sand-coloured city, sat with minarets pricked, like a fat, white, watchful cat.'

Other writers, however, have called it unimaginative and graceless and compared it to a toad. The glitzy clock in the central courtyard, a gift from King Louis-Philippe of France in return for the obelisk that adorns the Place de la Concorde in Paris, arrived damaged and was never repaired.

Mosque of An Nasir Mohammed MOSQUE

(Map p82) Dwarfed by Mohammed Ali's mosque, in the citadel complex, this beautiful 1318 mosque is the only Mamluk work that Mohammed Ali didn't demolish – instead, he used it as a stable. Before that, Ottoman sultan Selim I stripped its interior of its marble, but the old wood ceiling and muqarnas show up nicely, and the twisted

TOP TIPS

- Early-morning, late-night and Friday-afternoon arrivals/departures at Cairo airport are preferable (to avoid traffic).
- Keep small coins and bills (E£5 and under) for change and tips in an easily accessible pocket.
- Strangers who approach you around Midan Talaat Harb, the Egyptian Museum and Khan al-Khalili almost certainly want to sell you something.
- Most Cairo residents drink the tap water. If your system can handle it, help yourself to cold water outside mosques to cut down on plastic-bottle use.

The Citadel

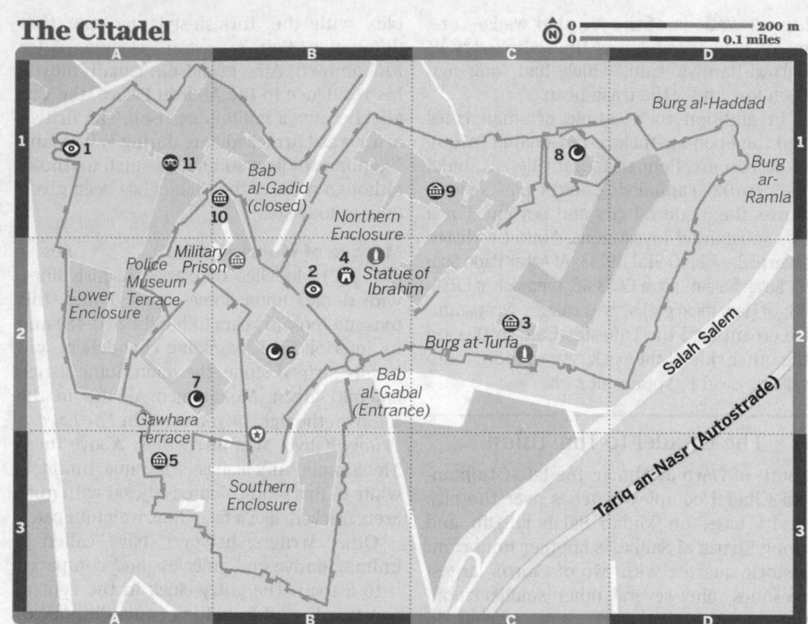

The Citadel

Sights

1 Bab al-Azab A1
2 Bab al-Qulla B2
3 Carriage Museum C2
4 Citadel B2
5 Gawhara Palace & Museum A3
6 Mosque of An-Nasir Mohammed B2
7 Mosque of Mohammed Ali A2
8 Mosque of Suleiman Pasha C1
9 National Military Museum C1
10 Police Museum B1
11 Site of the Massacre of the Mamluks A1

finials of the minarets are interesting for their covering of glazed tiles, something rarely seen in Egypt.

Police Museum MUSEUM
(Map p82) The quirky but flyblown Police Museum, located within the Citadel, includes displays on famous political assassinations, complete in some cases with the murder weapon. The main interest is its grand terrace with superb views all the way to the Pyramids of Giza. Immediately below, in the Citadel's Lower Enclosure (closed to the public), is Bab al-Azab, the site of the infamous massacre of the Mamluks.

Gawhara Palace & Museum MUSEUM
(Map p82) South of Mohammed Ali's mosque, in the citadel, is the Gawhara Palace & Museum, a lame attempt to evoke 19th-century court life, but it's most often closed. There are excellent views over the city from the terrace outside Gawhara.

National Military Museum MUSEUM
(Map p82) Mohammed Ali's one-time Harem Palace, within the citadel, is now the lavish National Military Museum and perhaps the best-tended exhibition in the country. Endless plush-carpeted halls are lined with dioramas depicting great moments in warfare, from Pharaonic times to the 20th-century conflicts with Israel – kitschy fun to start, then eventually a bit depressing. There is a cafeteria nearby.

★Mosque-Madrassa of Sultan Hassan MOSQUE
(Map p84; Midan Salah ad-Din; admission E£40, combination ticket with Mosque of ar-Rifa'i; ⏲8am-4.30pm) Massive yet elegant, this great structure is regarded as the finest piece of early-Mamluk architecture in Cairo. It was built between 1356 and 1363 by Sultan Hassan, a grandson of Sultan Qalaun; he took the throne at the age of 13, was deposed and reinstated no less than

three times, then assassinated shortly before the mosque was completed. Beyond the striking, recessed entrance, a dark passage leads into a peaceful courtyard surrounded by soaring walls.

The square courtyard is surrounded by four iwans (vaulted halls) dedicated to teaching the four main schools of Sunni Islam. At the rear of the eastern iwan, an especially beautiful mihrab is flanked by stolen Crusader columns. To the right, a bronze door leads to the sultan's mausoleum. During construction one of the minarets collapsed and killed some 300 onlookers.

Mosque of ar-Rifai MOSQUE

(Map p84; Midan Salah ad-Din; admission E£40, combination ticket with Mosque-Madrassa of Sultan Hassan; ⌚8am-4.30pm) Opposite the grand Mosque-Madrassa of Sultan Hassan (p82), the Mosque of ar-Rifai is constructed on a similarly grand scale, begun in 1869 and not finished until 1912. Members of modern Egypt's royal family, including Khedive Ismail and King Farouk, are buried inside, as is the last shah of Iran. Their tombs lie to the left of the entrance.

Amir Taz Palace HOUSE

(Map p84; ☎2514 2581; 17 Sharia Suyufiyya; ⌚9am-4pm) FREE Walking west along busy Sharia al-Saliba eventually leads to the Mosque of Ibn Tulun. A short detour north on Sharia Suyufiyya brings you to this restored home of one of Sultan Mohammed an-Nasr's closest advisers, who later controlled the throne through Sultan Hassan. Now used as a cultural centre, the home is not as extensive as Beit el-Suhaymi (p72), but admission is free, and it's less cluttered than the Gayer-Anderson Museum.

Museo Mevlevi MUSEUM

(Sama'khana; Map p84; Sharia Suyufiyya; ⌚9am-2pm) FREE Just north of the Amir Taz Palace, behind a green door with an Italian Institute sign, this museum is essentially a meticulously restored Ottoman-era theatre for whirling dervishes. Hidden behind stone facades, the beautiful wood structure feels like a little jewel box. Downstairs, see the remains of the madrassa that forms the building's foundation; the thorough notes are a rare model of thoughtful excavation.

Mosque of Ibn Tulun MOSQUE

(Map p84; Sharia al-Saliba; ⌚8am-4pm) FREE The city's oldest intact, functioning Islamic monument is easily identified by its high walls topped with neat crenellations that resemble a string of paper dolls. It was built between AD 876 and 879 by Ibn Tulun, who was sent to rule the outpost of Al-Fustat in the 9th century by the Abbasid caliph of Baghdad. It's also one of the most beautiful mosques in Cairo, and its geometric simplicity is best appreciated from the top of the minaret.

The mosque covers 2.5 hectares, large enough for the whole community of Al-Fustat to assemble for Friday prayers. An outer, moatlike courtyard, originally created to keep the secular city at a distance, was at one time filled with shops and stalls. Ibn Tulun drew inspiration from his homeland, particularly the ancient Mosque of Samarra (Iraq), on which the spiral minaret is modelled, as well as the use of brick. The minaret is accessed from the moat. He also added some innovations of his own: according to architectural historians, this is the first structure to use the pointed arch, a good 200 years before the European Gothic arch.

Gayer-Anderson Museum MUSEUM

(Beit al-Kritliyya, the House of the Cretan Woman; Map p84; ☎2364 7822; Sharia ibn Tulun; adult/student E£40/25, video E£20; ⌚9am-4pm) Through a gateway to the south of the main entrance of the Mosque of Ibn Tulun, this quirky museum gets its current name from John Gayer-Anderson, the British major and army doctor who restored the two adjoining 16th-century houses between 1935 and 1942, filling them with lovely antiquities, artworks and knick-knacks acquired

OFF THE BEATEN TRACK

A WALK THROUGH AL-KHALIFA

A map on the wall opposite the main entrance to the Mosque of Ibn Tulun, shows the sights under restoration in the area of Al-Khalifa. Al-Khalifa, also known as Al-Mashahed, is the area where the important descendants of Prophet Mohammed were buried. Today a major restoration project is under way to restore their mausoleums. The area retains an authentic if downtrodden atmosphere, with markets and workshops. The *moulids* of the people buried here are still celebrated some time before Ramadan.

The Citadel to Ibn Tulun

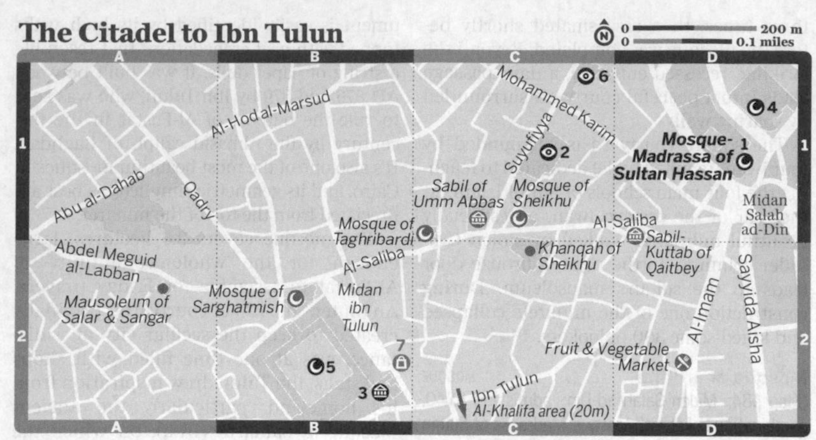

The Citadel to Ibn Tulun

Top Sights
1 Mosque-Madrassa of Sultan Hassan.......D1

Sights
2 Amir Taz Palace.......C1
3 Gayer-Anderson Museum.......B2
4 Mosque of ar-Rifai.......D1
5 Mosque of Ibn Tulun.......B2
6 Museo Mevlevi.......C1

Shopping
7 Khan Misr Touloun.......B2

on his travels in the region. The house was used as a location in the James Bond film *The Spy Who Loved Me.*

On his death in 1945, Gayer-Anderson bequeathed the lot to Egypt. The puzzle of rooms is decorated in a variety of styles: the Persian Room has exquisite tiling, the Damascus Room has lacquer and gold, and the Queen Anne Room displays ornate furniture and a silver tea set. The enchanting *mashrabiyya* gallery looks down onto a magnificent *qa'a* (reception hall) which has a marble fountain, decorated ceiling beams and carpet-covered alcoves. The rooftop terrace has been lovingly restored, with more complex *mashrabiyya.* Across the street, Khan Misr Touloun is a good handicrafts emporium.

From here, it's rewarding to keep walking another 750m west to the popular quarter of Sayyida Zeinab, where there's a metro station.

Northern Cemetery

The Northern Cemetery is half of a vast necropolis called Al-Qarafa or, more common among tourists, the City of the Dead. The titillating name conjures a vision of morbid slums, of tomb structures bursting with living families. But the area is more 'town' than 'shanty', complete with power lines, a post office and multistorey buildings. Thanks to a near complete absence of cars, it's also a fairly peaceful part of the city, with a friendly neighbourhood feel and some flawless Mamluk monuments.

The easiest way to the Northern Cemetery is walking east from Midan al-Hussein along Sharia al-Azhar. At Sharia Salah Salem, cross via the overpass. In addition to the three main monuments, several others have been well restored, but are not reliably open.

★Mosque of Qaitbey MOSQUE
(Map p86; 9am-4pm) FREE Sultan Qaitbey was as ruthless as any Mamluk sultan, but he was also something of an aesthete. His mosque, completed in 1474 as part of a much larger funerary complex, is widely agreed to mark the pinnacle of Islamic architecture in Cairo. The interior is one of the most pleasant places to sit and relax, but the true glory is the exterior of the dome, carved with the finest, most intricate floral designs anywhere in the Islamic world.

Qaitbey ruled for 28 years and was the last Mamluk leader with any real power in Egypt. He was a prolific builder, and with some 80 buildings in his name, he truly refined the Mamluk style. Behind the boldly striped facade, the interior has four iwans around a central court lit by large, lattice-screened windows. The interior is panelled in cool marble with a mesmerising decorative wood ceiling. The adjacent tomb chamber contains the cenotaphs of Qaitbey and his two sisters. The elegant and slender stone minaret, carved with a star pattern, and an intricate floral arabesque, is one of the city's most beautiful. Climb up for the best view.

Khanqah-Mausoleum of Farag Ibn Barquq TOMB

(Map p86; 9am-4pm) FREE Built by a son of Sultan Barquq, whose great madrassa and mausoleum stand on Bein al-Qasreen, this tomb complex was completed in 1411 because Barquq had wished to be buried near some particular illustrious Sufi sheikhs. The *khanqah*, a sort of monastery for a Sufi order, is a fortresslike building with high, sheer facades and twin minarets and domes, the largest stone domes in Cairo. Inside the ceilings are painted in mesmerising red-and-black geometric patterns.

Complex of Sultan Ashraf Barsbey RELIGIOUS SITE, TOMB

(Map p86) Enclosed by a stone wall midway between Barquq's tomb and the Mosque of Qaitbey is the funerary complex of Barsbey, who ruled from 1422 to 1438 and also built a mosque on Sharia al-Muizz, at the corner of Sharia al-Muski. Most of the compound is crumbling, but the dome of his mausoleum is carved with a beautiful star pattern, and there is some fine marble flooring and an ivory-inlay minbar (pulpit). The guard will let you in for baksheesh.

Gezira & Zamalek

Uninhabited until the mid-19th century, Gezira (Arabic for 'island') was a narrow strip of alluvial land rising up out of the Nile. After he built modern-day Downtown, Khedive Ismail dedicated his energy to a great palace on the island, with the rest of the land as a royal garden. During the development boom of the early 20th century the palace grounds were sold off, while the palace was made into a hotel. Much of the island is occupied by sports clubs and parks, while the northern third is stylish Zamalek, a leafy neighbourhood of old embassy mansions and 1920s apartment blocks. It has few tourist sites, but it's a pleasant place to wander around and an even better place to eat, drink and shop.

Museum of Modern Egyptian Art MUSEUM

(Map p94; 2736 6667; www.modernartmuseum.gov.eg) This vast collection of 20th- and 21st-century Egyptian art is set in the green, well-groomed Gezira Exhibition Grounds, across from the Cairo Opera House. The museum's highlights are Mahmoud Mukhtar's deco-elegant bronze *Bride of the Nile*, along with Mahmoud Said's painting *Al Madina* (The City, 1937). The museum was closed for maintenance at the time of research. Nearby are the Hanager Arts Centre and the Palace of arts, all closed for maintenance at the time of research.

★ Cairo Tower MONUMENT

(Burg Misr; Map p94; 2735 7187; www.cairotower.net; Sharia Hadayek al-Zuhreya; adult/child under 6yr E£70/free, video E£20; 8am-midnight, to

THE CITY OF THE DEAD

Some estimates put the number of living Cairenes in the Northern and Southern Cemeteries at half a million; others, perhaps more realistic, guess only 50,000. As Max Rodenbeck notes in *Cairo: The City Victorious,* some of the tomb dwellers, especially the paid guardians and their families, have lived here for generations. Others have moved in more recently – there was a spike in 1992, following the earthquake that flattened cheaply built high-rises, and others may have opted for a more central Qarafa home over forced relocation to a bleak low-income suburb. On Fridays and public holidays visitors flock here to picnic and pay their respects to the dead – a lively time to visit.

The cemetery first appealed to Mamluk sultans and emirs because it afforded ample building space. The vast mausoleums they built were more than just tombs; they were also meant as places for entertaining – a continuation of the Pharaonic tradition of picnicking among the graves. Even the humblest family tombs included a room for overnight visitors. The dead hoped they would be remembered; the city's homeless thanked them for free accommodation. This coexistence of the living and the dead was happening as far back as the 14th century, though these days in some tomb-houses, cenotaphs serve as tables and washing is strung between headstones.

Northern Cemetery

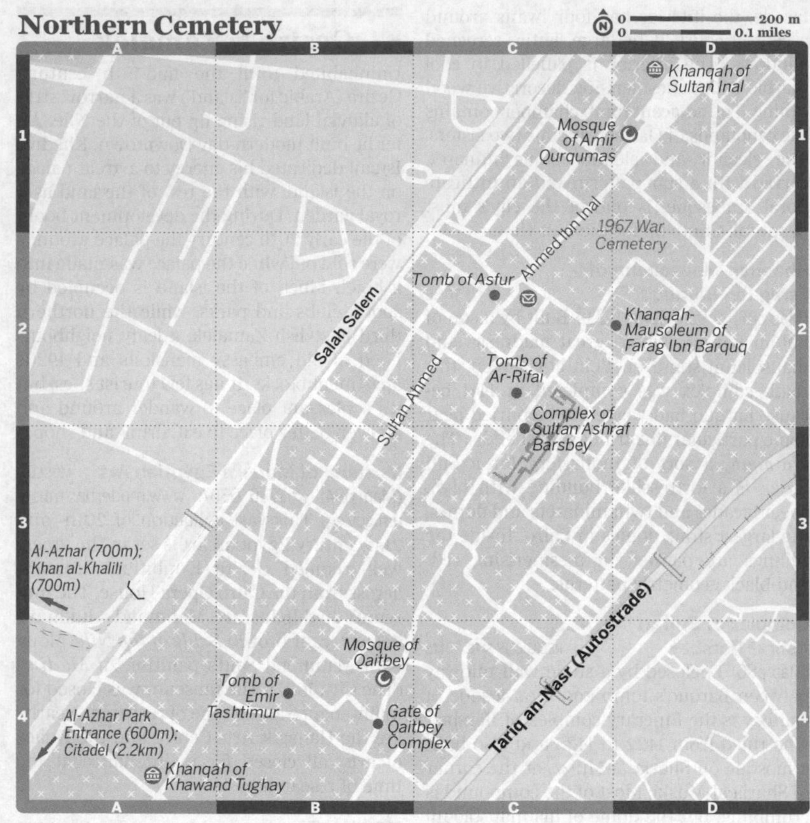

1am summer) This 187m-high tower is the city's most famous landmark after the Pyramids. Built in 1961, the structure, which resembles a stylized lotus plant with its latticework casing, was a thumb to the nose at the Americans, who had given Nasser the money used for its construction to buy US arms. The 360-degree views from the top are clearest in the late morning, after the haze burns off, or late afternoon.

You might encounter a queue for the elevator at dusk, as the tower is extremely popular with Cairenes. The **Sky Garden** cafe, one floor down from the observation deck, serves not-too-exorbitant drinks and food (beer E£30, sandwiches E£50). The **Revolving Restaurant** just below that is a bit pricier, with a E£200 minimum.

Cairo Marriott PALACE
(Map p88; Sharia Saray al-Gezira) Never mind that this is a luxury hotel: its core is a lavish palace built by Khedive Ismail to house Empress Éugenie when she visited for the opening of the Suez Canal in 1869. A stroll inside gives a sense of its original grandeur. Head straight through and down the stairs to grand old sitting rooms, then into the garden and right to the next entrance and the fantastic former ballroom, with triple-height ceilings and an enormous staircase for making that dramatic entrance.

Museum of Islamic Ceramics MUSEUM
(Map p88; 2737 3298; 1 Sharia Sheikh al-Marsafy, Zamalek; adult/student E£25/15; 10am-1.30pm & 5.30-9pm Sat-Thu) This beautiful small museum was closed for renovation at the time of research (admission and hours are approximate). But when it reopens, it's worth a peek for its collection of colourful plates, tiles and even 11th-century hand grenades. Equally appealing is the gorgeous 1924 villa it's housed in.

What is still open: the garden and back of the building, which are given over to the

Gezira Arts Centre (Map p88), with several galleries hosting rotating contemporary exhibitions.

Andalus Garden GARDENS
(Hadeeqat al-Andalus; Map p94; Sharia Saray al-Gezira; admission E£2; ⏲7am-10pm) One of several formal gardens in the area that are popular strolling spots for couples in the evening. This one's small, but adjacent to the Nile, and also nice during the day as it has plenty of shade from palm trees and vine-covered pergolas. Across Midan Saad Zaghloul, on the southwest side, is the entrance to the grandly named **Garden of Freedom and Friendship** (Map p94; admission E£2; ⏲7am-10pm), much larger but without the river views.

★**Mahmoud Mukhtar Museum** MUSEUM
(Map p94; ☎2736 6665; Sharia Tahrir; admission E£15; ⏲10am-2pm & 5-10pm Tue-Sun) Mukhtar (1891–1934) was the sculptor laureate of independent Egypt, responsible for Saad Zaghloul on the nearby roundabout and the *Egypt Reawakening* monument outside the Giza Zoo. Collected in this elegant, little-visited museum, his work ranges from tiny caricatures (look for *Ibn al-Balad,* a spunky city kid) to life-size portraits. Mukhtar's tomb sits in the basement.

The museum also houses some interesting temporary exhibitions.

Mohandiseen, Agouza & Doqqi

A map of Cairo in Baedecker's 1929 guide to Egypt shows nothing on the Nile's west bank other than a hospital and the road to the Pyramids. The hospital is still there, set back from the corniche, but it's now hemmed in on all sides by midrise buildings. This is the sprawl of Giza governorate – in administrative terms, not even part of Cairo at all – and it reaches all the way out to the foot of the Pyramids (they're not isolated in the desert, as you might have imagined). In the 1960s and 1970s, the neighbourhoods of Mohandiseen, Agouza and Doqqi, the closest areas to the Nile, were created to house Egypt's emerging professional classes. They remain middle-class bastions, home to families who made good under Sadat's open-door policy – though some pockets of Mohandiseen are Cairo's ritziest.

Unless you happen to find concrete and traffic stimulating, the main reason to come here are some good restaurants, a few embassies and upscale shopping on Sharia Suleiman Abaza and Sharia Libnan.

What little history there is since the pharaohs floats on the river in the form of **houseboats**, moored off Sharia el-Nil just north of Zamalek Bridge in Agouza. These

'GARBAGE CITY'

Looking around some parts of Cairo, you might think garbage is never collected – but it certainly is, by some 65,000 people known as *zabbaleen,* mostly Coptic Christians. Until 2004 the *zabbaleen* collected rubbish from Cairene homes, sorted through it, and made a living from selling the salvaged materials to wholesalers, while the organic waste was fed to their pigs, whose meat also brought them an extra income. In 2004, under Mubarak, the waste collection was handed out to multinationals but this ended in failure. In early 2014 the government officially reinstated the *zabaleen* role, giving vehicles and uniforms to around 60 *zabaleen* companies. They receive training and are paid a fixed sum.

The *zabaleen* live mostly in their district at the base of the Muqattam Hills, known as Manshiyet Nasr or Madeenat az-Zabbaleen. The area is pretty extraordinary, and in the middle of it is one of the most surprising churches in the country. The **Church of St Simeon the Tanner** (Kineesat Samaan al-Kharraz; Map p58; ☎2512 3666; Manshiyet Nasr), on a ridge above 'Garbage City', seats 5000 and is ringed with biblical scenes carved into the rock. Look over the ridge and you can see the whole sprawling city; look down, and you see all the city's refuse, sorted into recyclable bits.

But this church is not old, nor are any of the others in the complex, though some are tucked in spooky hermits' caves. Completed in 1994, St Simeon is a belated honour for a 10th-century ascetic who prayed to make Muqattam move at the behest of Fatimid caliph Al-Muizz li-Din Allah (per Matthew 17:20: 'If ye have faith as a grain of mustard seed, ye shall say unto this mountain, Remove hence to yonder place; and it shall remove...'). Today the church is a major site of Coptic pilgrimage.

Mohandiseen, Agouza & Zamalek

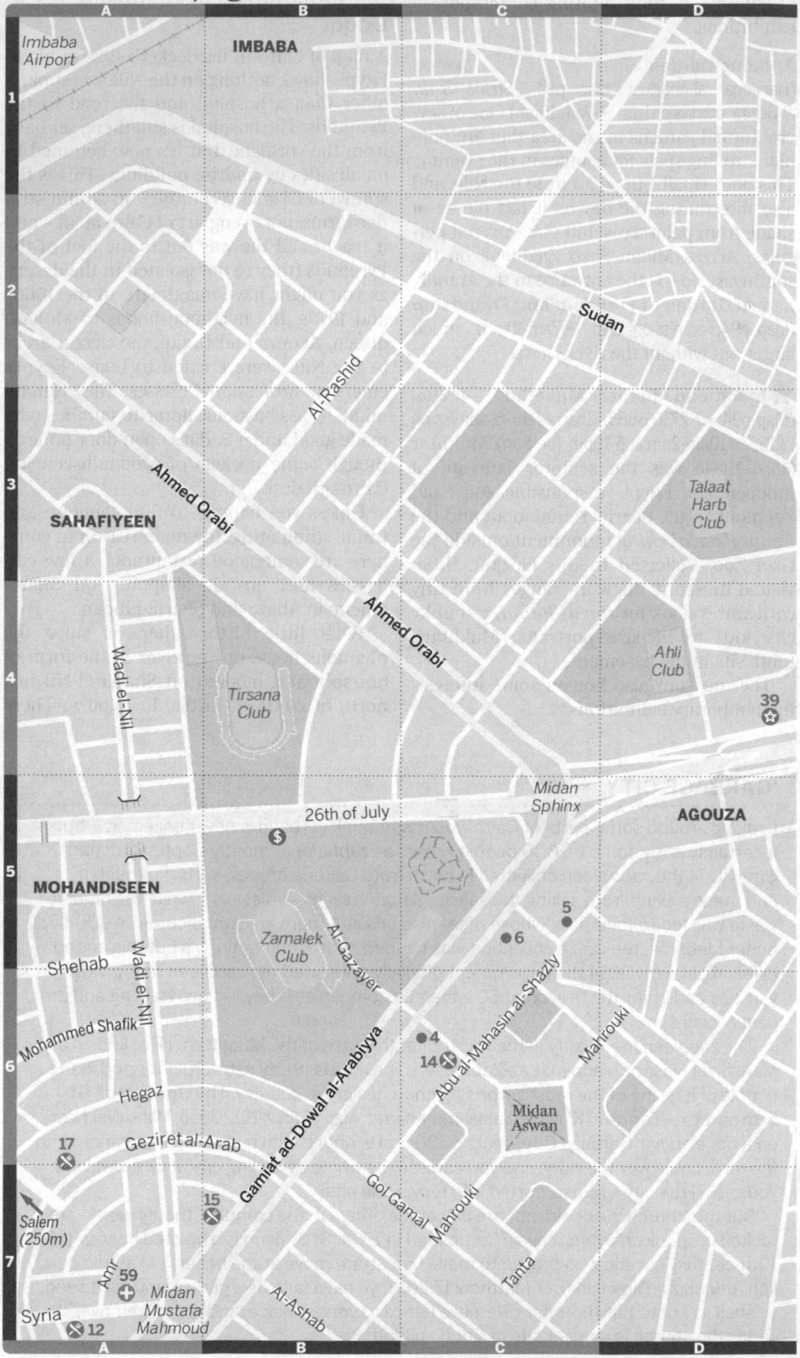

A B C D
1 2 3 4 5 6 7

Imbaba Airport
IMBABA
Sudan
Al-Rashid
Ahmed Orabi
Talaat Harb Club
SAHAFIYEEN
Ahmed Orabi
Ahli Club
Wadi el-Nil
Tirsana Club
39
Midan Sphinx
26th of July
AGOUZA
MOHANDISEEN
5
6
Zamalek Club
Al-Gazayer
Shehab
Wadi el-Nil
Abu al-Mahasin al-Shazly
Mahrouki
Mohammed Shafik
4
14
Gamiat ad-Dowal al-Arabiyya
Hegaz
Midan Aswan
17
Geziret al-Arab
Gol Gamal
Mahrouki
15
Salem (250m)
Tanta
Amr
59
Midan Mustafa Mahmoud
Al-Ashab
Syria
12

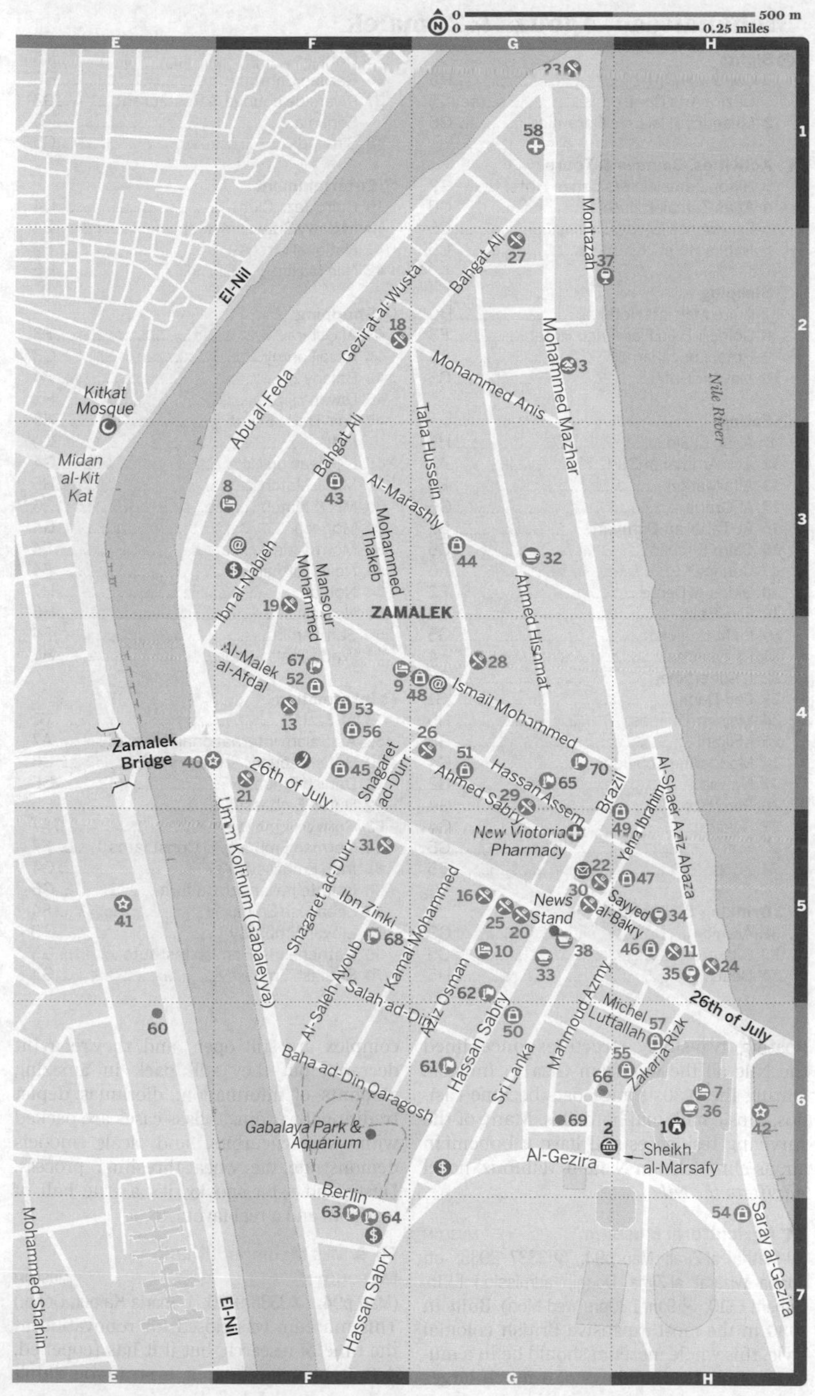
0 500 m
0 0.25 miles
E
F
G
H
1
2
3
4
5
6
7
El-Nil
Kitkat Mosque
Midan al-Kit Kat
Abu al-Feda
Gezirat al-Wusta
Bahgat Ali
Mohammed Anis
Taha Hussein
Montazah
Mohammed Mazhar
Nile River
Al-Marashly
Mohammed Thakeb
Mansour Mohammed
Ibn al-Nabieh
ZAMALEK
Ahmed Hishmat
Al-Malek al-Afdal
Ismail Mohammed
Zamalek Bridge
26th of July
Shagaret ad-Durr
Ahmed Sabry
Hassan Assem
Brazil
Yehia Ibrahim
Al-Shaer Aziz Abaza
New Victoria Pharmacy
Umm Kolthum (Gabaleyya)
Ibn Zinki
Kamal Mohammed
News Stand
Sayyed al-Bakry
Al-Saleh Ayoub
Salah ad-Din
Aziz Osman
Hassan Sabry
Sri Lanka
Mahmoud Azmy
Michel Lutfallah
Zakaria Rizk
Baha ad-Din Qaragosh
Gabalaya Park & Aquarium
Al-Gezira
Sheikh al-Marsafy
Berlin
Saray al-Gezira
Mohammed Shahin

Mohandiseen, Agouza & Zamalek

Sights
1 Cairo Marriott H6
Gezira Arts Centre .... (see 2)
2 Museum of Islamic Ceramics G6

Activities, Courses & Tours
3 Hilton Zamalek Residence Hotel G2
4 Atlas Zamalek Hotel C6
5 Experience Egypt C5
6 Nabila Hotel C5

Sleeping
7 Cairo Marriott Hotel H6
8 Golden Tulip Flamenco Hotel F3
9 Hotel Longchamps F4
10 Mayfair Hotel G5

Eating
11 Abou El Sid H5
12 Abu Ammar al-Suri A7
13 Alfa Market F4
14 Al-Omda C6
15 At-Tabei ad-Dumyati B7
16 Cairo Kitchen G5
17 Cedars A6
18 Didos Al Dente F2
19 Five Bells F3
20 La Mezzaluna G5
21 La Taverna F4
22 L'Aubergine G5
23 Left Bank G1
24 Maison Thomas H5
25 Makani G5
26 Mandarine Koueider G4
27 Nawab G2
28 Rigoletto G4
29 Sekem G4
30 Sufi G5
31 Zööba F5

Drinking & Nightlife
32 Arabica G3
33 Cilantro G5
34 Deals H5
35 Drinkies H5
36 Garden Café H6
37 Riverside Lounge & Restaurant G2
Sequoia .... (see 23)
38 Simonds G5

Entertainment
39 Cairo Jazz Club D4
40 El Sawy Culture Wheel E4
41 National Circus E5
42 Nile Maxim H6

Shopping
43 Al Qahira F3
44 Azza Fahmy G3
45 Balady F4
46 Diwan H5
47 Fair Trade Egypt H5
Loft .... (see 30)
48 L'Oiseau du Nil G4
49 Mix & Match H5
50 Mix & Match G6
51 Mobaco G4
52 Mom & Me F4
53 Nevin Altmann F4
54 Nomad H7
55 Nostalgia H6
56 Sami Amin F4
57 Wady Craft Shop H6

Information
58 Al-Ezaby G1
59 As-Salam International Hospital A7
60 British Council & Library E6
61 Danish Embassy G6
62 Dutch Embassy G5
63 German Embassy F7
64 German Embassy & Consulates F7
65 Irish Embassy G4
66 Istituto Italiano di Cultura G6
67 Lebanese Embassy F4
68 Libyan Embassy F5
69 Netherlands-Flemish Institute G6
70 Spanish Embassy G4

floating two-storey structures once lined the Nile all the way from Giza to Imbaba. During the 1930s some boats became casinos, music halls and bordellos. Many of the surviving residences still have a bohemian air, as chronicled in Naguib Mahfouz' novel *Adrift on the Nile*.

★ Agricultural Museum MUSEUM
(Al-Mathaf al-Zirai; Map p94; ☎3337 2933; off Sharia Wizarat al-Ziraa, Doqqi; admission E£15, camera E£10; ⏲9am-1.30pm Wed-Mon) Built in 1930 in the most expansive British colonial style, this whole museum should be in a museum. Only two buildings of a much larger complex are still open, and they're a bit decrepit, but they still pack in amazing amounts of information: dioramas depict traditional weddings, glass cases are packed with wax cucurbits, and scale models demonstrate the wheat-threshing process. Dusty and a bit spooky, it's a true hall of wonders and a real favourite.

Mr & Mrs Mahmoud Khalil Museum MUSEUM
(Map p94; ☎3338 9720; 1 Sharia Kafour, Doqqi) This museum was closed for renovation at the time of research, but if it has reopened, definitely make the trek, even if you didn't

come to Egypt to see 19th- and 20th-century European and Japanese art. Mahmoud and the missus, Emiline Lock, hobnobbed with European artists at the turn of the last century and amassed an impressive collection: Delacroix, Gauguin, Toulouse-Lautrec, Monet and more. The museum is just a few minutes' walk south from the Cairo Sheraton.

Activities

Boat Rides

One of the most pleasant things to do on a warm day is to go out on a **felucca**, Egypt's ancient broad-sail boat, with a supply of beer and a small picnic just as sunset approaches. Because it's near a wider spot in the river, the best place for hiring is the **Dok Dok landing stage** (Map p94; Corniche el-Nil), and the dock just to the south, on the corniche in Garden City, across from the Four Seasons. Subject to haggling, a boat and captain should cost between E£70 and E£100 per hour; your captain will appreciate additional baksheesh.

Once night falls, light-festooned **party boats** crowd the docks near Maspero, the east bank of the Nile north of 6th of October Bridge. A 45-minute or hour-long ride usually costs E£6 or so per person, and boats go whenever they're full.

Swimming

Finding a place to cool off in the city can be difficult. Cairenes who can afford it swim in members-only clubs. Some hotels do allow day use for nonguests, at a price. The best bargains are in Mohandiseen, where a minimum charge at the cafes at **Atlas Zamalek Hotel** (Map p88; ☎3346 7230; www.atlaszamalek.com; 20 Sharia Gamiat ad-Dowal al-Arabiyya; minimum E£70) and **Nabila Hotel** (Map p88; ☎3303 0302; 4 Sharia Gamiat ad-Dowal al-Arabiyya; minimum E£50; ⏲10am-5pm) give you access to their small rooftop pools.

For a bigger day outing, **Mohamed Ali Club** (☎02-3345 0228, 0122 211 3681; Km 13, Upper Egypt Agriculture Rd; day use E£100) is a major social scene – a mix of expats and

CAIRO FOR CHILDREN

Cairo can be exhausting for kids, but there is much they will enjoy. Most children will like an excursion on a Nile **felucca** or a night-time party boat, gawking at Tut's treasures in the Egyptian Museum (p132) and investigating the Pyramids of Giza (p121) and the brilliant solar barque at the nearby Cheops Boat Museum (p123), as well as the mazelike market of Khan al-Khalili (p70). Also check out smaller, uncrowded attractions like the Agricultural Museum (p90) and the Postal Museum (p61).

Overlooking Islamic Cairo, Al-Azhar Park (p80) has one of the few children's playgrounds in the central city, though the gardens in **Gezira** and **Ezbekiyya** also give room to run. When only bribery will help, try Mandarine Koueider (p102) for delectable, distracting ice cream. Or cut straight to toys at **Mom & Me** (Map p88; ☎2736 5751; 20A Sharia Mansour Mohammed, Zamalek). If you're staying a while, it's worth buying *Cairo, the Family Guide*, by Lesley Lababidi and Lisa Sabbahy (AUC Press, E£100), revised in 2010.

A few more ideas:

Cairo Puppet Theatre (Masrah al-Ara'is; Map p62; ☎2591 0954; Ezbekiyya; admission E£25; ⏲6pm Thu & Fri) Shows are in Arabic, but colourful and animated enough to entertain all ages.

National Circus (Balloon Theatre; Map p88; ☎3347 0612; Sharia el-Nil, Agouza; admission E£30-120; ⏲box office 11am-10pm, performances 6pm & 8pm) One-ring show with clowns, acrobats, lions and lots of glitter, usually running during the cooler months. Go early to get good seats. It's very traditional (including in its use of animals), and usually runs during the cooler months.

Giza Zoo (Guineenat al-Haywanet; Map p94; ☎3570 8895; www.gizazoo-eg.com; Midan al-Gamaa, Giza; admission E£20; ⏲9am-4pm, to 5pm in summer) It's in rather sorry shape these days, but you're going not for the animals, but for a chance to mingle with local children.

Dr Ragab's Pharaonic Village (☎3572 2533; www.pharaonicvillage.com; 3 Sharia al-Bahr al-Azam, Moneib; admission from E£150; ⏲9am-5pm) Full-tilt tourist trap, and a little tattered, but good for sparking the imagination about what life in ancient Egypt was like. Ticket window closes at 5pm. On the west bank of the Nile, 3.5km south of the Giza Zoo.

DIY WALKING CAIRO

Contrary to first impressions, Cairo is an excellent city for walking. The terrain is level, the scenery changes quickly, and you'll never accidentally wander into a 'bad' neighbourhood. We encourage getting a little lost in Cairo's back lanes, and, at least once, accepting a stranger's invitation to tea. These are some of the best places to stroll over the course of a day.

Islamic Cairo in the Morning

Start before 7am with tea at Fishawi's (p106) cafe and watch the khan slowly wake up. Take a quick peek at Bein al-Qasreen (p73) to admire the buildings without the crush of commerce, then head south: follow Sharia al-Muizz li-Din Allah (p72) and at Bab Zuweila (p78) take a left towards Darb al-Ahmar and Al-Azhar Park (p80), roughly following the old walls built by Saladin. Tiny workshops here produce shoes, parquet flooring, mother-of-pearl inlay boxes and more. But it's also a residential district, where families on upper floors run baskets down to the *ba'al* (grocer) for supplies, and knife-sharpeners and junk traders (the men who shout 'Beee-kya!') roll through the lanes. Keeping your bearings with the park to your left, you can wander all the way to the Citadel (p81). To loop back to Sharia al-Azhar, go via Sharia al-Khayamiyya.

Garden City at Twilight

The interlocking circles that form the streets of Garden City are maddening if you want to get anywhere, but they're perfect for admiring the crumbling mansions in this colonial-era district. The best time to visit is the hour before sundown, when the dust coating the architectural curlicues turns a warm gold and the starlings shrill in the trees.

Start at the north end (get the brutalist concrete Canadian embassy behind you right away!), keeping an eye out for wrought-iron dragons on cobwebbed gates, a rare Turkish-style wood-front home and the last real garden in Garden City, behind the Four Seasons hotel. Nearby at 10 Sharia Tulumbat is **Grey Pillars**, the British residency during WWII, with a beautiful birdcage elevator inside. Stop for a coffee at the peaceful **Falak** (Map p94; ☎0109 589 5850; 7 Sharia Gamal ad-Din Abu al-Mahasin, Garden City; ⏱Mon-Sun 10am-12am) cafe. You wind up, conveniently, near the Dok Dok felucca landing stage (p91) for a sailboat ride.

Downtown after Midnight

A jaunt Downtown is less walking than cafe-hopping. Here the air is cool and the streets are thronged. Start at Midan Orabi, where you can perch on any random planter and someone will come and sell you tea. From here Sharia Alfy and the smaller streets on either side are your playground for snacking, sheesha-smoking and maybe even some lavish tipping of belly dancers. For a younger scene, head to the pedestrian streets around the stock exchange. No matter how late you're out, you can wind up the night at the 24-hour Odeon Palace Hotel (p105) bar.

Egyptians – with house music, good Lebanese food (E£30 to E£50) and beers (E£35). It's located 3km south on the west bank, about even with Ma'adi. The **Hilton Zamalek Residence Hotel** (Map p88; ☎2737 0055; 21 Sharia Mohammed Mazhar, Zamalek; day use E£150; ⏱9am-sunset) has a sculpted dip pool with a Nile view. For a similar price, you can swim for the day at **Cataract Pyramids Resort** (☎3771 8060; www.cataracthotels.com; Harraniyya Rd, Giza; day use d E£200), located due east of the Pyramids on the road to Saqqara.

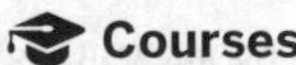

Courses

Art & Crafts

Darb 1718 (p69) organises many art as well as craft workshops. Next door is the Azza Fahmy Design Studio (p69) which has several excellent courses in jewellery making, attracting foreign teachers and students, as well as locals.

Belly-Dancing

The more service-minded tourist hotels can arrange classes, and this is the most flexible option. Some of the city's gyms and health centres offer group courses:

try **Tawazon Studio** (Map p62; ☎0109 555 7266; www.tawazonstudio.com; apt 23, 2nd floor, 5 Sharia Youssef al-Guindi, Bab El Louk), where drop-in classes cost E£60 when they're running. **Yasmina of Cairo** (☎0122 746 5185; www.yasminaofcairo.com; Giza) organises belly-dance classes, workshops and tours. She runs a small studio in her Doqqi apartment, where either she or one of her protégés will give you (or a group, if you can get one together) lessons.

Tours

Numerous companies and individuals offer tours of sights in and around Cairo. For private outings to ancient sites, we recommend **Hassan Saber** (☎0100 515 9857; hassansaber@hotmail.com), whose years of experience include an appearance on Anthony Bourdain's *No Reservations*. Also excellent is the experienced female guide **Manal Helmy** (☎0122 313 9045; noula.helmy@gmail.com), who comes recommended. Witty and enthusiastic **Ahmed Seddik** (☎0100 676 8269; www.ahmed-seddik.com; day-long tour E£200) runs a busy itinerary of group tours; check his website for the schedule. He's strongest on the Egyptian Museum and Saqqara. **Samo Tours** (☎2299 1155; www.samoegypttours.com) is also reliable, with excellent English-speaking guides, Egyptologists and drivers.

To hire a taxi for the day and dispense with a guide, try **Aton Amon** (☎0100 621 7674; aton_manos@yahoo.com; full day E£320), who speaks English and French; he also does airport pickups. Friendly **Fathy el-Menesy** (☎2486 4251; full day E£320) speaks English and owns a well-maintained Peugeot. The first female cabbie in Cairo **Nour Gaber** (☎0114 888 5561; ♿) is setting up an academy for female taxi drivers to improve their English, mental strength and driving skills, partly as a reaction against the sexual harassment against women.

Drivers (and sometimes guides) will often try to push you into shopping add-ons – the spurious perfume store that claims to supply the Body Shop; the illustrious papyrus 'museum' – for which they'll receive a commission. Many drivers factor this into their daily earnings, so it can be hard to dissuade them. Be firm, and if you're truly desperate, offer to pay the difference yourself. It may be the only way to convey the message that tourists are often happier without these shopping detours.

Festivals & Events

Moulid of Sayyidna al-Hussein RELIGIOUS

On the square in front of the Mosque of al-Hussein, this Sufi gathering celebrates the birthday of the prophet's grandson. If the crowds get too intense, you can watch from one of the rooftop cafes. It's near the end of the Islamic month of Rabei al-Tani (February 2015 and 2016).

Moulid of Sayyida Zeinab RELIGIOUS

The last week of the Islamic month of Ragab (May 2015 and 2016), this veneration of the prophet's granddaughter is a great neighbourhood event, behind the mosque of the same name.

D-CAF ART, PERFORMING ARTS

(Downtown Contemporary Arts Festival; d-caf.org; ⏲March & April) Going from strength to strength, the contemporary arts festival draws the focus on Downtown Cairo with first-rate multidisciplinary events in numerous venues.

Sleeping

Cairo is chock-a-block with budget crash pads, including a few exceptionally good ones, but midrange gems are rarer. On the upper end, impressive luxury hotels line the banks of the Nile. If your wallet has adequate padding, this is one city where you may want to enjoy these establishments. (The Ritz-Carlton was expected to join the party at some point in 2015, in the refurbished Nile-side property that was once the Hilton, on Midan Tahrir.) At least feel free to treat these hotels as locals do: as places of respite from the city din, with clean bathrooms and other comforts. Rates at the high end fluctuate according to season, and rarely include taxes or breakfast.

It pays to make reservations in advance, at least for your first night or two. Cairo is no place to haul your luggage around while comparing room rates, and online rates are often better.

Downtown

This is primarily budget territory, though there are a few noteworthy upper-end sleeps. Either way, you'll be in the thick of things and near great cheap eateries. Most hotels are located on or around Sharia Talaat Harb in old apartment blocks. Don't be alarmed by grimy stairs and shaky elevators – they aren't necessarily a reflection of

Doqqi, Giza & Gezira

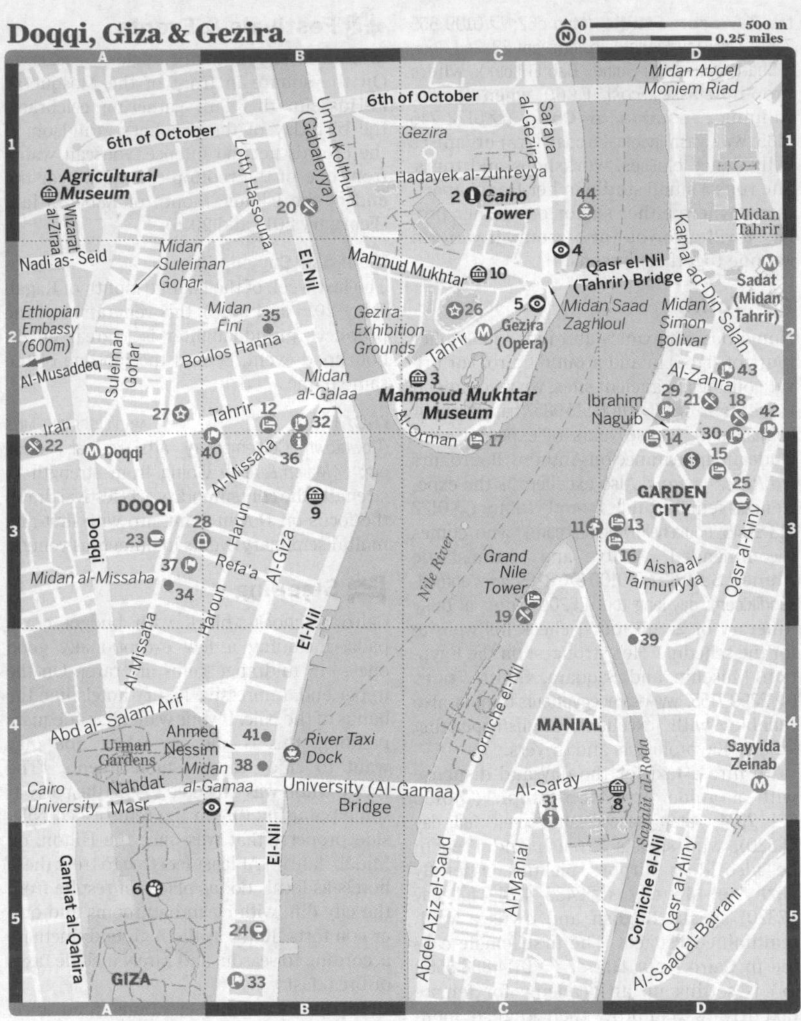

the hotels above. Many have balconies and windows overlooking noisy main streets; request a rear room if you're a light sleeper, with earplugs as backup.

★Pension Roma PENSION $

(Map p62; ☎2391 1088; www.pensionroma.com.eg; 4th fl, 169 Sharia Mohammed Farid; s E£109, d E£155-200, with air-con s E£164, d E£249-258; ❄📶) Run by a French-Egyptian woman with impeccable standards, the Roma brings dignity, even elegance, to the budget-travel scene. The towering ceilings, antique furniture and filmy white curtains create a feeling of timeless calm. Most rooms have shared bath, and some rooms have showers. Rooms in the new extension on a higher floor have ensuite bathrooms and air-con, and are quieter.

You'll never be pressured to buy a tour here (they're not even an option). Book ahead, as the place is popular with repeat guests, many of whom could afford more expensive places but prefer the old-Cairo atmosphere here.

Dina's Hostel HOSTEL $

(Map p62; ☎2396 3902; www.dinashostel.com; 5th fl, 42 Sharia Abdel Khalek Sarwat; d E£210, dm/s/d

Doqqi, Giza & Gezira

Top Sights

1	Agricultural Museum	A1
2	Cairo Tower	C1
3	Mahmoud Mukhtar Museum	C2

Sights

4	Andalus Garden	C2
5	Garden of Freedom and Friendship	C2
6	Giza Zoo	A5
7	Giza Zoo Entrance	B4
8	Manial Palace	D4
9	Mr & Mrs Mahmoud Khalil Museum	B3
10	Museum of Modern Egyptian Art	C2

Activities, Courses & Tours

11	Dok Dok Landing Stage	C3

Sleeping

12	El Tonsy	B2
13	Four Seasons at Nile Plaza	D3
14	Kempinski Nile	D3
15	Mandarin Hotel	D3
16	Nile Season	D3
17	Sofitel El Gezirah	C3

Eating

18	Mahrous	D2
	Osmanly	(see 14)
19	Revolving Restaurant	C3
20	Sea Gull	B1
21	Taboula	D2
22	Yemen Restaurant	A3

Drinking & Nightlife

	Buddha Bar	(see 17)
23	Cilantro	A3
24	Club 35	B5
25	Falak	D3

Entertainment

26	Cairo Opera House	C2
27	Cinema Tahrir	A2

Shopping

28	Nagada	A3

Information

29	British Embassy	D2
30	Canadian Embassy	D3
31	Egyptian Student Travel Services	C4
32	Ethiopian Embassy	B2
33	French Embassy & Consulate	B5
34	Goethe Institut	A3
35	Instituto Cervantes	B2
36	International Travel Bureau of Egypt	B3
37	Iranian Embassy	A3
38	Israeli Embassy	B4
39	Italian Embassy	D4
40	Jordanian Embassy	B3
41	Saudi Arabian Embassy	B4
42	Sudanese Embassy	D2
43	US Embassy	D2

Transport

44	Felucca Mooring Point	C1

without bathroom E£50/125/160;) Tranquil and tidy, Dina's is a good hostel option, not least because it's woman-owned and low on pressure tactics. It's also easy on the eyes, with warm colours, Egyptian appliqué pillows and soaring ceilings. The place has more private rooms than dorm beds, but it stays true to hostel roots with a gleaming shared kitchen.

The building entrance is down a passage just east of Stephenson's pharmacy.

Hotel Luna HOSTEL $

(Map p62; 2396 1020; www.hotellunacairo.com; 5th fl, 27 Sharia Talaat Harb; s/d/tr from E£150/200/250, without bathroom E£100/140/180, de luxe E£190/290/350;) Modern, backpacker-friendly Luna offers three options: simple, slightly aged rooms with shared bath; basic private-bath rooms; and the quieter 'Bella Luna' rooms with thicker mattresses and soothing pastel colour combos. Regardless, the fastidious owner has provided many small comforts, such as bedside lamps and bathmats. Resident tour organiser Sam gets high marks from readers, and there's an excellent shared kitchen.

Berlin Hotel HOSTEL $

(Map p62; 2395 7502; berlinhotelcairo@hotmail.com; 4th fl, 2 Sharia Shawarby; s/d E£120/150, with air-con E£147/197;) Berlin is pleasantly old-fashioned and very low on pressure tactics. Here, though, the knowledgable owner can arrange airport pickup and reasonably priced tours. Most of the 11 colour-saturated rooms (green! pink!) have air-con and private showers (but shared toilets); three rooms have fan only. There's a shared kitchen too, and good long-stay rates.

Sara Inn Hostel HOSTEL $

(Map p62; 0122 767 7592, 2392 2940; www.sarainnhostel.com; 21 Sharia Youssef al-Guindi; dm E£70, s/d from E£150/190, without bathroom E£100/130;) A decent option offering both dorms and private rooms for shoestring travellers. The Sara Inn is a small but personable place where you can easily get to know the staff. Plenty of well-strewn rugs and tapestries give a relaxed and cosy feel.

African House Hostel HOSTEL $
(Map p66; ☎2591 1744; www.africanhousehostel.com; 3rd fl, 15 Sharia Emad ad-Din; s/d/tr US$22/26/35, without bathroom US$16/22/29; 📶) The African House offers an affordable way to stay in one of the city's most gorgeous mid-19th-century buildings. Rooms on the 4th floor have dimmer halls, but big balconies. The shared kitchen is a bit grotty, and the toilets occasionally run, but the staff are very nice.

Meramees Hostel HOSTEL $
(Map p62; ☎2396 2318; 5th fl, 32 Sharia Sabri Abu Alam; s/d/tr E£125/150/185, dm/s/d/tr without bathroom E£41/75/110/130; ❄📶) This well-positioned hostel is easygoing, and the rooms have high ceilings, wooden floorboards, large windows and balconies – though those on the 5th floor are noticeably better kept than on the 6th. Communal bathrooms and a kitchen are kept clean, and the management seems to have travellers' interests in mind.

★**Hotel Royal** BOUTIQUE HOTEL $$
(Map p62; ☎2391 7203; cairohotelroyal.com; 1st fl, 10 Sharia Elwy; s/d/ste US$35/45/65; ❄📶) The Royal's owner brought back a minimalist all-white Scandinavian sensibility after living in Norway, all brightened with a touch of Egyptian glitz. All rooms have niceties like mini-fridges, comfy office-style desk chairs and bunches of flowers on bedside tables. It's smack in the middle of a lively late-night cafe scene, but away from main-street traffic noise.

Hotel Osiris HOTEL $$
(Map p62; ☎0100 531 1822, 2794 5728; www.hotelosiris.fr; 12th fl, 49 Sharia Nubar; s/d/tr from €25/40/50; ❄📶) On the top floor of a commercial building, the Osiris' rooms enjoy views across the city. The French-Egyptian couple who run the place keep the tile floors and white walls spotless, and the pretty hand-sewn appliqué bedspreads tidily arranged on the plush mattresses. Breakfast involves fresh juice, crêpes and omelettes. Its location in Bab al-Luq is quiet at night.

Golden Hotel HOTEL $$
(Map p62; ☎2390 3815; goldenhotelegypt.com; 13 Sharia Talaat Harb ; s/d €30/40; ❄📶) In an old building and very central location, this recently renovated hotel offers comfortable clean rooms, with high ceilings, fridges and ensuite bathrooms. The communal areas are quite

CAIRO HOTEL SCAMS

In short, all scams are attempts to distract you from your lodging of choice. Hotels do not open and close with any great frequency in Cairo, and if it's a known place, it is very unlikely to have gone out of business by the time you arrive.

At the airport, you may be approached by men or women with an official-looking badge, claiming to be government tourism representatives. (There are no such true reps at the airport.) They'll ask if you've booked a hotel, then offer to call to confirm that a room is waiting for you. Of course, they don't call the hotel – they call a friend, who says there is no booking and that his establishment is full. Concerned, the tout will offer to find you an alternative…

Some taxi drivers will stall by saying they don't know where your hotel is. In that case tell them to let you out at Midan Talaat Harb – from here it's a short walk to most budget hotels. Other lines include telling you the hotel you're heading for is closed/very expensive/horrible/a brothel and suggesting a 'better' place, for which they earn a commission, which will then be added to your bill.

The most elaborate scam is when a stranger (often on the airport bus) chats you up and asks your name and where you're staying. Then the person says goodbye and isn't seen again. What they next do is call a friend, who goes and stands outside the hotel you've booked. When you arrive, he or she will ask 'Are you…?', using the name you volunteered back at the airport. Then you'll be told that the hotel has been closed by the police/flooded due to plumbing issues/totally booked out and that the owners have organised a room for you elsewhere.

Finally, when checking in without a prior reservation, never pay for more than a night in advance. No decent hotel will ask for more, and this gives you recourse if the place doesn't meet your needs.

small, but the rooms are colourful. The friendly Egyptian-French and Swiss management will help with organising your time in Cairo.

Carlton Hotel HOTEL **$$**

(Map p62; 2575 5022; www.carltonhotelcairo.com; 21 Sharia 26th of July; s/d from E£221/315;) This centrally located hotel is a perfect base for a few days sightseeing in Cairo. If you get one of the renovated ('class A') rooms, this is a gem with a whiff of yesteryear, with the perk of an excellent rooftop bar. Most of the rooms have now been renovated but check before you book.

Victoria Hotel HOTEL **$$**

(Map p66; 2589 2290; www.victoriahotel-egypt.com; 66 Sharia al-Gomhuriyya; s/d from €40/54;) Not far from Ramses Station, the Victoria is a grand old palace with the happy addition of silent air-con, as well as comfy beds and satellite TV. Off long halls lined with clouded mirrors, the rooms have antique furniture and nice high ceilings. Two hitches: internet access isn't free, and the only nearby restaurant is At-Tabei ad-Dumyati (p99). Very close to the Orabi metro stops.

Windsor Hotel HOTEL **$$**

(Map p62; 2591 5810; www.windsorcairo.com; 19 Sharia Alfy; s/d from US$46/59, with shower & hand basin US$37/47;) Rooms at the Windsor are dim, many with low ceilings and noisy air-conditioners, and management is prone to adding surprise extra charges. But with the beautifully maintained elevator, worn stone stairs and a hotel restaurant where the dinner bell chimes every evening at 7.30pm, the place is hard for nostalgia buffs to resist.

Cairo City Center HOTEL **$$**

(Map p62; 0127 777 6383; www.cairocitycenterhotel.com; 14 Sharia Champollion; s/d US$30/40;) Don't judge it by the dingy, claustrophobic lobby – rooms here are fine, with high ceilings, shiny tile floors, new bathrooms and good-quality mattresses. The sitting area has a beautiful terrace looking straight down Sharia Mahmoud Bassiouni.

Cosmopolitan Hotel HOTEL **$$**

(Map p62; 2392 3845; 1 Sharia Ibn Taalab; s/d US$83/103;) Gloomy dark furniture, mysteriously spotted carpeting and reports of surly service would normally get this art-nouveau place dropped from the list. But its prime location, on a pedestrian street, is tough to beat. If you could choose anywhere in Cairo, this might not be it – but if it's booked as part of a package, you could do worse.

Talisman Hotel BOUTIQUE HOTEL **$$$**

(Map p62; 2393 9431; www.talisman hotel.com; 5th fl, 39 Sharia Talaat Harb; s/d from US$85/95;) The boutique Talisman has great style – jewel-tone rooms with a dash of Oriental kitsch – but its rooms aren't as well kept as they ought to be. The cocooning silence afforded by double-pane windows counts for a lot, while friendly staff make clients feel at home, and are helpful with travel arrangements.

Garden City

Just south of Midan Tahrir, this area is a lot quieter and much less congested, but there aren't many hotels to choose from.

Mandarin Hotel HOTEL **$$**

(Map p94; 2115 1145; Al-Sabah tower, 8 Sharia Ibrahim Naguib; s/d E£20-26;) Not quite as sleek as its website suggests, but still showing a bit of style, with a red-and-gold colour scheme and balconies off every room. Perks include fridges and a small but functional shared kitchen. With only 18 rooms, it fills up fast – book ahead.

Finding it in Garden City's web is a bit tricky – turn off Sharia Qasr el-Aini at the Co-op petrol station, and make the first left, and the next soft left after that. The hotel is in the same building as the Arab-African Bank.

Nile Season HOTEL **$$**

(Map p94; 0122 424 9896; www.juliana-hotel.com; 1087 Corniche an-Nil, 20 Sharia Aisha Timoria; s/d/tr US$45/55/65;) The location on the corniche is excellent. The spacious rooms are comfortable and clean, if lacking a bit in character, with good hot showers and a safe box.

Four Seasons at Nile Plaza LUXURY HOTEL **$$$**

(Map p94; 2791 7000; www.fourseasons.com/caironp; 1089 Corniche el-Nil; r from US$310;) Of the two Four Seasons in Cairo (the other is in Giza), this one has a more modern vibe (check out the cool Omar Nagdi painting behind reception), and a handier location, 15 minutes' walk from the Egyptian Museum. The impeccable rooms have windows that actually open (unfortunately rare in luxury hotels). Plus: three (!) swimming pools.

Kempinski Nile LUXURY HOTEL $$$

(Map p94; ☎2798 0000; www.kempinski.com; 12 Sharia Ahmed Ragab; r from US$140;) The Nileside tower nearly rivals its neighbour, the Four Seasons, for comfort, but the rooms are more or less half the price. Rooms are a bit smaller too, but all have balconies, and internet access is free. Service is good and friendly, and location fairly central and on the Nile. The swimming pool is a bit small.

Islamic Cairo

The negatives: no immediate metro access, touts like locusts, nowhere to get a beer and more than the usual number of mosques with loudspeakers. But this is the place to plunge in at Cairo's deep end.

El Hussein HOTEL $

(Map p76; ☎2591 8089; Midan al-Hussein; s/d E£155/180;) Off either side of an open-ended hallway where street noise reverberates, the rooms here are dreary and service surly. But the view from the front-facing ones with balconies affords mesmerising people-watching on the square below. There's a top-floor restaurant too. Entrance is in the back alley, one block off the square.

Arabian Nights HOTEL $

(Map p58; ☎2924 0924; www.arabiannights.hostel.com; 10 Sharia al-Addad; s/d/tr US$18/21/24, without bathroom US$14/17/19;) This midrange hotel is distinctly out of the tourist fray. Some rooms are quite dark and you need to check that the air-con works, but standards are generally good. The challenge is finding it: turn north on Sharia al-Mansouria (east along Sharia al-Azhar from Midan Hussein); 300m on, turn left at the ruined shell of cinema Kawakeb.

Le Riad BOUTIQUE HOTEL $$$

(Map p72; ☎2787 6074; www.leriadhotel.com; 114 Sharia al-Muizz li-Din Allah; ste from US$250;) Le Riad wouldn't be out of place in Damascus or Marrakech. In Cairo, though, it's alone in its amazing style – and, it must be said, its price. Nonetheless, the rooms are marvellous confections of Egyptian folk and Oriental fantasy, with rich colours, eye-popping fabrics and beaded lamps galore. Great views from the rooftop terrace.

Zamalek

The relatively quiet enclave of Zamalek offers the best night's sleep in the city, if not the cheapest. Many of Cairo's best restaurants, shops, bars and coffee shops are here, but sights are a taxi ride away over traffic-jammed bridges.

Mayfair Hotel HOTEL $

(Map p88; ☎2735 7315; www.mayfaircairo.com; 2nd fl, 9 Sharia Aziz Osman; s/d from E£275/320, without bathroom E£190/215;) The cheapest sleep in the neighbourhood, on a quiet street, with a fine large terrace. Double rooms are clean and a good size, with balconies, TVs and fridges. Some single rooms are cramped, and the young staff perfectly nice but perhaps a tad too attentive to female guests.

★Hotel Longchamps HOTEL $$

(Map p88; ☎2735 2311; hotellongchamps.com; 5th fl, 21 Sharia Ismail Mohammed; s/d/tr from US$80/106/126;) The old-style Hotel Longchamps is very much a favourite of returning visitors to Cairo, a home away from home – it's like staying in a smart Cairene apartment – with a friendly and extremely helpful owner. The comfortable, stylish rooms are spacious and well maintained, and if you want your own balcony and a small bathtub, get an 'executive' room.

This hotel is one where you usually need to book ahead. Guests gather to chat on the greenery-covered, peaceful rear balcony around sunset, or lounge in the restaurant.

Golden Tulip Flamenco Hotel HOTEL $$

(Map p88; ☎2735 0815; www.flamencohotels.com; 2 Sharia Gezirat al-Wusta; s/d/tr from US$87/97/128;) This popular place is a reasonable alternative to five-star heavyweights. Rooms are comfortable and well equipped, if slightly cramped in standard configuration. The extra US$10 for 'superior' class gives you interior space and a balcony overlooking the houseboats on the Nile.

Sofitel El Gezirah LUXURY HOTEL $$$

(Map p94; ☎2737 3737; www.sofitel.com; Sharia al-Orman; r from US$150;) Tired from travelling? Rest up here in a sumptuous room with superb views, and let the staff look after you. This hotel, on the tip of Gezira island, is delightfully quiet compared to other hotels in the area, but it can be hard to get a cab out. There are several good restaurants, one of them a favourite of ours, and the Buddha Bar.

Cairo Marriott Hotel LUXURY HOTEL $$$
(Map p88; ☎2728 3000; www.marriott.com/caieg; 16 Sharia Saray al-Gezira; r from US$155; P❄📶🏊) Historic atmosphere is thick in the lobby and public areas, which all occupy a 19th-century palace. The rooms are all in two modern towers, and many have tiny bathrooms, but touches like plasma-screen TVs and extra-plush beds make up for it. It also has a popular garden cafe, a great place to people-watch, and a good pool.

Doqqi

An upscale option, the Cairo Sheraton, was undergoing renovation at the time of research, and was set to reopen in early 2015.

El Tonsy HOTEL $$
(Map p94; ☎3337 6908; 143 Sharia Tahrir; s/d US$45/60; ❄📶) This smart, modern place is often used by groups, but it's also handy for the independent traveller who prefers to stay in a less touristy neighbourhood. The carpeted rooms are a little spare, but some have huge balconies (with Nile views for US$10 more), and there's a great terrace bar from which you can spy the Pyramids.

Eating

In Cairo, you can spend E£5 or E£500 on dinner. At one end of the spectrum are the street carts, *kushari* counters, and fruit-and-veg markets where the majority of Cairenes feed themselves. One step up are the Egyptian fast-food operations – forget 'Kentucky' and Pizza Hut – that serve some of the most delicious and cheap meals you'll have. As with the hotel scene, reliable mid-range options are in short supply, but the few good ones offer great value, especially for traditional food.

At the upper end, Cairo dining can be quite cosmopolitan, with the chefs usually imported straight from the relevant country, along with all the ingredients. Dinner reservations are generally recommended.

Many restaurants double as bars and nightclubs, with guests proceeding from multicourse meals into boozing and grooving.

Too tired to leave the hotel? You can get just about anything delivered, and even order online through **Otlob.com** (www.otlob.com), with service from more than 120 of the city's most popular restaurants.

Downtown

This is predominantly cheap-and-cheerful territory, plus a few nostalgic favourites. It's by far the best place to get good authentic Egyptian food.

★ **At-Tabei Ad-Dumyati** EGYPTIAN $
(Map p66; ☎2579 7533; 31 Sharia Orabi, Tewfikiya; dishes E£5-25; ⏲7am-1am; 🖉) This place offers some of the cheapest meals in Cairo – and also some of the freshest and most delicious, both sit-down and takeaway. Start by picking four salads from a large array, then order shwarma or ta'amiyya, along with some lentil soup or fuul. There are branches on **Talaat Harb** (Map p62; Talaat Harb Complex, Sharia Talaat Harb; dishes E£5-25; ⏲9am-midnight) and in Mohandeseen (p104).

Abu Tarek EGYPTIAN $
(Map p62; 40 Sharia Champollion; dishes E£5-12; ⏲8am-midnight; 🖉) 'We have no other branches!' proclaims this temple of *kushari*. No, the place has just expanded, decade by decade, into the upper storeys of its building, even as it has held onto the unofficial 'Best Kushari' title. It's worth eating in to check out the elaborate decor upstairs. You must pay in advance, either at the till downstairs (for takeaway) or with your waiter.

Akher Sa'a EGYPTIAN FAST FOOD $
(Map p62; ☎2575 1668; 14 Sharia Abdel Khalek, Sarwat; dishes E£2-10; ⏲24hr) A frantically busy fuul and ta'amiyya takeaway joint with a no-frills cafeteria next door, Akher Sa'a has a limited menu but its food is fresh and good. This branch in Sarwat has a fast-food-style set-up downstairs (note the genius giant-ta'amiyya 'burger') but glacial table service upstairs. There is also a branch on **Sharia Alfy** (Map p62; 8 Sharia Alfy; dishes E£2-10 ; ⏲24hr).

BUS STATION SNACK

If you're just passing through Cairo Gateway bus station and need a meal, take a short walk to **Hamada** (Map p66; Sharia al-Sahafa; kushari from E£5) for exceptionally good *kushari*. Turn right out the front of the bus station, then make a left at the first intersection; Hamada is on the right, midway down, with a red sign.

El-Abd BAKERY $

(Map p62; 25 Sharia Talaat Harb; pastries E£2-10; 8.30am-midnight) For pastries head for Cairo's most famous bakery, easily identified by the crowds of people outside tearing into their croissants, sweets and savoury pies. It's a great place to augment your ho-hum hotel breakfast. There is another branch at **Talaat Harb** (Map p62; 35 Sharia Talaat Harb; pastries E£2-10; 8.30am-midnight).

Fatatri at-Tahrir EGYPTIAN FAST FOOD $

(Map p62; 166 Sharia Tahrir; dishes E£9-20; 7am-1am) This tiny place just off Midan Tahrir has been serving sweet and savoury *fiteer* (flaky pizza) to Downtown residents and legions of backpackers for decades. It's reliable and delicious, though it can get very crowded in the afternoon.

Koshary Goha EGYPTIAN FAST FOOD $

(Map p62; 4 Sharia Emad ad-Din; kushari E£5, pasta E£13; 10am-midnight) Solid *kushari* in a gorgeous vintage-Cairo setting. But the real treat is the *makaroneh bi-lahm,* a baked pasta casserole with spicy tomato sauce. The staff sometimes calls it lasagne.

Sudan Restaurant NORTH AFRICAN $

(Map p62; Haret al-Sufi; dishes E£8-22; 10am-10pm) One of several Sudanese restaurants and cafes in this alley, this is the tidiest and perhaps serves the most delicious dishes. Try *salata iswid* ('black salad'), a spicy mix of eggplant and peanuts, and *qarassa,* stew served in a bread bowl, among other treats.

It's in the alley connecting Sharia Adly and Sharia Abdel Khalek Sarwat, in a courtyard off the southern end. Sign is Arabic only – yellow letters on a red background.

★ **Fasahat Soumaya** EGYPTIAN $$

(Map p62; 0100 9873 8637; 15 Sharia Youssef al-Guindi; mains E£28-30; 1-10.30pm;) Down a little pedestrian alley is this sweet restaurant with only a few tables. All the staples are here, prepared like an Egyptian mom would make: various stuffed vegies, hearty stews and extra odd bits (rice sausage, lamb shanks) on Thursdays. The sign is in Arabic only, green on a white wall, with a few steps down to the basement space.

★ **Café Riche** EGYPTIAN, EUROPEAN $$

(Map p62; 2392 9793; 17 Sharia Talaat Harb; dishes E£30-50; 10am-midnight;) This narrow restaurant, allegedly the oldest in Cairo, was once the favoured drinking spot of the intelligentsia. A certain old guard still sits under the ceiling fans, along with tourists who like the historic ambience. It's a reliable and nostalgic spot to enjoy a cold beer (E£12) and a meal of slightly Frenchified Egyptian dishes.

Kafein EUROPEAN, VEGETARIAN $$

(Map p62; 0100 302 5346; 28 Sharia Sherif; 7am-1.30am;) A great addition to Downtown eateries is this air-conditioned cafe-restaurant on two floors, with a small terrace in the little alley off Sharia Sherif. Many a foreign journalist enjoys the cool, free wi-fi and good coffee (E£8) here. On offer are delicious sandwiches (E£24 to E£30), fresh salads (E£25), milk shakes, teas served in a pot (E£15) and fresh juices.

Greek Club GREEK, EGYPTIAN $$

(Map p62; 2575 0822; 28 Sharia Mahmoud Bassiouni; E£30 min charge & E£5 cover charge for non-Greek; dishes E£10-45; 5pm-midnight) The Greek Club is a Downtown institution and a popular hangout with liberal Egyptians, artists and expats. A cold beer (E£12) on the outdoor terrace is joy during summer months. The food is nothing special but more than adequate, and the main dining room oozes vintage charm with high ceilings and tall columns.

Le Bistro FRENCH $$

(Map p62; 2392 7694; 8 Sharia Hoda Shaarawi; mains E£35-75; noon-11pm) Tucked away below street level, Le Bistro is a surprisingly fancy outpost Downtown. The food may not quite match its European ideal, but Cairenes love it, and steak *frites* can make a nice change from kebab. The restaurant entrance is to the right; you can also order off the food menu at the bar (enter to the left).

Felfela Restaurant EGYPTIAN $$

(Map p62; 2392 2833; 15 Sharia Hoda Shaarawi; dishes E£22-55; 8am-midnight;) Attracting tourists, coach parties and locals since 1963, Felfela is an institution that can deliver a reliable, if not wildly delicious, meal with good service. A bizarre jungle theme rules the decor, but the food is straight-down-the-line Egyptian and consistently decent, especially the mezze and grilled chicken.

Hati al-Geish GRILL $$

(Map p62; 23 Sharia Falaki; mains E£25-65; 11am-11pm) Carnivores will salivate upon entering this place, where the air is heavy with the smell of charcoal-cooked meat. The *kastileeta* (lamb chops) are splendid, and the tender *moza* (shanks) good for gnawing – the *moza fatta*, with a side of rice-and-pita casserole, is very good. No beer, but good fresh juices, and the waiters are quite dapper too.

Gad EGYPTIAN $$

(Map p62; ☎ 2576 3583; 13 Sharia 26th of July, Downtown; sandwiches E£4-18, mains E£25-60; ⏰ 9am-2am; 🖉) Gad's lighthouse logo is fitting: it's a beacon in the night for hungry Cairenes. The ground floor is for takeaway: *fiteer*, shwarma and salads. Order and pay at the till, then take the receipts to the relevant counters. Or sit upstairs and order off the menu.

The branch on **Sarwat** (Map p62; Sharia Abdel Khalek Sarwat at Shawarby; sandwiches E£4-18, mains E£25-60; ⏰ 9am-2am) is typically less crowded. There are also branches on **Sharia al-Azhar** (Map p78; Sharia al-Azhar; sandwiches E£4-18, mains E£25-60; ⏰ 9am-2am) and **Midan Falaki** (Map p62; Midan Falaki; sandwiches E£4-18, mains E£25-60; ⏰ 24hr).

Estoril EGYPTIAN $$

(Map p62; ☎ 2574 3102; off Sharia Talaat Harb; mezze E£12-45, mains E£37-78; ⏰ noon-midnight) There are clouds of cigarette smoke and tables crammed with Cairo's arts-and-letters set here, but once seated you'll feel like one of the club, scooping up simple mezze and ordering cold beer after beer. Women can come alone here, and the bar in the back is a good place to perch too. Food is nothing special but the atmosphere is old school.

Abu al-Hassan al-Haty GRILL $$

(Map p62; 3 Sharia Halim; mains E£20-55; ⏰ 11am-12am) With its foggy mirrors, dusty chandeliers and waiters who look older than the building itself, this is a beautiful relic of Downtown – it's often used as a set for period TV shows. The food (mostly grilled items) is a bit secondary, but perfectly palatable.

Gomhouriya EGYPTIAN $$

(Map p62; 42 Sharia Falaki; pigeons E£35; ⏰ noon-midnight) Roast, stuffed pigeon is the star of the show here – just tell the waiter how many birds you want, and they arrive crisp and hot, along with salad and all-you-can-drink mugs of peppery, lemony broth. The small English sign says 'Shalapy'.

Self-Catering

Souq at-Tawfiqiyya MARKET

(Sharia at-Tawfiqiyya; Map p62; ⏰ 7am-9pm) Blocks-long fruit-and-veg market, open late. Good dairy store at corner with Talaat Harb selling fresh cheese.

Souq Bab al-Luq MARKET

(Map p62; Midan Falaki; ⏰ 7am-7pm) Big indoor neighbourhood market with produce and meat; surrounding shops sell dry goods.

Garden City

This is the place to come for a formal feast. The luxury hotels lining the banks of the Nile here have some truly excellent restaurants.

Mahrous EGYPTIAN $

(Map p94; Sharia al-Haras; meals E£15; ⏰ 4pm-4am; 🖉) Perhaps Cairo's best fuul, and worth elevating to dinner status (note the atypical hours). With each plate of beans, you get a big spread of salads and fresh potato chips. It's just a tiny stand on a residential block. Turn in to Garden City at the Co-op gas station, make the first left, then a hard left at the next intersection.

Taboula LEBANESE $$

(Map p94; ☎ 2792 5261; www.taboula-eg.com; 1 Sharia Latin America; mezze E£15-35, mains E£37-85; ⏰ noon-1am) The Lebanese food at this basement joint isn't as good as Sabaya's, but the atmosphere is more fun – here it's all big groups of Cairenes celebrating birthdays around giant communal tables, with lots of cocktails to go around. Mezze like the *tomiyya* (garlic sauce) are your best bet, but skip the meatballs.

Osmanly TURKISH $$$

(Map p94; ☎ 2798 0000; Kempinski Nile, Corniche el-Nil; mezze E£40, mains E£130-240; ⏰ noon-midnight; 🖉) Exceptionally good Turkish food, served with elan, starting with handwashing in jasmine-scented water and moving on to a dazzling selection of cold mezze, and impeccably grilled meat. The four-course set menu is a relative steal at E£395.

★ Sabaya LEBANESE $$$

(Map p62; ☎ 2795 7171; Semiramis InterContinental, Corniche el-Nil; mezze E£25-75, mains E£80-180; ⏰ 7.30pm-1am) Delicious Lebanese food in a sumptuous but relaxed atmosphere. Diverse and delicate mezze come with fresh-baked pillows of pita, and mains such as *fatta* are served in individual cast-iron pots. The setting is very sleek, but considering portion sizes are generous and sharing is the norm, the prices are not as high as you would expect.

Bird Cage THAI $$$

(Map p62; ☎2795 7171; Semiramis InterContinental, Corniche el-Nil; mains E£75-145; ⏲noon-midnight) This soothing, wood-panelled space is a favourite with wealthy Cairenes. Grilled foods don't have the proper char, but other preparations, such as whole sea bass wrapped in banana leaves, are good and beautifully presented. The chef will make it truly Thai-spicy if you ask.

Revolving Restaurant FRENCH $$$

(Map p94; ☎2365 1234; www.grandniletower.com; Grand Nile Tower; mains E£190-320; ⏲7pm-midnight) Start with *terrine de foie gras* as you peer at the Pyramids from the 41st floor. By the time your *filet d'agneau* with tomato confit and a sweet garlic doughnut arrives, you'll be looking east to the Citadel. Sure, it's a gimmick, but the Revolving Restaurant at least has good French haute cuisine as well. Unlike in the rest of this Saudi-run hotel, alcohol is served.

Coptic Cairo

Elfostat Tivoli EGYPTIAN $$

(Map p68; Sharia Hassan al-Anwar; ⏲9:30am-7pm) The best place to rest up after a Coptic Cairo tour, though there's no real local feel as it's part of the built-for-tourists Souq al-Fustat complex. Still, prices are reasonable considering the garden setting.

Islamic Cairo

There are plenty of fast-food joints around Midan al-Hussein but the restaurants in this part of town are limited – you really have to like grilled meat, and not be too squeamish about hygiene.

Citadel View MIDDLE EASTERN $$

(Map p58; ☎2510 9151; Al-Azhar Park; mains E£42-130; ⏲noon-midnight; ✎) Eating at this gorgeous restaurant in Al-Azhar Park – on a vast multilevel terrace, with the whole city sprawled below – feels great. Fortunately the prices are not so stratospheric, and the food is good, with dishes like spicy sausage with pomegranate syrup and grilled fish with tahini. On Friday, only a buffet (E£150) is on offer. No alcohol.

Al-Halwagy EGYPTIAN $

(Map p76; ☎2591 7055; Midan al-Hussein; dishes E£6-30; ⏲24hr) Not directly on the square, but just behind a row of buildings, this good ta'amiyya, fuul and salad place has been around for nearly a century. You can eat at pavement tables or hide away upstairs.

Farahat EGYPTIAN $$

(Map p76; 126A Sharia al-Azhar; pigeons E£30; ⏲noon-midnight) In an alley off Sharia Al-Azhar, this place is legendary for its pigeon, available stuffed or grilled. It doesn't look like much – just plastic chairs outside – but once you start nibbling the succulent, spiced birds, you'll believe the hype.

Khan el-Khalili Restaurant & Mahfouz Coffee Shop EGYPTIAN $$

(Map p76; ☎2590 3788; 5 Sikket al-Badistan; snacks E£15-40, mains E£35-105; ⏲10am-2am) The luxurious Moorish-style interiors of this restaurant and adjoining cafe are a popular haven from the khan's bustle. The place may be geared to tourists but the food is good, the air-con is strong and the toilets are clean. Look for the metal detector in the lane, immediately west of the medieval gate.

Lakeside Cafe INTERNATIONAL $$

(Map p78; ☎2510 9162; Al-Azhar Park, Sharia Salah Salem; mezze E£12-25, mains E£19-59; P ❄ 📶 👪) Relaxing views over the lake and the minarets and domes of the old city of Cairo. Stick to the mezze, which are delicious, and the Egyptian specials, as the European dishes are less tasty. The views are superb.

Zamalek

Zamalek has some of Cairo's best and most stylish restaurants. Cheap dining is not one of the island's fortes, but there are a few possibilities, such as the **Baraka shwarma stand** on Sharia Brazil.

Mandarine Koueider ICE CREAM $

(Map p88; ☎2735 5010; 17 Sharia Shagaret ad-Durr; per scoop E£5; ⏲9am-11pm) The place to get your fix of delectable ice cream and sorbet. Definitely try the *zabadi bi-tut* (yoghurt with blackberry).

Rigoletto ICE CREAM $

(Map p88; ☎0102 666 3110; www.rigolettoicecream.com; Yamama Center, 3 Sharia Taha Hussein; per scoop E£8; ⏲10am-midnight; ❄) Delicious ice cream; try the *mastik* (Arabic gum) or mango ice, or bite into the brownies or carrot cake.

★**Zööba** EGYPTIAN $$

(Map p88; ☎3345 3980; www.ZoobaEats.com; Sharia 26th of July; salads E£12-15, mains E£13-19, desserts E£3-15; ⏰8am-1am) Small eatery serving fresh street food prepared with a gourmet twist; the delicious dishes can also be taken away – ideal for a picnic. Fresh juices, salads, whole-wheat *kushari* and fabulous salads. Keep space for the more-ish desserts like rice pudding with sweet potatoes and cinnamon. All is served at a zinc-clad table in the funkiest and most eclectic of decors.

Cairo Kitchen EGYPTIAN $$
(Map p88; ☎2735 4000; www.cairokitchen.com; 118 Sharia 26th of Jul; salads E£9-25, mains E£23-55; ⏰10am-midnight) Cairo Kitchen is a contemporary restaurant serving up traditional wholesome Egyptian home cooking. Order from the counter – a salad plate, a brown-rice *kushari* or a typical Egyptian stew of the day. The decor is colourful, prices are good and the place is popular with Cairenes. The cook book is already out too. Entrance on Sharia Aziz Osman.

L'Aubergine BISTRO $$
(Map p88; ☎2738 0080; 5 Sharia Sayyed al-Bakry; mains E£39-95; ⏰noon-2am; 🍸) This snug, white-walled, candlelit restaurant devotes half its menu to global vegetarian dishes, such as Turkish stewed aubergine and gnocchi with blue cheese. You can't go wrong with most of the cheesier, creamier items, and the chill-out soundtrack is a nice respite from Cairo street noise. At 10pm the DJ turns up the music, and a younger crowd arrives. Book ahead.

Didos Al Dente ITALIAN $$
(Map p88; ☎2735 9117; 26 Sharia Bahgat Ali; pasta E£18-42, pizza E£26-29; ⏰11am-2am) A noisy, crowded pizza-and-pasta joint with a small outdoor space, Didos rings with the clatter of dishes and often has crowds waiting out front for a table. It's popular with students from the nearby AUC dorm. No alcohol.

Abou El Sid EGYPTIAN $$
(Map p88; ☎2735 9640; www.abouelsid.com; 157 Sharia 26th of July; mezze E£15-35, mains E£37-90; ⏰noon-2am) Cairo's first hipster Egyptian restaurant (and now a national franchise), Abou El Sid is as popular with tourists as it is with upper-class natives. You can get better *molokhiyya* (garlicky leaf soup) elsewhere, but here you wash it down with a cocktail and lounge on kitschy gilt 'Louis Farouk' furniture.

The entrance is down a street off 26th of July, on the west side of the Baehler's Mansions complex; look for the tall wooden doors. Reservations are a good idea.

Maison Thomas EUROPEAN $$
(Map p88; ☎2735 7057; 157 Sharia 26th of July; sandwiches E£30-70, pizzas E£47-78; ⏰24hr) A little slice of the Continent, with loads of brass and mirrors, and waiters in long white aprons serving crusty baguette sandwiches. But this institution is best known for its pizza, with generous toppings.

Sufi CAFETERIA $$
(Map p88; ☎2738 1643; www.sufiegy.com; 12 Sharia Sayyed al-Bakry; dishes E£18-30; ⏰10am-midnight; 📶) Very popular in the evening with young Cairenes, serving healthy salads, filling sandwiches, pasta and both Oriental and Continental breakfast. The cafeteria is set in the bookshop; the cool interior was designed by Loft (p112) next door, and there is space for exhibitions and film screenings.

La Mezzaluna ITALIAN $$
(Map p88; ☎2735 2655; Sharia Aziz Osman; mains E£28-78; ⏰8am-11pm; 🍸) Head down a tiny alley to find this cool dual-level space that's frequented by Cairo bohemians. The menu is roughly Italian, from conventional combos such as tomato and basil to others like dill-and-salmon ravioli. Salads are enormous. No alcohol is served, but the little patio out front is a quiet place to take coffee.

Left Bank BRASSERIE, BAKERY $$
(Map p88; ☎2735 0014; www.leftbankonline.com; 53 Sharia Abu al-Feda; mains E£35-120; ⏰8am-midnight; P ❄) A great place for breakfast on the Nile, with a stylish indoor space, a wonderful terrace and a fabulous bread counter. The delicious Cairo breakfast (E£36) comes with eggs, fuul, falafel, feta, chick-pea salad and fresh juice. Later in the day there is a wide selection of salads, pastas, pizza and Mediterranean dishes. Popular with the Zamalek crowd.

Nawab INDIAN $$
(Map p88; ☎2736 0433; 21B Sharia Bahgat Ali; mains E£45-78; ⏰noon-10pm; 🍸) If you want some Indian spice without the trek to the Mena House in Giza, come to this good-value neighbourhood spot for butter chicken, lamb korma and a solid vegetarian selection.

Five Bells EGYPTIAN $$
(Map p88; ☎2735 8980; 13 Sharia Ismail Mohammed; mezze E£19-47; ⏰12.30pm-1am) A pretty place to rest up after a long stroll through Zamalek, this atmospheric garden restaurant serves traditional Egyptian mezze to a soundtrack of Edith Piaf and other wistful

European tunes. Snack on hot meatballs, fresh fried potato crisps and cold beer (E£18). Very popular at night.

La Taverna INTERNATIONAL **$$**
(Map p88; ☎2738 0936; 140 Sharia 26th of July; mains E£18-45; ⏲8am-midnight) Thanks to its proximity to El Sawy Cultural Wheel, there's usually an interesting crowd of Egyptians at this casual restaurant, and a buzz of big concepts being discussed. The food itself (club sandwiches, pasta) isn't astounding, but it's reasonably priced for Zamalek, and there's outside seating or cool air-con indoors.

Makani CAFE, SUSHI **$$**
(Map p88; ☎2736 1486; 118 Sharia 26th of July; ⏲10am-2am) Sushi and croissants aren't a standard combo, but both the Japanese flavours and the sandwiches are quite good, and the atmosphere is great for either hanging out over coffee and delicious carrot cake, or for a longer meal.

Self-Catering

Several shops on 26th of July sell very good quality produce.

Alfa Market SUPERMARKET
(Map p88; ☎2737 0801; 4 Sharia al-Malek al-Afdal; ⏲8am-10pm) Local foods and imported items.

Sekem SELF-CATERING
(Map p88; ☎2738 2724; www.sekem.com; 8 Sharia Ahmed Sabry; ⏲9am-8pm) Organic products and tofu.

Mohandiseen & Doqqi

These concrete suburbs look bland and flavourless, but it's possible to find some excellent restaurants – and don't discount the Nile views.

Al-Omda EGYPTIAN FAST FOOD **$**
(Map p88; ☎02-3346 2701; 6 Sharia al-Gazayer, Mohandiseen; dishes E£8-30; ⏲24hr; ❄📶) A mini-empire taking up the better part of a block, Al-Omda offers numerous ways to put grilled meats into your system. At the takeout joint on the corner, get a *shish tawooq* (marinated chicken grilled on skewers) sandwich with spicy pickles.

Or else you can sit down in the old-style 'Oriental' restaurant around the corner to your left, or head upstairs to the neon-lit cafe and get a sheesha with the trendy crowd.

At-Tabei ad-Dumyati EGYPTIAN FAST FOOD **$**
(Map p88; ☎3304 1124; 17 Sharia Gamiat ad-Dowal al-Arabiyya, Mohandesseen; dishes E£5-25; ⏲7am-1am) A branch of the Downtown fast-food experts.

Yemen Restaurant MIDDLE-EASTERN **$**
(Map p94; ☎3338 8087; 10 Sharia Iran, Doqqi; dishes E£15-45; ⏲24hr) This fluorescent-lit place has all the ambience of a car showroom, but it does have great authentic Yemeni dishes, served without cutlery, and huge rounds of flaky flatbread for scooping. Everything-in-the-pot salta (stew) is standard, but most everything on the cryptic menu is richly spiced, even the 'choped meat'. Sharia Iran is one block north of Midan Doqqi, running west.

Abu Ammar al-Suri SYRIAN **$**
(Map p88; ☎3336 0887; 8 Sharia Syria, Mohandiseen; sandwiches E£12-20, mains E£27-65; ⏲24hr) At this crowded fast-food operation, pantalooned men work the shwarma skewers, folding meat slices into huge pieces of Syrian-style *saj* flatbread. It does good lentil soup too.

Cedars LEBANESE **$$**
(Map p88; ☎3345 0088; 42 Sharia Geziret al-Arab, Mohandiseen; mezze E£20-37, mains E£46-80; ⏲10am-1am) This chic Lebanese restaurant is a favourite with Mohandiseen's lunching ladies, then with a younger crowd later in the evening. Rattan chairs dot the spacious terrace, where there's sheesha along with the better-than-average food: peppery *mouhamarra* (walnut and pomegranate syrup dip), fresh *ayran* (yogurt drink) and sandwiches stuffed with French fries. You can also get meals from the grill.

Sea Gull SEAFOOD **$$$**
(Map p94; ☎3749 4244; 106 Sharia el-Nil, Agouza; meals E£100-170; ⏲11am-1am) There's no menu here, just select your fish from the iced-down display, then retire to your table to admire the view and tuck into a spread of salads while everything is grilled. The crowd is almost entirely Egyptian families. Outside seating is great on a balmy night; there's air-con inside if you want it.

Drinking & Nightlife

Cairo isn't a 'dry' city, but locals tend to run on caffeine by day, available at both traditional ahwas and European-style cafes. Drinking alchohol typically doesn't start till the evening hours, and then it's limited to Western-style bars, most with a lot of expats mixed in, and some cheaper, more locals-only dives. For the former, Zamalek is the best place to go boozing; the latter are all Downtown.

Liquor is expensive, local wine is drinkable but not great, but beer is widely available and cheap. Beers range from around E£10 to E£25; cocktails are typically only at more upscale bars and range from E£40 to E£90. The fancier places can have door policies as strict as the nightclubs, so dress well and go in mixed groups. Many places also have full menus, so you can snack as you go.

Downtown

Vent BAR
(Map p62; ☎2574 7898; 6 Sharia Qasr el-Nil; ⏰noon-2am) Cairo's most happening and coolest art-space-cum-bar with live music sessions by international and local hip-hop and grime artists. There are screenings of experimental films and other events. This was formerly the Arabesque restaurant.

Odeon Palace Hotel BAR
(Map p62; ☎2577 6637; www.hodeon.com; 6 Sharia Abdel Hamid Said; ⏰24hr) Its fake turf singed by sheesha coals, this slightly dilapidated rooftop bar is favoured by Cairo's heavy-drinking theatre and cinema clique, and is a great place to watch the sun go down (or even better, come up).

Zahret al-Bustan COFFEEHOUSE
(Map p62; Sharia Talaat Harb; tea & sheesha E£9; ⏰8am-2am) This traditional ahwa is a bit of an intellectuals' and artists' haunt, though also firmly on many backpackers' lists, so be alert to scam artists. It's in the lane just behind Café Riche.

Windsor Bar BAR
(Map p62; ☎2591 5810; 19 Sharia Alfy; ⏰6pm-1am) Alas, most of the Windsor's regular clientele has passed on, leaving a few hotel guests, a cordial, polyglot bartender and a faint soundtrack of swing jazz and Umm Kolthum. Colonial history has settled in an almost palpable film on the taxidermist's antelope heads, the barrel-half chairs and the dainty wall sconces. Solo women will feel comfortable here.

Le Grillon BAR
(Map p62; ☎2574 3114; 8 Sharia Qasr el-Nil; ⏰11am-2am) Nominally a restaurant, this bizarre faux patio is all about beer, sheesha and gossip about politics and the arts scene. The illusion of outdoors is created with wicker furniture, fake vines and lots of ceiling fans. The entrance is in the back of a courtyard between two buildings.

Cilantro CAFE
(Map p62; 31 Sharia Mohammed Mahmoud; coffees & teas E£8-35, sandwiches E£15-50; ⏰9am-2am; 📶) Egypt's answer to Starbucks and Costa, this popular chain does all the usual coffee drinks, teas and juices, plus packaged sandwiches and cakes. If it weren't for the gaggles of headscarf-wearing teenage girls who crowd the banquettes after school, it would be easy to forget you're in Egypt.

There are other branches just about everywhere you turn: **Zamalek** (Map p88; Shorouk Bookstore, 17 Sharia Hassan Sabry, Zamalek; coffees & teas E£8-35, sandwiches E£15-50; ⏰10am-11pm), **Heliopolis** (4 Sharia Ibrahim; coffees & teas E£8-35, sandwiches E£15-50; ⏰24hr) and **Doqqi** (Map p94; Midan al-Missaha, Doqqi; coffees & teas E£8-35, sandwiches E£15-50; ⏰7am-1am),

FIND YOUR OWN AHWA

Cairo's ahwas – traditional coffeehouses – are essential places to unwind, chat and breathe deeply over a sheesha. Dusty floors, rickety tables and the clatter of dominoes and *towla* (backgammon) define the traditional ones. But newer, shinier places – where women smoke as well – have expanded the concept, not to mention the array of sheesha flavours, which now include everything from mango to bubblegum.

There's an ahwa for every possible subculture. We list a couple of the most famous ones here but half the joy of the ahwa is discovering 'yours'. Look in back alleys all over Downtown. Sports fans gather south of Sharia Alfy; intellectuals at Midan Falaki. There's a nice traditional joint down the lane behind Al-Azhar Mosque, and a cool mixed crowd next to Townhouse Gallery (p67). Young activists have claimed the pedestrian streets around the stock exchange. Even some mall food courts can be surprisingly fun. Most ahwas are open from 8am to 2am or so, and you can order a lot more than tea and coffee: try *karkadai* (hibiscus, hot or cold), *irfa* (cinnamon), *kamun* (cumin, good for colds), *yansun* (anise) and, in winter, hot, milky *sahlab*.

BALADI BAR CRAWL

Bar-hopping in Cairo typically takes you to Western-style lounges. But there's a parallel drinking culture in cheaper *baladi* (local) bars. These 'cafeterias', as they're often signed, have a slightly seedy, old-fashioned air. Renovations funded by beer company Stella have taken a layer of grime off a few, and now there's even an online guide at www.baladibar.com. Entrances are often hidden or screened off. Beers cost E£8 to E£12, and waiters expect tips. A few Downtown classics:

Cafeteria El Horreya (Map p62; ☎2392 0397; Midan Falaki; ⌚8am-2am) A Cairo institution, and quite wholesome as it's big, brightly lit and welcoming to women. No beer served on the side with the chessboards.

Cafeteria Stella (Map p62; cnr Sharia Hoda Shaarawi & Sharia Talaat Harb; ⌚1pm-midnight) Ceilings are higher than the room is wide, with tables crammed with a mix of characters from afternoon on. Look for the entrance behind a kiosk. Free nibbles are served with beer.

Cap d'Or (Map p62; ☎2123 8957; Sharia Abdel Khalek Sarwat; ⌚4pm-2am) Quite run-down and lit with fluorescent bulbs. The staff are used to seeing foreigners, but usually male-only.

Greek Club (p100) Cool beer on a terrace, and an air-kissing crowd talking about art, revolution and politics.

Cairo (Map p62; ☎2574 1479; 3 Sharia Saray al-Ezbekiyya; beer E£9.75; ⌚10am-3am) Walk through the grill restaurant to the 1st-floor bar. The sign is in Arabic only, blue letters on a red background.

Gemaica (Map p62; 16 Sharia Sherif; ⌚11am-2am) That's Egyptian for 'Jamaica'. In the pedestrian area around the stock exchange.

to name a few. All offer free wi-fi, strong air-con and usually clean restrooms.

Groppi's CAFE
(Map p62; Midan Talaat Harb; coffee & pastries from E£7; ⌚8am-11pm) Distinctly *not* part of the new coffee wave, Groppi's high point was more than 50 years ago when it was one of the most celebrated patisseries this side of the Mediterranean. Today, the offerings are poor and overpriced, and the tearoom reeks of cheap tobacco, but it nevertheless continues to appeal to hardcore nostalgia buffs.

Soma Caffe COFFEEHOUSE
(Map p62; 11 Sharia Saray al-Ezbekiyya; ⌚24hr) An ahwa dedicated to Kawkab al-Sharq ('Star of the Orient'), an epithet for the famous Egyptian singer Umm Kolthum. Look for the huge busts of the singer out front. Complement it with a visit to **Al-Andaleeb**, dedicated to singer/composer Mohammed Abd al-Wahhab, down the block at the corner with Sharia Mohammed Farid.

Drinkies LIQUOR STORE
(Map p62; ☎19930; 41 Sharia Talaat Harb) Spiffy modern booze sellers; no need to sneak behind a curtain, and even offers delivery.

Islamic Cairo

Fishawi's COFFEEHOUSE
(Map p76; Khan al-Khalili; ⌚24hr, during Ramadan 5pm-3am) Probably the oldest ahwa in the city, and certainly the most celebrated, Fishawi's has been a great place to watch the world go by since 1773. Despite being swamped by foreign tourists and equally wide-eyed out-of-town Egyptians, it is a regular ahwa, serving up *shai* (tea) and sheesha to stallholders and shoppers alike. Prices vary so confirm with your waiter.

Coffeeshop Al-Khatoun COFFEEHOUSE
(Map p78; Midan Al-Khatoun; tea & sheesha E£15; ⌚3pm-1am) Tucked away in a quiet square behind Al-Azhar, this modern outdoor ahwa is a great place to rest up after a walk, with tea and snacks and comfortable pillow-strewn benches. In the evenings it attracts an arty crowd – students from the Arabic Oud House school on the square and others.

Zamalek & Gezira

Sequoia LOUNGE
(Map p88; ☎2576 8086; www.sequoiaonline.ne; 3 Sharia Abu al-Feda, Zamalek; beer E£34, minimum charge Sun-Wed E£125, Thu-Sat E£150; ⌚1pm-

1am) At the very northern tip of Zamalek, this sprawling Nileside lounge is a swank scene, with low cushions for nursing a sheesha, snacking on everything from Egyptian-style mezze (E£25 to E£60) to sushi and sipping a cocktail (E£48 to E£83). We don't recommend it for main meals. Bring an extra layer – evenings right on the water can be surprisingly cool.

Simonds CAFE

(Map p88; ☎2735 9436; 112 Sharia 26th of July, Zamalek; coffees & pastries from E£10; ⊙7am-10pm) The recent overhaul of this century-old French-style cafe has divided locals: some say it's been sterilised, while others welcome the fresh coat of paint. Regardless, it's still a Cairene tradition to sit on a rickety chair and read the paper over a flaky, buttery pastry. Order and pay at the cash register, then take your ticket to the barista.

Garden Café CAFE

(Map p88; ☎2728 3000; Cairo Marriott, 16 Sharia Saray al-Gezira, Zamalek; ⊙6.30am-10pm) The Marriott's garden terrace is one of the most comfortable spots in town to relax over a drink. Big cane chairs, fresh air and good-quality wine and beer make it deservedly popular. The food is pricey and not very special.

Arabica CAFE

(Map p88; ☎2735 7982; 20 Sharia al-Marashly, Zamalek; fresh juices E£12-16, breakfast E£12-20, fiteer E£18-45; ⊙10am-midnight) Funky and lived-in, this upstairs cafe hosts a young crowd who doodle on the paper-topped tables. Unlike at slicker competitors, you can actually get some Egyptian food here along with your latte: fuul and *shakshuka* (scrambled eggs, peppers and tomatoes) for breakfast, and *fiteer* anytime.

Riverside Lounge & Restaurant LOUNGE

(Map p88; ☎0121 280 1290; www.riversidecairo.com; 16 Sharia al-Montazah, Zamalek; ⊙noon-1am) Super-fashionable lounge and restaurant in a top spot in Zamalek. Expect expensive cocktails and good sushi, but the thing here is to see and be seen. A few boutique hotel rooms are in the making.

Deals BAR

(Map p88; ☎2736 0502; 2 Sharia Sayyed al-Bakry; ⊙8am-2am; 📶) A small bar that never looks open but actually gets too packed for comfort late in the evening and at weekends. It's pleasant enough at quieter times. Also check out its larger new venue next door – a chic tea room with 'Louis Farouk' furniture and breakfast (E£25 to E£30), coffees and bistro meals (mains E£40 to E£65) throughout the day.

Buddha Bar LOUNGE

(Map p94; ☎2737 3737; Sofitel El Gezirah, Sharia al-Orman, Gezira; ⊙5pm-2am) The Cairo outpost of the world-famous Buddha Bar is where you can party with the beautiful people while sipping lychee martinis and listening to chill-out beats, all with great Nile views.

Drinkies LIQUOR STORE

(Map p88; ☎19330; 157 Sharia 26th of July, Zamalek) Cold beer, wine and more to take away.

Boulaq

Tamarai CLUB, LOUNGE

(Map p58; ☎2461 9910; Nile City Towers, 2005C Corniche el-Nil; minimum charge Thu-Sat E£250; ⊙8pm-2am) Strawberry-guava martinis, gorgeous lighting, an edgy pharaonic-goes-industrial interior and even alleged Paris Hilton sightings have put this restaurant/lounge/dance palace at the top of the nightlife list. Seeing and being seen are top activities, but this is also the best house music in the city. Definitely book a table ahead.

It's on the east bank of the Nile, about even with the north end of Zamalek.

☆ Entertainment

Cairenes thrive after sundown, so it's no surprise there's plenty of nightlife: lounges, a growing live-music scene and some bellydancing. Not that you need to go inside – street life can be entertainment enough. Lots of Cairenes take an evening stroll along the Nile corniche Downtown or on Qasr el-Nil bridge. Pop up tea kiosks provide refreshments.

Live Music

Many venues are eclectic, changing musical styles and scenes every night. Many also start as restaurants and shift into club mode after midnight, at which point the door policy gets stricter. Big packs of men (and sometimes even single men) are always a no-no – go in as mixed a group as you can, and ideally make reservations.

★Makan TRADITIONAL MUSIC

(Map p58; ☎2792 0878; egyptmusic.org; 1 Sharia Saad Zaghloul, Mounira) The Egyptian Centre for Culture & Art runs this intimate space dedicated to folk music. Don't miss the traditional women's *zar,* a sort of musical trance and healing ritual (Wednesday, 9pm; E£25); Tuesday has various performances of folk music, often an Egyptian-Sudanese jam session. To find the space, walk south on Sharia Mansour.

After Eight LIVE MUSIC, DJ
(Map p62; ☎2574 0855; www.after8cairo.com; 6 Sharia Qasr el-Nil, Downtown; minimum charge Wed-Sun E£60, Thu-Sat E£100; ⏰8pm-3am) A hip, poorly ventilated venue that gets packed for everything from Nubian jazz to the wildly popular DJ Dina, who mixes James Brown, '70s Egyptian pop and the latest cab-driver favourites on Tuesdays; the clientele is equally eclectic. Reserve online. Check the website for the regular belly-dance night with the Scottish Belly Lorna.

Cairo Opera House OPERA
(Map p94; ☎2739 8144; www.cairoopera.org; Gezira Exhibition Grounds, Gezira) Performances by the Cairo Opera and the Cairo Symphony Orchestra are held in the 1200-seat Main Hall, where jacket and tie are required for men (travellers have been known to borrow them from staff). The Small Hall is casual. Check the website for the schedule; note that some events are at a theatre near Abdeen Palace, or in Alexandria.

Al-Tannoura Egyptian Heritage Dance Troupe DANCE
(Map p76; ☎2512 1735; Wikala of Al-Ghouri, Sharia Mohammed Abduh, Islamic Cairo, off Sharia al-Azhar; ⏰performances at 8pm Mon, Wed & Sat) FREE Egypt's only Sufi dance troupe – more raucous and colourful than white-clad Turkish dervishes – puts on a mesmerising performance at the Wikala of Al-Ghouri near Al-Azhar, and occasionally other venues. It's a great opportunity to see one of the medieval spaces in use; arrive about an hour ahead to secure a seat.

CITY READS

- *Cairo: The City Victorious* by Max Rodenbeck
- *Cairo's Street Stories* by Lesley Lababidi
- *Understanding Cairo: The Logic of a City out of Control* by David Sims
- *Taxi* by Khalid Al-Khamissy

El Sawy Culture Wheel LIVE MUSIC
(El Sakia; Map p88; ☎2736 8881; www.culturewheel.com; Sharia 26th of July, Zamalek; ⏰8am-midnight) The most popular young Egyptian rock and jazz bands play at this lively and very active complex of a dozen performance spaces and galleries tucked under a bridge overpass. The main entrance is on the south side of 26th of July; there's a nice outdoor cafe by the Nile too.

Cairo Jazz Club JAZZ, DJ
(Map p88; ☎02-3345 9939; www.cairojazzclub.com; 197 Sharia 26th of July, Agouza; ⏰5pm-3am) The Cairo Jazz Club has kept up with the beat, and it has one of the city's liveliest stages, with modern Egyptian folk, electronica, fusion and more, seven nights a week, usually starting around 10pm. You must book a table ahead (online is easiest), and no one under 25 is admitted.

El Tanboura Hall TRADITIONAL MUSIC
(Map p62; ☎2392 6768; www.el-mastaba.org; 30A Sharia al-Balaqsa, Abdeen; ⏰doors open at 8pm) Regular shows by Rango, a trance-y Sudanese folk group (Thursday, 9.30pm; E£20), and El Tanboura Band (Friday, 9.30pm; E£20), playing *simsimiyya,* a musical style from the Suez Canal region, and occasionally other folk bands from Egypt (check the website for listings).

El Genaina CONCERT VENUE
(Map p78; ☎2363 7081; www.mawred.org; Sharia Salah Salem, Islamic Cairo) Al-Azhar Park's 300-seat open-air theatre hosts touring Western artists, stars from the Middle East and locals. Shows are often free (though you must pay the park entrance fee). Check their Facebook page for listings.

Belly-Dancing

If you see only one belly dancer in your life, it had better be in Cairo, the art form's true home. The best dancers perform at Cairo's five-star hotels, usually to an adoring crowd of wealthy Gulf Arabs. Shows typically begin around midnight, although the star might not take to the stage until 2am or later. Admission is steep; expect to pay upwards of E£250, which includes food but not drinks. Cairo's divas are often getting in tiffs with their host hotels or their managers, so their venues may change.

At the other end of the scale, you can watch a less nuanced expression of the art form for just a few pounds at several clubs around Sharia Alfy in Downtown Cairo.

They're seedy (prostitution is definitely a sideline), the mics are set on the highest reverb, and most of the dancers have the grace of amateur wrestlers. But it can be fun, especially if you can maintain enough of a buzz to join in the dancing onstage (a perk if you shower the dancer and the band with enough E£5 notes), but not so fun if you fall for the myriad overcharging tactics, such as fees for unordered snacks and even napkins (expect to pay about E£20 to E£25 for a Stella, after about E£10 cover charge). As at the hotels, nothing happens till after midnight.

★Shahrazad CABARET
(Map p62; 1 Sharia Alfy, Downtown; admission E£5; ⏲10pm-2am) Worth visiting for the gorgeous interior alone, this old-school hall got a makeover in recent years, and its Orientalist fantasia, complete with red-velvet drapes, feels substantially less seedy than other Downtown dives. This doesn't necessarily inspire a classier air in the patrons, however. Occasionally the venue hosts a DJ night for an artier crowd.

Palmyra CABARET
(Map p62; off Sharia 26th of July, Downtown; cover charge E£10, minimum charge E£30; ⏲10pm-2am) One of the seediest and most bygone-glory belly-dance venues is Palmyra, a cavernous, dilapidated 1950s dancehall in an alley off Sharia 26th of July. It has a full Arab musical contingent, belly dancers get (marginally) better the more money is thrown at them. It's in a courtyard behind shopfronts; once back here, go under the marquee marked 'Meame'.

Nile Maxim CABARET
(Map p88; ☎2738 8888; www.maximrestaurants.com; Sharia Saray al-Gezira, Zamalek, opposite Cairo Marriott Hotel; minimum charge E£180; ⏲sailings at 7.30pm & 10.45pm) The best of the Nile cruise boats, run by the Marriott, is a relatively economical way to see a big-name star such as Randa or Asmahan, along with an à la carte menu. Go for the later sailing, as the show is less rushed.

Haroun El-Rashid Nightclub CABARET
(Map p62; ☎3795 7171; Semiramis InterContinental, Corniche el-Nil, Garden City; ⏲11pm-4am Tue-Thu & Sun) This old-fashioned-looking five-star club – all red curtains and white marquee lights – is where the famous Dina has been known to undulate.

DYING ART OF BELLY-DANCING

The past few years have been tough on belly dancers in Egypt. Since the 2011 revolution the numbers of tourists have dwindled, particularly in Cairo, and the terrible economic situation gives little cause for celebration in Egypt; most Egyptians have no disposable income. Madame Raqia, the best known belly-dance choreographer, despairs that Mursi and the Brotherhood finished off the art of belly-dancing. She has closed down her website; some venues have closed too, a few belly dancers have given up, and the scene has become more sleazy. However some foreign dancers perform at top hotels and upmarket clubs, such as Lorna at After Eight (p108); many perform in more conservative dress.

Cinema

Cairo is the centre of film production for the Middle East, so there's quite a lot on. Check listings in *Al-Ahram Weekly* or online at www.yallabina.com. Tickets typically cost around E£25 and can be cheaper at daytime sessions (when more women attend shows at the lower-rent places). Also check schedules at the many cultural centres. Cinema Metro, Cinema Tahrir and Citystars Centre (p131) all regularly screen English-language films.

Zawya CINEMA
(Map p62; ☎0128 320 0888; www.zawyacinema.com; Cinema Odeon, 4 Sharia Abdel Hamid Said, off Sharia Talaat Harb, Downtown) Wonderful arthouse cinema showing both local and international films, but mainly from North Africa and the Middle East, with English subtitles.

Cinema Metro CINEMA
(Map p62; ☎2393 7061; 35 Sharia Talaat Harb, Downtown) Once Cairo's finest, this 1930s palace has been spruced up enough to show 3D blockbuster movies.

Cinema Tahrir CINEMA
(Map p94; ☎3335 4726; 122 Sharia Tahrir, Doqqi) Comfortable, modern cinema where single females shouldn't receive hassle.

Shopping

Faced with the mountains of chintzy souvenirs and the over-eager hustlers trying to sell them to you over endless glasses of tea, it's tempting to keep your wallet firmly shut in Cairo. But then you'd be missing out on some of Egypt's most beautiful treasures. The trick is knowing where to look.

Though they're touristy and stocked with goods from China, the tiny shops of Khan al-Khalili do yield a few specific finds. Downtown along Sharia Qasr el-Nil has cheap, mass-market fashion. Sharia al-Marashly and Sharia Mansour Mohammed in Zamalek have some gem boutiques for housewares and clothing, and not all of them are as expensive as you'd expect. For everything else, head to Citystars (p131), Cairo's best mall.

Downtown

★Oum El Dounia HANDICRAFTS
(Map p62; ☎2393 8273; 1st fl, 3 Sharia Talaat Harb; ⏰10am-9pm) At a great central location, Oum El Dounia sells an exceptionally tasteful and good-value selection of locally made crafts. These include glassware, ceramics, jewellery, clothes and other interesting trinkets. Illustrated postcards by cartoonist Golo make a nice change. One room is dedicated to books on Egypt, in French and in English.

American University in Cairo (AUC) Bookshop BOOKS
(Map p62; ☎2797 5929; www.aucpress.com; Sharia Sheikh Rihan; ⏰ 9am-4pm Sun-Thu, 10am-4pm Sat) The best English-language bookshop in Egypt, with two floors of material on the politics, sociology and history of Cairo, Egypt and the Middle East. Plenty of guidebooks and maps, and some fiction.

Lehnert & Landrock BOOKS
(Map p62; ☎2392 7606; lehnertandlandrock.net/; 44 Sharia Sherif; ⏰10am-7pm Mon-Sat) Old maps, books about Cairo and Egypt (some secondhand), great vintage postcards and reprints of wonderful old photographs.

Sono Cairo MUSIC
(Sawt al-Qahira; Map p62; Midan Opera; ⏰10am-11pm) In an arcade off Sharia al-Gomhurriya; stocks the classic Arab crooners.

Ezbekiyya Book Market BOOKS
(Map p62; Ezbekiyya Gardens) The 50 or so stalls here yield occasional finds, and some stock fun gift items such as Arabic alphabet posters.

Kartmo SOUVENIRS
(Map p62; 13 Sharia Mahmoud Bassiouni) In the passage cutting through to Sharia Qasr el-Nil, this enamel-sign maker sells snazzy 'Midan Tahrir' street plaques for E£200 – a nice revolutionary souvenir. You can also order custom designs, which take about a week.

Bulaq

Wikalat al-Balah CLOTHING, MARKET
(Souq Bulaq, Bulaq Market; Map p58; north of Sharia 26th of July; ⏰8am-6pm) This street market specialises in secondhand clothing, mostly well organised, clean and with marked prices (especially on Sharia al-Wabur al-Fransawi). It starts a few blocks west of the 6th of October overpass.

Coptic Cairo

Souq al-Fustat HANDICRAFTS, MARKET
(Map p68; Sharia Mar Girgis; ⏰8am-4pm) Brilliant shopping complex with various good craft shops, respectable vendors of carpets, modern ceramics, spices, richly embroidered *galabiyyas* (long Egyptian dress for men and women) and wooden toys along with a branch of Abd El Zaher (p110). Look out for **Association for the Protection of the Environment** (APE; Map p68; ☎0122 911 1937; www.ape.org.eg; Souq al-Fustat; ⏰10am-8pm) shop selling embroideries from Akhmim. Prices are marked (though occasionally negotiable), and sales pressure is pleasantly low.

Islamic Cairo

★Abd El Zaher GIFTS
(Map p76; 31 Sharia Mohammed Abduh; ⏰9am-11pm) Cairo's last working bookbinder also makes beautiful leather- and oil-paper-bound blank books, photo albums and diaries. Gold monogramming is included in the prices, which are heartbreakingly low considering the work that goes into them. Getting your own books bound starts around E£30 and takes a few days.

Abd al-Rahman Harraz FOOD
(Map p58; ☎2512 6349; 1 Midan Bab al-Khalq; ⏰10am-10pm) Established 1885, this is one of the most esteemed spice traders in Cairo, with a brisk business in medicinal herbs as well (upstairs, herbalists diagnose and prescribe). There's no English sign: look for dioramas of

CAIRO CRAFTS: WHAT & WHERE

These are the best districts for certain goods.

Appliqué Best buys are at the Tentmakers Market (p79), south of Bab Zuweila.

Backgammon and sheesha pipes Shops that stock ahwas line Sharia al-Muizz (p72) around Bein al-Qasreen. Another set of sheesha dealers are just east and west of Bab Zuweila (p78).

Carpets The carpet bazaar south of the Mosque-Madrassa of Al-Ghouri (p77) has imports; flat-weave Bedouin rugs are the only local style.

Gold and silver Head to the gold district on the west end of Khan al-Khalili (p70).

Inlay Artisans in Darb al-Ahmar sell out of their workshops.

Muski glass Available everywhere, but interesting to see the glassblowing studios in the district north of Bab al-Futuh (p75).

Perfume In addition to the southwest corner of Khan al-Khalili, try shops around Midan Falaki.

Spices Most dealers in the Khan are more trouble than they're worth. Try Abd al-Rahman Harraz (p110) or shops around Midan Falaki.

Egyptian village life in the corner shop windows. It's about 450m west of Bab Zuweila.

Souq al-Gomaa MARKET
(Friday Market; Map p58; Southern Cemetery; 6am-noon Fri) South of the Citadel, this sprawling weekly market is all the craziness of a medieval bazaar in a modern setting. Under a highway flyover, expect bicycles, live donkeys and broken telephones. Savvy pickers can find some funky objects and vintage clothes. Go before 10am to avoid the crush of people. Tell the taxi driver 'Khalifa', the name of the neighbourhood.

Atlas CLOTHING, HANDICRAFTS
(Map p76; 2591 8833; Sikket al-Badistan; 10am-8pm) In business since 1948, the Atlas family specialises in silk moiré kaftans and slippers. You can also order the fabric by the yard, or in custom-tailored clothing.

Khan Misr Touloun HANDICRAFTS
(Map p84; 2365 2227; Midan ibn Tulun; 10am-5pm Mon-Sat) This shop opposite the Mosque of Ibn Tulun is stacked with a desirable jumble of reasonably priced crafts, wooden chests, jewellery, pottery, puppets and scarves. Closes for vacation in August.

Mahmoud Abd El Ghaffar ACCESSORIES
(Map p76; 2589 7443; 73 Sharia Gawhar al-Qaid, Al Wikalah; 11am-11pm) One of the best dealers in belly-dancing outfits in the city. Look for the entrance at the end of a short lane just off the main street, and walk upstairs where the really good stuff is.

Karama BEAUTY
(Map p76; 2590 2386; 112 Sharia al-Azhar) Very popular with Cairenes for scent copies as well as its own blends and basic essences; look for the open-sided corner shop at the corner of Sharia al Muizz.

Zamalek

★Diwan BOOKS, MUSIC
(Map p88; 2736 2578; www.diwanegypt.com; 159 Sharia 26th of July; 9am-11.30pm) Fabulous: English, French and German titles, from novels to travel guides to coffee-table books. It also has a kids' section, a large music wing and a small cafe.

Fair Trade Egypt HANDICRAFTS
(Map p88; 2736 5123; fairtradeegypt.org/; 1st fl, 27 Sharia Yehia Ibrahim; 9am-8pm) Crafts sold here are produced in income-generating projects throughout the country. Items for sale include Bedouin rugs, hand-woven cotton, pottery from Al-Fayoum and beaded jewellery from Aswan. The cotton bedcovers and shawls are particularly lovely, and prices are very reasonable.

Azza Fahmy JEWELLERY
(Map p88; 0106 664 2365; www.azzafahmy.com; 15C Sharia Dr Taha Hussein, cnr of Sharia Marashly; 10am-10pm) World renowned contemporary jeweller inspired by Islamic and Pharaonic designs. Azza Fahmy also organises design workshops (p69) to make fabulous jewellery.

ANTIQUES ROADSHOW: CAIRO EDITION

Evidence of Cairo's glam years can be found in dusty warehouses and glittery shops. These are some of the best.

Ahmed El Dabba & Sons (Map p76; ☎2590 7823; 5 Sikket al-Badistan, Islamic Cairo) The most respected antiques dealer in Khan al-Khalili, filled with Louis XV furniture, jewellery and snuff boxes.

Amgad Naguib (Map p62; ☎0128 668 0908; off Sharia Mahmoud Bassiouni, Downtown) Make an appointment to visit Amgad's dusty treasure house Downtown. Along with vintage sunglasses, movie posters and groovy glass, you get some great stories.

Kerop (Map p62; 116 Mohammed Farid, Downtown; ⏱9am-1pm Mon-Fri) Vintage Cairo photos, from original plates, in a time-warp office.

King Saleh Bazaar (Map p72; 80 Sharia al-Muizz li-Din Allah, Islamic Cairo) Immediately south of the Madrassa & Mausoleum of Qalaun. The more you look through the dust, the more pops out.

Nostalgia (Map p88; 6 Sharia Zakaria Rizk, Zamalek) From framed Arabic ad prints to escargot forks.

L'Orientaliste (Map p62; ☎2575 3418; www.orientalecairo.com; 15 Sharia Qasr el-Nil, Downtown; ⏱10am-8pm) FInd rare books on Egypt and the Middle East, as well as lithographs, maps and engravings.

Al Qahira HOMEWARES

(Map p88; ☎0111 313 3932; 1st fl, Sharia Bahgat Ali; ⏱noon-9pm) Al Qahira sells quality Egyptian crafts, often with a quirky element. Brilliant jewellery by Suzanne El Masry, embroidered jewellery, fabrics printed with vintage photos of movie stars and some fun homewares.

Nevin Altmann CLOTHES

(Map p88; ☎2736 5431; www.nevinaltmann.com; 3 Sharia Hassan Assem; ⏱10am-10pm) Delightful intricately embroidered accessories, on cotton and linen, all made in different regions in Egypt. Look out for the beautiful fabric dolls too, which make great gifts.

Nomad HANDICRAFTS, JEWELLERY

(Map p88; ☎2736 1917; www.nomadgallery.ne; 1st fl, 14 Sharia Saray al-Gezira; ⏱9am-8pm) Specialists in jewellery and traditional Bedouin crafts and costumes. Items include appliqué tablecloths and cushion covers, dresses made in the oases, woven baskets, silk slippers and chunky silver jewellery. To find it, go past the Egyptian Water Works office to the 1st floor and ring the bell. There is a smaller branch in the Cairo Marriott.

L'Oiseau du Nil GIFTS, CLOTHES

(Asfour el Nil; Map p88; ☎2735 1458; www.asfourelnil.com; 23a Sharia Ismail Mohammed; ⏱11am-10pm Sat-Thu) Original gifts made in Egypt, great cotton clothing and the wonderful Egyptian cotton bed linen by Malaika.

Balady HANDICRAFTS

(Map p88; ☎0127 942 0300; 13 Sharia Mansour Mohammed; ⏱10am-10pm) Great assortment of hip gift items: Umm Kolthum laptop cases, handmade soaps, good-quality essential oils.

Sami Amin ACCESSORIES, HOMEWARES

(Map p88; ☎2738 1837; www.sami-amin.com; 15A Sharia Mansour Mohammed; ⏱10.30am-10pm Mon-Sat) Cool chunky brass-and-enamel jewellery as well as various leather goods for the home. Just down the street, at number 13, are leather bags, belts and other accessories, many imprinted with tribal patterns, and all very well priced.

Loft ANTIQUES, HOMEWARES

(Map p88; ☎2736 6931; www.loftegypt.com; 1st fl, 12 Sharia Sayyed al-Bakry; ⏱10am-10pm Mon-Sat) In a rambling apartment, this eclectic store stocks local regional curiosities from small brass candlesticks to antique divans, as well as large painted tabletop trays as seen in chic restaurants around town.

Mix & Match CLOTHING

(Map p88; ☎2736 4640; 11 Sharia Brazil; ⏱10am-8pm) Well made and locally designed, these separates for women in wool, silk and cotton are reasonably priced and often feature subtle Middle Eastern details. A **branch** (Map p88; 11 Sharia Hassan Sabry; ⏱10am-8pm), two blocks south, stocks larger sizes.

Wady Craft Shop HANDICRAFTS

(Map p88; ☎2738 4350; www.wadycrafts.com/shop; 5 Sharia Michel Luffallah; ⏰9am-1pm & 2-5pm) This charity store run by the Anglican church sells work done by refugee organisations: cotton bags, aprons, tablecloths, inlay coasters and silk-screened tea towels. Enter the church complex on Michel Lutfallah, and head to the northeast corner.

Mobaco CLOTHING

(Map p88; ☎2738 2790; 8 Sharia Ahmed Sabry) Sporty designs, inexpensive and with a great range of colours. There's always a flattering long skirt available, and men can choose from a rainbow of polo shirts sporting a camel logo. There are stores throughout the city, including at the Semiramis InterContinental.

Doqqi

Nagada CLOTHING, CERAMICS

(Map p94; ☎3748 6663; www.nagada.net; 13 Sharia Refa'a; ⏰10am-6.30pm) High-quality handwoven, colour-saturated silks, cottons and linens are the mainstay of this delightful shop. Buy by the yard, or in boxy, drapey women's and men's apparel. There's also very pretty pottery from Al-Fayoum.

Information

CULTURAL CENTRES

British Council & Library (Map p88; ☎3300 1666; www.britishcouncil.org.eg; 192 Sharia el-Nil; ⏰8am-8pm) Organises performances, exhibitions and talks and has a useful library. There is also one in Heliopolis (☎19789; www.britishcouncil.org.e; 4 Sharia el-Minia, off Sharia Nazih Khalifa; ⏰9am-7pm Sat-Thu).

Centre Français de Culture et de Coopération (Map p58; ☎2794 7679; institutfrancais-egypte.com; 1 Sharia Madrassat al-Huquq al-Fransiyya; ⏰11am-7pm Sun-Tue, Thu & Fri, 11am-8pm Wed; Ⓜ Saad Zaghloul) Regular films, lectures and exhibitions. Also in Heliopolis (☎2419 3857; institutfrancais-egypte.com; 5 Sharia Shafik al-Dib, Ard al-Golf; ⏰10am-10pm Sun-Thu).

Goethe Institut (Map p62; ☎2575 9877; www.goethe.de; 5 Sharia al-Bustan; ⏰library 1-7pm Sun-Wed) Seminars and lectures in German on Egyptology and other topics, plus visiting music groups, art exhibitions and film screenings. The library has more than 15,000 (mainly German) titles. The Doqqi location focuses on language classes.

Instituto Cervantes (Map p94; ☎3760 1746; elcairo.cervantes.es; 20 Sharia Boulos Hanna, Doqqi; ⏰9am-6pm Sun-Thu) Spanish language and cultural institute, screening films and organising lectures.

Istituto Italiano di Cultura (Map p88; ☎2735 8791; www.iiccairo.esteri.it; 3 Sharia Sheikh al-Marsafy, Zamalek; ⏰library 10am-4pm Sun, Tue & Thu) A busy program of films and lectures (sometimes in English) and art exhibitions, plus a library.

Netherlands-Flemish Institute (NVIC; Map p88; ☎2738 2520; www.nvic.leidenuniv.nl; 1 Sharia Mahmoud Azmy, Zamalek; ⏰9am-2pm Sun-Thu, lectures every Thu 6pm) This centre hosts art exhibitions and is well regarded for its weekly lectures and film series, almost always in English.

DANGERS & ANNOYANCES

Despite a rise in petty crime following the 2011 revolution, Cairo is still a pretty safe city, with crime rates likely much lower than where you're visiting from. In recent years sexual harassment of women in the street has increased, so women on their own should be vigilant particularly at night. There are reports of single women hassled late at night around Midan Tahrir and in the Islamic quarter of the city.

Theft

Pickpockets are rare in Cairo, but do sometimes operate in crowded spots such as Khan al-Khalili, the metro and buses. There have been incidents of bag theft. If anything does get stolen go straight to the tourist police.

Bogus Tours

Cairo's worst scams are associated with tours. Rather than making arrangements in Cairo, you are almost always better off booking tours in the place you'll be taking them. Stick with reputable agencies. Even your hotel is not a good place to book anything except typical day trips from Cairo. Never book with a random office Downtown (many are fronts) or with the help of someone you meet on the street.

Street Hassle

Contrary to media reports, women are generally safe walking alone in Cairo. After about 11pm, however, it's preferable to have some male accompaniment, and at all times avoid the cheapest buses (notorious for frottage, to female commuters' chagrin) and large groups of aimless men: political demonstrations and any kind of football-related celebration can bring out the testosterone. Also be a bit wary of men (or boys) who want to escort you across a street – it's a prime groping opportunity. Women should use a female cabbie at night; call Nour Gaber (p93).

EMERGENCY

In case of an accident or injury, call the As-Salam International Hospital. For anything more serious, contact your embassy.

The **main tourist police office** (Map p62; ☎216, 2395 9116; Sharia Adly) is on the 1st floor of a building in the alley just left of the main tourist office in Downtown. Come here first for minor emergencies, including theft; there are other offices by the Pyramids, across from Mena House and in Khan al-Khalili.

Ambulance (☎123)

Fire Department (☎180)

Police (☎122)

INTERNET ACCESS

The most conveniently located, all charging about E£5 per hour:

Concord (Map p62; 28 Sharia Mohammed Mahmoud, Downtown; per hr E£5; ⏲10am-2am) Handy for southern Downtown.

InterClub (Map p62; ☎2579 1860; 12 Sharia Talaat Harb, Downtown; ⏲8am-2am) Printing, faxing and scanning services; in alley next to Estoril restaurant.

Intr@net (Map p62; 1st fl, 36 Sharia Sherif, Downtown; ⏲24hr) Full service; walk back into the shopping arcade and upstairs.

Sigma Net (Map p88; Sharia Gezirat al-Wusta, Zamalek; per hr E£8; ⏲24hr) Opposite Golden Tulip Flamenco Hotel. Good air-con.

Zamalek Center (Map p88; ☎2736 4004; 25 Sharia Ismail Mohammed, Zamalek; ⏲24hr) Best rates in the area; other business services too.

MEDICAL SERVICES

Hospitals

Many of Cairo's hospitals suffer from antiquated equipment and a cavalier attitude to hygiene, but there are several exceptions. Your embassy should be able to recommend doctors and hospitals. Other options:

As-Salam International Hospital (Map p88; ☎2524 0250, emergency 19885; www.assih.com; Corniche el-Nil, Ma'adi) In the southern suburb of Ma'adi.

Badran Hospital (Map p58; ☎3337 8823; www.badranhospital.com; 3 Sharia al-Ahrar, Doqqi) Just northwest of 6th of October in Doqqi.

Pharmacies

These pharmacies operate 24 hours, have English-speaking staff and will deliver to your hotel.

Al-Ezaby (Map p88; ☎19600; www.pharmacyincairo.com; 46 Sharia Bahgat Ali, Zamalek) Other branches all over Cairo, open 24hr, and delivery to your hotel.

Ali & Ali (☎Downtown 2365 3880, Mohandiseen-3302 1421) Delivery only.

New Victoria Pharmacy (Map p88; ☎2735 1628; 6 Sharia Brazil, Zamalek)

Seif Pharmacy (☎19199; seifgroup.com/pharmacies) Delivery to your hotel.

MONEY

Hotel bank branches can change cash, but rates are slightly better at independent exchange bureaus, of which there are several along Sharia Adly in Downtown and on Sharia 26th of July in Zamalek. These tend to be open from 10am to 8pm Saturday to Thursday. ATMs are numerous, except in Islamic Cairo – the most convenient machine here is below El Hussein hotel in Khan al-Khalili.

American Express (Map p62; ☎2574 7991; 15 Sharia Qasr el-Nil, Downtown; ⏲9am-3pm Sat-Thu)

Citibank (Map p94; ☎2795 1873, 16644; www.citibankegypt.com; 4 Sharia Ahmad Pasha) Also in Zamalek (Map p88; ☎2736 5622; 4A Sharia al-Gezira).

Thomas Cook (Map p62; ☎2574 3955, emergency 0100 140 1367; www.thomascookegypt.com; 17 Sharia Mahmoud Bassiouni, Downtown; ⏲8am-4.30pm Sat-Thu) Other branches are located at Heliopolis (☎2416 4000; 7 Sharia Baghdad, Korba; ⏲8am-4.30pm Sat-Thu), the airport (☎emergency 2265 3147; www.thomascookegypt.com; Airport; ⏲24hr) and Zamalek (Map p88; ☎2696 2101, emergency 0100 538 9968; www.thomascookegypt.com; 3A Sharia Ismail Mohammed; ⏲8am-4.30pm Sat-Thu).

NEWS STANDS

One (Map p88) on the corner of Sharia 26th of July and Hassan Sabry in Zamalek has by far the best stock. All the major hotels have decent shops.

POST

Marked with green-and-yellow signs, post offices are numerous, though not all have signs in English explaining which window is meant for what business.

Express Mail Service (EMS; Map p62; ☎2390 5874; Sharia Baidaq, Behind Central Fire Department, Ataba; ⏲24hr) The main office is near the Ataba central office.

Main Post Office (Map p62; ☎2391 2614; Midan Ataba, Downtown; ⏲8am-6pm Sat-Thu) Stamps and letters at front entrance; parcels at the back entrance.

Post Traffic Centre (Map p66; ☎2575 0713; Midan Ramses; ⏲9am-2pm Sat-Thu) Another place to mail packages.

Poste Restante and Parcels (Map p62; ⏲24hr) On the back end of the main post office. Mail is held for three weeks; take your passport. For parcels, leave your package unsealed for inspection; the staff will tape it up. Boxes are for sale; rates for slowest service are E£170 for the first kilo, E£50 for each thereafter.

TELEPHONE

Telephone Centrale (Map p62; fax 2578 0979; 13 Midan Tahrir; 24hr) Also branches on Sharia Adly (8 Sharia Adly, Downtown; 24hr) and in Zamalek (Map p88; Sharia 26th of July).

TOILETS

Clean toilets in Cairo are a bit hard to come by, though most large museums and monuments have passable facilities. In Khan al-Khalili, head for the Khan el-Khalili Restaurant & Mahfouz Coffee Shop (p102). You can also nip in to fast-food places like Gad, where the toilets usually have an attendant; tip E£1 or E£2.

TOURIST INFORMATION

Ministry of Tourism (Main tourist office; 2391 3454; 5 Sharia Adly; 9am-6pm) Branches also at the Pyramids (p129) and Ramses Station (Tourist Office and Police; 2492 5985; Ramses Station; 9am-7pm).

TRAVEL AGENCIES

The streets around Midan Tahrir teem with travel agencies, but watch out for dodgy operators. Along with those listed below, **Amex** (Amex; Map p62; info 569 3299, www.americanexpress.com.eg; Midan Tahrir, Nile Hilton; 9am-5pm Sat-Thu) and Thomas Cook (p114) are reliable.

Backpacker Concierge (0106 350 7118; www.backpackerconcierge.com) Culturally and environmentally responsible desert trips and Nile cruises, plus more focused custom trips such as food tours. No walk-in office, but can communicate via phone, email, Facebook and Twitter.

Egypt Panorama Tours (2359 0200; www.eptours.com; 4 Rd 79, Ma'adi; 9am-5pm) Opposite Ma'adi metro station, this is one of the best-established agencies in town. It will book tickets, tours and hotel rooms and courier the documents to you, if necessary. It's good for four- and five-star hotel deals and tours within Egypt and around the Mediterranean. Note that separate departments handle flights and excursions.

Misr Travel (Map p62; 2393 0010; www.misrtravel.net; 1 Sharia Talaat Harb, Downtown) The official Egyptian government travel agency, which also has offices in most of the luxury hotels.

International Travel Bureau of Egypt (Map p94; 3760 1370; www.itbe-egypt.com; apt 97, Orman Tower, 48 Sharia al-Giza, Doqqi) Reliable small and family-run travel agency.

Getting There & Away

AIR

Cairo International Airport (flight info 0900 77777, Mobile flight info 27777; www.cairo-airport.com) Terminal 1 (2265 5000) and Terminal 2 (closed at time of research) are on the northeastern fringes of Heliopolis, 20km northeast of the city centre. Terminal 3 (16707; al-Matar al-Gideed) services EgyptAir's international and domestic flights and a few other international airlines. Terminal 1 services British Airways and other international airlines.

EgyptAir (2696 6798; Airport Terminal 3) Also branches on Sharia Talaat Harb (Map p62; 2393 0381; www.egyptair.com; cnr Sharia Talaat Harb & Sharia al-Bustan) and Sharia Adly (Map p62; 2390 0999; 6 Sharia Adly; 9am-8pm).

BUS

The main bus station, for all destinations in the Suez Canal area, Sinai, the deserts, Alexandria and Upper Egypt, is **Cairo Gateway** (Turgoman Garage; Sharia al-Gisr, Bulaq ; M Orabi), 400m west of the Orabi metro stop.

CAIRO AIRPORT TERMINALS & AIRLINES

TERMINAL	AIRLINES	SERVICES
Terminal 1, Arrivals 1	Al-Masria, British Airways, Emirates, Etihad, Kenya, Nile Air, Qatar, Royal Air Maroc, Sudan, Yemenia	ATM before immigration and to right just before exit doors; shuttle service to right after customs
Terminal 1, Arrivals 3	Alitalia, Air France, Delta, Eritrean, Ethiopian, KLM, Kuwait Airlines, Middle East Airlines, Oman Air, Royal Jordanian, Saudi Arabia	ATM to left; info desk to right; limo service straight ahead
Terminal 3	Aegean, Austrian, BMI, Egypt Air (domestic and international), Lufthansa, Singapore, Swiss, Turkish Airlines	ATMs to right; info desk in centre by escalators; car desks to right

Tickets are sold at different windows according to company and destination. Suez and Sinai tickets are to the right; Alexandria and towns in Upper Egypt to the left. It is advisable to book most tickets in advance, particularly for popular routes such as Sinai, Alexandria and Marsa Matruh in summer.

Companies operating here are **East Delta Travel Co** (☎ 2419 8533) for Suez and the Sinai; **West & Mid Delta Bus Co** (☎ 2432 0049; westmidbus-eg.com) for Alexandria, Marsa Matruh and Siwa; **Super Jet** (☎ 3572 5032, 2290 9017) for some Sinai resort towns; and **Upper Egypt Travel Co** (☎ 2576 0261) to Western Desert oases and Luxor (though for the latter, the train is better). They don't offer student discounts. There are also bus services to Libya, Israel and Jordan.

At the time of research several bus companies were setting up office at **Ramses Train Station** (Mahattat Ramses; ☎ 2575 3555; Midan Ramses, Downtown; Ⓜ Al-Shohadaa), but the only one established was Go Bus, with buses to major cities in Egypt leaving from Ramses Station. A few smaller bus stations run more frequent service. Head here if the Cairo Gateway departure times aren't ideal.

Go Bus (☎ 19567; www.gobus-eg.com; Ramses Station, Midan Ramses) Tickets – and even specific seats – on buses to major cities in Egypt can be booked online. Excellent service.

Abbassiyya Bus Terminal (Sinai Station; Map p58; Sharia Ramses, Abbassiyya; Ⓜ Abbassiyya) A few buses from Sinai still terminate here, 4km northeast of Ramses; take the nearby metro to the centre.

BUSES FROM CAIRO GATEWAY

DESTINATION	COMPANY	PRICE	DURATION	TIMES
Al-Arish	East Delta	E£35	5hr	7.30am, 4pm
Al-Kharga	Upper Egypt Travel	E£70	8-10hr	9.30pm, 10.30pm
Al-Quseir	Upper Egypt Travel	E£70–80	10hr	5.30am, 11pm, 1.30am
Alexandria	West & Mid Delta	E£30-50	3hr	hourly 5am-12.05am
Bahariya (Bawiti)	Upper Egypt Travel	E£35	4-5hr	6.30am, 8am
Dahab	East Delta	E£90	9hr	8am, 1.30pm, 7.30pm, 11.45pm
Dakhla	Upper Egypt Travel	E£75-90	8-10hr	7pm, 8.30pm
Farafra	Upper Egypt Travel	E£45-55	8-10hr	7am, 8am
Hurghada	SuperJet	E£68	6hr	7.30am, 2.30pm, 11.10pm
Ismailia	East Delta	E£20	4hr	every 30min 6am-7pm
Luxor	Upper Egypt Travel	E£100-120	11hr	9pm
Marsa Matruh	West & Mid Delta	E£65–75	5hr	6.15am, 8.30am, 11am, 4.30pm, 7.30pm, 10pm, 11.30pm
Port Said	East Delta	E£25	4hr	hourly 6.30am–9.30pm
Sharm	East Delta	E£65–80	7hr	10.30am, 4.30pm, 11pm, 1am
Sharm	SuperJet	E£85-98	7hr	7.30am, 1.15pm, 10.45pm
Siwa	West Delta	E£80	11hr	7.30pm, 11.30pm
St Katherine's	East Delta	E£50	7hr	11am
Suez	East Delta	E£15–20	2hr	every 30min 6am-7pm
Taba & Nuweiba	East Delta	E£80–100	8hr	9.30am, 11.30pm

Ramses Station

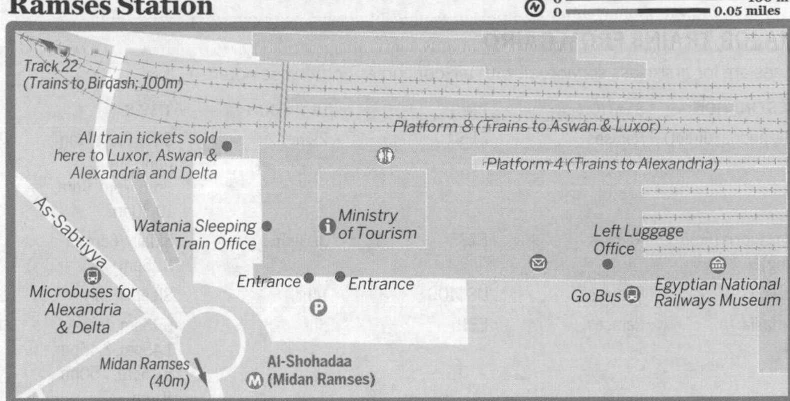

Abboud (Khazindar; Sharia al-Tir'a al-Boulaqia, Shubra; M Mezallat) Services to the Delta and Wadi Natrun, 5km north of Ramses. Walk east from Mezallat metro, about 800m.

MICROBUS & SERVEES

You can get a seat in a shared van or taxi to most destinations from the blocks between Ramses Station and Midan Ulali. For Al-Fayoum and the western oases, head to Moneib, on Sharia el-Nil in Giza, under the ring road overpass (take a taxi or walk 800m east from the Sakkiat Mekki metro stop). Midan al-Remaya in Giza, near the Pyramids, is another starting pointing for Al-Fayoum and western Delta towns; hop on a microbus from the Giza metro station.

TRAIN

Trains to Alexandria, Upper Egypt and major towns in the Delta are the most efficient and comfortable. Train travel to smaller towns is recommended for rail-fans only, as it's often quite slow and scruffy. Ramses Station (p116) is Cairo's main train station. It was under renovation at the time of research, but should have a left luggage office, a post office, ATMs and a tourist information office.

Secondary stations include Giza, for the sleeper to Upper Egypt; Giza Suburban, next to the metro stop of the same name, for Al-Fayoum; and Ain Shams, in the northeast part of the city, for Suez.

For 1st-class services, visit www.enr.gov.eg, where you can check schedules and purchase 1st-class tickets for trains on the main Alexandria–Aswan line. Purchasing tickets at Ramses requires getting to the right set of windows for your destination and knowing the time and/or train number you want. Confirm at the information desk, where the clerk can write your preference in Arabic to show the ticket seller.

Alexandria

The best trains are the Special and Spanish trains, which make fewer stops than the French ones. First class *(ula)* gets you a roomier, assigned seat and usually a much cleaner bathroom.

Luxor & Aswan

Tourists used to be restricted to travelling on the sleeper train to Luxor and Aswan. If you do encounter a desk clerk who does not want to sell you a ticket, you can always purchase a ticket on board from the conductor, for a small additional fee, or in advance online.

The overnight wagon-lits service to Luxor and Aswan is operated by a private company, Watania (p495). You can purchase tickets at the point of departure, Giza Station, in the trailer to the right of the entrance, or at Ramses in the larger sleeping train ticket office, which keeps longer hours and can take credit cards (for a surcharge), as well as cash in euros, dollars or Egyptian pounds. It's possible to book online too. Book before 6pm for the same day, but in high season (October to April), book several days in advance.

Marsa Matruh

Watania (p495) runs a train to the Mediterranean coast three times a week during the summer season.

Suez Canal

Delays on this route are common; going by bus is more efficient. If you're determined to travel by train, the best option is to Ismailia.

MAJOR TRAINS FROM CAIRO

Prices are for first-class service, all with air-con, unless otherwise noted.

DESTINATION	STATION	PRICE	DURATION	TIMES
Alexandria (direct)	Ramses	E£50	2½hr	8am, 9am, 11am, noon, 2pm, 6pm, 7pm, 9pm, 10.30pm
Alexandria (stopping)	Ramses	E£35	3–3½hr	8 daily, 6am–8.15pm
Aswan	Ramses	US$100	14hr	Sleeper only
Ismailia	Ramses	E£15	3hr	6.15am, 1pm, 1.45pm, 2.45pm, 5.45pm, 7.50pm, 10pm
Luxor & Aswan	Giza	US$100	9½hr (Luxor), 13hr (Aswan)	Sleeper only
Luxor	Ramses	E£90	10½hr	8am, noon, 7pm, 8pm, 1am
Marsa Matruh (sleeper)	Giza	US$43/E£252	7hr	11pm Sat, Mon, Wed, mid-Jun–mid-Sep
Port Said	Ramses	E£28	4hr	6.15am, 1.45pm, 7.50pm
Tanta	Ramses	E£18	1–1½hr	6am, 8.15am, 10am, 11am, noon, 2.10pm, 3.10pm, 4pm, 5.15pm
Zagazig	Ramses	E£15	1½hr	5.15am, 6.15am, 1pm, 1.45pm, 3.40pm, 7.50pm, 10pm

Getting Around

TO/FROM THE AIRPORT

Cairo International Airport (p115) is 20km northeast of the centre. The terminology is a bit confusing: Terminal 1 is three buildings, all within view of each other, though only arrival halls 1 and 3 receive commercial flights. Opened in 2009, Terminal 3 is 2km south. Terminal 2 was being renovated at the time of research, and slated for completion in early 2015. A blue-and-white shuttle bus connects terminals 1 and 3.

There's no left-luggage service, but there is free wi-fi. You can pick up a SIM card in Terminal 3 at the Vodafone kiosk, or inside the convenience store, both to the far right as you come out of customs.

Bus

Don't believe anyone who tells you there is no bus to the city centre. Air-con bus 27 or 356 (E£4, plus E£2 per large luggage item, one hour) runs at 20-minute intervals from 7am to midnight between Midan Abdel Moniem Riad (behind the Egyptian Museum) in central Cairo and the airport. After hours, the only option is bus 400 (E£1). Minibus 324 (E£1) goes to Midan Ramses. And, should you need them, buses depart for Alexandria hourly (E£40 to E£48, four hours).

Blue shuttle buses connect air terminals and the bus station. At Terminal 1, arrivals 1, the shuttle stops in the first lane of the car park, a little to your right as you come out the doors. In arrivals 3, bear left outside – the shuttle stops in the outer lane, under the skybridge to the Air Mall. The shuttle stops across the road from the bus complex just after you turn right at the petrol station. In Terminal 3, bear right out the doors, to the far end of the outer lane. From here, the shuttle drives straight into the bus terminal.

Taxi

The going rate to central Cairo is about E£95; metered cabs are seldom seen at this end, so you'll need to negotiate with one of the mob of drivers clustered around the door when you exit. It's better to get away a bit before starting negotiations, as just walking can sometimes bring the price down. Triple-check the agreed fare, as there is an irritating tendency for drivers to nod at what you say and claim a higher fare later. (Heading to the airport from the centre, you can easily get a meter taxi; you'll have to pay E£5 to enter the airport grounds.)

For a smoother arrival at almost the same price, arrange a car through your hotel, or call or book online **Cairo Airport Shuttle Bus** (☎19970; www.cairoshuttlebus.com; E£110 to Downtown), which runs small vans and has a desk at Terminals 1 and 3, arrivals 1 (though it can pick you up anywhere). In Terminal 1, arrivals 3, at the car-rental desk in the centre, **Star Choice** (☎0100 313 0020) offers rides for E£110; most airport limo services offer similar rates.

In the traffic-free early hours of the morning, the journey to central Cairo takes 20 minutes. At busier times of the day it can take more than an hour.

BUS & MINIBUS

Cairo is thoroughly served by a network of lumbering sardine-cans-on-wheels and smaller, shuttle-size minibuses (on which, theoretically, there's no standing allowed), but visitors will find only a few uses for them: they're good for a slow but cheap trip to the Pyramids or from the airport, but elsewhere you can travel more efficiently and comfortably by metro and/or taxi. Signs are in Arabic only, so you'll have to know your numerals. There is no known map of any of the city's bus routes. Just hop on and pay the conductor when he comes around selling tickets, which cost between 75pt and E£2 depending on distance and whether there's air-con (mint-green buses sometimes have it, as do the big white CTA buses).

Major bus hubs are Midan Abdel Moniem Riad, behind the Egyptian Museum and Midan Ataba.

CAR

Driving in Cairo can't be recommended – not only is it harrowing, but you're only contributing to the hideously clogged streets. Lane markings are ignored and traffic lights are discretionary unless enforced by a policeman.

At night some drivers use their headlights exclusively for flashing oncoming vehicles. But Cairo drivers do have road rules: they look out for each other and are tolerant of driving that elsewhere might provoke road rage. Things only go awry when an inexperienced driver – like an international visitor, perhaps – is thrown into the mix.

Hire

The only reason we expect you might rent a car is to drive directly out of the city. Finding a cheap deal with local operators is virtually impossible; you're much better off organising ahead via the web. The major options:

Avis (☎0100 107 7400; www.avisegypt.com; Airport)

Budget (☎2265 2395; www.budget.com; Terminal 1, Cairo Airport)

Europcar (☎0106 661 1027; www.europcar.com/car-EGYPT.html; Terminal 1, Cairo Airport)

Hertz (☎0180 000 822; www.hertzegypt.com; Airport) 24hr call centre; also has a branch Downtown (Map p62; ☎2575 8914; www.hertz-egypt.com; Ramses Hilton, Corniche el-Nil).

METRO

The metro is blissfully efficient, inexpensive and, outside rush hours (7am to 9am and 3pm to 6pm), not too crowded. Given the impossible car traffic in Cairo, if you can make even a portion of your journey on the metro, you'll save time and aggravation. Three lines are now in operation. Line 1 stretches 43km along the east bank of the Nile. Line 2 crosses to the west bank, passing through Downtown and across Gezira en route. Long-awaited Line 3 has opened partly from Abbassiya to Haroun station in Heliopolis, and eventually will connect the city to the airport (2019) and Ataba with Kitkat via Zamalek (2015).

Metro stations have signs with a big red 'M' in a blue star. Tickets cost E£1 to any stop; keep yours handy to feed into the turnstile on the way out. At the time of research, a stored-value card was in the works to replace tickets. Trains run every five minutes or so from around 6am until 11.30pm.

Two carriages in the centre of each train are reserved for women. Look for the blue 'Ladies' signs on the platform marking where you should stand.

TO & FROM THE CITADEL

Walking from Midan Ataba is feasible, but long: to the Citadel's entrance gate, it's almost 4km along Sharia al-Qala'a and its continuation, Sharia Mohammed Ali. At Midan Salah ad-Din, walk along Sharia Sayyida Aisha to Sharia Salah Salem, turn left to reach the main gate. Alternatively, minibus 150 (E£2) runs from Midan Ataba to Midan Salah ad-Din, still a 15-minute walk from the entrance; a second microbus can take you from Salah ad-Din to Sayyida Aisha at Salah Salem. Taking a taxi is only marginally quicker due to the complicated traffic-flow on Salah Salem. Leaving the Citadel, walk downhill and away from the main entrance to hail a cab.

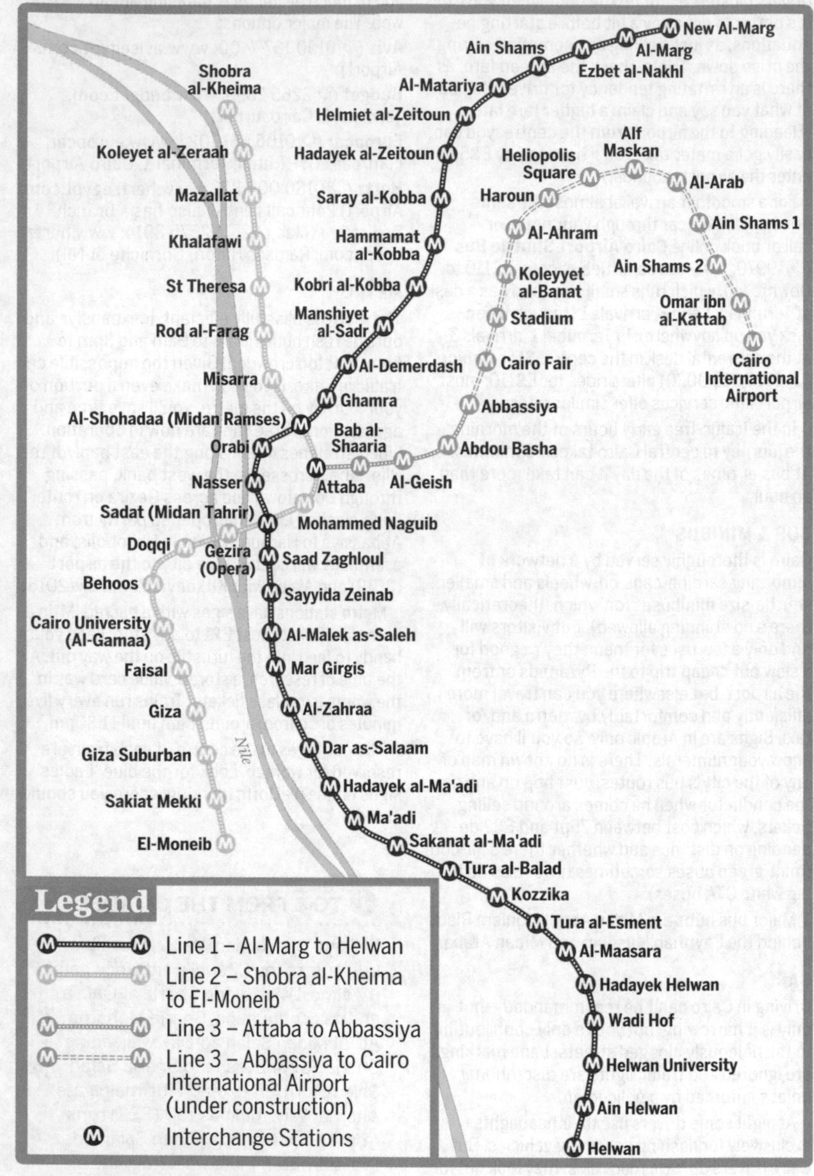

MICROBUS

Cairenes use the private microbus *(meekrobas)* – a small van with 12 or so seats – as much as the public bus. No destinations are marked, which can make them hard to use at first. But they're quite useful for major routes: from the Giza metro to near the Pyramids and Midan al-Remaya for long-distance microbuses, and from Ataba to Sayyida Aisha for the Citadel. Locals use coded hand gestures to communicate their destination to passing microbuses; if the van has a free seat, it will stop. Fares vary according to distance, from 75pt to E£4, paid after you take your seat. This often requires passing your money to passengers ahead and receiving your change the same way (which is always done scrupulously).

RIVER BUS

It's of limited utility, but it's scenic; the river bus runs from the corniche near Downtown Cairo to Giza by the zoo and Cairo University. The Downtown terminal is located at Maspero, 250m north of the Ramses Hilton, in front of the big round TV building. Boats depart every 15 minutes for Giza from near the zoo. The trip takes 30 minutes and the fare is E£1.

TAXI

Outside the mid-afternoon rush, taxis are readily available and will come to a screeching halt with the slightest wave of your hand. The whole Cairo cab experience has been transformed by new white taxis with meters and even, on occasion, air-con. Older unmetered, black-and-white taxis still ply the streets, but although there's potential for getting a cheaper fare in them, the discomfort and near-inevitable argument at the end make them not worth your while.

Meter rates start at E£2.50, plus E£1.25 per kilometre and E£0.25 waiting. A tip of 10% or so is very much appreciated, and it's good to have small change on hand, as drivers are often short of it. Some people have reported taxis with suspiciously fast-running meters, or drivers who claim the meter is broken. If you encounter either situation, simply stop the car, get out and flag down another – the vast majority are legitimate and won't give you trouble.

Hiring a taxi for a longer period runs from E£30 to E£40 per hour, depending on your bargaining skills; E£300 to E£400 for a full day is typical. Nour Gaber (p93), can be booked in advance, offers good rates and speaks English.

USEFUL METRO STATIONS

Ataba Convenient for Downtown.

Bab al-Shaaria Closest to Islamic Cairo, on the north side.

Gezira (Opera) By the Cairo Opera House, closest to Zamalek.

Giza Next to Giza train station, handy for buses to the Pyramids.

Mar Girgis In the middle of Coptic Cairo.

Mohammed Naguib Close to Abdeen Palace and the Museum of Islamic Art.

Al-Shohadaa Beneath Midan Ramses and Ramses Railway Station.

Nasser Sharia 26th of July and Sharia Ramses; closest to Downtown nightlife.

Sadat Beneath Midan Tahrir, close to the Egyptian Museum.

GREATER CAIRO

Giza

Technically all of Cairo on the west bank of the Nile is Giza, though the name is inextricably linked with the Pyramids, 9km from the river, on the edge of the desert. Truly time-strapped sightseers could stay out here and bypass Cairo entirely, but that's missing a lot of the fun. More realistically, you'll probably come out here on a day outing. Sharia al-Haram or Pyramids Rd leads straight to the site, and the village of Nazlet as-Samaan at its base and south of Pyramids Rd.

★ Pyramids of Giza ARCHAEOLOGICAL SITE

(Map p122; adult/student E£80/40; ⏲8am-4pm)

For nearly 4000 years, the extraordinary shape, impeccable geometry and sheer bulk of the Giza Pyramids have invited the obvious question: 'How were we built, and why?'

Centuries of research have given us parts of the answer. We know they were massive tombs constructed on the orders of the pharaohs by teams of workers tens-of-thousands strong. This is supported by the discovery of a pyramid-builders' settlement, complete with areas for large-scale food production and medical facilities.

Ongoing excavations on the Giza Plateau have provided more evidence that the workers were not the slaves of Hollywood tradition, but an organised workforce of Egyptian farmers. During the flood season, when the Nile covered their fields, the same farmers could have been redeployed by the highly structured bureaucracy to work on the pharaoh's tomb. In this way, the Pyramids can almost be seen as an ancient job-creation scheme. And the flood waters made it easier to transport building stone to the site.

But despite the evidence, some still won't accept that the ancient Egyptians were capable of such achievements. So-called pyramidologists point to the carving and placement of the stones, precise to the millimetre, and argue the numerological significance of the structures' dimensions as

The Giza Plateau

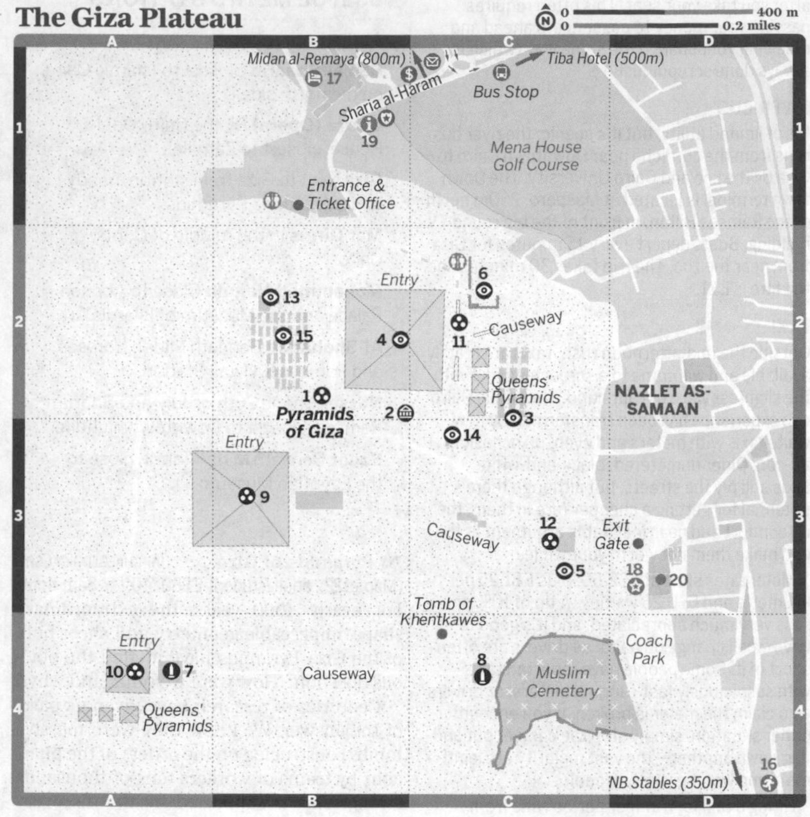

The Giza Plateau

Top Sights
1 Pyramids of Giza B2

Sights
2 Cheops Boat Museum B2
3 Eastern Cemetery C2
4 Great Pyramid of Khufu B2
5 Khafre's Valley Temple C3
6 King Farouk's Rest House C2
7 Menkaure's Funerary Temple A4
8 Menkaure's Valley Temple C4
9 Pyramid of Khafre B3
10 Pyramid of Menkaure A4
11 Solar Barque Pits C2
12 Sphinx C3
13 Tomb of Senegemib-Inti B2
14 Tomb of Seshemnufer IV C3
15 Western Cemetery B2

Activities, Courses & Tours
16 FB D4

Sleeping
17 Mena House Hotel B1

Eating
Khan al-Khalili .... (see 17)
Moghul Room .... (see 17)

Entertainment
18 Sound and Light Show D3

Information
19 Ministry of Tourism B1
20 Sound & Light Ticket Office D3

evidence that the Pyramids were constructed by angels or aliens. It's easy to laugh at these out-there ideas, but when you see the monuments up close, especially inside, you'll better understand why so many people believe such awesome structures must have unearthly origins.

➡ Great Pyramid of Khufu

(Great Pyramid of Cheops; Map p122; E£200; ⏲8am-4pm) The oldest pyramid in Giza and the largest in Egypt, Khufu's Great Pyramid stood 146m high when it was completed around 2570 BC. After 46 windy centuries, its height has been reduced by 9m.

There isn't much to see inside the pyramid, but the experience of climbing through the ancient structure is unforgettable – though impossible if you suffer the tiniest degree of claustrophobia. The elderly and unfit should not attempt the climb, as it is very steep.

First you clamber up the face of the pyramid a bit, up rudimentary stairs to the left of the entrance. Leave your camera with the guard if you have one, then crouch down to enter. At a juncture in the tunnel, a passage descends to an unfinished tomb (usually closed) about 100m along and 30m deep in the bedrock. From here, another passage, 1.3m high and 1m wide, ascends for about 40m to reach the Great Gallery, an impressive narrow space 47m long and 8.5m high. At the start of the gallery, a small horizontal passage leads into the so-called Queen's Chamber.

As you climb up through the Great Gallery, notice how precisely the blocks in the ceiling fit together. In the 10m-long King's Chamber at the end, the walls are built of red granite blocks. The ceiling itself consists of nine huge slabs of granite, which weigh more than 400 tonnes. Above these slabs, four more slabs are separated by gaps, which are designed to distribute the enormous weight away from the chamber. Good airflow from the modern ventilation system (built into two ancient tiny air shafts) will help you breathe easier as you contemplate the tremendous weight suspended above you.

East of the pyramid is a ruin of a different era: **King Farouk's Rest House**, a grand neo-Pharaonic structure built in 1946 by Mustafa Fahmy. It's now an unfortunate shambles, but there's a good view of the city from the adjacent yard.

Along the pyramid's east face, three small structures some 20m high resemble piles of rubble. These are the **Queens' Pyramids**, the tombs of Khufu's wives and sisters. You can enter some of them, but they're quite steamy inside. In the eastern cemetery behind, one or two tombs are occasionally open, and you can still see the perfectly smooth limestone facing along the bases of some structures. Note also the solar barque pits between the pyramids, which held giant ritual boats.

➡ Cheops Boat Museum

(Map p122; adult/student E£50/25; ⏲9am-4pm Oct-May, 9am-5pm Jun-Sep) Immediately south of the Great Pyramid is this fascinating museum with exactly one object on display: one of Cheops five solar barques (boats), buried near his pyramid, and unearthed in 1954. This huge stunning ancient wood vessel, possibly the oldest boat in existence, was carefully restored from 1200 pieces of Lebanese cedar and encased in this museum to protect it from the elements. Visitors to the museum must help this process by donning protective footwear to keep sand out.

Five large pits were found near the Great Pyramid of Khufu. They contained the pharaoh's solar barques, which may have been used to convey the mummy of the dead pharaoh across the Nile to the valley temple, from where it was brought up the causeway and into the tomb chamber. The boats were then buried around the pyramid to provide transport for the pharaoh in the next world.

This boat was put back together for this museum, but the others were buried again after their discovery.

➡ Pyramid of Khafre

(Pyramid of Chephren; Map p122; adult/student E£40/20; ⏲8am-4pm) The second pyramid, of Khafre, seems larger than that of his father, Khufu. At just 136m high, it's not, but it stands on higher ground and its peak is still capped with the original polished limestone casing. Originally all three pyramids were totally encased in this smooth white stone, which would have made them gleam in the sun. Over the centuries, this casing has been stripped for use in palaces and mosques, exposing the softer inner-core stones to the elements.

At the time of research, the interior of the pyramid was closed; it usually alternates opening with the Pyramid of Menkaure. The chambers and passageways of this pyramid are less elaborate than those in the Great Pyramid, but are almost as claustrophobic.

PYRAMIDS PRACTICALITIES

Entrance & Tickets

The main **entrance** (Map p122) is at the end of Pyramids Rd (Sharia al-Haram), though if you come on a tour bus, you may enter through a gate below the Sphinx, in the village of Nazlet as-Samaan; you can also exit here on foot.

Additional tickets are required for the Cheops Boat Museum and the pyramid interiors. The Great Pyramid is always open, along with one of the other two (they alternate every year or so). Pyramid interior tickets are purchased at the main entrance. Secondary-pyramid tickets are sold all day. At peak times Great Pyramid tickets (300 available in summer, 500 in winter) are sold in two lots, first thing in the morning and at 1pm. In winter, you may need to queue, especially on Wednesday and Thursday, when tour groups come from the Red Sea. At the time of research, with fewer tourists in Egypt, tickets were available all day, without queues. If you exit the site to purchase afternoon interior tickets, let the guards know so there's no trouble when you come back through.

Cameras are allowed all over the site, including in the museum, but not inside pyramids and tombs. Guards will watch your camera at the pyramid entrances, in exchange for E£5 or so baksheesh; some will also permit photos inside tombs for a tip.

Facilities & Food

Clean bathrooms are outside the main entrance (tip the attendant E£2 or so). On the plateau, there's one decent one in the Cheops Boat Museum, and another in a dodgy trailer near the Great Pyramid. At the base of the Sphinx, the open-air **cafe** (drinks E£20, sandwiches E£25-65) also has some. For food, it's grossly overpriced, and the waiters are easily 'confused' when making change. For the same amount, you can refresh at the nearby Pizza Hut or far lovelier Mena House, though this means a hike back up the hill to the main entrance. For cheap eats, walk a bit northeast on the main road through Nazlet as-Samaan, and you'll pass various snack options.

Horses & Camels

Considering the pressure, it's tempting to ignore the camel touts; however, the distance between the three pyramids is significant, so the service is a real one. 'Official' prices (E£35 per hour) exist, but, as one tourist police officer said with an apologetic shrug, 'You're still expected to bargain'. Realistically, you can't ride an animal any distance for less than E£50, and E£20 is the minimum for a short trot and photo op. Choose only healthy-looking animals, and if you're asked to pay more than agreed before you're let down, call over the nearest tourist police, or go to the office by the Mena House and complain. For longer rides, hiring a horse from one of the village stables is a far better option than taking one at the Pyramids.

The entrance descends into a passage and then across to the burial chamber, which still contains Khafre's large granite sarcophagus.

Back outside, to the east of the pyramid, are the substantial remains of Khafre's funerary temple and the flagged paving of the causeway that provided access from the Nile to the tomb.

➡ Pyramid of Menkaure

(Pyramid of Mycerinus; Map p122; adult/student E£40/20; ⌚8am-4pm) At 62m (originally 66.5m), this pyramid is the smallest of the trio, only about one-tenth the bulk of the Great Pyramid. The pharaoh Menkaure died before the structure was finished – around the bottom are several courses of granite facing that was never properly smoothed. The pyramid alternates opening with the Pyramid of Khafre. Inside, you descend into three distinct levels – the largest surprisingly vast – and you can peer into the main tomb.

Outside the pyramid you'll see the excavated remains of **Menkaure's Funerary Temple** and, further east, the ruins of his **valley temple**. To the south is another set of **Queens' Pyramids**. If you hike this far, horse and camel touts will want to lure you out in the desert for better photo ops of all three pyramids. If you go, keep your general-admission ticket handy in case police ask for it when you return.

➡ Khafre's Valley Temple

(Map p122) You approach the Sphinx through this temple that once sat at the edge of a small artificial lake, connected to the Nile by a canal – it was in this way that construction materials were brought to the area at the start, and, later, worshippers came to visit the temple. The sturdy building is filled with beautiful pink granite columns and alabaster floors.

Look in the corners, where the pink granite facing stones are fit together like pieces of a jigsaw puzzle. The temple originally held 23 statues of Khafre, which were illuminated with the ancient version of mood lighting, through slits between the top of the wall and the flat roof. Only one of these statues, all carved in the hard black stone diorite, has been found intact – it is now in the Egyptian Museum.

➡ Sphinx

(Map p122) Known in Arabic as Abu al-Hol (Father of Terror), this sculpture of a man with the haunches of a lion was dubbed the Sphinx by the ancient Greeks because it resembled their mythical winged monster who set riddles and killed anyone unable to answer them. A geological survey has shown that it was most likely carved from the bedrock at the bottom of the causeway, during Khafre's reign, so it probably portrays his features.

As is clear from the accounts of early Arab travellers, the nose was hammered off sometime between the 11th and 15th centuries, although some still like to blame Napoleon for the deed. Part of the fallen beard was carted off by 19th-century adventurers and is now on display in the British Museum in London. These days the Sphinx has potentially greater problems: pollution and rising groundwater are causing internal fractures, and it is under a constant state of repair.

Legends and superstitions abound about the Sphinx, and the mystery surrounding its long-forgotten purpose is almost as intriguing as its appearance. On seeing it for the first time, many visitors agree with English playwright Alan Bennett, who noted in his diary that seeing the Sphinx is like meeting a TV personality in the flesh: he's smaller than one had imagined.

➡ Cemeteries & Tombs

(Map p122) Private cemeteries are tucked into the hill alongside the causeways, as well as arrayed in neat rows around the Pyramids in a grid pattern – the **Eastern Cemetery** next to the Great Pyramid, as well as the **Western Cemetery**. Only a few of the tombs are open to the public at any given time, but the **Tomb of Seshemnufer IV**, just southeast of the Great Pyramid, is almost always open. Just inside the columned entrance, carved deer adorn the walls of the entrance room, and there's a burial chamber you can climb down into.

At the north end of the western cemetery, the **Tomb of Senegemib-Inti**, contains interesting inscriptions, including a rather vicious-looking hippopotamus, rippling with muscle.

Wissa Wassef Art Centre — ARTS CENTRE

(☎ 3381 5746; www.wissawassef.com; Saqqara Rd, Harraniyya; ⏲ 10am-5pm daily, studios closed Fri) The artisans of the Wissa Wassef Art Centre who work in open studios are known for their distinctive tapestries depicting rural scenes. Crude imitations are standard in souvenir shops; the ones for sale and on display in the museum here are in a completely different class, like paintings in wool. There's pottery and batik fabric, done to equally good effect. The place has the feeling of a sanctuary – quiet and refreshingly green, especially after a dusty Pyramids visit.

The center is housed in a beautiful mudbrick complex, the work of its founder, architect Ramses Wissa Wassef. It won an Aga Khan prize for its refined traditional style.

To get here, take a Saqqara-bound microbus (E£1) or taxi from Pyramids Rd at Maryutia Canal – a giant flyover runs above it. Get off when you see the blue 'Harraniyya' sign, after about 3.5km, and about 600m after the flyover turns away. The centre is by the canal on the west side of the road.

Kerdassa — SHOPPING CENTRE

(Tir'at al-Maryutia (Canal)) We mention this spot only because it is sometimes pushed as an insider shopping destination where you can buy scarves and *galabeyes* direct from the 'factory'. But the dismal setting of semi-rural poverty adjacent to a new strip mall, plus the price of a taxi ride (at least E£20 to E£25 from the Pyramids), cancels out the minor savings. The village is about 5.5km north of Pyramids Rd (roughly 15 minutes).

The Pyramids of Giza

Constructed more than 4000 years ago, the Pyramids are the last remaining wonder of the ancient world. The giant structures – the **Great Pyramid of Khufu** ❶, the smaller **Pyramid of Khafre** ❷ and the **Pyramid of Menkaure** ❸ – deservedly sit at the top of many travellers' to-do lists. But the site is challenging to explore, with everything, including the smaller **Queens' Pyramids** ❹ and assorted tombs such as the **Tomb of Senegemib-Inti** ❺, spread out in the desert under the hot sun. And it all looks, at fi rst glance, a bit smaller than you might have thought.

It helps to imagine them as they were: originally, the Pyramids gleamed in the sun, covered in a smooth white limestone casing. These enormous mausoleums, each devoted to a single pharaoh, were part of larger complexes. At the east base of each was a 'funerary temple', where the pharaoh was worshipped after his demise, with daily rounds of offerings to sustain his soul. In the ground around the pyramids, wooden boats – so-called solar barques – were buried with more supplies to transport the pharaoh's soul to the afterlife (one of these has been reconstructed and sits in the **Cheops Boat Museum** ❻). From each funerary temple, a long stone-paved causeway extended down the hill.

At the base of the plateau, a lake covered the land where the village of Nazlet as-Samaan is now – this was fed by a canal and enlarged with fl ood waters each year. At the end of each causeway, a 'valley temple' stood at the water's edge to greet visitors. Next to Khafre's valley temple, the lion-bodied **Sphinx** ❼ stands guard.

So much about the Pyramids remains mysterious – including the whereabouts of the bodies of the pharaohs themselves. But there's still plenty for visitors to see. Here we show you both the big picture and the little details to look out for, starting with the **ticket booth and entrance** ❽.

ZORA O'NEILL

Pyramid of Khafre

Khufu's son built this pyramid, which has some surviving limestone casing at the top. Scattered around the base are enormous granite stones that once added a snappy black stripe to the lowest level of the structure.

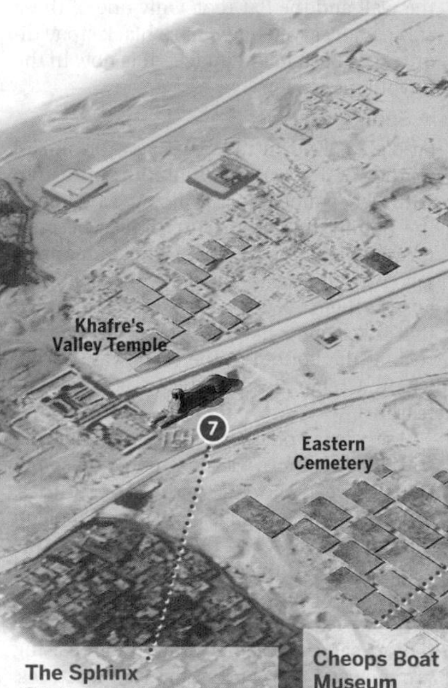

The Sphinx

This human-headed beast, thought to be a portrait of Khafre, guards the base of the plateau. The entrance is only through Khafre's valley temple. Come early or late in the day to avoid the long queue.

ZORA O'NEILL

Cheops Boat Museum

Preserved in its own modern tomb, this 4500-year-old cedar barge was dug up from in front of the Great Pyramid and reassembled by expert craftsmen like a 1224-piece jigsaw puzzle.

ZORA O'NEILL

ZORA O'NEILL

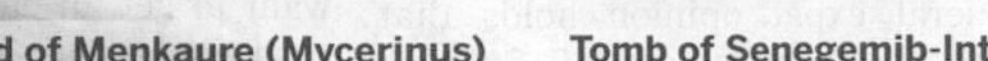

ZORA O'NEILL

Pyramid of Menkaure (Mycerinus)

This pyramid opens alternately with the Pyramid of Khafre. The gash in the exterior is the folly of Sultan al-Aziz Uthman, who tried to dismantle the pyramid in 1196.

Tomb of Senegemib-Inti

The Giza Plateau is dotted with small tombs like this one. Opening schedules vary each year. Duck inside to look for delicate wall carvings and enjoy a bit of shade.

3

2

Western Cemetery

Khafre's Funerary Temple

Ticket Booth & Entrance

Buy tickets, marked with a hologram sticker, here and only here. All other options are counterfeit. Clean bathrooms, the only good facilities, are in a building just to the east.

6

5

1

8

4

Great Pyramid of Khufu (Cheops)

Clamber inside the corridors to marvel at the precision engineering of the seamless stone blocks, each weighing 2.5 tonnes. Pause to consider the full weight of 2.3 million of them.

Queens' Pyramids

These smaller piles were built as the tombs of Khufu's sister, mother and wife. They're in bad shape, but some show the original limestone casing at the base – feel how smoothly the stones are fitted.

ZORA O'NEILL

ZORA O'NEILL

Activities

There's only one thing to do around the Pyramids, and you'll never stop hearing about it. But a desert **horse ride** at sunset, with the Pyramids as a background, is unforgettable.

All of the stables are strung along the road south of the coach park by the Sphinx gate. General expat opinion holds that some of the best stables are **NB Stables** (☎3382 0435), owned by Naser Breesh, who's praised for his healthy steeds and good guides; his place is just behind the Sphinx Club, further south than the others. **FB** (Map p122; ☎0106 507 0288; www.fbstables-giza.co.uk; Sharia Gamal Abdul Nasser) is also recommended.

Expect to pay around E£100 per person per hour at a good place; a reputable operation won't ask for money till the end of the ride. Others may charge less, but often their horses are very poorly kept. Tip your guide an additional E£10 to E£15, and keep your Pyramids site ticket or you'll be charged again to enter. Moonlit rides around the Pyramids are another favourite outing but under new regulations you can't ride anywhere close to the site after 6pm.

Sleeping

A Pyramids-area hotel may appeal if you want to get an early start at the site, and treat yourself a bit while you're at it. Plus, the only camping option in the Cairo area is out this way.

Salma Motel CAMPGROUND $
(☎0100 270 4442; Saqqara Rd, Harraniyya; campsites per person E£25, cabins E£100) The only camping option in Cairo is miles from the centre, adjacent to the Wissa Wassef Art Centre on the Maryutia Canal. To get here, take a microbus or taxi from Pyramids Rd in the direction of Saqqara and get off when you see the blue 'Harraniyya' sign.

Coming by car, take the Ring Rd freeway west, then exit at Maryutia Rd and head south.

THE PYRAMIDS HUSTLE

Usually crammed with buses, postcard vendors and gargling camels, the Pyramids is an intense tourist scene, and many visitors find it the most gruelling part of their trip. Unfortunately, until the site is better managed and the people in the village by the Pyramids have some other income besides selling horse and camel rides, there is no way to avoid the sales pressure and scam attempts. It does help, however, to know what you're up against. These days, with fewer tourists around, there are less vendors, but the despair to make some money by the ones who are left, is even greater.

The hustle can start before you even leave your hotel, where someone tries to sell you a 'sunrise tour' of the Pyramids: really just a way of delivering you early to the horse touts, as you can't enter the site before 8am. En route, someone will chat you up at the Giza metro, or a man will jump in your taxi while it's stuck in traffic on Pyramids Rd. The road ahead is closed, he warns, and the best way to proceed is on a horse. (The road *is* closed, sort of; about 1km from the site, all outbound traffic must detour north on Sharia al-Mansouria. Don't panic – you'll loop back to the Pyramids soon.) Nearer the gate, others will try to convince you the entrance has moved, or point you to a secret back route. Counterfeit tickets aren't unheard-of – buy yours only from the ticket windows at the main gate.

Once through the turnstiles, police might direct you to a waiting man, or men will ask for your ticket in an official tone. Ignore them, as they're just attempting to become your guide. You need only show your additional tickets at the Great Pyramid and whichever secondary pyramid is open (and guards should take only half the ticket, not the whole thing). Guards also usually check your general ticket at the Sphinx to make sure you haven't slipped through the downhill gate. Attendants at smaller tombs will ask for a ticket, hoping you'll assume you need to buy one – flash your general ticket, and you should be fine.

Even knowing all this won't stop touts from approaching you, and no matter how tersely and frequently you say no, these guys won't stop – it's the only job they've got. So it's key for your own happiness not to snap, but to smile and just keep walking. It also helps to remember that the Pyramids have been attracting tourists since day one, and a local was probably already waiting to sell a souvenir.

Barceló HOTEL $$
(☎3582 3300; www.barcelo.com; 229 Pyramids Rd; r from €40;) Well placed – and well priced – for a strategic visit to the Pyramids, without totally giving up on the city. The Giza metro stop is about 3km away, and the Pyramids are 4km. It's a standard chain, but all new as of 2010, with good breakfast and a nice rooftop pool.

Tiba Hotel HOTEL $$
(☎3358 1659; www.tibapyramidshotel.com; Pyramids Rd; r from E£257;) The best deal within walking distance of the Pyramids, though still not great quality. The traffic noise is intense as it's at a major intersection. Only stay here if you're on a budget and planning a surgical strike on the Pyramids.

Mena House Hotel LUXURY HOTEL $$$
(Map p122; ☎3377 3222; www.menahousehotel.com; Pyramids Rd; s/d garden wing from US$175/285, s/d/ste palace wing from US$245/335/690;) Built in 1869 as Khedive Ismail's hunting lodge, Mena House dazzles with intricate gold decoration and air that perpetually smells of jasmine. The grandest palace-wing rooms are borderline-kitschy Arabian Nights style, but the view of the Great Pyramid filling your window is a treat. Rooms in the garden wing are more typically modern. The swimming pool is suitably capacious.

Eating & Drinking

Andrea EGYPTIAN $$
(☎3383 1133; 59 Tir'at al-Maryutia; mains E£35-50; noon-midnight) Pleasant garden restaurant where women pat out bread dough at the entrance, and tend the spit-roasted chicken the place is justly famous for. It makes a great post-Pyramids lunch with salads and a few cold Stellas. (Make sure your driver doesn't take you to the unrelated Andrea Gardenia, south of Pyramids Rd.) Definitely worth the trip.

Located 1.5km north of Pyramids Rd on the west side of Maryutia Canal (you must drive north about 2km, below the flyover, then loop around to come down the other side of the canal; if you reach onramps to the elevated highway above, you've gone plenty far).

Khan al-Khalili EGYPTIAN, EUROPEAN $$
(Map p122; Mena House Hotel, Pyramids Rd; mains E£60-105; 24hr) The casual restaurant at Mena House has huge windows opening onto the Pyramids – a great place to rest up after a day of sightseeing, even if the food is a bit bland. But the menu is broad enough – from spaghetti to Indian dishes – that it's a crowd pleaser. A Stella costs E£29.

Moghul Room INDIAN $$$
(Map p122; ☎3377 3222; Mena House Hotel, Pyramids Rd; mains E£95-170; 7-11pm ;) Cairo's best Indian restaurant specialises in mild North Indian–style curries and kebabs, with an emphasis on tandoori dishes. Though it's a long taxi ride from Downtown, the opulent decor, good food and live sitar music make it worthwhile. There's a wide range of vegetarian options (from E£70 to E£85). Not entirely authentic but pleasant and beautiful surroundings.

Club 35 CLUB, LOUNGE
(Map p94; ☎3573 8500; club35lounge.com; Four Seasons at the First Residence, 35 Sharia al-Giza; 7pm-3am) If you go before midnight, the place doesn't look all that promising, as it's still in soft-jazz Asian-fusion-bistro mode. But later, a mixed crowd packs in for dancing, even though there's no actual dance floor. The sushi is pretty good.

THE PYRAMIDS AFTER DARK

Narrated by the Sphinx, the **sound and light show** (Map p122; ☎02-3385 7320; www.soundandlight.com.eg; Sphinx Entrance; admission E£75, translation headset E£10; winter shows at 7pm, 8pm & 9pm, summer at 7.30pm, 8.30pm & 9.30pm) is a rather dated spectacular. It's not worth a special trip, but fine if you're in the area – it is neat to see the Pyramids so dramatically lit. Though there's officially no student discount, some readers report negotiating a small one. Check the website or book ahead, as a minimum of 10 people is needed per show; if not it's canceled. The entrance is on the Sphinx side.

Information

EMERGENCY

Tourist Police (Map p122; ☎126; Pyramids Rd) Across from Mena House Hotel.

TOURIST INFORMATION

Ministry of Tourism (Map p122; ☎3383 8823; Pyramids Rd; 8.30am-5pm) Across from Mena House.

Getting There & Away

The most efficient traffic-beating way to reach the Pyramids is to go via metro to Giza, then by taxi (about E£15 to E£20), microbus or bus.

Microbuses cluster at the bottom of the west-side stairs from the metro (drivers are yelling 'Haram'). The fare is E£3. You can get off where the van turns off Pyramids Rd (at Sharia al-Mansouria, with the Tiba Hotel on the southeast corner), and walk 1km straight to the entrance.

Buses (usually E£1) stop on the north side of Pyramids Rd, just west of the underpass. Hop on any headed for Midan al-Remaya and get off at Sharia al-Mansouria, or look out for **355 or 357**, which terminate in front of Mena House (Map p122), about 250m from the site entrance.

Returning to Cairo, taxis will try to convince you to go for a flat fare, rather than on the meter. Walking out further helps. You could also take a tuk-tuk from the Sphinx side out to Pyramids Rd for about E£3.

Heliopolis

This pretty suburb shows a different, more relaxed side of the city, and is a nice antidote to central Cairo's tourist pressure. With all its trees and outdoor cafes, it's a pleasant place for an evening's wander. Many Egyptians think so too, as Heliopolis has become 'Downtown' for people living in dull satellite cities further east. It's also reasonably close to the airport, so you can get a taste of Cairo even if you're just on a pit stop in an airport-area hotel before an early flight.

Belgian industrialist and baron Édouard Empain laid out Heliopolis in the early 20th century as a 'garden city' for the colonial officials who ruled Egypt. Its whitewashed Moorish-style buildings with dark wood balconies, grand arcades and terraces are the European vision of the 'Orient' set in stone. Since the 1950s, overcrowding has filled in the green spaces between the villas with apartment buildings festooned with satellite dishes, but the area still has a relaxed, vaguely Mediterranean air.

THE END OF THE LINE

In March 2014 a bomb exploded on the long-suffering tram in Heliopolis, near the Presidential Palace. The old tram line was closed down, and the government is set to begin working on a complete overhaul of the existing tram system. The first stage is set to be completed by 2016, and will connect Heliopolis with New Cairo settlements.

Heliopolis

Sights

1 Uruba Palace C2

Eating

2 Abu Ammar al-Suri D1
3 Arabiata El Shabrawy D1
4 Mangiamo C1

Drinking & Nightlife

5 Cilantro D1
6 L'Amphitrion C2

Information

7 Centre Français de Culture et de Coopération B2

Sights

Sharia al-Ahram runs through Korba, 'downtown' Heliopolis. At the south end, **Uruba Palace** (Sharia al-Ahram) was once a grand hotel graced by the likes of King Albert I of Belgium and then appropriated as the presidential offices – at least until Mubarak got the boot in 2011. From the palace, at the first intersection with Sharia Ibrahim Laqqany (detour left for some pretty arcades), is the open-air cafeteria **L'Amphitrion** (2258 1379; 181 Sharia Ibrahim Laqqany; 10am-2am), as old as Heliopolis itself and a popular watering hole for Allied soldiers during the world wars. At the end of Sharia al-Ahram, the Basilica is a miniature version of Istanbul's famous Aya Sofya, dubbed the 'jelly mould' by local expats. Baron Empain is buried here.

Empain lived in a fantastical Hindu-look mansion, bedecked with geishas, elephants and serpents. The so-called **Baron's Palace** (Qasr al-Baron) is due east from the basilica, on Sharia al-Uruba (Airport Rd). It's not worth a dedicated trip, as you can't enter, but keep an eye out for it on your way to or from the airport. It has been locked tight since 1997, when 'Satanists' were allegedly holding rituals here – turns out they were a bunch of upper-class teenage metalheads.

Some might say similar delusions surround the **October War Panorama** (2402 2317; Sharia al-Uruba; admission E£30; shows 11am, 12.20pm, 6pm & 7.30pm Wed-Mon), a commemoration of the 1973 'victory' over Israel, built with slightly sinister flair by North Korean artists. A large circular mural and diorama depicts the Egyptian forces' breaching of the

Heliopolis

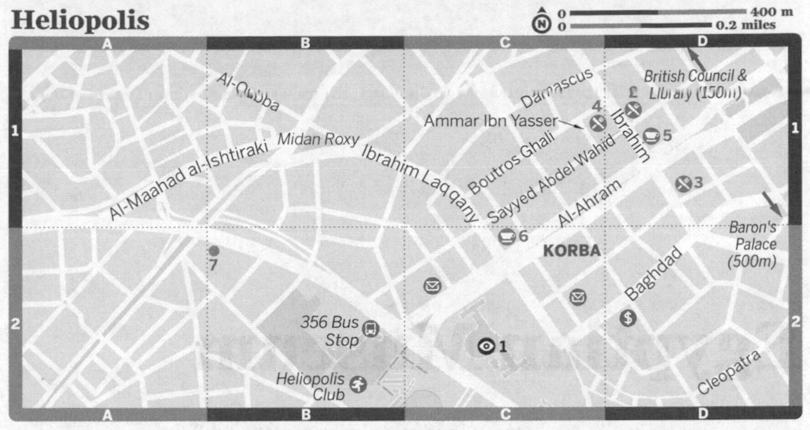

Bar Lev Line on the Suez Canal, while a stirring commentary (in Arabic only) recounts the heroic victories. It neatly skips over the successful Israeli counterattacks. The exhibition is about 2.5km southwest of the Baron's Palace, on the same road; you can flag down a bus on Sharia al-Uruba or get a taxi.

Eating & Drinking

In addition to the restaurants listed below, the L'Amphitrion (p130) is great for a beer and sheesha and to use the wi-fi.

Abu Ammar al-Suri SYRIAN $
(2258 6998; 19 Sharia Ibrahim; sandwiches E£14-20, mains E£19-45; 24hr) A branch of the tasty operation in Mohandiseen. Look for the lit-up plastic shwarma on the corner.

Arabiata El Shabrawy EGYPTIAN FAST FOOD $
(16919; 10 Sharia Ibrahim; sandwiches E£1.75-4.5; 8am-2am) One of the most popular cheap snack places in Heliopolis, with take-out or seats upstairs.

Mangiamo EGYPTIAN, ITALIAN $$
(2623 0119; 100 Sharia Ammar ibn Yasser; mains E£18-52; 10am-2am) Tucked away on a residential corner, Mangiamo feels a little like a private club, and its garden is a lovely quiet place to sit, with all the Heliopolis ladies out for lunch. The menu does all the Egyptian staples, plus good pizza and pasta.

Entertainment

Citystars Centre CINEMA
(2480 2013; Sharia Omar ibn Khattab, Nasr City) Megaplex at the mall with 12 screens.

Shopping

Citystars Centre SHOPPING CENTRE
(2480 0500; www.citystars-heliopolis.com.eg; Sharia Omar ibn Khattab, Nasr City; 11am-1am) Cairo's most lavish mall is the current landing spot for every new international chain, from Starbucks to Wagamama. There's a kids' theme park and a big cinema. It's about 12km east of Downtown. Just hop in a taxi and say, 'Citystars'.

Getting There & Away

The fastest route is the metro to Saray al-Kobba (exit on the east side of the tracks), then a taxi; tell the driver 'Korba'. Also, airport bus 356 goes from Midan Abdel Moniem Riad. The ride takes about 45 minutes. Get off outside the Heliopolis Club (the first stop after reaching the street with tram tracks). Buses usually run every 20 minutes.

Egyptian Museum

Includes ➡

One of the world's most important collections of ancient artefacts, the Egyptian Museum takes pride of place in Downtown Cairo, on the north side of Midan Tahrir. Inside the great domed, pinkish building, the glittering treasures of Tutankhamun and other great pharaohs lie alongside the grave goods, mummies, jewellery, eating bowls and toys of Egyptians whose names are lost to history. To walk around the museum is to embark on an adventure through time.

This is in part due to the museum structure itself. There's nary an interactive touch screen to be found; in fact many of the smaller items are in the same vitrines in which they were first placed when the museum opened in 1902. The lighting is so poor in some halls that by late afternoon you have to squint to make out details and read the words on the cryptic, typed display cards placed on a few key items.

In this way, the Egyptian Museum documents not just the time of the pharaohs, but also the history of Egyptology. Some display cards have turned obsolete as new discoveries have busted old theories. And the collection rapidly outgrew its sensible layout, as, for instance, Tutankhamun's enormous trove and the tomb contents of Tanis were both unearthed after the museum opened, and then had to be shoehorned into the space. Now more than 100,000 objects are wedged into about 15,000 sq metres.

Like the country itself, the museum is in flux. Most objects are still on display, although some are being moved to the Grand Egyptian Museum (p138). While some rooms are being refurbished the objects are deposited elsewhere in the museum, usually in the room next door. This museum will remain a major sight, very much the same as it is now with many of the master pieces but less clutter. However, it is not clear just how much will stay the same, and when the GEM will open.

All this makes the Egyptian Museum somewhat challenging to visit. One of the most rewarding strategies is simply to walk around and see what catches your eye. But it's hard to shake the sense that something even more stunning is waiting in the next room. We recommend some highlights but be sure to stop and see some of the lesser items, as they often do just as well if not better in bringing the world of the pharaohs back to life.

MUSEUM PRACTICALITIES

Entrance & Tickets

Getting into the Egyptian Museum (p132) is an exercise in queuing: at peak times, you ll wait to have your bag X-rayed, to buy tickets, to check your camera, to pass the turnstiles and to have your bag checked again. And a line forms at the exit (off the northwest corner) at closing time. Last tickets are sold one hour before closing time.

Additional tickets for the **Royal Mummies Halls** (1st fl, Rooms 56 & 46; adult/student E£100/60) are purchased upstairs near Room 56.

Cameras must be checked at the front gate, in the kiosk adjacent to the first X-ray machine. A small tip (E£1 or E£2) is nice when you claim your items. Return promptly at closing time, or you may find the room locked up.

Timing

Usually the museum is very crowded through most of the winter and on all public holidays, but at the time of writing the crowds were few. When it does get crowded, it's better to visit after lunchtime. Friday afternoons, when the museum closes earlier, are also quieter. The museum can be quite dim near dusk; you may want to bring a small torch.

Guides

Quite a few official guides troll for business in the garden area. No doubt they will approach you if you are not in a group, and will suggest to take you around for upwards of E£60 per hour. Some are better than others, but many have a fairly standard knowledge of what's on show at the museum. For those with more than a passing interest in Egyptology, wanting to go a bit deeper into the history, a visit in the company of one of Ahmed Seddik (p93), Manal Helmy (p93) or Hassan Saber (p93) is highly recommended.

Facilities & Food

Rest rooms are on the mezzanine of each southern staircase. A sign says tips are not accepted but, well, they are – E£1 or E£2 is good. The plaza on the west side of the building holds a basic **cafe**, with cold drinks, ice cream (from E£15) and basic sandwiches. You can only re-enter the museum at the front, and with much sweet-talking of the guards.

History

The current museum has its origins in several earlier efforts at managing Egypt's ancient heritage, beginning in 1835, when Egyptian ruler Mohammed Ali banned the export of antiquities. Not that anyone heeded this – French archaeologist Auguste Mariette was busy shipping his finds from Saqqara to the Louvre when he was empowered to create the Egyptian Antiquities Service in 1858.

Mariette's growing collection, from some 35 dig sites, bounced around various homes in Cairo until 1902, when the current building was erected, in a suitably prominent position in the city. There it has stood, in its original layout, a gem of early museum design. But the lack of upkeep, and the ever-expanding field of Egyptology, has strained the place. For decades, the museum's basement store was a notorious morass, as neglected sculptures sank into the soft flooring and needed to be excavated all over again.

Until 1996, museum security involved locking the door at night. When an enterprising thief stowed away overnight and helped himself to treasures, the museum authorities installed alarms and detectors, at the same time improving the lighting on many exhibits. During the 2011 revolution, the museum was broken into and a few artefacts went missing. To prevent further looting, activists formed a human chain around the building to guard its contents. By most reports, they were successful.

MUSEUM TOUR: GROUND FLOOR

Before entering the museum, wander through the garden. To your left lies the **tomb of Auguste Mariette** (1821–81), with a statue of the archaeologist, arms folded, shaded under a spreading tree. Mariette's tomb is overlooked by an **arc of busts** of two dozen Egyptological luminaries including Jean-François Champollion, who cracked the code of the hieroglyphs; Gaston Maspero, Mariette's successor as director of the Egyptian Antiquities Service; and Karl Lepsius, the pre-eminent 19th-century German Egyptologist.

The ground floor of the museum is laid out roughly chronologically in a clockwise fashion starting at the entrance hall.

Room 43 – Atrium

The central atrium is filled with a miscellany of large and small Egyptological finds. In the area before the steps lie some of the collection's oldest items. In the central cabinet No 8, the double-sided **Narmer Palette**, found at the Temple of Horus in Kom al-Ahmar near Edfu, is of great significance. Dating from around the 1st dynasty, it depicts Pharaoh Narmer (also known as Menes; c 3100 BC) wearing, on one side, the crown of Upper Egypt and, on the other side, the crown of Lower Egypt, suggesting the first union of Upper and Lower Egypt under one ruler. Egyptologists take this as the birth of ancient Egyptian civilisation and Narmer's reign as the first of the 1st dynasty. This, then, is the starting point of more than 3000 years of Pharaonic history in which more than 170 rulers presided over 30 dynasties and produced almost everything in this building. In this sense, the Narmer Palette is the foundation stone of the Egyptian Museum. In the sexagonal cabinet to the right is a small clay head from the 4th millenium BC, one of the earliest human representations found in Egypt. There are several other exquisite objects from the pre-Pharaonic period.

Room 48 – Early Dynastic Period

In glass cabinet No 16 is the **limestone statue of Zoser** (Djoser; 2667–2648 BC), the 3rd-dynasty pharaoh whose chief architect Imhotep designed the revolutionary Step Pyramid at Saqqara. The statue, discovered in 1924 in its *serdab* (cellar) in the north-eastern corner of the pyramid, is the oldest statue of its kind in the museum. The seated, near-life-size figure has lost its original inlaid eyes but is still impressive in a tight robe and striped head cloth over a huge wig.

Rooms 47 & 46 – Old Kingdom

Look for the three exquisite **black schist triads** that depict the pharaoh Menkaure (Mycerinus; 2532–2503 BC), builder of the smallest of the three Pyramids of Giza, flanked either side by a female figure. The hardness of the stone makes the sculptor's skill all the greater and has helped ensure the triads' survival through the ages. The figure to the pharaoh's right is the goddess Hathor, while each of the figures on his left represents a nome (administrative division) of Egypt, the name of which is given by the symbol above their head. These triads (plus one other that is not held by this museum) were discovered at the pharaoh's valley temple, just east of his pyramid at Giza.

Rooms 42, 37 & 32 – Masterpieces of the Old Kingdom

In the centre of Room 42 is one of the museum's masterpieces, a smooth, black **statue of Khafre** (Chephren; 2558–2532 BC). The builder of the second pyramid at Giza sits on a lion throne, and is protected by the wings of the falcon god Horus. The use of the stone diorite, which is harder than marble or granite, suggests the pharaoh's power. In fact, Khafre had 23 identical pieces carved for his valley temple at the Giza Plateau, though this is the only survivor.

Slightly to the left in front of Khafre, the core of the stunning **wooden statue of Ka-Aper** (No 40) was carved out of a single piece of sycamore (the arms were ancient additions; the legs, modern restorations). The sycamore was sacred to the goddess Hathor, while Ka-Aper's belly suggests his prosperity. His eyes are amazingly lifelike, set in copper lids with whites of opaque quartz and corneas of rock crystal, drilled and filled with black paste to form the pupils. When this statue was excavated at Saqqara in 1870, local workmen named him Sheikh al-Balad (Headman), for his resemblance to their own local leader. Behind you, to the left of the door, sits the **Seated Scribe** (No 44), a wonderful painted limestone figure, hand poised as if waiting to take dictation, his inlaid eyes set in an asymmetrical face giving him a very vivid appearance.

Egyptian Museum

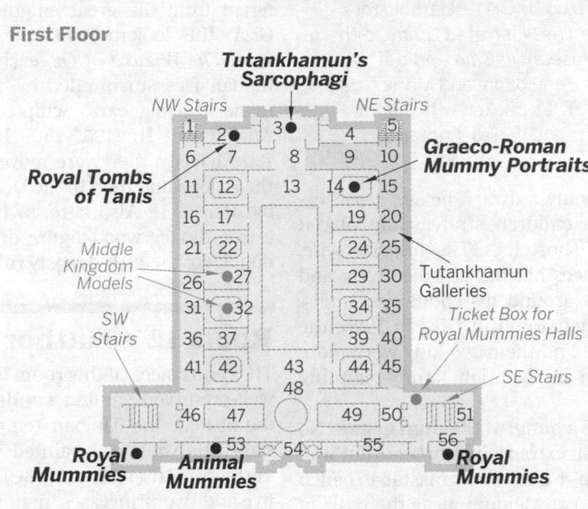

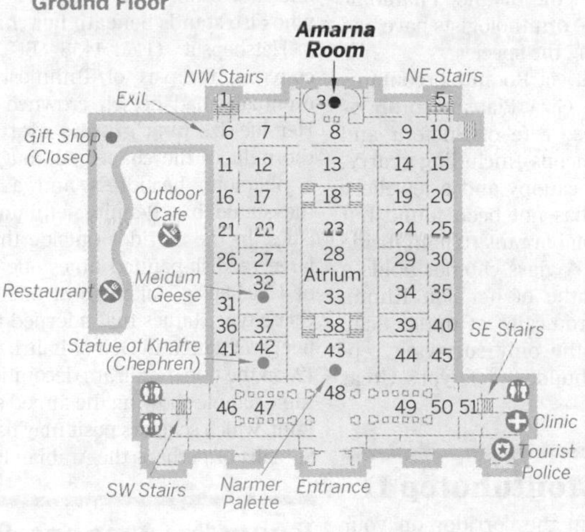

Room 32 is dominated by the beautiful **statues of Rahotep and Nofret** (No 27), a noble couple from the 4th-dynasty reign of Sneferu, builder of the Bent and the Red Pyramids at Dahshur. Almost life-size with well-preserved painted surfaces, the limestone sculptures have simple lines making them seem almost contemporary, despite having been around for a staggering 4600 years.

In a cabinet off to the left, a limestone group shows **Seneb**, 'chief of the royal wardrobe', and his family (No 39). Seneb is

EXTRA GUIDANCE

To make the most of an Egyptian Museum visit, stop by the AUC Bookstore and pick up *The Illustrated Guide to the Egyptian Museum in Cairo,* edited by Alessandro Bongioanni and Maria Croce Sole (E£180). It's packed with colour photographs and varied itineraries.

notable for being a dwarf: he sits cross-legged, his two children strategically placed to cover his short legs. His full-size wife, Senetites, places her arms protectively and affectionately around his shoulders. Rediscovered in their tomb in Giza in 1926, the happy couple and their two kids were more recently used in Egyptian family-planning campaigns.

Also here is a **panel of Meidum geese** (No 138), part of an extraordinarily beautiful wall painting from a mud-brick mastaba (bench above a tomb) at Meidum, near the oasis of Al-Fayoum. Though painted around 2500 BC, the pigments remain vivid and the degree of realism, even within the distinct Pharaonic style, is astonishing – ornithologists have had no trouble identifying the species.

Room 37, entered via Room 32, contains furniture from the Giza Plateau **tomb of Queen Hetepheres**, wife of Sneferu and mother of Khufu (Cheops), including a carrying chair, bed, bed canopy and a jewellery box. Her mummy has not been found but her shrivelled internal organs remain inside her Canopic chest. A glass cabinet holds a miniature ivory statue of her son Khufu, found at Abydos. Ironically, at under 8cm, this tiny figure is the only surviving representation of the builder of Egypt's Great Pyramid.

Room 26 – Montuhotep II

The seated statue in the corridor on your right, after leaving Room 32, represents Theban-born **Montuhotep II** (2055–2004 BC; No 136), first ruler of the Middle Kingdom period. He is shown with black skin (representing fertility and rebirth) and the red crown of Lower Egypt. This statue was discovered by Howard Carter under the forecourt of the pharaoh's temple at Deir al-Bahri in Thebes in 1900, when the ground gave way under his horse – a surprisingly common means of discovery in the annals of Egyptology.

Rooms 21 & 16 – Sphinxes

These **grey-granite sphinxes** are very different from the great enigmatic Sphinx at Giza – they look more like the Cowardly Lion from *The Wizard of Oz,* each with a fleshy human face surrounded by a great shaggy mane and big ears. Sculpted for Pharaoh Amenemhat III (1855–1808 BC) during the 12th dynasty, they were moved to Avaris by the Hyksos and then to the Delta city of Tanis by Ramses II. Also here, in Room 16, is an extraordinary wood figure of the ka (spirit double) of the 13th-dynasty ruler Hor Auibre.

Room 12 – Hathor Shrine

The centrepiece of this room is a remarkably well-preserved vaulted **sandstone chapel**, found near the Theban temple of Deir al-Bahri. Its walls are painted with reliefs of Tuthmosis III (1479–1425 BC), his wife Meritre and two princesses, making offerings to Hathor, who suckles the pharaoh. The life-size cow statue suckles Tuthmosis III's son and successor Amenhotep II (1427–1400 BC), who also stands beneath her chin.

Hatshepsut (1473–1458 BC), who was co-regent for part of Tuthmosis III's reign, eventually had herself crowned as pharaoh. Her life-size **pink granite statue** stands to the right of the chapel. Although she wears a pharaoh's headdress and a false beard, the statue has definite feminine characteristics. In the corridor outside this room, the large reddish-painted limestone head is also of Hatshepsut, taken from one of the huge Osiris-type statues that adorned the facade of her great temple at Deir al-Bahri. Also in Room 12, on the north wall, are decorations from the same temple showing the famed expedition to Punt, which scholars posit may be current-day Somalia or perhaps the Arabian Peninsula.

Room 3 – Amarna Room

Akhenaten (1352–1336 BC), the 'heretic pharaoh', did more than build a new capital at Tell al-Amarna, close the temples of the traditional state god Amun and promote the sun god Aten in his place. He also ushered in a period of great artistic freedom, as a glance around this room will show. Compare these great torsos with their strangely bulbous bellies, hips and thighs, their elongated faces and thick lips, with the sleek, hard-edged Middle Kingdom sculpture of previous rooms.

Perhaps most striking of all is the **unfinished head of Nefertiti** (No 161, in the left alcove), wife of Akhenaten. Worked in brown quartzite, it's an incredibly delicate and sensitive portrait and shows the queen to have been extremely beautiful – unlike some of the relief figures of her elsewhere in the room, in which she appears with exactly the same strange features as her husband. The masterpiece of this period, the finished bust of Nefertiti, can be seen in the Neues Museum in Berlin.

Room 10 – Ramses II

At the foot of the northeast stairs is a fabulous large, **grey-granite representation of Ramses II** (1279–1213 BC), builder of the Ramesseum and Abu Simbel. But here in this statue he is tenderly depicted as a child with his finger in his mouth nestled against the breast of a great falcon, in this case the Canaanite god Horus.

Room 34 – Graeco-Roman Room

It is best to visit these last rooms after seeing the 1st floor, because this is the end of the ancient Egyptian story. By the 4th century BC, Egypt had been invaded by many nations, most recently by the Macedonian Alexander the Great. Egypt's famously resistant culture had become porous, as will be obvious from the **statue** situated immediately to the left as you enter this room: a typically Greek face with curly beard and locks, but wearing a Pharaonic-style headdress.

Nearby on the right-hand wall, you'll see a large **sandstone panel** inscribed in three languages: official Egyptian hieroglyphics; the more popularly used demotic; and Greek, the language of the new rulers. This trilingual stone is similar in nature to the more famous Rosetta Stone that is now housed in London's British Museum. A **cast of the Rosetta Stone** stands near the museum entrance (Room 48).

HIGHLIGHTS OF THE EGYPTIAN MUSEUM

The following are our favourite, must-see exhibits, for which you need at least half a day but preferably a little more.

Tutankhamun Galleries (1st fl) Top on everyone's list, King Tut's treasures occupy a large chunk of the museum's upper floor. Go first to Room 3 to see his sarcophagi while the crowds are light.

Old Kingdom Rooms (Ground fl, Rooms 42, 37 & 32) After peeking at Tutankhamun, return to the ground floor for a chronological tour. Look out for the statue of the well-muscled Khafre – you may also recognise him from the Sphinx.

Amarna Room (Ground fl, Room 3) Stepping into this room feels like visiting another museum entirely – the artwork commissioned by Akhenaten for his new capital at Tell al-Amarna is dramatically different in style from his predecessors. Say hi to his wife, Nefertiti, while you're here.

Royal Tombs of Tanis (1st fl, Room 2) While everyone else is gawking at Tutankhamun's treasure down the hall, this room of gem-encrusted gold jewellery, found at the largest ruined city in the Nile Delta, is often empty.

Graeco-Roman Mummy Portraits (1st fl, Room 14) An odd interlude in mummy traditions, from very late in the ancient Egypt game, these wood panel portraits were placed over the faces of embalmed dead, staring up in vividly realistic style.

Animal Mummies (1st fl, Rooms 53 & 54) Tucked in an odd corner of the museum, this long, dim room contains the bundled remains of the ancients' beloved pets, honoured gods and even their last meals.

Middle Kingdom Models (1st fl, Rooms 32 & 27) When you've had your fill of gold and other royal trappings, stop in these rooms to get a picture of common life in ancient Egypt, depicted in miniature dioramas made to accompany the pharaoh to the other world.

Royal Mummies Halls (1st fl, Rooms 56 & 46) Visit these around lunch or near closing time to avoid the crowds – they don't require more than half an hour, but they do put a human face on all the stunning objects you've seen.

MUSEUM TOUR: FIRST FLOOR

Exhibits here are grouped thematically and can be viewed in any order, but if you come up the southeast stairs, you'll enter the Tutankhamun Galleries at Room 45 and experience the pieces in roughly the same order that they were laid out in the tomb (a poster on the wall outside Room 45 illustrates the tomb and treasures). But first, directly above the stairs, are the Royal Mummies Halls (p133).

Rooms 56 & 46 – Royal Mummies Halls

These rooms house the remains of some of Egypt's most illustrious pharaohs and queens from the 17th to the 21st dynasties, 1650 to 945 BC. They lie in individual glass showcases (kept at a constant 22°C) in two rooms at either corner of the museum. The mood is suitably sombre, and talking above a hushed whisper is forbidden (somewhat counterproductively, a guard will bellow 'silence' from time to time). Tour guides are not allowed to enter, although some do.

Displaying dead royalty has proved controversial. Late President Anwar Sadat took the royal mummies off display in 1979 for political reasons, but the subsequent reappearance of 11 of the better-looking mummies in 1994 did wonders for tourism figures, inspiring the opening of a second mummy room with second-tier but no less interesting personages. The ticket price is steep, but you certainly won't see so many mummies in any other single museum, nor get to peer at them so closely. Parents should be aware that the mummies can be frightening for young children.

Room 56

Take time to study some of the first room's celebrated inmates, beginning with the brave Theban pharaoh **Seqenenre Taa II** who died violently, possibly during struggles to reunite the country at the end of the Second Intermediate Period, around 1560 BC. His wounds are still visible beneath his curly hair, and his twisted arms reflect his violent death. The perfectly wrapped mummies of **Queen Merit Amun** and **Amenhotep I** (1525–1504 BC) show how all royal mummies would once have looked, bedecked with garlands.

On the opposite side of the room, **Tuthmosis II** (1525–1504 BC) lies next to his sister-wife, **Hatshepsut** – the great queen and female pharaoh, rendered so grandly in stone in Room 12, is here reduced to an 'obese female with bad teeth', according to the descriptive text. Their son, **Tuthmosis III** (1479–1425 BC), occupies the last case, looking not too bad considering he'd been severely damaged by grave robbers centuries ago.

In the centre of the room, **Ramses II** is strikingly well preserved, his haughty profile revealing the family's characteristic curved nose, his grey hair tinged with henna and his fingernails long. By contrast, his 13th son and successor, **Merenptah** (1213–1203 BC), has a distinctly white appearance caused by the mummification process. **Amenhotep II** rests in the next case, finally settled after a particularly tumultuous century of being shipped up and down the Nile and stolen from his tomb in the Valley of the Kings. **Tuthmosis IV** (1400–1390 BC) sports beautifully styled hair; he was also the first pharaoh to have his ears pierced. With his smooth black skin and square chin, **Seti I** (1294–1279 BC) rivals Ramses II in flawless preservation.

THE (NOT-SO-)GRAND EGYPTIAN MUSEUM

In 2002, amid much pomp and circumstance, then-President Hosni Mubarak laid the ceremonial foundation for the Grand Egyptian Museum (p138), the cornerstone of an ambitious project aimed at redefining the Giza Plateau. More than 10 years on, the project looks like one of the more blatant boondoggles of the dictator's reign, as plenty of cash was thrown at it, but virtually no progress has been made towards opening it.

Located 2km from the Great Pyramids, the GEM is meant to be a state-of-the-art showcase for the country's finest antiquities. But since the 2011 revolution, the fate of the project, so linked with Mubarak and his ousted antiquities chief Zahi Hawass, has been uncertain. Now the statue of Ramses, removed from Midan Ramses in 2006, stands alone guarding the site. Slowly, certain pieces are being moved from the old to the Grand museum, but no one knows exactly what will eventually be shown where. In the meantime, enjoy the fresh paint job here in the Downtown Egyptian Museum – that's likely the only real improvement in antiquities exhibits that tourists will see for a while.

Room 46

The second mummy room (same ticket) is located across the building, off Room 47. The corridor display relates some of the most famous mummy discoveries, including the 1881 Deir al-Bahri cache, and displays the body of **Queen Tiy**, with long flowing hair. Many of the mummies in this section date from the 20th and 21st dynasties, the end of the New Kingdom and the start of the Third Intermediate Period (c 1186–945 BC). You first pass **Ramses III** (1184–1153 BC) and **Ramses IV** (1153–1147 BC), and around the corner, the face of **Ramses V** (1147–1143 BC) is marked with small raised spots, likely caused by smallpox. In the centre of the room, **Nedjmet** (c 1070–946 BC) wears a lavish curly wig and has black-and-white stones for eyes. Next to her, **Queen Henettawy** (c 1025 BC), in a linen shroud painted with an image of Osiris, is a product of modern restorers, who repaired her cheeks, which had burst from overpacking by ancient embalmers. In the final section, the mummy of **Queen Nesikhonsu** still conveys the queen's vivid features, while **Queen Maatkare** lies with her pet baboon.

Tutankhamun Galleries

The treasures of the young New Kingdom pharaoh Tutankhamun, who ruled for only nine years during the 14th century BC (1336–1327 BC), are among the world's most famous antiquities. English archaeologist Howard Carter unearthed the tomb in 1922. Its well-hidden location in the Valley of the Kings, below the much grander but ransacked tomb of Ramses VI, had long prevented its discovery. Many archaeologists now believe that up to 80% of these extraordinary treasures were made for Tutankhamun's predecessors, Akhenaten and Smenkhkare – some still carry the names of the original owners. Perhaps with Tutankhamun's death everything connected with the Amarna Period was simply chucked in with him to be buried away and forgotten.

About 1700 items are spread throughout a series of rooms on the museum's 1st floor, and although the gold shines brightest, sometimes the less grand objects give more insight into the pharaoh's life.

Room 45

Flanking the doorway as you enter are two life-size **statues of Tutankhamun**, found in the tomb antechamber. The statues are made of wood coated in bitumen, their black skin suggesting an identification with Osiris and the rich, black river silt, symbolising fertility and rebirth.

Rooms 35 & 30

The **pharaoh's lion throne** (No 179) is one of the museum's highlights. Covered with sheet gold and inlaid with lapis, cornelian and other semiprecious stones, the wooden throne is supported by lion legs. The colourful tableau on the chair back depicts Ankhesenamun applying perfume to her husband, under the rays of the sun (Aten), the worship of which was a hangover from the Amarna Period. Evidence of remodelling of the figures suggests that this was actually the throne of Akhenaten, Tutankhamun's father and predecessor. The royals' robes are modelled in beaten silver, their hair made of glass paste.

Opposite the throne, on the east wall, **Tutankhamun's wig box** is made of dark wood, with strips of blue and orange inlay. The mushroom-shaped wooden support inside once held the pharaoh's short curly wig.

Many **golden statues** were placed in the tomb to help the pharaoh on his journey in the afterlife, including a series of 28 gilt-wood protective deities and 413 shabti, attendants who would serve the pharaoh in the afterlife. Only a few of them are displayed here.

Room 20

This room contains exquisite **alabaster jars** and **vessels** carved into the shape of boats and animals. Some critters have lifelike pink tongues sticking out – as if the artist just wanted to show he could render such a thing in stone.

Rooms 10 & 9

The eastern end of this gallery is filled with the pharaoh's three elaborate **funerary couches**, one supported by the cow-goddess Mehetweret, one by two figures of the goddess Ammit, 'the devourer' who ate the hearts of the damned, and the third by the lioness god Mehet. The huge **bouquets** of persea and olive leaves in Room 10, near the top of the stairs, were originally propped up beside the two black and gold guardian statues in Room 45. A cross-section plan on the wall next to the stairs shows how all the furniture was arranged in the tomb.

At the west end of Room 9, an alabaster chest contains four **Canopic jars**, the stoppers of which are in the form of Tutankhamun's head. Inside these jars, four miniature gold coffins (now in Room 3) held the pharaoh's internal organs. The chest was placed inside the golden Canopic shrine with the four gilded goddesses: Isis, Neith, Nephthys and Selket, all portrayed with protective outstretched arms.

Most people walk right past Tutankhamun's amazing **wardrobe**, laid out along the south wall. The pharaoh was buried with a range of sumptuous tunics covered in gold discs and beading, ritual robes of 'fake fur', a large supply of neatly folded underwear and split-toe socks to be worn with the 47 pairs of flip-flop-type sandals. From these and other objects, the Tutankhamun Textile Project has worked out that the pharaoh's vital statistics were: chest 79cm (31in), waist 74cm (29in) and hips 109cm (43in).

Rooms 8 & 7

These galleries just barely accommodate four massive **gilded wooden shrines**. These fitted one inside the other, like a set of Russian dolls, encasing at their centre the sarcophagi of the boy pharaoh.

Room 3

Everybody wants to see this room as it contains the pharaoh's golden sarcophagus and jewels; at peak times, prepare to queue. Tutankhamun's astonishing **death mask** has become an Egyptian icon. Made of solid gold and weighing 11kg, it covered the head of the mummy, and lay inside a series of three sarcophagi. The mask is an idealised portrait of the young pharaoh; the eyes are fashioned from obsidian and quartz, while the outlines of the eyes and the eyebrows are delineated with lapis lazuli. No less wondrous are the two **golden sarcophagi**, the inner two of the burial. The outermost coffin, along with the pharaoh's mummy, remains in his tomb in the Valley of the Kings. The smallest coffin is, like the mask, cast in solid gold and inlaid in the same fashion. It weighs 110kg. The slightly larger coffin is made of gilded wood.

Room 4 – Ancient Egyptian Jewellery

Even after Tutankhamun's treasures, this stunning collection of **royal jewellery** takes the breath away. The collection covers the period from early dynasties to the Romans and includes belts, inlaid beadwork, necklaces, semiprecious stones and bracelets. Among the most beautiful is a piece from the

KING TUT GOES TO THE LAB

Though we have much concrete evidence of the pharaoh Tutankhamun, in the form of his tomb contents, the boy king still remains elusive in some ways. How did he die? Who were his parents? Who was his wife? Advances in DNA analysis finally inspired a test of Tut and other mummies thought to be his relatives, and the results were revealed in 2010.

The DNA tests confirmed the predominant theory that Tut's grandparents were Amenhotep III and Queen Tiy. This in turn showed that Tut's father was almost certainly the 'heretic' pharaoh Akhenaten. Finally, the team was able to confirm that another unidentified mummy was Tut's mother – as well as Akhenaten's sister.

The researchers also looked for congenital disease markers. Had Tut and his forebears suffered from an ailment that caused the distorted face shape and androgynous look depicted so famously in Akhenaten's portraiture? In fact, the DNA showed no such abnormality – so Akhenaten's odd appearance may have been just a stylistic choice. But Tutankhamun was likely affected by inbreeding all the same. Two mummified foetuses buried with him are almost certainly his unborn daughters. And a separate theory posits that his wife was Ankhesamun, his half-sister. This all suggests the foetuses were too deformed to live.

Finally, while preparing Tutankhamun's mummy for the DNA analysis, a CT scan revealed a club foot and necrosis in one toe – which accounts for the numerous canes found in his tomb, despite his death at age 19. The samples also tested positive for parasites associated with malaria, which may have killed him.

So not every mystery is yet solved – but researchers are still at work on other mummies, which may untangle more of Tutankhamun's complex family history.

Pyramid of al-Lahun: the **diadem of Queen Sit-Hathor-Yunet**, a golden headband with a rearing cobra inset with semiprecious stones. Also of note are Pharaoh Ahmose's gold dagger and Seti II's gold earrings.

Room 2 – Royal Tombs of Tanis

This glittering collection of gold- and silver-encrusted objects came from six intact 21st- and 22nd-dynasty tombs unearthed at the Delta site of Tanis by the French in 1939. The tombs rivalled Tutankhamun's in riches, but news of the find was overshadowed by the outbreak of WWII. The gold **death mask of Psusennes I** (1039–991 BC), with thick black eyeliner, is shown alongside his silver inner coffin and another silver coffin with the head of a falcon belonging to the pharaoh Shoshenq II (c 890 BC).

Room 14 – Graeco-Roman Mummy Portraits

This room contains a small sample of the stunning portraits found on Graeco-Roman mummies, popularly known as the **Fayoum Portraits**. Painted on wooden panels, often during the subject's life, and placed over the mummies' embalmed faces, these portraits express the personalities of their subjects better than the stylised elegance of most other ancient Egyptian art, and are recognised as the link between ancient art and the Western portrait tradition.

Room 34 – Pharaonic Technology

Interesting for gadget buffs, this room contains a great number of everyday objects that helped support ancient Egypt's great leap out of prehistory. Some, such as the hand tools for farming, are still in use in parts of Egypt today, and others – needles and thread, combs, dice – look remarkably like our own. **Pharaonic boomerangs** were apparently used for hunting birds.

Room 43 – Yuya & Thuyu Rooms

Before Tutankhamun's tomb was uncovered, the tomb of Yuya and Thuyu (the parents of Queen Tiy, and Tutankhamun's great-grandparents) had yielded the most spectacular find in Egyptian archaeology. Found virtually intact in the Valley of the Kings in 1905, the tomb contained a vast number of treasures, including five ornate sarcophagi and the remarkably well-preserved mummies of the two commoners who became royal in-laws. Among many other items on display is the fabulous gilded and bead-trimmed **death mask of Thuyu**, at the front of the room.

Room 53 – Animal Mummies

Animal cults grew in strength throughout ancient Egypt, as the mummified cats, dogs, crocodiles, birds, monkeys and jackals in Room 53 suggest. Tucked in a dim, dusty wing of the museum, their rigid forms are a bit creepier than their human counterparts. Some edible beasts became 'victual mummies', preserved as food and 'browned' with resin, to offer the pharaoh an eternal picnic.

Room 37 – Model Armies

Discovered in the Asyut tomb of governor Mesheti and dating from about 2000 BC (11th dynasty), these are two sets of 40 **wooden warriors** marching in phalanxes. The darker soldiers (No 72) are Nubian archers from the south of the kingdom, each wearing brightly coloured kilts of varying design, while the lighter-skinned soldiers (No 73) are Egyptian pikemen.

Rooms 32 & 27 – Middle Kingdom Models

These lifelike **models** were mostly found in the tomb of Meketre, an 11th-dynasty chancellor in Thebes, and, like some of the best Egyptian tomb paintings, they provide a fascinating portrait of daily life almost 4000 years ago. They include finely modelled servants (especially in Room 32), fishing boats, kitchens and carpentry and weaving workshops. In Room 27, a model of Meketre's house includes fig trees in the garden, and a 1.5m-wide scene shows Meketre sitting with his sons, four scribes and others, counting cattle.

Cairo Outskirts & the Delta

Includes ➡

Best Places for History

- Memphis (p144)
- Imhotep Museum (p145)
- Bent Pyramid (p151)
- Pyramid of Meidum (p156)
- Tanis (p162)

Best Sights Off the Beaten Track

- Tunis (p155)
- Serapeum (p148)
- Qasr Qarun (p154)
- Wadi Rayyan (p154)
- Birqash Camel Market (p160)

Why Go?

Typical Egypt itineraries rarely take in the area right around Cairo because little of it can honestly be put in the 'must-see' category, except of course for the majestic ancient site of Saqqara, which lies on the city's southern edge. Thanks to speedy microbuses and good trains through the Delta, it's easy to get from Cairo's confines to open green fields; ancient sites you'll have all to yourself; modern Coptic monasteries with roots 17 centuries deep; and the not-for-the-squeamish action of a live camel market with camels that come from deepest Sudan. Every destination here can be visited as an easy day trip or a leisurely overnight excursion from the capital.

When to Go

Medinat al Fayoum

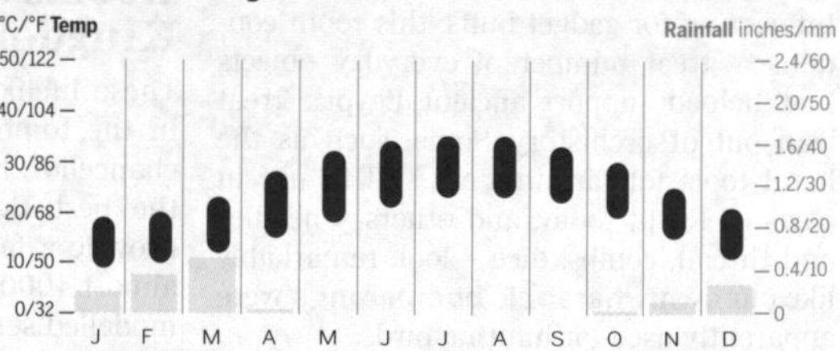

Dec–Feb The best time to visit shadeless Saqqara and other pyramids.

Jun–Aug Summer heat can be paralysing in Cairo. Cool off at Lake Qarun in Al-Fayoum.

Oct The *moulid* (saints' festival) of Al-Sayyed Badawi in Tanta draws a million Egyptians.

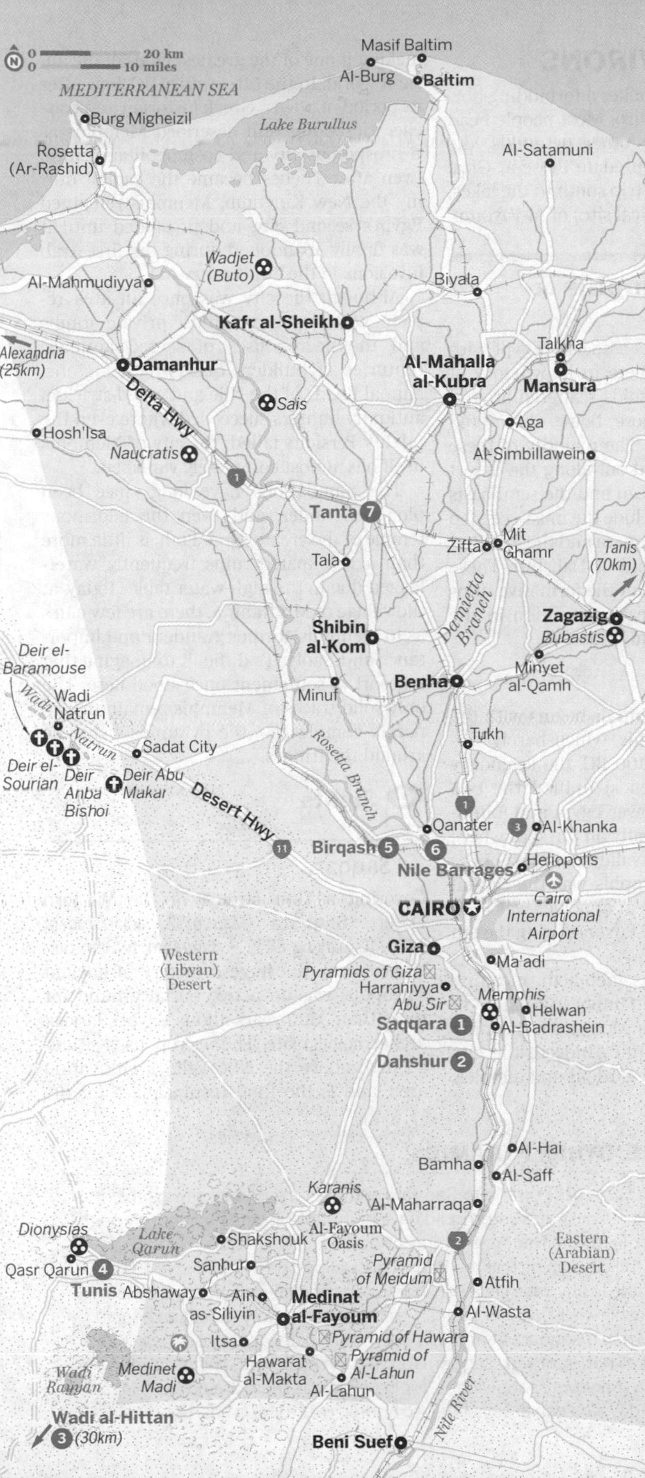

Cairo Outskirts & the Delta Highlights

1. Explore the half-buried ruins and amazing Old Kingdom art at **Saqqara** (p144)
2. Penetrate the heart of the Red Pyramid at **Dahshur** (p144)
3. Go sandboarding and fossil-spotting in the desert sands of **Wadi al-Hittan** (p155)
4. Chill out in the funky arts colony of **Tunis** (p155)
5. Immerse yourself in the sights, sounds and smells of the **Birqash Camel Market** (p160)
6. Pile on to a merry boat of day trippers to see the **Nile Barrages** (p160) at Qanater
7. Take a comfortable train trip to the Delta city of **Tanta** (p161), just to eat some sweets and enjoy the view

DESERT ENVIRONS

The Western Desert makes a forbidding border on this edge of Cairo. Most people head out this way for the 'other pyramids', the stone structures that predate those at Giza, but it's also worth the trip south to the lakes, dunes and archaeological sites of Al-Fayoum.

Saqqara, Memphis & Dahshur

Although most tourists associate Egypt with the Pyramids of Giza, there are known to be at least 118 ancient pyramids scattered around the country, with more being discovered every few years or so. The majority of these monuments are spread out along the desert between the Giza Plateau and the semi-oasis of Al-Fayoum. They include the must-see Step Pyramid of Zoser at Saqqara and the Red Pyramid and Bent Pyramid of Dahshur. These three pyramids represent the formative steps of architecture that reached fruition in the Great Pyramid of Khufu (p123).

History

The story of these pyramids begins with the ancient city of Memphis, which barely survives today. Around 3100 BC, the legendary pharaoh Narmer (Menes) unified the two lands of Upper and Lower Egypt and founded Memphis, symbolically on the spot where the Nile Delta met the valley. For most of the Pharaonic period Memphis was the capital of Egypt, though the seat of power was later moved to Thebes (now Luxor) during the era of the New Kingdom.

Originally known as Ineb-hedj, meaning 'white walls', the contemporary name of Memphis derives from Men-nefer, meaning 'established and beautiful'. Indeed, the city was filled with palaces, gardens and temples, making it one of the greatest cities of the ancient world. In the 5th century BC, long after its period of power, Greek historian and traveller Herodotus still described Memphis as 'a prosperous city and cosmopolitan centre'. Even after Thebes became the capital during the New Kingdom, Memphis remained Egypt's second city, and prospered until it was finally abandoned during the first Arab invasions in the 7th century AD.

Although the city was once an area replete with royal pyramids, private tombs and the necropolises of sacred animals, centuries of builders quarrying for stone, annual floods of the Nile and greed-stricken antiquity hunters succeeded where even the mighty Persians failed: the city of Memphis itself has almost completely vanished.

The foundations have long since been ploughed under, and even the enormous temple of the creator god, Ptah, is little more than a few sparse ruins frequently waterlogged due to the high water table. Today, at the village of Mit Rahina, there are few clues as to Memphis' former grandeur and importance and, sadly, it's difficult to imagine that any sort of settlement once stood here. The only solid traces of Memphis remain the funerary complexes – the pyramids – that lie around the fringes.

Sights

Saqqara

Covering a 7km stretch of the Western Desert, **Saqqara** (Map p152; adult/student E£80/40, parking E£5; 8am-4pm, to 3pm during Ramadan), the huge cemetery of ancient Memphis, was an active burial ground for more than 3500 years and is Egypt's largest archaeological site. The necropolis is situated high above the Nile Valley's cultivation area, and is the final resting place for de-

VISITING THE 'OTHER PYRAMIDS'

After the Pyramids of Giza (p121), a trip to Saqqara and the surrounding sites is the most popular day outing from Cairo, and you should have no trouble arranging a tour through your accommodation. For more freedom, simply hire a taxi for the day.

Just getting out of the city can be half the battle, so ideally go on a Friday or Saturday, when the traffic is lighter. In any case get a very early start. In winter, when daytime temperatures are manageable, visit Dahshur first, as it's the furthest away (about an hour in light traffic). Then you reach Saqqara at midday, when many of the tour buses have moved on. But if the day is at all hot, start with Saqqara to avoid the peak heat, and pace yourself.

Pack a picnic lunch (takeaway sandwiches, for instance), as there are no real places to eat; at the end of the day, you can always head to Andrea (p129) for a heartier meal.

READING THE PHARAONIC SCENES

When visiting temples and tombs, the endless scenes of pharaohs – standing sideways, presenting a never-ending line of gods with the same old offerings – can start to get a bit much. Look closer, however, and these scenes can reveal a few surprises.

As the little figures on the wall strike their eternal poses, a keen eye can find anything from pharaohs ploughing fields to small girls pulling at each other's hair. A whole range of activities that we consider modern can be found among the most ancient scenes, including hairdressing, perfumery, manicures and even massage – the treasury overseer Ptahhotep certainly enjoyed his comforts. There are similar scenes of pampering elsewhere at Saqqara, with a group of men in the Tomb of Ankhmahor enjoying both manicures and pedicures.

With the title 'overseer of royal hairdressers and wigmakers' commonly held by the highest officials in the land, hairdressing scenes can also be found in the most unexpected places. Not only does Ptahhotep have his wig fitted by his manservants, similar hairdressing scenes can even be found on coffins, as on the limestone sarcophagus of 11th-dynasty Queen Kawit (in Cairo's Egyptian Museum), which shows her wig being deftly styled.

Among its wealth of scenes, the Theban Tomb of Rekhmire, on Luxor's West Bank, shows a banquet at which the female harpist sings, 'Put perfume on the hair of the goddess Maat.' And nearby in the Deir al-Medina tomb of the workman Peshedu, his family tree contains relatives whose hair denotes their seniority: the eldest shown has the whitest hair.

As in many representations of ancient Egyptians, black eye make-up is worn by both male and female, adult and child. As well as its aesthetic value, it was also used as a means of reducing the glare of the sun – think ancient sunglasses. Even manual workers wore it: the Deir al-Medina Tomb of Ipy once contained a scene in which men building the royal tombs were having eye paint applied while they worked.

Professor Joann Fletcher

ceased pharaohs and their families, administrators, generals and sacred animals. The name Saqqara is most likely derived from Sokar, the Memphite god of the dead.

Old Kingdom pharaohs were buried within Saqqara's 11 major pyramids, while their subjects were buried in the hundreds of smaller tombs. Most of Saqqara, except for the Step Pyramid, was buried in sand until the mid-19th century, when the great French Egyptologist Auguste Mariette uncovered the Serapeum. Since then, it has been a gradual process of rediscovery: the Step Pyramid's massive funerary complex was not exposed until 1924, and it is in a constant state of restoration. French architect Jean-Philippe Lauer, who began work here in 1926, was involved in the project for an incredible 75 years until his death in 2001. More recently, there has been a string of new discoveries, including a whole slew of mummies and even a new pyramid.

★Imhotep Museum — MUSEUM

(Map p152) In the complex at the entrance to the site is this beautiful collection of some of the best finds from Saqqara, and one of the finest small museums in Egypt. It is framed as a tribute to the architect Imhotep, who served Pharaoh Zoser and is credited with creating ancient Egypt's first comprehensive vision of stone architecture (he also happens to be considered the world's first physician). His solid wood coffin is on display in one room.

There's also a good installation of the turquoise-green faience tiles from inside Zoser's pyramid and the striking carvings of starving people, complete with bony ribs and sagging breasts, found on the causeway of Unas. You'll also see some beautifully realistic portrait heads and statues, and a mummy (Merenre I) with his toes and head exposed – the oldest complete royal mummy, from 2292 BC.

As an interesting counterpoint to the ancient stuff, one room is a recreation of the library of Jean-Philippe Lauer, who spent most of his life excavating Saqqara. 'At times, I spoke to Imhotep,' the archaeologist said of his sometimes-desperate reconstruction process.

Step Pyramid of Zoser — MONUMENT

(Map p152) In the year 2650 BC Pharaoh Zoser (2667–2648 BC) asked his chief architect Imhotep (later deified), to built him a Step Pyramid. This is the world's earliest stone monument, and its significance cannot be overstated. The Step Pyramid is surrounded by a vast funerary complex, enclosed by a 1645m-long panelled limestone wall, and covers 15 hectares. Part of the enclosure wall survives today, and a section near the entrance was restored to its original 10m height.

Previously, temples were made of perishable materials, while royal tombs were usually underground rooms topped with a mud-brick mastaba (a structure in the shape of a bench above tombs that was the basis for later pyramids). However, Imhotep developed the mastaba into a pyramid and built it in hewn stone. From this flowed Egypt's later architectural achievements.

The pyramid was transformed from mastaba into pyramid through six stages of construction, the builders gaining confidence in their use of the new medium and mastering techniques required to move, place and secure the huge blocks. This first pyramid rose in six steps to a height of 60m, and was encased in fine white limestone.

You enter the complex at the southeastern corner via a colonnaded corridor and a broad **hypostyle hall**. The 40 pillars in the corridor are 'bundle columns', ribbed to resemble a bundle of palm or papyrus stems. The walls have been restored, but the protective ceiling is modern concrete. After the entrance, you pass through a large, false, half-open ka (attendant spirit) door when you enter – note the stone 'hinge' near the bottom. There were 14 such doors in the complex, in previous eras made of wood but here carved for the first time from stone and painted to resemble wood. They allowed the pharaoh's ka to come and go at will.

The hypostyle hall leads into the **Great South Court**, a huge open area flanking the south side of the pyramid, with a section of wall featuring a frieze of cobras (the rest are in the Imhotep Museum). The cobra (uraeus) represented the goddess Wadjet, a fire-spitting agent of destruction and protector of the pharaoh. It was a symbol of Egyptian royalty, and a rearing cobra always appeared on the brow of a pharaoh's headdress or crown.

TOP TIP

Microbuses and trains are the best way to travel just outside of Cairo, or rent a taxi for a day.

Near the base of the pyramid is an altar, and in the centre of the court are two stone D-shaped boundary markers, which delineated the ritual race the pharaoh had to run, a literal demonstration of his fitness to rule. The race was part of the Jubilee Festival (Heb-Sed), which usually occurred after 30 years' reign and showed the pharaoh's symbolic rejuvenation and the recognition of his supremacy by officials from all over Egypt. The construction of the Heb-Sed within Zoser's funerary complex was therefore intended to perpetuate his revitalisation for eternity.

The buildings on the eastern side of the pyramid are also connected with the royal jubilee, and include the **Heb-Sed (Jubilee) Court**. Buildings on the east side of the court represent the shrines of Lower Egypt, and those on the west represent Upper Egypt. All were designed to house the spirits of Egypt's gods when they gathered to witness the rebirth of the pharaoh during his jubilee rituals.

North of the Heb-Sed Court are the **House of the South Court** and **House of the North Court**, representing the two main shrines of Upper and Lower Egypt, and symbolising the unity of the country. The heraldic plants of the two regions were chosen to decorate the column capitals: papyrus for the north and lotus for the south.

The House of the South also features one of the earliest examples of tourist graffiti. In the 47th year of Ramses II's reign, nearly 1500 years after Zoser's death, Hadnakhte, a treasury scribe, recorded his admiration for Zoser while 'on a pleasure trip west of Memphis' in about 1232 BC. His hieratic script, written in black ink, is preserved behind perspex just inside the building's entrance.

A stone structure right in front of the pyramid, the *serdab* (a small room containing a statue of the deceased to which offerings were presented) contains a slightly tilted wooden box with two holes drilled into its north face. Look through these and you'll have the eerie experience of coming face to face with Zoser himself. Inside is a lifelike statue of the long-dead pharaoh, gazing stonily out towards the stars. However, this is only a copy – the original is in Cairo's Egyptian Museum.

The original entrance to the Step Pyramid is directly behind the *serdab*, and leads down to a maze of subterranean tunnels and chambers quarried for almost 6km through the rock. The pharaoh's burial chamber is vaulted in granite, and others are decorated with reliefs of the jubilee race and feature some exquisite blue faience tile decoration. Although the interior of the pyramid is unsafe and closed to the public, part of the blue-tiled decoration can be seen in the Imhotep Museum at the site entrance.

Pyramid of Userkaf MONUMENT
(Map p152) Northeast of the Step Pyramid is the Pyramid of Userkaf, the first pharaoh of the 5th dynasty (closed to the public for safety reasons). Although the removal of its limestone casing has left it a mound of rubble, it once rose to a height of 49m. Furthermore, its funerary temple was once decorated with the most exquisite naturalistic relief carvings, judging from one of the few remaining fragments (now in the Egyptian Museum) showing birds by the river.

Pyramid of Unas MONUMENT
(Map p152) To the southwest of Zoser's funerary complex is the Pyramid of Unas, last pharaoh of the 5th dynasty (2375–2345 BC). Built only 300 years after the inspired Step Pyramid, this unassuming pile of loose blocks once stood 43m high, and its interior marked the beginning of a significant development in funerary practices. For the first time, the royal burial chamber was decorated, its ceiling adorned with stars and its white alabaster lined walls inscribed with beautiful blue hieroglyphs.

The aforementioned hieroglyphs are some of the earliest examples of the funerary inscriptions that are now known as the **Pyramid Texts** (later compiled into the *Egyptian Book of the Dead*). Covering the walls of a number of the pyramids at Saqqara, the hieroglyphs are 'spells' to protect the soul of the deceased. Of the 283 separate phrases in Unas' tomb, most are prayers and hymns and lists of items, such as food and clothing the pharaoh would require in the afterlife.

The 750m-long **causeway** running from the east side of Unas' pyramid to his valley temple (now marked by little more than a couple of stone columns at the side of the road leading up to the site) was originally roofed and decorated with a great range of painted relief scenes, including a startling image of people starving, thought to be due to a famine during Unas' reign. A portion of the relief is on display in the Imhotep Museum.

The two 45m-long **boat pits** of Unas lie immediately south of the causeway, while on either side of the causeway are numerous **tombs** – more than 200 have been excavated. Of the several better-preserved examples usually open to visitors are the tombs of one of Unas' queens, Nebet, and that of Princess Idut, who was possibly his daughter. There are also several brightly painted tombs of prominent 5th- and 6th-dynasty officials. These include the Tomb of Mehu, the royal vizier (minister), and the Tomb of Nefer, the supervisor of singers.

North Saqqara

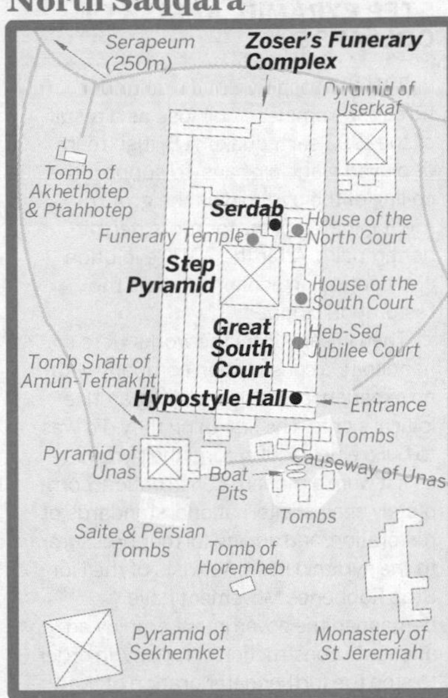

Several beautiful tombs have been cleared in the area east of the Pyramid of Unas. Although not quite as famous as the tombs north of the Step Pyramid, this set includes a number of interesting Pharaonic attendants. These include the joint **Tomb of Niankhkhnum and Khnumhotep**, overseers of the royal manicurists to Pharaoh Nyuserra; the **Tomb of Neferherenptah**, the overseer of the royal hairdressers; and the **Tomb of Irukaptah**, overseer of the royal butchers.

Around the sides of the Pyramid of Unas are several **large shaft tombs** built much later, in the Saite era (664–525 BC) and the Persian period (525–404 BC). These are some of the deepest tombs in Egypt, although as with just about everywhere else in the country, precautions against grave robbers failed. However, the sheer size of the tombs and the great stone sarcophagi within, combined with their sophisticated decoration, demonstrate

STEP PYRAMID: AT RISK OF COLLAPSE

In 2011 the Step Pyramid was under threat of 'imminent' collapse as a result of the 1992 earthquake. A British team deployed giant 'air-bags' to support the ceiling of the pyramid as the government initiated plans for more permanent repairs. After the 2011 revolution and continuing economic crisis the restoration stopped.

Then in early 2014 the works were handed to a construction company with no experience at all in restoring archaeological sights. The first thing they did was to build a new wall around the pyramid as if it were a modern construction, completely against international standards of restoration, and adding further pressure to the pyramid itself. Activists of the Non-Stop Robberies Movement have demanded the government employ an adequate construction company, in order to stop the further deterioration of the site. However, the government's answer was that the worries were unfounded, and nothing more than rumours spread by the deposed Muslim Brotherhood. The future for the oldest pyramid in the world is sadly very unsure.

that the technical achievements of the later part of ancient Egyptian history were equal to those of earlier times.

Monastery of St Jeremiah ARCHAEOLOGICAL SITE

(Map p152) Uphill from the causeway of Unas, southeast of the boat pits, are the half-buried remains of this Coptic monastery, which dates from the 5th century AD. Unfortunately, little is left of the structure, which was ransacked by invading Arabs in 950. More recently, the wall paintings and carvings were removed to the Coptic Museum (p66) in Cairo.

Pyramid of Sekhemket MONUMENT

(Map p152) Closed to the public because of its dangerous condition, the unfinished pyramid of Zoser's successor Sekhemket (2648–2640 BC) is a short distance west of the ruined Monastery of St Jeremiah. The project was abandoned for unknown reasons when the great limestone enclosure wall was only 3m high, despite the fact that the architects had already constructed the underground chambers in the rock beneath the pyramid as well as the deep shaft of the south tomb.

An unused travertine sarcophagus was found in the sealed burial chamber, and gold and jewellery and a child's body were discovered in the south tomb. Recent surveys have also revealed another mysterious large complex to the west of Sekhemket's enclosure, but this remains unexcavated.

Tomb of Horemheb TOMB

(Map p152) Originally designated as the final resting place of General Horemheb, this tomb became irrelevant in 1323 BC when its intended occupant seized power from Pharaoh Ay. Soon afterwards, Pharaoh Horemheb (1323–1295 BC) commissioned the building of a new tomb in the Valley of the Kings (p199). The tomb at Saqqara was never put to use, but it has yielded a number of exquisite reliefs that are currently displayed around the world.

Tomb of Akhethotep & Ptahhotep TOMB

(Map p152) This joint mastaba for Akhethotep and his son Ptahhotep has two burial chambers, two chapels and a pillared hall. The painted reliefs in Ptahhotep's section of the tomb are particularly beautiful, and portray a wide range of animals, from lions and hedgehogs to the domesticated cattle and fowl that were brought as offerings to the deceased. Ptahhotep himself is portrayed resplendent in a panther-skin robe inhaling perfume from a jar.

Akhethotep and his son Ptahhotep were senior royal officials during the reigns of Djedkare (2414–2375 BC) and Unas at the end of the 5th dynasty. Akhethotep served as vizier, judge and supervisor of pyramid cities and supervisor of priests, though his titles were eventually inherited by Ptahhotep, along with his tomb.

Philosophers' Circle MONUMENT

(Map p152) This is quite a sad-looking group of Greek statues, which are arranged in a semi-circle and sheltered by a spectacularly ugly concrete shelter. It's the remnant of a collection of philosophers and poets set up as a wayside shrine by Ptolemy I (323–283 BC) as part of his patronage of learning. From left to right are Plato, Heraclitus, Thales, Protagoras, Homer, Hesiod, Demetrius of Phalerum and Pindar.

Serapeum TOMB

(Map p152) The Serapeum, dedicated to the sacred Apis bull, is one of the highlights of visiting Saqqara. The first Apis burial took place in the reign of Amenhotep III (1390–1352 BC), and the practice continued until 30 BC. The enormous granite and limestone coffins weighed up to 80 tonnes each. When it died, the bull was mummified at Memphis, then carried in a stately procession to the subterranean galleries of the Serapeum at Saqqara, and placed in a huge stone sarcophagus.

The Apis, it was believed, was an incarnation of Ptah, the god of Memphis, and was the calf of a cow struck by lightning from heaven. The Apis bulls were by far the most important of the cult animals entombed at Saqqara. Once divinely impregnated, the cow could never again give birth, and her calf was kept in the Temple of Ptah at Memphis and worshipped as a god. The Apis was always portrayed as black, with a distinctive white diamond on its forehead, the image of a vulture on its back and a scarab-shaped mark on its tongue.

Until the mid-19th century, the existence of the sacred Apis tombs was known only from classical references. In 1851, Auguste Mariette, after finding a half-buried sphinx at Saqqara, and using the description given by the Greek historian Strabo in 24 BC, uncovered the avenue leading to the Serapeum. However, only one Apis sarcophagus was found intact.

★Mastaba of Ti — TOMB

(Map p152) The Mastaba of Ti was discovered by Auguste Mariette in 1865. It is perhaps the grandest and most detailed private tomb at Saqqara, and one of our main sources of knowledge about life in Old Kingdom Egypt. Its owner, Ti, was overseer of the Abu Sir pyramids and sun temples (among other things) during the 5th dynasty. In fact, the superb quality of his tomb is in keeping with his nickname, Ti the Rich. This is Old Kingdom art at its best.

A life-size statue of the deceased stands in the tomb's offering hall (as with the Zoser statue, the original is in the Egyptian Museum). Ti's wife, Neferhetpes, was priestess and 'royal acquaintance'. Together with their two sons, Demedj (overseer of the duck pond) and Ti (inspector of royal manicurists), the couple appears throughout the tomb alongside detailed scenes of daily life. As men and women are seen working on the land, preparing food, fishing, building boats, dancing, trading and avoiding crocodiles, their images are accompanied by chattering hieroglyphic dialogue, all no doubt familiar to Ti during his career as a royal overseer: 'Hurry up, the herdsman's coming', 'Don't make so much noise!', 'Pay up – it's cheap!'

Pyramid of Teti — MONUMENT

(Map p152) The Pyramid of Teti (2345–2323 BC), the first pharaoh of the 6th dynasty, was built in step form and cased in limestone, but today only a modest mound remains. In the interior can be seen portions of the hieroglyphic spells of the Pyramid Texts up close, as well as a shower of stars. Within the intact burial chamber, Teti's basalt sarcophagus is well preserved, and represents the first example of a sarcophagus with inscriptions.

Tomb of Kagemni — TOMB

(Map p152) The plump-looking chief justice under Teti, Kagemni appears in his own mastaba tomb as if he enjoyed the riches of the land, if the splendid and lively friezes inside are anything to go by. Look for catfish and eels thriving in the Nile, cows being milked, men feeding puppies, even dragonflies and other insects. Particularly vivid are the scenes of a crocodile and hippo fighting, and a row of vigorous dancers and acrobats.

Next door, the tombs of **Mereruka** (Map p152) and **Ankhmahor** (Map p152) contain similarly precise scenes, but they have since been closed due to deteriorating conditions.

SAQQARA PRACTICALITIES

- The main monuments are in an area around the Step Pyramid (p145) known as North Saqqara.
- About 1km south of the Step Pyramid is a group of monuments known as South Saqqara, with no official entry fee or opening hours.
- The only toilets at the site are at the main entrance to North Saqqara.
- Pack a lunch, as there are no food outlets at Saqqara aside from people selling cold drinks.
- Check at the ticket office to see which monuments are open – this constantly changes.
- Saqqara is one of the most popular attractions in the Cairo area, and because of the distances involved, independent visitors are rare.

South Saqqara

South Saqqara (Map p152) is home to several Old Kingdom tombs, pyramids and mounds of rubble, interesting to the more dedicated pyramid fans.

The most remote site in South Saqqara is the unusual funerary complex called the **Mastaba of al-Faraun** (Map p152), also called the Pharaoh's Bench. It belongs to the last 4th-dynasty pharaoh, the short-lived Shepseskaf (2503–2498 BC). Shepseskaf was the son of Menkaure (builder of Giza's third great pyramid), though he failed to emulate the glory of his father. Occupying an enclosure once covering 700 sq metres, Shepseskaf's rectangular tomb was built of limestone blocks, and originally covered by a further layer of fine, white limestone and a lower layer of red granite. Inside the tomb, a 21m-long corridor slopes down to storage rooms and a vaulted burial chamber.

Working your way back north, you pass the **Pyramid of Pepi II** (Map p152). The pharaoh's 94-year reign (2278–2184 BC) at the end of the 6th dynasty was probably the longest in Egyptian history. Despite Pepi's longevity, his 52m-high pyramid was of the same modest proportions as those of his predecessor, Pepi I. The exterior is little more than a mound of rubble, but the interior is decorated with more passages from the Pyramid Texts.

BEST OF SAQQARA

If you keep up a good pace, you can see the high points of Saqqara in about half a day.

➡ Start with a quick visit to the Imhotep Museum, to get the lay of the land.

➡ Head for **Zoser's funerary complex**, entering through the **hypostyle hall**, and gaze on the **Step Pyramid**, the world's oldest pyramid.

➡ Walk south towards the **Causeway of Unas**.

➡ Drive to the **Pyramid of Teti** to see some of the famous Pyramid Texts inside, and then pop into the nearby **Tomb of Kagemni**.

➡ End with the most wonderful tomb of all, the **Mastaba of Ti**, with its fascinating reliefs of daily life.

South Saqqara is also home to the pyramids of **Djedkare** (Map p152), **Merenre** (Map p152) and **Pepi I** (Map p152). Known as the 'Pyramid of the Sentinel', the 25m-high Djedkare pyramid contains the remains of the last ruler of the 5th dynasty, and can be penetrated from the north side. The pyramids of Merenre and Pepi I are little more than slowly collapsing piles of rock, though the latter is significant as 'Memphis' appears in one of its names.

Dahshur

About 10km south of Saqqara lies this impressive 3.5km-long **field** (adult/student E£60/30, parking E£5; ⌚8am-4pm, to 3pm during Ramadan) of 4th- and 12th-dynasty pyramids. Although there were originally 11 pyramids here, only the two Old Kingdom ones remain intact. Pharaoh Sneferu (2613–2589 BC), father of Khufu, built Egypt's first true pyramid here, the Red Pyramid, as well as an earlier version, the Bent Pyramid. These two striking pyramids are the same height, and together are also the third-largest pyramids in Egypt after the two largest at Giza.

The pyramids here are just as impressive as their counterparts at Giza, but the site is much more peaceful (no camel touts in sight). Before founding the necropolis at Dahshur, Sneferu also began the Pyramid of Meidum in Al-Fayoum. The area surrounding the Bent Pyramid is still a militarised zone, so it can only be admired at a distance. Fortunately, the wonderful Red Pyramid is open to visitors. Tickets are purchased at a small gatehouse on the edge of the site; there are no other facilities.

Red Pyramid MONUMENT

(North Pyramid) The world's oldest true pyramid is the Red Pyramid, which probably derives its name from the red tones of its weathered limestone, after the better-quality white limestone casing was removed. The architects had learned from their experiences building the rather deformed Bent Pyramid, so carried on where they had left off, building the Red Pyramid at the same 43-degree angle as the Bent Pyramid's more gently inclining upper section. Penetrating its somewhat dank interior is a true Indiana Jones-esque experience.

The entrance – via 125 extremely steep stone steps up, up, up, then down again, plus a 63m-long passage – takes you down to two antechambers with stunning 12m-high corbelled ceilings and a 15m-high corbelled burial chamber in which fragmentary human remains, possibly of Sneferu himself, were found. Also look for charcoal graffiti, left by British explorers in the early 19th century. Take your ticket to the entrance, along with a little baksheesh (tip) for the bored attendant.

Bent Pyramid MONUMENT

Trying to create a true, smooth-sided pyramid, Sneferu's architects began with the same steep angle and inward-leaning courses of stone they used to create step pyramids. When this began to show signs of stress and instability around halfway up its eventual 105m height, they had to reduce the angle from 54 degrees to 43 degrees and begin to lay the stones in horizontal layers. This explains why the structure has the unusual shape that gives it its name.

Most of its outer casing is still intact, and inside (closed to visitors) are two burial chambers, one of which retains its original ancient scaffolding of great cedar beams to counteract internal instability. There's also a small subsidiary pyramid to the south and the remains of a small funerary temple to the east. About halfway towards the cultivation to the east are the ruins of Sneferu's valley temple, which yielded some interesting reliefs.

Black Pyramid MONUMENT

You can only peer at this structure from the parking area by the Bent Pyramid. The oddly shaped, towerlike pyramid was built by Amenemhat III (1855–1808 BC), but has completely collapsed. The mud-brick remains contain a maze of corridors and rooms designed to deceive tomb robbers. Thieves did manage to penetrate the burial chambers but left behind a number of precious funerary artefacts that were discovered in 1993.

Memphis

Mit Rahina MUSEUM

(Memphis; adult/student E£40/20, parking E£5; 8am-4pm, to 3pm during Ramadan) The only remaining evidence of Memphis is this noteworthy open-air museum, built around a magnificent fallen colossal limestone **statue of Ramses II**. Its position on its back gives a great opportunity to inspect the carving up close – even the pharaoh's nipples are very precise. Its twin is the statue that stood in Midan Ramses in Cairo until 2006 that was moved to stand guard by the Grand Egyptian Museum (p138) construction site.

Other highlights of the museum include an alabaster sphinx of the New Kingdom, two statues of Ramses II that originally adorned Nubian temples, and the huge stone beds on which the sacred Apis bulls were mummified before being placed in the Serapeum at Saqqara.

Abu Sir

Surrounded by sand dunes, the pyramids of **Abu Sir** (Map p152; off Saqqara Rd; admission free; 8am-4pm) FREE form the necropolis of the 5th dynasty (2494–2345 BC). Most of the remains are less impressive than those in Giza or Saqqara, but it is bliss to enjoy a moment of peace at the humble ruins, and revel in the serene desolation of the surrounding desert. Of the four pyramid complexes at Abu Sir, Sahure's is the most complete.

Pyramid of Sahure MONUMENT

(Map p152) Sahure (2487–2475 BC) was the first of the 5th-dynasty pharaohs to be buried at Abu Sir. His pyramid, originally 50m high, is now badly damaged. From the entrance you can walk through a 75m-long corridor before crawling 2m on your stomach through Pharaonic dust and spiderwebs to reach the burial chamber. Sahure's funerary temple must have been an impressive temple, with black-basalt-paved floors, red-granite date-palm columns and walls decorated with 10,000 sq metres of superbly detailed reliefs.

It was connected by a 235m-long causeway to the valley temple, which was built at the edge of the cultivation and bordered by water. From the pyramid, on a clear day you can see some 10 other pyramids stretching out to the horizon. There is an official gatehouse at the site, but no set ticket price. In lieu of this, ad hoc guides lounge out front and will show you around for baksheesh. Don't count on a toilet here – there is one, but there's no guarantee it's working or that you'll be allowed to use it.

Pyramid of Nyuserra MONUMENT

(Map p152) The most dilapidated of the finished pyramids at Abu Sir belonged to Nyuserra (2445–2421 BC). Originally some 50m high, this pyramid has been heavily quarried over the millennia. In fact, Nyuserra reused his father Neferirkare's valley temple, and then redirected the causeway to lead not to his father's pyramid, but to his own.

The Pyramids of Abu Sir & Saqqara

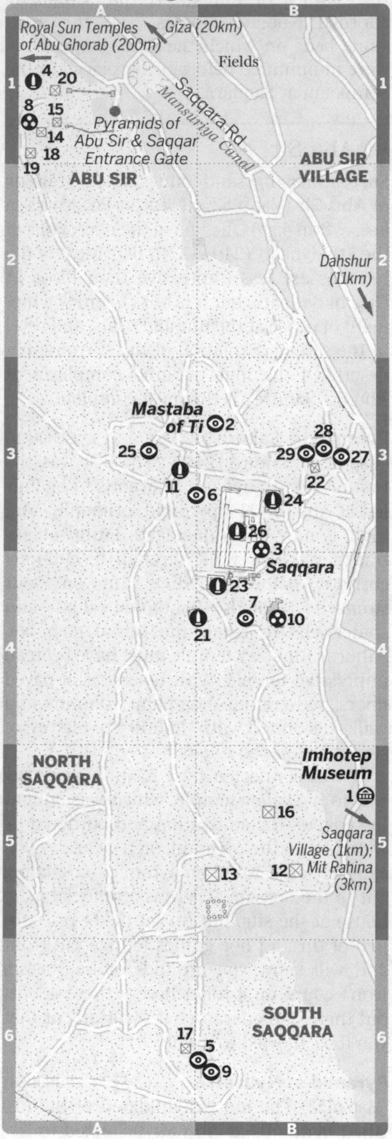

The Pyramids of Abu Sir & Saqqara

Top Sights

1	Imhotep Museum	B5
2	Mastaba of Ti	B3
3	Saqqara	B3

Sights

4	Abu Sir	A1
5	Mastaba of al-Faraun	B6
6	Monastery of St Jeremiah	B4
7	Philosophers' Circle	A3
8	Pyramid of Djedkare	B5
9	Pyramid of Merenre	B5
10	Pyramid of Neferirkare	A1
11	Pyramid of Nyuserra	A1
12	Pyramid of Pepi I	B5
13	Pyramid of Pepi II	A6
14	Pyramid of Queen Khentkawes II	A1
15	Pyramid of Raneferef	A1
16	Pyramid of Sahure	A1
17	Pyramid of Sekhemket	B4
18	Pyramid of Teti	B3
19	Pyramid of Unas	B4
20	Pyramid of Userkaf	B3
21	Royal Sun Temples of Abu Ghorab	A1
22	Serapeum	A3
23	South Saqqara	B6
24	Step Pyramid of Zoser	B3
25	Tomb of Akhethotep & Ptahhotep	B3
26	Tomb of Ankhmahor	B3
27	Tomb of Horemheb	B4
28	Tomb of Kagemni	B3
29	Tomb of Mereruka	B3

Information

The Pyramids of Abu Sir & Saqqar Main Entrance & Ticket Office	(see 1)
The Pyramids of Abu Sir & Saqqara Tourist Police	(see 1)

Pyramid of Neferirkare MONUMENT

(Map p152) Neferirkare (2475–2455 BC) was the third pharaoh of the 5th dynasty and Sahure's father. His burial place originally resembled the Step Pyramid at Saqqara. However, the present-day complex is only the core as the original outer casing has been stripped away, reducing the pyramid from its original planned height of 72m to today's 45m.

In the early 20th century in Neferirkare's funerary temple, archaeologists found the so-called Abu Sir Papyri, an important archive of Old Kingdom documents written in hieratic script, a shorthand form of hieroglyphs. They relate to the cult of the pharaohs buried at the site, recording important details of ritual ceremonies, temple equipment, priests' work rotas and the temple accounts.

South of Neferirkare's pyramid lies the badly ruined **Pyramid of Queen Khentkawes II** (Map p152), wife of Neferirkare and mother of both Raneferef and Nyuserra. In her nearby funerary temple, Czech archaeologists discovered another set of papyrus documents. In addition, two virtually destroyed pyramids to the south of the queen's pyramid may have belonged to the queens of Nyuserra.

Pyramid of Raneferef MONUMENT
(Pyramid of Neferefre; Map p152) The Pyramid of Raneferef (2448–2445 BC), who is believed to have reigned for four years before Nyuserra, is unfinished, and was only completed as a mastaba. In the adjoining mud-brick cult building, Czech archaeologists found fragments of statuary, including a superb limestone figurine of Raneferef protected by Horus (now in the Egyptian Museum) along with papyrus fragments relating to the Abu Sir temple archives.

Royal Sun Temples of Abu Ghorab MONUMENT
(Map p152) Just northwest of the Abu Sir pyramids lies the site of Abu Ghorab, which is home to two temples dedicated to the worship of Ra, the sun god of Heliopolis. Built for Pharaohs Userkaf (2494–2487 BC) and Nyuserra, these temples follow the traditional plan of a valley temple, and contain a causeway and a large stone enclosure. This enclosure contains a large limestone obelisk standing some 37m tall on a 20m-high base.

In front of the obelisk, the enormous alabaster altar can still be seen. Made in the form of a solar disc flanked by four 'hotep' signs (the hieroglyphic sign for 'offerings' and 'satisfied'), the altar itself reads: 'The sun god Ra is satisfied.'

Tours

For experienced riders, a popular outing is a horse or camel ride from Giza to Saqqara, a trip of about three hours. At Saqqara, it's also possible to hire a camel, horse or donkey from near the Serapeum to take you on a circuit of the sites for between E£75 and E£100. You'll need to pay more the further into the desert away from North Saqqara you go.

Getting There & Away

You can reach Saqqara and Mit Rahina by public transport, but only with a great deal of trouble; Dahshur and Abu Sir are not at all accessible this way. For this reason, the area is typically visited as part of an organised tour or with a private taxi from Cairo hired for the day (about E£320 to E£400, plus parking at each site). Moreover, the sites of Saqqara and Dahshur are quite vast, and it's an asset to have a car to drive you around them.

For the truly determined: take a microbus or bus down Pyramids Rd in Cairo to Maryutia Canal (under the ring-road flyover), then hop on a microbus bound for Saqqara village; ask to be let off at 'Haram Saqqara'. It's a 1.5km walk to the ticket office, though you may be able to get a tuk-tuk to take you there, and even down the road to Mit Rahina.

Al-Fayoum

084 / POP 2.5 MILLION

This large fertile basin, about 70km wide and 60km long, is often referred to as an oasis, though technically it's watered not by springs but by the Nile via hundreds of capillary canals, many dug in ancient times. The area harbours a number of important archaeological sites, as the pharaohs built pleasure palaces here and the Greeks, who believed the crocodiles in Lake Qarun were sacred, built temples where pilgrims could feed the beasts. The region is famous for its lush fields and orchards, so it's a good place to revel in fresh produce, and the lake is a popular weekend spot for vacationing Cairenes.

As a visitor, you'll deal primarily with two towns in the oasis. Medinat al-Fayoum, a city of half a million, is built along one of the largest canals and offers the usual Egyptian urban chaos. It's the main transit hub and has all the services you might need, including hotels. The downtown area is along the Bahr Yusuf, the main canal through the oasis. The village of Tunis, an arts colony on the west edge of Al-Fayoum, is the more typical place to spend the night – or on the nearby shores of Lake Qarun.

Sights

Lake Qarun LAKE
(Ptolemaic Temple adult/student E£25/15; Ptolemaic Temple 8am-4pm) Lake Qarun is a popular weekend spot for Cairenes looking to cool down, and the lake edge is dotted with cafes and wedding pavilions. It's not a big swimming spot, but even the sight of an expansive lake on the edge of the desert is refreshing, and you can rent a rowing boat. The lake is now an important bird area where thousands of migratory birds rest during their winter migration pattern south, including large numbers of flamingos.

Prior to the 12th-dynasty reigns of Sesostris III and his son Amenemhat III, the area that's now known as Al-Fayoum was entirely covered by Lake Qarun. In an early effort at land reclamation, both pharaohs

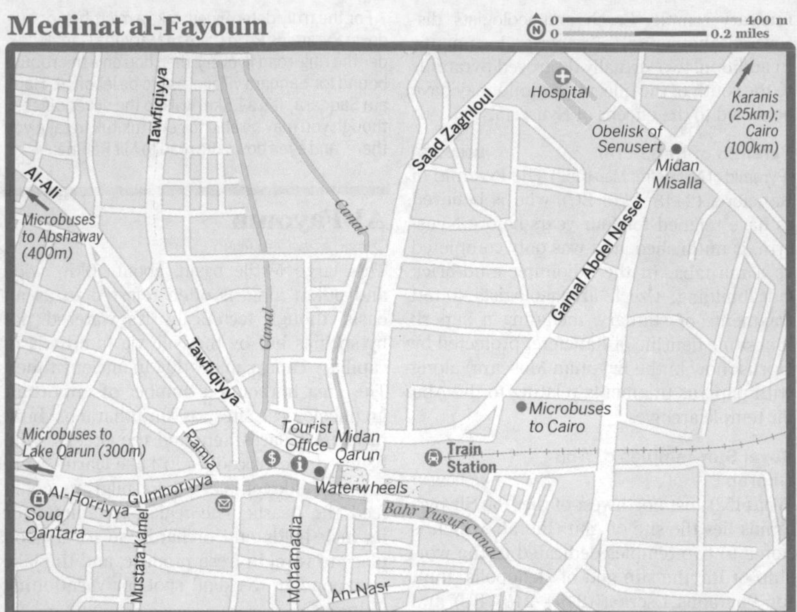

dug a series of canals linking Qarun to the Nile, and drained much of the lake.

Over the past few centuries, the lake has regained some of its former grandeur due to the diversion of the Nile to create more agricultural land, and it now stretches for 42km. However, since it presently sits at 45m below sea level, the water has suffered from increasing salinity. Remarkably, the wildlife has adapted, and today the self-proclaimed 'world's most ancient lake' supports a unique ecosystem. Chances are that you'll spot countless varieties of birds here, particularly in autumn, including a large colony of flamingos, grey herons, spoonbills and many duck species.

Qasr Qarun MONUMENT

FREE At the western end of Lake Qarun, just east of the village of Qasr Qarun, are the ruins of ancient Dionysias, once the starting point for caravans to the Western Desert oasis of Bahariya. All that remains of the ancient settlement is a Ptolemaic temple, known as Qasr Qarun, built in 4 BC and dedicated to Sobek, the crocodile-headed god of Al-Fayoum. There are excellent views from the rooftop.

The temple is built of blocks of yellow limestone, but unusually for Egypt there are no inscriptions, except over the entrance, where there is a winged sun, and on the roof, where there's a headless relief of Sobek on the left and a king on the right. The internal structure has been reinforced, so if you're feeling adventurous explore the amazing maze of chambers, tunnels and stairways. Take a torch or candles.

Wadi Rayyan Protected Area PARK

(admission per person E£20 plus per vehicle E£10, camping per person E£15) The 'Waterfalls' in the Wadi Rayyan Protected Area are the area's major attraction as a weekend picnic spot for Cairenes. Increasingly, visitors also head to another part of Wadi Rayyan, Wadi al-Hittan, a valley with the earliest prehistoric whale fossils ever discovered. The area is rich in wildlife, including white gazelles, Egyptian gazelles, sand foxes and fennec foxes, as well as rare species of resident birds, migrant birds and various kinds of eagles and falcons.

In the 1960s, Egyptian authorities created three lakes in the Wadi Rayyan depression, southwest of Lake Qarun, to hold excess water from agricultural drainage. This was intended to be the first step in an ambitious land-reclamation project, though not everything went to plan when the water started to become increasingly brackish. On the bright side, Wadi Rayyan is particularly conducive to large colonies of birds, and today the entire depression is administered as a national park.

Wadi Rayyan's waterfalls are about 20km away from the reserve's gate on the left side of the road. The waterfalls, where one lake drains into another, are beautiful but very popular, so we recommend spending time exploring the rest of the fascinating area. Big wooden rowboats take, for about E£50 to E£75, a one-hour trip out to the middle of the lake and then back up close to the falls. Along the main lakefront is a visitors centre, toilets and some cafes serving cold drinks and light meals. Five kilometres away is the stunning Jabal al-Modawara, which is fairly easy to climb and a great place to spot eagles or falcons. From Jabal al-Modawara, it's a 30km drive east on a dirt road to Wadi al-Hittan.

Wadi al-Hittan PARK

Part of Wadi Rayyan Protected Area is Wadi al-Hittan (Valley of the Whales), a Unesco World Heritage site, with more than 400 whale skeletons, about 40 million years old. These are the fossilised remains of the basilosaurus, some up to 18m long, and the smaller dorodontus, both rather fierce water predators. They show the clear evolution of land-based mammals into sea-going ones, as they have vestigial front and back legs.

The sands are also studded with the remains of manatees, big bony fish and plenty of shark teeth – which look very out of place in what is now a vast desert. The Valley of the Whales is criss-crossed by a small network of walking tracks leading out to more than a dozen skeletons, in addition to a wilderness campground complete with basic toilets and fire pits. It doesn't sound like much, but the desert setting is dramatic, and it's a great destination for a day or overnight outing, usually combined with Wadi Rayyan. Unesco is building the Wadi el Hitan Fossil and Climate Change Museum here to further protect the fossils.

Karanis ARCHAEOLOGICAL SITE

(adult/student E£30/15; ⏲8am-4pm) At the edge of the oasis depression, 25km north of Medinat al-Fayoum on the road to Cairo, lie the ruins of ancient Karanis. Founded by Ptolemy II's mercenaries in the 3rd century BC, the town was once a mud-brick settlement with a population in the thousands. Today, little of the ancient city remains intact aside from a few walls, though Karanis is home to two well-preserved **Graeco-Roman temples**.

The larger and more interesting temple was built in the 1st century BC and is dedicated to two local crocodile gods, Pnepheros and Petesouchos. In front of the east entrance is a large square container – essentially a giant swimming pool for the holy crocs. Inside, niches in the wall are where crocodile mummies would have been stowed, and a blocklike structure was the 'house' for the gods. The temple is also adorned with inscriptions dating from the reigns of the Roman emperors Nero, Claudius and Vespasian.

It's a trek to the north temple, and there is far less structure here – but you can see an ancient pigeon tower, off to the east, not so different from the ones that dot Al-Fayoum today. In the ruined domestic area north of the temple, you'll find a bathtub adorned with frescos.

There's a museum on-site, next to Lord Cromer's one-time field house, but it has been closed indefinitely. To get here, catch one of the Cairo-bound buses from Medinat al-Fayoum (E£6 to E£10), but it may be better to find a taxi to take you there and back.

Tunis VILLAGE

Near the southwest end of Lake Qarun, this village has been a getaway for Cairene artists and intellectuals since the 1970s, and it's also well known as a pottery centre. It's relatively quiet and green, and many people have built in the curvaceous mud-brick style of Hassan Fathy, Egypt's most influential modern architect. It has a few delightful simple hotels to while away a few days. The village holds an annual **festival** in early November for pottery and crafts.

Established in the 1970s by Swiss artists, Evelyne Porret and Michel Pastore, **Fayoum Pottery School** (☎084-682 0405; ⏲10am-6pm daily) FREE, which trains children and adults in the local potting traditions, is set in a beautiful mud-brick compound. Its architecture – very much in the Egyptian vernacular style – is as attractive as the students'

BEST READS

- *The Fayoum: History and Guide* by R Neil Hewison
- *In an Antique Land* by Amitav Ghosh, about life in a Delta village
- *Coptic Monasteries, Egypt's Monastic Art and Architecture* by Gawdat Gabra

THE FAYOUM PORTRAITS

Al-Fayoum may not be famous for much these days, but it was here that caches of what are some of the world's earliest portraits were found. These extraordinarily lifelike representations, known as the Fayoum Portraits, were painted on wooden panels and put over the faces of mummies, or painted directly onto linen shrouds covering the corpses. This fusion of ancient Egyptian and Graeco-Roman funerary practices laid the foundation for the Western tradition of realistic portraiture.

Dating from between 30 BC and AD 395, the paintings were executed in a technique involving a heated mixture of pigment and wax. Remarkable for the skill of the anonymous artists who painted them, the realistic and eerily modern-looking faces bridge the centuries. The haunting images are made all the more poignant by their youth (some are only babies) – a reflection of the high infant-mortality rates at the time.

More than a thousand of these portraits have been found, not just in Al-Fayoum but also throughout Egypt. They now reside in numerous museums around the world, including the Egyptian Museum in Cairo.

creations from clay, which are on sale here. From the school, ask for directions to the workshop of **Ahmed Abou Zeid**, another noted local potter. Pots are available in Cairo at Nagada (p113).

The **Fayoum Art Center Residency** project run by painter Mohamed Abla (see p457) hosts classes and resident artists from around the world. Also on the grounds is the **Caricature Museum**, a great collection of Egyptian political cartoons – interesting if you can read Arabic. Still, pop in just for the feel of the place – like the pottery school, it's a beautiful space, and you never know what you'll find here.

Medinet Madi ARCHAEOLOGICAL SITE

FREE This ancient city is one of the most isolated in Al-Fayoum, but this is also part of its appeal, as you're often alone out in the blowing sand that drifts over the heads of the stone sphinxes. Medinet Madi (Arabic for 'City of the Past') is noted for a well-preserved Middle Kingdom temple, few of which have survived in Egypt. It is dedicated to the crocodile god Sobek and the cobra goddess Renenutet, built by Amenemhat III and Amenemhat IV.

Italian excavations in the early 20th century uncovered an archive of Greek texts, which refer to the city as Narmouthis. They also found a separate crocodile-cult temple where the beasts appear to have been bred in captivity – a cache of eggs was found, along with bodies of the creatures in various stages of development. Often they were sacrificed when still quite young.

Visiting really requires a 4WD vehicle, as there is no real track to the site. If you take a taxi here, you'll have to walk 2km across the sand from the highway near Abu Gandir, the nearest village.

Pyramid of Meidum ARCHAEOLOGICAL SITE

(adult/student E£30/15; ⌚8am-4pm) About 30km northeast of Medinat al-Fayoum is the ruin of the first true pyramid attempted by the ancient Egyptians. It began as an eight-stepped structure, with the steps later filled in and an outer casing added to form the first pyramid shell. There were design flaws and, sometime after completion (possibly as late as the last few centuries BC), the pyramid's own weight caused the sides to collapse. Today, only the core stands, though it is still an impressive sight.

Pharaoh Huni (2637–2613 BC) commissioned the pyramid, although it was his son Sneferu who was responsible for the actual building. Sneferu's architects then went on to build the more successful Bent Pyramid and Red Pyramid at Dahshur.

The guard will unlock the entrance of the pyramid, from where steps lead 75m down to the empty burial chamber. Near the pyramid are the large mastaba tombs of some of Sneferu's family and officials, including his son Rahotep and wife Nofret.

The pyramid is hard to reach. The best option is to hire a taxi and visit as part of a larger tour.

Pyramid of Hawara ARCHAEOLOGICAL SITE

(adult/student E£30/15; ⌚8am-4pm) About 8km southeast of Medinat al-Fayoum, on the north side of the Bahr Yusuf, the canal that connects Al-Fayoum to the Nile, stands the dilapidated second pyramid of Amenemhat III, built at a gentler angle than his first one (the towerlike Black Pyramid at Dahshur). Herodotus described this temple (300m by 250m) as a 3000-room labyrinth that surpassed even the Pyramids of Giza. Strabo claimed it had as many rooms as there were provinces.

Although the Pyramid of Hawara was originally covered with white limestone casing, sadly only the mud-brick core remains today, and even the once-famous temple has been quarried. The interior of the pyramid, now closed to visitors, revealed several technical developments: corridors were blocked using a series of huge stone portcullises; the burial chamber is carved from a single piece of quartzite; and the chamber was sealed by an ingenious device using sand to lower the roof block into place.

Microbuses between Medinat al-Fayoum and Beni Suef pass through the town of Hawarat al-Makta. From here, it is just a short walk to the pyramid. Alternatively, you can visit in a taxi as part of a circuit.

Pyramid of Al-Lahun ARCHAEOLOGICAL SITE
(adult/student E£30/15; ⊙8am-4pm) About 10km southeast of Hawara are the ruins of this mud-brick pyramid, built by Pharaoh Sesostris II (1880–1874 BC). It's not worth a separate trip, but if you're driving by, look out for its strangely lumpen shape, set on an existing rock outcropping for extra stature. Ancient tomb robbers stripped it of all its rock and treasures, except for the amazing solid-gold cobra that is now displayed in the jewellery room (Room 4) of the Egyptian Museum in Cairo.

Waterwheels LANDMARK
(Medinat al-Fayoum, Bahr Yusuf) Al-Fayoum is famous for its more than 200 waterwheels, which have become a prominent symbol of the town and the oasis. The Greeks invented the waterwheel, and the first depictions of them are seen in Ptolemaic Egyptian sources, so it's quite likely that since Pharaonic times these devices have kept the town well irrigated despite its irregular topography of rolling hills and steep depressions. There is a rickety version in the centre of Medinat al-Fayoum.

Tours

Wadi al-Hittan is best visited as part of a tour, as a quality vehicle is required. The charge is about E£500 for four people for the day.

Hany Zaki TOUR
(☎0100 166 6979; www.facebook.com/Rahhala-Expeditions) Hani Zaki, founder of Rahhala Expeditions, has over 30 years' experience in the Western Desert, and organises bird-watching trips, desert safari and sand-boarding on the dunes. He can provide transport to see sights around Al-Fayoum.

Etman Abood TOUR
(☎0100 133 3781) Etman Abood can organise sandboarding and trips into the desert around Al-Fayoum and Wadi Rayyan.

Sleeping & Eating

Bedding down in Medinat al-Fayoum is not the most scenic option; it's far better, to head to Lake Qarun or Tunis. All the lodges have their own restaurants, and in Medinat al-Fayoum there are plenty of standard Egyptian snack joints, though nothing particularly remarkable.

Zad al-Mosafer BUNGALOW $
(☎084-682 0180, 0100 639 5590; Tunis; s/d E£100/120, without bathroom E£75/95) The quintessential groovy hang-out in Tunis, this is a somewhat ad hoc 'ecolodge' that's been around for years. It shows its age a bit, and it's on the main Lake Qarun road, so not exactly quiet, but the food and company are excellent.

Sobek Lodge BUNGALOW $
(☎0106 888 5423; sobekvilla@hotmail.com; Tunis; s/d E£150/200) A few basic but clean rooms are part of a larger potters' compound in the village of Tunis, in a nice green spot with plenty of space to lounge around. One major perk is the home-cooked meals.

Kom el Dikka Agri Lodge ECOLODGE $$
(☎0122 244 0012; komeldikkaagrilodge@gmail.com; Tunis; house sleeping 6 per night from $250) An 18-hectare organic olive farm overlooking Lake Qarun which has been recently developed into an agritourism lodge. There are two houses available on the estate with several rooms for rent.

New Panorama Village HOTEL $$
(☎084 6830 746; newpanorama.village@gmail.com; near Shakshouk, Lake Qarun; s/d from E£250/275; ❄@≋) Good value, if lacking a little in character, this collection of modern balcony-lined chalets looks over the lake. The Dananir restaurant specialises in fresh fish and fowl from the area, and has in- and outdoor seating.

SECURITY IN AL-FAYOUM

Al-Fayoum was long notorious for its heavy-handed security for independent travellers. In recent years, however, this seems to have lifted, and few travellers have reported issues. Police at checkpoints seldom inspect passports (though you should carry yours just in case), and often if you're a lone tourist in a microbus full of Egyptians, you're waved on through without question. Occasionally individual travellers may be appointed a police escort, but this rarely happens these days. If you avoid Medinat al-Fayoum and head for the sights elsewhere in the area, you may not be troubled by anything at all.

Lazib Inn RESORT **$$$**
(☎0122 950 1621; www.lazibinn.com) Lazib Inn Resort is near Tunis village in Al-Fayoum, overlooking Lake Qarun, with eight suites, a swimming pool, Jacuzzi and spa.

Helnan Auberge Fayoum LUXURY HOTEL **$$$**
(☎084-698 1200; www.helnan.com; near Shakshouk, Lake Qarun; s/d from US$100/120; ❄📶🏊) Built in 1937 as King Farouk's private hunting lodge, this hotel was where world leaders met after WWII to decide the borders of the Middle East. These days it remains an elegant refuge, so long as you focus on the colonial glamour and don't expect perfectly suave service.

Information

Fayoum Tourism Authority (☎634 2313; www.fayoumegypt.com; Medinat al-Fayoum, Bahr Yusuf) The Fayoum Tourism Authority has an office next to the waterwheels in Al-Fayoum's main town, but it's not always staffed; the same goes for a kiosk by the Helnan Auberge Fayoum on Lake Qarun.

Getting There & Away

Microbuses (E£10 to E£15, 1½ to two hours) are the quickest way to travel from Cairo to Al-Fayoum. Catch them at Midan al-Remaya in Giza, from Ulali near Ramses Station or from the ring-road underpass in Moneib. In Medinat al-Fayoum, ask to be dropped at Bahr Yusuf. If you're heading for Lake Qarun or Tunis, take a microbus direct from Midan al-Remaya in Giza to Abshaway, just south of the lake; from there you can take another microbus onward.

Returning, microbuses leave Medinat al-Fayoum from north of the train station and head to various main stations in Cairo; the fare depends on the destination.

Getting Around

For the lakes, Tunis and the various archaeological sites, you can hire a taxi in Al-Fayoum for between E£300 and E£400 for the day, in which time you could feasibly visit Karanis, Lake Qarun and Wadi Rayyan, with a short stop in Tunis.

If you want to spend more time in the desert or visit Wadi al-Hittan, you're probably better off going on an organised trip.

Microbuses connect most of the smaller villages with Medinat al-Fayoum – you can get to Shakshouk, for instance, the closest settlement to the good hotels on Lake Qarun, for E£1. To reach Qasr Qarun or Tunis, you'll likely have to switch microbuses in Abshaway (E£1).

Wadi Natrun

Wadi Natrun, about 100km northwest of Cairo, is known for its Coptic monasteries where thousands of Christians escaped from Roman persecution in the 4th century. Of the 60 or so original compounds in the valley, only four remain. These monastery buildings are impressive, as they were fortified after Arab raids in 817, but the art inside is not as striking as at the Monastery of St Anthony in the Eastern Desert. Your experience will largely depend on when you visit – most days are quiet, but visitors mob the churches on Christian and public holidays, yielding a glimpse into contemporary Coptic traditions. The monastic tradition is thriving, and the Coptic pope is still chosen from the Wadi Natrun monks.

The area was also important to the ancient Egyptians because the valley's salt lakes dry up in the summer and leave natron, a substance crucial to the mummification process. Today, natron is used on a larger scale by the chemical industry.

Wadi Natrun lies on the desert side of the eight-lane Cairo–Alexandria Desert Hwy, which roughly separates the green fields of the Delta and the harsh sands of the Western Desert, though the area is now dotted with farms and new satellite towns.

Sights

Deir Anba Bishoi MONASTERY
(☎02-2591 4448; ⌚9am-6pm, 7pm in summer) FREE St Bishoi came to the desert in AD

340 and founded two monasteries in Wadi Natrun: this one and neighbouring Deir el-Sourian. Deir Anba Bishoi is built around a church that contains the saint's body, said to be perfectly preserved in its tubelike container. Each year on 15 July, the tube is carried in procession around the church. According to the monks, the bearers clearly feel the weight of a whole body.

The fortified keep is entered via a drawbridge, passing into an area with a vegetable garden, well, kitchens, two churches and storerooms that can hold provisions for a year. On the roof (men only can climb up), trapdoors open to small cells that acted as makeshift tombs for those who died during frequent sieges. Adjacent is an enormous new cathedral. Outside the keep in a separate building is a shop selling monastery products: olive oil, honey, candles and, oddly, cleaning supplies.

Deir el-Sourian MONASTERY
(02-2590 5161; www.st-mary-alsourian.com; 9am-6pm, 7pm in summer) FREE About 500m northwest of Deir Anba Bishoi, Deir el-Sourian is the most picturesquely situated of the monasteries. It is named after wandering Syrian monks who bought the monastery from the Copts in the 8th century, though the Copts took it back in the 16th century. Its Church of the Virgin contains **11th-century wall paintings** and older icons with the eyes scratched out, including one saint in a distinctly Pharaonic-looking robe.

The church itself was built around the 4th-century cave where St Bishoi resided and tied his hair to the ceiling to keep himself awake during prayers. Elsewhere in the compound is a second ancient church, the tamarind tree of St Ephraim, allegedly sprung from the Syrian holy man's cane, and some slightly unfortunate mannequins of monks illustrating daily life at the monastery.

Deir Abu Makar MONASTERY
(02-2577 0614; www.stmacariusmonastery.org; 9am-6pm, closed during fasting periods) FREE Deir Abu Makar is the most secluded of the monasteries, so it's wise to confirm first at the bigger monasteries that it's open. It was founded around the cell where St Makarios spent his last 20 or so years. Structurally, it suffered more than other monasteries at the hands of raiding Bedouin, but it is famous as most of the Coptic popes have been selected from among its monks, and most are buried here.

Deir al-Baramouse MONASTERY
(info 02-592 2775; 9am-6pm Fri-Sun, closed during fasting periods) FREE Once quite isolated due to a bad road, Deir al-Baramouse now has more than 100 monks in residence, plus six modern churches in addition to its restored medieval fortress (not open to the public). There are also remnants of **13th-century wall frescos** in its oldest church, the Church of the Virgin Mary.

Activities

El-Hammra Eco-Lodge's pool is open for day use.

Sleeping

In addition to El-Hammra Eco-Lodge, men are welcome to spend the night at any of the monasteries, but must have written consent from the Cairo offices (see below). Even if you're not devout, it is good manners to attend religious services, and to leave a generous donation with the monks on departure.

El-Hammra Eco-Lodge LODGE $
(045 355 0944, 0100 660 5060; www.elhamraeco-lodge.com; s/d per person E£150/125, with 3 meals E£200/175;) Windblown and fairly run-down, this collection of rustic cottages isn't as 'green' as some would hope. But it's quiet, the owner is a character, and the food is good (breakfast is included). The pool is open for day use (E£75 for up to four people, including access to a bungalow, or E£80 per person with lunch).

Information

Some of the monasteries close during the three major fasting periods: Lent (40 days before Easter Week), Advent (40 days before Christmas) and the Dormition (two weeks in August), so it's worth checking with their Cairo offices:

Deir Abu Makar (02-2577 0614; www.stmacariusmonastery.org)
Deir Anba Bishoi (02-2591 4448)
Deir el-Baramouse (02-2592 2775)
Deir el-Sourian (02-2590 5161; www.st-mary-alsourian.com)

Getting There & Away

Alexandria-bound West & Mid Delta Co buses from Cairo Gateway can drop you on the Desert Hwy close to Wadi Natrun (tell the driver you want to get off at Master Mall and Rest), but charge the full price to Alex (E£36). Cheaper are the microbuses (E£9, one hour) from Midan al-Remaya near the Pyramids of Giza, or West

& Mid Delta Co buses from Abboud (E£13); the buses go into the less-than-lovely town of Wadi Natrun. Tuk-tuks and taxis wait at the highway and the bus depot. A tuk-tuk to Deir Anba Bishoi and Deir el-Sourian (you can walk between the two), with pick-up a couple of hours later, will cost E£25. To visit all four monasteries, you'll need a taxi; expect to pay around E£25 per hour.

A taxi from Cairo should cost about E£320 there and back, including a couple of hours driving around to all the monasteries.

THE NILE DELTA

North of Cairo, the Nile River divides into two branches that enter the Mediterranean at the old ports of Damietta and Rosetta, forming one of the most fertile and most cultivated regions in the world. Laced with countless waterways, the lush, fan-shaped Delta region is a relaxing counterpoint to Cairo's grit and the desert's austerity. Very few tourists make it here, and there is little infrastructure in the way of hotels and information offices; police may even be a bit suspicious of your motives. But just a day visit on a train or bus can be rewarding for travellers who prefer aimless exploration to actual sightseeing.

Birqash Camel Market

Egypt's largest **camel market** (Souq al-Gimaal; admission E£25, camera E£20; ⏲6am-noon Fri & Sun) is held at Birqash (pronounced Bir'ash), a small village 35km northwest of Cairo, just on the edge of the Delta's cultivated land. The camel market is not for the faint of heart – these beasts are not treated like beloved pets. But it can make an unforgettable day trip, especially if you're a keen photographer. Hundreds of camels are sold here every market day, with the liveliest action between 7am and 10am.

Most of the animals are brought up the Forty Days Rd from western Sudan to just north of Abu Simbel by camel herders, and from there to the market in Daraw in Upper Egypt. Unsold camels are then hobbled and crammed into trucks for the 24-hour drive to Birqash. By the time they arrive, many are emaciated, fit only for the knacker's yard, and some expire at the market itself. Traders stand no nonsense and camels that get out of line are beaten relentlessly.

In addition to those from Sudan, there are camels from various parts of Egypt (including Sinai, the west and the south) and sometimes from as far away as Somalia. They are traded for cash or other livestock, such as goats, sheep and horses, and sold for farm work or slaughter. Smaller camels go for as little as E£750, but bigger beasts can sell for E£6000 and up.

ℹ Information

While at the market, watch out for pickpockets. Women should dress conservatively – the market is very much a man's scene, with the only female presence being the local tea-lady. But traders here are accustomed to tourists and are generally happy to answer questions and have their photos taken if you ask nicely. Always be alert to bolting camels – even hobbled, they can move pretty fast.

ℹ Getting There & Away

Microbuses and trucks (E£2) run from the site of the old camel market at Imbaba. To get to Imbaba, take a microbus from Midan Abdel Moniem Riad in Downtown Cairo, then ask around for a connecting service to the old market – Imbaba airport *(matar Imbaba)* is the nearest landmark. Or you could take a taxi to the old market site. Returning to Cairo, microbuses for Imbaba leave when full.

The easiest option is to simply hire a taxi from Cairo, with waiting time – one hour in the market is usually enough for most people. The full trip will cost around E£200. You could also combine this with a trip to the Nile Barrages and have the taxi drop you there, then return on the river bus.

Nile Barrages

Half the appeal of Qanater ('Barrages') is the two-hour trip on a ramshackle river bus, best done on Fridays or public holidays. Large groups of young people and smaller family parties pack the boats, and the scraggly public gardens at Qanater, a 1km patch of land between the two branches of the Nile where the 19th-century barrages are handsome pieces of engineering. On the boats, Arabic pop blares and the younger passengers sing along, clap, dance and decorously flirt.

It's an enjoyable, sociable jaunt, though prepare yourself for attention. Tourists are a rare and intriguing sight, and Qanater is a popular destination for young males, who relish cruising the promenade between the two barrages on their motor scooters. The barrages themselves are a series of basins and locks built to guarantee a year-round flow of water into the Delta region, thus leading to a great increase in cotton production. The barrage on the Damietta branch consists of 71 sluices stretching 521m across the river; the Rosetta Barrage is 438m long with 61 sluices.

Getting There & Away

River buses (E£12) go from the dock in front of the TV building (Maspero), just north of the Ramses Hilton in central Cairo. They depart when full, from 7am to about 10am. You can return by microbus (E£20) if the boat departures aren't convenient, or if you need a little quiet. Qanater is very close to Birqash, so you could hire a taxi to drive you to the market, then leave you at Qanater, and take the boat back; pay about E£170 to E£200.

Tanta

040 / POP 429,000

The largest city in the Delta, Tanta is an easy place to sample slower-paced Delta life, as it's accessible by good trains. It's a major centre for Sufism, and home to a large mosque dedicated to Al-Sayyed Ahmed al-Badawi, a Moroccan Sufi who fought the Crusaders in the 13th century. The *moulid* (saints' festival) held in his honour follows the cotton harvest, usually the last week in October. It is one of the biggest in Egypt, drawing crowds of more than a million people for the eight days of chanting, rituals and sweets for which Tanta is best known.

If visiting during the *moulid,* prepare yourself for mayhem (women should not go alone as sexual harassment is rife) and book accommodation well in advance.

History

This area of the western Delta was once home to the ancient cities of Sais, Naucratis and Wadjet. Although these cities have been wiped off the map, anyone with a historical interest in the Delta region might be intrigued as to where they once stood. A museum in Tanta allegedly holds some treasures, but it is perpetually closed for 'renovation'.

Northwest of Tanta, on the east bank of the Rosetta branch of the Nile, once stood the legendary city of **Sais** (Sa al-Hagar), Egypt's 26th-dynasty capital. Sacred to Neith, goddess of war and hunting, and protector of embalmed bodies, Sais dates back to the start of Egyptian history, and was replete with palaces, temples and royal tombs. However, the city was destroyed in 525 BC by the Persian emperor Cambyses, who reportedly exhumed the mummies of previous rulers from the ground and had them publicly whipped and burned.

West of Tanta, more than halfway along the road to Damanhur, is where the city of **Naucratis** once stood. The city was given to the Greeks to settle during the 7th century BC.

Northeast of Damanhur and northwest of Tanta was the Egyptian cult centre of **Wadjet** (known as Buto to the Greeks), which honoured the cobra goddess of Lower Egypt. Cobras were once worshipped here by devout followers.

Sights

The **Mosque of al-Sayyed Ahmed al-Badawi** (24hr) FREE is 300m from the train station – bear right across the parking area in front of the station and then you'll see the mosque at the end of the first major street. Al-Badawi, born in Morocco, came to Tanta in 1234, and founded one of Egypt's largest Sufi orders, the Badawiya. Inside the mosque to the left, al-Badawi's shrine is lit with green fluorescent lights and circled by pilgrims snapping photos on their mobile phones.

Behind the mosque is Tanta's **old market district**, good for an aimless stroll. The road to the mosque is lined with **sweets-sellers**; the local speciality is a type of nougat studded with nuts or dried chickpeas.

Tanta Museum MUSEUM

(0433 19003; Sharia Mustafa al-Guindi; 9am-4pm Sun-Wed) The Tanta Museum houses a good collection of artefacts found in the area around Tanta, from the ancient sites of Sais, Naucratis and Buto. Excavations from these sites have yielded statues, pottery and other objects now in the museum collection.

Sleeping & Eating

Most visitors to Tanta generally pass through by day, though Tanta has a decent range of accommodation.

New Arafa Hotel HOTEL $$

(340 5040; www.newarafahotel.com; Midan al-Mahatta; s/d from E£180/320;) Hotels cluster around the train station in Tanta, and the best of the lot is the not-so-new New Arafa Hotel. Arriving passengers are greeted with modern rooms that are well insulated from the bustling city streets, and there is a decent bar and restaurant on the premises.

Getting There & Away

From Ramses Station in Cairo, a comfortable air-con train (E£35 to E£60, one to 1½ hours) runs to Tanta eight times a day (three morning departures give you time for a day trip) and deposits you directly in the centre. The fastest return trains go at 5pm and 6pm; the last goes at 10pm. This is far preferable to a bus, as it's not subject to traffic whims.

Zagazig & Bubastis

055 / POP 279,000

Just outside the city of Zagazig (Egyptians say 'za'-a-*zi*') are the ruins of Bubastis, one of the country's most ancient cities. Serious Egyptology buffs will enjoy a visit to the temple that's dedicated to the resident deity, the elegant cat goddess Bastet. It's an easy outing to combine with the larger Tanis. Zagazig is only 80km northeast of Cairo, and serves as an easy day trip from the capital.

Sights

Temple of Bubastis ARCHAEOLOGICAL SITE

(adult/student E£15/10; 8am-4pm) Festivals held at the Temple of Bubastis attracted more than 700,000 revellers who sang, danced, feasted, consumed great quantities of wine and offered sacrifices to the goddess Bastet. Khufu and Khafre started building the temple during the 4th dynasty, but additions were made over about 17 centuries. Now it is just a pile of rubble, but the nearby **cat cemetery**, a series of underground galleries where many bronze statues of cats were found, is morbidly fun to explore.

Sleeping

Marina HOTEL $$

(231 3934; 58 Sharia Gamal Abdel Nasser; s/d from E£290/350;) Marina is a somewhat upmarket affair near the Al-Fatr Mosque that caters to local business travellers. Fairly standard rooms are comfortable despite being unmemorable, though the views from the nearby bridge are very attractive, particularly when the mosque is lit up at night.

Getting There & Away

The cheapest and fastest way to go to Zagazig is by bus or microbus. There are frequent departures in both directions between Zagazig's train station and Cairo's Abboud terminal (E£5 to E£6, one to two hours).

Tanis

Just outside the village of San al-Hagar, 70km northeast of Zagazig, are the partly excavated ruins of Tanis, a city known as Djanet to the ancient Egyptians and Zoan to the Hebrews. The site rightly falls low on the priority list for Egyptology fans, but it is striking because it sits on the edge of lush green plantations.

Tanis ARCHAEOLOGICAL SITE

FREE Some call it the Saqqara of the Delta, due to its impressive scale – though it is not so well preserved as the desert ruins. For several centuries Tanis was one of the largest cities in the Delta, and became a site of great importance after the end of the New Kingdom, especially during the Late Period (747–332 BC). Cinema buffs are also quick to point out that Tanis is where Indiana Jones discovered the 'Lost Ark'.

The earliest buildings at Tanis are from the reign of Psusennes I (1039–991 BC), who surrounded the Temple of Amun with a great enclosure wall. His royal tomb and five others from the 21st dynasty were unearthed by the French in 1939, and the treasures are some of the most spectacular ever found in Egypt. The tombs at the site are now quite empty, as the trove, which includes gorgeous jewellery, is on view in the Egyptian Museum. Psusennes I and later kings reused blocks and statues from earlier eras – so much of the stone actually dates from the Old and Middle Kingdoms. His successors added a temple to Mut, Khons and the Asiatic goddess Astarte, together with a sacred lake, and temple building continued until Ptolemaic times.

Getting There & Away

To reach Tanis, take a microbus or East Delta bus from Ulali or Abboud in Cairo (E£7 to E£15, one to two hours) to the town of Faqus, which is about 35km south of Tanis. From Faqus, take a service taxi or bus (E£2) to the village of San al-Hagar, or alternatively hire a taxi (E£35) to take you to the site.

Alternatively, and much more slowly and with much more dust, the train takes about 3½ hours to get to Abu Kabir (adult/student E£20/15), the nearest station to Faqus. These old, non-air-con trains leave from the far east end of Cairo's Ramses Station (ask for 'Sharq' or 'Limun') approximately every two hours.

If you're coming from Zagazig, the train is slightly more appealing. It takes just 45 minutes to Abu Kabir, and there are more options, with service every hour or so.

Nile Valley: Beni Suef to Qena

Includes ➡

Why Go?

If you're in a hurry to reach the treasures and pleasures of the south, it is easy to dismiss this first segment of Upper Egypt between Cairo and Luxor. But the less touristed parts of the country almost always repay the effort of a visit.

Much of this part of the valley is less developed than the other valleys but people here also have to grapple with the issues of modernity, with water and electricity shortages, and since the downfall of the Muslim Brotherhood, with sectarian tension and security issues.

However much a backwater this region might seem, it played a key role in Egypt's destiny as its many archaeological sites bear witness – from the lavishly painted tombs of the early provincial rulers at Beni Hasan to the remains of Akhetaten, where Tutankhamun was brought up, and the Pharaonic-inspired monasteries of the early Christian period.

Note: due to security concerns, research was conducted remotely by the author for this chapter, except for Dendera, Abydos and Qena.

Best Places to Eat

- Koshary Nagwa (p168)
- Dahabiyya Houseboat & Restaurant (p168)
- Al-Watania Palace Hotel (p174)

Best Places to Stay

- Al-Safa Hotel (p177)
- Al-Watania Palace Hotel (p174)
- City Center Hotel (p166)
- Horus Resort (p168)
- House of Life (p180)

When to Go

Asyut

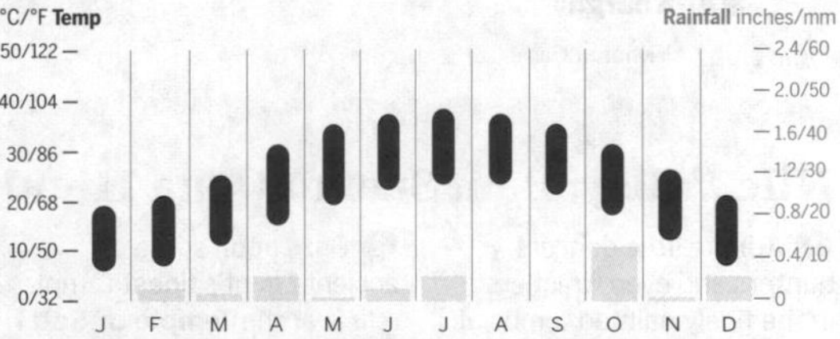

Apr Sham el Nessim, the spring festival, is celebrated in style in the region.

Aug Millions of people arrive to celebrate the Feast of the Virgin outside Minya.

Oct-Nov The ideal touring time, with the light being particularly beautiful.

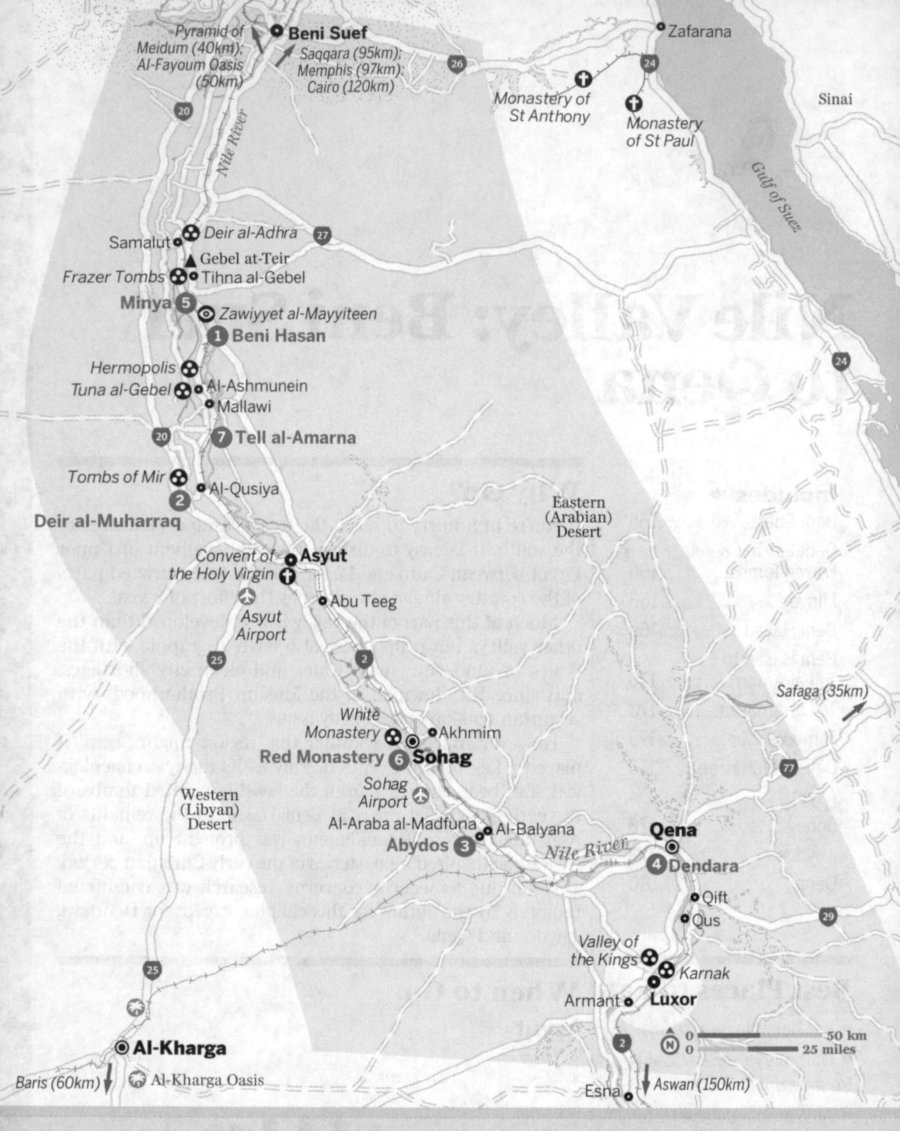

Nile Valley: Beni Suef to Qena Highlights

1. Admire lithe dancers, hunters and even wrestlers in the finely painted tombs at **Beni Hasan** (p169).

2. Visit the Coptic monastery of **Deir al-Muharraq** (p173) to see why Copts claim to be heirs to the ancient Egyptians.

3. Gaze upon some of ancient Egypt's finest temple reliefs at the **Temple of Seti I** (p178) in Abydos.

4. Marvel at one of the best-preserved temple complexes in Egypt in Dendara's magnificent **Temple of Hathor** (p180).

5. Hang out in the colonial-era centre of **Minya** (p166).

6. See the frescos at the **Red Monastery** (p176), one of the finest buildings from late antiquity.

7. Wander through the lush countryside around Akhetaten in **Tell al-Amarna** (p170), site of the doomed city of the heretic king Akhenaten.

History

For ancient Egyptians, Upper Egypt began south of the ancient capital of Memphis, beyond present-day Saqqara.

Egyptians divided the area that stretched between Beni Suef and Qena into 15 nomes (provinces), each with its own capital. Provincial governors and notables built their tombs on the desert edge. Abydos, located close to modern Sohag, was once the predominant religious centre in the region as well as one of the country's most sacred sites and a place of pilgrimage: Egypt's earliest dynastic rulers were interred there and it flourished well into the Christian era.

When New Kingdom Pharaoh Akhenaten tried to break the power of the Theban priesthood, he moved his capital to a new city, Akhetaten (near modern Mallawi), one of the few places along the Nile not already associated with a deity.

Christianity arrived early in Upper Egypt. Sectarian splits in Alexandria and the popularity of the monastic tradition established by St Anthony in the Eastern Desert encouraged priests to settle in the provinces. The many churches and monasteries that continue to function in the area are testament to the strength of the Christian tradition: this area has the largest Coptic communities outside Cairo.

Dependent on agriculture, much of the area remained a backwater throughout the Christian and Islamic periods, although Qena and Asyut flourished as trading hubs: Qena was the jumping-off point for the Red Sea port of Safaga, while Asyut linked the Nile with the Western Desert and the Darb al-Arba'een/Sudan caravan route.

Today much of the region remains poor. Agriculture is still the mainstay of the economy, but cannot absorb the population growth. The lack of any real industrial base south of Cairo has caused severe economic hardship, particularly for young people who drift in increasing numbers into the towns and cities in search of work. Resentment at their lack of hope was compounded by the loss of remittances from Iraq: many people from this region who had found work there in the 1980s lost it with the outbreak of the first Gulf War. Religious militants exploited the violence that exploded in the 1990s, directing it towards the government in a bid to create an Islamic state. The insurrection was violently crushed. The Muslim Brotherhood found much support here after 2011 and there was renewed violence after the downfall of President Morsi. Whoever rules in Cairo will need to address the causes of the unrest – poverty and thwarted hopes.

Dangers & Annoyances

Travel restrictions, in place since the 1990s Islamic insurrection, had eased by late 2012, but the violent protests of Muslim Brotherhood supporters in the summer of 2013 has made this one of the most difficult regions to travel through, with many foreign governments recommending their citizens stay away. Nile cruises between Cairo and Luxor, which had resumed, are again on hold. But the siutation is fluid and some areas, particularly south of Sohag (Abydos and Dendara, for instance), can be visited without trouble.

ℹ Getting There & Away

Trains are recommended for getting in and out of this part of the country. There are frequent services heading north to Cairo and south to Luxor and Aswan. At some stations, the old edict that foreigners can only buy tickets for selected services is still enforced. But in practice, if you can't buy a ticket at the station, you ought to be able to buy one on the train. Buses, private vehicles and taxis are alternatives now that security measures have been eased, but it can be very slow leaving Cairo by road.

ℹ Getting Around

Trains are the best way of moving between the cities in this part of Egypt and microbuses are the best way of making shorter journeys. If the security situation changes, the police may put them off limits to foreigners or you might find yourself being escorted by armed police.

Beni Suef

☎082 / POP 193,535

Beni Suef is a provincial capital, 120km south of Cairo. From antiquity until at least the 16th century it was famous for its linen. In the 19th century it was still sufficiently important to have an American consulate, but there is now little to capture the traveller's interest beyond the sight of a provincial city at work. It is, however, a transport hub between Cairo and Luxor, and the Red Sea and Al-Fayoum.

Sights

Beni Suef Museum MUSEUM
(adult/student E£20/10; ⏲9am-4pm) Next to the governorate building and behind the zoo, this museum is Beni Suef's main attraction. There is a small but worthwhile collection of objects from the Old Kingdom to the Mohammed Ali period with good Ptolemaic carvings, Coptic weavings and 19th-century table-settings.

Sleeping & Eating

There are cheap *kushari*, *fuul* (fava beans) and *ta'amiyya* (mashed, deep-fried fava beans) stands around the train station and Sharia 26th of July.

City Center Hotel HOTEL $$
(☎236 7273; www.citychotel.com; Midan al-Mahatta; s/d E£115/160; ❄📶) Around the corner from the forlorn Semiramis Hotel and across the square from the train station, this three-star, 45-room hotel is popular with managers and white-collar workers posted to Beni Suef. The 6th-floor restaurant serves a mixed menu including pizzas, chicken and pigeons for lunch and dinner, although you might need to order in advance.

Information

Bank of Alexandria (43 Sharia 26th of July) Just off Midan al-Gomhuriyya.
Post Office (Sharia Safiyya Zaghloul)

Getting There & Away

BUS

The bus station is along the main road, Sharia Bur Said, south of the town centre. Buses run from about 6am to 6pm to Cairo, Minya and Al-Fayoum. There is also a daily bus to Zafarana (E£30, three to four hours). The bus will stop at the turn-off to the Monastery of St Anthony, about 130km east of Beni Suef. From here it is a further 12km to the monastery. Microbuses also run the same routes.

TRAIN

There are frequent train connections north to Cairo and Giza (90 minutes to two hours), and south to Minya (one hour 25 minutes).

Gebel at-Teir & Frazer Tombs

The clifflike Gebel at-Teir (Bird Mountain) rises on the east bank of the Nile, some 93km south of Beni Suef and 20km north of Minya. **Deir al-Adhra** (Monastery of the Virgin) is perched 130m above the river. The mountain takes its name from a legend that all Egyptian birds paused here on the monastery's annual feast day. The monastery was formerly known as the Convent of the Pulley, a reminder of the time when rope was the only way of reaching the cliff top.

Coptic tradition claims that the Holy Family rested here for three days on their journey through Egypt. A cave-chapel built on the site in the 4th century AD is ascribed to Helena, mother of Byzantine Emperor Constantine. A 19th-century building encloses the cave, whose icon of the virgin is said to have miraculous powers. The monastery, unvisited for most of the year, is mobbed by many thousands of pilgrims during the week-long Feast of the Assumption, culminating on 22 August.

You can get to the monastery by public transport (*servees* or microbus from Minya to Samalut and a boat across the river), but a private taxi from Minya shouldn't cost more than E£100 to E£150 for the return trip.

Five kilometres south of Tihna al-Gebel, the **Frazer Tombs** date back to the 5th and 6th dynasties. These Old Kingdom tombs are cut into the east-bank cliffs, overlooking the valley. Only two tombs are open, and both, very simple, contain eroded images and hieroglyphs but no colourful scenes and are likely to appeal only if you have a passion for rarely visited sites.

Minya

☎086 / POP 235,234

Minya, the 'Bride of Upper Egypt' (Arousa as-Sa'id), sits on the boundary between Upper and Lower Egypt. A provincial capital 245km south of Cairo, it was the capital of the Upper Egyptian cotton trade, but its factories now process sugar and produce soap and perfume.

When Minya was caught up in the Islamist insurgency of the 1990s, the government sent tanks and armoured personnel carriers, as they did again in 2013 to quell the pro-Muslim Brotherhood protests. Security has since stepped down, which is good news for visitors because Minya has one of the most pleasant town centres in Upper Egypt. With broad tree-lined streets, a wide corniche and some great, if shabby, early-20th-century buildings, central Minya has retained the feel of a more graceful era. At the time of our visit, this was one of the most relaxed places to visit between Cairo and Luxor.

Minya

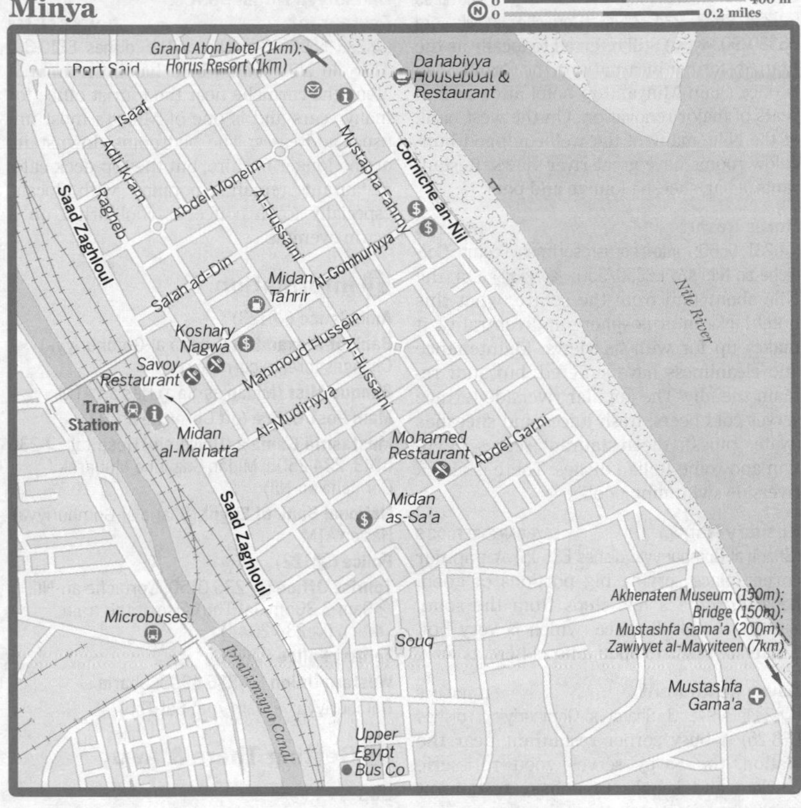

Sights

Beyond the pleasure of walking around the town centre and watching the Nile flow against the background of the Eastern Hills, Minya doesn't have many sights although that will change when the new museum opens. There is a **souq** (market) at the southern end of the town centre and the streets that run from it to Midan Tahrir are among the liveliest.

Hantours (horse-drawn carriages; per hour E£25 to E£35) can be rented for a leisurely ride around the town centre or along the corniche. **Feluccas** (Egyptian sailing boats; per hour E£30) can be rented at the landing opposite the tourist office for trips along the river and to Banana Island, which is good for a picnic.

Akhenaten Museum MUSEUM

The new Akhenaten Museum, on the east bank, is heading towards completion and will open, although no date has been set. If seems likely it will be home, for some months at least, to the iconic bust of Queen Nefertiti (now in Berlin) as well as other treasures from nearby Tell al-Amarna.

Zawiyyet al-Mayyiteen CEMETERY

On the east bank about 7km southeast of town, the large Muslim and Christian cemetery Zawiyyet al-Mayyiteen (Place of the Dead), consists of several hundred mudbrick mausoleums. Stretching for 4km from the road to the hills and said to be one of the largest cemeteries in the world, it is an interesting sight.

Sleeping & Eating

Minya has a decent selection of hotels, but these days many are not accepting foreigners or are suffering from the lack of custom. Eating options are few. Your best bet might be to eat in the hotels.

Grand Aton Hotel HOTEL $$

(☎234 2993, 234 2994; Corniche an-Nil; s/d US$80/90; ❄ ≋) Still referred to locally as the Etap (its former incarnation), the Grand Aton is once again Minya's top hotel after several years of major renovation. On the west bank of the Nile, many of the well-equipped bungalow rooms have great river views. Restaurants, a bar, sheesha lounge and pool.

Horus Resort HOTEL $$

(☎231 6660; info@horusresortmenia.com; Corniche an-Nil; s/d E£350/550; ❄ ≋) On the Nile about 1km from the centre, what this hotel lacks in atmosphere and centrality, it makes up for with its views. Maintenance and cleanliness have suffered, but staff remain friendly. The popular riverside terrace serves cold beers, fresh juices and sheeshas (water pipes); the restaurant serves Egyptian and some Italian dishes. There is also a riverside swimming pool.

Koshary Nagwa EGYPTIAN FAST FOOD $

(Sharia al-Gomhuriyya; dishes E£5-15) A popular corner place serving big portions of good, basic *kushari* a few steps from the souq. Beware the chilli sauce, which is very hot. There are plans to open a hotel here as well.

Savoy Restaurant EGYPTIAN $

(☎234 3494; 3 Sharia al-Gomhuriyya; dishes E£8-25) A busy corner restaurant near the station, the Savoy serves good rotisserie chicken and kebabs in a busy restaurant (with air-con). It also does takeaway.

Mohamed Restaurant EGYPTIAN $

(Sharia al-Hussaini; dishes E£5-15) This popular restaurant serves basic grills and salads on a street packed with food options, from juice stands to a bakery and patisserie.

Dahabiyya Houseboat & Restaurant FLOATING CAFE $$

(☎236 5596; Corniche an-Nil; dishes E£10-30) This old Nile sailing boat has been moored along the corniche near the tourist office for many years and is one of Minya's most unusual addresses. The bedrooms downstairs are no longer for hire, but the top-deck cafe-restaurant remains popular with locals, especially for a coffee or cool drink on a warm evening.

Information

Ambulance (☎123)

Bank of Alexandria (Sharia al-Gomhuriyya) Changes foreign currency.

Banque Misr (Midan as-Sa'a) Has an ATM.

Main Post Office (off Corniche an-Nil)

Mustashfa Gama'a (University Hospital; ☎236 6743, 234 2505; Midan Suzanne Mubarak/Corniche an-Nil)

National Bank of Egypt (Sharia al-Gomhuriyya) Has an ATM.

Police (☎122)

Tourist Office (☎236 0150; Corniche an-Nil; ⌚9am-3.30pm Sat-Thu) Also at the train station (☎234 2044).

Tourist Police (☎126)

Western Union (☎236 4905; Sharia al-Gomhuriyya; ⌚9am-7pm Sat-Thu)

Getting There & Away

BUS

The **Upper Egypt Bus Co** (☎236 3721; Sharia Saad Zaghloul) has hourly services to Cairo (E£12, four hours) from 6am. Buses leave for Hurghada at 10.30am and 10.30pm (E£50, six hours).

PLUNDERING THE PAST

Antiquity theft is nothing new in Egypt – people have been taking from tombs and other sites for millennia. But in the security void that followed Mubarak's 2011 downfall, many sites were plundered across the country. With continuing economic hardship giving more people a motive to go digging, looting continues to be widespread throughout Egypt. Famous sites, including the Egyptian Museum in Cairo, have suffered losses, but many lesser-known places, including El Hibeh and Mallawi's museum, have been plundered too. The unit of the Egyptian government charged with recovering antiquities has struggled to cope with the challenge, although some major pieces have been recovered from salesrooms abroad. One of the loudest defenders is Dr Monica Hanna, an Egyptologist who was at the Mallawi Museum in August 2013 when most of its 1000-plus antiquities were looted (more than half have since been recovered). Dr Hanna has since created Egypt's Heritage Taskforce, one of several organisations helping to protect antiquities, but the threat remains.

MICROBUS & SERVEES

A seat in a microbus or *servees* will cost E£30 to Cairo and E£15 to Asyut.

TRAIN

The tourist office (p168) in the station may be able to help with information. Trains to Cairo (three to four hours) have only 1st- and 2nd-class carriages and leave at least every 1½ hours starting at 4.25am. Trains heading south also leave fairly frequently, with the fastest trains departing from Minya between 11pm and 1am. Seven 1st-/2nd-class trains go all the way to Luxor (six to eight hours) and Aswan (eight to 11 hours), stopping at Asyut two hours), Sohag (three to four hours) and Qena (five to seven hours).

Beni Hasan

The necropolis of **Beni Hasan** (adult/student E£40/20; ⏲8am-5pm) occupies a range of east-bank limestone cliffs some 20km south of Minya. It is a superb and important location and has the added attraction of a rest house, occasionally open for drinks. Most tombs date from the 11th and 12th dynasties (2125–1795 BC), the 39 upper tombs belonging to nomarchs (local governors). Many remain unfinished and only four are currently open to visitors, but they are worth the trouble of visiting for the glimpse they provide of daily life and political tensions of the period.

A guard will accompany you from the ticket office, so baksheesh (tips) is expected (at least E£10). Try to see the tombs chronologically.

Sights

Tomb of Baqet (No 15) TOMB

Baqet was an 11th-dynasty governor of the Oryx nome. His rectangular tomb chapel has seven tomb shafts and some well-preserved wall paintings. They include Baqet and his wife on the left wall watching weavers and acrobats – mostly women in diaphanous dresses in flexible poses. Further along, animals, presumably possessions of Baqet, are being counted. A hunting scene in the desert shows mythical creatures among the gazelles.

The back wall shows a sequence of wrestling moves that are still used today. The right (south) wall is decorated with scenes from the nomarch's daily life, with potters, metalworkers and a flax harvest, among others.

Tomb of Kheti (No 17) TOMB

Kheti, Baqet's son, inherited the governorship of the Oryx nome from his father. His tomb chapel, with two of its original six papyrus columns intact, has many vivid painted scenes that show hunting, linen production, board games, metalwork, wrestling, acrobatics and dancing, most of them watched over by the nomarch. Notice the yogalike positions on the right-hand wall, between images of winemaking and herding. On the west-facing wall are images of 10 different trees.

Tomb of Amenemhat (No 2) TOMB

Amenemhat was a 12th-dynasty governor of Oryx. His tomb is the largest and possibly the best at Beni Hasan and, like that of Khnumhotep, its impressive facade and interior decoration mark a clear departure from the more modest earlier ones. Entered through a columned doorway and with its six columns intact, it contains beautifully executed scenes of farming, hunting, manufacturing and offerings to the deceased, who can also be seen with his dogs.

As well as the fine paintings, the tomb has a long, faded text in which Amenemhat addresses the visitors to his chapel: 'You who love life and hate death, say: Thousands of bread and beer, thousands of cattle and wild fowl for the ka of the hereditary prince…the Great Chief of the Oryx Nome…'

Tomb of Khnumhotep (No 3) TOMB

Khnumhotep was governor during the early 12th dynasty, and his detailed 'autobiography' is inscribed on the base of walls that contain the most detailed painted scenes. The tomb is famous for its rich, finely rendered scenes of plant, animal and bird life. On the left wall farmers are shown tending their crops while a scribe is shown recording the harvest. Also on the left wall is a representation of a delegation bringing offerings from Asia – their clothes, faces and beards are all distinct.

Speos Artemidos MONUMENT

(Grotto of Artemis) If the guardian agrees, you can follow a cliffside track that leads southeast for about 2.5km, then some 500m into a wadi to the rock-cut temple called the Speos Artemidos and referred to locally as Istabl Antar (Stable of Antar, an Arab warrior-poet and folk hero), but actually dedicated to the ancient Egyptian lion-goddess Pasht.

Dating back to the 18th dynasty, the small temple was started by Hatshepsut (1473–1458 BC) and completed by Tuthmosis III (1479–1425 BC). There is a small hall with roughly hewn Hathor-headed columns and an unfinished sanctuary. On the walls are scenes of Hatshepsut making offerings and, on its upper facade, an inscription describing how she restored order after the Hyksos, even though she reigned long after the event. Expect to be accompanied by a police escort and a guard (who will want baksheesh).

Getting There & Away

It may be possible to take a microbus from Minya to the east bank and then another heading south to Beni Hasan, but as elsewhere, this will take time. A taxi from Minya will cost anything from E£100 to E£200, depending on your bargaining skills and how long you stay at the site.

Beni Hasan to Tell al-Amarna

Forty kilometres south of Minya, near the town of Al-Ashmunein, **Hermopolis** is the site of the ancient city of Khemenu. Capital of the 15th Upper Egyptian nome, its name (Eight Town) refers to four pairs of snake and frog gods that, according to one Egyptian creation myth, existed here before the first earth appeared out of the waters of chaos. This was also an important cult centre of Thoth, god of wisdom and writing, whom the Greeks identified with their god Hermes, hence the city's Greek name, 'Hermopolis'.

Little remains of the wealthy ancient city, the most striking ruins being two colossal 14th-century-BC quartzite statues of Thoth as a baboon. These supported part of Thoth's temple, which was rebuilt throughout antiquity. A Middle Kingdom temple gateway and a pylon of Ramses II, using stone plundered from nearby Tell al-Amarna, also survive. The most interesting ruins are from the Coptic basilica, which reused columns and even the baboon statues, though first removing their giant phalluses.

Several kilometres south of Hermopolis and then 5km along a road into the desert, **Tuna al-Gebel** (Map p171; adult/student E£15/10; ⏲8am-5pm) was the necropolis of Hermopolis. Given the lack of tourists in the area, check with the Minya tourist office that the site is open.

At one time Tuna al-Gebel belonged to Akhetaten, the short-lived capital of Pharaoh Akhenaten, and along the road you pass one of 14 stelae marking the boundary of the royal city. The large stone stele carries Akhenaten's vow never to expand his city beyond this western limit of the city's farmlands and associated villages, nor to be buried anywhere else, although it seems he was eventually buried in the Valley of the Kings at Luxor. To the left, two damaged statues of the pharaoh and his wife Nefertiti hold offering tables; the sides are inscribed with figures of three of their daughters.

South of the stele, which is located about 5km past the village of Tuna al-Gebel, are the **catacombs** (Map p171) and tombs of the residents and sacred animals of Hermopolis. The dark catacomb galleries once held millions of mummified ibis, the 'living image of Thoth', and thousands of mummified baboons, sacrificed and embalmed by the Ptolemaic and Roman faithful. The subterranean cemetery extends for at least 3km, perhaps even all the way to Hermopolis. You need a torch to explore the galleries.

The nearby **Tomb of Petosiris** (Map p171) was built by a high priest of Thoth from the early Ptolemaic period. His templelike tomb, like his sarcophagus in the Egyptian Museum in Cairo, shows early Greek influence. The wonderful coloured reliefs of farming and the deceased being given offerings also show Greek influence, with the figures wearing Greek dress.

The guard may open several other tombs (for a baksheesh), the most interesting being the **Tomb of Isadora** (Map p171), a wealthy woman who drowned in the Nile during the rule of Antoninus Pius (AD 138–161). The tomb has few decorations, but does contain the unfortunate woman's **mummy**, with its teeth, hair and fingernails clearly visible.

The slow village service from Minya stops at Mallawi and from there a network of microbuses runs around the villages here. But unless you have time to burn, the only viable way to get around these sites is by taxi from Minya, perhaps continuing on to Asyut. Expect to pay E£100 to E£200, depending on the time you want to spend and your bargaining skills.

Tell al-Amarna

In the fifth year of his reign, Pharaoh Akhenaten (1352–1336 BC) and his queen Nefertiti abandoned the gods and priests of Karnak and established a new religion based on the worship of Aten, god of the sun disc.

They also built a new city, **Akhetaten** (Horizon of the Aten), on the east bank

Hermopolis, Tuna al-Gebel & Tell al-Amarna

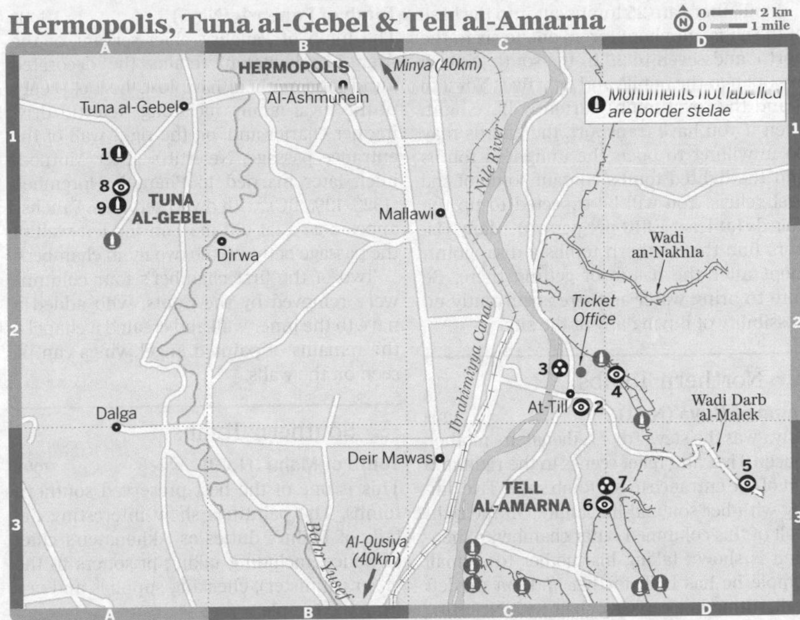

of the Nile, in the area now known as Tell al-Amarna, a beautiful yet solitary crescent-shaped plain, which extends about 10km from north to south. Bounded by the river and backed by a bay of high cliffs, this was the capital of Egypt for some 30 years.

Akhetaten was abandoned for all time after Akhenaten's death. His successor, a son by a minor wife, changed his name from Tutankhaten to Tutankhamun (1336–1327 BC), moved the capital back to Thebes, re-established the cult of Amun at Thebes, restored power to the Theban priesthood and brought an end to what is known as the Amarna Period. Akhetaten fell into ruin, its palaces and temples quarried during the reign of Ramses II for buildings in Hermopolis and other cities.

Archaeologists value the site because, unlike most places in Egypt, it was occupied for just one reign. Many visitors are attracted by the romance of Akhenaten's doomed project but the ruins, scattered across the desert plain, are hard to understand, the tombs nowhere near as interesting or well preserved as others along the Nile (although the remains of the north palace and the Great Temple of Aten can still be identified), and the visit can be disappointing.

Hermopolis, Tuna al-Gebel & Tell al-Amarna

Sights

1	Catacombs	A1
2	Great Temple of Aten	C2
3	North Palace	C2
4	Northern Tombs	D2
5	Royal Tomb of Akhenaten	D3
6	Southern Tombs	C3
7	Tell al-Amarna Necropolis	D3
	Tomb of Isadora	(see 8)
8	Tomb of Petosiris	A1
9	Tuna al-Gebel	A1

Sights

Two groups of cliff tombs, about 8km apart, make up the **Tell al-Amarna necropolis** (Map p171; adult/student E£25/15; 8am-4pm Oct-May, to 5pm Jun-Sep), which features some coloured, though defaced, wall paintings of life during the Aten revolution. Remains of temples and private or administrative buildings are scattered across a wide area: this was, after all, an imperial city.

There used to be a bus for touring the site but it was not running at the time of our visit. As the site is so large, the only viable way of visiting is to come by private taxi or with your own car.

In all, there are 25 tombs cut into the base of the cliffs, numbered from one to six in the north, and seven to 25 in the south. Not all are open to the public and only five (Nos 3 to 6 and the royal tomb) currently have light. Even if you have transport, the guards may be unwilling to open the unlighted tombs and the lighted tombs contain some of the best reliefs. You will be expected to tip the guards (at least E£10 per person). Many visitors find the southern tombs a disappointment after the hassle of getting there. Be sure to bring water as there is currently no possibility of buying any at the site.

Northern Tombs

Tomb of Huya (No 1) — TOMB

Huya was the steward of Akhenaten's mother, Queen Tiye, and relief scenes to the right and left of the entrance to his tomb show Tiye dining with her son and his family. On the right wall of this columned outer chamber, Akhenaten is shown taking his mother to a small temple he has built for her and, on the left wall, sitting in a carrying chair with Nefertiti.

Tomb of Meryre II (No 2) — TOMB

Meryre II was superintendent of Nefertiti's household, and to the left of the entrance, you will find a scene that shows Nefertiti pouring wine for Akhenaten.

Tomb of Ahmose (No 3) — TOMB

Ahmose's title was 'Fan-Bearer on the King's Right Hand'. Much of his tomb decoration was unfinished: the left-hand wall of the long corridor leading to the burial chamber shows the artists' different stages. The upper register shows the royal couple on their way to the Great Temple of Aten, followed by armed guards. The lower register shows them seated in the palace listening to an orchestra.

Tomb of Meryre I (No 4) — TOMB

High priest of the Aten, Meryre is shown, on the left wall of the columned chamber, being carried by his friends to receive rewards from the royal couple. On the right-hand wall, the royal couple are shown making offerings to the Aten disc; note here the rare depiction of a rainbow.

Tomb of Pentu (No 5) — TOMB

Pentu, the royal physician, was buried in a simple tomb. The left-hand wall of the corridor is decorated with images of the royal family at the Great Temple of Aten and of Pentu being appointed their physician.

Tomb of Panehsy (No 6) — TOMB

The tomb of Panehsy, chief servant of the Aten in Akhetaten, retains the decorated facade most others have lost. Inside, scenes of the royal family, including Nefertiti driving her chariot and, on the right wall of the entrance passage, Nefertiti's sister Mutnodjmet, later married to Pharaoh Horemheb (1323–1295 BC), with dwarf servants. Panehsy appears as a fat old man on the left wall of the passage between the two main chambers.

Two of the first chamber's four columns were removed by the Copts, who added a nave to the inner wall and created a chapel – the remains of painted angel wings can be seen on the walls.

Southern Tombs

Tomb of Mahu (No 9) — TOMB

This is one of the best preserved southern tombs. The paintings show interesting details of Mahu's duties as Akhenaten's chief of police, including taking prisoners to the vizier (minister), checking supplies and visiting the temple.

Tomb of Ay (No 25) — TOMB

This is the finest tomb at Tell al-Amarna. The images here reflect the importance of Ay and Tiyi, with scenes including the couple worshipping the sun and Ay receiving rewards from the royal family, including red-leather riding gloves. Ay wasn't buried here, but in the west valley beside the Valley of the Kings at Thebes.

Ay's titles were simply 'God's Father' and 'Fan-Bearer on the King's Right Hand' and he was vizier to three pharaohs before becoming one himself (he succeeded Tutankhamun and reigned from 1327 to 1323 BC). His wife Tiyi was Nefertiti's wet nurse.

Royal Tomb of Akhenaten

Akhenaten's own **tomb** (Map p171; additional ticket adult/student E£20/10) is in a ravine about 12km up the Royal Valley (Wadi Darb al-Malek), the valley that divides the north and south sections of the cliffs and where the sun was seen to rise each dawn. A well-laid road leads up the bleak valley. The guard will need to start up the tomb's generator. Very little remains inside. The right-hand chamber has damaged reliefs of Akhenaten and his family worshipping Aten. A raised rectangular outline in the burial chamber once held the sarcophagus, which is now in the Egyptian

Museum in Cairo (after being returned from Germany). Akhenaten himself was probably not buried here, although members of his family certainly were. Some believe he was buried in KV 55 in Luxor's Valley of the Kings, where his sarcophagus was discovered. The whereabouts of his mummy remains are a mystery.

Getting There & Away

Even if the security situation allows it, getting to Tell al-Amarna by public transport remains a challenge, and until the site bus starts running, it's pointless: the site is so large that it is impossible to visit on foot. So for now you need to take a taxi from Asyut, Minya or Mallawi and a long drive down the east bank of the river, or a crossing on the irregular car ferry (per car E£20). Expect to pay as much as E£150 to E£250 depending on where you start and how long you want to stay. Be sure to specify which tombs you want to visit or your driver may refuse to go to far-flung sites.

Tombs of Mir

The necropolis of the governors of Cusae, the **Tombs of Mir** (adult/student E£25/15; 9am-5pm Sat-Wed), as they are commonly known (sometimes also Meir), were dug into the barren escarpment during the Old and Middle Kingdoms. Nine tombs are decorated and open to the public; six others were unfinished and remain unexcavated.

Tomb No 1 and the adjoining **tomb No 2** are inscribed with 720 Pharaonic deities, but as the tombs were used as cells by early Coptic hermits, many faces and names of the gods were destroyed. In **tomb No 4** you can still see the original grid drawn on the wall to assist the artist in designing the layout of the wall decorations. **Tomb No 3** features a cow giving birth.

About 50 minutes' drive from Asyut towards Minya, the bus will drop you at Al-Qusiya. Few vehicles from Al-Qusiya go out to the Tombs of Mir, so you'll have to hire a taxi to take you there. Expect to pay at least E£50, depending on how long you spend at the site. A taxi from Asyut to Mir will cost E£70 to E£100. Ideally, you could combine this with a visit to Deir al-Muharraq.

Deir al-Muharraq

Deir al-Muharraq (Burnt Monastery), an hour's drive northwest of Asyut, is a place of pilgrimage, refuge and vows, where the strength of Coptic traditions can be experienced. The 120 resident monks believe that Mary and Jesus inhabited a cave on this site for six months and 10 days after fleeing from Herod. This was their longest stay at any of the numerous places where they are said to have rested in Egypt. Coptic tradition claims the **Church of al-Azraq** (Church of the Anointed) that sits over the cave and is the world's oldest Christian church, consecrated around AD 60. More certain is the presence of monastic life here since the 4th century. The current building dates from the 12th to 13th centuries. Unusually, the church contains two iconostases. The one to the left of the altar came from an Ethiopian Church of Sts Peter and Paul, which used to sit on the roof. Other objects from the Ethiopians are displayed in the hall outside the church.

The **keep** beside the church is an independent 7th-century tower, rebuilt in the 12th and 20th centuries. Reached by drawbridge, its four floors can serve as a mini-monastery, complete with its own small **Church of St Michael**, a refectory, accommodation and even burial space behind the altar.

Monks believe the monastery's religious significance is given in the Book of Isaiah.

> In that day there will be an altar to the Lord in the midst of the land of Egypt, and a pillar to the Lord at its border. It will be a sign and a witness to the Lord of Host in the land of Egypt; when they cry to the Lord because of oppressors he will send them a saviour, and will defend and deliver them. And the Lord will make himself known to the Egyptians; and the Egyptians will know the Lord in that day and worship with sacrifice and burnt offering, and they will make vows to the Lord and perform them.
>
> Isaiah 19:19–21

The monastery has done much to preserve Coptic tradition: monks here spoke the Coptic language until the 19th century (at that time there were 190 of them) and while other monasteries celebrate some of the Coptic liturgy in Arabic (for their Arabic-speaking congregation), here they stick to Coptic.

Also in the compound, the **Church of St George** (Mar Girgis) was built in 1880 with permission from the Ottoman sultan, who was still the official sovereign of Egypt. It is decorated with paintings of the 12 apostles and other religious scenes, its iconostasis is made from marble, and many of the icons are in Byzantine style. Tradition has it that the icon showing the Virgin and Child was painted by St Luke.

Remember to remove shoes before entering either church and respect the silence and sanctity of the place. For a week every year (usually 21–28 June), thousands of pilgrims attend the monastery's annual feast, a time when visitors may not be admitted.

You will usually be escorted around the monastery and, while there is no fee, donations are appreciated. Visits sometimes finish with a brief visit to the new church built in 1940 or the nearby gift shop or with a cool drink in the monastery's reception room.

About 50 minutes' drive from Asyut towards Minya, the bus will drop you at Al-Qusiya. From there, you may be able to get a seat in the local microbus (E£5) to the monastery.

Asyut

☎088 / POP 389,307

Asyut, 375km south of Cairo, was settled during Pharaonic times on a broad fertile plain bordering the west bank of the Nile and has preserved an echo of antiquity in its name. As Swaty, it was the ancient capital of the 13th nome of Upper Egypt. Surrounded by rich agricultural land and sitting at the end of one of Africa's great caravan routes, from sub-Saharan Africa and Sudan to Asyut via Al-Kharga Oasis, it has always been important commercially, if not politically. For centuries one of the main commodities traded here was slaves: caravans stopped here for quarantine before being traded, a period in which slavers used to prepare some of their male slaves for the harem.

Much of modern Asyut is an agglomeration of high-rises that carry neither trace nor reminder of the ancient Egyptian entrepôt. In the late 1980s this was one of the earliest centres of Islamist fomentation and there has been trouble here more recently. In the summer and autumn of 2000, it was also the scene of an apparition in which the Virgin Mary appeared to Copts and Muslims, in the words of one witness, 'with flashes of heavenly lights and spiritual doves'.

The standard of hotels has dropped significantly in the past few years so, although transport links make it a popular stopover between Minya and Luxor (as does its reputation for fruit and juices), you will find better hotels elsewhere along the Nile.

Sights

For a city of such history, Asyut has surprisingly little to show for itself, partly because most of the city still remains unexcavated and the ancient tombs in the hills on the edge of the irrigation are currently unvisited.

Asyut Barrage — LANDMARK

Until the Nile-side **Alexan Palace**, one of the city's finest 19th-century buildings, has been renovated and reopened, the most accessible monument to Asyut's period of wealth is the Asyut Barrage. Built over the Nile between 1898 and 1902 to regulate the flow of water into the Ibrahimiyya Canal and assure irrigation of the valley as far north as Beni Suef, it also serves as a bridge across the Nile.

As the barrage still has strategic importance, photography is forbidden, so you should keep your camera out of sight.

Banana Island — ISLAND

(Gezirat al-Moz) Banana Island, to the north of town, is a shady, pleasant place to picnic. You'll have to bargain with a felucca captain for the ride: expect to pay at least E£40 an hour.

Convent of the Holy Virgin — CONVENT

At Dirunka, some 11km southwest of Asyut, this convent was built near a cave where the Holy Family are said to have taken refuge during their flight into Egypt. Some 50 nuns and monks live at the convent, built into a cliff situated about 120m above the valley. One of the monks will be happy to show you around. You will need to go by taxi (E£20 to E£40).

During the Moulid (saints' festival) of the Virgin (held in the second half of August), many thousands of pilgrims come to pray here, carrying portraits of Mary and Jesus.

Sleeping

As a large provincial centre, Asyut has a selection of hotels but many are overpriced and noisy.

YMCA — HOSTEL $

(☎230 3018; Sharia el-Nemis; s/d E£30/50; ❄) This hostel, with a large garden, offers basic rooms (with fridges) that get booked out by Egyptian youth groups. Worth calling ahead to book.

Al-Watania Palace Hotel — HOTEL $$

(☎228 7981; Sharia al-Gomhuriyya; s/d US$60/80; ❄📶) The newest, smartest and largest hotel in Asyut has spacious rooms, an impressive lobby, various function rooms and more stars than anywhere else around. There is a choice of restaurants, although only the rooftop grill is currently operating. What you lose in location and atmosphere is made up for with comfort and service.

Assiutel Hotel HOTEL $$
(☎ 231 212; 146 Corniche an-Nil (Thawra); s US$47 & 67, d US$66 & 86; ❄) Overlooking the Nile and the noisy corniche, this was long the best place in town. It has two levels of rooms, neither particularly welcoming, the cheaper ones worn, but all with satellite TV, fridge and private bathroom. There is a dull restaurant (mains E£15 to E£30) and one of Asyut's only bars.

Eating

The mid-priced rooftop restaurant at Al-Watania Palace Hotel is among the more reliable places to eat, while the Assiutel is currently the only place in town serving alcohol. There are the usual fuul and ta'amiyya stands around the train station and some more upmarket options along the Nile, plus a very friendly cafe.

Kushari Galal EGYPTIAN FAST FOOD $
(Sharia Talaat Harb; dishes from E£5) The most reliable carbohydrate intake place in town – delicious, convenient and open late.

Casablanca Sweet Restaurant EGYPTIAN FAST FOOD $
(☎ 088 231 2727; Sharia Mohamed Tawfiq Khashba; dishes E£7-12) Come here for savoury *fiteer* (Egyptian flaky pizza), pizzas (though nothing to do with the Italian variety) and sweet crêpes.

Information

Ambulance (☎ 123)
Bank of Alexandria (Sharia Port Said; ⏲ 9am-2pm & 6-8pm Sun-Thu) Has an ATM.
Banque du Caire (Midan Talaat Harb) Has an ATM.
Banque Misr (Midan Talaat Harb) Has an ATM.
Gama'a Hospital (☎ 233 4500; University of Asyut)
Main Post Office (Sharia al-Geish)
Police (☎ 122)
Tourist Office (☎ 231 0010; Governorate Bldg, Corniche an-Nil (Thawra)) The very welcoming staff at the tourist office can provide maps of the city and help arrange onward travel.
Tourist Police (☎ 126)

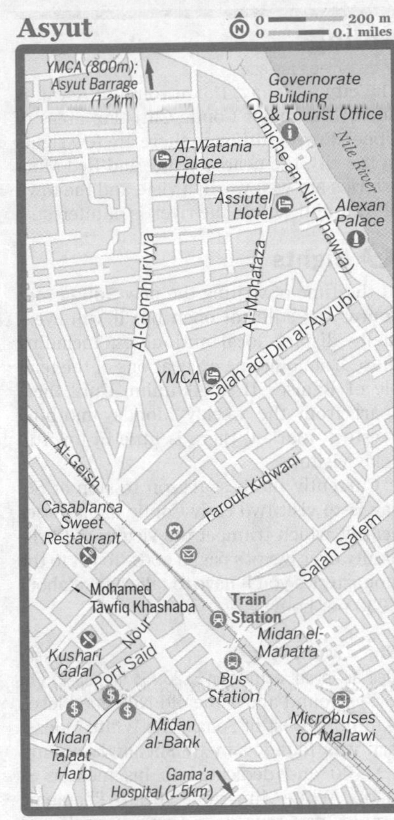

Getting There & Away

Asyut is a major hub for all forms of transport, although if you want to go by road to Luxor and the south you will have to change at Sohag.

AIR

Asyut's airport, 35km west of the city, has been reopened and there are now several flights a week to Cairo and the Gulf.

BUS

The **bus station** (☎ 233 0460) near the train station has services to Cairo, west to Dakhla and elsewhere in the New Valley, and to Hurghada.

MICROBUS & TAXI

There are no microbuses to Luxor, but there are to Mallawi. A private taxi to Luxor will cost at least E£150 each way.

TRAIN

There are several daytime trains to Cairo (four to five hours) and Minya (one hour), and about 10 daily south to Luxor (five to six hours) and Aswan (eight to nine hours). All stop in Sohag (one to two hours) and Qena (three to four hours).

Sohag

☎093 / POP 189,638

The city of Sohag, 115km south of Asyut, is one of the major Coptic Christian areas of Upper Egypt. Although there are few sights in the city, the nearby White and Red Monasteries are well worth a visit, and the town of Akhmim, across the river, is of interest.

Sights

At the time of writing the new **Sohag Museum** was still not open but it will eventually display local antiquities, including those from ongoing excavations of the temple of Ramses II in Akhmim. Until then, apart from the weekly Monday morning livestock market, there is little in town to delay visitors.

Currently the best reason to stop at Sohag is to visit two early Coptic monasteries nearby, which trumpet the victory of Christianity over Egypt's pagan gods. To get to the monasteries you'll have to take a taxi (about E£30 per hour).

White Monastery MONASTERY

(Deir al-Abyad; admission E£20; ⏲7am-dusk) On rocky ground above the old Nile flood level, 6km northwest of Sohag, the White Monastery was founded by St Shenouda around AD 400 and dedicated to his mentor, St Bigol. White limestone from Pharaonic temples was reused, and ancient gods and hieroglyphs still look out from some of the blocks. The design of the outer walls echoes ancient temples.

The monastery once supported a huge community of monks and boasted the largest library in Egypt. Research is finally underway on the manuscripts, while the monastery is currently home to 23 monks. The fortress walls still stand though they failed to protect the interior, most of which is in ruins.

Nevertheless, it is easy to make out the plan of the church inside the enclosure walls. Made of brick and measuring 75m by 35m, it follows a basilica plan, with a nave, two side aisles and a triple apse. The nave and apses are intact, the domes decorated with the Dormition of the Virgin and Christ Pantocrator. Nineteen columns, taken from an earlier structure, separate the side chapels from the nave. Visitors wanting to assist in services may arrive from 4am.

★**Red Monastery** MONASTERY

(Deir al-Ahmar; admission E£20; ⏲7am-midnight) The Red Monastery, 4km southeast of the White Monastery and hidden at the rear of a village, is one of the most remarkable Christian buildings in Egypt. Founded by Besa, a disciple of St Shenouda who, according to legend, was a thief who converted to Christianity, it was dedicated to St Bishoi.

The older of the monastery's two chapels, the Chapel of St Bishoi and St Bigol, dates from the 4th century AD and some 80% of its surfaces are still covered with painted plaster and frescos. An extensive restoration by the American Research Center in Egypt and USAID has revealed them in full glory. The quality and extent of the surviving work has led this chapel to be likened to the Hagia Sophia in İstanbul and the church of Ravenna as one of the great surviving monuments of late antiquity. The Chapel of the Virgin, across the open court, is a more modern and less interesting structure.

Akhmim TOWN

The satellite town of Akhmim, on Sohag's east bank, covers the ruins of the ancient Egyptian town of Ipu, itself built over an older predynastic settlement. It was dedicated to Min, a fertility god often represented by a giant phallus, equated with Pan by the Greeks (who later called the town Panopolis). A taxi to Akhmim should cost around E£30 per hour. The microbus costs E£4 and takes 15 minutes.

The current name echoes that of the god Min, but more definite links to antiquity were uncovered in 1982 when excavations beside the Mosque of Sheikh Naqshadi revealed an 11m-high statue of Meret Amun. This is the tallest statue of an ancient queen to have been discovered in Egypt. Meret Amun (Beloved of the Amun) was the daughter of Ramses II, wife of Amenhotep and priestess of the Temple of Min. She is shown here with flail in hand, wearing a ceremonial headdress and large earrings. Nearby, the remains of a seated statue of her father still retain some original colour.

Little is left of the temple itself, and the statue of Meret Amun now stands in a huge excavation pit, among the remains of a Roman settlement and houses of the modern town. Another excavation pit has been dug across the road and a more extensive excavation is underway nearby.

Akhmim was famed in antiquity for its textiles – one of its current weavers calls it 'Manchester before history'. The tradition continues today and opposite the statue of Meret Amun, across from the post office, a green door leads to a small weaving factory (knock if it is shut). Here you can see weavers at work and buy hand-woven silk and cotton textiles straight from the bolt (silk E£75 to E£100 per metre, cotton E£40) or packets of ready-made tablecloths and serviettes.

Sleeping & Eating

Sohag doesn't have the charm of Minya or the facilities of Luxor, but it does have a good hotel. The best food options are in the two main hotels. Budget *kushari,* fuul and ta'amiyya places line the roads near the train station. For something fancier, try the **floating cafe** tied up on the east bank, south of the bridge, which is good for grills. More romantic is a cafe on Gezira Island, reached by boat from the north side of the Hotel al-Nil.

Al-Safa Hotel HOTEL **$$**
(☎230 7701, 230 7702; Sharia al-Gomhuriyya, West Bank; s/d E£220/330; ❄ 📶) A well-placed west-bank spot across the river from the new museum and the best hotel in town (which isn't saying much). Rooms are comfortable and the riverside terrace is very popular in the evening for snacks, soft drinks and water pipes. Prices vary according to demand.

Hotel al-Nil HOTEL **$$**
(☎460 6253; Sharia al-Gamah, East Bank; s/d with Nile view E£300/325; ❄) The newest hotel in town, on the east bank near the new museum, across the water from Al-Safa. Most rooms have Nile views, but the standard of service, food and cleanliness are disappointing. The large riverside terrace is popular for tea and *sheesha*.

Information

Bank of Alexandria (Sharia al-Gomhuriyya; ⏲9am-2pm & 6-8pm Sun-Thu) Has an ATM; changes cash and travellers cheques.

Banque du Caire (Sharia al-Gomhuriyya) Has an ATM; changes cash and travellers cheques.

Post Office (Sharia al-Gomhuriyya)

Tourist Office (☎460 4913; Governorate Bldg; ⏲8.30am-3pm Sun-Thu) This helpful office, in the building beside the new museum on the east bank, can help arrange visits to the monasteries.

Tourist Police (☎460 4800)

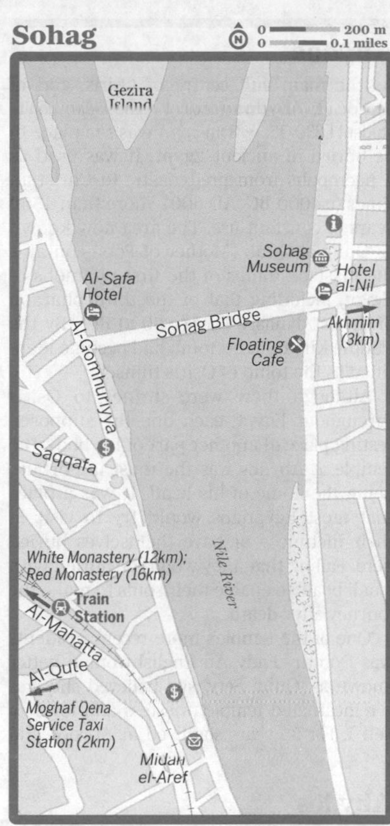

Getting There & Around

Train and private taxi remain the easiest way of moving around.

AIR

Since 2010, Sohag has had an international airport, with direct flights to Cairo and the Gulf.

MICROBUS

Microbus services are an option to the north and to Qena, but the station (ask for 'Moghaf Qena') is out of the centre and hard to find. You will need to change in Qena to get to Luxor. There are also microbuses from here to Al-Balyana for Abydos.

TRAIN

There is frequent train service north and south along the Cairo–Luxor main line, with a dozen daily trains to Asyut (one to two hours) and Luxor (three to four hours). The service to Al-Balyana (3rd-class only; one to two hours) is very slow.

Abydos

As the main cult centre of Osiris, god of the dead, **Abydos** (ancient name Ibdju; adult/student E£30/15; ⏲8am-5pm) was *the* place to be buried in ancient Egypt. It was used as a necropolis from predynastic to Christian times (c 4000 BC–AD 600), more than 4500 years of constant use. The area now known as Umm al-Qa'ab (Mother of Pots) contains the mastaba tombs of the first pharaohs of Egypt, including that of the third pharaoh of the 1st dynasty, Djer (c 3000 BC). By the Middle Kingdom his tomb had become identified as the tomb of Osiris himself.

Although there were shrines to Osiris throughout Egypt, each one the supposed resting place of another part of his body, the temple at Abydos was the most important, being the home of his head. It was a place that most Egyptians would try to visit in their lifetime – or have themselves buried here. Failing that, they would be buried with small boats to enable their souls to make the journey after death.

One of the temple's more recent residents was Dorothy Eady. An Englishwoman better known as 'Omm Sety', she believed she was a reincarnated temple priestess and lover of Seti I. For 35 years she lived at Abydos and provided archaeologists with information about the working of the temple, in which she was given permission to perform the old rites. She died in 1981 and was buried in the desert.

Sights

★Temple of Seti I MONUMENT

(Cenotaph; adult/student E£40/20) The first structure you'll see at Abydos is the striking Cenotaph or Great Temple of Seti I, which, after a certain amount of restoration work, is one of the most complete temples in Egypt. With beautiful decoration and plenty of atmosphere, it is the main attraction here, although the nearby Osireion is also wrapped in mystery and the desert views are spectacular.

This great limestone structure, unusually L-shaped rather than rectangular, was dedicated to the six major gods – Osiris, Isis and Horus, Amun-Ra, Ra-Horakhty and Ptah – and also to Seti I (1294–1279 BC) himself. In the aftermath of the Amarna Period, it is a clear statement of a return to the old ways. As you roam through Seti's dark halls and sanctuaries an air of mystery surrounds you.

The temple is entered through a largely destroyed pylon and two courtyards, built by Seti I's son Ramses II, who is depicted on

Abydos

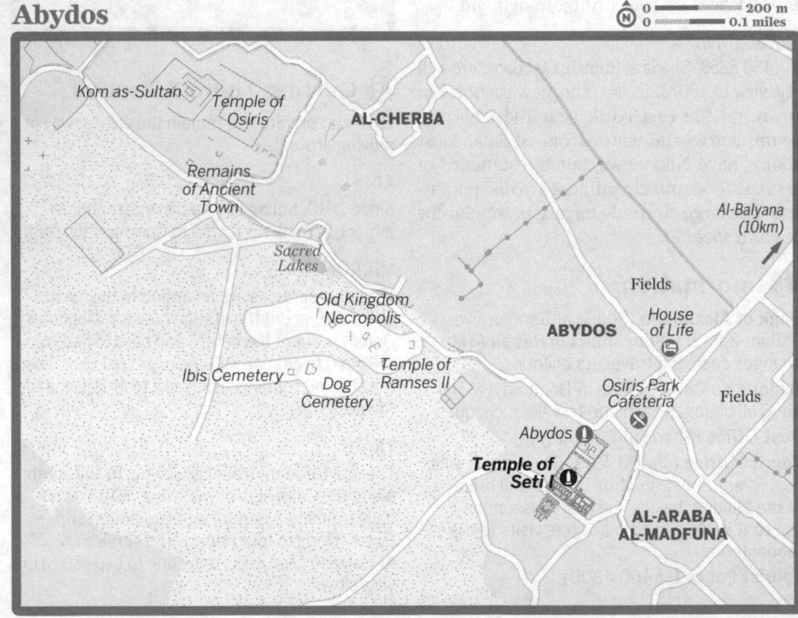

DON'T MISS

THE OSIREION

Directly behind the Temple of Seti I, the Osireion is a weird and wonderful building that continues to baffle Egyptologists, though it is usually interpreted as a cenotaph to Osiris. Originally thought to be an Old Kingdom structure, on account of the great blocks of granite used in its construction, it has now been dated to Seti's reign; its design is believed to be based on the rock-cut tombs in the Valley of the Kings. At the centre of its columned 'burial chamber', which lies at a lower level than Seti's temple, is a dummy sarcophagus. This chamber was originally surrounded by water, but thanks to a rising water table, the entire structure is now flooded, making inspection of the funerary and ritual texts carved on its walls hazardous.

the portico killing Asiatics and worshipping Osiris. Beyond is the first hypostyle hall, also completed by Ramses II. Reliefs depict the pharaoh making offerings to the gods and preparing the temple building.

The second hypostyle hall, with 24 sandstone papyrus columns, was the last part of the temple to have been decorated by Seti, although he died before the work was completed. The reliefs that were finished are of the highest quality. Particularly outstanding is a scene on the rear right-hand wall showing Seti standing in front of a shrine to Osiris, upon which sits the god himself. Standing in front of him are the goddesses Maat, Renpet, Isis, Nephthys and Amentet. Below is a frieze of Hapi, the Nile god.

At the rear of this second hypostyle hall are sanctuaries for each of the seven gods (right to left: Horus, Isis, Osiris, Amun-Ra, Ra-Horakhty, Ptah and Seti), which once held their cult statues. The Osiris sanctuary, third from the right, leads to a series of inner chambers dedicated to the god, his wife and child, Isis and Horus, and the ever-present Seti. More interesting are the chambers off to the left of the seven sanctuaries: here, in a group of chambers dedicated to the mysteries of Osiris, the god is shown mummified with the goddess Isis hovering above him as a bird, a graphic depiction of the conception of their son Horus.

Immediately to the left of this, the corridor known as Gallery of the Kings is carved with the figures of Seti I with his eldest son, the future Ramses II, and a long list of the pharaohs who preceded them.

Temple of Ramses II MONUMENT

Just northwest of Seti I's temple is the smaller and less-well-preserved structure built by his son Ramses II (1279–1213 BC). Although following the rectangular plan of a traditional temple, it has sanctuaries for each god Ramses considered important, including Osiris, Amun-Ra, Thoth, Min, the deified Seti I and, of course, Ramses himself. Although the roof is missing, the reliefs again retain a significant amount of their colour, clearly seen on figures of priests, offering bearers and the pharaoh anointing the gods' statues. You may not be allowed to visit this site.

Temple of Seti I

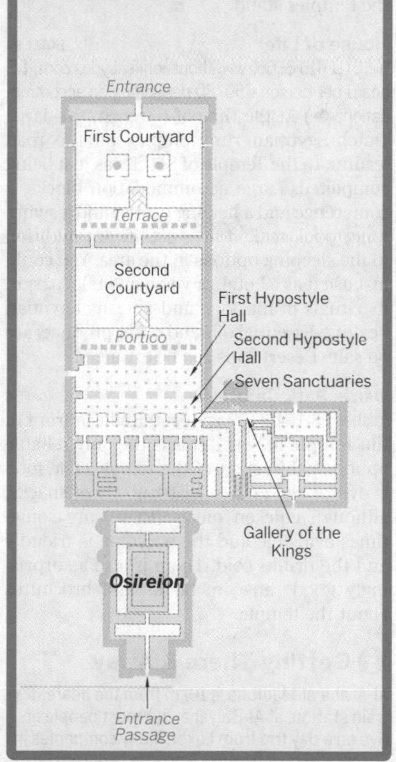

THE CULT OF OSIRIS

The most familiar of all ancient Egypt's myths is the story of Isis and Osiris, preserved in the writings of the Greek historian Plutarch (c AD 46–126) following a visit to Egypt. According to Plutarch, Osiris and his sister-wife Isis ruled on earth, bringing peace and prosperity to their kingdom. Seething with jealousy at their success, their brother Seth invited Osiris to a banquet and tricked him into climbing inside a chest. Once Osiris was inside, Seth sealed the coffin and threw it into the Nile, drowning his brother. Following the murder, the distraught Isis retrieved her brother-husband's body, only to have it seized back by Seth who dismembered it, scattering the pieces far and wide. But Isis refused to give up and, taking the form of a kite, searched for the separate body parts, burying each piece where she found it, which explains why there are so many places that claim to be Osiris' tomb.

Another version of the story has Isis collecting the parts of Osiris and reassembling them to create the first mummy, helped by Anubis, god of embalming. Then, using her immense magic, she restored Osiris to life for long enough to conceive their son Horus. Raised to avenge his father, Horus defeated Seth. While Horus ruled on earth, represented by each pharaoh, his resurrected father ruled as Lord of the Afterlife. A much-loved god, Osiris came to represent the hope for salvation after death, a concept as important to life-loving ancient Egyptians as it was to early Christians.

Sleeping & Eating

There are a couple of hotels and cafes in Al-Araba al-Madfuna, the village in which the temples stand.

House of Life HOTEL $$

(☎0111 415 6666; www.houseoflifeabydos.com; full board per person €50/80 depending on accommodation; @) At the time of our visit, this large Dutch-Egyptian–run complex on the road leading to the Temple of Seti I was just being completed. Large accommodation blocks, a conference and a healing centre, and a swimming pool, make this a significant addition to the sleeping options in the area. You could just use it as a hotel, or you could take part in its rituals of massage and ancient Egyptian healing. Essential oils and other products are on sale. Desert trips can be arranged.

Osiris Park Cafeteria CAFE $

(dishes E£20-40; ⌚7am-10pm) Right in front of the Temple of Seti I, this is the only reliable option within sight of the temple. The food is overpriced and consists mostly of snacks, although chicken meals (E£40) are sometimes available and the welcome is friendly and the drinks cold. There is also a surprisingly good range of books and brochures about the temple.

Getting There & Away

Al-Araba al-Madfuna is 10km from the nearest train station, at Al-Balyana, but most people arrive on a day trip from Luxor. Many companies in Luxor offer coach tours. A private taxi from Luxor should cost from E£300 return, depending on how long you want at the temple. A train leaves Luxor at 8.25am (1st-/2nd-class E£34/21, three hours). A private taxi from Al-Balyana to the temple will cost about E£50 depending on the wait time. A microbus from Al-Balyana costs E£3.

Qena

☎096 / POP 201,191

Ninety-one kilometres east of Al-Balyana, and 62km north of Luxor, Qena sits on a huge bend of the river and at the intersection of the main Nile road and the road running across the desert to the Red Sea towns of Port Safaga and Hurghada. A market town and provincial capital, it is a useful junction for a visit to the spectacular temple complex at Dendara, located just outside the town. It's also the place to be on the 14th of the Islamic month of Sha'ban, when the city's 12th-century patron saint, Abdel Rehim al-Qenawi, is celebrated.

Sights

Dendara TEMPLE

(adult/student E£40/20; ⌚7am-6pm) Dendara was an important administrative and religious centre as early as the 6th dynasty (c 2320 BC). Although built at the very end of the Pharaonic period, the **Temple of Hathor** (adult/student E£35/20; ⌚8am-5pm) at her cult site of Dendara is one of the iconic Egyptian buildings, mostly because it remains virtually intact, with a great stone roof and columns, dark chambers, underground crypts and twisting stairways all carved with hieroglyphs.

The goddess Hathor had been worshipped here since the Old Kingdom. But this great temple was only begun in the 30th dynasty, with much of the building undertaken by the Ptolemies and completed during the Roman period.

Few deities have such varied characteristics. Hathor was the goddess of love and sensual pleasures, patron of music and dancing: the Greeks appropriately associated her with their goddess Aphrodite. Like most Egyptian gods, Hathor was known by a range of titles, including 'the golden one', 'she of the beautiful hair' and 'lady of drunkenness', representing the joyful intoxication involved in her worship. As the 'Lady of the West' she was also protector of the dead. She is usually represented as a woman, a cow, or a woman with a headdress of cow's horns and sun disc, as she was the daughter of the sun-god Ra. She was also a maternal figure and as wife of Horus was often portrayed as the divine mother of the reigning pharaoh. In a famous statue from Deir al-Bahri in Luxor she even appears in the form of a cow suckling Amenhotep II (1427–1400 BC). Confusingly, she shared many of these attributes with the goddess Isis, who was also described as the mother of the king. In the end Isis essentially overshadowed Hathor as an ubermother when the legend of Isis and Osiris expanded to include the birth of Horus.

Dendara is 4km southwest of Qena on the west side of the Nile. Most visitors arrive from Luxor. A return taxi from Luxor will cost about E£200. There is also a day cruise to Dendara from Luxor. If you arrive in Qena by train, you will need to take a taxi to the temple (E£40 to the temple and back with some waiting time).

Sleeping & Eating

Qena is close enough to Luxor for most people not to need to stay over. Downtown and around the train station are restaurants and cafes serving fuul, *kushari* and pizza.

Dendara

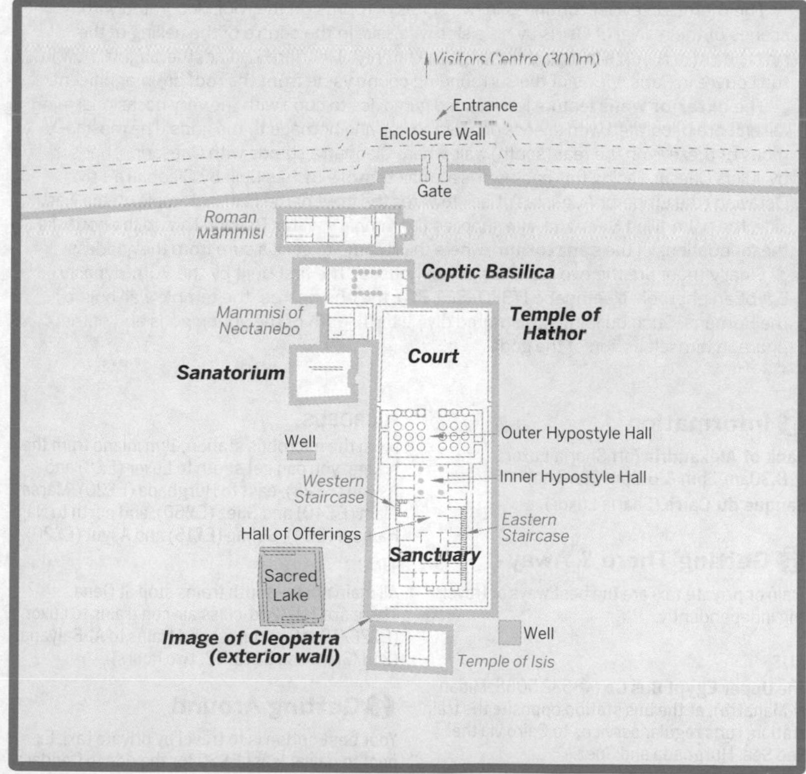

DENDARA: TOURING THE TEMPLE OF HATHOR

All visitors must pass through the **visitors centre**, with ticket office and bazaar. Beyond the towering gateway and mud walls, the temple was built on a slight rise. The entrance leads into the **outer hypostyle hall**, built by Roman emperor Tiberius, the first six of its 24 great stone columns adorned on all four sides with Hathor's head, defaced by Christians but still an impressive sight. The walls are carved with scenes of Tiberius and his Roman successors presenting offerings to the Egyptian gods: the message here, as throughout the temple, is the continuity of tradition, even under foreign rulers.

The inner temple was built by the Ptolemies. The smaller **inner hypostyle hall** again has Hathor columns and walls carved with scenes of royal ceremonials, including the founding of the temple. But notice the 'blank' cartouches that reveal much about the political instability of late Ptolemaic times – with such a rapid turnover of pharaohs, the stonemasons seem to have been reluctant to carve the names of those who might not be in the job for long. Things reached an all-time low in 80 BC when Ptolemy XI murdered his more popular wife and stepmother Berenice III after only 19 days of co-rule. The outraged citizens of Alexandria dragged the pharaoh from his palace and killed him in revenge.

Beyond the second hypostyle hall, you will find the **Hall of Offerings** leads to the **sanctuary**, the most holy part of the temple, home to the goddess' statue. A further Hathor statue was stored in the crypt beneath her temple, and brought out each year for the New Year Festival. It was carried into the Hall of Offerings, where it rested with statues of other gods before being taken to the roof. The **western staircase** is decorated with scenes from this procession. In the open-air kiosk on the southwestern corner of the roof, the gods awaited the first reviving rays of the sun-god Ra on New Year's Day. The statues were later taken down the **eastern staircase**, which is also decorated with this scene.

The theme of revival continues in two suites of rooms on the roof, decorated with scenes of the revival of Osiris by his sister-wife, Isis. In the centre of the ceiling of the **northeastern suite** is a plaster cast of the famous 'Dendara Zodiac', the original now in the Louvre in Paris. Views of the surrounding countryside from the roof are magnificent.

The **exterior walls** feature lion-headed gargoyles to cope with the very occasional rainfall and are decorated with scenes of pharaohs paying homage to the gods. The most famous of these is on the rear (south) wall, where Cleopatra stands with Caesarion, her son by Julius Caesar. Facing this back wall is a small **temple of Isis** built by Cleopatra's rival Octavian (the Emperor Augustus). Back towards the front of the Hathor temple on the west side, the palm-filled **Sacred Lake** supplied the temple's water. Beyond this, to the north, lie the foundations of the **sanatorium**, where the ill came to seek a cure from the goddess.

Finally there are the two *mammisi* (birth houses), the first built by the 30th-dynasty Egyptian pharaoh, Nectanebo I (380–362 BC), the one nearest the temple wall built by the Romans. Such buildings celebrated divine birth, both of the young gods and of the pharaoh himself as son of the gods.

Information

Bank of Alexandria (off Sharia Luxor; 8.30am-2pm & 6-8pm Sun-Thu)

Banque du Caire (Sharia Luxor)

Getting There & Away

Train or private taxi are the best ways of travelling independently.

BUS

The **Upper Egypt Bus Co** (532 5068; Midan al-Mahatta), at the bus station opposite the train station, runs regular services to Cairo via the Red Sea, Hurghada and Suez.

MICROBUS

From the microbus station, 1km inland from the bridge, you can get south to Luxor (E£8) and Aswan (E£28), east to Hurghada (E£20), Marsa Alam (E£40) and Suez (E£60), and north to Nag Hamadi (E£4), Sohag (E£15) and Asyut (E£20).

TRAIN

All main north–south trains stop at Qena. There are 1st-/2nd-class air-con trains to Luxor (E£26/18, 40 minutes) and trains to Al-Balyana (2nd/3rd class E£18/12, two hours).

Getting Around

Your best option is to travel by private taxi. Expect to pay at least E£50 for the ride to Dendara.

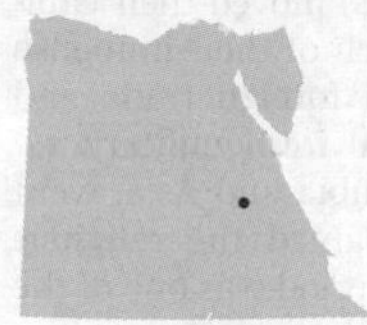

Nile Valley: Luxor

095 / POP 484,132

Includes ➡

Best Places to Eat

- Sofra Restaurant & Café (p222)
- Al-Moudira (p223)
- Silk Road (p223)
- Nile Valley Hotel (p223)
- As-Sahaby Lane (p222)

Best Places to Sleep

- Al-Moudira (p221)
- Hilton Luxor Resort & Spa (p218)
- Nefertiti Hotel (p216)
- Beit Sabée (p219)
- La Maison de Pythagore (p217)

Why Go?

Luxor is often called the world's greatest open-air museum, but that comes nowhere near describing this extraordinary place. Nothing in the world compares to the scale and grandeur of the monuments that have survived from ancient Thebes.

The setting is breathtakingly beautiful, the Nile flowing between the modern city and west-bank necropolis, backed by the enigmatic Theban escarpment. Scattered across the landscape is an embarrassment of riches, from the temples of Karnak and Luxor in the east to the many tombs and temples on the west bank.

Thebes' wealth and power, legendary in antiquity, began to lure Western travellers from the end of the 18th century. Depending on the political situation, today's traveller might be alone at the sights, or be surrounded by coachloads of tourists. Whichever it is, a little planning will help you get the most from the magic of the Theban landscape and its unparalleled archaeological heritage.

When to Go

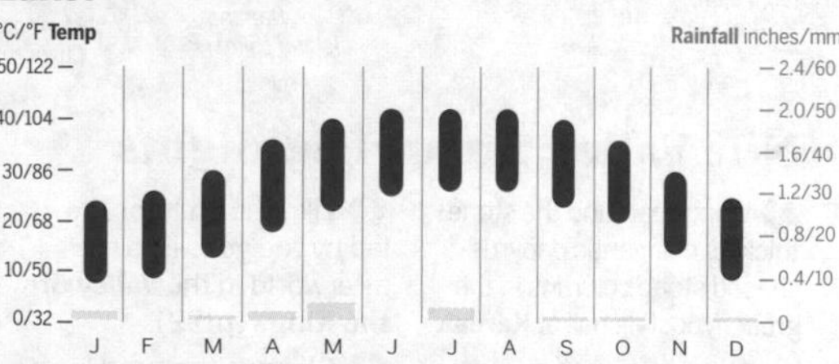

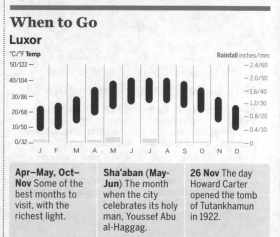

Apr–May, Oct–Nov Some of the best months to visit, with the richest light.

Sha'aban (May–Jun) The month when the city celebrates its holy man, Youssef Abu al-Haggag.

26 Nov The day Howard Carter opened the tomb of Tutankhamun in 1922.

History

Thebes (ancient Waset) became important in the Middle Kingdom period (2055–1650 BC). The 11th-dynasty Theban prince Montuhotep II (2055–2004 BC) reunited Upper and Lower Egypt, made Thebes his capital and increased Karnak's importance as a cult centre to the local god Amun with a temple dedicated to him. The 12th-dynasty pharaohs (1985–1795 BC) moved their capital back north, but much of their immense wealth from expanded foreign trade and agriculture, and tribute from military expeditions made into Nubia and Asia, went to Thebes, which remained the religious capital. This 200-year period was one of the

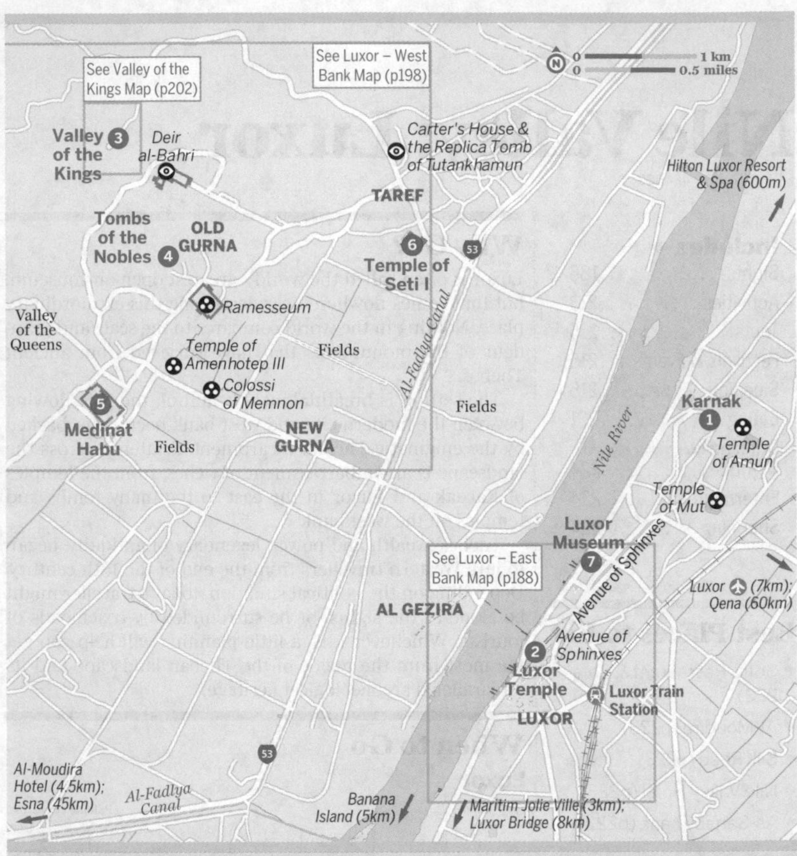

Nile Valley: Luxor Highlights

1. Wander around the stone thickets of gigantic papyrus-shaped stone columns in the great hypostyle hall at **Karnak** (p186).
2. Marvel at the stunning architecture of the **Luxor Temple** (p193) and return later at night to see the beautifully lit carvings on the walls.
3. Like the pharaoh, be led by the gods into the afterworld in the **Valley of the Kings** (p199).
4. Glimpse the good life of an ancient Egyptian aristocrat on the tomb walls in the **Tombs of the Nobles** (p197).
5. Wander through the best-preserved Theban temple, **Medinat Habu** (p208), in the soft, late-afternoon light.
6. Sense the spirituality of the rarely visited **Temple of Seti I** (p210).
7. Visit the numerous treasures of the compact **Luxor Museum** (p195).

LUXOR IN...

Two Days

If you've only got two days in Luxor, your schedule will be full on. Spend the first day on the east bank, starting early morning with a visit of the **Temples of Karnak** (p186). After Karnak stroll along the corniche to the **Luxor Museum** (p195). After a late lunch at Sofra (p222), visit **Luxor Temple** (p193) in the golden glow of the afternoon sun. Return after dinner to see the temple floodlit. The next day take a taxi for a day to the west bank, and start early again to avoid the crowds at the **Valley of the Kings** (p199). On the way back visit **Howard Carter's Hous**e (p210), with its brilliant replica of Tutankhamun's tomb, and the **Memorial Temple of Hatshepsut** (p206). After lunch visit the **Tombs of the Nobles** (p197), or the wonderful temple of Ramses III at **Medinet Habu** (p208).

Four Days

Four days allows for a more leisurely schedule. Allow one extra day on the west bank to visit the **Tombs of the Nobles** (p197), the **Ramesseum** (p209) and the **Temple of Seti I** (p210), and take a day trip to the amazing **temples of Dendara** (p180) and **Abydos** (p178).

richest times throughout Egyptian history, which witnessed a great flourishing of architecture and the arts, and major advances in science.

It was the Thebans again, under Ahmose I, who, after the Second Intermediate Period (1650–1550 BC), drove out the ruling Asiatic Hyksos and unified Egypt. Because of his military victories and as the founder of the 18th dynasty, Ahmose was deified and worshipped at Thebes for hundreds of years. This was the beginning of the glorious New Kingdom (1550–1069 BC), when Thebes reached its apogee. It was home to tens of thousands of people, who helped construct many of its great monuments.

The greatest contributor of all to Thebes was probably Amenhotep III (1390–1352 BC). He made substantial additions to the temple complex at Karnak, and built his great palace, Malqata, on the west bank, with a large harbour for religious festivals and the largest memorial temple ever built. Very little of the latter is left beyond the so-called Colossi of Memnon, the largest monolithic statue ever carved. His son Amenhotep IV (1352–1336 BC), who later renamed himself Akhenaten, moved the capital from Thebes to his new city of Akhetaten (Tell al-Amarna), worshipped one god only (Aten the solar god), and brought about dramatic changes in art and architecture. After his death, the powerful priesthood was soon reinstated under Akhenaten's successor, Tutankhamun (1336–1327 BC), who built very little but became the best-known pharaoh ever when his tomb was discovered full of treasure in 1922. Ramses II (1279–1213 BC) may have exaggerated his military victories, but he too was a great builder and added the magnificent hypostyle hall to Karnak, other halls to Luxor Temple, and built the Ramesseum and two magnificent tombs in the Valley of the Kings for himself and his many sons.

The decline of Pharaonic rule was mirrored by Thebes' gradual slide into insignificance: when the Persians sacked Thebes, it was clear the end was nigh. Mud-brick settlements clung to the once mighty Theban temples, and people hid within the stone walls against marauding desert tribes. Early Christians built churches in the temples, carved crosses on the walls and scratched out reliefs of the pagan gods. The area fell into obscurity in the 7th century AD after the Arab invasion, and the only reminder of its glorious past was the name bestowed on it by its Arab rulers: Al-Uqsur (The Fortifications), giving modern Luxor its name. By the time European travellers arrived here in the 18th century, Luxor was little more than a large Upper Egyptian village, known more for its 12th-century saint, Abu al-Haggag, buried above the mound of Luxor Temple, than for its half-buried ruins.

The growth of Egyptomania changed that. Napoleon arrived in 1798 wanting to revive Egypt's greatness and, with the publication of the *Description de l'Egypte,* did manage to revive interest in Egypt. European exhibitions of mummies, jewellery and other spectacular funerary artefacts from Theban tombs (often found by plundering adventurers rather than enquiring scholars) made Luxor an increasingly popular destination for travellers. By 1869, when Thomas Cook brought his first group of tourists to Egypt, Luxor was one of the highlights. Mass tourism had arrived and Luxor regained its place on the world map.

The 1960s saw the start of modern mass tourism on the Nile with Luxor as its epicentre, with more hotels and sights than anywhere else in southern Egypt. The town has since grown into a city of several hundred thousand people, almost all of them dependant on tourism. In the past couple of decades, there have been booms and crashes, the latest crash brought on by the riots that ended the presidency of Hosni Mubarak. Tourist numbers have been down since then and people in Luxor and elsewhere in the south have suffered.

Sights

Luxor sights are spread on the east and west banks of the Nile. Start on the east bank, where visitors will find most of the hotels, the modern town of Luxor and the temple complexes of Luxor and Karnak. The west bank, traditionally the 'side of the dead', is where the mortuary temples and necropolis are located.

East Bank

Temples of Karnak

More than a temple, **Karnak** (238 0270; Sharia Maabad al-Karnak; adult/student E£65/40; 6am-6pm; P) is an extraordinary complex of sanctuaries, kiosks, pylons and obelisks dedicated to the Theban gods and the greater glory of pharaohs. Everything is on a gigantic scale: the site covers over 2 sq km, large enough to contain about 10 cathedrals, while its main structure, the Temple of Amun, is one of the world's largest religious complexes. This was where the god lived on earth, surrounded by the houses of his wife Mut and their son Khonsu, two other huge temple complexes on this site. Built, added to, dismantled, restored, enlarged and decorated over nearly 1500 years, Karnak was the most important place of worship in Egypt during the New Kingdom, when it was called Ipet-Sut, meaning 'The Most Esteemed of Places'.

The most important place of worship was the massive Amun Temple Enclosure (Precinct of Amun), dominated by the great Temple of Amun-Ra, with its famous hypostyle hall, a spectacular forest of giant papyrus-shaped columns. On its southern side is the **Mut Temple Enclosure**, once linked to the main temple by an avenue of ram-headed sphinxes. To the north is the Montu Temple Enclosure, which honoured the local Theban war god. The 3km paved avenue of human-headed sphinxes that once linked the great Temple of Amun at Karnak with Luxor Temple is now again being cleared. Most of what you can see was built by the powerful pharaohs of the 18th to 20th dynasties (1570–1090 BC), who spent fortunes on making their mark in this most sacred of places. Later pharaohs extended and rebuilt the complex, as did the Ptolemies and early Christians. The further into the complex you venture, the older the structures.

Wandering through this gigantic complex is one of the highlights of any visit to Egypt. The light is most beautiful in the early morning or later afternoon, and the temple is quieter then, as later in the morning the tour groups and loads of day trippers from Hurghada arrive. It pays to visit more than once, to make sense of the overwhelming jumble of ancient remains.

RESOURCES

Luxor Egypt (www.luxoregypt.org) Has information on Luxor.

Theban Mapping Project (www.thebanmappingproject.com) has history, images and news from the Valley of the Kings

Flats in Luxor (www.flatsinluxor.com) Accommodation, guide and tour bookings.

Luxor Times (http://luxortimesmagazine.blogspot.co.uk) The local English-language paper.

★ **Amun Temple Enclosure** TEMPLE

(Map p190; Karnak; adult/student E£80/40) Amun-Ra was the local god of Karnak (Luxor) and during the New Kingdom, when the princes of Thebes ruled Egypt, he became the preeminent state god, with a temple that reflected his status. At the height of its power, the temple owned 421,000 head of cattle, 65 cities, 83 ships and 2764 sq km of agricultural land and had 81,000 people working for it. The shell that remains, sacked by Assyrians and Persians, is grand, beautiful and inspiring.

The **Quay of Amun** was the dock where the large boats carrying the statues of the gods moored during festivals. From paintings in the tomb of Nakht and elsewhere we know that there were palaces to the north of the quay and that these were surrounded by lush gardens. On the east side, a ramp slopes down to the processional **avenue of ram-headed sphinxes**. These lead to the massive unfinished **first pylon**, the last to be built, during the reign of Nectanebo I (30th dynasty). The inner side of the pylon still has the massive mud-brick construction ramp, up which blocks of stone for the pylon were dragged with rollers and ropes. Napoleon's expedition recorded blocks still on the ramp.

➡ Great Court

Behind the first pylon lies the Great Court, the largest area of the Karnak complex. To the left is the **Temple of Seti II** with three small chapels that held the sacred barques of Mut, Amun and Khonsu during the lead-up to the Opet Festival. In the southeastern corner (far right) is the well-preserved **Temple of Ramses III**, a miniature version of the pharaoh's temple at Medinat Habu. The temple plan is simple and classic: pylon, open court, vestibule with four Osirid columns and four columns, hypostyle hall with eight columns and three barque chapels for Amun, Mut and Khonsu. At the centre of the court is a 21m column with a papyrus-shaped capital – the only survivor of 10 columns that originally stood here – and a small alabaster altar, all that remains of the Kiosk of Taharka, the 25th-dynasty Nubian pharaoh.

The **second pylon** was begun by Horemheb, the last 18th-dynasty pharaoh, and continued by Ramses I and Ramses II, who also raised three colossal red-granite statues of himself on either side of the entrance; one is now destroyed.

➡ Great Hypostyle Hall

Beyond the second pylon is the extraordinary Great Hypostyle Hall, one of the greatest religious monuments ever built. Covering 5500 sq metres (enough space to contain both Rome's St Peter's Basilica and London's St Paul's Cathedral) the hall is an unforgettable forest of 134 towering stone pillars. Their papyrus shape symbolises a swamp, of which there were so many along the Nile. Ancient Egyptians believed that these plants surrounded the primeval mound on which life was first created. Each summer when the Nile began to flood, this hall and its columns would fill with several feet of water. Originally, the columns would have been brightly painted – some colour remains – and roofed, making it pretty dark away from the lit main axis. The size and grandeur of the pillars and the endless decorations are overwhelming: take your time, sit for a while and stare at the dizzying spectacle.

The hall was planned by Ramses I and built by Seti I and Ramses II. Note the difference in quality between the delicate raised relief in the northern part, by Seti I, and the much cruder sunken relief work, added by Ramses II in the southern part of the hall. The cryptic scenes on the inner walls were intended for the priesthood and the royalty who understood the religious context, but the outer walls are easier to comprehend, showing the pharaoh's military prowess and strength, and his ability to bring order to chaos.

On the back of the **third pylon**, built by Amenhotep III, to the right the pharaoh is shown sailing the sacred barque during the Opet Festival. Tuthmosis I (1504–1492 BC) created a narrow court between the **third** and **fourth pylons**, where four obelisks stood, two each for Tuthmosis I and Tuthmosis III (1479–1425 BC). Only the bases remain except for one, 22m high, raised for Tuthmosis I.

➡ Inner Temple

Beyond the fourth pylon is the **Hypostyle Hall of Tuthmosis III** built by Tuthmosis I in precious wood, and altered by Tuthmosis III with 14 columns and a stone roof. In this court stands one of the two magnificent

DON'T MISS

THE BEST TOMBS

With so many tombs to choose from, the following are the highlights of the Theban necropolis:

Valley of the Kings

- ➡ Tuthmosis III
- ➡ Amenhotep II
- ➡ Horemheb

Valley of the Queens

- ➡ Amunherkhepshef

Tombs of the Nobles

- ➡ Nakht
- ➡ Sennofer
- ➡ Ramose

Deir al-Medina

- ➡ Sennedjem

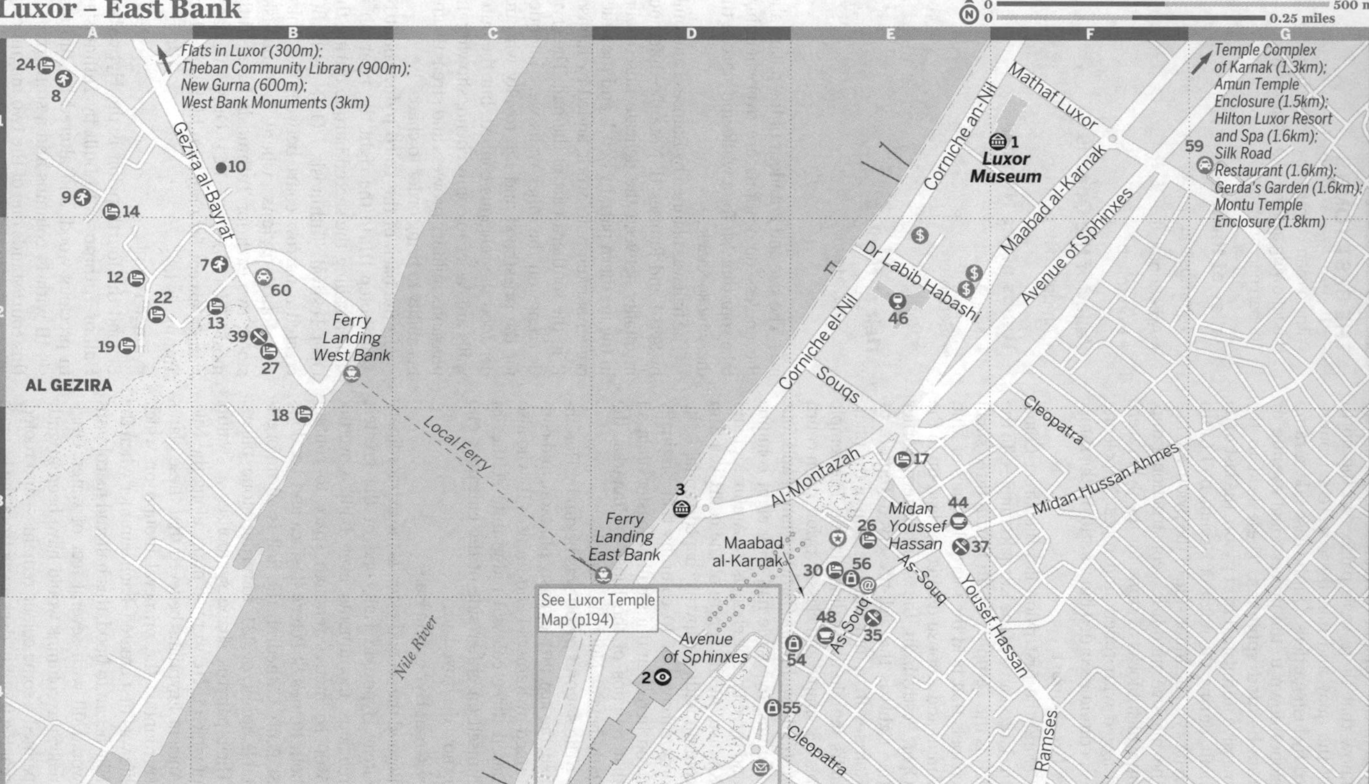
Luxor – East Bank
0 500 m
0 0.25 miles
A
B
C
D
E
F
G
1
2
3
4
Flats in Luxor (300m); Theban Community Library (900m); New Gurna (600m); West Bank Monuments (3km)
Temple Complex of Karnak (1.3km); Amun Temple Enclosure (1.5km); Hilton Luxor Resort and Spa (1.6km); Silk Road Restaurant (1.6km); Gerda's Garden (1.6km); Montu Temple Enclosure (1.8km)
Gezira al-Bayrat
AL GEZIRA
Ferry Landing West Bank
Local Ferry
Nile River
Ferry Landing East Bank
See Luxor Temple Map (p194)
Avenue of Sphinxes
Maabad al-Karnak
Al-Montazah
Corniche el-Nil
Corniche an-Nil
Souqs
Dr Labib Habashi
Mathaf Luxor
Maabad al-Karnak
Avenue of Sphinxes
1 Luxor Museum
Cleopatra
Midan Hussan Ahmes
Midan Youssef Hassan
As-Souq
Yousef Hassan
Ramses
Cleopatra
1
2
3
7
8
9
10
12
13
14
17
18
19
22
24
26
27
30
35
37
39
44
46
48
54
55
56
59
60

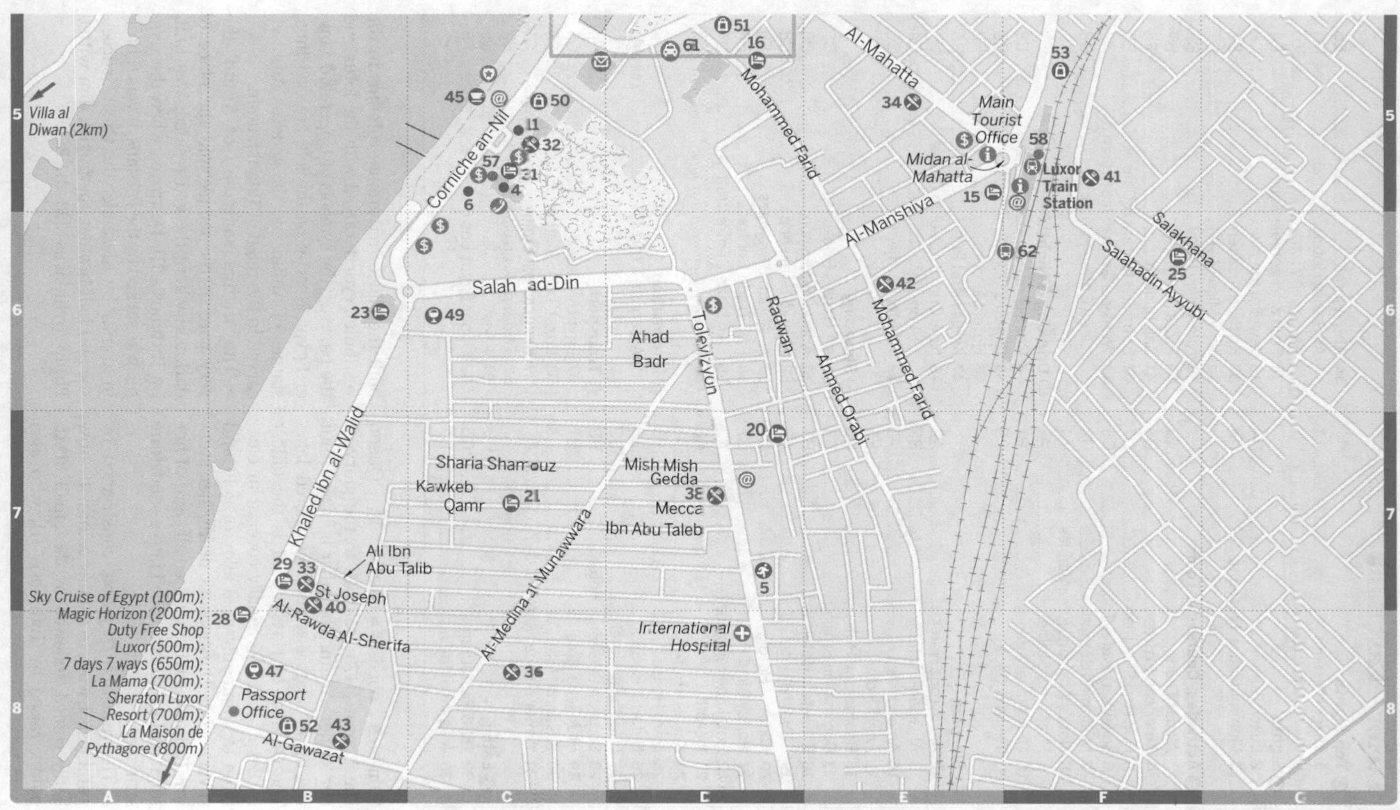

Villa al Diwan (2km)
45
50
51
61
16
53
Al-Mahatta
34
Main Tourist Office
58
Midan al-Mahatta
Luxor Train Station
41
15
62
Mohammed Farid
Corniche an-Nil
11
32
57
31
4
6
Al-Manshiya
Salakhana
25
Salahadin Ayyubi
42
Salah ad-Din
23
49
Televizyon
Radwan
Ahmed Orabi
Mohammed Farid
Ahad
Badr
20
Sharia Sharmouz
Kawkeb Qamr
21
Mish Mish Gedda
38
Mecca
Ibn Abu Taleb
Khaled ibn al-Walid
Al-Medina al-Munawwara
Ali Ibn Abu Talib
29
33
St Joseph
40
5
Al-Rawda Al-Sherifa
28
International Hospital
36
47
Passport Office
52
43
Al-Gawazat
Sky Cruise of Egypt (100m); Magic Horizon (200m); Duty Free Shop Luxor(500m); 7 days 7 ways (650m); La Mama (700m); Sheraton Luxor Resort (700m); La Maison de Pythagore (800m)
A
B
C
D
E
F
G
5
6
7
8

Luxor – East Bank

Top Sights
1 Luxor Museum ... F1

Sights
2 Luxor Temple ... D4
3 Mummification Museum ... D3

Activities, Courses & Tours
Aladin Tours ... (see 26)
4 American Express ... C5
5 Hod Hod Suleiman ... D7
6 Jolley's Travel & Tours ... C5
7 Mohamed Setouhy ... B2
8 Nobi's Arabian Horse Stables ... A1
9 Pharaoh's Stables ... A1
10 QEA Travel Agency ... B1
11 Thomas Cook ... C5

Sleeping
12 Al-Fayrouz Hotel ... A2
13 Al-Gezira Hotel ... B2
14 Amon Hotel ... A1
15 Anglo Hotel ... E5
16 Boomerang Hotel ... D5
17 Domina Inn Emilio ... E3
18 El-Mesala Hotel ... B3
19 El-Nakhil Hotel ... A2
20 Fontana Hotel ... D7
21 Happy Land Hotel ... C7
22 Hotel Sheherazade ... A2
23 Iberotel Luxor ... B6
24 Kareem Hotel ... A1
25 Mara House ... F6
26 Nefertiti Hotel ... E3
27 Nile Valley Hotel ... B2
28 Sonesta St George Hotel ... B8
29 St Joseph Hotel ... B7
30 Susanna Hotel ... E3
31 Winter Palace Hotel ... C5

Eating
32 1886 Restaurant ... C5
33 A Taste of India ... B7
34 Abu Ashraf ... E5
Al-Gezira Hotel ... (see 13)
As-Sahaby Lane ... (see 26)
35 Fruit & Vegetable Souq ... E4
36 Jewel of the Nile ... C8
37 Koshari Alzaeem ... E3
38 New Mish Mish ... D7
39 Nile Valley Hotel ... B2
40 Pizza Roma.It ... B7
41 Salahadeen ... F5
42 Sofra Restaurant & Café ... E6
43 Wenkie's German Ice Cream & Iced Coffee Parlour ... B8

Drinking & Nightlife
44 Chez Omar ... E3
45 Cilantro ... C5
46 Hotel Mercure ... E2
47 Kings Head Pub ... B8
48 New Oum Koulsoum Coffee Shop ... E4
49 Tutotel Partner Hotel ... C6

Shopping
50 AA Gaddis Bookshop ... C5
51 Aboudi Bookshop ... D5
52 Aboudi Bookshop ... B8
53 Al-Ahram Beverages ... F5
54 Fair Trade Centre ... E4
55 Fair Trade Centre Craft ... D4
56 Habiba ... E3

Information
American Express ... (see 4)

Transport
57 EgyptAir ... C5
58 Luxor Train Station ... F5
59 Service Taxi Station ... G1
60 Taxi & pick-up parking lot ... B2
61 Taxis ... D5
62 Upper Egypt Bus Co ... F6

30m-high obelisks erected by Queen Hatshepsut (1473–1458 BC) to the glory of her 'father' Amun. The other is broken but the upper shaft lies near the sacred lake. The **Obelisk of Hatshepsut** is the tallest in Egypt, its tip originally covered in electrum (a commonly used alloy of gold and silver). After Hatshepsut's death, her stepson Tuthmosis III eradicated all signs of her reign and had them walled into a sandstone structure.

The ruined **fifth pylon**, constructed by Tuthmosis I, leads to another colonnade now badly ruined, followed by the small **sixth pylon**, raised by Tuthmosis III, who also built the pair of red-granite columns in the vestibule beyond, carved with the lotus and the papyrus, the symbols of Upper and Lower Egypt. Nearby, on the left, are two huge statues of Amun and the goddess Amunet, carved in the reign of Tutankhamun.

The original **sanctuary of Amun**, the very core of the temple and the place of darkness where the god resided, was built by Tuthmosis III. Destroyed when the temple was sacked by the Persians, it was rebuilt in granite by Alexander the Great's successor and half-brother, the fragile, dim-witted Philip Arrhidaeus (323–317 BC).

East of the shrine of Philip Arrhidaeus is the oldest-known part of the temple, the **Middle Kingdom Court**, where Sesostris I built a shrine, the foundation walls of which have been found. On the northern wall of the court is the **Wall of Records**, a running tally of the organised tribute the pharaoh exacted in honour of Amun from his subjugated lands.

➡ Great Festival Hall of Tuthmosis III

At the back of the Middle Kingdom Court is the Great Festival Hall of Tuthmosis III. It is an unusual structure with carved stone columns imitating tent poles, perhaps a reference to the pharaoh's life under canvas on his frequent military expeditions abroad. The columned vestibule that lies beyond, generally referred to as the Botanical Gardens, has wonderful, detailed relief scenes of the flora and fauna that the pharaoh had encountered during his campaigns in Syria and Palestine, and had brought back to Egypt.

➡ Secondary Axis of the Amun Temple Enclosure

The courtyard between the Hypostyle Hall and the **seventh pylon**, built by Tuthmosis III, is known as the **cachette court**, as thousands of stone and bronze statues were discovered here in 1903. The priests had the old statues and temple furniture they no longer needed buried around 300 BC. Most statues were sent to the Egyptian Museum in Cairo, but some remain, standing in front of the seventh pylon, including four of Tuthmosis III on the left.

The well-preserved **eighth pylon**, built by Queen Hatshepsut, is the oldest part of the north–south axis of the temple, and one of the earliest pylons in Karnak. Carved on it is a text she falsely attributed to Tuthmosis I, justifying her taking the throne of Egypt.

East of the seventh and eighth pylons is the **sacred lake**, where, according to Herodotus, the priests of Amun bathed twice daily and nightly for ritual purity. On the northwestern side of the lake is part of the Fallen Obelisk of Hatshepsut showing her coronation, and a Giant Scarab in stone dedicated by Amenhotep III to Khepri, a form of the sun god.

In the southwestern corner of the enclosure is the **Temple of Khonsu**, god of the moon, and son of Amun and Mut. It can be reached from a door in the southern wall of the Hypostyle Hall of the Temple of Amun, via a path through various blocks of stone. The temple, mostly the work of Ramses III and enlarged by later Ramesside rulers, lies north of **Euergetes' Gate** and the avenue of sphinxes leading to Luxor Temple. The temple pylon leads via a peristyle court to a hypostyle hall with eight columns carved with figures of Ramses XI and the High Priest Herihor, who effectively ruled Upper Egypt at the time. The next chamber housed the sacred barque of Khonsu.

Mut Temple Enclosure TEMPLE

From the 10th pylon, an avenue of sphinxes leads to the partly excavated southern enclosure – the Precinct of Mut, the consort of Amun. The Temple of Mut was built by Amenhotep III and consists of a sanctuary, a hypostyle hall and two courts. It has been restoed and officially opened to the public, included in the ticket to the Temple of Amun. Access, however, is not always granted.

Amenhotep also set up more than 700 black-granite statues of the lioness goddess Sekhmet, Mut's northern counterpart, which are believed to form a calendar, with two statues for every day of the year, receiving offerings each morning and evening.

Montu Temple Enclosure TEMPLE

A gate, usually locked, on the wall near the Temple of Ptah (in the Amun Temple Enclosure) leads to the Montu Temple Enclosure. Montu, the falcon-headed warrior god, was one of the original deities of Thebes. The main temple was built by Amenhotep III and modified by others. The complex is very dilapidated.

Open-Air Museum MUSEUM

(Map p192; tickets at main ticket office, adult/student E£25/15; ⌚6am-5.30pm summer, 6am-4.30pm winter) Off to the left (north) of the first court of the Amun Temple Enclosure is Karnak's open-air museum. The term 'museum' and the fact that there is so much else to see in Karnak means that most visitors skip this collection of stones, statues and shrines, but it is definitely worth a look.

TOP TIP

Coaches bringing day trippers from the Red Sea arrive in Luxor around 10am, heading either for the Valley of the Kings or the Temple of Karnak, so avoid those sights late morning if you don't like being overrun.

Amun Temple Enclosure

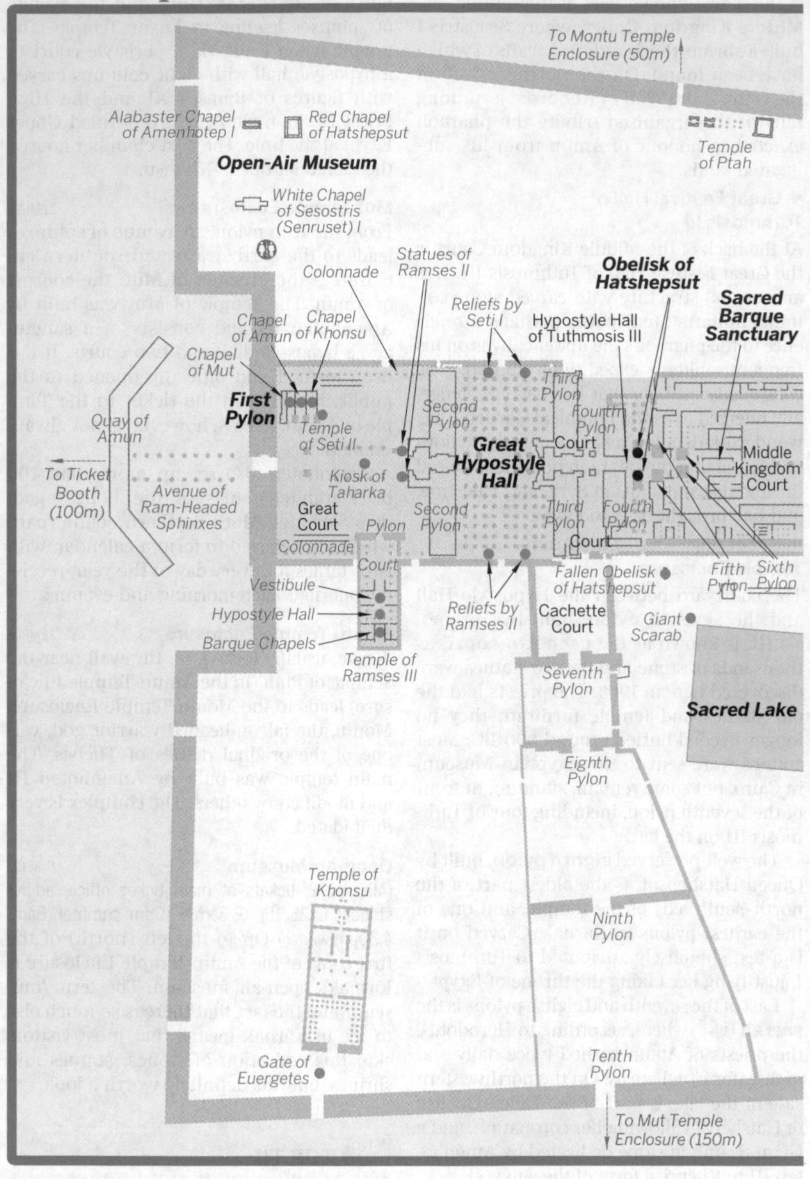

The well-preserved chapels include the **White Chapel of Sesostris I**, one of the oldest and most beautiful monuments in Karnak, which has wonderful Middle Kingdom reliefs; the **Red Chapel of Hatshepsut**, its red quartzite blocks reassembled in 2000; and the **Alabaster Chapel of Amenhotep I**. The museum also contains a collection of statuary found throughout the temple complex.

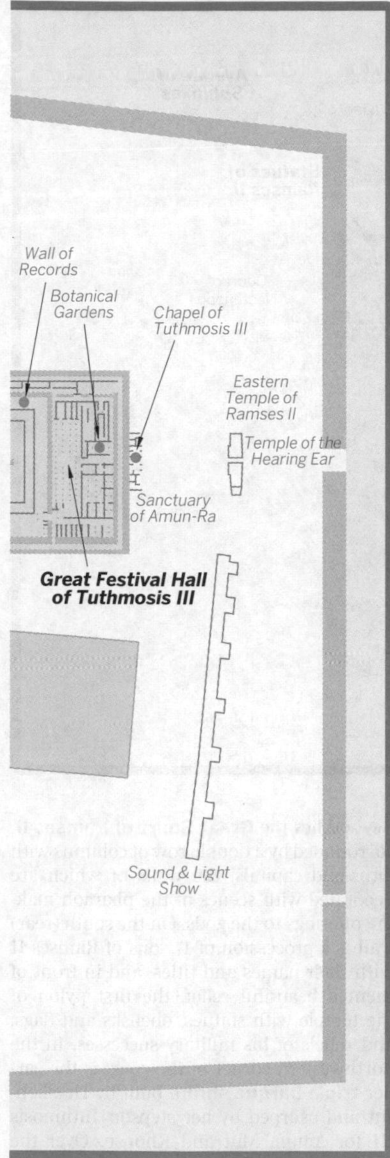

Karnak Sound and Light Show SHOW
(☎02-3385 7320; www.soundandlight.com.eg; E£100, video camera E£35; ⏱shows at 7pm, 8pm & 9pm in winter, at 8pm, 9pm & 10pm in summer) This highly kitsch sound-and-light show is a 1½-hour Hollywood-style extravaganza that recounts the history of Thebes and the lives of the many pharaohs who built here in honour of Amun. It's worth a visit particularly for a chance to walk through the beautifully lit temple at night. The shows (1st/2nd/3rd) run as follows:

DAY	SHOW 1	SHOW 2	SHOW 3
Monday	English	French	Spanish
Tuesday	English	Japanese	German
Wednesday	German	English	French
Thursday	English	French	Arabic
Friday	English	French	(no 3rd show)
Saturday	French	English	German
Sunday	German	English	Italian

Luxor Temples & Museums

Luxor Temple TEMPLE
(Map p30; ☎237 2408; Corniche an-Nil; adult/student E£60/30; ⏱6am-9pm) Largely built by the New Kingdom pharaohs Amenhotep III (1390–1352 BC) and Ramses II (1279–1213 BC), this temple is a strikingly graceful monument in the heart of the modern town. Also known as the Southern Sanctuary, it was largely built for the Opet celebrations, when the statues of Amun, Mut and Khonsu were brought from Karnak, along the Avenue of Sphinxes, and reunited here during the inundation.

Visit early when the temple opens, before the crowds arrive, or later at sunset when the stones glow. Whenever you go, be sure to return at night when the temple is lit up, creating an eerie spectacle as shadow and light play off the reliefs and colonnades.

Amenhotep III greatly enlarged an older shrine built by Hatshepsut, and rededicated the massive temple as Amun's southern *ipet* (harem), the private quarters of the god. The structure was further added to by Tutankhamun, Ramses II, Alexander the Great and various Romans. The Romans constructed a military fort around the temple that the Arabs later called Al-Uqsur (The Fortifications), which was later corrupted to give modern Luxor its name.

In ancient times the temple would have been surrounded by a warren of mud-brick houses, shops and workshops, which now lie under the modern town, but after the decline of the city people moved into the – by then – partly covered temple complex and built their city within it. In the 14th century, a mosque was built in one of the interior courts for the local sheikh (holy man) Abu

Luxor Temple

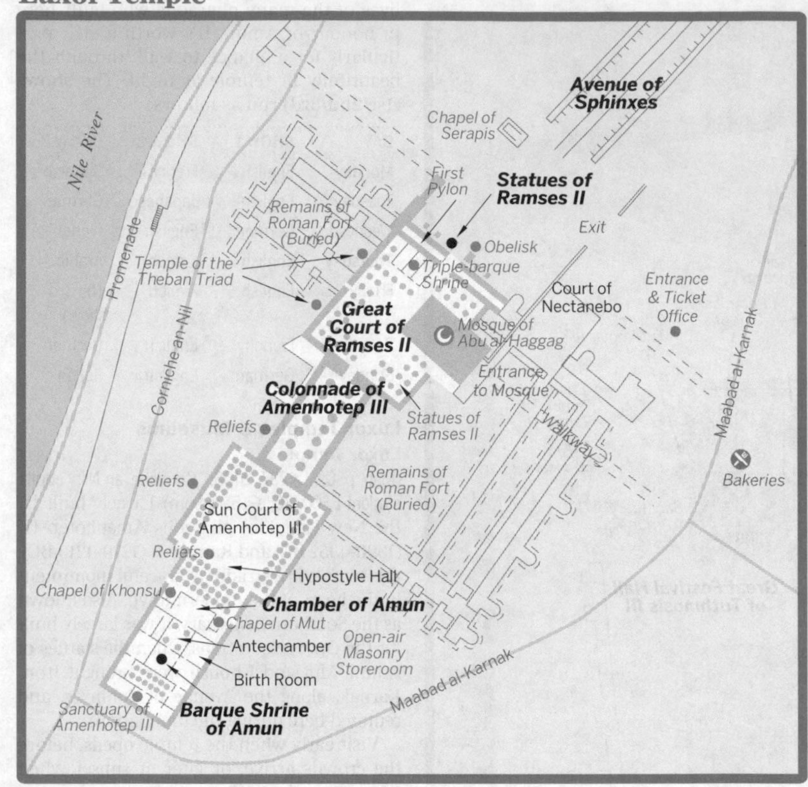

al-Haggag. Excavation works, begun in 1885, have cleared away the village and debris of centuries to uncover what can be seen of the temple today, but the mosque remains and has recently been restored after a fire.

The temple is less complex to understand than Karnak, but here again you walk back in time the deeper you go into it. In front of the temple is the beginning of the **avenue of sphinxes** that ran all the way to the temples at Karnak 3km to the north, and is now almost entirely excavated.

The massive 24m-high **first pylon** was raised by Ramses II and decorated with reliefs of his military exploits, including the Battle of Kadesh. The pylon was originally fronted by six colossal statues of Ramses II, four seated and two standing, but only two of the seated figures and one standing remain. Of the original pair of pink granite obelisks that stood here, one remains while the other stands in the Place de la Concorde in Paris.

Beyond lies the **Great Court of Ramses II**, surrounded by a double row of columns with lotus-bud capitals, the walls of which are decorated with scenes of the pharaoh making offerings to the gods. On the south (rear) wall is a procession of 17 sons of Ramses II with their names and titles, and in front of them a beautiful relief, the first pylon of the temple with statues, obelisks and flags, and reliefs of his military successes. In the northwestern corner of the court is the earlier **triple-barque shrine** built by Hatshepsut and usurped by her stepson Tuthmosis III for Amun, Mut and Khonsu. Over the southeastern side hangs the 14th-century **Mosque of Abu al-Haggag**, dedicated to a local sheikh, entered from Sharia Maabad al-Karnak, outside the temple precinct.

Beyond the court is the older splendid **Colonnade of Amenhotep III**, built as the grand entrance to the Temple of Amun of the Opet. The walls behind the elegant open papyrus columns were decorated during the reign of the young pharaoh Tutankhamun and celebrate the return to Theban orthodoxy following the wayward reign of the previous pharaoh, Akhenaten. The Opet Festival is depicted in lively detail, with the pharaoh, nobility and common people joining the triumphal procession. Look out for the drummers and acrobats doing back bends.

South of the Colonnade is the **Sun Court of Amenhotep III**, once enclosed on three sides by double rows of towering papyrus-bundle columns, the best preserved of which, with their architraves extant, are those on the eastern and western sides. In 1989 workmen found here a cache of 26 statues, buried by priests in Roman times, now displayed in the Luxor Museum.

Beyond lies the **Hypostyle Hall**, the first room of the original Opet temple, with four rows of eight columns each, leading to the temple's main rooms. The central chamber on the axis south of the Hypostyle Hall was the **cult sanctuary of Amun**, stuccoed over by the Romans in the 3rd century AD and painted with scenes of Roman officials: some of this is still intact and vivid. Through this chamber, either side of which are chapels dedicated to Mut and Khonsu, is the four-columned antechamber, where offerings were made to Amun, and immediately behind it the **Barque Shrine of Amun**, rebuilt by Alexander the Great, with reliefs portraying him as an Egyptian pharaoh.

To the east a doorway leads into two rooms. The first is Amenhotep III's **'birth room'** with scenes of his symbolic divine birth. You can see the moment of his conception, when the fingers of the god touch those of the queen and 'his dew filled her body', according to the accompanying hieroglyphic caption. The **Sanctuary of Amenhotep III** is the last chamber; it still has the remains of the stone base on which Amun's statue stood, and although it was once the most sacred part of the temple, the busy street that now runs directly behind it makes it less atmospheric.

★ Luxor Museum — MUSEUM

(Map p188; Corniche an-Nil; adult/student E£100/50; ⌚9am-5pm) This wonderful museum has a well-chosen and brilliantly displayed and explained collection of antiquities dating from the end of the Old Kingdom right through to the Mamluk period, mostly gathered from the Theban temples and necropolis. The ticket price puts many off, but don't let that stop you: this is one of the most rewarding sights in Luxor.

The **ground-floor gallery** has several masterpieces including a well-preserved limestone relief of Tuthmosis III (No 140), an exquisitely carved statue of Tuthmosis III in greywacke from the Temple of Karnak (No 2), an alabaster figure of Amenhotep III protected by the great crocodile god Sobek (No 155) and, one of the few examples of Old Kingdom art found at Thebes, a relief of Unas-ankh (No 183), found in his tomb on the west bank.

A **new wing** was opened in 2004, dedicated to the glory of Thebes during the New Kingdom period. The highlight, and the main reason for the new construction, is the two royal mummies, Ahmose I (founder of the 18th dynasty) and the mummy some believe to be Ramses I (founder of the 19th dynasty and father of Seti I), beautifully displayed without their wrappings in dark rooms. Other well-labelled displays illustrate the military might of Thebes during the New Kingdom, the age of Egypt's empire building, including chariots and weapons. On the upper floor the military theme is diluted with scenes from daily life showing the technology used in the New Kingdom. Multimedia displays show workers harvesting papyrus and processing it into sheets to be used for writing. Young boys are shown learning to read and write hieroglyphs beside a display of a scribe's implements and an architect's tools.

Back in the old building, moving up via the ramp to the **1st floor**, you come face-to-face with a seated granite figure of the legendary scribe Amenhotep (No 4), son of Hapu, the great official eventually deified in Ptolemaic times and who, as overseer of all the pharaoh's works under Amenhotep III (1390–1352 BC), was responsible for many of Thebes' greatest buildings. One of the most interesting exhibits is the Wall of Akhenaten, a series of small sandstone blocks named *talatat* (threes) by workmen – probably because their height and length was about three hand lengths – that came from Amenhotep IV's contribution at Karnak before he changed his name to Akhenaten and left Thebes for Tell al-Amarna. His building was demolished and about 40,000 blocks used to fill in Karnak's ninth pylon were found in the late 1960s and partially reassembled here. The scenes showing Akhenaten, his wife Nefertiti and temple life are a rare example of decoration from a Temple of Aten. Further highlights are treasures from Tutankhamun's tomb, including *shabti* (servant) figures, model boats, sandals, arrows and a series of gilded bronze rosettes from his funeral pall.

A ramp back down to the **ground floor** leaves you close to the exit and beside a black-and-gold wooden head of the cow deity Mehit-Weret, an aspect of the goddess Hathor, which was also found in Tutankhamun's tomb.

On the left just before the exit is a **small hall** containing 16 of 22 statues that were uncovered in Luxor Temple in 1989. All are magnificent examples of ancient Egyptian sculpture but pride of place at the end of the hall is given to an almost pristine 2.45m-tall quartzite statue of a muscular Amenhotep III, wearing a pleated kilt.

Mummification Museum MUSEUM

(Map p188; Corniche an-Nil; adult/student E£60/30; ⌚9am-2pm) Housed in the former visitors centre on Luxor's corniche, the Mummification Museum has well-presented exhibits explaining the art of mummification, and a range of mummified creatures. But the museum is small and some may find the entrance fee overpriced.

On display are the well-preserved mummy of a 21st-dynasty high priest of Amun, Maserharti, and a host of mummified animals. Vitrines show the tools and materials used in the mummification process – check out the small spoon and metal spatula used for scraping the brain out of the skull. Several artefacts that were crucial to the mummy's journey to the afterlife have also been included, as well as some picturesque painted coffins. Presiding over the entrance is a beautiful little statue of the jackal god, Anubis, the god of embalming who helped Isis turn her brother-husband Osiris into the first mummy.

West Bank

The west bank is a world away from the noise and bustle of Luxor town on the east bank. Taking a taxi across the bridge, 6km south of the centre, or crossing on the old ferry, you are immediately in the lush countryside, with bright-green sugarcane fields along irrigation canals and clusters of colourful houses, all against the background of the desert and the Theban hills. Coming towards the end of the cultivated land you start to notice huge sandstone blocks lying in the middle of fields, gaping black holes in the rocks and giant sandstone forms on the edge of the cultivation below. Magnificent memorial temples were built on the flood plains here, where the pharaoh's cult could be perpetuated by the devotions of his priests and subjects, while his body and worldly wealth, and the bodies of his wives and children, were laid in splendidly decorated hidden tombs excavated in the hills.

From the New Kingdom onwards, the necropolis also supported a large living population of artisans, labourers, temple priests and guards, who devoted their lives to the construction and maintenance of this city of the dead, and who protected the tombs full of treasure from eager robbers. The artisans perfected the techniques of tomb building, decoration and concealment, and passed the secrets down through their families. They all built their tombs here.

Until a generation ago, villagers used tombs to shelter from the extremes of the desert climate and, until recently, many lived in houses built over the Tombs of the Nobles. These beautifully painted houses were a picturesque sight to anyone visiting the west bank. However, over the past 100 years or so the Supreme Council of Antiquities has been trying to relocate the inhabitants of Al-Gurna. In spring 2007 their houses were demolished, and the families were moved to a huge new village of small breeze-block houses 8km north of the Valley of the Kings.

Tickets

The **Antiquities Inspectorate ticket office** (Map p198; main road, 3km inland from ferry landing; ⌚6am-5pm), near Medinat Habu, sells tickets to most sites on the West Bank except for the Temple at Deir al-Bahri, the Assasif Tombs (available at Deir al-Bahri ticket office), the Valley of the Kings and the Valley of the Queens. Check here first to see which tickets are available, and which tombs are open. All sites are officially open from 6am to 5pm. Photography is not permitted in any tombs and guards may confiscate film or memory cards.

Tickets are valid only for the day of purchase and no refunds are given. Prices (adult/student):

Dra Abu'l Naga (Roy & Shuroy) E£20/10

Deir al-Medina Temple & Tombs (except Peshedu) E£40/20

Medinat Habu (Temple of Ramses III) E£40/20

Ramesseum E£40/20

Temple of Merenptah E£20/10

Temple of Seti I E£30/15

Carter's House & the Replica Tomb of Tutankhamun E£50/25

Tomb of Peshedu (Deir al-Medina) E£15/8

Tombs of the Nobles E£20/10 to E£40/20 per group of tombs

Tombs of the Nobles — TOMB

(Map p198; ⌚6am-5pm) The tombs in this area are some of the best, but least visited, attractions on the west bank. Nestled in the foothills opposite the Ramesseum are more than 400 tombs belonging to nobles from the 6th dynasty to the Graeco-Roman period. The tombs that are open to the public are divided into groups and each requires a separate ticket from the Antiquities Inspectorate ticket office near Medinat Habu.

Where the pharaohs decorated their tombs with cryptic passages from the Book of the Dead to guide them through the afterlife, the nobles, intent on letting the good life continue after their death, decorated their tombs with wonderfully detailed scenes of their daily lives.

➡ Tombs of Khonsu, Userhet & Benia

(Nos 31, 51 & 343; adult/student E£20/10) Khonsu was First Prophet in the memorial temple of Tuthmosis III (1479–1425 BC). Inside the first chamber of Khonsu's tomb are scenes of the Montu festival at Armant, about 20km south of Luxor, the festival of the god of war over which he presided. The sacred barque with the shrine of Montu is towed by two smaller boats. The gods Osiris and Anubis are also honoured, and in many scenes Khonsu is seen making offerings to them. The ceiling is adorned with images of ducks flying around and nests with eggs. Next door is the less preserved tomb of Userhet, a priest during the time of Seti I (1294–1279 BC).

The tomb of Benia, just behind that of Khonsu, is even more colourful. Benia was a boarder in the Royal Nursery and chief treasurer also during the reign of Tuthmosis III. There are many scenes of offering tables piled high with food and drinks overlooked by Benia, and sometimes by his parents. In a niche cut out at the end of the tomb is a statue of Benia flanked by his parents, all three with destroyed faces.

➡ Tombs of Menna, Nakht & Amenenope

(Nos 52, 69 & 148; adult/student E£30/15) The beautiful and highly colourful wall paintings in the tomb of Menna and the tomb of Nakht emphasise rural life in 18th-dynasty Egypt. Menna was an estate inspector and Nakht was an astronomer of Amun. Their finely detailed tombs show scenes of farming, hunting, fishing and feasting. The tomb of Nakht has a small museum area in its first chamber. Although this tomb is so small that only a handful of visitors are able to squeeze in at a time, the walls have some of the best-known examples of Egyptian tomb paintings.

The tomb of Amenemope is one of the most recent to be opened for visitors. The large funerary complex has been open since antiquity and lost most of its decoration. Among the more recent materials found when archaeologists arrived were early Coptic manuscripts and Howard Carter's copy of the *Spectator* from 1912. Amenemope (c 1186–1069 BC) lived in the reigns of Ramses III, IV and V. His titles included Third Prophet of Amon and Greatest of the Seers of Re in Thebes. The sarcophagus in the upper corridor was dragged from the lower burial chamber.

➡ Tombs of Ramose, Userhet & Khaemhet

(Nos 55, 56 & 57; adult/student E£40/20) The tomb of Ramose, a governor of Thebes under Amenhotep III and Akhenaten, is fascinating because it is one of the few monuments dating from that time, a period of transition between two different forms of religious worship. The exquisite paintings and low reliefs show scenes in two different styles from the reigns of both pharaohs, depicting Ramose's funeral and his relationship with Akhenaten. The tomb was never actually finished, perhaps because Ramose died prematurely.

Next door is the tomb of Userhet, one of Amenhotep II's royal scribes, with fine wall paintings depicting daily life. Userhet is shown presenting gifts to Amenhotep II; there's a barber cutting hair on another wall; other scenes include men making wine and people hunting gazelles from a chariot.

The tomb of Khaemhet, Amenhotep III's royal inspector of the granaries and court scribe, has scenes on the walls showing Khaemhet making offerings, the pharaoh depicted as a sphinx, the funeral ritual of Osiris and images of daily country life as well as official business.

➡ Tombs of Sennofer & Rekhmire

(Nos 96 & 100; adult/student E£30/15) The most interesting parts of the tomb of Sennofer, overseer of the Garden of Amun under Amenhotep II, are to be found deep underground,

Luxor – West Bank

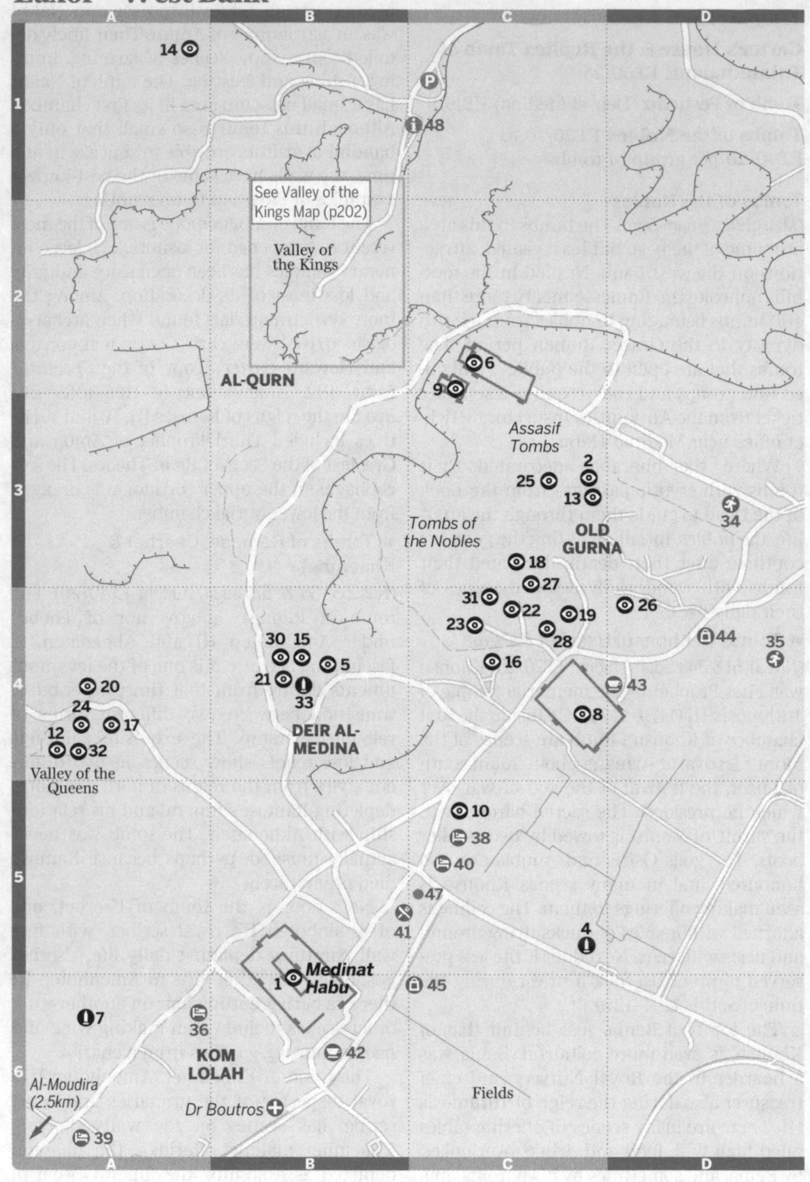

in the main chamber. The ceiling there is covered with clear paintings of grapes and vines, while most of the vivid scenes on the surrounding walls and columns depict Sennofer and all the different women in his life, including his wife, daughters and wet nurse.

The tomb of Rekhmire, vizier under Tuthmosis III and Amenhotep II, is one of the best preserved in the area. In the first chamber, to the extreme left, are scenes of Rekhmire receiving gifts from foreign lands. The panther and giraffe are gifts from Nu-

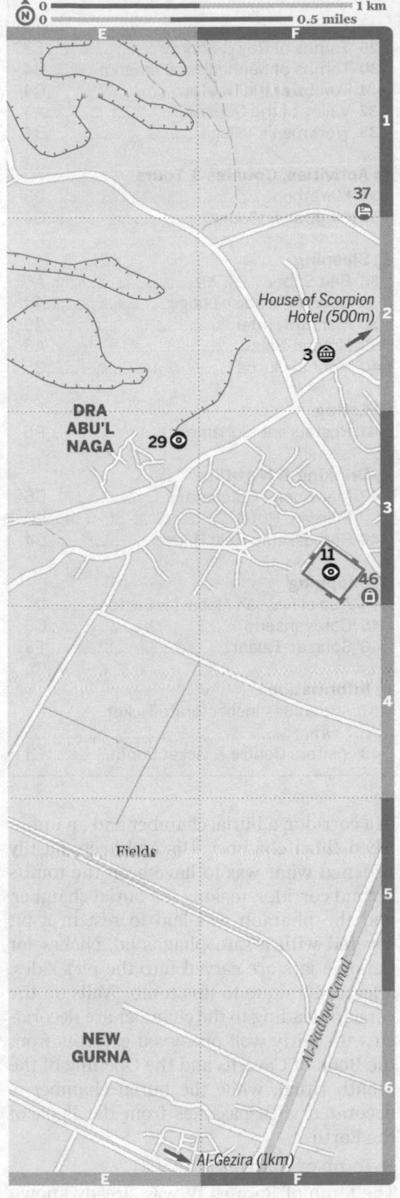

bia; the elephant, horses and chariot are from Syria; and the expensive vases come from Crete and the Aegean Islands. The opposite chamber (right) has good hunting scenes. The central chamber is long, narrow and, unusually, slopes upwards towards a false door. The west wall shows Rekhmire inspecting the production of metals, bricks, jewellery, leather, furniture and statuary (you can see workers on scaffolding carving a massive statue), while the east wall painting shows banquet scenes, complete with lyrics (the female harpist sings 'Put perfume on the hair of the goddess Maat').

➡ Tombs of Neferronpet, Dhutmosi & Nefersekheru

(Nos 178, 295 & 296; adult/student E£30/15) Discovered in 1915, the highlight of the brightly painted tomb of Neferronpet (also known as Kenro), the scribe of the treasury under Ramses II, is the scene showing Kenro overseeing the weighing of gold at the treasury. Next door, the tomb of Nefersekheru, an officer of the treasury during the same period, is similar in style and content to his neighbours. The ceiling is decorated with a huge variety of elaborate geometric patterns. From this long tomb, a small passage leads into the tomb of Dhutmosi, which is in poor condition.

★Valley of the Kings TOMB

(Wadi Biban al-Muluk; Map p202; www.thebanmappingproject.com; adult/student for 3 tombs excl Ramses VI, Ay & Tutankhamun E£100/50; ⏲6am-4pm) The west bank of Luxor had been the site of royal burials since around 2100 BC, but it was the pharaohs of the New Kingdom period (1550–1069 BC) who chose this isolated valley dominated by the pyramid-shaped mountain peak of Al-Qurn (The Horn). Once called the Great Necropolis of Millions of Years of Pharaoh, or the Place of Truth, the Valley of the Kings has 63 magnificent royal tombs, each quite different from the other.

The tombs have suffered greatly from treasure hunters, floods and, in recent years, from mass tourism: carbon dioxide, friction and humidity produced by the average of 2.8g of sweat left by each visitor have affected the reliefs and the pigments of the wall paintings. The Department of Antiquities has installed dehumidifiers and glass screens in the worst-affected tombs, and introduced a rotation system for opening tombs to the public while restoring others. The entry ticket gains access to three tombs, with an extra ticket to see the tombs of Ay, Tutankamun and Ramses VI.

The road into the Valley of the Kings is a gradual, dry, hot climb, so be prepared, especially if you are riding a bicycle. Be preared to run the gaunlet of the tourist

Luxor – West Bank

Top Sights
1 Medinat Habu....B6

Sights
2 Assasif Tombs....C3
3 Carter's House & the Replica Tomb of Tutankhamun....F2
4 Colossi of Memnon....C5
5 Deir al-Medina....B4
6 Memorial Temple of Hatshepsut....C2
7 Palace of Amenhotep III....A6
8 Ramesseum....C4
9 Temple of Mentuhotep....C2
10 Temple of Merenptah & Museum....C5
11 Temple of Seti I....F3
12 Tomb of Amunherkhepshef....A4
13 Tomb of Ankhhor....C3
14 Tomb of Ay....A1
15 Tomb of Ipy....B4
16 Tomb of Khaemhet....C4
17 Tomb of Khaemwaset....A4
18 Tomb of Menna....C3
19 Tomb of Nakht....C4
20 Tomb of Nefertari....A4
21 Tomb of Peshedu....B4
22 Tomb of Rekhmire....C4
23 Tomb of Sennofer....C4
24 Tomb of Titi....A4
25 Tombs of Kheruef & Mntophaat....C3
26 Tombs of Khonsu, Userhet & Benia....D4
27 Tombs of Neferronpet, Dhutmosi & Nefersekheru....C3
28 Tombs of Ramose & Userhet....C4
29 Tombs of Roy & Shuroy....E3
30 Tombs of Sennedjem & Inherka....B4
31 Tombs of the Nobles....C4
32 Valley of the Queens....A4
33 Workmen's Village....B4

Activities, Courses & Tours
34 Marathon....D3
35 Sindbad Balloons....D4

Sleeping
36 Beit Sabée....A6
37 Desert Paradise Lodge....F1
38 Marsam Hotel....C5
39 Nour al-Balad....A6
40 Nour al-Gurna....C5

Eating
41 Restaurant Mohammed....B5

Drinking & Nightlife
42 Maratonga Cafeteria....B6
Marsam Hotel....(see 38)
43 Ramesseum Rest House....D4

Shopping
44 Abo el Hassan Alabaster Factory....D4
45 Caravanserai....C6
46 Souq at-Talaat....F3

Information
47 Antiquities Inspectorate Ticket Office....C5
48 Visitors Centre & Ticket Booth....C1

bazaar, which sells soft drinks, ice creams and snacks alongside the tat. The air-conditioned visitors centre has a good model of the valley, a movie about Carter's discovery of the tomb of Tutankhamun, and toilets (there are Portacabins higher up, but this is the one to use). A *tuf-tuf* (a little electrical train) ferries visitors between the visitors centre and the tombs (it can be hot during summer). The ride costs E£4. It's worth having a torch to illuminate badly lit areas.

Most tombs described here are usually open to visitors. They are listed in the order that they are found when entering the site. The best source of information about the tombs, their decoration and history is the **Theban Mapping Project** (www.thebanmappingproject.com).

➡ Tomb of Ramses VII (KV 1)

Near the main entrance is the small, unfinished tomb of Ramses VII (1136–1129 BC). Only 44.3m long (short for a royal tomb because of Ramses' sudden death), it consists of a corridor, a burial chamber and an unfinished third chamber. His architects hastily widened what was to have been the tomb's second corridor, making it a burial chamber, and the pharaoh was laid to rest in a pit covered with a sarcophagus lid. Niches for Canopic jars are carved into the pit's sides, a feature unique to this tomb. Walls on the corridor leading to the chamber are decorated with fairly well preserved excerpts from the Book of Caverns and the Opening of the Mouth ritual, while the burial chamber is decorated with passages from the Book of the Earth.

➡ Tomb of Ramses IV (KV 2)

The tomb of Ramses IV was already known in Ptolemaic times, evident from the graffiti on the walls dating back to 278 BC. Ramses IV (1153–1147 BC) died before the tomb was completed. The paintings in the burial chamber have deteriorated, but there is a wonderful image of the goddess Nut, stretched across the blue ceiling, and it is the only tomb to contain the text of the Book of Nut, with a description of the daily path taken by the sun every day. The red-granite sarcophagus, though empty, is one of the largest in the valley. The discovery of an ancient plan of the tomb on papyrus (now in the Turin Museum) shows the sarcophagus was originally enclosed by four large shrines similar to those in Tutankhamun's tomb. The mummy of Ramses IV was later reburied in the tomb of Amenhotep II (KV 35), and is now in the Egyptian Museum in Cairo.

➡ Tomb of Ramses IX (KV 6)

Opposite Ramses II is the most visited tomb in the valley, the tomb of Ramses IX (1126–1108 BC), with a wide entrance, a long sloping corridor, a large antechamber decorated with the animals, serpents and demons from the Book of the Dead, and then a pillared hall and short hallway before the burial chamber. On either side of the gate on the rear wall are two figures of priests, both dressed in panther-skin robes and sporting a ceremonial sidelock. The walls of the burial chamber feature the Book of Amduat, the Book of Caverns and the Book of the Earth; the Book of the Heavens is represented on the ceiling. Although it is unfinished, it was the last tomb in the valley to have so much of its decoration completed, and the paintings are relatively well preserved.

➡ Tomb of Ramses II (KV 7)

As befits the burial place of one of Egypt's longest-reigning pharaohs (67 years, from 1279 to 1213 BC), KV 7 is one of the biggest tombs in the valley. However, flash floods destroyed much of what must have been spectacular decoration, so it is unlikely to open anytime soon. Based on the decorative scheme in his father Seti I's superb tomb, the walls of Ramses II's tomb would once have been just as brightly coloured, featuring scenes from the Litany of Ra, Book of Gates, the Book of the Dead and other sacred texts. In one of the side chambers off the burial chamber is a statue of Osiris similar to one found by Dr Kent Weeks in KV 5, giving him yet more evidence for his theory that KV5 belongs to the many sons of Ramses.

➡ Tomb of Merenptah (KV 8)

Ramses II lived for so long that 12 of his sons died before he did, so it was finally his 13th son Merenptah (1213–1203 BC) who succeeded him in his 60s. The second-largest tomb in the valley, Merenptah's tomb has been open since antiquity and has its share of Greek and Coptic graffiti. Floods have damaged the lower part of the walls of the long tunnel-like tomb, but the upper parts have well-preserved reliefs. The corridors are decorated with the Book of the Dead, the Book of Gates and the Book of Amduat. Beyond a shaft is a false burial chamber with two pillars decorated with the Book of Gates. Although much of the decoration in the burial chamber has faded, it remains an impressive room, with a sunken floor and brick niches on the front and rear walls.

The pharaoh was originally buried inside four stone sarcophagi, three of granite (the lid of the second still in situ, with an effigy of Merenptah on top) and the fourth, innermost, sarcophagus of alabaster. In a rare mistake by ancient Egyptian engineers, the outer sarcophagus did not fit through the tomb entrance and its gates had to be hacked away.

➡ Tomb of Tutankhamun (KV 62)

(adult/student E£100/50) The story of the celebrated discovery of the famous tomb and all the fabulous treasures it contained far outshines its actual appearance, and it is one of the least impressive tombs in the valley. Tutankhamun's tomb is small and bears all the signs of a rather hasty completion and inglorious burial, as well as significant damage to the decorations. The son of Akhenaten and one of Akhenaten's sisters, he ruled briefly (1336–1327 BC) and died young, with no great battles or buildings to his credit, so there was little time to build a tomb.

The Egyptologist Howard Carter slaved away for six seasons in the valley, believing that he would find the tomb of Tutankhamun intact with all its treasures. The first step was found on 4 November 1922, and on 5 November the rest of the steps and a sealed doorway came to light. Carter wired Lord

TACKLING THE WEST BANK

Take more than a day to visit the west bank, if you can. Plan your day in advance as tickets for most sights must be bought from the central ticket office, and are only valid for that day. Early-morning visits are ideal, but that is unfortunately when most tour groups visit the Memorial Temple of Hatshepsut or the Valley of the Kings. So try to leave these two to the afternoon to avoid the crowds and visit other sights such as Tombs of the Nobles or the Ramesseum in the morning.

Valley of the Kings

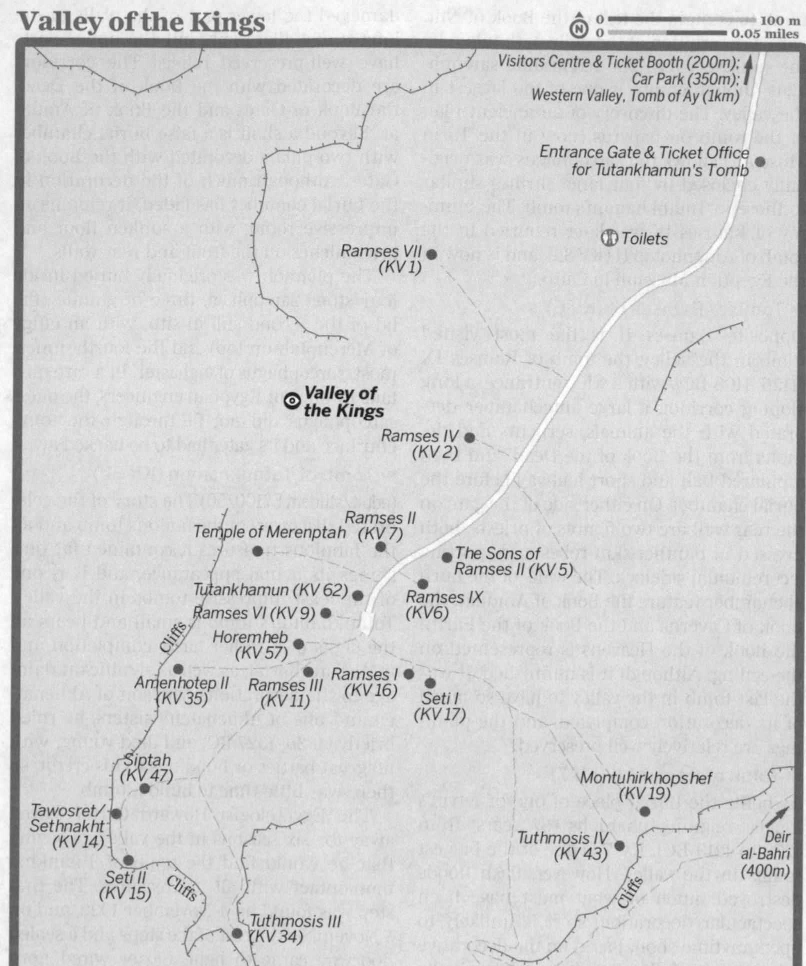

Carnarvon to join him in Egypt immediately for the opening of what he believed was the completely intact tomb of Tutankhamun.

The tomb had been partially robbed twice in antiquity, but its priceless cache of treasures vindicated Carter's dream beyond even his wildest imaginings. Four chambers were crammed with jewellery, furniture, statues, chariots, musical instruments, weapons, boxes, jars and food. Even the later discovery that many had been stuffed haphazardly into the wrong boxes by necropolis officials 'tidying up' after the ancient robberies does not detract from their dazzling wealth. Some archaeologists believe that Tutankhamun was perhaps buried with all the regalia of the unpopular Amarna royal line, as some of it is inscribed with the names of his father Akhenaten and the mysterious Smenkhkare (1388–1336 BC), who some Egyptologists believe was Nefertiti ruling as pharaoh.

Most of the treasure is in the Cairo Museum, with a few pieces in Luxor Museum: only Tutankhamun's mummy in its gilded wooden coffin is in situ. The burial-chamber walls are decorated by chubby figures of the pharaoh before the gods, painted against a yellow-gold background. The wall at the foot end of the sarcophagus shows scenes of the pharaoh's funeral; the 12 squatting apes from the Book of Amduat, representing the 12 hours of the night, are featured on the opposite wall.

An exact replica of the tomb and sarcophagus, as well as a full explanation of the rediscovery of the tomb, has been installed in the grounds of Howard Carter's house (p210).

➡ Tomb of Ramses VI (KV 9)

(adult/student E£60/30) The intactness of Tutankhamun's tomb is largely thanks to the existence of the tomb of Ramses VI. The tomb was actually begun for the ephemeral Ramses V (1147–1143 BC) and continued by Ramses VI (1143–1136 BC), with both pharaohs apparently buried here; the names and titles of Ramses V still appear in the first half of the tomb. Following the tomb's ransacking a mere 20 years after burial, the mummies of both Ramses V and Ramses VI were moved to Amenhotep II's tomb, where they were found in 1898 and taken to Cairo.

Although the tomb's plastering was not finished, its fine decoration is well preserved, with an emphasis on astronomical scenes and texts. Extracts from the Book of Gates and the Book of Caverns cover the entrance corridor. These continue into the midsection of the tomb and well room, with the addition of the Book of the Heavens. Nearer the burial chamber the walls are decorated with extracts from the Book of Amduat. The burial chamber is beautifully decorated, with a superb double image of Nut framing the Book of the Day and Book of the Night on the ceiling. This nocturnal landscape in black and gold shows the sky goddess swallowing the sun each evening to give birth to it each morning in an endless cycle of new life designed to revive the souls of the dead pharaohs. The walls of the chamber are filled with fine images of Ramses VI with various deities, as well as scenes from the Book of the Earth, showing the sun god's progress through the night, the gods who help him and the forces of darkness trying to stop him reaching the dawn; look out for the decapitated, kneeling figures of the sun god's enemies around the base of the chamber walls and the black-coloured executioners who turn the decapitated bodies upside down to render them as helpless as possible.

➡ Tomb of Ramses III (KV 11)

Ramses III (1184–1153 BC), the last of Egypt's warrior pharaohs, built one of the longest tombs in the Valley of the Kings. His tomb, started but abandoned by Sethnakht (1186–1184 BC), is 125m long, much of it still beautifully decorated with colourful painted sunken reliefs featuring the traditional ritual texts (Litany of Ra, Book of Gates etc) and Ramses before the gods. Unusually here are the secular scenes, in the small side rooms of the entrance corridor, showing foreign tributes such as highly detailed pottery imported from the Aegean, the royal armoury, boats and, in the last of these side chambers, the blind harpists that gave the tomb one of its alternative names: 'Tomb of the Harpers'.

In the chamber beyond is an aborted tunnel where ancient builders ran into the neighbouring tomb. They shifted the axis of the tomb to the west and built a corridor leading to a pillared hall, with walls decorated with scenes from the Book of Gates. There is also ancient graffiti on the rear right pillar describing the reburial of the pharaoh during the 21st dynasty (1069–945 BC). The remainder of the tomb is only partially excavated and structurally weak.

Ramses III's sarcophagus is in the Louvre in Paris, its detailed lid is in the Fitzwilliam Museum in Cambridge and his mummy – found in the Deir al-Bahri cache – was the model for Boris Karloff's character in the 1930s film *The Mummy*. The mummy is now in Cairo's Egyptian Museum.

➡ Tomb of Horemheb (KV 57)

This tomb was discovered filled with ransacked pieces of the royal funerary equipment, including a number of wooden figurines that were taken to the Egyptian Museum in Cairo. Horemheb (1323–1295 BC), a general and military strongman under Tutankhamun, brought stability after the turmoil of Akhenaten's reign. He had already built a lavish tomb in Saqqara, but abandoned it for this tomb. The various stages of decoration in the burial chamber give a fascinating glimpse into the process of tomb decoration.

From the entrance, a steep flight of steps and an equally steep passage leads to a well shaft decorated with superb figures of Horemheb before the gods. Notice Hathor's blue-and-black striped wig and the lotus crown of the young god Nefertum, all executed against a grey-blue background. The six-pillared burial chamber decorated with part of the Book of Gates remains partially unfinished, showing how the decoration was applied by following a grid system in red ink over which the figures were drawn in black prior to their carving and painting. The pharaoh's empty red-granite sarcophagus carved with protective figures of goddesses with outstretched wings remains in the tomb; his mummy is missing.

➡ **Tomb of Amenhotep II (KV 35)**

One of the deepest structures in the valley, this tomb has more than 90 steps down to a modern gangway, built over a deep pit designed to protect the inner, lower chambers from both thieves (which it failed to do) and the water from flash floods.

Stars cover the entire ceiling in the huge burial chamber and the walls feature, as if on a giant painted scroll, text from the Book of Amduat. While most figures are of the same sticklike proportions as in the tomb of Amenhotep's father and predecessor Tuthmosis III, this is the first royal tomb in the valley to also show figures of more rounded proportions, as on the pillars in the burial chamber showing the pharaoh before Osiris, Hathor and Anubis. The burial chamber is also unique for its double level; the top level was filled with pillars, the bottom contained the sarcophagus.

Although thieves breached the tomb in antiquity, Amenhotep's (1427-1400 BC) mummy was restored by the priests, put back in his sarcophagus with a garland of flowers around his neck, and buried with 13 other royal mummies in the two side rooms, including Tuthmosis IV (1400–1390 BC), Amenhotep III, Merenptah, Ramses IV, V and VI, and Seti II (1200–1194 BC), most of which are now at the Egyptian Museum.

➡ **Tomb of Tuthmosis III (KV 34)**

Hidden in the hills between high limestone cliffs and reached only via a steep staircase that crosses an even steeper ravine, this tomb demonstrates the lengths to which the ancient pharaohs went to thwart the cunning of the ancient thieves.

Tuthmosis III (1479–1425 BC), an innovator in many fields, and whose military exploits and stature earned him the description 'the Napoleon of ancient Egypt', was one of the first to build his tomb in the Valley of the Kings. As secrecy was his utmost concern, he chose the most inaccessible spot and designed his burial place with a series of passages at haphazard angles and fake doors to mislead or catch potential robbers.

The shaft, now traversed by a narrow gangway, leads to an antechamber supported by two pillars, the walls of which are adorned with a list of more than 700 gods and demigods. As the earliest tomb in the valley to be painted, the walls appear to be simply giant versions of funerary papyri, with scenes populated by stick men. The burial chamber has curved walls and is oval in shape; it contains the pharaoh's quartzite sarcophagus that is carved in the shape of a cartouche.

➡ **Tomb of Siptah (KV 47)**

Discovered in 1905, the tomb of Siptah (1194–1188 BC) was never completed but the upper corridors are nonetheless covered in fine paintings. The tomb's entrance is decorated with the sun disc, and figures of Maat, the goddess of truth, kneel on each side of the doorway. There are further scenes from the Book of Amduat, and figures of Anubis, after which the tomb remains undecorated.

➡ **Tomb of Tawosret/Sethnakht (KV 14)**

Tawosret was the wife of Seti II and after his successor Siptah died she took power herself (1188–1186 BC). Egyptologists think she began the tomb for herself and Seti II but their burials were removed by her successor, the equally short-lived Sethnakht (1186–1184 BC), who completed the tomb by adding a second burial chamber for himself. The change of ownership can be seen in the tomb's decoration; the upper corridors show the queen, accompanied by her stepson Siptah, in the presence of the gods. Siptah's cartouche was later replaced by Seti II's. But in the lower corridors and burial chambers images of Tawosret have been plastered over by images or cartouches of Sethnakht.

The tomb has been open since antiquity and although the decoration has worn off in some parts, the colour and state of the burial chambers remains good, with astronomical ceiling decorations and images of Tawosret and Sethnakht with the gods. The final scene from the Book of Caverns adorning Tawosret's burial chamber is particularly impressive, showing the sun god as a ram-headed figure stretching out his wings to emerge from the darkness of the underworld.

➡ **Tomb of Seti II (KV 15)**

Adjacent to the tomb of Tawosret/Sethnakht is a smaller tomb where it seems Sethnakht buried Seti II (1200–1194 BC) after turfing him out of KV 14. Open since ancient times judging by the many examples of classical graffiti, the tomb's entrance area has some finely carved relief scenes, although the rest was quickly finished off in paint alone. The walls have extracts from the Litany of Ra, the Book of Gates and the Book of Amduat and, unusually, on the walls of the well room, images of the type of funerary objects used in pharaohs' tombs, such as golden statuettes of the pharaoh within a shrine.

➡ Tomb of Ramses I (KV 16)

Ramses I (1295–1294 BC) only ruled for a year so his tomb is a very simple affair. It has the shortest entrance corridor leading to a single, almost square, burial chamber, containing the pharaoh's open pink granite sarcophagus. Only the chamber is superbly decorated, very similar to Horemheb's tomb (KV 57), with extracts from the Book of Gates, as well as scenes of the pharaoh in the presence of the gods, eg the pharaoh kneeling between the jackal-headed 'Soul of Nekhen' and the falcon-headed 'Soul of Pe', symbolising Upper and Lower Egypt.

➡ Tomb of Seti I (KV 17)

As befits such an important pharaoh, Seti I (1294–1279 BC), son and heir of Ramses I, has one of the longest (137m) and most beautiful tombs in the valley. Its discovery by Giovanni Belzoni in 1817 generated almost the same interest as the discovery of Tutankhamun's tomb a century later. As the first royal tomb to be decorated throughout, its raised, painted relief scenes are similar to those found in the pharaoh's beautifully decorated temple at Abydos and the quality of the work is superb. Two of its painted reliefs showing Seti with Hathor are now in the Louvre in Paris and Florence's Archaeological Museum, while Seti's alabaster sarcophagus was bought by Sir John Soane, and it can still be seen in the basement of his London house-turned-museum.

The tomb is indefinitely closed for restoration (ongoing since 1991), but there is a plan to create a replica of the tomb that will include copies of the missing parts held in foreign museums.

➡ Tomb of Montuhirkopshef (KV 19)

The tomb of Ramses IX's son (c 1000 BC), whose name translates as 'The Arm of Montu is Strong', is located high up in the valley's eastern wall. It is small and unfinished but has fine paintings and few visitors. Its entrance corridor is adorned with life-size reliefs of various gods, including Osiris, Ptah, Thoth and Khonsu, receiving offerings from the young prince, who is shown in all his finery, wearing exquisitely pleated fine linen robes and a blue-and-gold 'sidelock of youth' attached to his black wig – not to mention his gorgeous make-up (as worn by both men and women in ancient Egypt).

➡ Tomb of Tuthmosis IV (KV 43)

The tomb of Tuthmosis IV (1400–1390 BC) is one of the largest and deepest tombs constructed during the 18th dynasty. It is also the first in which paint was applied over a yellow background, beginning a tradition that was continued in many tombs. It was discovered in 1903 by Howard Carter, 20 years earlier than the tomb of Tuthmosis IV's great-grandson, Tutankhamun. It is accessed by two long flights of steps leading down and around to the burial chamber, where there's an enormous sarcophagus covered in hieroglyphs. The walls of the well shaft and antechamber are decorated with painted scenes of Tuthmosis before the gods, and the figures of the goddess Hathor are particularly fetching in a range of beautiful dresses decorated with beaded designs.

On the left (south) wall of the antechamber there is a patch of ancient Egyptian graffiti dating back to 1315 BC, written by government official Maya and his assistant Djehutymose and referring to their inspection and restoration of Tuthmosis IV's burial on the orders of Horemheb following the first wave of robbery in the eighth year of Horemheb's reign, some 67 years after Tuthmosis IV died.

➡ Tomb of Ay (KV 23)

(adult/student E£25/15) Although he succeeded Tutankhamun, Ay's brief reign from 1327 to 1323 BC tends to be associated with the earlier Amarna period and Akhenaten (some Egyptologists have suggested he could have been the father of Akhenaten's wife Nefertiti). Ay abandoned a grandiose tomb in Amarna and took over another in the West Valley here. The West Valley played an important part in the Amarna story, as it was chosen as a new burial ground by Amenhotep III for his own enormous tomb (KV 22, partway up the valley), and his son and successor Akhenaten also began a tomb here, before he relocated the capital at Amarna, where he was eventually buried. It seems Tutankhamun too planned to be buried in the West Valley, until his early death saw his successor Ay 'switch' tombs. Tutankhamun was buried in a tomb (KV 62) in the traditional section of the Valley of the

Kings, while Ay himself took over the tomb Tutankhamun had begun at the head of the West Valley. The tomb is accessed by a dirt road leading off from the car park at the Valley of the Kings that winds for almost 2km up a desolate valley past sheer rock cliffs. Recapturing the atmosphere (and silence) once found in the neighbouring Valley of the Kings makes it worth the visit.

Although only the burial chamber is decorated, it is noted for its scenes of Ay hippopotamus hunting and fishing in the marshes (scenes usually found in the tombs of nobles not royalty) and for a wall featuring 12 baboons, representing the 12 hours of the night, after which the West Valley or Wadi al-Gurud (Valley of the Monkeys) is named.

Tickets for the tomb of Ay must be bought from the Antiquities Inspectorate office near Medinat Habu.

Memorial Temple of Hatshepsut TEMPLE

(Map p198; Deir al-Bahri; adult/student E£50/25; ⏲6am-5pm) At Deir al-Bahri, the eyes first focus on the dramatic rugged limestone cliffs that rise nearly 300m above the desert plain, a monument made by nature, only to realise that at the foot of all this immense beauty lies a human-made monument even more extraordinary, the dazzling Temple of Hatshepsut. The almost modern-looking temple blends in beautifully with the cliffs from which it is partly cut; a marriage made in heaven. Most of what you see has been painstakingly reconstructed.

Continuous excavation and restoration since 1891 have revealed one of ancient Egypt's finest monuments, but it must have been even more stunning in the days of Hatshepsut (1473–1458 BC), when it was approached by a grand sphinx-lined causeway instead of today's noisy tourist bazaar, when the court was a garden planted with exotic trees and perfumed plants, and when it was linked due east across the Nile to the Temple of Karnak. Called Djeser-djeseru (Most Holy of Holies), it was designed by Senenmut, a courtier at Hatshepsut's court and perhaps also her lover. If the design seems unusual, note that it did in fact feature all the things a memorial temple usually had, including the rising central axis and a three-part plan, but had to be adapted to the chosen site almost exactly on the same line with the Temple of Amun at Karnak, and near an older shrine to the goddess Hathor.

The temple was vandalised over the centuries: Tuthmosis III removed his stepmother's name whenever he could, Akhenaten removed all references to Amun, and the early Christians turned it into a monastery, Deir al-Bahri (Monastery of the North), and defaced the pagan reliefs.

Deir al-Bahri has been designated as one of the hottest places on earth, so an early morning visit is advisable, also because the reliefs are best seen in the low sunlight. The complex is entered via the **great court**, where original ancient tree roots are still visible. The colonnades on the lower terrace were closed for restoration at the time of writing. The delicate relief work on the **south colonnade**, left of the ramp, has reliefs of the transportation of a pair of obelisks commissioned by Hatshepsut from the Aswan quarries to Thebes, and the **north** one features scenes of birds being caught.

A large ramp leads to the two upper terraces. The best-preserved reliefs are on the **middle terrace**. The reliefs in the **north colonnade** record Hatshepsut's divine birth and at the end of it is the Chapel of Anubis, with well-preserved colourful reliefs of a disfigured Hatshepsut and Tuthmosis III in the presence of Anubis, Ra-Horakhty and Hathor. The wonderfully detailed reliefs in the **Punt Colonnade** to the left of the entrance tell the story of the expedition to the Land of Punt to collect myrrh trees needed for the incense used in temple ceremonies. There are depictions of the strange animals and exotic plants seen there, the foreign architecture and strange landscapes as well as the different-looking people. At the end of this colonnade is the **Hathor Chapel**, with two chambers both with Hathor-headed columns. Reliefs on the west wall show, if you have a torch, Hathor as a cow licking Hatshepsut's hand, and the queen drinking from Hathor's udder. On the north wall is a faded relief of Hatshepsut's soldiers in naval dress in the goddess' honour. Beyond the pillared halls is a three-roomed chapel cut into the rock, now closed to the public, with reliefs of the queen in front of the deities, and with a small figure behind the door of Senenmut, the temple's architect and some believe Hatshepsut's lover.

The **upper terrace**, restored by a Polish-Egyptian team over the last 25 years, had 24 colossal Osiris statues, some of which are left. The central pink-granite doorway leads into the **Sanctuary of Amun**, which is hewn out of the cliff.

On the south side of Hatshepsut's temple lie the remains of the **Temple of Montuhotep**, built for the founder of the 11th dynasty

Memorial Temple of Hatshepsut

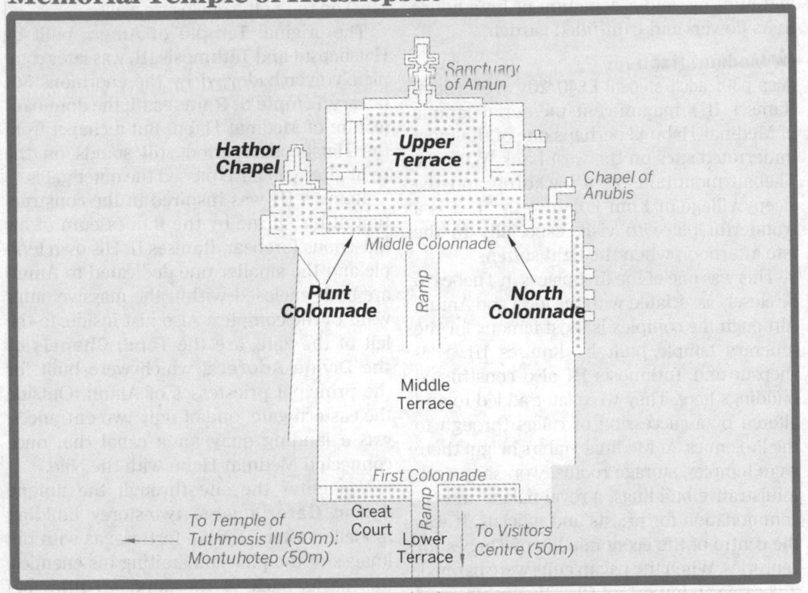

and one of the oldest temples so far discovered in Thebes, and the **Temple of Tuthmosis III**, Hatshepsut's successor. Both are in ruins.

Deir al-Medina TEMPLE

(Monastery of the Town; Map p198; adult/student E£40/20, extra ticket for Tomb of Peshedu adult/student E£15/10; 6am-5pm) This site takes its name from a Ptolemaic temple, later converted to a Coptic monastery, but the real attraction is the unique ruined settlement, the **Workmen's Village**. Many of the workers and artists who created tombs in the Valley of the Kings and Valley of the Queens lived and were buried here. Archaeologists have uncovered more than 70 houses in this village and many tombs, the most beautiful of which are now open to the public.

About 1km off the road to the Valley of the Queens and up a short, steep paved road, the small Ptolemaic-era temple, measuring only 10m by 15m, was built between 221 and 116 BC. It was dedicated to Hathor, the goddess of pleasure and love, and to Maat, the goddess of truth and personification of cosmic order. In front of the temple are the remains of the workers' village, mostly low walls although there are also remains of ancient irrigation pipes. More impressive, however, are the nearby tombs.

The beautifully adorned **tomb of Inherka** (No 359) belonged to a 19th-dynasty servant who worked in the Place of Truth, the Valley of the Kings. The one-room tomb has magnificent wall paintings, including the famous scene of a cat (representing the sun god Ra) killing a snake (representing the evil serpent Apophis) under a sacred tree, on the left wall. There are also beautiful domestic scenes of Inherka with his wife and children. Right next to it is the **tomb of Sennedjem** (No 1), a stunningly decorated 19th-dynasty tomb that contains two small chambers and some equally exquisite paintings. Sennedjem was an artist who lived during the reigns of Seti I and Ramses II and it seems he ensured his own tomb was as finely decorated as those of his masters. Due to the popularity and small size of both these tombs, only 10 people at a time are allowed inside; it's likely you'll find yourself in a queue.

While you wait, take a look at the 19th-dynasty **tomb of Peshedu** (No 3) just up the slope from the other two tombs. Peshedu was another servant in the Place of Truth and can be seen in the burial chamber praying under a palm tree beside a lake.

Close by is the **tomb of Ipy** (No 217), a sculptor during the reign of Ramses II. Here scenes of everyday life eclipse the usual emphasis on ritual, with scenes of farming and hunting, and a depiction of Ipy's house in its flower- and fruit-filled garden.

★Medinat Habu TEMPLE

(Map p30; adult/student E£40/20; ⏲6am-5pm)

Ramses III's magnificent memorial temple of Medinat Habu is perhaps one of the most underrated sites on the west bank. With the Theban mountains as a backdrop and the sleepy village of Kom Lolah in front, it is a wonderful place to visit, especially in the late afternoon when the light softens.

This was one of the first places in Thebes to be closely associated with the local god Amun. Although the complex is most famous for the funerary temple built by Ramses III, Hatshepsut and Tuthmosis III also constructed buildings here. They were later added to and altered by a succession of rulers through to the Ptolemies. At Medinat Habu's height there were temples, storage rooms, workshops, administrative buildings, a royal palace and accommodation for priests and officials. It was the centre of the economic life of Thebes for centuries. When the pagan cults were banned, it became an important Christian centre, and was still inhabited as late as the 9th century AD, when a plague was thought to have decimated the town. You can still see the mud-brick remains of the medieval town that gave the site its name (medina means 'town' or 'city') on top of the enclosure walls.

The original **Temple of Amun**, built by Hatshepsut and Tuthmosis III, was later completely overshadowed by the enormous **Funerary Temple of Ramses III**, the dominant feature of Medinat Habu. But a chapel from the Hatshepsut period still stands on the right after you have passed the outer gates.

Ramses III was inspired in the construction of his shrine by the Ramesseum of his illustrious forebear, Ramses II. His own temple and the smaller one dedicated to Amun are both enclosed within the massive outer walls of the complex. Also just inside, to the left of the gate, are the **Tomb Chapels of the Divine Adorers**, which were built for the principal priestesses of Amun. Outside the eastern gate, one of only two entrances, was a landing quay for a canal that once connected Medinat Habu with the Nile.

You enter the site through the unique **Syrian Gate**, a large two-storey building modelled after a Syrian fortress: as with the images of the pharaoh smiting his enemies, this harks back to the famous battles between Egyptians and Hittites, particularly at the time of Ramses II. If you follow the wall to the left you will find a staircase leading to the upper floors. There is not much to see in the rooms but you'll get some great views

Medinat Habu

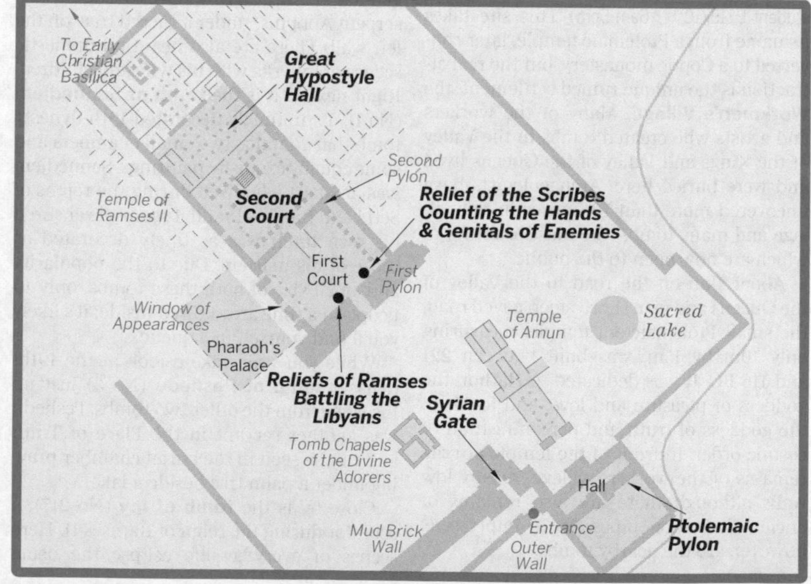

Rameseum

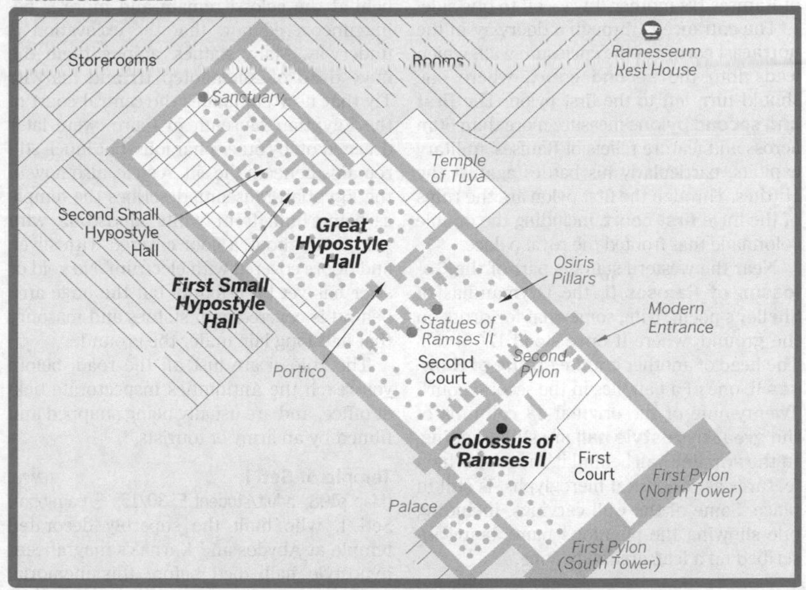

out across the village in front of the temple and over the fields to the south.

The well-preserved **first pylon** marks the front of the temple proper. Ramses III is portrayed in its reliefs as the victor in several wars. Most famous are the fine reliefs of his victory over the Libyans (who you can recognise by their long robes, sidelocks and beards). There is also a gruesome scene of scribes tallying the number of enemies killed by counting severed hands and genitals.

To the left of the **first court** are the remains of the **Pharaoh's Palace**; the three rooms at the rear were for the royal harem. There is a window between the first court and the Pharaoh's Palace known as the **Window of Appearances**, which allowed the pharaoh to show himself to his subjects.

The reliefs of the **second pylon** feature Ramses III presenting prisoners of war to Amun and his vulture-goddess wife, Mut. Colonnades and reliefs surround the **second court**, depicting various religious ceremonies.

If you have time to wander about the extensive ruins around the funerary temple you will see the remains of an **early Christian basilica** as well as a small **sacred lake** and, on the south side of the temple, the outline of the palace and the window, looking into the temple courtyard, where Ramses would appear.

Ramesseum TEMPLE
(Map p198; adult/student E£40/20; ⌚6am-5pm)
Ramses II called his massive memorial temple 'the Temple of Millions of Years of User-Maat-Ra'; classical visitors called it the tomb of Ozymandias; and Jean-François Champollion, who deciphered hieroglyphics, called it the Ramesseum. Like other memorial temples it was part of Ramses II's funerary complex. His tomb was built deep in the hills, but his memorial temple was on the edge of the cultivation on a canal that connected with the Nile and with other memorial temples.

Unlike the well-preserved structures that Ramses II built at Karnak and Abu Simbel, his memorial temple has not survived the times very well. It is mostly in ruins, despite extensive restoration – a fact that would no doubt disappoint Ramses II. The Ramesseum is famous for the scattered remains of fallen statues that inspired the English poet Shelley's poem 'Ozymandias', using the undeniable fact of Ramses' mortality to ridicule his aspirations to immortality.

Although more elaborate than many other temples, the layout of the Ramesseum is fairly orthodox, consisting of two courts, hypostyle halls, sanctuary, accompanying chambers and storerooms. What is unusual is that the rectangular floor plan was altered to incorporate an older, smaller temple – that of Ramses II's mother, Tuya – off to one side.

The entrance is through a doorway in the northeast corner of the enclosure wall, which leads into the **second court**, where one should turn left to the first pylon. The **first and second pylons** measure more than 60m across and feature reliefs of Ramses' military exploits, particularly his battles against the Hittites. Through the first pylon are the ruins of the huge **first court**, including the double colonnade that fronted the royal palace.

Near the western stairs is part of the **Colossus of Ramses II**, the Ozymandias of Shelley's poem, lying somewhat forlornly on the ground, where it once stood 17.5m tall. The head of another granite **statue of Ramses II**, one of a pair, lies in the second court. Twenty-nine of the original 48 columns of the **great hypostyle hall** are still standing. In the **smaller hall** behind it, the roof, which features astronomical hieroglyphs, is still in place. Some of the wall carvings, including one showing the pharaoh's name being inscribed on a leaf, are finely done.

Colossi of Memnon MONUMENT

(Map p198) FREE The two faceless Colossi of Memnon, originally representing Pharaoh Amenhotep III and rising majestically about 18m from the plain, are the first monuments tourists see when they visit the west bank. Yet few visitors have any idea that these giant enthroned figures are set in front of the main entrance to an equally impressive funerary temple, the largest in Egypt, the remains of which are slowly being brought to light.

The colossi, each cut from a single block of stone and weighing 1000 tonnes, were already a great tourist attraction during Graeco-Roman times, when the statues were attributed to Memnon, the legendary African king who was slain by Achilles during the Trojan War. The Greeks and Romans considered it good luck to hear the whistling sound emitted by the northern statue at sunrise, which they believed to be the cry of Memnon greeting his mother Eos, the goddess of dawn. She in turn would weep tears of dew for his untimely death. All this was probably due to a crack in the colossus' upper body, which appeared after the 27 BC earthquake. As the heat of the morning sun baked the dew-soaked stone, sand particles would break off and resonate inside the cracks in the structure. After Septimus Severus (AD 193–211) repaired the statue in the 3rd century AD, Memnon's plaintive greeting was heard no more.

Some tiny parts of the temple that stood behind the colossi remain and more is being uncovered now that the excavation is underway. Many statues, among them the huge dyad of Amenhotep III and his wife Tiy that now dominates the central court of the Egyptian Museum in Cairo, were later dragged off by other pharaohs, but much still remains beneath the silt. A stele, also now in the Egyptian Museum, describes the temple as being built from 'white sandstone, with gold throughout, a floor covered with silver, and doors covered with electrum'. No gold or slver has yet been found, but the huge area behind is covered with statues and masonry that had long lain under the ground.

The colossi are just off the road, before you reach the Antiquities Inspectorate ticket office, and are usually being snapped and filmed by an army of tourists.

Temple of Seti I TEMPLE

(Map p198; adult/student E£30/15; ⏲6am-5pm) Seti I, who built the superbly decorated temple at Abydos and Karnak's magnificent hypostyle hall, died before this memorial temple was finished, so it was completed by his son Ramses II who had a heavier hand. At the northern end of the Theban necropolis, this temple sees few visitors, despite its picturesque location near a palm grove.

The temple was severely damaged by floods in 1994 and has been extensively restored. The entrance is through a small door in the northeast corner of the reconstructed fortresslike enclosure wall. The first and second pylons and the court are in ruins, as is the pharaoh's palace: recent excavations have revealed its foundations, just south of the court. The earliest found example of a palace within a memorial temple, its plan is similar to the better-preserved palace at the memorial temple of Ramses III at Medinat Habu.

The walls of the columned portico at the west facade of the temple, and those of the hypostyle court beyond it, contain some superbly executed reliefs. Off the hypostyle are six shrines and to the south is a small chapel dedicated to Seti's father, Ramses I, who died before he could build his own mortuary temple.

Carter's House & the Replica Tomb of Tutankhamun MUSEUM

(Map p198; adult/student E£50/25; ⏲9am-5pm; P 👪) The domed house where Howard Carter lived during his search for Tutankhamun's tomb is surrounded by a garden on what is otherwise a barren slope above the road from Deir al-Bahri to the Valley of the Kings. The house has been restored and decorated with pictures and tools of the excavation. An exact replica of Tutankhamun's burial chamber has been constructed on the edge of the garden along with an exhibition relating to the discovery of the tomb.

The replica has faithfully copied the shape of the original tomb, but only the burial (right-hand side) has been reproduced here. The work is intended to challenge assumptions about our desire to see original objects and to take some of the pressure off the original tomb. Although the young pharaoh's mummy has not been included, every detail of the chamber has been exactly reproduced, including some dust and pitting on the walls to the wooden railing, and cracks in the sarcophagus. The left-hand storeroom (not open in the original tomb) has been used to mount displays explaining how the tomb was discovered and reproduced.

There is a cafe space on the side of Carter's House which, when it reopens, will make this a peaceful place to stop for refreshment.

Assasif Tombs TOMB

(Map p198; Kheruef & Mntophaat adult/student E£40/20, Pabasa E£30/15) This group of tombs, located near Deir al-Bahri, belongs to 18th-dynasty nobles, and 25th- and 26th-dynasty nobles under the Nubian pharaohs. The area is under excavation by archaeologists, but of the many tombs here only some are open to the public, including the Tombs of Kheruef and Mntophaat and of Pabasa. Tickets are available at the ticket office of Deir al-Bahri (Temple of Hatshepsut).

The tomb of Kheruef is the largest 18th-dynasty noble's tomb here in Thebes, and it has some of the finest examples of New Kingdom relief, unfortunately mostly in poor condition. Among the images are some showing the jubilee celebration of Amenhotep III. The tomb of Pabasa, a 26th-dynasty priest, has wonderful scenes of agriculture, including bee-keeping, hunting and fishing.

Dra Abu'l Naga TOMB

(adult/student E£20/10; 6am-5pm) Hidden in the desert cliffs north of Deir al-Bahri lies yet another necropolis, Dra Abu'l Naga, with more than 100 tombs of rulers and officials. Most of these date from the 17th dynasty to the late period (c 1550–500 BC), but in the summer of 2014 it was announced that a royal tomb from the 11th dynasty had been found (c 2081–1938 BC). The area has been extensively plundered but two tombs escaped with their paintings mostly intact.

The **tomb of Roy** (No 234), a royal scribe and steward of Horemheb, is small with scenes of funerary offerings and agriculture, and a beautifully painted ceiling. A few metres away, the T-shaped **tomb of Shuroy** (No 13) contains some finely executed, but in places heavily damaged, paintings of Shuroy and his wife making offerings to the gods and a funeral procession led by a child mourner.

Valley of the Queens TOMB

(Biban al-Harim; Map p198; adult/student E£50/25, Nefertari E£100; 6am-5pm) There are at least 75 tombs in the Valley of the Queens, which sits at the southern end of the Theban hillside. They belonged to queens of the 19th and 20th dynasties as well as to other members of the royal families, including princesses and the Ramesside princes. The most famous of these, the tomb of Nefertari, is only occasionally opened, but others are worth the visit.

➡ Tomb of Nefertari (No 66)

Hailed as the finest tomb in the Theban necropolis (and in all of Egypt for that matter) the tomb of Nefertari was completely restored and reopened, but closed again. It is occasionally possible to visit. A replica of the tomb is planned to be installed, alongside the replica of Tutankhamun's burial chamber, near Howard Carter's house.

Nefertari was one of the five wives of Ramses II, the New Kingdom pharaoh known for his colossal monuments, but the tomb he built for his favourite queen is a shrine to her beauty and, without doubt, an exquisite labour of love. Every centimetre of the walls in the tomb's three chambers and connecting corridors is adorned with colourful scenes of Nefertari in the company

AVENUE OF SPHINXES

A 3km-long alley of sphinxes connecting Luxor and Karnak is being excavated. Most of the buildings covering the sphinxes have been destroyed, including some that were important to the development of 19th- and early-20th-century Luxor. The avenue will evenutally be completely revealed although it remains to be seen how many people will want to walk from Luxor to Karnak temples.

WHAT TO BRING

When visiting the west-bank sights, bring plenty of water (it is available at some sights, but you should overestimate the amount you will need). A sun hat, sunglasses and sunscreen are also essential. Small change for baksheesh is much needed, as guardians rely on tips to augment their pathetic salaries; E£5 or E£10 should be enough for them to either leave you in peace, or to open a door or reflect light on a particularly beautiful painting. A torch (flashlight) can come in handy.

of the gods and with associated text from the Book of the Dead nearby. Invariably, the 'Most Beautiful of Them', as Nefertari was known, is depicted wearing a divinely transparent white gown and a golden headdress featuring two long feathers extending from the back of a vulture. The ceiling of the tomb is festooned with golden stars.

Like most of the tombs in the Valley of the Kings, this one had been plundered by the time it was discovered by archaeologists. Only a few fragments of the queen's pink-granite sarcophagus remained, and of her mummified body, only traces of her knees were left.

➡ Tomb of Amunherkhepshef (No 55)

The valley's showpiece is now the tomb of Amunherkhepshef, with its beautiful, well-preserved reliefs. Amunherkhepshef, the son of Ramses III, was in his teens when he died. On the walls of the tomb's vestibule, Ramses holds his son's hand to introduce him to the gods that will help him on his journey to the afterlife. Amunherkhepshef wears a kilt and sandals, with the sidelock of hair typical of young boys.

The mummified five-month-old foetus on display in the tomb is the subject of many an inventive story, among them the suggestion that the foetus was aborted by Amunherkhepshef's mother when she heard of his death. It was found by Italian excavators in a valley to the south of the Valley of the Queens.

➡ Tomb of Khaemwaset (No 44)

Another son of Ramses III, Khaemwaset died young; there is little information about his age or cause of death. His tomb is filled with well-preserved, brightly coloured reliefs. Like Amunherkhepshef's tomb, it follows a linear plan, and is decorated with scenes of the pharaoh introducing his son to the gods, and scenes from the Book of the Dead. The vestibule has an astronomical ceiling, showing Ramses III in full ceremonial dress, followed by his son wearing a tunic and the sidelock of hair signifying his youth.

➡ Tomb of Titi (No 52)

Egyptologists are not sure which Ramesside pharaoh Titi was married to; in her tomb she is referred to as the royal wife, royal mother and royal daughter. Some archaeologists believe she was the wife of Ramses III, and her tomb is in many ways similar to those of Khaemwaset and Amunherkhepshef, perhaps her sons. The tomb has a corridor leading to a square chapel, off which is the burial chamber and two other small rooms. The paintings are faded but you can still make out a winged Maat kneeling on the left-hand side of the corridor, and the queen before Toth, Ptah and the four sons of Horus opposite. Inside the burial chamber are a series of animal guardians: a jackal and lion, two monkeys and a monkey with a bow.

New Gurna VILLAGE

(www.fathyheritage.com) Hassan Fathy's mud-brick village lies just past the railway track on the road from the ferry to the Antiquities Inspectorate ticket office. Although built to rehouse the inhabitants of Old Gurna, who lived on and around the Tombs of the Nobles, the village became a showcase of utilitarian mud-brick design.

The stunning buildings had Hassan Fathy's signature domes and vaults, thick mud-brick walls and natural ventilation, but the project failed in its original intention because most inhabitants of Old Gurna refused to move into the houses. Today much of Fathy's work is in tatters, the original houses replaced with breeze block although the beautiful mud-brick mosque and theatre survive. Unesco has recognised the need to safeguard the village, but its plans have stalled.

Theban Community Library LIBRARY

(☎0100 523 8113; http://www.thebanmappingproject.com/about/TMP-April-2013-Progress-Report.pdf; near New Gourna; ⏲1-8pm winter, 2-10pm summer;) FREE The latest project from Kent Weeks and the Theban Mapping Project is the first open library in Luxor. Opened in 2011, the free service has general books in Arabic and English, and a good collection on archaeology and issues related to conservation. There are regular evening lectures.

More information is available from the librarian, Ahmed Hassan.

Open to all, the library is used by local archaeologists and guides, school children (there is no other library that serves them) and people from the villages. The latest additions include books on diet and prenatal care for local mothers. The library is self-funding and welcomes donations of books and of funding.

Activities

Ballooning

Hot-air ballooning to see the sun rise over the ancient monuments on the west bank and Theban mountains is a great way to start the day. **Horus** (0111 015 1241, 228 2670; www.horusballoon.com), **Hod Hod Suleiman** (Map p188; 0122 115 8593, 227 1116; Sharia Omar Ali, off Sharia Televizyon), **Magic Horizon** (227 4060; www.visitluxorinhotairballoon.com; Sharia Khaled Ibn al-Walid; from E£900) and **Sindbad Balloons** (Map p198; 227 2960, 0100 330 7708; www.sindbadballoons.com) all offer morning flights at varying prices, often depending on how many people are on board. Expect to pay from €80 to €150 per person, although it is possible to bargain, particularly out of season.

Donkey, Horse & Camel Rides

Riding a horse, a donkey or a camel through the fields and seeing the sunset behind the Theban hills is wonderful. Boys at the local ferry dock on the west bank offer donkey and camel rides for about E£30 to E£40 for an hour. There are many reports of women getting hassled, and of overcharging at the end. Some west-bank hotels also offer camel trips, which include visits to nearby villages for a cup of tea, and donkey treks around the west bank. These trips, which start at around 7am (sometimes 5am) and finish near lunchtime, cost a minimum of about E£50 per person.

Excellent horses can be found at **Nobi's Arabian Horse Stables** (Map p188; 0100 504 8558, 231 0024; www.luxorstables.com; approx per hour for camel or horse with helmet E£35, for donkey LE£25; 7am-sunset), which also provides riding hats, English saddles and insurance (E£35 an hour). Nobi, one of the best-established and most reliable operators, also has camels at the same price and donkeys at E£25 an hour. He has the expertise to organise longer horse-riding and camping trips into the desert, or a week from Luxor to Kom Ombo along the west bank. Call ahead to book, and he can arrange a hassle-free transfer to make sure you arrive at the right place, as often taxi drivers will try and take you to a friend's stable instead. Around the corner is **Pharaoh's Stables** (Map p188; 0100 632 4961, 231 2263; per hour E£30-35; 7am-sunset) with horses, donkeys and camels (all E£30 to E£40 per hour).

Volunteering

Those distressed by the state of the horses in Luxor streets may like to visit **ACE** (Animal Care in Egypt; 928 0727; www.ace-egypt.org.uk; at the start of Sharia al-Habil, near traffic police; donations welcome; 8am-noon & 1-5pm). It's a veterinary hospital and animal-welfare centre seeing up to 200 animals a day. Treatment for the working animals of Egyptians, particularly donkeys and horses, is free. Volunteers are welcome.

KV5: THE GREATEST FIND SINCE TUTANKHAMUN

In May 1995, American archaeologist Dr Kent Weeks discovered the largest tomb in Egypt, believed to be the burial place of the many sons of Ramses II. It was immediately hailed as the greatest find since that of Tutankhamun, or as one London newspaper put it: 'The Mummy of all Tombs'.

In 1987, Weeks located the entrance to tomb KV 5, which Howard Carter had uncovered but dismissed as destroyed. Weeks' team cleared the entrance chambers, finding pottery, fragments of sarcophagi and wall decorations, which led him to believe it was the tomb of the sons of Ramses II. Then in 1995 Weeks unearthed a doorway leading to an incredible 121 chambers and corridors, making the tomb many times larger and more complex than any other found in Egypt. Clearing the debris from this unique and enormous tomb is a painstaking and dangerous task. Not only does every bucketful have to be sifted for fragments of pottery, bones and reliefs, but major engineering work has to be done to shore up the structure of the 440m-long tomb. Progress is slow but Weeks speculates that it has as many as 150 chambers. The excavation can be followed on the excellent website www.thebanmappingproject.com.

FEMALE PHARAOHS

Pharaoh was an exclusively male title and in early Egyptian history there was no word for a queen regent, but records show there actually were a few female pharaohs. From early dynastic times it seemed common practice that on the death of the pharaoh, if his heir was too young to rule or there was no heir, his wife, often also his stepsister or sister, would be appointed regent. It's not clear if this role was limited to a regency, or if they were created pharaoh, but what is sure is that they were often buried with all the honours reserved for a pharaoh.

The first queen to have ruled independently is thought to have been Merneith, who was the wife of the 1st-dynasty Pharaoh Djer (c 3000 BC), and mother of Den who ruled after her. Her name was found on a clay seal impression with all the names of the early kings, and she was buried with full royal honours at Abydos. Almost every dynasty had a woman who ruled for a short while under the title of 'King's Mother'. The 12th-dynasty Sobeknofru, daughter of Amenemhat III and wife and half sister of Amenhotep IV, is thought to have ruled Egypt from 1799 to 1795 BC, and her titles included Female Horus, King of Upper and Lower Egypt, and Daughter of Ra.

Hatshepsut is the most famous of Egypt's female pharaohs. When her husband and half-brother Tuthmosis II died in 1479 BC, Hatshepsut became regent with her stepson Tuthmosis III. Later, with the support of the Amun priesthood, she declared herself pharaoh, and her rule (1473–1458 BC) marked a period of peace and internal growth for Egypt. Sometimes she is shown in the regalia of the male pharaoh, including the false beard, sometimes she is clearly female. When Tuthmosis III finally took control in 1458 BC, he ordered all reference to her be wiped from Egyptian history, so her mummy has never been found, and her name and images were almost all erased.

Nefertiti, wife of the rebel pharaoh Akhenaten, was clearly involved in her husband's policies and is often depicted wearing kingly regalia. Some believe that she was in fact the mysterious Smenkhkare, known to have ruled for a few years after Akhenaten's death in 1336 BC. After Seti II died, his wife Tawosret became coregent with her stepson Siptah, and later proclaimed herself pharaoh (1188–1186 BC). She was buried in the Valley of the Kings.

About 1000 years later Cleopatra came to the throne at the age of 17, in 51 BC. It's thought that she first ruled jointly with her father Ptolemy XII and, after his death, with her younger brother Ptolemy XIII. To keep Egypt independent, she allied herself with the Roman Julius Caesar, whom she married and whose son she bore. After Caesar's death, she famously married another powerful Roman, Marc Antony, and fell with him to the might of Augustus Caesar.

Felucca Rides

As elsewhere in Egypt, the nicest place to be late afternoon is on the Nile. Take a felucca from either bank, and sail for a few hours, catching the soft afternoon light and the sunset, cooling in the afternoon breeze and calming down after sightseeing. Felucca prices range from E£30 to E£50 per boat per hour, depending on your bargaining skills.

A popular felucca trip is upriver to Banana Island, a tiny isle dotted with palms about 5km from Luxor. The trip takes two to three hours. Plan it in such a way that you're on your way back in time to watch a brilliant Nile sunset from the boat. Be sure to agree in advance exactly what is included. Beware that some captains have been charging a fictitious 'entry fee' to the island (it's free).

Swimming

After a hot morning of tombs and temples, a dip in a pool can be heavenly. Most bigger hotels and some budget places have swimming pools. The **Iberotel Luxor** (Map p188; Sharia Khaled ibn al-Walid) has a great pool on a pontoon on the Nile that can be used for E£100. The Hilton (p218) will usually allow you to swim if you are staying for lunch (check beforehand). The St Joseph (p218) and Domina Inn Emilio (p217) hotels have small rooftop pools that you can use for E£20. In the current downturn, most other east-bank hotels will also allow access for a fee. On the west bank the **Al-Moudira Hotel** (☎0122 325 1307; www.moudira.com; Daba'iyya; ❄@📶🏊) has a wonderful pool set in a peaceful garden on the edge of the desert; nonresidents can use it for E£75.

Because of the bargaining and hassle involved, some people may find independent travel challenging at times, and a day tour in an air-conditioned tour bus, taking in the main sights, might be just the thing. These tours offer a good introduction to the city.

Most small budget hotels aggressively promote their own tours. Some of these are better than others and there have been complaints from a number of travellers that they ended up seeing little more than papyrus shops and alabaster factories from a sweaty car with no air-con. If you do decide to take one of these tours, expect to pay about E£75 to E£100 per person.

Several of the more reliable travel agents are all next to each other, next door to the Winter Palace Hotel (p218). All offer the same kind of tours, so you can easily compare the prices. Aladin Tours (p215) at the Nefertiti Hotel also organises day cruises to Dendara from E£460 per person.

Aladin Tours CULTURAL TOUR
(Map p188; 237 2386, 0100 601 6132; http://nefertitihotel.com/tours; Nefertiti Hotel, Sharia as-Sahbi; 10am-6pm) This very helpful travel agency, run by the young, energetic Aladin, organises sightseeing tours in Luxor and around as well as in the Western Desert, plus boat trips and ferry tickets to Sinai.

American Express CULTURAL TOUR
(Map p188, 237 8333; luxor@amexfranchise.com; Corniche an-Nil, next to Winter Palace Hotel; 8am-8pm) Offers a large menu of tours in and around Luxor. Prices range from E£250 to E£400 per person for a half-day.

Jolley's Travel & Tours CULTURAL TOUR
(Map p188; 237 2262; www.jolleys.com; 9am-10pm) This reputable company, next to the Winter Palace Hotel, also runs day trips to the main sites.

QEA Travel Agency CULTURAL TOUR
(Map p188; 0100 294 3169; http://questforegyptianadventure.com; Gezira al-Bayrat) A different approach from this British-run agency that runs tailor-made tours in and around Luxor, as well as further afield to the Red Sea or the Western Desert. A percentage of its profits go towards charitable projects in Egypt.

Thomas Cook CULTURAL TOUR
(Map p188; 237 2196; www.thomascookegypt.com; 8am-8pm) Next to the Winter Palace, and offers an array of tours. Prices range from E£150 to E£400 per person for a half-day.

Festivals & Events

The town's biggest traditional festival is the **Moulid of Abu al-Haggag** (p23), a raucous five-day carnival that takes place in the third week before Ramadan.

In late January or early February each year a **marathon** (Map p198; 02-2260 6930, 0122 214 8839; www.egyptianmarathon.com) is held on the west bank. It begins at Deir al-Bahri and loops around the main antiquities sites before ending back where it began.

Sleeping

Luxor has a wide range of hotels for all budgets. Most package-tour hotels are on the east bank, as are most shops, restaurants and hectic town life. The west bank is developing at a fast rate and is certainly no longer entirely rural. But it is still a tranquil place, where

THE BEAUTIFUL FESTIVAL OF THE OPET

The most important annual religious festival in Thebes and Egypt was the **Opet Festival**, when the barque shrines of the Theban triad Amun, Mut and Khonsu were taken in a procession from the Karnak temples to their home at Luxor Temple. The festival lasted two to four weeks during the summer, the second month of the Nile flood, and was particularly important during the New Kingdom. The cult images were carried on the shoulders of the priests along the avenue of sphinxes, stopping for ceremonies and to rest at six barque shrines on the way, or taken by boat up the Nile, as seen on the reliefs in Amenhotep III's Colonnade in Luxor Temple and the outer wall of the Temple of Ramses III in the Great Court in Karnak. The statue of Amun was reunited with his ithyphallic form Amenemopet, symbolising fertility and rejuvenation. The ceremony reaffirmed the pharaoh's authority and his close ties with the 'King of Gods' Amun. The pharaoh, after all, was the living embodiment of the god Horus on earth. One of the highlights of the modern *moulid* (saint's festival) of Abu al-Haggag is when a felucca is pulled in procession through town, circling the temple, a modern echo of the ancient Opet Festival.

THE RETURN OF THE MUMMY

In 1881 Egypt's antiquities authority made the greatest mummy find in history: the mummies of 40 pharaohs, queens and nobles, just south of Deir al-Bahri in tomb No 320. It seems that 21st-dynasty priests had them moved as a protection against tomb robbers to this communal grave, after 934 BC. The mummies included those of Amenhotep I, Tuthmosis I, II and III, Seti I and Ramses II and III, many of which are now on display at the Egyptian Museum in Cairo. Their removal from the tomb and procession down to the Nile, from where they were taken by barge to Cairo, was accompanied by the eerie sound of black-clad village women ululating to give a royal send-off to the remains. The episode makes for one of the most stunning scenes in Shadi Abdel Salam's 1969 epic *Al-Mummia* (The Mummy), one of the most beautiful films made in Egypt.

However, the cache had already been found a decade earlier by the Abdel Rassoul family from Gurna, who were making a tidy sum by selling contents from it. Mummies, coffins, sumptuous jewellery and other artefacts made their way to Europe and North America. One of the mummies ended up in a small museum in Niagara Falls, Canada, until the late 1990s, when the crossed arms and excellent state of the body were recognised by an Egyptologist as signs of possible royalty. When the museum closed in 1999, the mummy was acquired by the Michael Carlos Museum in Atlanta. CT scans, X-rays, radiocarbon dating and computer imaging attempted to identify the mummy, and although they could only suggest that it was from later than the Ramesside period, an uncanny resemblance to the mummified faces of Seti I and Ramses II was seized upon by some Egyptologists as proof that this was the missing mummy of Ramses I. As a gesture of goodwill, the museum returned the mummy to Egypt in 2003, and it is now in the Luxor Museum.

the pace of life is much slower and where evenings are more often than not blissfully quiet. Since the 2011 revolution, tourism to Luxor has dropped dramatically and several places have closed their doors. If the slump continues, it may be possible to bargain.

At all costs avoid hotel touts, who may pounce on you as you get off the train or bus; they will get a 25% to 40% commission for bringing you to a hotel, but that will be added to your bill. Many budget and midrange hotels offer free or cheap transfers from the airport or train station, so to avoid touts and bargaining with taxi drivers call ahead and arrange to be picked up.

Luxor has a good selection of budget places. Many boast both roof gardens and washing machines. Budget hotels on the west bank are particularly good value, much quieter and often offer a more authentic encounter with locals. There is an ever-growing selection of midrange hotels on both banks, many catering to families.

If you are looking for a hotel with character, then check out the small mud-brick, traditional-style hotels on the west bank. East bank hotels are often modern places, popular with budget and adventure tour groups. There are some excellent bargains in this category, with good facilities at attractive rates. Out of season some incredibly cheap packages can be found, including flights from the UK.

East Bank

★Nefertiti Hotel HOTEL $

(Map p188; ☎237 2386; www.nefertitihotel.com; Sharia as-Sahabi, btwn Sharia Maabad al-Karnak & Sharia as-Souq; s/d/tr E£160/200/270; ⊖❄📶) Aladin as-Sahabi runs his family's hotel with care and passion, offering recently renovated, midrange facilities at budget prices. No wonder this hotel is popular with our readers: rooms are simple but very cosy and come with kettles and tea/coffee, the small private bathrooms are spotless, and an excellent breakfast is served on the roof terrace. One of the best budget options.

Larger new rooms on the top floors are decorated in local style. The rooftop is great for a drink or a bite, with great views of the west bank, Luxor Temple and Avenue of Sphinxes, all lit up at night. The Aladin Tours travel agency is also in the building.

★Boomerang Hotel HOTEL $

(Map p188; ☎228 0981; www.boomerangluxor.com; Mohamed Farid; dm E£25, d E£45-120; ❄📶) If the 1970s exist in Luxor it is in the Boomerang (although it was not actually here in the '70s) – a happy mix of Australia and Egypt with a range of budget rooms, some with air-con and en suite bathrooms, lounge and terrace, Aussie BBQ, tour booking, free wi-fi and just about everything else you could need.

Happy Land Hotel HOSTEL $
(Map p188; ☎227 1828; www.luxorhappyland.com; Sharia Qamr; s/d E£85/90, without bathroom E£75/80;) The Happy Land, a backpackers' favourite, offers clean rooms and spotless bathrooms, as well as very friendly service, a copious breakfast with fruit and cornflakes, and a rooftop terrace. Competition among Luxor's budget hotels is fierce, and the Happy Land comes out well almost every time. It doesn't need to send touts to the station!

Bikes can be rented for E£10 per day, and wi-fi and laundry facilities are free. Mr Ibrahim tries his utmost to make everyone appreciate his town. It sells ISIC cards.

Fontana Hotel HOSTEL $
(Map p188; ☎228 0663, 010 733 3238; www.fontanaluxorhotel.com; Sharia Radwan, off Sharia Televizyon; s/d/tr E£40/60/75, without bathroom E£30/50/65;) An old stalwart of the budget-hotel scene, this 25-room hotel has clean rooms, a washing machine for guest use, a luggage storage room, a rooftop terrace and a kitchen. Bathrooms are large and clean, and toilet paper and towels are provided. The owner, Magdi Soliman, is helpful. Beware extra breakfast charges.

Anglo Hotel HOTEL $
(Map p188; ☎238 1679; Midan al-Mahatta; s/d/tr E£60/110/140;) Across the road from the train station, so noisy at times, but right in the centre of town. Reception is worn, but old-style rooms are clean and excellent value with air-con, satellite TV, private bathroom, telephone and free wi-fi. The bar in the basement is popular with locals.

★**La Maison de Pythagore** GUESTHOUSE $$
(☎0100 535 0532; www.louxor-egypte.com; Al-Awamiya; s/d/tr €35/50/60;) This small guesthouse with seven rooms in a traditional Egyptian house is tucked away in the village behind the Sheraton Hotel, close to the tourist facilities and the Nile, but a world away from Luxor's hustle. Run by the Belgian Anne and her son Thomas, it's a great place to stay for a few days.

The soft traditional architecture encloses simple but cosy rooms, stylishly painted in earthy colours mixed with turquoise and blue. Some rooms have air-con, others fans, but all have large bathrooms. The garden is a small oasis with date palms, flowers, fruit trees and a fall of bougainvillea. Breakfast is served on the large roof terrace. Lunch and dinner, made with local seasonal produce, are available to order and can be taken in the garden or on the roof. Mother and son are both passionate about Egypt, and run their own tailor-made half-day to one-week tours and adventures for their guests and others.

Mara House GUESTHOUSE $$
(Map p188; ☎0100 757 1855; www.egyptwithmara.com; Sharia Salahadin Ayyubi, off Sharia Salakhana; r per person US$50;) Irish Mara wanted to open a home for travellers and seems to have succeeded with spacious rooms, each decorated in local style, and including a sitting area and a clean bathroom. Some of the accommodation is small flats, particularly good for families. This is a very popular option so book well ahead in the winter season.

The modern house, in a real Egyptian neighbourhood right behind the train station, can be hard to find but call for instructions or a free transfer. Mara also runs Salahadeen, a popular Egyptian restaurant where the food is served as it is in Egyptian homes.

Sonesta St George Hotel HOTEL $$
(Map p188; ☎238 2575; www.sonesta.com/luxor; Sharia Khaled ibn al-Walid; s/d city view from US$50, Nile view from US$75;) This 322-room marble-filled hotel, with faux Pharaonic columns and a flamelike fence around the roof, has a kitsch value that should not be overlooked. It is a good, lively place to stay. The hotel is well managed, has friendly staff, comfortable rooms with great views, a heated swimming pool, business centre and a good selection of restaurants.

Susanna Hotel HOTEL $$
(Map p188; ☎236 9915; www.susannahotelluxor.com; 52 Sharia Maabad al-Karnak; s/d/tr city view US$30/35/50, Nile view US$40/45/60;) Set between the Luxor Temple and the souq, this modern 45-room hotel has comfortable beds, wi-fi, air-con, satellite TV and great views. There is a good rooftop restaurant with views over Luxor Temple and the Nile, perfect for a sunset drink as alcohol is available – also a small rooftop pool.

Domina Inn Emilio HOTEL $$
(Map p188; ☎237 6666; www.emiliotravel.com; Sharia Yousef Hassan; s/d $30/45;) A good midrange hotel, the Emilio has 101 spacious rooms, all fully equipped with

SELF-CATERING RENTAL

Families or those planning a prolonged stay in Luxor might consider a self-catering option. Flat rental is mushrooming in Luxor, on both banks; it is cheap, and many foreigners are getting involved in the business. The downside of self-catering is sex tourism, as there is very little control as to whom people can bring in, whereas in hotels foreigners are not allowed to take guests back to their room.

Several companies can arrange flat rentals, including **Flats in Luxor** (010 356 4540; www.flatsinluxor.com; per night from $50;) run by a British-Egyptian couple who started renting out their own flats but now also manage others. The websites www.luxor-westbank.com and www.luxor4flats.com also have a wide selection of flats and houses available.

Villa al Diwan (227 4852, 0100 160 1214; www.al-diwan.fr; waterfront, west bank; per week from €900;) is a wonderful six-bedroom rental villa in traditional style overlooking the Nile and easily accommodating 12 people. The well-appointed rooms are on the 1st floor, while the ground floor has a kitchen, dining and sitting room and a terrace garden with a new pool. The rooftop terrace is a great place to watch the Nile and the surrounding countryside. It's located on the waterfront on the west bank, about 10 minutes south of the ferry landing.

minifridge, satellite TV, private bathroom, air-con and 24-hour room service. Other extras include an AstroTurfed roof terrace with plenty of shade and a large pool, a sauna and a business centre.

St Joseph Hotel HOTEL **$$**
(Map p188; 238 1707; stjosephhotel@yahoo.com; Sharia Khaled ibn al-Walid; s/d US$25/30;) This popular and well-run three-star hotel has been a favourite with small groups for years thanks to its simple but comfortable rooms with satellite TV, air-con and clean private bathrooms. All rooms have some Nile views, although the front rooms with a full view are quite noisy. There is also a small (heated) rooftop pool, a bar and a restaurant. The breakfast buffet is quite basic.

★Hilton Luxor Resort and Spa LUXURY HOTEL **$$$**
(239 9999; www.hiltonluxor.com; New Karnak; r from US$220;) The Luxor Hilton is the slickest, most luxurious resort in Luxor. Located 2km north of Luxor centre, past the Karnak temples, the large Nileside rooms are elegant and tastefully decorated in a warm Asian-inspired style with lots of neutral colours and wood. Communal areas exude calm and tranquillity and the spa is impressive, more Thailand than Egypt.

The large grounds include two Nile-view infinity swimming pools with submerged sun loungers, a Technogym, and several top-class restaurants, including the Mediterranean Olives and a chic Asian bistro, Silk Road. The staff and management are young and very hands-on. This hotel is almost a destination in itself, albeit not very family oriented.

Winter Palace Hotel HISTORIC HOTEL **$$$**
(Map p188; 237 1197; www.sofitel.com; Corniche an-Nil; old wing r from $160, ste from $450;) The Winter Palace was built to attract the aristocracy of Europe and is one of Egypt's most famous historic hotels. A wonderfully atmospheric Victorian pile, it has high ceilings, lots of gorgeous textiles, fabulous views over the Nile, an enormous garden with exotic trees and shrubs, a huge swimming pool and a tennis court.

Rooms vary in size and decor, but all are very comfortable, and the service is generally excellent. Food can be variable, with afternoon tea (E£150) a disappointment, but grand dining still a pleasure. The newer Pavillion Wing in the garden has more functional rooms, but use of the same public areas. Plans to upgrade the old building into a more luxurious version of itself were on hold at the time of writing.

Maritim Jolie Ville Kings Island RESORT **$$$**
(227 4855; www.jolieville-hotels.com; Kings Island; s/d/tr US$90/120/160;) Set amid lush gardens on its own island, 4km south of town, this is a great family hotel with a minizoo and playground in addition to several large swimming pools, tennis courts, spa and feluccas. There are 647 well-furnished and comfortable rooms in octagonal buildings throughout the extensive grounds. Offers a motorboat and bus shuttle to the centre of town.

Sheraton Luxor Resort RESORT $$$
(227 4544; www.sheratonluxor.com; Sharia Khaled ibn al-Walid; s/d from US$100;) This secluded three-storey building is set amid lush gardens at the far southern end of Sharia Khaled ibn al-Walid – close enough to walk to some restaurants but away from the street noise. Rooms are well appointed and those overlooking the Nile have great views. A popular hotel with a high repeat rate.

The hotel charges for internet in the rooms. The rundown garden bungalows should be avoided. The Italian restaurant, La Mama, remains popular.

West Bank

Marsam Hotel HISTORIC HOTEL $
(Map p198; 237 2403, 231 1603; www.marsamluxor.com; Old Gurna; s/d €15/25, without bathroom €12/20;) The oldest hotel on the west bank, the Marsam was originally built in the 1920s as a house for archaeologists from the University of Chicago, but was later turned into a hotel by Sheikh Ali of the local Abd el Rasoul family. The family have run it ever since. Work in 2013 left the hotel looking its best.

Twenty of the 36 rooms have en suite bathrooms and air-con, the others fans, but all retain the simple mud brick design and bare furnishings. The courtyard, open to fields and the excavations of the Temple of Amenhotep III, is a lovely, shaded place to sit – a delicious breakfast with home-baked bread is served here. Atmospheric and quiet, and close to almost all the west-bank sights, it remains popular with archaeologists, so you need to book ahead, particularly during the dig season (roughly from October to March). If you can't get a room, stop by for lunch, or a cold beer at the end of a hot day seeing the tombs.

Al-Gezira Hotel HOTEL $
(Map p188; 231 2505; www.el-gezira.com; Gezira al-Bayrat; s/d/tr E£100/150/210;) This hotel, in a modern building, is very much a home away from home – literally so for quite a few archaeologists during the winter season. The charming owners make everyone feel welcome, so that the hotel is often full. The 11 homey rooms are pristine, all with private bathrooms, overlooking the lake or a dried-up branch of the Nile.

The upstairs rooftop restaurant, where breakfast is served, has great Nile views as well as cold beer (E£12) and good traditional Egyptian food (set menu E£50). The same family also owns the nearby Gezira Garden (same website), a slightly newer building (s/d €25/35).

Kareem Hotel HOTEL $
(Map p188; 0100 184 2083; www.hotelkareem-lxr.com; Al-Gezira; s/d/tr E£130/210/280, 3-room flat per week E£1000;) Newly opened hotel with 12 simple but very clean rooms in a quiet residential area. The owner is young and helpful and keeps the place spotless. The hotel has little character otherwise but offers good value, and has a little garden and a splendid rooftop terrace with a restaurant where the owner's sister cooks.

Al-Fayrouz Hotel HOTEL $
(Map p188; 0122 277 0565, 231 2709; www.elfayrouz.com; Al-Gezira; s/d/tr/q E£95/150/190/240;) This tranquil hotel with 22 brightly painted rooms, overlooking fields, is a good base for exploring the monuments of the west bank. Under Egyptian-German management, the simple, nicely decorated rooms are spotless and most have balconies.

The more expensive rooms (count on E£25 more per person) are larger, have a sitting area and more character. Meals are served on the comfortable roof terrace or in the popular garden restaurant.

★ **Beit Sabée** BOUTIQUE HOTEL $$
(Map p198; 0111 837 5604; www.beitsabee.com; Bairat; d €30-80;) More like a house than a hotel, Beit Sabee has appeared in design magazines for its cool use of Nubian colours and local furnishings with a twist. Near the farms around Medinat Habu, it offers quiet accommodation, a closer contact with rural Egypt and fabulous views of the desert and Medina Habu from the rooftop.

Set in a traditional-style two-storey mudbrick house, the 15 bedrooms with en suite bathrooms are effortlessly chic and stylish, although some are larger and brighter than others. The bigger ones could easily take a third person (extra €10 per night). Breakfast is served in the courtyard or on the roof, and lunch and dinner can be served (E£50 for a meal with meat, E£30 for vegetarian). This is a good place to spend a calm few days.

Nile Valley Hotel HOTEL $$
(Map p188; 231 1477, 0122 796 4473; www.nilevalley.nl; Al-Gezira; s/d/tr/ste E£195/255/310/330;) A delightful Dutch-Egyptian-run hotel in a modern block right near the ferry

landing. The comfortable rooms almost all have ultraclean private bathrooms, satellite TV and air-con. Upstairs is a good rooftop bar-restaurant with fantastic views of the Nile and Luxor Temple, and there is a pool and children's pool in the garden.

Some rooms have Nile views but those overlooking the rear garden are quieter and slightly bigger. This hotel is particularly family friendly, and often has families staying here for a week or more. Staff also organise social events some evenings on the rooftop. Nonresidents can use the pool for E£50.

Hotel Sheherazade HOTEL **$$**
(Map p188; ☎0100 611 5939, 231 1228; www.hotelsheherazade.com; Al-Gezira; s/d/tr E£200/280/350, flat E£400; E£45; ❄📶) Mohamed El Sanuoy's dream of building a hotel has culminated in one of the most welcoming of west bank hotels and somewhere he takes great pride in. The 28 comfortable and spacious rooms are decorated with local colour and furnishings and all have en suite bathrooms with water heated by solar panels. The Moorish-style building is surrounded by a garden.

There are two restaurants (3-course meals per person), a well-tended garden and a small Arabic school.

El-Mesala Hotel GUESTHOUSE **$$**
(Map p188; ☎231 5105, 0122 352 4523; www.hotelelmesala.com; Al-Gezira, near ferry landing; s/d/tr/flat €20/30/37/40; ❄📶🏊) One of the better small, family-oriented hotels in Al-Gezira on the west bank. The hotel is on the Nile, a stone's throw from the ferry landing, and therefore perfectly located for visits on both banks. It has 17 immaculate rooms with comfortable beds, and with balconies looking at Luxor Temple and the Nile.

The staff and the manager Mr Ahmed are all extremely welcoming, and everything is absolutely spotless. The restaurant is in the front garden, and there's a great rooftop terrace for sunbathing.

Amon Hotel GUESTHOUSE **$$**
(Map p188; ☎231 0912, 0100 639 4585; www.amonhotel.com; Al-Gezira; s/d/tr/family €25/30/40/50; ❄📶) Charming family-run hotel in a modern building with spotless rooms, free wi-fi, a wonderful lush exotic garden where it's pleasant to have breakfast, lunch or a drink, extremely helpful staff and delicious home-cooked meals. This hotel is popular with archaeologists in winter, so book ahead.

In the new wing the rooms are large with private bathrooms, ceiling fans, air-con and balconies overlooking the courtyard. In the old wing, some of the small rooms have private bathrooms, and all have air-con. On the top floor are three triple rooms with an adjoining terrace and stunning views over the Theban Hills and the east bank. There are some single and doubles with shared bathroom at €5 less.

Desert Paradise Lodge LODGE **$$**
(Map p198; ☎231 3036; www.desertparadiselodge.com; Qabawi; s/d €40/70; ❄@🏊) Far from the crowds, off the road to the Valley of the Kings and on the edge of the desert, this is a place for those who want to do the west bank slowly and calmly. This beautiful small lodge, built in traditional style, has spacious domed rooms, lots of communal space, a garden and terraces overlooking the Theban hills.

It's 1.5km from the crossroads to Valley of the Kings, on the first left after Carter House.

El-Nakhil Hotel HOTEL **$$**
(Map p188; ☎231 3922, 0122 382 1007; www.elnakhil.com; Gezira El Bairat; s/d/tr €25/35/45; ❄📶) Nestled in a palm grove, the Nakhil (Palm Tree) is on the edge of Al-Gezira. This resort-style hotel has 17 spotless, well-finished domed rooms, all with private bathrooms and air-con. It also has family rooms, baby cots, and three rooms that can cater for disabled guests. The large rooftop restaurant has great views over the Nile.

House of Scorpion GUESTHOUSE **$$**
(☎0100 512 8732; tayeb.saket@yahoo.com; Al-Taref; r E£240-280, ste E£400; ❄📶) Charming little guesthouse in a mud-brick house with seven differently themed rooms, all large with tiled bathrooms and small salons in Arab style. Tayeb, who runs the place, is very helpful and friendly. It's away from the crowds and mainly works by word of mouth. It is essential to call or book ahead for food as well as for sleeping.

Nour al-Gurna GUESTHOUSE **$$**
(Map p198; ☎0100 129 5812, 231 1430; www.nourelgournahotel.com; Old Gurna; s E£150, d E£200-250, ste E£300) Set in a palm grove, Nour al-Gurna has large mud-brick rooms, with fans, mosquito nets, small stereos, locally made furniture and tiled bathrooms. Romantic and original, with friendly management, this is a lovely centrally located hotel convenient for visiting west-bank sites.

Nour al-Balad GUESTHOUSE $$
(Map p198; ☎206 0111; www.nourelgournahotel.com; Ezbet Bisily; s/d/ste E£200/250/300; ❄) The sister hotel to Nour al-Gurna is even quieter and has more spacious rooms. To get here, follow the track behind Medinat Habu for 500m.

★ **Al-Moudira** LUXURY HOTEL $$$
(☎0122 392 8332, 095 255 1440; www.moudira.com; Daba'iyya; r/ste US$285/355; ❄@📶🏊) Al-Moudira is a luxury hotel with a style and individuality so often lacking in Egypt. A Moorish fantasy of pointed arches and soaring domes, surrounded by lush green and birdsong, the hotel has 54 rooms grouped around a small garden courtyard, a large pool and hammam (bathhouse). It has a tranquil courtyard restaurant and vibrant bar, and excellent and friendly service.

Each room is different in shape, size (all are very large) and decoration, each having its own hand-painted trompe l'œil theme and with Egyptian antiques. Cushioned benches and comfortable antique chairs invite pashalike lounging and the enormous vaulted bathrooms feel like private hammams. Public spaces are even more spectacular with traditional *mashrabiyya* (wooden lattice) combined with work by contemporary 'orientalist' artists. The staff are friendly and very helpful. Set on the edge of the cultivated land and the desert, this hotel is spectacular and unique. Don't let its isolation put you off: transport is quick and easy.

Eating

Most people come to Luxor for monuments and not for its fine cuisine – a good thing as most restaurants, particularly in the hotels, have long been mediocre. But the food is improving, particularly where restaurants serve traditional Egyptian food. Outside of hotels, few places serve alcohol or accept credit-card payment; exceptions are noted in the reviews. Unless otherwise noted, restaurants tend to open from about 9am until midnight.

Luxor has a number of good bakeries. Try the ones on Sharia Ahmed Orabi, at the beginning of Sharia Maabad al-Karnak and on Sharia Gedda. On the west bank try the food and fruit shops on the main street in Al-Gezira, or head for the wonderful weekly market Souq at-Talaat (p225), in Taref opposite the Temple of Seti I.

East Bank

★ **Wenkie's German Ice Cream & Iced Coffee Parlour** ICE CREAM $
(Map p188; ☎0128 894 7380; www.facebook.com/wenkies; Sharia al-Gawazat; scoops from E£2; ⏲2-8pm Sat-Thu) For people who only opened a shop in February 2014, Ernst and Babette Wenk have quickly become legends, serving the freshest, most delicious ice cream in Luxor – some are saying even in the world. Using organic buffalo milk and local fresh fruits, they make and sell ices and sorbets from a small shop/parlour near the passport office, opposite the Nile Palace. The secret to their success is the quality of the product, the distinctly local flavours (among them hibiscus, mango and doum palm ices) and the price: E£2 for a small scoop, E£4 for a big one. Wenkie's also serves iced coffee, milkshakes and waffles. It tends to close on holidays and for a couple of months in the summer. Their ices are also available at the Crepe Cafe near Luxor station.

Koshari Alzaeem EGYPTIAN FAST FOOD $
(Map p188; Midan Youssef Hassan; E£5-15; ⏲24hr) Probably the best *kushari* (noodles, rice, black lentils, fried onions and tomato sauce) in town. The few tables tend to fill up fast. There is a second, larger branch near the junction of Televizyon and Al-Manshiya streets.

Abu Ashraf EGYPTIAN FAST FOOD $
(Map p188; ☎237 5936; Sharia al-Mahatta; dishes E£15-30; ⏲8am-11pm) This large, popular restaurant and takeaway is just down from the train station. It serves roasted chicken (E£16), pizzas (E£20), good *kushari* (E£4 to E£10) and kebabs (E£20).

Fruit & Vegetable Souq MARKET $
(Map p188; Sharia as-Souq) This is the best place for fruit and veg, although the good stuff sells out early in the morning. On either side of the main street are little shops selling produce and groceries throughout the day.

New Mish Mish EGYPTIAN FAST FOOD $
(Map p188; ☎228 1756, 0100 810 5862; Sharia Televizyon; dishes E£5-40; ⏲8am-midnight; ❄) A long-standing budget-traveller haunt, Mish Mish has a contemporary and air-conditioned fast-food-style interior, serving good sandwiches (E£8 to E£20), salads (E£5 to E£15), grilled meats (E£25 to E£35) including shwarma, mixed grill and stuffed pigeon, and good grilled and fried-fish dishes

(E£25 to E£40). There's no alcohol, but there is a selection of fresh fruit juices (E£5).

★Sofra Restaurant & Café EGYPTIAN $$

(Map p188; ☎235 9752; www.sofra.com.eg; 90 Sharia Mohamed Farid; mains E£20-60; ⊙11am-midnight) Sofra remains our favourite restaurant in Luxor. Located in a 1930s house, away from all the tourist tat, it is as Egyptian as can be, in menu, decor and even in price. The large menu features all the traditional Egyptian dishes such as stuffed pigeon and excellent duck, as well as a large selection of salads, dips (E£4) and mezze.

The ground floor has three small private dining rooms and a salon, giving the feeling of being in someone's home. There is also a spacious covered rooftop terrace, which is also a cafe where you can come for a drink. The house is filled with antique oriental furniture, chandeliers and traditional decorations, all simple but tasteful. Alcohol is not available, but there are delicious juices on offer, as fresh as the food, and with friendly staff and sheesha to finish, the place is a real treat, recommended by many.

★As-Sahaby Lane EGYPTIAN $$

(Map p188; ☎095 236 5509; www.nefertitihotel.com/sahabi.htm; Sharia as-Sahaby, off Sharia as-Souq; mains E£45-70; ⊙9am-11.30pm) Great alfresco restaurant in the lane running between the souq and the street to the Karnak temples. Fresh and well-prepared Egyptian dishes like *fiteer* (flaky pizza) and *tagen* (stew cooked in earthenware pots) are served alongside good pizzas and salads, although the chef is constantly expanding his range: look out for the new camel with couscous.

The young staff are both friendly and efficient and the terrace is a great place to watch the world go by, or relax after shopping in the souq. The same menu is served on the hotel's rooftop terrace, which has great views over Luxor Temple and the Thebes mountains, both floodlit at night.

Pizza Roma.It ITALIAN $$

(Map p188; ☎0111 879 9559; Sharia St Joseph; dishes E£40-60) The most popular Italian restaurant in Luxor. Run by an Italian woman and her Egyptian partner, the small orange-painted restaurant serves a long list of pastas and pizzas, as well as some classic Italian meat dishes. All are reliable, made as closely as possible to the Italian way.

The restaurant attracts a mix of locals, tourists, expats and visiting Cairenes. It doesn't serve alcohol, but you can bring your own. For dessert, head around the corner for ice cream from Wenkie's.

Salahadeen EGYPTIAN $$

(Map p188; ☎0100 757 1855; www.salahadeen.com; Mara Hotel, Sharia Salahadin Ayyubi, off Sharia Salakhana; dishes E£18-60; ⊙6pm-midnight; ❄) Salahadeen offers a set three-course menu of fresh home-cooked Egyptian food. Most dishes consist of vegetables, and the vegetarian options are not cooked in a meat broth as in so many other places. It is essential to book ahead. Alcohol is served.

The food is served as if in an Egyptian home – knives and forks are offered but guests are encouraged to eat in the Egyptian way by dipping bread in the various dishes.

Gerda's Garden EGYPTIAN, EUROPEAN $$

(☎235 8688, 0122 534 8326; www.luxor-german-restaurant.com; opp Hilton Luxor, New Karnak; dishes E£15-45; ⊙6.30-11pm; ❄) Gerda is one half of a German-Egyptian couple whose restaurant has built a strong following with European residents and regular visitors to Luxor. The decor is homely provincial European bistro, but the menu features both Egyptian specials like kebab and delicious grilled pigeon, and very European comfort food for those slightly homesick, such as goulash and potato salad. They also serve an excellent grilled duck (E£55), as well as fish when they can get it fresh from the Mediterranean (E£50-65).

Jewel of the Nile BRITISH, EGYPTIAN $$

(Map p188; ☎0106 252 2394; Sharia al-Rawda al-Sherifa; mains E£40-60, set menu E£75-85; ⊙noon-midnight; ❄📶🍸) Laura and Mahmud have survived the tourist downturn by offering traditional Egyptian food using organic vegetables from their farm, as well as British food for homesick Brits: steaks, cottage pie, apple crumble and an all-day English breakfast (E£25). On Sundays a traditional lunch is served all day with roast beef and Yorkshire pudding (E£50), and on Saturdays and Wednesdays at 5.30pm there is a popular quiz night in aid of local charities. The menu features a good selection of vegetarian dishes. The dining room is air-conditioned and there is a small space outside. Alcohol available. It's 300m off Sharia Khaled ibn al-Walid.

A Taste of India INDIAN $$

(Map p188; ☎0109 373 2727; Sharia St Joseph; dishes E£35-80; ⊙noon-11pm; ❄🍸) A small British-run Indian restaurant in neutral colours with plain wooden tables and chairs. On the menu are European versions of Indian dishes such as korma, spinach masala and *jalfrezi* (marinated meat curry with tomato, pepper and onion), as well as original Indian specials such as madras and vindaloo curries. For those not too fond of spice, a few international (read British) dishes such as steak and pastas are available. The place is popular with expat Brits, as well as vegetarians who come for spicy vegetable dishes. The building, under the sign of Asia House, also has a Thai and Chinese restaurant. It's off Sharia Khaled ibn al-Walid.

Silk Road ASIAN $$$

(☎237 4933; www.hiltonluxor.com; New Karnak; dishes E£70-120; ⏲6.30-11pm; ❄) Silk Road is one of the most sophisticated dining experiences in Luxor, offering an exotic cuisine, rich in spices, sourced from India, Thailand, China and all over Asia and prepared by the wonderful Indian chef. The setting is Asian minimal chic. If you are at a loss with the large-ish menu, ask for a degustation of several dishes (from E£240). Good wine list, and perfect for a romantic dinner.

1886 Restaurant MEDITERRANEAN $$$

(Map p188; ☎238 0425; Winter Palace Hotel, Corniche an-Nil; mains E£160-310; ⏲7-11pm; ❄) The 1886 is the fanciest restaurant in the town centre, serving inventive Mediterranean-French food and a few Egyptian dishes with a twist, all in a grand old-style dining room with formal, white-gloved waiters. Guests are expected to dress up for the occasion – men wear a tie and/or jacket (some are available for borrowing). A grand evening out!

The menu changes with the seasons, but expect delicacies such as grilled spine lobster in a butter sauce, or risotto of prawns and truffle. Pressed duck is a speciality and there is an extensive (and expensive) wine list.

Little Britain

The area around the Sonesta St George Hotel (p217), on Sharia Khaled Ibn al-Walid, slightly away from Luxor centre, has a large concentration of British pubs and restaurants. Every other restaurant is run by a British-Egyptian couple; most are clean and serve decent British-European food as well as a few Egyptian specialities. If you are yearning for a good pizza, pasta or steak, then this is the place to head. A Sunday roast of beef with Yorkshire pudding is on most menus.

West Bank

Restaurant Mohammed EGYPTIAN $

(Map p108; ☎0120 325 1307, Kom Lolah; set meals E£35-60) Mohammed's is a blast of old-time Luxor, a simple, family-run restaurant attached to the owner's mud-brick house, where charming Mohammed Abdel Lahi serves with his son Azab, while his wife cooks. The small menu includes meat grills, delicious chicken and duck as well as stuffed pigeon, a local speciality. Stella beer is usually available as well as Egyptian wine.

With an outdoor terrace and laid-back atmosphere, it is a great place to recharge batteries in the middle of a day exploring temples and tombs, or to linger in the evening, but call ahead to make sure it is open. They can also organise a picnic in the desert or on a felucca upon demand.

★Nile Valley Hotel INTERNATIONAL $$

(Map p188; Al-Gezira; meals E£40-60; ⏲8am-11pm) A popular rooftop restaurant with a bird's-eye view of the west bank's waterfront, the river and Luxor Temple, the Nile Valley has a wide-ranging menu of Egyptian and international specialities. It is also a good place to relax with a cold beer (E£16).

Al-Gezira Hotel EGYPTIAN $$

(Map p188; ☎231 0034; Al-Gezira; set menu E£35) This comfortable rooftop restaurant serves a set menu with Egyptian specialities, such as the popular *molokhiyya* (stewed leaf soup) and *mahshi kurumb* (stuffed cabbage leaves cooked with dill and spices) that must be ordered in advance. There are great views over the Nile and the bright lights of Luxor beyond. Cool beers (E£12) and Egyptian wine (E£85) are on offer.

★Al-Moudira MEDITERRANEAN $$$

(☎0120 325 1307; Daba'iyya; mains E£75-110; ⏲8am-midnight) In keeping with its flamboyant decor, Al-Moudira has the most sophisticated and most expensive food on the west bank, with great salads and grills at lunchtime. The more elaborate dinner menu, which changes daily, has delicious Mediterranean-Lebanese cuisine. This is a great place for a romantic dinner in the courtyard, or by the fire in the winter. Reserve ahead.

Ramesseum Rest House CAFE $

After visiting the tombs of the Nobles or the Ramesseum, take a break on the terrace of the rest-house restaurant right next to the Ramesseum temple that is called, not surprisingly, **Ramesseum Rest House** (Map p198; ☎0100 945 0789; beside the Ramesseum, Gurna; ⏰7am-1am). It is a great place to relax and have a cool drink, even a beer, or something simple to eat. You can leave your bike here while exploring the surroundings.

Drinking & Nightlife

East Bank

Even without booming tourism, Luxor is busy at night. Luxor Temple is open until 10pm and worth seeing at night; the souq is open late as well and more lively at night than in the day. In summer lots of locals stroll along the corniche.

However, this is not exactly the place for clubbing, even if you're into dancing to outmoded disco music. There are some bars with decent atmosphere, and most of the larger hotels put on a folkloric show several times each week, depending on the season and number of tour groups around.

You'll find discos at **Tutotel Partner Hotel** (Map p188; ☎237 7990), one of the more popular options, and **Hotel Mercure** (Map p188; ☎238 0944) but they were closed at the time of writing, and might reopen when there is more stability.

Cilantro CAFE
(Map p188; lower level, Corniche an-Nil) A pleasant, popular outdoor cafe, right on the Nile, in front of the Winter Palace Hotel. The former Metropolitan is now part of the Egyptian coffee chain Cilantro, serving dull though usually reliable snacks and good coffee. Away from the hassle of the corniche, right by the waterline, it is a good place to while away a moment.

New Oum Koulsoum Coffee Shop CAFE
(Map p188; http://oumkolsoumcaffe.com; Sharia as-Souq; ⏰24hr) Pleasant ahwa (coffeehouse) right in the heart of the souq, on a large terrace with welcoming mist machines, where you can recover from shopping and haggling and watch the crowds without any hassle. On the menu are fresh juices (E£10 to E£20), hot and cold drinks and a good sheesha (E£15), as well as 'professional Nespresso' coffee (E£15).

Chez Omar CAFE
(Map p188; Sharia Yousef Hassan) This relaxed cafe terrace in a small garden off the main souq, with bamboo furniture, is perfect to take a break from the buzz around. A good place to have a fresh juice, smoke a sheesha or eat a snack. Inside is Chez Omar II, a cool laid-back eatery with Egyptian dishes such as kebab and pigeon stew (E£30).

Kings Head Pub PUB
(Map p188; ☎0106 510 2133; Sharia Khaled ibn al-Walid) A relaxed and perennially popular place to have a beer (E£15), shoot pool and watch sports on a big screen, the Kings Head tries to capture the atmosphere of an English pub without being twee. The laid-back atmosphere also means that women can come here without being harassed.

West Bank

There are no real bars on the west bank; drinking is done at restaurants or not at all, but these are three very pleasant places for a drink.

Maratonga Cafeteria CAFE
(Map p198; ☎231 0233; Kom Lolah; ⏰6am-11pm) This friendly outdoor cafe-restaurant, in front of Medinat Habu, is the best place to sip a cold drink under a big tree after wandering through Ramses III's magnificent temple, or to have a delicious *tagen* (E£40) or salad for lunch. The view is superlative and the atmosphere is relaxing.

Marsam Hotel CAFE
(Map p198; www.marsamluxor.com; Old Gurna; 📶) The old hotel has a beautiful, shaded garden courtyard, a very pleasant place for a drink, day or night.

☆ Entertainment

If you want to avoid the bright lights of the town, the west bank is the place to be. Nobi's Arabian Horse Stables (p213) and QEA Travel Agency (p215) arrange evening desert BBQs for groups of 10 or more and sometimes put on a horse-dancing show.

Shopping

A whole range of Egyptian souvenirs are available in Luxor town, but for alabaster it is best to head for the west bank. The alabaster is mined about 80km northwest of the Valley of the Kings, and although the alabaster factories near the Ramesseum and Deir al-Bahri sell cheap handmade cups, vases and lights in the shape of Nefertiti's head, it is possible to find higher-quality bowls and vases, often unpolished, which are great buys. Take care when buying, as sometimes what passes for stone is actually wax with stone chips. Avoid going with a tour guide as his commission will invariably be added to your bill.

The *tagen* (clay pots) that are used in local cooking make a more unusual buy. Very practical, they can be used to cook on top of the stove or in the oven and they look good on the table too. Prices start at E£10 for a very small pot and go up to about E£40. They're on sale on the street just beside the police station in Luxor's east bank.

★Caravanserai CRAFT
(Map p198; ☎0122 327 8771; www.caravanserailuxor.com; Kom Lolah; ⏲8am-10pm) This delightful shop, the only one of its kind on the west bank, is kept by the friendly Hamdi and his family in their newly refurbished house near Medinat Habu. Recognising that making crafts was one of the few things poor Egyptian women could do to earn money, he decided to set up a shop to encourage and help them.

Hamdi buys almost everything people make, telling them what sells well, suggesting ways of improving their designs; above all he loves the people's creativity. His newly enlarged shop is sumptuous and spacious and has beautiful pottery from the Western Oases, Siwan embroideries, amazing appliqué bags and many other crafts that can be found almost nowhere else in Egypt.

Habiba CRAFT
(Map p188; ☎0100 124 2026, 235 7305; www.habibagallery.com; Sharia Sidi Mahmoud, off Sharia as-Souq; ⏲10am-10pm) Run by an Australian woman who wants to promote the best of Egyptian crafts, Habiba sells an ever-expanding selection of Bedouin embroidery, jewellery, leather work, wonderful Siwan scarves, cotton embroidered scarves from Sohag, the best Egyptian cotton towels (usually only for export), mirrors, brass lights and much more – and all at fair-trade fixed prices.

This tiny shop goes from strength to strength, offering the best selection of crafts on the east bank. It is a world away from what is available in the nearby souq. Another **branch** (Sharia Hilton; ⏲10am-10pm) has opened in New Karnak near the Hilton Luxor.

DON'T MISS

CONTEMPORARY LUXOR

With so many world-class monuments it is easy to lose sight of contemporary Luxor, particularly when time is limited. Take some time to stroll through the Luxor souq (p221). Be sure to venture beyond the tourist bazaar just off Sharia al-Mahatta, where locals shop for fabrics, food and household goods – liveliest in the early evening. There you get a glimpse into a world far away from the temples. On the west bank, **Souq at Talaat** (Map p198; ⏲Tue mornings) is a rural-style weekly market, little visited by tourists. It is held on Tuesday mornings in Taref near the also little-visited Temple of Seti I. Instead of taking a taxi across the bridge, head for the local ferry opposite Luxor Temple to go across, and take a taxi, pick-up or bicycle, all available near the west-bank ferry landing.

Fair Trade Centre CRAFT
(Map p188; ☎236 0870, 0100 034 7900; Sharia Maabad al-Karnak; ⏲9am-10.30pm) A shop that markets handicrafts from NGO projects throughout Egypt. It has well-priced hand-carved wood and pottery from the nearby villages of Hejaza and Garagos, aromatic oils from Quz, beadwork from Sinai, hand-blown glass, Akhmim table linen, beading from the west bank in Luxor, and recycled glass and paper from Cairo. Another **branch** (Map p188; Sharia Maabad Luxor; ⏲9am-10.30pm) has opened behind Luxor Temple, next to McDonalds.

Abo el Hassan Alabaster Factory CRAFT
(Map p198; ☎0106 733 3081; West Bank, opposite Tombs of the Nobles; ⏲8am-4pm) Mohamed Yousef's shop looks nothing from the outside, but he has a wide range of alabaster and other carved stone on sale. Unlike many other alabaster shops, he will admit that the stone doesn't come from the Theban hills, but from Asyut and Minya. Prices range from E£100 to E£1000, there is no hard sell and the shop is air-conditioned.

AA Gaddis Bookshop SOUVENIRS, BOOKS
(Map p188; ☎238 7042; www.gaddis-and-co.co.uk; Corniche an-Nil; ⏲10am-9pm Mon-Sat, 10.30am-9pm Sun, closed Jun & Jul) Next door to the Winter Palace Hotel, as it has been for generations; extensive selection of books on Egypt, postcards and souvenirs.

Aboudi Bookshop BOOKS
(Map p188; ☎237 2390, 0111 117 4764; www.aboudi-bookstore.com; Sharia Maabad al-Karnak; ⏰9.30am-10pm) Has an excellent selection of guidebooks, English-language books on Egypt and the Middle East, maps, postcards and fiction. It's behind Luxor Temple.

Aboudi Bookshop BOOKS
(Map p188; ☎237 3390, 213 9117; Sharia al Gawazat, off Sharia Khaled ibn al-Walid; ⏰9.30am-10pm) Part of the same family as the Aboudi Bookshop on Sharia Maabad al-Karnak, this bookshop also has a great selection of English-language books on Egypt and the Middle East, maps and postcards. Behind the post office.

Duty Free Shop Luxor DRINK
(Sharia Awamaya; ⏰10am-2pm & 7-11pm) Shop for cigarettes and alcohol at the downtown duty free, which has a good selection of the main brands. You need to bring your passport and come within 48 hours of arrival in Egypt. The branch at the Karnak temples was closed at the time of writing.

Al-Ahram Beverages DRINK
(Map p188; ☎237 2445; Sharia Ramses) This is the Luxor outlet for the country's monopoly beer and wine producer.

ℹ Information

DANGERS & ANNOYANCES

Luxor has long been considered the 'hassle capital' of Egypt and with so little business around, this has not improved. Some *calèche* (horse-drawn carriage) drivers can be particularly aggressive, pushed by the need to feed their horses, many of them quite malnourished. This hassle is a sign of desperation caused by the difficult financial situation that Egypt, and particularly Luxor, is in.

The most common scams are asking for extra baksheesh at the monuments, overcharging for a *calèche* or felucca, charging European prices for taxi rides, and touts in the souq or station targeting new arrivals. A frequent scam is for taxi or *calèche* drivers to tell tourists there is a local souq that is less touristy than the souq behind the Luxor Temple. They then drive around town and pull up at the same old souq. The tourist office or the tourist police will need a written report from you if anything happens, and will try to take action.

In recent years Luxor has also become a known destination for female sex tourism, popular with some often-older Western women looking for sex with young Egyptians. Individual women travellers looking for nothing more risqué than an ancient temple or a desert sunset can find themselves hassled.

EMERGENCY

Ambulance (☎123)

Police (Map p188; ☎122, 237 2350; cnr Sharia Maabad al-Karnak & Sharia al-Matafy)

Tourist Police (Map p188; ☎237 6820; Corniche an-Nil; ⏰8am-3pm & 8pm-midnight) On the walkway below the corniche, opposite the Winter Palace Hotel.

INTERNET ACCESS

You can find internet access everywhere in Luxor. Many hotels now also have wi-fi, and it's mostly free in budget and midrange hotels. Prices in internet cafes range from E£4 to E£10 per hour.

Gamil Centre (Map p188; lower level, Corniche an-Nil; ⏰24hr) In front of the Winter Palace Hotel.

Heroes Internet (Map p188; Sharia Televizyon; ⏰24hr)

Lotus Internet Café (Map p188; ☎238 0419; Sharia as-Souq; ⏰9am-midnight) Located next door to the restaurant of the same name.

Salem Net (Map p188; ☎236 4652; ⏰24hr) Good connection and air-conditioned room next to the train station, opposite the Anglo Hotel.

MEDICAL SERVICES

Dr Boutros (Map p198; ☎231 0851; Kom Lolah) Excellent English- and French-speaking doctor, who works on the west bank.

Dr Ihab Rizk (☎0122 216 0846) English-speaking cardiologist, who will come to your hotel, on the east bank.

International Hospital (Map p188; ☎228 0192, 228 0194; Sharia Televizyon) The best place in town.

MONEY

Most major Egyptian banks have branches in Luxor. Unless otherwise noted, usual opening hours are 8.30am to 2pm and 5pm to 6pm Sunday to Thursday. ATMs can be found all over town, including at most banks and five-star hotels.

American Express (Map p188; ☎237 8333; Corniche an-Nil; ⏰9am-4.30pm) Beside the entrance to the Winter Palace Hotel.

Banque du Caire (Map p188; Corniche an-Nil) Near the Winter Palace Hotel and Egyptair.

Banque Misr (Map p188; Corniche an-Nil) Near Luxor Temple.

Broxelles Exchange (Map p188; ☎237 1300; Sharia al-Mahatta; ⏰9am-9pm) Better exchange rates than the bank.

HSBC (Map p188; Corniche an-Nil) Near the Iberotel Luxor.

National Bank of Egypt (Map p188; Corniche an-Nil) Near the Winter Palace Hotel and Egyptair.

Thomas Cook (Map p188; ☎237 2196; Corniche an-Nil; ⏰8am-8pm) Below entrance to Winter Palace Hotel.

POST

Main post office (Map p188; Sharia al-Mahatta; ⏰8.30am-2.30pm Sat-Thu)

TELEPHONE

There are card phones scattered throughout the town. Cards are available from kiosks and shops. There are several mobile-phone shops on Sharia al-Mahatta and Sharia Televizyon that sell cheap tourist SIM cards.

Telephone office (Map p188; Corniche an-Nil; ⏰8am-8pm) Below the entrance to Winter Palace Hotel.

TOURIST INFORMATION

Airport office (☎237 2306; ⏰8am-8pm)

Main tourist office (Map p188; ☎237 3294, 237 2215; Midan al-Mahatta; ⏰9am-8pm) Very helpful and well-informed tourist information opposite the train station, run by Taher Eladesy. There is also an office for hotel bookings, tours and tickets for the sound-and-light show in Karnak. There's a branch (Map p188; ☎237 0259; Train Station; ⏰8am-8pm) in the train station too.

ℹ Getting There & Away

AIR

EgyptAir (Map p188; ☎238 0581; www.egyptair.com, Winter Palace Hotel, Corniche an-Nil; ⏰8am-8pm) operates flights to Cairo, Abu Simbel (via Aswan) and Sharm el-Sheikh. A one-way ticket to Cairo costs between E£370 and E£720. The staff here are efficient and friendly.

BUS

With bus travel along the Nile restricted, the obvious services to use are for the Red Sea coast (Hurghada) and on to Cairo. The **Zanakta bus station** (☎0128 436 663) is out of town on the road to the airport – about 1km before it. A taxi from the town to the bus station will cost around E£25 to E£35.

Tickets for the **Upper Egypt Bus Co** (Map p188; ☎232 3218, 237 2118; Midan al-Mahatta) buses can be bought at its office in town, just south of the train station. Some buses leave from there as well. Buses heading to Cairo leave at 6.30pm from the town office and 7pm from the bus station (E£100, 10 to 11 hours), but booking ahead is essential.

Six daily buses head from the bus station to Hurghada (E£35, five hours) from 8.30am to 8pm. All stop in Qena (E£8, one to two hours) and Safaga (E£30 to E£35, four to 4½ hours) and go on to Suez (E£70 to E£80, 10 hours).

For Al-Quseir and Marsa Alam, change at Safaga. We do not reocmmend the bus to Sharm el-Sheikh because of the unrest in Sinai.

There are frequent buses to Qena (E£5 to E£7) between 6.30am and 8pm, but you pay for the taxi to get to the bus station so it's cheaper to take the servees (service taxi). There is a daily bus to Port Said at 7.30pm (E£80, 12 hours) via Ismailia (E£75).

To go to the Western Desert oases take a train to Asyut, from where there are several buses a day to Kharga (E£18) and Dakhla (E£30).

Super Jet (☎236 7732) runs buses from Luxor bus station at 8pm to Cairo (E£110, 10 to 12 hours) via Hurghada (E£40, four hours).

FELUCCA

You can't take a felucca from Luxor to Aswan; most feluccas leave from Esna because of the Esna Lock. But unless you have a strong wind, it can take days to go more than a few kilometres in this direction. We recommend taking a felucca downstream from Aswan.

MICROBUS

The station for microbuses on the east bank is behind the train station. Foreigners can take servees from Luxor to Aswan (E£20) via Esna (E£5), Edfu (E£9), Kom Ombo (E£15), Hurghada (E£20) and Qena (E£4). There is no service to Asyut. Drivers are always ready to privatise a car to make special trips up the Nile to Aswan, stopping at the sights on the way; expect to pay around E£500. To Asyut or to Hurghada, the going rate is about E£500. It is possible to take a private servees to Kharga via the direct road, avoiding Asyut, at E£700 for the car (maximum seven people).

TRAIN

Luxor Station (Map p188; ☎237 2018; Midan al-Mahatta) has a tourist office, plenty of card phones and a post office.

The **Watania Egypt Sleeping Train** (☎02-2574 9474, 237 2015; www.wataniasleepingtrains.com) goes daily to Cairo at 7.15pm and 10.30pm (single/double including dinner and breakfast US$100/120, child four to nine years US$85, nine hours). No student discounts; tickets can be paid for in US dollars, euros or Egyptian pounds.

For day trains headed north to Cairo (E£95/45 in 1st/2nd class), the best are 981, at 8.25am, stopping at Qena (for Dendara; E£28/19 in 1st/2nd class), Balyana (for Abydos; E£34/21, three hours) and Asyut (for the Western Desert; E£53/30).The slower 983 leaves at 10.30am, and the 935 at noon.

There are several trains daily to Aswan (adult E£25/15 in 1st/2nd class, three hours): the 996 at 1am, the 1902 at 9.30am and the 980 at 6pm, as well as to Cairo (E£90/46 in 1st/2nd class): the 981 at 8.45am, the 983 at 10.30am, the 935

WEST BANK TRANSPORT

Most tourists cross to the west bank by bus or taxi via the bridge, about 8km south of town. But the river remains the quickest way to go. The *baladi* (municipal) ferry costs E£1 for foreigners and leaves from a dock in front of Luxor Temple. Small motor launches (locally called *lunches*) also leave from wherever they can find customers and will take you across for E£10 to E£20 for a small group.

On the west bank, the taxi lot is near the ferry landing. Voices call out the destinations of *kabouts* (pick-up trucks). If you listen out for Gurna you'll be on the right road to the ticket office (50pt). Pick-ups run back and forth between the villages, so you can always flag one down on your way to one of the sites, although you will have to walk from the main road to the entrance, which, in the case of the Valley of the Kings or Queens is quite far. If you want to have an entire pick-up for yourself, it'll cost around E£10. The driver is likely to stick to his normal route.

To hire a private taxi for the day, expect to pay between E£150 and E£250 per day, depending on the season, the state of tourism and your bargaining skills. Past the taxi lot are bicycles for rent for E£15/20 per day.

Donkeys and camels with guides can also be rented at the landing, but it's safer to rent them from a recognised stable.

For an idea of the distances involved, from the local ferry landing it is 3km straight ahead to the ticket office, past the Colossi of Memnon; 4km to the Valley of the Queens; and 8km to the Valley of the Kings.

at noon, the 887 at 6.25pm, the 977 at 7pm, the 1903 at 7.45pm, the 997 at 11.10pm and the 989 at midnight. All train tickets are best bought in advance, but if you buy your ticket on the train there is a surplus of E£6.

Getting Around

TO/FROM THE AIRPORT

Luxor airport is 7km east of town. There is no longer an official price for taxis from Luxor airport into town, so the drivers set their prices, often about E£70 to E£100 or more. Quite often there is not enough work for all the drivers, so when you try to take a taxi, a fight between drivers may erupt. In short, it is a major hassle, so if you want peace of mind ask the hotel to arrange your transfer. There is no bus between the airport and the town.

BICYCLE

The compact town lends itself to cycling, and distances on the generally flat west bank are just far enough to provide some exercise but not be exhausting (except when the weather is too hot). Cycling at night is discouraged given the local habit of driving without headlights.

Many hotels rent out bikes. Prices vary, as does the quality of bikes. You might find one for E£20 a day, or E£10 an hour. Be sure to check roadworthiness – there's nothing worse than getting stuck with a broken chain halfway to the Valley of the Kings.

You can take bikes across to the west bank on the *baladi* ferry or pick one up from **Mohamed Setouhy** (☎ 0100 223 9710; E£10 per hour) on the west bank.

FELUCCA

There is a multitude of feluccas to take you on short trips around Luxor, leaving from various points all along the river. How much you pay depends on your bargaining skills, but expect about E£30 to E£40 for an hour of sailing.

HORSE-DRAWN CARRIAGES

Known as *calèche* or *hantour*, horse-drawn carriages cost from E£20 to E£100 per hour depending on your haggling skills and the desperation of the driver. Expect to pay about E£30 to get to Karnak.

PICK-UP TRUCKS & MICROBUSES

Kabout (pick-up trucks) and microbuses are often the quickest and easiest way to get about in Luxor. They ply fixed routes and will stop whenever flagged down. To get to the Karnak temples, take a microbus from Luxor station or from behind Luxor Temple for 50pt. Other routes run inside the town.

TAXI

There are plenty of taxis in Luxor, but passengers still have to bargain hard for trips. A short trip around town is likely to cost at least E£10. Taxis can also be hired for day trips around the west bank; expect to pay at least E£200, depending on the length of the excursion and your bargaining skills.

Nile Valley: Esna to Abu Simbel

Includes ➡

Why Go

The Nile south of Luxor is increasingly hemmed in by the Eastern Desert, its banks lined with grand, well-preserved Graeco-Roman temples at Esna, Edfu and Kom Ombo, and its lush fields punctuated by palm-backed villages – it's the ideal place to sail through on a Nile boat. The once-great city of Al-Kab provides the perfect contrast to the grandeur of the temples, while at Gebel Silsila the river passes through a gorge sacred to the ancients, who used the quarry to build the temples in Luxor. Aswan, the ancient ivory-trading post, has a laid-back atmosphere and plenty of things to see.

South of Aswan, the land is dominated by Lake Nasser, the world's largest artificial lake. On its shores is one of ancient Egypt's most awesome structures: the Great Temple of Ramses II at Abu Simbel.

Best Places to Stay

- ➡ Sofitel Old Cataract Hotel & Spa (p250)
- ➡ Eskaleh (p264)
- ➡ Philae Hotel (p249)
- ➡ Bet al-Kerem (p249)
- ➡ Mövenpick Resort Aswan (p250)

Best Activities

- ➡ Sailing in a dahabiyya (p31)
- ➡ Birdwatching in Aswan (p248)
- ➡ Taking felucca trip around the islands in Aswan (p247)
- ➡ Visiting the Daraw camel market (p240)

When to Go

Aswan

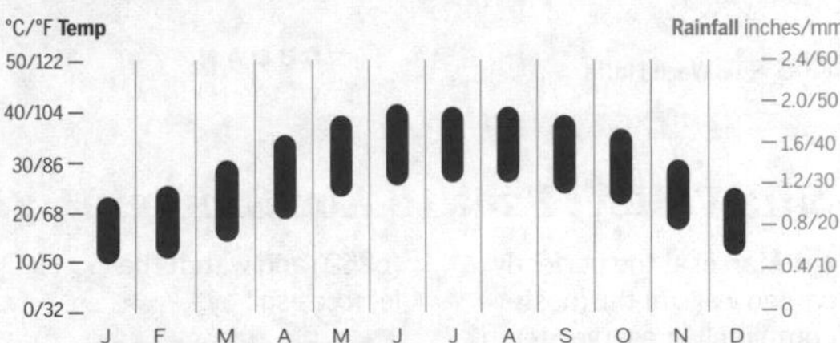

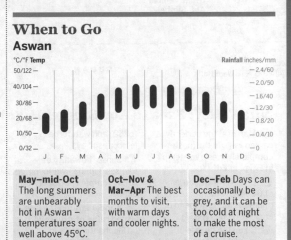

May–mid-Oct The long summers are unbearably hot in Aswan – temperatures soar well above 45°C.

Oct–Nov & Mar–Apr The best months to visit, with warm days and cooler nights.

Dec–Feb Days can occasionally be grey, and it can be too cold at night to make the most of a cruise.

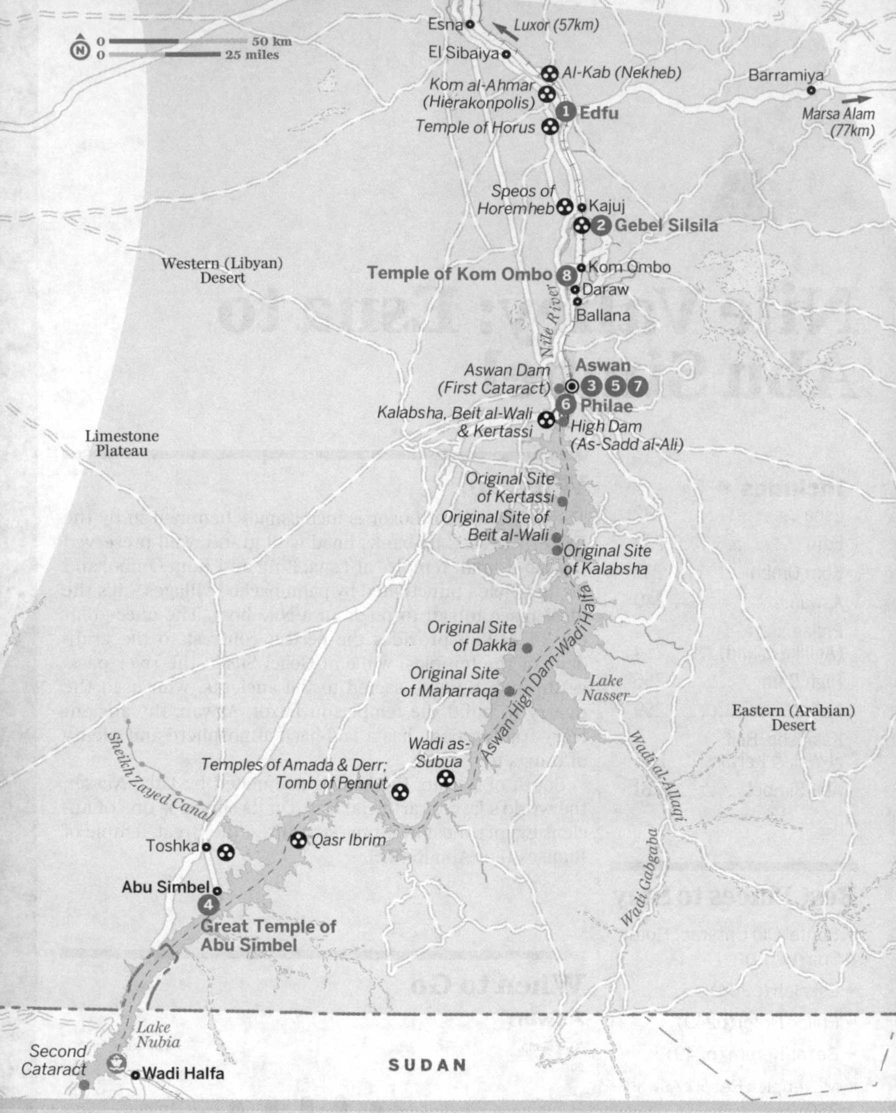

Nile Valley: Esna to Abu Simbel Highlights

1. Marvel at the perfectly carved walls of the most completely preserved temple in Egypt at **Edfu** (p235).
2. Discover the quarries of **Gebel Silsila**, where the pharaohs found stone to build ancient Thebes (p237).
3. Sit on the terrace of Aswan's **Old Cataract Hotel** (p250) and watch the feluccas sail by.
4. Sense the vanity of Ramses II in the awe-inspiring **Great Temple** (p262) of Abu Simbel.
5. Wander around the little-visited **ruins of Abu** (p243) on Elephantine Island.
6. Take a boat out to the marvellous **Temple of Isis** (p254) at Philae.
7. Stroll through the **botanical gardens** (p245) of Kitchener's Island in the afternoon sun.
8. See the unusual double **Temple of Kom Ombo** (p238) in the morning light.

History

The Nile Valley between Luxor and Aswan was the domain of the vulture and crocodile gods, a place of harsh nature and grand landscapes. Its cult places – centres such as Al-Kab and Kom al-Ahmar – date back to the earliest periods of Egyptian history. The Narmer Palette, the object around which the origins of the 1st dynasty have been constructed, was found here, as was one of the earliest-known Egyptian temples, made of wood not stone. The area's Lascaux-type rock carvings and human remains have opened a window onto Egypt's remotest, predynastic past.

Yet most of what one can see between Luxor and Aswan dates from the last period of ancient Egyptian history, when the country was ruled by the descendants of Alexander the Great's Macedonian general, Ptolemy I (323–283 BC). They ruled for some 300 years. Although they were based in Alexandria and looked out to the Mediterranean, the Ptolemies respected the country's ancient traditions and religion, setting an example to the Romans who succeeded them. They ensured peaceful rule in Upper Egypt by erecting temples in honour of the local gods, building in grand Pharaonic style to appease the priesthood and earn the trust of the people. The riverside temples at Esna, Edfu, Kom Ombo and Philae are as notable for their strategic locations, on ancient trade routes or at key commercial centres, as for their artistic or architectural merit.

Aswan's history was always going to be different. However much Theban, Macedonian or Roman rulers in the north may have wanted to ignore the south, they dared not neglect their southern border. Settlement on Elephantine Island, located in the middle of the Nile at Aswan, dates back to at least 3000 BC. Named Abu (Ivory) after the trade that flourished here, it was a natural fortress positioned just below the First Nile Cataract, one of six sets of rapids that blocked the river between Aswan and Khartoum. At the beginning of Egypt's dynastic history, in the Old Kingdom (2686–2125 BC), Abu became capital of the first Upper Egyptian *nome* (province) and developed into a thriving economic and religious centre, its strategic importance underlined by the title accorded to its rulers, Keepers of the Gate of the South. By the end of ancient history, with Egypt part of a larger Roman Empire, the southern frontier town was seen as a place of exile for anyone from the north who stepped out of line.

Climate

Heading south from Luxor, the fertile, green Nile Valley narrows considerably and becomes more and more enclosed by the desert. The climate also changes and becomes increasingly desert-like, with mostly warm, dry days in winter (December to February) – with an average temperature of about 26°C during the day – but often surprisingly cold nights. Summer (June to August) days are dry but often very hot, with temperatures hovering between 38°C and 45°C, making it difficult to visit sights outdoors. At the height of summer, temperatures hardly seem to drop during the night.

HENNA TATTOOS

Henna is the natural dye derived from the leaves of the *Lawsonia inermis* shrub, grown in southern Egypt and Nubia for millennia – traces of it have even been found on the nails of mummified pharaohs.

Like their ancestors, Nubian women use henna powder for their hair and also to decorate hands and feet prior to getting married. The intricate red-brown designs adorn the skin for a fortnight or so before fading away.

Women visitors will be offered henna 'tattoos' on their hands (or feet or stomachs, from E£30 per tattoo) at some of the Nubian villages on Elephantine Island or on the west bank of Aswan or in the souq. It looks great and you get to spend time with Nubian women. Always check who will apply the tattoos; this is women's work, but would-be Lotharios see this as a great opportunity to get close to a bit of foreign flesh.

Foreigners tend to prefer black to the traditional red henna tattoos, but beware: this is in fact natural henna darkened with the very toxic hair dye PPD, which is banned in Europe. Avoid black henna completely, and visit www.hennapage.com to see the damage the dye can cause, from a light allergic reaction to chemical burns and sometimes even death.

Getting There & Away

There are currently no buses between Aswan and Luxor. There are several trains daily between Luxor and Aswan, which preferably should be booked in advance, although tickets are for sale on board for an extra E£6. Microbuses run regularly between the two cities and are now the best way of reaching the places in between. But the most inspiring way of seeing this part of the country is the slow way, sailing on a felucca (traditional canvas-sailed boat) or a dahabiyya (houseboat), taking in the sights and this most glorious stretch of river.

There is still a convoy system in place between Aswan and Abu Simbel, and foreigners are only allowed to travel by bus, taxi or minibus in an armed convoy that leaves twice a day. The other option is to fly, or to take a cruise on Lake Nasser.

Getting Around

Foreigners are no longer restricted when travelling between towns in the far south of Egypt, except between Aswan and Abu Simbel. Minibuses run between towns, although in some places they will drop you a kilometre or more from the sights. The easiest way to visit the sights between Luxor and Aswan is to privately hire a taxi for a day and visit sights en route, or to privately hire one once you are in the town and want to go to the sight. Security tightens inevitably if there has been any kind of incident, even if it's not necessarily related to tourists or terrorism.

SOUTHERN UPPER EGYPT

Esna

095 / POP 67,220

Most visitors come to Esna, 64km south of Luxor on the west bank of the Nile, for the Temple of Khnum, but the busy little farming town itself is quite charming. Beyond the small bazaar selling mainly tourist souvenirs are several examples of 19th-century provincial architecture with elaborate *mashrabiyya* (wooden lattice screens). Immediately north of the temple is a beautiful but run-down **Ottoman caravanserai**, the Wekalat al-Gedawi, once the commercial centre of Esna. Merchants from Sudan, Somalia and central Africa stayed on the 2nd floor here, and a market was held regularly in the courtyard, with Arab gum, ostrich feathers, elephant tusks and other exotica for sale. Opposite the temple is the Fatimid-era **Emari minaret**, one of the oldest in Egypt, which escaped the mosque's demolition in 1960. An old oil mill, in the covered souq south of the temple, presses lettuce seed into oil, considered an aphrodisiac since ancient times.

Until the early 20th century, Esna was an important stop on the camel-caravan route between Sudan and Cairo, and between the Western Desert oases and the Nile Valley. It is now also known for the barrage through which all cruise boats have to pass. The town makes for a pleasant morning excursion from Luxor, or a stop between Luxor and Aswan.

Esna

The **tourist police office** (☎240 0686) is in the tourist souq near the temple. There is a busy souq, particularly on Mondays, on both sides of the canal.

Sights

Temple of Khnum TEMPLE

(adult/student E£30/15; ⏲6am-5pm) The Ptolemaic-Roman Temple of Khnum is situated about 200m from the boat landing, at the end of the tourist souq. The temple today sits in a 9m-deep pit, which represents 15 centuries of desert sand and debris, accumulated since it was abandoned during the Roman period. Most of the temple, which was similar in size to the temples of Edfu and Dendara, is still covered. All that was excavated in the 1840s, what you see now, is the Roman hypostyle hall.

Khnum was the ram-headed creator god who fashioned humankind on his potter's wheel using Nile clay. Construction of the temple dedicated to him was begun, on the site of an earlier temple, by Ptolemy VI Philometor (180–145 BC). The Romans added the hypostyle hall that can be visited today, with well-preserved carvings from as late as the 3rd century AD. A quay connecting the temple to the Nile was built by Roman emperor Marcus Aurelius (AD 161–180).

➡ Touring the Temple

The central doorway leads into the dark, atmospheric vestibule, where the roof is supported by 18 columns with wonderfully varied floral capitals in the form of palm leaves, lotus buds and papyrus fans; some also have bunches of grapes, a distinctive Roman touch. The roof is decorated with astronomical scenes, while the pillars are covered with hieroglyphic accounts of temple rituals. Inside the front corners, beside the smaller doorways, are two hymns to Khnum. The first is a morning hymn to awaken Khnum in his shrine, and the second is a wonderful 'hymn of creation' that acknowledges him as creator of all, even foreigners: 'All are formed on his potter's wheel, their speech different in every region but the lord of the wheel is their father too.'

On the walls, Roman emperors dressed as pharaohs make offerings to the local gods of Esna. The northern wall has scenes of Emperor Commodus catching fish in a papyrus thicket with the god Khnum and, next to this, presenting the temple to the god.

The back wall, to the northeast, constructed during the Ptolemaic Period, features reliefs of two Ptolemaic pharaohs, Ptolemy VI Philometor and Ptolemy VIII Euergetes (170–116 BC). A number of Roman emperors, including Septimus Severus, Caracalla and Geta, added their names near the hall's rear gateway. Outside, an underground pump struggles to move groundwater away from the structure.

Eating & Drinking

Few people linger in Esna; for most it's a stop on the road between Luxor and Aswan. There is nowhere to stay but there are a few ahwas (coffeehouses) with terraces, where drinks and some basic food are served, opposite the temple.

Getting There & Away

Trains are a pain because the train station is on the opposite (east) bank of the Nile, away from the town centre, but *kabouts* (pick-up trucks) shuttle between the two. The busy *kabout* station is beside the canal, and a block further north is the *microbus* station. A seat in a microbus to Luxor costs E£5, to Edfu E£5 and to Aswan E£12. Arrivals are generally dropped off on the main thoroughfare into town, along which *hantour* (horse-drawn carriage) drivers congregate in the hope of picking up a fare. They ask E£30 for the five- to 10-minute ride to the temple and return.

UNCOVERING ANCIENT PAINTINGS

Most Egyptian temples were once as colourful as the tombs in Luxor, their walls, pillars and ceilings completely painted. It was long believed that the colours had been lost to time and the abrasive winds. But work inside the hypostyle hall at the Temple of Khnum shows that the colours are still there. Using a cocktail of chemicals, archaeologists have delicately removed millennia of dust and dirt to confirm that all figures were completely painted and all backgrounds were white. There is now a debate among Egyptologists as to whether the entire temple – and other temples – should be restored, or whether the majority should be left covered, and therefore protected, for future generations.

Al-Kab & Kom al-Ahmar

Between Esna and Edfu are the ruins of two settlements, both dating back more than 3000 years, with traces of even earlier habitation.

Originally known as Nekheb, **Al-Kab** grew from a prehistoric settlement to become one of the most important cities of ancient Egypt, home to Nekhbet, the vulture goddess of Upper Egypt, one of two deities who protected the pharaoh right back to the Old Kingdom.

Further east into the desert from Al-Kab, if you have transport, you'll see several temples dedicated to Nubian gods. You'll find a Ptolemaic temple with a staircase leading up to two columned vestibules before a chapel carved into the rock. Further south is a small chapel, locally known as Al-Hammam (The Bathhouse), built by Setau, Viceroy of Nubia under Ramses II. At the centre of the wadi is a large vulture-shaped crag covered in inscriptions from predynastic times to the Old Kingdom. Some 3.5km further east into the desert is the small chapel of Nekhbet, built by Amenhotep III (1390–1352 BC) as a way station for the vulture goddess's cult statue when she passed through 'The Valley'. Her protective influence was no doubt appreciated, as this was one of the supply routes to the goldmines that gave Egypt much of its wealth.

Across the river lies **Kom al-Ahmar** (closed to the public), ancient Nekhen or Hierakonpolis, home of the falcon god Nekheny, an early form of Horus. Although little remains of this important city, recent excavations have revealed a large settlement (with Egypt's earliest brewery!), a predynastic cemetery dating from around 3400 BC with elephant and cattle burials, together with the site of Egypt's earliest-known temple, a large timber-framed structure fronted by 12m-high imported wood pillars. A century ago, within this sacred enclosure, archaeologists discovered a range of ritual artefacts, among them two items of huge historical significance: the Narmer Palette and a superb gold falcon head of the god Horus, both now among the highlights of Cairo's Egyptian Museum.

Sights

Nekheb MONUMENT

FREE The ancient city of Nekheb is still being excavated, so is off limits, but the most impressive remains above ground are the mud-brick city walls – 11m high, 12m thick and 550m long each side – which form a square that you can walk around from the outside. They were last rebuilt in the 4th century BC.

Note how the walls were built in sections: if the Nile flood was particularly high, there was a chance the walls might fall. Building this way meant that sections could be repaired without rebuilding the entire wall. The oldest of the sandstone temples within the walls, dedicated to the god Thoth, was built by Ramses II (1279–1213 BC) and the adjoining Temple of Nekhbet was built during the Late Period. Both reused blocks from much earlier temples from the Early Dynastic Period (from c 3100 BC) and the Middle Kingdom (2055–1650 BC).

Al Kab Tombs MONUMENT

(adult/student E£40/20; 8am-4pm) Cut into the ridge above Al Kab is a row of tombs. The most interesting (No 2), from the New Kingdom (1550–1069 BC) belonged to Ahmose, 'Captain-General of Sailors' under Pharaoh Ahmose I (1550–1525 BC). Another Ahmose, son of Ebana, left a detailed account of his bravery in the battle against the Hyksos. All have well-preserved and beautiful images.

To the north of the New Kingdom tombs, and not open to visitors, are a series from the Old Kingdom. The oldest, including one on the top of the ridge, date to around 2700 BC.

Getting There & Away

Al-Kab and Kom al-Ahmar are 26km south of Esna. Microbuses will drop you off, but you might struggle to find one to move on from here. The best way of seeing Al-Kab is to take a private taxi from Esna or Edfu, or to stop on the way between Luxor and Aswan. Dahabiyyas and some feluccas travelling from Aswan to Esna stop here too, but bigger cruise boats are not able to dock.

Edfu

097 / POP 69,000

Built on a rise above the broad river valley, the Temple of Horus at Edfu, having escaped destruction from Nile floods, is the most completely preserved Egyptian temple. One of the last ancient attempts at building on a grand scale, the temple dominates this west-bank town, 53km south of Esna. Its well-preserved reliefs have provided archaeologists with much valuable information about temple rituals and the power of the priesthood. Walking through the large, gloomy chambers, visitors are sometimes overwhelmed by a sense of awe at the mysteries of ancient Egypt.

Modern Edfu, a centre for sugar and pottery, is a friendly, buzzing provincial centre. Although it is an agricultural town, tourism is the biggest money-earner; almost everyone seems to have an interest in the tourist shops, and all visitors must brave them in order to reach the temple.

Sights

Temple of Horus TEMPLE

(adult/student E£60/30; 7am-7pm) This Ptolemaic temple, built between 237 and 57 BC, is one of the best-preserved ancient monuments in Egypt, and perhaps the world. Preserved by desert sand, which filled the place after the pagan cult was banned, the temple is dedicated to Horus, the avenging son of Isis and Osiris. It is very similar in style to the Temple of Hathor in Dendara. With its roof intact, it is also one of the most atmospheric of ancient buildings.

Edfu was a settlement and cemetery site from around 3000 BC onward. It was the 'home' and cult centre of the falcon god Horus of Behdet (the ancient name for Edfu), although the Temple of Horus as it exists today is Ptolemaic. Started by Ptolemy III (246–221 BC) on 23 August 237 BC, on the site of an earlier and smaller New Kingdom structure, the sandstone temple was completed some 180 years later by Ptolemy XII Neos Dionysos, Cleopatra VII's father. In conception and design it follows the general plan, scale, ornamentation and traditions of Pharaonic architecture, right down to the Egyptian attire worn by Greek pharaohs depicted in the temple's reliefs. Although it is much newer than cult temples at Luxor or Abydos, its excellent state of preservation helps to fill in many historical gaps; it is, in effect, a 2000-year-old example of an architectural style that was already archaic during Ptolemaic times.

Two hundred years ago the temple was buried by sand, rubble and part of the village of Edfu, which had spread over the roof. Excavation was begun by Auguste Mariette in the mid-19th century. Today the temple is entered via a long row of shops selling tourist tat, and a new visitors centre that houses the ticket office, clean toilets, a cafeteria and a room for showing a 15-minute film on the history of the temple in English.

➡ Touring the Temple

Beyond the Roman *mammisi* (birth house), with some colourful carvings, the massive 36m-high **pylon** (gateway) is guarded by two huge but splendid granite statues of Horus as a falcon. The walls are decorated with colossal reliefs of Ptolemy XII Neos Dionysos,

DON'T MISS

VICTORY PARADE IN THE TEMPLE OF HORUS

Exit the hypostyle hall to the east of the sanctuary and you come to a narrow passage between the temple and its outer enclosure wall. This ambulatory, the passage of victory, contains scenes of the dramatic battle between Horus and Seth at the annual Festival of Victory. Throughout the conflict, Seth is shown in the form of a hippopotamus, his tiny size rendering him less threatening.

Edfu

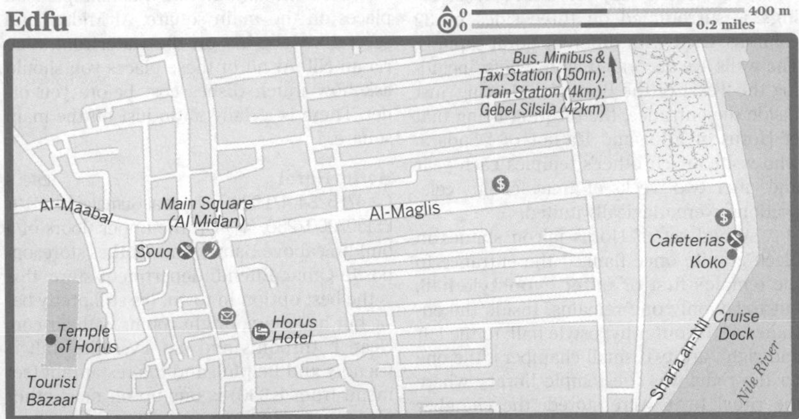

Temple of Horus

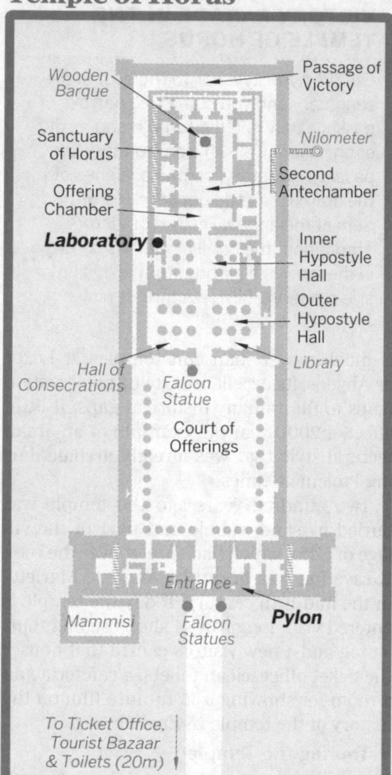

who is holding his enemies by their hair before Horus and is about to smash their skulls; this is the classic propaganda pose of the almighty pharaoh.

Beyond this pylon, the **court of offerings** is surrounded on three sides by 32 columns, each with different floral capitals. The walls are decorated with reliefs, including the 'Feast of the Beautiful Meeting' just inside the entrance, the meeting being that of Horus of Edfu and Hathor of Dendara, who visited each other's temples each year and, after two weeks of great fertility celebrations, were magically united.

A second set of Horus falcon statues in black granite once flanked the entrance to the temple's first or **outer hypostyle hall**, but today only one remains. Inside the entrance of the outer hypostyle hall, to the left and right, are two small chambers: the one on the right was the temple library where the ritual texts were stored; the chamber on the left was the hall of consecrations, a vestry where freshly laundered robes and ritual vases were kept. The hall itself has 12 columns, and the walls are decorated with reliefs of the temple's founding.

The **inner hypostyle hall** also has 12 columns, and in the top left part of the hall is perhaps this temple's most interesting room: the temple laboratory. Here, all the necessary perfumes and incense recipes were carefully brewed up and stored, their ingredients listed on the walls.

Exit the inner hypostyle hall through the large central doorway to enter the **offering chamber**, or first antechamber, which has an altar where daily offerings of fruit, flowers, wine, milk and other foods were left. On the west side, 242 steps lead up to the rooftop and its fantastic view of the Nile and the surrounding fields. (The roof is closed to visitors.)

The **second antechamber** gives access to the sanctuary of Horus, which contains the polished-granite shrine that once housed the gold cult statue of Horus. Created during the reign of Nectanebo II (360–343 BC), this shrine, or house of the god, was reused by the Ptolemies in their newer temple. In front of it stands a replica of the wooden barque in which Horus' statue would be taken out of the temple in procession during festive occasions: the original is now in the Louvre, Paris.

On the eastern enclosure wall, look for the remains of the Nilometer, which measured the level of the river and helped predict the coming harvest.

Sleeping & Eating

There is a kebab joint and other simple food places on the main square, Al Midan, and several **cafeterias** on the waterfront, Sharia an-Nil. At all of these places you should ask how much dishes cost before you order. There is a daily **souq** just off the main square.

Horus Hotel HOTEL $

(☎ 471 5284, 471 5286; Sharia al-Gumhuriya; s/d/tr E£150/200/250; ❄) On the upper floors of a building above Baby Home clothes store, opposite Omar Effendi department store, this is the best option in town. It's still pretty basic but has clean, bright rooms with air-con, clean bathrooms and old TVs. The staff is friendly and helpful, and the restaurant (set menu from E£50) is one up on most other places to eat in town.

Information

As in other Egyptian towns, the main street of Edfu (Sharia al-Maglis) is lined with mobile-phone shops. A large **Telephone centrale** sits on the southern side of the square and the **post office** is behind it, just south of here, along the first street off to the left. The **Banque du Caire** (Sharia al-Maglis) has an ATM.

On the waterfront where the cruise boats dock are bazaars, the Bank of Alexandria, the **Bank al-Ahli al-Masri** and internet cafe **Koko** (Sharia an-Nil; per hr E£10).

Getting There & Away

Edfu train station is on the east bank of the Nile, about 4km from the town. There are frequent trains heading to Luxor and Aswan throughout the day, although most are 2nd and 3rd class only. To get to the town, you must first take a *kabout* from the train station to the bridge, then another into town. Each costs 50pt.

The bus and microbus station is at the entrance to town, next to the bridge over the Nile. There are no longer any buses along the Aswan–Luxor Nile road (they take the road through the desert). The only current option for driving along the Nile (unless you go by taxi) is to go by microbus: to Luxor (E£10, two hours), Kom Ombo (E£5, 45 minutes), Aswan (E£10, 1½ hours) and Marsa Alam on the Red Sea (E£25, four to five hours).

Hantours take passengers from the waterfront to the temple or vice versa for E£25 to E£30, but you will have to bargain.

Gebel Silsila

At Gebel Silsila, about 42km south of Edfu, the Nile narrows considerably to pass between steep sandstone cliffs that are cluttered with ancient rock stelae and graffiti. Known in Pharaonic times as Khenu (Place of Rowing), it was an important centre for the cult of the Nile: every year at the beginning of the inundation season, sacrifices were made here to ensure the fertility of the land. The Nile at its height flowing through the narrow gorge must have been a particularly impressive sight, and noisy, which no doubt explains why the location was chosen as a cult centre. The gorge also marks the change in the bedrock of Egypt, from limestone to sandstone. The sandstone quarries here were worked by thousands of men from the 18th dynasty or earlier through to the Roman period. The quarries were for centuries the main source in Egypt of sandstone for temple building.

Sights

Speos of Horemheb MONUMENT

(adult/student E£40/20; 8am-5pm) Several stelae lead to the Speos of Horemheb, a rock-hewn chapel started by Horemheb (1323–1295 BC) and finished by the officials of the later Ramesside kings.

Ancient Quarries MONUMENT

The proximity of the river to the hillside, with its quality sandstone, made this an obvious place for ancient Egyptians to cut stone for their temples. The quarries were in use from an early age but systematically worked during the New Kingdom, when huge teams of cutters hacked out blocks that were floated down to Luxor to be used in buildings such as the temple complex of Karnak and the Ramesseum.

The most attractive monuments are on the west bank, where the rocks are carved with inscriptions and tiny shrines from all periods, as well as adorned with larger chapels. The southern side of the site is marked by a massive pillar of rock, known as the 'Capstan', so called because locals believe there was once a chain – *silsila* in Arabic, from which the place takes its name – that ran from the east to the west bank. Nearby are the three shrines built by Merenptah, Ramses II and Seti I during the New Kingdom. Further north, the main quarry has clear masons' marks and a group of elaborate private memorial chapels. Several stelae, including a large Stelae of Shoshenq I, mark the northern limit of the quarry.

The east bank is mostly out of bounds, but looking across from the west bank one gets a real sense of the grandeur and scale of what the pharaohs undertook, especially the huge passageway cut into the hillside.

Getting There & Away

The best way to get to Gebel Silsila is by felucca or dahabiyya between Aswan and Esna. Alternatively, hire a private taxi at Edfu and take the west-bank valley road to Silsila.

Kom Ombo

097 / POP 71,600

The fertile, irrigated sugar-cane fields around Kom Ombo, 65km south of Edfu, support not only the original community of fellaheen (peasant farmers), but also a large population of Nubians displaced from their own lands by the creation of Lake Nasser. It's a pleasant

LASCAUX ON THE NILE

Canadian archaeologists working in the 1960s in the area of Qurta, some 15km north of Kom Ombo, discovered what they thought to be extremely old petroglyphs. Paleolithic, they thought. Ridiculous, said the experts. The matter was dropped, the site forgotten. But the images were rediscovered in 2005 by a team of archaeologists led by Dr Dirk Huyge of the Royal Museum of Art and History, Brussels (Belgium). This time the archaeologists discovered other petroglyphs that were partly covered by sediment and other deposits. These were recently dated in Belgium to the Pleistocene period of rock art, making them at least 15,000 years old, and therefore both chronologically and stylistically from the same period as the images in Lascaux, France.

The images are carved into the side of huge Nubian sandstone rocks. Most of these fine carvings are of wild horned cows in different positions, although there are also gazelles, birds, hippos and fish in a naturalistic style, and a few stylised human figures with pronounced buttocks but no other particular features. These discoveries do not just represent some of the largest and finest examples of rock art ever found in Egypt. They also pose a challenging question. How can there be such similarities between images found in Egypt and France? Was there some sort of cultural exchange between the people of Lascaux and Qurta?

Work is continuing at Qurta and no doubt more discoveries will be found. Dr Huyge believes that the Qurta art is part of an evolution and that even older work will be found. The guarded site is not currently open to the public.

little place, easily accessible en route between Aswan and Luxor. A huge cattle market is held on the outskirts of town, near the railway line, on Thursdays. The main attraction these days, however, is the unique riverside temple to Horus the Elder (Haroeris) and Sobek and its attached Crocodile Museum, about 4km from the town's centre, on a promontory overlooking the Nile.

In ancient times Kom Ombo was known as Pa-Sebek (Land of Sobek), after the crocodile god of the region. It became important during the Ptolemaic period, when its name was changed to Ombos and it became the capital of the first Upper Egyptian nome during the reign of Ptolemy VI Philometor. Kom Ombo was an important military base and a trading centre between Egypt and Nubia. Gold was traded here, but more importantly it was a market for African elephants brought from Ethiopia, which the Ptolemies needed to fight the Indian elephants of their long-term rivals the Seleucids, who ruled Alexander's former empire to the east of Egypt.

Sights

Temple of Kom Ombo TEMPLE
(adult/student E£40/20; 7am-7pm) Standing on a promontory at a bend in the Nile, where in ancient times sacred crocodiles basked in the sun on the riverbank, is the Temple of Kom Ombo, one of the most beautifully sited temples. Unique in Egypt, it is dedicated to two gods, and has some lovely images. The newly opened Crocodile Museum, included in the ticket price, has a beautifully lit and well-explained display of crocodile mummies and inscriptions.

The temple was dedicated to the local crocodile god Sobek and to Haroeris (from har-wer), meaning Horus the Elder. This is reflected in the temple's plan: perfectly symmetrical along the main axis of the temple, there are twin entrances, two linked hypostyle halls with carvings of the two gods on either side, and twin sanctuaries. It is assumed that there were also two priesthoods. The left (western) side of the temple was dedicated to the god Haroeris, and the right (eastern) half to Sobek.

Reused blocks suggest an earlier temple from the Middle Kingdom period, but the main temple was built by Ptolemy VI Philometor, though most of its decoration was completed by Cleopatra VII's father, Ptolemy XII Neos Dionysos. The temple's spectacular riverside setting has resulted in the erosion of some of its partly Roman forecourt and outer sections, but much of the complex has survived and is very similar in layout to the Ptolemaic temples of Edfu and Dendara, albeit smaller.

➡ Touring the Temple

Passing into the temple's forecourt, where reliefs are divided between the two gods, there is a **double altar** in the centre of the court for both gods. Beyond are the shared **inner and outer hypostyle halls**, each with 10 columns. Inside the outer hypostyle hall, to the left is a finely executed relief showing Ptolemy XII Neos Dionysos being presented to Haroeris by Isis and the lion-headed goddess Raettawy, with Thoth looking on. The walls to the right show the crowning of Ptolemy XII by Nekhbet (the vulture goddess worshipped at the Upper Egyptian town of Al-Kab) and Wadjet (the snake goddess based at Buto in Lower Egypt), with the dual crown of Upper and Lower Egypt, symbolising the unification of Egypt.

Reliefs in the **inner hypostyle** hall show Haroeris presenting Ptolemy VIII Euergetes with a curved weapon, representing the sword of victory. Behind Ptolemy is his sister-wife and co-ruler Cleopatra II.

From here, three **antechambers**, each with double entrances, lead to the sanctuaries of Sobek and Haroeris. The now-ruined chambers on either side would have been used to store priests' vestments and liturgical papyri. The walls of the sanctuaries are now one or two courses high, allowing you to see the secret passage that enabled the priests to give the gods a 'voice' to answer the petitions of pilgrims.

The **outer passage**, which runs around the temple walls, is unusual. Here, on the left-hand (northern) corner of the temple's back wall, is a puzzling scene, which is often described as a collection of 'surgical instruments'. It seems more probable that these were some of the accoutrements used during the temple's daily rituals, although the temple was certainly a place of healing, the nearest thing to an ancient hospital.

Near the Ptolemaic gateway on the southeast corner of the complex is a small shrine to Hathor, while a small **mammisi** stands in the southwest corner. Beyond this to the north you will find the deep well that supplied the temple with water, and close by is a small pool in which crocodiles, Sobek's sacred animal, were raised.

The path out of the complex leads to the new **Crocodile Museum**. It's well worth a visit for its beautiful collection of mummified crocodiles and ancient carvings, which is well lit and well explained. The museum is also dark and air-conditioned, which can be a blessing on a hot day.

Sleeping & Eating

There still isn't anywhere worth staying in Kom Ombo: it is too close to Aswan for anyone to open a tourist hotel.

Snacks and drinks can be bought at the series of cafeterias and tourist bazaars that line the Nile by the temple. **Cafeteria Venus**

Temple of Kom Ombo

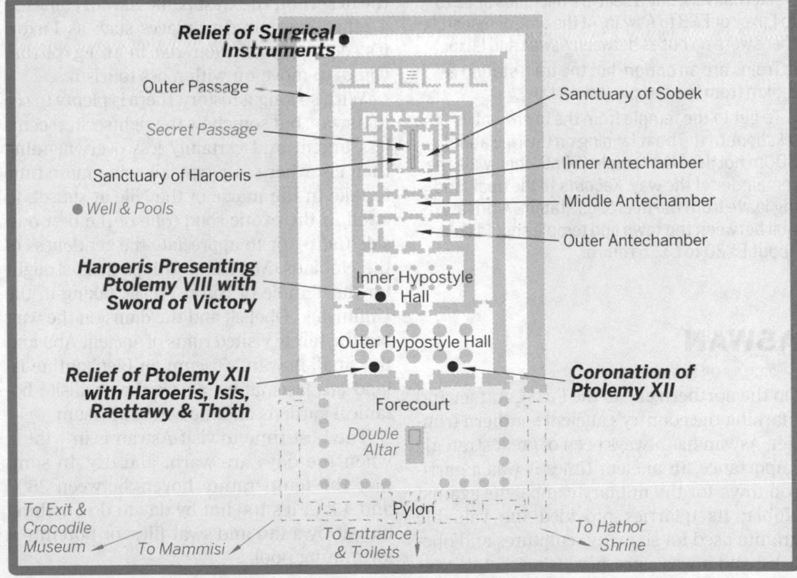

WORTH A TRIP

DARAW

Just south of Kom Ombo is the village of Daraw, which has a remarkable camel market.

Daraw Camel Market (Souq al-Gimaal; ⏲ mornings Tue & Thu) Most of the camels come in caravans from Sudan's Darfur and Kordofan along the Darb al-Arba'een (Forty Days Rd) to just north of Abu Simbel before being trucked to Daraw. Here they spend two days in quarantine before being sold by their Sudanese owners. Most go on to the camel market in Birqash, about 35km northwest of Cairo, where they are either sold to Egyptian farmers, exported to neighbouring countries or slaughtered for meat. This is no place for the squeamish.

Camels are sold here each day of the week, but the main market days are Tuesday and Thursday, when sometimes as many as 2000 camels are brought from Abu Simbel.

Hosh al-Kenzi (Kenzian House; ☎273 0970; Sharia al-Kunuz; donations welcome; ⏲8am-noon) The Nubian museum Hosh al-Kenzi, located opposite Dar Rasoul Mosque, was built in 1912 by the father of the current resident, Haj Mohammed Eid Mohammed Hassanein. The house is worth seeing for its construction, in traditional Nubian style, and for its decoration with objects mostly made from palm trees. Next door is a workshop where the beaded curtains made from date pips, pieces of palm frond or various seeds are still produced for Nubian houses.

on the north side of the temple sometimes serves cold beers in a pleasant garden setting.

Getting There & Around

The best way to visit the temple is on a tour or by private taxi. A private taxi from Luxor taking in both Edfu and Kom Ombo and returning in the evening can cost from about E£500 to E£700; moving on to Aswan instead of returning to Luxor will cost between E£500 and E£600. A private taxi from Aswan will cost from E£250 to E£300.

Alternatively, buy a seat in a microbus at E£15 to Luxor or E£3 to Aswan. At the time of research, there were no buses between Aswan and Luxor.

Trains are an option, but the train station is 3.5km from the temple (take a taxi).

To get to the temple from the town centre, take a *kabout* to the boat landing on the Nile about 800m north of the temple (50pt), then walk the remainder of the way. *Kabouts* to the boat landing leave from the microbus station. A private taxi between the town and temple should cost about E£20 to E£25 return.

ASWAN

☎097 / POP 265,000

On the northern end of the First Cataract and marking the country's ancient southern frontier, Aswan has always been of great strategic importance. In ancient times it was a garrison town for the military campaigns against Nubia; its quarries provided the valuable granite used for so many sculptures and obelisks; and it was a prosperous marketplace at the crossroads of the ancient caravan routes. Today, slower than most places in Egypt, laid-back and pleasant, it is the perfect place to linger for a few days, to rest and recover from the rigours of travelling along the Nile. The river is wide, languorous and stunningly beautiful here, flowing gently down from Lake Nasser, around dramatic black-granite boulders and palm-studded islands. Colourful, sleepy Nubian villages run down to the water and stand out against the backdrop of the desert on the west bank. Aswan comes as a relief, compared to places such as Luxor: it's seemingly off the radar in an Egypt that wants to move on with mass tourism.

With so long a history, there is plenty to see in Aswan, but somehow the sightseeing seems less urgent and certainly less overwhelming than elsewhere in Egypt, allowing more time to take in the magic of the Nile at sunset, to stroll in the exotic souq (one of the best outside Cairo), or to appreciate the gentleness of the Nubians. Most tour groups head straight for the Temple of Isis at Philae, taking in the Unfinished Obelisk and the dams on the way, but the rarely visited ruins of ancient Abu and the small Aswan Museum on Elephantine Island are fascinating, as are the exquisite botanical gardens and the Nubia Museum.

The best time to visit Aswan is in winter, when the days are warm and dry. In summer the temperature hovers between 38°C and 45°C; it's too hot by day to do anything but sit by a fan and swat flies, or flop into a swimming pool.

Sights

Aswan's sights are spread out, mostly to the south and west of the town. The souq cuts right through the centre of town, parallel to the Nile. The Nubia Museum is within walking distance, just, but all other sights require transport. The sites on the islands and on the west bank involve a short boat trip.

Town & East Bank

Corniche WATERFRONT

(Map p244) Walking along the Corniche and watching the sunset over the islands and the desert on the other side of the Nile is a favourite pastime in Aswan. The view from riverside cafe terraces may be blocked by cruise boats, but plans are under way to relocate them all to a dock that is under construction at the northern end of town; for now the best place to watch the sunset is from the Old Cataract Hotel terrace, or from the Sunset restaurant.

Sharia as-Souq MARKET

(Map p244) Starting from the southern end, Sharia as-Souq appears very much like the tourist bazaars all over Egypt, with slightly less persistent traders than elsewhere in the country trying to lure passers-by into their shops to buy scarves, perfume, spice and roughly carved copies of Pharaonic statues. But a closer look reveals more exotic elements.

Traders sell Nubian talismans for good luck, colourful Nubian baskets and skull caps, Sudanese swords, African masks, and enormous stuffed crocodiles and desert creatures. Aswan is famous for the quality of its fuul sudani (peanuts), henna powder (sold in different qualities) and dried hibiscus flowers (used to make the much-loved local drink *karkadai*). The pace is slow, particularly in the late afternoon; the air has a slight whiff of sandalwood; and, as in ancient times, you may feel that Aswan is the gateway to Africa.

★**Nubia Museum** MUSEUM

(Map p242; ☎319 333; www.numibia.net/nubia/intro.htm; el Fanadek St; adult/student E£60/30; ⏲9am-1pm & 5-9pm winter, 6-10pm summer) The little-visited Nubia Museum, opposite Basma Hotel, is a treat, a showcase of the history, art and culture of Nubia. Established in 1997, in cooperation with Unesco, the museum is a reminder of what was lost beneath Lake Nasser. Exhibits are beautifully displayed in huge halls, where clearly written explanations take you from 4500 BC through to the present day.

The exhibits start with prehistoric artefacts and objects from the Kingdom of Kush and Meroe. Coptic and Islamic art displays lead to a description of the massive Unesco project to move Nubia's most important historic monuments away from the rising waters of Lake Nasser, following the building of the Aswan High Dam. Among museum highlights are 6000-year-old painted pottery bowls and an impressive quartzite statue of a 25th-dynasty priest of Amun in Thebes with distinct Kushite (Upper Nubian) features. The stunning horse armour found in tombs from the Ballana period (5th to 7th centuries BC) shows the sophistication of artisanship during this brief ascendancy. A fascinating display traces the development of irrigation along the Nile, from the earliest attempts to control the flow of the river, right up to the building of the old Aswan Dam. A model of a Nubian house, complete with old furniture and mannequins wearing traditional silver jewellery, attempts to portray the folk culture of modern Nubia.

Unfinished Obelisk ARCHAEOLOGICAL SITE

(Map p242; adult/student E£40/20; ⏲8am-5pm) Aswan was the source of Egypt's finest granite, the hard stone ancient Egyptians used to make statues, and to embellish temples, pyramids and obelisks. In the **Northern Quarries**, about 1.5km from town opposite the Fatimid Cemetery, is a huge discarded obelisk, which would have been the largest of all, but was abandoned before it was completely extracted. Microbuses will drop you within a few minutes' walk. Private taxis will charge about E£15.

The unfinished obelisk has given archaeologists valuable insights into how these monuments were created. Three sides of the shaft, which is nearly 42m long, were completed except for the inscriptions. At 1168 tonnes, the completed obelisk would have been the single heaviest piece of stone the Egyptians ever fashioned. A flaw appeared in the rock at a late stage in the process, however, so it lies where the disappointed stonemasons abandoned it, still partly attached to the parent rock.

Upon entering the quarry, steps lead down into the pit of the obelisk, where there are ancient pictographs of dolphins and ostriches or flamingos, thought to have been painted by workers at the quarry.

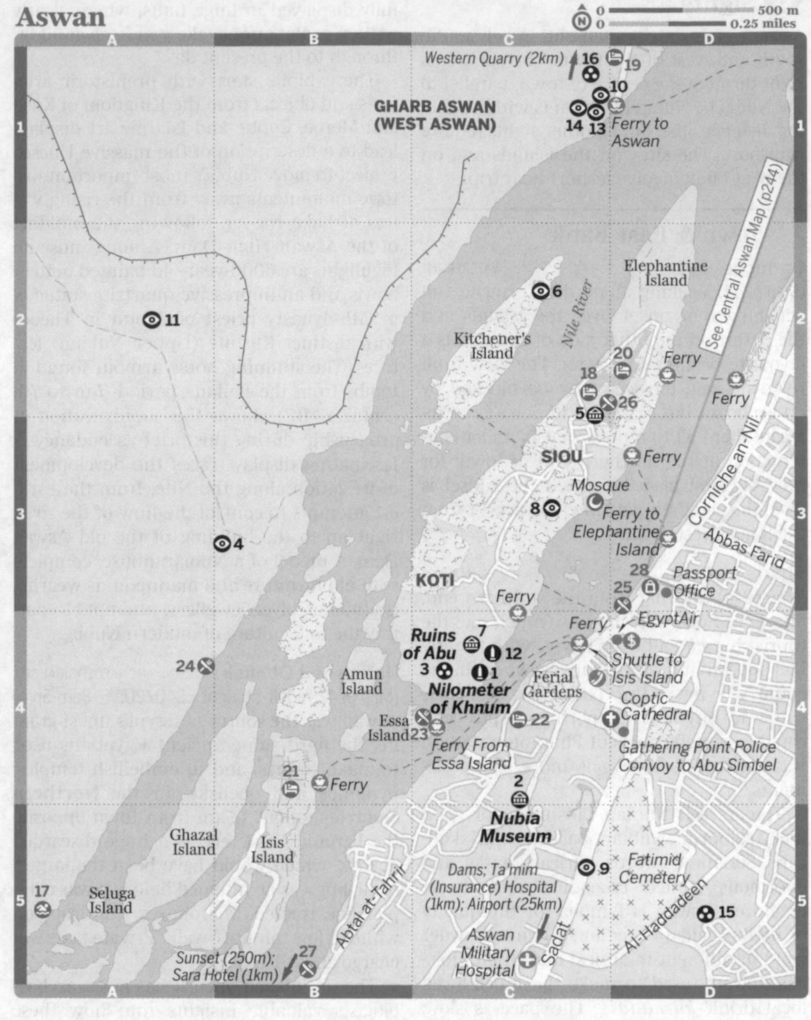

Fatimid Cemetery CEMETERY

(Map p242) Among the modern graves in this vast cemetery are some ruined mud-brick domed tombs, some of which go back to the 9th century. The domes are built on a drum with corners sticking out like horns, a feature unique to southern Egypt. Tombs decorated with flags belong to local saints; you may see Aswanis circumambulating a tomb, praying for the saint's intercession.

The municipality of Aswan has fenced off the Fatimid Cemetery. Enter from the main gate, a 10-minute walk from the Corniche along the road to the airport, and walk right through the cemetery to join the road to the Unfinished Obelisk; just aim for the four-storey building facing the back of the cemetery. The site's caretaker will often accompany you and show you the best-preserved tombs, for which he should be given a baksheesh (tip) of a few pounds.

The River

Elephantine Island ISLAND

(Map p242) Elephantine Island lies opposite the town centre, just north of the First Cataract. The island's southern end comprises

Aswan

the site of the ancient settlement of Abu (p245). Its name meant both 'elephant' and 'ivory' in ancient Egyptian, a reminder of the important role the island once played in the ivory trade. The island's Nubian villages of **Siou** and **Koti** make a surprising counterpoint to the bustle of the city across the water. A recent building boom has changed the nature of the island, but it remains calm and essentially rural.

At the beginning of the 1st dynasty (about 3000 BC) a fortress was built on the island to establish Egypt's southern frontier. Abu soon became an important customs point and trading centre. It remained strategically significant throughout the Pharaonic period as a departure point for the military and commercial expeditions into Nubia and the south. During the 6th dynasty (2345–2181 BC) Abu gained its strength as a political and economic centre and, despite occasional ups and downs, the island retained its importance until the Graeco-Roman period.

As well as being a thriving settlement, Elephantine Island was the main cult centre of the ram-headed god Khnum (at first the god of the inundation, and from the 18th dynasty worshipped as the creator of humankind on his potter's wheel), Satet (Khnum's wife, and guardian of the southern frontier) and their daughter Anket. Each year the rushing of the waters of the flood were first heard here on Elephantine Island. Over time religious complexes took over more and more of the island, so residential areas moved either further north on the island or to the east bank. The temple town of Abu received its coup de grâce in the 4th century AD, when Christianity was established as the imperial Roman religion. From then on, worship of the ancient gods was gradually abandoned and defensive fortifications were moved to the east bank, today's city of Aswan.

Siou and Koti villages lie between the ruins in the south and the Mövenpick Resort, which fills the northern end of the island. A north–south path crosses the middle of the island and links the two villages. Close to the wall separating the Mövenpick Resort from Siou village, facing Kitchener's Island, is **Baaba Dool** (Map 242; ☎0100 497 2608; Siou) FREE, a gorgeous painted Nubian house, where the owner Mustapha serves tea, sells Nubian handicrafts and can arrange live music and dancing performed by local women. The roof terrace is the perfect place to watch the sunset on the west bank, with a multitude of birds flying around the island opposite. Also in the villages is Animalia (p246), a charming Nubian museum.

Western women should be respectful of local tradition and wear modest clothes. More and more visitors prefer to enjoy the traditional set-up of the villages, and rent flats or houses here for a few days.

★Aswan Museum & the Ruins of Abu
ARCHAEOLOGICAL SITE

(Elephantine Island; adult/student E£35/15; ⌚8am-5pm) The fascinating ruins of the original town of Abu and the Aswan Museum lie at the southern end of Elephantine

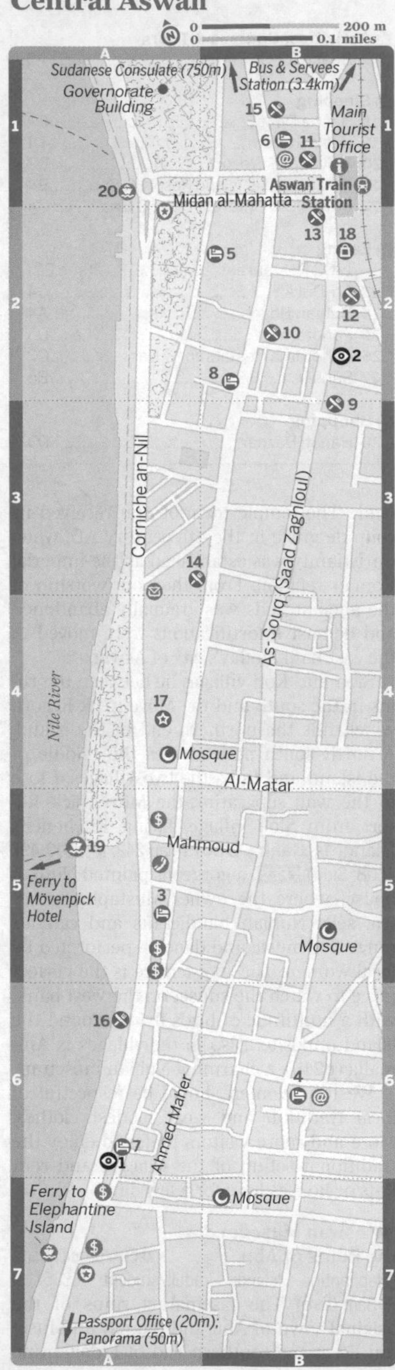

Central Aswan

Sights

1 Corniche....A6
2 Sharia as-Souq....B2

Sleeping

3 Hathor Hotel....A5
4 Keylany Hotel....B6
5 Marhaba Palace Hotel....B2
6 Nuba Nile Hotel....B1
7 Philae Hotel....A6
8 Ramses Hotel....B2

Eating

9 Al-Madina....B3
10 Al-Makka....B2
11 Biti Pizza....B1
12 Chef Khalil....B2
13 El-Tahrer Pizza....B2
14 Haramein Foul & Ta'amiyya....A3
15 Koshary Aly Baba Restaurant....B1
16 Salah Ad-Din....A6

Entertainment

17 Palace of Culture....A4

Shopping

18 Nubia Tourist Book Centre....B2

Transport

19 Ferry....A5
20 Ferry to West Aswan & Tombs of the Nobles....A1

Island. The ruins have been the subject of extensive excavation and a walkway has been arranged over some of them. The museum was closed for renovation at the time of writing.

Aswan Museum

(Map p242; Elephantine Island) The main part of the Aswan Museum is housed in the villa of Sir William Willcocks, architect of the old Aswan Dam. Built in 1898, the villa became a museum in 1912, and houses antiquities discovered in Aswan and Nubia. The modern annexe has a delightful collection of objects, from weapons, pottery and utensils to statues, encased mummies and sarcophagi from predynastic to late Roman times, found in the excavations on Elephantine Island.

Although most of the Nubian artefacts rescued from the temples flooded by Lake Nasser were moved to the Nubia Museum (p241), there are some well-displayed objects here, with excellent labels in English and Arabic. Artefacts are organised in separate glass cases, each explaining a particular facet of life on the island in ancient times:

death, trade, religion, weaving, hunting, farming, cooking and so on. At the right of the main entrance, in a room by itself, lies the sarcophagus and mummy of a sacred ram, the animal associated with Khnum.

➡ **Ruins of Abu**

(Map p242; Elephantine Island) A path through the garden behind the Aswan Museum leads to the evocative ruins of ancient Abu. Numbered plaques and reconstructed buildings mark the island's long history from around 3000 BC to the 14th century AD. The largest structure in the site is the partially reconstructed Temple of Khnum (plaque numbers 6, 12 and 13). Built in honour of the god of inundation during the Old Kingdom, it was added to and used for more than 1500 years before being extensively rebuilt in Ptolemaic times.

Other highlights include a small 4th-dynasty step pyramid, thought to have been built by Sneferu (2613–2589 BC; father of Khufu of Great Pyramid fame); a tiny Ptolemaic chapel (number 15), reconstructed from the Temple of Kalabsha (which is now just south of the High Dam); a reconstructed 18th-dynasty temple (number 2), built by Hatshepsut (1473–1458 BC) and dedicated to the goddess Satet; a cemetery for sacred rams (number 11), thought to have been the living embodiment of the god Khnum; and the ruins of an Aramaic Jewish colony dating from the 5th century BC.

The **Nilometer of the Temple of Khnum** (Map p242; Ruins of Abu, Elephantine Island; number 7) is below the southern balustrade of the Khnum temple. Heavenly portents and priestly prophecies aside, in ancient times only a Nilometer could give a real indication of the likelihood of a bountiful harvest. Built in the 26th dynasty, the Nilometer of Khnum has stone stairs leading down to a small basin for measuring the Nile's maximum level. When the Nilometer here in the southern frontier town recorded a high water level of the river, it meant a good harvest, which in turn meant more taxes. Another stairway, with a scale etched into its wall, leads to the water from the basin's northern end.

Descending to the river's edge from beneath a sycamore tree near the Aswan Museum is the **Nilometer of the Satet Temple** (Map p242; Ruins of Abu, Elephantine Island; number 10). Built in late Ptolemaic or early Roman times and restored in the 19th century, its staircase is roofed over and niches in the walls would have had oil lamps to provide light. If you look hard as you descend to the river, you can see the names of Roman prefects carved into the left-hand wall.

Aswan Botanical Gardens GARDENS

(Map p242; admission E£20; ⏲8am-6pm) Kitchener's Island, to the west of Elephantine Island, was given to Lord Horatio Kitchener in the 1890s when he was commander of the Egyptian army. Indulging his passion for beautiful palms and plants, Kitchener turned the entire island into the stunning Aswan Botanical Gardens, importing plants from the Far East, India and parts of Africa.

Covering 6.8 hectares, the gardens are filled with birds as well as hundreds of species of flora. While it may have lost some of its former glory, its majestic trees are still a stunning sight, particularly just before sunset when the light is softer and the scent of sandalwood floats on the breeze. Avoid coming here on Fridays, when the place is invaded by picnicking extended families with stereos.

The island is most easily seen as part of a felucca tour. Alternatively, take the northernmost ferry to Elephantine Island and walk through the village to the other side of the island, where a few little feluccas wait on the western edge to take visitors across to the gardens. Expect to pay at least E£20 to E£25 for a round trip.

West Bank

It is easiest to visit the west bank as part of a felucca tour. The longer way is to take a ferry from Elephantine Island across to the landing for the Monastery of St Simeon. To get to the Tombs of the Nobles, or Gharb Aswan Nubian village, take the public ferry that leaves from a landing opposite the train station, on the east bank.

Aga Khan Mausoleum TOMB

(Map p242; ⏲closed to the public) The elegant **Tomb of Mohammed Shah Aga Khan** belongs to the 48th imam (leader) of the Ismaili sect. In his illustrious life he was hugely influential in the partition of India and the creation of Pakistan, and was father-in-law to Rita Hayworth. The Aga Khan liked to winter in Aswan for his health and was buried here after his death in 1957.

His fourth wife, Frenchwoman Yvonne Labrousse, known as Begum Om Habibeh, died in 2000 and is also buried here. The family's white villa is in the garden beneath

DON'T MISS

THE UNOFFICIAL NUBIAN MUSEUM

Animalia (Map p242; ☎ 097-231 4152, 0100 545 6420; main street, Siou, Elephantine Island; admission E£5, incl guided tour E£10; ⏰ 8am-7pm) This is a small but charming museum run by Mohamed Sobhi, a Nubian guide, and his family, who have dedicated part of their large house to the traditions, flora, fauna and history of Nubia. It has a collection of stuffed animals found in Nubia, samples of sedimentary rocks, great pictures of Nubia before it was flooded by Lake Nasser, a small shop selling Nubian crafts at fixed prices, and a lovely roof terrace where drinks and lunch are served overlooking the gardens.

Mohamed Sobhi is passionate and knowledgeable about Nubian culture and the natural world. He also takes people around Elephantine Island, and on early morning birdwatching (p248) trips.

the tomb. The begum was known for her charitable work: the Om Habibeh Foundation continues to work to improve healthcare in Aswan.

Monastery of St Simeon MONASTERY
(Deir Amba Samaan; Map p242; adult/student E£30/15; ⏰ 8am-4pm) Resembling a fortress, the 7th-century Monastery of St Simeon was first dedicated to the local saint Anba Hedra, who renounced the world on his wedding day. It was rebuilt in the 10th century and dedicated to St Simeon. From here the monks travelled into Nubia, in the hope of converting the Nubians to Christianity. To get there, take a private boat across the Nile, scramble up the desert track on foot (about 25 minutes) or hire a camel to take you up (expect to pay about E£30).

Surrounded by desert sands, the monastery was built on two levels – the lower level of stone and the upper level of mud brick – surrounded by 10m-high walls. At its height, the monastery may have housed as many as 1000 monks, but it was partially destroyed by the troops of Saladin (Salah ad-Din) in 1173. The basilica has traces of frescos. The cells still have their *mastaba* (bench) beds. The last room on the right includes graffiti from Muslim pilgrims who stayed here en route to Mecca.

An alternative way to get here is to take the ferry to the Tombs of the Nobles and ride a camel or donkey from there. Remember to bring water.

Tombs of the Nobles TOMB
(Map p242; adult/student E£30/15; ⏰ 8am-4pm) The high cliffs opposite Aswan, just north of Kitchener's Island, are honeycombed with the tombs of the governors, the Keepers of the Gate of the South, and other dignitaries of ancient Elephantine Island. The tombs, known as the Tombs of the Nobles, are still being excavated: significant finds were made in 2014. Six decorated tombs are open to the public.

The tombs date from the Old and Middle Kingdoms and most follow a simple plan, with an entrance hall, a pillared room and a corridor leading to the burial chamber. A set of stairs cutting diagonally across the hill goes up to the tombs from the ferry landing.

The adjoining tombs of father and son **Mekhu and Sabni** (tomb numbers 25 and 26), both governors, date from the long reign of 6th-dynasty Pharaoh Pepi II (2278–2184 BC). The reliefs in Sabni's tomb record how he led his army into Nubia, to punish the tribe responsible for killing his father during a previous military campaign, and to recover his father's body. Upon his return, Pepi II sent him his own royal embalmers and professional mourners, to show the importance accorded to the keepers of the southern frontier. Several reliefs in Sabni's tomb retain their original colours, and there are some lovely hunting and fishing scenes depicting him with his daughters in the pillared hall.

Sarenput was the local governor and overseer of the priesthood of Satet and Khnum under 12th-dynasty Pharaoh Amenemhat II (1922–1878 BC). The **tomb of Sarenput II** (number 31) is one of the most beautiful and best-preserved tombs, its colours still vivid. A six-pillared entrance chamber leads into a corridor with six niches holding statues of Sarenput. The burial chamber has four columns and a niche with wall paintings showing Sarenput with his wife (on the right) and his mother (on the left), as well as hunting and fishing scenes.

The **tomb of Harkhuf** (number 34), governor of the south during the reign of Pepi II, is hardly decorated, except for remarkable hieroglyphic texts about his three trading expeditions into central Africa, right of the entrance. Included here is Pepi II, then only a boy of eight, advising Harkhuf to take extra care of the 'dancing pygmy' he had obtained on his travels, as the pharaoh was very keen to see him in Memphis. 'My majesty desires to see this pygmy more than the gifts of Sinai or of Punt,' Harkhuf writes. Look carefully to see the tiny hieroglyph figure of the pygmy several times in the text.

Hekaib, also known as Pepinakht, was overseer of foreign soldiers during the reign of Pepi II. He was sent to quell rebellions in both Nubia and Palestine, and was even deified after his death, as is revealed by the small shrine of Hekaib built on Elephantine Island during the Middle Kingdom (c 1900 BC). Inside the **tomb of Hekaib** (number 35), fine reliefs show fighting bulls and hunting scenes.

The court of the **tomb of Sarenput I** (number 36), grandfather of Sarenput II and governor during the 12th-dynasty reign of Sesostris I (1965–1920 BC), has the remains of six pillars, decorated with reliefs. On each side of the entrance Sarenput is shown being followed by his dogs and sandal-bearer, his flower-bearing harem, his wife and his three sons.

Qubbet al-Hawa TOMB

(Map p242) On the hilltop above the Tombs of the Nobles lies this small domed tomb, constructed for a local sheikh or holy man. The steep climb up is rewarded with stunning views of the Nile and the surrounding area.

Gharb Aswan VILLAGE

(Map p242; West Aswan) Gharb Aswan is no longer a sleepy village, as Aswan expands ever quicker, but the Nubian settlement just north of the Tombs of the Nobles remains a tranquil place. It is particularly pleasant at night, after the souqs near the ferry landing have closed. Bet al-Kerem (p249) is a recommended place to stay for a few nights.

Western Quarry ARCHAEOLOGICAL SITE

(Map p242) Isolated in the desert to the west of the Tomb of the Nobles is the ancient Western Quarry, where stone for many ancient monuments – possibly including the Colossi of Memnon – was quarried. A large **unfinished obelisk**, made for Seti I (1294–1279 BC), was decorated on three sides of its apex before it was abandoned.

Expect to pay at least E£90, after bargaining, for the camel ride from the boat landing, 30 minutes each way. Take plenty of water, and watch for snakes.

Near the obelisk, the ancient quarry face and marks are clearly visible, along with tracks on which the huge blocks were dragged down to the Nile.

Activities

Feluccas

The Nile looks fabulous and magical at Aswan, and few things are more relaxing than hiring a felucca before sunset and sailing between the islands, the desert and the huge black boulders, listening to the flapping of a sail and to Nubian boys singing from tiny dugouts. On days when cruise boats dock together in town, hundreds of feluccas circle the islands, so it's a good time to take a felucca a bit further out towards Seheyl Island. The tourist office suggests felucca rates are around E£70 per hour, motor boats E£80.

The trustworthy **Gelal** (☎0122 415 4902), who hangs out near Panorama (p250) restaurant and the ferry landing, offers hassle-free tours on his family's feluccas at a fixed price (E£35 per boat for an hour, E£50 for a motor boat). Gelal is from Seheyl Island and can also arrange a visit to the island and lunch (E£40) in his house, as well as a swim on a safe beach.

Lake Nasser Day Trips

Lake Nasser is usually glimpsed from the top of the Aswan Dam or seen over several

CROCODILES IN THE NILE?

The Nile was once synonymous with crocodiles, particularly the large ones that carry the river's name. The Nile crocodile is the world's second-largest reptile: an adult grows to between 4m and 4.5m – and some get as large as 6m. It's commonly held that there are none north of the Aswan Dam. Is this true? Not according to the Egyptian Environmental Affairs Agency's Crocodile Management Unit.

There is a well-known adult crocodile living around the river at Aswan. Others have been released from restaurants and houses in Aswan, where they were kept as pets while they were little – though even a small one can take off your finger. Plus there may be as many as 20,000 of them in Lake Nasser. Just when you thought it was safe to go back in the water...

DON'T MISS

BIRDWATCHING IN ASWAN

Birdwatchers have long flocked to Aswan to watch its flocks of migrating birds. But being on the Nile very early in the morning, gliding along the edge of the islands, watching birds and hearing how they fit into ancient Egyptian history or into Nubian traditions, will appeal to a much wider audience than just specialists.

Mohamed Arabi (☎0122 324 0132; www.touregypt.net/featurestories/aswanbirding.htm; per person from US$50) Mohamed Arabi is known as the 'Birdman of Aswan' and no bird escapes his eye. He has been taking twitchers and documentary-makers on the Nile for many years, but is also happy to take amateurs. Call him direct.

His small speedboat glides into the channels between the islands while he points out the vegetation; sunbirds; hoopoes; purple, squacco, striated and night herons; pied kingfishers; little and cattle egrets; redshanks; and many other birds.

Mohamed Sobhi (☎097-231 4152, 0100 545 6420; per person US$25) Mohamed Sobhi, the owner of Nubian museum Animalia (p246), takes twitchers and others on nature tours along the Nile using a large motor boat.

days from a cruise boat, but there is nothing to stop you going out for a rewarding day trip. **African Angler** (☎230 9748; www.african-angler.net; from per person $185 incl rods & lunch) has small boats and offers day fishing for perch with a fishing guide, or a mini eco-safari looking at wildlife on or along the shores of the lake. Everything is arranged for the day, including transfers to and from your hotel. Prices include rods and lunch, and get cheaper the bigger the group.

Swimming

Aswan is a hot place, and often the only way to cool down, apart from hiding in your air-conditioned room, is to swim. Joining the local kids splashing about in the Nile is not a good idea. Schistosomiasis (an infection of the bowel and bladder caused by a freshwater fluke) can be caught in stagnant water; boatmen know where the current is strong enough (but not too strong) for it to be safe for swimming, among them a **beach** (Map p242) on the west bank opposite Seluga Island, for which you will need to rent a motor boat.

Some hotels open their swimming pools to the public, generally from 9am to sunset and particularly if occupancy rates are low. The Mövenpick Resort on Elephant Island charges nonguests E£120 to use its pools.

Tours

Small hotels and travel agencies arrange day tours of the area's major sights. Half-day guided tours usually include the Temple of Isis at Philae, the Unfinished Obelisk and the High Dam, and start at E£300 (per person with three to five people), including admission to all sites. Some budget hotels offer cheaper tours but are not licensed to guide groups. Travel agencies will also arrange felucca trips to Elephantine and Kitchener's Islands, but it is cheaper to deal directly with the boatmen.

All travel agencies and most hotels in Aswan offer trips to Abu Simbel, but watch out for huge price differences, and check that the bus is comfortable and has air-con. Thomas Cook charges about E£1000 per person, including a seat in an air-con minibus, admission fees and guide, and E£1400 by air, including transfers, fees and guide. By contrast, budget hotels offer tours for about E£300 to E£400 in a smaller bus, though often not including the entrance fee or guide.

Sleeping

Most visitors to Aswan stay on their cruise boats, so there has been little investment in hotels recently, but things are slowly changing. Prices vary greatly depending on the season; high-season rates run from October through to April, but peak in December and January. In the low season, and even until early November, you'll have no trouble finding a room at lower prices.

Hotel touts at the train station try to convince tired travellers that the hotel they have booked is now closed, so that they can take them to another hotel and collect a commission. Ignore them, as their commission will be added to your bill.

Baaba Dool GUESTHOUSE $
(Map p242; ☎0100 497 2608; Siou, Elephantine Island; r without bathroom per person €10) A

great place to unwind for a few days. A few rooms in this beautiful mud-brick house are painted in Nubian style, and have superb views over the Nile and the botanical gardens. Rooms are very basic but clean (bring a sleeping bag) and there are shared hot showers. Mustapha can arrange meals. Book ahead.

Nuba Nile Hotel HOTEL $

(Map p244; ☎231 3553; www.nubanilehotel.com; Sharia Abtal at-Tahrir; s/d/tr/q E£150/180/220/250; ❄📶🌅) This friendly family-run hotel is one of the more reliable of Aswan's budget hotels, conveniently located just north of the train station and beside a popular ahwa and internet cafe. Check the room before you agree, as they vary considerably, but all have private bathrooms and air-con and some have been repainted. Wi-fi costs E£30 a day.

Hathor Hotel HOTEL $

(Map p244; ☎231 4580; www.hathorhotel.com; Corniche an-Nil; ❄📶🌅) The Hathor was closed at the time of research, but is to reopen with 36 good-value rooms. The rooftop terrace has a small swimming pool and spectacular Nile views.

★Philae Hotel HOTEL $$

(Map p244; ☎0100 222 9628, 231 2090; www.philae-hotel.com; Corniche an-Nil; s/d/tr US$80/100/120; ❄📶) The well-established Philae Hotel is by far the best midrange hotel in town. The tasteful and cosy rooms are decorated in fabrics with Arabic calligraphy and elegant local furnishings. The hotel restaurant serves mainly vegetarian organic food from its own gardens, and at very reasonable prices for the quality (mains from E£55 to E£70). The Philae is no longer a secret, so book ahead.

Bet al-Kerem GUESTHOUSE $$

(Map p242; ☎0122 391 1052, 0122 384 2218; www.betelkerem.com; Gharb Aswan, west bank; s/d with shared bathroom €30/40; ❄) This modern hotel on the west side of the Nile overlooking the desert and the Tomb of the Nobles is a great find, offering nine quiet and comfortable rooms with very clean shared bathrooms. The hotel boasts a wonderful rooftop terrace overlooking the Nile and Nubian village, and the staff are both friendly and proud to be Nubian. Call ahead and Shaaban will come and fetch you or explain how to get there. The restaurant serves delicious meals (from €7 to €10).

Marhaba Palace Hotel HOTEL $$

(Map p244; ☎233 0102; www.marhaba-aswan.com; Corniche an-Nil; s/d US$60/80; ❄) The Marhaba has small but cosy and tastefully decorated rooms, with comfortable beds, sumptuous bathrooms (for this price range) and satellite TV. Bright and welcoming, it overlooks a park on the Corniche and has two restaurants, friendly staff and a roof terrace with excellent Nile views.

Keylany Hotel HOTEL $$

(Map p244; ☎231 7332; www.keylanyhotel.com; 25 Sharia Keylany; s/d/tr US$23/34/45; ❄@📶🌅) This great little hotel used to come at budget prices, but costs have gone up and some find it expensive for what is on offer. The simple but comfortable rooms are furnished with pine furniture, and have spotless bathrooms with proper showers and hot water. The management and staff are friendly and helpful.

The roof terrace doesn't have Nile views but there is a burlap sunshade and furniture made from palm fronds, and it is a great place to hang out.

★Sofitel Old Cataract Hotel & Spa HISTORIC HOTEL $$$

(Map p242; ☎231 6000; www.sofitel-legend.com; Sharia Abtal at-Tahrir; s & d from US$295-320; ❄🌅) The grande dame of Aswan hotels, the Cataract is a destination in itself and brings you back to the days of Agatha Christie, who is said to have written part of her novel

ASWAN HOUSE RENTALS

A number of flats are for rent on the west bank of Aswan, or on Elephantine Island, offering a good-value option for a longer stay, or even just for a night. Simply walk around on Elephantine Island and you will be offered houses for rent.

If you want to book ahead, check **Bet al-Kerem** for Nubian houses, or ask Mohamed Sobhi at Animalia (p246). Mohamed Arabi has three amazing **houses** (☎0122 324 0132; per night from €100) for rent in his 4-hectare garden and orchard on the west bank, all tastefully decorated in Nubian style, but with cool marble floors, clean bathrooms and a sitting room. These houses are very peaceful, and, at night, dinner with garden produce is served on a terrace on the Nile.

Death on the Nile here (the hotel certainly featured in the movie). The splendid buildings and well-tended gardens command fantastic views of the Nile and the desert.

The Old Cataract reopened at the end of 2011 having been completely refitted. The original building, now known as the Palace Wing, has 76 rooms, of which more than half are suites. But the biggest change has been brought to the 1960s annexe, the Garden Wing, where all rooms have stunning Nile views. The 1902 Restaurant (p251) serves some of the fanciest food on the Nile, while Kebabgy and Saraya serve simpler food in a more relaxed atmosphere. The large pool looks onto the river and ruins of Elephantine Island, while the two-floor spa has a fitness centre, hammam, sauna and Thai therapists.

Pyramisa Isis Island Resort & Spa HOTEL **$$$**
(Map p242; ☎231 7400; www.pyramisaegypt.com; r garden/Nile view €120/150; ❄@≋) An imposing four-star resort hotel on its own island (there are regular free shuttle boats to town) with 477 big, well-appointed rooms overlooking the Nile or the garden. Popular with tour groups, it has two huge swimming pools and several restaurants – usually with long queues at the enormous buffets. Very friendly staff.

Sara Hotel HOTEL **$$$**
(☎232 7234; www.sarahotel-aswan.com; s/d US$120/180; ❄≋) Built on a clifftop overlooking the Nile about 2km beyond the Nubia Museum, the Sara is isolated but has fantastic views over the First Cataract and the Western Desert. It's worth putting up with the kitsch pastel decor for the 60 spotlessly clean rooms with satellite TV, a friendly staff and a good-sized pool overlooking the Nile.

Corner rooms have huge balconies. The cafeteria is hugely popular with Aswanis. A shuttle bus runs into town hourly. If you want to stay in Aswan for a few days of peace and quiet, the Sara is a good choice, unless the in-house disco revives.

Mövenpick Resort Aswan RESORT **$$$**
(Map p242; ☎230 3455; www.moevenpick-aswan.com; Elephantine Island; s/d from US$90/144; ❄@≋) Hidden in a large, lush garden but dominated by an eyesore tower, the Mövenpick sits on the northern end of Elephantine Island. The hotel recently had a total makeover and has very comfortable rooms, decorated in Nubian style and colours. The swimming pool is great, as is the tower-top restaurant and bar.

Guests are transported to and from the town centre by a free ferry. There are best rates via the website.

Eating

Aswan is a sleepy place and most tourists eat on board the cruise boats, but there are a few laid-back restaurants. Outside the hotels, few serve alcohol and few accept credit cards.

Panorama EGYPTIAN **$**
(Map p242; ☎231 6169; Corniche an-Nil; dishes E£10-30) With its pleasant Nile-side terrace, this is a great place to chill and sip a herbal tea or fresh juice. It also serves simple Egyptian stews cooked in clay pots, with salad, mezze (a selection of starters) and rice or chips, or an all-day breakfast. Not to be confused with the restaurant of the same name in the Mövenpick Resort.

Al-Makka GRILL **$$**
(Map p244; ☎230 3232; Sharia Abtal at-Tahrir; mains E£35-50; ⏰noon-2am) Popular with meat-eating local families, this place is famous for its excellent fresh kebabs and kofta (mincemeat and spices grilled on a skewer), as well as pigeon and chicken. Everything comes with bread, salad, tahini and TV. It's opposite the Ramses Hotel.

Its sister-restaurant **Al-Madina** (Map p244; ☎230 5696; Sharia as-Souq) serves a similar menu.

Salah Ad-Din INTERNATIONAL **$$**
(Map p244; ☎231 0361; Corniche an-Nil; mains E£40-80; ⏰noon-late) One of the best of the Nile-side restaurants, with several terraces and a freezing air-conditioned dining room. The menu has Egyptian, Nubian and international dishes, a notch better than most restaurants in Aswan. The service is efficient and the beers are cool (E£18). There is also a terrace to smoke a sheesha.

Nubian Beach EGYPTIAN **$$**
(Map p242; west bank; set menu per person E£65) Nubian cafe-restaurant set in a quiet garden on the west bank of the Nile, against the backdrop of a towering sand dune and near a popular swimming spot. During the heat of the day or on cold winter nights, there is a beautifully painted room indoors. The food is simple but good, and beer is sometimes served.

LOCAL KNOWLEDGE

LOCAL CUISINE

Along Sharia as-Souq and Sharia Abtal at-Tahrir there are plenty of small restaurants and cafes, where you can take in the lively atmosphere of the souq and sample local flavours.

Haramein Foul & Ta'amiyya (Map p244; Sharia Abtal at-Tahrir; E£3-10) A tiny takeaway place hidden among the low-rise apartment blocks. This is where Aswanis go when they want good fuul (fava bean paste) and ta'amiyya (felafel).

Koshary Aly Baba Restaurant (Map p244; Sharia Abtal at-Tahrir; kushari E£5-10) A good *kushari* place (*kushari* is a mix of noodles, rice, black lentils, fried onions and tomato sauce) that also sells takeaway shwarma and *kofta* (mincemeat and spices grilled on a skewer).

El-Tahrer Pizza (Map p244; Midan al-Mahatta; dishes E£25-40) Just off the souq in front of the train station, El-Tahrer Pizza is a popular cafe serving pizza and *fiteer* (Egyptian flaky pizza) at rock-bottom prices. Tea and sheesha (E£5) are also served.

Chef Khalil EGYPTIAN $$
(Map p244; ☎231 0142; Sharia as-Souq; meals E£80-130; ⏰noon-1am) Small but popular fish restaurant, a short walk from the train station into the souq. It serves fish from Lake Nasser and the Red Sea, chosen from a chilled display, charged by weight and grilled, baked or fried to your choice and served with salad and rice or French fries. Sometimes it also serves lobster (E£130).

Ad-Dukka EGYPTIAN $$
(Map p242; ☎231 8293; Essa Island; mains E£45-60; ⏰6.30-10pm) This Nubian restaurant, set on an island just beyond Elephantine Island, continues to serve excellent Nubian food, in large and lavishly decorated portions. It can be a wonderfully atmospheric place to spend an evening. To get here, there's a free ferry from the dock opposite the EgyptAir office.

Biti Pizza PIZZA $$
(Map p244; Midan al-Mahatta; dishes E£30-38; ⏰10am-midnight; ❄) Biti is a popular air-conditioned restaurant that serves good Western-style pizzas. Even more recommended are the delicious sweet and savoury *fiteer* (Egyptian flaky pizza), including the excellent tuna *fiteer* or the fruit-and-nut dessert version. Watch out for the more expensive English-language tourist menu with the offer of any topping for E£38. The main menu is cheaper.

Sunset PIZZA $$
(Map p242; ☎233 0601; Sharia Abtal at-Tahrir, Nasr City; set menu E£40-50; ⏰9am-3am) A cafe terrace and restaurant to head for at sunset (if you can't get to the Cataract Hotel) for its spectacular views over the First Cataract. Sit on the huge shady terrace for a mint tea, or enjoy the small selection of excellent grills or pizzas (E£40 to E£50). Take a taxi here after dark. Very popular with locals later at night.

★Panorama Restaurant & Bar INTERNATIONAL $$$
(Map p242; ☎230 3455; www.moevenpick-hotels.com; Mövenpick Resort Aswan, Elephantine Island; mains E£90-160) The Panorama is the best thing to open in Aswan, and in the Mövenpick's eyesore tower, in a long time. The food is good, service friendly and efficient, the room is elegant; but the real draw is the 360-degree view of Aswan, the river and the desert, spectacular at sunset, glittering at night.

The menu is mostly North African – mezze, tagines, kebab, Red Sea fish – and also includes curries and some Italian dishes. The three-course set menu costs E£250. There is a long cocktail menu and a full wine list.

1902 Restaurant FRENCH $$$
(Map p242; ☎231 6000; www.sofitel-legend.com; Sharia Abtal at-Tahrir; mains E£150-250; ⏰7-11pm) The revamped Old Cataract Hotel has several top-end outlets, but none grander than the 1902. Under its Moorish-inspired dome, the chefs – trained here and in France – serve some of the finest food in the country. The outcome is sophisticated, expensive and mostly nouvelle cuisine.

There is usually duck from France, fresh fish from the Red Sea, perhaps some foie gras, good Italian oils and cheese, a serious wine list from around the world…Service is as attentive as the room is grand, and guests are invited to play their part by dressing for the occasion. As a dining experience, there is simply nothing else like this south of Cairo.

Drinking & Nightlife

Strolling along the Corniche, watching the moon rise as you sit at a rooftop terrace or having a cool drink at one of the Nile-side restaurants is about all that most travellers get up to in Aswan at night.

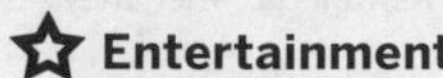

Entertainment

Between October and February/March, Aswan's folkloric dance troupe sporadically performs Nubian tahtib (dance performed with wooden staves) and songs depicting village life at the **Palace of Culture** (Map p244; ☎231 3390; Corniche an-Nil). Call to check about performances, as the venue was closed at the time of writing.

Nubian shows are sometimes performed at the Mövenpick Resort Aswan and smaller hotels such as Bet al-Kerem. If you're lucky, you may be invited to a Nubian wedding on a weekend night. Foreign guests are deemed auspicious additions to the ceremony, but don't be surprised if you're asked to help defray the huge costs of the band and the food.

Shopping

Aswan's famous souq (p241) is a good place to pick up souvenirs and crafts. Handmade Nubian skullcaps (from E£20), colourful scarves (E£25 to E£50), and traditional baskets and trays (E£80 to E£200) in varying sizes are popular. The spices and indigo powder prominently displayed are also good buys, and most spice shops sell dried hibiscus, used to make the refreshing drink *karkadai* and of the best quality in Aswan. Beware that what is often sold as saffron is in fact safflower. Egyptians have been using it to dye textiles and food for millennia, but it does not have the same taste as saffron. Aswan is also famous for the quality of its henna powder and its delicious roasted peanuts. The higher grade of the latter goes for E£30 per kilogram.

International newspapers and magazines are usually available from the newsstand near the Philae Hotel on the Corniche.

Hanafi Bazaar HANDICRAFTS
(Map p242; ☎231 4083; Corniche an-Nil; ⌚9am-8pm) With its mock Pharaonic facade, this is the oldest, no doubt also the dustiest, and best bazaar in town, with genuine Nubian swords, baskets, amulets, silk kaftans and beads from all over Africa, run by the totally laid-back Hanafi brothers.

Nubia Tourist Book Centre BOOKS
(Map p244; Sharia as-Souq; ⌚9am-10pm) Good, air-conditioned bookshop near the train station with loads of books on Aswan and Egypt. This branch was closed at the time of our visit, but there is another well-stocked branch in the tourist bazaar at the Unfinished Obelisk (p241).

Information

EMERGENCY

Ambulance (☎123)

Police (Map p244; ☎230 2043; Corniche an-Nil) Near Thomas Cook.

Tourist Police (Map p244; ☎231 4393, 230 3436; Corniche an-Nil) Contact the tourist office first to help with translation.

INTERNET ACCESS

Internet prices range from E£10 to E£15 per hour.

Aswanet Internet Café (Map p244; 25 Sharia Keylany; ⌚9am-11pm) Next to Keylany Hotel.

Nuba Nile Internet (Map p244; Sharia Abtal at-Tahrir; per hr E£10; ⌚24hr) Next to Nuba Nile Hotel.

MEDICAL SERVICES

Aswan Military Hospital (Map p242; ☎231 4739, 231 7985; Sharia Sadat) The top hospital in town.

Ta'mim (Insurance) Hospital (☎231 5112, 231 6510; Sharia Sadat) Newest hospital, with a good reputation.

MONEY

Unless otherwise noted, banking hours are 8.30am to 2pm and 5pm to 8pm Sunday to Thursday. There are ATMs and exchange booths along the Corniche and around Sharia as-Souq, as well as at the train station.

American Express (Map p242; ☎230 6983; Corniche an-Nil; ⌚9am-5pm)

Bank of Alexandria (Map p244; Corniche an-Nil)

Banque du Caire (Map p244; Corniche an-Nil) Branch and ATM.

Banque Misr (Map p244; Corniche an-Nil; ⌚8am-3pm & 5-8pm) ATM and foreign-exchange booth next to main building.

Thomas Cook (Map p244; ☎230 4011; Corniche an-Nil; ⌚8am-2pm & 5-9pm)

POST

Main Post Office (Map p244; Corniche an-Nil; ⌚8am-8pm Sat-Thu, 1-5pm Fri)

TELEPHONE

There are **cardphones** (Map p244) along the Corniche and at the train station.

Telephone Centrale (Map p242; Corniche an-Nil; ⌚24hr)

TOURIST INFORMATION

Main Tourist Office (Map p244; ☎ 231 2811; Midan al-Mahatta; ⏰ 8am-3pm & 7-9pm Sat-Thu) This tourist office has little material, and little access to any, but staff can advise on timetables, and give an idea of prices for taxis and feluccas.

Getting There & Away

AIR

Daily flights are available with **EgyptAir** (Map p242; ☎ 231 5000; Corniche an-Nil; ⏰ 8am-3pm & 7-9pm Sat-Thu) from Aswan to Cairo (one way from E£358, 1¼ hours). If tourist demand increases, the flight to Luxor may be reinstated. There are several 45-minute flights to Abu Simbel each week.

BOAT

Five-star cruise boats and fishing safaris operate on Lake Nasser.

BUS

The bus station is 3.5km north of the train station. Buses currently do not run along the Nile and therefore the service to Luxor is not recommended. Buses to Abu Simbel (E£25, four hours) leave at 8am and 5pm. A direct bus to Cairo (E£110, 14 hours) leaves at 3.30pm and 4pm daily, via Hurghada (Al-Ghardaka; E£60). A bus to Marsa Alam (E£25) leaves at 6am.

MICROBUS

Microbuses leave from the bus station, 3.5km north of the train station. A taxi there will cost E£15, or 50pt in a communal taxi, from downtown. A seat in a microbus costs: Luxor E£20, Kom Ombo E£3, Edfu E£10, Esna E£15 and Qena E£25.

TRAIN

From **Aswan Train Station** (☎ 231 4754; Midan al-Mahatta) a number of daily trains run north to Cairo from 5am to 9.10pm (E£120, 14 hours). Tickets should be bought in advance, but can be bought on the train for an additional fee.

All trains heading north to Luxor (E£25) stop at Daraw, Kom Ombo, Edfu and Esna. Student discounts are available on all of these trains.

Watania Egypt Sleeping Train (☎ 230 2124; www.wataniasleepingtrains.com; s/d cabin per person incl dinner & breakfast US$120/100, per child US$85) has two daily services to Cairo at 4pm and 7pm. No student discount.

POLICE CONVOYS

Driving north from Aswan to Luxor no longer needs to be done in convoy, but there is still a twice-daily (4am and 11am) convoy to Abu Simbel, compulsory for foreigners. **Armed convoys** (Map p242) congregate at the beginning of Sharia Sadat, near the Coptic Cathedral. Be there at least 15 minutes in advance. It takes at least three hours to reach Abu Simbel.

Getting Around

TO/FROM THE AIRPORT

The airport is located 25km southwest of town. A taxi to/from the airport costs about E£50 to E£70 depending on your bargaining skills.

BICYCLE

Aswan is not a great town for cycling. However, there are a few places at the train-station end of Sharia as-Souq where you can hire bicycles for about E£15 a day. Bet al-Kerem (p249) runs cycling trips in the countryside.

FERRY

Two public ferries (E£1) run to Elephantine Island; the one departing across from EgyptAir goes to the Aswan Museum, while the one across from Thomas Cook goes to Siou. A third public ferry (E£1) goes from the ferry landing across from the train station to West Aswan and the Tombs of the Nobles. Foreigners might be expected to pay more.

TAXI

A taxi tour that includes Philae, the High Dam and the Unfinished Obelisk near Fatimid Cemetery costs from E£200 to E£300 for five to six people, excluding entry tickets. A taxi anywhere within the town costs E£5 to E£15.

Microbuses (50pt) run along the major roads in Aswan.

AROUND ASWAN

Aswan Dam

At the end of the 19th century, Egypt's fast-growing population made it imperative to cultivate more agricultural land. This would only be possible by regulating the flow of the Nile, which would also ensure the river did not burst its banks during the flood. The British engineer Sir William Willcocks started construction of the original Aswan Dam in 1898 above the First Cataract. When completed in 1902, it was the largest dam in the world, measuring 2441m

Around Aswan

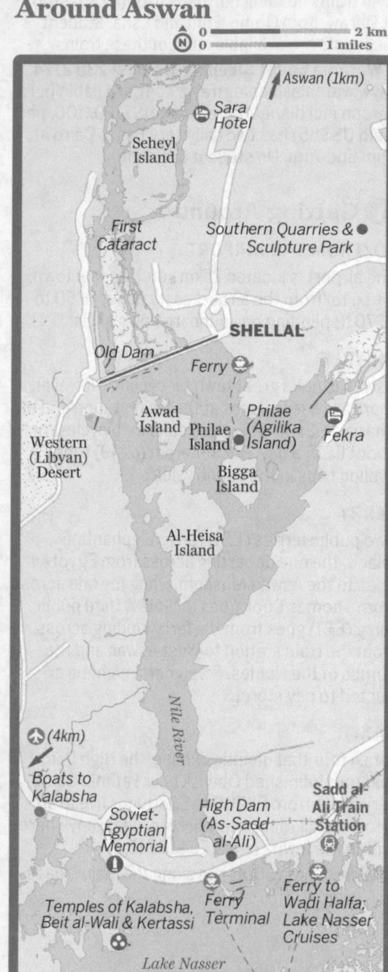

across, 50m high and 30m wide, and was made almost entirely of Aswan granite.

It was raised twice to meet the demand, not only to increase the area of cultivable land but also to provide hydroelectric power. With the opening of the 1960s High Dam, the old dam now only generates hydroelectricity for a nearby factory producing fertilisers, and otherwise serves as a tourist attraction on the way to the High Dam, 6km upstream. The road to the airport and all trips to Abu Simbel by road include a drive across the Aswan Dam.

Seheyl Island

The large island situated just north of the old Aswan Dam, **Seheyl** (adult/child E£25/15; 7am-4pm Oct-Apr, to 5pm May-Sep) was sacred to the goddess Anukis. Prior to the dam's construction, the Nile would rush noisily through the granite boulders that emerged from the riverbed just south of here, forming the First Cataract, called Shellal by the Egyptians. Herodotus reported that an Egyptian official had told him that this was the source of the Nile, which flowed north and south from there. Now the waters flow slowly and Seheyl makes an ideal destination for a slightly longer felucca trip.

On the island's southern tip is a cliff with more than **200 inscriptions**, most dating to the 18th and 19th dynasties, of princes, generals and other officials who passed by on their journey to Nubia. The most famous is the so-called 'famine stele' from the 3rd dynasty that recounts a terrible seven-year famine during the reign of Zoser (2667–2648 BC), which the pharaoh tried to end by making offerings to the Temple of Khnum on Elephantine Island.

Next to the inscriptions is a friendly Nubian village with brightly coloured houses. Several houses now welcome visitors, selling tea and good Nubian lunches as well as local crafts. It's a pleasant place to stroll around.

Philae (Agilika Island)

Sights

Temple of Isis TEMPLE
(adult/child E£60/30; 7am-4pm Oct-May, to 5pm Jun-Sep) Perched on the island of Philae (fee-*leh*), the Temple of Isis attracted pilgrims for thousands of years and was one of the last pagan temples to operate, after the arrival of Christianity. One of Egypt's most seductive sights, the temple was saved after it was moved to higher ground following the building of the Aswan High Dam.

The cult of Isis at Philae goes back at least to the 7th century BC, but the earliest surviving remains date from the reign of the last native king of Egypt, Nectanebo I (380–362 BC). The most important ruins were begun by Ptolemy II Philadelphus (285–246 BC) and added to for the next 500 years until the reign of Diocletian (AD 284–305). By Roman times Isis had become the most popular of all the Egyptian gods, worshipped across the Roman Empire even as far as Britain.

Indeed, as late as AD 550, well after Rome and its empire embraced Christianity, Isis was still being worshipped at Philae. Early Christians eventually transformed the main temple's hypostyle hall into a chapel and defaced the pagan reliefs, their inscriptions later vandalised by early Muslims.

After 1902 and the building of the old Aswan Dam, the temple was flooded for six months each year, allowing travellers to row boats among the partially submerged columns to peer down through the translucent green at the wondrous sanctuaries of the mighty gods below.

After the completion of the High Dam, the temple would have entirely disappeared had Unesco not intervened. Between 1972 and 1980, the massive temple complex was disassembled stone by stone. It was then reconstructed 20m higher on nearby Agilika Island, which was landscaped to resemble the original sacred isle of Isis.

➡ Touring the Temple

The boat across to the temple leaves you at the base of the Kiosk of Nectanebo, the oldest part of the Philae complex. Heading north, you walk down the outer temple court, which has colonnades running along both sides; the western one is the most complete, with windows that originally overlooked the island of Bigga. At the end is the entrance of the Temple of Isis, marked by the 18m-high towers of the first pylon with reliefs of Ptolemy XII Neos Dionysos smiting enemies.

In the central court of the Temple of Isis, the *mammisi* is dedicated to Horus, son of Isis and Osiris. Successive pharaohs reinstated their legitimacy as the mortal descendants of Horus by taking part in rituals celebrating the Isis legend and the birth of her son Horus in the marshes.

The second pylon leads to a hypostyle hall, with superb column capitals, and

Philae (Agilika Island)

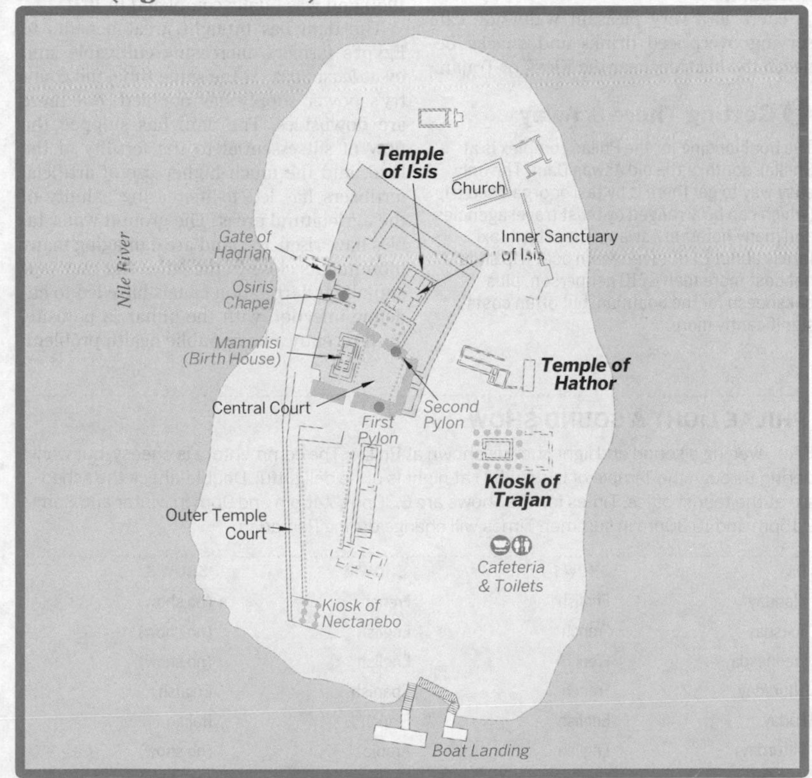

beyond lie three vestibules, leading into the **Inner Sanctuary of Isis**. Two granite shrines stood here, one containing a gold statue of Isis and another containing the barque in which the statue travelled, but those were long ago moved to Florence and Paris, and only the stone pedestal for the barque remains, inscribed with the names of Ptolemy III and his wife, Berenice. Take a side door west out of the hypostyle hall to the **Gate of Hadrian** where there is an image of the god Hapi, sitting in a cave at the First Cataract, representing the source of the river Nile.

East of the second pylon is the delightful **Temple of Hathor**, decorated with reliefs of musicians (including an ape playing the lute) and Bes, the god of childbirth. South of this is the elegant, unfinished pavilion by the water's edge, known as the **Kiosk of Trajan** (or 'Pharaoh's Bed'), perhaps the most famous of Philae's monuments and one that was frequently painted by Victorian artists, whose boats were moored beneath it.

There is a very pleasant waterside cafe serving overpriced drinks and snacks beneath the big tree, near the Kiosk of Trajan.

Getting There & Away

The boat landing for the Philae complex is at Shellal, south of the old Aswan Dam. The only easy way to get there is by taxi or organised trip (which can be arranged by most travel agencies and many hotels in Aswan). The return taxi fare is about E£60. The return boat trip should not cost more than E£10 per person, plus baksheesh for the boatman, but often costs significantly more.

Aswan High Dam

Egypt's modern example of construction on a monumental scale, the controversial **Aswan High Dam** (as-Sadd al-Ali; adult/child E£20/10; P) contains 18 times the amount of material used in the Great Pyramid of Khufu and it created Lake Nasser, the world's largest artificial lake.

From the 1940s, it was clear that the old Aswan Dam, which only regulated the flow of water, was not big enough to counter the unpredictable annual flooding of the Nile. In 1952, when Gamal Abdel Nasser came to power, plans were drawn up for a new dam, 6km south of the old one, but from the start there were political and engineering difficulties. In 1956, after the World Bank refused the promised loan for the project, Nasser ordered the nationalisation of the Suez Canal, which sparked the Suez Crisis in which France, the UK and Israel invaded the canal region. But Nasser got his way and also won additional funding and expertise from the Soviet Union. Work on the dam started in 1960 and was finally completed in 1971.

The dam has brought great benefits to Egypt's farmers, increasing cultivable land by at least 30%. At the same time, the country's power supply has doubled. But there are downsides. The dam has stopped the flow of silt essential to the fertility of the land, and the much higher use of artificial fertilisers has led to increasing salinity of the agricultural areas. The ground water tables have risen, too, and are damaging many monuments close to the Nile. The now perennially full irrigation canals have led to endemic infection with the bilharzia parasite, until recently a huge public health problem.

PHILAE LIGHT & SOUND SHOW

Each evening a sound and light show is shown at Philae. The commentary is cheesy, but wandering through the Temple of Isis (p254) at night is quite delightful. Double-check the schedule at the tourist office. Times for the shows are 6.30pm, 7.45pm and 9pm in winter and 8pm, 9.15pm and 10.30pm in summer. Times will change during Ramadan.

DAY	SHOW 1	SHOW 2	SHOW 3
Monday	English	French	(no show)
Tuesday	French	English	(no show)
Wednesday	French	English	(no show)
Thursday	French	Spanish	English
Friday	English	French	Italian
Saturday	English	Arabic	(no show)
Sunday	German	English	(no show)

FEKRA CULTURAL CENTRE

Fekra (www.fekraculture.com; Gebal Shisha, Shellal) is a farm located on 40,000 sq metres of land on the lake between the old and the High Dam, and overlooks Philae Island. The Fekra Cultural Centre – *fekra* means thought or idea in Arabic – is a fascinating project of artists from around the world, aiming to support Nubian and Upper Egyptian artists, and to promote an international cultural exchange through organising artistic events and workshops. It's a magical place for its energy and wonderful location.

A Nubian-style mud-brick house right on the lake, it's perfectly peaceful and a great place for swimming. It has midrange accommodation for 12 people and a few extra Bedouin tents, with shared bathrooms, but were not welcoming guests at the time of research.

Most people visit the High Dam, 13km south of Aswan, as part of an organised trip to sights south of Aswan. There is a small pavilion with displays detailing the dimensions and the construction of the dam, and on the western side is a monument honouring Soviet-Egyptian friendship and cooperation. Video cameras and zoom lenses cannot be used, although nobody seems to police this.

LOWER NUBIA & LAKE NASSER

For thousands of years, the First Cataract marked the border between Egypt and Nubia, the land that stretched from Aswan to Khartoum. The Nile Valley on the Egyptian side was fertile and continuously cultivated, while the banks further south in Nubia were more rugged, with rocky desert cliffs and sand separating small pockets of agricultural land.

The building of the Aswan and High Dams irrevocably changed all that, and much of Nubia disappeared under the waters of Lake Nasser. The landscape now is dominated by the contrast of smooth desert and the calm green-brown water of the lake. Apart from the beauty and the peace of the lake itself, the main attraction of this region is the temples that were so painstakingly moved above the flood waters in the 1960s.

The area between the First and the Second Cataracts is generally known as Lower Nubia (ancient Egyptian Wawat), and further south between the Second and Sixth Cataracts is Upper Nubia (Kush).

To the ancient Egyptians, Nubia was Ta-Sety, the Land of Bowmen, after the weapon for which the Nubians were famous. It was a crucial route for the trade with sub-Saharan Africa, and it was the source of much-needed raw materials, such as copper, ivory, ebony and gold. The modern name is thought to come from the ancient Egyptian word *nbw*, meaning 'gold'.

Egypt was always interested in Nubia and its riches, and the two peoples' histories were always connected: when Egypt was strong it dominated Nubia and aggressively exploited its natural resources; when Egypt was weak, the Nubians enjoyed periods of growth and development.

Evidence of 10,000-year-old settlements has been found in northern Nubia. At Nabta Playa, located some 100km west of Abu Simbel, archaeologists have recently discovered the remains of houses, sculpted monoliths and the world's oldest calendar, made of small standing stones, dating from around 6000 BC.

Until 3500 BC Nubia and Egypt both developed in roughly the same way, domesticating animals, growing crops and gradually adopting permanent settlements. Both people were ethnically linked, but the darker-skinned Nubians had more African features and spoke a Nilo-Saharan language, while the ancient Egyptian language is Afro-Asiatic.

With the unification of the land north of Aswan around 3100 BC, Egypt started to impose its authority on Nubia. From the beginning of the Old Kingdom, for nearly 5000 years, expeditions were sent to extract the region's considerable mineral wealth. During the First Intermediate Period (2160–2025 BC), central authority in Egypt collapsed, while Nubia became stronger, and Nubian soldiers played an important role in Egypt's civil war.

The reunification of Egypt, at the start of the Middle Kingdom, saw Lower Nubia again annexed and a chain of fortresses built at strategic points along the Nile to safeguard trade.

During the New Kingdom, instead of fortresses, the Egyptians built temples in

Nubia, dividing the whole of the region into five nomes, ruled on the pharaoh's behalf by his viceroy, who took the title King's Son of Kush. Taking advantage of Egypt's political disunity during the Third Intermediate Period (1069–945 BC), the tables were turned and Nubians extended their authority far to the north, ruling Egypt for a century as the 25th Kushite dynasty (747–656 BC). The 25th dynasty ended with the Assyrian invasion of Egypt, after which Nubian action was guided by its own best interests, sometimes siding with foreign invaders, sometimes with its Egyptian neighbours.

Christianity gradually spread to Nubia after the 5th century AD and lasted long after Islam had spread along the Egyptian Nile. In AD 652 Egypt's new Muslim authorities made a peace treaty with the Christian king of Nubia. That treaty lasted more or less until the 13th century, when Egyptians moved south again: the last Christian king of Nubia was deposed in 1305 and most of the population converted to Islam. In the 19th century Nubia was again important to Egyptian ambitions as the route for its supply of slaves. The rise of the Mahdist state in Sudan at the end of the 19th century led to Nubia being divided for the last time: with the defeat of the Mahdi and his successor, and the establishment of the Anglo-Egyptian government in Sudan in 1899, a border between Egypt and Sudan was established 40km north of Wadi Halfa.

Modern Nubia

Following the completion of the old Aswan Dam in 1902, and again after its height was raised in 1912 and 1934, the high-water level of the Nile in Lower Nubia gradually rose from 87m to 121m, partially submerging many of the monuments in the area and, by the 1930s, totally flooding a large number of Nubian villages. With their homes flooded, some Nubians moved north where, with government help, they bought land and built villages based on their traditional architecture. Most of the Nubian villages close to Aswan, such as Elephantine, Gharb Aswan (West Aswan) and Seheyl, are made up of people who moved at this time. Those who decided to stay in their homeland built houses on higher land, assuming they would be safe, but they saw their date plantations, central to their economy, destroyed. This meant that many Nubian men were forced to search for work further north, leaving the women behind to run the communities.

NUBIAN MUSIC

It's one of those strange quirks, but it's almost easier to hear and buy Nubian music in the West than it is in Egypt (Aswan is the exception). Nubian music, very different to the more popular Egyptian music, is rarely heard on national TV and radio, and hard to find in music stores in Cairo. But Nubian artists sell CDs by the rackload in Europe and play to sell-out audiences.

The biggest name is Ali Hassan Kuban. A former tillerman from a village near Aswan, Kuban grew up playing at weddings and parties and made the leap to a global audience after performing at a Berlin festival in 1989. Before his death in 2001 he released several CDs on the German label Piranha (www.piranha.de), including *Walk Like a Nubian*.

The Nubian sound is easily accessible, particularly to a Western audience familiar with African music. It is rhythmic, warm and exotic, mixing simple melodies and soulful vocals. This can be heard at its best on a series of CDs by a loose grouping of musicians and vocalists recording under the name Salamat. Look out especially for *Mambo al-Soudani* (again on the Piranha label).

A slightly different facet of Nubian music is represented by Hamza ad-Din, a Sufi-inspired Nubian composer born in Wadi Halfa in 1929 and widely respected in the West for his semiclassical compositions written for the oud (lute). You can find ad-Din's *Escalay* (The Waterwheel) in a recording by the composer himself, or in an excellent version by the Kronos Quartet on their CD *Pieces of Africa*.

The best places to pick up CDs of Nubian music are from the music stores in the Aswan souq (p241), where the sales assistants are happy to let you listen to different musicians. To hear authentic live Nubian music, try to get yourself invited to a Nubian wedding in Aswan. You can also head to Eskaleh (p264) in Abu Simbel, where the renowned Nubian musician Fikry el Kashef plays with his friends.

Less than 30 years later, the building of the High Dam forced those who had stayed to move. In the 1960s, 50,000 Egyptian Nubians were relocated to government-built villages around Kom Ombo, 50km north of Aswan.

Nubian Culture

The Nubians have paid the highest price for Egypt's greater good. They have lost their homes and their homeland, and with a new generation growing up far from the homeland, as Egyptians, or even Europeans and Americans, they are now also gradually losing their distinctive identity and traditions.

What is left of Nubian culture then seems all the more vibrant. Nubian music, famous for its unique sound, was popularised in the West by musicians such as Hamza ad-Din, whose oud (lute) melodies are ethereally beautiful. In addition to the oud, two basic instruments give the music its distinctive rhythm and harmony: the *douff,* a wide, shallow drum or tabla that musicians hold in their hands; and the *kisir,* a type of stringed instrument.

Less known abroad is Nubia's distinctive architecture, which was the main influence on Egyptian mud-brick architect Hassan Fathy. Traditional Lower Nubian houses are made with mud bricks; unlike the Upper Egyptian houses, they often have domed or vaulted ceilings, and further south the houses usually have a flat split-palm roof. They are plastered or whitewashed and covered with decorations, including ceramic plates. The basic forms of these houses can be seen in the Nubian villages around Aswan and in Ballana, near Kom Ombo.

Nubians also have their own marriage customs. Traditionally, wedding festivities lasted for up to 15 days, although nowadays they are a three-day affair. On the first night of the festivities, the bride and groom celebrate separately with their respective friends and families. On the second night, the bride takes her party to the groom's home and both groups dance to traditional music until the wee hours. Then the bride returns home and her hands and feet are painted with beautiful designs in henna. The groom will also have his hands and feet covered in henna but without any design. On the third day, the groom and his party walk slowly to the bride's house in a *zaffer* (procession), singing and dancing the whole way. Traditionally the groom will stay at the bride's house for three days before seeing his family. The couple then set up home.

Getting There & Away

Although all the sights except Qasr Ibrim have roads leading to them, the only sites foreigners are currently allowed to drive to are Kalabsha, Beit al-Wali and Kertassi. The road to Abu Simbel from Aswan is open, but foreigners are only allowed to travel in a police convoy. Abu Simbel can be reached by plane from Aswan or Cairo.

For the moment, the rest of the sights can only be reached by boat, which is in any case the best way to see Lake Nasser's dramatic monuments. African Angler (p248) operates boats on the lake, running fishing safaris and safaris around the shore.

Lake Nasser

Lake Nasser, the world's largest artificial lake, covers an area of 5250 sq km, and is 510km long and between 5km and 35km wide. On average it contains some 135 billion cu metres of water, of which an estimated six billion are lost each year to evaporation. Its maximum capacity is 157 billion cu metres of water, which was reached in 1996 after heavy rains in Ethiopia, forcing the opening of a special spillway at Toshka, about 30km north of Abu Simbel, the first time it had been opened since the dam was built. The Egyptian government has since embarked on a controversial project to build a new canal and irrigate thousands of hectares in what is now the Nubian Desert between Toshka and the New Valley, a project ex-president Mubarak likened to the Suez Canal and Aswan High Dam in its scale.

Numbers aside, the contrast between this enormous body of water and the remote desert stretching away on all sides makes Lake Nasser a place of austere beauty. Because the level of the lake fluctuates it has been difficult to build settlements around its edges. Instead the lake has become a place for birds to rest on their long migratory journeys north and south. Gazelles, foxes and several types of snake (including the deadly horned viper) live on its shores. Many species of fish live in its waters, including the enormous Nile perch. Crocodiles – some reportedly up to 5m long – and monitor lizards also live in the lake's shallows. The main human presence here, apart from the fast-growing population of Abu Simbel town and the few tourists who visit, is limited to the 5000 or so fishers who spend up to six months at a time in small rowing boats, together catching about 50,000 tonnes of small fish each year.

Kalabsha, Beit al-Wali & Kertassi

As a result of a massive Unesco effort, the temples of Kalabsha were transplanted from a now-submerged site about 50km south of Aswan. The new site is on the west bank of Lake Nasser just south of the High Dam.

When the water level is low you can sometimes walk across to the site; otherwise you can find a motor boat on the western side of the High Dam (around E£30 for the return trip and an hour to visit).

Sights

Kalabsha Temple MONUMENT
(adult/concession E£40/20 incl Beit al-Wali & Temple of Kertassi; ⌚8am-5pm) Kalabsha Temple is an impressive Ptolemaic and Roman structure, not unlike nearby Philae in its layout. The early-19th-century Swiss traveller Burckhardt (who rediscovered Abu Simbel) thought it was 'amongst the most precious remains of Egyptian antiquity'.

The Temple of Kalabsha, started in the late Ptolemaic period and completed during the reign of Emperor Augustus (30 BC–AD 14), was dedicated to the Nubian solar god Merwel, known to the Greeks as Mandulis. Later it was used as a church.

An impressive stone causeway leads from the lake to the first pylon of the temple, beyond which are the colonnaded court and the eight-columned hypostyle hall. Inscriptions on the walls show various emperors or pharaohs in the presence of gods and goddesses. Just beyond the hall is the sanctuary, consisting of three chambers. Stairs from one chamber lead up to the roof, from where there are superb views of Lake Nasser and the High Dam, across the capitals of the hall and court. An inner passage, between the temple and the encircling wall, leads to a well-preserved Nilometer. The temple's original outer stone gateway was given by the Egyptian government to Germany in 1977, in thanks for helping to move this building. It is now in the Egyptian Museum, Berlin.

Beit al-Wali MONUMENT
(adult/concession E£40/20 incl Temples of Kalabsha & Kertassi; ⌚8am-5pm) Nearby the Temple of Kalabsha, the Temple of Beit al-Wali, mostly built by Ramses II, is cut into the rock and fronted by a brick pylon. On the walls of the forecourt, several fine reliefs detail the pharaoh's victory over the Nubians (on the south wall) and wars against the Libyans and Syrians (on the north wall). Ramses is gripping the hair of his enemies prior to smashing their brains while women plead for mercy.

The finest scenes are those of Ramses on his throne, receiving the tribute paid by the defeated Nubians, including leopard skins, gold rings, elephant tusks, and exotic animals.

Temple of Kertassi MONUMENT
(adult/concession E£40/20 incl Temple of Kalabsha & Beit al-Wali; ⌚8am-5pm) Just north of the Temple of Kalabsha are the scant but picturesque remains of the Temple of Kertassi, with two Hathor columns, a massive architrave and four fine papyrus columns.

Wadi as-Subua

The temples of Wadi as-Subua were moved to this site, about 4km west of the original and now-submerged Wadi as-Subua, between 1961 and 1965. Wadi as-Subua means 'Valley of Lions' in Arabic and refers to the avenue of sphinxes leading to the Temple of Ramses II.

Sights

Temple of Ramses II MONUMENT
(adult/student E£35/20 incl Temple of Dakka & Temple of Maharraqa) Built during the reign of the energetic pharaoh, the interior of the Temple of Ramses II was hewn from the rock and fronted by a stone pylon and colossal statues. Behind the pylon is a court featuring 10 more statues of the pharaoh, beyond which lie a 12-pillared hall and the sanctuary. The central niche was once carved with relief scenes of Ramses making offerings to Amun-Ra and Ra-Horakhty. In Christian times this part was converted into a church, the pagan reliefs plastered over and painted with saints, so that now, with part of the plaster fallen away, Ramses II appears to be adoring St Peter!

Temple of Dakka MONUMENT
(adult/student E£35/20 incl Temple of Ramses II & Temple of Maharraqa) About 1km to the north of the Temple of Ramses II are the remains of the Temple of Dakka, begun by the Nubian pharaoh Arkamani (218–200 BC) using materials from much earlier structures and adapted by the Ptolemies and the Roman emperor Augustus. Originally situated 50km north of here, it is dedicated to the god of wisdom, Thoth, and is notable for its 12m-high pylon, which you can climb for great views of the lake and the surrounding temples.

Temple of Maharraqa MONUMENT

(⌚ adult/student E£35/20 incl Temple of Ramses II & Temple of Dakka) The Temple of Maharraqa, the smallest of the three at Wadi as-Subua, originally stood 40km north at the ancient site of Ofendina. Dedicated to Isis and Serapis, the Alexandrian god, its decorations were never finished and all that remains is a small hypostyle hall, where in the northeast corner an usual spiral staircase of masonry leads up to the roof.

Amada

Situated around 180km south of the High Dam there are two temples and a tomb at Amada.

Sights

Temple of Amada MONUMENT

(adult/student E£35/20 incl Tomb of Pennut & Temple of Derr) The Temple of Amada, moved about 2.6km from its original location, is the oldest surviving monument on Lake Nasser. It was built jointly by 18th-dynasty pharaohs Tuthmosis III (1479–1425 BC) and his son Amenhotep II, with a hypostyle hall added by his successor, Tuthmosis IV (1400–1390 BC). Dedicated, like many temples in Nubia, to the gods Amun-Ra and Ra-Horakhty, it has some of the finest and best-preserved reliefs of any Nubian monument and contains two important historical inscriptions.

The first of these, on a stele at the left (north) side of the entrance, describes the unsuccessful Libyan invasion of Egypt (1209 BC) during Pharaoh Merenptah's reign. A second stele on the back wall of the sanctuary describes Amenhotep II's military campaign (1424 BC) in Palestine. Both were no doubt designed to impress upon the Nubians that political opposition to the powerful Egyptians was useless.

Temple of Derr MONUMENT

(adult/student E£35/20 incl Tomb of Amada & Tomb of Pennut) The rock-cut Temple of Derr, built by Ramses II, stood on a curve of the Nile. The pylon and court have disappeared, but there are some well-preserved reliefs in the ruined pillared hall, illustrating the Nubian campaign of Ramses II, with the usual killing of his enemies, accompanied by his famous pet lion. Following cleaning, many of the scenes are once again brightly coloured.

Tomb of Pennut TOMB

(adult/student E£35/20 incl Tomb of Amada & Temple of Derr) The small rock-cut Tomb of Pennut, viceroy of Nubia under Ramses VI (1143–1136 BC), was originally situated at Aniba, 40km southwest of Amada. This well-preserved Nubian tomb consists of a small offering chapel and a niche at the rear, with reliefs depicting events and personalities from Pennut's life, including him being presented with a gift by Ramses VI. It's a five-minute walk from the Temple of Derr.

Qasr Ibrim

The only Nubian monument visible on its original site, Qasr Ibrim once sat on top of a 70m-high cliff, about 60km north of Abu Simbel, but now has water lapping at its edges.

There is evidence that Ibrim was a garrison town from 1000 BC onward, and that around 680 BC the 25th-dynasty Pharaoh Taharka (690–664 BC), a Nubian by birth, built a mud-brick temple dedicated to Isis. During Roman times the town was one of the last bastions of paganism, its six temples converting to Christianity two centuries later than the rest of Egypt. It then became one of the main Christian centres in Lower Nubia and held out against Islam until the 16th century, when a group of Bosnian mercenaries, part of the Ottoman army, occupied the site. The mercenaries stayed on and eventually married into the local Nubian community, using part of the cathedral as a mosque.

Among the structural remains, the most impressive is an 8th-century sandstone cathedral built over Taharka's temple. The site is closed to visitors because of ongoing archaeological work.

Abu Simbel

☎ 097

Laid-back and quiet, the town of Abu Simbel lies 280km south of Aswan and only 40km north of the Sudanese border. Few tourists linger more than the few hours needed to visit the colossal temples for which it is famous. But anyone interested in Lake Nasser, in seeing the temples without the crowds, in wandering around a small nontouristy Nubian town without a police escort, or in listening to Nubian music might choose to hang around for a day or two.

Sights & Activities

Temples of Abu Simbel TEMPLE

(adult/student incl guide fee E£100/50; ⏲6am-5pm Oct-Apr, to 6pm May-Sep) Overlooking Lake Nasser, the two temples of Abu Simbel are among the most famous and spectacular monuments in Egypt.

➡ Great Temple of Ramses II

Carved out of the mountain on the west bank of the Nile between 1274 and 1244 BC, Ramses II's imposing temple was as much dedicated to the deified pharaoh himself as to Ra-Horakhty, Amun and Ptah. The four colossal statues of the pharoah, which front the temple, are like gigantic sentinels watching over the incoming traffic from the south, undoubtedly designed as a warning of the strength of the pharaoh.

Over the centuries both the Nile and the desert sands shifted, and this temple was lost to the world until 1813, when it was rediscovered by chance by the Swiss explorer Jean-Louis Burckhardt. Only one of the heads was completely showing above the sand, the next head was broken off and, of the remaining two, only the crowns could be seen. Enough sand was cleared away in 1817 by Giovanni Belzoni for the temple to be entered.

From the temple's forecourt, a short flight of steps leads up to the terrace in front of the massive rock-cut facade, which is about 30m high and 35m wide. Guarding the entrance, three of the four famous **colossal statues** stare out across the water into eternity – the inner left statue collapsed in antiquity and its upper body still lies on the ground. The statues, more than 20m high, are accompanied by smaller statues of the pharaoh's mother, Queen Tuya, his wife Nefertari and some of his favourite children. Above the entrance, between the central throned colossi, is the figure of the falcon-headed sun god Ra-Horakhty.

The roof of the **large hall** is decorated with vultures, symbolising the protective goddess Nekhbet, and is supported by eight columns, each fronted by an Osiride statue of Ramses II. Reliefs on the walls depict the pharaoh's prowess in battle, trampling over his enemies and slaughtering them in front of the gods. On the north wall is a depiction of the famous Battle of Kadesh (c 1274 BC), in what is now Syria, where Ramses inspired his demoralised army, so that they won the battle against the Hittites. The scene is dominated by a famous relief of Ramses in his chariot, shooting arrows at his fleeing en-

SAVING NUBIA'S MONUMENTS

When plans were finalised for the creation of the Aswan High Dam, worldwide attention focused on the many valuable and irreplaceable ancient monuments doomed by the waters of Lake Nasser. Between 1960 and 1980 the Unesco-sponsored Nubian Rescue Campaign gathered expertise and financing from more than 50 countries, and sent Egyptian and foreign archaeological teams to Nubia. Necropolises were excavated, many portable artefacts and relics were removed to museums and, while some temples disappeared beneath the lake, 14 were salvaged.

Ten of the temples, including the complexes of **Philae** (adult/student E£50/25; ⏲7am-4pm), Kalabsha (p260) and Abu Simbel (p262), were dismantled stone by stone and painstakingly rebuilt on higher ground. Four others were donated to the countries that contributed to the rescue effort, including the splendid Temple of Dendur, now reconstructed in the Metropolitan Museum of Art in New York.

Perhaps the greatest achievement of all was the preservation of the temples at Abu Simbel. Ancient magnificence and skill met with equally impressive modern technology as, at a cost of about US$40 million, Egyptian, Italian, Swedish, German and French archaeological teams cut the temples up into more than 2000 huge blocks, weighing from 10 to 40 tonnes each, and reconstructed them inside an artificially built mountain, 210m away from the water and 65m above the original site. The temples were carefully oriented to face the original direction, and the landscape of their original environment was recreated on and around the dome-shaped concrete mountain.

The project took just over four years. The temples of Abu Simbel were officially reopened in 1968, while the sacred site they had occupied for more than 3000 years disappeared beneath Lake Nasser. A plaque to the right of the temple entrance eloquently describes this achievement: 'Through this restoration of the past, we have indeed helped to build the future of mankind.'

Great Temple of Ramses II

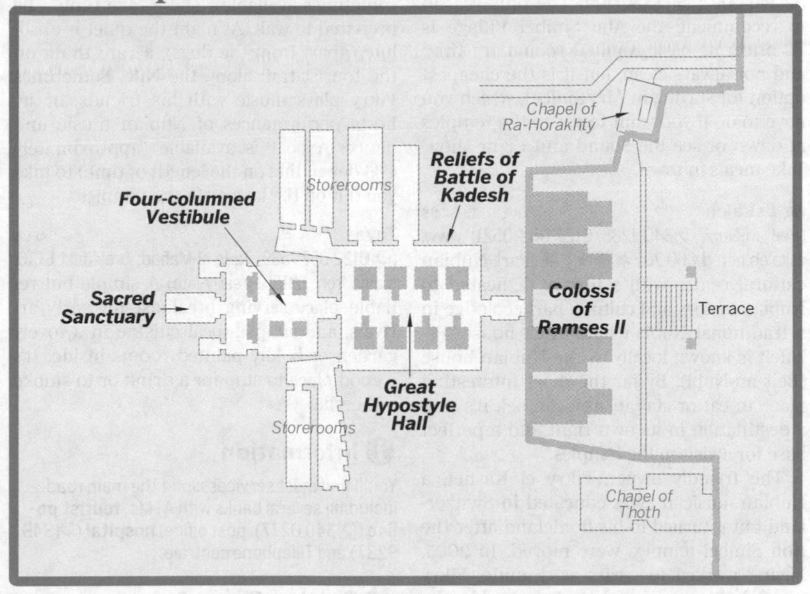

emies. Also visible is the Egyptian camp, walled off by its soldiers' round-topped shields, and the fortified Hittite town, surrounded by the Orontes River.

The next hall, the **four-columned vestibule** where Ramses and Nefertari are shown in front of the gods and the solar barques, leads to the sacred sanctuary, where Ramses and the triad of gods of the Great Temple sit on their thrones.

The original temple was aligned in such a way that each 21 February and 21 October, Ramses' birthday and coronation day, the first rays of the rising sun moved across the hypostyle hall, through the vestibule and into the sanctuary, where they illuminate the figures of Ra-Horakhty, Ramses II and Amun. Ptah, to the left, was never supposed to be illuminated. Since the temples were moved, this phenomenon happens one day later.

➡ Temple of Hathor

Next to the Great Temple of Ramses II is the much smaller Temple of Hathor, with a rock-cut facade fronted by six 10m-high standing statues of Ramses and Nefertari, with some of their many children by their side. Nefertari here wears the costume of the goddess Hathor, and is, unusually, portrayed as the same height as her husband (instead of knee-height, as most consorts were depicted).

Inside, the six pillars of the hypostyle hall are crowned with capitals in the bovine shape of Hathor. On the walls the queen appears in front of the gods very much equal to Ramses II, and she is seen honouring her husband. The vestibule and adjoining chambers, which have colourful scenes of the goddess and her sacred barque, lead to the sanctuary, which has a weathered statue of Hathor as a cow emerging from the rock. The art here is softer and more graceful than in the Great Temple.

➡ Sound & Light Show

(www.soundandlight.com.eg; adult/child E£100/50; ⏲ shows 6pm Oct-Apr, 8pm May-Sep) A sound and light show is performed nightly at Abu Simbel. Headphones are provided, allowing visitors to listen to the commentary in various languages. While the text is flowery and forgettable, the laser show projected onto the temples is stunning and well worth the detour.

Sleeping & Eating

Few people stay the night in Abu Simbel, but there are a couple of places dedicated to package tours and a couple of others for those looking for ultimate peace and quiet.

Along Abu Simbel's main road is a line-up of cheap cafes, with the Nubian Oasis and Wadi el-Nil among the most popular.

Abu Simbel Village HOTEL $

(☎340 0092; s/d E£80/100) The only reason to recommend the Abu Simbel Village is its price: its basic, vaulted rooms are tired and not always clean, but it is the cheapest option for staying in Abu Simbel, which you have to do if you want to get to the temples at dawn or see the Sound and Light show. Take meals in town.

★ **Eskaleh** GUESTHOUSE $$

(Beit an-Nubi; ☎340 1288, 0122 368 0521; www.eskaleh.net; d €60-70;) Part Nubian cultural centre with a library dedicated to Nubian history and culture, part ecolodge in a traditional Nubian mud-brick house, Eskaleh is known locally as the Nubian house (Beit an-Nubi). By far the most interesting place to eat or stay in Abu Simbel, it's also a destination in its own right and a perfect base for a visit to the temples.

The friendly owner, Fikry el Kashef, a Nubian musician, was educated in Switzerland but returned to his homeland after the Abu Simbel temples were moved. In 2005, having worked for years as a guide, Fikry created this wonderful enclave beside the lake with the idea of sharing the Nubian experience with interested foreigners. Simple but comfortable rooms have local furniture, fans, air-con and good private bathrooms. Some also have a private terrace. Nubian kitchen staff prepare delicious home-cooked meals (three-course lunch or dinner from €7 to €11) with organic produce from Fikry's garden and fish from the lake (and beer is sometimes available). These take time – be prepared to wait. At night the quiet is absolute (apart from the dogs), a rare thing on the tourist trail along the Nile. Sometimes Fikry plays music with his friends, or he hosts performances of Nubian music and dance. A boat is available (approximately €35 depending on the length of time) to take you out on the lake or to the temples.

Toya CAFE $

(☎0122 357 7539; Tariq al-Mabad; breakfast E£10, mains from E£15; early-late) A simple but reliable place serving breakfast for early arrivals, and simple, local cuisine in a lovely garden or boldly painted rooms inside. It's a good place to stop for a drink or to smoke a sheesha.

Information

You'll find most services along the main road, including several banks with ATMs, **tourist police** (☎340 0277), post office, **hospital** (☎349 9237) and Telephone centrale.

Getting There & Away

Buses from Abu Simbel to Aswan (E£25, four hours) leave at 8am and 4pm from Wadi el-Nil restaurant on the main road. There's no advance booking, and tickets are purchased on board. There is usually a police escort. EgyptAir has several flights daily from Abu Simbel to Aswan with connections to Cairo.

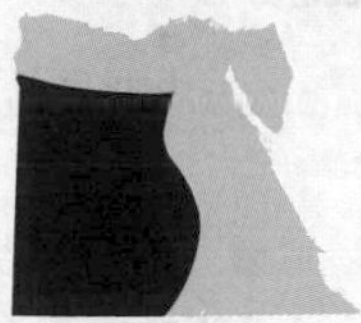

Siwa Oasis & the Western Desert

Includes ➡

Why Go?

Older than the Pyramids, as sublime as any temple, Egypt's Western Desert is a vast sweep of elemental beauty. The White Desert's shimmering vista of surreal rock formations and the ripple and swell of the Great Sand Sea's mammoth dunes are simply bewitching.

Within this intense landscape five oases, shaded by palm plantations and blessed by a plethora of natural hot and cold springs, provide a glimpse of rural Egyptian life. Get lost exploring Al-Qasr's squiggling narrow lanes in Dakhla. Watch sunset sear across the countryside atop Gebel al-Ingleez in Bahariya. Take a stroll amid Siwa's sprawling date palms. Then once you've finished adventuring, kick back and just enjoy the laid-back pace of oasis life.

Best Natural Spring Soaks

- ➡ Cleopatra's Bath (p295)
- ➡ Bir Wahed (p295)
- ➡ Ain Gomma (p291)
- ➡ Bir al-Gebel (p278)

Best Places to Stay

- ➡ Camping in the White Desert (p284)
- ➡ Adrère Amellal (p300)
- ➡ Al-Babinshal (p299)
- ➡ Shali Lodge (p299)
- ➡ Under the Moon Camp (p291)

When to Go

Siwa

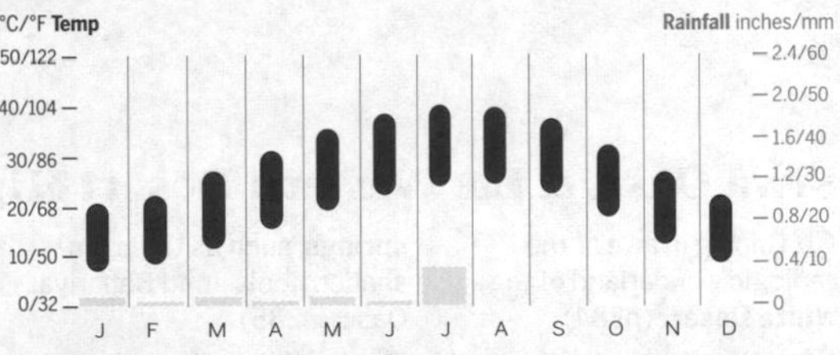

Apr–May After winter, travellers thin out. See the White Desert without the crowds.

Sep–Oct Wander the oases' palm groves as the date harvest commences.

Nov–Mar Desert-expedition high season. Don your explorer hat and hit the dunes.

Siwa Oasis
Qara Oasis
Qattara Depression
Az-Zeitun
Siwa
Areg Oasis
Lake Qarun
Cairo (70km)
Al-Fayoum Oasis
Medinat al-Fayoum
Beni Suef
Bahariya Oasis
Bawiti
Gebel az-Zuqaq
Gebel Gala Siwa
Eastern (Arabian) Desert
Minya
Mallawi
Deir Mawas
Black Desert
White Desert
Qasr al-Farafra
Quss Abu Said
Farafra Oasis
Ghard Abu Muhariq
Nile River
Abu Minqar
Western (Libyan) Desert
Qasr el-Labakha
Al-Qasr
Dakhla Oasis
Abu Tartur Plateau
Mut
Al-Kharga
Al-Kharga Oasis
Bulaq
Jaja
Baris
Great Sand Sea
Gilf Kebir
Gebel Uweinat
Lake Nasser
0 100 km
0 50 miles

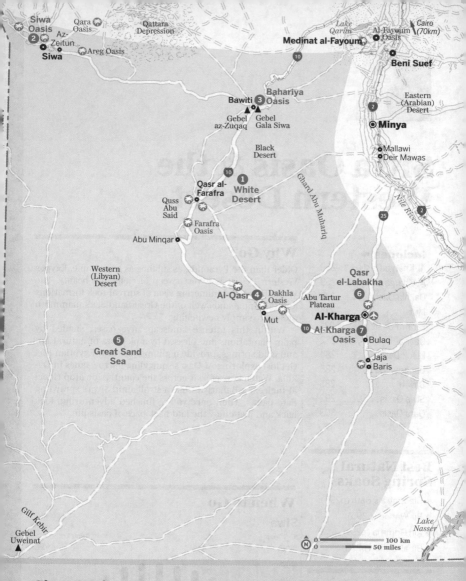

Siwa Oasis & the Western Desert Highlights

1. Gaping in awe at the geologic wonderland of the **White Desert** (p284).
2. Hitting the end of the road at **Siwa Oasis** (p292) to revel in the far-from-anywhere vibe and delve into the unique Siwan culture.
3. Soaking off the dust in one of the region's **natural springs**, such as the palm-shaded pools amid Bahariya Oasis (p285).
4. Wandering through the lost-in-time, labyrinthine mud-brick town of **Al-Qasr** (p280).
5. Putting on your explorer garb to take a multiday safari among the endless dunes of the **Great Sand Sea** (p303).
6. Scrambling around the old Roman fort at **Qasr el-Labakha** (p274).
7. Exploring the fascinating, and rarely visited, early Christian ruins of **Al-Kharga Oasis** (p269).

History

As with the Sahara and other deserts that stretch across northern Africa, the Western Desert was once a savannah that supported all manner of wildlife. Giraffes, lions and elephants roamed here in Palaeolithic times, when the landscape is thought to have looked much like the African Sahel. All that you see in the desert – the huge tracts of sand, the vast gravel plains, the fossil beds and limestone rocks – were once the happy hunting grounds that supported nomadic tribes. Gradual climate change led to desertification and turned this vast area into the arid expanse seen today. Only depressions in the desert floor have enough water to support wildlife, agriculture and human settlement.

The ancient Egyptians understood the nature of the desert, which they saw as being synonymous with death and exile. Seth, the god of chaos who killed his brother Osiris, was said to rule here. It is believed the ancient Egyptians maintained links with the oases throughout the Pharaonic era, and with the accession of a Libyan dynasty (22nd dynasty; 945–715 BC), focus increased on the oases and the caravan routes linking the Nile Valley with lands to the west.

The oases enjoyed a period of great prosperity during Roman times, when new wells and improved irrigation led to the production of wheat and grapes for export to Rome. Garrisoned fortresses that protected the oases and trade routes can still be seen in the desert around Al Kharga and Bahariya, and Roman-era temples and tombs lie scattered across all the oases.

When the Romans withdrew from Egypt, the trade routes became a target for attacking nomadic tribes. Trade suffered, the oases went into gradual decline, and the population of settlements shrank. By medieval times, raids by nomads were severe enough to bring Mamluk garrisons to the oases. The fortified villages built to defend the population can still be seen in Dakhla (Al-Qasr, Balat) and Siwa (Shali).

The biggest change to the oases after the departure of the Romans occurred in 1958, when President Nasser created the so-called New Valley to relieve population pressure along the Nile. Roads were laid between the previously isolated oases, irrigation systems were modernised and an administration was established. The New Valley Governorate is the largest in Egypt and one of the least densely populated: there has never been enough work to draw significant numbers away from the Nile.

The Western Desert region has remained mostly unscathed throughout Egypt's recent years of political upheaval. Even during the 2011 revolution, Al-Kharga was the only Western Desert oasis town to throw itself into the anti-Mubarak fray; after police fired into a crowd of protesters, the protesters set fire to the police station, a courthouse and other buildings. Three demonstrators were reported killed, with about 100 injured. More recently though, the difficulties involved in maintaining security in such a vast region have come to the fore. Two attacks on a military checkpoint in Farafra Oasis occurred in 2014, including an attack in July which left 22 army personnel dead.

Long-Range Desert Safaris

Going on safari in the Western Desert can be one of the most rewarding experiences Egypt has to offer. It can also be one of the most frustrating. Each oasis has good local guides, but many of them operate on a shoestring and have neither the expertise nor the equipment to pull off a long-range expedition. This may not stop them from trying to persuade you they can do it. Included among the Western Desert's more challenging routes are the **Great Sand Sea** and remote **Gilf Kebir** (in Egypt's southwest corner), where you'll find the Cave of the Swimmers – made famous by *The English Patient* – and **Gebel Uweinat**, a 2000m-high peak trisected by the Egyptian, Libyan and Sudanese borders. These adventures require extensive organisation, quality equipment and plenty of experience to properly execute; the consequences of mishaps are severe, sometimes fatal. Military permits, which are available locally for short desert treks, must be procured in Cairo for longer trips.

Choose one of the operators that have solid international reputations, are among the more reliable in Egypt, and will treat the desert with the respect it deserves. Multiday expeditions run only between October and April.

Al-Badawiya DESERT TOUR
(☎Cairo 02-2390 6429, Farafra 092-751 1163; www.badawiya.com; 21 Sharia Youssef el-Gendy, Downtown, Cairo) The three Ali brothers are Bedouin from Farafra, who have built up a significant business operating out of their Farafra-based hotel and an office in downtown Cairo. With considerable experience in

KNOW YOUR DUNES

Classification of sand dune shapes was made in the 1970s, when scientists examined photographs of dune fields taken from space. Of the five typical shapes, four are found in Egypt.

Seif

Named for the Arabic word for sword, these long dunes form parallel to the prevailing wind. They are primarily found in the Great Sand Sea and the northern Western Desert. Usually on the move, they will even fall down an escarpment, reforming at its base.

Barchan

These are crescent-shaped dunes, with a slip face on one side. They are as wide as they are long and are usually found in straight lines with flat corridors between them. They can travel as far as 19m in one year. They are predominant in Al-Kharga and Dakhla Oases and in the Great Sand Sea.

Star

Created by wind blowing in different directions, these dunes are usually found alone. Instead of moving, they tend to build up within a circle. They are rare in Egypt.

Crescent

These hill-like dunes, also called whale-back dunes, form when smaller dunes collide and piggyback on one another. With their sides pointing in different directions, these distinctive shapes can be seen between Al-Kharga and Dakhla Oases.

the Western Desert, they can mount tailored camel or jeep safaris from three to 28 days in length. They have tents, cooking equipment and bedding.

Dabuka Expeditions DESERT TOUR
(☎02-2525 7687; www.dabuka.de; 2 Osman Bldg, Corniche el-Nil, Maadi, Cairo) This German-based company specialises in North African desert travel through Egypt, Libya, Sudan, Tunisia and Jordan. In Egypt it arranges multiday safaris into the Great Sand Sea, Gebel Uweinat and Gilf Kebir, as well as specialised tours led by scientists and archaeologists. It can also organise 4WD rental and logistics for desert do-it-yourselfers.

Hisham Nessim DESERT TOUR
(☎0100 667 8099; www.raid4x4egypt.com) Rally driver and owner of the Aquasun hotels in Farafra and Sinai, Hisham Nessim has been driving in the desert for many years. With satellite phones, GPS and six 4WDs specially rigged for long-range desert travel, he is prepared to go to all corners of Egypt. He offers 12 programs of two to 20 days, or will tailor-make tours.

Khalifa Expedition DESERT TOUR
(☎0122 321 5445; www.khalifaexpedition.com; Lotus House, Bawiti, Bahariya) Khaled and Rose-Maria Khalifa have been running camel and jeep tours throughout the Western Desert from their base in Bahariya Oasis for more than 15 years. Rose-Maria is a qualified speech therapist and foot masseuse, which perhaps explains why they also offer meditation-retreat desert tours for people more interested in communing with nature than looking at antiquities.

Pan Arab Tours DESERT TOUR
(☎02-2418 4409; www.panarabtours.com; 5 Saudi-Egyptian Bldg, Sharia el-Nozha, Heliopolis, Cairo) With more than 30 years' experience, Pan Arab Tours has developed expertise in taking visitors into Egypt's deserts. Used by archaeologists as well as tourists, the company has a number of specially equipped vehicles and offers nine desert itineraries throughout the country, from four to 18 days as well as tailor-made tours. It also rents 4WDs.

Zarzora Expedition DESERT TOUR
(☎0100 118 8221; www.zarzora.com; 5 Sharia Tahrir, Mut, Dakhla) Captained by the experienced Ahmed Al-Mestekawi, a retired colonel who used to conduct military desert patrols, Zarzora does expeditions to Siwa, Gilf Kebir and the Great Sand Sea. Ahmed has in-depth knowledge of the area and moonlights as a lecturer on the desert's environment and history.

AL-KHARGA OASIS

☎092 / POP 74,490

As the closest of the oases to the Nile Valley, Al-Kharga used to have the unenviable role as a place of banishment for mischievous Nile Valley citizens. Its remote location, punishing summer heat and destructive winds meant that the oasis was synonymous with misery and exile. It may seem strange, then, that its chief town, Al-Kharga, was chosen as the capital of the New Valley Governorate in the 1950s. Life in the oasis has improved somewhat since then, and the smattering of ancient sites here means it's a decent stopover if you want to dip your toes in the desert lands after a Nile Valley trip.

Lying in a 220km-long and 40km-wide depression, Al-Kharga Oasis was at the crossroads of vital desert trade routes, including the famous Darb al-Arba'een (p270). This influential location brought it great prosperity, and with the arrival of the Romans, wells were dug, crops cultivated and fortresses built to protect caravan routes. Even as late as the 1890s, British forces were using lookout towers here to safeguard the 'back door' into Egypt.

Al-Kharga

The bustling city of Al-Kharga is the largest town in the Western Desert and also the poster-child of the government's efforts to modernise the oases. The town's wide, bare boulevards rimmed by drab concrete housing blocks are definitely not what most travellers conjure up when they picture an oasis idyll. Despite the less than picturesque surroundings, the town is a good base for exploring a handful of unique, gently crumbling sights found around this oasis valley floor.

Sights

★Necropolis of Al-Bagawat ARCHAEOLOGICAL SITE

(Map 269; adult/student E£35/15 incl Monastery of Al-Kashef; 8am-5pm) It may not look like much from afar, but this necropolis is one of the earliest surviving and best-preserved Christian cemeteries in the world. About 1km north of the Temple of Hibis, it's built on the site of an earlier Egyptian necropolis, with most of the 263 mud-brick chapel-tombs appearing to date from the 4th to the 6th centuries AD. Some have interiors decorated with murals of biblical scenes and boast ornate facades.

Al-Kharga Oasis

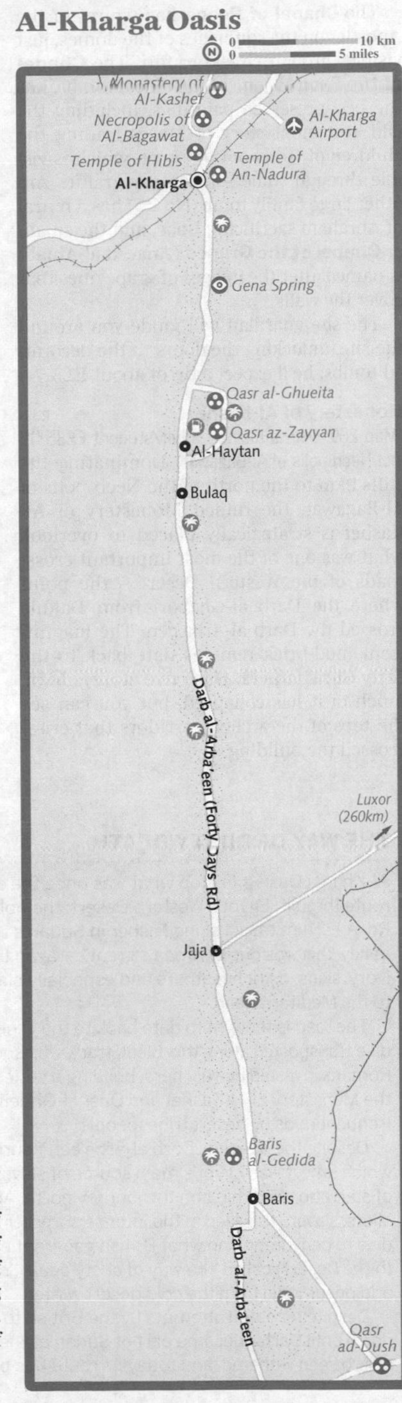

The **Chapel of Peace** has figures of the Apostles on the squinches of the domes, just visible through Greek graffiti. The **Chapel of the Exodus**, one of the oldest tombs, has the best-preserved paintings, including the Old Testament story of Moses leading the children of Israel out of Egypt, which is visible through some 9th-century graffiti. Another large family tomb (**No 25**) has a mural of Abraham sacrificing Isaac, and the smaller **Chapel of the Grapes** (Anaeed al-Ainab) is named after the images of grapevines that cover the walls.

The site guardian will guide you around the site, unlocking the doors to the decorated tombs; he'll expect a tip of about E£5.

Monastery of Al-Kashef RUIN

(Map 269; Deir al-Kashef; adult/student E£35/15 incl Necropolis of Al-Bagawat) Dominating the cliffs 2km to the north of the Necropolis of Al-Bagawat, the ruined Monastery of Al-Kashef is strategically placed to overlook what was one of the most important crossroads of the Western Desert – the point where the Darb al-Ghabari from Dakhla crossed the Darb al-Arba'een. The magnificent mud-brick remains date back to the early Christian era. Once five storeys high, much of it has collapsed, but you can see the tops of the arched corridors that crisscrossed the building.

To get here, walk or drive on the left-hand track from the Necropolis of Al-Bagawat for about 2km.

Temple of Hibis TEMPLE

(Map 269; adult/student E£40/20) The town of Hebet ('the Plough', now corrupted into Hibis) was the capital of the oasis in antiquity, but all that remains today is the well-preserved limestone Temple of Hibis. It's 2km north of town, just to the left of the main road; pick-ups (E£1) heading to Al-Munira pass this way. Once sitting on the edge of a sacred lake, the temple was dedicated to Amun of Hibis (the local version of the god, who was sometimes given solar powers, becoming Amun-Ra).

Amun-Hibis appears here with his usual companions Mut and Khons. Look for reliefs in the **hypostyle hall** showing the god Seth battling with the evil serpent Apophis. There's also an avenue of sphinxes, a court and an inner sanctuary. Construction of the temple began during the 25th dynasty, though the decorations and a colonnade were added over the following 300 years.

Temple of An-Nadura RUIN

Located on a hill to the right of the main road when heading north from Al-Kharga town, the Temple of An-Nadura has strategic views of the area and once doubled as a fortified lookout. It was built during the reign of Roman emperor Antoninus Pius

THE WAY OF DUSTY DEATH

Al-Kharga Oasis sits atop what was once the only major African north–south trade route through Egypt's Western Desert: the notorious **Darb al-Arba'een**, or Forty Days Rd. A 1721km track linking Fasher in Sudan's Darfur province with Asyut in the Nile Valley, this was one of Africa's great caravan trails, bringing the riches of Sudan – gold, ivory, skins, ostrich feathers and especially slaves – north to the Nile Valley and beyond to the Mediterranean.

The road is thought to date back to the Old Kingdom. The richness of the merchandise transported along this bleak track was such that protecting it was a priority. The Romans invested heavily here, building a series of fortresses – such as Qasr ad-Dush, the Monastery of Al-Kashef and Qasr al-Ghueita – to tax the caravans and try to foil the frequent raids by desert tribespeople.

Despite the dangers, Darb al-Arba'een flourished until well into the Islamic era, by which time it was Egypt's main source of slaves. Untold numbers of human cargo died of starvation and thirst on the journey north. According to 19th-century European travellers, slavers travelled in the intense summer heat, preferring to expose their merchandise to dehydration on what British geographer GW Murray (author of the 1967 *Dare Me to the Desert*) called 'the way of dusty death', rather than risk the possibility of bronchitis and pneumonia from the cold desert winter.

Despite repeated attempts by the British to suppress the trade, slaves were brought north until Darfur became part of Sudan at the beginning of the 20th century. The Darb al-Arba'een withered, and today its route has been all but lost.

Al-Kharga

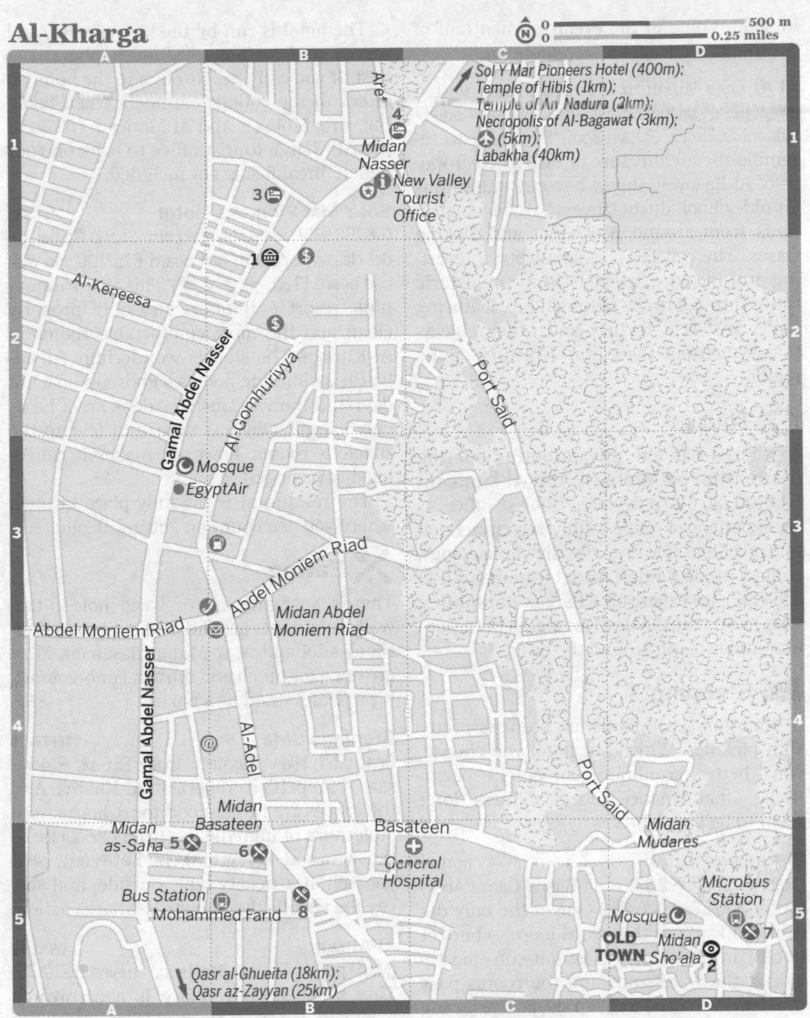

(AD 138–161) to protect the oasis. Now badly ruined, but the superb vistas here are ideal for sunset adulation.

Midan Sho'ala Market MARKET

(Map p271; Midan Sho'ala) Stock up on all your fresh produce at this truly local market that runs through the alleyways off Midan Sho'ala. You'll find everything from plastic-fantastic houseware to clucking chickens piled high in boxes. Traditional cobblers and metal-workers, and local dates by the barrelful, sit between stalls selling bawdy, cheap clothing and chintzy-tat. It's brilliant and there's not a singing toy camel or pyramid snow-globe

Al-Kharga

Sights

1 Al-Kharga Museum of Antiquities B2
2 Midan Sho'ala Market D5

Sleeping

3 El-Radwan Hotel B1
4 Kharga Oasis Hotel B1

Eating

5 Al-Ahram A5
6 Crepiano Cafe B5
7 Pizza Ibn al-Balad D5
8 Wembe B5

in sight. Come in the evening when half of Al-Kharga seems to be here shopping.

Al-Kharga Museum of Antiquities MUSEUM
(Map p271; Sharia Gamal Abdel Nasser; adult/student E£25/15; ⏲8am-3pm) Designed to resemble the architecture of nearby Necropolis of Al-Bagawat, this two-storey museum is an old-school, dusty trove of archaeological finds from around Al-Kharga and Dakhla Oases. The collection is small but interesting and includes artefacts from prehistoric times through to the Ottoman era, featuring tools, jewellery, textiles and other objects that sketch out the cultural history of the region.

Tours

Al-Kharga has few private outfits offering desert trips, but **Mohsen Abd Al Moneam** (☎0100 180 6127), from the tourist office, is an experienced guide highly recommended by travellers. If you really dig archaeology, contact guide **Sameh Abdel Rihem** (☎0100 296 2192), an expert on Kharga's antiquities, who has a palpable love for sights both popular and esoteric around the oasis.

Sleeping

Al-Kharga's accommodation scene is pretty slim pickings. Whichever hotel you choose, you'd better recalibrate your hotel expectations – maintenance and cleanliness don't seem to be top priorities.

El-Radwan Hotel HOTEL $
(Map p271; ☎792 1716; off Sharia Gamal Abdel Nasser; s/d E£90/120; ❄) One of the only decent (and we use that word loosely) budget hotels in Al-Kharga. The air-con mostly works, the water runs and the rooms pass muster if you need a cheap sleep. The facade looks like it's about to fall down but, oh well, it does get better on the inside. Breakfast is not included.

Kharga Oasis Hotel HOTEL $
(Map p271; ☎792 1206, 0126 866 6299; Midan Nasser; r €10, bungalow €15; ❄) This homage to the 1960s' love of concrete blocks is your best bet for bedding down for the night in Al-Kharga. The main building sports large rooms with decent beds and bathrooms, but opt for one of the traditionally styled domed bungalows out back, set around a tranquil and lush palm-filled garden (beware the mosquitoes) for a bit more style.

The hotel is run by the government, and service and maintenance are haphazard at best. If you can't get through to the hotel on either of the contact numbers when booking, ring Mohsen Abd Al Moneam (p272) of the Al-Kharga tourist office to book on your behalf. Breakfast is not included.

Sol Y Mar Pioneers Hotel HOTEL $$$
(☎792 9751; www.solymar.com; Sharia Gamal Abdel Nasser; s/d with half board €75/100, ste with half board €120; ❄@📶≋) This vast salmon-pink resort still offers the only properly clean and the most comfortable rooms in Al-Kharga. The staff is wonderfully friendly; the swimming pool is a godsend on a hot day; and the vast, lush gardens are a heavenly escape. Obvious wear and tear to the spacious rooms, however, makes it ridiculously overpriced.

The restaurant is the only place in town where you can count on getting alcohol.

Eating

There's a smattering of basic hole-in-the-wall restaurants around Midan Sho'ala, Sharia al-Adel and near Midan Basateen. Most are open for lunch and dinner. For breakfast, hit a felafel stand or a bakery.

Crepiano Cafe CREPERIE $
(Map p271; Midan Basateen; mains E£6-12; ⏲4pm-late; ✎) Yep. It's a creperie in Al-Kharga. And the crepes are rather good too. Choose from a plethora of ingredients (from chocolate to sausage and everything in between); seat yourself at a rickety table outside; and survey the chaotic downtown Al-Kharga action.

Al-Ahram GRILL $$
(Map p271; Sharia Basateen; mains E£10-35) This small, friendly place is a carnivore's favourite. It serves roast chicken and kofta (mincemeat and spices grilled on a skewer) accompanied by modest salads and vegetable dishes. The smell of grilled meat will lure you in. Look for the sign above with pictures of the pyramids *(al-ahram)* to find it.

Wembe EGYPTIAN $$
(Map p271; Midan Basateen; meals E£20-35) This busy joint gets the thumbs up from Al-Kharga locals for serving simple but tasty Egyptian feasts of grilled meats, salads, rice and vegetable dishes. It's one of the town's most solid choices for a decent meal. The sign above says 'Wimpy'.

Pizza Ibn al-Balad EGYPTIAN FAST FOOD $$
(Map p271; Midan Sho'ala; pizzas E£20-40; 5pm-late;) If you're pining for a change from grilled meat and salad, make a beeline for this little place that rustles up some of the best *fiteer* (Egyptian flaky pizza) in the oases. Choose from cheese, vegetarian, tuna or beef toppings.

Information

Banque du Caire (Map p271; off Sharia Gamal Abdel Nasser) Has an ATM.

General Hospital (Map p271; 792 0777; Sharia Basateen) Only to be used in extreme emergencies.

Main Post Office (Map p271; Sharia Abdel Moniem Riad; 8am-2.30pm Sat-Thu)

National Bank of Egypt (Map p271; Sharia Gamal Abdel Nasser) Across from the museum; has an ATM.

New Valley Tourist Office (Map p271; 792 1206; Midan Nasser; 9am-2pm Sat-Thu) Speak to Mohsen Abd Al Moneam (p272), a motherlode of knowledge about Al-Kharga Oasis. He can arrange private transport to sights and also to Luxor. Call his mobile.

Telephone Centrale (Map p271; Sharia Abdel Moniem Riad; 24hr)

Tourist Police (Map p271; 792 1367; Sharia Gamal Abdel Nasser) Next door to Al-Kharga tourist office.

Getting There & Away

AIR

The airport is 5km north of town. The Petroleum Service Company (usually) has Monday and Thursday flights on a 15-seat plane, leaving Cairo at 8am and returning from Al-Kharga at 3pm (E£600 one way, 1½ hours). Contact the Al-Kharga tourist office for schedules and bookings.

BUS

From the **bus station** (Map p271; 792 4587; Sharia Mohammed Farid), Upper Egypt Bus Co operates buses to Cairo (E£65, eight to 10 hours) daily at 9pm and 10pm. There are three services to Asyut (E£25, three to four hours) at 6am, 7am and 9am. The bus heading north to Dakhla Oasis (E£25, three hours) leaves at 2pm.

There's no direct bus service to Luxor. You can either catch a bus to Asyut and change there, or hire a private taxi.

MICROBUS

Head to the **microbus station** (Map p271; Midan Sho'ala) to pick up services to Dakhla (E£25, three hours) or Asyut (E£25, three to four hours). Microbuses only leave when full.

TAXI

Private taxis can get you to/from Luxor (via Jaja) in about four hours using the Darb al-Arba'een (Forty Days Rd). This will set you back about E£550, but if you can get a few people to share costs it's an excellent alternative to the bus if you want to combine a trip to the Western Desert with the Nile Valley. If you want private transport to Cairo, a taxi will cost E£1350. Contact Mohsen Abd Al Moneam (p272) at the Al-Kharga tourist office to arrange a car for you.

Getting Around

Al-Kharga is fairly spread out, with the bus station in the south-central part of town, the minibus stand in the southeast near the souq, and most hotels a fair hike away from both. Microbuses (50pt) run along the main streets of Al-Kharga, especially Sharia Gamal Abdel Nasser. Taxis for trips in town cost between E£3 to E£6.

Around Al-Kharga

The most popular monuments near Al-Kharga lie along the good asphalt road that stretches south to Baris, but there are a few intriguing, harder-to-reach destinations north of town; though less visited, they are hands-down the best day or overnight trips you can make around the oasis.

Qasr al-Ghueita & Qasr az-Zayyan

Although you wouldn't guess it from the arid dusty landscape, during antiquity this area, some 18km south of Al-Kharga, was the centre of a fertile agricultural community renowned for its grapes and winemaking. Settlement here has been dated back to the Middle Kingdom period when it was known as Perousekh. Today two sturdy forts from its later Roman period survive here, lording-it-up over the plains, and were probably utilised as garrison buildings for troops.

Sights

Qasr al-Ghueita FORT
(adult/student E£25/15; 8am-5pm) From the main road to Baris, an asphalted track leads 2km to this imposing mud-brick fortress. The garrison's massive outer walls enclose a 25th-dynasty sandstone temple, dedicated to the Theban triad Amun, Mut and Khons. In later centuries, the fortress served as the perimeter for a village, with some houses surviving along the outer wall. Within the

hypostyle hall a series of reliefs show Hapy, the pot-bellied Nile god, holding symbols of the nomes (provinces) of Upper Egypt.

Its name means 'Fortress of the Small Garden', which harks back to the days when this area was a fertile agricultural community.

Qasr az-Zayyan FORT
(adult/student E£25/15; ⊙8am-5pm Oct-Apr) The remnants of the fortress of Qasr az-Zayyan encloses a temple, but not much remains of the building and unless you're a die-hard archaeology fanatic, it's easy to give this one a miss. The fort is 4km south from Qasr al-Ghueita.

Getting There & Away

If you don't have your own vehicle, you can get to the forts from Al-Kharga by taking a microbus heading for Baris (E£8) or a covered pick-up going to Bulaq (E£2.50). From the highway an asphalt road links the forts, running up the desert incline for 3km to Qasr al-Gueita, and then it's another 4km to Qasr az-Zayyan. It's an extremely long, hot hike if you're on foot – be sure to take plenty of water.

Baris

Although once one of the most important trading centres along the Darb al-Arba'een (Forty Days Rd), Baris has little to show for its illustrious commercial history; today it's hard to imagine it was once the centre of anything. If you're peckish there are a few kiosks selling fuul (fava bean paste) and felafel.

Sights

Baris al-Gedida ARCHITECTURE
The mud-brick houses of Baris al-Gedida lie about 2km north of the original town. Hassan Fathy, Egypt's most influential modern architect, designed the houses using traditional methods and materials, intending Baris al-Gedida to be a model for other new settlements. Work stopped at the outbreak of the Six Day War of 1967, and only two houses and some public spaces have ever been completed. The site was abandoned and never lived in.

Qasr ad-Dush FORT
(adult/student E£30/15; ⊙8am-5pm) About 13km to the southeast of Baris, Qasr ad-Dush is an imposing Roman temple-fortress completed around AD 177 on the site of the ancient town of Kysis. A 1st-century sandstone temple abutting the fortress was dedicated to Isis and Serapis. The gold decorations that once covered parts of the temple and earned it renown have long gone, but there is still some decoration on the inner stone walls.

Dush was a border town strategically placed at the intersection of five desert tracks and was one of the southern gateways to Egypt. It may also have been used to guard the Darb al-Dush, an east–west track to the Esna and Edfu temples in the Nile Valley. As a result it was solidly built and heavily garrisoned, with four or five more storeys lying underground.

Getting There & Away

Baris is 90km south of Al-Kharga. The frequent microbuses and pick-up trucks are the best public transport option between Al-Kharga and Baris, and cost about E£8. To cover the 15km between Qasr ad-Dush and Baris, negotiate a special ride with a covered pick-up, usually available for E£40, depending on waiting time. Hiring a private car for a day to see all the sights between Al-Kharga and Dush costs about E£300; this is best arranged through the tourist office in Al-Kharga.

Qasr el-Labakha

Set amid a desertscape of duney desolation, Qasr el-Labakha is a micro-oasis some 40km north of Al-Kharga. Scattered among sandy swells and rocky shelves are the remains of a towering four-storey **Roman fortress**, two **temples**, and a vast **necropolis** where more than 500 mummies have been unearthed (you can still see human remains in the tombs). Day and overnight trips to Labakha can be arranged by Al-Kharga's tourist office, with prices starting at around US$120 per vehicle.

A small camp here, which is a perfect outpost for exploring the area, is run by the gentle-natured Sayed Taleb, who cleaned out the site's ancient aqueducts and uses them to water his garden.

West of Qasr el-Labakha

About 20km west of Labakha lie the impressive fort ruins of **Ain Umm el-Dabadib**, which sit on a ridge rising grandly out of the desert plains. It has one of the most complex underground aqueduct systems built in this area by the Romans.

Keep going another 50km and you'll reach **Ain Amur** up on the Abu Tartur Plateau, the highest spring in the Western Desert. It's small so plan on a dunk rather than a swim.

Trips to both these sites qualify as serious desert excursions that require a 4WD and experienced drivers, who can be contacted through Al-Kharga's tourist office. Expect to pay around US$220 per vehicle (which may include a back-up 4WD, for safety) to Ain Amur and back.

DAKHLA OASIS

☎092 / POP 80,230

With more than a dozen fertile hamlets sprinkled along the Western Desert circuit road, Dakhla lives up to most visitors' romantic expectations of oasis life. Lush palm groves and orchards support traditional villages, where imposing, ancient mud-brick forts still stand guard over the townships and allude to their less tranquil past.

The region has been inhabited since prehistoric times, with fossilised bones hinting at human habitation dating back 150,000 years. In Neolithic times, Dakhla was the site of a vast lake, and rock paintings show that elephants, zebras and ostriches wandered its shores. As the area dried up, inhabitants migrated east to become the earliest settlers of the Nile Valley. In Pharaonic times, Dakhla retained several settlements and was a fertile land producing wine, fruit and grains. The Romans, and later Christians, left their mark by building over older settlements, and during medieval times the towns were fortified to protect them from Bedouin and Arab raids. Al-Qasr (p280) is the best-preserved of these towns – and among the most enchanting places – anywhere in the Western Desert.

Mut

At the centre of the oasis lies the town of Mut, named after the god Amun's consort, settled since Pharaonic times. Now a modern Egyptian town of squat block concrete buildings, it has decent facilities and makes the most convenient base for travellers. You will, however, have a richer experience of Dakhla by staying in or around Al-Qasr. Mut's slumping old town remnants and the proximity of the palm groves help to give it a touch of charm – though only a touch.

Sights

Ethnographic Museum MUSEUM

(Map p276; Sharia as-Salam; admission E£5; ⏲by request) Dakhla's wonderful museum is only opened on request: ask at the tourist office (or call) and Omar Ahmad will arrange a time for your visit with the museum's manager, Ibrahim Kamel. The museum is laid out as a traditional home, with different areas for men, women and visitors. Displays of clothing, baskets, jewellery and other domestic items give an insight into oasis life.

Old Town of Mut RUIN

(Map p276) For much of old Mut's existence, the villagers lived with the threat of raiding Bedouin. Most houses here have no outside windows, thus protecting against intruders and keeping out the heat and wind of the desert. The labyrinth of mud-brick houses and lanes that wind up the slopes of the hill is definitely worth exploring, even if you may sometimes stumble into a trash heap.

Dakhla Oasis

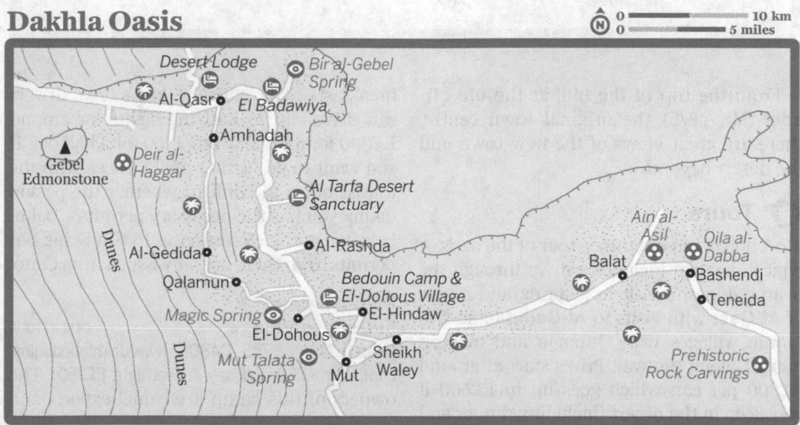

Mut

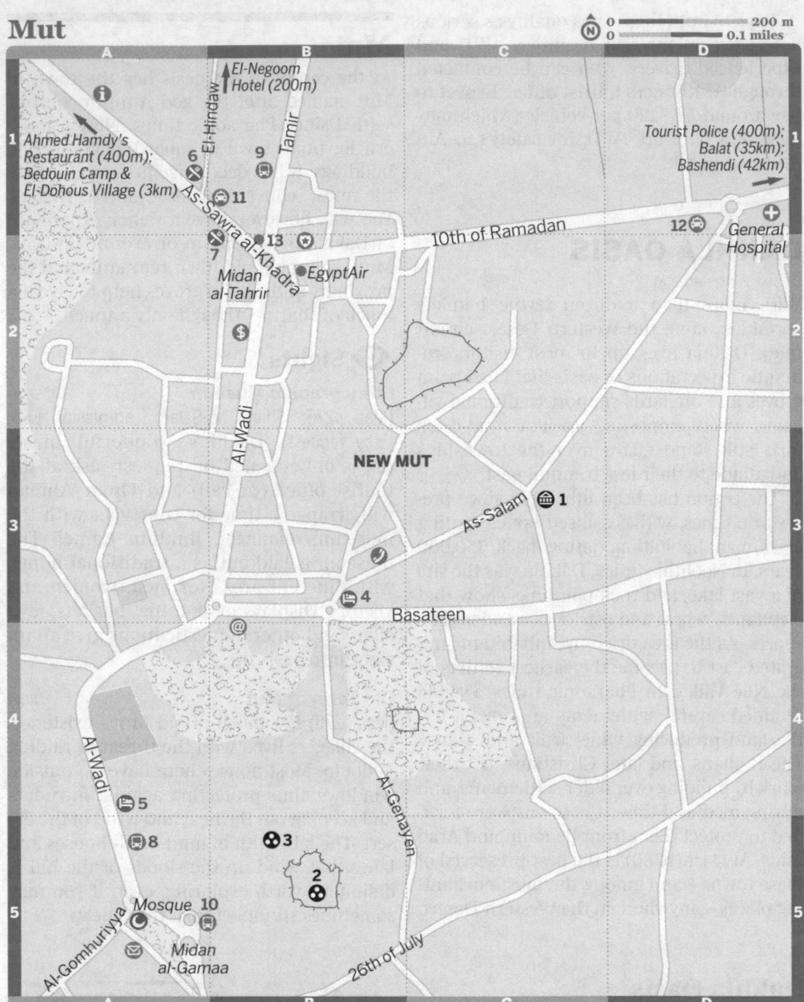

From the top of the hill, at the **old citadel** (Map p276), the original town centre, there are great views of the new town and the desert beyond.

Tours

Most hotels can organise a tour of the oasis. A typical day trip includes a drive through the nearby dunes, a visit to a spring and a tour of **Al-Qasr** with visits to **Al-Gedida** and **Qalamun**, villages with Ottoman and modern houses, along the way. Prices start at around E£300 per car, which goes up to E£500 if you sleep in the desert (including dinner and breakfast). Alternatively, Mut's taxi drivers can drive you to outlying sights for around E£300 for a full day or E£150 for a half day. If you want to go further afield, check with the tourist office to confirm whether the person taking you has the necessary permits – Dakhla is one of the closest oases to Gilf Kebir, but permits to go there are only issued from Cairo.

Bedouin Camp & El-Dohous Village DESERT TOUR

(Map p275; ☎785 0480; www.dakhlabedouins.com; 2hr E£60, full day & overnight E£250) The owners of this camp are camel experts and

Mut

Sights

1 Ethnographic Museum C3
2 Old Citadel B5
3 Old Town of Mut B5

Sleeping

4 Anwar Hotel B3
5 El Forsan Hotel A4

Eating

El Forsan Cafe .... (see 5)
6 Fatri el-Wadi A1
7 Said Shihad B2

Transport

8 Bus Station A5
9 Microbuses & Servees B1
10 Microbuses to Farafra and Al-Kharga Oases A5
11 Pick-Ups to Al-Qasr B1
12 Pick-Ups to Balat & Bashendi D1
13 Upper Egypt Bus Co Booking Office B2

can arrange both short jaunts and longer camel trips into the desert around Dakhla. If you're a serious camel-aficionado, they can train you in handling your trusty steed at their camel school and will also organise multiday safaris between the oases.

Sleeping

Mut has a decent selection of hotels, although most crowd the budget end of the spectrum.

You should be able to camp near the dunes west of Mut or by Al-Qasr (on a starlit plateau just north of town), but check first with the tourist office in Mut.

El Forsan Hotel HOTEL $

(Map p276; ☎782 1343; Sharia al-Wadi; s/d E£135/180, bungalow without air-con E£90/135; ❄📶) Ignore the creepy horror-movie corridor as you enter because El Forsan is the best budget deal in town. A recent paint job and new bed linen (including duvets) has smartened up the air-con rooms, while out the back within the garden there are domed mud-brick (rather worn) bungalows. Friendly manager Zaqaria whips up great breakfasts.

El-Negoom Hotel HOTEL $

(☎782 0014; s/d E£90/120; ❄📶) On a quiet street behind the tourist office, north of Sharia as-Sawra al-Khadra, this friendly hotel has a homey lobby and a span of sparsely furnished and rather old-fashioned but tidy little abodes with bathrooms – some even have TV.

Anwar Hotel HOTEL $

(Map p276; ☎782 0070; Sharia Basateen; s/d/tr from E£50/75/100; ❄) Friendly Mr Anwar runs this family establishment with gusto and offers flexibly priced, relatively clean rooms with shared or private bathroom options. Noise from the nearby mosque can be an issue, and the younger Anwars are a bit overeager to sell their tours.

Bedouin Camp & El-Dohous Village HOTEL $$

(Map p275; ☎785 0480; www.dakhlabedouins.com; Al-Dohous; s/d half board E£170/250; 📶🏊) El-Dohous Village, 3km from Mut centre, has a huge variety of domed and curvy rooms that give off good vibes, all decorated with local crafts. The hilltop restaurant has outstanding views; there are plenty of cushioned chill-out areas strewn about the place; and there's a hot spring on-site. The friendliness of the staff is just one more reason to stay.

Eating

There is no fancy dining in Mut, but there is some decent, fresh food (mostly of the chicken/kebab/rice variety) to be had. Most felafel takeaways close by noon.

El Forsan Cafe EGYPTIAN $$

(Map p276; El Forsan Hotel, Sharia al-Wadi; meals E£30-45; 🚭) Behind El-Forsan Hotel (you can walk through the hotel to enter), this surprisingly lush patch of grass is home to a garden cafe that serves up mammoth feasts of simple but fresh Egyptian flavours, including all manner of mahshi (stuffed vegetables) and the usual grilled meat. Locals hang out drinking tea here until the wee hours of the morning.

Said Shihad EGYPTIAN $$

(Map p276; Sharia as-Sawra al-Khadra; meals E£20-35) Owner Said is on to a good thing here: grilling up a meat-centric feast nightly for a dedicated following of hungry locals. The shish kebab is the thing to go for – perfectly succulent and served with potatoes in a tomato sauce, rice and beans.

Ahmed Hamdy's Restaurant EGYPTIAN $$

(☎782 0767; Sharia as-Sawra al-Khadra; meals E£20-30) On the main road into town is Ahmed Hamdy's popular place serving delicious chicken, kebabs, vegetables and a few other small dishes inside or on the terrace. The freshly squeezed lime juice is excellent and you can request beer (E£12) and sheesha.

Fatri el-Wadi EGYPTIAN FAST FOOD **$$**
(Map p276; Sharia as-Sawra al-Khadra; mains E£20-60; ⌚dinner) Fresh-from-the-oven *fiteer*, made to order by a friendly crew.

Information

Mut is a great place to practise life off-grid. Internet connections here have been known to approach courier-pigeon speed.

Bank Misr (Map p276; Sharia Al-Wadi; ⌚8.30am-2pm Sun-Thu) Has an ATM, exchanges cash and makes cash advances on Visa and MasterCard.

Internet Cafe (Map p276; Sharia Basateen; per hr E£2; ⌚11am-midnight) Gets you online, if you're patient.

General Hospital (Map p276; ☎782 1555; Sharia 10th of Ramadan) Passes muster in an emergency.

Main Post Office (Map p276; Midan al-Gamaa; ⌚8am-2pm Sat-Thu)

Telephone Centrale (Map p276; Sharia as-Salam; ⌚24hr)

Tourist Office (Map p276; ☎782 1685, 0122 179 6467; Sharia as-Sawra al-Khadra; ⌚8am-3pm) Friendly tourist-office director Omar Ahmad can help with all your oasis queries. He can be contacted anytime on his mobile: ☎0122 179 6467.

Tourist Police (☎782 1687; Sharia 10th of Ramadan)

Getting There & Away

BUS

From Mut's **bus station** (Map p276; ☎782 4366; Sharia al-Wadi), Upper Egypt Bus Co runs buses to Cairo (E£90, 10 hours) via Al-Kharga Oasis (E£25, two to three hours) and Asyut (E£50, five hours) at 7pm and 7.30pm.

You can also travel to Cairo via Farafra Oasis (E£35, four hours) and Bahariya Oasis (E£60, seven hours) at 6am and 6pm.

All buses pick up passengers from the bus station first and then at Midan al-Tahrir, across the roundabout from the bus **booking office** (Map p276; Sharia as-Sawra al-Khadra) kiosk.

MICROBUS

Microbuses to Al-Kharga (E£25), Farafra (E£40) and Cairo (E£90; night runs only) leave when full – which isn't often – from the old part of Mut, near the mosque.

Getting Around

Most places in Dakhla are linked by crowded pick-ups or microbuses, but working out where they all go requires a degree in astrophysics. Those heading to Al-Qasr (E£1.50) depart from Sharia as-Sawra al-Khadra. You can take pick-ups to Balat and Bashendi from in front of the hospital for E£1.50. Most others depart from the *servees* (service taxi) station on Sharia Tamir.

It may prove easier on occasion to bargain for a 'special' pick-up. A taxi to Al-Qasr should cost E£80 with waiting time.

Around Mut

The slumping mud-brick villages and palmaries, speckled with hot springs, that surround Mut capture the essence of slow-paced oasis life and are some of the Western Desert's most evocative sights.

Sights & Activities

A few kilometres out past the southern or western end of Mut you can have a roll around in sand dunes which, while not the most spectacular in the desert, are easy to reach for people without their own transport (if on foot, count on at least an hour's walk each way). Almost every hotel and restaurant in Mut offers day trips that include a sand-dune stop. Sunset camel rides out to the dunes can also be arranged.

Bir al-Gebel SPRING
(admission E£10) Set among breathtaking desert scenery, Bir al-Gebel is a gorgeous place for a soak. During the day in winter and spring any ambience here is overwhelmed by day-tripping school groups and blaring music. Come in the evening when the groups have left and the stars blaze across the sky. A sign marks the turn-off 20km north of Mut, from where it's about another 5km to the springs.

If you do arrive during a busy period, there's a more serene natural spring about 500m before Bir al-Gebel on the right, concealed behind a brick pump house.

Mut Talata SPRING
(admission E£10) There are several hot sulphur pools around the town of Mut, but the easiest to reach is Mut Talata. It's at the site of the small Mut Inn, so unless you are staying there, you've got to pay to take a dip. The pool's funny-coloured water is both warm and relaxing, though it may stain clothes.

LOCAL KNOWLEDGE

ETIQUETTE FOR A SPRING SOAK

There's nothing better after a hard day's rambling along the dusty tracks of the desert than a soak or swim in one of the many natural springs. If you're planning to bathe in the public waterholes that speckle the oases, it's important to be mindful of generally accepted spring etiquette:

- If local men are bathing, women should wait until they finish before entering the water.
- At springs within towns, women should wear a baggy T-shirt and shorts or, preferably, pants over their bathing suit. Use your best (conservative) judgement, and don't swim if the vibe is leery.
- Men should leave the Speedos at home.

Magic Spring SPRING
(admission E£10) Off the road to Qalamun is the so-called Magic Spring, a cool, rock-lined pool where you can relax with soft drinks (E£5 to E£10) served at a small cafeteria under a couple of palm trees.

Rock Carvings HISTORIC SITE
Carved into the weird rock formations 45km towards Al-Kharga, where two important caravan routes once met, are prehistoric petroglyphs of camels, giraffes and tribal symbols. The site has recently suffered from the attentions of less-scrupulous travellers who have all but ruined most of these curious images with their own graffiti. 4WD and a good driver are necessary to get here.

Balat

For a captivating glance into life during medieval times, pay a visit to the Islamic village of Balat, 35km east of Mut. Built during the era of the Mamluks and Turks on a site that dates back to the Old Kingdom, charismatic winding lanes weave through low-slung corridors past Gaudí-like moulded benches. Palm fronds are still used for shelter as smoothly rounded walls ease into each other. The tiny doors here were designed to keep houses cool and confuse potential invaders. A guide will happily take you onto the roof of one of the three-storey mud-brick houses for commanding views (a small tip is expected).

Sights

Qila al-Dabba RUIN
(Map 275; adult/student E£25/15; 8am-5pm) Qila al-Dabba is Balat's ancient necropolis. The five *mastabas* (mud-brick structures above tombs that were the basis for later pyramids) here, the largest of which stands more than 10m high, date back to the 6th dynasty. Four are ruined, but one has been restored and is open to the public. To get here, take the dirt track that meets the main road 200m east of Balat and head north. The necropolis is 3.5km along the road, past Ain al-Asil.

Originally all five *mastabas* would have been clad in fine limestone, with three thought to have belonged to important Old Kingdom governors of the oasis. If the *mastaba* is locked, the site guardian can usually be found in the nearby buildings.

Ain al-Asil RUIN
Ain al-Asil, or Spring of the Origin, is the site of a ruined Old Kingdom fortress that's unfortunately much less interesting than its name suggests. It's 2km along the dirt track on the way to Qila al-Dabba.

Getting There & Away

To get to Balat, take a pick-up from near the general hospital in Mut (E£1.50).

Bashendi

This small village north of the main Dakhla–Al-Kharga road takes its name from Pasha Hindi, the medieval sheikh buried nearby.

Sights

Tomb of Kitines TOMB
(adult/student incl Tomb of Pasha Hindi E£25/15; 8am-5pm) This sandstone tomb was occupied by Senussi soldiers during WWI and by a village family after that. Nevertheless, some funerary reliefs have survived and show the 2nd-century AD notable meeting the gods Min, Seth and Shu.

Tomb of Pasha Hindi SHRINE
(adult/student incl Tomb of Kitines E£25/15) The Tomb of Pasha Hindi is covered by an Islamic-era dome, which sits over a Roman

structure, clearly visible from inside the building. Locals make pilgrimages to pray for the saint's intercession.

Carpet-Making Cooperative CULTURAL CENTRE
(admission E£3; ⏲9am-1pm Sun-Thu) In Bashendi's carpet-making cooperative you can see rugs being woven and browse through the showroom.

Al-Qasr

One of the must-see sights in the western oases is the extraordinary medieval/Ottoman town of Al-Qasr, which lies on the edge of lush vegetation at the foot of pink limestone cliffs marking the northern edge of the oasis. Portions of the old village have been thoughtfully restored to provide a glimpse of how other oasis towns looked before the New Valley development projects had their way with them; the effect is pure magic. Several hundred people still live in the town that not so long ago was home to several thousand.

Al-Qasr is also a prime spot to romp around in the desert without a guide. Just north of town the plateau is textured with shallow, sandy wadis (valleys or dry riverbeds) that weave around rocky benches and weirdly hewn hills. The ground is littered with fossils, including sharks' teeth. For what may be the most sweeping vistas in any of the oases, hike to the top of the high bluffs that rise from the plateau – just choose the massive ramp of sand that looks most promising, and trek on up! Running back down hundreds of feet of sand is an instant regression to childhood glee. From Al-Qasr, it takes about two hours to reach the top, and longer if you dawdle, so bring enough water and snacks for the round trip. If the moon is full, set out before sunset and return by moonlight.

Sights

If you have your own vehicle, or driver, there are a handful of sights on the secondary road between Al-Qasr and Mut that are worthy of a visit. The ruined village of **Amhadah** has several tombs nearby dating from the 2nd century. Further along towards Mut, the road passes through the sleepy villages of **Al-Gedida** and **Qalamun**, both of which are home to plenty of traditional mud-brick architecture.

★Al-Qasr Old Town HISTORIC SITE
Al-Qasr's mud-brick maze of an old town is built on the ancient foundations of a Roman city and is thought to be one of the oldest inhabited areas of the oases. Most of what you can see today dates to the Ottoman period (1516–1798), though its creaky, picturesque labyrinth of narrow, covered streets harks back to its ancient origins. During its heyday, this was probably the capital of the Dakhla Oasis, easily protected by barring the fort's quartered streets.

The winding lanes manage to remain cool in the scalding summer and also serve to protect their inhabitants from desert sandstorms. Entrances to old houses can be clearly seen and some are marked by beautiful **lintels** – acacia beams situated above the door. Carved with the names of the carpenter and the owner of the house, the date and a verse from the Quran, these decorative touches are wonderfully preserved. The size of the houses here and the surviving fragments of decoration suggest a puzzling level of wealth and importance given to this town by the Ottomans.

There are 37 lintels in the village, the earliest of which dates to the early 16th century. One of the finest is above the Tomb of Sheikh Nasr ad-Din inside the **old mosque**, which is marked by a restored 12th-century mud-brick minaret. Adjoining it is **Nasr ad-Din Mosque**, with a 21m-high minaret. Several buildings have been renovated, including the old **madrassa**, a school where Islamic law was taught and which doubled as a town hall and courthouse: prisoners were tied to a stake near the entrance.

Also of interest is the restored **House of Abu Nafir**. A dramatic pointed arch at the entrance frames a huge studded wooden door. Built of mud brick, and on a grander scale than the surrounding houses, it incorporates massive blocks from an earlier structure, possibly a Ptolemaic temple, decorated with hieroglyphic reliefs.

Other features of the town include the **pottery factory**, a **blacksmith's forge**, a **waterwheel**, an **olive press** and a huge **old corn mill** that has been fully restored to function with Flintstone-like efficiency when its shaft is rotated. Near the entrance is the **Ethnographic Museum** (admission E£3; ⏲9am-sunset). Occupying Sherif Ahmed's house, which itself dates back to 1785, the museum's everyday objects try to give life to the empty buildings around them.

The Supreme Council for Antiquities has taken responsibility for the town, but doesn't charge an entrance fee. It's helpful to hook up with one of the Antiquities guards (if they're about) for a tour; they will expect a 'donation' of E£10. There are signposts scattered around the alleys but some of the highlights are tricky to find. A note to photographers: midday is actually a good time to take pictures here, since that's when the most light penetrates the canyon-like corridors.

Sleeping

Al-Qasr Hotel HOSTEL $
(Map 275; ☎787 6013; Main Highway, Al-Qasr; r without bathroom E£30) This old backpacker favourite sits above a cafe-restaurant on the main highway through Al-Qasr. Rooms are as basic as they get but there's a breezy upstairs communal sitting area where you can play games or relax, and for E£5 you can sleep on a mattress on the roof. Owner Mohamed has a long history of fine hospitality.

El Badawiya HOTEL $$
(Map 275; ☎772 7451; www.badawiya.com; s/d €44/56;) Perched above the fork in the road to Bir al-Gebel, this family friendly hotel features comfortable domed rooms of stone, mud and tile that could do with a touch of maintenance, but the mesmerising views of the oasis and desert from the private balconies make up for it. The swimming pool is an added bonus after a hot desert tour.

★Al Tarfa Desert Sanctuary BOUTIQUE HOTEL $$$
(Map 275; ☎910 5007; www.altarfa.net; s/d full board €360/440;) Taking the high end to unheard-of heights in Dakhla, Al Tarfa is flat-out desert-fabulous. The traditionally inspired decor is superbly tasteful and impeccably rendered, down to the smallest detail – from the embroidered bedspreads that look like museum-quality pieces to the mud-plastered walls that don't show a single crack. Private transfers to the hotel's isolated site, north of Al-Qasr, can be arranged.

Even the golden dunes that flow behind the resort seem like they've been landscaped to undulating perfection. Each suite is unique; the pool is like a liquid sapphire; and the spa features massage therapists brought in from Thailand.

Desert Lodge BOUTIQUE HOTEL $$$
(Map 275; ☎772 7061; www.desertlodge.net; Al-Qasr; s/d/tr half board US$90/150/210;) This thoughtfully designed, ecofriendly mud-brick fortress of a lodge crowns the hilltop at the eastern edge of Al-Qasr, overlooking the old town. Rooms are decorated in minimalist desert style incorporating tranquil pastel blues, pinks and greens. The restaurant is adequate, and there is also a bar, a private hot spring, and a painting studio on the desert's edge.

Getting There & Away

Pick-ups to Al-Qasr leave from opposite Said Shihad restaurant in Mut and cost E£1.50, or take a microbus from Mut's microbus stand (E£1.50).

Deir al-Haggar

This restored sandstone **temple** (Map 275; adult/student E£25/15; 8am-sunset) is one of the most complete Roman monuments in Dakhla. Dedicated to the Theban triad of Amun, Mut and Khons, as well as Horus (who can be seen with a falcon's head), it was built between the reigns of Nero (AD 54–68) and Domitian (AD 81–96). Some relief panels are quite well preserved, though most are covered in bird poop.

The temple is signposted 7km west of Al-Qasr; from the turn-off it's a further 5km.

If you look carefully in the adjacent Porch of Titus you can see the names of the entire team of Gerhard Rohlfs, the 19th-century desert explorer, carved into the wall. Also visible are the names of famous desert travellers Edmonstone, Drovetti and Houghton.

FARAFRA OASIS

Blink and you might just miss dusty Farafra, the least populated and most remote of the Western Desert's oases. Its exposed location made it prone to frequent attacks by Libyans and Bedouin tribes, many of whom eventually settled in the oasis and now make up much of the population. In recent years, the government has been increasing its efforts to revitalise this region, and the production of olives, dates, apricots, guavas, figs, oranges, apples and sunflowers is slowly growing.

Farafra is light on tourist infrastructure or any real attractions. In the past couple of decades a trickle of travellers attracted by the oasis' proximity to the White Desert (only 20km away), a torpid pace of life and extensive palm gardens began to use Farafra as their base for further desert explorations. Since the 2011 revolution, though, that steady trickle has dried up and August 2014's armed attack on the Farafra police checkpoint (p267) looks set to keep it that way for the near future.

Qasr al-Farafra

The only real town in Farafra Oasis, Qasr al-Farafra remains a barely developed speck on the Western Desert circuit. The town's tumbledown Roman fortress was originally built to guard this part of the desert caravan route, though these days all it has to show for it is a mound of rubble. Some small, mud-brick houses still stand in the back alleys, their doorways secured with medieval peg locks and their walls painted with verses of the Quran.

The main reason for a stopover here is a trip to the White Desert (Sahra al-Beida), but independent travellers will find tours much easier to organise from Bahariya Oasis.

Sights & Activities

Take a stroll through the palm gardens just west of 'downtown'. They're truly lovely, and full of activity during the date harvest (September/October).

Badr's Museum MUSEUM
(Map p283; ☎751 0091; off Sharia al-Mardasa; donation E£10; ⊙8.30am-sunset) Badr Abdel Moghny is a self-taught artist whose gift to his town has become its only real sight. Badr's Museum showcases his work, much of which records traditional oasis life. His distinctive style of painting and sculpture in mud, stone and sand has won him foreign admirers; he exhibited successfully in Europe in the early 1990s and later in Cairo.

Bir Sitta SPRING
(Well No 6) This sulphurous hot spring 6km west of Qasr al-Farafra is a popular pit stop. Water gushes into a jacuzzi-sized concrete pool and then spills out into a larger tank. This is a good place for a night-time soak under the stars.

Ain Bishay SPRING
The Roman spring of Ain Bishay bubbles forth from a hillock on the northwest edge of Qasr al-Farafra. It has been developed into an irrigated grove of date palms together with citrus, olive, apricot and carob trees, and is a cool haven.

Abu Nuss Lake LAKE
During the stifling heat of summer, a plunge in Abu Nuss Lake offers instant relief from hot and sweaty afternoons. There's some interesting bird life here, too. The turn-off for the lake is approximately 11km north of Qasr al-Farafra along the main road to Dakhla.

Tours

Farafra is nearer than Bahariya to the White Desert but there is a very limited choice of desert outfits. A dearth of tourists since the 2011 revolution also means that it's not likely independent travellers will find others to hook up with for a tour. The Al-Badawiya, Sunrise and Al-Waha hotels can usually organise excursions around Farafra and the White Desert, with prices starting at around E£400 per vehicle; however, with the tourism slow-down it would be prudent to contact them before your arrival to check prices and tour possibilities.

Sleeping

Sunrise Hotel & Safari HOTEL $
(Map p283; ☎0122 720 1387; wahafarafra@yahoo.com; Bahariya–Dakhla rd; r E£150) The Sunrise has gone for the Bedouin domed motif, and has installed refrigerators and TVs in brick bungalows that surround a rectangular courtyard. Some of the rooms have a strong septic stench, so check out a few. The family

Farafra Oasis

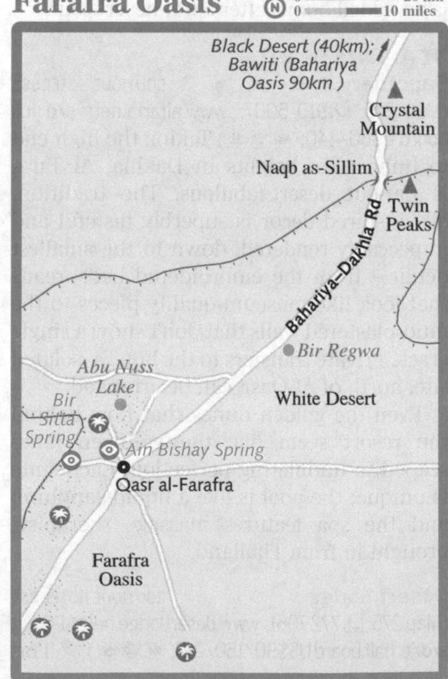

who run this place also run Farafra's other cheapie hotel option – the Al-Waha Hotel.

Al-Waha Hotel HOTEL $
(Map p283; ☎0122 720 0387; wahafarafra@yahoo.com; off Sharia al-Mardasa; r E£75, without bathroom E£60) This small, spartan hotel has acceptably clean, well-worn rooms with faux-oriental rugs. In summer the cement walls throb with heat.

Al-Badawiya Safari & Hotel HOTEL $$
(Map p283; ☎751 0060; www.badawiya.com; Bahariya–Dakhla rd; s/d US$25/35, ste with air-con US$35/50; ❄📶🏊) Al-Badawiya dominates Farafra tourism with its hotel and safari outfit. Comfortable domed rooms have plenty of traditional Bedouin style, though they could do with a lick of maintenance. There's a refreshing (albeit small) pool and a restaurant. The White and Western Desert tours are thoroughly professional.

Eating

Eating choices are limited in Farafra. Anyone looking for a change from the chicken/grilled meat combo is pretty much out of luck. The Al-Badawiya hotel also has a restaurant.

Al-Abeyt EGYPTIAN $
(Map p283; Sharia al-Mishtafa Nakhaz; felafel & fuul E£1-5) Nothing fancy. Just a friendly joint dishing up cheap-as-chips felafel and fuul.

Samir Restaurant EGYPTIAN $$
(Map p283; Sharia al-Balad; meals E£25-35) Samir's is the most atmospheric choice out of Farafra's slim pickings of dining options. Set meals of grilled meat and chicken are the same as other restaurants in town, but your table comes complete with the fine-dining flourish of a tablecloth.

El-Aseil EGYPTIAN $$
(Map p283; Sharia al-Mishtafa Nakhaz; meals E£20-25) Grilled meat with the full caboodle of rice, salad, tahini and bread is the order of the day at this spartan place.

Hussein's Restaurant EGYPTIAN $$
(Map p283; Sharia al-Balad; meals E£20-30) Hussein's does – surprise, surprise – chicken and grilled-meat staples with soup, salad and bread.

Information

For tourist information, contact the tourist office in Mut. For internet, you might be able to get online at either the computer shop or mobile (cellphone) shop on the main drag.

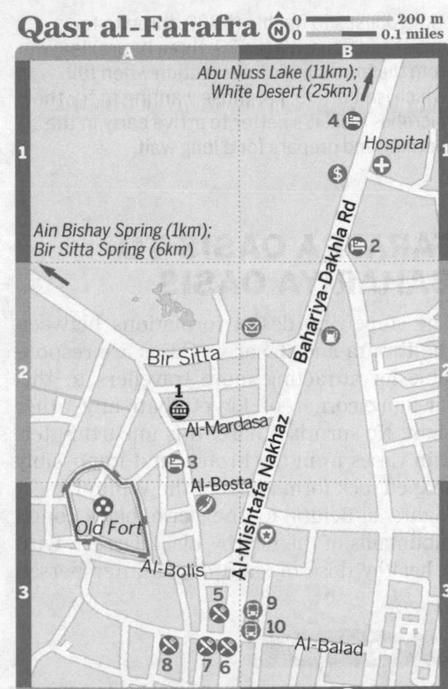

Qasr al-Farafra

Sights
1 Badr's Museum A2

Sleeping
2 Al-Badawiya Safari & Hotel B1
3 Al-Waha Hotel A2
4 Sunrise Hotel & Safari B1

Eating
5 Al-Abeyt A3
6 El-Aseil A3
7 Hussein's Restaurant A3
8 Samir Restaurant A3

Transport
9 Buses to Bahariya & Cairo B3
10 Microbuses to Dakhla and Bahariya B3

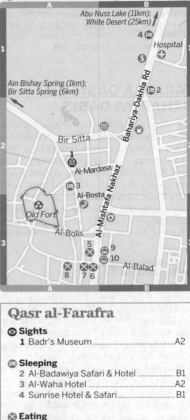

Bank Misr (Map p283; Bahariya–Dakhla rd) Has an ATM, though best not to depend on it.
Hospital (Map p283; ☎751 0047; Bahariya–Dakhla rd) For dire emergencies only.

Getting There & Away

There are Upper Egypt Bus Co buses from Farafra to Cairo (E£45, eight to 10 hours) via Bahariya (E£25, three hours) at 10am and 10pm. Buses from Farafra to Dakhla (E£25, four hours) leave around 2pm or 3pm and around 2am. Tickets are bought from the conductor.

Microbuses to Dakhla (E£20, three to four hours) and Bahariya (E£20, three hours) leave from the town's main intersection when full (which isn't often). For those wanting to try their microbus luck, it's better to arrive early in the morning and prepare for a long wait.

FARAFRA OASIS TO BAHARIYA OASIS

The stupefying desert formations between the Farafra and Bahariya Oases are responsible for attracting more travellers to this far-flung corner of Egypt than any other sight. No surprises here: this unearthly terrain varies from the bizarre and impossibly shaped rock formations of the White Desert (Sahra al-Beida) to the eerie black-coned mountains of the nearby Black Desert, with a healthy dose of sand dunes interspersed for good measure. These regions are relatively easy to get to from either Farafra or Bahariya Oases and are immensely popular with one-day and overnight safari tours.

Black Desert

The change in the desert floor from beige to black, 50km south of Bawiti, signals the beginning of the Black Desert (Sahra Suda). Formed by the erosion of the mountains, which have spread a layer of black powder and rubble over the peaks and plateaus, it looks like a landscape straight out of Hades. The Black Desert is a popular stop-off for tours running out of Bahariya Oasis and is usually combined with a White Desert tour.

Other sights in the region include **Gebel Gala Siwa**, a pyramid-shaped mountain that was formerly a lookout post for caravans coming from Siwa, and **Gebel az-Zuqaq**, a moun-

DON'T MISS

EGYPT'S MIND-BENDING WHITE DESERT

Upon first glimpse of the **White Desert National Park** (Sahra al-Beida; park entry US$5), you'll feel like Alice through the looking-glass. About 20km northeast of Farafra, on the highway's east side, blinding-white rock spires sprout almost supernaturally from the ground, each frost-coloured lollipop licked into ever odder shapes by the dry desert winds. They are best viewed at sunrise or sunset, when the sun lights them with orangey-pink hues, or under a full moon, which gives the landscape a ghostly Arctic appearance.

As you get further into the 300-sq-km national park, you'll notice that the surreal shapes start to take on familiar forms: chickens, ostriches, camels and other uncanny shapes abound. The sand around the outcroppings is littered with quartz and different varieties of deep-black iron pyrites, as well as small fossils.

On the west side of the highway, away from the wind-hewn sculptures, chalk towers called inselbergs burst from the desert floor like a smaller, more intimate (and, naturally, whiter) version of Arizona's Monument Valley. Between them run grand boulevards of sand, like geologic Champs-Élysées. No less beautiful than the east side of the road, the shade and privacy here make it a great area to camp.

About 50km north are two flat-topped mountains known as the **Twin Peaks**, a key navigation point for travellers. A favourite destination of local tour operators, the view from the top of the surrounding symmetrical hills, all shaped like giant ant-hills, is spectacular. Just beyond here, the road climbs a steep escarpment known as **Naqb as-Sillim** (Pass of the Stairs); this is the main pass that leads into and out of the Farafra depression and marks the end of the White Desert.

A few kilometres further along, the desert floor changes again and becomes littered with quartz crystals. If you look at the rock formations in this area you'll see that they are also largely made of crystal. The most famous of the formations is the **Crystal Mountain**, actually a large rock made entirely of quartz. It sits right beside the main road some 24km north of Naqb as-Sillim, and is easily recognisable by the large hole through its middle.

As well as the national park entry fee, you pay a E£10 fee for each night you sleep here. If you come as part of a group, the fees are included in your tour. You can usually buy tickets at the entrance to the park, but don't worry about going in without one; you can just pay the rangers when they find you.

tain known for the red, yellow and orange streaks in its limestone base. There is an easily climbed path leading to the mountain's peak.

Getting There & Away

Ordinary vehicles are able to drive the first kilometre or so off the Bahariya–Dakhla road into the White or Black Deserts, but only 4WD vehicles can advance deeper into either area. Some travellers simply get off the bus and take themselves into the White Desert – but be sure you have adequate supplies, and remember that traffic between the neighbouring oases is rarely heavy. The megaliths west of the highway are easy to access by foot, as are the so-called mushrooms to the east; the weirdest wonderland of white hoodoos is quite far to the east, and walking there would be a real haul. Bir Regwa, a small spring situated along the highway at one of the park entrances, usually has water; it's good to know where it is (just in case), though best not to rely on it.

There are plenty of safari outfits that can take you around these sights by jeep, by camel or on foot (note the camel and walking trips are vehicle-supported). If you're mainly interested in the White Desert, 4WD trips historically have been significantly cheaper from Farafra than from Bahariya; however, due to a lack of tourism there in recent years, desert tours are much easier to organise in Bahariya.

BAHARIYA OASIS

☎02 / POP 33,340

Bahariya is one of the more fetching of the desert circuit oases, and at just 365km from Cairo it's also the most accessible. Much of the oasis floor here is covered by sprawling shady date palms and speckled with dozens of natural springs, which beg to be plunged into. The surrounding landscape of rocky, sandy mesas is a grand introduction to the Western Desert's barren beauty.

The conical hills that lie strewn around the valley floor may have once formed islands in the lake that covered the area during prehistoric times. During the Pharaonic era, the oasis was a centre of agriculture, producing wine sold in the Nile Valley and as far away as Rome. Its strategic location on the Libya–Nile Valley caravan routes ensured it prospered throughout later ages. In recent years, stunning archaeological finds, such as that of the Golden Mummies, and easy access to the White and Black Deserts have earned Bahariya a firm spot on the tourist map.

Bawiti

Take one look at Bawiti's dusty, unappealing main road, and you'll wonder why you came. You have to scratch beneath the surface of this town to find its charms. Stroll through its fertile palm groves, soak in one of the many hot springs or explore its quiet back streets, where you'll meet truly friendly, hospitable people.

Until recently, Bawiti was a quiet town dependent on agriculture, but it's become a tourist hub for trips to the White and Black Deserts, with the Golden Mummies an added draw. Be warned that upon arrival you may be accosted by overzealous safari guides before you even step off the bus.

Sights & Activities

★Qarat Qasr Salim ARCHAEOLOGICAL SITE
(Map p288; Sharia Yusef Salim; Bawiti joint site ticket adult/student E£60/30; ⏲8.30am-4pm) This small mound amid the houses of Bawiti is likely to have been built upon centuries of debris. There are two well-preserved 26th-dynasty tombs here that were robbed in antiquity and reused as collective burial sites in Roman times. Both are home to some excellently preserved and colourful wall paintings.

The rock-cut **Tomb of Zed-Amun-ef-ankh** gives a glimpse of Bahariya in its heyday, the vibrant tomb paintings hinting at the wealth of its former occupant. Next to it lies the **Tomb of Bannentiu**, Zed-Amun-ef-ankh's son. Consisting of a four-columned burial chamber with an inner sanctuary, it is covered in fine reliefs depicting Bannentiu with the god Khons and goddesses Isis and Nephthys.

YOUR TICKET TO ANTIQUITIES

Bahariya's authorities issue a one-day ticket that gives entry to five of the Bahariya Oasis' ancient sites: the Golden Mummies Museum (p286), the Tomb of Zed-Amun-ef-ankh (p285), the Tomb of Bannentiu (p285), the Ain el-Muftella (p290) and the Temple of Alexander (p291). Tickets are available at the **ticket office** (Map p288; Sharia al-Mathaf, Bawiti, beside Golden Mummies Museum; adult/student E£60/30; ⏲8am-4pm) of the museum so stop there first. Yup, you gotta pay for 'em all, even if you only visit one.

Bahariya Oasis

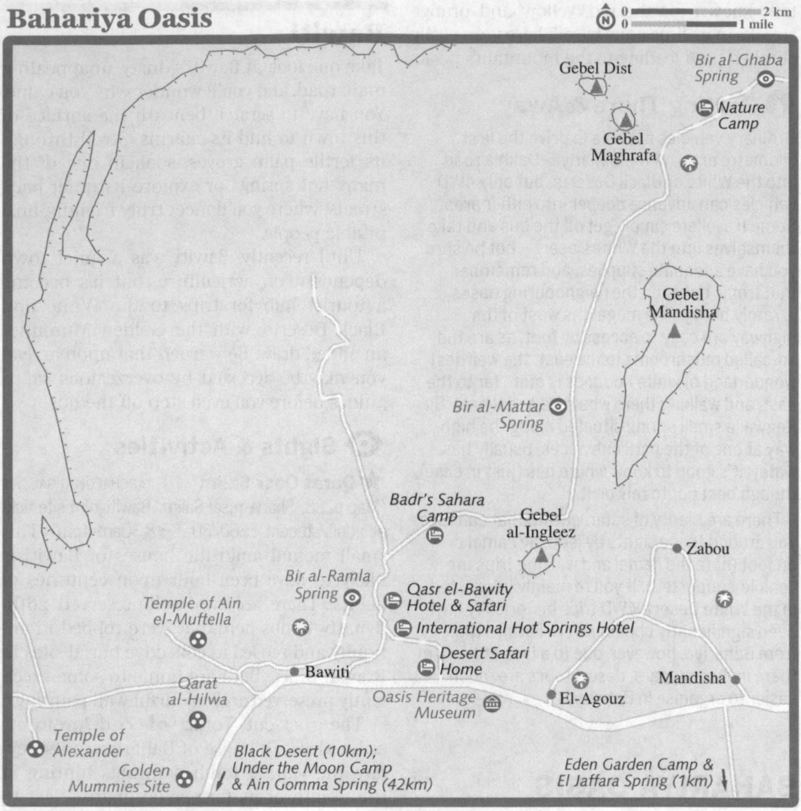

0 2 km
0 1 mile

Gebel Dist
Bir al-Ghaba Spring
Nature Camp
Gebel Maghrafa
Gebel Mandisha
Bir al-Mattar Spring
Badr's Sahara Camp
Gebel al-Ingleez
Zabou
Bir al-Ramla Spring
Qasr el-Bawity Hotel & Safari
Temple of Ain el-Muftella
International Hot Springs Hotel
Desert Safari Home
Bawiti
Mandisha
Qarat al-Hilwa
Oasis Heritage Museum
El-Agouz
Temple of Alexander
Golden Mummies Site
Black Desert (10km); Under the Moon Camp & Ain Gomma Spring (42km)
Eden Garden Camp & El Jaffara Spring (1km)

Golden Mummies Museum MUSEUM

(al-Mathaf; Map p288; Sharia al-Mathaf; Bawiti joint site ticket adult/student E£60/30; 8am-2pm) Only 10 of Bahariya's richly decorated cache of mummies are exhibited here. While the motifs are formulaic and the work is second-rate, the painted faces show a move away from stylised Pharaonic mummy decoration towards Fayoum portraiture.

The museum doesn't have a sign. Look for the building resembling a wartime bunker behind a low cream-coloured wall topped with guard turrets. The ticket office (p285) for all of Bawiti's sites is just inside the entrance gate.

Underneath the wrappings, the embalmers' work appears to have been sloppy: in some cases the bodies decayed before embalming began, which suggests that these mummies mark the beginning of the end of mummification. Sadly, the exhibit embodies that spirit, and is entirely underwhelming.

El-Beshmo SPRING

(Map p288) The closest springs to central Bawiti are the so-called Roman springs, known as El-Beshmo, beside El-Beshmo Lodge. The view over the oasis gardens and the desert beyond is wonderful, but unfortunately the spring is not suitable for swimming.

Oasis Heritage Museum MUSEUM

(3847 3666; Bahariya–Cairo rd; admission E£5-10; hours vary) That giant sandcastle-looking-thing, 3km east of town on the road to Cairo, is Mahmoud Ed's Oasis Heritage Museum. Inspired by Badr's Museum in Farafra, its creator captures, in clay, scenes from traditional village life, among them men hunting, women weaving and a painful-looking barber/doctor encounter. There's also a display of old oasis dresses and jewellery.

Sleeping

There is a decent selection of budget and mid-priced hotels in Bawiti, but if you want to catch the mellow oasis vibe, head for one of the camps outside of town.

It makes sense to sort out accommodation in Bawiti before you arrive, especially in high season, to avoid dealing with the touts that swarm each bus arrival.

Old Oasis Hotel HOTEL $
(Map p288; ☎3847 3028; www.oldoasis.hostel.com; s/d/tr E£120/180/220, without air-con E£90/120/180; ❄📶🏊) One of the most charming places to stay in Bawiti town sits among a pretty garden of palm and olive trees. It has 13 simple but impeccable fan rooms, plus a few fancier stone-wall air-con rooms. A large pool receives steaming hot water from the nearby spring; the run-off waters the garden, where there's a shady restaurant-cafe. The hotel is located by El-Beshmo spring.

New Oasis Hotel HOTEL $
(Map p288; ☎0122 847 4171; max_rfs@hotmail.com; s/d E£100/200, without air-con E£65/150; ❄) A study in curvaceous construction, this small, homey hotel has several tear-drop-shaped rooms, some with balconies overlooking the expansive palm groves nearby. Inside, the rooms are in good shape, though someone seems to have been a little overzealous with the powder-blue paint. It's one of the nicer budget options in town, located next to El-Beshmo spring.

BAHARIYA TOURS

There is furious competition throughout the oases – and even in Cairo – for tour business, but it is particularly intense in Bahariya. Here, every hotel offers tours, as do a number of eager young men who have taken out bank loans to pay for their cars. The battle for customers is so fierce that buses arriving in Bahariya are sometimes greeted by a tourist-police officer, who escorts foreigners through the throng of aggressive touts to the safe haven of the tourist office. Here Mohamed Abd el-Kader can give you up-to-date information about local hotels and tour operators. If you're feeling overwhelmed, check with him first.

A typical itinerary will take you to the sights in and around Bahariya (Temple of Alexander (p291), Temple of Ain el-Muftella (p290), Gebel Dist (p290) and Gebel al-Ingleez (p290)) then out through the Black Desert (p284), with a stop at the **Crystal Mountain** and then into the White Desert (p284).

A full day exploring the local sights of Bahariya runs from E£250 to E£400; a half-day Black Desert trip costs E£400; a one-night camping trip into the White Desert will cost E£800 to E£1200. If you're travelling into the remote corners of the desert on a multiday excursion, you'll be looking at E£1000 to E£1500 per day. One of the variables is how much of the distance is covered off-road. Remember, cheaper isn't always better. A reliable car and driver are well worth a few extra pounds.

Before signing up, check vehicles to make sure they're roadworthy; confirm how much food and drink is supplied (and what this will be); confirm start and end times (some operators start late in the afternoon and return early in the morning but charge for full days); and try to talk with travellers who have just returned from a trip to get their feedback.

Many cheap Cairo hotels and hostels push their White Desert tours, but it's a much better idea to arrange things in Bawiti, where you can meet the people who will be responsible for your experience before forking over any cash. There are some well-established local safari outfits.

Helal Travel (☎0122 423 6580; www.helaltravel.com; Under the Moon Camp, Bahariya Oasis) One of Bawiti's most highly reputable tour operators, Helal Travel offers White and Black Desert trips and can arrange a whole swag of other desert safaris.

White Desert Tours (☎0122 321 2179; www.whitedeserttours.com; International Hot Spring Hotel, Bahariya Oasis) Operating since 1995, this German-owned tour company specialises in the White Desert and the area around Bahariya Oasis, but can also tailor-make multiday safaris.

Eden Garden Tours (☎0100 071 0707; www.edengardentours.com; Eden Garden Camp, Bahariya Oasis) This local tour operator's White Desert tours have been highly recommended by past travellers.

Bawiti

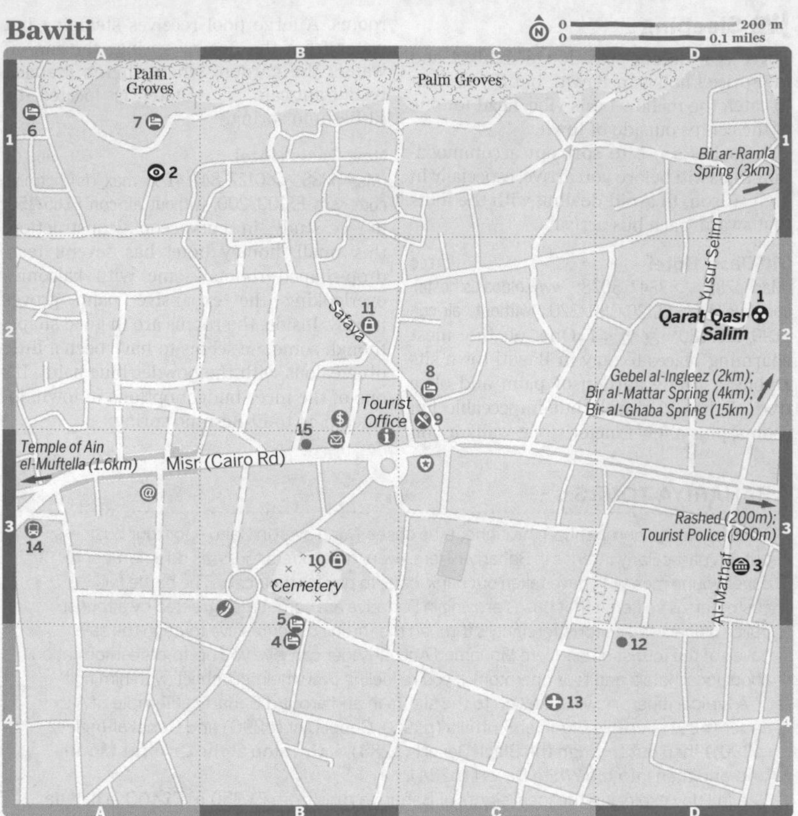

Desert Safari Home HOTEL $

(☎0122 731 3908; www.desertsafarihome.com; s/d E£100/150, without bathroom E£70/100; ❄@) This decent budget option is inconveniently located 2km from the centre of town but has good rooms. Owner Badry Khozam willingly picks up guests from the bus station.

Alpenblick Hotel HOTEL $$

(Map p288; ☎3847 2184; www.alpenblick-hotel-oasis.com; s/d €13/22, d without air-con €16; ❄) This granddaddy of the Bahariya hotel scene keeps getting dragged out of retirement by its consecutive owners; the current ones give a warm welcome. The rooms are spick-and-span though simple, and there's a large shaded courtyard where you can hang out and meet other travellers.

To find it, follow the signs from the turn-off opposite the tourist information building.

Western Desert Hotel HOTEL $$

(Map p288; ☎0122 301 2155; www.westerndeserthotel.com; Sharia Safaya; s/d E£175/300; ❄📶) Right in the middle of town, this concrete block has well-kept rooms with powerful air-con and beds that even boast two sheets. It's a solid, safe choice with a supremely convenient location. When it's not busy, you'll get a discount if you ask.

Eating

The market area on Sharia Misr houses several good and cheap roasted chicken and kebab joints that fire up after dusk. Fresh veggies can be found along the street between Sharia Misr and Telephone centrale. As for restaurants, the scene is feeble.

Popular Restaurant EGYPTIAN $$

(Map p288; ☎3847 2239; Sharia Safaya; set meals E£45) Popular is Bawiti's main restaurant op-

Bawiti

Top Sights
1 Qarat Qasr Salim D2

Sights
2 El-Beshmo A1
3 Golden Mummies Museum D3

Sleeping
4 Alpenblick Hotel B4
5 Nature Camp B3
6 New Oasis Hotel A1
7 Old Oasis Hotel A1
8 Western Desert Hotel C2

Eating
9 Popular Restaurant C2

Shopping
10 Girls Work Shop B3
11 Horass Handcraft B2

Information
12 Antiquities Inspectorate Ticket Office D4
13 Hospital C4

Transport
14 Hilal Coffeehouse & Bus Stop A3
15 Upper Egypt Bus Co Ticket Kiosk B3

tion, but standards have slipped and its set meals are now hugely overpriced. On a good note, the service is superfriendly and there's icy cold beer.

Rashed EGYPTIAN $$
(Sharia Misr; meals E£25) Big and clean, Rashed serves set multicourse meals that revolve around the usual meaty grill options. Head east for about 400m from the tourist information building, along the main road, to find it.

Shopping

Girls Work Shop HANDICRAFTS
(Map p288; ⏲10am-1pm Sat-Thu) This little store sells only crafts made in Bahariya Oasis, providing local women with skills and much-needed work. Unique items include hand-embroidered greeting cards. It's located south of Sharia Misr.

Horass Handcraft HANDICRAFTS
(Map p288; Sharia Safaya; ⏲8am-8pm) Sells some locally made crafts, including hand-decorated pouches cleverly marketed as 'mobile phone holders' or, our favourite, 'guidebook holders'. It also has standard adorned traditional Bedouin costumes and camel-hair socks. If the shop is closed, knock on the door directly across the street.

Information

Hospital (Map p288; ☎3847 2390) Head to Cairo except in dire emergency.

National Bank of Development (Map p288; ⏲9am-2pm Sun-Thu) Has an ATM and changes cash. Off Sharia Misr.

Tourist Office (Map p288; ☎3847 3039; Sharia Misr; ⏲8am-2pm & 7-9pm Sat-Thu) Run by helpful Mohamed Abd el-Kader, who can also be contacted on ☎0122 373 6567.

Tourist Police (☎3847 3900; Sharia Misr)

Getting There & Away

BUS

From the **bus ticket kiosk** (Map p288; ☎3847 3610; Sharia Misr; ⏲9am-1pm & 7-11pm), near the post office, Upper Egypt Bus Co has services to Cairo (E£40, five hours) at 6.30am, 10am and 3pm. They are often full, so it's strongly advised to buy tickets the day before travelling. There are two more Cairo-bound buses that originate in Dakhla and pass through Bawiti around noon and midnight, stopping at the **Hilal Coffeehouse** (Map p288; Sharia Misr) at the western end of town. For those, hope there are seats and buy your ticket on the bus.

If you're heading to Farafra (E£20, two hours) and Dakhla (E£40, four to five hours), you can hop on one of the buses headed that way from Cairo. They leave Bahariya around noon and 11.30pm from the bus ticket kiosk and also pick up passengers at Hilal Coffeehouse.

MICROBUS

Whenever they're full, microbuses run from Bawiti to Cairo (E£40), ending near the Moneib metro station in Giza. Microbuses to Farafra (E£25) and Dakhla (E£45) are rare, and are best caught an hour or so before the night bus departs. All leave from Hilal Coffeehouse.

There is no public transport to Siwa down the desert road. To take this road you have to hire a private 4WD. Expect to pay around E£1500 per car. If there's a 4WD from Siwa that's returning empty, you might be able to ride with it for half that amount. Permits (E£140 per person) are required and are usually organised by your driver. The tourist office can also help with permits.

BAHARIYA'S GOLDEN MUMMY CACHE

Put it down to the donkey: until 1996, no one had any idea of the extent of Bahariya's archaeological treasure trove. Then a donkey stumbled on a hole near the temple of Alexander the Great, and its rider saw the face of a golden mummy peering through the sand. Or so the story goes. (Some locals wink knowingly at what they assert is a much-popularised myth.) Nevertheless, since then archaeologists have done extensive research in a cemetery that stretches over 3 sq km. Radar has revealed more than 10,000 mummies, and excavation has revealed more than 250 of them in what has come to be called the Valley of the Golden Mummies.

These silent witnesses of a bygone age could shed new light on life in this part of Egypt during the Graeco-Roman period, a 600-year interlude marking the transition between the Pharaonic and Christian eras. Bahariya was then a thriving oasis and, with its rich, fertile land watered by natural springs, was a famous producer of wheat and wine. Greek and, later, Roman families set up home here and became a kind of expatriate elite.

Research has shown that after a brief decline when Ptolemies and Romans fought for control of the oasis, Roman administrators embarked on a major public works program, expanding irrigation systems, digging wells, restoring aqueducts and building roads. Thousands of mud-brick buildings sprang up throughout the oasis. Bahariya became a major source of grain for the empire and was home to a large garrison of troops; its wealth grew proportionately. Researchers are hoping that continued excavation of the necropolis will provide more answers about the region's early history and its inhabitants.

Around Bawiti

While there are some antiquities outside Bawiti that are arguably worth seeing, the main attractions are the natural ones, including immense palm gardens, many fed by springs ideal for a night-time soak. Further afield lies wild desert scenery; the Black Desert, Gebel Dist and Gebel Maghrafa can be seen on a day trip or overnight safari.

Sights

A number of sights in Bahariya can be included as part of a tour by the many safari operators in Bawiti. Some can also be done on foot, if the weather is cool.

★Gebel al-Ingleez MOUNTAIN

Clearly visible from the road to Cairo, flat-topped Gebel al-Ingleez, also known as Black Mountain, takes its name from a WWI lookout post. From here Captain Williams, a British officer, monitored the movements of Libyan Senussi tribesmen. At the top are the modest remains of Captain Williams' lookout post. But the real reason to come up here is for the fantastic panoramic views, which roll out across the oasis and to the desert beyond.

Head here to watch sunset for the most atmospheric experience. A dirt track winds up to a plateau near the top, from where a footpath leads across the ridge to the summit (about a five-minute walk).

Temple of Ain el-Muftella TEMPLE

(Bawiti joint site ticket adult/student E£60/30; ⏱8am-4pm) These four 26th-dynasty chapels, approximately 2km west of Bawiti, together form the Temple of Ain el-Muftella. The bulk of the building was ordered by 26th-dynasty high priest Zed-Khonsu-ef-ankh, whose tomb (closed to the public) has been discovered under houses in Bawiti. Archaeologists suspect that the chapels could have been built during the New Kingdom, significantly expanded during the Late Period, and added to during Greek and Roman times. All have been restored and given wooden roofs to protect them from the elements.

Gebel Dist MOUNTAIN

Gebel Dist is an impressive pyramid-shaped mountain visible from most of the oasis. A local landmark, it is famous for its fossils; dinosaur bones were found here in the early 20th century, disproving the previously held theory that dinosaurs only lived in North America. In 2001 researchers from the University of Pennsylvania found the remains of a giant dinosaur here: *Paralititan stromeri.*

The discovery of this huge herbivore, which the team deduced was standing on the edge of a tidal channel when it died 94 million years ago, makes it likely that Bahariya was once a swamp similar to the Florida everglades. About 100m away is **Gebel Maghrafa** (Mountain of the Ladle).

Qarat al-Hilwa RUIN

(Bawiti joint site ticket adult/student E£60/30; 8am-4pm) This ancient necropolis includes the 18th-dynasty Tomb of Amenhotep Huy. Overall it's a rather uninspiring site that will only interest the most avid of archaeology fans.

Temple of Alexander TEMPLE

(Bawiti joint site ticket adult/student E£60/30; 8am-4pm) The Temple of Alexander, southwest of Bawiti, is the only place in Egypt where Alexander the Great's cartouche has been found. Despite this fame, the site itself is small and unimpressive.

Gebel Mandisha MOUNTAIN

Gebel Mandisha is a ridge capped with black dolomite and basalt that runs for 4km behind the village of the same name, just east of Bawiti.

Hot & Cold Springs

★Ain Gomma SPRING

Ain Gomma, 45km south of Bawiti, is one of the most magnificent springs around. Cool, crystal-clear water gushes into this small pool surrounded by the vast desert expanse, and the funkiest cafe in all of the oases sits beside it. Situated near the town of El-Hayz, you can take a Dakhla-bound bus here, but it's difficult to get back without your own transport. Many safari trips to the White Desert will stop here en route.

Bir al-Ghaba SPRING

One of the most satisfying springs to visit is Bir al-Ghaba, located about 15km northeast of Bawiti. It's quite a trek to get out here but there is nothing quite like a moonlit hot bath on the edge of the desert.

El Jaffara SPRING

A few kilometres south of the Bahariya-Cairo road, about 7km from Bawiti, lies the mini-oasis of El Jaffara, where two springs – one hot, one cold – make this a prime spot in winter or summer. It's near Eden Garden Camp.

Bir al-Mattar SPRING

At Bir al-Mattar, 7km northeast of Bawiti, cold springs pour into a viaduct, then down into a concrete pool, in which you can splash around during the hot summer months. As with all Bawiti's springs, the mineral content is high and the water can stain clothing.

Bir al-Ramla SPRING

The sulphurous spring of Bir al-Ramla, 3km north of town, is very hot (45°C) and suitable for a soak, though you may feel a bit exposed to the donkey traffic passing to and fro. Women should stay well covered.

Sleeping

Badr's Sahara Camp HUT $

(0122 792 2728; www.badrysaharacamp.com; s/d E£60/100) A couple of kilometres from Bawiti, Badr's Sahara Camp has a handful of bucolic, African-influenced huts, each with two beds and small patios out front. Hot water and electricity can't always be counted on, but cool desert breezes and knockout views of the oasis valley can. Pick-ups are available.

★Under the Moon Camp BUNGALOW $$

(0122 423 6580; www.helaltravel.com; El-Hayz; huts s/d half board E£200/250, bungalows s/d half board E£300/350) Isolated in the small oasis hamlet of El-Hayz, 45km south of Bawiti, this beautiful camp features several round, stone huts (no electricity) and some new mud-brick bungalows (with lights) scattered around a garden compound. The accommodation is as simple as it gets, but the hospitality and the setting can't be beat.

The lovely Ain Gomma spring is nearby and there's a cold spring pool right in the camp, with desert views. Helal, the Bedouin owner who once trained Egyptian military units in desert navigation, runs highly recommended safari trips and arranges free pick-ups from Bawiti.

Nature Camp BUNGALOW $$

(Map p288; 0127 718 8476; naturecamps@hotmail.com; Bir al-Ghaba; r half board per person E£150) At the foot of Gebel Dist, 17km north of Bawiti, Nature Camp sets new standards for environmentally focused budget accommodation. The peaceful cluster of candlelit and intricately designed thatch huts looks out onto the expansive desert beside Bir al-Ghaba. The food is very good (meals E£25) and the owner, Ashraf Lotfe, is a skilled desert hand.

Transport to and from Bawiti can be arranged.

Eden Garden Camp HUT $$

(0100 071 0707; www.edengardentours.com; hut per person full board E£125, s/d full board €35/45;) Located 7km east of Bawiti, in the small, serene oasis of El Jaffara, Eden Garden is a superfriendly place with African-style huts, shaded lounge areas, fresh food and, best of all, two springs just outside its gates: one hot and one cold. Its desert safaris have a good reputation, and pick-ups from Bawiti are free.

International Hot Spring Hotel HOTEL $$
(☎ 02-3847 3014, 0122 321 2179; www.whitedesert-tours.com; s/d half board per person US$50/40) About 3km outside Bawiti on the road to Cairo, this spa resort has 36 very comfortable rooms and eight chalets, built around a hot spring and set in a delightful garden. There's also a rooftop lounge and a good restaurant. German owner Peter Wirth is an old Western Desert hand and organises recommended trips in the area.

Qasr el-Bawity Hotel & Safari BOUTIQUE HOTEL $$
(☎ 3847 1880; www.qasrelbawity.com; r with half board from €60;) Qasr el-Bawity offers an intimate hotel experience amid a sumptuous desert setting. Stone-clad rooms sport ornate domed roofs and furniture with arty, frilly touches. There are two pools (one natural and one chlorinated), and the restaurant is suitably good.

SIWA OASIS

☎ 046 / POP 21,690

Siwa is the stuff of desert daydreams. Just 50km from the Libyan border this fertile basin, sitting about 25m below sea level and brimming with olive and palm trees, epitomises slow-paced oasis life. Set between the shady groves, squat, slouching mud-brick hamlets are connected by winding dirt lanes where trundling donkey carts are still as much a part of the street action as puttering motorbikes and 4WDs. Scattered throughout the oasis are crystal-clear springs, which are a heavenly respite from the harsh heat. At the edge of the oasis, the swells of the Great Sand Sea roll to the horizon, providing irresistible fodder for desert exploration.

Siwa's geographic isolation helped protect a unique society that stands distinctly apart from mainstream Egyptian culture. Originally settled by Berbers (roaming North African tribes), Siwa was still practically independent only a few hundred years ago. For centuries the oasis had contact with only the few caravan traders that passed along this way via Qara, Qattara and Kerdassa (near Cairo), and the occasional determined pilgrim seeking the famous Oracle of Amun. Today, local traditions and Siwi, the local Berber language, still dominate.

Well worth the long haul to get out here, Siwa casts a spell that's hard to resist.

History

Siwa has a long and ancient past: in late 2007, a human footprint was found that is thought to date back three million years, making it one of the oldest known human prints in the world. Flints discovered in the oasis show that it was inhabited in Palaeolithic and Neolithic times, but beyond that Siwa's early history remains a mystery.

The oldest monuments in the oasis, including the Temple of the Oracle, date from the 26th dynasty, when Egypt was invaded by the Assyrians. Siwa's Oracle of Amun was already famous then, and Egyptologists suspect it dates back to the earlier 21st dynasty, when the Amun priesthood became prominent throughout Egypt.

Such was the fame of Siwa's oracle that its prophecies threatened the Persians, who invaded Egypt in 525 BC and ended the 26th dynasty. One of the Western Desert's most persistent legends is of the lost army of Persian king Cambyses, which was sent to destroy the oracle but disappeared completely in the desert (see p296). This only helped increase the oracle's prestige, reinforcing the political power of the Amun priesthood.

The oracle's power – and with it, Siwa's fame – grew throughout the ancient world. The young conqueror Alexander the Great led a small party on a perilous eight-day journey across the desert in 331 BC. It is believed that the priests of Amun, who was the supreme god of the Egyptian pantheon and later associated with the Greek god Zeus, declared him to be a son of the god.

The end of Roman rule, the collapse of the trade route and the gradual decline in the influence of oracles in general all contributed to Siwa's gentle slide into obscurity. While Christianity spread through most of Egypt, there is no evidence that it ever reached Siwa, and priests continued to worship Amun here until the 6th century AD. The Muslim conquerors, who crossed the desert in AD 708, were defeated several times by the fierce Siwans. However, there was a cost to this isolation: it is said that by 1203 the population had declined to just 40 men, who moved from Aghurmi to found the new

Siwa Oasis

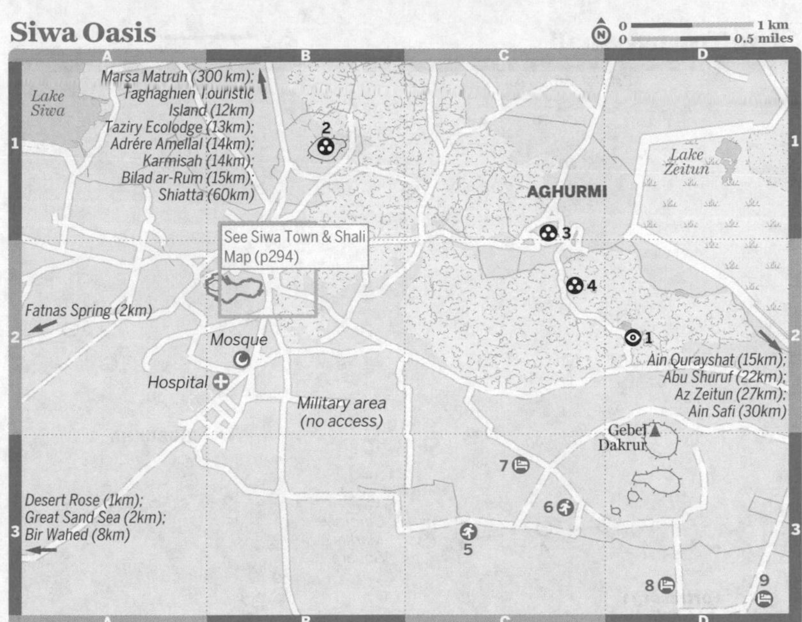

fortress-town of Shali. The oasis finally converted to Islam around the 12th century, and gradually built up wealth trading date and olive crops along the Nile Valley, and also with Libyan Fezzan and the Bedouins.

European travellers arrived at the end of the 18th century – WG Browne in 1792 and Frederick Hornemann in 1798 – but most were met with a hostile reception, and several narrowly escaped with their lives. Siwa was again visited in WWII, when the British and Italian/German forces chased each other in and out of Siwa and Jaghbub, 120km west in Libya. By then Siwa was politically incorporated into Egypt, but the oasis remained physically isolated until an asphalt road connected it to Marsa Matruh in the 1980s. As a result, Siwans still speak their own Berber dialect and have a strong local culture, quite distinct from the rest of Egypt. The oasis is now home to some 21,000 Siwans and about 2000 Egyptians.

Siwa Oasis

Sights

1 Cleopatra's Bath D2
2 Gebel al-Mawta B1
3 Temple of the Oracle C1
4 Temple of Umm Ubayd C2

Activities, Courses & Tours

5 Am Agbenek Siwa Inn Hotel C3
6 Sherif Sand Bath C3
Tala Ranch .... (see 9)

Sleeping

7 Qasr Alzaytuna C3
8 Siwa Shali Resort D3
9 Tala Ranch Hotel D3

Sights & Activities

Even though there are some fascinating sights hidden in the dense palm greenery of this oasis, Siwa's main attraction is its serene atmosphere. Strolling through the palm groves or riding a bike to a cool spring for a swim is all part of this oasis' slow, soothing, far-from-anywhere charm. Hang out with other travellers; have a picnic; ride a donkey cart; explore the dunes by 4WD; and soak it all in.

One of Siwa's most impressive sights is the oasis itself, which boasts more than 300,000 palm trees, 70,000 olive trees and a great many fruit orchards. The vegetation is sustained by more than 300 freshwater springs and streams, and the area attracts an amazing variety of bird life, including quail and falcons.

Siwa Town & Shali

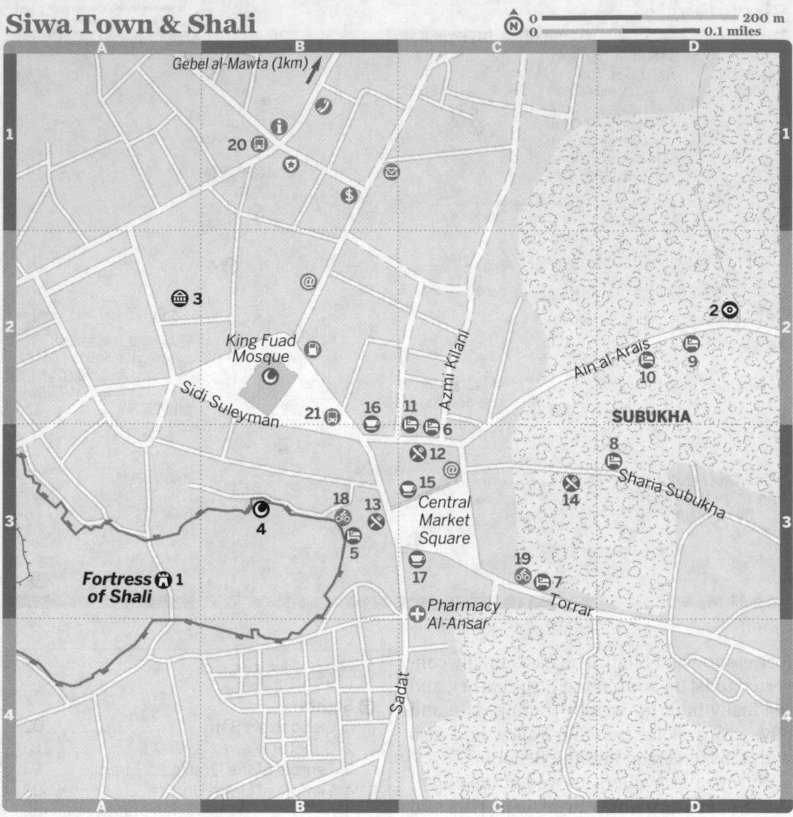

Siwa Town & Shali

Top Sights
1 Fortress of Shali A3

Sights
2 Ain al-Arais D2
3 House of Siwa Museum A2
4 Old Mosque B3

Sleeping
5 Al-Babinshal B3
6 Kelany Hotel C3
7 Palm Trees Hotel C3
8 Shali Lodge D3
9 Siwa Safari Gardens Hotel D2
10 Siwa Safari Paradise D2
11 Yousef Hotel C2

Eating
12 Abdu's Restaurant C3
13 Abo Ayman Restaurant B3
Al-Babinshal Restaurant ..... (see 5)
Kenooz Siwa ..... (see 8)
14 Nour al-Waha C3

Drinking & Nightlife
15 Abdu Coffeeshop C3
16 Shaqraza B2
17 Zeytouna C3

Transport
18 Bicycle Repair Shop B3
19 Bicycle Repair Shop C3
20 Bus Stop & West & Middle Delta Bus Co Ticket Office B1
21 Microbuses to Marsa Matruh B2

Siwa Town

Siwa is a pleasant little town centred on a **market square**, where roads skedaddle off into the palm groves in nearly every direction. The proliferation of motorcycles zooming around the main square may mean it's not as peaceful as it once was but rural ambience still abounds.

★ Fortress of Shali — FORTRESS

(Map p294) FREE Central Siwa is dominated by the spectacular organic shapes of the remains of this 13th-century mud-brick fortress. Built from *kershef* (chunks of salt from the lake just outside town, mixed with rock and plastered in local clay), the labyrinth of huddled buildings was originally four or five storeys high and housed hundreds of people. A path leads over the slumping remnants, past the **Old Mosque** (Map p294) with its chimney-shaped minaret, to the top for panoramic views.

For centuries, few outsiders were admitted inside the fortress – and even fewer came back out to tell the tale. But three days of rain in 1926 caused more damage than any invader had managed and, over the last decades, inhabitants moved to newer and more comfortable houses with running water and electricity. Now only a few buildings around the edges are occupied or used for storage.

House of Siwa Museum — MUSEUM

(Map p294; adult/student E£10/5; ⏲9am-2.30pm Sun-Thu) This small museum contains an interesting display of traditional clothing, jewellery and crafts typical of the oasis. It's worth the entry fee just to check out the wedding dresses. It's a block northwest of the King Fuad Mosque.

Gebel al-Mawta — ARCHAEOLOGICAL SITE

(Map p293; adult/student E£25/15; ⏲9am-5pm) This small hill, at the northern end of Siwa Town, is honeycombed with rock tombs peppered with wall paintings. Its name, Gebel al-Mawta, means 'Mountain of the Dead' and most of the tombs here date back to the 26th dynasty, Ptolemaic and Roman times. Only 1km from the centre of town, the tombs were used by the Siwans as shelters when the Italians bombed the oasis during WWII.

The best paintings are in the **Tomb of Si Amun**, where beautifully coloured reliefs portray the dead man – thought to be a wealthy Greek landowner or merchant – making offerings and praying to Egyptian gods. Also interesting are the unfinished **Tomb of Mesu-Isis**, with a beautiful depiction of cobras in red and blue above the entrance; the **Tomb of Niperpathot**, with inscriptions and crude drawings in the same reddish ink seen on modern Siwan pottery; and finally the **Tomb of the Crocodile**, whose badly deteriorating wall paintings include a yellow crocodile representing the god Sobek.

Hot & Cold Springs

Siwa has no shortage of active, bubbling springs hidden among its palm groves. At all of the springs in town, women should swim in pants and a shirt and use general good judgement concerning modesty.

Cleopatra's Bath — SPRING

(Spring of the Sun; Map p293) Following the track that leads to the Temple of the Oracle and continuing past the Temple of Umm Ubayd will lead you to Siwa's most famous spring, Cleopatra's Bath. The crystal-clear water gurgles up into a large stone pool, which is a popular bathing spot for locals as well as tourists. A couple of cafes beside the spring have comfortable shaded lounging areas and serve soft drinks; bring your own picnic if you want to hang out for a while.

Bir Wahed — SPRING

A favourite Siwa excursion is the freshwater lake at Bir Wahed, 15km away on the edge of the Great Sand Sea. Once over the top of a dune, you come to a hot spring, the size of a large Jacuzzi, where sulphurous water bubbles in a pool and runs off to irrigate a garden. Cooling down in the lake, then watching the sun setting over the dunes while soaking in a hot spring, is a surreal experience.

The thorns in this rose are the mosquitoes that bite at sunset and the fact that a permit is necessary to vist Bir Wahed (see p302). Because it's far from town, women can wear bathing suits here without offending locals. Bir Wahed can only be reached by 4WD, so if you don't have your own, you'll need to hire a guide and car.

Fatnas Spring — SPRING

(Lake Siwa) This fairly secluded pool is on a small island in the salty Birket Siwa, accessible across a narrow causeway. Nicknamed 'Fantasy Island' for its idyllic setting, the pool is about 6km from Siwa Town, and

THE LOST ARMY OF CAMBYSES

Persian king Cambyses invaded Egypt in 525 BC, overthrowing Egyptian pharaoh Psamtek III and signalling the beginning of Persian rule for the next 193 years. This success, however, did not continue. In the years immediately following his conquest of Egypt, Cambyses mounted several disastrous offensives. In one, he sent a mercenary army down the Nile into Kush (now Sudan) that was so undersupplied it had to turn to cannibalism to survive, and the soldiers returned in disgrace without even encountering the enemy.

Cambyses' most famous failure remains his attempt to capture the Oracle of Amun in Siwa. Herodotus recounts how the oracle predicted a tragic end for Cambyses, and so the ruler dispatched an army of 50,000 men from Thebes, supported by a vast train of pack animals carrying supplies and weapons. The army is purported to have reached Farafra before turning west to cover the 325km of open desert to Siwa – a 30-day march without any shade or sources of water. Legend has it that after struggling through the Great Sand Sea, the men were engulfed by a fierce sandstorm, which buried the entire army.

Over the centuries, dozens of expeditions have searched in vain for a trace of Cambyses' soldiers. Perhaps one day the shifting sands will reveal the remnants of this ancient army.

surrounded by palm trees and lush greenery. It's an idyllic place to watch the sunset, and there's a small cafe among the palms, which is good for a spot of tea or a puff of sheesha.

A Ministry of Agriculture project to try to improve the lake's drainage has left the 'island' high and dry, so sometimes the cafe may look out over salty mudflats rather than water. A donkey cart round trip from town will cost about E£25, with time to swim and hang out.

Ain al-Arais SPRING

(Map p294) The closest spring to central Siwa is Ain al-Arais, a cool, inviting waterhole with a grotto-like bottom, just five minutes' walk from the main market square. A casual cafe-restaurant is right beside the spring.

Aghurmi

Before Shali was founded in the 13th century, Siwa's main settlement was at Aghurmi, 4km east of the present town of Siwa. It was here that in 331 BC Alexander the Great consulted the famed oracle.

Temple of the Oracle RUIN

(Map p293; adult/student E£25/15; ⌚9am-5pm) The 26th-dynasty Temple of the Oracle sits in the northwest corner of the ruins of Aghurmi village. Built in the 6th century BC, probably on top of an earlier temple, it was dedicated to Amun (occasionally referred to as Zeus or Jupiter Ammon) and was a powerful symbol of the town's wealth. One of the most revered oracles in the ancient Mediterranean, its power was such that some rulers sought its advice while others sent armies to destroy it.

Although treasure hunters have been at work here and the buttressed temple was poorly restored in the 1970s, it remains an evocative site, steeped in history. Surrounded by the ruins of Aghurmi, it has awesome views over the Siwan oasis palm-tops.

Temple of Umm Ubayd RUIN

(Map p293) This almost totally ruined temple was dedicated to Amun. It was originally connected to the Temple of the Oracle by a causeway and was used during oracle rituals. Nineteenth-century travellers got to see more of it than we can; a Siwan governor blew up the temple in 1896 in order to construct the town's modern mosque and police building. Only part of a wall covered with inscriptions survives. It's located about 200m along the track from the Temple of the Oracle.

Around Siwa

There are a few villages, ruins and springs around Siwa that are worth a trip if you've got the time. To visit these sights you'll need your own vehicle. Mahdi Hweiti at the Siwa tourist office organises trips, as does almost every restaurant and hotel in town. None of the sights, with the exception of Shiatta, require permits.

Shiatta LAKE

Sixty kilometres west of Siwa Town, this stunning salt lake on the edge of the Great Sand

Sea is ringed by palm trees. It's a popular stopover for migratory birds – including flamingos – and gazelles may be seen here too. The lake once reached all the way to Siwa Town, and an ancient boat lies somewhere 7m below the surface. These days this area is mainly used by Bedouin tribes for grazing livestock, and it has first-rate desert views.

Ain Qurayshat SPRING

Ain Qurayshat, about 20km east from Siwa Town, has the largest free-flowing spring in the oasis. The best way to reach the spring is via the causeway across salty Lake Zeitun, which has striking views.

Abu Shuruf SPRING

Abu Shuruf, a clean spring said by locals to have healing properties, is 27km east of Siwa Town and 7km east of Ain Qurayshat spring in the next palm thicket. The clear water here is deliciously cold, but the ambience is somewhat spoilt by the sight and noise of the nearby Hayat water-bottling plant.

Az-Zeitun RUIN

Roughly 30km east of Siwa Town, this abandoned mud-brick village, beaten by the sand and wind, sits alone on the sandy plain. Hundreds of Roman-era tombs have been discovered about 2km beyond Az-Zeitun and are currently under excavation, although little of interest has so far been found.

Ain Safi VILLAGE

Three kilometres east of the abandoned village of Az-Zeitun, this is the last human vestige before the overwhelming wall of desert dunes that stretches for hundreds of kilometres, all the way south to Al-Kharga Oasis. Some 30 Bedouin remain here.

Kharmisah VILLAGE

About 15km northwest of Siwa Town, this village has five natural springs and is renowned for the quality of its olive gardens.

Bilad ar-Rum RUIN

Just north of Kharmisah, around 17km northwest of Siwa Town, the City of the Romans has about 100 tombs cut into the rock of the nearby hills and the ruins of a stone temple, among the spots rumoured to be the final resting place of Alexander the Great. Nearby is **Maraqi**, where Liana Souvaltzi, a Greek archaeologist, claimed in 1995 to have found Alexander's tomb. Her findings proved controversial and the Egyptian authorities revoked her permit and closed the site.

Tours

Almost all restaurants and hotels in Siwa offer tours, ranging from half a day in the desert around Siwa Town to a full five- or six-day safari. Abdu's Restaurant (p300) and the Palm Trees Hotel (p299) have established a good reputation for their trips. The tourist office is also an excellent place to get help with organising tours.

All desert trips require permits, which cost E£140 per person, per day and are usually obtained by your guide from the tourist office. Trip prices vary according to itineraries but the average cost of a car and driver for a full day to visit the sights around Siwa is E£200. One of the most popular half-day trips takes you to the cold lake and hot springs at Bir Wahed, on the edge of the Great Sand Sea. Palm Trees offers this with an overnight option, but you'll sleep in a camp on the edge of town, not in the dunes.

GAY SIWA?

Much attention has been paid to Siwa's unique history of intimate male relations. Back when Siwa's citizens still lived in the Fortress of Shali, young men between the ages of 20 and 40 were expected to spend their nights outside the fortress to tend to the fields and protect the town from attack. These men of Siwa had a notorious reputation, not only for their bravery (they were known as *zaggalah,* or 'club bearers'), but for their love of palm wine, music and openly gay relations. Single-sex marriages were still practised in Siwa right up until WWII, although they had been outlawed in Egypt decades earlier.

Even though Siwa has been listed as a place to visit in several gay travel directories, the situation today is quite different. Residents of Siwa vehemently deny that local gay men exist in their town, and international travellers coming to Siwa in hope of 'hooking up' have been faced with increasingly homophobic sentiments. Siwan men are not amused at being propositioned by passing strangers – they are much more likely than foreigners to bear the brunt of anti-gay attitudes. Violent attacks on local men accused of homosexuality are not unheard of.

Other popular half-day itineraries include a tour of the springs Ain Qurayshat, Abu Shuruf, Az-Zeitun and Ain Safi (E£150 for two people, E£200 for a bigger group); and a tour of Siwa Town and its environs (Temple of the Oracle, Gebel al-Mawta, Cleopatra's Bath, Fortress of Shali and Fatnas). Overnight trips vary in length according to destination. Most trips are done by 4WD, so ensure that the vehicle is roadworthy before you set out and that you have enough water.

Ghazal Safari DESERT TOUR

(☎0100 277 1234) If you're looking to explore the area of the Great Sand Sea surrounding Siwa, we highly recommend Ghazal Safari. Driver/guide Abd El-Rahman Azmy has a kick-ass vehicle and a love for Siwa that's contagious.

Tala Ranch DESERT TOUR

(Map p293; ☎0100 588 6003; talaranchsiwa@hotmail.com; Gebel Dakrur) If you dream of riding camels, Sherif Fahmy of Tala Ranch can arrange it, at E£350 for a day trip, including lunch, or E£400 for an overnight in the desert (with at least four people) including lunch, dinner, and breakfast in the morning. These trips are virtually impossible to arrange in summer, since daytime temperatures are too hot.

Am Agbenek Siwa Inn Hotel HORSE RIDING

(Map p293; ☎0100 333 2042, 0128 245 0981; www.amagbeneksiwa.over-blog.com) You can ride horses through the dunes or to various springs from the new stables at Am Agbenek Siwa Inn Hotel. Trip lengths range from one-hour jaunts (E£70) to three-day safaris.

Festivals & Events

Occasionally on Thursday nights, after the evening prayer, local Sufis of the Arusiya order gather near the tomb shrine of Sidi Suleiman, behind the King Fuad Mosque in the centre of Siwa Town, for a *zikr* (a long session of dancing, swaying and singing repetitive songs in praise of God) and they don't mind the odd foreigner watching.

Moulid at-Tagmigra RELIGIOUS

(Aug) Once a year, just after the corn harvest in late summer, Siwa Town's small tomb shrine of Sidi Suleiman is the scene of a *moulid* (saints' festival), known in Siwi as the Moulid at-Tagmigra. Banners announce the *moulid*, and *zikrs* are performed outside the tomb.

Siyaha Festival CULTURAL

(Oct) For three days around October's full moon, Gebel Dakrur is the scene of the Siyaha festival. Thousands of Siwans gather to celebrate the date harvest, renewing friendships and settling any quarrels that broke out over the previous year. Unfortunately, the festival has been cancelled for the past couple of years. Check with the tourist office to find out if it's taking place.

During the festival all Siwans, no matter what their financial or social standing, eat together at a huge feast after the noon prayer each day. The festival is intertwined with Sufism, and each evening, hundreds of men form a circle and join together in a *zikr*. Siwan women do not attend the festivities, although girls up to about the age of 12 are present until sunset.

SAND BATHING AT GEBEL DAKRUR

If you thought a soak in a hot spring was invigorating, wait until you try a dip in one of the scalding-hot sand baths of **Gebel Dakrur**, several kilometres southeast of Siwa Town. From July to September, people flock here from all over the world to take turns at being immersed up to their necks in a bath of very hot sand for up to 20 minutes at a time. Local doctors claim that a treatment regime of three to five days can cure rheumatism and arthritis – and judging by the number of repeat customers they get they might just be on to something. There are several places around the western slope of the mountain where you can get therapeutically sand-dunked. **Sherif Sand Bath** (Map p293; ☎0100 366 1905; treatments E£115-160; Jun-Sep) has a good reputation. Expect to pay E£115 to E£160 for each treatment, which includes food and overnight lodging.

The mountain also supplies the oasis with the reddish-brown pigment used to decorate Siwan pottery. Siwans believe that the mountain is haunted and claim that *afrit* (spirits) can be heard singing in the gardens at night.

Sleeping

Siwa Town has a great collection of places to bed down in, with everything from competitively priced budget pads to dazzling top-end options. Many midrange and top-end sleeping options can also be found further afield in Siwa Oasis, around Gebel Dakrur and Sidi Jaafar.

The police here are jittery about people camping close to town. If you want to sleep in the desert, it's best to organise a tour with a local guide.

Siwa Town

Kelany Hotel HOTEL $
(Map p294; ☎0102 336 9627; Sharia Azmi Kilani; s/d/tr E£80/120/150;) Kelany's small rooms may be showing their age but they're still a step above other budget places in Siwa; if you're looking for a cheap sleep with air-con and working wi-fi, this is your best bet. The rooftop restaurant (meals E£35) features views of the Fortress of Shali, Gebel Dakrur and everything in between. Breakfast is not included.

Palm Trees Hotel HOTEL $
(Map p294; ☎460 1703, 0122 104 6652; m_s_siwa@yahoo.com; Sharia Torrar; s/d E£35/50, without bathroom E£25/35, bungalow s/d E£50/70, r with air-con E£75;) If you can handle the mosquitoes (seriously, bring bug-spray), then this popular budget hotel is a lovely place to stay It has sufficiently tidy rooms boasting screened windows, fans and balconics. The shady garden with date-palm furniture is delightful and the few ground-level bungalows have porches spilling onto the greenery.

Yousef Hotel HOTEL $
(Map p294; ☎460 0678; Central Market Sq; s/d E£30/40, without bathroom E£20/30) This old-timer on the Siwa scene is still going strong. Yes, the rooms are tattered, but the rooftop has great views of the oasis, and if you're saving your *guinay* for desert exploits, you really can't beat the price. The central location means noise can be an issue and during summer only heat-masochists need apply.

★ Al-Babinshal BOUTIQUE HOTEL $$
(Map p294; ☎460 1499; www.siwa.com/accommodations.html; s/d E£285/365; Sep-Jun) This gorgeous, curvy mud-brick hotel is seamlessly grafted onto Shali fortress with its labyrinthine architecture all built from *kershef* bricks like the original fort. A maze of tunnels and stairways connects the spacious and cool rooms. Decor is distinctly desert style with date palm furniture, local textiles and traditional wooden-shuttered windows used in abundance to add to the local vibe.

★ Shali Lodge BOUTIQUE HOTEL $$
(Map p294; ☎0101 118 5820; www.siwa.com/accommodations.html; Sharia Subukha; s/d/tr/ste E£285/375/475/550; Sep-Jun;) This tiny, beautiful mud-brick hotel, owned by environmentalist Mounir Neamatallah, nestles in a lush palm grove about 100m from Siwa's main square. The large, extremely comfortable rooms have lots of curvacious mud-brick goodness, exposed palm beams, rock-walled bathrooms and cushioned sitting nooks. Tasteful and quiet, this is how small hotels should be.

Siwa Safari Gardens Hotel HOTEL $$
(Map p294; ☎460 2801; www.siwagardens.com; Sharia Ain al-Arais; s/d/tr half board E£270/370/470;) This simple but supremely tidy hotel gets all the little things right: superclean, bright rooms and a serene palm-shaded courtyard with a gleaming spring-fed pool. Ground-floor rooms are surprisingly plain, so bag a dome-ceilinged 2nd-floor room for more character. The staff here goes out of the way to help.

LOCAL KNOWLEDGE

RESPECTING LOCAL CUSTOMS

Take a look around, and when you see Siwan women, you probably won't glimpse more than an eye peeking out from behind a shawl. Modesty is serious business. When Western women wear shorts and tank tops here, it's about the same as walking naked around a stranger's home – in other words, you probably wouldn't do it. Perhaps even more than elsewhere in Egypt, travellers should dress conscientiously in Siwa. Women should cover legs, upper arms, and cleavage and men should stick to long pants rather than shorts. Displays of affection between couples should be saved for the hotel room. As with anywhere in the country, showing respect earns respect.

Desert Rose GUESTHOUSE $$
(☎0122 440 8164; ali_siwa@hotmail.com; r €15-40, bungalow €45-65;) This secluded guesthouse, overlooking the dunes, has spotless rooms (all share bathrooms) in a funky octagonal building and five bungalows in the garden, which has a clear spring-water pool. There are no electric lights, but a small generator can charge cameras and phones. The guests' kitchen makes it good for families and groups of friends.

Siwa Safari Paradise HOTEL $$
(Map p294; ☎460 1590; www.siwaparadise.com; Sharia Ain al-Arais; s/d E£350/450, bungalow US$67/75, with air-con US$96/124;) Laid out along a maze of garden paths, this resort-style hotel mainly attracts northern Europeans looking to sunbake by the natural spring pool. The spacious air-con bungalows are the pick of the bunch here with dome ceilings and little lounge areas. The cheaper rooms in the main building are rather bland and formulaic.

Sidi Jaafar

★**Adrère Amellal** LUXURY HOTEL $$$
(☎02-2736 7879; www.adrereamellal.net; Sidi Jaafar, White Mountain; s/d full board incl desert excursions US$460/605, ste from US$800;) Backed by the dramatic White Mountain (called Adrère Amellal in Siwi), this impeccable retreat lies in its own oasis, 13km from Siwa Town, with stunning views over Birket Siwa salt lake and the Great Sand Sea's dunes. It offers the ultimate in spartan-chic. Elegantly simple suites showcase traditional architecture techniques and there's no electricity; rooms are lit by candlelight and gardens by hurricane lamps.

When sandy adventures are done for the day, guests loll by the natural-spring swimming pool until it's time for a gourmet dinner eaten under the stars. This truly magnificent – and highly romantic – hideaway is one of Egypt's most special and innovative places to stay.

Taziry Ecolodge BOUTIQUE HOTEL $$$
(☎02-3337 0842, 0101 633 3200; www.taziry.com; Gaary; s/d/tr US$115/145/230, chalet from US$260;) This peaceful hotel 12km west of Siwa Town was designed and built by its friendly owners, an artist and an engineer, both from Alexandria. Large natural-material rooms are decorated with local crafts and Bedouin rugs. Tranquil and laid-back, with no electricity and a natural-spring pool overlooking the lake, it is a great place to unwind and experience Siwa's magic. Families can choose their own adobe chalet.

Gebel Dakrur

Qasr Alzaytuna HOTEL $
(Map p293; ☎0122 222 4209; www.alzaytuna.com; s/d/tr E£150/200/240;) Perfect for those who want a restful getaway, Qasr Alzaytuna has neat-as-a-pin rooms (some with dinky balconies) and a tranquil date-palm garden complete with spring-fed swimming pool. The important things are done right, like nice mattresses and modern bathrooms, and your host, Sammia, is as welcoming as could be. It's a great choice for families, and lies roughly 2km southeast of Siwa Town.

Tala Ranch Hotel BOUTIQUE HOTEL $$
(Map p293; ☎0100 588 8003; www.talaranch-hotel.com; s/d E£300/400) This low-key place offers generous helpings of hush and is as relaxing as things get with just six stylish, comfortable rooms and only the camels, desert and wind for distractions. Owner Sherif can organise camel safaris for guests, while his wife, Siham, prepares commendable Egyptian food served in a Bedouin tent (four-course dinner E£120). It's 5km southeast of Siwa's centre.

Siwa Shali Resort RESORT $$
(Map p293; ☎0100 630 1017; www.siwashaliresort.com; s/d/ste half board €26/52/70;) This self-contained village of traditionally styled bungalows snakes its way along a 500m spring-fed pool. While the rooms are nothing special, suites have sitting rooms with two mattresses, perfect for young kids. It's popular with European tour groups on all-inclusive packages, as it's 4km from town.

Eating

Most of the restaurants and cafes in Siwa cater to tourists and are open from about 8am until late. There are a couple of felafel/fuul joints plus an *aysh* (flatbread) bakery about 50m off the main square past the Kelany Hotel. For travellers looking for oasis ambience, there are several cosy palm-garden restaurants around Siwa serving the usual combination of Egyptian and Western fare.

★**Abdu's Restaurant** INTERNATIONAL $
(Map p294; ☎460 1243; Central Market Sq; dishes E£5-30; ⊙8.30am-midnight) Before wi-fi and

smartphones, there were places like this – a village hub where people gathered nightly to meet, catch up and swap stories. The longest-running restaurant in town remains the best eating option thanks to its friendly on-the-ball staff and a huge menu of breakfast, pasta, traditional dishes, vegetable stews, couscous, roasted chickens and pizza.

Abdu's is also prime territory for organising safaris and day trips with staff happy to dish out advice and information on all things 'Siwa'.

Nour al-Waha INTERNATIONAL **$**
(Map p294; ☎046 460 0293; Sharia Subukha; mains E£5-20; ⊙noon-midnight) This popular hang-out, in a palm grove opposite Shali Lodge, has shady tables and plenty of tea and games on hand for those who just want to while away the day in the shade. The food is a mixture of Egyptian and Western, and is generally fresh and good.

Al-Babinshal Restaurant EGYPTIAN **$$**
(Map p294; Fortress of Shali; mains E£20-55; ⊙8am-late Sep-Jun) On the roof of the hotel of the same name, this might just be the most romantic dining spot in the oases. Moodily lit in the evenings, it's practically attached to the Fortress of Shali and has sweeping views over all of Siwa. This is the place in town to try camel-meat stew.

Kenooz Siwa EGYPTIAN **$$**
(Map p294; ☎046 460 1299; Shali Lodge, Sharia Subukha; mains E£15-25; ⊙8am-midnight Sep-Jun) On the roof terrace of Shali Lodge, this cafe-restaurant is a great place to hang out while enjoying a mint tea or a cold drink. Mains include some unique Siwan specialities, such as baked lentils and eggplant with pomegranate sauce.

Abo Ayman Restaurant GRILL **$$**
(Map p294; off Sharia Sadat; meals E£13-23; ⊙11am-midnight) Roasted on a hand-turned spit over coals in an old oil drum, the chickens at Abo Ayman are the juiciest in Siwa. They're well seasoned, and served with salad, tahini and bread. You can sit inside at low tables, but we like the tables outside with street views.

Drinking & Nightlife

Many of the cafes around town are no-name places where Siwan men gather to watch TV and chat, but no alcohol is served. A couple of the most enjoyable cafes are found next to Cleopatra's Bath.

Shaqraza CAFE
(Map p294; Sharia Sidi Suleyman; 📶) The hippest cafe-restaurant in Siwa sits on a shaded rooftop overlooking the central square. Choose a regular table with chairs or lounge on cushions. Browse an extensive list of coffees, teas and juices, plus a full food menu (mains from E£5 to E£30). Throw in the wifi and this place seems like a sure hit.

Taghaghien Touristic Island BAR
(☎921 0060; admission E£25; ⊙10am-10pm) Desperate for a beer? This small island 12km northwest of Siwa Town and connected by a causeway is one of the few places selling the amber nectar (for a whopping E£35 a bottle). Shaded tables, paddleboat rentals and sweet sunset vistas make it great for a day trip or picnic. You'll need your own transport to get here.

Abdu Coffeeshop COFFEEHOUSE
(Map p294; Central Market Sq) Abdu's packs out nightly with local men smoking sheesha, downing tea and slapping backgammon pieces with triumphant vigour.

Zeytouna COFFEEHOUSE
(Map p294; Central Market Sq) Right in town, Zeytouna is a favourite evening haunt for local men drinking tea and coffee. Its tables often spill out onto the town square.

Shopping

Siwa's rich culture is well represented by the abundance of traditional crafts that are still made for local use as well as for tourists. There are a tonne of shops around Siwa Town selling very similar items, so browse around a bit before you buy. Happy haggling!

Siwan women love to adorn themselves with heavy silver jewellery and you should be able to find some interesting pieces around town. Local wedding dresses are famous for their red, orange, green and black embroidery, often embellished with shells and beads. Look for black silk *asherah nazitaf* and white cotton *asherah namilal* dresses.

A variety of baskets are woven from date-palm fronds. You can spot old baskets by their finer workmanship and the use of silk or leather instead of vinyl and polyester. The *tarkamt,* a woven plate that features a red leather centre, is traditionally used for serving sweets, the larger *tghara* is used for storing bread. Smaller baskets include the *aqarush* and the red-and-green silk-tasselled *nedibash*. You'll also find pottery coloured with pigment from Gebel Dakrur, used locally as water jugs, drinking cups and incense burners.

Siwa is also known for its dates and olives, found in every other shop around the main square. Ask to taste a few different varieties; you really can't go wrong.

Information

EMERGENCY

Tourist Police (Map p294; ☎460 2047; Siwa Town) Across the road from the tourist information office.

INTERNET ACCESS

There's a sprinkling of computers around the centre of town, most for E£10 per hour.

Al-Waha Internet (Map p294; Central Market Sq, Siwa Town; ⏲noon-midnight) Pay E£10 to E£15 per day for a wi-fi connection that works all around the centre of town, even into some of the hotels, giving you 24-hour internet access from your laptop. Good speeds.

Desert Net Cafe (Map p294; Siwa Town; per hr E£3; ⏲11am-3pm & 7pm-3am) The cheapest internet access in town, usually with decent connection speeds. It's on the street between King Fuad Mosque and the bank.

MEDICAL SERVICES

Hospital (Map p293; ☎460 0459; Sharia Sadat, Siwa Town) Only for emergencies.

Pharmacy Al-Ansar (Map p294; ☎460 1310; Sharia Sadat, Siwa Town; ⏲8am-2pm & 4pm-2am)

MONEY

Banque du Caire (Map p294; Siwa Town; ⏲8.30am-2pm & 5-8pm) Two-hundred metres north from the King Fuad Mosque, this bank is purported to be the only all-mud-brick bank in the world. The ATM usually works but – just in case – you're better off bringing enough money to Siwa with you. It's a long way to the next bank.

PERMITS

A permit is needed to venture off the beaten track from Siwa, but this is easily arranged by local guides. Mahdi Hweiti at the tourist office can also help arrange permits quickly (but not on Fridays). Permits cost E£140 per person, per day. The same rate applies for the permit needed to travel from Siwa to Bahariya. You'll need copies of your passport.

POST & TELEPHONE

Main Post Office (Map p294; Siwa Town; ⏲8am-2pm Sat-Thu) Twenty metres north of Banque du Caire.

Telephone Centrale (Map p294; Siwa Town; ⏲24hr) Just north of the tourist information office.

TOURIST INFORMATION

Tourist Office (Map p294; ☎460 1338; mahdi_hweiti@yahoo.com; Siwa Town; ⏲9am-2pm Sat-Thu, plus 5-8pm Oct-Apr) Siwa's tourist officer, Mahdi Hweiti, is extremely knowledgeable about the oasis and can help arrange desert safaris or trips to surrounding villages. His mobile number is ☎0100 546 1992. The office is opposite the bus station.

Getting There & Away

BUS

Siwa's **bus stop** (Map p294) and ticket office is opposite the tourist police station; when you arrive into town, however, you'll be let off near the central market square. It's sensible to buy your ticket ahead of time as buses are often full.

From the bus stop West & Middle Delta Bus Co buses depart for Alexandria (E£55, eight hours), via Marsa Matruh (E£30, four hours) at 7am, 10am and 10pm. The 10pm service costs E£10 more. The daily Cairo–Siwa direct bus service had been temporarily suspended while we were in town, meaning travellers had to change buses in Alexandria. We were assured it should be back on the schedule by the time you read this and will cost E£120.

MICROBUS

Microbuses going to Marsa Matruh (E£30) leave from the main square near the King Fuad Mosque. They are more frequent and *way* more comfortable than the West & Middle Delta bus, and the same price.

4WD

The Siwa–Bahariya road construction began in 2005 and, after many delays, is now nearly completely asphalted, except for a small gravel portion about halfway along that is still being finished. The whole distance (about 400km) can be crossed in five hours. A 4WD is necessary and there is no public transport along the route. Drivers and the required permits to journey this way are easy to arrange at either end. You'll pay about E£1500 per car, so team up with others to share the cost. If you can afford it, it's totally worth it, both for the scenery and to avoid the buzzkill of going through Alexandria and Cairo just to travel from one oasis to the next. Ensure that the vehicle is a roadworthy 4WD and that you have plentiful food and water.

TO/FROM LIBYA

Though Siwa is only about 50km from the Libyan border, it's currently illegal to leave or enter either country along this stretch of the frontier.

Getting Around

BICYCLE

Bicycles are one of the best ways to get around and can be rented from several sources, including most hotels and a number of shops dotted around the town centre. Getting a bike from one of the bicycle repair shops gives you a better chance of finding a bike in good condition. The going rate is E£15 to E£20 per day.

DONKEY CART

Caretas (donkey carts) are a much-used mode of transport for Siwans and can be a more amusing, if slower, way to get around than bicycles or cars. Some of the boys who drive the carts speak English and can be fierce hagglers. Expect to pay about E£30 for two to three hours, or E£10 for a short trip.

MOTORCYCLE

Though not as enjoyable or tranquil as bicycles, motorbikes can also be rented. You can pick one up from the bike shop next to Al-Babinshal Hotel, or at Palm Trees Hotel. Expect to pay between E£100 and E£200 per day.

SERVEES

Pick-up trucks serve as communal taxis linking Siwa Town with surrounding villages. To get to Bilad ar-Rum costs E£1 each way. If you want to hire your own to get to more remote sites, Mahdi Hweiti at the tourist office will be able to help, or head for the petrol station and talk directly to drivers. One reliable, English-speaking driver with a good-quality vehicle is Anwar Mohammed (☎ 0122 687 3261). Prices are per truck, not per passenger, and depend on the duration of the trip, the distance to be covered and, of course, your haggling skills.

BEYOND SIWA

Qara Oasis

Qara (pronounced 'Ghara') Oasis lies about 120km northeast of Siwa as the crow flies, near the Qattara Depression. This remote oasis is home to 317 Berbers who, like the Siwans, built their fortresslike town on top of a mountain. The old clifftop fortress, no longer inhabited, is in a decent state of preservation; there are springs to swim in; and the palm gardens are beautiful (but the mosquitoes are fierce).

There are a number of legends as to how the population here remained constant over the years: according to one, mystical forces kept things in balance, so for every birth or new arrival, someone living in the village would die. Needless to say, visitors to Qara were discouraged from spending the night! Nowadays this superstition is largely disregarded, but there aren't any hotels and most travellers visit on a day trip.

A car and driver from Siwa should cost E£800 for a round trip; when the new road out here is finally finished this price will probably drop to E£400 to E£500.

Note: some locals in Siwa may suggest bringing candies for the local kids in Qara, but we strongly discourage this, both because it's bad for their teeth and because we've seen what happens in places where kids learn to think every tourist is laden with sweets.

Great Sand Sea

One of the world's largest dune fields, the Great Sand Sea straddles Egypt and Libya, stretching over 800km from its northern edge near the Mediterranean coast south to Gilf Kebir. Covering a colossal 72,000 sq km, it contains some of the largest recorded dunes in the world, including one that is 140km long. Aerial surveys and expeditions have helped the charting of this vast expanse, but it remains one of the least-explored areas on the planet.

Crescent, *seif* (sword) and *barchan* dunes are found here in abundance, and have challenged desert travellers and explorers for hundreds of years. The Persian king Cambyses is thought to have lost an army here, while the WWII British Long Range Desert Group spent months trying to find a way through the impenetrable sands to launch surprise attacks on the German army.

The Great Sand Sea is not a place to go wandering on a whim, and you will need permits as well as good preparation. Guides can take you to the edges of the Great Sand Sea from Siwa, and many safari outfits will take you on expeditions that skirt the area. Remember that you don't need to penetrate far into the desert in order to feel the isolation, beauty and enormous scale of this amazing landscape.

Alexandria & the Mediterranean Coast

Includes ➡

Best Places to Eat

- Picnic at Agiba Beach (p335)
- Zephyrion (p330)
- Kadoura (p323)
- Mohammed Ahmed (p322)
- Greek Club (p323)

Best Places to Stay

- Cecil Hotel (p321)
- Egypt Hotel (p321)

Why Go?

Egypt's northern coastline runs for 500km along Mediterranean shores. Its sandy beaches and turquoise-hued sea lures floods of Egyptians here during the summertime. Most travellers, however, make a beeline straight to the once-great port city of Alexandria. Eulogised through the centuries, this faded old dame of a metropolis continues to be celebrated today in Egyptian music and literature despite its well-worn facade. By far Egypt's most atmospheric city, Alexandria's fresh sea air, fantastic seafood, ancient history and crumbling gems of belle époque buildings imbue it with an urban pulse distinctly different from that of Cairo.

To delve deeper into this region, take a pilgrimage to the sobering, beautifully kept WWII war memorials of El Alamein. Or amble the souq streets of Rosetta, edged by Ottoman-era architecture and brimming with time-stood-still ambience.

When to Go

Alexandria

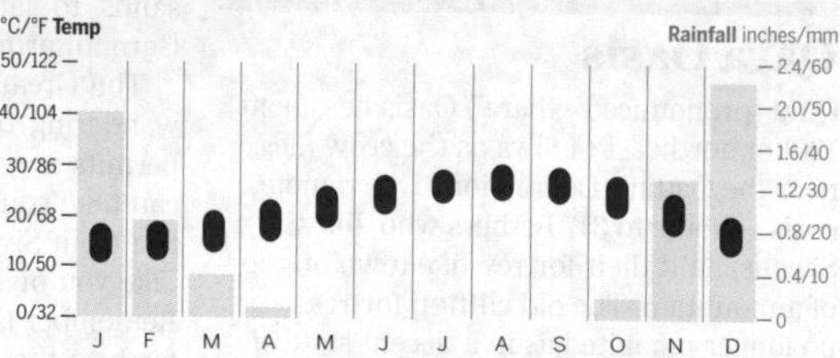

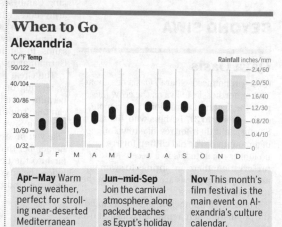

Apr–May Warm spring weather, perfect for strolling near-deserted Mediterranean shores.

Jun–mid-Sep Join the carnival atmosphere along packed beaches as Egypt's holiday season begins.

Nov This month's film festival is the main event on Alexandria's culture calendar.

ALEXANDRIA

☎03 / POP 4.1 MILLION

Founded by none other than Alexander the Great and once the seat of Queen Cleopatra, the city of Alexandria (Al-Iskendariyya) is the stuff that legends are made of. Its harbour entrance was once marked by the towering Pharos lighthouse (one of the Seven Wonders of the Ancient World) and its Great Library was renowned as the ultimate archive of ancient knowledge. Alas, fate dealt the city a spate of cruel blows. The Pharos lighthouse collapsed. The literary treasures of the Great Library were torched. Today no sign remains of the great Alexander himself and the city of Cleopatra has been mostly swallowed up by the ocean. To add insult to injury, Egypt's subsequent Muslim rulers moved the capital to Cairo, ignobly thrusting the once-influential metropolis into near obscurity for centuries.

In the 19th century Alexandria was revived by a cosmopolitan makeover that flirted with European-style decadence. The city's renaissance, as one of the Mediterranean's key commercial hubs, brought with it a new, swaggering fame, lauded by writers and poets. This revival, though, was cut short in the 1950s by President Nasser's nationalism. Today the peeling, faded and scarred remnants of this later period pockmark the once-grand seafront Corniche, ingraining the city with an aching sense of abandoned glory. Alexandria is a champion survivor, however, and today is striving to forge a new identity as Egypt's cultural capital. Legions of young local artists and writers are finding their voices here, and the modern library of Alexandria is probably the most innovative cultural landmark in the country.

But for many visitors, Alexandria remains a city of ambience rather than sights. After you've deciphered its mind-boggling history amid museums and monuments, it's the ideal place to spend time sipping coffee in old-world cafes, and meandering the harbour area to gaze up at belle époque architecture

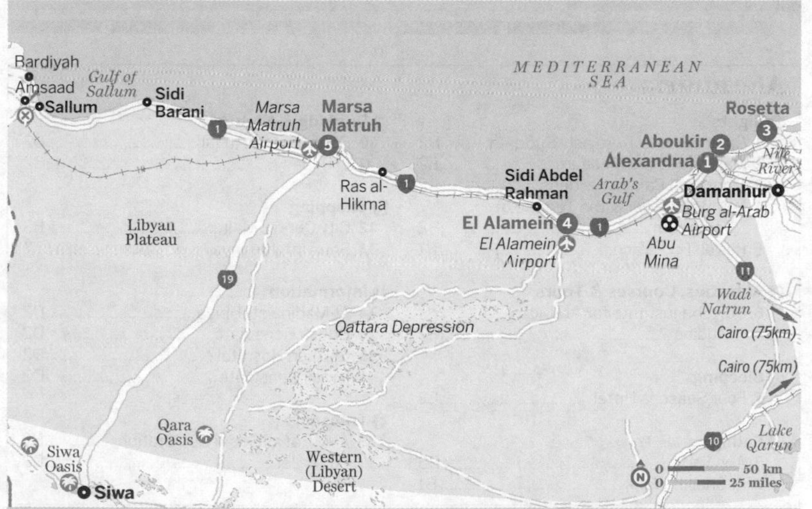

Alexandria & the Mediterranean Coast Highlights

1. Tour the modern incarnation of an ancient wonder at the **Bibliotheca Alexandrina** (p313), tasting the last drops of 19th-century grandeur at a period cafe, and stroll the streets and souqs of soulful Anfushi at night in **Alexandria**.
2. Eat your fill of fresh seafood along the shore at **Aboukir** (p330).
3. Amble through the dusty, donkey-filled streets of **Rosetta** (Ar-Rashid; p330), where narrow lanes are rimmed by restored Ottoman-era architecture.
4. Remember the desert battles of WWII's North Africa campaign at the poignant war memorials of **El Alamein** (p331).
5. Splashing about in stunning aqua waters at the beaches near **Marsa Matruh** (p335).

Alexandria

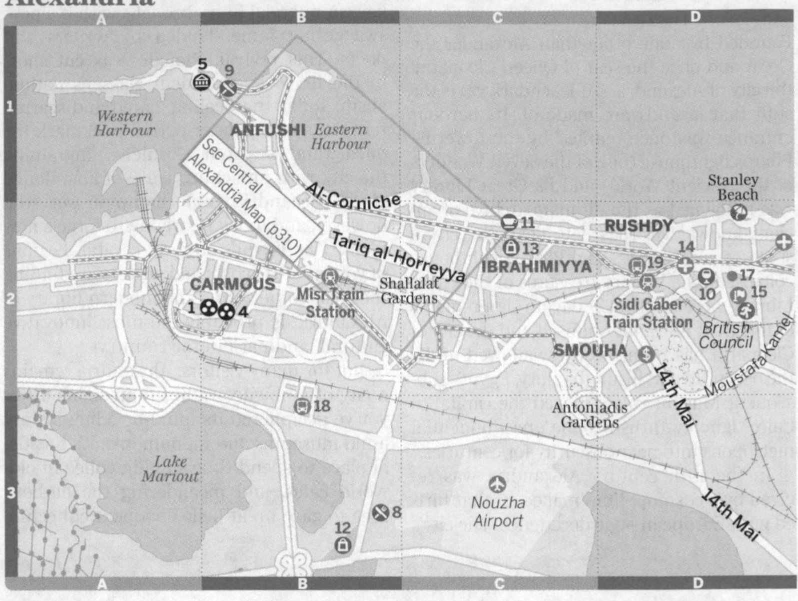

Alexandria

Sights
1 Catacombs of Kom ash-Suqqafa B2
2 Mahmoud Said Museum......................E2
3 Montazah Palace Gardens G2
4 Pompey's Pillar & the Temple of Serapeum B2
5 Ras el-Tin Palace.................................B1

Activities, Courses & Tours
6 Qortoba Institute for Arabic Studies F2

Sleeping
7 Four Seasons Hotel E2

Eating
8 Abo Faris B3
9 El-Sheikh Wafik B1

Drinking & Nightlife
10 Centro de Portugal..............................D2
11 El Rehany C2

Shopping
12 City Center Mall B3
13 Souq Ibrahimiyya C2

Information
14 Al-Madina at-Tibiya.............................D2
15 British Consulate................................D2
16 German Hospital D2
17 Israeli Consulate.................................D2

Transport
18 Al-Mo'af al-Gedid Bus Station B3
19 Super Jet D2

and ponder the ghosts of the past. The facade of this city may have tarnished down the centuries but its allure has not diminished.

History

Alexandria's history bridges the time of the pharaohs and the days of Islam. The city gave rise to the last great Pharaonic dynasty (the Ptolemies); provided the entry into Egypt for the Romans; nurtured early Christianity; then rapidly faded into near obscurity when Islam's invading armies passed it by to set up camp on a site along the Nile that later became Cairo.

The city was conceived by Alexander the Great, who arrived from Sinai having had his right to rule Egypt confirmed by the priests of Memphis. Here, on the shores of his familiar sea, he chose a fishing village as the site for a new city that he hoped would link the old Pharaonic world and the new world of the Greeks. Foundations were laid

in 331 BC, and almost immediately Alexander departed for Siwa in order to consult the famous oracle, before then marching for Persia. His conquering army went as far as India, and after his death at Babylon in 323 BC the rule of Egypt fell to the Macedonian general Ptolemy. Ptolemy won a struggle over Alexander's remains and buried them somewhere around Alexandria.

Ptolemy masterminded the development of the new city, filling it with architecture to rival Rome or Athens and establishing it as the cultural and political centre of his empire. To create a sense of continuity between his rule and that of the Pharaonic dynasties, Ptolemy made Alexandria look at least superficially Egyptian by adorning it with sphinxes, obelisks and statues scavenged from the old sites of Memphis and Heliopolis. The city developed into a major port and became an important halt on the trade routes between Europe and Asia. Its economic wealth was equally matched by its intellectual standing. Its famed library stimulated some of the great advances of the age: this was where Herophilus discovered that the head, not the heart, is the seat of thought; Euclid developed geometry; Aristarchus discovered that the earth revolves around the sun; and Eratosthenes calculated the earth's circumference. A grand tower, the Pharos, one of the Seven Wonders of the Ancient World, was built on an island just offshore and served as both a beacon to guide ships entering the booming harbour and an ostentatious symbol of the city's greatness.

During the reign of its most famous regent, Cleopatra (51–30 BC), Alexandria rivalled Rome in everything but military power – a situation that Rome found intolerable and was eventually forced to act upon. Under Roman control, Alexandria remained the capital of Egypt, but during the 4th century AD, civil war, famine and disease ravaged the city's populace and it never regained its former glory. Alexandria's fall was sealed when the conquering Muslim armies swept into Egypt in the 7th century and bypassed Alexandria in favour of a new capital on the Nile.

Alexandria remained in decline through the Middle Ages and was even superseded in importance as a seaport by the nearby town of Rosetta (Ar-Rashid). Over the centuries its monuments were destroyed by earthquakes and their ruins quarried for building materials, so much so that one of the greatest cities of the classical world was reduced to little more than a fishing village (now Anfushi), with a population of less than 10,000.

ALEXANDRIA IN...

Two Days

Start day one sipping coffee at one of the city's many period cafes, then get a taste of the past at the excellent **Alexandria National Museum** (p309). Follow that up with lunch at the bustling **Mohammed Ahmed** (p322), deservedly regarded as the king of fuul (fava bean paste) and felafel. Having gained a sense of the city's history, explore the future at the iconic **Bibliotheca Alexandrina** (p313), checking out several of its must-see museums and exhibits. When done, head across the street to **Selsela Cafe** (p324) for some tea or ahwa (coffee), as the waves of the bay roll in alongside. Hop into a microbus and ride the length of the Corniche, all the way down to **Fort Qaitbey** (p313), a scenic spot for sunset, then walk back to the centre of town through the streets and souqs of **Anfushi**, stopping for a seafood dinner sooner – at **Kadoura** (p323) – or later – at **Farag** (p323).

On day two, get an early start at the **Anfushi Fish Market** (p327), one of the liveliest souqs in Egypt. Stop off for breakfast at **Delices** (p325), then decide: if you want ancient sights, head to **Kom al-Dikka** (p310) and the underground **Catacombs of Kom ash-Shuqqafa** (p316); but if you're up for the **beach** (p319) – and some great people-watching – head for one of the sandy strips along the shore to the east. For dinner, try something different at casual grilled-quail joint **Malek es-Seman** (p322). Finish off your day with an evening drink at the atmospheric **Cap d'Or** (p324), or tea and a sheesha at **El Tugareya** (p324).

Four Days

Follow the two-day itinerary, then add a day trip to **Rosetta** (Ar-Rashid; p330) and the mouth of the Nile, and on the fourth day head to **El Alamein** (p331) and spend the afternoon on the beach in **Sidi Abdel Rahman** (p334).

The turning point in Alexandria's fortunes came with Napoleon's invasion of 1798; recognising the city's strategic importance, he initiated its revival. During the subsequent reign of the Egyptian reformist Mohammed Ali, a new town was built on top of the old one. Alexandria once more became one of the Mediterranean's busiest ports and attracted a cosmopolitan mix of people, among them wealthy Turkish-Egyptian traders, Jews, Greeks, Italians and many others from around the Mediterranean. Multicultural, sitting on the foundations of antiquity, perfectly placed on the overland route between Europe and the East, and growing wealthy from trade, Alexandria took on an almost mythical quality and served as the muse for a new string of poets, writers and intellectuals. But the wave of anticolonial, pro-Arab sentiment that swept Colonel Gamal Abdel Nasser to power in 1952 also spelt the end for Alexandria's cosmopolitan communities. Those foreigners who didn't stream out of the country in the wake of King Farouk's yacht found themselves forced out a few years later following the Suez Crisis, when Nasser confiscated foreign properties and nationalised many foreign-owned businesses.

Since that time the character of the city has changed completely. In the 1940s some 40% of the city's population was made up of foreigners, while now most of its residents are native Egyptians. Where there were 300,000 residents in the 1940s, Alexandria is now home to more than four million.

Many people credit events that happened here with lighting the fuse that exploded into the 2011 revolution. In June 2010 a 28-year-old man named Khaled Said was beaten to death by police in Alexandria, apparently after he posted videos on the internet showing police pocketing drugs confiscated in a bust. Soon after the murder, a Facebook page called 'We are all Khaled Said' was created, showing photos of the young man's horribly smashed face and publicly exposing police accounts of his death as blatant fabrications. Outraged, tens of thousands of Egyptians 'friended' the page. A series of protests were held in Alexandria demanding justice. Khaled Said's killing, and the subsequent cover-up, became a symbol of everything believed to be wrong with the regime under President Mubarak. By January 2011, nearly 380,000 people had joined the Facebook page, and its moderator, Google executive Wael Ghonim, used it as a virtual megaphone to call for the demonstrations in Cairo's Tahrir Sq that ultimately ousted Mubarak. Alexandria itself saw some of the largest and most intense protests in the entire country during the 2011 revolution, forcing a complete retreat of the police from the city's streets.

Sights

Modern Alexandria lies protracted along a curving shoreline, stretching for 20km and rarely extending more than 3km inland. The centre of the city arcs around the Eastern Harbour, almost enclosed by two spindly promontories. The city's main tram station at Midan Ramla, where most lines terminate, is considered the epicentre of the city. Two of the city centre's main shopping streets, Sharia Saad Zaghloul and Sharia Safiyya Zaghloul, run off this square. Just west of the tram station is the larger and more formal square, Midan Saad Zaghloul, with a popular garden facing the seafront. Around these two midans are the central shopping areas, the tourist office, restaurants and the majority of the cheaper hotels.

Northwest of this central area is the older, atmospheric neighbourhood of Anfushi; southwest is Carmous, which has some notable Roman ruins. Heading east, a succession of newer districts stretches along the coast to the upmarket residential area of Rushdy and the trendy suburbs of San Stefano, and further on to Montazah, with its palace and gardens, which marks the eastern limits of the city. The Corniche (Al-Corniche) is the long coastal road that connects nearly all parts of the city, though crossing it involves playing chicken with swarms of hurtling buses and taxis.

If you're spending significant time in the city, the street map produced by Mohandes Mostafa el Fadaly (p327) is very useful.

Central Alexandria

'Like Cannes with acne' was Michael Palin's verdict on Alexandria's sweeping seafront **Corniche** (in his book *Around the World in 80 Days*). Right in the middle of the broad Corniche is the legendary Cecil Hotel (p321) overlooking Midan Saad Zaghloul. Built in 1930, it's an Alexandrian institution and a memorial to the city's raffish heyday, when guests included the likes of Somerset Maugham, Noël Coward and Winston Churchill, and the British Secret Service operated out of a suite on the 1st floor. The hotel was eternalised in Lawrence Durrell's *Alexandria Quartet*.

★ **Alexandria National Museum** MUSEUM
(Map p310; 110 Sharia Tariq al-Horreyya; adult/student E£40/25; ⌚9am-4.30pm) This excellent museum sets a high benchmark for summing up Alexandria's past. With a small, thoughtfully selected and well-labelled collection singled out from Alexandria's other museums, it does a sterling job of relating the city's history from antiquity until the modern period.

Housed in a beautifully restored Italianate villa, it stocks several thousand years of Alexandrian history, arranged chronologically

THE PHAROS

The Egyptian coast was a nightmare for ancient sailors, the flat featureless shoreline making it hard to steer away from hidden rocks and sandbanks. To encourage trade, Ptolemy I (323–283 BC) ordered a great tower to be built, one that could be seen by sailors long before they reached the coast. After 12 years of construction, the Pharos was inaugurated in 283 BC. The structure was added to until it acquired such massive and unique proportions that ancient scholars regarded it as one of the Seven Wonders of the Ancient World.

In its original form the Pharos was a simple marker, probably topped with a statue, as was common at the time. The tower became a lighthouse, so historians believe, in the 1st century AD, when the Romans added a beacon, probably an oil-fed flame reflected by sheets of polished bronze. According to descriptions from as late as the 12th century, the Pharos had a square base, an octagonal central section and a round top. Contemporary images of the Pharos still exist, most notably in a mosaic in St Mark's Basilica in Venice and another in a church in eastern Libya, and in two terracotta representations in Alexandria's Graeco-Roman Museum.

In all, the Pharos withstood winds, floods and the odd tidal wave for 17 centuries; however, in 1303 a violent earthquake rattled the entire eastern Mediterranean and the Pharos was finally toppled. More than a century later the sultan Qaitbey quarried the ruins for the fortress that still stands on the site.

Central Alexandria

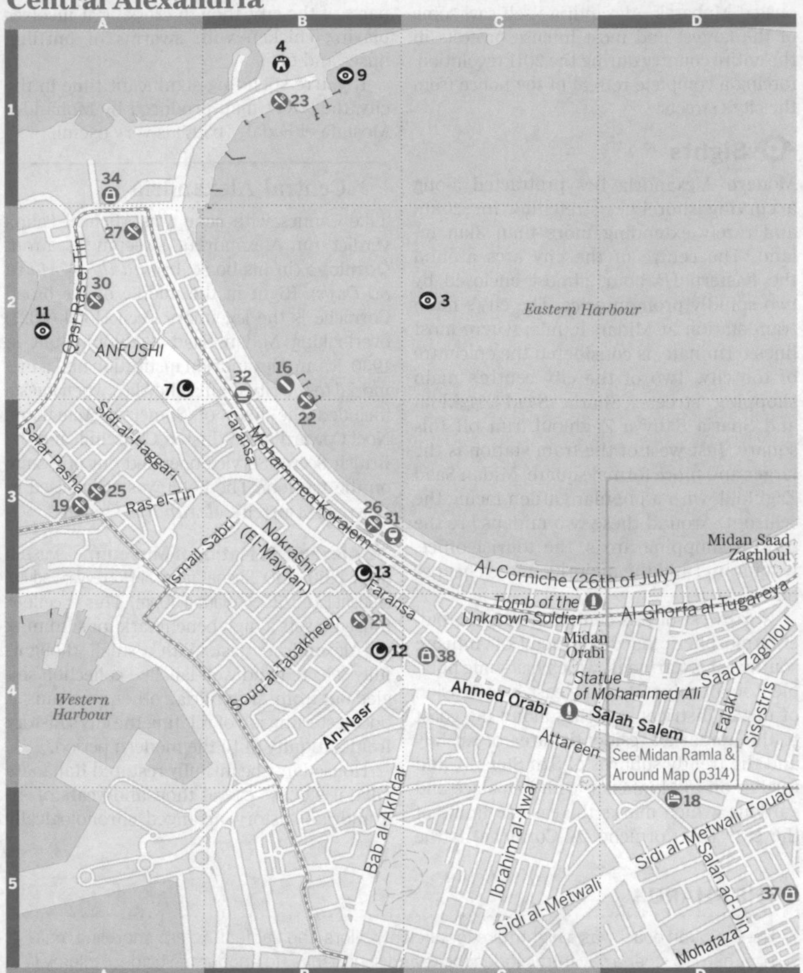

over three floors. Well-written information panels throughout provide useful insights into the life and beliefs of Alexandrians through the centuries.

The **ground floor** is dedicated to Graeco-Roman times, and highlights include a sphinx and other sculptures found during underwater excavations at Aboukir. Look for the small statue of the Greek god Harpocrates with a finger to his lips (representing silence); he was morphed from the original Egyptian god Horus. Also check out the beautiful statue of a Ptolemaic queen, with Egyptian looks and a Hellenistic body.

The **basement** covers the Pharaonic period, with finds from all over Egypt. The **top floor** displays artefacts from the Byzantine, Islamic and modern periods, with coins, Ottoman weapons and jewels. Don't miss the exquisite silver shield. Early coexistence of Alexandria's major religions is represented by a carved wooden cross encircled by a crescent.

Kom al-Dikka ARCHAEOLOGICAL SITE
(Map p310; Sharia Yousri; adult/student E£30/15; ⌚9am-4.30pm) This site was discovered when foundations were being laid for an

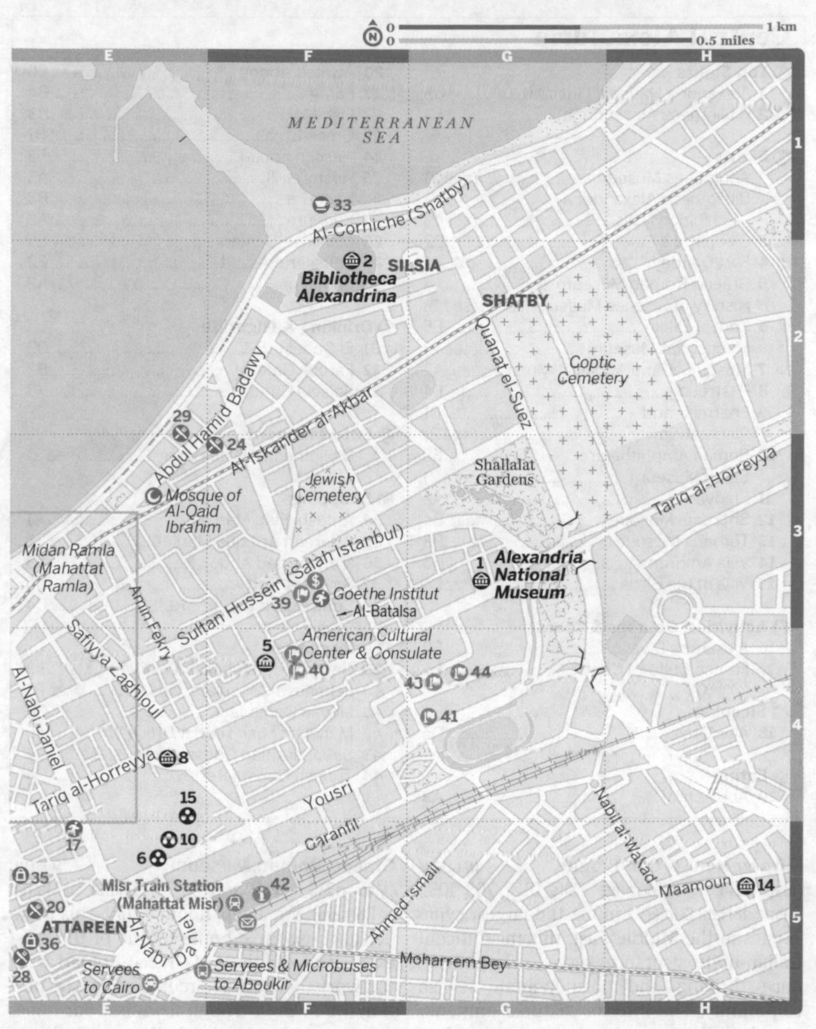

apartment building on a site known unceremoniously as Kom al-Dikka (Mound of Rubble). In Ptolemaic times this area was known as the Park of Pan, a pleasure garden where citizens of Alexandria could indulge in various lazy pursuits. Although the ruins aren't terribly impressive, they remain a preserved ode to the days of the centurion and include the 13 white-marble terraces of the only **Roman amphitheatre** found in Egypt.

In the same complex is the **Villa of the Birds**, a wealthy urban dwelling that dates to the time of Hadrian (AD 117–138). Despite being redecorated at least four times in antiquity before being destroyed by fire in the 3rd century AD, its floor mosaic of pigeons, peacocks, quails, parrots and water hens remains astonishingly well preserved. Additional mosaics feature a panther, and a stylised flower design known as a rosette. To see the villa, buy a separate ticket at the site entrance.

Excavations continue to uncover more in the area. In early 2010 the ruins of a Ptolemaic-era temple were uncovered along with statues of gods and goddesses, including a number of the cat goddess Bastet.

Central Alexandria

Top Sights
- 1 Alexandria National Museum G3
- 2 Bibliotheca Alexandrina F2

Sights
- Antiquities Museum .... (see 2)
- Bibliotheca Alexandrina Exhibition Halls .... (see 2)
- 3 Cleopatra's Palace C2
- 4 Fort Qaitbey B1
- 5 Graeco-Roman Museum F4
- History of Science Museum .... (see 2)
- 6 Kom al-Dikka E5
- Manuscript Museum .... (see 2)
- 7 Mosque of Abu Abbas al-Mursi A2
- 8 Pastroudis E4
- 9 Pharos Island B1
- Planetarium .... (see 2)
- 10 Roman Amphitheatre E5
- Sadat Museum .... (see 2)
- 11 Shipyards A2
- 12 Shorbagi Mosque B4
- 13 Terbana Mosque B3
- 14 Villa Ambron H5
- 15 Villa of the Birds E4

Activities, Courses & Tours
- 16 Alexandra Dive B2
- 17 French Cultural Centre E5

Sleeping
- 18 Alex Otel D5

Eating
- 19 Abu Ashraf A3
- 20 Awalad Abdou E5
- 21 Farag B4
- 22 Fish Market B3
- 23 Greek Club B1
- 24 Hassan Fouad F3
- 25 Hosny Grill A3
- 26 Kadoura B3
- 27 Kadoura A2
- 28 Malek es-Seman E5
- 29 Patisserie Assad E2
- 30 Samakmak A2

Drinking & Nightlife
- 31 El Qobesi B3
- 32 Farouk Cafe B2
- 33 Selsela Cafe F1

Entertainment
- Bibliotheca Alexandrina .... (see 2)

Shopping
- 34 Anfushi Fish Market A1
- 35 Attareen Antique Market E5
- 36 Mohammed Abdo E5
- 37 Sayed el-Safty D5
- 38 Souq District C4

Information
- 39 German Consulate F3
- 40 Lebanese Consulate F4
- 41 Libyan Consulate G4
- 42 Mahattat Misr Tourist Office F5
- 43 Saudi Arabian Consulate G4
- 44 Turkish Consulate G4

Eliyahu Hanavi Synagogue SYNAGOGUE

(Map p314; ☎to arrange visits 0122 703 1031; Sharia al-Nabi Daniel) Among the largest synagogues in the Middle East, this magnificent Italian-built structure served Alexandria's once thriving and cosmopolitan Jewish community. The interior features immense marble columns and space for more than 700 people, with brass name plates still affixed to the regular seats of male worshippers. Since the wars with Israel and the 1956 Suez Crisis, the community has dwindled and rarely musters the 10 men necessary to hold a service.

Visits to this poignant and moving reminder of the city's multicultural past must be arranged through Ben Youssef Gaon, president of the local Jewish community and, aged in his 50s, among its youngest current members. Call Ben Youssef's mobile; if you can't make contact this way, try asking at the front gate. A donation of E£10 to E£20 is appreciated but not required.

Graeco-Roman Museum MUSEUM

(Map p310; ☎483 6434; 5 Sharia al-Mathaf ar-Romani) We keep hoping that this wonderful museum – home to one of the most extensive collections of Graeco-Roman art in the world – will have reopened by the next time we swing through town but our hopes continue to be thwarted. The restoration of this site has been dragging on for years and there is no official completion date for the work. Check with the tourist office when you arrive for any up-to-date information.

Anfushi & Fort Qaitbey

Charismatic Anfushi, the old Turkish part of town, was where stuffy Alexandria oncecame to let down its hair. While Midan Ramla and the Midan Tahrir area were developed along the lines of a European model in the 19th century, Anfushi remained untouched, an indigenous quarter standing in counterpoint to the new cosmopolitan city. This is where writer Lawrence Durrell's characters came in search of prostitutes and a bit of rough trade. Today it remains one of the poorer parts of the city, where a huge number of people live squeezed into atmospheric but old and decaying buildings, many of which seem to be teetering on the verge of collapse.

Fort Qaitbey FORTRESS
(Map p310; Eastern Harbour; adult/student E£25/15; ⏲9am-4pm) The Eastern Harbour is dominated by the bulky walls of Fort Qaitbey, built on a narrow peninsula over the remains of the legendary Pharos lighthouse by the Mamluk sultan Qaitbey in 1480. Finely restored, there is a warren of rooms to explore, and the walk here is just as rewarding. From Midan Ramla it's a 30- to 45-minute stroll along the Corniche with spectacular harbour views along the way. Alternatively, take yellow tram 15 from Midan Ramla or flag down a microbus along the Corniche. Taxi should cost E£5.

The Pharos lighthouse, which had been in use for some 17 centuries, was destroyed by an earthquake and lay in ruins for more than 100 years before Qaitbey ordered the fortification of the city's harbour. Material from the fallen Pharos was reused, and if you get close to the outer walls you can pick out some great pillars of red granite, which in all likelihood came from the ancient lighthouse. Other parts of the ancient building are scattered around the nearby seabed.

Mosque of Abu Abbas al-Mursi MOSQUE
(Map p310; Sharia Mohammed Koraiem) This stately mosque was originally the tomb of a 13th-century Sufi saint from Murcia in Spain. Today, it dominates a large midan (square) that covers an entire city block, which is easily visible and accessible from the Corniche. Several successive mosques have been built and rebuilt on the site; though the current structure dates to the modern era, it's still an attractive octagonal building with a soaring central tower and an interior decorated with eye-catching Islamic mosaics, tiling and woodwork.

Leave your shoes at the entrance and slip the attendant a little baksheesh (tip) when you collect them. Visitors can join devotees who still flock to **Al-Mursi's shrine** under the main floor. On summer nights a carnival-like atmosphere surrounds the mosque, where there's everything from pony rides to bumper cars to merry-go-rounds.

Terbana Mosque MOSQUE
(Map p310; Sharia Faransa) The beautiful little Terbana Mosque stands at the junction of Sharia Faransa and Wokalet al-Limon. This entire quarter, known as Gumruk, stands on land that was underwater in the Middle Ages. Late-17th-century builders incorporated bits of ancient Alexandria in the mosque's structure, reusing two classical columns to support the minaret. The red-and-black-painted brickwork on the facade is typical of Delta-style architecture. The **Shorbagi Mosque** (Map p310; Sharia Nokrashi), nearby, is also built with salvaged remnants of antiquity.

Shipyards WATERFRONT
(Map p310; Ras el-Tin) Where northern Anfushi hits the sea, you can wander among huge wooden vessels in various states of construction. In small workshops, craftspeople make accessories for the boats, such as intricately carved helms (steering wheels) and cabinets.

Ras el-Tin Palace HISTORIC BUILDING
(Map p306) Along Alexandria's western shore, past the shipyards, you'll spot Ras el-Tin Palace. Originally built in the 1830s for Mohammed Ali, it's now part of a naval base and was an official presidential residence. It was here that King Farouk signed his abdication papers in 1952. Unfortunately it's not open to visitors.

Eastern Suburbs

★Bibliotheca Alexandrina MUSEUM
(Map p310; ☎483 9999; www.bibalex.org; Al-Corniche, Shatby; adult/student combined ticket E£70/5; ⏲10am-4pm Sun-Thu) Alexandria's ancient library was one of the greatest of all

LOCAL KNOWLEDGE

FINDING ALEXANDRIA'S ANCIENT CORE

Interestingly, modern Alexandria is built directly on top of the ancient city and often follows the ancient street pattern. The street now known as Tariq al-Horreyya was the ancient Canopic Way, extending from the city's Gate of the Sun in the east to the Gate of the Moon in the west. The centre of town was where it crossed the Street of the Soma (now Sharia al-Nabi Daniel). In other words, if you stop at Vinous Cafe (p325), you can sip coffee right where the heart of the ancient city used to be.

Midan Ramla & Around

classical institutions, and while replacing it might seem a Herculean task, the new Bibliotheca Alexandrina manages it with aplomb. Opened in 2002, this impressive piece of modern architecture is a deliberate attempt to rekindle the brilliance of the original centre of learning and culture. The complex has become one of Egypt's major cultural venues, a stage for numerous international performers, and is home to a collection of museums.

The building takes the form of a gigantic angled discus embedded in the ground, evoking a second sun rising out of the Mediterranean. The granite exterior walls are carved with letters, pictograms, hieroglyphs and symbols from more than 120 different human scripts. Inside, the jaw-dropping main reading room can accommodate eight million books and 2500 readers under its sloping roof, with windows specially designed to let sunlight flood in but keep out rays that might harm the collection.

In addition to the main reading room, there are four specialised libraries (a children's library for ages six to 11; a youth library for ages 11 to 17; a multimedia library; and a library for the blind) and a huge array of other diversions. There are four permanent museums, a planetarium, a conference centre, a range of temporary and permanent exhibitions, and a full schedule of events. To fully explore this very worthy attraction, you should allot half a day, though to gape at the astounding main reading room and do a tour, you'll need an hour or so.

Tickets to the library can be bought outside the main entrance, where all bags must be checked. Audio guides are also available in English, Arabic and French.

Note that while the library has a wide range of kid-friendly activities and diversions, little ones under the age of six are not admitted to the library complex. Helpfully, day care is available during opening hours.

Midan Ramla & Around

Sights
1 Cavafy Museum ... D3
2 Eliyahu Hanavi Synagogue ... C2

Sleeping
3 Cecil Hotel ... B2
4 Egypt Hotel ... D1
5 Hotel Crillon ... B2
6 Hotel Union ... B2
7 Metropole Hotel ... C2
8 Swiss Canal Hotel ... A3
9 Triomphe Hotel ... B2
10 Windsor Palace Hotel ... B2

Eating
11 Abu Nasr ... B2
12 Chez Gaby ... D4
China House ... (see 3)
13 Gad ... C4
14 Gad ... D1
15 La Varanda ... C2
16 Mohammed Ahmed ... C2
17 Taverna ... D2

Drinking & Nightlife
18 Ahwa Sayed Darwish ... D3
19 Athineos ... D1
20 Cap d'Or ... A3
21 Delices ... C2
22 Drinkies ... B2
23 El Tugareya ... A2
24 Freshat Juice Bar ... D1
25 Imperial Cafe & Restaurant ... C2
26 Sofianopoulos Coffee Store ... A3
27 Spitfire ... A3
28 Trianon ... C2
29 Vinous ... D4

Entertainment
30 Alexandria Opera House ... D4

Shopping
31 Al-Maaref Bookshop ... C2
32 Mohandes Mostafa el Fadaly ... D2

Information
33 French Consulate ... A2
34 Italian Consulate ... C1
35 Main Tourist Office ... C2
36 Passport Office ... B4

Transport
Airport Bus Departures ... (see 3)
Avis ... (see 3)
37 EgyptAir ... D1
38 No 1 Minibus to Sidi Gaber ... C2
39 West & Mid Delta Bus Co ... C2

The library is on the seafront, and you can easily get there by taxi, microbus or by walking along the Corniche.

➡ The Museums

A beautifully displayed collection of ancient texts, antiquarian books and maps are hosted in the **Manuscript Museum**, including a copy of the only surviving scroll from Alexandria's ancient library.

The **Antiquities Museum** has a well-curated exhibition of artefacts that romp from the Egyptian, through the Greek and Roman periods, and into the Byzantine and Islamic eras. The focus though is on the Graeco-Roman period. The highlight display is of the antiquities discovered during underwater excavations in the harbour and at Aboukir. Also, the collection of finds unearthed when the foundations of the library were dug are particularly interesting, including a fine Roman mosaic of a dog.

In the **Sadat Museum**, ex-president Anwar Sadat's time in office is documented using a series of multimedia displays of the leader's speeches, photographs and information on the Egypt–Israel peace process that he brokered.

The **History of Science Museum** underneath the Planetarium is targeted at children of school age and covers the contribution to science of three key historic eras – Pharaonic Egypt, Hellenistic Alexandria and the Islamic era.

The Bibliotheca's **exhibition halls** are home to several permanent exhibitions including a hall showcasing the work of contemporary Arabic artists; a fascinating heritage collection with gorgeously displayed textiles, folk art and Arabic science equipment from the Medieval period; and the wonderful Impressions of Alexandria Exhibition, which does a sterling job of tracing the city's long history through drawings, maps and early photographs. There's also a video program on Egyptian history called the *Culturama*, displayed on nine screens.

The **Planetarium** is a futuristic neon-lit sphere looming on the plaza in front of the library, like a mini Death Star from *Star Wars*. It shows 3D films hourly on a rotating schedule (see website), and has an Exploratorium as well as the aforementioned History of Science Museum, which are both great for kids.

THE GREAT LIBRARY OF ALEXANDRIA

The original Library of Alexandria was the greatest repository of books and documents in all of antiquity. Ptolemy I (323–283 BC) established the library in 283 BC as part of a larger research complex known as the Mouseion (Shrine of the Muses; the source of today's word 'museum'). This dedicated centre of learning housed more than 100 full-time scholars and boasted lecture areas, gardens, a zoo, shrines and the library itself. Uniquely, this was one of the first major 'public' libraries and was open to all persons with the proper scholarly qualifications.

Demetrius Phalereus, a disciple of Aristotle, was charged with governing the library, and together with Ptolemy I and his successors he established the lofty goal of collecting copies of all the books in the world. Manuscripts found on ships arriving at Alexandria's busy port were confiscated by law and copied, and merchants were sent to scour the markets of other Mediterranean cities looking for tomes of all descriptions. Most books back then consisted of papyrus scrolls, often translated into Greek and rolled and stored in the library's many labelled pigeonholes. At its height the library was said to contain more than 700,000 works, which indicated some duplication, as this was believed to be more than the number of published works in existence. The library soon exceeded its capacity and a 'daughter library' was established in the Temple of Serapeum (p318) to stock the overflow. The vast collection established Alexandria's position as the pre-eminent centre of culture and civilisation in the world.

It is uncertain exactly who was responsible for the destruction of the ancient world's greatest archives of knowledge, though there are several suspects. Julius Caesar is the first. In his scrap with Pompey in 48 BC, Caesar set fire to Alexandria's harbour, which also engulfed the part of the city in which the library stood. Then in AD 270, Zenobia, Queen of Palmyra (now Syria), captured Egypt and clashed with Roman Emperor Aurelian here, the resulting siege destroying more of the library. At this time, Alexandria's main centre of learning moved to the daughter library in the Serapeum. Early Christians are next in line for the blame: the daughter library was finally destroyed as part of an anti-pagan purge led by Christian Roman Emperor Theodosius in AD 391.

Montazah Palace Gardens GARDENS
(Map p306; admission gardens/beach E£8/15) Khedive Abbas Hilmy (1892–1914) built Montazah as his summer palace, a refuge for when Cairo was too hot. It's designed in a pseudo-Moorish style, which has been given a Florentine twist with the addition of a tower modelled on one at Florence's Palazzo Vecchio. The palace itself is off limits but the surrounding lush gardens are prime strolling territory. The simplest way to get here is to stand on the Corniche or on Sharia Tariq al-Horreyya and flag down a microbus; when it slows, shout 'Montazah'; if it's going that way (most are), it'll stop and you can jump on.

There's an attractive sandy cove here with a semiprivate beach well suited to kids, although it's not particularly clean, and an eccentric Victorian-style bridge running out to a small island of pylons. In all, it's a pleasant escape from the city centre. A second royal residence on the grounds, known as the Salamlek and built in an Austrian style, has been converted into a luxury hotel.

Mahmoud Said Museum MUSEUM
(Map p306; 6 Sharia Mohammed Pasha Said, Gianaclis) Little known outside his home country, Mahmoud Said (1897–1964) was one of Egypt's finest 20th-century artists. A judge by profession, he moonlighted as a painter and became a key member of a group of sophisticates devoted to forging an Egyptian artistic identity in the 1920s and '30s. This museum presents about 40 of his works in the Italianate villa in which he once lived. The museum has been closed for restoration for a few years so check with the tourist office before making the trip out here. From the San Stefano tram stop (line 2), cross the tracks and go up the steps to the raised road (opposite the huge mall). Go right and Sharia Mohammed Pasha Said is a short distance away on the left.

Carmous

Catacombs of Kom ash-Suqqafa ARCHAEOLOGICAL SITE
(Map p306; adult/student E£40/25; 9am-5pm) Discovered accidentally in 1900 when a don-

key disappeared through the ground, these catacombs are the largest known Roman burial site in Egypt and one of the last major works of construction dedicated to the religion of ancient Egypt.

Demonstrating Alexandria's hallmark fusion of Pharaonic and Greek styles, the architects used a Graeco-Roman approach. The catacombs consist of three tiers of tombs and chambers cut into bedrock to a depth of 35m (the bottom level is flooded and inaccessible).

As impressive as all this sounds, if you've been to the tombs on Luxor's west bank, Kom ash-Shuqqafa will surely leave you underwhelmed: most of the walls are unadorned, nearly all the paintings faded to invisibility.

Entry is through a spiral staircase; the bodies of the dead would have been lowered on ropes down the centre of this circular shaft. The staircase leads off to a **rotunda** with a central well piercing down into the gloom of the flooded lower level. When the catacombs were originally constructed in the 2nd century AD, probably as a family crypt, the rotunda would have led only to the **triclinium** (to your left) and **principal tomb chamber** (straight ahead). But over the 300 years that the tomb was in use, more chambers were hacked out until it had developed into a hive that could accommodate more than 300 corpses.

The triclinium was a banqueting hall where grieving relatives paid their last respects with a funeral feast. Mourners, who returned to feast after 40 days and again on each anniversary, reclined on the raised benches at the centre of the room around a low table.

Back in the rotunda, head down the stairs to the principal tomb, the centrepiece of the catacombs. Here, an antechamber with columns and pediment leads through to an inner sanctum. The typical Alexandrian-style decoration shows an odd synthesis of ancient Egyptian, Greek and Roman funerary iconography. The doorway to the inner chamber is flanked by figures representing Anubis, the Egyptian god of the dead, but he

THE SIGHTS UNDER THE SEA

Alexandria has sunk between 6m and 8m since antiquity, so most of what remains of the ancient city lies hidden beneath the modern city or the waters of the Mediterranean. On land, much has been destroyed as the city has grown. But underwater the story is different, and each year reveals more finds from the Ptolemaic period.

So far, exploration has been concentrated around the fortress of Qaitbey, where the Pharos is believed to have stood; the southeastern part of the Eastern Harbour, where parts of the submerged Ptolemaic royal quarter were found; and Aboukir, where remains of the two sunken cities of Herakleion (Thonis) and Menouthis were found. Some of the recovered treasures can be seen in the Bibliotheca Alexandrina's Antiquities Museum (p315) and in the Alexandria National Museum (p309) but divers can also explore the submerged harbour sites with local company Alexandra Dive (p318).

If you feel like a bit of Indiana-Jones-under-the-sea action, the following are Alexandria's top dive sites:

Cleopatra's Palace (Map p310) This royal-quarter area in the Eastern Harbour has yielded some of Alexandria's most interesting underwater antiquities. Today divers can see a couple of large, enigmatic sphinxes as well as red-granite columns, platforms and pavements that archaeologists speculate formed part of a former palace. There's also a remarkably complete shipwreck here that has been carbon dated to between 90 BC and AD 130. Depth: 5m. Rating: novice.

Pharos Island (Map p310) This site, just offshore from Fort Qaitbey, contains sphinxes, columns, capitals and statues dating from the Pharaonic, Greek and Roman eras as well as giant granite blocks believed to be remnants of the Pharos Lighthouse, broken as if by a fall from a great height. Depth: 8m to 15m. Rating: novice.

Heracleion-Thonis For archaeologists the discovery of the port of Heracleon-Thonis in Aboukir has been a triumph of a discovery. Excavations have revealed a huge amount of treasures including giant 5m-high statues (raised from the site), remnants of temple buildings, and gold coins and jewellery. For the nonarchaeologist diver, though, the major sight in this area is the *L'Orient* wreck (Napoleon's flagship that sank in 1798). Depth: 14m. Rating: intermediate.

is dressed as a Roman legionary and sports a serpent's tail representative of Agathos Daimon, a Greek divinity.

From the antechamber a couple of short passages lead to a large U-shaped chamber lined with loculi – the holes in which the bodies were placed. After the body (or bodies, as many of the loculi held more than one) had been placed inside, the small chamber was sealed with a plaster slab.

Back up in the rotunda, four other passageways lead off to small clusters of tombs. One of these gives access to an entirely different complex, known as the **Hall of Caracalla**. This had its own staircase access (long since caved in) and has been joined to Kom ash-Shuqqafa, which it pre-dates, by industrious tomb robbers who hacked a new passageway. Beside the hole in the wall, a painting shows the mummification of Osiris and the kidnapping of Persephone by Hades, illustrating ancient Egyptian and Greek funerary myths.

You can easily walk to the catacombs from Pompey's Pillar, which is also located in Carmous. If walking from the pillar, start from in front of the ticket office. With your back to the entrance, take the small street to the right, slightly uphill and away from the tram tracks. Follow this street for several hundred metres past a small mosque on the left; the entrance to the catacombs is in the next block on your left. A taxi from Midan Saad Zaghloul to the catacombs costs around E£20.

Pompey's Pillar & the Temple of Serapeum ARCHAEOLOGICAL SITE

(Map p306; adult/student E£30/15; ⏲9am-4.30pm) This massive 30m column looms over the debris of the glorious ancient settlement of Rhakotis, the original township from which Alexandria grew. Known as Pompey's Pillar, for centuries the column, hewn from red Aswan granite, has been one of the city's prime sights: a single, tapered shaft, 2.7m at its base and capped by a fine Corinthian capital. The column rises out of the sparse ruins of the Temple of Serapeum, a magnificent structure that stood here in ancient times.

The column was named by travellers who remembered the murder of the Roman general Pompey by Cleopatra's brother, but an inscription on the base (presumably once covered with rubble) announces that it was erected in AD 291 to support a statue of the Emperor Diocletian.

Underneath the column, steps lead downwards to the great temple of Serapis, the god of Alexandria. Also here was the 'daughter library' of the Great Library of Alexandria, which was said to have contained copies and overflow of texts. These scrolls could be consulted by anyone using the temple, making it one of the most important intellectual and religious centres in the Mediterranean.

In AD 391 Christians launched a final assault on pagan intellectuals and destroyed the Serapeum and its library, leaving just the lonely pillar standing. The site is now little more than rubble pocked by trenches and holes, with a couple of narrow shafts from the Serapeum to explore below, a few sphinxes (originally from Heliopolis) and a surviving Nilometer (a structure used to measure and record the level of the Nile in ancient times). The pillar on top is the only ancient monument remaining whole and standing today in Alexandria.

When taking a taxi here, ask for it by the Arabic name, Amoud el-Sawari. The fare should be E£15 to E£20 from Midan Saad Zaghloul.

Activities & Tours

Alexandra Dive DIVING

(Map p310; ☎483 2045; www.alex-dive.com; Corniche, Anfushi; 2-dive package €80, with own equipment €60) Alexandria's diving experts, headed up by Dr Ashraf Sabry, who has been exploring the coastline here for decades. The company offers dive packages to the underwater archaeological sites in and around Alex, as well as to the WWI and WWII wreck dives offshore.

Be aware that visibility in the harbour waters can be an issue. Several divers have reported that poor visibility in the bay (as little as 1m depending on the time of year) affected their enjoyment of the harbour dives.

Tamer Zakaria GUIDED TOUR

(☎0122 370 8210; tamerzakaria@yahoo.com) A highly recommended English-speaking guide and Egyptologist, friendly and knowledgable, available for day guiding. He can also organise trips.

Festivals & Events

Bibliotheca Alexandrina International Summer Festival MUSIC

(www.bibalex.org; Bibliotheca Alexandrina; ⏲Aug) This month-long program of concerts is Alexandria's prime summer event, organised and taking place in the concert halls and performance spaces of the Bibliotheca Alexandrina. The program takes in the breadth of musical genres, from orchestral to traditional folk troupes.

Alexandria International Film Festival FILM
(http://alexandriafilm.org; ⌚Nov) The Alexandria International Film Festival takes place every November, and is a key event in Egypt's cinematic calendar. Independent film-makers from across the world showcase their work here. Screenings and Q&As with the directors take place at several cinemas and historic buildings around town.

Sleeping

Alexandria continues to suffer from a dearth of midrange hotels. Budget accommodation is well represented, with hotels running the gamut from downright seedy to decent. The selection of places to rest your head then quickly shoots straight into the top-end category with several five-star hotel chains and a handful of historic hotels along the seafront.

The summer months of June to September are Alexandria's high season, when half of Cairo seems to decamp here to escape the heat of the capital. Prebooking during this period is advised.

Quite a few of the budget hotels front at least partly onto the Corniche. One of the pleasures of staying in Alexandria is pushing open the shutters in the morning to get a face full of fresh air off the Mediterranean, but light sleepers may want to consider a room off the Corniche due to the unrelenting din of traffic. At any of Alexandria's budget hotels, it's wise to bring along your own soap, towel and toilet paper, as supplies can be erratic.

Hotel Union HOTEL $
(Map p314; ☎480 7312; 5th fl, 164 Al-Corniche; s E£120-230, d E£180-250, s/d without bathroom E£80/100; ❄📶) The Union is one of Alexandria's best budget options in the city centre and is always bustling with a mix of Egyptian holidaymakers and foreign travellers. The simple rooms (which come in a bewildering mix of bathroom/view/air-con rates) are well maintained, and cleanliness here far exceeds the city's usual haphazard hotel standards. It's a safe and solid backpacker choice.

Triomphe Hotel HOTEL $
(Map p314; ☎480 7585; adalabaza@hotmail.com; 3rd fl, Sharia Gamal ad-Din Yassin; d/tr E£150/180,

LOCAL KNOWLEDGE

HITTING THE BEACH IN ALEXANDRIA

If you want to get in the water, there are plenty of public and private beaches along Alexandria's waterfront. But the shoreline between the Eastern Harbour and Montazah can be grubby and packed to the rafters in summer, and most locals head for beaches on the North Coast for the high season. Women should note that at everywhere but the beaches owned by Western hotels, modesty prevails and covering up when swimming is strongly recommended – wear a baggy T-shirt and shorts over your swimsuit. At these and any city beaches, expect to pay an entrance fee and more for umbrellas and chairs, if desired.

Mamoura Beach (Map p306; area/beach entry E£4/8) About 1km east of Montazah, Mamoura is the 'beachiest' of Alexandria's beaches. There's a cobblestone boardwalk with a few ice-cream shops and food stalls, but what really makes this feel different from other beaches is the 800m between it and the main road, meaning there's no noisy speedway behind you. To get here, flag down an Aboukir-bound microbus along the Corniche and let the driver know you want Mamoura. Local authorities are trying to keep this suburb exclusive by charging everyone who enters the area, though you might not have to pay if you walk in. A much less crowded private beach is next to the main beach, with nice frond-type umbrellas and a E£40 per person entry fee.

Miami Beach (Map p306) Miami Beach (me-ami) has a sheltered cove with a water slide and jungle gym set-up in the sea for kids to frolic on, but note that these get almost comically crowded during peak season. It's 12.5km east of Midan Saad Zaghloul along the Corniche.

Stanley Beach (Map p306) This spectacular beach, on a tiny bay with Stanley Bridge soaring above it, has a modest patch of sand for bathing backed by three levels of beach cabins. The sight of the sea crashing against the bridge's concrete supports is dramatic, but this beach is not very suitable for kids due to the wave action.

LITERARY ALEXANDRIA

Alexandria is better known for its literature and writers than for any bricks-and-mortar monuments, and many a traveller arrives at Misr Train Station with a copy of Lawrence Durrell's *Alexandria Quartet* in hand. Unlike the Alexandria of ancient days past, the Alexandria evoked by Durrell, EM Forster and the Alexandrian-Greek poet Constantine Cavafy can still be seen draped over the buildings of the city's central area.

Born of Greek parents, Cavafy (1863–1933) lived all but a few of his 70 years in Alexandria. In some poems he resurrects figures from the Ptolemaic era and classical Greece; in others he captures fragments of the city through its routines or chance encounters. He was born into one of the city's wealthiest families, but a reversal of fortune forced him to spend most of his life working as a clerk for the Ministry of Public Works.

Cavafy was first introduced to the English-speaking world by EM Forster (1879–1970), the celebrated English novelist who'd already published *A Room with a View* and *Howards End* when he arrived in Alexandria in 1916. Working for the Red Cross, Forster spent three years in the city and, although it failed to find a place in his subsequent novels, he compiled what he referred to as an 'antiguide'. His *Alexandria: A History & Guide* was intended, he explained, as a guide to things not there, based on the premise that 'the sights of Alexandria are in themselves not interesting, but they fascinate when we approach them from the past'.

The guide provided an introduction to the city for Lawrence Durrell (1912–90), who arrived in Egypt 22 years after Forster's departure. Durrell had been evacuated from Greece and resented Alexandria, which he called a 'smashed up broken down shabby Neapolitan town'. But as visitors discover today, first impressions are misleading; between 1941 and 1945 Durrell found great distraction in the slightly unreal air of decadence and promiscuity engendered by the uncertainties of the ongoing desert war, which led to the writing of his most famous work.

Travellers on a literary pilgrimage may want to hunt down these lesser-seen sights:

Cavafy Museum (Map p314; ☎486 1598; 4 Sharia Sharm el-Sheikh; adult/child E£15/free; ⏰10am-4pm Tue-Sun) Cavafy spent his last 25 years in an apartment, above a brothel, on the former Rue Lepsius (now Sharia Sharm el-Sheikh). With a Greek church (St Saba Church) around the corner and a hospital opposite, Cavafy thought this was the ideal place to live; somewhere to cater for the flesh, somewhere to provide forgiveness for sins, and a place in which to die. Now preserved as the Cavafy Museum, two of the six rooms are arranged as Cavafy kept them. Editions of the poet's publications and photocopies of his manuscripts, notebooks and correspondence lie spread out on tables throughout the rooms.

Villa Ambron (Map p310; 19 Sharia Maamoun) Committed fans of the *Alexandria Quartet* might like to search out Villa Ambron, where Durrell lived and wrote during the last two years of WWII. Gilda Ambron, whose name appeared in the Quartet's 'Balthazar', painted with her mother in a studio in the garden that they shared with their neighbour Clea Badaro, who provided inspiration for the character of Clea in the *Quartet*. Durrell's room was on top of an octagonal tower in the garden. Sadly the place has deteriorated badly over the past couple of decades but if you're up for a pilgrimage anyway, from Misr Train Station walk southeast down Sharia Moharrem Bey, then at the little square at the end turn left onto Sharia Nabil al-Wakad. Sharia Maamoun is about 200m along on the right. Villa Ambron is at No 19.

Pastroudis (Map p310; Sharia Tariq al-Horreyya) If possessed by literary nostalgia, you can make a detour to the place where the famous Pastroudis Cafe once stood. Now closed, this was a meeting point for the characters of Lawrence Durrell's *Alexandria Quartet*.

s/d without bathroom E£75/130) The homely Triumph has a leafy lobby that feels like you've wandered into someone's living room. Spacious rooms cling to shreds of former elegance, with high ceilings and dark-wood furniture, though some are ageing more gracefully than others. It's worth paying extra for the en suite doubles (which have balconies with side sea views) even if you're travelling solo.

Hotel Crillon HOTEL **$**
(Map p314; ☎480 0330; 3rd fl, 5 Sharia Adib Ishaq; s without bathroom E£133-150, d without bathroom E£176-205) This old-timer has oodles of char-

acter but is rough around the edges. Sea-facing rooms boast million-dollar harbour vistas, balconies, high ceilings and a bizarre hotchpotch of furniture. That said, shared bathrooms are shabby, and if you're offered a room that isn't on the 3rd floor, view before committing – some look like they haven't been cleaned since the 1970s.

Swiss Canal Hotel HOTEL $
(Map p314; ☎480 8373; 14 Sharia al-Bursa al-Qadima; s/d E£100/120) The Swiss Canal's salmon pink rooms pass muster if you're looking for a cheap bed and the budget hotels along the Corniche are full. Double rooms are large, light filled and generally clean (for Alexandria) though extremely basic with spongy soft beds and sparse furnishings. Don't bother with the pokey singles.

★Egypt Hotel HOTEL $$
(Map p314; ☎481 4483; 1 Sharia Degla; s/d/tr US$65/70/80; ❄📶) The Egypt fills a desperate need for decent midrange digs. A noticeable step up from the budget choices, it's set in a renovated 100-year-old Italian building right on the Corniche. Smallish rooms have old-school-style high beds with crisp white linen, wood floors, lovely dark-wood furniture, clean bathrooms, powerful air-con and small balconies with sea or street views.

Staff here are a lot more on the ball with information than you'll find elsewhere in the city. Don't worry about the dingy street entrance. Once inside (a clunky elevator ride up to the 3rd floor), it's a neat-as-a-pin, charmingly peaceful oasis.

Alex Otel HOTEL $$
(Alexander the Great Hotel; Map p310; ☎487 2141; www.alexotel.com; 5 Sharia Oskofia; s/d/f US$30/40/60) In a quiet position – beside St Katherine School – the Alex Otel may have no grand harbour views but its squeaky-clean rooms come with excellent air-con, copious hot water in the bathrooms and office-style furniture. We're impressed with the little touches like kettles in the rooms. If you're travelling with children in tow, the studio-style suites are good value.

★Cecil Hotel HISTORIC HOTEL $$$
(Map p314; ☎487 7173; http://en.steigenberger.com/Alexandria/Steigenberger-Cecil-Hotel; 16 Midan Saad Zaghloul; s/d/tr €122/134/146; ❄📶) The historic Cecil Hotel is a true Alexandria legend, though a series of refits over the years have unfortunately erased most of the days-gone-by lustre from when Durrell and Churchill propped up the famous bar here. Rooms are elegantly attired in red and cream. Bag a seafront one to make the most of the sweeping views over the Eastern Harbour.

Monty's Bar (now on the 1st floor) and the grand lobby retain a fraction of their historic glory, but the creaky old-fashioned elevator still trundles between floors.

Windsor Palace Hotel HISTORIC HOTEL $$$
(Map p314; ☎480 8123; www.paradiseinnegypt.com; 17 Sharia ash-Shohada; r with sea/street view US$120/100, ste from US$140) This bejewelled Edwardian gem has been keeping a watchful eye on the Med since 1907. In the 1990s the Windsor was given a much-needed nip and tuck. Thankfully the wonderful old elevators and grand lobby were retained, and rooms still boast the sort of old-world, green-and-gold pizazz that wouldn't be out of place on the *Orient Express*. Pick a seafront room for old-world atmosphere.

Four Seasons Hotel LUXURY HOTEL $$$
(Map p306; ☎581 8000; www.fourseasons.com; 399 Al-Corniche, San Stefano; r US$170-220, ste from US$270; ❄@📶🏊) The much-loved old Casino San Stefano made way for this grand edifice, with gleaming towers that dwarf neighbouring buildings. Inside no expense has been spared: the marble lobby gleams; the army of staff is eager to please; and the rooms – decked out in soft lemon – sport modern conveniences while reflecting Alexandria's Egyptian, Greek and French heritage. An infinity pool overlooks the sea, and a tunnel under the Corniche leads to a private beach. Kids will be happy too, with their own pool, babysitting services and entertainment.

Metropole Hotel HISTORIC HOTEL $$$
(Map p314; ☎486 1467; www.paradiseinnegypt.com; 52 Sharia Saad Zaghloul; s/d with sea view US$119/129, r with street view US$99; ❄📶) The Metropole is like a high-class lady fallen on hard times. Although it was entirely revamped in the 1990s – including a magnificently tacky lobby with Parthenon-style friezes – there's definite wear and tear beyond its hilarious gilded doors, panelled walls and over-the-top chandeliers in the mammoth rooms. Still, the place has atmosphere in spades.

Eating

Alexandria is all about seafood. One of the great dining pleasures here is tucking into the day's fresh catch, straight out of the Mediterranean, in one of the seafood restaurants overlooking the Eastern Harbour. After dinner it's de rigueur to spend a lazy evening sitting in one of the city-centre cafes, watching the world go by. Note that many restaurants don't serve alcohol. For a beer with your meal, you'll have to head to one of the luxury hotels or upmarket restaurants.

Central Alexandria

★Mohammed Ahmed EGYPTIAN FAST FOOD $
(Map p314; ☎483 3576; 17 Sharia Shakor Pasha; dishes E£2-8; ⏲24hr; ✎) Looking for us at lunchtime in Alex? We're usually scoffing fuul (fava bean paste) and felafel here. Mohammed Ahmed is the undisputed king of spectacularly good and cheap Egyptian standards. Select your fuul (we recommend *iskandarani*), add some felafel, choose a few accompanying salads, and let the feasting begin. Note that the street sign on the corner of Saad Zaghloul calls this Abdel Fattah el-Hadary St.

There's an English menu to help your selection. The tahini, *banga* (beetroot) and *torshi* (bright-pink pickled vegetables) are all good choices to add to your meal.

Taverna EGYPTIAN FAST FOOD $
(Map p314; ☎487 8591; Mahattat Ramla; mains E£9-35; ⏲7am-1am; ✎) This deservedly popular establishment serves up some of the best shwarma in town plus excellent hand-thrown sweet or savoury *fiteer* (Egyptian flaky pizza) – we're rather partial to the chocolate and banana one. It also does a fine Western-style pizza if you're hankering for Italian. Eat in or take away.

Awalad Abdou SANDWICHES $
(Map p310; Sharia Mohafaza; sandwiches E£2-5; ⏲24hr) With only minor concessions made to hygiene, this uberbudget place is nonetheless a smashing find. These guys will whip up microsandwiches with a scrumptious, meaty filling of your choice. Just point to what looks good and quaff it down while standing at the counter. It can be a challenge to find – there's no sign; look for a small shop with hanging cured meats, near Sharia Attareen.

Gad EGYPTIAN FAST FOOD $
(Map p314; Sharia Saad Zaghloul; mains E£8-30; ✎) Egypt's answer to (although a vast improvement on) McDonald's, this chain of absurdly popular takeaway joints has people flocking (think gadflies) day and night. It serves a huge range of filled sandwiches, kebabs, ta'amiyya (Egyptian variant of felafel), and mouth-watering shwarma. The *makarna firin* (oven-baked macaroni and cheese) is perfect comfort food. There's also a second central branch of **Gad** (Map p314; Sharia Mohammed Azmy Tossoun).

Abu Nasr EGYPTIAN FAST FOOD $
(Map p314; cnr Sharia Ibn el-Roumi & Al-Ghorfa al-Tugareya; mains E£5) This unusually tidy place serves good, filling *kushari* (mix of noodles, rice, black lentils, fried onions and tomato sauce). Don't forget to douse your dish with liberal lashings of vinegar and spicy sauce. There's no sign in English, so look for the gleaming gold bowls.

Patisserie Assad BAKERY $
(Map p310; 14 Sharia Abdul Hamid Badawy; pastries E£2-5; ⏲9.30am-4am) Just east of Midan Saad Zaghloul, this hole-in-the-wall bakery does good sweets, *fiteer* and croissants, sold by weight. It also offers a selection of hard-to-find local honey and olive oil. There's no sign, so look for the honey stacked in the window.

Hassan Fouad SELF-CATERING $
(Map p310; ☎485 9213; cnr Sharia Abdul Hamid Badawy & Moursi Gamil Aziz; ⏲9.30am-4am) This tiny and incredibly tidy market offers beautifully displayed produce, such as grapes from Lebanon and tasty Egyptian mangoes, and a good selection of imported staples such as digestive biscuits. There's no sign in English; look for the place with artfully stacked fruits and a bright-red sign.

Malek es-Seman EGYPTIAN $$
(Map p310; ☎390 0698; 48 Midan el-Soriyin Masguid el-Attarine; dishes E£25; ⏲8pm-3am) By day this is a small courtyard clothes market; by night it's an open-air restaurant doing one thing very, very well: quail. Birds are served grilled or stuffed. Both ways are delicious, but we especially like the charred and crispy flavour when grilled. Orders come with bread and six different salads. It's off Sharia Attareen, just south of the junction with Sharia Mohafaza. To find it look for a painted sign with a small bird. Serves beer.

La Varanda EUROPEAN $$
(Map p314; ☎486 1432; 46 Sharia Saad Zaghloul; mains E£25-60; 📶) Next door to famous tearoom Delices (and run by the same people), La Varanda is a cosy little place that specialises in Greek and French cuisine. This is a great place if you fancy a steak, or give the *yuvetsi* (Greek pasta) or meatballs a try. Dessert is taken care of by Delices' mammoth patisserie selection. Beer and Egyptian wine are served.

Fish Market SEAFOOD **$$**
(Map p310; Al-Corniche; mains E£35-80) An Alexandria institution for the hoity-toity set, Fish Market's dining room is in a prime position slap on the Med and is one of the city's most popular spots for a seafood splurge. Choose from a dazzling array of fishy mains displayed in the cabinets and dive into the fantastic mezze (served with excellent Lebanese-style bread) while you wait.

China House CHINESE **$$**
(Map p314; 487 7173; top fl, Cecil Hotel, 16 Midan Saad Zaghloul; mains E£30-70; 11am-11.30pm;) Need a change from shwarma and kebabs? Atop the Cecil Hotel, this rooftop restaurant serves decent Asian flavours complete with lovely service, dangling lanterns and stunning views over the harbour. The ambience is breezy; the chicken dumplings and grilled beef with garlic are first rate; and the banana fritters are a scrumptious treat. Beer and Egyptian wine are served.

Chez Gaby ITALIAN **$$**
(Map p314; 487 4404; Sharia Tariq al-Horreyya; mains E£25-55; Sun-Thu) This old-fashioned taverna is like stepping back in time. We love the intimate atmosphere, complete with chequered tablecloths, friendly service, and a menu of pasta and pizza. Alcohol is served.

Anfushi

For some authentic Alexandrian flavour and atmosphere, head for the simple, good-value streetside restaurants in Anfushi. Sharia Safar Pasha is lined with a dozen places where fires crackle and flame under the grills barbecuing meat and fish. You could chance a table at any of them and probably come away satisfied. Don't hesitate to bring the kids to any of the places we recommend; most are filled with families. All are open well past midnight.

El-Sheikh Wafik DESSERTS **$**
(Map p306; 279 9570; Qasr Ras el-Tin; desserts E£3-9) This unassuming and breezy corner cafe serves up some of the best desserts in town. You can get the usual ice cream in several flavours, but the real treats are Egyptian classics such as *couscousy* (E£8) – a yummy mix of couscous, shredded coconut, nuts, raisins and sugar, topped with hot milk.

★ **Greek Club** GREEK **$$**
(White and Blue Restaurant; Map p310; 480 2690; top fl, Greek Nautical Club, Al-Corniche; mains E£20-70;) The Greek Club's wide terrace is just the ticket for catching the evening breeze and watching the lights along Alex's legendary bay. The moussaka and the souvlaki are both easy menu winners, and the seafood selection (priced by weight) is excellent too. Order your fish Greek-style – oven baked with lemon, olive oil and oregano.

This is one of the best places in the city for a sundowner beer or cocktail. Minimum charge in the restaurant is E£75.

★ **Kadoura** SEAFOOD **$$**
(Map p310; 480 0405; 33 Sharia Bairam at-Tonsi; mains E£35-80) Pronounced 'Adora', this is one of Alexandria's most authentic fish restaurants, where food is served at tables in the narrow street. Pick your fish from a huge ice-packed selection, usually including sea bass, red and grey mullet, bluefish, sole, squid, crab and prawns. A selection of mezze is served with all orders (don't hope for a menu).

Most fish costs E£40 to E£80 per kilo, prawns E£180 per kilo. It has a second, air-conditioned (less atmospheric) branch along the **Corniche** (Map p310; Al-Corniche).

Farag SEAFOOD **$$**
(Map p310; 481 1047; 7 Souq al-Tabakheen; mains E£35-75; noon-3pm & 6pm-late) This very local spot is deep in the heart of the souq. Sit outdoors under the awning or inside in the air-conditioned dining room to feast on perfectly cooked and seasoned seafood. It's a bit hard to find – the sign is high above street level. If you do miss it, just ask around; everyone knows it.

Samakmak EGYPTIAN **$$**
(Map p310; 481 1560; 42 Qasr Ras el-Tin; mains E£50-120; 1-4pm & 6pm-2am) Owned by Zizi Salem, the retired queen of the Alexandrian belly-dancing scene, Samakmak is one step up from the other fish eateries in Anfushi. The fish is as fresh as elsewhere, but customers flock to this place for its specials, including crayfish, marvellous crab *tagen* (a stew cooked in a deep clay pot) and a great spaghetti with clams.

Abu Ashraf SEAFOOD **$$**
(Map p310; 481 6597; 28 Sharia Safar Pasha; mains E£35-60) Make your selection from the day's catch, then take a seat under the awning and watch it being cooked. Sea bass stuffed with garlic and herbs is a speciality, as is the creamy prawn *kishk* (casserole). Price is determined by weight and type of fish, ranging from grey mullet at E£45 per kilo to jumbo prawns at E£200 per kilo.

Hosny Grill GRILL $$
(Map p310; ☎481 2350; Sharia Safar Pasha; mains E£30-50) Hosny Grill is a semi-outdoor place specialising in tasty grilled chicken, kebabs and other meat dishes, all served with the usual triumvirate of vegetables, salad and rice. You'll have to roll out the door after eating here. It's opposite Abu Ashraf restaurant.

Outside the Centre

Abo Faris KEBAB $
(Map p306; mains E£10-20) This excellent restaurant specialises in Syrian-style shwarma, a mouth-watering concoction of spicy grilled lamb or chicken, slathered in garlicky mayonnaise and pickles, rolled up inside roasted *shammy* (pita-like bread). A full menu is available, and seating is indoors or in a garden patio. It's about 500m before Alexandria's City Centre Mall, on the left as you're coming from the city. Taxi drivers should know it. Takeaway available.

Drinking & Nightlife

During summer the 20km length of the Corniche from Ras el-Tin to Montazah seems to become one great strung-out ahwa (coffeehouse). With a few exceptions, these are not the greatest places – they're catering for a passing holiday trade and tend to overcharge. Nevertheless, Alexandria is a great place to get in some quality sheesha time. While many ahwas remain the exclusive domain of backgammon-playing men, those we recommend are family friendly unless otherwise mentioned.

Those looking for an alcoholic tipple are less in luck. Sixty years ago Alexandria was so famous for its Greek tavernas and divey watering holes that the 1958 movie *Ice Cold in Alex* was entirely based around a stranded WWII ambulance crew struggling through the desert, dreaming of making it back to Alexandria to sip a beer. These days Alex isn't much of a drinking town and there are few places worth crossing the desert for.

Central Alexandria

★ **Selsela Cafe** CAFE
(Map p310; Chatby Beach, Al-Corniche) At this fantastic cafe across from the Bibliotheca Alexandrina you can sip tea and smoke sheesha to the sound of waves rolling in, and smell sea air instead of petrol fumes (yay). Directly on the water, it has rustic palm-frond-shaded tables replete with twinkling coloured lights, set on a small curving beach where you can hardly hear the traffic.

It's a great place to relax in the sultry breeze, enjoying the Mediterranean vibe. To find it, look for the modern sculpture with three white needles, directly across the Corniche from the library. Walk past the sculpture towards the sea; the entrance is down the steps to the right.

★ **Cap d'Or** BAR
(Map p314; ☎487 5177; 4 Sharia Adbi Bek Ishak; ⌚10am-3am) The Cap d'Or, just off Sharia Saad Zaghloul, is one of the only surviving typical Alexandrian bars. With beer flowing generously, stained-glass windows, a long marble-topped bar, plenty of ancient memorabilia decorating the walls and crackling tapes of old French *chanson* (a type of traditional folk music) or Egyptian hits, it feels like a throwback to Alex's cosmopolitan past.

Bohemian crowds come to drink cold Stella beer, snack on great seafood, and just hang out at the bar talking or playing guitar with fellow drinkers. Thursday and Friday nights are more 'open-minded' than most nights in Alexandria.

El Tugareya COFFEEHOUSE
(Map p314; Al-Corniche; ⌚9am-late) Although it may not look like much to the uninitiated (it doesn't even sport a sign), this 90-year-old institution is one of the most important ahwas in town. It's an informal centre of business and trade (the name roughly translates to 'commerce'), where deals are brokered in time-honoured tradition – over a glass of *shai* (tea) or ahwa (coffee).

The cafe is separated into multiple rooms, covering a whole block. The southern side is a male-dominated area dedicated to games and informal socialising, while along the Corniche you're likely to be part of a rambunctious mix of writers, film-makers, students, expats and courting couples filling the hall with a cacophony of animated conversation.

Imperial Cafe & Restaurant CAFE
(Map p314; Midan Saad Zaghloul; ⌚10am-late; wi-fi) This classic cafe has been tastefully refitted to become a chic yet comfortable space with air-con, wi-fi and a list of espresso-based coffees, smoothies and fancy juices. There's a full menu (E£20 to E£40) featuring burgers, sandwiches and fajitas. You can also sit out on the pavement at an umbrella-covered table. It's a great place to take a break.

DON'T MISS

CAFE CULTURE

In case you hadn't noticed, Alexandria is a cafe town – and we're not talking Starbucks double-decaf-soy-low-fat-vanilla-grande lattes here. Ever since the first half of the 20th century, Alexandria's culture has revolved around cafes, where the city's diverse population congregated to live out life's dramas over pastries and a cup of tea or coffee. Famous literary figures met here, chattering and pondering the city they could not quite grasp. Many of these old haunts remain, and even though the food and drink in many aren't up to scratch, they are definitely worth a visit, to experience them as living relics of times past and to catch a glimpse of their grand decor. Here's a rundown of classic java joints where you can get a sip of the old days. Most open early and close late.

Delices (Map p314; 46 Sharia Saad Zaghloul; 9am-late;) This enormous old tearoom has been in business since 1922, and with its suited waiters and high-ceilinged halls, it drips with atmosphere. The patisserie here once supplied Egypt's royalty and the cafe was a favourite haunt of Allied soldiers during WWII. The coffee's not brilliant but the tarts, pastries, desserts, and cheesecakes (from E£12 to E£16) are to die for.

On a hot day, order the speciality Deliccino drink (ice cream and espresso milkshake). There's also a full menu of crêpes, pasta and sandwiches (from E£23 to E£30).

Sofianopoulos Coffee Store (Map p314; 484 5469; 21 Sharia Saad Zaghloul) You can smell the coffee from half a block away. This old-fashioned coffee retailer would be in a museum anywhere else in the world. Dominated by huge silver coffee grinders, stacks of glossy beans and the wonderful, faintly herbal aroma of roasted java, it's caffeine heaven and it serves ahwa (coffee) fit for a king.

Trianon (Map p314; 56 Midan Saad Zaghloul; 9am-midnight) Trianon was a favourite haunt of the Greek poet Cavafy, who worked in offices on the floor above. Stop here to admire the 1930s grandeur of its sensational ornate ceiling and grab one of its decent but expensive continental-style breakfasts.

Athineos (Map p314; 486 8131; 21 Midan Saad Zaghloul) Opposite Midan Ramla, this place lives and breathes nostalgia. The cafe part still has its original 1940s fittings. Come for the period character; skip the food.

Vinous (Map p314; 486 0956; cnr Sharia al-Nabi Daniel & Tariq al-Horreyya) Vinous is an old-school patisserie with more grand art deco styling than you can poke a puff pastry at. You can sense some of its old glory in the decorative (if worn) details.

Spitfire BAR

(Map p314; 7 Sharia L'Ancienne Bourse; 2pm-1.30am Mon-Sat) Just north of Sharia Saad Zaghloul, Spitfire has a rough-and-ready feel and a reputation as a sailors' hang-out. Walls are plastered with shipping-line stickers, rock-and-roll memorabilia and photos of drunk regulars. It's a great place for a fun evening out drinking with a mixed clientele of locals, expats, and passers-through.

Freshat Juice Bar JUICE BAR

(Map p314; 18 Sharia Amin Fekry; 9am-late) This sparkling little find has a cornucopia of different juices on offer, including all the standards plus some interesting and hard-to-find traditional drinks. If you're keen to try something new, ask the friendly owner, Ayman. All juices can be made without sugar on request.

Ahwa Sayed Darwish COFFEEHOUSE

(Map p314; Sharia Abu Shusha; 11am-late) Named for the composer of Egypt's national anthem, this tiny and highly enjoyable local coffeeshop, near Sharia al-Nabi Daniel, is set on a quiet and leafy side street around the corner from the Cavafy Museum. The chairs are comfortably padded, and the sheesha is clean. The clientele is exclusively men.

Drinkies LIQUOR STORE

(Map p314; delivery 480 6309; Sharia al-Ghorfa al-Tugareya; noon-midnight) Takeaway beer is available in the city centre at this aptly named place. It also delivers.

Anfushi

El Qobesi JUICE BAR

(Map p310; 486 7860; 51 Al-Corniche; 24hr) El Qobesi has crowned itself the 'king of

CULTURAL CENTRES

Many of the city's cultural centres operate libraries and organise programs of films, lectures, exhibitions and performances. Take along your passport as you may have to show it before entering.

British Council (Map p306; ☎545 6512; www.britishcouncil.org.eg; 11 Sharia Mahmoud Abu al-Ela, Kafr Abdu, Rushdy; ⏰11am-7pm Sat-Thu)

French Cultural Centre (Map p310; ☎391 8952; 30 Sharia al-Nabi Daniel; ⏰9am-9pm Mon-Sat) Has a bookshop with extensive French and some English-language titles.

Goethe Institut (Map p310; ☎487 9870; www.goethe.de/kairo; 10 Sharia al-Batalsa, Azarita; ⏰9am-1pm Mon-Thu, to 2pm Sun)

mango' but take one sip and you will bow down a loyal peon. Slivers of several ripe mangoes are cajoled nearly whole into a tall, chilled glass to make some of the best mango juice we've ever tried. Open around the clock, and always bustling.

Sit streetside and watch the chaos: locals often pull up for a quick in-car slurp, and we've even seen full microbuses stop by.

Farouk Cafe COFFEEHOUSE
(Map p310; ☎480 3103; Sharia Ismail Sabry) This venerable sheesha joint looks like it hasn't changed an iota since opening in 1928. It's a delightfully ramshackle old place, with dusty bronze lanterns outside, and charmingly fusty old men arguing and playing board games at the tables under huge photos of the former king.

Outside the Centre

Centro de Portugal BAR
(Map p306; ☎0122 336 5608; 42 Sharia Abd al-Kader; admission E£25; ⏰3pm-1am) This hard-to-find expat haven off Sharia Kafr Abdou has a garden bar on a leafy patio, darts and pool, plus a tiny disco complete with mirrored ball. Best of all, the beverages are very cold. Drinks are purchased via an unusual card system: E£75 gets you enough credits for a choice of five beers, three glasses of wine, two cocktails or 10 soft drinks.

The food menu (mains E£35 to E£70) offers Western standards, and there's a small playground for kids (who get free admission). It's a great place to unwind and meet local expats while sucking down an icy gin and tonic.

El Rehany COFFEEHOUSE
(Map p306; ☎590 5521; cnr Al-Corniche & Sharia Ismail Fangary, Camp Chesar) This expansive and breezy Alexandrian classic is reputed to have the best sheesha in town, served with a flourish by attentive boys in smart two-toned waistcoats while waiters in black and white bring tea in silver urns. The decor is eclectically elegant, including lofty ceilings etched with elaborate floral patterns, tables and chairs in Islamic designs, and burgundy tablecloths.

Check out the bizarre assortment of knick-knacks in the glass displays in the back too. There's no sign in English, so look for the place with green awnings, next to the Premiere Wellness and Fitness Centre.

☆ Entertainment

Alexandria's cultural life has never really recovered from the exodus of Europeans and Jews in the 1940s and '50s, but in recent years things have started to change for the better. Since the opening of the Bibliotheca Alexandrina, the town is once again trying to compete with Cairo as the proprietor of Egyptian arts.

The free monthly booklet *Alex Agenda*, available at some hotels, is extremely useful for its extensive list of concerts, theatre events and live gigs throughout Alexandria; its Facebook page also has links about some events.

Bibliotheca Alexandrina PERFORMING ARTS
(Map p310; ☎483 9999; www.bibalex.org; Corniche al-Bahr, Shatby) The Bibliotheca Alexandrina is the most important cultural venue in town, hosting major music festivals, international concerts and performances. Check the website to see what's happening while you're in town.

Alexandria Opera House OPERA
(Map p314; ☎486 5106; www.cairoopera.org/sayed_darwish.aspx; 22 Sharia Tariq al-Horreyya) The former Sayed Darwish Theatre has been refurbished and now houses the city's modestly proportioned but splendid opera house.

Alexandria Centre of Arts PERFORMING ARTS
(Map p314; ☎495 6633; info@aca.org.eg; 1 Sharia Tariq al-Horreyya; ⏰9am-9pm Sat-Thu) This active cultural centre, housed in a whitewashed villa, hosts contemporary-arts exhibitions,

poetry readings and occasional free concerts in its theatre. There is also an art studio, a library and a cinema on the 1st floor.

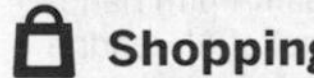

Shopping

The city's main souq district is just west of Midan Tahrir.

Attareen Antique Market ANTIQUES
(Map p310; 10am-late) Antique collectors will have a blast diving through the confusion of backstreets and alleys of this antique market. Many items found their way here after the European upper class was forced en masse to make a hasty departure from Egypt following the 1952 revolution.

Sayed el-Safty ANTIQUES
(Map p310; 392 2972; 63 Sharia Attareen; 11am-late) Probably the most interesting antique shop in the city. Well worth a browse.

Mohammed Abdo SMOKING
(Map p310; cnr Attareen & Mohafaza) Build your own sheesha like the locals do.

Al-Maaref Bookshop BOOKS
(Map p314; 487 3303; 32 Midan Saad Zaghloul) Has a small English-language section that includes titles on Egypt and Alexandria.

Mohandes Mostafa el Fadaly MAPS
(Map p314; 2nd fl, 49 Sharia Safiyya Zaghloul; 9am-4pm Sat-Thu) A *mohandes* (engineer) who created and sells a street map of Alexandria (E£30), indispensable if you're spending any significant time in the city. Find Mostafa above the Mr Sanyo clothes store.

Information

DANGERS & ANNOYANCES

Since the 2011 revolution both anti- and pro-government protests have become a regular occurrence in Alexandria. As protests have been known to erupt with little or no warning into violent clashes, travellers should steer clear of any areas where demonstrations are taking place. It's important to note that protests tend to be extremely localised activities: even when a march or demonstration is happening in one part of the city, the rest of Alexandria is generally calm.

LOCAL KNOWLEDGE

TOP SOUQS

Although you won't find the sort of antediluvian bazaars here that you do in Cairo, Alexandria has several busy souqs that are ideal spots to immerse yourself in some lively market action.

Anfushi Fish Market (Map p310, Qasr Ras el Tin) In a city that devours more fish than a hungry seal, you'd expect to find a pretty impressive fish market – and Alexandria delivers. At the northern tip of Anfushi, this market bustles daily with flapping seafood that's literally just been thrown off the boat. Get here early, when it's busiest. Things die down by midmorning.

Souq District (Map p310) At the western end of Midan Tahrir, the battered, grand architecture switches scale to something more intimate as you enter the city's main souq district. It's one long, heaving bustle of produce, fish and meat stalls, bakeries, cafes and sundry shops selling every imaginable household item. This is a great area to check out at night.

Sharia Faransa begins with cloth, clothes and dressmaking accessories. The tight weave of covered alleys running off to the west are known as Zinqat as-Sittat (the alley of the women). Here you'll find buttons, braid, baubles, bangles, beads and much more, from junk jewellery to frighteningly large padded bras. Beyond the haberdashery you will find the gold and silver dealers, then the herbalists and spice vendors. A couple of blocks west of Sharia Faransa, Sharia Nokrashi (also known as El-Maydan) starts at Midan Nasr and runs for about a kilometre through the heart of Anfushi.

Souq Ibrahimiyya (Map p306; Sharia Omar Lofty) This is one of our favourite markets for peeking into Egyptian life. Down several tiny, covered side streets near the Sporting Club, it's packed with fresh produce, piles of still-wet seafood, and stalls selling poultry and meats, both before and after they've seen the butcher's block. It's best in the morning, when the vendors are at their most vocal and enthusiastic.

EMERGENCY

Tourist Police (Map p314; ☎485 0507; Midan Saad Zaghloul) Upstairs from the main tourist office.

INTERNET ACCESS

Farous Net Café (Map p314; Tariq al-Horreyya; per hr E£3; ⏰10am-midnight)

Hightop Internet Café (Map p314; ☎484 0192; 71 Sharia al-Nabi Daniel; per hr E£3; ⏰10am-midnight)

MEDICAL SERVICES

Al-Madina at-Tibiya (Alexandria Medical City Hospital; Map p306; ☎543 7402, 543 2150; Sharia Ahmed Shawky, Rushdy; ⏰24hr) Well-equipped private hospital.

Central Pharmacy (Map p314; ☎486 0744; 19 Sharia Ahmed Orabi; ⏰9am-10pm) This 100-year-old establishment is worth visiting just for the soaring ceilings and beautiful display cabinets.

German Hospital (Map p306; ☎584 0757; 56 Sharia Abdel Salaam Aarafa, Glymm; ⏰8am-10pm) Near Saba Basha tram stop (line 2) and next to Al-Obeedi Hospital. Staffed by highly qualified doctors, and has a day clinic for nonemergency patients.

MONEY

There are dozens of banks and ATMs in central Alexandria, particularly on Sharia Salah Salem and Sharia Talaat Harb, the city's banking district.

If changing cash or cashing travellers cheques, it's simplest to use one of the many exchange bureaus on the side streets between Midan Ramla and the Corniche.

American Express (Amex; Map p306; ☎420 2288; www.americanexpress.com.eg; Elsaladya Bldg, Sharia 14th Mai, Smouha; ⏰9am-4pm Sun-Thu) Changes cash and travellers cheques, and is also a travel agency.

Banque du Caire (Map p314; Sharia Salah Salem) Also has a branch on Sharia Talaat Harb. (Map p314; cnr Sharia Sisostris & Talaat Harb)

HSBC (Map p310; 47 Sharia Sultan Hussein; ⏰8.30am-5pm Sun-Thu) Has an ATM.

Thomas Cook (Map p314; ☎484 7830; Midan Ramla; ⏰8am-5pm) Money exchange and also changes travellers cheques.

POST

DHL (Map p314; 9 Sharia Salah Salem; ⏰9am-5pm Sat-Thu)

Main post office (Map p314; Sharia al-Bursa al-Qadima; ⏰9am-9pm Sat-Thu) Just east of Midan Orabi; several other branches are dotted around the city.

TOURIST INFORMATION

Mahattat Misr Tourist Office (Map p310; ☎392 5985; Platform 1, Misr Train Station; ⏰8.30am-6pm) The staff is eager to help, even if they don't have much actual information.

Main tourist office (Map p314; ☎485 1556; Midan Saad Zaghloul; ⏰8.30am-6pm) Hands out a good brochure (with map) of Alexandria sights and has friendly staff.

ℹ Getting There & Away

AIR

All flights to Alexandria arrive at Burg al-Arab Airport, about 45km southwest of the city. Smaller Nouzha Airport, 7km southeast, is in the process of a drawn-out renovation. When it reopens, domestic flights will likely be routed here.

BUS

All long-distance buses leave from **Al-Mo'af al-Gedid Bus Station** (New Garage; Map p306). It's several kilometres south of Midan Saad Zaghloul; to get there either catch a microbus from Misr Train Station (E£2) or grab a taxi from the city centre (E£25). The main companies operating from here are **West & Mid Delta Bus Co** (Map p314; ☎480 9685; Midan Saad Zaghloul; ⏰9am-9pm) and **Super Jet** (Map p306; ☎543 5222; Sidi Gaber Train Station; ⏰8am-10pm); both have central-city booking offices.

Cairo

Super Jet has hourly buses to Cairo (E£35 to E£40, 2½ hours), also stopping at Cairo airport, from early morning. Services stop in the late evening, though there may be a single late service. West & Mid Delta also has hourly departures (E£35).

North Coast & Siwa

West & Mid Delta has hourly departures to Marsa Matruh (E£30, four hours); a few of these buses continue on to Sallum (E£35 to E£45, nine hours) on the border with Libya. Three services daily go to Siwa (E£55, nine hours) at 8.30am, 11am and 10pm. Super Jet runs five buses to Marsa Matruh (E£35) daily during summer (June to September), the last one generally leaving in the late afternoon. Most Marsa Matruh buses stop in El Alamein (one hour), and will stop at Sidi Abdel Rahman if you want to get off, though you will have to pay the full Marsa Matruh fare.

Sinai

West & Mid Delta has one daily service to Sharm el-Sheikh (E£100, eight to 10 hours) at 9pm.

Suez Canal & Red Sea Coast

Super Jet has a daily evening service to Hurghada (E£100, nine hours). West & Mid Delta has four services per day to Port Said (E£30, four to five hours), two to Ismailia (E£35, five hours) and four to Suez (E£45, five hours). It also has an 8am and 6.30pm bus to Hurghada (E£95).

SERVEES & MICROBUS

Servees (service taxis) and microbuses for Aboukir (Map p310), and *servees* for Cairo (Map p310), depart from outside Misr Train Station; all others leave from Al-Mo'af al-Gedid Bus Station out at Moharrem Bey. Fares cost around E£25 to Cairo or Marsa Matruh. Sample fares to more-local destinations include Zagazig (E£10), Tanta (E£10), Mansura (E£12), Rosetta (E£6) and Aboukir (E£4).

TRAIN

There are two train stations in Alexandria. The main terminal is **Misr Train Station** (Mahattat Misr ; ☎ 426 3207; Sharia Al-Nabi Daniel) about 1km south of Midan Ramla. **Sidi Gaber Train Station** (Mahattat Sidi Gaber; ☎ 426 3953) serves the eastern suburbs. Trains from Cairo stop at Sidi Gaber first and most locals get off here but if you're going to the city centre around Midan Saad Zaghloul, make sure you stay on until Misr Train Station.

There are 10 trains daily between Alexandria and Cairo, from 8am to 10pm. Services at 9am, noon, 2pm, 3pm, 4.45pm, 8pm and 10pm (E£50/35 in 1st/2nd class, 2½ hours) make fewer stops. Trains departing at 8.15am, 1pm, and 3.30pm (E£41/25 in 1st/2nd class, 3½ hours) make multiple stops. There are two daily trains to Luxor at 5pm and 10pm (E£129/69 in 1st/2nd class), with the 5pm train continuing to Aswan (E£148/77 in 1st/2nd class).

At Misr Train Station, 1st- and 2nd-class tickets to Cairo are sold at the ticket office along platform 1; 3rd- and 2nd-class tickets to destinations other than Cairo are purchased in the front hall. If you're getting a taxi from the station, it's advisable to bypass the drivers lurking outside the entrance as they're renowned for overcharging new arrivals – instead walk out onto the street and flag one down.

Getting Around

As a visitor to Alexandria, you'll rarely use the buses, and while the tram is fun, it's painfully slow. Taxis and microbuses are generally the best options for getting around.

TO/FROM THE AIRPORT

Transport to Burg al-Arab Airport is via the air-conditioned airport bus (one way E£6 plus E£1 per bag, one hour), leaving outside the Cecil Hotel on Midan Saad Zaghloul three hours before all flight departures; confirm the exact bus departure time at the Cecil. A taxi to/from the airport should cost between E£100 and E£150. You can also catch bus 475 (E£4, one hour) from Misr Train Station.

If you do need to get to/from Nouzha Airport, a taxi should cost no more than E£25. There are also minibuses from Midan Orabi and Midan Ramla.

CAR

Car hire starts from US$40 per day (including 100km). If you do rent, ensure that you're especially scrupulous with the initial and return inspections, to avoid any compensation claims for very minor vehicle damage. The price of using a car and driver service can be comparable, and saves the headache of negotiating traffic yourself.

Avis (Map p314; ☎ 485 7400; Cecil Hotel, Midan Saad Zaghloul; ⊙ 8am-6pm) Avis has a full range of cars, with drivers available for an additional US$20 per day.

MICROBUS

Want to travel like the locals? Hop on a microbus. The most useful are the ones zooming along the Corniche. There are no set departure points or stops, so when one passes, wave and shout your destination; if it's heading that way it will stop to pick you up. It costs anywhere from 50pt for a short trip to E£2 to go all the way to Montazah.

TAXI

There are no working taxi meters in Alexandria. Locals simply pay the correct amount as they get out of the taxi, but since fares are both unpublished and subjective, this can be a challenge for a visitor to pull off (especially considering many drivers expect visitors to pay higher fares and won't hesitate to aggressively argue the point). Negotiate a price before you get in and try to give the driver the exact amount.

Some sample fares: Midan Ramla to Misr Train Station E£10; Midan Saad Zaghloul to Fort Qaitbey E£5; Midan Saad Zaghloul to the Bibliotheca Alexandrina E£10; Hotel Cecil to Montazah E£25.

TRAM

Alexandria's rumbling, clackety old trams are fun to ride, but they can be almost unbearably slow and hence not the best option for getting around.

The central tram station, Mahattat Ramla, is at Midan Ramla; from here lime-yellow-coloured trams go west and blue-coloured ones travel east. Check the easy-to-read route maps at the stations to find the line you're looking for. The line numbers on each tramcar are in Arabic, but you can tell which line it is by the colour of the sign at the front and then match that to the colour of the line number on the route map. Some trams have two or three carriages, in which case one of them is reserved for women. Fares range from 25pt to E£1.

Tram 14 goes to Misr Train Station; tram 15 goes through Anfushi; trams 1 and 25 go to Sidi Gaber Train Station.

AROUND ALEXANDRIA

Aboukir

Aboukir (pronounced abu-eer), a small coastal town 24km east of Alexandria, shot to fame in 1798 when the Battle of the Nile saw the British admiral Horatio Nelson administer a crushing defeat over Napoleon's French fleet. Just offshore, underwater excavations over the past decade have revealed the sunken city of legendary Herakleion (Thonis), which was swallowed by the Mediterranean about 1200 years ago (p317).

The beach isn't the cleanest but local Alexandrians head here in droves for summer lunches at one of the excellent fish restaurants. If you feel like some slap-up seafood, we highly recommend the seafront **Zephyrion** (03-562 1319; fish per kg E£40-160; lunch & dinner). This old Greek fish taverna (the name is Greek for 'sea breeze') was founded in 1929 and serves first-class fish on the sweeping blue-and-white terrace that overlooks the bay. Beer is available.

The easiest way to get to Aboukir is by flagging down an east-bound microbus along the Corniche (E£2). It will drop you at a roundabout; the sea is to your left as you face the large mosque beyond the roundabout.

Alternatively, a taxi from Alexandria's city centre should cost around E£50 to E£60 each way.

Rosetta (Ar-Rashid)

045 / POP 69,000

Poor old Rosetta. Today it's hard to believe that this dusty town, squatting on the western branch of the Nile, 65km northeast of Alexandria, was once Egypt's most significant port. Locally known as Ar-Rashid, Rosetta was founded in the 9th century and outgrew Alexandria in importance during that town's 18th- and 19th-century decline. Alas, as Alexandria got back on its feet and regained power in the late 19th century, Rosetta was thrust into near irrelevance.

Today its backwater appeal strikes a contrast with the modern hustle of nearby Alexandria. Here the streets are packed with donkeys pulling overloaded carts, and the souq area has an atmosphere of centuries past with basket-weavers artfully working fronds and blacksmiths hammering away in medieval-looking shop fronts.

Rosetta may be most famous as the discovery place of the stone stele that provided the key to deciphering hieroglyphics but its main draw is its striking Islamic architecture, in the form of beautifully crafted Ottoman-era merchants' houses. There are at least 22 of them tucked away along the streets. Unfortunately most are not open to visitors, although you can admire their decorated facades.

Sights

Built in the traditional Delta style using small, flat bricks painted alternately red and black, Rosetta's Ottoman houses are generally three-storey structures with the upper floor slightly overhanging the lower. At ground level the doorways often feature intricate painted floral designs, while jutting and ornate *mashrabiyya* (lattice) windows decorate the walls.

You can admire some excellent examples of this local architecture along the main souq, which runs the length of Sharia Port Said from the microbus station and town square.

The **Beit Killi** museum on the main square is closed, as is **Hammam Azouz**, and there's no official reopening date for either.

House of Amasyali HISTORIC BUILDING

(Sharia al-Anira Feriel; adult/student incl entry to House of Abu Shaheen E£15/10; 9am-4pm) The House of Amasyali is one of the most impressive of all Rosetta's fine buildings. The facade has beautiful, small lantern lights and vast expanses of *mashrabiyyas*, which circulate cool breezes around the house. The main reception room upstairs is overlooked by a screened wooden gallery behind which the women would sit, obscured from view. To get here from the central souq, take the second left-hand turn down Sharia Port Said and walk four blocks.

House of Abu Shaheen HISTORIC BUILDING

(Mill House; off Sharia al-Anira Feriel; adult/student incl entry to House of Amasyali E£15/10; 9am-4pm) The House of Abu Shaheen has a reconstructed mill on the ground floor, featuring enormous wooden beams and planks. You can actually see the gears and teeth rotate, which 200 years ago would have been pushed in an endless circle by a bored draught animal. In the courtyard, the roof of the stables is supported by granite columns with Graeco-Roman capitals. It's right next door to the House of Amasyali, entry to which is included on the same ticket.

THE ROSETTA STONE

Now a crowd-pulling exhibit at the British Museum in London, the Rosetta Stone is the most significant find in the history of Egyptology. Unearthed in 1799 by a French soldier doing his duty improving the defences of Fort St Julien near Rosetta, the stone is the lower half of a large, dark granitic stele. It records a decree issued in 196 BC by the priests of Memphis, establishing the religious cult of Ptolemy V and granting the 13-year-old pharaoh status as a deity – in exchange for tax exemptions and other priestly perks. In order to be understood by Egyptians, Greeks and others then living in the country, the decree was written in the three scripts current at the time – hieroglyphic, demotic (a cursive form of hieroglyphs) and Greek, a language that European scholars would have read fluently. The trilingual inscription was set up in a temple beside a statue of the pharaoh. At the time of its discovery, much was known about ancient Egypt, but scholars had still not managed to decipher hieroglyphs. It was quickly realised that these three scripts would make it possible to compare identical texts, and therefore to crack the code and recover the lost world of the ancient Egyptians.

When the British defeated Napoleon's army in 1801, they wrote a clause in the surrender document insisting that antiquities be handed to the victors, the Rosetta Stone being foremost among them. The French made a cast and the original was shipped to London, where Englishman Thomas Young established the direction in which the hieroglyphs should be read, and recognised that hieroglyphs enclosed within oval rings (cartouches) were the names of royalty.

But in 1822, before Young devised a system for reading the mysterious script, Frenchman Jean François Champollion recognised that signs could be alphabetic, syllabic or determinative, and established that the hieroglyphs inscribed on the Rosetta Stone were actually a translation from the Greek, and not the other way around. This allowed him to establish a complete list of signs with their Greek equivalents. His obsessive work not only solved the mystery of Pharaonic script but also contributed significantly to a modern understanding of ancient Egypt.

Fort of Qaitbey FORTRESS
(adult/student E£15/8; ⏲8am-5pm) About 5km north of Rosetta along the Nile, this fort was built in 1479 to guard the mouth of the Nile 6km further on. It was on this spot that the famous Rosetta Stone was found; we'll wager that this is now the site of the lamest historical exhibit in the world, especially in relation to the importance of the discovery that was made here. A round trip by taxi should cost E£15.

ℹ Getting There & Away

There are regular microbuses (E£6, one hour) to Rosetta from Al-Mo'af al-Gedid Bus Station in Alexandria. Rosetta's microbus station is right on the square that leads into the main souq. A private car with driver or a taxi to Rosetta from Alexandria should cost you around E£170 return.

MEDITERRANEAN COAST

Almost the entire stretch of coastline between Alexandria and Sidi Abdel Rahman is jam-packed with resorts paying homage to the modern gods of concrete construction. This is where well-to-do Cairenes and the top brass of Egypt's military establishment come to escape the oppressive city heat of the summer. Virtually all of these developments are private villa-resorts owned or rented by Egyptian families and there's little for the independent traveller.

Halfway down the coast to Libya, El Alamein is home to several poignantly beautiful memorials to the WWII battles that took place here. Further on, the striking coastline is less developed, although resorts are creeping along the shore all the way to the Egyptian summer-holiday town of Marsa Matruh.

El Alamein

☎046

This small coastal outpost is famed for the decisive victory doled out here by the Allies during WWII. More than 80,000 soldiers were killed or wounded in the series of desert battles fought nearby, which helped cement Allied control of North Africa. The thousands

OFF THE BEATEN TRACK

THE SIGHTS OF ST MENA

St Mena was an Egyptian soldier in the Roman Legion who was martyred for not renouncing his Christian faith. During the late 4th century the area surrounding St Mena's tomb, on the outskirts of modern-day Burg al-Arab, 45km southwest of Alexandria, became synonymous with miraculous acts. By the 5th century pilgrims were flocking here from as far away as Europe and the area became the bustling city of Martyroupolis – only Jerusalem rivalled it as a place of pilgrimage. After the Arab armies conquered Alexandria in AD 641, Martyroupolis fell into obscurity and many of the churches were destroyed. In the early 20th century, Martyroupolis (now known as Abu Mena) was rediscovered by archaeologists and the modern Monastery of St Mena the Miracle Giver was founded nearby.

Abu Mena

Thanks to Bedouin raids and marble pilfering not much remains of the once-grand Byzantine pilgrimage centre of Martyroupolis, although the outline of the mammoth basilica is still easily recognisable. A modest wooden chapel has been built over the basilica's altar with the altar stone still in place. A piece of St Mena's body is kept in a cabinet here. From the chapel a row of stubby column remnants leads to the saint's tomb. Changes in the water table have caused degradation to the excavations and the site has been placed on Unesco's endangered monuments list. Despite the damage to the site, travellers interested in Egypt's Coptic history will find Abu Mena (Burg al-Arab) sheds some light on Egypt's leading role in the early Christian era. The site is accessed by a desert track (accessible by normal vehicles) just to the south of the Monastery of St Mena. If you're unsure of directions, ask at the monastery.

Monastery of St Mena the Miracle Giver

This **monastery** (Deir Mar-Mena; Burg al-Arb), built in 1959, is a major pilgrimage site for Egyptian Coptic Christians. Aswan granite and marble were used to build the large cathedral. Skilled monk artisans created the interior's resplendent mosaic tilework dome and ornate wooden panel iconostasis that grace the interior. Behind the cathedral is the tomb of Pope Kyrillos VI, who founded the monastery.

of graves in the Commonwealth, German and Italian war cemeteries in the vicinity of the town are a bleak reminder of the losses.

Much cheerier are the fine sands and heavenly water of the nearby beaches. Finding a place to access the sea is easier if you're staying at one of the local resorts, but there are also a few places where independent visitors can get in the water.

It's possible to stay overnight here and in nearby Sidi Abdel Rahman, but El Alamein is easiest visited as a day trip from Alexandria.

Sights

War Museum MUSEUM

(☎410 0021; adult/student E£20/10; ⏰9am-2pm) This museum is an excellent introduction to the North African campaigns of WWII, including the Battle of El Alamein. There's a collection of memorabilia, uniforms, photos and maps, with explanations in Arabic, English, German and Italian. A range of tanks, artillery and hardware from the fields of battle is displayed outside. The turn-off to the museum is along the main highway; just look for the large tank in the middle of the road.

Commonwealth War Cemetery CEMETERY

(⏰7am-2.30pm) The Commonwealth War Cemetery is a haunting place where more than 7000 tombstones stand in regimented rows between beautifully tended desert plants. Soldiers from the UK, Australia, New Zealand, France, Greece, South Africa, East and West Africa, Malaysia and India who fought for the Allied cause all lie here. As you enter, a separate memorial commemorating the Australian contingent is to your right. The cemetery is about 1km east of El Alamein's War Museum.

At the Australian memorial a small plaque, with a relief map, gives an overview of the key battlefield locations. The cemetery itself was a rear area during the fighting; the front line ran from the Italian memorial and wound its way 65km south to the Qattara Depression.

The cemetery is supposedly visitable outside of regular hours via a key left outside the gate, but this may not be reliable.

German War Memorial MEMORIAL

About 7km west of El Alamein, what looks like a hermetically sealed sandstone fortress overlooking the sea is actually the German War Memorial. Inside this silent but unmistakable reminder of war lie the tombs of approximately 4000 German servicemen and, in the centre, a memorial obelisk. To reach the memorial, take the marked turn-off from the main highway; the entrance to the memorial is locked, but if you wait for a moment the friendly Bedouin keeper will let you in.

From the memorial, there's a panoramic view of the stretch of shore in this area.

German Memorial Beach BEACH

Across 2km of desert directly in front of the German war memorial is the tiny and glorious German Memorial Beach, which is relatively rubbish free. The sea here is multiple shades of blue, and you'll feel miles away from Alexandria's teeming beaches. To get there, ask the Bedouin keeper at the memorial to open the gate leading to the sand tracks – he'll urge you to first get permission from the Coast Guard post (visible from the memorial, but well out of the way if on foot). He may offer to accompany you.

There's also a road direct to the beach from the Alexandria–Matruh highway. It's an unmarked sand track, leading over some low hills to the beach. The turn-off is 150m east of the road to the German War Memorial.

Italian Memorial MEMORIAL

About 11km west of El Alamein, the Italian memorial has a wide path rimmed by flowering shrubs leading up to a tall, slender tower. This was roughly where the front line between the opposing armies ran in WWII's North Africa campaign.

Inside the tower, the simple design of square white marble slabs covering the walls, engraved only with the names of the dead, is a moving experience. The tower is kept locked but the Bedouin caretaker will appear and open it up for you soon after you arrive.

At the roadside entrance to the memorial there is a small one-room **museum** with some interesting maps, artillery, photos and memorabilia from the battle. Most of the information is in Italian only, although there are a couple of translations into English and Arabic. On a practical note, the Italian memorial has the only clean toilets in El Alamein.

Before reaching the memorial, you'll notice on the left (south) side of the road what appears to be a large rock milestone.

TURNING POINT AT EL ALAMEIN

For a brief period in 1942, the tiny railway station at El Alamein commanded the attention of the entire world. Since 1940 the British had battled the Italians and Germans for control of North Africa; fighting raged back and forth from Tunisia to Egypt as first one side and then the other seized the advantage.

By 1942, Axis units under Field Marshal Erwin Rommel, the celebrated 'Desert Fox', had pushed the Allies back to the last defensible position before Cairo – a line running from El Alamein 65km south to the impassable Qattara Depression. The situation appeared hopeless. British staffers burnt their papers to prevent them from falling into enemy hands; the Germans were expected in Alexandria any day; and Mussolini flew to Egypt to prepare for his triumphal entry into Cairo.

In desperate fighting, however, the Allies repulsed the next German thrust by late July. In early September, galvanised by the little-known general Bernard Law Montgomery, the Allies parried a second attack that focused on the famous Alam al-Halfa ridge.

Monty gathered his strength for an all-out counteroffensive, which he launched on 23 October 1942. Intense fighting raged for 13 days, with each side suffering appalling losses, until the Axis line at last crumbled. Rommel's routed legions retreated westward, never to return to Egypt. The Desert Fox was recalled to Germany to spare him the disgrace of defeat, but 230,000 of his soldiers eventually surrendered in Tunisia.

Monty was knighted, and became the most famous British general of the war. In 1946 he was made First Viscount Montgomery of Alamein, a title he used for the rest of his life. Of the battle, Winston Churchill famously said, 'Before Alamein we never had a victory. After Alamein we never had a defeat.'

Inscribed on it is the Italian summary of the battle: '*Mancò la fortuna, non il valore*' ('We were short on luck, not on bravery').

Tours

If you spend time in town, you may field offers of desert excursions to visit key battle sites, such as **Ruweisat Ridge**; however, if you want to explore the World War II sites fully, you should consider opting for a specialised tour. Aside from the fact that millions of landmines were planted during the fighting and no one seems to know how many remain, officially you must obtain approval from the Egyptian military in order to access the battlefields. It's a controlled area, and if you're caught without permission you risk serious trouble; what's more, if anything goes wrong in the desert, you will not be able to rely on the authorities for assistance.

As well as visiting the battle sites, a specialist tour operator will be able to take you to other areas that played important roles during the fighting. These include the Egyptian Railway workers' building known as the **blockhouse** which, during the worst of the fighting, served as a hospital where German and Australian doctors worked alongside each other treating the wounded of both sides.

Wilderness Ventures Egypt GUIDED TOUR
(www.wilderness-ventures-egypt.com) This highly recommendable tour company runs excellent three-day El Alamein tours, camping at night on the Qattara Depression. Tours take in all the important sites in the area including the major battlefields of Ruweisat Ridge, Tel el Eissa and Point 29, along with sites such as the blockhouse and the war memorials.

Sleeping & Eating

The store beside the War Museum has a small cafeteria where you can get a good spread of fuul, ta'amiyya and salads. It may be possible to camp on the beaches nearby but you'll have to hunt around for the police and attempt to get a *tasreeh* (camping permit).

The luxury hotels along the coast from here to Sidi Abdel Rahman are an alternative, if you don't mind parting with a wad of cash.

Getting There & Away

The easiest option is to organise your own car and driver. A taxi will charge around E£350 to E£450 to take you from Alexandria to the War Museum, ferry you between the cemeteries, make a stop at a beach and bring you back to Alexandria.

Alternatively, catch any of the Marsa Matruh buses or microbuses from Al-Mo'af al-Gedid Bus Station in Alexandria. You'll be dropped on the main road about 200m down the hill from the War Museum.

Sidi Abdel Rahman

☎046

The gorgeous beaches of Sidi Abdel Rahman are the raison d'être for this growing resort hamlet, and with charter flights between Europe and nearby El Alamein (23km east), development is likely to continue. Several resorts take prime position on the sparkling waters and white sands of the Mediterranean and are the major draw – though there is little else to see or do here.

Sights

Shaat al-Hanna BEACH
This gorgeous beach is a real find, with irresistible milky-blue water that's great for swimming. Even out here, conservative dress for women applies. The main free beach is, unfortunately, more trashy than it used to be, so if that turns you off, pay E£50 per person for the clean, private beach, which has umbrellas and lounge chairs. Heading west along the Alexandria–Marsa Matruh road, the turn-off for the beach is marked by three rusting yellow signs 1.9km after the 155km to Marsa Matruh milestone.

The road is part paved and part sand, but fine for regular cars.

Sleeping & Eating

Ghazala Regency RESORT $$$
(☎419 0060; www.ghazalaregencyalamein.com; Km140 on Alexandria–Marsa Matruh rd, Ghazala Bay; s/d €93/107; ❄ 📶 🏊) The Ghazala Regency caters to European families on package tours. The rooms are large, but the decor uninspired, the housekeeping variable and the buffet meals bland. The beach, however, is out of this world. If you're looking to lie on a beautiful beach with tanned Italians in skimpy swimwear (we're not talking about the ladies), this fits the bill.

Getting There & Away

Buses and microbuses to Marsa Matruh from Al-Mo'af al-Gedid Bus Station in Alexandria can drop you here, but it's quite a trek to the resort from the road. It's better to arrive by private car or taxi.

Marsa Matruh

046 / POP 120,600

During summer the Mediterranean town of Marsa Matruh is the real-deal Egyptian resort-town experience. From June to September it can seem like half of the lower Nile Valley has decamped here for their holidays. The brilliant-white, sandy beaches are squeezed full of families; the dusty streets buzz with people well into the wee hours of the morning; throngs of street stalls sell hot food and souvenirs; and impromptu street musicians bang out rhythmic tunes.

For the rest of the year, Marsa Matruh presses the snooze button and returns to its usual near-comatose state. The city's turquoise bays lie empty and the only visitors are Bedouins and Libyans stocking up on goods.

Whatever the time of year, few foreign tourists make the trip out here, except to break the journey to Siwa.

Sights & Activities

The luminescence of the water along this stretch of coast is marred only by the town's overflowing hotel scene. The beaches on the east side of town, near the bridge over to Rommel's Beach, have calm, shallow water great for small kids, plus palm-frond shade cubicles. At any of the town beaches expect to pay from E£5 to E£10 for a chair and umbrella.

Further away, the water is just as nice and you can still find a few places where the developers have yet to start pouring cement. During the hot summer months women cannot bathe in swimsuits, unless they can handle being the object of intense harassment and ogling. The exceptions are the private beaches of the top-end hotels, although even here most Egyptian women remain fully dressed and in the shade.

Lido BEACH

(Map p336) Marsa Matruh's main beach has decent sand and clear water, but during summer you'll have trouble finding space to throw down your towel.

Cleopatra's Beach BEACH

Possibly the most beautiful piece of coastline in the area, Cleopatra's Beach sits about 14km west of Marsa Matruh around the bay's thin tentacle of land. The sea here is an exquisite hue and the rock formations are worth a look. You can wade to Cleopatra's Bath, a natural pool where legend has imagined the queen and Mark Antony enjoying a dip, but you can't actually swim, due to the waves and rocks just offshore.

Shaati al-Gharam BEACH

(Map p337) At the tip of the tentacle of land west of Marsa Matruh you'll find Shaati al-Gharam (Lovers' Beach). Unsurprisingly, the water here is sublime, but the sand is only marginally less busy than at the main city beaches. In summer boats (E£3) shuttle back and forth from the Lido beach across the bay. Taxis charge about E£20 each way.

Rommel's Beach BEACH

Right at the tip of Marsa Matruh's eastern peninsula, this quiet but rocky piece of shore is good for swimming. Just before the beach is the cave system where Colonel Rommel planned the Axis forces' military operations during WWII. The caves are now home to **Rommel's Cave Museum** (9am-2pm Sun-Thu), which displays some of Rommel's personal effects and the maps he drew up here.

Agiba Beach BEACH

Agiba means 'miracle' in Arabic, and Agiba Beach, about 24km west of Marsa Matruh, is just that. It is a small, spectacular cove, accessible only via a path leading down from the clifftop. The water here is a dazzling, clear turquoise. It's packed in summer and near empty the rest of the year. Note it isn't ideal for toddlers, as the waves roll in strongly. Microbuses (Map p336; E£2) to Agiba leave from in front of the National Bank of Egypt.

About 1km to 2km east of the hilltop above Agiba there's a long expanse of accessible beach, with fine sand and deep blue water, which is far less crowded than the cove. Confusingly, this stretch of shore is also known as Agiba Beach. To get here, take the turn-off marked by a blue, white and yellow sign (in Arabic) 3km west of Carol's Beau Rivage resort. This paved road leads to the beachfront; the entrance is gated, but at the time of writing there was no fee.

Sleeping

The accommodation situation in Marsa Matruh leaves a lot to be desired. With a few exceptions, hotels generally specialise in mediocrity at unreasonable rates, but demand for rooms over summer is such that hoteliers really don't need to try hard.

Marsa Matruh

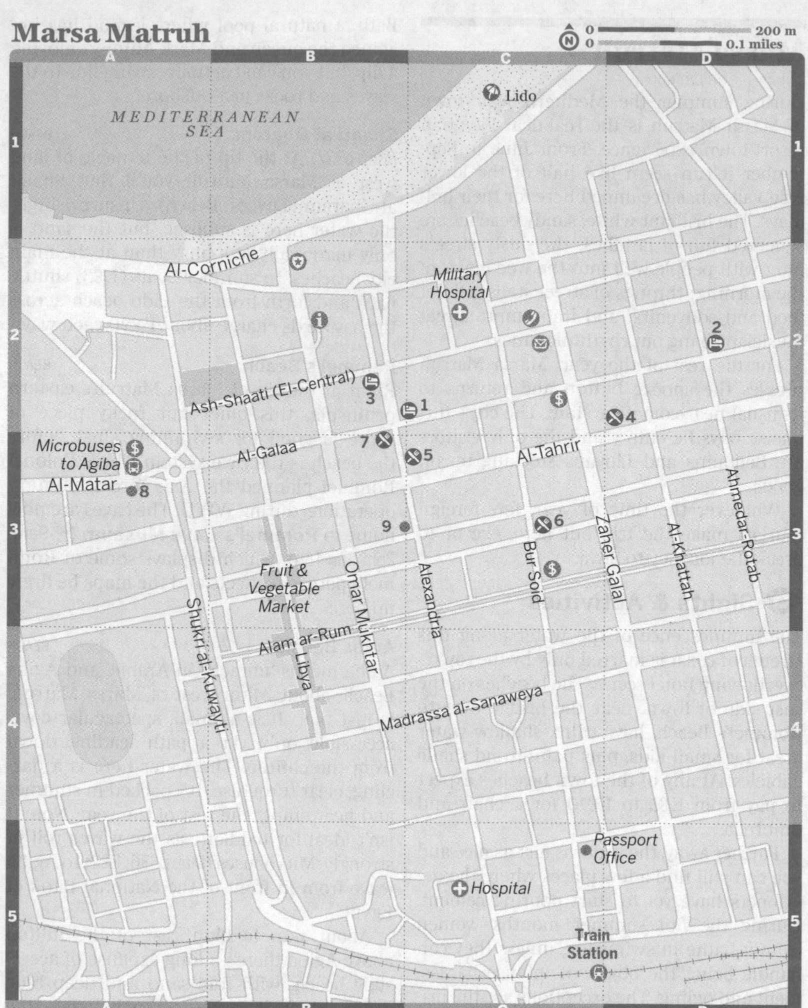

Prices fluctuate wildly from winter to summer. From June to September, you're advised to book well ahead. Note that many hotels will make you pay for a double room even if you are travelling solo. Note that, outside of peak season, it's best to ring ahead to check that your hotel is open, as some choose to shut up shop during the quiet months.

Hotel des Roses INN $

(Map p336; ☎493 2755; Sharia al-Galaa; per person E£85; ⏲mid-Jul–mid-Sep) This charming old hotel feels almost like a country inn, with more character than any other place in town. Oil paintings cover the walls downstairs; bed frames look like hospital surplus; and the pipe-smoking owner has a true bohemian air. Not the most modern, and no air-conditioning, but we like it anyway.

Riviera Palace Hotel HOTEL $$

(Map p336; ☎0127 465 666; Sharia Alexandria; s/d E£200/450; ❄📶) Schizophrenic lobby decor ahoy. We're not sure how the stuffed toy tigers go with the 1950s chintz theme but at least it's far from bland and boring. Rooms are quite large and, despite the obvious wear

Marsa Matruh

Sleeping

Eating

Information

Transport

and tear, good value with crisp white linen on the beds and big bathrooms.

Reem Hotel HOTEL $$
(Map p337; ☎493 3605; Al-Corniche; s/d E£250/400, with air-con E£400/500; ❄) On the plus side this is a hop, skip and jump across the Corniche from the beach. On the negative, upkeep is severely lacking for the price and the rooms are straight out of a 1980s how-to-decorate-your-cheap-motel catalogue. But it's tidy enough, and the location can't be beaten.

El-Lido HOTEL $$
(Map p336; ☎493 2248; Sharia Alexandria; s/d E£150/300; ❄) This centrally located 1970s cement-block hotel has dimly lit rooms complete with crazy red wallpaper. It's quiet, well run and decently clean (for Marsa Matruh). The fan-only rooms have balconies overlooking the street while the air-con rooms (same price) are pokier.

Jaz Almaza Beach Resort RESORT $$$
(☎436 0000; www.jaz.travel/destinations/egypt/mersa-matruh-hotels/jaz-almaza-beach-resort.aspx; s/d US$250/300; ❄@📶🏊) Serious luxury-resort seekers should look no further. On a remote stretch of seafront 37km east of Marsa Matruh, this resort features a sweep of supreme sand fronting the palm-tree-strewn grounds, fantastic restaurants, and all the bells and whistles a sun-worshipper needs. Little ones are well looked after here with kids clubs and child-friendly pools.

Carol's Beau Rivage RESORT $$$
(www.carolsbeaurivage.com; s/d US$200/300; ❄@📶🏊) Set around a delightful bay with glowing aquamarine water, 15km west of Marsa Matruh on Sallum highway, this resort has comfortable rooms in a safari theme, with elephant paintings, dark-wood furnishings and cane chairs on the balconies. The overall feel is a bit institutional, but the beach is certainly one of the nicest in the area.

Negresco Hotel HOTEL $$$
(Map p337; ☎493 4491, 493 4492; Al-Corniche; s/d E£650/1000; ❄📶) Slap bang on the Corniche, the Negresco is a solid, safe choice. The large rooms are ridiculously overpriced for their sparse furnishings, but all have powerful air-con, great showers (in roomy bathrooms), flat-screen TVs, comfortable beds and little balconies. Off-season prices are significantly lower (single/double E£400/550).

Eating

Marsa Matruh is a great town for self-catering, as it's centred on the outdoor food market. Pick up bread, cheese and fruit along with dates and olives from Siwa Oasis for a perfect beach picnic.

Felfela FELAFEL $
(Map p336; Sharia Port Said; meals E£2-15; ✎) The best fuul and felafel joint in town, this is the spot vegetarians – or anyone looking to fill up cheaply – should seek out.

Kamana Restaurant GRILL $
(Map p336; Sharia al-Galaa; meals E£8-20) This simple restaurant does a roaring trade in grilled chicken and kebabs. Follow your nose at the intersection with Sharia Alexandria and you can't miss it.

Around Marsa Matruh

Abdu Kofta GRILL **$$**
(Map p336; ☎0122 314 4989; Sharia al-Tahrir; dishes E£7-60) Locals will swear that this is the best restaurant in town. In the clean and cool 1st-floor room, it serves *kofta* (mincemeat and spices grilled on a skewer) or grilled meat by the weight, served with good mezze and salads.

Abou Aby Pizza PIZZERIA **$$**
(Map p336; Sharia Alexandria; mains from E£15; ⊙lunch & dinner; ✎) This popular place serves up tasty Western-style pizza. Upstairs seating offers good views onto the street action below.

Information

There are several exchange bureau on Sharia al-Galaa.

Banque Misr (Map p336; Sharia al-Galaa; ⊙9am-2.30pm Sun-Thu) Has an ATM.

CIB Bank (Map p336; Sharia Port Said; ⊙8am-3pm Sun-Thu) Has an ATM.

Military Hospital (Map p336; ☎493 5286; Sharia ash-Shaati)

Passport Office (Map p336; ☎493 5351; ⊙8am-3pm Sat-Thu) Off Sharia Alexandria. No sign; look for the yellow/brown building with a line in front, or ask for the *gawezaat.*

SpeedNet (Map p336; 7 Sharia Alexandria; per hour E£2) Internet cafe with hot and soft drinks.

Tourist office (Map p336; ☎493 1841; Sharia Omar Mukhta; ⊙8.30am-7pm Jun-Sep, to 5pm Oct-May) One block off the Corniche. Staff are eager despite lack of information on offer.

Tourist Police (Map p336; ☎493 5575; cnr Sharia Omar Mukhtar & Al-Corniche)

LIBYAN BORDER-CROSSING WARNING

At the time of writing entering Libya overland from Egypt's Amsaad border near Sallum was not possible for foreign travellers due to the ongoing political instability in Libya's Cyrenaica region, which runs from the Egypt–Libya border west to Benghazi. Travellers were not being issued with a tourist visa and those that had been issued with a tourist visa prior to travel were not being allowed to enter Libya through this border. The Libyan government has no control over much of this region and kidnappings, rebel roadblocks and car jackings are common along the main coastal highway from the border. If the situation improves and overland travel again becomes possible, those wishing to cross here should heed government travel advisories and follow the situation on the ground closely.

Getting There & Away

AIR

EgyptAir (Map p336; ☎493 6573; Sharia al-Matar) has twice-weekly flights (Thursdays and Sundays) between Cairo and Marsa Matruh from June to September. Tickets cost about E£700 one way.

BUS

Marsa Matruh's **bus station** (Sharia Alexandria) is 2km south of town. Expect to pay E£10 for a taxi to the town centre. Microbuses (50pt) cruise Sharia Madrassa al-Sanaweya, around where the fruit-and-vegetable market dead-ends, and head to the bus station.

West & Mid Delta Bus Co has hourly services to Alexandria from 7am to 2am (E£35, four hours). During summer it runs buses to Cairo (E£65, five to six hours) at 7.30am, 10.30am, noon, 3.30pm, 5.30pm, 10pm and midnight. In winter buses leave for Cairo at noon and 3.30pm. There are four buses daily to Sallum (E£20, three hours) at 7am, 1.30pm, 4.30pm and 8pm. For Siwa (E£35, four hours) buses leave at 1.30pm and 4pm. Note that the West & Mid Delta buses running between Alexandria and Marsa Matruh seem like the oldest fleet in the country and breakdowns aren't uncommon.

From June to September Super Jet runs daily bus services to Alexandria and Cairo from the bus station; its fleet is – in general – better maintained than West & Mid Delta.

Between June and September there's a ticket booking office for **West & Mid Delta Bus Co** (Map p336; ☎490 5079; Sharia Alexandria) open in the centre of town.

MICROBUS

The microbus lot is beside the bus station. Microbuses to Siwa, if there are enough passengers, cost E£35; they are much more comfortable and efficient than West & Mid Delta buses on the same route but you may have to wait for an hour or two for them to fill up. Other fares include El Alamein (E£20), Alexandria (E£35), Cairo (E£50) and Sallum (E£20).

TRAIN

From 15 June to 15 September three **sleeper trains** (☎02-3748 9488; www.wataniasleepingtrains.com; per person s/d cabin US$60/43) run weekly between Cairo and Marsa Matruh (seven hours). Trains depart Cairo Monday, Wednesday and Saturday at 11.30pm, arriving in Marsa Matruh at 6.30am. For the return journey, trains leave Marsa Matruh on Sunday, Tuesday and

Thursday at 10pm, arriving in Cairo at 5.40am. Make reservations by phone in Cairo or buy your ticket on the train.

Between June and September there are also two air-conditioned 1st-/2nd-class express trains running daily between Cairo and Marsa Matruh (E£58/34 in 1st/2nd class, seven hours).

Ordinary 2nd-/3rd-class trains without air-con run year-round between Marsa Matruh and Alexandria (6½ hours), but these are not recommended – even those working at the station have described the trains as 'horrible'.

Getting Around

Get to or from the airport in one of the EgyptAir minibuses, which leave from several pick-up points along the Corniche.

Private taxis or pick-ups can be hired for the day, but you must bargain aggressively, especially in summer. Expect to pay E£80 to E£150, depending on the distance.

A taxi from the bus station to the Corniche costs between E£10 and E£15.

Bikes can be rented from makeshift rental places along Sharia Alexandria during high season for E£10 to E£20 per day.

Sallum

☎046

Look up 'middle of nowhere' in the dictionary and you might find the town of Sallum, a mere 12km from the Libyan frontier. Nestled at the foot of Gebel as-Sallum and lying on the Gulf of Sallum, the town was once the ancient port of Baranis. While a few Roman wells testify to its history, it is now mostly a rough-and-ready Bedouin trading post that sees few international visitors, though it does have an extremely numerous and enthusiastic population of flies.

The sea here, as along the rest of this stretch of coast, is crystal clear and aquamarine in colour, but don't think about frolicking in the water – dumped rubbish lines the sand, government property surrounds the town, permits are needed to be on the beach after 5pm and the whole town reeks like stale garbage.

On the eastern entrance to the town there is a modest WWII Commonwealth War Cemetery, commemorating the destruction of hundreds of British tanks by the Germans at nearby 'Hell Fire' pass.

Sleeping & Eating

Sallum's accommodation scene is best avoided. There are a few simple food stands speckled around serving up fuul, felafel and kebabs.

El-Gezira Hotel HOTEL $
(☎480 0616; s/d E£100/150) Probably the best bet for bedding down for the night in Sallum (which isn't saying much), El-Gezira has basic rooms with TVs – which may or may not work. It's directly behind the bus stand.

Sirt Hotel HOTEL $
(☎480 1113; s/d E£150/250) The Sirt is flat-out basic, and insanely overpriced for what you get, but is doable for a night. It's about 700m east of the bus stand.

Information

The money changers on the street by Sallum bus stand swap Egyptian pounds for Libyan dinars.

National Bank of Egypt (☎480 0590; 9am-2pm Sun-Thu) The ATM here works and the bank will exchange foreign currency into Egyptian pounds but not Libyan dinars.

Getting There & Away

There are buses and microbuses heading to Sallum from Alexandria and Marsa Matruh.

From Sallum, buses for Marsa Matruh (E£20, three hours) depart at 6am, 10am, noon, 7pm and 9pm. A 10pm bus goes to Alexandria (E£55, eight hours) and Cairo (E£70, eleven hours) or just take a Marsa Matruh service and change there. A *servees* or microbus to Marsa Matruh will cost E£20 to E£30.

Servees (E£5, or E£35 for a whole car) to the Libyan border crossing at Amsaad depart when full.

Suez Canal

Includes ➡

Best Places to Eat

- ➡ El Borg (p344)
- ➡ Pizza Pino (p344)
- ➡ Nefertiti (p347)

Best Places to Stay

- ➡ Mercure Forsan Island (p346)
- ➡ Holiday Hotel (p343)

Why Go?

The Suez Canal, Egypt's glorious triumph of engineering over nature, dominates this region, slicing through the sands of the Isthmus of Suez for 163km, not only severing mainland Egypt from Sinai but also Africa from Asia. The canal was the remarkable achievement of Egypt's belle époque, an era buoyed by grand aspirations and finished by bankruptcy and broken dreams. This period also gave birth to the canalside cities of Port Said and Ismailia. Today their streets remain haunted by this fleeting age of grandeur, their distinctive architecture teetering on picturesque disrepair.

Although this region is often bypassed by all but the most rampant supertanker-spotters, anyone with an interest in Egypt's modern history will enjoy the crumbs of former finery on display. And while the Canal Zone may have no vast ruins or mammoth temples, there's a slower pace to life here that will be appreciated by those travelling with time up their sleeve.

When to Go

Port Said

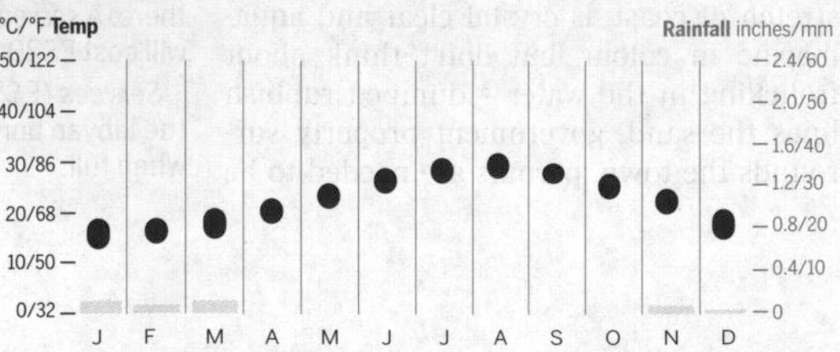

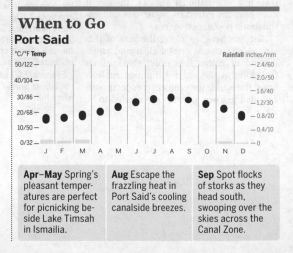

Apr–May Spring's pleasant temperatures are perfect for picnicking beside Lake Timsah in Ismailia.

Aug Escape the frazzling heat in Port Said's cooling canalside breezes.

Sep Spot flocks of storks as they head south, swooping over the skies across the Canal Zone.

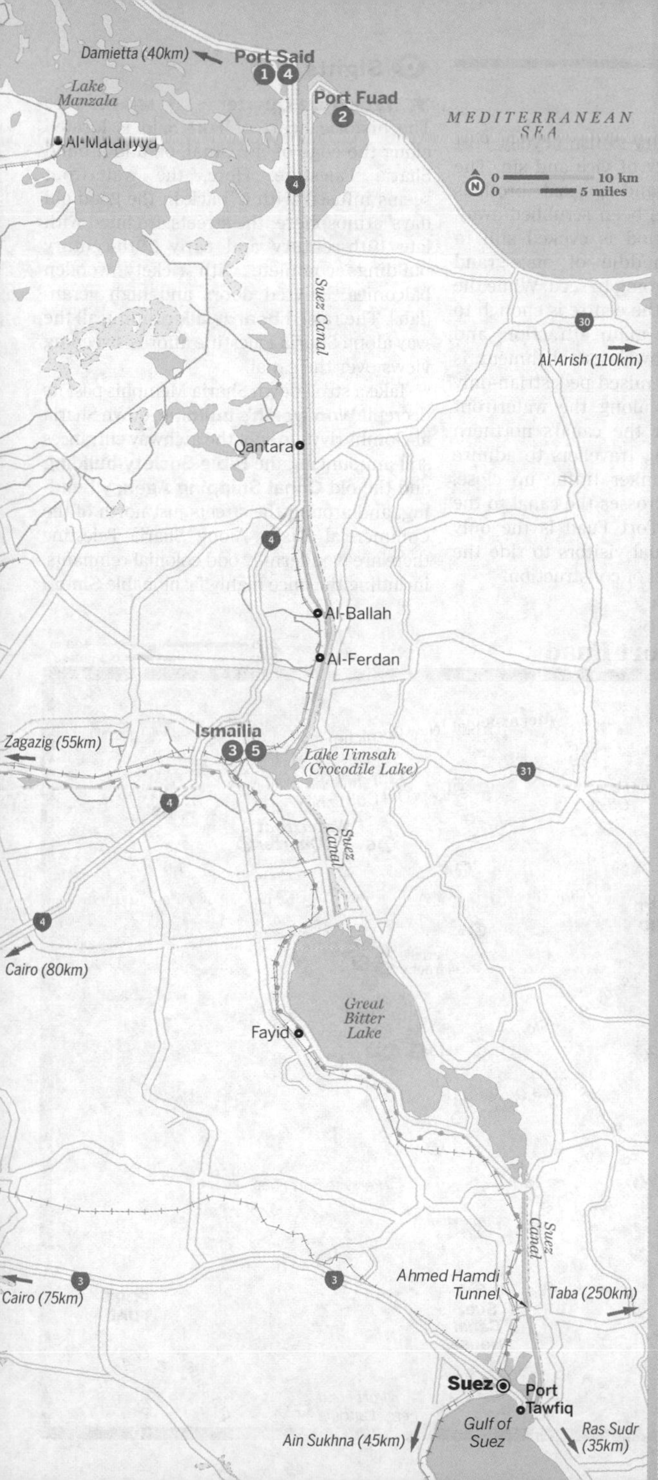

Suez Canal Highlights

1. Exploring the faded grandeur of Port Said's **waterfront quarter** (p342) and then feasting on superfresh seafood along the Corniche.
2. Commuting from Africa to Asia in 15 minutes flat: jump on the ferry from Port Said to **Port Fuad** (p345) to sample life on the canal.
3. Taking a break from Egypt's usual hectic pace among the colonial-era villas of slumberous **Ismailia** (p345).
4. Making peace with your inner supertanker-spotting geek, with a walk along the canalside boardwalk of **Port Said** (p342).
5. Admiring more than 4000 objects from Pharaonic and Graeco-Roman times at the rarely visited **Ismailia Museum** (p345).

Port Said

066 / POP 570,600

In its late-19th-century raffish heyday, Port Said was Egypt's city of vice and sin. The boozing seafarers and packed brothels may have long since been scrubbed away, but this louche period is evoked still in the waterfront's muddle of once-grand architecture slowly going to seed. While the yesteryear allure of the centre is enough to prompt a visit, the main attraction, and the reason for the town's establishment, is the Suez Canal. The raised pedestrian-only boardwalk running along the waterfront provides views over the canal's northern entry point, allowing travellers to admire the passing supertanker traffic up close. The free ferry that crosses the canal to the languid suburb of Port Fuad is the only opportunity for casual visitors to ride the waters of this marvel of construction.

Sights

★Waterfront Quarter NEIGHBOURHOOD

The historic heart of Port Said is located along the edge of the canal, on and around Sharia Palestine. Here, the waterfront seems infused with a 'back in the good old days' atmosphere; the streets are lined with late 19th-century and early 20th-century buildings complete with rickety wooden balconies, louvred doors and high verandahs. The raised **boardwalk** running all the way along Sharia Palestine affords sweeping views over the canal.

Take a stroll down Sharia Memphis past its decrepit **Woolworth's building**, down Sharia al-Gomhuriyya to spot the archway entrances still announcing the **Bible Society building** and the old **Canal Shipping Agency building**, and around the streets just north of the Commercial Basin. Along Sharia Palestine there are wonderfully odd colonial remnants, including the once highly fashionable **Simon**

Port Said & Port Fuad

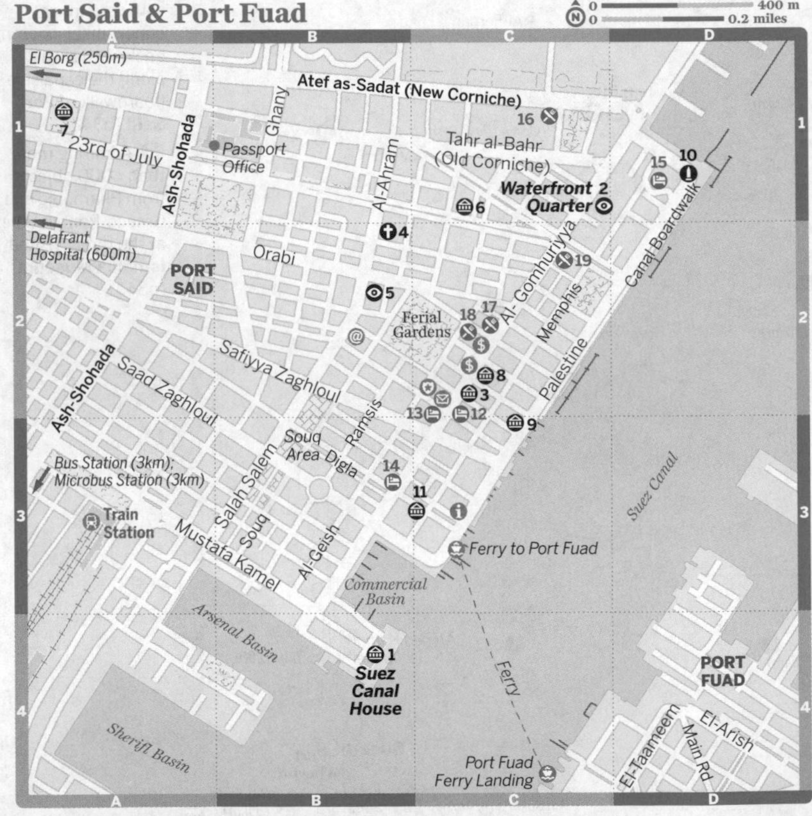

Arzt department store. At the very northern end of Sharia Palestine is a large **stone plinth**, originally to have been the site of what's now known as the Statue of Liberty (p347) and which instead once held a statue of Ferdinand de Lesseps, until it was torn down in 1956 with the nationalisation of the Suez Canal.

East of here, on Sharia 23rd of July, is the **Italian consulate building**, erected in the 1930s and adorned with an engraved piece of the propaganda of fascist dictator Benito Mussolini: 'Rome – once again at the heart of an empire'.

Several blocks inland, on and around Sharia Salah Salem, there is an impressive collection of churches, including the **Coptic Orthodox Church of St Bishoi of the Virgin** and the **Franciscan compound**.

★**Suez Canal House** HISTORIC BUILDING
(Commercial Basin) If you've ever seen a picture of Port Said, it was probably of the striking green domes of the Suez Canal House, which was built in time for the inauguration of the canal in 1869. At the time of writing it was fenced off (and not open to the public), so the best way to get a good look at the building's famous facade is by hopping on the free ferry to Port Fuad (p345).

Port Said & Port Fuad

Top Sights
1 Suez Canal House B4
2 Waterfront Quarter C1

Sights
3 Bible Society Building C2
4 Coptic Orthodox Church B2
5 Franciscan Compound B2
6 Italian Consulate C1
7 Military Museum A1
8 Old Canal Shipping Agency Building C2
9 Simon Arzt Department Store Building C3
10 Stone Plinth D1
11 Woolworth's Building C3

Sleeping
12 Holiday Hotel C2
13 Hotel de la Poste C2
14 New Continental B3
15 Resta Port Said Hotel D1

Eating
16 Abou Essam C1
17 Galal C2
18 Metro Supermarket C2
19 Pizza Pino C2

Military Museum MUSEUM
(322 4657; Sharia 23rd of July; admission E£5; 10am-3pm Sat-Thu) This little museum is worth a peek for its information on the canal and also for some rather bizarre exhibits (complete with toy soldiers) documenting the 1956 Suez Crisis and the 1967 and 1973 wars with Israel. In the museum gardens you can view a few captured US tanks with the Star of David painted on them, as well as an odd collection of UXOs (unexploded ordnance).

Sleeping

New Continental HOTEL $
(322 5024; 30 Sharia al-Gomhuriyya; s/d E£150/220;) Friendly management makes this typical Egyptian budget hotel stand out from the crowd. Light-filled rooms have teensy balconies and come in a range of sizes, so ask to see a few. All come with TV and an astounding clutter of furniture. We particularly love the hilarious gold palm-tree mural decor in the hallways.

Hotel de la Poste HISTORIC HOTEL $
(322 4048; 42 Sharia al-Gomhuriyya; s/d E£75/95;) This faded classic still manages to maintain a hint of its original colonial charm, though you will have to use your imagination. Clean, basic rooms (balconies cost an extra E£15) and a decent ground-floor restaurant are good perks.

★**Holiday Hotel** HOTEL $$
(322 0711; Sharia al-Gomhuriyya; s/d E£235/320;) The Holiday has had a rather swish makeover that includes a new cafe fronting the entrance and smallish, refitted rooms freshly decked out in soothing shades of beige and boasting Ikea-style furniture. It's all surprisingly modern and tasteful. Plenty of company employees from the ships stay here, so the friendly staff are used to foreigners.

Resta Port Said Hotel HOTEL $$$
(332 5511; www.restahotels.com; off Sharia Palestine; s/d US$120/130; P) The rooms at the Resta are about as snazzy as Port Said gets, although it's well overdue for refurbishment. The pool area has views out to the canal, while the business-style rooms are well sized and comfortable. Make sure you ask for a room overlooking the canal.

Eating & Drinking

Self-caterers will find all the groceries they need at **Metro Supermarket** (Sharia al-Geish; ⌚9am-10pm). For fruit and vegetables, try the lively market around Sharia Souq, three blocks north of Sharia al-Gomhuriyya.

★El Borg SEAFOOD **$$**
(☎332 3442; Beach Plaza, off Sharia Atef as-Sadat; mains E£20-50; ⌚10am-3am) This massive Port Said institution is always buzzing with families on a night out. There's a small menu of grills if you don't feel like fish, but the good-value fresh seafood is really what the crowds flock here for. Eat on the shorefront terrace in the evening for superb beach-promenade people-watching.

★Pizza Pino ITALIAN **$$**
(Sharia al-Gomhuriyya; mains E£20-50) This art deco–style bistro has plenty of cosy appeal and attentive staff. Pizza Pino is a local favourite for its hearty portions of pasta, good pizzas and decently priced grills. If only the background music didn't make you feel like you're stuck in an elevator with Kenny G.

Galal EGYPTIAN **$$**
(60 Sharia al-Gomhuriyya; mains E£20-50) Good for a lunch stop in between gazing at the crumbling relics of Port Said's architecture, the friendly Galal has shaded streetside seating and a menu covering all the usual Egyptian favourites from *shish tawooq* (marinated chicken grilled on skewers) to pigeon.

Abou Essam SEAFOOD **$$**
(☎323 2776; Sharia Atef as-Sadat; mains E£30-60) This flashy glass-fronted place does a great selection of fish, pasta and grilled meat, and has a popular serve-yourself salad bar.

Information

Port Said was declared a duty-free port in 1976. In theory, everyone must pass through customs when entering and leaving the city, though in practice this is seldom enforced. Regardless, be sure to have your passport with you.

Most banks and important services are on Sharia al-Gomhuriyya, two blocks inland from the canal.

Delafrant Hospital (☎322 2663; Sharia Orabi; ⌚24hr) Decent, centrally located hospital.

Main post office (Sharia al-Geish; ⌚8.30am-2pm Sat-Thu)

National Bank of Egypt (Sharia al-Gomhuriyya; ⌚8.30am-2.30pm Sun-Thu) Has an ATM.

Tourist office (☎323 5289; 8 Sharia Palestine; ⌚10am-7pm Sat-Thu) Enthusiastic staff and good maps of town.

Tourist police (☎322 8570; Sharia al-Geish; ⌚8am-2pm Sun-Thu) Beside the main post office.

Getting There & Away

BOAT

For Africa overlanders with vehicles it may be possible to journey by cargo ship from Port Said (or nearby Damietta) to Turkey. **Salem Al Makrani Cargo Co** (☎Turkey +90 324-239 22 00; murat@almakrani.com.tr) officially operates sailings every Thursday and Sunday from Damietta to Mersin (cabin per person US$270, car US$600). **Sisa Shipping** (☎Turkey +90 326-613 4374; www.sisashipping.com) supposedly operates weekly sailings from Port Said to Iskenderun or Mersin (per person for pullman seat/two-bed berth US$180/275, motorbike/

THE PORT SAID STADIUM MASSACRE

Port Said was thrown into the international media spotlight in February 2012 when a riot broke out at Port Said Stadium after a football game between rival teams Al-Masry (Port Said) and Al-Ahly (Cairo). Al-Masry supporters attacked Al-Ahly supporters, leaving 74 Al-Ahly fans dead and more than 1000 injured in Egypt's biggest football disaster. Claims that the massacre had been organised by Egypt's security forces hung over the investigation afterwards; however, these have never been proven. The official government inquiry into the incident concluded that lax security and Al-Masry fans were equally to blame. Further furore erupted in Port Said when 21 of the 73 defendants on trial for involvement in the riot were sentenced to death in March 2013, with supporters and lawyers of some of the accused claiming that many of the defendants were scapegoats for those really responsible. As a comparison, many pointed to the fact that the largest sentence handed down for the police officials indicted in the incident was a 15-year jail term. In the wake of the trial, violent antigovernment protests wracked Port Said, Ismailia and Suez throughout early 2013. These left dozens dead and hundreds injured, and the army was finally deployed in the Suez region to restore order.

car US$230/550); unfortunately in reality these services are erratic at best and travellers have been stuck at either end awaiting a boat for up to a month. Sisa Shipping's agent in Port Said is **Kadmar** (☎334 4016; for reservations in Egypt medhat@kadmar.com; El Mahrousa Bldg, Sharia Mahmoud Sedkey), which can organise reservations for Egypt departures.

BUS & MICROBUS

The bus station is about 3km from the town centre at the beginning of the road to Cairo (about E£10 in a taxi).

Super Jet (☎372 1779) has buses every two hours to Cairo (E£25, four hours) and a bus to Alexandria (E£30, four hours) at 4.30pm daily.

East Delta Travel Co (☎372 9883) runs the following services:

Alexandria E£30, four to five hours, departing 7am, 11am, 2pm, 4pm, 6pm and 8pm

Cairo E£25, four hours, hourly from 5am to 9pm daily

Ismailia E£10, one to 1½ hours, hourly from 6am to 11am then 2pm to 6pm

Suez E£15, 2½ to three hours, departing 6am, 10am, 2pm and 4pm

The microbus and *servees* (service taxi) station is next door to the bus station. Sample fares: Cairo (E£25), Ismailia (E£10) and Suez (E£15).

TRAIN

Services to Cairo (E£21/11 in 1st/2nd class, five hours), via Ismailia (E£11/4, two hours), run at 5.30am, 1pm and 5.30pm. There's also a 2nd-class-only service at 7.30pm. Delays are common and buses are, in general, a quicker and way more comfortable option.

Getting Around

Microbuses run along main arteries such as Sharia Orabi and Sharia ash-Shohada, and cost 50pt to E£1 for a short ride.

There are plenty of blue-and-white taxis around Port Said. Fares for short trips within the town centre average E£5.

> **DON'T MISS**
>
> **CROSSING THE CANAL**
>
> Keen to travel across the waters of the Suez Canal but don't have your own yacht? Not best buddies with the captain of a supertanker? Stroll down to the ferry terminal at the southwestern end of Sharia Palestine in Port Said and hop aboard the free ferry to **Port Fuad**. Ferries leave about every 10 minutes throughout the day and the quick journey offers panoramic views of all the canal action.
>
> Once deposited in Port Fuad, founded in 1925, head south from the quayside mosque to explore boulevards lined with sprawling French-inspired residences. Although the streets are now mired in litter and many of the villas teeter on the brink of decay, their sloping tiled roofs, lush gardens and wooden balconies hung with colourful washing still invoke the genteel splendour of a bygone era.

Ismailia

☎064 / POP 293,180

Ismailia was founded by and named after Pasha Ismail, khedive of Egypt in the 1860s while the Suez Canal was being built. The city was also the temporary home of Ferdinand de Lesseps, the director of the Suez Canal Company, who lived here until the canal was completed. Not surprisingly, Ismailia grew in the image of the French masters who had ensconced themselves in Egypt during the colonial era. Today, Ismailia's historic town centre, with its elegant colonial streets, expansive lawns and late-19th-century villas, is one of the most peaceful and picturesque neighbourhoods in Egypt. The heart of Ismailia and the area most worth exploring is the old European quarter around Sharia Thawra and the central square, Midan al-Gomhuriyya.

Sights & Activities

Ismailia Museum MUSEUM

(☎391 2749; Mohammed Ali Quay; adult/child E£15/5; ⏰8am-4pm, closed for noon prayers Fri) More than 4000 objects from Pharaonic and Graeco-Roman times are housed in this small but interesting museum on the eastern edge of town. The collection includes statues, scarabs, stelae and records of the first canal, built between the Bitter Lakes and Bubastis by the Persian ruler Darius. The highlight is a 4th-century-AD mosaic depicting Phaedra sending a love letter to her stepson Hippolytus, while below Dionysus rides a chariot driven by Eros.

Garden of the Stelae MONUMENT

(Mohammed Ali Quay) Just southwest of Ismailia's museum is a garden containing a rather forlorn little sphinx from the time of Ramses II (1279–1213 BC). You need permission from the museum to visit the garden but you are able to see the unremarkable statue from the street.

Ismailia

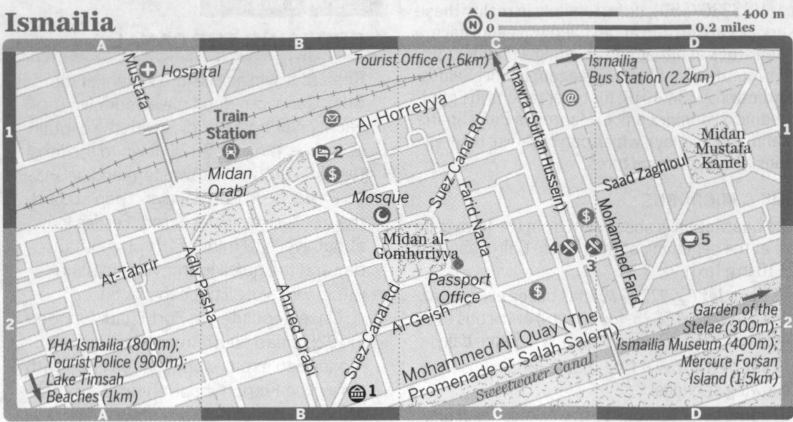

De Lesseps' House HISTORIC BUILDING

(Mohammed Ali Quay) Unfortunately unless you're a guest of the Suez Canal Authority (the house is their private guesthouse) you can only admire the exterior of the one-time residence of the French consul to Egypt from the road outside. Inside the grounds de Lesseps' private carriage has been encased in glass and remains in impeccable condition. The house is located near the corner of Sharia Ahmed Orabi.

Lake Timsah BEACH

There are several beaches around Lake Timsah, on the southeastern edge of town. The better ones are owned by the various clubs dotting the shore and you'll need to pay to use them (on average about E£20); the public beaches charge between E£3 and E£5. For a taxi between town and the beaches expect to pay E£5.

Sleeping

New Palace Hotel HISTORIC HOTEL $

(☎391 7761; Midan Orabi; s/d E£120/160; ❄📶) This old-timer hotel is home to clean, simple rooms that have a decent dose of old-fashioned flair. Grab one of the front-facing rooms for the best deal; some have charming touches such as dark furniture and barrel chairs. Interior-facing rooms are far plainer and pokier but will save you E£20.

YHA Ismailia HOSTEL $

(☎392 2850; Lake Timsah Rd; s/d E£47/52; ❄) This cement block on the shore of the lake doesn't look like much, but its sparkling-clean (if institutional) rooms are decent sized and all come with their own bathrooms, so it's a budget steal. The hostel is a E£5 taxi ride from the centre; ask the driver for Beit Shebab.

Ismailia

Sights
1 De Lesseps' House B2

Sleeping
2 New Palace Hotel B1

Eating
3 Nefertiti C2
4 Thebes Patisserie C2

Drinking & Nightlife
5 El-Mestkawu D2

★ **Mercure Forsan Island** RESORT $$$

(☎391 6316; www.mercure.com; Gezirat Forsan; s/d from €93/103; ❄📶🏊) Occupying its own island 1.6km southeast from Ismailia's centre, the Mercure's private beach and gardens make it a tranquil haven. The snazzy rooms outfitted with modern bathrooms and brightened by colourful textiles are worth splashing out for. Even if you're not staying, stop by for a swim (day passes available for E£160) or a gourmet dinner by the water.

Eating & Drinking

Takeaway and budget places are concentrated on and around Sharia Thawra and around Midan Orabi.

Thebes Patisserie DESSERTS $

(Sharia Thawra; pastries E£3-10; ⏲11am-10pm) Thebes dishes out the best desserts in town and is a great ice-cream stop on a hot day.

★Nefertiti SEAFOOD **$$**
(☎391 0494; Sharia Thawra; mains E£20-45) This dinky place, with walls covered in quirky decorations (everything from Chinese posters to papyrus), has a tasty menu serving up fresh seafood, grills and a bit of pasta. The grilled shrimp is delicious.

El-Mestkawu COFFEEHOUSE
(Sharia Al-Geish; ⏲noon-late) A fabulous shaded verandah cafe where the old-timers of town gossip, drink coffee and watch the world go by while smoking a sheesha.

Information

Banque Misr (Sharia Thawra; ⏲8.30am-2.30pm Sun-Thu) Has an ATM.

Hospital (☎337 3902, 337 3903; Sharia Mustafa; ⏲24hr) Local public hospital. Fine for an emergency.

Main post office (Sharia al-Horreyya; ⏲8.30am-2pm Sat-Thu)

Tourist office (☎332 1078; 1st fl, New Governorate Bldg, Sharia Tugary, Sheikh Zayeed area; ⏲8.30am-3pm Sat-Thu) About 1.5km northeast of Midan Orabi.

Tourist police (☎333 2910; ⏲8am-2pm Sun-Thu) About 2.5km south of Midan Orabi, situated in the Lake Timsah beach area.

Getting There & Away

BUS

Ismailia's **bus station** (Sharia Mohammed Sabry) is about 3km north of the old quarter; taxis to the town centre cost around E£5. From here **East Delta Travel Co** (☎332 1513) has buses to the following destinations:

Alexandria E£35, five hours, twice daily at 7am and 2.30pm

Cairo E£25, four hours, every 30 minutes between 6am and 8pm

Dahab E£65, seven to eight hours, daily at 10.30pm

Port Said E£10, one hour, hourly from 6am to 11am and 1pm to 5pm

Sharm el-Sheikh E£55, six hours, twice daily at 2pm and 10.30pm

Suez E£10, 1½ hours, hourly from 6.30am to 11.30am and 1.30pm to 6.30pm

TRAIN

Services to Cairo (E£15/8 in 1st/2nd class, four to five hours) run at 11am, 2.20pm, 4.15pm and 5.20pm. The 5.20pm service is 2nd class only. Three trains daily run to Port Said (1st/2nd class E£10/4) at 9.45am, 11.15am and 2.15pm. Six 2nd-class-only trains head daily to Suez (E£1.50) at 7am, 8.10am, 10.30am, 1.15pm, 3.15pm and 6pm.

Getting Around

Microbuses ply the main arteries of the city. Fares cost between 50pt and E£1. Taxis are plentiful. Short trips cost from E£3 to E£7.

Suez

☎062 / POP 485,340

Poor old Suez; the heavy thumping delivered during the 1967 and 1973 wars with Israel wiped out most of its colonial relics and so it has none of the nostalgic appeal of Port Said and Ismailia. Instead, a sprawl of grim and gritty concrete blocks overwhelms much of the city, with the additional piles of festering rubbish sprouting along most of the streets simply enhancing the down-and-out air. There are a few old remnants along a couple of streets in Port Tawfiq, which managed to escape the bombing, but nothing of note to deserve a stopover. If you do get stuck here, note that overzealous security measures have made canal-viewing here a no-go; plenty of barbed wire and bored guards stop any wannabe sightseers from snapping photos.

Sleeping

Endeavouring to avoid spending the night in Suez is the preferable option.

Medina Hotel HOTEL **$**
(☎322 4056; Sharia Talaat Harb; s/d E£75/125; ❄) If you don't mind migraine-inducing candy-cane-painted walls and a lack of windows, the Medina is reasonably clean and well cared for.

LADY LIBERTY ON THE CANAL

New York's famous *Statue of Liberty* has its origins in Egypt. The empty plinth at the end of Port Said's Sharia Palestine was originally meant to host a colossal lighthouse in statue form to celebrate the incredible achievement of completing the Suez Canal. French sculptor Frédéric-Auguste Bartholdi designed a torch-bearing Egyptian woman, who would tower over the canal's entrance to symbolise 'Egypt carrying the light of Asia'. Sketches were drawn and models were made but the statue was ultimately abandoned due to costs. Instead Bartholdi's grandiose vision found new life on a completely different continent. With some tweaking, the 'Light of Asia' statue design eventually morphed into New York's Lady Liberty.

Red Sea Hotel HOTEL $$
(☎319 0190; 13 Sharia Riad, Port Tawfiq; s/d E£405/500; ❄📶) In a quiet location near the yacht basin, the Red Sea's decent-sized rooms are home to a range of rough-around-the-edges furniture and ugly brown carpets.

Hotel Green House HOTEL $$
(☎319 1553, 319 1554; greenhouse-suez@hotmail.com; Sharia al-Geish; s/d from E£500/628; ❄@🏊) Although ridiculously overpriced, Hotel Green House is still the nicest place to bed down in Suez (there's not much competition). Rooms are large but desperately dated.

Eating

For inexpensive favourites such as ta'amiyya (Egyptian variant of felafel) and shwarma, take a wander around the Sharia Talaat Harb area.

Koshary Palace EGYPTIAN FAST FOOD $
(Sharia al-Geish; meals E£3-5) Clean and friendly, lots of local flavour and good *kushari* (mix of noodles, rice, black lentils, fried onions and tomato sauce), all in your choice of sizes.

Al-Khalifa Fish Centre SEAFOOD $$
(☎333 7303; Midan Nesima; mains E£20-50) Tucked away on the edge of Midan Nesima in

Suez

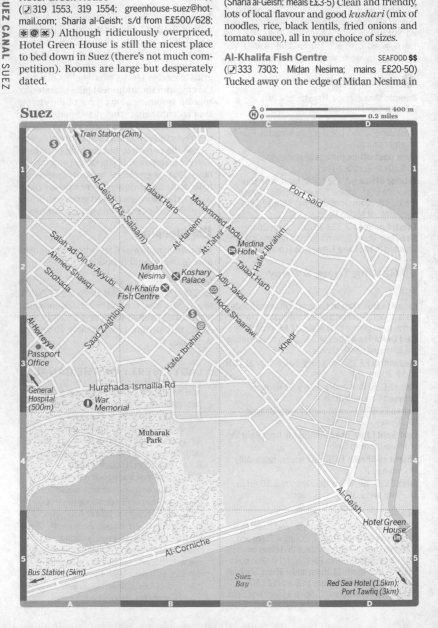

THE SUEZ CANAL

The Suez Canal represents the culmination of centuries of effort to enhance trade and expand the empires of Egypt by connecting the Red Sea with the Mediterranean Sea, but it was Ferdinand de Lesseps, the French consul to Egypt, who pursued the idea through to its conclusion. In 1854 de Lesseps presented his proposal to the Egyptian khedive Said Pasha, who authorised him to excavate the canal; work began in 1859.

A decade later the canal was completed amid much fanfare. When two small fleets, one originating in Port Said and the other in Suez, met at the new town of Ismailia on 16 November 1869, the Suez Canal was declared open and Africa was officially severed from Asia.

Ownership of the canal remained in French and British hands for the next 86 years until, in the wake of Egyptian independence, President Gamal Abdel Nasser nationalised the Suez in 1956. The two European powers, in conjunction with Israel, invaded Egypt in an attempt to retake the waterway by force. In what came to be known as the 'Suez Crisis', they were forced to retreat in the face of widespread international condemnation.

Today, the Suez Canal remains one of the world's most heavily used shipping lanes. In August 2014 plans to further increase traffic along the canal were announced by Egypt's President Sisi. A new 35km-long channel is to be constructed running parallel to the original canal, basically turning the canal into a two-lane water highway for part of its length. With more than 50 ships passing through the Suez each day and yearly toll revenues amounting to US$5 billion, the Suez remains one of the largest contributors to the Egyptian state coffers and a vital component of the country's economy.

the congested town centre, this no-frills place sells the day's ocean catch by weight; you can pick out your fish, then wait for it to be grilled.

Information

Banque Misr (Sharia al-Geish; 8.30am-2.30pm Sun-Thu) Has an ATM.

General Hospital (333 1190; Sharia al-Baladiya; 24hr) Ok for an emergency.

Main post office (Sharia Hoda Shaarawi; 8.30am-2pm Sat-Thu)

Getting There & Away

BUS & MICROBUS

The **bus station** (Cairo–Suez rd) is 5km out of town along the road to Cairo. **East Delta Travel Co** (356 4853) operates to the following:

Cairo E£15 to E£20, two hours, every 30 minutes from 6am to 9pm

Dahab E£60, seven hours, daily at 11am

Ismailia E£10, 1½ hours, every 30 minutes from 6am to 4pm

Port Said E£20, 2½ hours, daily at 7am, 9am, 11am, 12.15pm and 3.30pm

Sharm el-Sheikh E£50, six hours, departing 8.30am, 11am, 1.30pm, 3pm, 4.30pm, 5.15pm and 6pm

St Katherine Protectorate E£35, four hours, daily at 2pm

Upper Egypt Bus Co (356 4258) runs buses to Hurghada (E£35 to E£40, four hours) almost hourly between 5am and 11pm, and to Luxor (E£60 to E£70, nine to 10 hours) via Qena (E£45 to E£50, five to six hours) at 8am, 2pm and 8pm

The microbus and *servees* station is beside the bus station. The only place in Sinai they serve is Al-Tor (E£15).

TRAIN

Six uncomfortable 2nd-class Cairo-bound trains depart Suez daily (E£15 to E£18, three hours) going only as far as Ain Shams, 10km northeast of central Cairo; the first Cairo-bound train leaves at 5.30am. There are also eight slow trains to Ismailia.

Getting Around

There are regular microbus services along Sharia al-Geish to Port Tawfiq. They will pick up or drop off anywhere along the route and they cost 50pt.

Taxis (painted blue) are easy to find almost everywhere. Expect to pay E£10 between the bus station and town, E£15 between the bus station and Port Tawfiq, and E£5 between Suez and Port Tawfiq.

Red Sea Coast

Includes ➡

Why Go?

Some of the most important sites in Christianity's early evolution lie in the Red Sea coast's northern barren mountains. Venture south of brashly loud and proud Hurghada and you'll not only find some of Egypt's best diving but also the epic, wild expanse of the Eastern Desert. Criss-crossed by trade routes dating back to the far reaches of prehistory, and scattered with ancient rock art and lonely ruins, this little-visited area is a desert-adventurer's dream.

Back on the 'Red Sea Riviera', famous (or infamous, depending on your view) for being a bargain bonanza of cheap package holidays, overdevelopment has pock-marked the coastline deeply, leaving a trail of megaresorts and half-finished hotels in its wake. Dig a little deeper into this region, though, and the Red Sea may just surprise you.

Best Places to Eat

- ➡ Zia Amelia (p356)
- ➡ Restaurant Marianne (p367)
- ➡ Le Garage (p356)

Best Places to Stay

- ➡ Wadi Lahami Village (p368)
- ➡ Captain's Inn (p354)
- ➡ Oberoi Sahl Hasheesh (p361)
- ➡ La Maison Bleue (p356)

When to Go

Hurghada

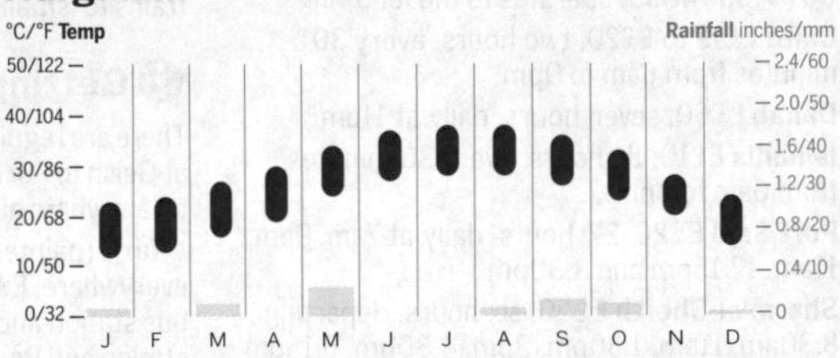

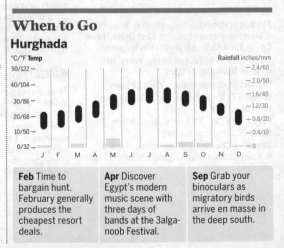

Feb Time to bargain hunt. February generally produces the cheapest resort deals.

Apr Discover Egypt's modern music scene with three days of bands at the 3alganoob Festival.

Sep Grab your binoculars as migratory birds arrive en masse in the deep south.

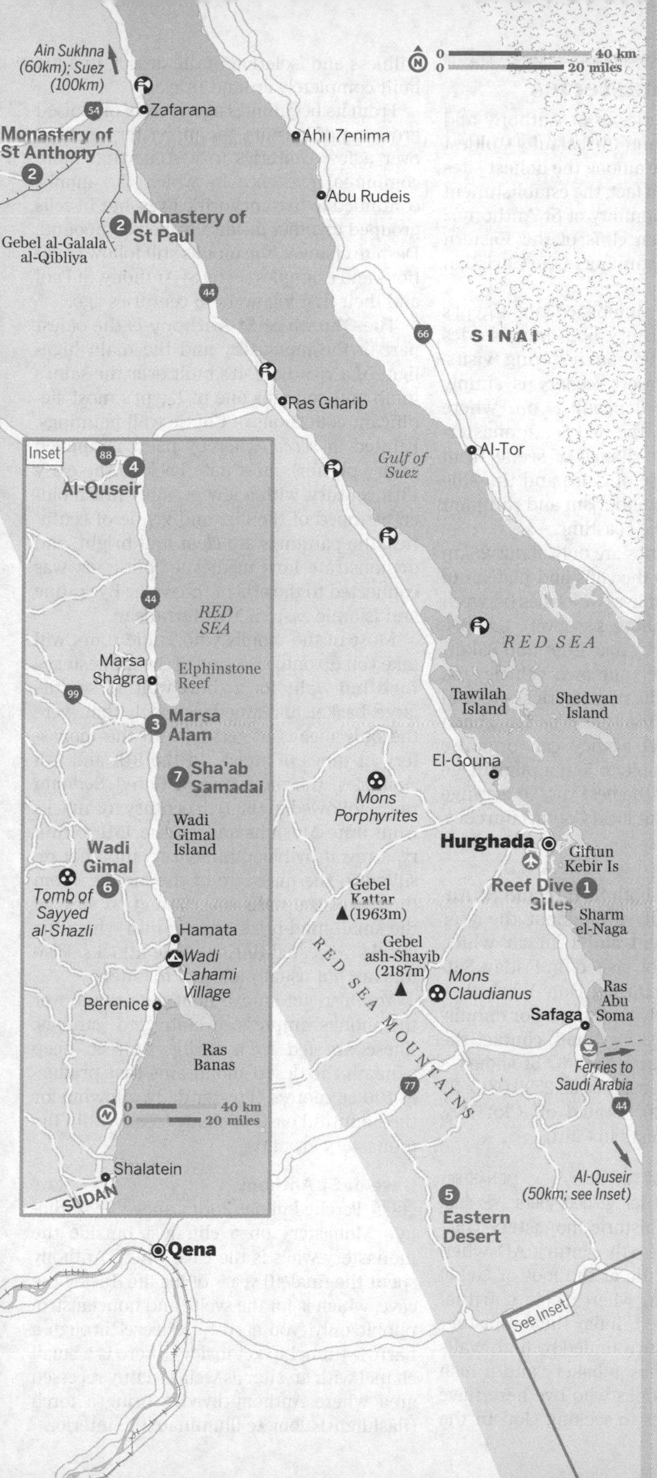

Red Sea Coast Highlights

1. Make a diving-date with the **world-class reefs** (p357) off Hurghada to discover why the Red Sea was catapulted onto the tourism stage.
2. Reflect on monasticism's centuries-old roots at the monasteries of **St Anthony** (p352) and **St Paul** (p353).
3. Flop down at one of the chilled-out beach camps around **Marsa Alam** (p368).
4. Wander the old town of **Al-Quseir**, (p365) where the streets are imbued with an evocative haze of yesteryear.
5. Trek through wadis, mountains and endless expanses of sand in the **Eastern Desert** (p369).
6. Explore remnants of Rome's mighty emerald mines in **Wadi Gimal** (p371).
7. Observe pods of spinner dolphins up close at the kaleidoscope reef of **Sha'ab Samadai** (p369).

Red Sea Monasteries

The Coptic monasteries of St Anthony and St Paul are Egypt's and Christianity's oldest monasteries, and are among the holiest sites in the Coptic faith. In fact, the establishment of the religious community of St Anthony's, hidden in the barren cliffs of the Eastern Desert, marks the beginning of the Christian monastic tradition.

If you're at all interested in Egypt's lengthy Christian history, both monasteries make for fascinating and inspiring visits. The surrounding desert scenery is simply breathtaking and, depending on where you're coming from, the Red Sea monasteries are a refreshing change of scene from the hassles and noise of Cairo and the Nile Valley, or the package tourism and rampant commercialism of the coastline.

The two monasteries are only about 25km apart, but thanks to the cliffs and plateau of Gebel al-Galala al-Qibliya (which lies between 900m and 1300m above sea level), the distance between them by road is around 85km.

If you don't have your own vehicle, the easiest way to visit the monasteries is to join an organised tour from Cairo or Hurghada (any hotel or travel agency can organise these). It's also possible to join a pilgrimage group from Cairo – the best way to arrange this is by enquiring at local Coptic churches.

Sights

The monasteries of both St Paul and St Anthony are open daily throughout the year except during Advent and Lent, at which time they can only be visited on Friday, Saturday and Sunday. During Holy Week they are closed completely to visitors. For enquiries or to confirm visiting times, contact the monasteries' **headquarters** (St Anthony's info 02-2590 6025, St Paul's info 02-2590 0218; 26 Al-Keneesa al-Morcosia), located off Clot Bey, south of Midan Ramses in Cairo.

★ Monastery of St Anthony MONASTERY

(donation appreciated for guided tours; 4am to 5pm) FREE This historic monastery traces its origins to the 4th century AD when monks began to settle at the foot of Gebel al-Galala al-Qibliya, where their spiritual leader, Anthony, lived. Today the monastery is a large complex surrounded by high walls with several churches, a bakery and a lush garden. The 120 monks who live here have dedicated their lives to seeking God in the stillness and isolation of the desert, in a life built completely around prayer.

From its beginnings as a loosely organised grouping of hermits, the monastery evolved over a few centuries to a somewhat more communal existence in which the monks continued to live anchoritic lives, but in cells grouped together inside a walled compound. Despite changes, the monks still follow traditions and examples set by St Anthony, St Paul and their first followers 16 centuries ago.

The **Church of St Anthony** is the oldest part of the monastery and the main highlight of a visit here. It's built over the saint's tomb and contains one of Egypt's most significant collections of Coptic wall paintings. Painted in *secco* (whereby paint is applied to dry plaster), most date back to the early 13th century, with a few possibly much older. Stripped of the dirt and grime of centuries, the paintings are clear and bright, and demonstrate how medieval Coptic art was connected to the arts of the wider Byzantine and Islamic eastern Mediterranean.

Most of the monks who guide tours will take you up onto a section of the monastery's **fortified walls** for a short walk to see the large basket and wooden winch that were the only means of getting into the monastery in times of attack. In the 8th and 9th centuries, the monastery suffered Bedouin raids, followed in the 11th century by attacks from irate Muslims and, in the 15th century, a revolt by bloodthirsty servants that resulted in the massacre of the monks. From the top of the walls you get a great view of the small mud-brick **citadel** into which the monks retreated during these attacks. Visitors are not usually allowed to enter.

You also get an excellent panorama over the monks' impressive cultivated gardens. These are fed by a spring sourced deep beneath the desert mountains that produces 100 cu metres of water daily, allowing for the bountiful oasis of shady trees within the monastery grounds.

Cave of St Anthony CAVE

FREE Perched about 300m above St Anthony's Monastery on a cliff just outside the monastery walls is the cave where Anthony spent the final 40 years of his life. Inside the cave, which is for the svelte and nonclaustrophobic only (you need to squeeze through a narrow tunnel to get inside), there is a small chapel with an altar as well as a tiny recessed area where Anthony lived – bring a torch (flashlight) along to illuminate the interior.

The climb up the 1158 wooden steps to the cave entrance is hot and steep and takes about half an hour if you're reasonably fit. At the top, as you catch your breath on a small ledge (littered with the graffiti of countless pilgrims), you can admire the wide vistas over the hills and valley below.

★ Monastery of St Paul MONASTERY
(donation appreciated for guided tours; ⌚6am-6pm) FREE Dating to the 4th century, the Monastery of St Paul began as a grouping of hermitages in the cliffs around the site where St Paul had his hermitage. The complex's heart is the **Church of St Paul**, which was built in and around the cave where Paul lived. It's cluttered with altars, candles, ostrich eggs (the symbol of the Resurrection) and murals representing saints and biblical stories. The **fortress** above the church was where the monks retreated during Bedouin raids.

St Paul's monastery is quieter and much more low-key than nearby St Anthony's, and is often bypassed in favour of its larger neighbour. But a visit is well worthwhile, and gives a glimpse into the life of silence, prayer and asceticism that has flowered here in the Eastern Desert for almost two millennia. Visitors are welcome and can wander freely around the monastery but taking a guided tour with an English-speaking monk will allow you to access many of the locked areas.

St Paul himself was born into a wealthy family in Alexandria in the mid-3rd century and originally fled to the Eastern Desert to escape Roman persecution. He lived alone in a cave here for more than 90 years, finding bodily sustenance in a nearby spring and palm tree. According to tradition, in AD 343 the then 90-year-old St Anthony had a vision of Paul. After making a difficult trek through the mountains to visit him, Paul died, and was buried by Anthony's hands.

Activities

Monastery Trail HIKING
It is possible to hike between the Monasteries of St Paul and St Anthony along a 30km (approximately) trail across the top of the plateau, taking one to two days to do so. Hiking this rugged area, commonly known as 'Devil's Country', is only for the fit and experienced, however, and should under no circumstances be attempted without a local guide. In 2001 a lone tourist attempting the walk died of thirst after losing his way. Those who have made the hike recommend starting from St Paul's.

Sleeping & Eating

There is no official accommodation for the general public at either monastery, although male pilgrims are allowed to spend the night in a dormitory at the Monastery of St Anthony with written consent from the monastery's Cairo headquarters. Since this is a major destination for Coptic Christians on religious pilgrimages, guests are expected

THE FATHER OF MONASTICISM

Although St Paul is honoured as the earliest Christian hermit, it is St Anthony who is considered the Father of Monasticism. Anthony was born around AD 251, the son of a provincial landowner from a small Upper Egyptian town near Beni Suef. Orphaned with his sister at the age of 18, he was already more interested in the spiritual than the temporal, and soon gave away his share of the inheritance to the poor. After studying with a local holy man, Anthony went into the Eastern Desert, living in a cave and seeking solitude and spiritual salvation. Word of his holiness soon spread and flocks of disciples arrived, seeking to imitate his ascetic existence.

After a brief spell in Alexandria ministering to Christians imprisoned under Emperor Maximinus Daia in the early 4th century, Anthony returned to the desert. Once again, he was pursued by eager followers, though he managed to flee even further into the desert in search of solitude. After establishing himself in a cave on a remote mountain, his disciples formed a loose community at its base, and thus was born the first Christian monastery.

The number of Anthony's followers grew rapidly, and within decades of his death, nearly every town in Egypt was surrounded by hermitages. Soon after, the whole Byzantine Empire was alive with monastic fervour, which by the next century had spread throughout Italy and France.

It is ironic that, for all his influence, Anthony spent his life seeking to escape others. When he died at the advanced age of 105, his sole wish for solitude was finally respected and the location of his grave became a closely guarded secret.

to attend prayer sessions, respect the atmosphere of the grounds and leave a donation at the time of departure. Both monasteries have canteens that sell snacks, drinks and simple meals.

Sahara Inn Motel MOTEL $$
(Cairo–Hurghada hwy; s/d from E£140/250;) If you haven't made reservations in advance, or your XX chromosome prevents you from bedding down in the monastery, you can spend the night in the nearby junction town of Zafarana. Here you'll find the Sahara Inn Motel, which offers up some bare-bones concrete cubicles and a restaurant.

Getting There & Away

Zafarana is located 62km south of Ain Sukhna and 150km east of Beni Suef on the Nile. Buses running between Cairo or Suez and Hurghada will drop you at Zafarana, but direct access to the monasteries is limited to private vehicles and to tour buses from Cairo or Hurghada.

To get to St Anthony's, start from the main Zafarana junction and follow the road west towards Beni Suef for 37km, where you'll reach the monastery turn-off. From here, it's 17km further south along a good road through the desert to St Anthony's.

The turn-off for St Paul's is about 27km south of the Zafarana lighthouse along the road to Hurghada (watch for a small signpost). Once at the turn-off, it's then 10km further along a good tarmac road to the main gate of the monastery, and about 3km further to the monastery itself.

Buses running between Suez and Hurghada can drop you along the main road at the turn-off, from where the only option is hitching. If you do decide to hitch (which isn't the best idea), don't go alone, and be sure you're properly equipped, especially with water, as it's a long, hot, dry and isolated stretch.

El-Gouna

065 / POP 10,000

If you're looking for a family-friendly beach resort far removed from the rough and tumble of real life, look no further. The brainchild of Egyptian billionaire Onsi Sawiris, El-Gouna is a self-contained holiday town frequented by Egypt's chichi set and by Europeans on package tours. Boasting 16 hotels, an 18-hole golf course, and boutique shopping and restaurants galore, it's about as far removed from Egypt's usual dusty hustle as you can get. The only local experience you are likely to have is smoking a sheesha (albeit on a marina terrace overlooking some mighty swanky yachts) but if you're simply after a place to laze on a beach and do some diving then you'll definitely enjoy your time here.

Sights & Activities

El-Gouna is a veritable paradise for water sports. The various dive operators and resort activity centres offer a laundry list of activities including sailing, ocean kayaking, fishing, parasailing, jet-skiing, windsurfing, kitesurfing and waterskiing. El-Gouna is increasingly used by divers as a base to explore the dive sites around Hurghada (p357).

Bibliotheca Alexandrina El-Gouna CULTURAL BUILDING
(Culturama; Kafr El-Gouna; admission E£10; 10am-10pm Sat-Thu) Linked to Alexandria's modern Bibliotheca Alexandrina library, this peaceful oasis is El-Gouna's cultural hub. A multimedia ('culturama') show takes visitors though Egypt's vast history – check the schedule for the various different language screenings – while in the library you can access a huge range of rare books via online links to the Alexandrian library. For those who have forgotten to bring a beach read, take advantage of the fiction lending library.

Emperor Divers DIVING
(0122 488 8779; www.emperordivers.com; Three Corners Ocean View Hotel, Abu Tig Marina; 1 day, 2 dives €59, 3 days, 6 dives €165) This highly reputable dive operator has been running Red Sea dive trips since 1992.

Sleeping

Advance bookings are the name of the game here. Walk-ins are practically unheard of and booking online, or through a travel agent, will score you a much better deal. Most of the accommodation is resort-style with all-inclusive packages the norm, but the Abu Tig Marina area has a clutch of smaller, more midrange options. Check out www.elgouna.com for more accommodation listings.

★**Captain's Inn** HOTEL $$
(358 0170; http://captainsinn.elgouna.com; Abu Tig Marina; s/d/tr from €35/45/58;) This superfriendly hotel is a favourite home away from home for divers and kitesurfers who are in town for thrills on the water rather than fancy rooms. The location, near to restaurants and the beach, is fantastic; the flower-filled courtyard is a great place to relax; and the rooms – decked out in natty blue and white – are light filled and comfortable.

COPTIC ART 101

Before you set foot into the Coptic monasteries of the Eastern Desert, here is a quick introduction to the history and tradition of Egyptian Coptic art.

Coptic art refers to the distinct Christian art of Egypt. Although it originated from the ancient Egyptian and Greek heritages, it has also been influenced by the Persians, Byzantines and Syrians. In fact, due to its myriad influences, the exact nature of Coptic art can be difficult to define, though it is fortunately easy to identify. Since early Christian artisans were extremely utilitarian in their aims, Coptic art typically manifests itself in daily items such as textiles and religious illustrations. Furthermore, Coptic art has a strong tradition of painting, particularly portraits and wall paintings.

Textiles

The Coptic Church inherited a strong tradition of textile-making from the ancient Egyptians, particularly loom and tapestry weaving. For the most part, Coptic textiles are made from linen, though there is some evidence of sophisticated silk-weaving. In regards to design, Coptic textiles borrow heavily from Greek-Egyptian themes, and include traditional pattern motifs such as cupids, dancing maidens and animals. These are typically incorporated with specific Christian motifs such as fish, grapes and biblical scenes, especially the Immaculate Conception.

Religious Illustrations

Religious illustration originated in ancient Egypt when pharaohs started adorning papyrus texts with liturgies and prayers. Coptic Christians retained this tradition, and early papyrus texts maintained the original Egyptian design of protective illustrations surrounded by elaborate borders and text. Like the Egyptians, Coptic artisans used bright colours for vignettes, and striking black ink for all texts. Later on, however, Coptic illustrations began to take on greater complexity as they started to incorporate religious imagery, landscapes and intricate geometric designs.

Portraits

In comparison to other early Christian movements, the Coptic Church is unique in regard to their abundance of martyrs, saints and ascetics. Since the actions and deeds of these individuals helped to form the foundation of the Church, their images were immortalised in portraits, and hung in every chapel and church throughout the land. In these paintings, the human figure is usually depicted in the front position, with placid, almond-shaped eyes and idealised expressions. Coptic portraits of Jesus Christ are unique in that they usually depict him enthroned by saints and angels as opposed to suffering on the cross.

Wall Paintings

Early Coptic wall paintings were unsophisticated in comparison to later endeavours, primarily because ancient Egyptian temples were being converted into churches. In order to complete the transformation, Pharaonic reliefs were covered with layers of plaster, and Christian themes were painted on top. As Coptic art developed and prospered, however, wall painting became increasingly complex, particularly following the mastery of dye mixing and gold stencilling. Some of the finest Coptic wall paintings depict spiritual scenes that are awash with vibrant colours and accented with gold.

Coptic Art Today

Long overshadowed by both ancient Egyptian and Islamic themes, Coptic art does not receive much attention in Egypt despite its lengthy history and established tradition. Fortunately, this cultural heritage has been preserved in museums, churches and monasteries throughout Egypt and the world, and the artistic traditions continue to flourish among communities of modern-day Coptics.

Mosaique HOTEL **$$**

(☎358 0077; http://mosaique.elgouna.com; Abu Tig Marina; s/d from €45/55; ❄📶🏊) We really like Mosaique's bright and breezy rooms with their balconies, comfortable beds and lots of blue-and-white textiles. The location on Abu Tig Marina makes it easy to go out and explore shops and restaurants, although the extremely tempting pool area may put plans for leaving the hotel on hold.

★**La Maison Bleue** HOTEL **$$$**

(☎0128 359 1116; www.lamaison-bleue.com; Kite Centre Rd; ste from €330; ❄📶🏊) Conjuring up an ambience of colonial decadence, La Maison Bleue's interior is all grand tiled floors, intricate wooden ceilings, and walls graced with a quirky mix of art deco and Egyptian motifs to create an opulent yet artistic aesthetic. As you'd expect, the suites here are superiorly comfortable with distinctive early-20th-century styling fit for royalty.

There's a sweep of private beach out front, and if a long, hard day on the beach gets too much, the hotel's gloriously sumptuous spa and hammam will soothe your sun-frazzled soul. If you're out to impress your other half with a romantic getaway, you really can't go wrong here.

Sheraton Miramar RESORT **$$$**

(☎354 5845; www.sheratonmiramarresort.com; El-Gouna; s/d from €150/180; ❄@🏊) Designed by well-known architect Michael Graves, this pastel-toned mammoth five-star resort is one of the signature properties of El-Gouna. The entire complex is strung along a series of beach-fringed private islands just offshore from town. It's a lovely place to stay if you just want to flop out on the beach.

Dawar el-Omda RESORT **$$$**

(☎358 0063; http://dawarelomda-elgouna.com; Kafr El-Gouna; s/d from €60/80; ❄📶🏊) In the heart of downtown El-Gouna, this tastefully decorated four-star resort eschews European design in favour of classic Egyptian lines and arches, and has cosy, well-appointed rooms and a convenient lagoonside location. There's no beach but shuttles are at the ready to whisk you away to the sands.

Eating

★**Zia Amelia** ITALIAN **$$**

(Kafr El-Gouna; mains E£40-80; ⏱1-11pm) El-Gouna's cutest restaurant is rustic done right with a charmingly intimate interior and an outdoor-dining area shaded by vine-covered trellis. The menu is home-style Italian with generous portions of lasagne, homemade pasta and seafood. Leave room for dessert because the tiramisu is decidedly wicked.

★**Le Garage** INTERNATIONAL **$$**

(Abu Tig Marina; mains E£30-90; ⏱4pm-midnight; 📶🖋) Flying the flag for the gourmet-burger craze in El-Gouna, Le Garage does everything from a straight-up burger to varieties such as tandoori chicken, blue cheese with walnuts and grapes, and a burger that's topped with truffles and edible gold leaf. There are a couple of decent veggie options too.

Upstairs INTERNATIONAL **$$**

(Kafr El-Gouna; mains E£40-90) A fine-dining experience for the carnivore in your life, Upstairs (which confusingly is not upstairs) has a menu packed to the rafters with French-influenced meat dishes. The signature dish is a delicious camel and pineapple curry but there's plenty of steak, seafood and other meaty delights if you're not feeling adventurous.

Getting There & Away

AIR

Hurghada Airport is 20km south along the main coastal highway.

BUS

Go Bus Co (☎355 6188, hot line 19567; www.gobus-eg.com) runs seven services daily to Cairo (E£75 to E£150, six hours) finishing at its office beside the Hilton Ramses, in Cairo's Tahrir Sq. Tickets are best booked a day in advance. The ticket office and bus stop in El-Gouna is on the main plaza in Kafr El-Gouna, opposite the tourist information centre.

To Hurghada, buses leave every 20 minutes between 7am and midnight from a bus stop also on the main plaza. Tickets cost E£5.

TAXI

Taxis run frequently between El-Gouna and Hurghada; fares range from E£60 to E£75, depending on your destination.

Getting Around

The El-Gouna sprawl is readily accessible by a comprehensive network of souped-up, decorative local buses known as Tuf Tuf shuttles. Day passes cost E£5 and a weekly pass E£20. Colourful tuk-tuks also whizz around the streets. Standard fares are E£5.

Hurghada

065 / POP 160,900

Plucked from obscurity and thrust into the limelight during the early days of the Red Sea's tourism drive, the tiny fishing village of Hurghada has long since morphed into today's dense band of concrete that marches relentlessly along the coastline for well over 20km. Rampant construction has left the town blighted by half-finished shells of pleasure palaces never realised. The coral reefs closest to the shore – which put Hurghada on the international hot-spot map originally – have been degraded by illegal landfill operations and irresponsible reef use. In recent years Hurghada's star has largely lost its lustre and many travellers have migrated to the newer, glossier resorts of El-Gouna and Sharm el-Sheikh.

There is hope, though. Further offshore there is still superb diving; local NGOs are now playing a leading role in getting the town to clean up its act; and the new resort area concentrated to the south of town and Sigala's swish new marina are bringing back some of Hurghada's sheen. If you want to combine a diving holiday with the Nile Valley sites, Hurghada is a convenient destination. Independent travellers, however, will probably prefer to press on to Dahab in Sinai.

Hurghada is split into three main areas. To the north is Ad-Dahar, the most 'Egyptian' part of the city, with lively backstreet neighbourhoods and a bustling souq. Separated from Ad-Dahar by a sandy mountain called Gebel al-Afish is the congested Sigala area, with shops and restaurants aplenty. South of Sigala, lining the coastal road, is the resort strip. Here you'll find an ever-growing row of mostly upmarket resorts.

Sights

Although many of Hurghada's beaches are bare and stark, developers have snapped up almost every available spot. Apart from the not-so-appealing **public beach** (Map p362; Sigala; admission E£2; 8am-sunset), the main option is to head to one of the resorts, most of which charge nonguests between E£25 and E£75 for beach access.

Dive Sites

The reefs close to Hurghada and El-Gouna have suffered heavy damage due to unfettered tourism development. Thanks to tireless campaigns by local NGOs, however, conservation measures have now been implemented and the situation around both towns is beginning to improve. Most dive sites are only accessible by boat and many diving-boat excursions are happy to take snorkellers along. For all diving tours, shop

RESCUING THE RED SEA

Conservationists estimate that more than 1000 pleasure boats and almost as many fishing boats ply the waters between Hurghada and the many reefs situated within an hour of the town. Fifteen years ago, there was nothing to stop captains from anchoring to the coral, or snorkellers and divers breaking off a colourful chunk to take home. Due largely to the efforts of the **Hurghada Environmental Protection & Conservation Association** (HEPCA; www.hepca.com), however, the Red Sea's reefs are at last being protected.

Set up in 1992 by 12 of the town's larger, more reputable dive companies, HEPCA's program to conserve the Red Sea's reefs includes public-awareness campaigns, direct community action and lobbying of the Egyptian government to introduce appropriate laws. Thanks to these efforts, the whole coast south of Suez Governorate is now known as the Red Sea Protectorate. One of the program's earliest successes was to establish a system of more than 570 mooring buoys at popular dive sites in the region to prevent boat captains dropping anchor on the coral.

While continuing in its efforts to ensure the Red Sea's diving sites are protected, in recent years HEPCA has branched out into even more ambitious conservation projects. In 2009 the NGO took over responsibility for waste management in the southern Red Sea, a service which had been sporadic and unregulated until then. Now Marsa Alam and its environs have a regular door-to-door rubbish-collection service and a recycling plant. The service was judged such a success that in 2010 it was expanded to include Hurghada as well, and is now seen as a model for solid waste management in Egypt.

For more information on safe diving practices or if you'd like to get involved with helping HEPCA protect the Red Sea by joining in a clean-up, check the organisation's website.

Hurghada Coast

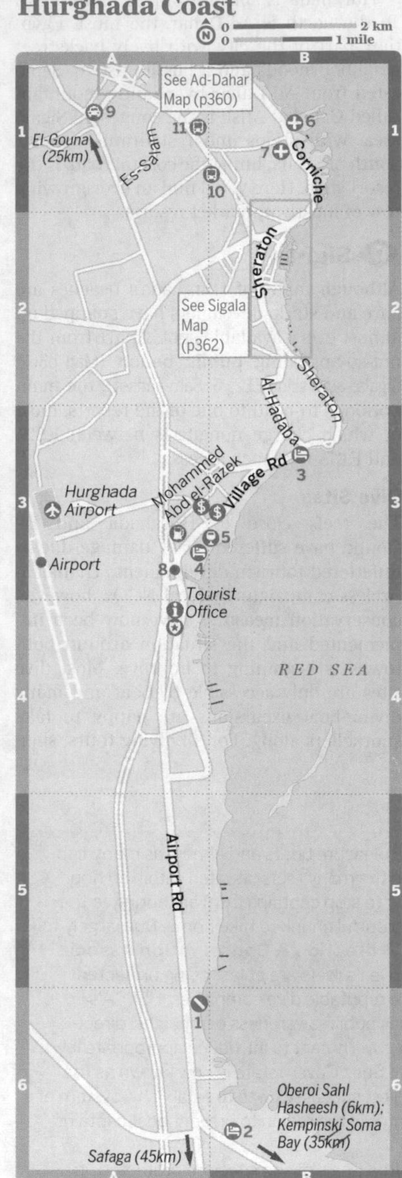

Hurghada Coast

Activities, Courses & Tours
1 Jasmin Diving Centre A6

Sleeping
2 Dana Beach Resort B6
3 Hurghada Marriott Beach Resort B3
4 Steigenberger Al Dau Beach Hotel A3

Drinking & Nightlife
5 Little Buddha B3

Information
6 As-Salam Hospital B1
7 Naval Hyperbaric & Emergency Medical Center B1

Transport
8 EgyptAir A3
9 Servees Station A1
10 Super Jet Bus Station B1
11 Upper Egypt Bus Co Bus Station A1

around a bit. Relying on your hotel may not be the best way to do things; travellers often complain about not getting everything they expected. For any boat trip, take your passport as you'll need to show it at the port.

Siyul Kebira DIVE SITE
(Southern Straits of Gubal) The reef's upper section is home to bannerfish, angelfish and snapper. If the current is strong, you can drift along the wall skirting the edges of huge coral outcroppings. Depth: 10m to 30m. Rating: intermediate.

Sha'ab al-Erg DIVE SITE
(off El-Gouna) Ease of access means this is an excellent dive site for beginners, though veteran divers will still enjoy the towering brain corals and fan-encrusted rock formations. Depth: 5m to 15m. Rating: novice.

Umm Qamar DIVE SITE
Umm Qamar, 9km north of Giftun Islands, has three coral towers that are swathed in purple, soft coral and surrounded by glassfish. Depth: 10m to 27m. Rating: intermediate.

Giftun Islands DIVE SITE
(off Hurghada) These islands are surrounded by a number of spectacular reefs teeming with marine life, including Hamda, Banana Reef, Sha'ab Sabrina, Erg Somaya and Sha'ab Torfa. Depth: 5m to 30m. Rating: intermediate.

Gota Abu Ramada DIVE SITE
An abundance of marine life is on display here, 5km south of Giftun Islands, making Gota Abu Ramada a popular spot for underwater photographers, snorkellers and night divers. Depth: 3m to 15m. Rating: novice.

Activities

Jasmin Diving Centre DIVING
(Map p358; ☎346 0334; www.jasmin-diving.com; Grand Seas Resort Hostmark, Resort Strip; 3 days, 3 dives €87, 2-day PADI Scuba Diver course from €175) This centre has an excellent reputation and was a founding member of Hurghada Environmental Protection & Conservation Association (HEPCA).

Subex DIVING
(Map p360; ☎354 7593; www.subex.org; Ad-Dahar; 1 day, 2 dives €92, 3 days (6 dives) €240) This well-known Swiss outfit is known for its professionalism.

Aquanaut Blue Heaven DIVING
(Map p362; ☎344 0892; www.aquanaut.net; Royal Regina Resort, Sigala; 1 day, 2 dives €33, 3 days, 6 dives €93, 1-day PADI Discover Scuba €80) Long-standing Hurghada dive centre, located off Sharia Sheraton.

Prince Diving Centre DIVING
(Map p360; ☎0111 742 7168; www.prince-diving.com; Sharia Sayyed al-Qorayem, Ad-Dahar; 1 day, 2 dives €35, 3 days, 6 dives €100, PADI Scuba Diver course €180) This backpacker favourite is recommended by past divers.

Tours

Tours to almost anywhere in Egypt can be organised from Hurghada. The most popular options are desert jeep safaris (from E£200); visits to either Mons Porphyrites (p370) or Mons Claudianus (p370); full-day excursions to Luxor or to the monasteries of St Paul and St Anthony (p352); camel treks, quad-bike trips (from E£250) and sunset desert excursions.

Falco Safari ADVENTURE TOUR
(☎0100 390 5492; www.falcosafari.com; quad-bike trip from €25, jeep/buggy safari €30/80) These guys run dune-buggy and quad-biking excursions, and jeep trips into the desert. Vehicle maintenance and safety are of a high standard. They will pick up and drop off at any hotel in the Hurghada or El-Gouna area.

Sleeping

Most budget accommodation is within Ad-Dahar not far from the sea, though the water is rarely within sight. Sigala is a convenient base but it's extremely congested and noisy, while the resort strip, which extends south of Hurghada along the coast, is home to the majority of the city's four- and five-star resorts.

European travel agencies offer significant reductions if you book resorts in advance, especially since prices fluctuate according to the season and state of the tourism industry. If you haven't booked, you can still show up and request a room, although accommodation is more expensive this way. Fortunately, supply outstrips demand, so there is always room for negotiation.

Ad-Dahar

El-Arosa Hotel HOTEL $
(Map p360; ☎0106 667 8765, 354 8434; elarosahotel@yahoo.com; off Corniche; s/d/tr E£100/120/180; ❄ 🏊) El-Arosa overlooks the sea from the inland side of the Corniche. Few of the quaintly old-fashioned rooms have ocean views but they boast decent amenities and there's even a pool (albeit located in the dining room). Staff are extremely sweet and the whole place has a homely feel. Guests get beach day use at a hotel across the road.

Seaview HOTEL $
(☎0127 200 0968; www.seaviewhotel.com.eg; Corniche; s/d/tr E£120/180/230; ❄ 📶) You may need sunglasses to deal with the garish yellow and orange hallways but this place is a great budget deal. Neat, bright rooms are painted an easier-on-the-eye white and green, and all have balconies and some superweird sci-fi-style paintings on the walls. Guests can use the beach at a hotel close by for a small fee.

4 Seasons Hotel HOSTEL $
(Map p360; ☎0122 714 3917; fourseasonshurghada@hotmail.com; off Sharia Sayyed al-Qorayem; s/d E£80/100; ❄ 📶) This long-standing backpacker favourite is run by Mohammed, who is always on hand to dish out advice and help. The rooms unfortunately are looking worse for wear these days though the air-con doubles with balconies are in better nick. There's definite room for negotiation on rates and guests can pay E£20 for beach day use at a nearby hotel.

Geisum Village RESORT $$
(Map p360; ☎354 6692; Corniche; s/d/tr US$25/35/39; ❄ @ 📶 🏊) This stalwart of the Hurghada scene isn't going to win any style awards but its surprisingly tidy and bright rooms (decked out in a cream and green combo) are great for a cheap beach break.

Ad-Dahar

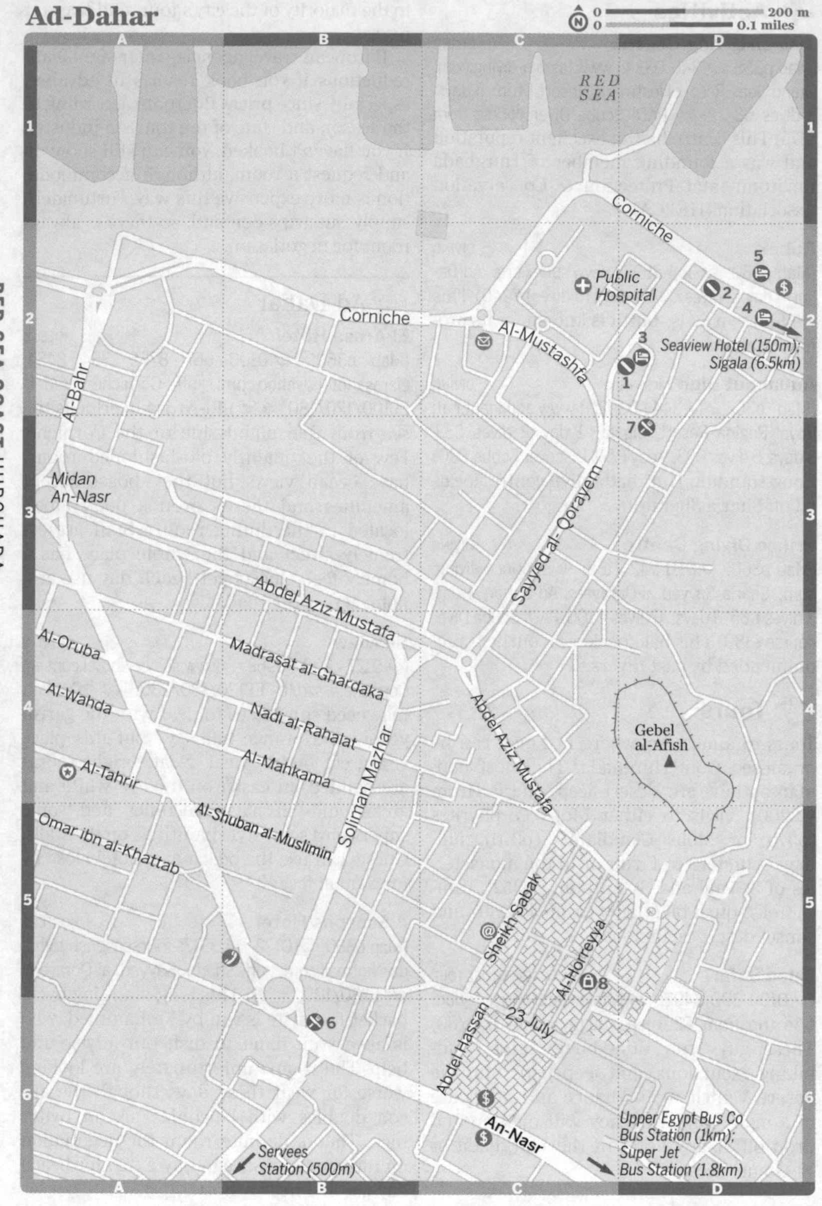

The centre of the action is the large swimming pool surrounded by well-tended gardens that run down to a minuscule patch of private beach.

It's extremely popular with Egyptian families up for boisterous fun in the sun, so don't expect a peaceful retreat.

Ad-Dahar

Activities, Courses & Tours
1 Prince Diving Centre D2
2 Subex D2

Sleeping
3 4 Seasons Hotel D2
4 El-Arosa Hotel D2
5 Geisum Village D2

Eating
6 Gad B6
7 Kanaria D3

Shopping
8 Ad-Dahar Souq C5

Sigala

White Albatross HOTEL $
(Map p362; ☎344 2519; walbatros53@hotmail.com; Sharia Sheraton; s/d E£120/150; ❄) If you want to be slap in the centre of the Sigala action, this small hotel has cosy, extremely clean and comfortable rooms with little homely touches. Unfortunately management here isn't as helpful as elsewhere, but if you're happy to fend for yourself, it's fantastic value.

Roma HOTEL $$
(Map p362; ☎344 8141; www.romahotel-hurghada.com; Sharia al-Hadaba; s/d/tr from US$39/50/64; ❄📶🏊) This business-style hotel has a glitzy lobby that promises much more than the simple rooms deliver, but everything is kept neat and clean, and some rooms have had a recent refit with fresh furnishings and new paint. The swimming pool and private beach are extra bonuses.

Resort Strip

Steigenberger Al Dau Beach Hotel RESORT $$
(Map p358; ☎346 5400; www.steigenberger-aldaubeach.com; Resort Strip; r half board from €67; ❄📶🏊) Large, tastefully decorated rooms, a mind-boggling amount of activities on offer and an absolutely mammoth pool make the Steigenberger a long-running favourite for a family holiday. The private beach is kept beautifully clean and the manicured gardens offer a shady retreat after a day in the sun.

Hurghada Marriott Beach Resort RESORT $$
(Map p358; ☎344 6950; www.marriott.com; Resort Strip; s/d €65/75; ❄@📶🏊) Within walking distance of the resort strip's nightlife and restaurants, the well-kept rooms here exude a modern, beachy feel. Some may be disappointed by the small beach area, but if you want the freedom to pick and choose where to eat, it's a good choice.

★ **Oberoi Sahl Hasheesh** LUXURY HOTEL $$$
(☎344 0777; www.oberoihotels.com; Sahl Hasheesh; ste full board from €225; ❄📶🏊) Peaceful, exclusive and opulent beyond your imagination, the Oberoi features palatial suites decorated in minimalist Moorish style. Each suite comes complete with sunken marble baths, private courtyards – some with pools – and panoramic sea views. Justifiably advertised as the most luxurious destination on the Red Sea, the Oberoi is world-class, and guests here are pampered to their hearts' content.

Kempinski Soma Bay RESORT $$$
(☎356 1500; www.kempinski.com/somabay; Soma Bay; r full board from €140; ❄@📶🏊) Kempinski don't do understated and this massive complex is no exception. From the palatial arabesque lobby to the immense beach and huge pool area, this is luxury firing on all five cylinders. Be aware that the Soma Bay resort area is a good 40km south of Hurghada, so this isn't a place for people who like popping into town.

Dana Beach Resort RESORT $$$
(Map p358; ☎346 0401; www.pickalbatros.com; Resort Strip; r full board from €215; ❄📶🏊) This megaresort serves up masses of amenities, making it a winner for families. There's a reef just offshore that's great for snorkelling, and the well-tended gardens, four swimming pools and a long strip of sand are prime fodder for kicking back and chilling out. Standard rooms are rather bland for the price.

Eating

If you're travelling on a budget, Ad-Dahar and Sigala have dozens of inexpensive local-style restaurants squirrelled away in the back streets.

Gad EGYPTIAN FAST FOOD $
(Map p362; Sharia Sheraton, Sigala; dishes E£5-45; 🖉) If you're looking for cheap, filling and tasty Egyptian staples, you can't go wrong with Egypt's favourite fast-food restaurant. The sprawling menu covers everything from felafel and shwarma to *fiteer* (Egyptian flaky pizza) and full kebab meals. There's another **branch** (Map p360; Sharia an-Nasr) in Ad-Dahar.

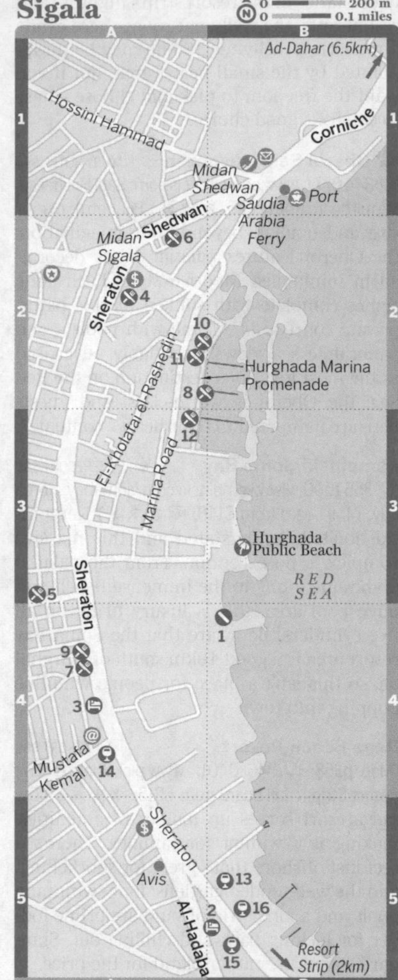

Sigala

Activities, Courses & Tours
1 Aquanaut Blue Heaven B4

Sleeping
2 Roma B5
3 White Albatross A4

Eating
4 Abu Khadigah A2
5 El Zahraa Bakery A3
6 El-Halaka A2
7 Gad A4
8 Ma'Sa'La A2
9 Moby Dick A4
10 Nubian Cafe A2
11 Restaurant B's A2
12 White Elephant A3

Drinking & Nightlife
13 Caribbean Beach Bar B5
14 El Mashrabia A4
15 Retro B5
16 South Beach B5

Abu Khadigah EGYPTIAN $
(Map p362; Sharia Sheraton, Sigala; meals E£10-20) For authentic Egyptian kebabs and other local staples, Abu Khadigah is just the ticket. It's known for its *kofta* (mincemeat and spices grilled on a skewer) and stuffed cabbage leaves.

El Zahraa Bakery SWEETS $
(Map p362; Sigala; sweets E£2-6;) Don't blame us if your dentistry bill skyrockets after a visit to this place. El Zahraa's myriad variations of baklava and *kunafa* (vermicelli-like pastry over a vanilla base, soaked in syrup) are mana for those inclined to a sweet tooth.

Ma'Sa'La INDIAN $$
(Map p362; Hurghada Marina Promenade, Sigala; mains E£45-75;) Dishing up a taste of the subcontinent in Hurghada, Ma'Sa'La is the place to head when you're hankering for a curry. The menu is Anglo-style Indian and the spice is tasty rather than hot but it's all executed brilliantly. Eat on the comfy sofas on the front terrace for blue-sea and flashy-boat views.

Moby Dick INTERNATIONAL $$
(Map p362; Sharia Sheraton, Sigala; mains E£35-100) People rave about Moby Dick's succulent steaks but it also does pasta and seafood as well, and has a fine line in crispy, fresh salads. There's a really nice vibe here and the helpful, chatty staff seem to really care about the food. Beer is also well priced at just E£10 per bottle.

White Elephant ASIAN $$
(Map p362; Hurghada Marina Promenade, Sigala; mains E£40-90;) After a hot day there's nothing like a spicy and zingy Thai feast to help you sweat it out. White Elephant doesn't scrimp on the heat factor either (though you can ask them to tone down the spice). Perfect for Thai-food fans. Serves sushi as well.

El-Halaka EGYPTIAN $$
(Map p362; Sharia Shedwan, Sigala; mains E£15-40) This place makes up for its understated location and interior with some superfresh seafood (the fish market is close by). Fish is priced by weight, but there are plenty of cheaper grills and seafood dishes on the menu.

Nubian Cafe EGYPTIAN $$
(Map p362; Hurghada Marina Promenade, Sigala; mains E£25-70;) In a town where international food rules, it's nice to see someone taking a stand for Egyptian cuisine. The Nubian Cafe does flavoursome *tagens* (a stew cooked in a deep clay pot), good mezze, including a scrumptious *baba ghanoog* (purée of grilled aubergines), and meaty grills. There's plenty for vegetarians to sink their teeth into too.

Kanaria INTERNATIONAL $$
(Map p360; off Shari Sayyed al-Qorayem, Ad-Dahar; small dishes E£7-10, mains E£20-35;) With its hotchpotch interior decoration – dolphin murals, Christmas tinsel, giant baby photos, 3D Mecca panorama – Kanaria is the most eclectic place to eat in Ad-Dahar. The menu can be as hit-and-miss as the decor, but pick the mixed grill and any other Egyptian-style dishes (the moussaka is great) and you can't go wrong.

Restaurant B's INTERNATIONAL $$$
(Map p362; Hurghada Marina Promenade, Sigala; mains E£95-165) With some creative Mediterranean-style starters and a mains menu packed full of meaty options taking their inspiration from around the globe, Restaurant B's has a lot more flair than other Hurghada options. For a slap-up feast, try the camel steak with chocolate chilli sauce, or the Persian-style lamb medallions.

Drinking & Nightlife

Thanks to its large community of resident dive instructors, tour guides, hotel employees and other foreigners, Hurghada has some of Egypt's liveliest nightlife.

South Beach BAR
(Map p362; Sharia Sheraton, Sigala; 10am-2pm) This beach bar has a lovely patch of sand, a good restaurant and plenty of live music to dance to in the evening. It's also home to Egypt's first ice bar. Yep, you don't get much more bizarre than walking out of blistering heat to don a coat and drink cocktails at -5°C.

El Mashrabia CAFE
(Map p362; Sharia Sheraton, Sigala; hot drinks E£4-14, juices E£12-14, sheesha E£2.50-10) This is our favourite pit stop in Hurghada for a juice, tea or sheesha. El Mashrabia is slap on Sigala's main road, with shady outdoor seating and a dimly lit cafe decorated in a mishmash of Chinese lanterns and Pharaonic art. It's easy to spot – the facade is decorated with fake *mashrabiyya* (wooden lattice screens used to screen windows).

Retro BAR
(Map p362; Sharia Sheraton, Sigala) This relaxed pub dishes up live music every Sunday and Wednesday and plays an eclectic mash of rock, blues and soul at other times. An easy-going vibe, decent bar menu and pool table make it an all-round winner.

Caribbean Beach Bar BAR
(Map p362; Sharia Sheraton, Sigala) If you're looking to chill out with a cocktail right next to the sea, this palm-thatched terrace right on the waterfront has a laid-back atmosphere made for lounging. Once the sun has set there's often live music or parties. You have to walk through the Bella Vista Hotel to get here.

Little Buddha CLUB
(Map p358; www.littlebuddha-hurghada.com; Village Rd, Resort Strip) Get your cocktails at the ready for Hurghada's top blingfest. Little Buddha has been the centre of resort-strip nightlife for years now. Beers start at E£20, mixed drinks from E£55 and if you're feeling more than a little flush a bottle of Moet goes for E£1950.

Shopping

Ad-Dahar Souq MARKET
(Map p360; off Sharia an-Nasr) Hurghada's souq area is a dusty sprawl of lanes crammed with shops selling silver and copper products, leather, papyrus and sheesha pipes. This is the place to put your haggling hat on and snag a bargain. It's best visited at night when the worst of the day's heat is done and the alleys are packed with people out for an evening stroll.

Information

DANGERS & ANNOYANCES

Although Hurghada is a resort town, this is still Egypt; both men and women will garner more respect, and receive less hassle, if they save their swimwear for the hotel beaches. Females should also note that topless bathing is illegal in Egypt. All travellers should dress modestly when walking around town, especially in the souq area of Ad-Dahar.

EMERGENCY

Ambulance (☎354 9982, 123)

Police (Map p362; ☎354 6303, 122; Sharia Shedwan, Sigala)

Tourist police (Map p360; ☎065 344 4774; Sharia al-Tahrir, Ad-Dahar) There's another tourist-police kiosk on the resort strip (Map p358; ☎344 4774; Resort Strip) next to the tourist office.

MEDICAL SERVICES

As-Salam Hospital (Map p358; ☎354 8785/6/7; Corniche) Just north of Iberotel Arabella.

Naval Hyperbaric & Emergency Medical Center (Map p358; ☎344 9150, 354 8450; Corniche) Has a hyperbaric chamber. Near Iberotel Arabella.

MONEY

There are ATMs all over the city.

Banque Misr (Map p360; Corniche, Ad-Dahar; ⏲8.30am-2.30pm Sun-Thu) Has an ATM.

HSBC (Map p362; Sharia Sheraton, Sigala; ⏲8.30am-2.30pm Sun-Thu) Also has an ATM on the resort strip (Map p358; Village Rd).

Thomas Cook (Map p362; ☎344 3338; Sharia Sheraton, Sigala; ⏲9am-3pm & 4-10pm) Also has branches in Ad-Dahar (Map p360; ☎354 1871/0; Sharia an-Nasr, Ad-Dahar; ⏲9am-2pm & 6-10pm) and on the resort strip (Map p358; ☎344 6830; Resort Strip; ⏲9am-5pm).

TOURIST INFORMATION

Tourist Office (Map p358; ☎344 4420; Resort Strip; ⏲8am-8pm Sat-Thu, 2-10pm Fri) Small kiosk in the middle of the resort strip.

Getting There & Away

AIR

Hurghada Airport (Map p358; ☎346 2722; Main Hwy), near the resort strip, receives plenty of (mostly charter) flights direct from European destinations. If you've booked a package deal from Europe, it's likely that a flight will be included in your deal.

EgyptAir (Map p358; ☎344 3592/3; www.egyptair.com; Resort Strip) has several daily flights to Cairo. Tickets can be as low as E£350 but prices tend to fluctuate greatly depending on the season.

BOAT

The ferry service between Hurghada and Sharm el-Sheikh stopped operating in 2010. Every year new plans are proposed to begin a new service but, so far, nothing has come of them. Check for an update when you arrive.

BUS

Hurghada doesn't have a central bus station. Instead, the major companies all depart from their own separate stations, which are strung out along Sharia An-Nasr in Ad-Dahar. Bus schedules change randomly, so check timings when booking.

Upper Egypt Bus Co (Map p358; ☎354 7582; off Sharia an-Nasr, Ad-Dahar) departures:

Al-Quseir E£15, 1½ hours, four per day (1.30am, 5am, 9.30am and 4pm). The first three services go on to Marsa Alam (E£25, four hours) and Shalatein.

Aswan E£45 to E£50, seven hours, two per day (10.30pm and 12.30am)

Cairo E£65, six to seven hours, eight per day

Luxor E£30, five hours, four per day (8pm, 10.30pm, 12.30am and 3.30am)

Sharm el-Sheikh E£90, 10 hours, daily (10.30pm)

Suez E£50, four to five hours, seven per day

Super Jet (Map p358; ☎355 3499; Sharia an-Nasr, Ad-Dahar) has daily buses to Cairo (E£70, six hours) departing at midday, 2.30pm, 5pm and midnight. The 2.30pm service also goes to Alexandria (E£100, nine hours). There's a service to Luxor (E£40, four hours) at 8.30am.

SERVEES

Servees (service taxis) leave from the **Servees Station** (Map p358; Ad-Dahar) when full. There are cars to Cairo (E£55 to E£70, six hours), Safaga (E£10, one hour) and Al-Quseir (E£10, 1½ hours). It is also possible to take a *servees* to Luxor (E£25, five hours).

Getting Around

TO/FROM THE AIRPORT

A taxi to downtown Ad-Dahar should cost between E£25 and E£35, but you'll need to bargain hard.

CAR

There are numerous car-rental agencies along Sharia Sheraton in Sigala, including **Avis** (Map p362; ☎344 7400; Sharia al-Hadaba).

MICROBUS

Microbuses run throughout the day from central Ad-Dahar south along the resort strip and along Sharia an-Nasr and other major routes. Rides cost between E£1 and E£3.

TAXI

Taxis from Ad-Dahar to the start of the resort strip (around the Marriott hotel) charge about E£15. Travelling from the bus station to the centre of Ad-Dahar, expect to pay E£10.

Safaga

☎065 / POP 33,720

Safaga is a rough-and-ready port town that keeps itself in existence through the export of phosphates from local mines. It's also a major local terminal for the ferry to Saudi Arabia, and during the hajj, thousands of pilgrims from the Nile Valley set off from here on their voyages to Mecca. Despite the turquoise waters and the reefs that lie offshore, the town itself is an unattractive grid of flyblown, litter-strewn streets. Unless you're into windsurfing (which is top-notch here) or diving and are staying at one of the beach hotels along the resort strip at the northern end of the bay, it's not worth a stopover.

The main road, Sharia al-Gomhuriyya, runs parallel to the waterfront. At the far-northern end of town, near the roundabout with the large dolphin sculpture, a road branches northeast leading to the resort strip.

Sights & Activities

Most people come to Safaga for the diving. It's also a famously windy place, with a fairly steady stream blowing in from the north, and most of the resort hotels have windsurfing centres, plus kitesurfing and other aquatic sports.

Panorama Reef DIVE SITE
(outer Safaga Bay) Panorama Reef is famous for its schooling barracuda, as well as numerous dolphins, eagle rays, grey reef sharks and silvertips. Depth: 3m to 40m. Rating: intermediate. Access by boat.

Salem Express DIVE SITE
(south Safaga Bay) The *Salem Express* is a stunning yet mournful sight. In 1991 this passenger ferry sank with hundreds of pilgrims returning from the hajj on board. While diving, take a moment to reflect on this watery graveyard. Depth: 15m to 30m. Rating: intermediate. Access by boat.

Mena Dive DIVING
(☎326 0060; www.menadive.com; Resort Strip, Safaga; 1 day, 2 dives €47, 3 days, 6 dives €129) Mena Dive has been the centre of Safaga's diving scene since the 1990s.

Orca Dive Club DIVING
(☎326 0111; www.orca-diveclub-safaga.com; Resort Strip, Safaga; 1 day, 2 dives €55, 3 days, 6 dives €156) One of the Red Sea's leading technical diving centres.

Sleeping & Eating

At the northern end of town are several inexpensive restaurants, though nothing is particularly noteworthy. Most travellers prefer to eat in their hotels, and all-inclusive plans are generally available.

Toubia Hotel HOTEL $
(☎0122 313 5676; Corniche; s/d E£150/240) This cement block may not look like much but owner Hakim and his welcoming family create a really homely atmosphere. All 22 simple rooms are kept scrupulously clean and there's a lovely swath of private beach just outside.

Menaville Resort RESORT $$
(☎326 0600; www.menaville-resort.com; Resort Strip; s/d half board per week €330/484; ❄@≋) This low-key four-star resort is very popular with European divers. The hotel fronts a wonderful stretch of sand, and accommodation is in whitewashed, bright and airy bungalows, set around a large pool.

Getting There & Away

The bus station is near the southern end of town. About 1.5km north of the bus station is the *servees* station, followed by the port entrance (for ferries to Saudi Arabia).

BOAT

There are regular passenger boats from Safaga to Duba (Saudi Arabia), and services to Jeddah (Saudi Arabia) during the hajj.

BUS

Safaga is located along the main coastal highway, 53km south of Hurghada. There are seven daily buses to Cairo (E£65 to E£75, seven to eight hours) and regular daily departures to Suez (E£40 to E£45, five to six hours), which also stop in Hurghada (E£10, one hour). There are also a few daily departures to Al-Quseir (E£10, one hour), Marsa Alam (E£25 to E£30, three hours) and Shalatein (E£50, seven hours).

SERVEES

Servees run to Cairo (E£55 to E£60 per person, seven hours), Hurghada (E£10, one hour), Al-Quseir (E£10, one hour) and Marsa Alam (E£15 to £20, two to three hours).

Al-Quseir

☎065 / POP 35,045

Far removed from the resort clamour of the rest of the Red Sea coast, the historic city of Al-Quseir is a muddle of colourful and creaky coral-block architecture, dating from the Ottoman era, that sadly is bypassed by most

Al-Quseir

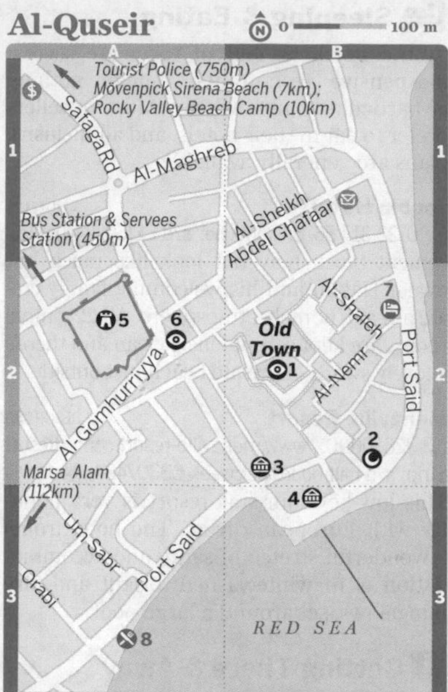

Al-Quseir

Top Sights

1 Old Town B2

Sights

2 Faran Mosque B2
3 Granary B2
4 Old Police Station B3
5 Ottoman Fortress A2
6 Shrine of Abdel Ghaffaar al-Yemeni A2

Sleeping

7 Al-Quseir Hotel B2

Eating

8 Restaurant Marianne A3

tourists. This charmingly sleepy seaside town has a history stretching back to Pharaonic times, when it was the main port for boats heading south to the fabled East African kingdom of Punt. Although nothing remains from this earliest era, strolling through Al-Quseir's photogenic old streets – backed by the battered ramparts of the Ottoman fortress and speckled with the domed tombs of various holy men who died en route to or from Mecca – provides a fascinating glimpse into this region before tourism took over.

History

Prior to the 10th century, Al-Quseir was one of the most important ports on the Red Sea and a major departure point for pilgrims travelling to Mecca for the hajj. It also served as a thriving centre of trade and export between the Nile Valley and the Red Sea and beyond. Even during its period of decline, the city remained a major settlement and was sufficiently important for the Ottomans to fortify it during the 16th century. Later the British beat the French for control of Al-Quseir and for some time it was the main import channel for the spice trade from India to Britain. The opening of the Suez Canal in 1869 put an end to all this, however, and the town's decline accelerated, with only a brief burst of prosperity as a phosphate-processing centre in the early decades of the 20th century.

Sights

Al-Quseir is a lesser-known dive destination; most operators are affiliated with hotels.

Ottoman Fortress FORTRESS

(Map p366; Sharia al-Gomhurriyya; admission E£15; 9am-5pm) Much of the original exterior wall of this small fortress remains intact, although it was modified several times by the French, as well as the British, who permanently altered the fortress by firing some 6000 cannonballs upon it during a heated battle in the 19th century. Inside some of the rooms there are interesting information boards documenting the history of Al-Quseir.

Shrine of Abdel Ghaffaar al-Yemeni SHRINE

(Map p366; Sharia al-Gomhurriyya) Just across from Al-Quseir's fortress is the 19th-century shrine of Yemeni sheikh Abdel Ghaffaar al-Yemeni, which is marked by an old gravestone in a niche in the wall.

El Qadim DIVE SITE

Located 7km north of Al-Quseir in a small bay abutted by the Mövenpick Resort, this dive site boasts a complex network of interconnecting caves and canyons. Depth: 5m to 30m. Rating: intermediate. Access from the shore.

El Kaf DIVE SITE

An easy plunge 10km south of Al-Quseir that appeals to divers of all skill levels, El Kaf is a canyon pitted with small caves and passages, and accented by massive coral boulders and sandy ravines. Depth: 18m to 25m. Rating: novice. Access from the shore.

Sleeping & Eating

★Al-Quseir Hotel HISTORIC HOTEL $
(Map p366; ☎333 2301; www.alquseirhotel.com; Sharia Port Said; r without bathroom E£138-158, with air-con E£198; ❄) If you're looking for atmosphere rather than amenities, this renovated 1920s merchant's house is a delightful place to stay. Sitting right on the seafront, Al-Quseir Hotel has just six simple but spacious rooms and is brimming full of character with its original narrow wooden staircase, high wooden ceilings and latticework on the windows.

Grab a seafront room for views. If you order ahead, meals can be provided. During summer this place practically throbs with heat, so is best avoided.

Rocky Valley Beach Camp BEACH CAMP $$
(☎333 5247; www.rockyvalleydiverscamp.com; 1 week full board incl diving per person €350) About 10km north of Al-Quseir, this camp is a veritable paradise for shoestringing scuba aficionados. Rocky Valley lures in divers by offering a variety of cheap all-inclusive packages, which include Bedouin-style tents, beachside barbecues, late-night beach parties and some incredible reefs right off the shore. It's a fun place where management works hard to foster a communal atmosphere.

Mövenpick Sirena Beach RESORT $$$
(☎335 0410; www.moevenpick-quseir.com; s/d US$130/185; ❄@🛜🏊) This low-set, domed ensemble 7km north of Al-Quseir centre is one of the most laid-back resorts along the coast. Its amenities include excellent food and the usual five-star facilities, diving centre, quiet evenings and a refreshing absence of glitz. The management is known for its environmentally conscious approach.

★Restaurant Marianne EGYPTIAN $$
(Map p366; ☎065 333 4386; Sharia Port Said; mains E£20-40) If you want to sample the bounty of the Red Sea, this local favourite has superfriendly service, a great menu featuring seafood as well as all the usual Egyptian favourites, and seating right on the sand.

Information

National Bank of Egypt (Map p366; Safaga Rd; ⊙8.30am-2.30pm Sun-Thu) Has an ATM.
Tourist police (☎335 0024; Safaga Rd)

Getting There & Away

The bus station is roughly 500m northwest from the old town. Buses run to Cairo (E£80, 10 hours) via Hurghada (E£20 to E£25, 1½ to two hours), departing at 8.30am, 1pm, 3.30pm and 10pm. Buses to Marsa Alam (E£15, two hours) leave at 4am, 6pm and 10pm, but the schedule changes frequently so check ahead.

The *servees* station is next door to the bus station. Cars leave, when full, to Hurghada (E£15 to E£20, 1½ hours) and Marsa Alam (E£15, two hours). Be prepared to haggle.

Getting Around

Microbuses go along Sharia al-Gomhuriyya; some also head to the bus and *servees* stations. Fares are between 50pt and E£1, depending on the distance travelled. A taxi from the bus station to the waterfront costs E£5 to E£7.

DON'T MISS

STROLLING AROUND THE OLD TOWN

Ringed in between Sharia Al-Gomhuriyya and the waterfront is Al-Quseir's **old town** (Map p366). It's a twisting labyrinth of alleyways where progress seems happy to hit the snooze button and local life is snail-paced. Within the squiggle of lanes, wind your way past pastel-washed houses, many boasting original *mashrabiyya* (wooden lattice) window screens and in various states of photogenic decay, while looking out for hand-painted hajj decorations and quirkily coloured doors.

A few historic buildings to look out for on your wandering:

Old Police Station (Map p366; Sharia Port Said) Originally an Ottoman *diwan* (council chamber), the once grand old police station on Al-Quseir's waterfront is now a picturesque but dilapidated shell.

Granary (Map p366) Just behind the old police station is the fortress-like facade of the granary. It dates to the early 19th century and was used to store wheat before being shipped to Mecca.

Faran Mosque (Map p366; Sharia Port Said) The Faran Mosque's minaret was built in 1704.

Marsa Alam & Around

065

In-the-know divers have been heading to Marsa Alam for years, attracted to the seas that offer up some of Egypt's best diving just off the rugged coastline. Despite this, the far-flung destination stayed well off the tourism radar for a long time. Now, however, the secret is out. The area is being heavily touted as the Red Sea Riviera's new tourist drawcard by the Egyptian government, and the last few years have seen a construction boom along the coastline. While the town of Marsa Alam itself is a rather nondescript place, which most of the development has passed by, the strip of coast to its north and south has been snapped up by eager developers and is now home to a plethora of resorts and half-built hotels.

Despite the construction, Marsa Alam's coastline is still a diving aficionado's dream and there are some long-standing beach camps here specifically for those who want to spend most of their time underwater. This is also the best base from which to venture into the southern reaches of Egypt's vast Eastern Desert, where gold and emeralds were once mined by the Romans in the barren, mineral-rich mountains just inland.

Sights

Elphinstone DIVE SITE
North of Marsa Alam, Elphinstone has steep reef walls covered with soft corals, and is washed by strong currents that are ideal for sharks – seven species reportedly frequent its waters. Depth: 20m to 40m. Rating: advanced.

Sha'ab Sharm DIVE SITE
Impressive topography and excellent marine life (hammerheads, barracuda, groper and yellowmouth moray eels) mark this large, kidney-shaped offshore reef 30km northeast of Wadi Gimal. Depth: 15m to more than 40m. Rating: advanced.

Hamada DIVE SITE
Atop an inshore reef 60km north of Berenice lies the wreck of this 65m-long cargo ship. Lying on her side in just 14m of water, *Hamada* is a fairly easy, extremely picturesque dive site. Depth: 6m to 14m. Rating: novice.

Sataya Reef DIVE SITE
Horseshoe-shaped Sataya, 50km north of Berenice, is the main reef of the Fury Shoals, and has steep walls leading down to a sandy slope scattered with a great variety of coral heads. Depth: 4m to more than 40m. Rating: intermediate.

Activities

Red Sea Diving Safari DIVING
(02-337 1833, 02-337 9942; www.redsea-divingsafari.com; Marsa Shagra; 5-day diving packages from €175) Run by environmentalist and longtime diver Hossam Hassan, who pioneered diving in the Red Sea's deep south, this operator is the diving expert for the region.

Festivals & Events

3alganoob Music Festival MUSIC
(0100 739 0971; www.3alganoob.org; Tondoba Bay, Marsa Alam; Apr) Egypt's only modern music festival, this three-day feast features the country's most interesting independent bands in everything from electronica to alternative rock. It's only been going since 2013 but has already developed a devoted following. Camping areas are set up for festival-goers, and activities such as yoga, film screenings, diving and even a beach clean-up are organised.

Sleeping

There are few places to stay in Marsa Alam village itself but north and south along the coast there's an ever-growing number of all-inclusive resorts, plus a handful of simpler, diver-oriented camps, many of which practice sustainable tourism.

Um Tondoba BEACH CAMP $$
(0111 181 2277; www.deep-south-diving.com; Marsa Alam; s/d full board hut €25/50, chalet €35/70) Stripping it right back to the basics of sun, sea and sand, Um Tondoba offers basic palm-thatch beach huts and domed concrete chalets (located across the road from the beach rather than on the shore), good diving packages and an exceptionally mellow atmosphere. It's 14km south of Marsa Alam along the main road.

★ **Wadi Lahami Village** BEACH CAMP $$$
(0122 391 3786, Cairo head office 02-3337 1833; www.redsea-divingsafari.com; Wadi Lahami; s/d full board tent €60/90, royal tent €65/100, chalet €80/120) Tucked into a remote mangrove bay 120km south along the main road from Marsa Alam, this hideaway is worth the extra effort it takes to get here. Diving is the main activity – the pristine reefs of the Fury Shoals are easily accessed by boat – but the

lonely location, and nearby mangroves, are a perfect setting for nature-lovers as well.

Wadi Lahami has a thorough environmental policy and recycles waste and water as well as supporting and promoting sustainable diving practices. It offers simple but spotless and comfortable accommodation in a choice of two-bed tents sharing bathroom facilities or stone chalets with en suite. A superb choice for those seeking beautiful vistas and lashings of tranquillity.

Marsa Shagra Village BEACH CAMP **$$$**
(☎0122 244 9073, Cairo head office 02-3337 1833; www.redsea-divingsafari.com; Marsa Shagra; s/d full board tent €65/100, royal tent €70/110, hut €75/110; 📶) This large-scale camp offers spectacular snorkelling and diving just offshore. Marsa Shagra was one of the first eco-minded places to open on the Red Sea and, despite the development that has gone on around it, has stayed true to its sustainable-tourism credentials. It's 24km north of Marsa Alam along the main road.

Oasis Resort RESORT **$$$**
(☎0100 505 2855; www.oasis-marsaalam.de; Marsa Shagra; s/d half board €65/106; ❄≋) Located 24km north of Marsa Alam along the main road, Oasis is smaller than many of the megaresorts along this stretch, and is unique for utilising local materials and traditional architecture rather than the usual concrete-splurge. Rooms here are spacious, airy and comfortable, offering great sea views.

Information

Hyperbaric Chamber (☎0109 510 0262, emergency VHF code 16 0122 218 7550) Located 24km north of Marsa Alam on the coastal road.

Tourist police (☎375 0000; Quaraya Hotel) On the coastal road.

Getting There & Away

AIR

Marsa Alam Airport (☎370 0021) is 67km north of Marsa Alam along the Al-Quseir road. There is no public transport, so you'll need to arrange a transfer in advance with your hotel.

Egypt Air has flights to Cairo four days per week. Prices tend to fluctuate wildly depending on the season and availability but the cheapest fares tend to be around E£900. The airport is also served by charter flights originating in Europe.

BUS

Marsa Alam bus station is just past the T-junction along the Edfu road. Buses to Cairo (E£85 to E£90, 10 to 11 hours) via Al-Quseir (E£15, two hours) and Hurghada (E£30 to E£35, 3½ to four hours) depart at 1.30pm and 8.30pm, but check beforehand as timetables change frequently. There are also a couple of services per day to Shalatein (E£20 to E£25, four hours).

SERVEES

The *servees* station is beside the bus station and has pretty regular services to Al-Quseir (E£15, two hours).

WORTH A TRIP

ENCOUNTERING DOLPHINS AT SAMADAI

Sha'ab Samadai (Samadai Dolphin Sanctuary; admission E£105), a lagoon 18km southeast of Marsa Alam, is home to three dive sites with a reef system full of interesting coral pinnacles and fish life. What makes Samadai so special, though, is the pod of spinner dolphins (numbering up to 480) which regularly visits the lagoon. As with any wildlife-watching, there is no guarantee that you'll see dolphins on your visit; however, the huge diversity of corals and other sealife here makes snorkelling or diving at Samadai a wonderful experience.

Samadai is managed by local conservation NGO HEPCA (p357; www.hepca.com), which has established a daily cap on visitor numbers to protect the dolphins and introduced an admission fee that goes towards maintaining the conservation of the lagoon.

Eastern Desert

This vast, desolate area, rimmed by the Red Sea Mountains to the east and the Nile Valley in the west, was once criss-crossed by ancient trade routes and dotted with settlements that played vital roles in the development of many of the region's greatest civilisations. Today the Eastern Desert's rugged expanses are filled with fascinating footprints of this history, including rock inscriptions, ancient gold and mineral mines, wells and watchtowers, and religious shrines and buildings. Time spent here is one of the highlights of any visit to the Red Sea coast; it's a world apart from the commercialised coastline.

None of the roads crossing the desert can be freely travelled – some are completely closed to foreigners – and all the sites require a guide. As a result, it is strongly advised (in fact necessary) that you explore the Eastern Desert with the aid of an experienced tour operator.

Sights

Mons Porphyrites RUIN

These ancient Roman porphyry quarries provided the precious white-and-purple crystalline stone used in sarcophagi, columns and other decorative work. It was transported across the desert along the Via Porphyrites to the Nile and then shipped across the Roman world. The quarries were under direct control of the imperial family in Rome, which had encampments, workshops and even temples built for workers here. Evidence of this quarry town can still be seen, although not much of it is standing. Tours can be easily arranged in Hurghada.

Mons Porphyrites is about 40km northwest of Hurghada. A road leading to the site branches off the main road about 20km north of town.

Mons Claudianus RUIN

This Roman granite quarry/fortress complex is one of the largest of the Roman settlements dotting the Eastern Desert. For Roman prisoners, brought to hack granite out of the barren mountains, this was the end of the line. It was more a concentration camp than a quarry – you can see the remains of the tiny cells that these unfortunates inhabited. There is also an immense cracked pillar, left where it fell 2000 years ago, and a small temple. Tours can be easily arranged in Hurghada.

There's a signposted turn-off about 40km along the Safaga–Qena road; from there it's another 25km northwest along a track of deteriorated tarmac.

Barrameya HISTORIC SITE

One of the most impressive rock-inscription collections in the Eastern Desert is at Barrameya, which fringes the Marsa Alam–Edfu road. Here, in the smooth, grey rock are hunting scenes with dogs chasing ostriches, depictions of giraffes and cattle, and hieroglyphic accounts of trade expeditions.

NOMADS OF THE EASTERN DESERT

Although the desert of the southern Red Sea may seem empty and inhospitable, the area has been home to nomadic Ababda and Besharin tribes for millennia. Members of the Beja, a nomadic tribe of African origin, they are thought to be descendants of the Blemmyes, the fierce tribespeople mentioned by classical geographers. Until well into the 20th century, the extent of the territory in which they roamed was almost exactly as described by the Romans, with whom they were constantly at war some 2000 years earlier.

Expert camel herders, the Ababda and Besharin lived a nomadic lifestyle that hardly changed until the waters of Lake Nasser rose and destroyed their traditional grazing lands. While most Besharin, many of whom do not speak Arabic, live in Sudan, most of the Arabic-speaking Ababda are settled in communities in the Nile Valley between Aswan and Luxor. A small number continue to live in their ancestral territory, concentrated in the area from Marsa Alam to Wadi Gimal, as well as on the eastern shores of Lake Nasser.

If you spend time in the region, you'll still likely see traditional Ababda huts, lined inside with thick, hand-woven blankets, or hear Ababda music, characterised by rhythmic clapping and drumming and heavy use of the five-stringed lyrelike *tamboura*. At the centre of Ababda social life is *jibena* – heavily sweetened coffee prepared from fresh-roasted beans in a small earthenware flask heated directly in the coals.

With the rapid expansion of tourism along the southern Red Sea, long-standing Ababda lifestyles have become increasingly threatened. Tourism has begun to replace livestock and camels as the main source of livelihood, and many Ababda men now work as guards or labourers on the resorts springing up around Marsa Alam, while others have started working with travel companies, offering camel safaris to tourists.

There are differing views on the impact of tourism in this region. On one hand, revenue from tourism can play a vital role in the development of the region, particularly through the sale of locally produced crafts or payment for services of a local guide. Indigenous tourism sometimes becomes exploitative, however, and visits can take on an unfortunate 'human zoo' quality. If you are considering a visit, ask questions about the nature of your trip and consider the potential positive and negative impact that it may have on the community.

OFF THE BEATEN TRACK

ON THE EMERALD TRAIL

Source of Egypt's famed emerald mines, the southern region of the Eastern Desert is a wild place of white-sand wadis and craggy peaks that are rarely visited. Starkly beautiful **Wadi Gimal Protectorate** extends inland for about 85km from its coastal opening south of Marsa Alam, and is home to a rich variety of bird life, gazelles and stands of mangrove. The tumbled remains of emerald and gold mines dating from the Pharaonic and Roman eras are scattered throughout the interior. This area provided emeralds that were used across the ancient world and was the exclusive source of the gem for the Roman Empire.

Some major remnants of the Roman's thirst for emeralds have been left in this harshly beautiful desert:

Sikait Sikait is thought to be the main settlement for the workers of the Roman emerald mines. It's about 80km southwest of Marsa Alam. The small Temple of Isis still stands while the remnants of buildings lie strewn across the hillside.

Nugrus The ruins of the actual emerald mines can be seen on the slopes of Nugrus, where the ground is littered with pottery fragments. The smaller ruins of **Geili** and **Appalonia** (both trading points) are nearby.

Karba Matthba This mysterious ruin of what must have once been a substantial villa or complex sit on top of an isolated desert ridge. From here there are incredible panoramas over the sprawling desert tracts.

Wadi Hammamat HISTORIC SITE

This rock-inscription collection is found along the high, smooth walls of Wadi Hammamat, about halfway along the road connecting Al-Quseir to the town of Qift. This remarkable graffiti dates from Pharaonic times down to Egypt's 20th-century King Farouk. The road through the wadi runs along an ancient trade route, and remains of old wells as well as other evidence of the area's long history can be seen along the way.

In Graeco-Roman times, watchtowers were built along the trail at short enough intervals for signals to be visible, and many of them are still intact on the barren hilltops on either side of the road.

Tomb of Sayyed al-Shazli TOMB

(Wadi Humaysara) The Eastern Desert is scattered with numerous Islamic tombs and shrines. One of the best known is that of Sayyed al-Shazli, a 13th-century sheikh, revered as an important Sufi leader. His followers believe that he wanted to die in a place where nobody had ever sinned. Evidently such a place was difficult to find, as the site (about 145km southwest of Marsa Alam) was a journey of several days from either the Nile Valley or the coast.

The tomb was restored under the orders of King Farouk in 1947, and there is now an asphalt road leading to it. His *moulid* (saints' festival), on the 15th of the Muslim month of Shawal, is attended by thousands of Sufis. Note that it's usually difficult (and often impossible) for tour operators to get permission for foreign travellers to visit the area the tomb is in.

 Tours

Although second-rate travel agencies occupy every corner of the tourist hub of Hurghada, it is recommended that you book a tour through a desert specialist.

Red Sea Desert Adventures DESERT TOUR

(0122 399 3860; www.redseadesertadventures.com; Marsa Shagra; per person from €60) This extremely professional safari outfit, run by Dutch geologist Karin van Opstal and Austrian Thomas Krakhofer, offers tailor-made walking, camel and jeep safaris throughout the Eastern Desert. Both have lived in Marsa Alam for over a decade. They are authorities on the geography, culture and history of this area and work closely with local Ababda tribespeople.

Tours start at approximately €60 per person, though cost varies depending on the specifications of your uniquely catered tour, the size of your party and the time of year. In order for the necessary permits to be organised for multiday desert safaris, try to book at least one month in advance. It also offers day tours to Shalatein (€80) and the emerald mines of Wadi Gimal (€90).

Getting There & Away

Apart from trips to Mons Claudianus and Mons Porphyrites, which are easily arranged in Hurghada, the only viable option for accessing the southern Eastern Desert sites is to go through a local tour operator, who can organise permissions and transport arrangements.

Berenice

The military centre and small port of Berenice, 150km south of Marsa Alam, was founded in 275 BC by Ptolemy II Philadelphus. From about the 3rd to the 5th century AD, it was one of the most important harbours and trading posts on the Red Sea coast, and is mentioned in the 1st-century-AD mariner's chronicle *Periplus of the Erythraean Sea*.

The remnants of the ancient town, including ruins of the **Temple of Serapis**, are located just south of the present-day village, and have been the subject of ongoing archaeological investigations. Between excavation seasons the ruins are covered up to aid preservation, meaning there is nothing to see. Just to the northeast of Berenice, jutting into the sea, is Ras Banas peninsula, which is an important military base. Because of this, and despite the slow encroachment of resorts skimming the coastline just to the north around Wadi Lahami, independent visits are not officially allowed. You can expect to be questioned by the tourist police, and to be accompanied by an escort even if you succeed in getting to Berenice.

The nearest accommodation is north of Berenice, along the coast around Hamata and Wadi Lahami.

Buses (E£50, nine hours) departing from Hurghada, bound for Shalatein, stop in Berenice. You will need to arrange your own transport in order to get out to the ruins.

Shalatein

This dusty outpost 90km south of Berenice marks the administrative boundary between Egypt and Sudan. With that said, Egypt considers the political boundary to be another 175km southeast, beyond the town of Halaib, a once-important Red Sea port that has long since fallen into obscurity. Sudan strongly disagrees, resulting in a large swath of disputed territory that is probably worth avoiding in the interest of personal safety.

As with Berenice, independent visitors are discouraged, and the area is sporadically closed to foreigners completely. You can expect to be questioned by the tourist police, and to be accompanied by an escort even if you succeed in getting to Shalatein. In contrast to the suspicion the authorities cast on sole travellers here, Shalatein has become a popular day-trip destination for large groups bussed in from Marsa Alam's resort area. A more sensitive approach to visiting this fascinating area, however, is by organising an excursion through Red Sea Desert Adventures (p371). If you do make it here as an independent traveller, be aware that there is no official accommodation in town and camping needs to be cleared with the police.

Buses (E£55, nine to 10 hours) departing from Hurghada via Berenice terminate in Shalatein.

Sights

Camel Market MARKET

The colourful daily camel market is the major highlight of a visit to Shalatein. This is a major stop on the camel-trading route from Sudan, which for many of the camels finishes in the Birqash camel market outside Cairo. Amid the dust and the vendors, Rashaida tribesmen in their lavender *galabeyas* mix with Ababda, Besharin and other peoples from southern Egypt and northern Sudan.

Shalatein Souq MARKET

Shalatein's old souq is worth a ramble for its intriguing atmosphere that's a world apart from the rest of Egypt. It's a tangle of haphazard wooden-plank shacks selling everything from traditional earthenware jugs used for making *jibena* (coffee) to the latest digital gadgetry displayed on dust-loaded rickety shelves.

Sinai

Includes ➡

Best Places to Eat

- ➡ Wadi Itlah (p406)
- ➡ Lakhbatita (p392)
- ➡ Fairuz (p385)
- ➡ Fares Seafood (p384)

Best Places to Stay

- ➡ Sawa Camp (p399)
- ➡ Al-Karm Ecolodge (p406)
- ➡ Alf Leila (p391)
- ➡ Camel Hotel (p383)
- ➡ Dahab Paradise (p391)

Why Go?

Rugged and starkly beautiful, the Sinai Peninsula's vast and empty desert heart has managed to capture imaginations throughout the centuries. Coveted for both its deep religious significance and its strategic position as a crossroads of empires, prophets and pilgrims, conquerors and exiles have all left their footprints on the sands here.

A springboard to the underwater wonders of the Red Sea, Sinai's seaside resorts serve up a medley of sun-drenched holiday fun that's a world apart from the rest of Egypt. Step away from the buzz of the coast, however, and Sinai's true soul can be found. Here amid the red-tinged, ragged peaks and endless never-never of sand, the Bedouin continue to preserve their proud traditions while dealing with the endless march of progress. On a star-studded night, surrounded by the monstrous silhouettes of mountains, travellers realise why Sinai continues to cast a spell over all who visit.

Note: due to security concerns, research was conducted remotely for this chapter, except Sharm el Sheikh.

When to Go

Dahab

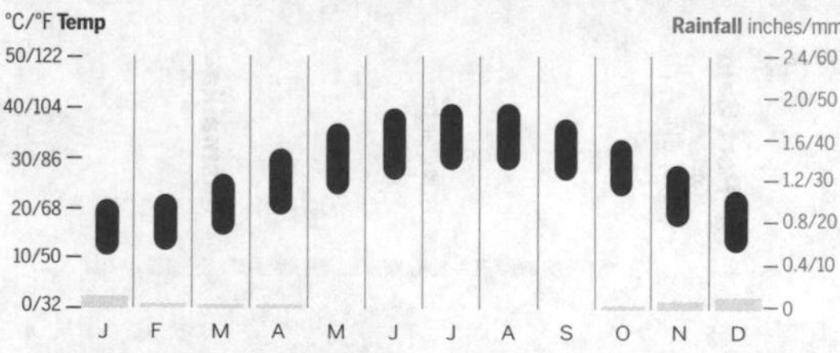

Mar In the desert, spring's colourful flurry of life carpets the sands.

Apr Celebrate all things Sinai at the Dahab Bedouin Festival.

Oct Sneak in some autumn sun along the coast.

Sinai Highlights

1. Dive into **Ras Mohammed** (p378), an underwater fantasia of coral mountains and ghostly shipwrecks.

2. Follow the footsteps of prophets and pilgrims on the time-worn rock stairs of Mt Sinai's **Steps of Repentance** (p404).

3. View one of the world's most important collections of early religious art and manuscripts at **St Katherine's Monastery** (p401).

4. Snorkel the **Lighthouse Reef** (p389) then relax with a beer, sheesha and new friends in the backpacker vortex of **Dahab.**

5. Escape the crowds to laze on a beach, with a to-do

list of nothing, at a **beach camp** (p399) north of Nuweiba.

6 Discover the raw beauty of **Ras Abu Gallum Protectorate** (p394) on a trek or camel safari with a Bedouin guide.

7 Explore the plunging chasm of South Sinai's **Blue Hole** (p390).

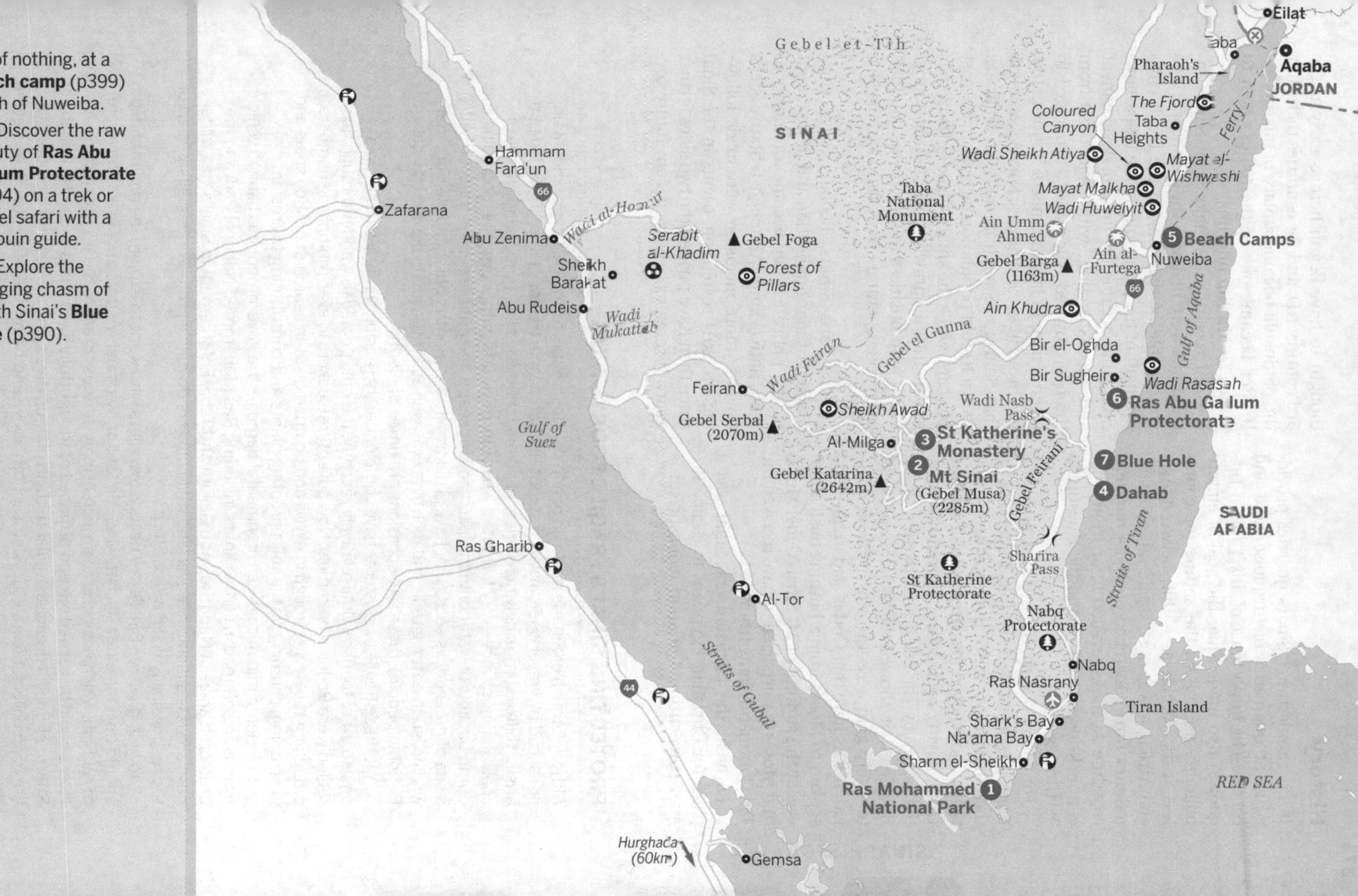

History

In Pharaonic times Sinai's quarries provided great quantities of turquoise, gold and copper. The importance of this 'Land of Turquoise' also made Sinai the goal of empire builders, as well as the setting for countless wars. Acting as a link between Asia and Africa, it was of strategic value – many military forces marched along its northern coastline as they travelled to or from what is now known as Israel and the Palestinian Territories.

For many people, Sinai is first and foremost the 'great and terrible wilderness' of the Bible, across which the Israelites are said to have journeyed in search of the Promised Land, having been delivered from the Egyptian army by the celebrated parting of the Red Sea that allowed the 'Children of Israel' to safely gain access to the dry land of Sinai. It was here that God is said to have first spoken to Moses from a burning bush and it was at the summit of Mt Sinai (Gebel Musa) that Moses is purported to have received the Ten Commandments from God.

Early in the Christian era, Sinai was a place for Christian Egyptians to escape Roman persecution. Christian monasticism is thought to have begun here as early as the 3rd century AD, and for centuries thereafter the peninsula became a place of pilgrimage. It later became one of the routes taken to Mecca by Muslim pilgrims.

Until recently the majority of Sinai's inhabitants were Bedouin, the only people who are capable of surviving in the harsh environment of the peninsula. In the 1990s, however, Sinai became the focus of development and 'reconstruction', with inhabitants from the overcrowded Nile Valley encouraged to resettle here in large numbers. Tourism, too, has brought great changes. Surveys estimate that Sharm el-Sheikh in southern Sinai has seen a 10-fold population increase in the past 20 years, while the small village of Dahab has grown into a sprawling beach-front tourist town, with business in both towns dominated by tour operators from Cairo and the Nile Valley.

For years Sinai's Bedouin have complained of marginalisation and ill-treatment by the police as they become a minority in their native land. Although tentative steps towards more inclusion were made following the 2011 revolution, events in the Sinai since then have pushed the two sides further apart. It remains to be seen if any future gov-

PROTECTING SINAI'S FRAGILE ECOSYSTEMS

Although much of Sinai is made up of hot, dry desert, it is full of life. Craggy mountains are sliced by gravel wadis in which sprout the odd acacia tree or clump of gnarled tamarisk, while a surprisingly rich variety of plants tenuously cling to the sandy flanks of coastal dunes. Once every few years, when storm clouds gather over the mountains and dump buckets of water onto this parched landscape, the entire scene is transformed into a sea of greenery as seeds that have lain dormant for months burst into life. For Sinai's wildlife, such as the gazelle and rock hyrax (as well as for the goats herded by local Bedouin people), these rare occasions are times of plenty.

Yet these fragile ecosystems have come under increasing threat from the rapid onslaught of tourism. Until relatively recently, the only people to wander through this region were Bedouin on camels. Now adventure-seekers in ever-multiplying numbers are ploughing their way through in 4WDs and on quad bikes in search of pristine spots and, in so doing, churning up the soil, uprooting plants and contributing to erosion.

In order to minimise the environmental damage, the government has banned vehicles from going off-road in certain areas, including Ras Mohammed National Park and the protected areas of Nabq, Ras Abu Gallum and Taba. Enforcement in Sinai's vast wilderness areas is difficult, however, and while rangers do patrol protectorates, a large part of the responsibility is left with visitors.

To help preserve Sinai's raw beauty, travellers who want to explore the region in depth should do it the old-fashioned way – on foot or by camel. Visitors should also be aware of rubbish, which has become an increasingly serious threat to Sinai's ecosystems. All litter should be carried out and disposed of thoughtfully. Dive clubs located in Dahab and Sharm el-Sheikh organise regular rubbish pick-up dives, and always find far more than they can collect. Sinai's ecosystems – both above and below the sea – should be treated with care.

ernment can manage to mend the bridge of mutual mistrust that has, up to now, dominated dialogue between Cairo and Sinai's traditional inhabitants.

Dangers & Annoyances

Because of the peninsula's unique position between cultures and continents, plus its mountainous terrain and – in more recent times – its tourist masses, Sinai is considered less safe for travellers than other parts of the country.

A string of bomb attacks in the mid-2000s thrust Sinai into the international spotlight. In 2004 three bomb attacks in Taba killed 34 people and injured more than 150. In 2005 a series of coordinated bombings in Sharm el-Sheikh killed 88 people and injured close to 200 and in 2006 three bombs exploded in Dahab, killing 23 people and injuring more than 75.

Security concerns have again come to the fore in the region since the 2011 revolution. Although much of the activity has occurred in northern Sinai – far from any tourist centre – and specifically targeting police and army facilities, a suicide attack on a tourist bus in Taba on 16 February 2014 that killed four and wounded 16 was firmly aimed at Sinai's tourism industry.

Separately, a spate of kidnapping incidents on the St Katherine–Sharm el-Sheikh and Taba–Dahab roads occurred in 2012 and 2013. On all these occasions the hostages were taken by Bedouin tribesmen in high-profile attempts to pressurise the Egyptian government to release jailed Bedouin. In all instances, the hostages were released unharmed after a short period of negotiation.

It is impossible to offer anything other than speculation regarding the possibility of future terrorist attacks in Sinai. The majority of travellers to South Sinai enjoy their visit without incident. This region, in particular the tourist centres of Sharm el-Sheikh, Dahab and St Katherine, has remained unaffected by the waves of protest in other parts of Egypt since the 2011 revolution.

However, due to security fears in the wider (mainly northern) Sinai region, many foreign government travel advisories warn against travel in all or parts of the Sinai Peninsula. Most still consider Sharm el Sheikh a safe destination. Travellers should read their embassy's advice for updates on the situation and keep informed of the latest events before making travel plans.

SINAI COAST

A barren coastline of extraordinary beauty, the Sinai Coast has seen some of history's most significant events over the past several millennia played out against its isolated shores. These days, however, the region is more renowned for its superb coral reefs, unique Bedouin culture and sandy beaches. South Sinai is both nirvana for members of the international diving fraternity and a famous package-tourism escape for Europeans looking for sun, sand and sea.

Ras Sudr

☎069

Ras Sudr (or simply Sudr) was originally developed as the base town for one of Egypt's largest oil refineries, though its coastline and proximity to Cairo have spurred its transition into a resort area for wealthy Cairene families. The town centre lies just off the main highway, while to the south and north lie a handful of ageing resorts interspersed with holiday villas. With near constant winds, blowing at mostly force five or six, Sudr also enjoys a fine reputation among windsurfers.

One of the most famous places for wind- and kite-surfing, **Moon Beach** (☎340 1500; www.moonbeachholidays.com; 7-day half-board s/d UK£440/750, 7-day windsurfing course incl kit hire UK£150) has beach-front bungalows with all the trimmings. Additionally, there's a professionally staffed and stocked wind- and kite-surfing centre and school. Nightly rates and shorter-stay packages are available.

East Delta has a bus station along the main road about 500m south of the main junction. Buses to Cairo (E£30, two to three hours) depart at 7.30am, 2pm and 4pm. A taxi from the bus station in Ras Sudr to Moon Beach costs about E£30.

Al-Tor

☎069 / POP 19,830

Al-Tor, also known as Tur Sinai, has been a significant port since ancient times, although today it primarily serves as the administrative capital of the South Sinai Governorate. Due to its stiff and constant breezes, Al-Tor has been trying in recent years to establish itself as a wind- and kite-surfing destination.

National Bank of Egypt has a branch with an ATM in the town centre near the post office. If you've overstayed your welcome in

Egypt, you can extend your visa at the Mogamma, the large administrative building on the main road in the town centre.

About 5km from town are some hot springs known as **Hammam Musa** (admission E£25), which tradition holds to have been one of the possible stopping points used by Moses and the Israelites on their journey through Sinai.

The East Delta bus station is along the main road at the northern edge of town opposite the hospital. Buses depart from 7am onward throughout the day to Sharm el-Sheikh (E£15 to E£20, two hours).

Ras Mohammed National Park

About 20km west of Sharm el-Sheikh on the road from Al-Tor lies the headland of **Ras Mohammed National Park** (admission per person €6; ⏲8am-5pm), named by local fishers for a cliff that resembles a man's profile. The waters surrounding the peninsula are considered the jewel in the crown of the Red Sea. The park is visited annually by more than 50,000 visitors, enticed by the prospect of marvelling at some of the world's most spectacular coral-reef ecosystems, including a profusion of coral species and teeming marine life. Most, if not all, of the Red Sea's 1000 species of fish can be seen in the park's waters, including sought-after pelagics, such as hammerheads, manta rays and whale sharks.

Ras Mohammed occupies a total of 480 sq km of land and sea, including the desert in and around the *ras* (headland), Tiran Island, and the shoreline between Sharm el-Sheikh harbour and Nabq Protectorate.

Sights & Activities

Those planning to dive in Ras Mohammed will need to arrive via a boat tour or a liveaboard, both of which typically depart from Sharm el-Sheikh or Dahab.

If arriving at the national park by private car, it's possible to follow a network of (colour-coded) tracks to a variety of wilderness beaches and to snorkel on offshore reefs – travellers need to bring your own snorkelling equipment.

Khashaba Beach BEACH

From Ras Mohammed visitors centre, a pink-signposted track leads to pretty Khashaba Beach, which has a designated camping area (permit required) nearby.

Marsa Bareika Beach BEACH

Yellow arrows point the way to the sandy beaches and calm waters of Marsa Bareika, an excellent sport for snorkelling and safe for children.

Main Beach BEACH

Aptly named Main Beach gets crowded with day-trippers from Sharm el-Sheikh, but with its vertical coral walls just offshore, it remains one of the best snorkelling destinations in Ras Mohammed National Park. Follow the blue-arrowed track to get here.

Aqaba Beach BEACH

A track (brown arrows) leads to Aqaba Beach. Just offshore is the Eel Garden dive site, named after an eel colony 20m down.

Shark Observatory Clifftop VIEWPOINT

This clifftop area, near Main Beach, has views over the dive-site area known as the Shark Observatory. Despite the name, you would be very lucky to spot a shark. The view though, spanning both the Straits of Gubal and the Straits of Tiran, is lovely.

Jolanda Bay BEACH

There's some excellent snorkelling at Jolanda Bay, which is reached by a track marked with red arrows.

Old Quay Beach BEACH

Old Quay beach is perfect for snorkelling; it has a spectacular vertical reef teeming with fish just offshore.

Mangrove Channel FOREST

Green arrows lead to Ras Mohammed's Mangrove Channel, one of the most northerly mangrove forests in the world. Nearby, you can see huge cracks (one of the largest is 40m long) in the earth's surface, caused by ancient earthquakes. The beach of **Hidden Bay** is also nearby.

Salt Lake LAKE

(Magic Lake) This stunningly aqua-blue salt lake is about 200m inland from Ras Mohammed's Mangrove Channel and is a popular swimming stop.

Diving & Snorkelling

Ras Za'atir DIVE SITE

(Marsa Bareika) Off the south lip of the mouth of Marsa Bareika, marking the start of the Ras Mohammed wall, Ras Za'atir has a series of caves and overhangs where black coral trees flourish. Depth: surface to more than 40m. Rating: intermediate. Access: boat.

Jackfish Alley DIVE SITE
(Ras Mohammed) A comparatively shallow site that is good for a second or third dive, Jackfish Alley has two enormous caves filled with shoaling glassfish. Depth: 6m to 20m. Rating: intermediate. Access: boat.

Shark & Jolanda Reefs DIVE SITE
(Ras Mohammed) This two-for-one special off the southern tip of Ras Mohammed is among the most famous dives in the Red Sea, and rated one of the top five dives in the world. Strong currents take divers on a thrilling ride along sheer coral walls, through vast schools of fish and eventually to the remains of the *Jolanda,* a Cypriot freighter that sank in 1980. Depth: surface to more than 40m. Rating: advanced. Access: boat.

Information

All visitors need to bring their passport to enter the park. Travellers who have been issued the 14-day free Sinai-only visa on entry to Sinai cannot go to Ras Mohammed overland but should not have any problem on Ras Mohammed dive-boat trips – check with the dive clubs to confirm.

The entrance to the park is about 20km from the beaches.

Visitors Centre (10am-sunset Sat-Thu) Ras Mohammed's visitors centre is clearly marked

Ras Mohammed National Park

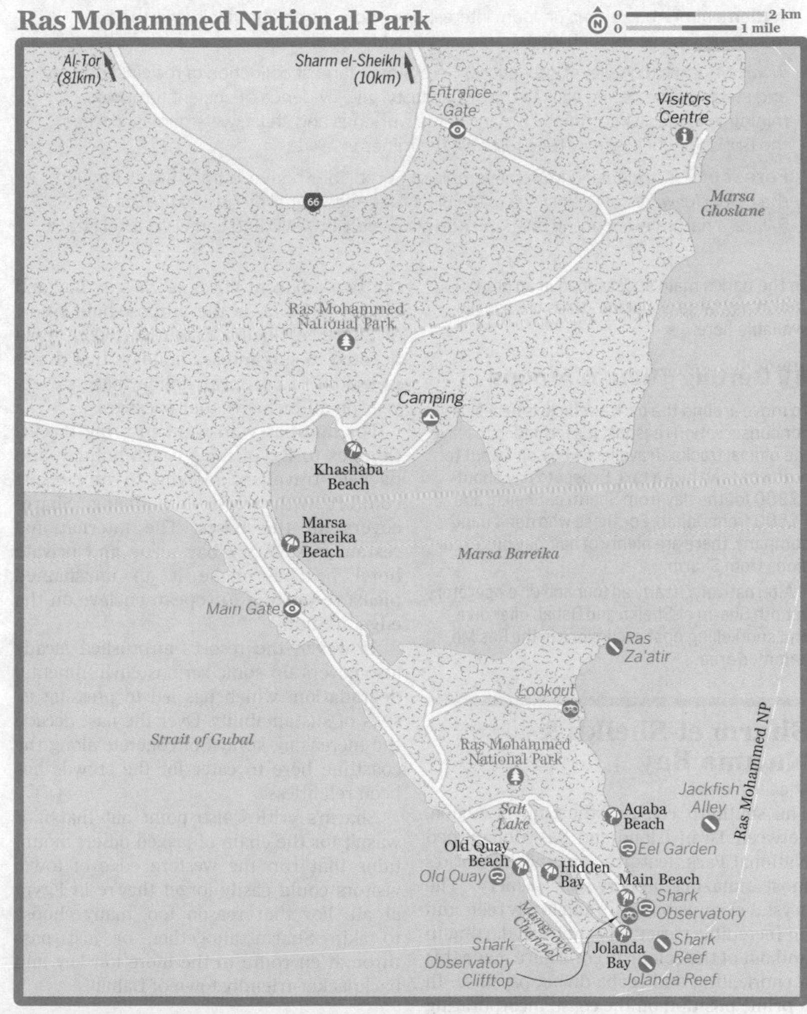

OFF THE BEATEN TRACK

FOLLOWING HISTORY'S FOOTPRINTS TO SERABIT AL-KHADIM

Sinai's rugged expanses are dotted with traces of early settlements and pilgrimage routes. A journey to the area around Serabit al-Khadim captures a sense of this ancient history and takes travellers into the rugged, desolate heartland of the region.

The most straightforward way to visit this area is to arrange a trip with a tour operator in Dahab (a two-day 4WD tour costs roughly E£700 per person).

Highlights of this lesser-seen part of Sinai:

Serabit al-Khadim One of Sinai's most impressive sites, this ruined Pharaonic temple is surrounded by ancient turquoise mines and starkly beautiful landscapes. Turquoise was mined here as far back as the Old Kingdom, and the temple, dedicated to the goddess Hathor, dates back to the 12th dynasty. Beside it is a New Kingdom shrine to Sopdu, god of the Eastern Desert. Inscriptions upon the temple court walls list the temple's benefactors, including Hatshepsut (1473–1458 BC) and Tuthmosis III (1479–1425 BC).

Serabit al-Khadim can be reached via an unsignposted track just south of the coastal settlement of Abu Zenima or, more interestingly, from a track branching north off the road running east through Wadi Feiran via Wadi Mukattab.

Wadi Mukattab (Valley of Inscriptions) Here Sinai's largest collection of rock inscriptions and stelae, some dating back to the 3rd dynasty, give evidence of ancient turquoise-mining activities. Unfortunately, many of the workings and stelae were damaged when the British unsuccessfully tried to revive the mines in 1901.

Forest of Pillars Inland from the temple of Serabit al-Khadim, a track heads through the colourful wadis of Gebel Foga to the cliffs that edge Gebel et-Tih and the Forest of Pillars, a naturally occurring phenomenon accessible by 4WD and camel via a long track.

on the park's main access road in an area known as Marsa Ghoslane. Maps are usually available here.

Getting There & Around

To move around the park a vehicle is necessary. For conservation reasons, it's forbidden to leave the official tracks. Travellers who don't want to rent a car can hire a taxi. Expect to pay about E£200 for the day from Sharm el-Sheikh, and E£500 from Dahab. For those who don't mind company, there are plenty of half-day bus excursions from Sharm.

Alternatively, nearly all tour and dive operators in both Sharm el-Sheikh and Dahab offer dive and snorkelling boat excursions in the Ras Mohammed area.

Sharm el-Sheikh & Na'ama Bay

☎069 / POP 38,480

The southern coast of the Gulf of Aqaba, between Tiran Island and Ras Mohammed National Park, features some of the world's most amazing underwater scenery. The crystal-clear waters, rare and lovely reefs and an incredible variety of exotic fish darting in and out of the colourful coral have made this a snorkelling and scuba-diving paradise. In a prime position on the coast, incorporating the two adjacent coves of Na'ama Bay and Sharm al-Maya, is the purpose-built resort of Sharm el-Sheikh, a tourism boom town devoted to sun-and-sea holidays that draws in legions of European holidaymakers every year on all-inclusive tour packages.

For families who want to bring the little ones to Egypt for a beach holiday, and package-travellers looking to mix resort comfort with world-class diving, Sharm covers all the bases. The international restaurants, buzzy bar scene and private hotel beaches make it an unashamed pleasure-seeking European enclave on the edge of Sinai.

However, the resort's airbrushed facade also covers up some serious environmental degradation, which has led to pressing issues of sustainability. Over the past decade the increasing sprawl of concrete along the coastline here to cater for the crowds has been relentless.

Sharm's critics also point out that if it wasn't for the chain of jagged desert mountains that rim the western edge of town, visitors could easily forget they're in Egypt at all. For that reason too, many choose to skip Sharm altogether, or just pass through en route to the more low-key and backpacker-friendly town of Dahab.

Sights

It's something of a tragedy that Sharm's truly exquisite diving has been overshadowed by unfettered tourist development; however, offshore dive sites in both Sharm and the adjacent Ras Mohammed National Park are easily accessible by live-aboards, or even from boat trips departing from Dahab.

Snorkelling in the waters around Sharm is excellent. While there are some easily accessed reefs in central Na'ama Bay, it's better to head to the more impressive Gardens or Ras Um Sid reefs.

Most resorts have beach access – either their own stretch of waterfront, or by agreement with another resort. Check when booking, as hotel beaches are fairly distant (up to 10km) from the hotel itself and can only be accessed via shuttle. Nearly all hotels allow day-access on their beaches.

Jackson Reef DIVE SITE
(Straits of Tiran) Home to sharks and large pelagic fish, Jackson Reef is crowned with the remains of a Cypriot freighter, the *Lara,* which ran aground here in 1985. Depth: surface to more than 40m. Rating: intermediate to advanced. Access: boat.

Thomas Reef DIVE SITE
(Straits of Tiran) The smallest, but easily the most spectacular of the Tiran reefs, Thomas is home to steeply plunging walls that are lined with soft coral, schooling fish and patrolling sharks. Depth: surface to more than 40m. Rating: advanced. Access: boat.

Gardens DIVE SITE
(btwn Shark's Bay & Na'ama Bay) At the perennially popular Gardens there are actually three sites in one. **Near Garden** (Map p382) is home to a lovely chain of pinnacles; **Middle Garden** (Map p382) features a fringing ridge that gently slopes down to a bed of sandy 'trails'; and **Far Garden** (Map p382) is home to the 'Cathedral', a colourful overhang in deep water. Depth: surface to more than 40m. Rating: intermediate. Access: shore or boat.

Ras Um Sid DIVE SITE
(Map p382) One of the best dive sites in the area, Ras Um Sid features a spectacular gorgonian forest along a dramatic drop-off that hosts a great variety of reef fish. It's opposite Hotel Royal Paradise. Depth: 15m to 40m. Rating: intermediate. Access: shore or boat.

Dunraven DIVE SITE
The *Dunraven* sunk in 1876 on her way from Bombay to Newcastle. Today the wreck, found at the southeast tip of Sha'ab Mahmud, is encrusted in coral and home to various knick-knacks including china plates, metal steins, and jars of gooseberries and rhubarb among the detritus. Depth: 15m to 28m. Rating: intermediate. Access: boat

Activities

Most resorts offer a range of water sports, including sailing, windsurfing, parasailing, pedalos and glass-bottom boats. Camel rides to 'traditional Bedouin villages' can be easily arranged with most hotels. Expect to pay US$40 to US$60 and to be part of a large group. Several top-end hotels offer horse riding from about US$30 to US$60 per hour.

Camel Dive Club DIVING
(Map p384; ☎360 0700; www.cameldive.com; Camel Hotel, King of Bahrain St; 1 day, 1 dive €40, 1 day, 2 dives €50-70) This highly professional and respected club is owned by Sinai diver Hisham Gabr. As well as being a 5-Star PADI Instructor Development Centre it is fully fitted out for wheelchair access and holds a PADI Accessibility Award.

Sinai Divers DIVING
(Map 384; ☎360 0697; www.sinaidivers.com; Ghazala Beach Hotel, Na'ama Bay Promenade; 1 day, 1 dive €37, 1 day, 2 dives €63) Based at the Ghazala Beach Hotel, this is one of Sharm el-Sheikh's most established dive centres.

Shark's Bay Diving Club DIVING
(☎360 0942; www.sharksbay.com; Shark's Bay Umbi Diving Village, Shark's Bay; house reef, 2 dives €50, 1 day, 2 dives €60) Shark's Bay is a Bedouin-run centre with years of experience and its own house reef.

Tours

Almost all travel agencies and large hotels organise jeep or bus trips to St Katherine's Monastery, Ras Mohammed National Park, and to desert attractions such as the Coloured Canyon. Be aware, however, that group sizes are often large.

Black Jack Bike CYCLING
(☎0122 370 3116; www.blackjackbike.com; tours from €50) This small company organises highly recommended mountain-bike tours into the Nabq Protectorate. Bikes are European standard, and tours include pick-up from hotel, helmet, water and a support van.

Sharm el-Sheikh & Na'ama Bay

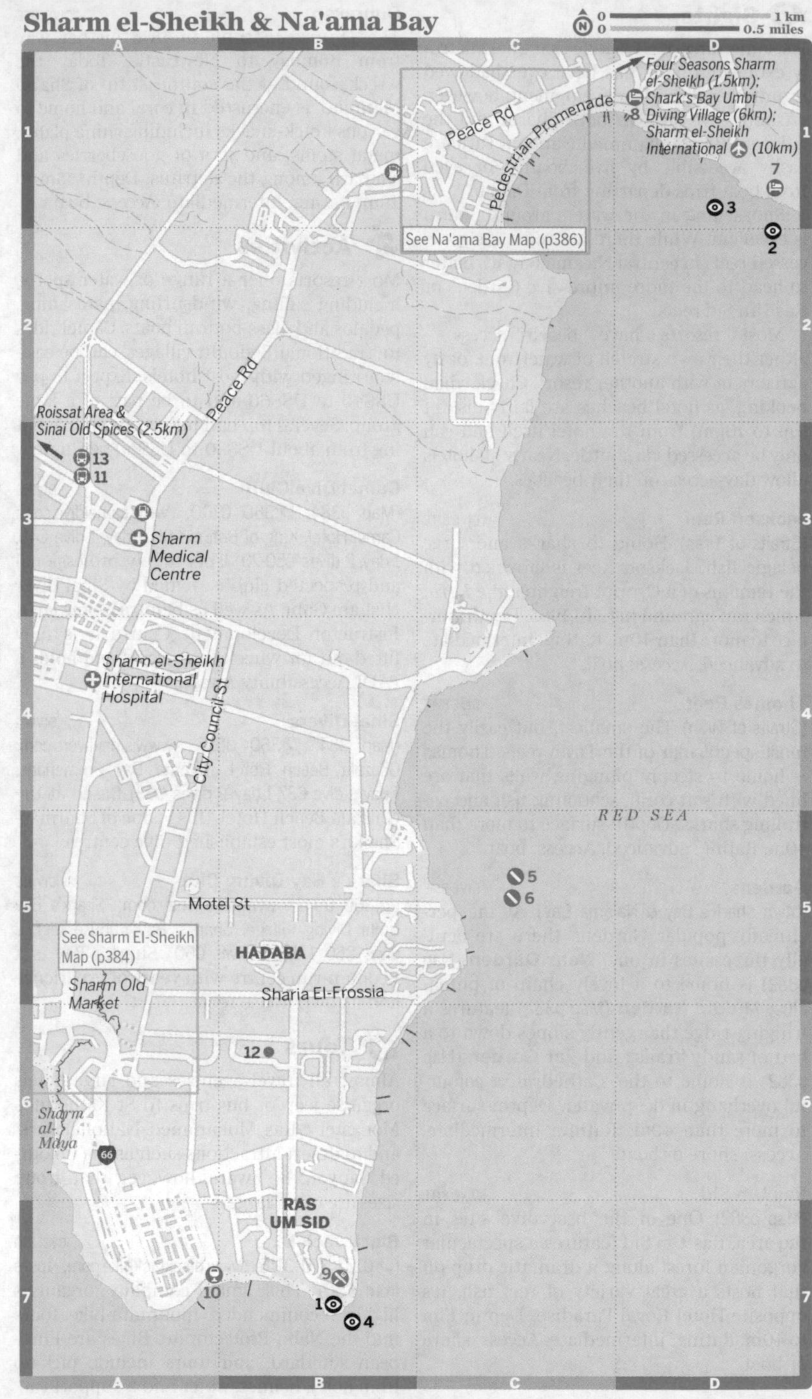

0 1 km
0 0.5 miles
Four Seasons Sharm el-Sheikh (1.5km); Shark's Bay Umbi Diving Village (6km); Sharm el-Sheikh International (10km)
Peace Rd
Pedestrian Promenade
See Na'ama Bay Map (p386)
Roissat Area & Sinai Old Spices (2.5km)
Sharm Medical Centre
Sharm el-Sheikh International Hospital
City Council St
RED SEA
Motel St
See Sharm El-Sheikh Map (p384)
HADABA
Sharm Old Market
Sharia El-Frossia
Sharm al-Maya
RAS UM SID

Sharm el-Sheikh & Na'ama Bay

Sights
Far Garden .... (see 2)
1 Lighthouse B7
2 Middle Garden D2
3 Near Garden D1
4 Ras Um Sid B7

Activities, Courses & Tours
5 Amphoras C5
6 Turtle Bay C5

Sleeping
7 Hyatt Regency Sharm el-Sheikh D1
8 Oonas Hotel D1

Eating
9 Al-Fanar B7
Sala Thai .... (see 7)

Drinking & Nightlife
10 Farsha Cafe A7

Transport
11 East Delta Bus Station A3
12 Hertz B6
13 Super Jet Bus Station A3

Black Jack also offers tailor-made tours for people interested in full-day or multiday trips and rents out bikes. Call or book online.

Sleeping

Sharm el-Sheikh and the surrounding area have one of the greatest concentrations of hotels in Egypt, with all-inclusive resorts being the standard rather than the exception. For anyone serious about pinching their pennies, it's probably wise to continue on to Dahab.

Be advised that the hotel scene in Sharm is changing rapidly and prices tend to be subject to wild fluctuations depending on the number of tourists in town. Also, despite high rack rates, most of the luxury resorts sell their rooms at much cheaper prices through European travel agencies as part of all-inclusive packages.

★ Sinai Old Spices B&B $
(☎0120 222 0509; www.sinaioldspices.com; Roissat area; s/d €15/24; P❄🛜) Hidden behind a terracotta wall, this charming B&B serves up quirky style using locally inspired architecture. The individually decorated rooms come with kitchenettes and fabulous modern bathrooms. It's a E£30 taxi ride from Sharm, so won't suit everyone, but offers a retreat from the bright lights of Na'ama Bay.

Phone beforehand to arrange a pick-up, or get directions; it's tricky to find.

Aida 2 HOTEL $
(Map 384; off Sultan Qabos St, Na'ama Bay; s/d US$20/28; ❄🛜🏊) Surprisingly quiet for being slap on the shopping drag, this cheapie hotel has decent-sized rooms set around a tiny pool. There's a strong smell of chlorine in the corridors (which also seem to be a prime cockroach party area) but the rooms themselves are a real budget find.

★ Camel Hotel HOTEL $$
(Map 384; ☎360 0700; www.cameldive.com; King of Bahrain St, Na'ama Bay; r from US$50; ❄🛜🏊) Attached to the dive centre of the same name, Camel Hotel is the smart choice to stay if diving is your main agenda in Sharm. Despite being in the heart of Na'ama Bay, the spacious, modern rooms, set around a lovely courtyard pool area, are gloriously quiet (thanks to soundproof windows), so you're guaranteed a good night's sleep. The hotel (and its dive centre) holds a PADI Accessibility Award; five of the rooms and all the common areas (including restaurant, bar and pool) have full wheelchair access.

Shark's Bay Umbi Diving Village HOTEL $$
(☎360 0942; www.sharksbay.com; Shark's Bay; s/d cabin €26/40, r €37/50, hut without bathroom €19/24; P❄🛜) This long-standing Bedouin-owned place is a tumble of cute chalets flowing down to the beach. Pine beach cabins are spick and span, if a bit of a squeeze, and larger rooms are built into the cliff above. Cheaper, spartan huts (with mattresses, mosquito nets and fans) are up on the clifftop. To get here, ask the taxi driver for 'Shark's Bay Umbi'.

Taxis cost approximately E£25 from Na'ama Bay and E£35 to E£45 from the bus station.

Oonas Hotel HOTEL $$
(Map p382; ☎360 0581; www.oonasdiveclub.com; Na'ama Bay; s/d/tr €45/60/84, ste s/d/tr €90/100/129; ❄🛜) Oonas is a combo dive centre and hotel with bland but well-equipped rooms and a prime spot along the promenade. Accommodation is cheaper if booked as part of a week-long dive package.

Sharm el-Sheikh

Four Seasons Sharm el-Sheikh RESORT $$$
(☎360 3555; www.fourseasons.com/sharmelsheikh; r from US$330; ❄@📶🏊) This palatial resort is the height of secluded luxury built around palm-fringed courtyards and manicured gardens overlooking the Straits of Tiran. Huge rooms seamlessly blend modern design with Arabesque accents boasting intricate lattice woodwork and ornate bronze fixtures.

Hilton Sharm el-Sheikh Fayrouz Resort RESORT $$$
(Map 384; ☎360 0136; www3.hilton.com; Peace Rd; s/d US$95/110; ❄@📶🏊) It may pale in comparison to the ostentatious shows of wealth found at competing hotels but the bungalows at this low-key, family-friendly resort are large and light-filled, and it has an enviable location right on Na'ama Bay's promenade.

Hyatt Regency Sharm el-Sheikh RESORT $$$
(Map p382; ☎360 1234; www.sharm.hyatt.com; Gardens Bay; r from US$145; ❄@📶🏊) With grand villa styling, superior service and vast landscaped gardens, the Hyatt is a serene retreat. Standard rooms are classically decorated and many have sweeping sea views.

Eating

Koshary El-Sheikh EGYPTIAN FAST FOOD $
(Map p384; King of Bahrain St, Sharm Old Market, Sharm al-Maya; meals E£5-10) Egypt's favourite carbohydrate-fuelled feast, *kushari* (mix of noodles, rice, black lentils, fried onions and tomato sauce), is dished up here.

★ **Fares Seafood** SEAFOOD $$
(Map p384; City Council St, Hadaba; mains E£35-100; ⏲noon-late; ❄) Always crowded with locals, Fares is a Sharm el-Sheikh institution for good-value seafood. Order fish priced by weight or choose from one of the pasta or *tagen* (stew cooked in a deep clay pot) options on the menu. We're pretty partial to the mixed *tagen* of calamari and shrimp.

El-Masrien EGYPTIAN **$$**
(Map p384; King of Bahrain St, Sharm Old Market, Sharm al-Maya; dishes E£8-40; noon-late) This old-fashioned restaurant is our top dining spot in Sharm Old Market. Its continued success is due to the simple fact it delivers succulent kebabs, *kofta* (mincemeat and spices grilled on a skewer) and all the usual Egyptian staples without the prices of fancier Sharm restaurants. Service here is superfriendly, too.

Tandoori INDIAN **$$**
(Map 384; Camel Hotel, King of Bahrain St, Na'ama Bay; dishes E£40-125; from 6.30pm) The courtyard of the Camel Hotel is home to what many consider Sharm's best Indian food. Granted, it leans towards Anglo-Indian (all the korma, butter chicken and madras dishes are there), but it's all executed brilliantly. There's a fantastic choice for vegetarians, too, with plenty of *paneer*- (Indian cottage cheese) and *palak*- (spinach) based curries.

Al-Fanar ITALIAN **$$**
(Map p382; Ras Um Sid; dishes E£40-150; 10am-10.30pm;) Thanks to a great slice of beach out front (home to one of Sharm's best snorkelling spots), lovely views from the terrace, and decent pasta and pizza on the menu, Al-Fanar is a long-standing Sharm el-Sheikh favourite.

Pomodoro ITALIAN **$$**
(Map 384; King of Bahrain St, Na'ama Bay; dishes E£48-150;) A great spot for casual dining, Pomodoro has a modern, buzzy, friendly vibe and a menu stuffed with pasta, pizza and a fair whack of seafood.

★ **Fairuz** MIDDLE EASTERN **$$$**
(Map 384; King of Bahrain St, Na'ama Bay; mezze dishes E£18-28, mains E£85-165;) This Levantine restaurant is a mouth-watering journey through the subtle flavours of the Middle East. Choose *batingan bi laban* (aubergine in garlicky yoghurt), *makinek* (spicy sausages) and *loubieh* (a green-bean stew) to share with delicious fresh-from-the-oven bread. The mezze set menu (E£105 per person, minimum two people) is the best way to sample an array of flavours.

Sala Thai THAI **$$$**
(Map p382; 360 1234; Hyatt Regency Sharm el-Sheikh; mains E£70-200; 6.30pm-10.30pm) Sala Thai is where we like to head for an extra-special treat in Sharm: sumptuous feasting on fiery curries and delicately spiced noodle dishes, personal service, and outstanding Red Sea views. Bookings are essential and the dress code is smart-casual, so leave your flip-flops behind.

Drinking & Nightlife

★ **Farsha Cafe** CAFE
(Map p382; Sharia el-Bahr, Ras Um Sid) All nooks and crannies, floor cushions, Bedouin tents and swinging lamps, Farsha is the kind of place that travellers come to for a coffee and find themselves lingering four drinks and a sheesha pipe later. Great for a lazy day full of lounging or a night of chilled-out music and cocktails.

Camel Roof Bar BAR
(Map 384; Camel Hotel, King of Bahrain St, Na'ama Bay; 3pm-2.30am) Camel is a favourite among dive instructors for its relaxed, casual vibe. This is the optimal place to start off the evening, especially for divers looking to swap stories from down under.

Pacha CLUB
(Map 384; www.pachasharm.com; King of Bahrain St, Na'ama Bay; tickets presale/at door E£140/180; 11pm-late) The hub of Sharm's nightlife, Pacha goes wild pretty much every night of the week. Watch for advertising around town to find out about upcoming events. Women gain free entry into the club before midnight.

Little Buddha CLUB
(Map 384; Sultan Qabos St, Na'ama Bay) DJs spin those proprietary Buddha Bar sounds well into the night.

Information

EMERGENCY

Tourist Police (360 0554, 366 0675; Na'ama Bay; 8am-2pm) In a booth next to Marina Sharm Hotel. There is also another branch (Map p384; 366 0311; City Council St, Hadaba) in Hadaba.

MEDICAL SERVICES

Sharm el-Sheikh Hyberbaric Medical Center (360 0865, emergency 0122 212 4292; hyper_med _center@sinainet.com.eg; main Sharm el-Maya rd; 24hr)
Sharm el-Sheikh International Hospital (Map p382; 366 0318; Peace Rd; 24hr)

MONEY

There are copious ATMs in Na'ama Bay, including several in the Na'ama Centre, and in the lobbies of all the larger hotels. Otherwise, all the major banks have branches in Hadaba.

Na'ama Bay

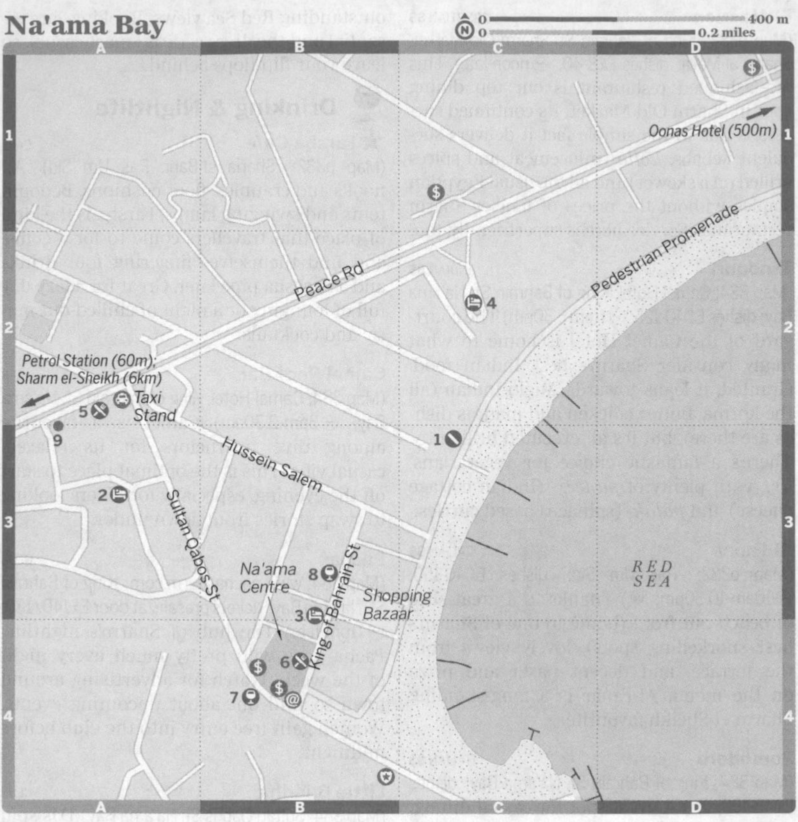

Na'ama Bay

Activities, Courses & Tours
Camel Dive Club ....(see 3)
1 Sinai Divers C3

Sleeping
2 Aida 2 .... A3
3 Camel Hotel B3
4 Hilton Sharm el-Sheikh Fayrouz Resort C2

Eating
5 Carrefour Supermarket A2
6 Fairuz B4
Pomodoro .... (see 3)
Tandoori .... (see 3)

Drinking & Nightlife
Camel Roof Bar .... (see 3)
7 Little Buddha B4
8 Pacha B3

Transport
9 Avis A3
Sixt Car Rental .... (see 4)

HSBC (☎360 0614; Na'ama Centre, Na'ama Bay; ⏰8.30am-2.30pm Sun-Thu) Has an ATM.

National Bank of Egypt (Map p384; Bank St, Hadaba; ⏰8.30am-2.30pm Sun-Thu) Also has a branch in Na'ama Bay (Na'ama Centre).

Thomas Cook (☎360 1808; Gafy Mall, Peace Rd, Na'ama Bay; ⏰9am-2pm & 6-10pm) Just west of Sinai Star Hotel.

Western Union (☎364 0466; Rosetta Hotel, Na'ama Bay; ⏰8.30am-2pm & 6-10pm Sat-Thu, 3-10pm Fri)

POST

Main Post Office (Map p384; Bank St, Hadaba; ⏰8.30am-2pm Sat-Thu)

Getting There & Away

AIR

Sharm el-Sheikh International Airport (☎362 3304; www.sharm-el-sheikh.airport-authority.com; Sharm-Na'ama Bay Rd) is Sinai's major travel hub. **Egypt Air** (Map p384; ☎366 1056; www.egyptair.com; Sharm al-Maya; 9am-9pm), opposite Sharm Old Market, has several flights per day to Cairo. Prices fluctuate wildly but fares to Cairo start from about E£450.

EasyJet (www.easyjet.com) operates three flights weekly to the UK and, if booked in advance, can be one of the cheapest ways to fly in or out of Egypt. There are also plenty of charter flights in and out of Sharm, which usually offer cut-price fares.

BOAT

The ferry service between Sharm el-Sheikh and Hurghada stopped operating in 2010. Plans for a new ferry are always talked about but have yet to come to fruition. Enquire at any of the hotels and travel agencies in Sharm el-Sheikh for up-to-date information. You could also contact the Sharm el-Sheikh **Port Office** (☎366 0217).

BUS

The **East Delta Travel Co bus station** (Map p382; ☎366 0660) is just off Peace Rd behind the Mobil petrol station. It runs 11 buses to Cairo (E£60 to E£80, seven hours) daily. Heading north, there are buses to Dahab (E£15, 1½ hours) at 7am, 9am, 3pm, 5pm and 9pm; the 9am and 5pm services carry on to Nuweiba (E£30, three hours) and Taba (E£55, 4½ hours).

Super Jet (Map p382; ☎366 1622) buses leave from behind the East Delta station. Buses run to Cairo (E£85, six to seven hours) at 11am, 1pm, 3pm and 11.30pm. The 3pm service continues on to Alexandria (E£110, eight to nine hours).

Getting Around

TO/FROM THE AIRPORT

Sharm el-Sheikh International Airport is 10km north of Na'ama Bay at Ras Nasrany; taxis generally charge from E£20 to E£25 from the airport to Na'ama Bay. Prepare to bargain hard.

CAR

Car-rental agencies include **Avis** (Map 384; ☎360 2400, 360 0979; Peace Rd, Na'ama Bay), just west of Carrefour Supermarket; **Hertz** (Map p382; ☎366 2299; Bank St, Hadaba) and **Sixt Car Rental** (Map 384; ☎360 0137; Hilton Fayrouz Resort, Peace Rd, Na'ama Bay). All charge about US$80 per day for a basic saloon, and US$120 and up for a roomier 4WD.

MICROBUS & TAXI

Blue-and-white microbuses regularly ply the stretch between central Na'ama Bay and Sharm el-Sheikh. The fare is E£2, although foreigners are often charged E£5. Taxis charge a minimum of E£15 between Sharm Old Market and Na'ama Bay.

Nabq Protectorate

Thirty-five kilometres north of Sharm el-Sheikh, Nabq is the largest coastal protectorate on the Gulf of Aqaba. Named after an oasis that lies within its boundaries, Nabq straddles 600 sq km of land and sea between the Straits of Tiran and Dahab. Less frequently visited than Ras Mohammed National Park further south, Nabq is a good place to see Sinai as it was before the arrival of mass tourism. Within the park are several hiking trails and snorkelling spots.

There is a visitors centre located off the road leading from Sharm el-Sheikh past the airport and Ras Nasrany. Nabq's main attraction is its mangrove forest, which runs along the shoreline at the mouth of Wadi Kid and is the most northerly mangrove stand in the world. Just inland from the mangrove forest are the dunes of Wadi Kid, which are home to one of the Middle East's largest stands of arak bushes (arak twigs were traditionally used by Bedouin to clean teeth). Offshore, rich reefs are easy to access, although visibility can be poor because of sediment from the mangroves. You'll need a vehicle to get here, or join an organised tour from Sharm el-Sheikh or Dahab.

Dahab

☎069

Low-key, laid-back and low-rise, Dahab is the Middle East's prime beach resort for independent travellers. The startling transformation from dusty Bedouin outpost to spruced-up tourist village is not without its detractors, who reminisce fondly of the days when beach bums dossed in basic huts by the shore. But for all the starry-eyed memories, there are plenty of plusses that have come with prosperity. Diving is now a much safer and more organised activity thanks to better regulation of operators; and the town is cleaner and more family-friendly, offering accommodation choices for everyone rather than just hardened backpackers.

Meaning 'gold' in Arabic – a reference to the area's sandy coastline (despite the main

Dahab

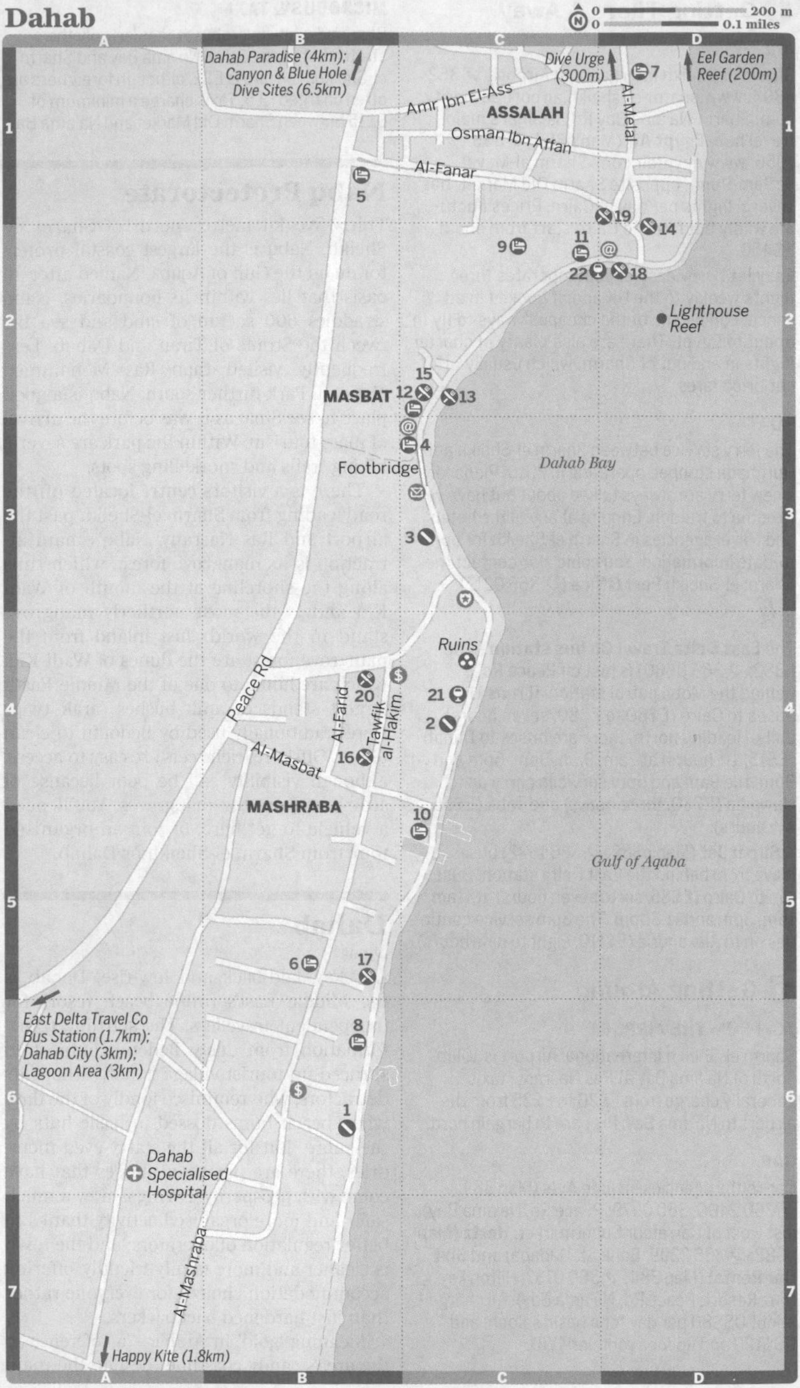

0 200 m
0 0.1 miles

Dahab Paradise (4km); Canyon & Blue Hole Dive Sites (6.5km)
Dive Urge (300m)
7
Eel Garden Reef (200m)
Amr Ibn El-Ass
ASSALAH
Al-Melal
Osman Ibn Affan
Al-Fanar
5
19
14
9
11
22
18
Lighthouse Reef
15
MASBAT
12
13
4
Footbridge
Dahab Bay
3
Ruins
20
21
2
Peace Rd
Al-Farid
Tawfik al-Hakim
16
Al-Masbat
MASHRABA
10
Gulf of Aqaba
6
17
East Delta Travel Co Bus Station (1.7km); Dahab City (3km); Lagoon Area (3km)
8
1
Dahab Specialised Hospital
Al-Mashraba
Happy Kite (1.8km)

Dahab

Activities, Courses & Tours

1 Big Blue Dive Centre ... B6
2 Nesima Dive Centre ... C4
3 Poseidon Divers ... C3
Red Sea Relax Dive Centre ... (see 11)

Sleeping

4 Alaska Camp & Hotel ... C3
5 Alf Leila ... B1
6 Bishbishi Garden Village ... B5
7 Blue Beach Club ... D1
8 Christina Beach Palace & Christina Pool ... B6
9 Dahab Coach House ... C2
10 Nesima Resort ... C5
11 Red Sea Relax ... C2
12 Seven Heaven ... C2

Eating

13 Ali Baba ... C2
14 Athanor ... D2
15 Blue House ... C2
16 King Chicken ... B4
17 Lakhbatita ... B5
18 Nirvana ... D2
19 Ralph's German Bakery ... D1
20 Seabride Restaurant ... B4

Drinking & Nightlife

Churchill's ... (see 11)
21 Tree Bar ... C4
22 Yalla Bar ... C2

tourist area having no golden sands to speak of) – Dahab is a great base from which to explore some of Egypt's most spectacular diving and snorkelling. Predominantly a Bedouin enclave at its heart, Dahab is also the preferred base for organising guided trekking and camel excursions into the interior deserts, as well as to the heights of Mt Sinai.

This is the one town in South Sinai where independent travellers are the rule rather than the exception and Dahab's growth has not destroyed its budget-traveller roots. Reeled in by a fusion of hippy mellowness and resort chic (where cappuccino and sushi are as much a part of the action as cheap rooms and herds of goats fossicking in the back alleys), many travellers plan a few nights here and instead stay for weeks.

Sights & Activities

Dahab's sights are all underwater. The best reefs for snorkelling are Lighthouse Reef and Eel Garden, both in Assalah. Snorkelling gear can be hired from all the dive centres and many other places for about E£25 to E£40 per day. Keep in mind that some of the reefs have unexpected currents – drownings have occurred – so keep your wits about you.

Note that despite the intimidating reputation of the Canyon and Blue Hole dive sites as danger zones for careless divers, the tops of the reefs are teeming with life, making them fine snorkelling destinations when the sea is calm. Most dive operators organise half-day Blue Hole trips and can also organise snorkelling trips and dive safaris to Ras Abu Gallum (p394), Nabq Protectorate (p387) and Ras Mohammed National Park (p378).

Canyon
DIVE SITE

One of the area's most popular dives, the Canyon is a long, narrow trench that runs perpendicular to the reef shelf, and is home to prolific hard and soft corals. It's on the north side of Dahab. Depth: 5m to 33m. Rating: intermediate. Access: shore.

Eel Garden
DIVE SITE

(Map p38) Eel Garden takes its name from the countless garden eels that carpet the sea floor. Other highlights include huge coral boulders and dense congregations of barracudas. Located north of Dahab. Depth: 5m to 20m. Rating: intermediate. Access: shore.

Lighthouse Reef
DIVE SITE

(Map p388; Assalah) This sloping reef is home to a bounty of fish life and is Dahab's main night-diving site. More-experienced divers can descend to the sandy bottom, where there's a profusion of coral towers. Depth: 5m to 30m. Rating: novice. Access: shore.

Islands
DIVE SITE

This underwater *Alice in Wonderland*-esque site south of Dahab offers an outstanding topography of coral alleyways, amphitheatres, valleys and gullies. Depth: 5m to 18m. Rating: novice. Access: shore.

Umm Sid
DIVE SITE

An impressive entrance through a wide corridor carved into a steeply sloping reef is a highlight of this dive site 15km south of Dahab. Further down you'll find table corals and two enormous gorgonians. Depth: 5m to 35m. Rating: intermediate to advanced. Access: shore.

DON'T MISS

DIVING THE BLUE HOLE

Carved into a reef just offshore, 8km north of Dahab, Blue Hole is Egypt's most infamous dive site. It is a gaping sinkhole that drops straight down – some say it's as deep as 130m.

Exploring the deeper depths should be left to experienced technical divers. There's plenty to discover close to the surface. The outer lip of the Blue Hole is full of marine life, and a reasonable plunge into the hole itself is somewhat akin to skydiving.

Depth: 7m to 27m. Rating: intermediate. Access: shore.

Entry is at the **Bells**, a narrow breach in the reef table that forms a pool close to shore. From here, divers descend through a chimney, exiting at 27m on a ledge that opens to the sea. Swimming south along the wall, a saddle in the reef at 7m allows entry to the Blue Hole. As long as divers monitor their depth carefully, they can finish up by swimming across the sinkhole towards shore.

Unfortunately, the site has claimed several lives, mainly thrill-seekers venturing well below the sport-diving limit. The trap is an archway at approximately 65m, which connects the sinkhole to the open ocean. Underprepared solo divers attempting to find this archway have succumbed to narcosis, missed the archway entirely, lost all sense of direction or simply run out of air.

Gabr el-Bint DIVE SITE

This dive 25km south of Dahab features a dramatic seascape highlighted by a 60m wall cut by numerous chasms, faults and sandy ravines. If you access the site by land, the journey combines a 4WD trip and a Bedouin-led camel convoy. Depth: 10m to 30m. Rating: intermediate. Access: boat or shore.

Dive Operators

Red Sea Relax Dive Centre DIVING

(Map p388; ☎364 1309; www.red-sea-relax.com; Red Sea Relax Hotel, Masbat; per shore dive €19, 1 day, 2-3 dives €68) Long-standing five-star PADI centre with an excellent reputation.

Poseidon Divers DIVING

(Map p388; ☎364 0091; www.poseidondivers.com; Crazy Camel Camp, Mashraba; 1 day, 2 dives €44) Award-winning PADI centre that consistently gets recommended by travellers.

Big Blue Dive Centre DIVING

(Map p388; ☎364 0045; www.bigbluedahab.com; Mashraba; 1 dive €33, 2 dives €55) Popular and friendly five-star PADI centre with a good reputation.

Dive Urge DIVING

(☎364 0957; www.dive-urge.com; Sharia al-Melal, Assalah; 1 day, 3 dives €72) Five-star PADI centre with commendable environmental credentials. The centre and adjoining resort are fully wheelchair accessible.

Nesima Dive Centre DIVING

(Map p388; ☎364 0320; www.nesima-resort.com; Nesima Resort, Mashraba; per dive €28, 1 day, 2 dives €55) A reputable club owned by local environmental activist and veteran diver Sherif Ebeid.

Camel & Jeep Safaris

Dahab is one of the best places in Sinai to arrange camel safaris into the dramatic mountains lining the coast, especially the spectacular Ras Abu Gallum Protectorate (p394). Further afield, the desert area around Nuweiba is home to some of the South Sinai coast's most interesting sights, including the Coloured Canyon (p398), a popular jeep safari from Dahab.

Nearly all hotels, dive centres and travel agencies offer jeep and camel safaris. When choosing who to go with, check to see if the tour operator works with the Bedouin. Local communities unfortunately have been generally excluded from the tourist industry, which tends to be dominated by migrants from the Nile Valley. Prices vary considerably depending on the time of year, distances covered and itinerary, but expect to pay around E£200 per person for an evening trip into the mountains with dinner at a Bedouin camp, and from about E£300 to E£400 per person per day for a safari including all food and water.

If opting for a private, custom-made camel or jeep safari rather than an organised trip, be sure that the guide registers with the police before beginning the safari.

Water Sports

There's no beach to speak of in Assalah – instead the rocky coastline leads straight out onto the reef. For the golden sands after which Dahab was named, you'll need to head down to the lagoon, where the luxury resorts are clustered. Most resorts offer day-access to their beaches starting from E£50, and pedalos and kayaks can be hired. The lagoon area is also Dahab's water-sport centre.

Club Mistral WATER SPORTS
(☎364 1577; www.club-mistral.com; Dahab Resort; 1hr windsurfing lesson €40) Club Mistral in the lagoon resort area offers both windsurfing and kitesurfing instruction, as well as equipment rental.

Happy Kite WATER SPORTS
(☎0109 224 4822; www.happy-kite.com; 1hr lesson €50) Located in the lagoon resort area, Happy Kite offers kitesurfing lessons, full-day courses and equipment rental.

Tours

All the tour operators in Dahab offer tours to Mt Sinai (p404) and St Katherine's Monastery (p401) for about E£150. Nearly all also offer one-day, whirlwind trips to either Petra in Jordan (US$200) or Jerusalem in Israel (US$90). Unless you are seriously strapped for time it's usually best to make your own independent arrangements for Jordan and Israel. If you do decide to take one of these international tours, be aware that most of your time will be spent travelling there and back, with very little time actually spent at the sights.

Festivals & Events

Dahab Bedouin Festival CULTURE
(www.bedouinfestival.com; Apr) This annual one-week festival inaugurated in 2011 seeks to celebrate Dahab's Bedouin culture and promote sustainable tourism. It brings a program of events ranging from desert excursions and diving trips to music concerts and handicraft markets.

Sleeping

Dahab boasts bedding-down options that range from cell-like cement huts to attractive backpacker palaces with cushioned seating shaded by palm groves. There's also a good mix of midrange resorts that are small enough for guests to catch the mellow Dahab vibe. Luxury accommodation is available at the lagoon resort area. New places are going up all the time, while older establishments are being knocked down. Most budget and many midrange hotel rates in Dahab do not include breakfast.

Alaska Camp & Hotel HOTEL $
(Map p388; ☎364 1004; www.dahabescape.com; Masbat; r E£100-140, with air-con E£170-200;) Easy on the wallet without sacrificing the small comforts, Alaska has a variety of spacious, bright, sparkling-clean, simple rooms with super-comfortable beds. The attractive courtyard garden is a welcoming, shady spot in which to relax and meet other travellers, and the central location means you're just a couple of steps from the promenade bustle.

Seven Heaven HOSTEL $
(Map p388; ☎364 0080; www.7heavenhotel.com; Masbat; dm E£15, r with/without air-con E£80/60, without bathroom E£40;) An all-in-one stalwart of the Dahab scene (combining a dive shop and tour office), Seven Heaven offers one of the best-value shoestringer deals in town. It has a huge range of rooms, which go up in price as you add in extras; the six-bed dorms, which come with air-con and bathroom, are a bargain.

Bishbishi Garden Village HOSTEL $
(Map p388; ☎364 0727; www.bishbishi.com; Sharia al-Mashraba, Mashraba; r with/without air-con €12/10, without bathroom €5;) A classic of the Dahab camp scene, Bishbishi continues to offer a winning mix of easy on the wallet rooms and lots of shaded communal areas for socialising.

★**Alf Leila** BOUTIQUE HOTEL $$
(Map p388; ☎364 0595; www.alfleilaboutiquehotel.com; cnr Peace Rd & Sharia al-Fanar, Masbat; s/d €33/46, ste €42-65;) With a nod towards its namesake *1001 Arabian Nights*, Alf Leila's seven rooms are a daydream of gorgeous tile-work and traditional textiles decorated using muted colours, stone and wood. The location (on the main road) isn't the best, but if you don't mind a walk to the beach, this place is worth it for sheer uniqueness.

★**Dahab Paradise** RESORT $$
(☎0100 700 4133; www.dahabparadise.com; s/d/tr €58/72/99;) This low-key resort, on a secluded sweep of bay on the main road to the Blue Hole, is the perfect getaway. Decorated in warm, earthy tones with accents of antique wood, the charming rooms have

a touch of understated beach-chic elegance. If all the peace and serenity gets too much, the bright lights of Masbat are a 10-minute taxi-ride away.

Red Sea Relax HOTEL $$
(Map p388; ☎364 1309; www.red-sea-relax.com; Masbat; dm €4, s/d/tr/f €37/46/56/74, d without bathroom €18; ❄📶≋) With rooms wrapped around a glistening pool, Red Sea Relax dishes up a winning formula of resort-like facilities for bargain prices. Rooms come with nice added extras such as tea- and coffee-making facilities and TVs. Plus there are free water fill-ups, a beckoning rooftop bar and an excellent dive centre. The dormitory means budgeteers get resort facilities for backpacker costs.

Dahab Coach House GUESTHOUSE $$
(Map p388; ☎0100 981 1321; www.dahabcoachhouse.dk; Masbat; s/d €40/42; ❄📶) What this place lacks in midrange resort facilities it more than makes up for with hugely helpful management and a genuinely welcoming atmosphere. The rooms are simple but comfortable, and the courtyard is the perfect place to chill out after a long day's diving.

Christina Beach Palace & Christina Pool HOTEL $$
(Map p388; ☎364 0390; www.christinahotels.com; Mashraba; s/d/tr US$40/53/70, with air-con US$50/66/87, in annexe US$29.50/45/45; ❄📶≋) This Swiss-run hotel offers a degree of efficiency unmatched in town. There is a range of rooms to suit your preference: Beach Palace rooms have lovely sea views, while the recently renovated poolside digs are more luxurious. Christina Residence annexe is a good-value option, set amid a leafy garden across the road.

Nesima Resort RESORT $$
(Map p388; ☎364 0320; www.nesima-resort.com; Mashraba; s/d/ste €47/61/84; ❄📶≋) A lovely compromise if you want resort living without being isolated from town. Set amid a mature garden of blooming bougainvillea, Nesima's cosy cottages have pleasing stone and wood overtones, domed ceilings and cute terraces.

Blue Beach Club RESORT $$
(Map p388; ☎364 0411; www.bluebeachclub.com; Assalah; s/d/ste €28/36/44; ❄📶≋) Blue Beach's spacious annexe rooms (across the road from the main resort) are bright, comfortably outfitted and boast the snazziest modern bathrooms in Dahab.

Eating

The waterfront is lined with Bedouin-style restaurants where you can relax on cushions while gazing out over the sparkling waters of the Gulf of Aqaba. None of the food served up is really standout fantastic; most places go for quantity (with menus that read like novellas) rather than quality, but the chilled-out ambience can't be beaten.

King Chicken FAST FOOD $
(Map p388; Sharia Tawfik al-Hakim, Mashraba; dishes E£15-25) Always crowded with locals, this cheap and cheerful little place hits the spot for budget chicken-dinner heaven.

★Lakhbatita ITALIAN $$
(Map p388; Mashraba; dishes E£65-120; ⏲6-11.30pm; ✎) We adore Lakhbatita's eccentric decoration, its friendly, personal service and its serene ambience, all of which bring to Dahab a little touch of Italian flair. The small menu of homemade pasta dishes, many featuring seafood, is a cut above what's served up elsewhere. Try the mushroom ravioli or the garlic and chilli prawns. No alcohol is served but diners are welcome to bring their own.

Seabride Restaurant SEAFOOD $$
(Map p388; Mashraba; meals E£40-60) Located away from the shorefront, this is the locals' favourite haunt for seafood. All meals come loaded with fish soup, rice, salad, *baba ghanoog* (purée of grilled aubergines), a delectably tangy tahini and bread. Fish is priced by weight (choose from the display downstairs) or order cheaper options off the menu. The spicy Bedouin calamari is seafood Dahab-style.

Blue House THAI $$
(Map p388; Masbat; mains E£40-80; ✎) An inspiring selection of authentic Thai cuisine keeps this breezy upstairs terrace packed with diners. Tuck into flavour-filled curries with a choice of tofu, chicken, beef or seafood and you'll understand why this place has so many fans.

Ralph's German Bakery CAFE $$
(Map p388; Sharia al-Fanar, Masbat; coffee E£10-18, pastries E£6-12, sandwiches & breakfasts E£20-30; ⏲7am-6pm; ✎) Singlehandedly raising the bar for coffee in Dahab, this place is caffeine heaven and is also Dahab's top stop for breakfast. People who have the willpower to not add one of the delectable Danish pastries onto their order are doing better than us.

Ali Baba INTERNATIONAL $$

(Map p388; Masbat; mains E£30-80; ⏲10am-late; 📶🖋) One of the most popular restaurants along the waterfront strip for good reason: this place adds flair to its seafood selection with some inspired menu choices. Great service, comfy sofas to lounge on, stylish lanterns and twinkly fairy lights add to the relaxed seaside ambience.

Nirvana INDIAN $$

(Map p388; Masbat; dishes E£45-75; 📶🖋) A slice of the subcontinent complete with direct beach access and sun-loungers. Although not particularly authentic, the meals are tasty all the same and the ice cream, with homemade waffle cone, is perfect to accompany a promenade stroll after dinner.

Athanor ITALIAN $$

(Map p388; Sharia al-Melal, Assalah; pizzas E£18-40; 📶🖋) Dahab's best thin-crust pizzas are served up here on the shady garden terrace.

Drinking & Nightlife

Tree Bar BAR

(Map p388; Mashraba; ⏲10pm-late) Two-for-one cocktail deals and a thumping soundtrack of urban, house and R&B make this open-air beachfront bar Dahab's top late-night party venue.

Churchill's BAR

(Map p388; Red Sea Relax, Masbat; beer E£10-14; 📶) Dahab's sports bar has a big-screen TV so fans won't miss their favourite team play, plus there's a breezy rooftop terrace that's perfect for sunset drinks.

Yalla Bar BAR

(Map p388; Masbat; beer E£10-12; 📶) This hugely popular waterfront bar-restaurant has a winning formula of friendly staff and excellent happy-hour beer prices (from 5pm to 9pm).

Information

DANGERS & ANNOYANCES

After the Dahab suicide bombing of April 2006 (which killed 23 people and injured dozens) the government pumped up security within Dahab and the town hasn't been targeted since. Dahab's location, however, within the greater South Sinai region, does mean that many government travel advisories currently warn against visiting. Although the potential for a future terrorist attack can never be wholly ruled out, it's important to emphasise that since the 2011 revolution Dahab has remained one of Egypt's most relaxed destinations and, within the town itself, has experienced no problems.

EMERGENCY

Police (Map p388; ☎364 0213, 364 0215; Mashraba)

INTERNET ACCESS

Wi-fi is widely available free at most hotels and many of the restaurants.

Aladdin Bookstore & Internet (Map p388; Masbat; per hr E£5) Also home to a second-hand bookshop.

MEDICAL SERVICES

Dahab Specialised Hospital (Map p388; ☎364 2714; Mashraba) An excellent private hospital with full hyperbaric-chamber facilities.

Dr Haikal (☎0100 143 3325; Dahab City) Local doctor whose surgery near the lagoon also has a hyperbaric chamber.

MONEY

There are plenty of ATMs scattered along the waterfront.

Banque du Caire (Map p388; Sharia al-Mashraba, Mashraba) Has an ATM.

National Bank of Egypt (Map p388; Sharia Tawfik al-Hakim, Mashraba) Has an ATM.

Getting There & Away

Buses leave from the **bus station** (☎364 1808) in Dahab City, well southwest of the centre of the action. Departure times change without notice. Check beforehand with the bus station. Destinations include:

Cairo E£90, nine hours, four daily at 9am, 12.30pm, 3pm and 10pm

Hurghada E£105, 10 hours, daily at 4pm

Luxor E£130, 18 hours, daily at 4pm

Nuweiba E£15, one hour, daily at 10.30am

Sharm el-Sheikh E£15 to E£20, two hours, 11 daily

Taba E£45, 2½ hours, daily at 10.30am

Although there is no public bus from Dahab to the St Katherine Protectorate, local transport

ONE TOKE OVER THE LINE

Dahab's hippy roots and generally backpacker-friendly atmosphere often go hand in hand with drug use. At some point here, travellers will likely be offered marijuana or hashish (and possibly harder stuff), and may see people openly using drugs. Some misinformed travellers have the attitude that toking is legal – it's not at all, and the penalty for being caught with drugs is harsh.

initiative **Bedouin Bus** (☎0101 668 4274; www.bedouinbus.com; one-way E£50) runs a twice-weekly minibus service from Dahab to St Katherine, which is an excellent option for independent travellers. The bus leaves every Tuesday and Friday at 5pm (check the website for bus stop details) and the journey takes two hours.

Taxi drivers at the bus station (and around town) charge E£100 to Sharm el-Sheikh and E£250 to St Katherine.

Getting Around

A variety of variously banged-up pick-ups operate as local taxis. From Masbat to the bus station costs between E£10 and E£15. To get to the Blue Hole independently you can negotiate with any of the pick-up drivers in town (E£60 to E£80 return). Don't forget to arrange a return time.

Bicycles are a great way to get around Dahab and can be hired from many hotels and travel agencies in town.

Ras Abu Gallum Protectorate

The starkly beautiful Ras Abu Gallum Protectorate covers 400 sq km of coastline between Dahab and Nuweiba, mixing coastal mountains, narrow valleys, sand dunes and fine-gravel beaches with several diving and snorkelling sites. Scientists describe the area as a 'floristic frontier', where Mediterranean conditions are influenced by a tropical climate. With its 165 plant species (including 44 found nowhere else in Sinai) and wealth of mammals and reptiles, this enviromentally important area is a fascinating place to visit.

Bedouin of the Mizena tribe live within the protectorate confines, fishing here as they have done for centuries (although this is now regulated by the protectorate).

Travel agencies in Dahab offer camel, jeep and walking excursions to Ras Abu Gallum. Hiking into the reserve by following the path from the Blue Hole is also popular. The track winds along the shoreline to Ras Abu Gallum village and El-Omeyid village (one hour), where it's possible to camp overnight in a hut. Most tour agencies in Dahab offer day trips to Ras Abu Gallum for around E£200 or overnight for E£350 (including return transport to the Blue Hole, lunch and snorkelling gear) or it can easily be hiked independently.

There are several walking trails in the reserve, and Bedouin guides and camels can be hired at either Ras Abu Gallum village or, if coming from the Nuweiba side, through the ranger house at the edge of Wadi Rasasah. Popular destinations within the protectorate include Bir el-Oghda, a now-deserted Bedouin village, and Bir Sugheir, a water source at the edge of the protectorate.

Nuweiba

☎069

Stretched over about 15km, Nuweiba lacks a defined centre and a cohesive ambience, and functions primarily as a port town for travellers catching the Aqaba-bound ferry to Jordan. For a brief period following the Egypt–Israel peace treaty of 1979, however, a thriving Israeli tourism trade here meant Nuweiba could claim rivalry to Dahab as Sinai's hippy beach paradise. Due to the vagaries of the regional political situation over recent decades, Israeli travellers have for the most part shunned Sinai, and while Sharm boomed under waves of foreign and domestic investment, and Dahab grew steadily into a low-key resort town, Nuweiba was left to go to seed. The downturn in tourism since the 2011 revolution has contributed further to Nuweiba's decline. As a result, Tarabin (Nuweiba's waterfront beach-camp area) has become ever-more ramshackle, which is a shame given that with a little sprucing up it could easily be the mellow beach-camp paradise that Dahab was a decade ago.

Sights & Activities

Dive Sites

The dive sites around Nuweiba tend to be less busy than others along the Gulf of Aqaba and host an impressive variety of marine life. Shallow reefs offshore are reasonable places for snorkelling, but the best spot is **Stone House Reef** just south of town.

Ras Shaitan DIVE SITE

(Map p38) The highlight of this dive 15km north of Nuweiba is undoubtedly the contoured topography, including narrow valleys, sand-filled depressions and deep chasms. Depth: 10m to 30m. Rating: intermediate. Access: shore.

Sinker DIVE SITE

(Map p38; Nuweiba) The Sinker is a massive submerged mooring buoy designed for cargo ships, which was sunk by mistake in the mid-1990s. Since then it has developed into a fantastic artificial reef, attracting a host of small, colourful species. The access point is 5km north of Nuweiba. Depth: 6m to 35m. Rating: intermediate. Access: shore.

THE BEDOUIN OF SINAI

Sinai's rugged tracts are home to desert dwellers, most of whom live in the north of the peninsula. The Bedouin – whose numbers are variously estimated to be between 80,000 and 300,000 – belong to 14 distinct tribes, most with ties to Bedouin in the Negev (Israel), Jordan and northern Saudi Arabia, and each with their own customs and culture. The Sukwarka, who live along the northern coast near Al-Arish, are the largest tribe. Others include the Tarabin, who have territory in both northern and southern Sinai; the Tyaha in the centre of the peninsula who, together with the Tarabin, trace their roots to Palestine; and the Haweitat, centred in an area southeast of Suez, and originally from the Hejaz in Saudi Arabia.

The seven Bedouin tribes in southern Sinai are known collectively as the Towara or 'Arabs of Al-Tor', the provincial capital. Of these, the first to settle in Sinai were the Aleiqat and the Suwalha, who arrived soon after the Muslim conquest of Egypt. The largest southern tribe is the Mizena, who are concentrated along the coast between Sharm el-Sheikh and Nuweiba. Some members of the tiny Jabaliyya tribe, centred in the mountains around St Katherine, are said to be descendants of Macedonians sent by Emperor Justinian to build and protect the monastery in the 6th century.

Thanks to centuries of living in the harsh conditions of Sinai, the Bedouin have developed a sophisticated understanding of their environment. Strict laws and traditions govern the use of precious resources. Water use is closely regulated and vegetation carefully conserved, as revealed in the Bedouin adage 'killing a tree is like killing a soul'. Local life centres on clans and their sheikhs (leaders), and loyalty and hospitality – essential for surviving in the desert – are paramount. Traditional tent dwellings are made of woven goat hair, sometimes mixed with sheep's wool. Women's black veils and robes are often elaborately embroidered, with the use of red signifying that they are married, and blue unmarried.

Sinai's original inhabitants have often been left behind in the race to build up the coast, and they are sometimes viewed with distrust because of their ties to tribes in neighbouring countries, and allegations of criminal activity and links to terrorist cells throughout Sinai. Bedouin traditions also tend to come second to the significant economical benefits brought by development in the peninsula – benefits that, according to Bedouin activists, Bedouins are yet to fully experience. Egyptian human rights organisations have also reported ongoing persecution of Bedouin people, including imprisonment without charges, and there have been regular demonstrations by Bedouin claiming mistreatment by the police. These concerns, as well as loss of traditional lands, pollution of fishing areas and insensitive tourism, have contributed to the sense of marginalisation and unrest.

Throughout the world – and especially in Egypt – tourism has the power to shape the destinies of communities. Travellers can limit any negative effects by seeking out Bedouin-owned businesses, buying locally, staying informed of prevalent issues and never being afraid to ask questions.

Ras Mumlach DIVE SITE

A sloping reef about 30km south of Nuweiba interspersed with enormous boulders and excellent table corals. Depth: 10m to 25m. Rating: intermediate. Access: shore.

Camel & Jeep Safaris

The desert around Nuweiba has plenty of lush oases and interesting rock formations to explore. Camps in Tarabin can organise trips to the outlying area. We recommend choosing a local Bedouin guide – not only does it benefit those typically marginalised by tour operators from the Nile Valley, but there have been some instances of travellers lost in the desert without water because their so-called guides didn't know the routes.

Itineraries – and, as a result, prices – are generally custom-designed, but expect to pay from about E£300 to E£400 per person per day for a safari including all food and water.

Sleeping

On the northern edge of town, Tarabin is essentially a pedestrian-only boardwalk that stretches along the waterfront for 1.5km. Unfortunately the lack of business in recent years has contributed to a lackadaisical attitude in both beach cleaning and camp repairs. The places we recommend are all in good shape.

Nuweiba

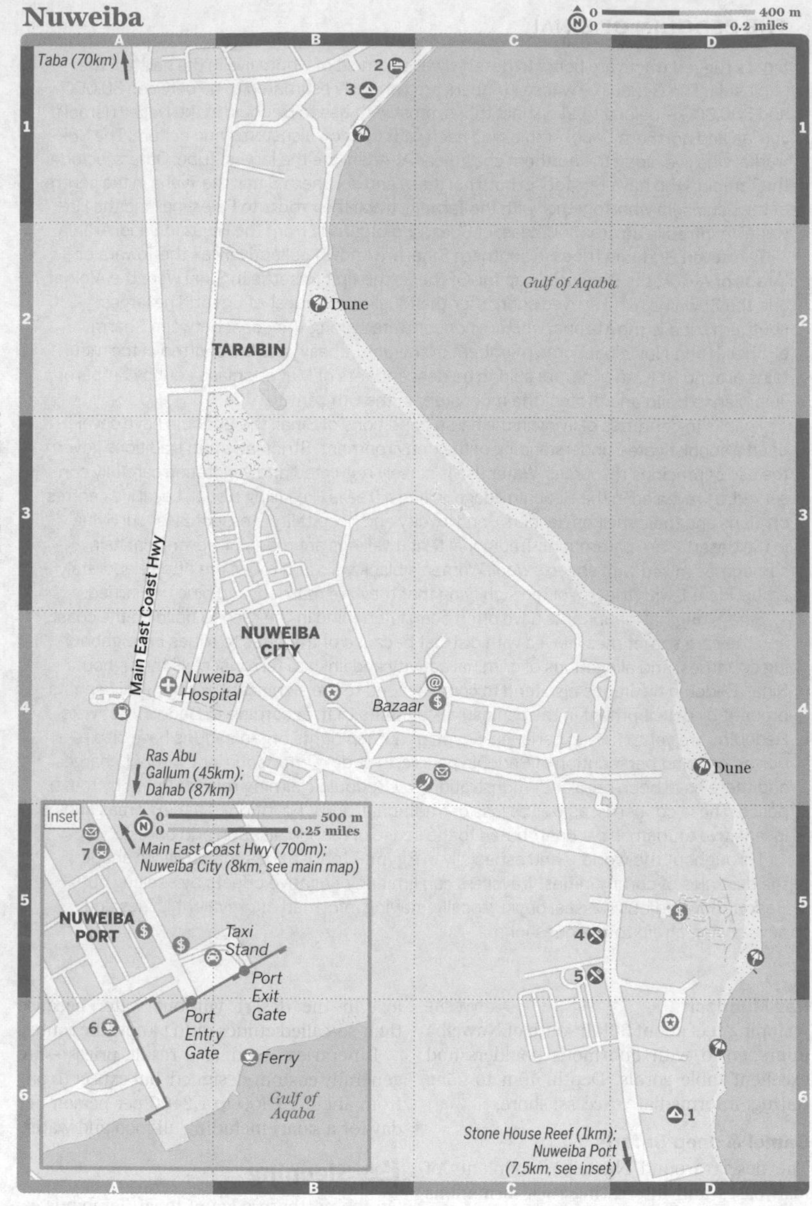

Petra Camp BEACH CAMP **$**
(☎0100 472 2001; mahmoud.sokhar@gmail.com; Tarabin; s/d hut E£44/88; ❄) One of the nicest camps in Tarabin. The centrepiece here is an atmospheric open-air restaurant that was constructed from recycled wood salvaged from a defunct Cairo theatre. Huts are simple but well cared for and most come with air-con. The communal bathrooms are clean, and the restaurant serves up a decent selection of Egyptian and international favourites.

Nuweiba

Sleeping

1 Habiba Village D6
2 Nakhil Inn B1
3 Petra Camp B1

Eating

4 Cleopatra Restaurant C5
5 Han Kang C5

Transport

6 AB Maritime Ferry Ticket Office A6
7 East Delta Travel Company Bus Station A5

★Nakhil Inn HOTEL $$
(☎350 0879; www.nakhil-inn.com; Tarabin; s/d €35/42; ❄📶) The friendly Nakhil is a cosy compromise for those who want hotel comforts without the crowds. The charming studio-style wooden cabins exude simple beach chic. Guests can snorkel the reef just a few metres from the shore, go kayaking or diving, or simply unwind while lazing about in one of the hammocks or seating spots along the private beach.

Habiba Village BEACH CAMP $$
(☎0122 217 6624; www.habibavillage.com; Nuweiba City; s/d/tr €29/39/49; ❄📶) The rooms are a little rough around the edges for the price but are set around a quiet courtyard that's a hop, skip and jump from a nice beach with a good snorkelling reef. Management is engaged in a local permaculture project and has set up an organic farm where interested long-stayers (three month minimum commitment) can volunteer.

Eating

At the port a cluster of places sell fuul (fava bean paste) and ta'amiyya (felafel) in the area behind the National Bank of Egypt and before the ticket office for Aqaba ferries.

Cleopatra Restaurant SEAFOOD $$
(Nuweiba City; dishes E£20-50) One of the more popular tourist restaurants in Nuweiba City, Cleopatra offers up the bounty of the sea along with a few Western fast-food favourites.

Han Kang ASIAN $$
(Nuweiba City; dishes E£20-40) This surprisingly good Chinese restaurant hits the spot, especially if you've been on the road for a while and can't bear to look at another felafel sandwich.

Information

Banks in Nuweiba will not handle Jordanian dinars.

Al-Mostakbal Internet Café (Nuweiba City; per hr E£1; ⏰9am-3am)

Banque du Caire (Nuweiba Port; ⏰8.30am-2.30pm Sun-Thu) Has an ATM.

Banque Misr (Nuweiba Port; ⏰8.30am-2.30pm Sun-Thu) Has an ATM.

Nuweiba Hospital (☎350 0302; Nuweiba City; ⏰24hr) Just off the Main East Coast Hwy to Dahab.

Tourist Police (Nuweiba City; ⏰8am-2pm Sat-Thu) There's another tourist police office (☎350 0231) near Habiba Village.

Getting There & Away

BOAT

Travellers who are definitely returning to Egypt, and not staying in Jordan for longer than eight days, can take the touristic ferry (p400) to Aqaba (Jordan) from Taba. It's infinitely more organised and more comfortable than the public ferries from Nuweiba.

AB Maritime runs two public ferries from Nuweiba to Aqaba. The so-called 'fast-ferry' service leaves Nuweiba from Sunday to Friday (supposedly) at 2pm and takes roughly two hours, assuming normal sea conditions. Heading back to Nuweiba, fast ferries depart from Aqaba at noon. One-way tickets cost US$80 for economy and US$100 for first class. Due to lack of business the fast-ferry service has been dropped and subsequently reinstated several times since the 2011 revolution. As the 'fast-ferry' is infinitely more comfortable than its sister 'slow' service, it's worthwhile for travellers to check locally if it's running before resigning themselves to the 'slow-ferry'.

The 'slow-ferry' service leaves Nuweiba at (again, supposedly) 3pm daily and arrives in Aqaba on average about four hours later. Heading back to Nuweiba, slow ferries depart from Aqaba at 1am. One-way tickets cost US$70.

A word of caution: the Nuweiba–Aqaba ferry service (both 'fast' and 'slow' ferries) is renowned for interminable delays. A small sampling of horror stories we have received from travellers includes a monumental 20-hour delay due to heavy thunderstorms and rough seas, as well as a truly epic three-day delay due to severe power outages. While the majority of travellers experience a delay of no more than two or three hours, it's best to leave some flexibility in onward Jordanian travel schedules in case of mishaps.

Tickets can be paid in either US dollars or Egyptian pounds. Egyptian departure tax (US$10/E£50) is paid at the time of purchase. Tickets can only be purchased on the day of departure, at the ferry ticket office (p490) in a small building near the port. Travellers must be at the port two hours before sailing in order to buy tickets and get through the shambolic departure formalities in the terminal building. Note that during the hajj, boats are booked weeks prior to departure. For travel during this period – the only exception to the rule – it's necessary to buy tickets as far in advance as possible.

To find the ticket office from the bus station, turn right when exiting the bus station, walking towards the water, and turn right again after the National Bank of Egypt. Continue along one block, and the sand-coloured ticket office building ahead is on the left.

Most nationalities are entitled to receive a free Jordanian visa upon arrival in Aqaba. Passports are handed to the immigration officials once onboard the ferry and collected again once arrived at the immigration building in Aqaba.

BUS

From the **bus station** (☎352 0371; Nuweiba Port), East Delta Travel Co has buses to Sharm el-Sheikh (E£30, three to four hours) via Dahab (E£15, one hour) at 6.30am and 4pm. Buses to Taba (E£15, one hour) leave at 9am, noon, and 3pm. The 9am and 3pm Taba services carry on to Cairo but due to security issues, foreign travellers are not allowed to travel on the Taba–Cairo road. Anyone attempting to travel to Cairo this way is likely to be made to get off the bus at either Taba bus station or Taba police check-point.

There is no public bus to St Katherine Protectorate but local transport initiative Bedouin Bus (p394) operates a twice weekly shuttle service between Nuweiba and St Katherine. It leaves Nuweiba every Wednesday and Sunday at 2pm (check the website for pick-up details).

TAXI

Taxis and a few *servees* (service taxis) hang out by the port. Unless you get there when the ferry has arrived from Aqaba, you'll have to wait a long time for a *servees* to fill up. A taxi to Dahab costs about E£150 and roughly E£100 to the further beach camps on the Nuweiba–Taba road.

Getting Around

Expect to pay E£10 to E£20 for a taxi from the port or bus station to Nuweiba City, depending on destination and negotiating powers, and from E£5 for the few kilometres between Tarabin and Nuweiba City.

Around Nuweiba

Home to some of Sinai's most interesting, and easily accessible, desert landscapes, the stretch of coastal desert around Nuweiba is prime camel- and jeep-safari territory. Safaris into this area are best arranged from Dahab, Nuweiba or the beach camps strung out along the Nuweiba–Taba road.

Sights

Coloured Canyon CANYON

This canyon derives its name from the layers of bright, multicoloured stones that resemble paintings on its steep, narrow walls. It's magnificently beautiful. As the canyon is sheltered from the wind, the silence is one of its most impressive features. It's a favourite day trip from both Dahab and Sharm el-Sheikh, so unfortunately the ambience can be destroyed somewhat if a couple of large bus tours arrive at the same time.

Mayet el-Wishwashi OASIS

The area around the spring of Mayat el-Wishwashi is great for hiking. The actual spring is hidden within a canyon and only has only a trickle of water, except after floods. Nearby is **Mayat Malkha**, a palm grove fed by the spring's waters and set amid colourful sandstone.

Ain Umm Ahmed OASIS

Picturesque Ain Umm Ahmed is the largest oasis in eastern Sinai, with lots of palms, Bedouin houses and a famous stream that becomes an icy river in the winter months.

Wadi Huweiyit CANYON

Wadi Huweiyit is an impressive sandstone canyon with lookouts that give panoramic views over to Saudi Arabia.

Ain Khudra OASIS

The spring of Ain Khudra oasis is where Miriam was supposed to have been struck by leprosy for criticising Moses.

Ain al-Furtega OASIS

This pretty palm-filled oasis is 16km northwest of Nuweiba.

Wadi Sheikh Atiya TOMB

The oasis area of Wadi Sheikh Atiya is named after the father of the Tarabin tribe – the largest tribe in the area – who lies buried here under a white dome. Bedouin frequently come on pilgrimage.

Gebel Barga MOUNTAIN

The climb up Gebel Barga is quite tricky but the summit affords stunning views over the mountains of eastern Sinai.

WORTH A TRIP

SINAI BEACH CAMPS

The coastline between Nuweiba and Taba is Egypt's last bastion of the traditional beach camp. For years this region's business came from Israelis looking for a closer-to-home Goa, but unfortunately political turmoil in recent years has kept them away, and other travellers are still to venture north and discover this tranquil beach-bum haven. Ideal for those who want to seriously veg out, this stretch of shore has yet to succumb to restaurant touts or rowdy bar music; lazing in a hammock is still the de rigueur activity.

We name just a small selection of the beach camps here. There are plenty more for those who want to explore. All the camps recommended have restaurants and can help organise desert treks for guests who tire of slothing out on the sand. For travellers who don't have their own transport and don't want to hire a taxi, the East Delta (p393) buses running between Dahab and Taba can drop people anywhere along this shore.

Sawa Camp (☎0100 272 2838; www.sawacamp.com; Mahash area; s/d hut E£95/160) A strip of perfect white beach, hammocks on every hut porch, solar-powered showers and a restaurant dishing up delicious meals: Sawa ticks all the boxes for a laid-back, family-friendly travel stop that's great for unwinding. Bedouin owner Salama has got all the little touches right. Simple *hoosha* (palm-thatch) huts all have electricity and the communal bathrooms are kept spotless.

Ayyash Camp (☎0122 760 4668; Ras Shaitan area; s/d hut E£40/80) Located on the rocky point of the frighteningly named Ras Shaitan (Satan's Head), Ayyash's stretch of sand is a bit stony and the facilities really are superbasic. Still, that doesn't dissuade its fans, who come here to flop out on seriously hippy vibes and cheap, chilled-out beach-bum living.

Basata (☎350 0481; www.basata.com; Ras Burgaa area; camp sites per person €12, s/d hut €23/40, 3-person chalets €80) Basata (meaning 'simplicity' in Arabic) is an ecologically minded settlement that uses organically grown produce and recycles its rubbish. Self-catering is the norm – there's a communal kitchen and cooking ingredients are available to buy – but it does serve dinner for those feeling lazy. The ambience is laid-back and family-friendly with a New Age twist.

Taba

☎069

Taba holds the dubious distinction of being the last portion of Sinai to be returned to Egypt under the terms of the 1979 Egypt–Israel peace treaty. Egypt argued that Taba was on the Egyptian side of the armistice line agreed to in 1949, while Israel contended that it was on the Ottoman side of a border agreed between the Ottomans and British Egypt in 1906, and therefore the lines drawn in 1949 and 1979 were in error. In 1988 the issue was submitted to an international commission, which ruled in Egypt's favour; Israel returned Taba to Egypt later that year.

As part of this agreement, Israeli travellers were permitted to visit Taba visa-free for up to 48 hours, which sparked tourism development throughout the town. Following a bomb attack in 2004 that killed and injured a large number of Israeli travellers, however, Taba's tourism dried up. In the early 2000s the flashy Taba Heights resort project, just south of town, attempted to reinvigorate the stagnant local economy, aiming squarely at the European package-tourist market.

Events here in 2014 have yet again brought Taba into the headlines for all the wrong reasons. On 16 February 2014 a bomb exploded on a tourist bus near Taba's Hilton Hotel, killing four and wounding 16. And in May 2014 a flash flood caused severe damage in the Taba area, destroying two hotels directly in the flood's path within the Taba Heights project and forcing others to close for several weeks for extensive repairs. Although Taba's tourism industry is endeavouring to get back on its feet, it will probably take a long time to fully recover.

Sights

Pharaoh's Island FORTRESS

(Gezirat Fara'un; adult/child E£20/10; ⏲9am-5pm) About 7km south of Taba and 250m off the Egyptian coast, this tiny islet in turquoise waters is dominated by the much-restored Castle of Salah ad-Din. The castle was originally a fortress built by the Crusaders in

1115, but was captured and expanded by Saladin in 1170 as a bulwark against feared Crusader penetration south from Palestine.

Information

The town centre is home to a couple of banks, a small hospital and various shops. Just inside the border you'll find an ATM and several foreign-exchange booths. Cash and travellers cheques can also be exchanged at the Taba Hilton. The Taba Heights resort area lies about 20km south of the main town.

DANGERS & ANNOYANCES

The Taba bus bombing on 16 February 2014 was directly aimed at tourists. In their statement claiming responsibility for the attack, Ansar Beit al-Maqdis militants pledged to continue on a campaign of attacks that directly affect Egypt's economic interests. In the aftermath most foreign governments issued travel warnings for the South Sinai area.

The Taba border remains the only reliable crossing between Egypt and Israel and overland travellers continue to cross here, just as a small number of package-tourists are continuing to holiday within the Taba Heights resort. Travellers heading this way should check the latest travel advisories and, more importantly, pay attention to local advice once on the ground.

Getting There & Away

The Taba–Eilat border is open 24 hours daily. Egyptian departure tax is E£75.

AIR

At the time of research, Taba International Airport was closed.

BOAT

Meenagate Marine Transport (in Aqaba 03-201 3100; www.meenagate.com; Sharia King Hussein bin Talal, Aqaba ; office 10am-7pm) operates a fast and efficient daily ferry service to Aqaba in Jordan. The ferry leaves Taba Marina (at Taba Heights resort area) at 6am and arrives in Aqaba at 6.30am. On the return leg, the ferry leaves from Aqaba's Royal Yacht Club port (rather than the public port) at 7.30pm and arrives in Taba at 8pm. Passengers should be at the ports one hour before departure time.

Only round-trip tickets (adult/child US$130/90) are allowed to be purchased. The return ticket is valid for eight days after departure. Egyptian departure tax is included in the ticket but not Jordanian departure tax (JD10). Independent travellers can book tickets through Meenagate's website. Bookings should be made at least 48 hours in advance.

BUS

Taba's **bus station** (353 0250) is along the main road about 800m south of the border. East Delta Travel Co buses to Nuweiba (E£15, one hour) leave at 3pm and 4pm. The 3pm service carries on to Dahab (E£30, 2½ hours) and Sharm el-Sheikh (E£45, four hours). There are also two buses daily to Cairo (E£80, six to seven hours) via the Nakhl–Suez road, but foreign travellers are not allowed to travel this route due to security issues. For travellers who've crossed the border from Eilat and want to journey directly to Cairo, the only option is to go via Sharm el-Sheikh.

MINIBUS & SERVEES

Minibuses and *servees* wait by the border for passengers. If business is slack, there may be a long wait for the vehicle to fill up – alternatively, travellers can pay the equivalent of all seven fares and leave immediately. Per-person fares are about E£15 to Nuweiba, E£30 to Dahab and E£45 to Sharm el-Sheikh. Bargaining power increases when the bus departure times are approaching.

SINAI INTERIOR

Sinai's rugged interior is populated by barren mountains, wind-sculpted canyons and wadis that burst into life with even the briefest rains. The rocks and desert landscapes turn shades of pink, ochre and velvet-black as the sun rises and falls, and what little vegetation there is appears to grow magically out of the rock. Bedouin still wander through the wilderness, and camels are the best way to travel, with much of the terrain too rocky even for a 4WD. Against this desolate backdrop some of the most sacred events in recorded human history are said to have taken place, which has consequently immortalised Sinai in the annals of Judaism, Christianity and Islam.

St Katherine Protectorate

069

The 4350-sq-km St Katherine Protectorate was created in 1996 to counteract the detrimental effects of rapidly increasing tourism on St Katherine's Monastery and the adjacent Mt Sinai. In addition to the area's unique high-altitude desert ecosystem, it protects a wealth of historical sites sacred to the world's three main monotheistic religions, and the core part around the monastery has been declared a Unesco World Heritage site.

Rising up out of the desert and jutting above the other peaks surrounding the monastery is the towering 2285m Mt Sinai (Gebel Musa). Tucked into a barren valley at the foot of Mt Sinai is the ancient St Katherine's Monastery. Approximately 3.5km from here is the small town of Al-Milga, which is also called Katroon and is known as the 'Meeting Place' by local Jabaliyya Bedouin.

Sights

★St Katherine's Monastery MONASTERY
(Cairo 02-2482 8513; 9am-noon Mon-Thu & Sat, except religious holidays) FREE This ancient monastery traces its founding to about AD 330, when the Byzantine empress Helena had a small chapel and a fortified refuge for local hermits built beside what was believed to be the burning bush from which God spoke to Moses. Today St Katherine's is considered one of the oldest continually functioning monastic communities in the world, and its chapel is one of early Christianity's only surviving churches.

The monastery is named after St Katherine, the legendary martyr of Alexandria, who was tortured on a spiked wheel and then beheaded for her faith. Tradition holds that her body was transported by angels away from the torture device (which spun out of control and killed the pagan onlookers) and onto the slopes of Egypt's highest mountain peak. The peak, which lies about 6km south of Mt Sinai, subsequently became known as Gebel Katarina. Katherine's body was 'found' about 300 years later by monks from the monastery in a state of perfect preservation.

In the 6th century Emperor Justinian ordered a fortress to be constructed around the original chapel, together with a basilica and a monastery, to provide a secure home for the monastic community that had grown there, and as a refuge for the Christians of southern Sinai.

Since then the monastery has been visited by pilgrims from throughout the world, many of whom braved extraordinarily difficult and dangerous journeys to reach the remote and isolated site. Today a paved access road has removed the hazards that used to accompany a trip here, and the monastery has become a popular day trip from Sharm el-Sheikh and Dahab.

Travellers visiting should remember that this is still a functioning monastery, which necessitates conservative dress – no one with shorts is permitted to enter, and women must cover their shoulders.

➡ Touring the Monastery

Inside the walled compound, the ornately decorated 6th-century **Church of the Transfiguration** has a nave flanked by massive marble columns and walls covered in richly gilded icons and paintings. At the church's eastern end, a gilded 17th-century iconostasis separates the nave from the sanctuary and the apse, where St Katherine's remains are interred (off limits to most visitors). High in the apse above the altar is one of the monastery's most stunning artistic treasures, the 6th-century mosaic of the transfiguration, although it can be difficult to see it past the chandeliers and the iconostasis. To the left of and below the altar is the monastery's holiest area, the Chapel of the Burning Bush, which is off limits to the public.

It's possible to see what is thought to be a descendant of the original **burning bush** in the monastery compound; however, due to visitors snipping cuttings of the bush to take home as blessings, the area surrounding it is now fenced off. Near the burning bush is the Well of Moses, a natural spring that is supposed to give marital happiness to those who drink from it.

Above the Well of Moses is the superb **Monastery Museum** (Sacred Sacristy; adult/student E£25/10), which has been magnificently restored. It has displays (labelled in Arabic and English) of many of the monastery's artistic treasures, including some of

TREAD LIGHTLY IN ST KATHERINE PROTECTORATE

To limit tourism impact on this special place, the following code is in force:

- Respect the area's religious and historical importance and the local Bedouin culture and traditions.
- Carry your litter out; bury your bodily waste; and burn your toilet paper.
- Do not contaminate or overuse water sources.

The following acts are illegal:

- Removing any object, including rocks, plants and animals.
- Disturbing or harming animals or birds.
- Cutting or uprooting plants.
- Writing, painting or carving graffiti.

St Katherine's Monastery

A HISTORY OF THE MONASTERY

4th Century With hermetic communities congregating in the area, a chapel is established around the site of Moses' miraculous **Burning Bush** ❶.

6th Century In a show of might, Emperor Justinian adds the monastery **fortifications** ❷ and orders the building of the basilica, which is graced by Byzantine art, including the **Mosaic of the Transfiguration** ❸.

7th Century The prophet Mohammed signs the **Ahtiname** ❹, a declaration of his protection of the monastery. When the Arab armies conquer Egypt in AD 641, the monastery is left untouched. Despite the era's tumultuous times, monastery abbot St John Klimakos writes his famed **Ladder of Divine Ascent** ❺ treatise, depicted in the Sacred Sacristy.

9th Century Extraordinary happenings surround the monastery when, according to tradition, a monk discovers the body of St Katherine on a mountain summit.

11th Century To escape the wrath of Fatimid caliph Al-Hakim, wily monks build a mosque within the monastery grounds.

15th Century Frequent raids and attacks on the monastery lead the monks to build the **Ancient Gate** ❻ to prevent the ransacking of church treasures and to keep the monastic community safe.

19th Century In 1859 biblical scholar Constantin von Tischendorf borrows 347 pages of the **Codex Sinaiticus** ❼ from the monastery, but fails to get his library books back on time. Greek artisans travel from the island of Tinos in 1871 to help construct the **bell tower** ❽.

20th Century Renovations inside the monastery reveal 18 more missing parchment leaves from the Codex Sinaiticus, proving that all the secrets hidden within these ancient walls may not yet be revealed.

SIMON BALSON/ALAMY ©

Fortifications

The formidable walls are 2m thick and 11m high. Justinian sent a Balkan garrison to watch over the newly fortified monastery, and today's local Jabaleyya tribe are said to be their descendents.

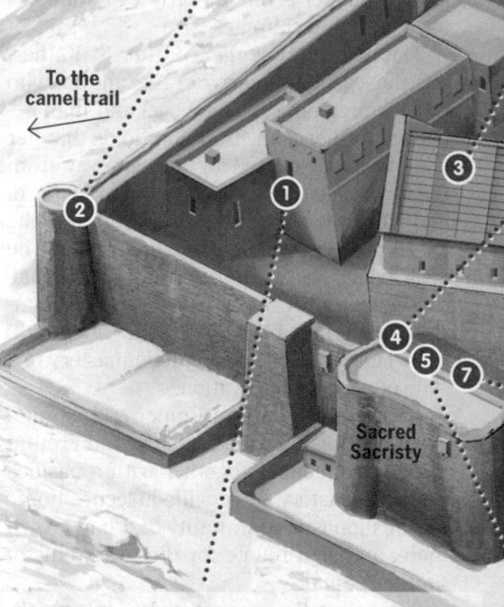

The Burning Bush

This flourishing bramble (the endemic Sinai shrub *Rubus Sanctus*) was transplanted in the 10th century to its present location. Tradition states that cuttings of the plant refuse to grow outside the monastery walls.

JESSICA LEE

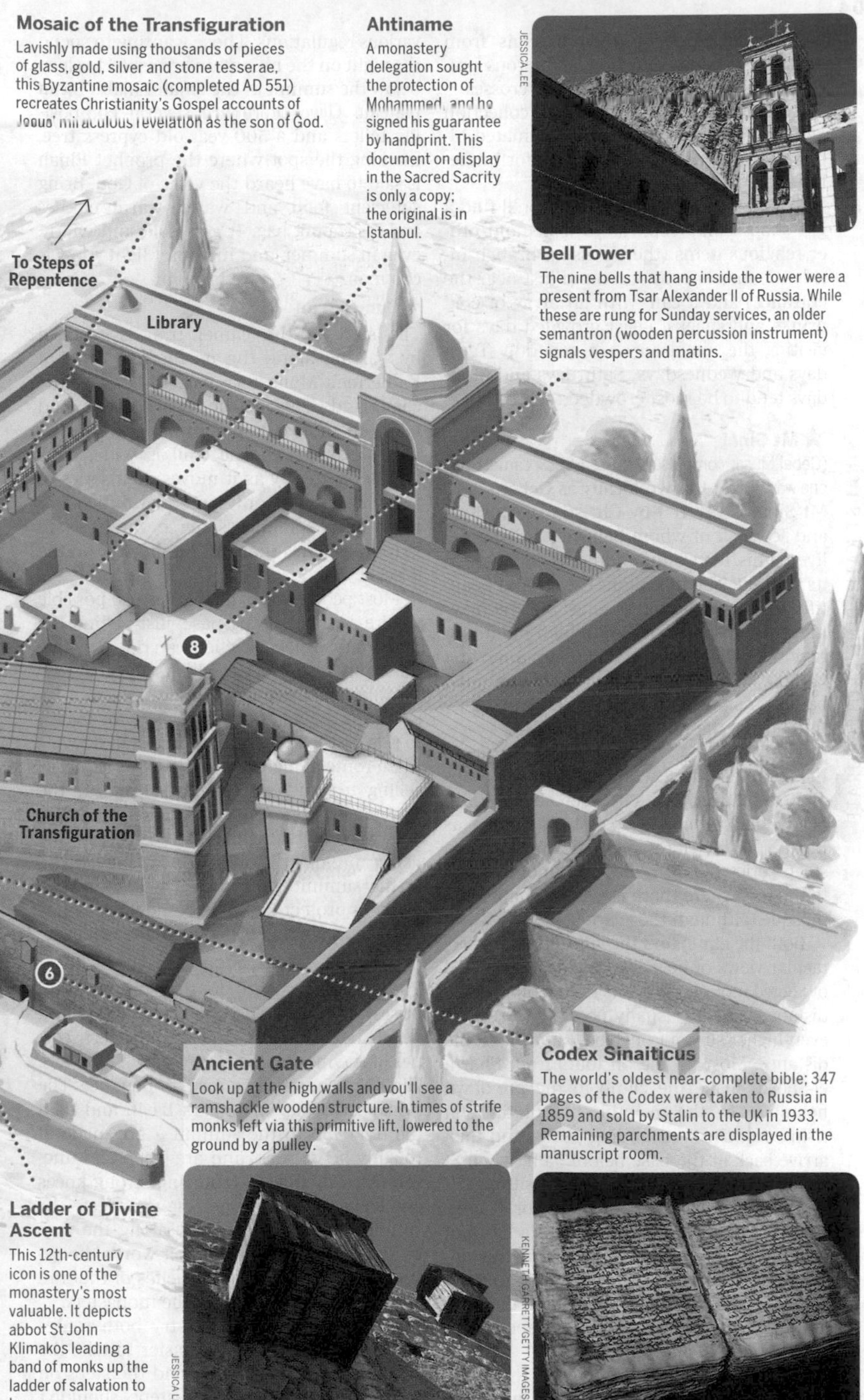

Mosaic of the Transfiguration
Lavishly made using thousands of pieces of glass, gold, silver and stone tesserae, this Byzantine mosaic (completed AD 551) recreates Christianity's Gospel accounts of Jesus' miraculous revelation as the son of God.
Ahtiname
A monastery delegation sought the protection of Mohammed, and he signed his guarantee by handprint. This document on display in the Sacred Sacrity is only a copy; the original is in Istanbul.
JESSICA LEE
Bell Tower
The nine bells that hang inside the tower were a present from Tsar Alexander II of Russia. While these are rung for Sunday services, an older semantron (wooden percussion instrument) signals vespers and matins.
To Steps of Repentence
Library
8
Church of the Transfiguration
6
Ancient Gate
Look up at the high walls and you'll see a ramshackle wooden structure. In times of strife monks left via this primitive lift, lowered to the ground by a pulley.
Codex Sinaiticus
The world's oldest near-complete bible; 347 pages of the Codex were taken to Russia in 1859 and sold by Stalin to the UK in 1933. Remaining parchments are displayed in the manuscript room.
Ladder of Divine Ascent
This 12th-century icon is one of the monastery's most valuable. It depicts abbot St John Klimakos leading a band of monks up the ladder of salvation to heaven.
JESSICA LEE
KENNETH GARRETT/GETTY IMAGES ©

the spectacular Byzantine-era icons from its world-famous collection, numerous precious chalices, and gold and silver crosses.

Although it contains a priceless collection of ancient manuscripts and illuminated bibles, the monastery's **library** is unfortunately closed to the general public.

Outside the monastery walls you'll find a gift shop selling replicas of icons and other religious items (there's also a branch inside the monastery compound just near the entrance) and a cafe with an array of cold drinks and snacks. Least crowded days for visiting the monastery are generally Tuesdays and Wednesdays; Saturdays and Mondays tend to be most crowded.

★Mt Sinai MOUNTAIN

(Gebel Musa; compulsory guide E£125, camel rides one way E£125) Known locally as Gebel Musa, Mt Sinai is revered by Christians, Muslims and Jews, all of whom believe that God delivered his Ten Commandments to Moses at its summit. The mountain is easy and beautiful to climb, and offers a taste of the magnificence of southern Sinai's high mountain region. For pilgrims, it also offers a moving glimpse into biblical times. All hikers must be accompanied by a local Bedouin guide (hired from the monastery car park).

There are two well-defined routes up to the summit – the camel trail and the Steps of Repentance – which meet about 300m below the summit at a plateau known as Elijah's Basin. Here, everyone must take a steep series of 750 rocky and uneven steps to the top, where there is a small chapel and mosque (although these are kept locked).

Both the climb and the summit offer spectacular views of nearby plunging valleys and of jagged mountain chains rolling off into the distance, and it's usually possible to see the even-higher summit of Gebel Katarina in the distance. Most people on tours from Sharm el-Sheikh make the climb in the pre-dawn hours to see the magnificence of the sun rising over the surrounding peaks, and then arrive back at the base before 9am, when St Katherine's Monastery opens for visitors.

An alternative is to walk up for sunset, when there are rarely more than a handful of other hikers on the summit. For this option, travellers must be comfortable making the descent down the camel trail in the dark and make sure they have sturdy shoes and a good torch (flashlight).

Due to the sanctity of the area, the Egyptian National Parks Office has instituted various regulations. Those wanting to spend the night on the mountain are asked to sleep below the summit at the small Elijah's Basin plateau. Here there are several composting toilets and a 500-year-old cypress tree, marking the spot where the prophet Elijah is said to have heard the voice of God. Bring sufficient food and water, warm clothes and a sleeping bag. It gets cold and windy, even in summer, and in winter light snow is common.

➡ Camel Trail

The start of the camel trail is reached by walking along the northern wall of St Katherine's Monastery past the end of the compound. This is the easier route, and takes about two hours to ascend, moving at a steady pace. The trail is wide, clear and slopes gently as it moves up a series of switchbacks. The only potential difficulty – apart from sometimes fierce winds – are gravelly patches that can be slippery on the descent.

Most people walk up, but it's also possible to hire a camel at the base, just behind the monastery, which travellers can ride to where the camel trail ends at Elijah's Basin. Those who decide to try this should note that it's easier on the anatomy (especially for males) to ride up the mountain, rather than down.

En route along the trail are several kiosks selling tea and soft drinks, and near the summit vendors rent out blankets (E£5) to help ward off the chill. For those ascending in the pre-dawn hours to wait for sunrise at the summit, these are a worthy investment to protect against the howling winds (though the blankets do smell like camels).

➡ Steps of Repentance

The alternative path to the summit comprises the taxing 3750 Steps of Repentance, which begin outside the southeastern corner of the monastery compound. They were laid by one monk as a form of penance. The steps – 3000 up to Elijah's Basin and then the final 750 to the summit – are made of roughly hewn rock, and are steep and uneven in many places, requiring strong knees and concentration in placing your feet. The stunning mountain scenery along the way, though, makes this path well worth the extra effort, and the lower reaches of the trail afford impressive views of the monastery.

For those who want to try both routes to Mt Sinai's summit, it's easier to take the camel trail on the way up and the steps on the way back down. The steps shouldn't be attempted in the dark though, so those heading to the summit for sunset and not staying overnight should go up via the steps and come down the easier camel trail.

Activities & Tours

The majority of visitors arrive at the St Katherine Protectorate on organised tours departing from either Sharm el-Sheikh or Dahab. Nevertheless, St Katherine's Monastery lies in the heart of South Sinai's high mountain region, and the surrounding area is an ideal trekking destination for anyone with a rugged and adventurous bent. It's easy to organise everything independently at Al-Milga.

Guided & Camel Treks

Guided treks and camel treks typically start at around €50 per day including food and equipment. You should buy firewood in Al-Miga in order to discourage destruction of the few trees in the mountains. Make sure you bring water-purification tablets, unless you want to rely on the mountain springs. You'll also need comfortable walking boots, a hat and sunglasses, sunblock, a warm jacket, a good sleeping bag and toilet paper. Keep in mind that it can get very cold at night – frost, and even snow, are common in winter. Treks range from half a day to a week or more, and can be done either on camel or on foot. Even if you decide to walk, you'll need at least one camel for your food and luggage. Whoever you go with, be sure to register with the police prior to leaving.

For detailed information on trekking in this area, check out www.discoversinai.net and www.st-katherine.net.

One of the most common circuits goes to the **Galt al-Azraq** (Blue Pools) and takes four to five days. The trail leaves Al-Milga via the constructed **Abu Giffa Pass** and goes through **Wadi Tubug**, taking a detour around **Wadi Shagg**, where there are springs, waterholes and *bustans* (lush, walled gardens). The walk then continues through the picturesque **Wadi Zuweitin** (Valley of the Olives), home to ancient olive trees said by local Bedouin to have been planted by the founder of the Jabaliyya tribe. The first night is often spent here, and there is a small stone hut in which hikers can sometimes sleep. The hike continues through **Wadi Gibal**, through high passes and along the valleys of **Farsh Asara** and **Farsh Arnab**.

Many hikers then climb either **Ras Abu Alda** or **Gebel Abu Gasba** before heading to the spring of **Ain Nagila** and the ruins of a Byzantine monastery at **Bab ad-Dunya** (Gate of the World). On the third day the trail leads to the crystal-clear, icy waters of the **Galt al-Azraq**, a deep, dramatic pool in the rock, before continuing on the fourth day through more dramatic wadis to a camel pass on **Gebel Abbas Basha**. A one-hour hike up a fairly easy but steep path leads to a ruined palace built by the 19th-century viceroy Abbas Hilmi I, and there are stunning views from the summit (2304m). The trail then goes back to Wadi Zuweitin and retraces its way to Al-Milga.

Other destinations include **Sheikh Awad**, home to a sheikh's tomb and Bedouin settlement; the **Nugra Waterfall**, a difficult-to-reach, rain-fed cascade about 20m high, which is reached through a winding canyon called Wadi Nugra; and **Naqb al-Faria**, a camel path with rock inscriptions. A shorter trip is the hike to the top of **Gebel Katarina**, Egypt's highest peak at 2642m. It takes about five hours to reach the summit along a straightforward but taxing trail. The views from the top are breathtaking, and the panorama can even include the mountains of Saudi Arabia on a clear day. The **Blue Valley**, given its name after a Belgian artist painted the rocks here blue some years ago, is another popular day trip.

Tour Operators

Mountain Tours Office DESERT TOUR
(☎347 0457; www.sheikmousa.com; El-Malga Bedouin Camp, Al-Miga, St Katherine Protectorate) The main hub for trekking activities in the St Katherine region, this office can organise anything from a short afternoon stroll to a multiday itinerary. It can also arrange yoga and meditation retreats, rock climbing and 4WD tours.

Wilderness Ventures Egypt DESERT TOUR
(☎0128 282 7182; www.wilderness-ventures-egypt.com) Working closely with local Jabaliyya Bedouin, this highly recommended company organises a variety of treks and activities inside St Katherine Protectorate, with a strong focus on Bedouin culture and local history. Of particular note, it organises hikes in the nearby Wadi Itlah gardens that include a slap-up lunch in one of the gardens and fascinating astronomy sessions.

It also runs Sinai's only proper camel-riding school (where travellers are taught how to properly handle their trusty steed before setting out on a trek).

Sleeping

Most hotels and guesthouses are based in the village of Al-Milga (Katreen), approximately 3.5km from St Katherine's Monastery.

★ Al-Karm Ecolodge LODGE $
(0100 132 4693; Sheikh Awaad; r without bathroom incl half/full board per person E£100/120;) Surrounded by lush gardens in a remote wadi, this Bedouin-owned ecolodge is the perfect spot to sample the tranquillity and rugged beauty of southern Sinai. It deserves kudos for its environmental efforts: solar-powered showers; composting toilets; and beautifully designed, simple stone and palm-trunk rooms decorated with local textiles, which blend into the scenery. Transport and lodge booking is easiest done through Mountain Tours Office (p405); minimal English is spoken at the lodge.

It is only accessible by 4WD. The turn-off is signposted 'Garaba Valley' about 20km from St Katherine on the Wadi Feiran road.

Lit only by the flicker of candlelight by night, this is a truly unique spot that is worth the effort to get here. There is plenty of good trekking that can be arranged by the lodge.

El-Malga Bedouin Camp HOSTEL $
(0100 641 3575; www.sheikmousa.com; Al-Milga; dm E£25, s/d E£100/150, without bathroom E£55/85;) This popular backpacker-friendly camp, run by the affable Sheikh Mousa, offers excellent quality for the price. The newly built en suite rooms are large and comfortable, while the cheaper rooms all share excellent bathroom facilities with hot water. At the base of the Mountain Tours Office, an easy 500m walk from the bus station.

Monastery Guesthouse GUESTHOUSE $$
(347 0353; St Katherine's Monastery; s/d US$35/60;) A favourite of pilgrims the world over, this guesthouse right next to St Katherine's Monastery offers well-kept rooms surrounding a pleasant courtyard. Meals at the on-site cafeteria are filling and tasty, and lunches can be arranged for a few extra dollars per person. Make sure to ask for a mountain-view rather than a courtyard-view room.

Daniela Village HOTEL $$
(347 0379; www.daniela-hotels.com; Al-Miga; s/d €33/44;) One of the nicest midrange hotels in Al-Milga, this three-star affair comprises stone-clad chalets that are scattered around attractive grounds. The on-site bar-restaurant is a popular tourist hang-out, and is especially good for those in need of a beer after an all-night trek. It's diagonally opposite the hospital and about 1.5km from the bus station.

Eating

Al-Milga has a bakery opposite the mosque, a couple of simple restaurants and several well-stocked supermarkets – perfect for stocking up on supplies before hitting the trails. Most tourists take their meals at their camp or hotel, or in the monastery's cafeteria.

If you are spending a little time in St Katherine, don't miss the opportunity of having lunch, surrounded by shady fruit trees, in the gardens of **Wadi Itlah**. Local tour company Wilderness Ventures Egypt (p405) can arrange this for you.

Information

The **St Katherine Protectorate Office** (347 0032), located near the entrance to Al-Milga, sometimes has informative booklets to four 'interpretive trails' established in the area, including one for Mt Sinai. These booklets take you through each trail, explaining flora and fauna as well as sites of historical and religious significance.

Banque Misr (10am-1pm & 5-8pm Sat-Thu) Beside the petrol station; has an ATM and also changes US dollars and euro.

Nahda Internet (Al-Milga; noon-late) Beside El-Malga Bedouin Camp.

Police (347 0046; Al-Milga) Beside the St Katherine Protectorate Office.

Post Office (Al-Milga; 8.30am-2pm Sat-Thu) Beside the bakery.

St Katherine Hospital (347 0263; Al-Milga; 24hr) Provides very basic care only.

Getting There & Away

The **bus station** (347 0250) is just off the main road in Al-Milga, behind the mosque. East Delta Travel Co runs one daily bus to Cairo (E£50, seven hours) at 6am via Wadi Feiran and Suez (E£40, five hours).

There is no public bus service between St Katherine and the Sinai coast but local transport initiative Bedouin Bus (p394) runs a twice-weekly bus service from Al-Milga to both Dahab and Nuweiba. To Dahab the bus departs every Tuesday and Friday at 11am, and to Nuweiba the bus leaves every Wednesday and Sunday at 8am. The bus leaves from in front of the bakery (opposite the mosque) on Al-Milga's main street. At other times, you'll need to hire a taxi to the Sinai coast. The rate per car is E£250 to either Dahab or Sharm el-Sheikh.

Taxis and pick-ups usually wait at the monastery car park for people coming down from Mt Sinai in the morning, and then again around noon when the monastery's visiting hours end. A lift to the village costs E£10 to E£15.

Wadi Feiran

This long valley serves as the main drainage route for the entire high mountain region into the Gulf of Suez. Sinai's largest oasis, it is lush and very beautiful, containing more than 12,000 date palms, as well as Bedouin communities representing all of Sinai's tribes. Stone walls surround the palms, and the rocky mountains on each side of the wadi have subtly different colours that stand out at sunrise and sunset, making the landscape even more dramatic.

Feiran also has biblical significance – it is believed to be the Rephidim mentioned in the Old Testament where the Israelites defeated their enemies. Because of this it later became the first Christian stronghold in Sinai. An extensively rebuilt early-Christian convent remains from this time, but you need permission from St Katherine's Monastery to visit.

The valley is an ideal spot from which to trek into the surrounding mountains. To the south, the 2070m **Gebel Serbal** (Mt Serbal), believed by early Christians to have been the real Mt Sinai, is a challenging six-hour hike to the summit along a track known as **Sikket ar-Reshshah**. Those who persevere are rewarded with fantastic panoramic views. You must be accompanied by a Bedouin guide for all hikes, which can be arranged either in Al-Milga (at St Katherine) or at the Bedouin Flower Garden Restaurant in Wadi Feiran itself.

NORTHERN SINAI

Rarely visited by tourists, northern Sinai has a barren desert interior, much of which is off limits to foreigners, and a palm-fringed Mediterranean coast backed by soft white sands sculpted into low dunes. As a crossroad between Asia and Africa, the coastal highway follows what must be one of history's oldest march routes. Known in ancient times as the Way of Horus, it was used by the Egyptians, Persians, Greeks, Crusaders and Arab Muslims. The Copts believe that the infant Jesus also passed along this route with his parents during their flight into Egypt.

Due to the lack of security in the region and frequency of militant attacks in the area, northern Sinai is a no-go zone on most foreign-government travel advisories. The situation on the ground is extremely fluid with random outbreaks of violence and bombing campaigns occurring with no prior warning. Travellers should heed travel advisories before planning any journeys here.

Al-Arish

068 / POP 140,000

Much of the north coast of Sinai between Port Fuad and Al-Arish is dominated by the swampy lagoon of Lake Bardawil, separated from the Mediterranean by a limestone

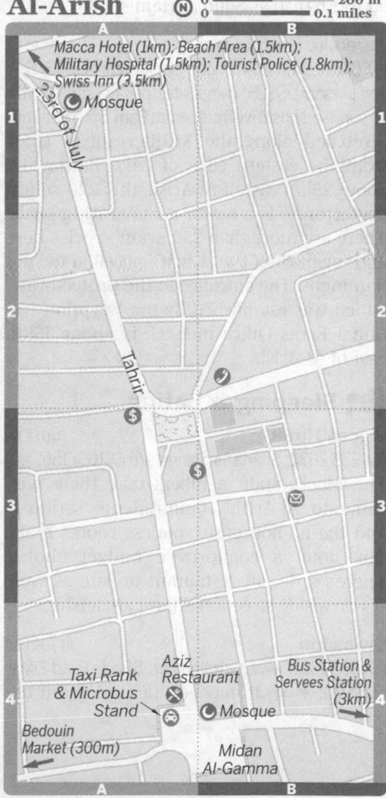

ridge. As a result of this inhospitable geography, Al-Arish is the only major city in the region, and by default the capital of North Sinai Governorate. The town's sprawl of ugly low-rise cement blocks wouldn't win any design awards and although the palm-fringed (though litter-strewn) coastline used to feature as a summer break spot for holidaying Cairenes, since the 2011 revolution Al-Arish has been wracked by waves of violence, with frequent militant attacks on police and army facilities, meaning even this modest tourism has dried up.

Sights & Activities

Bedouin Market MARKET
(9am-2pm Thu) Bedouin arrive en masse for Al-Arish's weekly market, selling silver, beadwork and embroidered dresses. Squeezing between the bleating goats, chicken cages and huge mounds of onions, while trying to manoeuvre through the crowds, is an experience itself. It's held at the southern edge of Al-Arish near the main market (signposted in English as Souq al-Hamis).

Zerenike Protectorate PARK
(0100 544 2641; per person/car US$5/5, r per person US$25, camp sites per person US$10; sunrise-sunset, visitors centre 9am-5pm Sat-Thu) Stretched along the Mediterranean coast from the eastern edge of Lake Bardawil t about 25km east of Al-Arish, this 220-sq-km protectorate is a haven for migrating birds. There are more than 250 avian species here and for most of the year it's possible to spot flamingos. The entrance to the protectorate, which was established by the Egyptian National Parks Office in 1985, is about 35km east of Al-Arish.

Sleeping & Eating

Macca Hotel HOTEL $$
(335 2632; Sharia as-Salam; s/d E£105/155;) The Macca staff members take their 'welcome to Al-Arish' commitments seriously and the no-nonsense, spotless rooms make this hotel a comfortable budget choice. There's a decent restaurant on-site as well. It's on a side street off Sharia al-Geish.

Swiss Inn RESORT $$
(335 1321; www.swissinn.net; Sharia Fuad Zikry; r US$90;) It may be a tad faded but the cheerful, tidy rooms here all have sea views and balconies.

Aziz Restaurant EGYPTIAN $
(Sharia Tahrir; dishes E£5-25) An affordable restaurant offering filling meals of fuul and ta'amiyya, as well as grilled chicken, *kofta*, rice and spaghetti.

Information

Banque Misr (off Sharia Tahrir; 8.30am-2.30pm Sun-Thu) Has an ATM.

Main Post Office (off Sharia Tahrir; 8.30am-2pm Sat-Thu)

Military Hospital (332 4018; coast rd; 24hr) Near the Governorate Building.

Tourist Police (336 1016; Sharia Fuad Zikry; 24hr)

Getting There & Away

The main bus and *servees* stations are next to each other, about 3km southeast of the town centre (about E£5 in a taxi).

From the **bus station** (332 5931), East Delta Travel Co buses depart to Cairo (E£40, five hours) at 8am and 4pm; and to Ismailia (E£20, three hours) at 7am, 10.30am, 11.30am, 2pm, 3pm and 4pm.

Getting Around

The main **taxi rank and microbus stand** is at Midan al-Gamma, near the market at the southern end of town. Microbuses shuttle regularly between here and the beach (50pt).

Rafah

068 / POP 31,500

This coastal town, 48km northeast of Al-Arish, marks the border with the Palestinian Territories' Gaza Strip, which was reopened on 28 May 2011 for the first time since Hamas took control of Gaza in 2007. Since then, the border has been closed, and again reopened, several times due to security fears and political changes in Cairo. The reopening of the border was part of the August 2014 Cairo-brokered ceasefire deal between Israel and Hamas, although in practice since then, due to a series of violent attacks by militants in the North Sinai area, the border has only been opened intermittently. It is absolutely not recommended for travellers to take this route.

Understand Egypt

Egypt Today

Egypt was long seen as the land of eternity, where nothing ever changed. That image has been shattered by recent events, but some things remain: Egypt's location, its huge population and its control of the Suez Canal ensure that it is still a major player in the region. Even with the turmoil following the downfall of two presidents in as many years, it still enjoys great prestige in diplomacy, the arts and as a moderate Islamic country.

Best on Film

Death on the Nile (1978) Agatha Christie's story about Poirot investigating the murder of a heiress on board a Nile cruiser, showing off Nile scenery at its best.

The Yacoubian Building (2006) Blockbuster Egyptian movie adapted from Alaa Al Aswany's novel, portraying the stories of the residents of one block of flats in downtown Cairo.

Ruby Cairo (1992) A wife tracks down her missing husband to a hideaway in Egypt.

The Spy Who Loved Me (1977) The Pyramids, Karnak and Islamic Cairo all provide glamorous backdrops for the antics of James Bond.

Best in Print

Taxi (Khaled Alkhamissi) Bestselling novel, and now also a play, of 58 fictional monologues by Cairo taxi drivers.

The Cairo Trilogy (Naguib Mahfouz) This epic trilogy tells the story of three generations of a Cairene family in the early decades of the 20th century.

The Yacoubian Building (Alaa Al Aswany) Bestselling exposé of Egyptian society during the 1990s.

Maryam's Maze (Mansoura Ez-Eldin) Brilliant story of an Egyptian woman trying to find her way in the confusion around her.

You Say You Want a Revolution...

It's all change in Egypt at the moment. After three decades of President Hosni Mubarak's regime, and almost another three before that under Presidents Nasser and Sadat, Egyptians broke the mould. There had been elections under President Mubarak, but they were severely compromised and designed to preserve the power of the ruling National Democratic Party. The election campaign that followed Mubarak's departure was dominated by the *felool* (Mubarak supporters) and the Muslim Brotherhood, the only other group that had countrywide organisation. In June 2012, Mohammed Morsi, a Muslim Brotherhood leader, became Egypt's first democratically elected president, winning 51.7% of the vote to defeat Ahmed Shafik, Mubarak's last prime minister.

Morsi's presidency was supposed to be a new beginning but he disappointed many Egyptians, failing to take measures to improve the economy, but giving himself unlimited powers. He also forced through a contentious Islamist constitution, which also gave more autonomy to the military. As the financial and security situation deteriorated, Egyptians took to the streets again and many demonstrations turned violent. At the end of June 2013, with millions attending some of the protests, the head of the military, Field Marshal Abdel Fattah al-Sisi, overthrew Morsi. Although Sisi declared that he did not seek power, in May 2014, he won a landslide victory in the presidential election. Whatever happens next, one thing is clear: if Egyptians fall out of love with Sisi, they will demand more change.

Even in revolutionary Egypt, some things remain unchanged, such as lingering over coffee in one of Alexandria's cosmopolitan cafes or sipping a calming glass of *shai* (tea) after a frenzied shopping episode in Cairo's Khan al-Khalili. Magnificent monuments are everywhere – the pointed perfection of the Pyramids and the majestic tombs and temples of Luxor are some of the wonders that generations of visitors have admired during their city sojourns, jaunts up and down the Nile and expeditions through spectacularly stark desert landscapes.

Pressing Problems

Modern Egypt is bursting at the seams. More than half a century on from the great Nasser-led revolution, Egypt is again in flux following the overthrow of two presidents in two years. Although Mubarak and Morsi have gone, the problems they allowed to grow remain: a booming population, notably high unemployment and a basket-case economy. Once home to the all-powerful pharaohs, the country has largely been reduced to dependency on the USA, the Gulf States, the European Union, the IMF...

The list of woes continues and includes torture and ill-treatment of prisoners in detention, described by Amnesty International as 'systematic'; the issue of child labour, particularly within the lucrative national cotton industry (Unicef reports that over one million children are believed to work in this industry alone); regularly reported cases of 'administrative detention' of individuals without trial, including many pro-democracy activists, which has brought criticism from both local media and international human-rights organisations; continuing restrictions on women under personal-status laws, which, for example, deny the freedom to travel without permission, now compounded by a growing problem of sexual harrassment; rampant inflation, leading to food shortages within the poorest communities; and constant environmental threats, with polluted waterways, overpopulation, unregulated emissions, a looming water crisis and soil salinity being of serious concern. Most obvious for the visitor is a crisis in tourism: the crowds which used to throng the temples and tombs now stay on the Red Sea beaches, or at home.

Eternally Egypt

One thing that can be said with certainty is this: the Egypt that is emerging from this tumultuous time is as fascinating as ever. The monuments that tell the story of the country's glorious past remain, as do the special talents that have always singled out the Egyptians: their ability to laugh and to improvise. Whether in the suffocating density of Cairo's city streets or the harsh elements of the open desert, they remain an incredibly resilient people who find humour and optimism in the most unlikely of circumstances. While your travels in Egypt might not always be easygoing or hassle-free, they'll certainly be eye-opening.

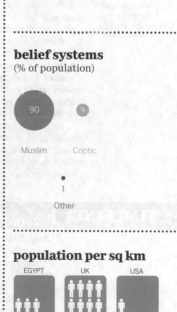

POPULATION: **APPROX 87 MILLION**

ANNUAL POPULATION GROWTH RATE: **1.8%**

INFLATION: **12%**

UNEMPLOYMENT: **13%**

AVERAGE ANNUAL INCOME: **US$5532**

if Egypt were 100 people

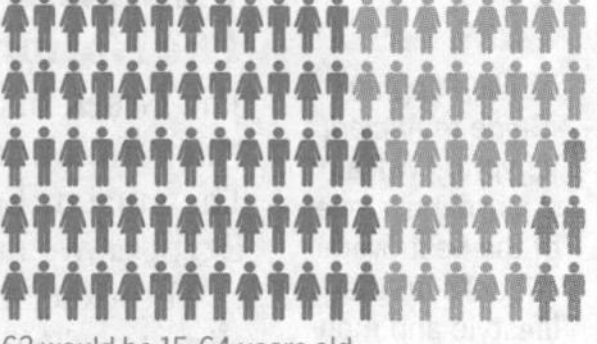

63 would be 15-64 years old
32 would be under 14 years old
5 would be over 64 years old

belief systems

(% of population)

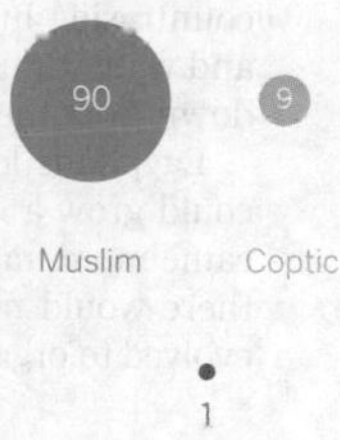

population per sq km

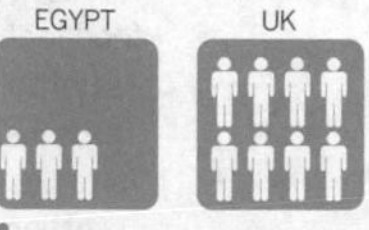

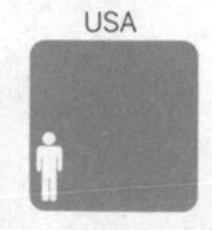

≈ 30 people

History

The history of Egypt is as rich as the land, as varied as the landscape and as long as the Nile, longer than most in the world. As recent events continue to show, it can also be as lively as the character of its people. While much of Europe was still wrapped in animal skins and wielding clubs, ancient Egyptians enjoyed a sophisticated life, dedicated to maintaining order in the universe and to making the most of their one great commodity, the Nile.

The Penguin Guide to Ancient Egypt by William J Murnane is one of the best overall books on the lifestyle and monuments of the Pharaonic period, with illustrations and descriptions of major temples and tombs.

The Nile

The Nation's Gift

The Greek historian Herodotus observed that Egypt was the gift of the Nile, and although it might now be a cliché, it also happens to be true. The ancient Egyptians called it simply *iteru,* the river. Without the Nile, Egypt as we know it would not exist.

The exact history is obscure, but many thousands of years ago the climate of North Africa changed dramatically. Patterns of rainfall also changed and Egypt, formerly a rich savannah, became increasingly dry. The social consequences were dramatic. People in this part of Africa lived as nomads, hunting, gathering and moving across the region with the seasons. But when their pastures turned to desert, there was only one place for them to go: the Nile.

Rainfall in east and central Africa ensured that the Nile in Egypt rose each summer; this happened some time towards the end of June in Aswan. The waters would reach their height around the Cairo area in September. In most years this surge of water flooded the valley and left the countryside hidden. As the rains eased, the river level started to drop and water drained off the land, leaving behind a layer of rich silt washed down from the hills of Africa.

Egyptians learned that if they planted seed on this fertile land, they could grow a good crop. As more people settled along the valley, it became more important to make the best use of the annual floodwater, or there would not be enough food for the following year. A social order evolved to organise the workforce to make the most of this 'gift', an order

TIMELINE

c 250,000 BC

Earliest human traces in Egypt. The valley savannah provides ample food for hunter-gatherers until climate change turns lush countryside to desert and forces settlement along the fertile Nile.

c 13,000 BC

The rock carvings at Qurta, near Kom Ombo, the oldest rock art in North Africa, had already been created.

c 3100 BC

Legend credits a pharaoh named Narmer with uniting the people between the Mediterranean and the First Cataract at Aswan. Memphis becomes capital of a united Upper Egypt and Lower Egypt.

that had farmers at the bottom, bureaucrats and governors in the middle and, at the top of this pyramid, the pharaoh.

Egyptian legend credited all this social development to the good king Osiris, who, so the story went, taught Egyptians how to farm, how to make the best use of the Nile and how to live a good, civil life. The myth harks back to an idealised past, but also ties in with what we know of the emergence of kingship: one of the earliest attributions of kingship, the predynastic Scorpion Macehead, found in Hierakonpolis around 3000 BC, shows an irrigation ritual. This suggests that even right back in early times, making use of the river's gift was a key part of the role of the leader.

The site of Luxor Temple has been a place of worship for the last 3500 years and remains one today: the Mosque of Abu al-Haggag is situated high above the great court.

Source Stories

The rise of the Nile was a matter of continual wonder for ancient Egyptians, as it was right up to the 19th century, when European explorers settled the question of the source. There is no evidence that ancient Egyptians knew where this lifeline came from. In the absence of facts, they made up stories.

One of the least convincing of all Egyptian myths concerning the rise of the Nile places the river's source in Aswan, beneath the First Cataract. From the cataract, the river was said to flow north to the Mediterranean and south into Africa.

The river's life-giving force was revered in many ways, most obviously as a god, Hapy. He was an unusual deity in that, contrary to the slim outline of most gods, Hapy was most often portrayed as a pot-bellied man with hanging breasts and a headdress of papyrus. Hapy was celebrated at a feast each year when the Nile rose. In later images he was often shown tying papyrus and lotus plants together, a reminder that the Nile bound together the north and south of the country.

But the most enduring and endearing of all Egyptian myths concerning the river is devoted to the figure of Isis, the mourning wife. Wherever the river originated, the annual rising of the Nile was explained as being tears shed by the mother goddess at the loss of the good king Osiris.

Ramses: The Son of Light by Christian Jacq is the first of a five-volume popular hagiography of the famous pharaoh. The prose is simplistic, but Jacq is an Egyptologist, so the basics are accurate.

Matters of Fact

Wherever it came from, the Nile was the beginning and end for most Egyptians. They were born beside it and had their first postnatal bath in its waters. It sustained them throughout their lives, made possible the vegetables in the fields, the chickens, cows, ducks and fish on their plates, and filled their drinking vessels when they were thirsty. When it was very hot or at the end of a day's work, it was the Nile that provided relief, a place to bathe. Later, when they died, if they had the funds, their body would be taken along the river to the cult centre at Abydos. And it was water from the Nile that the embalmers used when they prepared

2650–2323 BC

This period of great pyramid building at Giza and Saqqara suggests that for at least part of each year, presumably when the Nile flooded, a substantial workforce was available for civic projects.

2125–1650 BC

Thebes emerges as capital of Upper Egypt and as the pre-eminent seat of religious power. When the Theban ruler Montuhotep II establishes the Middle Kingdom, Thebes becomes its capital.

1650–1550 BC

The Hyksos – western Asian tribes who settled in northern Egypt – control the valley, ushering in the Second Intermediate Period, a time of great technological and social innovation.

1550–1186 BC

Ahmose, prince of Thebes, defeats the Hyksos c 1532 BC and begins a period of expansion into Nubia and Palestine. Over the next two centuries, his successors expand the empire.

the body for burial. But burial was a moment of total separation from this life source for, if you were lucky, you were buried away from the damp, where the dry sands and rocks of the desert would preserve your remains throughout eternity.

Coptic Egypt by Christian Cannuyer tells the story from the earliest preachings by Mark the Evangelist in 1st century AD Alexandria to 21st century Christianity in Egypt.

Not everything about the river was generous – it also brought dangers in many forms: the crocodile, the sudden flood that washed away helpless children and brought the house down on one's head, the diseases that thrived in water, and the creatures (among them the mosquito) that carried them. The river also dictated the rhythm of life and everything started with the beginning of the inundation: New Year fell as the waters rose. This was a time of celebration and also, for some, of relaxation. As the land was covered with water and a boat was needed to travel from one village to the next, farmers found time to catch up on long-neglected chores, fixing tools and working on their houses. This was also the period of the corvée, the labour system by which it is thought many civic projects were built, among them the pyramids, the canal cut through from the Nile to the Red Sea and, in the 19th century, the Suez Canal.

The river also brought the taxman, for it was on the level of flood that the level of the annual tax was set. The formula was simple. Bureaucrats watched the rise of the river on Elephantine Island, where a gauge had been cut along the side of the rock. Each year's flood was recorded at its height. If the water rose to the level of 14 cubits, there would be enough food to go around. If it rose to 16, there would be an abundance – and abundance meant higher taxation. And if there were, say, only eight cubits, then it was time to prepare for the worst because famine would come and many would follow Osiris to the land of spirits beyond the valley.

MARTYRS & HEROES

Alexandria's history is scarred by fights between devotees of different religions, as St Mark discovered to his cost: the man who brought Christianity to Egypt was executed for speaking out against the worship of the city's pagan god Serapis. Many decrees came from Rome that litigated against Christians, the worst coming from Emperor Diocletian. The persecution was so extreme and cost so many lives (some Coptic historians have estimated 144,000) that the Coptic Church calendar, the Era of Martyrs, begins with the year of Diocletian's accession, AD 284. But change was not far away.

In AD 293 Diocletian found himself sharing power with Constantine. In 312, just as Constantine went into battle against his opponents, he had a vision of a cross blazing in the sky, on which was written 'In This Conquer'. When he emerged victorious, becoming ruler of the empire, Constantine converted to Christianity and, in 324, made Christianity the imperial religion.

1352–1336 BC

Akhenaten establishes monotheism at his new capital, Akhetaten. After his death around 1335 BC, his heir, Tutankhamun, returns the capital to Thebes again and power is restored to the priests of Amun.

1294–1279 BC

Seti I restores the empire and initiates a period of neoconservatism: his temple at Abydos copies Old Kingdom styles. He then constructs the finest tomb in the Valley of the Kings.

1279–1213 BC

Seti's son, Ramses II, constructs more buildings than any other pharaoh. He makes Avaris, his home town, the centre of Egyptian trade, but adds to the glory of Thebes.

1184–1153 BC

Ramses III provides a stable moment in an unstable century, controlling the Libyans, defeating the 'Sea People' and suppressing internal dissent. After his death, power slips from the throne.

Old Habits

Even when the old gods were long dead, and roads and railways ran alongside the river, the Nile exerted its magic and its power. In the 18th and 19th centuries it was the way in which foreigners uncovered the mysteries of the past, sailing upriver when the winds blew from the north, and finding themselves face to face with unimaginable splendour. Even then, Egyptians clung to their habits and their dependence on the river. In the 1830s the British Orientalist Edward Lane recorded that 17 June was still called the Night of the Drop. 'It is believed', he wrote, 'that a miraculous drop then falls into the Nile; and causes it to rise.' Lane also recorded the custom of creating a figure of a girl, the 'Bride of the Nile', out of mud, which was then washed away as the river rose, an echo of an ancient ceremony in which effigies – and perhaps also young women – were sacrificed to the rising river.

Some 100 years later, in 1934, the Egyptologist Margaret Murray spent a mid-September night in a Coptic village, celebrating the night of the high Nile, giving thanks 'to the Ruler of the river, no longer Osiris, but Christ; and as of old they pray for a blessing upon their children and their homes'.

This kind of spiritual bond with the river was broken when dams and barrages stopped the annual flood. But Egyptians, whether they live along the river or in one of the new satellite cities in the desert, remain as dependent on the Nile as ever. Now, instead of praying to the 'Ruler of the river', they put their faith in engineers, who, like kings of old, help them make the most of the water; and in politicians, who are currently renegotiating water-sharing agreements with Nile-basin neighbours. Wherever they pin their hopes, they know that, as ever, their happiness, their very existence, depends on water flowing past Aswan on its way to the Mediterranean.

The best source for accurate plans of the Theban tombs can be found in Nicholas Reeves and Richard H Wilkinson's *The Complete Valley of the Kings*, or online at Kent Weeks' Theban Mapping Project (www.thebanmappingproject.com).

Christian Egypt

In the Beginning...

Coptic tradition states that Christianity arrived in Egypt in AD 45 in the form of St Mark. According to this tradition, St Mark, originally from Cyrene in modern-day Libya, was in Alexandria when his sandal broke. He took it to a cobbler, Ananias, who hurt his hand while working on the sandal and shouted 'O One God', at which St Mark recognised his first convert to the new religion. While there is no way to prove the story, there is no denying the basic truth that Christianity arrived early in Egypt, direct from Palestine.

The country had long been open to foreign religious influences and nowhere more so than in Alexandria. At the height of their power, ancient Egyptians had exported their religions – Amun of Thebes was known and feared throughout the Mediterranean. And even in times

945–715 BC

Libyan settlers become increasingly powerful in the Delta, eventually taking power as the 22nd and 23rd dynasties, but the Egyptian Nile is divided among a series of princes.

663 BC

Ashurbanipal, King of the Assyrians, attacks Egypt, sacks Thebes and loots the Temple of Amun. Devastated Egypt is ruled by Libyan princes from Sais in the Delta.

610–595 BC

Late Period pharaoh Necho encourages foreign trade by strengthening ties (and his navy) in the Mediterranean, cutting a canal to the Red Sea and sending an expedition to sail around Africa.

525 BC

The Persian king Cambyses makes Egypt part of his empire and rules as pharaoh, launching an attack against Nubia and then on Siwa, in which his army disappears into the desert.

of weakness, the cult of the goddess Isis spread throughout the Roman Empire. But Egyptians were also open to foreign religious ideas. The Persians did little to impose their gods on the country when they sacked Thebes in the 6th century BC and made Egypt part of their empire. Two centuries later, Alexander the Great viewed things differently, at least in the north of the country: while he built shrines to Amun at Karnak and was happy to be welcomed as pharaoh by the priests at Memphis, he also encouraged Greeks and Jews to bring their gods to his new city. Alexandria, under the Macedonian's successors, the Ptolemies, became a centre for multiculturalism, where people of many different beliefs and religions lived and worshipped side by side.

The Early Church

Egypt's Coptic Christians absorbed much from both the form and the content of the ancient pagan religion. It is impossible to make direct parallels, but the rise of the cult of Mary appears to have been influenced by the popularity of Isis: both were said to have conceived through divine intervention. According to the late Coptic musicologist Dr Ragheb Moftah, the way in which the Coptic liturgy was performed seems to have evolved from ancient rites and in it, even today, we can hear an echo of ancient Egypt's rituals. Even the physical structure of Coptic churches echoes the layout of earlier pagan temples in the use of three different sacred spaces, the innermost one containing the altar reserved for priests. This is hidden from the rest of the congregation by the iconostasis, with its images of saints, just as ancient priests were hidden behind walls decorated with gods and pharaohs.

The early need to hold hidden prayer, the desire to follow Jesus' example of retreat from the world, the increasing difficulty of reconciling

ST ANTHONY: CREATOR OF MONASTICISM

St Anthony was the son of wealthy landowners, but found himself orphaned at an early age. As an adult, he sold his inheritance, gave the proceeds to the poor and retreated to the desert near St Paul. Other Christians soon followed, inspired by his example and perhaps also to escape persecution. The hermit moved further up into the hills, hiding alone in a cave, while leaving his followers to a life of collective retreat – the first monastery – in the valley below.

There may have been earlier religious communities in the desert, especially one in Palestine, but St Anthony is credited with creating this new way of living, one that sought salvation through retreat. It was left to St Pachomius, born around AD 285, to order the life of these hermits into what we would now recognise as monasteries, which has proved to be one of the most important movements in Christianity.

521–486 BC
Persian king Darius I appeases Egyptians by building temples and promoting trade, completing Necho's canal to the Red Sea.

331 BC
Alexander invades Egypt and visits the capital, Memphis, and the oracle at Siwa. He lays out a city, Alexandria, that will become the pivot of Hellenic culture in the Mediterranean.

323 BC
On Alexander's death in Babylon, his general Ptolemy is given control of Egypt. Alexander's body is buried in Alexandria, where Ptolemy builds the Museion and Library and perhaps also the Pharos.

c 310–250 BC
Under Ptolemaic patronage and with access to a library of 700,000 written works, scholars in Alexandria calculate the earth's circumference, discover it circles the sun and compile the definitive edition of Homer's poems.

spiritual values with the demands and temptations of urban life, and perhaps also the memory of pagan hermits, led some Christians to leave the Nile Valley and seek spiritual purity in the desert. The man credited with being the first is St Paul, born in Alexandria in AD 228. He fled to the Eastern Desert to escape the persecutions around 250. The desert life obviously suited him for he is said to have survived there for almost a century, dying around 343. Although there are 5th-century accounts of the man, there is still some controversy as to whether St Paul existed. There is no such problem with the man he is said to have inspired.

Egypt's Christians played a decisive role in the evolution of the young religion. In a series of meetings with Christians from across the empire, Copts argued over the nature of divinity, the duties of a Christian, the correct way to pray and many other aspects of religious life. In one matter in particular, Copts found themselves isolated. Many Christians argued that, as Jesus was born, there must have been a time when he was not divine and part of God. The Coptic clergy, particularly one Athanasius, argued that this idea of a dual nature was a throwback to polytheism. The crunch came in 325 at a council in Nicea, organised by the emperor, at which the Alexandrians triumphed: the Nicene Creed stated unequivocally that Father and Son are one. With this success, Alexandria confirmed its status as the centre of Mediterranean culture.

The sixth Fatimid caliph, El Hakim, was notorious for his unusual behaviour: convinced that a woman's place was in the home, he banned the manufacture of women's shoes.

Death of the Old Gods

In 391 AD Emperor Theodosius issued an edict that banned people from visiting pagan temples, but also even looking at pagan statues. While the edict was ignored in some places, it was taken seriously in Alexandria, where the Temple of Serapis still stood in the city centre. The golden statue of the god remained in his sanctuary, adored by the faithful, until the Christian patriarch of Alexandria stirred a crowd and led them in an attack on the temple: the god was toppled from his plinth – proving false the prophets who foresaw doom should he be damaged – and then dragged through the streets and burned. The crowd is also believed to have set fire to the temple library, which had contained one of the largest collections of scrolls in the world since the Alexandrian 'mother library' had been burned during an attack by Julius Caesar. The patriarch then built a church over the ruins.

Constantine had moved his capital to the city of Byzantium, renamed Constantinople (now Istanbul), in 330 and from that moment power seeped from Alexandria. More than a century later, in 451, the Egyptians were officially sidelined at the Council of Chalcedon. Refusing to accept that Jesus was one person but had two natures, which again seemed a revival of polytheism, the Egyptians split with the rest of Christianity, their patriarch was excommunicated and soon after Alexandria was sacked.

255 BC

The Greek astrologer Eratosthenes of Cyrene (Libya) settles in Alexandria, from where he makes the first accurate calculation of the world's circumference.

246–221 BC

Ptolemy III Euergetes I begins a building program that includes the Serapeum in Alexandria and the Temple of Horus at Edfu. His successor continues his work.

196 BC

A block of granodiorite stone is carved with a decree in three scripts: hieroglyph, demotic and Greek. Later it will be uncovered in the town of Rosetta and provide the key for deciphering the ancient language.

170–116 BC

Ptolemy VIII Euergetes II's reign is characterised by violence and brutality, but also by the opening of the Edfu Temple and by building at Philae and Kom Ombo.

Ancient Egypt: The Great Discoveries by Nicholas Reeves is a chronology of 200 years of marvellous finds, from the Rosetta Stone (1799) to the Valley of the Golden Mummies (1999).

Yet in spite of the religious split, Egypt was still part of the Byzantine Empire, ruled by a foreign governor, and its fortunes were tied to the empire. This caused ever-greater tension, which peaked in the reign of Emperor Justinian (528–565). Alexandrians stoned the emperor's governor, who retaliated by sending his army to punish the people. In 629 a messenger travelled to the emperor in Byzantium from Arabia. He had been sent by a man named Mohammed to reveal a new religion, Islam. The messenger was murdered on the way. Ten years later, Arab armies invaded Egypt.

After Byzantium

Under their brilliant general Amr ibn al-As, the Arabs swept through a badly defended and ill-prepared Egypt, defeated the Byzantine army near Babylon and found the gates of Alexandria opened to them without a fight.

Amr didn't force Egyptians to convert to the new religion, but did levy a tax on nonbelievers and showed preference to those who did convert. Slowly, inevitably, the population turned, although how fast is open to dispute. Eventually, however, some monasteries emptied and Coptic writing and language, the last version of the language of the pharaohs, stopped being spoken in public. Christian communities remained strongest in the new capital, Cairo, and in the valley south as far as the ancient capital, Thebes (Luxor). Increasingly Christians also fell back on the monasteries. In places such as Wadi Natrun and studded along the Nile Valley, monastic communities hid behind their high walls, preserving the old language, the old traditions and, in their libraries, some of the old wisdom.

By the middle of the 19th century, even the monasteries were under threat and European travellers sailing up the Nile were shocked to discover monks swimming naked up to their boats to beg for food and money. The decline continued until the 20th century. By then, only around 10% of Egyptians were Christians and the great monasteries were at their lowest ebb. Ironically, Christianity responded to these threats by enjoying something of a revival. Modernising influences in the early 20th century sparked a cultural renewal that breathed new life into, among other things, the long-defunct tradition of icon painting. Islamist violence aimed at Copts in the 1980s and 1990s had the effect of significantly increasing the number of monks. At St Anthony's Monastery numbers rose from 24 in 1960 to 69 in 1986, and in St Bishoi from 12 to 115.

The election of a Muslim Brotherhood–led government in 2012, in the wake of the downfall of President Mubarak, did nothing to ease tensions and Copts continued to find themselves targeted with impunity. Many wealthier Copts chose to emigrate to the US, Canada or Australia. Also in 2012, the popular Coptic Pope Shenouda III died. He was succeeded by His Holiness Pope Theodoros II, the 118th Patriarch of Alexandria.

48 BC

The fire that Julius Caesar lit to destroy the fleet in Alexandria harbour spreads through the city and burns down the Great Library.

30 BC

After Antony and Cleopatra are defeated at Actium, Ptolemaic rule ends and Roman rule starts, with Egypt initially the personal property of Octavian (the future emperor Augustus Caesar).

AD 45

According to Coptic tradition, St Mark arrives in Alexandria and converts an Alexandria cobbler. Christianity is certainly established in Egypt by the end of the century.

130–131

The Roman Emperor Hadrian spends eight to 10 months touring in Egypt, a journey that turns sour when his favourite, Antinoos, drowns in the Nile. The youth is deified and a temple is dedicated to him at Antinoopolis.

The Coming of the Arabs

Around 628 AD a man called Mohammed, the leader of a newly united Arab force, wrote to some of the most powerful men in the world, including the Byzantine Emperor Heraclius, inviting them to convert to his new religion. The emperor, who had never heard of Islam and who regarded the people of Arabia as nothing more than a mild irritant on the edge of his mighty empire, declined. By the time of Heraclius' death in 641, Arab armies had conquered much of the Byzantine Empire, including Syria and most of Egypt, and were camped outside the walls of the Egyptian capital, Alexandria.

Many of the tales recounted each night by Sheherazade in *The Thousand and One Nights* are set in Mamluk-era Egypt, particularly in Cairo, referred to as 'Mother of the World'.

The Victorious

Egyptians were used to foreign invaders but had never before experienced any like the Arabs, who came with religious as well as political intentions. After Alexandria fell, the Arab general Amr wrote to his leader, the Caliph Omar, to say that he had captured a city of 4000 palaces, 4000 baths, 400 theatres and 12,000 sellers of green vegetables. Omar, perhaps sensing danger in such sophistication, ordered his army to create a new Muslim capital. The site chosen was beside the Roman fort of Babylon, at the place where the Nile fanned out into the delta. Initially a tented camp known as al-Fustat, Arabic for 'the tents', it soon grew into one of the region's key cities, until it was eclipsed by newer neighbouring settlements – the 8th-century Abbassid city al-Askar, the 9th-century Tulunid city Al-Qatai and, finally, the 10th-century Fatimid city al-Qahira, Arabic for 'victorious' and the origin of the word Cairo.

FOREIGN INVADERS

The story of ancient Egypt is the story of Egypt's relationships with its neighbours, for its wealth attracted some and its strategic location on the Mediterranean and Red Seas, and on the trade routes between Africa and Asia, attracted others. When it was strong, it controlled the gold of Nubia and the trade route across the Levant – not for nothing was the image of Ramses II crushing the Hittites at Kadesh splashed across so many temple walls. When it was weak, it caught the attention of the power of the moment. In 663 BC the Assyrian leader Ashurbanipal sacked Thebes. A century later the Persians were in control of the Nile. In 331 BC Alexander the Great moved against the Egyptians and incorporated them into his Hellenic empire. In 30 BC Octavian, the future Roman emperor Augustus Caesar, annexed the country as his own property. Arab armies stormed through in the 7th century AD just as Ottoman ones did in the 16th century and Egypt remained officially a part of the Ottoman Empire until 1919.

c 271

St Anthony begins his retreat from the world, living in a cave in the Eastern Desert. He soon attracts others, whom he organises into a loose community, Christianity's first monks.

391

Fifty years after the Byzantine emperor Constantine spoke against the religion of the pharaohs, his successor Theodosius makes paganism a treasonable offence and Alexandria's Temple of Serapis burns.

451

At the Council of Chalcedon, Egyptian Christians refuse to accept that Jesus Christ had two natures, human and divine, and the Coptic Church separates from the rest of Christianity.

640

An Arab army under Amr ibn al-As sweeps through Egypt and establishes a base at the Roman fort of Babylon (now part of Cairo). The following year, Amr captures the Byzantine capital, Alexandria.

Arabs & Egyptians

The majority of Egyptians were Christian at the time of the Arab conquest, none of whom Amr forcibly converted. The new religion was prepared to cohabit with the older ones. In order to uphold their beliefs, Copts and other non-Muslims were obliged to pay a tax, but this was initially less than they had had to pay to the Byzantine emperor. Yet there was a gradual move towards conversion and by the 10th century the majority of people in Egypt were Muslims.

The Great Pyramid of Khufu (built in 2570 BC) remained the tallest artificial structure in the world until the building of the Eiffel Tower in 1889.

Sunni or Shia?

The shift of Egypt's capitals was matched by instability in the Arab empire, whose power centre moved from Mecca to Damascus and then Baghdad. This also reflected the shifting nature of the caliphate, the leadership of Islam, divided between the Sunni and the Shiite factions. The earlier Arab dynasties were Sunni. The Fatimids, who conquered Egypt in the 10th century and created the city of al-Qahira, were Shiite. At the centre of their new city was a mosque, Al-Azhar, whose sheikh became the country's main authority on religious matters. But Saladin (Salah ad-Din), who took power in Egypt in 1171 and created the Ayyubid dynasty, was a Sunni. From then on, and ever since, the sheikhs of Al-Azhar have taught Sunni orthodoxy. The majority of Egyptians today are Sunni.

The Mamluks

One of the last rulers of Saladin's Ayyubid dynasty, a man named Sultan as-Salih, brought the innovation of a permanent Turkic slave-soldier class. Most sultans relied on friends and relatives to provide a measure of security. As-Salih was so despised by all that he thought it wise to provide his own protection and did so by purchasing a large number of slaves from the land between the Urals and the Caspian. These men were freed on arrival in Egypt – their name, Mamluks, means 'owned' or 'slave' – and formed into a warrior class, which came to rule Egypt.

QAITBEY

The contradictions in the Mamluk constitution are typified in the figure of Sultan Qaitbey, who ruled between 1468 and 1496. Bought as a slave-boy by one sultan, he witnessed the brief reigns of nine others before clawing his way to power. As sultan he rapaciously taxed all his subjects and dealt out vicious punishments with his own hands, once tearing out the eyes and tongue of a court chemist who had failed to transform lead into gold. Yet Qaitbey marked his ruthless reign with some of Cairo's most beautiful monuments, notably his madrassa and tomb in the Northern Cemetery.

832

The caliph Al-Mamun, son of Haroun ar-Rashid, arrives to suppress a Coptic uprising. He also forces a way into the Pyramid of Cheops, although no treasure is recorded as being found.

868

Ahmed ibn Tulun, the son of a Turkish Mamluk, takes control of Egypt, creating a new dynasty (Tulunid) and a new capital, Al-Qatai, in Cairo, of which only his mosque survives.

969

The Shiite general Jawhar lays the foundations for a new palace-city, Al-Qahira (Cairo), and founds a new university-mosque, Al-Azhar. Two years later the Fatimid caliph, Al-Muizz, settles here from Tunis.

996

Fatimid caliph Al-Hakim ushers in one of the least tolerant of all regimes, forbidding women to leave their houses, discriminating against Christians and Jews, banning the sale of grapes and having all dogs in Cairo killed.

Mamluks owed their allegiance not to a blood line but to their original owner, the emir. New purchases maintained the groups. There was no system of hereditary lineage; instead it was rule by the strongest. Rare was the sultan who died of old age. Natural-born soldiers, Mamluks fought a series of successful campaigns that gave Egypt control of all of Palestine and Syria, the Hejaz and much of North Africa, the largest Islamic empire of the late Middle Ages. Because they were forbidden to bequeath their wealth, Mamluks built on a grand scale, endowing Cairo with exquisite mosques, schools and tombs. During their 267-year reign (1250–1517), the city became the intellectual and cultural centre of the Islamic world.

At the Battle of the Pyramids, Napoleon's forces took just 45 minutes to rout the Mamluk army, killing 1000 for the loss of 29 of their own men.

The funding for the Mamluks' great buildings came from trade. A canal existed that connected the Red Sea with the Nile at Cairo, and thus the Mediterranean, forming a vital link in the busy commercial route between Europe and India and east Asia. In the 14th and 15th centuries, the Mamluks worked with the Venetians to control east–west trade and both grew fabulously rich from it.

The end of these fabled days came about for two reasons at the beginning of the 16th century: Vasco da Gama's discovery of the sea route around the Cape of Good Hope freed European merchants from the heavy taxes charged by Cairo; and the Ottoman Turks emerged as a mighty new force, looking to unify the Muslim world. In 1516 the Mamluks, under the command of their penultimate sultan Al-Ghouri, were obliged to meet the Turkish threat. The battle, which took place at Aleppo in Syria, resulted in complete defeat for the Mamluks. In January of the following year the Turkish sultan Selim I entered Cairo and although the Mamluks remained in power in Egypt, they never again enjoyed their former prominence or autonomy.

Modern Times

Napoleon & Description de l'Egypte

When Napoleon and his musket-armed forces blew apart the scimitar-wielding Mamluk cavalry at the Battle of the Pyramids in 1798, which he claimed he was doing with the approval of the Ottoman sultan, he dragged Egypt into the age of geopolitics. Napoleon professed a desire to revive Egypt's glory, free it from the yoke of tyranny and educate its masses, but there was also the significant matter of striking a blow at Britain. Napoleon found a way to strike at British interests by capturing Egypt and in the process taking control of the quickest route between Europe and Britain's fast-growing empire in the East.

Famed as an American icon, the monument now known as the Statue of Liberty was originally intended to stand at the mouth of the Suez Canal.

Napoleon's forces weren't always successful. In 1798, a British fleet under Admiral Nelson had been criss-crossing the Mediterranean trying

1171

Saladin, a Kurdish Sunni, seizes power and establishes the Ayyubid dynasty. In 1176 he begins work on a citadel in Cairo, home to the city's rulers for the next seven centuries.

1249

The start of the Fifth Crusade, directed against Egypt and led by Louis IX. The following year, the French king is taken captive by the Egyptians and ransomed for a huge sum.

1250

Mamluk slave warriors, most of Turkish or Kurdish origin, seize control of Egypt. Although their rule is often harsh and anarchic, they build some of Cairo's most impressive and beautiful monuments.

1260

The Mamluk Baybars becomes sultan. Having created a strong alliance at home, he moves against the last Crusaders in the Holy Land, capturing their Syrian stronghold of Krak des Chevaliers in 1271.

to find the French force and, on 1 August, they found them at anchor in Aboukir Bay, off the coast of Alexandria. Only three French warships survived the ensuing Battle of the Nile. Encouraged by the British, the Ottoman sultan sent an army that was trounced by the French, which put paid to any pretence that the French were in Egypt with the complicity of Constantinople. Despite these setbacks, the French still maintained rule.

Favoured punishments employed by the Mamluks included *al-tawsit*, in which the victim was cut in half at the belly, and *al-khazuq* (impaling).

During Napoleon's time in the newly conquered Egypt, he established a French-style government, revamped the tax system, brought in Africa's first printing press, implemented public-works projects and introduced new crops and a new system of weights and measures. He also brought 167 scholars and artists, whom he commissioned to make a complete study of Egypt's monuments, crafts, arts, flora and fauna, and of its society and people. The resulting work was published as the 24-volume *Description de l'Egypte*, which did much to stimulate the study of Egyptian antiquities.

However, relations between the occupied and occupier deteriorated rapidly and there were regular uprisings against the French in Cairo. When the British landed an army, also at Aboukir, in 1801, the French agreed to an armistice and departed.

The Albanian Kings

The French and then British departure left Egypt politically unstable, a situation that was soon exploited by a lieutenant in an Albanian contingent of the Ottoman army, named Mohammed Ali. Within five years of the French evacuation, he had fought and conspired his way to become pasha (governor) of Egypt. Although he was nominally the vassal of Constantinople, like so many governors before him, he soon realised that the country could be his own.

The sultan in Constantinople was too weak to resist this challenge to his power. And once he had defeated a British force of 5000 men, the only threat to Mohammed Ali could come from the Mamluk beys (leaders). Any danger here was swiftly and viciously dealt with. On 1 March 1811, Mohammed Ali invited some 470 Mamluk beys to the Citadel to feast his son's imminent departure for Mecca. When the feasting was over the Mamluks mounted their lavishly decorated horses and were led in procession down the narrow, high-sided defile below what is now the Police Museum. As they approached the Bab al-Azab, the great gates were swung closed and gunfire rained down from above. After the fusillades, Mohammed Ali's soldiers waded in with swords and axes to finish the job. Legend relates that only one Mamluk escaped alive, leaping over the wall on his horse.

Zayni Barakat by Gamal al-Ghitani is full of intrigue, backstabbing and general Machiavellian goings-on in the twilight of Mamluk-era Cairo.

Mohammed Ali's reign is pivotal in the history of Egypt. Having watched the old Mamluk army flounder against superior European

1468

Mamluk sultan Qaitbey begins a 27-year reign that brings stability and wealth to the country. Qaitbey constructs a tomb complex in Cairo and a fort over the Pharos in Alexandria.

1517

Turkish sultan Selim I takes Cairo, executes the last Mamluk sultan and makes Egypt a Turkish province. For almost 300 years it will be ruled, however weakly, from Istanbul.

1768

Scottish laird James Bruce arrives in Cairo on his way in search of the source of the Nile; later he returns to Britain having secured permission for European ships to sail up the Red Sea to Suez.

1798

Napoleon invades, bringing a group of scholars who produce the first full description of Egypt's antiquities. The British force the French out but the French (and European) fascination with ancient Egypt lives on.

weapons and tactics, he recognised the need to modernise his new army, as well as his new country. Under his uncompromising rule, Egypt abandoned its medieval-style feudalism and looked to Europe for innovation. In his long reign (he died in 1848), Mohammed Ali modernised the army, built a navy, built roads, cut a new canal linking Alexandria with the Nile, introduced public education, improved irrigation, built a barrage across the Nile and began planting Egypt's fields with the valuable cash crop, cotton. His heirs continued the work, implementing reforms and social projects, foremost of which were the building of Africa's first railway, opening factories and starting a telegraph and postal system. Egypt's fledgling cotton industry boomed as production in the USA was disrupted by civil war, and revenues were directed into ever-grander schemes. Grandest of all was the Suez Canal, which opened in 1869 to great fanfare and an audience that included European royalty, including Empress Eugenie of France.

Khedive Ismail, Mohammed Ali's grandson, had taken on more debt than even Egypt's booming economy could handle and European politicians and banks were quick to exploit his growing weakness. Six years after opening the canal, Ismail was forced to sell his controlling share to the British government and soon after that, bankruptcy and British pressure forced him to abdicate. This sort of foreign involvement in Egyptian affairs created great resentment, especially among a group of officers in the Egyptian army, who moved against the new khedive. In 1882, under the pretext of restoring order, the British fleet bombarded Alexandria, and British soldiers defeated a nationalist Egyptian army.

The Complete Pyramids: Solving the Ancient Mysteries by Mark Lehner and Richard H Wilkinson is a readable reference to the famous threesome of Giza and the other 70-plus triangular-sided funerary monuments besides.

The Veiled Protectorate

The British had no desire to make Egypt a colony: their main reason for involvement was to ensure the safety of the Suez Canal. So they allowed the heirs of Mohammed Ali to remain on the throne, while the real power was concentrated in the hands of the British agent Sir Evelyn Baring. By appointing British 'advisors' to Egyptian ministries and himself advising the khedive, Baring operated what became known as the veiled protectorate, colonisation by another name.

British desire to ensure the safety of their passage to India coloured Egyptian policy for the next few decades. For instance, it became increasingly obvious that controlling Egypt meant controlling the Nile and therefore an Egyptian force was sent to protect that interest in Sudan. When they came up against the Islamist uprising of the Mahdi, and following the death of General Charles Gordon in Khartoum in 1885, British troops became involved on the middle Nile.

Under the 'veiled protectorate' the Suez Canal was secured, Egypt's finances bolstered, the bureaucracy and infrastructure improved, and there

1805

An Albanian mercenary, Mohammed Ali, exploits the power vacuum left by the French to seize power and establish a new 'Egyptian' dynasty; his modernisation program transforms the country.

1833

Mohammed Ali's new army moves through the Levant and crushes the Ottoman army at Konya. Constantinople is exposed, but the European powers force the Egyptians to withdraw.

1856

Africa's first railway, between Tanta and Cairo, is built by British engineer Robert Stephenson. The line, extended to Suez in 1858, carries Europeans heading east until the opening of the Suez Canal.

1858

The British explorers Richard Burton and John Hanning Speke reach Lake Victoria and recognise it as the main source of the White Nile.

PACKAGING TOURISM

In 1869, with the opening of the Suez Canal, the Khedive (Viceroy) Ismail announced that Egypt was now part of Europe, not Africa. Wherever it was, the massive amounts the khedive spent on developing and promoting his country boosted the number of people who wanted to see the treasures along the Nile. So at the same time as the British Prince and Princess of Wales were sailing the royal dahabiyya (houseboat), Thomas Cook took the first organised package tour up the Nile by steamer. It was the start of an industry that has since become one of Egypt's core businesses – mass tourism.

were some social advances. But the situation became ever more frustrating for Egyptians with the outbreak of WWI, when Turkey's alliance with Germany allowed Britain to make Egypt an official protectorate.

The Egyptians' desire for self-determination was strengthened by the Allies' use of the country as a barracks during a war that most Egyptians regarded as having nothing to do with them. Popular national sentiments were articulated by riots in 1919 and, more eloquently, by the likes of Saad Zaghloul, the most brilliant of an emerging breed of young Egyptian politicians, who said of the British, 'I have no quarrel with them personally but I want to see an independent Egypt'. The British allowed the formation of a nationalist political party, called the Wafd (Delegation), and granted Egypt its sovereignty, but this was seen as an empty gesture. King Fuad enjoyed little popularity among his people and the British still kept a tight rein on the administration.

The British and their Allies came to Egypt in greater numbers following the outbreak of WWII. The war wasn't all bad news for the Egyptians – certainly not for shopkeepers and businessmen who saw thousands of Allied soldiers pouring into the towns and cities with money to burn on 48-hour leave from the desert. But there was a vocal element who saw the Germans as potential liberators. Students held rallies in support of Rommel, and a small cabal of Egyptian officers, including future presidents Nasser and Sadat, plotted to aid the German general's advance on their city.

The Rise and Fall of Ancient Egypt by Toby Wilkinson gives an authoritative overview of ancient Egypt.

Rommel pushed the Allied forces back almost to Alexandria, which had the British hurriedly burning documents in such quantities that the skies over Cairo turned dark with the ash, but the Germans did not break through. Instead, the British maintained a military and political presence in Egypt until a day of flames almost seven years after the war.

1859

Ferdinand de Lesseps, a French engineer, sees work begin on his project to build a canal between the Mediterranean and Red Seas, making it the quickest way from Europe to the East. The canal takes 10 years to complete.

1869

Khedive Ismail, Mohammed Ali's grandson, opens the Suez Canal. The British, who had preferred a railway, soon take control of the waterway as the quickest route to their Eastern empire.

1879

Having bankrupted the country, running up debts of more than £100 million, Khedive Ismail is forced to abdicate but not before selling his shares in the Suez Canal to Britain.

1882

British troops invade to suppress nationalist elements in the army. Although they officially restore power to the khedive, Britain effectively rules Egypt in what becomes the 'veiled protectorate'.

Independent Egypt

Emerging from the Ashes

After years of demonstrations, strikes and riots against foreign rule, in 1952 an Anglo Egyptian showdown over a police station in the Suez Canal zone provided the spark that ignited the capital. Shops and businesses owned or frequented by foreigners were torched by mobs and many landmarks of 70 years of British rule were reduced to charred ruins within a day.

While the smoke cleared, the sense of agitation remained, not just against the British but also against the monarchy that most Egyptians regarded as too easily influenced by the British. King Farouk assumed the monarchy would survive the turmoil because it could count on the support of the Egyptian army. But a faction within the officer corps, known as the Free Officers, had long been planning a coup. On 20 July 1952, the leader of the Free Officers, Colonel Gamal Abdel Nasser, heard that a new minister of war knew of the group and had planned their arrest. Two nights later, army units loyal to the Free Officers moved on key posts in the capital and by the following morning the monarchy had fallen. King Farouk, descendant of the Albanian Mohammed Ali, departed from Alexandria harbour on the royal yacht on 26 July 1952, leaving Egypt to be ruled by Egyptians for the first time since the pharaohs.

Colonel Nasser became president in elections held in 1956. With the aim of returning some of Egypt's wealth to its much-exploited peasantry, but also in an echo of the events of Russia in 1917, the country's landowners were dispossessed and many of their assets nationalised. Nasser also moved against the country's huge foreign community and, although he did not force them to emigrate, his new measures persuaded many to sell up and ship out.

In the year of his inauguration, Nasser successfully faced down Britain and France in a confrontation over the Suez Canal, which was mostly owned by British and French investors. On 26 July, the fourth anniversary of King Farouk's departure, Nasser announced that he had nationalised the Suez Canal to finance the building of a great dam that would control the flooding of the Nile and boost Egyptian agriculture. When a combined British, French and Israeli invasion force, sent to take possession of the canal, was forced into an undignified retreat after the UN and US applied pressure, Nasser emerged from the conflict a hero of the developing world. He was seen as a sort of Robin Hood and Ramses rolled into one, and the man who had finally and publicly shaken off the colonial yoke.

As a young Egyptian officer during WWII, Anwar Sadat was imprisoned by the British for conspiring with German spies.

1902
Inauguration of the Aswan Dam and the Asyut Barrage, which help control the Nile flood. The Egyptian Museum is also opened on what is now Cairo's Midan Tahrir.

1914
When Turkey sides with Germany in the war, Britain moves to make Egypt an official British protectorate. A new ruler, Hussein Kamel, takes the title of Sultan of Egypt.

1922
Britain grants Egypt independence, but reserves the right to defend Egypt, its interests in Sudan and, most importantly, the Suez Canal, where Britain continues to maintain a large military presence.

1922
Howard Carter discovers the tomb of Tutankhamun. The first great Egyptological discovery in the age of mass media, the tomb contains more than 3000 objects and takes 10 years to excavate.

Neighbours & Friends

Nasser's show of strength in 1956 led to many years of drum-beating and antagonism between Egypt and its Arab friends on one side, and their unwelcome neighbour Israel on the other.

The opera *Aida* was originally commissioned for the opening ceremony of the Suez Canal, but Verdi was late delivering. *Rigoletto* was performed in 1869 and *Aida* first performed on Christmas Eve, 1871, two years after the opening.

Relations with Israel had been hostile ever since its founding in 1948. Egypt had sent soldiers to fight alongside Palestinians against the newly proclaimed Jewish state and ended up on the losing side. Although privately Nasser acknowledged that the Arabs would probably lose another war against Israel, for public consumption he gave rabble-rousing speeches about liberating Palestine. But he was a skilled orator and by early 1967 the mood engendered throughout the Arab world by these speeches was beginning to catch up with him. Soon other Arab leaders started to accuse him of cowardice and of hiding behind the UN troops stationed in Sinai since the Suez Crisis. Nasser responded by ordering the peacekeepers out and blockading the Straits of Tiran, effectively closing the southern Israeli port of Eilat. He gave Israel reassurances that he wasn't going to attack but meanwhile massed his forces east of Suez. In June, Israel struck first, launching a surprise attack that destroyed the Egyptian airforce before it was airborne and following up with a ground assault.

When the shooting stopped six days later, Israel controlled all of the Sinai Peninsula and had closed the Suez Canal (which didn't reopen for another eight years). A humiliated Nasser offered to resign, but in a spontaneous outpouring of support, the Egyptian people wouldn't accept this move and he remained in office. However, it was to be for only another three years; abruptly in November 1970, the president died of a heart attack.

Anwar Sadat, another of the Free Officers and Egypt's next president, instigated a reversal of foreign policy. Nasser had looked to the Soviet Union for inspiration, but Sadat looked to the US, swapping socialist principles for capitalist opportunism. Having kept a low profile for a decade and a half, the wealthy resurfaced and were joined by a large, new, moneyed middle class who grew rich on the back of Sadat's much-touted *al-infitah* (open-door policy). Sadat also believed that to revitalise Egypt's economy he would have to deal with Israel.

In November 1977, a time when Arab leaders still refused to talk publicly to Israel, Sadat travelled to Jerusalem to negotiate a peace treaty with Israel. The following year, he and the Israeli premier signed the Camp David Agreement, in which Israel agreed to withdraw from Sinai in return for Egyptian recognition of Israel's right to exist. There was shock in the Arab world, where Sadat's rejection of Nasser's pan-Arabist principles was seen as a betrayal. As a result, Egypt lost much prestige among the Arabs, who moved the HQ of the Arab League out of Cairo,

1936

The Anglo-Egyptian treaty commits British troops to confine themselves to the Suez Canal and to leave Egypt within 20 years.

1942

The German Field Marshal Rommel pushes his tanks corps across the Libyan coast and into Egypt, causing panic in Cairo. His adversary, British General Montgomery, pushes him back from El Alamein to Tunisia.

1952

Anti-British sentiment leads to many foreign buildings in Cairo being burned. By the summer, Nasser and his fellow Free Officers have overthrown King Farouk and established the Republic of Egypt.

1956

After President Nasser nationalises the Suez Canal, British, French and Israeli forces attack the canal zone, but are forced to retreat.

and Sadat lost his life. On 6 October 1981, at a parade commemorating the 1973 war, one of his soldiers, a member of an Islamist group, broke from the marching ranks and sprayed the presidential stand with gunfire. Sadat was killed instantly.

Two centuries of the adventures and interests of foreigners in Egypt, up to the 1956 Suez crisis, are brilliantly evoked in Lonely Planet author Anthony Sattin's *Lifting the Veil.*

Mubarak & the Rise of the Islamist Movement

Sadat was succeeded by Hosni Mubarak, a former airforce chief of staff and vice president. Less flamboyant than Sadat and less charismatic than Nasser, Mubarak was regarded as unimaginative and indecisive, but managed to carry out a balancing act on several fronts, abroad and at home. To the irritation of more hard-line states such as Syria and Libya, Mubarak rehabilitated Egypt in the eyes of the Arab world without abandoning the treaty with Israel. At the same time, he managed to keep the lid on the Islamist extremists at home. In the early 1990s the lid blew off.

Theories abound regarding the rise of fundamentalist Islamist groups in Egypt. Some believe it had more to do with harsh socio-economic conditions, despite the use of religion by Islamist groups. More than 30 years after the revolution, government promises had failed to keep up with the population explosion and a generation of youths was living in squalid, overcrowded housing, without jobs and many feeling little or no hope for the future. With a political system that allowed little chance to voice legitimate opposition, many felt the only hope lay with Islamist parties such as the Muslim Brotherhood and their calls for change. Denied recognition by the state as a legal political entity, in the 1980s and 1990s the Islamists turned to force. There were frequent attempts on the life of the president and his ministers, and clashes with the security forces. The matter escalated from a domestic issue to a matter of international concern when Islamists began to target one of the state's most vulnerable and valuable sources of income: tourists.

Several groups of foreign tourists were shot at, bombed or otherwise assaulted throughout the 1990s, including the 1997 fire-bomb attack on a tour bus outside the Egyptian Museum in Cairo, followed a few weeks later by the killing of holidaymakers at the Temple of Hatshepsut in Luxor by members of the Gama'a al-Islamiyya (Islamic Group), a Muslim Brotherhood splinter group.

The brutality of the massacre and its success at deterring foreign visitors destroyed grassroots support for militants, and the Muslim Brotherhood declared a ceasefire the following year. Things were relatively quiet until October 2004, when bombs at Taba, on the border with Israel, and the nearby Ras Shaytan camp, killed 34 and signalled the start of an unsettled 12 months.

1967

Egypt, Syria and Jordan are defeated by Israel in the Six Day War. Egypt loses control of the Sinai Peninsula and Nasser resigns, but is returned to power by popular demand.

1970

Fifty-two-year-old Gamal Abdel Nasser, Egyptian president since 1956, dies of a heart attack and is replaced by his fellow revolutionary, Anwar Sadat.

1971

The Aswan High Dam is completed. Eleven years in the making, it extends Lake Nasser to some 510km and Egypt's farmland by 30%. Around 50,000 Nubians and many monuments are relocated.

1973

In October, Egyptian forces attack and cross Israeli defences along the Suez Canal. Although the Egyptians are repulsed and Israel threatens Cairo, the war is seen as an Egyptian success.

First Elections

The Modern History of Egypt by PJ Vatiokis is the best one-volume history of the 19th and 20th centuries. Jason Thompson's *A History of Egypt* is the latest attempt to tell the whole 5000-year story.

In 2005 President Mubarak bowed to growing international pressure to bring the country's political system in line with Western-style democracy, and proposed a constitutional amendment (subsequently approved by parliament and ratified at a national referendum) that aimed to introduce direct and competitive presidential elections. While some pundits saw this as a step in the right direction, others suspected it was a sham, particularly as popular opposition groups such as the Muslim Brotherhood were still banned and other independent candidates were required to have the backing of at least 65 members of the lower house of parliament. As the lower house was dominated by the National Democratic Party (NDP), the possibility of real change was slight. When the Kifaya! (Enough!) coalition of opposition groups protested at these restrictions, security forces cracked down. Ayman Nour, the leader of the popular Ghad (Tomorrow) party, was jailed on forgery charges. Local human rights organisations questioned the validity of the charges and expressed concern for Nour's safety, while the US released a statement declaring it was 'deeply troubled' by the conviction.

At this stage the banned Muslim Brotherhood began holding its own rallies and there were two isolated terrorist incidents in Cairo aimed at foreign tourists, both carried out by members of the same pro-Islamist family. Soon afterwards, three bombs at the popular beach resort of Sharm el-Sheikh claimed the lives of 88 people, most of them Egyptian. Various groups claimed responsibility, tourism took an immediate hit and Egyptians braced themselves for the possibility of further terrorist incursions and domestic unrest.

In 2005 Mubarak won the country's first multicandidate presidential election with 89% of the vote, after a turnout of just 23% of the 32 million registered voters. There were many reports from observers, such as the Egyptian Organization for Human Rights (EOHR), of disorganisation, intimidation and abusive security forces at the polls, and opposition parties and candidates (including Ayman Nour) alleged the vote was unfair and the result invalid. Still, other observers noted the process was a great improvement on previous elections.

Cairo: The City Victorious by Max Rodenbeck is the most authoritative and entertaining read on the convoluted and picturesque 1000-year history of the Egyptian capital.

In subsequent parliamentary elections in November 2005, Muslim Brotherhood independents won 88 seats in the 444-seat national parliament (six times the number they had previously held), making the Brotherhood a major player on the national political scene despite its officially illegal status.

Egypt Now

On 11 February 2011, President Mubarak resigned as president. The most obvious reason for his departure, 30 years into his presidency, was the hundreds of thousands of people who had been demonstrating for

1981

President Sadat is assassinated, an event precipitated by his having signed the Camp David peace accord with Israel in 1978. He is replaced by Vice President Hosni Mubarak.

1988

Naguib Mahfouz becomes the first Arab to win the Nobel Prize for Literature. His nomination is the cause of great national pride.

1997

Sixty-two foreign tourists and Egyptians are gunned down at the Temple of Hatshepsut in Luxor, an event that sparks a security crackdown and a tourism crisis.

2011

Mubarak resigns as president after mass protests against his regime throughout the country, most notably in Cairo's Midan Tahrir. He is replaced by a ruling council of his former generals.

months, most notably in an 18-day occupation of Cairo's Midan Tahrir. Mubarak's loss of support among the Egyptian military and the US may have been equally significant. Economic problems and the prospect of Gamal Mubarak succeeding his ailing father were among many reasons for the loss of popularity.

The euphoria that followed Mubarak's departure was heightened by the fact that security forces had not fired on protestors. The army was seen as the protector of the revolution and people in Tahrir chanted 'the people, the army, one hand'. Mubarak's old generals, including former minister for defence and head of armed forces Field Marshal Tantawi, took power and formed a ruling council.

The Supreme Council of the Armed Forces (SCAF) presented itself as an honest broker to usher the country towards democracy, but before elections were held, ensured autonomy for the armed forces by passing a decree that future governments would not be able to select the head of the armed forces or intervene in the military's internal or economic affairs.

Egypt's first open presidential and parliamentary elections in 2012 confirmed the rise of the Muslim Brotherhood and Salafist parties. The Brotherhood's Mohammed Morsi became Egypt's first democratically elected president. The euphoria that greeted his election soon faded after he pushed through a pro-Islamist constitution, granted himself unlimited powers, put himself beyond the law and suppressed public protests. By the summer of 2013 Egypt's economic crisis had created huge queues at petrol stations and daily power cuts to homes and business. Millions took to the streets to demand his resignation. When that failed, the army stepped in.

Morsi's defence minister, Abdel Fatah al-Sisi, who was behind the regime change, insisted he had no desire for power. But in spring 2014, with an interim government in place, Sisi resigned from the army, with the rank of field marshal, and announced his candidacy. Only one person opposed him, left-wing politician Hamdeen Sabahi. Sisi won around 96% of the votes. But although he had called for 40 million Egyptians, some 75% of the electorate, to turn out to vote, more than half of them abstained. Although he could claim to have the backing of more Egyptians than Morsi ever had, Sisi's position was weakened by the low turnout. Not that this will matter, if he is able to deal with the issue that brought so many people onto the streets: the continuing economic crisis. Mubarak and Morsi failed to do so. Egypt's future stability depends on the ability of the country's new ruler to meet the aspirations of an increasingly empowered and overwhelmingly young population.

Both Egypt and Israel were able to claim victory in the October 1973 war. The Egyptians boast of having broken the Israeli hold on Sinai while the Israelis were fighting their way towards Cairo when the UN imposed a ceasefire. This sense of victory helped make the Camp David peace talks possible.

The trilogy of *The Mummy* (1999), *The Mummy Returns* (2001) and *The Scorpion King* (2002) was written by Stephen Sommers. The films feature fabulous art direction and far-fetched plots set in ancient and early-20th-century Egypt.

2012

The Muslim Brotherhood emerges from Egypt's first democratic parliamentary elections with 235 of the 508 seats. The biggest surprise is the 121 seats won by the extreme Islamist Salafi party, Nour.

2013

The Brotherhood's Mohammed Morsi is overthrown after only a year as president following mass demonstrations across the country.

2013

Protest sit-ins outside the Rabaa al-Adaweya and al-Nahda mosques in Cairo are broken up by security forces. Casualty figures are disputed but at least 600 protesters die that day and thousands are injured.

2014

In June, Field Marshal Abdel Fatah al-Sisi is sworn in as president after a landslide victory in an election where less than half of the electorate turned out to vote.

Ancient Egypt & the Pharaohs

Co-authored by Professor Joann Fletcher

Despite its rather clichéd image, there is so much more to ancient Egypt than temples, tombs and Tutankhamun. As the world's first nation-state, predating the civilisations of Greece and Rome by several millennia, Egypt was responsible for some of the great achievements in human history – it was one of the places where writing was invented in 3200BC, the first stone monuments were erected and an entire culture set in place, one that remained largely unchanged for thousands of years.

Professor Joann Fletcher, of the University of York, is an Egyptologist, a writer and a consultant to museums and the media.

Eternal life

All of Egypt's achievements were made possible by the Nile River, which brought life to this virtually rainless land. In contrast to the vast barren 'red land' of desert, which the Egyptians called *deshret*, the narrow river banks were known as *kemet* (black land), a reference to the rich silt deposited by the river's annual floods. Abundant harvests grown in this red earth were then gathered as taxes by a highly organised bureaucracy working on behalf of the pharaoh. They used this wealth to run the administration and to fund ambitious building projects designed to enhance royal status.

The survival of these pyramids, temples and tombs often give the misleading impression that Egyptians were a morbid bunch obsessed with religion and death. In fact it seems they, or at least the elite, loved life so much that they went to enormous lengths to ensure the fun continued forever.

This longing for eternity suffused almost every aspect of ancient Egyptian life and gave the culture its incredible coherence and conservatism. Egyptians believed they had to appease their gods so the gods would take care of them. The pharaoh, who ruled by divine approval, ensured order in a world of chaos, and was the intermediary between the people and the gods. Absolute monarchy was therefore integral to Egyptian culture.

Although successive invaders took over Egypt from the end of the New Kingdom (around 1069 BC), Egypt's indigenous culture was so deeply rooted that they could not escape its influence. Libyans, Nubians and Persians all came to adopt traditional Egyptian ways, and their kings and emperors continued to build temples to the Egyptian gods, and to proclaim their divine birth on the temple walls. It was only at the end of the 4th century AD, when the Roman Empire adopted Christianity, that this ancient Egyptian belief system finally collapsed: their gods were taken from them, their temples were closed and all knowledge of the 'pagan' hieroglyphs that transmitted their culture was lost, until it was recovered in the 19th century.

The Great Monuments

Ancient Egyptians built a stunning array of monumental buildings along the Nile. They had very little wood, so they mainly used sun-baked mudbrick for their houses, fortresses and palaces. Of these, little remains today.

For their tombs and temples, however, they used quarried sandstone, limestone or granite, which in many cases have really withstood the test of time

Temples

Many gods had their own cult centres, but they were also worshipped at various temples throughout Egypt. Built on sites considered sacred, existing temples were added to by successive pharaohs to demonstrate their piety. This is best seen at the enormous complex of Karnak, the culmination of 2000 years of reconstruction.

Surrounded by huge enclosure walls of mudbrick, the stone temples within were regarded as houses of the gods, where daily rituals were performed on behalf of the pharaoh. As the intermediary between gods and humans, the pharaoh was high priest of every temple, although in practice these powers were delegated to each temple's high priest.

As well as temples to house the gods (cult temples), there were also funerary (mortuary) temples where each pharaoh was worshipped after death. Eventually sited away from their tombs for security reasons, the best examples are on Luxor's West Bank, where pharaohs buried in the Valley of the Kings had huge funerary temples built closer to the river. These include Ramses III's temple at Medinat Habu, Amenhotep III's once-vast temple marked by the Colossi of Memnon, and the best-known example built by Hatshepsut into the cliffs of Deir al-Bahri.

Pyramids

Initially, tombs were created to differentiate the burials of the elite from the majority, whose bodies were placed directly into the desert sand.

By around 3100 BC the mound of sand heaped over a grave was replaced by a more permanent structure of mudbrick; the structure's characteristic bench-shape is known as a mastaba, after the Arabic word for bench.

HOW TO WRAP A MUMMY

Mummification was used by many ancient cultures, but the Egyptians were the masters of this highly complex procedure, which they refined over thousands of years. At first bodies were simply buried in the desert away from cultivation. The hot, dry conditions and aridity of the sand allowed body fluids to drain away while preserving the skin, hair and nails intact.

As society developed, those who would once have been buried in a hole in the ground demanded tombs befitting their status. But as the bodies were no longer in direct contact with the sand, they rapidly decomposed. An alternative means of preservation was therefore required. After a long process of experimentation, and a good deal of trial and error, the Egyptians seem to have finally cracked it around 2600 BC when they started to remove the internal organs, where putrefaction begins.

All the organs were removed except the kidneys, which were hard to reach, and the heart, considered to be the source of intelligence. The brain was generally removed by inserting a metal probe up the nose and whisking until it had liquefied sufficiently to be drained down the nose. All the rest – lungs, liver, stomach and intestines – were removed through an opening cut in the left flank. Then the body and its separate organs were covered with natron salt (a combination of sodium carbonate and sodium bicarbonate) and left to dry out for 40 days, after which they were washed, purified and anointed with a range of oils, spices and resins. All were then wrapped in layers of linen, with the appropriate amulets set in place over the various parts of the body as priests recited the necessary incantations.

With each of the internal organs placed inside its own burial container (one of four Canopic jars), the wrapped body with its funerary mask was placed inside its coffin. It was then ready for the funeral procession to the tomb, where the vital Opening of the Mouth ceremony reanimated the soul and restored its senses. The essential offerings of food and drink then sustained the soul of the deceased that resided within the mummy as it was finally laid to rest inside the tomb.

As stone replaced mudbrick, the addition of further levels to increase height created the pyramid, the first built at Saqqara for King Zoser. Its stepped sides soon evolved into the familiar smooth-sided structure, with the Pyramids of Giza the most famous examples.

The worldly goods buried with the mummies for use in the afterlife give valuable details about everyday life and how it was lived, be it in the bustling, cosmopolitan capital Memphis or in the small rural settlements scattered along the banks of the Nile.

Pyramids are generally surrounded by the mastaba tombs of officials wanting burial close to their pharaoh in order to share in an afterlife, which was still the prerogative of royalty.

Rock-Cut Tombs

When the power of the monarchy broke down at the end of the Old Kingdom, the afterlife became increasingly accessible to those outside the royal family, and as officials became more independent they began to opt for burial in their home towns.

With little room for grand superstructures along many of the narrow stretches beside the Nile, an alternative type of tomb developed, tunnels cut into the cliffs that border the river. Most were built on the west bank, the traditional place of burial where the sun was seen to sink down into the underworld each evening. These simple rock-cut tombs consisting of a single chamber gradually developed into more elaborate structures complete with an open courtyard, offering a chapel and entrance facade carved out of the rock, with a shaft leading down into a burial chamber.

The most impressive rock-cut tombs were those built for the kings of the New Kingdom (1550–1069 BC), who relocated the royal burial ground south to the religious capital Thebes (modern Luxor), in a remote desert valley on the west bank, now known as the Valley of the Kings. There is evidence suggesting the first tomb (KV 39) here may have been built by Amenhotep I. The tomb of his successor Tuthmosis I was built by royal architect Ineni, whose biographical inscription states that he supervised its construction alone, 'with no one seeing, no one hearing'. In a radical departure from tradition, the offering chapels that were once part of the tomb's layout were now replaced by funerary (mortuary) temples built some distance away to preserve the tomb's secret location.

The tombs themselves were designed with a long corridor descending to a network of chambers decorated with scenes to help the deceased reach the next world. Many of these were extracts from the Book of the Dead, the modern term for ancient funerary works including the Book of Amduat (literally, 'that which is in the underworld'), the Book of Gates and the Litany of Ra. These describe the sun god's nightly journey through the darkness of the underworld, the realm of Osiris, with each hour of the night regarded as a separate region guarded by demigods. In order for Ra and the dead souls who accompanied him to pass through on their way to rebirth at dawn, they had to know the demigods' names in order to get past them.

Pharaonic Who's Who

Egypt's Pharaonic history is based on the regnal years of each pharaoh, a word derived from *per-aa,* meaning palace. Among the many hundreds of pharaohs who ruled Egypt over a 3000-year period, the following are some of the names found most frequently around the ancient sites.

Narmer (Menes) c 3100 BC First king to unite Lower and Upper Egypt. Narmer from south (Upper) Egypt is portrayed as victorious on the famous Narmer Palette in the Egyptian Museum. He is perhaps to be identified with the semimythical King Menes, founder of Egypt's ancient capital city Memphis.

Zoser (Djoser) c 2667–2648 BC As second king of the 3rd dynasty, Zoser was buried in Egypt's first pyramid, the world's oldest monumental stone building, designed by the architect Imhotep. Zoser's statue in the foyer of the Egyptian Museum shows a long-haired king with a slight moustache.

Sneferu c 2613–2589 BC The first king of the 4th dynasty, and held in the highest esteem by later generations, Sneferu was Egypt's greatest pyramid builder.

He was responsible for four such structures, and his final resting place, the Red (Northern) Pyramid at Dahshur, was Egypt's first true pyramid and a model for the more famous pyramids at Giza.

Khufu (Cheops) c 2589–2566 BC As Sneferu's son and successor, Khufu was the second king of the 4th dynasty. Best known for Egypt's largest pyramid, the Great Pyramid at Giza, his only surviving likeness is Egypt's smallest royal sculpture, a 7.5cm-high figurine in the Egyptian Museum.

Khafre (Khephren, Chephren) c 2558–2532 BC Khafre was a younger son of Khufu who succeeded his half-brother to become fourth king of the 4th dynasty. He built the second of Giza's famous pyramids and is best known as the model for the face of the Great Sphinx.

Menkaure (Mycerinus) c 2532–2503 BC As the son of Khafre and fifth king of the 4th dynasty, Menkaure built the smallest of Giza's three huge pyramids. He is also well represented by a series of superb sculptures in the Egyptian Museum.

Amenhotep I c 1525–1504 BC As second king of the 18th dynasty, Amenhotep I ruled for a time with his mother Ahmose-Nofretari. They founded the village of Deir el-Medina for the workers who built the tombs in the Valley of the Kings, and Amenhotep I may have been the first king to be buried there.

Hatshepsut c 1473–1458 BC As the most famous of Egypt's female pharaohs, Hatshepsut took power at the death of her brother-husband Tuthmosis II and initially ruled jointly with her nephew-stepson Tuthmosis III.

Tuthmosis III c 1479–1425 BC As sixth king of the 18th dynasty, Tuthmosis III (the Napoleon of ancient Egypt) expanded Egypt's empire with a series of foreign campaigns into Syria. He built extensively at Karnak, added a chapel at Deir al-Bahri and his tomb was the first in the Valley of the Kings to be decorated.

Amenhotep III c 1390–1352 BC As ninth king of the 18th dynasty, Amenhotep III's reign marks the zenith of Egypt's culture and power. He is the creator of Luxor Temple and the largest ever funerary temple marked by the Colossi of Memnon, and his many innovations, including Aten worship, are usually credited to his son Amenhotep IV (later 'Akhenaten').

Akhenaten (Amenhotep IV) c 1352–1336 BC Changing his name from Amenhotep to distance himself from the state god Amun, Akhenaten relocated the royal capital to Amarna with his wife Nefertiti. While many still regard him as a monotheist and benign revolutionary, the evidence suggests he was a dictator whose reforms were political rather than religious.

Nefertiti c 1338–1336 BC (?) Famous for her painted bust in Berlin, Nefertiti ruled with her husband Akhenaten, and while the identity of his successor remains controversial, this may have been Nefertiti herself, using the throne name 'Smenkhkare'.

Tutankhamun c 1336–1327 BC As the 11th king of the 18th dynasty, Tutankhamun's fame is based on the great quantities of treasure discovered in his tomb in 1922. The son of Akhenaten by one of Akhenaten's sisters, Tutankhamun reopened the traditional temples and restored Egypt's fortunes after the disastrous reign of his father.

Horemheb c 1323–1295 BC As a military general, Horemheb restored Egypt's empire under Tutankhamun and after the brief reign of Ay, eventually became king himself, marrying Nefertiti's sister Mutnodjmet. His tomb at Saqqara was abandoned in favour of a royal burial in a superbly decorated tomb in the Valley of the Kings.

Seti I c 1294–1279 BC The second king of the 19th dynasty, Seti I continued to consolidate Egypt's empire with foreign campaigns. Best known for building Karnak's Hypostyle Hall, a superb temple at Abydos and a huge tomb in the Valley of the Kings.

Ramses II c 1279–1213 BC As son and successor of Seti I, Ramses II fought the Hittites at the Battle of Kadesh and built temples including Abu Simbel and the Ramesseum, once adorned with the statue that inspired poet PB Shelley's 'Ozymandias'.

Ramses III c 1184–1153 BC As second king of the 20th dynasty, Ramses III was the last of the warrior kings, repelling several attempted invasions portrayed in scenes at his funerary temple Medinat Habu.

Taharka 690–664 BC As fourth king of the 25th dynasty, Taharka was one of Egypt's Nubian pharaohs and his daughter Amenirdis II was high priestess at

The funerary texts in the tombs gave the deceased all the knowledge that would be needed to reach the afterlife: knowledge of the power of those in the underworld, knowledge of the hidden forces, knowledge of each hour and each god, knowledge of the gates the deceased must pass through and knowledge of how the powerful enemies could be destroyed.

Karnak, where Taharka undertook building work. A fine sculpted head of the king is in Aswan's Nubian Museum, and he was buried in a pyramid at Nuri in southern Nubia.

Alexander the Great 331–323 BC Alexander invaded Egypt in 331 BC, founded Alexandria, visited Amun's temple at Siwa Oasis to confirm his divinity and after his untimely death in Babylon in 323 BC, his mummy was eventually buried in Alexandria.

Ptolemy I 323–283 BC As Alexander's general and rumoured half-brother, Ptolemy seized Egypt at Alexander's death and established the Ptolemaic line of pharaohs. Ruling in traditional style for 300 years, they made Alexandria the greatest capital of the ancient world.

Cleopatra VII 51–30 BC As the 19th ruler of the Ptolemaic dynasty, Cleopatra VII ruled with her brothers Ptolemy XIII, then Ptolemy XIV before taking power herself. A brilliant politician who restored Egypt's former glories, she married Julius Caesar then Mark Antony, whose defeat at Actium in 31 BC led to the couple's suicide.

Thirty royal dynasties ruled over a 3000-year period, now divided into the Old, Middle and New Kingdoms separated by intermittent periods of unrest (Intermediate periods) when the country split into north (Lower Egypt) and south (Upper Egypt).

Gods & Goddesses

Initially representing aspects of the natural world, Egypt's gods and goddesses grew more complex through time. As they began to blend together and adopt each other's characteristics, they started to become difficult to identify, although their distinctive headgear and clothing can provide clues as to who they are. The following brief descriptions should help travellers spot at least a few of the many hundreds who appear on monuments and in museums.

Amun The local god of Thebes (Luxor) who became the state god of New Kingdom Egypt. Originally he may have been associated with the power of the wind, and he was a creator god. Later he became closely associated with the fertility god Min and combined with the sun god to create Amun-Ra, king of the gods. He is generally portrayed seated on a throne with a double-plumed crown and sometimes the horns of his sacred ram to accentuate his procreative vigour.

Anubis The funerary god who deals with burial and afterlife. Anubis is the god of mummification, the patron of embalmers and guardian of cemeteries, and is generally depicted as a black jackal or a jackal-headed man.

Apophis The huge snake embodying darkness and chaos was the enemy of the sun god Ra. It tried to destroy him every night during his journey through the underworld, to prevent him reaching the dawn. Seth speared the serpent, and the blood stain that was left explained the red sky at sunset and sunrise.

Aten The solar disc whose rays end in outstretched hands was worshipped as a god during the 18th dynasty, and became chief deity under the reign of Akhenaten.

Atum Creator god of Heliopolis who rose from the primeval waters and ejaculated (or sneezed, depending on the myth) to create gods and humans. He was also the god who would destroy everything at the end of times. Generally depicted as a man wearing the double crown, but sometimes also with the head of a ram or a scarab, Atum represented the setting sun.

Bastet Cat goddess whose cult centre was Bubastis; ferocious when defending her father Ra the sun god, she was often shown as a friendly deity, a symbol of motherhood, personified by the domestic cat.

Bes A household deity, Bes was a grotesque yet benign dwarf god fond of music and dancing; he kept evil from the home and protected women in childbirth by waving his knives and sticking out his tongue.

Geb God of the earth associated with vegetation and fertility, he is generally depicted as a green man lying beneath his sister-wife Nut, the sky goddess, supported by their father Shu, god of air. He is the father of Osiris, Isis, Seth and Nephtys.

Hapy God of the Nile flood and the plump embodiment of fertility shown as an androgynous figure with sagging breasts and a swollen belly, sometimes shown with a clump of papyrus on his head.

Hathor Goddess of love, sexuality and pleasure represented as a cow, or a woman with a crown of horns and sun's disc in her guise as the sun god's daughter. Patron of music and dancing whose principle cult centre was at Dendara, she was known as 'she of the beautiful hair' and 'lady of drunkenness'. She was the wife of Horus.

Horus Falcon god of the sky and son of Isis and Osiris, he avenged his father to rule on earth and was personified by the ruling pharaoh. He can appear as a falcon or a man with a falcon's head, and his eye *(wedjat)* was a powerful amulet. Horus, the husband of Hathor, was closely associated with kingship and is often seen hovering as a falcon over the pharaoh's head.

Isis Goddess of magic and protector of her brother-husband Osiris and their son Horus. She represented the ideal wife, made the first mummy of Osiris' body and was a protector of the dead. As symbolic mother of the pharaoh she appears as a woman with a throne-shaped crown, or sometimes with Hathor's cow horns. She is often seen suckling the infant Horus.

Khepri God of the rising sun represented by the scarab beetle, whose habit of rolling balls of dirt was likened to the sun's journey across the sky.

Khnum Ram-headed god who created life on a potter's wheel; he also controlled the waters of the Nile flood from his cave at Elephantine and his cult centre was Esna.

Khons Young god of the moon and son of Amun and Mut. He is generally depicted in human form wearing a crescent moon crown and the 'sidelock of youth' hairstyle.

Maat Goddess of cosmic order, truth and justice, depicted as a woman wearing an ostrich feather on her head, or sometimes by the feather alone.

Mut Amun's consort and one of the symbolic mothers of the king; her name means both 'mother' and 'vulture' and she is generally shown as a woman with a vulture headdress.

Nekhbet Vulture goddess of Upper Egypt worshipped at el-Kab; she often appears with her sister-goddess Wadjet the cobra, protecting the pharaoh.

Nut Sky goddess usually portrayed as a woman whose star-spangled body arches across tomb and temple ceilings. She swallows the sun each evening to give birth to it each morning.

Osiris God of death, fertilty and resurrection whose main cult centre was at Abydos. As the first mummy created, he was magically revived by Isis to produce their son Horus, who took over the earthly kingship, while Osiris became ruler of the underworld and symbol of eternal life. He represented good, while his brother Seth represented evil.

Ptah Creator god of Memphis who brought the world into being by his thoughts and spoken words. He is patron of craftsmen, wears a tight-fitting robe and a skullcap, and usually clutches a tall sceptre (resembling a 1950s microphone).

Ra The supreme deity in the Egyptian pantheon, the sun god is generally shown as a man with a falcon's head topped by a sun disc, although he can take many forms (eg Aten, Khepri) and other gods merge with him to enhance their powers (eg Amun-Ra, Ra-Atum). In his underworld aspect he can be shown with a ram's head. Ra travelled through the skies in a boat, sinking down into the underworld each night before re-emerging at dawn to bring light.

Sekhmet Lioness goddess of Memphis whose name means 'the powerful one'. As a daughter of sun god Ra she was capable of great destruction and was the bringer of pestilence; her priests functioned as doctors, and her statues were erected to protect Egypt from the plague.

Seth God of chaos and confusion personified by a mythological, composite animal. In pre-Dynastic times the king was revered as the incarnation of both Horus and Seth. However, during the Old Kingdom, the myth arose that after murdering his brother Osiris he was defeated by Horus, and from then on he was regarded as evil, too dangerous to be depicted on temple walls, even as a hieroglyph.

Sobek Crocodile god representing Pharaonic might, he was worshipped at Kom Ombo and Fayyum. Both sites had sacred lakes with crocodiles.

Taweret Hippopotamus goddess who often appears upright to scare evil from the home and protect women in childbirth.

Thoth God of knowledge and writing, and patron of scribes. He is portrayed as an ibis or baboon, or most frequently as an ibis-headed man holding a scribe's palette, and his cult centre was at Hermopolis. He was closely identified with the moon, and was considered the guardian of the deceased in the underworld.

The ancient Egyptians' secret to a contented life is summed up by the words of one of their poems: 'it is good to drink beer with happy hearts, when one is clothed in clean robes'.

CHRONOLOGY OF THE PHARAOHS

EARLY DYNASTIC PERIOD	
1st Dynasty	**3100–2890 BC**
Narmer (Menes)	c 3100 BC
2nd Dynasty	**2890–2686 BC**
OLD KINGDOM	
3rd Dynasty	**2686–2613 BC**
Zoser	2667–2648 BC
Sekhemket	2648–2640 BC
4th Dynasty	**2613–2494 BC**
Sneferu	2613–2589 BC
Khufu (Cheops)	2589–2566 BC
Djedefra	2566–2558 BC
Khafre (Chephren)	2558–2532 BC
Menkaure (Mycerinus)	2532–2503 BC
Shepseskaf	2503–2498 BC
5th Dynasty	**2494–2345 BC**
Userkaf	2494–2487 BC
Sahure	2487–2475 BC
Neferirkare	2475–2455 BC
Shepseskare	2455–2448 BC
Raneferef	2448–2445 BC
Nyuserra	2445–2421 BC
Unas	2375–2345 BC
6th Dynasty	**2345–2181 BC**
Teti	2345–2323 BC
Pepi I	2321–2287 BC
Pepi II	2278–2184 BC
7th–8th Dynasties	**2181–2125 BC**
FIRST INTERMEDIATE PERIOD	
9th–10th Dynasties	**2160–2025 BC**
MIDDLE KINGDOM	
11th Dynasty	**2055–1985 BC**
Montuhotep II	2055–2004 BC
Montuhotep III	2004–1992 BC
12th Dynasty	**1985–1795 BC**
Amenemhat I	1985–1955 BC
Sesostris I	1965–1920 BC
Amenemhat II	1922–1878 BC
Sesostris II	1880–1874 BC
Sesostris III	1874–1855 BC
Amenemhat III	1855–1808 BC
Amenemhat IV	1808–1799 BC
13th–14th Dynasties	**1795–1650 BC**

SECOND INTERMEDIATE PERIOD	
15th–17th Dynasties	**1650–1550 BC**
NEW KINGDOM	
18th Dynasty	**1550–1290 BC**
Ahmose	1550–1525 BC
Amenhotep I	1525–1504 BC
Tuthmosis I	1504–1492 BC
Tuthmosis II	1492–1479 BC
Tuthmosis III	1479–1425 BC
Hatshepsut	1473–1458 BC
Amenhotep II	1427–1400 BC
Tuthmosis IV	1400–1390 BC
Amenhotep III	1390–1352 BC
Akhenaten	1352–1336 BC
Tutankhamun	1336–1327 BC
Horemheb	1323–1295 BC
19th Dynasty	**1295–1186 BC**
Ramses I	1295–1294 BC
Seti I	1294–1279 BC
Ramses II	1279–1213 BC
Seti II	1200–1194 BC
20th Dynasty	**1186–1069 BC**
Ramses III	1184–1153 BC
THIRD INTERMEDIATE PERIOD	
21st Dynasty	**1069–945 BC**
Psusennes I	1039–991 BC
22nd–23rd Dynasties	**945–712 BC**
24th–26th Dynasties	**727–525 BC**
LATE PERIOD	
27th Dynasty	**525–404 BC**
Cambyses	525–522 BC
Darius	521–486 BC
28th–31st Dynasties	**404–332 BC**
GRAECO-ROMAN PERIOD	
Macedonian and Ptolemaic	**332–30 BC**
Alexander the Great	332–323 BC
Ptolemy I	305–282 BC
Ptolemy III	246–222 BC
Ptolemy VIII	170–163 and 145–116 BC
Cleopatra VII	51–30 BC
Roman	**30–313 BC**
Augustus	30 BC–AD 14
Hadrian	117–138
Diocletian	284–305

Art in Life & Death

Ancient Egyptian art is instantly recognisable, its distinctive style remaining largely unchanged for more than three millennia. With its basic characteristics already in place at the beginning of the Pharaonic Period c 3100 BC, the motif of the king smiting his enemies on the Narmer Palette was still used in Roman times.

The vast quantities of food and drink offered in temples and tombs were duplicated on surrounding walls to ensure a constant supply for eternity. The offerings are shown piled up in layers, sometimes appearing to float in the air if the artist took this practice too far.

The Purpose of Art

Despite being described in modern terms as 'works of art', the reasons for the production of art in ancient Egypt are still very much misunderstood. Whereas most cultures create art for purely decorative purposes, Egyptian art was primarily functional, and closely linked to religion and ideology. All ancient Egyptian art was part of a unified system of representation; there was no tradition of an individual artistic expression. To represent an object in art was to make it eternal, to give it permanence. There was also a standard repertoire of funerary scenes, from the colourful images that adorn the walls of tombs to the highly detailed vignettes illuminating funerary texts. Each image, whether carved on stone or painted on papyrus, was designed to serve and protect the deceased on their journey into the afterlife.

The majority of artefacts were produced for religious and funerary purposes and, despite their breathtaking beauty, would have been hidden away from public gaze, either within a temple's dark interior or, like Tut's mask, buried in a tomb with the dead. This only makes the objects – and those who made them – even more remarkable. Artists regarded the things they made as pieces of equipment to do a job rather than works of art to be displayed and admired.

The Egyptians believed it was essential that the things they portrayed had every relevant feature shown as clearly as possible. Then when they were magically reanimated through the correct rituals they would be able to function as effectively as possible, protecting and sustaining the unseen spirits of both the gods and the dead.

Figures needed a clear outline, with a profile of nose and mouth to let them breathe, and the eye shown whole as if seen from the front, to allow the figure to see. This explains why eyes were often painted on the sides of coffins to allow the dead to see out and why hieroglyphs such as snakes or enemy figures were sometimes shown in two halves to prevent them causing damage when re-activated.

Art & Nature

While working within very restrictive conventions, the ancient artists still managed to capture a feeling of vitality. Inspired by the natural world around them, they selected images to reflect the concept of life and rebirth, as embodied by the scarab beetles and tilapia fish thought capable of self-generation. Since images were also believed to be able to transmit the life force they contained: fluttering birds, gambolling cattle and the speeding quarry of huntsmen were all favourite motifs. The life-giving properties of plants are also much in evidence, with wheat, grapes, onions and figs stacked side by side with the flowers the Egyptians loved so much. Particularly common are the lotus (water lily) and papyrus, the heraldic symbols of Upper and Lower Egypt often shown entwined to symbolise a kingdom united.

The Meaning of Colour

Egypt was represented politically by the White Crown of Upper Egypt and the Red Crown of Lower Egypt, fitted together in the dual crown to represent the unification of the two lands.

The country was also represented by the colours red and black, the red desert wastes of *deshret* contrasting with the fertile black land of *kemet*. For Egyptians, black was the colour of life, and black was the colour of choice to represent Osiris, the god of fertility and resurrection, in contrast to the redness associated with his brother Seth, god of chaos. Sometimes Osiris is also shown with green skin, the colour of vegetation and new life. Some of his fellow gods are blue to echo the ethereal blue of the sky, and the golden yellow of the sun is regularly employed for its protective qualities.

Human figures were initially represented with different-coloured skin tones, the red-brown of men contrasting with the paler, yellowed tones of women, and although this has been interpreted as indicating that men spent most of the time working outdoors whereas women led a more sheltered existence, changes in artistic convention meant everyone was eventually shown with the same red-brown skin tone.

The texts for the afterlife give various visions of paradise, from joining the sun god Ra in his journey across the sky, to joining Osiris in the underworld or rising up to become one of the Imperishable Stars, the variety of final destinations reflecting the ancient Egyptians' multifaceted belief system.

Romancing the Stone

Sculptors worked in a variety of different mediums, with stone often chosen for its colour – white limestone and alabaster (calcite), golden sandstone, green schist (slate), brown quartzite and both black and red granite. Smaller items could be made of red or yellow jasper; orange carnelian or blue lapis lazuli; metals such as copper, gold or silver; or less costly materials such as wood or highly glazed blue faïence pottery.

All these materials were used to produce a wide range of statuary for temples and tombs, from 20m-high stone colossi to gold figurines a few centimetres tall. Amulets and jewellery were another means of ensuring the security of the dead. While their beauty would enhance the appearance of the living, each piece was also carefully designed as a protective talisman or a means of communicating status. Even when creating such small-scale masterpieces, the same principles employed in larger-scale works of art applied, and little of the work that the ancient craftsmen produced was either accidental or frivolous.

Texts for the Afterlife

Initially, the afterlife was restricted to royalty and the texts meant to guide the pharaohs towards eternity were inscribed on the walls of their burial chambers. Since the rulers of the Old Kingdom were buried in pyramids, the accompanying funerary writings are known as the **Pyramid Texts**.

In the hope of sharing in the royal afterlife, Old Kingdom officials built their tombs close to the pyramids until the pharaohs lost power at the end of the Old Kingdom. No longer reliant on the pharaoh's favour, the officials began to use the royal funerary texts for themselves. Inscribed on their coffins, they are known as **Coffin Texts** – a Middle Kingdom version of the earlier Pyramid Texts, adapted for nonroyal use.

This 'democratisation' of the afterlife evolved even further when the Coffin Texts were literally brought out in paperback, inscribed on papyrus and made available to the masses during the New Kingdom. Referred to by the modern term the **Book of the Dead**, the Egyptians knew this as the Book of Coming Forth by Day, with sections entitled 'Spell for not dying a second

MAGIC SIGNS

The small figures of humans, animals, birds and symbols that populate the script were believed to infuse each scene with divine power. In fact certain signs were considered so potent they were shown in two halves to prevent them causing havoc should they magically reanimate. Yet the ancient Egyptians also liked a joke, and their language was often onomatopoeic – for example, the word for cat was miw after the noise it makes, and the word for wine was *irp*, after the noise made by those who drank it.

time', 'Spell not to rot and not to do work in the land of the dead' and 'Spell for not having your magic taken away'. These spells and instructions acted as a kind of guidebook to the afterlife, with some of the texts accompanied by maps, and images of some of the gods and demons that would be encountered en route together with the correct way to address them.

Royal vs Nonroyal Tomb Decoration

The New Kingdom royal tombs in the Valley of the Kings are decorated with highly formal scenes showing the pharaoh in the company of the gods and all the forces of darkness defeated. Since the pharaoh was always pharaoh, even in death, there was no room for the informality and scenes of daily life that can be found in the tombs of lesser mortals.

The nonroyal tombs show a much more relaxed, almost eclectic nature of scenes, which feature everything from eating and drinking to dancing and hairdressing. But here again, these apparently random scenes of daily life carry the same message found throughout Egyptian art – the eternal continuity of life and the triumph of order over chaos. As the pharaoh is shown smiting the enemy and restoring peace to the land, his subjects contribute to this continual battle of opposites in which order must always triumph for life to continue.

A common tomb scene is the banquet at which guests enjoy generous quantities of food and drink. Although no doubt reflecting some of the pleasures the deceased had enjoyed in life, the food portrayed was also meant to sustain their souls, as would the accompanying scenes of bountiful harvests which would ensure supplies never ran out. Even the music and dance performed at these banquets indicate much more than a party in full swing – the lively proceedings were another way of reviving the deceased by awakening their senses.

The culmination of this idea can be found in the all-important Opening of the Mouth ceremony, performed by the deceased's heir (either the next king or the eldest son). The ceremony was designed to reanimate the soul (*ka*), which could then go on to enjoy eternal life once all its senses had been restored. Noise and movement were believed to reactivate hearing and sight, while the sense of smell was restored with incense and flowers. The essential offerings of food and drink sustained the soul that resided within the mummy as it was finally laid to rest inside the tomb.

THE HUNTING SCENE

In one of the most common nonroyal tomb scenes, the tomb owner is seen hunting on the river. On a basic level one can see this as the deceased enjoying a day out boating with his family. However, the scene is far more complex than it first appears. The tomb owner, shown in a central position in the prime of life, strikes a formal pose as he restores order amid the chaos of nature all around him. In his task he is supported by the female members of his family, from his small daughter to the wife standing serenely beside him. Dressed far too impractically for a hunting trip on the river, his wife wears an outfit more in keeping with a priestess of Hathor, goddess of love and sensual pleasure. Yet Hathor is also the protector of the dead and capable of great violence as defender of her father, the sun god Ra, in his eternal struggle against the chaotic forces of darkness.

Some versions of this riverside hunting scene also feature a cat. Often described as a kind of 'retriever' (whoever heard of a retriever cat?), the cat is one of the creatures who was believed to defend the sun god on his nightly journey through the underworld. Similarly, the river's teeming fish were regarded as pilots for the sun god's boat and were themselves potent symbols of rebirth. Even the abundant lotus flowers are significant since the lotus, whose petals open each morning, is the flower that symbolised rebirth. Once the coded meaning of ancient Egyptian art is understood, such previously silent images almost scream out the idea of 'life'.

Hieroglyphs

Hieroglyphs, meaning 'sacred carvings' in Greek, are the pictorial script used by the ancient Egyptians. It is generally agreed that writing was invented in Sumer, Mesopotamia. Egyptian hieroglyphs differ greatly from Mesopotamian cuneiform, but some suggest that the Egyptians took the concept of writing from the Sumerians, and developed their own script. Others believe that the Egyptians developed the world's first script. For 3500 years it remained fairly unchanged, only written by a very small literary elite, while the spoken language underwent huge changes.

The earliest recorded hieroglyphs have been found on a bone label from a Predynastic tomb at Abydos from 3150 BC. The last hieroglyphic inscription was carved on a temple wall in Philae on 24 August AD 394.

The Privilege of Writing

It is very possible that the overall literacy rate in ancient Egypt was less than 1% of the entire population, but the impact of hieroglyphs on Egyptian culture cannot be overestimated, as they provided the means by which the state took shape. They were used by a civil service of scribes working on the king's behalf to collect taxes and organise vast workforces.

During the Old Kingdom literary works included funerary texts, letters, hymns and poems, and by the early Middle Kingdom narrative Egyptian literature was created by the growing intellectual class of scribes.

Within a few centuries, day-to-day transactions were undertaken in a shorthand version of hieroglyphs known as hieratic, whereas hieroglyphs remained the perfect medium for monumental inscriptions. Covering every available tomb and temple surface, hieroglyphs were regarded as 'the words of the Thoth', the ibis-headed god of writing and patron deity of scribes, who, like the scribes, is often shown holding a reed pen and ink palette.

Reading Hieroglyphs

Hieroglyphs may at first appear deceptively simple, but they are best understood if divided into three categories – logograms (ideograms), determinatives and phonograms. Logograms represent the thing they depict (eg the sun sign meaning 'sun'), while determinatives are simply placed at the ends of words to reinforce their meaning (eg the sun sign in the verb 'to shine'). Phonograms are less straightforward and represent either one, two or three consonants.

The 26 signs usually described in simple terms as 'the hieroglyphic alphabet' are the single consonant signs (eg the owl pronounced 'm', the zig-zag water sign 'n'). Another 100 or so signs are biconsonantal (eg the bowl sign read as 'nb'), and a further 50 are triconsonantal signs (eg 'nfr' meaning good, perfect or beautiful). There are no actual vowels as such.

It can be a bit tricky to read ancient Egyptian texts. Scribes usually wrote hieroglyphs from right to left, and in columns which needed to be read from top to bottom. But sometimes they wrote from left to write. To complicate matters further, no punctuation was used. The way human figures or animals face is usually a pointer to the way one should read the text.

What's in a Name?

The majority of hieroglyphic inscriptions are endless repetitions of the names and titles of the pharaohs and gods, surrounded by protective symbols. Names were of tremendous importance to the Egyptians and as vital to an individual's existence as their soul, and it was sincerely believed that 'to speak the name of the dead is to make them live'.

THE LADY OF THE HOUSE

The home was very much the female domain. The most common title for women of all social classes was *nebet per* (lady of the house), emphasising their control over most aspects of domestic life. Although there is little evidence of marriage ceremonies, monogamy was standard practice for the majority, with divorce and remarriage relatively common and initiated by either sex. With the same legal rights as men, women were responsible for running the home and although there were male launderers, cleaners and cooks, it was mainly women who cared for the children, cleaned the house, made clothing and prepared food in small open-air kitchens adjoining the home.

Royal names were also followed by epithets such as 'life, prosperity, health', comparable to the way in which the name of the Prophet Mohammed is always followed by the phrase 'peace be upon him'. For further protection, royal names were written inside a rectangular fortress wall known as a *serekh,* which later developed into the more familiar oval-shaped cartouche (the French word for cartridge).

Although each pharaoh had five names, cartouches were used to enclose the two most important ones: the 'prenomen' or 'King of Upper and Lower Egypt' name assumed at the coronation and written with a bee and a sedge plant; and the 'nomen' or 'Son of Ra' name, which was given at birth and written with a goose and a sun sign.

As an example, Amenhotep III is known by his nomen or Son of Ra name 'Amun-hotep' (meaning Amun is content), although his prenomen or King of Upper and Lower Egypt name was Neb-maat-Re (meaning Ra, lord of truth). His grandson had the most famous of all Egyptian names, Tut-ankh-amun, which literally translates as 'the living image of Amun', yet he had originally been named Tut-ankh-aten, meaning 'the living image of the Aten' – a change in name that reflects the shifting politics of the time.

The loss of one's name meant permanent obliteration from history, and those unfortunate enough to incur official censure included commoners and pharaohs alike. At times it even happened to the gods themselves, a fate which befell the state god Amun during the reign of the 'heretic' pharaoh Akhenaten, who in turn suffered the same fate together with his god Aten when Amun was later restored.

In order to prevent this kind of obliteration, names were sometimes carved so deeply into the rock it is possible to place an outstretched hand right inside each hieroglyph, as is the case of Ramses III's name and titles at his funerary temple of Medinat Habu.

The Greeks were so impressed with the ancient culture that they regarded Egypt as the 'cradle of civilisation', and even the occupying Romans adopted the country's ancient gods and traditions.

Gods were incorporated into the names of ordinary people, and as well as Amunhotep there was Rahotep (the sun god Ra is content) and Ptahhotep (the creator god Ptah is content). By changing 'hotep' (meaning 'content') to 'mose' (meaning 'born of'), the names Amenmose, Ramose and Ptahmose meant that these men were 'born of' these gods.

In similar fashion, goddesses featured in women's names. Hathor, goddess of love, beauty and pleasure, was a particular favourite, with names such as Sithathor (daughter of Hathor). Standard male names could also be feminised by the simple addition of 't', so Nefer (good, beautiful or perfect) becomes Nefert, which could be further embellished with the addition of a verb, as in the case of the famous name Nefertiti (goodness/beauty/perfection has come).

Others were known by their place of origin, such as Panehesy (the Nubian), or could be named after flora and fauna – Miwt (cat), Debet (hippopotamus) and Seshen (lotus), which is still in use today as the name Susan.

Everyday Living

With ancient Egypt's history focused on its royals, the part played by the rest of the ancient population is frequently ignored. The great emphasis on written history also excludes the 99% of the ancient population who were unable to write, and it can often seem as if the only people who lived in ancient Egypt were pharaohs, priests and scribes.

The silent majority are often dismissed as little more than illiterate peasants, although these were the very people who built the monuments and produced the wealth on which the culture was based.

Fortunately Egypt's climate, at least, is democratic, and has preserved the remains of people throughout society, from the mummies of the wealthy in their grand tombs to the remains of the poorest individuals buried in hollows in the sand.

Laundry marks were found on ancient garments; male launderers were employed by the wealthy, and even a few ancient laundry lists have survived, listing the types of garments they had to wash in the course of their work.

Domestic Life

In Egypt's dry climate, houses were traditionally built of mudbrick, whether they were the narrow back-to-back homes of workers or the sprawling palaces of the royals. The main differences were the number of rooms and the quality of fixtures and fittings. The villas of the wealthy often incorporated walled gardens with stone drainage systems for small pools, and some even had ensuite bathroom facilities – look out for the limestone toilet seat found at Amarna and now hanging in the Egyptian Museum in Cairo.

Just like the mudbrick houses in rural Egypt today, ancient homes were warm in winter and cool in summer. Small, high-set windows reduced the sun's heat but allowed breezes to blow through, and stairs gave access to the flat roof where the family could relax or sleep.

Houses were often whitewashed on the outside to deflect the heat, but interiors were usually painted in bright colours, the walls and floors of wealthier homes further enhanced with gilding and inlaid tiles. Although the furniture of most homes would have been quite sparse – little more than a mudbrick bench, a couple of stools and a few sleeping mats – the wealthy could afford beautiful furniture, including inlaid chairs and footstools, storage chests, beds with linen sheets and feather-stuffed cushions. Most homes also had small shrines for household deities and busts of family ancestors, and a small raised area seems to have been reserved for women in childbirth.

The staple food was bread, produced in many varieties, including the dense calorie-laden loaves mass-produced for those working on government building schemes. Onions, leeks, garlic and pulses were eaten in great quantities along with dates, figs, pomegranates and grapes. Grapes were also used, along with honey, as sweeteners. Spices, herbs, nuts and seeds were also added to food, along with oil extracted from native plants and imported almonds and olives. Although cows provided milk for drinking and making butter and cheese, meat was only eaten regularly by the wealthy and by priests allowed to eat temple offerings once the gods had been satisfied. This was mostly beef, although sheep, goats

THE WISE SCRIBE

A huge civil service of scribes worked on the pharaoh's behalf to record taxes and organise workers. Taught to read and write in the schools attached to temples where written texts were stored and studied, the great majority of scribes were male. However, some women are also shown with documents and literacy would have been necessary to undertake roles they are known to have held, including overseer, steward, teacher, doctor, high priestess, vizier and even pharaoh on at least six occasions.

and pigs were also eaten, as were game and wild fowl. Fish was generally dried and salted and, because of its importance in workers' diets, a fish-processing plant existed at the pyramid builders' settlement at Giza.

Although the wealthy enjoyed wine (with the best produced in the vineyards of the Delta and western oases, or imported from Syria), the standard beverage was a rather soupy barley beer, which was drunk throughout society by everyone, including children.

The Egyptian calendar was based on the annual cycle of the Nile, with three seasons – *akhet* (inundation), *peret* (spring planting) and *shemu* (summer harvest). As the flood waters receded by October, farmers planted their crops in the silt left behind, using irrigation canals to water their crops until harvest in April.

At Work

The majority of ancient Egyptians were farmers, whose lives were based around the annual cycle of the Nile. Agriculture was so fundamental to life in both this world and the next that it was one of the dominant themes in tomb scenes. The standard repertoire of ploughing, sowing and reaping is often interspersed with officials checking field boundaries or calculating the grain to be paid as tax in this pre-coinage economy. The officials are often accompanied by scribes busily recording all transactions, with hieroglyphs now known to have been first developed c 3250 BC as a means of recording produce.

Closely related to the scribe's profession were the artists and sculptors who produced the stunning artefacts synonymous with ancient Egypt. From colossal statues to delicate jewellery, all were fashioned using simple tools and natural materials.

Building stone was hewn by teams of labourers supplemented by prisoners, with granite obtained from Aswan, sandstone from Gebel Silsila, alabaster from Hatnub near Amarna and limestone from Tura near modern Cairo. Gold came from mines in the Eastern Desert and Nubia, and both copper and turquoise were mined in the Sinai. With such precious commodities being transported large distances, trade routes and border areas were patrolled by guards, police (known as *medjay*) and the army, when not out on campaign.

Men also plied their trade as potters, carpenters, builders, metalworkers, jewellers, weavers, fishermen and butchers, with many of these professions handed down from father to son: this is especially well portrayed in the tomb scenes of Rekhmire. There were also itinerant workers such as barbers, dancers and midwives, and those employed for their skills as magicians. Men worked alongside women as servants in wealthy homes, performing standard household duties, and thousands of people were employed in the temples, which formed the heart of every settlement as a combination of town hall, college, library and medical centre.

Clothing & Jewellery

As well as priests and priestesses, temples employed their own scribes, butchers, gardeners, florists, perfume-makers, musicians and dancers, many of whom worked on a part-time basis.

Personal appearance was clearly important to the Egyptians, with wigs, jewellery, cosmetics and perfumes worn by men and women alike. Garments were generally linen, made from the flax plant before the introduction of cotton in Ptolemaic times. Status was reflected in the fineness and quantity of the linen, but as it was expensive, surviving clothes show frequent patching and darning.

The most common garment was the loincloth, worn like underpants beneath other clothes. Men also wore a linen kilt, sometimes pleated, and both men and women wore the bag-tunic made from a rectangle of linen folded in half and sewn up each side. The most common female garments were dresses, most wrapped sari-like around the body, although there were also V-neck designs cut to shape, and detachable sleeves for easy cleaning.

Linen leggings have also been found, as well as socks with a gap between the toes for wearing with sandals made of vegetable fibre or leather. Plain headscarves were worn to protect the head from the sun or during messy work; the striped *nemes* (headcloth) was only worn by the pharaoh, who also had numerous crowns and diadems for ceremonial occasions.

Jewellery was worn by men and women throughout society for both aesthetic and magical purposes. It was made of various materials, from gold to glazed pottery, and included collars, necklaces, hair ornaments, bracelets, anklets, belts, earrings and finger rings.

Hair styles

Wigs and hair extensions were popular, at least from c 3400 BC, as was the use of henna *(Lawsonia inermis)* as a hair dye. Many people shaved or cropped their hair for cleanliness and to prevent head lice (which have been found in the hair of pharaohs). The clergy had to shave their heads for ritual purity and children's heads were partially shaved to leave only a side lock of hair as a symbol of youth.

Pharaonic Glossary

akh	usually translated as 'transfigured spirit', produced when the *ka* (soul) and *ba* (spirit) united after the deceased was judged worthy enough to enter the afterlife
Ammut	composite monster of the underworld who was part crocodile, part lion and part hippo, and ate the hearts of the unworthy dead; her name means 'The Devourer'
ba	usually translated as 'spirit', which appeared after death as a human-headed bird, able to fly to and from the tomb and into the afterlife
Book of the Dead	modern term for the collection of ancient funerary texts designed to guide the dead through the afterlife, developed at the beginning of the New Kingdom and partly based on the earlier Pyramid Texts and Coffin Texts
Canopic jars	containers usually made of limestone or calcite to store the preserved entrails (stomach, liver, lungs and intestines) of mummified individuals
cartouche	the protective oval shape (the name derived from the French word for cartridge), which surrounded the names of kings, queens and occasionally gods
cenotaph	a memorial structure set up in memory of a deceased king or queen, separate from their tomb or funerary temple
Coffin Texts	funerary texts developed from the earlier Pyramid Texts, which were then written on coffins during the Middle Kingdom
coregency	a period of joint rule by two pharaohs, usually father and son
cult temple	the standard religious building(s) designed to house the spirits of the gods and accessible only to the priesthood, usually located on the Nile's east bank
deshret	'red land', referring to barren desert
djed pillar	the symbolic backbone of Osiris, bestowing strength and stability and often worn as an amulet
false door	the means by which the soul of the deceased could enter and leave the world of the living to accept funerary offerings brought to their tomb
funerary (mortuary) temple	the religious structures where the souls of dead pharaohs were commemorated and sustained with offerings, usually built on the Nile's west bank
Heb-Sed festival	the jubilee ceremony of royal renewal and rejuvenation, which pharaohs usually celebrated after 30 years' rule
Heb-Sed race	part of the Heb-Sed festival when pharaohs undertook physical feats such as running to demonstrate their prowess and fitness to rule
hieratic	ancient shorthand version of hieroglyphs used for day-to-day transactions by scribes
hieroglyphs	Greek for 'sacred carvings', referring to ancient Egypt's formal picture writing used mainly for tomb and temple walls

hypostyle hall	imposing section of temple characterised by densely packed monumental columns
ka	Usually translated as 'soul', this was a person's 'double', which was created with them at birth and which lived on after death, sustained by offerings left by the living
kemet	'black land', referring to the fertile areas along the Nile's banks
king lists	chronological lists of each king's names kept as a means of recording history
lotus (water lily)	the heraldic plant of Upper (southern) Egypt
mammisi	the Birth House attached to certain Late Period and Graeco-Roman temples and associated with the goddesses Isis and Hathor
mastaba	Arabic word for bench, used to describe the mudbrick tomb structures built over subterranean burial chambers and from which pyramids developed
name	an essential part of each individual given at birth, and spoken after their death to allow them to live again in the afterlife
naos	sanctuary containing the god's statue, generally located in the centre of ancient temples
natron	mixture of sodium carbonate and sodium bicarbonate used to dry out the body during mummification and used by the living to clean linen, teeth and skin
nemes	the yellow-and-blue striped headcloth worn by pharaohs, the most famous example found on Tutankhamun's golden death mask
nomarch	local governor of each of Egypt's 42 nomes
nome	Greek term for Egypt's 42 provinces – 22 in Upper Egypt and later 20 added in Lower Egypt
obelisk	monolithic stone pillar tapering to a pyramidal top that was often gilded to reflect sunlight around temples and usually set in pairs
Opening of the Mouth ceremony	the culmination of the funeral, performed on the mummy of the deceased by their heir or funerary priest using spells and implements to restore their senses
Opet festival	annual celebration held at Luxor Temple to restore the powers of the pharaoh at a secret meeting with the god Amun
papyrus	the heraldic plant of Lower (northern) Egypt whose reedlike stem was sliced and layered to create paperlike sheets for writing
pharaoh	term for an Egyptian king derived from the ancient Egyptian word for palace, *per-aa*
pylon	monumental gateway with sloping sides forming the entrance to temples
Pyramid Texts	funerary texts inscribed on the walls of late Old Kingdom pyramids and restricted to royalty
sacred animals	living creatures thought to represent certain gods – eg the crocodile (identified with Sobek), the cat (identified with Bastet) – and often mummified at death
sarcophagus	derived from the Greek for 'flesh eating' and referring to the large stone coffins used to house the mummy and its wooden coffin(s)
scarab	the sacred dung beetle believed to propel the sun's disc through the sky in the same way the beetle pushes a ball of dung across the floor
serapeum	vast network of underground catacombs at Saqqara in which the Apis bulls were buried, later associated with the Ptolemaic god Serapis
serdab	from the Arabic word for cellar, a small room in a mastaba tomb containing a statue of the deceased to which offerings were presented
shabti (or ushabti)	small servant figurines placed in burials designed to undertake any manual work in the afterlife on behalf of the deceased

shadow	an essential part of each individual, the shadow was believed to offer protection, based on the importance of shade in an extremely hot climate
sidelock of youth	characteristic hairstyle of children and certain priests in which the head is shaved and a single lock of hair allowed to grow
solar barque	the boat in which the sun god Ra sailed through the heavens, with actual examples buried close to certain pyramids for use by the spirits of the pharaohs
Uraeus	an image of the cobra goddess Wadjet worn at the brow of royalty to symbolically protect them by spitting fire into the eyes of their enemies
Weighing of the Heart (The Judgement of Osiris)	the heart of the deceased was weighed against the feather of Maat with Osiris as judge; if light and free of sin they were allowed to spend eternity as an *akh*, but if their heart was heavy with sin it was eaten by Ammut and they were damned forever

The Egyptians

A badge worn by a Cairene woman soon after President Mubarak stepped down read 'Egyptian and proud'. Understanding what it means to be Egyptian has never been easier, nor more difficult because there are now so many possibilities. But one characteristic that still links the majority of Egyptians, from the university professor in Alexandria to the shoeshine boy in Luxor, is an immense pride in simply being Egyptian, pride in their extraordinary history and in some of their recent achievements.

The people of the south – anywhere south of Minya and down as far as Aswan – are known as Saidis (pronounced sai-eed-ees). They tend to be more traditional than people in the north.

Sense of Community

It's hard sometimes for outsiders to see where the Egyptians' sense of pride comes from, given the pervasive poverty, low literacy levels, high unemployment, housing shortages, infrastructure failings and myriad other pitfalls that face the country. But aiding each Egyptian in the daily struggle is every other Egyptian, and indeed there is a real sense that everybody's in it together. Large extended families and close-knit neighbourhoods act as social support groups, strangers fall easily into conversation with each other, and whatever goes wrong, somebody always knows someone somewhere who can help fix it.

Comforters

For Egyptians, religion cushions life's blows. Religion permeates Egyptian life, although for many, President Morsi's brand of Islam was too strident. Egyptians love enjoying themselves too much to welcome an authoritarian, politicised version of Islam. But religion is always there in the background. Ask after someone's health and the answer, from a Christian or a Muslim, is *Alhamdulallah* (Fine. Praise to God). Arrange to meet tomorrow and it's *Inshallah* (God willing). Then, if your appointee fails to turn up, God obviously didn't mean it to be.

And when all else fails – and it so often fails – there's humour. Egyptians are renowned for it. Jokes and wisecracks are the parlance of life. Comedy is the staple of the local cinema industry and the backbone of TV scheduling. The stock character is the little guy who through wit and a sharp tongue

SILENT COMMUNICATION IN EGYPT

Egyptians have an array of nonverbal ways of getting a point across – and if you know some of them, you'll be much less likely to get offended, run over or neglected in a restaurant.

First, 'no' is often communicated with a simple upward nod or a brusque *tsk* sound – which can seem a bit rude if you're not expecting it. But if you use it casually to touts on the street, they're more likely to leave you alone.

Another signal that can be misinterpreted by foreigners is a loud hissing sound. That guy might be trying to get your attention so you don't get trampled by his donkey cart coming down the narrow lane. But he might also be insulting you by implying you are a prostitute.

But the most essential gesture to learn is the one for asking for the bill at a restaurant. Make eye contact with your waiter, hold out your hand palm up, then make a quick chopping motion across it with the side of your other hand, as if to say 'Cut me off'. Works like a charm.

BACKHAND ECONOMY

Baksheesh means tip, but it's more than just a reward for services rendered. Salaries and wages in Egypt are much lower than in Western countries, so baksheesh is an essential means of supplementing income. Even Egyptians have to constantly dole out the baksheesh – to park their cars, receive mail and ensure they get fresh produce at the grocers.

For travellers not used to tipping, demands for baksheesh for pointing out the obvious in museums can be quite irritating. But services such as opening a door, delivering room service or carrying your bags warrant baksheesh. This may only be a few Egyptian pounds, but will always be welcome.

We suggest carrying lots of small change with you (trust us – you'll need it!) and also to keep it separate from bigger bills. And remember, there is only one immutable rule and that is that you can never give too much.

always manages to prick pomposity and triumph over the odds. Laughter lubricates the wheels of social exchange and one of the most enjoyable aspects of travelling in Egypt is how much can be negotiated with a smile.

Lifestyle

There's no simple definition of Egyptian society. There are obviously differences between someone living off their land in the Nile Delta and someone working in Cairo. But even among the latter, there are extremes of experience. On the one hand there's religious conservatism, where women wear the long, black, all-concealing *abeyya* and men wear the gownlike *galabeya*. In traditional circles, cousins marry cousins; going to Alexandria constitutes the trip of a lifetime; and all is 'God's will'. On the other hand, there are sections of society whose members order out from McDonald's; whose daughters wear slinky black numbers and flirt outrageously; who think nothing of regular trips to the USA; and who never set foot in a mosque until the day they're laid out in one. The bulk of the Egyptian populace falls somewhere between these two extremes.

A City Story

The typical urban family lives in an overcrowded suburb in a six-floor breeze-block apartment building with cracking walls and dodgy plumbing. If they're lucky they may own a small car. Otherwise the husband will take the metro to work or, more likely, fight for a handhold on one of the city's sardine-can buses. He may well be a university graduate (about 40,000 people graduate each year), although a degree is no longer any guarantee of a job – graduate unemployment has shot up in the past decade. He may also be one of the million-plus paper-pushing civil servants, earning a pittance to while away each day in an undemanding job. This at least allows him to slip away from work early each afternoon to borrow his cousin's taxi for a few hours to bring in some much-needed supplementary income. His wife remains at home cooking, looking after the three or more children, and swapping visits with his mother, her mother and various other family members.

The official site of the Egyptian Tourist Authority (www.egypt.travel) has magazine-type features, news and a huge range of resources and links, while the State Information Service (www.sis.gov.eg) provides information on everything from geography to the economy.

The Country Scene

Life in rural Egypt is undergoing a transformation. Just over half the country's population lives there, creating some of the most densely populated agricultural land in the world. What little land remains is divided into small plots (averaging just 0.6 hectares), which don't even support a medium-sized family. Just under one third of Egyptians make their living off the land. Returns are small – agriculture accounts for just 14% of Egypt's GDP. The small size of plots prevents mechanisation and improved yields. As a result, farmers increasingly rely on animal husbandry or look for other ways of surviving. The farmer you see working his field may spend his afternoons working as a labourer or selling cigarettes from a homemade kiosk to make ends meet.

Egypt has a strong national team of swimmers and tennis players; tennis being ex-president Mubarak's favourite sport.

The countryside remains the repository of traditional culture and values. Large families are still the norm, particularly in Upper Egypt, and extended families still live together. High rates of female illiteracy are standard. All of this is gradually changing.

Sport

Egypt is football-obsessed. The country hosts the Egyptian Premier League, which is regarded as one of the top 20 most competitive leagues in the world. The two most popular clubs are Ahly and Zamalek; both are located in Cairo and both inspire fervent loyalty in their fans. The Egyptian national team hasn't qualified for the FIFA World Cup since 1990 (and its 2009 loss to Algeria in a qualifier match sparked passionate protests and riots in Egypt and abroad). But it has won the African Nations Cup six times, including in 2008.

Multiple Identities

Most Egyptians will proudly tell you that they are descendants of the ancient Egyptians and, while there is a strand of truth in this, any Pharaonic blood still flowing in modern veins has been seriously diluted. The country has weathered invasions of Libyans, Persians, Greeks, Romans and, most significantly, the 4000 Arab horsemen who invaded in AD 640. In the centuries following the Arab conquest, there was significant Arab migration and intermarriage with the indigenous population. The Mamluks, rulers of Egypt between the 13th and 16th centuries, were of Turkish and Circassian origins, and then there were the Ottoman Turks, rulers and occupiers from 1517 until the latter years of the 18th century.

THE MOULID

A cross between a funfair and a religious festival, a *moulid* celebrates the birthday of a local saint or holy person – typically Muslim, but in Egypt, there are Coptic *moulid*s too. They are often a colourful riot of celebrations attended by hundreds of thousands of people. Visitors from out of town set up camp in the streets, close to the saint's tomb, where children's rides, sideshows and food stalls are erected. In the midst of the chaos, barbers perform mass circumcisions; snake charmers induce cobras out of baskets; and children are presented at the shrine to be blessed and the sick to be cured.

*Tartour*s (cone-shaped hats) and *fanous* (lanterns) are made and sold to passers-by and in the evenings local Sufi orders usually hold hypnotic *zikr*s (literally 'remembrance') in colourful tents. In a *zikr* the *mugzzabin* (Sufi followers who participate in *zikr*s) stand in straight lines and sway from side to side to rhythmic clapping that gradually increases in intensity over a period of hours. Other *zikr*s are formidable endurance tests where troupes of musicians perform for hours in the company of ecstatic dancers.

Most *moulid*s last for about a week, with one night, the *leila kebira* (big night), being the rowdiest. Much of the infrastructure is provided by 'professional' *mawladiyya*, or *moulid* people, who spend their lives going from one *moulid* to another.

For visitors, the hardest part about attending a *moulid* is ascertaining dates. Events are tied to either the Islamic or Gregorian calendars and dates can be different each year. The country's biggest *moulid*, for al-Sayyed al-Badawi, in Tanta, does have a fixed date, in the last week of October. Cairo hosts several *moulid*s, and there are a number of smaller *moulid*s in the area around Luxor.

If you do attend the festivities, be prepared for immense crowds (hold on to your valuables) and incredible noise. These are typically family events, so crowds are usually mixed, but women should always be escorted by a male.

Desert Tribes

Beside the Egyptians of the Nile Valley, there is a handful of separate indigenous groups with ancient roots. The ancestors of Egypt's Bedouins are believed to have migrated from the Arabian Peninsula, before settling the Western and Eastern Deserts and Sinai. But their nomadic way of life is under threat as the interests of the rest of the country increasingly intrude on their once-isolated domains.

In the Western Desert, particularly in and around Siwa Oasis, are a small number of Berbers who have retained much of their own identity. They are quite easily distinguished from other Egyptians by the dress of the women, who usually don the *meliyya* (head-to-toe garment with slits for the eyes). Although many speak Arabic, they have preserved their own native tongues.

People of the South

In the south, the tall, dark-skinned Nubians originate from Nubia, the region between Aswan in southern Egypt and Khartoum in Sudan. Their homeland almost completely disappeared in the 1970s when the High Dam created Lake Nasser. Some of Egypt's Nubians emigrated to Cairo, but the majority were resettled in towns and villages between Edfu and Aswan. Their cultural identity has survived, however, and whether in the way they decorate their homes or play their music, Nubians are recognisably distinct from other Egyptians.

Religion

Some 90% of Egypt's population is Muslim. Islam prevails in Egyptian life at a low-key, almost unconscious level, and yet almost all men heed the amplified call of the muezzin (mosque official) each Friday noon, when the crowds from the mosques block streets and footpaths. The vast majority of the 10% of Egypt that isn't Muslim is Coptic Christian. The two communities have a mixed history, with periodic flare-ups. One of the most inspiring images of the 2011 Tahrir protests was the sight of Muslims protecting Christians while they prayed, and vice versa. The Muslim Brotherhood government under President Morsi was criticised for inciting violence towards Copts and for not stepping in to help when communities or churches were attacked.

One of the most influential Islamic authorities in Egypt is the Grand Sheikh of Al-Azhar, a position appointed by the Egyptian president and currently held by Sheikh Ahmed al-Tayeb. It is his role to define the official Egyptian Islamic line on any particular matter, from organ donations to heavy-metal music.

Islam

Islam, the predominant religion of Egypt, shares its roots with Judaism and Christianity. Adam, Abraham (Ibrahim), Noah and Moses are all prophets in Islam; Jesus is recognised as a prophet, but not the son of God. Muslim teachings correspond closely to the Torah (the foundation book of Judaism) and the Christian Gospels. The essence of Islam is the Quran, which Muslims believe is the last and truest message from God, delivered by the Archangel Gabriel to the Prophet Mohammed.

The Life of Mohammed

Islam was founded in the early 7th century by Mohammed, who was born around AD 570 in Mecca. Mohammed is said to have received his first divine message at about the age of 40. The revelations continued for the rest of his life and were transcribed to become the holy Quran. To this day not one dot of the Quran has been changed, making it, Muslims believe, the direct word of God.

Mohammed started preaching in 613, three years after the first revelation, but could only attract a few dozen followers. Having attacked the ways of Meccan life, especially the worship of a wealth of idols, he made many enemies. In 622 he and his followers retreated to Medina, an oasis town some 360km from Mecca. This Hejira, or migration, marks the start

The Coptic church was influential in shaping the rituals of the early Christian church. Some, including the hidden altar and use of incense, were adapted from existing pagan practices.

of the Muslim calendar. Mohammed died in 632 but the new religion continued its rapid spread, reaching all of Arabia by 634 and Egypt in 642.

…men in Egypt …eived the vote … 1956. Six years later, Hakmet abu Zeid became the first woman in the Egyptian cabinet.

Pillars of Islam

Islam means 'submission' and this principle is visible in the daily life of Muslims. The faith is expressed by observance of the five 'pillars of Islam', which oblige Muslims to:

- Publicly declare that 'there is no god but God, and Mohammed is His Prophet'.
- Pray five times a day: at sunrise, noon, mid-afternoon, sunset and night.
- Give *zakat* (alms) for the propagation of Islam and to help the needy.
- Fast during daylight hours during the month of Ramadan.
- Complete the hajj (the pilgrimage to Mecca).

The first pillar is accomplished through prayer, which is the second pillar and an essential part of the daily life of a believer. Five times a day the muezzins sing out the call to prayer through speakers on top of the minarets. It is perfectly permissible to pray at home or elsewhere; only the noon prayer on Friday is meant to be conducted in the mosque. Women typically pray at home; when they go to the mosque, there is a separate section for them.

The fourth pillar, *sawm* (fasting), is done during the ninth month of the Muslim calendar, Ramadan, when all believers fast during the day. Pious Muslims do not allow anything to pass their lips in daylight hours. Although many Muslims do not follow the injunctions to the letter, most conform to some extent. The impact of the fasting is often lessened by a shift in waking hours (aided by the cancellation of daylight saving time in Egypt when necessary), and people tend to sleep late if they can, or nap in the afternoon. They then live much of their social life until sunrise.

Far from being a month of austerity, Ramadan is a joyous time, with great camaraderie among fellow fasters. The evening meal during Ramadan, called *iftar* (breaking the fast), is always a celebration. In some parts of town, tables are laid out in the street as charitable acts by the wealthy to provide food for the less fortunate. Evenings are imbued with a party atmosphere and there's plenty of street entertainment, often until sunrise.

Christianity

The majority of Egyptian Christians are known as Copts. The term is the Western form of the Arabic *qibt,* derived from the Greek *aegyptios* (Egyptian), which in turn comes from the ancient Egyptian language.

Although Christianity did not become the official religion of Egypt until the 4th century, Egypt was one of the first countries to embrace the new faith. St Mark, companion of the apostles Paul and Peter, is said to have begun preaching Christianity in Egypt around AD 45. From the closure of the pagan temples to the arrival of Islam, Christianity was the predominant religion in Egypt.

The Monophysite Controversy

Egyptian Christians split from the Orthodox Church of the Eastern (or Byzantine) Empire, of which Egypt was then a part, after the main body of the church described Christ as both human and divine. Dioscurus, the patriarch of Alexandria, refused to accept this description, and embraced the theory that Christ is totally absorbed by his divinity and that it is blasphemous to consider him human.

The Coptic Church is ruled by a patriarch (presently Pope Shenouda III), other members of the religious hierarchy and an ecclesiastical council of laypeople. It has a long history of monasticism and in fact the first Christian monks, St Anthony and St Pachomius, were Copts.

The Coptic language, which has its origins in Egyptian hieroglyphs and ancient Greek, is still used in religious ceremonies, sometimes in conjunction with Arabic for the benefit of the congregation. Today the Coptic language is based on the Greek alphabet with an additional seven characters taken from hieroglyphs.

The Copts

The Copts have long provided something of an educated elite in Egypt, filling many important government and bureaucratic posts. They're perceived as being an economically powerful minority, and a good number of Copts are wealthy and influential. With that said, there are also a lot of Copts at the very bottom of the heap: the *zabbalin,* the garbage-pickers of Cairo, who sort through much of the city's rubbish, have always been Copts.

The Copts have suffered as a result of recent upheavals. Many churches and Coptic homes and businesses have been destroyed in the past few years and, faced with a lack of protection, many Copts have chosen to emigrate.

On their ret[illegible] from a wome[illegible] suffrage confe[illegible] ence in Rome in 1923, pioneer Arab feminists Huda Sharawi and Saiza Nabarawi threw away their *abeyyas* at Ramses Station in Cairo. Many in the crowd of women who had come to welcome them home followed suit.

Other Denominations

Other Christian denominations are represented in Egypt, each by a few thousand adherents. In total, there are about one million members of other Christian groups. Among Catholics, apart from Roman Catholics of the Latin rite, the whole gamut of the fragmented Middle Eastern rites is represented, including the Armenian, Syrian, Chaldean, Maronite and Melkite rites. The Anglican communion comes under the Episcopal Church in Jerusalem. The Armenian Apostolic Church has around 10,000 members, and the Greek Orthodox Church is based in Alexandria.

Women in Egypt

Some of the biggest misunderstandings between Egyptians and Westerners occur over the issue of women. Half-truths and stereotypes exist on both sides: many Westerners assume all Egyptian women are repressed victims, while many Egyptians see Western women as sex-obsessed and immoral.

For many Egyptians of both genders, the role of a woman is specifically defined: she is the mother and the matron of the household. The man is the provider. But there are thousands of middle- and upper-middle-class professional women in Egypt who, like their counterparts in the West, juggle work and family responsibilities. Among the working classes, where adherence to tradition is theoretically strongest, it's certainly the ideal for women to concentrate on home and family, but economic reality means that millions of women are forced to work at the same time as being responsible for all domestic chores.

The issue of sex is big, naturally. Premarital sex (or any sex outside marriage) is taboo in Egypt. But marriage is an expensive business, so men must often put it off until well into their 30s. This leads to a frustration that can often seem palpable in the streets. For women the issue is potentially far more serious. Women are typically expected to be virgins when they marry and a family's reputation can still rest on this point. Thus the social restrictions placed on young women are meant to protect her for marriage.

This has long had the effect of dampening discussions of sexual abuse and harassment. But in 2008, a woman for the first time sued a man who had attacked her in the street, and the perpetrator was sentenced to jail. Women were targeted by gangs during some of the protests in Tahrir Square and there were many incidents of harrassment and rape. In June 2014, newly elected President al-Sisi pushed the issue into the limelight when he went to visit a rape victim in hospital to apologise on behalf of the nation. As with so many aspects of Egyptian life since the revolution, the role of women is in flux.

The Arts

While Egyptian culture has not had much impact in the West, many Egyptian actors and musicians are revered cultural icons all over the Arab world. The 2011 revolution spawned a cultural outpouring like no other, and several visual artists have been successful in the global art market. Egypt's cultural identity and the right of all Egyptians to be active participants in the cultural process is one of the big achievements of the 2011 revolution.

Literature

Naguib Mahfouz, who won a Nobel Prize for his work, was for many years just about the only Egyptian writer frequently read in the West. Things are changing. In the last decade several new writers have tried to define a new Egyptian novelistic style, striving for a fresh language and style. Many of these are now being translated into English.

20th-Century Writing

Awarded the Nobel Prize for Literature in 1988, Naguib Mahfouz was one of the most important 20th-century writers of Arabic literature. Born in 1911 in Cairo's Islamic quarter, Mahfouz began writing when he was 17 and published over 50 novels and 350 short stories, as well as movie scripts, plays and journalism. His first efforts were influenced by the European greats, but over the course of his career he developed a voice that was uniquely Egyptian, and drew its inspiration from the talk in the coffeehouses and the dialect of Cairo's streets. In 1994 he was the victim of a knife attack that left him partially paralysed. The attack was a response to a book Mahfouz had written, which was a thinly disguised allegory of the life of the great religious leaders including Prophet Mohammed. Mahfouz died in 2006 after falling and sustaining a head injury.

Beyond Mahfouz

On the strength of what's available in English, it's easy to view Egyptian literature as beginning and ending with Mahfouz, but other respected writers include Taha Hussein, a blind author and intellectual who spent much of his life in trouble with whichever establishment happened to be in power; the Alexandrian playwright Tawfiq al-Hakim; and Yousef Idris, a writer of powerful short stories.

Egypt's women writers are also enjoying international success. Feminist and activist Nawal al-Saadawi's fictional work *Woman at Point Zero* has been translated into 28 languages. An outspoken critic on behalf of women, she is marginalised at home – her nonfiction book *The Hidden Face of Eve,* which criticises the role of women in the Arab world, is banned in Egypt. Those interested in learning more about her fascinating and inspirational life should read her autobiography *Walking Through Fire,* which was published in 2002.

Born in Cairo, Ahdaf Soueif writes in English as well as Arabic, but most of her work has yet to appear in Arabic. Her most successful novel, *The Map of Love*, set in Egypt, was short-listed for the Booker prize, and her other novels are *Aisha, Sandpiper* and *In the Eye of the Sun.* In early 2012 she published her memoir: *Cairo: My City, Our Revolution.*

Egyptian Classics

➡ *Beer in the Snooker Club* by Waguih Ghali is a fantastic novel of youthful angst set against a backdrop of 1950s revolutionary Egypt and literary London. It's the Egyptian *Catcher in the Rye.*

➡ *The Cairo Trilogy* by Naguib Mahfouz is usually considered Mahfouz' masterpiece; this generational saga of family life is rich in colour and detail, and has earned comparisons with Dickens and Zola.

➡ *Love in Exile* and *Sunset Oasis* by Bahaa Taher, one of the most respected living writers in the Arab world, have both won awards.

➡ *The Harafish* by Naguib Mahfouz would be our desert-island choice if we were allowed only one work by Mahfouz. This is written in an episodic, almost folkloric style that owes much to the tradition of *The Thousand and One Nights.*

➡ *Proud Beggars, The Colours of Infamy* and *The Jokers* by Albert Cossery were all recently translated and published following the author's death in 2008. His novels were written in French, and have a cult following among Egyptophiles.

➡ *Zayni Barakat* by Gamal al-Ghitani is a drama set in Cairo during the waning years of the Mamluk era. It was made into an extremely successful local TV drama in the early 1990s.

Egyptian Contemporary Novels

As well known globally as Naguib Mahfouz, contemporary dentist-turned-novelist Alaa Al-Aswany writes about Egyptians, poverty and class differences. His 2002 blockbuster *The Yacoubian Building* is a bleak but compelling snapshot of contemporary Cairo seen through the stories of the occupants of a Downtown building. The world's biggest-selling novel in Arabic, it is reminiscent (though not at all derivative) of the novels of Rohinton Mistry.

Author Al-Aswa[ny] *(The Yacou[bian] Building)* is a p[ro]fessional denti[st] whose first office was located in the real-life Yacoubian Building, at 34 Sharia Talaat Harb in Downtown Cairo.

A NEW GENERATION OF AUTHORS

➡ Mansoura Ez-Eldin – This journalist, activist and writer was a voice of the 2011 revolution and her novel *Maryam's Maze* is considered a masterpiece of imagination and literary form.

➡ Khaled Al Khamissi (www.khaledalkhamissi.com) – His wonderful novel *Taxi* consists of essays of the conversations with Cairene taxi drivers, highlighting the Egyptian passion and sense of humor. His second novel is *Noah's Ark*.

➡ Muhammad Aladdin (http://alaaeldin.blogspot.com) – This young novelist and activist is very much part of the new literary scene in Cairo, and his second novel, *The Gospel According to Adam*, set in Midan Tahrir, examines a society that has lost all certainties. His latest novel, *A Well-Trained Stray*, was published in Arabic in 2014.

➡ Ahmed Alaidy – The author of *Being Abbas El Abd* writes with profound cynicism and humour about the despair of Egypt's youth.

➡ Ibrahim Abdel Meguid – *No One Sleeps in Alexandria* is an antidote to the mythical Alexandria of Lawrence Durrell. The first book in a trilogy, it portrays the city in the same period as the Quartet but as viewed by two poor Egyptians. His latest novel, the last in the trilogy, is *Clouds over Alexandria*.

➡ Miral al-Tahawy – *The Tent* is a bleak but beautiful tale of the slow descent into madness of a crippled Bedouin girl.

➡ Nael El Toukhy – His latest novel, *Women of the Karentina* (2013), describing an imaginary underworld in Alexandria, contains a rich mix of humour and misery.

The story is an elaborate soap opera, but is remarkable for the way it depicts Egypt towards the end of Mubarak's rule and for introducing archetypes that hadn't previously been captured in Arabic literature. Al-Aswany's subsequent writing – *Chicago,* a novella, and *Friendly Fire,* a collection of short stories – both have a strong focus on contemporary Egypt. His most recent books, *The Automobile Club of Egypt* and *The Republic As If,* have not yet been translated into English.

Salwa Bakr tackles taboo subjects such as sexual prejudice and social inequality. Her work includes the novels *The Golden Chariot* and the excellent *The Man from Bashmour*.

One of the most promising of a very vibrant new generation of writers is Mansoura Ez-Eldin, whose novel *Maryam's Maze* is the wonderfully written story of a woman trying to find her way in the confusion all around her.

…ther-and-… team of …reenwriter …is Hamed and …rector Marwan Hamed adapted Alaa Al-Aswany's bestselling *The Yacoubian Building* for the screen. The budget of over US$3 million was the largest ever seen in Egypt.

Egypt in Western Novels

The Alexandria Quartet by Lawrence Durrell is essential reading perhaps, but to visit Alexandria looking for the city of the *Quartet* is a bit like heading to London hoping to run into Mary Poppins.

Baby Love by Louisa Young is a smart, hip novel that shimmies between Shepherd's Bush in London and the West Bank of Luxor, as a former belly dancer, now single mother, skirts romance and a violent past.

City of Gold by Len Deighton is a thriller set in wartime Cairo, elevated by solid research. The period detail is fantastic and brings the city to life.

Death on the Nile by Agatha Christie draws on Christie's experiences of a winter in Upper Egypt. An absolute must if you're booked on a cruise.

Although the well-known film of the same name bears little resemblance to the novel, Michael Ondaatje's *The English Patient* – a story of love, desert and destiny in WWII – remains a beautifully written, poetic novel.

Egypt during the war serves as the setting for the trials and traumas of a despicable bunch of expats in *The Levant Trilogy* by Olivia Manning. It has some fabulous descriptions of life in Cairo during WWII, and was filmed by the BBC as *Fortunes of War* starring Kenneth Branagh and Emma Thompson.

Moon Tiger by Penelope Lively is an award-winning romance, very moving in parts, with events that occurred in Cairo during WWII at its heart.

The Photographer's Wife by Robert Sole is one of three historical romances by this French journalist set in late-19th-century Egypt. They're slow-going but worth it for the fine period detail and emotive stories.

Cinema

In the halcyon years of the 1940s and 1950s, Cairo's film studios turned out more than 100 movies annually, filling cinemas throughout the Arab world with charming musicals that are still classics of regional cinema. Until recently Cairo remained a major player in the film industry, but only about 20 films are made each year. The chief reason for the decline, according to the producers, was excessive government taxation and restrictive censorship. Asked what sort of things are censored, one film industry figure replied, 'Sex, politics, religion – that's all'. However, at least one Cairo film critic has suggested that another reason for the demise of local film is that so much of what is made is of poor quality. The ingredients of the typical Egyptian film are shallow plot lines, farcical slapstick humour, over-the-top acting and perhaps a little belly dancing.

One Egyptian director who consistently stood apart from the mainstream was Youssef Chahine (1926–2008). He directed over 35 films, has been called Egypt's Fellini and was honoured at Cannes in 1997 with a lifetime achievement award. His later and more well-known works are

1999's *Al-Akhar* (The Other), 1997's *Al-Masir* (Destiny) and 1994's *Al-Muhagir* (The Emigrant). Others to look out for are *Al-Widaa Bonaparte* (Adieu Bonaparte), a historical drama about the French occupation and *Iskandariyya Ley?* (Alexandria Why?), an autobiographical meditation on the city of Chahine's birth.

Since the 2011 revolution a new wave of filmmakers has entered the Egyptian cinema scene and are taking Egyptian cinema into exciting and unchartered territory. In early 2014 Zawya, a new cinema in downtown Cairo, opened, showing art-house movies and work by young Egyptian filmmakers.

Music

Forty years after her death, the 'Star of the Orient', Umm Kolthum, still provokes huge emotion in Egypt. But the new kids on the block are making a loud noise. The latest sound heard in Cairo is *mahraganat*, created by artists from some of the poorest suburbs and slums, who are shouting about their disenchantment with their situation.

Classical

Classical Arabic music peaked in the 1940s and '50s. These were the golden days of a rushing tide of nationalism and then, later, of Nasser's rule when Cairo was the virile heart of the Arab-speaking world. Its singers were icons and, through radio, their impassioned words captured and inflamed the spirits of listeners from Algiers to Baghdad.

Chief among them was Umm Kolthum, the most famous Arab singer of the 20th century. Her protracted love songs and *qasa'id* (long poems) were the very expression of the Arab world's collective identity. Egypt's love affair with Umm Kolthum was such that on the afternoon of the first Thursday of each month, streets would become deserted as the whole country sat beside a radio to listen to her regular live-broadcast performances. She had her male counterparts in Abdel Halim Hafez and Farid al-Attrache, but they never attracted anything like the devotion accorded

I Loved You Your Voice by Selim Nassib is a delightful historical novel based on the romantic obsession of the Egyptian poet and lyricist Ahmad Rami for singer Umm Kolthum. He writes despairing poems that become the lyrics she sings. Their relationship is never consummated and as she becomes famous, he becomes increasingly pathetic.

NEW EGYPTIAN CINEMA

Several new Egyptian films have won international awards, although some are banned in Egypt for being critical of the new regime.

- Jehane Noujaim's *The Square* was shortlisted for the Best Documentary Award at the 2014 Oscars. It was shown in cinemas around the world but was banned in Egypt. This brilliant film documents events in Tahrir from the first 18 days of the revolution until President Morsi's exit.
- The master filmmaker Mohamed Khan has made a comeback with *Fatat El-Masnaa* (Factory Girl), a film about women seeking independence in a society that barely allows them to breathe.
- In *Harag W' Marag* (Chaos, Order) Mohamed Khan's daughter Nadine Khan tells a story of two tough youths vying for a girl in a poor but lively and exotic-looking Cairo neighborhood.
- *Rags and Tatters* by Ahmad Abdalla, another brilliant award-winning film, is an honest take on the Egyptian revolution, and unusual, as it is for the most part silent.
- *Villa 69*, director Ayten Amin's debut film, shows how Hussein (Khaled Abul-Naga), a solitary man in his 50s who lives alone in a beautiful but dilapidated villa, is forced to deal with reality when his sister and her grandson come to stay.
- *Coming Forth By Day*, the debut feature film by writer-director Hala Lotfy, shows a small family being worn down by the indignities of everyday life: sickness, money problems, rejection, restlessness, frustration.

'As-Sitt' (the Lady). She retired after a concert in 1972. When she died three years later, millions of grieving Egyptians poured onto the streets of Cairo. The Umm Kolthum Museum opened in Cairo in 2002.

…he interested …ontemporary …rt should visit the Mashrabia and Townhouse galleries in Cairo.

Popular

Ahmed Adawiyya did for Arabic music what punk did to popular music in the West. Throwing out traditional melodies and melodramas, his backstreet, streetwise and, to some, politically subversive songs captured the spirit of the times and dominated popular culture throughout the 1970s. He set the blueprint for a new kind of music known as *al-jeel* (the generation), characterised by a clattering, hand-clapping rhythm overlaid with synthesised twirling and a catchy, repetitive vocal. This evolved into a more Western-style pop, helmed by Amr Diab, who is often described as the Arab world's Ricky Martin.

Adawiyya's legacy also spawned something called *shaabi* (from the word for popular), much cruder than *al-jeel*, and often with satirical or politically provocative lyrics. The acceptable face of *shaabi* is TV-friendly Hakim, whose albums regularly sell around the million mark. In 2010 *shaabi* singer Mohamed Mounir brought out a song *Ezay?* (How?), that was banned for being too political; he brought it out again with the backdrop of the people in Midan Tahrir during the 2011 revolution.

The uprisings of the revolutionary youth in Cairo and elsewhere was fuelled by rap and hip-hop music, the so-called *shebabi* (youth) music. The sound of Cairo now is *mahraganat*, a relentless mix of drumbeats and auto-tuned rap that started in Cairo's slums but has been likened to grime music. The artists often record at home, and spread their music via the internet. Diesel, AKA Mohamed Saber, is one of *mahraganat's* most innovative artists, while Sadat, AKA al-Sadat Abdelaziz, is its biggest star. The music expresses the reality of young people, using their slang to express their struggle. They sing about revolution, drugs and sexual harassment, and mainly perform live in street weddings.

Visual Arts

Visual artists have been documenting the people's uprising, first in Midan Tahrir, and then across galleries in Cairo. The artist and musician Ahmed Bassiouny, killed on the third day of the uprising against Mubarak, had his work shown posthumously at the 2011 Venice Biennale. The

SOUNDTRACK OF THE REVOLUTION

The following songs and bands form part of the soundtrack of the 2011 revolution. Some are available internationally; all are on YouTube.

➡ *Irhal* (Leave) by Ramy Essam – This song made Ramy Essam one of the stars of the revolution; he sang it on stage on 11 February, when it was announced that Mubarak had gone.

➡ *Eid Fi Eid* (Hand in Hand) by The Arabian Knightz – One of the first Egyptian rap bands to release music about the revolution, they filmed a video for their track in Midan Tahrir.

➡ *Rebel* by The Arabian Knightz, featuring Lauryn Hill – This track was recorded during the first days of the revolution.

➡ *Thawra* by Rayess Bek – Lebanese band sings about and for the revolution with a background of the slogan '*as-shab yurid thawra*' ('the people want revolution') chanted in Midan Tahrir.

➡ *Sout el Hurriya* (Voice of Freedom) by Amir Eid, Hany Adel, Hawary and Sherif – The YouTube clip shows the song sung by people in Midan Tahrir.

CONTEMPORARY EGYPTIAN ARTISTS

- Chant Avedissian (www.chantavedissian.com) – Armenian-Egyptian artist whose stencils of iconic celebrities from the past have become very much in demand with Middle Eastern art collectors.
- Youssef Nabil (www.youssefnabil.com) – Egyptian artist living in New York who makes hand-coloured gelatin silver prints of photographs of Egyptian and international celebrities.
- Ghada Amer (www.ghadaamer.com) – Egyptian artist who embroiders on abstract canvases that deal with female sexuality and eroticism.
- Lara Baladi – Egyptian-Lebanese multimedia artist who works with personal and collective memory.
- Mohamed Abla (www.ablamuseum.com) – His work on social injustice was not exhibited in Egypt during the Mubarak years.
- Wael Shawky – One of the most powerful and poignant voices coming out of Egypt, Wael Shawky reinterprets faith, myth and history through video installations.

art scene is energetic and has enjoyed a chaotic freedom since 2011, with many other Egyptian artists now enjoying international acclaim.

With the outbreak of revolution, graffiti artists have made the streets their canvas. As an Egyptian graffiti artist said in an interview: 'Creating graffiti involves taking ownership of the streets, just like we did during the uprising. And so of course it's political, and illegal.' Now, in post-revolution Cairo, street art spreads rapidly and is often painted over almost as fast. Many graffiti artists now get commissions from art galleries. Ganzeer, possibly Egypt's most famous street artist, was briefly arrested in May 2011, months after the revolution, over a poster criticising the military's repression of freedom. Another excellent graffiti artist is Keizer (check his Facebook page). The Cairo street art map on Google maps hasn't been updated for a while, but for more information on graffiti in Egypt check out the blog: http://suzeeinthecity.wordpress.com

One of Egypt's most famous belly dancers, Soheir el-Babli, renounced show business and adopted the Islamic veil in 1993, setting off a wave of religiously motivated resignations among the country's belly-dance artists.

Belly Dancing

Tomb paintings in Egypt prove that the tradition of formalised dancing goes back as far as the pharaohs. During medieval times the *ghawazee,* a cast of dancers, travelled with storytellers and poets and performed publicly. In the 19th century the Muslim authorities were outraged that Muslim women were performing for 'infidel' men on their Grand Tour, and dancers were banished from Cairo to Esna. Belly dancing began to gain credibility and popularity in Egypt with the advent of cinema, which imbued belly dancing with glamour and made household names of a handful of dancers.

Since the early 1990s Islamist conservatives have patrolled weddings in poor areas of Cairo and forcibly prevented women from dancing or singing, cutting off a vital source of income for lower-echelon performers. At the same time, a number of high-profile entertainers donned the veil and retired, denouncing their former profession as sinful. Now few Egyptian belly dancers perform in public, and their place has been taken by foreigners mainly dancing for tourists. The future for Egyptian belly dancing looks uncertain.

Egyptian Cuisine: Bi'l Hana wa-Shifa!

***Bi'l hana wa-shifa* means bon appétit, or more literally 'with health and gratification'! Compared to the highly regarded regional cuisines of Lebanon, Turkey and Iran, Egyptian food might seem to lack refinement and diversity. But the food here is good, fresh, honest peasant fare that packs an occasional sensational punch. Pulses feature large on the menu, and come cooked in a stew (for breakfast, lunch or dinner), as a soup or fried in patties (*ta'amiyya*). Egyptians love meat, if they can afford it, and lamb and chicken are always available.**

Staples & Specialities

Egyptian meals typically centre on stews and vegetables, with meat increasingly becoming a luxury. There's plenty of coastline to reel in the fruits of the Mediterranean and Red Seas, although much fish also comes from the Nile. Street food is what most Egyptians can afford, and they happily wait in line at the best *koshari* (heady mix of macaroni, rice, lentils, fried onions and a spicy tomato sauce) eateries or stalls selling hot and crispy *ta'amiyya* (Egyptian name for felafel), the ubiquitous Middle Eastern vegetarian staple. Egyptians love to eat lots, so there is always room for something sweet.

DIY Food

http://egyptian-food.org/ and www.foodofegypt.com: loads of recipes for tasty Egyptian dishes

www.foodby-country.com: a basic overview of Egyptian food and recipes

Mezze

Largely vegetable-based and always bursting with colour and flavour, mezze (a selection of hot and cold starters) aren't strictly Egyptian, as many standards hail from the Levant or Turkey. But they have been customised here in a more limited and economical form. They're the perfect start to any meal, and it's usually perfectly acceptable for diners to order an entire meal from the mezze list and forego the mains.

Bread

A'aish (bread) is the most important staple of the national diet. *A'aish baladi*, the traditional bread, is made from a combination of plain and

TRAVEL YOUR TASTEBUDS

- *Fatta* – Rice and bread soaked in a garlicky-vinegary sauce with lamb or chicken, then oven cooked in a *tagen* (clay pot). It's very heavy; after eating retire to a chaise longue.
- *Mahshi kurumb* – These rice- and meat-stuffed cabbage leaves are decadently delightful when correctly cooked with plenty of dill and *samna* (clarified butter).
- *Molokhiyya* – A slightly slippery but delicious soup made from jute leaves, served with rabbit (or chicken) and plenty of garlic.
- *Hamam mahshi* – Roast pigeon stuffed with *fireek* (green wheat) and rice. This dish is served at all traditional restaurants and can be fiddly to eat; beware the plentiful little bones.

A TABLE OF MEZZE

- Hummus – A paste of mashed chickpeas with lemon, garlic and tahini
- Tahini – A paste of sesame seeds with oil, garlic and lemon, served with pita bread or grilled fish.
- *Baba ghanoog* – A puree of grilled aubergines with garlic and oil.
- *Wara ainab* – Vine leaves stuffed with rice, herbs and meat, cooked in a broth.
- *Bessara* – Cold broad-bean puree.
- *Kibbeh* – Fried patty of bulgur wheat stuffed with minced lamb and pine nuts.
- *Sambusas* – Cheese- or meat-filled mini pies.
- *Torshi* – Crunchy pickled cucumbers, carrots and turnips.

wholemeal flour with sufficient leavening to form a pocket and soft crust, and is cooked over an open flame. Locals use it in lieu of cutlery to scoop up dips, and rip it into pieces to wrap around morsels of meat. *A'aish shammy*, a bigger version made with plain white flour only, is the usual wrapping for *ta'amiyya*. In the countryside, the women bake a round leavened bread with three handles – the same shape in which the ancient Egyptians made bread. Bakeries also sell a sweetish white Western-style roll, called *kaiser*, often served in restaurants or hotels for breakfast.

The New Book of Middle Eastern Food (1968) by Egyptian-born Claudia Roden brought the cuisines of the region to the attention of Western cooks. It's still an essential reference, now updated and expanded, as fascinating for its cultural insights as for its great recipes.

Salads

Simplicity is the key to Egyptian salads, which are eaten as a mezze or as an accompaniment to a meat or fish main. The standard *salata baladi* of chopped tomatoes, cucumber, onion and pepper sometimes gets a kick from peppery arugula. The Middle East's delicious and healthy signature salad, tabbouleh (bulgur wheat, parsley and tomato, with a sprinkling of sesame seeds, lemon and garlic), is also common. Seasonal vegetables, such as beetroot or carrots, are often boiled and served cold with a tangy oil-and-lemon dressing.

Vegetables & Soups

The archetypal Egyptian veg is *molokhiyya*, a leafy green of the jute plant, that was known to be part of the pharaohs' diet. It has a similar sticky texture to okra, and Egyptians prepare it as a slimy and surprisingly sexy soup with a bright, nourishing flavour. Traditionally served as an accompaniment to rabbit, it inspires an almost religious devotion among locals. The most popular soup is *sharbat ads* (lentil soup), made with red split lentils and served with cumin and wedges of lemon. *Fuul nabed* (broad-bean soup) is also common.

Meats

Kofta and kebab are two of the most popular meat dishes in Egypt. *Kofta*, spiced minced lamb or beef peppered with spices and shaped into balls, is skewered and grilled. It is the signature element of the Egyptian favourite *daoud basha,* meatballs cooked with pine nuts and tomato sauce in a *tagen* (clay pot). Kebab is skewered and flame-grilled chunks of meat, normally lamb (the chicken equivalent is called *shish tawooq*). The meat usually comes on a bed of *baqdounis* (parsley), and you eat it with bread, salad and tahini.

Firekh (chicken) roasted on a spit is common, and in restaurants is typically ordered by the half. *Hamam* (pigeon) is also extremely popular, and is eaten stuffed and roasted, grilled or as a *tagen* with onions, tomatoes and rice.

P PICKS

➜ Kadoura (p323; Alexandria) Some of the best seafood in the country, especially when the sea has been bountiful.

➜ Farahat (p102; Cairo) Legendary stuffed, roasted pigeon joint, wedged in an alley.

➜ Sofra (p222; Luxor) Original Egyptian decor and a cool roof terrace complement the wonderful Egyptian food and good choice of fresh juices at this charming house restaurant.

➜ 1902 Restaurant (p251; Aswan) The grand dining experience of the Sofitel Cataract Hotel has old-world charm, style and some very fine French- and Italian-inspired cuisine. Somewhere to dress up for.

➜ Citadel View (p102; Cairo) Grand setting overlooking the city, with an eclectic menu featuring rarely seen Egyptian dishes.

Ancient Egyptians believed that when Osiris was chopped into pieces by his brother Seth, his wife Isis found the pieces strewn all over Egypt. She found all but one: his penis had been swallowed by a catfish. Even today some Egyptians are reluctant to eat catfish.

Fish & Seafood

When in Alexandria, along the Red Sea and in Sinai, you'll undoubtedly join the locals in falling hook, line and sinker for the marvellous array of fresh seafood on offer. Local favourites are *kalamaari* (squid), *balti* (fish that are about 15cm long, flattish and grey with a light belly), and the larger, tastier *bouri* (mullet). You'll also commonly find sea bass, seabream, red mullet, bluefish, sole and *subeit* or *gambari* (shrimp) on restaurant menus. The Red Sea is famous for its spiny lobsters, while the tilapia from Lake Nasser is a delight. The most popular ways to cook fish are to grill them over coals or fry them in olive oil.

Copts are very fond of *fesikh,* sun-dried, salted and fermented grey mullet, traditionally eaten during the Sham an-Nessim festival, a spring celebration that goes back to ancient times. The shops selling *fesikh* are recognisable by the smell; the flavour is an acquired taste.

Desserts & Sweets

The prince of local puds is *mahallabiye,* made using rice flour, milk, sugar and rose or orange water, topped with chopped pistachios and almonds. Almost as popular are *ruz bi laban* (rice pudding) and *omm ali* (layers of *fiteer* pastry with nuts and raisins, soaked in cream and milk, and baked in the oven).

Best of all are the pastries, including *kunafa,* a vermicelli-like pastry soaked in syrup, or rolled and stuffed with nuts. The most famous of all pastries is baklava, made from delicate filo drenched in syrup. Variations on baklava are flavoured with fresh nuts or stuffed with wickedly rich clotted cream *(ishta).*

Drinks

Many Egyptians may not drink alcohol in accordance with Islamic traditions, but there are plenty of non-alcoholic beverages to please the palette, from hot herbal teas, Arabic chai and coffee, to delicious seasonal fresh juices.

Water

Egyptians say that once you drink water from the Nile, you will always come back. Once you drink water from the tap, however, you might not feel like going anywhere – the stuff can be toxic. The exception is in Cairo, where, if you have a hardier constitution, you can usually drink it without injury – most locals do, even if it tastes heavily of chlorine. Bottled water is cheap and readily available in even the smallest towns.

Tea & Coffee

Drinking *shai* (tea) is the signature pastime of the country, and it is seen as strange and decidedly antisocial not to sip the tannin-laden beverage at regular intervals throughout the day. *Shai* usually comes as a strong brew of local leaves, ground fine and left in the bottom of the glass, or served 'English'-style, as a teabag plonked in a cup or glass of hot water. It is usually served sweet; to moderate this, order it *sukar khafif* – with 'a little sugar'. If you don't want any sugar, ask for *min ghayr sukar*. Far more refreshing is *shai* served with mint leaves: ask for *shai bi-na'na*. In winter locals love to drink sweet *shai bi-haleeb* (tea with milk).

Arabic coffee (ahwa), traditionally served in coffeehouses, is a thick and powerful Turkish-style brew that's served in small cups and drunk in a couple of short sips. As with tea, you have to specify how much sugar you want: *ahwa mazboot* is a moderate amount of sugar, *ahwa saada* is without sugar, and *ahwa ziyada* (extra sweet) will likely make your teeth fall out on contact. Traditionally you can tell your future from the coffee mud left at the bottom. In hotels and Western-style restaurants you are more likely to be served instant coffee (always called *neskafe*), although upmarket places increasingly serve Italian-style espressos and cappuccinos.

For younger readers, www.historyforkids.org has a great overview of food in ancient Egypt.

Before There Was Starbucks

The coffeehouse, known as ahwa (the Arabic word for coffee is now synonymous with the place in which it's drunk), is one of the great Egyptian social institutions. Traditionally ahwas have been all-male preserves, but it's now common to see young, mixed-sex groups of Egyptians in ahwas, especially in Cairo and Alexandria. The ahwa is a relaxed and unfussy place where regulars go every day to sip a glass of tea, meet friends, talk about politics or wind down for the night.

A feature of coffeehouses from Alexandria to Aswan, sheesha is a pastime that's as addictive as it is magical. Most people opt for tobacco soaked in apple juice *(tuffah)* but in trendier places it's also possible to order strawberry, melon, cherry or mixed-fruit flavours. A decorated glass pipe filled with water will be brought, hot coals will be placed in it to get it started and you will be given a disposable plastic mouthpiece to slip over the pipe's stem. The only secret to a good smoke is to take a puff every now and again to keep the coals hot. Bliss!

The delicious drink *karkadai* or hibiscus is famous for 'strengthening the blood' (lowering blood pressure).

FAST FOOD, EGYPTIAN STYLE

Once you've sampled the joys of the traditional Egyptian fast food you'll be hooked. These are the staples:

- *Fuul* – The national dish, often eaten for breakfast, is an unassuming peasant dish of slow-cooked fava beans with garlic, parsley, olive oil, lemon, salt, black pepper and cumin.
- *Ta'amiyya* (also known as felafel) – Ground broad beans and spices rolled into patties and deep fried.
- *Shwarma* – Strips of lamb or chicken sliced from a vertical spit, sizzled on a hot plate with chopped tomatoes and garnish, and then stuffed into *shammy* bread.
- *Kushari* – A vegetarian's best friend: noodles, rice, black lentils, chickpeas and fried onions, with a tangy tomato sauce. Many *kushari* shops also sell *makaroneh bi-lahm*, a baked pasta-and-lamb casserole.
- *Fiteer* – The Egyptian pizza has a thin, flaky pastry base, and is topped with salty haloumi cheese and olives, or comes sweet with jam, coconut and raisins.

Of course, it's worth mentioning that even though the smoke from sheesha is filtered through water and tastes nothing like the tobacco from cigarettes, it's smoke nevertheless, and the nicotine hit you'll get is far more intense.

ooks for Cooks

yptian Cooking: A Practical Guide by Samia Abdennour

The Complete Middle Eastern Cookbook by Tess Mallos

Apricots on the Nile: A Memoir with Recipes by Colette Rossant

Beer & Wine

For beer in Egypt just say 'Stella'. Not to be confused with the Belgian lager, it's light and perfectly drinkable. It now has sister brews in crisp, lower-alcohol Sakara Gold and the dangerous Sakara King (10%). Most locals just stick to the unfussy basic brew – it's the cheapest (around E£20 in restaurants) and, as long as it's cold, it tastes fine.

Over the past decade, the quality and choice of wine in Egypt has improved significantly. For the better wines, such as the Château des Rêves cabernet sauvignon, the grapes are imported from Lebanon. The Gianaclis whites are serviceable. These wines average between E£100 and E£150 per bottle in restaurants throughout the country. Imported wines are both harder to find and significantly more expensive.

Other Drinks

Over the hot summer months many ahwa-goers opt for cooler drinks such as chilled, crimson-hued *karkadai,* a wonderfully refreshing drink boiled up from hibiscus leaves (it's also served hot in winter). Another refresher is fresh *limoon* (lemon juice), sometimes blended with mint (*bi-nana*). In winter many prefer *sahlab,* a thick warm drink made with the starch from the orchid tuber, milk and chopped nuts; *helba,* a fenugreek tea; or *yansoon,* a digestive aniseed drink.

Juice stands are recognisable by the hanging bags of netted fruit (and carrots) that adorn their facades and are an absolute godsend on a hot summer's day. Standard juices *(asiir)* include *moz* (banana), *guafa* (guava), *limoon, manga* (mango), *bortuaan* (orange), *rumman* (pomegranate; say *min ghayr sukar* to avoid sugar overload), *farawla* (strawberry) and *asab* (sugar cane). A glass costs between E£3 and E£10 depending on the fruit used.

Where & When to Eat & Drink

Unfortunately for visitors, the best food in Egypt is invariably in private homes. If you are lucky enough to be invited to share a home-cooked meal, take up the offer (bring a box of sweets for the hostess). But you will most likely be stuffed to the point of bursting – the minute you look close to cleaning your plate, you will be showered with more food, which no amount of protesting can stop.

In restaurants, stick with Egyptian standards and you'll be well fed, if not dazzled by variety. The only place we'd recommend trying other

DOS & DON'TS

- Remember to always remove your shoes before sitting down on a rug or carpet to eat or drink tea.
- Avoid putting your left hand into a communal dish if you're eating Egyptian style – your left hand is used for, well, wiping yourself in the absence of toilet paper.
- If you need to blow your nose in a restaurant, leave the dining area and go outside or to the toilet.
- Make sure you refrain from eating, drinking or smoking in public during the daytime in the holy month of Ramadan (international hotels are an exception to this rule).
- Always sit at the dinner table next to a person of the same sex unless your host or hostess suggests otherwise.

RAMADAN NIGHTS

Ramadan is the Muslim holy month of fasting from sunrise to dusk, but it is also a month of feasting and eating well at night. *Iftar,* the evening meal prepared to break the fast, is a special feast calling for substantial soups, chicken and meat dishes, and other delicacies. It's often enjoyed communally in the street or in large, specially erected tents. Like other celebrations it is also accompanied by a flurry of baking of sweet pastries.

regional cuisines is Cairo, as well as the tourist zones of Luxor, Sharm el-Sheikh and Dahab. In Alexandria, follow locals' lead and dine out in the seafood restaurants – they're some of the best in the region.

Egyptians usually dine at a later hour than in the West; it's usual to see diners arrive at a restaurant at 10pm or even later in the cities, particularly in summer. They also dine in large family groups, smoke like chimneys and linger over their meals.

Unless it's a special occasion, the main meal of the day is usually lunch for standard restaurant and cafe business hours. At night, Egyptians typically eat lighter or grab snacks. Portion sizes can be enormous at any time, so order with restraint – wasting food is not appreciated.

Omm ali is said to have been introduced into Egypt by Miss O'Malley, an Irish mistress of Khedive Ismail; another tradition has it that it was prepared to mark the murder of Omm Ali (Mother of Ali), the wife of a 13th-century sultan of Egypt, by her rival.

Vegetarians & Vegans

Though it's usual for Egyptians to eat lots of vegetables, the concept of voluntary vegetarianism is quite foreign. Observant Copts follow a vegan diet much of the year (hence the popularity of *kushari*), but more standard Egyptian logic is, 'why would you not eat meat if you can afford it?'

Fortunately, it's not difficult to order vegetable-based dishes. You can eat loads of mezze and salads, *fuul, ta'amiyya,* the occasional omelette, or oven-baked vegetable *tagens* with okra and eggplant. When in doubt, you can always order a stack of pita bread and a bowl of hummus. If you do eat fish, note that fresh seafood is nearly always available in tourist towns and along the coasts.

The main cause of inadvertent meat eating is meat stock, which is often used to make otherwise vegetarian *tagens* and soups. Your hosts or waiter may not even consider such stock to be meat, so they will reassure you that the dish is vegetarian.

Habits & Customs

Egyptians eat a standard three meals a day. For most people breakfast consists of bread and cheese, maybe olives or a fried egg at home, or a *fuul* sandwich on the run to work. Lunch is the day's main meal, taken from 2pm onwards, but more likely around 3pm or 4pm when dad's home from work and the kids are back from school. Whatever's served, the women of the house (usually the mother) will probably have spent most of the morning in the kitchen preparing it, it'll be hot and there'll probably be plenty to go around. Whatever's left over is usually served up again later in the evening as supper.

Environment

Egypt, as the ancient historian Herodotus knew, is the gift of the Nile, and the country is entirely dependent on the river as its only source of irrigation, as it never rains. Most wildlife is found in the desert and coral reefs of the Red Sea, as the Nile Valley is already overcrowded with humans. The narrow strip of fertile land between the desert and river faces many threats, particularly from overpopulation, from the salinisation of the land and from rising ground-water levels caused by the building of the High Dam in Aswan.

The Land

Egypt has four of the world's five officially identified types of sand dunes, including the *seif* (sword) dunes, so named because they resemble the blades of curved Arab swords.

The Nile Valley is home to most Egyptians, with some 90% of the population confined to the narrow strip of fertile land bordering the great river. To the south the river is hemmed in by mountains and the agricultural plain is narrow, but as the river flows north the land becomes flatter and the valley widens to between 20km and 30km.

To the east of the valley is the Eastern Desert (this is also known as the Arabian Desert), a barren plateau bounded on its eastern edge by a high ridge of mountains that rises to more than 2000m and extends for about 800km. To the west is the Western Desert (also known as the Libyan Desert), which officially comprises two-thirds of the land surface of Egypt. If you ignore the political boundaries on the map, the Western Desert stretches right across the top of North Africa under its better-known and highly evocative name, the Sahara (Arabic for 'desert').

Cairo also demarcates Egyptian geography as it lies roughly at the point where the Nile splits into several tributaries and the valley becomes a 200km-wide delta. Burdened with the task of providing for the entire country, this Delta region ranks among the world's most intensely cultivated lands.

To the east, across the Suez Canal, is the triangular wedge of Sinai. It's a geological extension of the Eastern Desert; the terrain here slopes from the high mountain ridges, which include Mt Sinai and Gebel Katarina (the highest mountain in Egypt at 2642m) in the south, to desert coastal plains and lagoons in the north.

Wildlife

Birding Egypt (www.birdinginegypt.com) serves the Egyptian birding community by listing top birding sites, rarities and travel tips.

Egypt is about 94% desert – such a figure conjures up images of vast, barren wastelands where nothing can live. However, there are plenty of desert regions where fragile ecosystems have adapted over millenniums to extremely hostile conditions.

Animals

Egypt is home to about 100 species of mammals, though you'd be lucky to see anything other than camels, donkeys, horses and buffalo. Although Egypt's deserts were once sanctuaries for an amazing variety of larger mammals, such as the leopard, cheetah, oryx, aardwolf, striped hyena and caracal, all of these have been brought to the brink of extinction through hunting. Creatures such as the sand cat, the fennec fox and the Nubian ibex are rarely sighted, and Egyptian cheetahs and leopards have most likely already been wiped out.

There were three types of gazelle in Egypt: the Arabian, dorcas and white. Unfortunately, Arabian gazelles are thought to be extinct, and there are only individual sightings of dorcas and white gazelles, though herds were common features of the desert landscape only 35 years ago.

The zorilla, a kind of weasel, lives in the Gebel Elba region. In Sinai you may see the rock hyrax, a small creature about the size of a large rabbit, which lives in large groups and is extremely sociable.

Less loveable are the 34 species of snake in Egypt. The best known is the cobra, which featured prominently on the headdress of the ancient pharaohs. Another well-known species is the horned viper, a thickset snake that has horns over its eyes. There are also plenty of scorpions, although they're largely nocturnal and rarely seen. Be careful if you're lifting up stones as they like to burrow into cool spots.

Natural Selections: A Year of Egypt's Wildlife, written and illustrated by Richard Hoath and published by the American University in Cairo Press, is a passionate account of the birds, mammals, insects and marine creatures that make Egypt their home.

Birds

About 430 bird species have been sighted in Egypt, about one-third of which actually breed there. Most of the others are passage migrants or winter visitors. Each year an estimated one to two million large birds migrate via certain routes from Europe to Africa through Egypt. Most large birds, including flamingos, storks, cranes, herons and all large birds of prey, are protected under Egyptian law.

The most ubiquitous birds are the house sparrow and the hooded crow, while the most distinctive is the hoopoe. This cinnamon-toned bird has a head shaped like a hammer and extends its crest in a dramatic fashion when it's excited. Hoopoes are often seen hunting for insects in gardens in central Cairo, though they're more common in the countryside.

Plants

The lotus that symbolises ancient Egypt can be found, albeit rarely, in the Delta area, but the papyrus reed, depicted in ancient art in vast swamps where the pharaohs hunted hippos, has disappeared from its natural habitats. Except for one clump found in 1968 in Wadi Natrun, papyrus is now found only in botanical gardens.

RESPONSIBLE TRAVEL

Tourism is vital to the Egyptian economy, and with fewer visitors the country is hitting rock bottom. At the same time, millions of visitors a year can't help but add to the ecological and environmental overload. As long as outsiders have been stumbling upon or searching for the wonders of ancient Egypt, they have also been crawling all over them, chipping bits off or leaving their own contributions engraved in the stones. Needless to say, this is not sustainable.

Mass tourism threatens to destroy the very monuments that visitors come to see. In the recent past, at sites such as the Valley of the Kings, thousands of visitors a day mill about in cramped tombs designed for one occupant. The deterioration of the painted wall reliefs alarms archaeologists, whose calls for limits on the number of visitors have largely fallen on deaf ears.

Even the Pyramids, which have so far survived 4500 years, are suffering. Cracks have begun to appear in inner chambers and, in cases such as these, authorities have been forced to limit visitors and to close the great structures periodically to give them some rest and recuperation. It is likely only a matter of time before similar measures are enforced elsewhere.

In the meantime it's up to the traveller to be aware of these serious concerns. Don't be tempted to baksheesh guards so you can use your flash in tombs. Don't clamber over toppled pillars and statues. Don't touch painted reliefs. It's all just common sense.

More than 100 varieties of grass thrive in areas where there is water, and the date palm can be seen in virtually every cultivable area. Along with tamarisk and acacia, the imported jacaranda and poinciana (red and orange flowers) have come to mark Egyptian summers with their vivid colours.

The Egyptian tortoise, native to the Mediterranean coastal desert, is one of the world's smallest tortoises; most males are less than 9cm long.

Environmental Issues

Cairo is close to claiming the dubious title of the world's most polluted city. The average Cairene inhales more than 20 times the acceptable level of air pollution every day, according to the World Health Organization. That means that every Cairo resident's daily air-pollution intake is akin to smoking a pack of cigarettes. A startling feature article by Ursula Lindsey published in *Cairo* magazine asserted that as many as 20,000 Cairenes die each year of pollution-related disease and that close to half a million contract pollution-related respiratory diseases.

The biggest culprits for the air pollution are the industrial plants, particularly those burning the heavy, low-quality *mazut* in generating plants. The increase of cement and steel factories, often established by Western countries in Egypt over the past two decades, is highly polluting, and have ruined the health of workers and nearby residents. A second factor is the desert storms as most of Egypt is desert. The growing number of vehicles adds to the problem. Some estimates place over two million cars in the greater Cairo area, and it's clear that this number is increasing every year. Very few run on unleaded petrol; most are poorly maintained diesel-run Fiats and Peugeots that spew out dangerous fumes.

ALTERNATIVE ENERGY: EGYPT'S WAVE OF THE FUTURE

One of Egypt's most acclaimed achievements is the High Dam in Aswan, which gave the country the opportunity to generate a large portion of its electricity cleanly and freely. For a country that still relies heavily on thermal power plants, increased reliance on hydropower was definitely a step in the right direction. Hydropower projects are underway in towns like Qanater and Nag Hammadi, and this will hopefully set a precedent for further investment in this industry.

Another form of alternative energy that has huge potential in Egypt is wind power; more precisely, large-scale wind farms. One of the largest wind farms in all of Africa and the Middle East is located in the town of Zafarana, approximately halfway between Cairo and Hurghada. Here, along the windswept Red Sea coast, the average wind speed is 9 metres per second, which allows a production capability of over 150MW.

There is also a growing business sector in Egypt for diverse forms of solar-power usage, particularly in remote areas that are unable to access the unified power grid. A good example of this is the use of photovoltaics, which are high-powered reflectors that can produce voltage when exposed to sunlight. Photovoltaics are extremely advantageous in that they can be easily utilised for anything from illuminating roads to strengthening scattered mobile-phone signals. Considering that Egypt basks in sunshine virtually year-round, there is an incredible amount of potential in this field.

Of course, despite the progress that has been made so far in the renewable-energy industry within Egypt, significant problems and obstacles for its development remain. There are still heavy government regulations within the energy industry that protect existing large companies and hinder entrepreneurial innovation. As more and more countries start to take drastic steps to reach sustainability in a time of depleting resources, there's reason to be optimistic that Egypt will follow suit. Furthermore, as an influential player in both Africa and the Middle East, Egypt is in a unique position to be able to induce a change in attitude beyond its borders.

Hassan Ansah is a freelance writer and journalist who has taught at the Western International University in Phoenix, Arizona, and at the American University in Cairo (AUC).

Though factories are officially required to undertake environmental-impact assessments and the government lays out a system of incentives and penalties designed to encourage industrial polluters to clean up their acts, few have done so and little is being done to prosecute offenders. Laws designed to have emission levels of vehicles tested don't appear to be regularly enforced. Organisations such as the US Agency for International Development (USAID) have tried to turn the situation around by funding initiatives such as the Cairo Air Improvement project, costing several hundreds of millions of US dollars.

The seriousness of the situation is particularly apparent each October and November, when the infamous 'black cloud' appears over the city. A dense layer of smog, which is variously blamed on thermal inversion, rice-straw burning in the Delta, automobile exhaust, burning rubbish and industrial pollution, it is a vivid reminder of an increasingly serious environmental problem.

You can download a Wadi Rayyan Protected Area atlas, which contains 15 chapters of photos and maps, at www.eiecop.org/ambiente2/projects_2/wadielrayan_atlas.htm.

Impact of Tourism

Ill-planned tourism development remains one of the biggest threats to Egypt's environment, particularly along the Red Sea coast and in Sinai. Following decades of frenzied development along the Red Sea coast, damaged coral reefs now run along most of its length. In Sinai, the coastline near Sharm el-Sheikh was the site of a building boom for many years: the downturn in tourism since 2011 has left half-finished resorts defacing the seafront. Whether the businesspeople investing here will make good on their promises to protect the reefs around the area remains to be seen.

Since the opening of the Nile bridge in Luxor (previously there was only a ferry) many more visitors visit the west-bank monuments, causing much damage in the fragile tombs. Several villages built over the tombs have been bulldozed as part of the project to make Luxor the largest open-air museum in the world. Large residential areas in Luxor have also been demolished to clear areas around historical sites, despite protests from some locals and organisations.

Fortunately, there have been some positive developments. A National Parks office has opened in Hurghada and is hoping to rein in some of the more grandiose development plans in the Marsa Alam area. And new 'green' guidelines for running hotels are being trialled under a joint US–Egyptian Red Sea Sustainable Tourism Initiative (RSSTI). Recommendations focus on energy use, water conservation, and the handling and disposal of waste, including simple measures such as installing foot-pedal taps at sinks, which make it harder to leave water running.

Finally, Egypt has an increasing number of high-profile eco-lodges. It started with the fabulous Basata in Sinai and Adrére Amellal at Siwa and they appear to have inspired a few others towards environmentally responsible tourism.

At www.hepca.com you can learn about the efforts of Hurghada Environmental Protection and Conservation Association (HEPCA) to conserve the Red Sea's reefs through public-awareness campaigns, direct community action and lobbying efforts.

National Parks

Egypt currently has 29 'protected areas' in a bid to protect the incredible range of biodiversity in the country, which ranges from river islands and underwater coral reefs to desert ecosystems. However, just what 'protected area' means varies wildly. Take, for instance, the Nile Islands Protected Area, which runs all the way from Cairo to Aswan: nobody is clear which islands are included and most are inhabited and cultivated without restriction. Other sites are closed to the public while some, such as Egypt's oldest national park, Ras Mohammed National Park in the Red Sea, are popular tourist destinations that have received international plaudits for their eco smarts. Even hunting is allowed in some of the protectorates if you have the right permit from Egyptian environmental authorities.

NOTABLE NATIONAL PARKS

Egypt has a number of notable national parks:

- **Lake Qarun Protectorate** (p153) Scenic lake important for wintering water birds.
- **Nabq Protectorate** (p387) Southern Sinai coastal strip with the most northerly mangrove swamp in the world.
- **Ras Mohammed National Park** (p378) Spectacular reefs with sheer cliffs of coral; a haven for migrating white storks in autumn.
- **Siwa Oasis** (p292) Three separate areas of natural springs, palm groves, salt lakes and endangered dorcas gazelles.
- **St Katherine Protectorate** (p400) Mountains rich in plant and animal life including Nubian ibex and rock hyrax.
- **Wadi Rayyan Protected Area** (p154) Uninhabited Saharan lake with endangered wildlife.
- **White Desert** (p284) White chalk monoliths, fossils and rock formations.
- **Zerenike Protectorate** (p408) A lagoon on Lake Bardawil that harbours migrating water birds.

The problem, as always, is a lack of funding. The Egyptian Environmental Affairs Agency (EEAA) has neither the high-level support nor the resources needed to provide effective management of the protectorates. Some help has arrived through foreign donors and assistance: the Italians at Wadi Rayyan; the EU at St Katherine; and USAID at the Red Sea coast and islands.

High Dam Effect

The Aswan High Dam and its sibling, Lake Nasser, have been a mixed blessing. They allowed more irrigation for farming, but stopped the rich deposits of silt that were left after the annual flood and fertilised the land. This has led to a serious degradation of Egypt's soil and has made agriculture in Egypt entirely dependent on fertilisers. The annual inundations also used to flush away the salts from the soil. But now that there is no annual flood, the biggest problem facing farmers is the high salinity of the soil.

Soil erosion has also become a major problem, particularly in the Delta region. The Nile has so little outflow and deposits so little silt that the Mediterranean is now gradually eating away the coastline. This also threatens the thriving fishing industry in the Delta lagoons. And, as the rich nutrients of the Nile no longer reach the sea, fish stocks there have been seriously reduced.

Another potentially catastrophic consequence of the dam and lake appears to be the rise in ground-water levels. With the water table higher, and salt levels raised, the sandstone blocks of many Egyptian monuments are being eaten away.

Survival Guide

Safe Travel

Itfadal

Egypt was one of the safest countries in the world to visit, until recently. Tales of exceptional hospitality were commonplace and if you happened to leave your wallet on a cafe table, the chances were that someone would come running down the street after you to hand it back. Similarly, you were – and still are – likely to be invited to join people at meals, for a cup of tea or in their homes. *Itfadal*, welcome, is still one of the most often heard words. But several years of social protest, bitterness following the killing of hundreds of people in August 2013 (when security forces broke up sit-ins in Cairo), a lack of regular policing, and economic hardship have changed things significantly in many ways, and it pays to be aware of this.

Social Unrest

A 2014 protest law has made it more difficult for crowds to gather. This was put through to deter Muslim Brotherhood supporters from gathering in large numbers, as they had been doing on a regular basis. It has also made it more difficult for any other group to gather en masse to protest.

But that doesn't mean that everything is quiet, and a quick look through the Egyptian daily press reveals a long list of continuing flashpoints and protests. Most of them are far from tourist sites, so it should not intrude on a holiday to Egypt. But in the current climate, it pays to be more than usually aware.

GOVERNMENT TRAVEL ADVICE

Many government websites offer travel advisories that have up-to-date information on current hot spots. It should be remembered, however, that these are often overly cautious.

Australian Department of Foreign Affairs & Trade (www.smarttraveller.gov.au)

British Foreign & Commonwealth Office (www.fco.gov.uk)

Canadian Department of Foreign Affairs & International Trade (www.dfait-maeci.gc.ca)

US State Department (www.travel.state.gov)

Terrorism

There has been a significant rise in terror attacks in Egypt since the downfall of President Morsi in 2013. Almost all of these have been aimed at security and government targets. The exception is in North Sinai, where Ansar Bayt al-Maqdis and other jihadi groups are fighting against Egyptian military forces: a tourist bus was attacked at Taba in 2014, leaving four dead, three of them tourists. There have been several bomb blasts in and around Cairo, including a bomb attack on the minister of interior's car, which killed two (not the minister) and injured 20 bystanders. Several small explosive devices have since been discovered in public places, particularly in Cairo, including one on the metro.

The Greatest Threat

The greatest threat to you on your journey in Egypt will be to your intestines. Many people visiting the country suffer from some sort of intestinal trouble and for a variety of reasons, from unfamiliar diet and lack of hygiene to contaminated food and water. The amount of food offered, usually considerably more than one eats at home, can also threaten your intestinal happiness. Eat moderately, at least at the

KEEPING SAFE & AVOIDING TROUBLE

Some dos...

- Be vigilant in cities, keeping clear of large public gatherings.
- Cooperate politely with security checks in hotel foyers and at road checkpoints.
- Keep up to date with news in English-language newspapers.
- Check the latest travel warnings online through your country's state department or foreign ministry.
- Consult your embassy/consulate on arrival if there have been recent public-order issues. Some countries operate a register, to ensure you receive notifications if trouble is expected.
- Be aware of the specific risks to women travellers (p487).
- Keep your passport and wallet in a safe place.
- Recognise that some taxi drivers, cafe owners and even hoteliers might try to charge you more than locals. Hotels, like museums, often have different rates for locals (this applies to international chains as much as bugdet hostels). Often this is something you have to accept.

Some don'ts...

- Don't lose a sense of proportion – the chances of running into trouble are very slim.
- Don't get involved: if you see political protests or civil unrest, leave as fast as possible.
- Don't strike up conversations of a stridently political nature with people you don't know.
- Avoid driving outside towns and cities at night: the majority of road incidents in Egypt happen after dark.
- Don't photograph military installations. Some other buildings are also prohibited, including old Aswan Dam. You can be arrested for doing so, however innocent you might be.

start of your trip. Always use bottled water, for drinking and for brushing your teeth. Wash your hands before eating. And make sure you drink enough water during the day.

Theft & Crime

In spite of all the media attention, crime in Egypt is still significantly less prevalent than in many Western countries. You can still usually leave your camera with the guard at the entrance to a tomb, or your bag with the concierge of a hotel without worrying whether it will be there, and intact, when you get back. Locals still have too much to lose by stealing in a country where thieving from guests is particularly frowned upon. Punishments are harsh and, with unemployment so high, the chance of losing one's job is something most Egyptians will not risk. But that doesn't mean that you should not take precautions. Here are some common scams that you should watch out for.

- Most Cairo taxis now have up-to-date meters, but in some places the old meters, with their fares in piastres, are still in use. Be sure that the meter is working, or that you know how much you will pay at the end. Otherwise, leave and look for another taxi.
- Shop owners and hawkers will sometimes claim that an item is locally crafted. Some are. But many things you will be offered in souqs, and particularly in shops around antiquity sites, are mass produced and imported.
- Most visitors to Egypt's sites are offered something that looks old. *Antika* is the word, with its suggestion of antiquity. Most things openly for sale are no older than the time it took for them to be covered in dust, or faded by the sun (months, perhaps, occasionally years). If you were to buy an actual antiquity and try to take it home, however innocently, you would be smuggling, a crime which can carry a prison sentence with hard labour, and a huge fine.
- In taxis and elsewhere, you might be told a hard-luck story involving a relative in hospital needing funds for drugs or an operation, or to buy materials to study, or increasingly, food to eat. You must decide for yourself whether it's better to give something, in case it's true (as it sometimes is) or turn away.

Minefields

There are still unexploded landmines left over from World War II, around El Alamein and elsewhere along the Mediterranean and Red Sea coasts. There are usually danger signs and the areas ought to be closed off. If in doubt, consult a local.

Women Travellers

Lots of women travel solo in Egypt and most have a great time in the country. Travelling alone as a female though is unfathomable to many Egyptians so expect a lot of attention. Some of this is welcome; as a lone female you're more likely, than a single male or travelling couple, to be befriended by families and local women and garner invites to people's houses. Unfortunately though, you're also more likely to encounter some unwelcome attention as well.

Egypt has a bad reputation for sexual harassment. For the most part, this comes in the form of wearying amounts of cat-calling, declarations of love, leering or being followed down the street, and minor groping in crowds or closed-in spaces such as buses or taxis. This can all put something of a dampener on your travels.

Street harassment is a major problem for Egyptian women. In a recent survey carried out by Egyptian NGO **HarassMap**, a staggering 99.3% of Egyptian women stated that they had been subjected to some form of harassment.

Attitudes are slowly changing. Sexual harassment was made a criminal offence in Egypt in June 2014 and in September 2014 Cairo University took the initiative to officially adopt an anti-sexual-harassment policy on campus. Both these unprecedented steps are a huge leap forward in recognising a problem that has been brushed under the carpet for years. In saying that, Egypt has a long road to travel in tackling its harassment issues head on.

TOP TIPS

- Expect copious questions about your marital status and number of children. Egyptians are highly family-orientated and talking about family is a normal conversation starter, particularly with strangers. If you're single and childless expect countless queries about why this is. Sometimes, to preserve your sanity, it's easier to make up a cover-story about your 'husband' and 'children' back home.
- Use the women-only carriages on the Cairo metro. Not only are they less crowded than the other carriages, but they're also a great opportunity to meet local women.
- Stock up on tampons and other female sanitary products in Cairo, Alexandria, Luxor, Sharm el-Sheikh and Hurghada. Outside of the main centres they can be expensive and more difficult to source.
- Trust your instincts. If you enter a hotel or restaurant and feel the atmosphere is leery, you're probably right. Don't grin and bear it. Just walk straight out.

Deciphering Cat-Calls

For many female travellers being cat-called in Egypt can be particularly unnerving if you can't understand what is being said. Once you know what the wannabe lotharios are actually muttering as you walk past, you may find it more cringeworthy than scary. Egypt's most common cat-calls are:

- **Muza** Hugely popular slang term for a curvaceous, pretty female. You're being compared to a *muz* (banana) for your curves.
- **Asal (honey)** Exactly the same as in English.
- **Sarokh (rocket)** In young male street-slang this means 'this girl is rocket', a compliment to your exceptional beauty.
- **Ishta (cream)** Going out of fashion but still occasionally heard; describing a good-looking female.

THE DARK SIDE OF EGYPT'S DEMONSTRATIONS

Since the 2011 Revolution, a huge number of sexual assaults and rapes have occurred at protests and rallies including a couple of high-profile attacks on foreign female journalists. Over the four-day protest period in July 2013 alone, which resulted in the ousting of President Morsi, Egyptian anti-sexual harassment groups reported 91 cases of serious sexual assault or rape of female demonstrators in Tahrir Square. In June 2014 a video of a female protester being attacked by a mob went viral, prompting a long-overdue nationwide debate on sexual assault in Egypt. Female travellers are advised to stay well away from any protests.

➡ **Mahallabiye** In a country of sweet-tooths it's not surprising that the popular dessert of *mahallabiye* (milk custard with pine nuts and almonds) has become a slang word for a pretty woman.

➡ **Gazelle** Although you may be slightly put out at being compared to a small desert-dwelling mammal of the antelope family, Egyptians consider gazelles their most beautiful native animal and being called one is supposed to be complimentary.

Adopting The Right Attitude

It's easier said than done, but ignoring most verbal harassment is usually the best policy. Very few will persist following or cat-calling for more than a few metres if you act as if you haven't noticed them. Walk and act confidently; persistent harassers tend to latch onto those who look like they don't know what they're doing.

Most importantly, don't presume that every man who wants to strike up a conversation is out to get you. Egyptians tend to be gregarious, naturally hospitable and extremely open to talking to strangers. As the majority of Egyptians who work in tourism are male, you'll miss out on some great local interactions if you're too scared to talk to them.

Appropriate Dress

Egypt is a highly conservative country by nature so this is not the place to be breaking out your hot pants and strappy tank tops. You will stick out less like a sore thumb if you dress modestly, covering shoulders, cleavage and knees. T-shirts (with a sleeve that covers upper arms), long pants and long skirts not only aid to deflect unwanted attention but also help in encouraging interactions with local women, some of whom wouldn't approach travellers wearing skimpier attire.

Bikinis and swimsuits are best left to the private beaches of hotels. On public beaches and in the desert hot springs wear a t-shirt and shorts over your swimsuit at the least.

Public Spaces To Be Wary Of

➡ Never sit in the front passenger seat of taxis, *servees* or microbuses.

➡ Don't go to *baladi* (local) bars unaccompanied.

➡ Some coffeehouses are strictly men-only affairs. Check out the scene before sitting down

➡ The evenings of Eid al-Fitr (the holiday at the end of Ramadan) seem to be an excuse for groups of young men to roam the streets harassing women. If you're in Luxor, Cairo or Alexandria at this time, it can be best to stay off the street after nightfall.

Responding to Persistent Harassment

For serious encounters and any incidences of physical contact, don't be afraid to create a scene. Saying '*haraam aleik!*' or '*ayb aleik!*' (both mean 'shame on you!') or the simpler '*imshi!*' ('go away!') is usually enough to stop most harassers. Don't hesitate to ask for help. Most Egyptians are hugely embarrassed and ashamed of the harassment problem their country has and bystanders will usually jump to your aid if prompted.

Also, report any harassment to **HarassMap** (www.harassmap.org). This NGO do excellent work in breaking the stereotypes that surround sexual harassment in Egypt by documenting the extent of incidents throughout the country.

What to Do in an Emergency

For help, counselling and legal advice if you have been seriously attacked you can contact the Egyptian women's rights organisations **El Nadeem Center for Victims of Violence and Torture** (☎0100 666 2404; info@elnadeem.org) or **Nazra for Feminist Studies** (☎0101 191 0917; info@nazra.org).

HarassMap (www.harassmap.org) are also an excellent resource for advice.

Directory A–Z

Accommodation

Rates

- The price ranges box indicates prices for rooms in the winter tourist high season, typically November to February. For budget and most midrange hotels, taxes are included; for high-end hotels, tax is typically separate. Breakfast is included in the room price unless indicated otherwise.
- Rates at budget and midrange places can be negotiable in off-peak seasons, generally March to September, except on the Mediterranean coast and during the middle of the week. Some last-minute booking websites sometimes have lower rates for top-end hotels.
- Many hotels will take US dollars or euros in payment, and some higher-end places even insist on it, though officially this is illegal. Lower-end hotels are usually cash only, though it's not a given that all upmarket hotels accept credit cards.
- Most top-end chains and a few midrange hotels in Egypt offer nonsmoking rooms, though you can't always count on one being available.

Seasons

- Rates often go up by around 10% during the two big feasts (Eid al-Fitr and Eid al-Adha) and New Year (20 December to 5 January). See p482 for more information.
- On the Mediterranean coast, prices may go up by 50% or more in the summer season (approximately 1 July to 15 September).

Types

- Egypt offers visitors the full spectrum of accommodation: hotels, resorts, pensions, B&Bs, youth hostels, cruise boats and even a few camping grounds and ecolodges.
- In Cairo, Alexandria, Luxor and Aswan, there are options for all budgets, from budget to superluxury.
- Elsewhere along the Nile options are more limited, with fairly bare-bones operations that mostly cater to Egyptian travellers.

BOOK YOUR STAY ONLINE

For more accommodation reviews by Lonely Planet authors, check out http://lonelyplanet.com/egypt/hotels/. You'll find independent reviews, as well as recommendations on the best places to stay. Best of all, you can book online.

SLEEPING PRICE RANGE

Accommodation options can be categorised as follows:

$ less than E£250

$$ E£250–750

$$$ more than E£750

- In the oases budget options range from decent to very good and backpacker friendly.
- The Red Sea coast and Sharm el-Sheikh are largely dedicated to package tourism. Resorts here typically offer all-inclusive rates that cover most drinks and some activities, though some also offer half- or full-board options (two or three meals). Booking well in advance can yield major discounts, as can booking at the last minute.

Camping

- Officially, camping is allowed at only a few places around Egypt, at a couple of camping grounds and at a few hotels; these facilities are extremely basic.
- To camp in the wilderness, you typically must be with a group. But it's possible to go DIY in a few places in national parks, such as the White Desert.

Hostels

- Egypt has eight hostels recognised by **Hostelling International** (HI; www.hihostels.com), where having a HI card will earn you a discount.
- There are also a number of independent operations offering dorm beds and small private rooms.
- Hostels tend to be noisy and often a bit grimy. In some there are rooms for mixed couples or families but on the whole the sexes are segregated.
- Most of the time you'll be better off staying at a budget hotel instead.
- Brace yourself for heavy sales pressure for guided tours, especially in Cairo.

Hotels

BUDGET

At the low end, there's little consistency in standards. You can spend as little as E£50 a night for a clean single room with hot water, or E£150 or more for a dirty room without a shower. Generally, rates include a basic breakfast, usually a couple of pieces of bread, a wedge of processed cheese, a serving of jam, and tea or coffee.

Competition among budget hotels in cities such as Cairo and Luxor is fierce, which keeps standards reasonably high and developing all the time. At this point, most rooms have private bathrooms, but some older hotels still have shared bathrooms only. Air-con is also an option, sometimes for an extra E£20–E£50. Places catering to backpackers often have welcoming lounges with satellite TV, internet access and backgammon boards.

Some hotels will tell you they have hot water when they don't. Turn the tap on and check, or look for an electric water heater when checking the bathroom. If there's no plug in your bathroom sink, try using the lid of a mineral-water bottle – it often fits well enough.

Some budget establishments economise on sheets and will change linens only on request. Toilet paper is usually supplied, but you'll often need to bring your own soap and shampoo.

MIDRANGE

Midrange options are surprisingly limited, particularly in Cairo and Alexandria, where investment is channelled into top-end accommodation. Moreover, many hotels in this category coast on package-tour bookings. As a result, you could wind up paying more for TV and air-con, in grungy surrounds.

Even if you typically travel in this price bracket, consider budget operations as well – some will be dramatically nicer, for half the price.

TOP END

- Most international luxury and business chains are represented, and amenities are (for the most part) up to international standards.
- Independent luxury hotels can be hit-and-miss, however, especially at the entry level of this price bracket, so you may want to inspect your room in person before committing any money.
- Most luxury lodging can be booked at a discount in advance, particularly in low season and these days while few tourists visit Egypt.
- Beware taxes: quoted rates often don't include them, and they can be as high as 24%.

Activities

For wilderness trips you may need military permits, required for the Eastern Desert south of Shams Alam, around Lake Nasser, between Bahariyya and Siwa, and off-road in the Western Desert. Safari companies can usually obtain them with two weeks' notice.

Customs Regulations

- Duty-free allowances on arrival: 1L alcohol, 1L perfume, 200 cigarettes and 25 cigars.
- Up to 48 hours after arrival, you can purchase another 3L alcohol plus up to US$200 in other duty-free articles at dedicated Egypt Free shops at the airport and in Cairo. (Touts in tourist areas may ask you to use your allotment to buy alcohol for them.)
- Customs Declaration Form D occasionally required for electronics, jewellery and cash.
- Prohibited and restricted articles include tools for espionage as well as books, pamphlets, films and photos 'subversive or constituting a national risk or incompatible with the public interest'. This needs to be taken seriously.

Discount Cards

The International Student Identity Card (ISIC) gives discounts on museum and site entries. Some travellers have also been able to get the discount with HI cards and Eurail cards. To get an **ISIC** (www.isicegypt.org) in Cairo, visit **Egyptian Student Travel Services** (Map p94; ☎02-2363 7251, 02-2531 0330; www.estsegypt.com; 23 Sharia al-Manial, Rhoda Island). You'll need a university ID card, a photocopy of your passport and one photo; cards can be bought online too. Beware counterfeit operations in Downtown Cairo.

Electricity

Electricity has become increasingly unreliable since 2011 and everywhere in Egypt, including the centre of Cairo, suffers regular, usually daily outages.

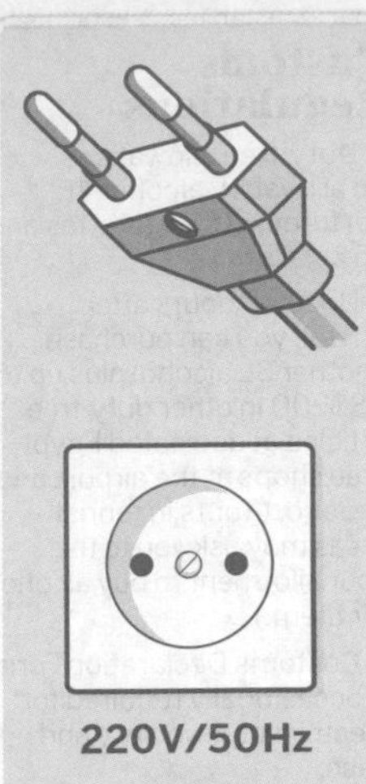

Embassies & Consulates

Australian Embassy (Map p58; ☎02-2770 6600; www.egypt.embassy.gov.au; 11th fl, World Trade Centre, 1191 Corniche el-Nil, Cairo; ⊙8am-4.15pm Sun-Wed, to 1.30pm Thu) Located 1km north of 26th of July Bridge, Cairo.

Canadian Embassy (Map p94; ☎02-2791 8700; www.canadainternational.gc.ca/egypt-egypte; 26 Sharia Kamel ash-Shenawy, Garden City, Cairo; ⊙8am-4.30pm Sun-Wed, to 1.30pm Thu)

Ethiopian Embassy (Map p94; ☎02-3335 3696; ethio@ethioembassy.org.eg; Villa 11, Midan Messaha, Doqqi, Cairo, Consular section: Consular section: 21 Sharia Sheikh Mohamed al-Ghazali, Doqqi, Cairo Street; ⊙Sun-Thu 8.30am-4.30pm)

French Embassy & Consulate (Map p94; ☎Consular Section Alexandria 03-3484 7950, Consular section Cairo 02-3567 3350, Embassy 02-3567 3200; www.ambafrance-eg.org; 29 av. Sharia Charles de Gaulle, Giza, Cairo, Consular section: 7 Sharia Abi Shammar, Giza, Cairo; 2 Midan Ahmed Orabi, Mansheya, Alexandria; ⊙Sun-Thu 9.30am-5pm) There is a French consular section in Alexandria. (Map p314; ☎484 7950; 2 Midan Orabi)

German Embassy & Consulates (Map p88; ☎Alexandria 03-4867503, Cairo 02-27282000, Hurghada 065-3443605; www.kairo.diplo.de; 2 Sharia Berlin, off Sharia Hassan Sabri, Zamalek, Cairo, 9 Sharia al-Fawatem, Mazarita, Alexandria; 365 Sharia al-Gabal ash-Shamali, Hurghada; ⊙Mon-Thu 12.30-2pm (Alexandria); Sun-Thu 9am-noon (Hurghada)) Alexandria (Map p310; ☎03-486 7503; 9 Sharia el-Fawatem); Cairo (Map p88; ☎02-2728 2000; www.kairo.diplo.de; 2 Sharia Berlin, Zamalek, Cairo); Hurghada (☎065-344 3605; 365 Sharia al-Gabal al-Shamali)

Iranian Embassy (Map p94; ☎02-3348 6492; 12 Sharia Refa'a, off Midan al-Misaha, Doqqi, Cairo; ⊙7.30am-2.30pm Sat-Thu)

Irish Embassy (Map p88; ☎02-2735 8264; www.embassyofireland.org.eg; 22 Hassan Assem, Zamalek, Cairo; ⊙9am-noon Sun-Thu)

Israeli Embassy & Consulate (☎02-33321500; www.embassies.gov.il; ⊙10am-12.30pm Sun-Thu) Alexandria (Map p306; ☎03-544 9501; 15 Sharia Mena, Rushdy); Cairo (Map p94; ☎02-3332 1500; 6 Sharia Ibn Malek, Giza)

Italian Embassy & Consulate (☎02-2794 3194; ambasciata.cairo@esteri.it; 15 Sh. Abdel Rahman Fahmy, Garden City, Cairo, Consulate: 24 Sh. El-Galaa, Boulak) Alexandria (Map p314; ☎03-487 9470; 25 Midan Saad Zaghloul); Cairo (Map p94; ☎02-2794 3194; www.ambilcairo.esteri.it; 15 Sharia Abd al-Rahman Fahmy, Garden City)

Jordanian Embassy (Map p94; ☎02-3749 9912; 6 Sharia Gohainy, Cairo)

Kenyan Embassy (Map p58; ☎02-2359 2159; www.kenemb-cairo.com; 7 Sharia al-Quds al-Sharif, Mohandiseen, Cairo) Located 800m northwest of Midan Mustafa Mahmoud.

Lebanese Embassy & Consulate (☎02-2738 2823; www.lebembassyegypt.org; 22 Mansour Mohamad, Zamalek; ⊙9am-noon Sun-Thu) Alexandria (Map p310; ☎03-484 6589; 64 Sharia Tariq al-Horreyya); Cairo (Map p88; ☎02-2738 2823; 22 Sharia Mansour Mohammed, Zamalek)

Libyan Embassy & Consulate (☎02-2735 1269; El Gabalaya, Zamalek) Alexandria (Map p310; ☎03-494 0877; 4 Sharia Batris Lumomba); Cairo (Map p88; ☎02-735 1269; 7 Sharia el-Saleh Ayoub, Zamalek, Cairo)

Dutch Embassy (☎02-2739 5500; http://egypt.nlembassy.org; 18 Sharia Hassan Sabry, Zamalek, Cairo; ⊙8am-4pm Sun-Thu) It's 1km north of 26th of July Bridge.

New Zealand Embassy (Map p58; ☎02-2461 6000; www.nzembassy.com; Level 8, North Tower, Nile City Towers, 2005 Corniche el-Nil, Cairo; 9am-3pm Sun-Thu)

Saudi Arabian Embassy & Consulates (☎02-3774 9800; egemb@mofa.gov.sa; 2 Ahmed Nessim, Giza; ⊙8am-3pm Sat-Thu) Alexandria (Map p310; ☎03-497 7951; 12 Sharia Jabarti); Cairo (Map p94; ☎02-3761 4308; 2 Sharia Ahmed Nessim, Giza); Suez (☎062-333 4016; 10 Sharia Abbas al-Akkad, Port Tawfiq)

South Sudan Embassy (☎02-2358 6513; www.errssegypt.com; 53 El Nadi, Maadi; ⊙9am-3pm Sun-Thu)

Spanish Embassy & Consulate (☎02-2735 6462; emb.elcairo@maec.es; 41 Ismail Mohamed, Zamalek) Alexandria (☎0100 340 7177; 101 Sharia Tariq al-Horreyya); **Cairo** (Map p88;☎02-2735 6462; embespeg@mail.mae.es; 41 Sharia Ismail Mohammed, Zamalek)

Sudanese Embassy & Consulate (3 El Ibrahimi, Garden City; ⊙9am-3pm Sun-Thu) Aswan; (☎097-230 7231; Bldg 20, Atlas) Cairo (Map p94;

02-2794 9661; 3 Sharia al-Ibrahimy. Garden City, Cairo)

Turkish Embassy & Consulate Alexandria (Map p310; 03-399 0700; 11 Sharia Kamel el-Kilany); Cairo (Map p58; 02-2797 8400; 25 Sharia Falaki, Mounira)

UK Embassy & Consulate (02-2791 6000; consular.cairo@fco.gov.uk; 7 Ahmed Ragheb, Garden City, 9am-2pm Sun-Thu); Alexandria; (03-546 7001; Sharia Mena, Rushdy; 10am-1pm Sun-Thu)- Cairo (Map p94; 02-2791 6000; www.ukinegypt.fco.gov.uk; 7 Sharia Ahmed Ragheb, Garden City, Cairo; 8am-3.30pm Sun-Wed, 8am-2pm Thu)

US Embassy (Map p94; 02-2797 3300; www.egypt.usembassy.gov; 5 Sharia Tawfiq Diab, Garden City, Cairo; 9am-4pm Sun-Thu)

Food

Many restaurants do not quote taxes (10%) in the menu prices, and will also add 12% for 'service', but this is typically used to cover waitstaff salaries and is not strictly a bonus. So an additional cash tip, paid directly to your server, is nice.

Overall, tipping is appreciated in budget places, advisable in midrange places and essential in all top-end restaurants.

Most budget restaurants do not serve alcohol.

EATING PRICE RANGES

The following price categories are for a typical main dish:

$ less than E£20

$$ E£20–E£80

$$$ more than E£80

Gay & Lesbian Travellers

Egypt is a conservative society that increasingly condemns homosexuality but, at the same time, plenty of same-sex activity goes on. The scene is strictly underground.

Tapping into it can be tricky because signals are ambiguous, as Egyptian men routinely hold hands, link arms and give each other kisses on greeting.

Typically, only the passive partner in a gay relationship is regarded as gay, so foreign male visitors may receive blatant and crudely phrased propositions from Egyptian men. Bar the occasional young crusader, few Egyptian men would openly attest to being gay.

Homosexuality is not strictly criminalised, but things are changing. Early in 2014 an Egyptian court sentenced four men convicted of the 'crime' of gay sex to a total of 28 years in prison, and about 80 more were arrested. The situation remains very tense, and the main Egyptian gay-and-lesbian site, www.gayegypt.com, has decided to deactivate its message forums in light of the spate of arrests in 2014.

Health

Before You Go

No vaccines are required for Egypt, but check the status of standard injections (diphtheria, tetanus, pertussis, polio, measles, mumps and rubella), as boosters in adulthood are now recommended for many. In addition, consider the following:

Hepatitis A and B Administered together or separately, at least two weeks before travel.

Rabies Only if you'll be in remote areas near animals.

Typhoid At least two weeks before travel.

Yellow fever Required if you're coming from or travelling to certain countries in southern Africa, including Sudan.

Travel insurance is highly recommended, particularly coverage with emergency evacuation services, as road accidents and the like are quite common. Also see your doctor and dentist before travelling. Consider registering with the **International Association for Medical Assistance to Travellers** (IAMAT; www.iamat.org) for a list of reputable doctors.

For longer trips, Lonely Planet's *Africa: Healthy Travel* is packed with advice on pretrip planning, emergency first aid, immunisation and disease information, as well as what to do if you get sick on the road.

TRAVEL HEALTH WEBSITES

Check these government sites before your trip for advice and news of possible outbreaks or seasonal concerns.

Australia (www.dfat.gov.au/travel)

Canada (www.travel-health.gc.ca)

UK (www.dh.gov.uk)

USA (www.cdc.gov/travel)

In Egypt

Health care Excellent standards in private and university hospitals, but patchier elsewhere. Dental care is variable. Be prepared to pay upfront for all medical and dental treatment.

Hospitals You may need to provide medicine and sterile dressings from a pharmacy. Nursing care may be rudimentary, as this is something families and friends are expected to provide.

Hygiene Standards are low. Always wash hands thoroughly before and after eating, and choose restaurants with high turnover.

Pharmacies For minor illnesses, consult a pharmacist first. They are well trained, speak English and can dispense all kinds of medication.

Water Generally not safe, but in Cairo tap water is heavily chlorinated and relatively drinkable. We recommend iodine or the **Steripen** (www.steripen.com) to reduce the use of plastic bottles.

Specific Health Risks

Heat exhaustion This is common, given the shadeless settings of most archaeological sites, as well as a lack of sanitary restrooms, which might lead you to drink less water than is required. Symptoms include headache, dizziness and tiredness and can progress to vomiting if untreated. Drink liquids (ideally sports drinks or water with rehydrating salts) before you're thirsty and wear a hat to keep off the sun. Treat yourself to an air-con hotel if necessary.

Heatstroke A much more serious condition, caused by a breakdown in the body's heat-regulating mechanism, which can cause death if untreated. This leads to irrational behaviour, a cessation of sweating and loss of consciousness. Rapid cooling with ice and water, plus intravenous fluid replacement, is required.

Insect bites and stings More annoying than toxic, but look out for sandflies on Mediterranean beaches, and mosquitoes. All bites are at risk of infection, so it's better to avoid them in the first place, with a DEET-based repellent.

Rift Valley fever A rare haemorrhagic fever spread through blood, including from infected animals. It causes a flulike illness with fever, joint pains and occasionally more serious complications. Complete recovery is possible.

Schistosomiasis (bilharzia) An infection of the bowel and bladder caused by a freshwater fluke. It can be contracted through the skin. Avoid all stagnant water, canals and slow-running rivers. Symptoms include a transient fever and rash and, in advanced cases, blood in the stool or in the urine. A blood test can detect antibodies if you have been exposed, and treatment is then possible.

Travellers' diarrhoea This and other mild food poisoning are virtually unavoidable, as food-hygiene standards are not high. The best cure is rest, fluids (best with oral rehydration salts, sold as Rehydran in Egypt) and a cool environment. Antinal pills, a widely available stomach disinfectant, can also help. If symptoms persist more than 72 hours or are accompanied by fever, see a doctor.

Tuberculosis TB is common in Egypt, though nowhere near as rampant as in sub-Saharan Africa. The respiratory infection is spread through close contact and occasionally through milk or milk products. Risk is high only for people in teaching positions or health care.

Typhoid Spread through contaminated food or water and marked by fever or a pink rash on the abdomen.

Yellow fever Mosquito-borne and extremely rare in Egypt. If you need a vaccination for onward travel to Sudan, you can obtain it at the medical clinic in Terminal 1 of Cairo airport, or at the Giza governorate building (next to the Giza Court by the train station). It costs approximately E£100.

Insurance

- Travel insurance to cover theft, loss and medical problems is a good idea.
- Some policies exclude 'dangerous activities', which can include scuba diving, motorcycling and trekking.
- Insure yourself to the gills if you're driving. Road conditions are hazardous.
- For the same reason, check that the policy covers ambulances and an emergency flight home.
- Worldwide travel insurance is available at www.lonelyplanet.com/bookings. You can buy, extend and claim online any time, even if you're already on the road.

Internet Access

- Widely available throughout Egypt, though not always fast.
- Internet cafes are common, if not rampant; rates are usually between E£5 and E£10 per hour.
- Free wi-fi is surprisingly rare in Cairo and Alexandria, but most hotels offer it (we mark these with 🛜 or @ if only a fixed connection is available).
- In Siwa and Dahab, there are pay-as-you-go services that offer wi-fi all around town for E£10 to E£15 per day.
- A mobile dongle (USB adaptor) for your laptop gives access anywhere with mobile-phone coverage. Vodafone charges E£125 for the USB stick and has various data price plans (from E£50).

Language Courses

Studying Arabic in Egypt is popular because the dialect is understood throughout the Arab world, and classes are plentiful and inexpensive. You're entitled to a student visa only if enrolled at an accredited university such as the American University in Cairo (AUC), so bear in mind the need for extending your tourist visa.

Alexandria

Qortoba Institute for Arabic Studies (Map p306; ☎03-556 2959; www.qortoba.net; cnr Muhammad Nabeel Hamdy & Khalid Bin Waleed, Miami; from per hour €5; ⌚9am-4pm Sun-Thu) Private tuition options as well as student apartments.

Cairo

Arabic Language Institute (ALI; Map p62; www.aucegypt.edu) For college students or postgrads, this department of the AUC is the strongest option, but the campus is isolated.

International House (International Language Institute ILI; Map p58; ☎02-3346 3087; www.arabicegypt.com; 4 Sharia Mahmoud Azmi, Mohandiseen; 4-week course from €245) The largest school in Cairo, so able to offer the biggest range of levels. Two-week and four-week sessions. Excellent Egyptian-colloquial textbooks. Also online courses.

Kalimat (Map p58; ☎02-3761 8136; www.kalimategypt.com; 22 Sharia Mohammed Mahmoud Shaaban, Mohandiseen; 4-week course from E£1440) Smaller than ILI, but more convenient Cairo location.

Luxor

Hotel Sheherazade (☎0100 611 5939; www.hotelsheherazade.com; Gezira al-Bayrat; 2-week course E£6000) Bespoke Arabic courses run by teachers trained by and using course books from DEAC (Institut Francais's Department for Teaching Contemporary Arabic). The price includes two weeks B&B at the Hotel Sheherazade, 40 hours of tuition, airport transfers and three sightseeing tours around Luxor.

Sinai

Magana Camp (☎012 795 2402; www.almagana.de) This beach camp between Taba and Nuweiba runs summer and winter programs, two to six weeks, with three hours of study a day. See the Magana Camp group on Facebook.

Legal Matters

Foreign travellers are subject to Egyptian laws and get no special consideration. If you are arrested you have the right to telephone your embassy immediately.

Bribes Egypt is notoriously corrupt, but don't assume this means you can pay your way through. You may encounter an official who'd like to exploit the awkward situation you're in, and of course, your bribe only perpetuates the system.

Drugs Drug use can be penalised by hanging, and you'll get no exemption just because you're a tourist. That said, you will no doubt be offered at least hashish during your travels, especially in backpacker-friendly zones. We can't recommend it.

Political activity Postrevolution, police are particularly suspicious of 'foreign agitators' or anyone who could be perceived as such, including journalists and people working for NGOs. Both writers and foreign students have been detained on charges of abetting violence. It's best to avoid political affiliation of any kind, and avoid taking photos of government buildings and other sensitive areas.

Maps

Nelles Verlag has one of the most complete general maps of Egypt (scale 1:2,500,000), including a map of the Nile Valley (scale 1:750,000) and a good enlargement of central Cairo. You can find it and a number of other good maps at the AUC bookshop in Cairo; elsewhere in Egypt, selection dwindles.

The top pick for drivers is the Kümmerly & Frey map, which covers all of Egypt on a scale of 1:825,000, though it was last updated in 2000. The Freytag & Berndt map is a lesser scale (1:1,200,000) but includes insets of Cairo and central Alexandria.

Money

Change There is a severe shortage of small change, which is invaluable for tips, taxi fares and more. Withdraw odd amounts from ATMs to avoid a stack of unwieldy E£200 notes, hoard small bills and always try to break big bills at fancier establishments.

Currency Egyptian pound (E£), *guinay* in Arabic, divided into 100 piastres (pt).

Exchange rate The government sets the exchange rate, and it is fairly stable, changing incrementally only every few years. There is no real black-market exchange.

Foreign currency Some tour operators and hotels insist on US dollars or euros, even though this is technically illegal. It's a good idea to travel with a small stash of hard currency, though increasingly you can pay by credit card.

Notes and coins Coins of 5pt, 10pt and 25pt are basically extinct; 50pt notes and coins are also on their way out. E£1 coins are the most commonly used small change, while E£5, E£10, E£20, E£50, E£100 and E£200 notes are commonly used.

TIPPING IN EGYPT

Baksheesh culture is strong – when in doubt, tip.

SERVICE	TIP
Ahwa or cafe	E£3-5
Hotel staff (collective)	E£15-20 per guest per day
Informal mosque or monument guide	E£10-20 (more if you climb a minaret)
Meter taxi	E£5
Restaurant	10-15%
Shoe attendant in mosque	E£5-10
Toilet attendant	E£5-10

Prices Produce markets and some other venues sometimes write prices in piastres: E£3.50 as 350pt, for example.

ATMs

Cash machines are common, except in Middle Egypt and the oases, where you may find only one. Then you'd be stuck if there's a technical problem, so load up before going somewhere remote. Banque Misr, CIB, Egyptian American Bank and HSBC are the most reliable.

Credit Cards

All major cards are accepted in midrange-and-up establishments. In remote areas they remain useless. You may be charged a percentage of the sale (anywhere between 3% and 10%).

Retain receipts to check later against your statements as there have been cases of shop owners adding extra zeros.

Visa and MasterCard can be used for cash advances at Banque Misr and the National Bank of Egypt, as well as at Thomas Cook offices.

Moneychangers

Money can be officially changed at Amex and Thomas Cook offices, as well as commercial banks, foreign exchange (forex) bureaux and some hotels. Rates don't vary much, but forex bureaux usually don't charge commission.

US dollars, euros and British pounds are the easiest to change (and can be changed back at the end of your stay). Inspect the bills you're given, and don't accept any badly defaced, shabby or torn notes because you'll have difficulty offloading them later.

Travellers Cheques

The only reliable place to cash travellers cheques in Egypt is at the issuing office (Amex or Thomas Cook) in Cairo, Alexandria, Luxor, Aswan, Hurghada and Sharm el-Sheikh. Forex bureaux don't handle them, and even the major banks are unreliable.

MAJOR ISLAMIC HOLIDAYS

The Islamic calendar is based on the lunar year, approximately 11 days shorter than the Gregorian calendar, so holidays shift through the seasons. These are the principal religious holidays in Egypt, which can cause changes to bus schedules and business openings.

Moulid an-Nabi The birthday of the Prophet Mohammed, and children receive gifts.

Eid al-Fitr (Feast of Fast-Breaking) The end of Ramadan, essentially a three-day feast.

Eid al-Adha (Feast of the Sacrifice) Commemorates Ibrahim's (Abraham's) sacrifice, and families that can afford it buy a sheep to slaughter. The holiday lasts four days, though many businesses reopen by the third day. Many families go out of town, so if you want to travel at this time, book your tickets well in advance.

Ras as-Sana (New Year's Day) A national day off, but only a low-key celebration.

Dates for Ramadan and Eid al-Fitr are approximate, as they rely on the sighting of the new moon.

HOLIDAY	2015	2016	2017	2018
Moulid an-Nabi	3 Jan & 23 Dec	12 Dec	1 Dec	20 Nov
Ramadan begins	17 Jun	7 Jun	27 May	16 May
Eid al-Fitr	17 Jul	7 Jul	26 Jun	15 Jun
Eid al-Adha	23 Sep	13 Sep	2 Sep	22 Aug
New Year begins	14 Oct (1437)	3 Oct (1438)	22 Sep (1439)	12 Sept (1437)

Opening Hours

The weekend is Friday and Saturday; some businesses close Sunday. During Ramadan, offices, museums and tourist sites keep shorter hours.

Banks 8.30am to 2.30pm Sunday to Thursday

Bars and clubs Early evening until 3am, often later (particularly in Cairo)

Cafes 7am to 1am

Government offices 8am to 2pm Sunday to Thursday. Tourist offices are generally open longer.

Post offices 8.30am to 2pm Saturday to Thursday

Private offices 10am to 2pm and 4pm to 9pm Saturday to Thursday

Restaurants Noon to midnight

Shops 9am to 1pm and 5pm to 10pm June to September, 10am to 6pm October to May

Photography

- Egyptians on the whole, and Egyptian women in particular, are relatively camera-shy, so you should always ask before taking pictures.
- Photos are theoretically prohibited inside ancient

tombs, though guards often encourage camera use in exchange for tips.

- To combat the glare of sun, a UV filter is recommended.
- A standard daylight filter helps keep dust off your lens. Also pack compressed air and cleaning cloths.
- Avoid taking photos of anything that could be considered of military or other strategic importance. Taking photos out of bus windows especially provokes suspicion.
- Lonely Planet's *Travel Photography*, by Richard I'Anson, provides excellent advice on gear and taking photos on the road.

Post

Parcels Surface mail to the USA, Australia or Europe costs roughly E£150 for the first kilogram, and E£40 for each thereafter. Usually only the main post office in a city will handle parcels; bring them unsealed so the contents can be inspected for customs. Clerks usually have cartons and tape on hand. Many shops provide shipping of goods for a relatively small fee.

Poste restante The service functions well and is generally free. If the clerk can't find your mail, ask him or her to check under Mr, Ms or Mrs in addition to your first and last names.

Service In recent years **Egypt Post** (☎0800 800 2800; www.egyptpost.org) has improved, and it's reasonably reliable. The express service (EMS) is downright speedy.

Stamps Available at yellow-and-green-signed post offices and some shops and hotels.

Public Holidays

Businesses and government offices also close on major Islamic holidays.

New Year's Day (1 Jan) Official national holiday but many businesses stay open.

Coptic Christmas (7 Jan) Most government offices and all Coptic businesses close.

January 25 Revolution Day (25 Jan)

Sham an-Nessim (Mar/Apr) First Monday after Coptic Easter, this tradition with Pharaonic roots is celebrated by all Egyptians, with family picnics. Few businesses close, however.

Sinai Liberation Day (25 Apr) Celebrating Israel's return of the peninsula in 1982.

May Day (1 May) Labour Day.

Revolution Day (23 Jul) Date of the 1952 coup, when the Free Officers seized power from the monarchy.

Armed Forces Day (6 Oct) Celebrating Egyptian successes during the 1973 war with Israel, with some military pomp.

RAMADAN: WHAT TO EXPECT

Travelling in Egypt during the month of Ramadan, when observant Muslims abstain from all food and drink (including water during daylight hours), presents some challenges but also affords visitors a unique insight into local culture – provided you can stay up late enough to enjoy it.

Most restaurants that serve Egyptians are closed during the day, and the only reliable place to eat is in hotels – the same goes for finding alcohol of any kind. Don't plan on taking desert tours, as guides will not want to venture far. Shop owners get cranky as the day wears on, and tend to shut by 2.30pm or so, so do your bargaining early. Avoid taking taxis close to sundown, as everyone wants to get home to their families.

Once night falls and everyone has nibbled on the customary dates, Egyptians regain their energy. Restaurants reopen and lay out a lavish fast-breaking feast called *iftar* (reserve ahead at high-end places). The streets are decked with glowing lanterns and thronged with families. The goal is to stay up – or at least catnap and get up again – for the *sohour,* another big meal just before dawn. In Cairo and Alexandria, there's a whole circuit of *sohour* scenes, from the funkiest fuul vendors trotting out their best spreads to chic waterside pavilions with DJs – think after-party, but with food.

The best way to cope is to keep sightseeing expectations low, don't eat in front of Muslims and take a long nap in the afternoon. Then put on your stretchy pants and accept any invitation to join the feast.

Safe Travel

The incidence of crime, violent or otherwise, in Egypt is negligible compared with most Western countries, and you're generally safe walking around day or night. Following the 2011 revolution, after which police activity was severely curtailed, there has been a spike in petty crime, though it is statistically still quite rare and easily avoided.

Apart from the issues discussed here, you should be aware that the Egyptian authorities take a hard view of illegal drug use.

Theft

Since 2011, bag and wallet snatchings have been on the rise, usually as drive-bys on mopeds, though very occasionally at knifepoint or gunpoint. Don't let this deter you: you're still more likely to lose your wallet in Barcelona. Simple street-smart precautions should suffice: carry your bag across your body or at least on the side away from the street, and keep it looped around a chair leg in restaurants. Don't walk on empty streets past 1am or 2am. Be aware of your surroundings when you take your wallet out, and don't go to an ATM alone at night.

More common theft, such as items stolen from locked hotel rooms and even from safes, continues, so secure your belongings in a locked suitcase.

Generally, though, unwary visitors are parted from their money through scams, and these are something that you really do have to watch out for (see p473 and p488 for more information).

THE ART OF BARGAINING

Haggling is part of the every day. It's essentially a kind of scaled pricing: it can be a discount for people who have more time than money, but if your time is too valuable to discuss a transaction over tea, then you're expected to pay more. Your relative affluence of course factors into the calculations as well.

Shopping this way can seem like a hassle, but it can be fun way of life in Egypt (though, it should be noted, it's never done if you don't consider it a game. The basic procedure:

- Shop around and check fixed-price stores to get an idea of the upper limit.
- Decide how much you would be happy to pay.
- Express a casual interest and ask the vendor the price.

From here, it's up to your own style. The steeliest hagglers start with well below half the starting price, pointing out flaws or quoting a competitor's price. A properly theatrical salesman will respond with indignant shouting or a wounded cry, but it's all bluster. We know one shopper who closed deals in less than five minutes by citing her intense gastrointestinal distress – although unfortunately this was not bluster on her part.

A gentler tactic is to start out just a bit lower than the price you had in mind, or suggest other items in the shop that might be thrown in to sweeten the deal. Resist the vendor's attempts to provoke guilt – he will never sell below cost. If you reach an impasse, relax and drink the tea that's perpetually on offer – or simply walk out, which might close the deal in your favour.

You're never under any obligation to buy – but you should never initiate bargaining on an item you don't actually want, and you shouldn't back out of an agreed-upon price. The 'best' price isn't necessarily the cheapest – it's the one that both you and the seller are happy with. Remember that E£5 or E£10 makes virtually no difference in your budget, and years from now, you won't remember what you paid – but you will have your souvenir of Egypt, and a good story of how you got it.

Shopping

So great is the quantity of junk souvenirs in Egypt that it can easily hide the good stuff, but if you persist you'll find some treasures. Shop owners have begun commissioning stylish home items from traditional artisans, with some beautiful results. Also look out for traditional Siwan, Bedouin and Nubian handicrafts, such as embroidery.

The undisputed shopping capital is Cairo's medieval souq, Khan al-Khalili, which is just as much a tourist circus as it is one of the Middle East's most storied markets. There are some treasures to be had, assuming you have the time (and the patience). Increasingly, fixed-price shops in Cairo stock familiar Egyptian crafts, often with better quality than you'd find in the souq. Prices are of course higher than you'd get through bargaining, but rarely outrageous.

Appliqué & Fabric

Embroidered cloth in intricate patterns and scenes is available as pillow cases, bedspreads and wall hangings. Stitches should be small and barely visible. Printed fabric used for tents is inexpensive when sold by the meter (about E£10) and a bit more if worked into a tablecloth.

Gold & Silver

A gold cartouche with a name in hieroglyphics is a popular gift, as is a silver pendant with a name in Arabic. Gold and silver are sold by weight. Check the international market price before you buy, then add in a bit extra for work.

Inlay

Wood boxes and other items are inlaid with mother-of-pearl and bone in intricate patterns. Surfaces should be smooth and not gummed with glue. An inlaid backgammon set, with pieces, should cost about E£70.

Muski Glass

This bubble-shot glass in blue, green and brown is made from recycled bottles and fashioned into cups and other home items. It's extremely fragile, so pack it well.

Papyrus

Papyrus dealers are as ubiquitous as perfume shops, and this Egyptian invention makes an easy-to-carry souvenir. True papyrus is heavy and difficult to tear; it should not feel delicate, and veins should be visible when it is held up to the light. Good artwork should be hand-painted, not stamped. A small painting on faux papyrus (made from banana leaves) can go for just E£10; a good-quality piece can easily be 10 times as much.

Perfume

You can't escape Egypt without visiting an essential-oils dealer. Most are less than essential, being diluted with vegetable oil. Be sceptical if a salesman drips more than a tiny drop on your arm, then rubs furiously. And watch when your bottles are packed up – make sure they're filled from the stock you sampled. *Sawsan* (lotus) and *full* (jasmine) are the most distinctively Egyptian scents.

Spices

Spices are a good buy, particularly *kuzbara* (coriander), *kamoon* (cumin), *shatta* (chilli), *filfil iswid* (black pepper) and *karkadai* (hibiscus). Buy whole spices, never ground, for freshness, and skip the 'saffron' – it's really safflower and tastes of little more than dust. The shops that sell these items *(attareen)* also deal in henna, soaps and herbal treatments. The best are neighbourhood dealers, not in tourist zones.

Telephone

Mobile Phones

Egypt's GSM network (on the 900MHz/1800MHz band) has thorough coverage, at least in urban areas. SIM cards from any of the three carriers (Vodafone, the largest; Mobinil; Etisalat) cost E£15. You can buy them as well as top-up cards from most kiosks, where you may be asked to show your passport. For pay-as-you-go data service (about E£5 per day or E£50 per month), register at a company phone shop.

Phone Codes

Area codes Leave off the initial zero when calling from outside Egypt.

Directory assistance ☎140 or ☎141

Egypt country code ☎20

International access code from Egypt ☎00

Public Phones

Payphones (from yellow-and-green Menatel and red-and blue Nile Tel) are card-operated. Cards are sold at shops and kiosks. Once you insert the card into the telephone, press the flag in the top left corner to get instructions in English.

Alternatively, a telephone centrale is an office where you book a call at the desk, pay in advance for three minutes, then take your phone call in a booth. Telephone centrales also offer fax services.

Time

➡ Egypt is two hours ahead of GMT/UTC.

➡ Egypt does observe Daylight Saving Time, but the clocks are turned back an hour during Ramadan, if it falls in the summer, to cut the day short for observers.

Toilets

➡ Few official public toilets exist, but it's acceptable to use one in a restaurant or hotel even if you're not a customer.

➡ Toilet paper is seldom in stalls – an attendant may provide it as you enter, for a tip.

➡ Do not flush paper – deposit it in the bin next to the toilet

➡ Many toilets have an integrated bidet tube, which unfortunately can get quite mucky. The knob for the bidet is usually to the right of the toilet tank – open it very slowly to gauge the pressure.

MOBILE-PHONE NUMBERS IN EGYPT

All mobile phone numbers have had 11 digits, beginning with 01, since October 2011, although you may still see old-format numbers in print. Use this table to determine the extra digit:

OLD PREFIX	NEW PREFIX
010	0100
011	0111
012	0122
014	0114
016	0106
017	0127
018	0128
019	0109

➡ Some toilets are of the 'squat' variety – use the hose (and bucket, if provided) to 'flush' and to wash your hands.

➡ In cities it's a good idea to make a mental note of all Western-style fast-food joints and five-star hotels, as these are where you'll find the most sanitary facilities.

➡ When you're trekking in the desert or camping on a beach, either pack out your toilet paper or burn it. Do not bury it – it will eventually be revealed by the wind.

Tourist Information

The **Egyptian Tourist Authority** (www.egypt.travel) has offices throughout the country. Individual office staff members may be helpful, but often they're just doling out rather dated maps and brochures.

The smaller towns and oases tend to have better offices than the big cities. In short, don't rely on these tourist offices, but don't rule them out either.

Travellers with Disabilities

Egypt is not well equipped for travellers with a mobility problem. Ramps are few, public facilities don't necessarily have lifts, curbs are high (except in Alexandria, which has wheelchair-friendly pavements), traffic is lethal and gaining entrance to some of the ancient sites – such as the Pyramids of Giza or the tombs on the West Bank near Luxor – is all but impossible due to their narrow entrances and steep stairs.

Despite all this, there is no reason why intrepid travellers with disabilities shouldn't visit Egypt. In general you'll find locals willing to assist with any difficulties. Anyone with a wheelchair can take advantage of the large hatchback Peugeot 504s that are often used as taxis (though they're rarer in Cairo now). One of these, together with a driver, can be hired for the day. Chances are the driver will be happy to help you in and out of the vehicle. For getting around the country, most places can be reached via comfortable internal flights.

The following businesses in Egypt make a special effort:

El-Nakhil Hotel (Map p188; ☎095-231 3922, 0122 382 1007; www.elnakhil.com; Gezira El Bairat; s/d/tr €25/35/45; ❄📶) Nestled in a palm grove, the Nakhil (Palm Tree) is on the edge of Al-Gezira. This resort-style hotel has 17 spotless, well-finished domed rooms, all with private bathrooms and air-con. It also has family rooms, baby cots, and three rooms that can cater for disabled guests. The large rooftop restaurant has great views over the Nile.

Camel Hotel and Dive Club (☎069-360 0700; www.cameldive.com; King of Bahrain St, Sharm El-Sheikh; s/d/tr €62/64/87; ❄📶🏊) Specific poolside accommodation and

PRACTICALITIES

➡ **Water** With the exception of Cairo, tap water in Egypt is not considered safe to drink. In Cairo, a steady diet of tap water can be hard on the stomach, but an occasional glass or ice cube isn't deadly.

➡ **Noise** Pack earplugs for noisy Cairo hotel rooms, loud movies on buses and the predawn call to prayer.

➡ **Weights & Measures** Egypt uses the metric system.

➡ **Checkpoints** Security checkpoints are common on highways outside Cairo. Carry your passport with you.

➡ **Smoking** Is common in Egypt, including in restaurants and bars. Nonsmoking facilities are rare. Sheesha (hookah or water pipe) is a common social pastime. It delivers substantially more nicotine than you might be used to.

➡ **Alcohol** Is available, though typically served only at higher-end restaurants. Drinking on the street is taboo, as is public drunkenness.

➡ **TV & DVD** International English-language TV news such as CNN and BBC World can be accessed in hotel rooms throughout the country. Egyptian DVDs are region 2 format, the same as Europe.

➡ **Radio** BBC World Service is on the Middle East shortwave schedule, broadcasting from Cyprus. See www.bbc.co.uk/worldservice for details. In Cairo, European-program 95.4FM/557AM runs news in English at 7.30am, 2.30pm and 8pm. Nile Radio 104.2FM (104.2kHz) has English-language pop music.

➡ **Newspapers & Magazines** The best English newspaper is ***Daily News Egypt***, (E£4), while the monthly ***Egypt Today*** (E£20; also online at www.egypttoday.com) covers social and economic issues.

other facilities for divers with disabilities.

Egypt for All (☎0122-396 1991; www.egyptforall.com; 334 Sharia Sudan, Mohandiseen, Cairo) Agency specialising in making travel arrangements for mobility-impaired visitors, from day trips to complete Egypt tours.

Visas & Permits

- Visas required for most foreigners.
- Available for most nationalities at airport on arrival, though check before departure.
- Visa fees:

Australia A$35

Canada C$25

Europe €25

Israel 65NIS

Japan ¥5,500

New Zealand NZ$45

UK UK£15

USA US$15

- When buying visas at the airport, payment is accepted in US dollars, UK sterling and euros.
- Airport visas typically valid for 30 days in Egypt. If you want more time, apply in advance or get an extension in Egypt.
- Overland from Jordan: visas available at the port in Aqaba.
- Overland from Israel: visas at border only if guaranteed by Egyptian travel agency; otherwise, apply in advance in Tel Aviv or at the consulate in Eilat (65NIS for US or German citizens; 100NIS for others).
- Travel in Sinai between Sharm el-Sheikh and Taba, including St Katherine's Monastery but not Ras Mohammed National Park, requires no visa, only a free entry stamp, good for a 15-day stay.
- Visa extensions used to be routine, but are now subject to scrutiny, especially after repeat extensions. Be polite and say you need more time to appreciate the wonders of Egypt.
- 14-day grace period for extension application, with E£100 late fee. If you leave during this time, you must pay E£135 fine at the airport.

VISA EXTENSIONS: WHERE TO GO

Wherever you apply, you'll need one photo and two copies each of your passport's data page and the visa page. The fee depends on where you apply, but it's no more than E£15.

Alexandria (Map p314; ☎03-482 7873; 2nd fl, 25 Sharia Talaat Harb; ⊙8.30am-2pm Mon-Thu, 10am-2pm Fri, 9am-11am Sat-Sun)

Aswan (Map p242; ☎097-231 2238; 1st fl, Police Bldg, Corniche an-Nil; ⊙8.30am-1pm Sat-Thu)

Cairo – Agouza (☎02-3338 4226; El Shorta Tower, Sharia Nawal; ⊙8am-1.30pm Sat-Wed)

Cairo – Downtown (Mogamma Bldg, Midan Tahrir; ⊙8am-1.30pm Sat-Wed)

Hurghada (Sharia an-Nasr, Ad-Dahar; ⊙8am-2pm Sat-Thu)

Ismailia (☎064-391 4559; Midan al-Gomhuriyya; ⊙8am-2pm Sat-Thu)

Luxor (Map p188; ☎095-238 0885; Sharia Khalid ibn al-Walid; ⊙8am-2pm Sat-Thu)

Minya (☎095-236 4193; 2nd fl, above main post office; ⊙8.30am-2pm Sat-Thu)

Port Said (Governorate Bldg, Sharia 23rd of July; ⊙8am-2pm Sat-Thu)

Suez (Sharia al-Horreyya; ⊙8.30am-3pm)

Women Travellers

In public anyway, Egypt is a man's world, and solo women will certainly receive comments in the street – some polite, others less so – and possible groping. As small consolation, street harassment is a major problem for Egyptian women as well. With basic smarts, the constant male attention can be at least relegated to background irritation.

- Wear a sturdy bra and conservative clothing: long sleeves and pants or skirts. Sunglasses also deflect attention.
- Carry a scarf to cover your head inside mosques.
- Outside of Red Sea resorts, swim in shorts and a T-shirt at the least.
- A wedding ring sometimes helps, but it's more effective if your 'husband' (any male travel companion) is present. Most effective: travel with a child.
- Keep your distance. Even innocent, friendly talk can be misconstrued as flirtation, as can any physical contact.
- Ignore obnoxious comments – if you respond to every one, you'll wear yourself out, and public shaming seldom gets satisfying results.
- Text incidents to **Harass map** (☎0106 987 0900; www.harassmap.org).

SCAMS & HUSTLES

Many Egyptians will greet you in the street and offer you tea and other hospitality, all out of genuine kindness. But in tourist hot spots, 'Hello, my friend' can be double-speak for 'This way, sucker'. Next thing you know, you're drinking tea with your new friend...in a perfume shop.

The smoothest operators don't reveal their motives immediately. A kindly professor wants to show you a good restaurant; a mosque 'muezzin' starts by showing off his skills; or a bystander warns you not to get caught up in a (fictitious) demonstration ahead. They adapt tactics rapidly. They've taken up the 'Don't you remember me?' line used in many other African countries, for instance, and use tales of the 2011 revolution as conversational bait.

It's all pretty harmless, and many are genuinely friendly and interesting to talk to. But it can be wearing to be treated like a walking wallet. Everyone works out a strategy to short-circuit a pitch, for when a smile and a quick stride fails. One travelling couple turned the tables: 'We'd love to come to your shop, but yesterday a man scammed us out of all of our money.' Claiming not to speak English, on the other hand, usually backfires, as polyglot touts can perform in nearly any language.

Aside from the hustling, there are touts who lie and misinform to divert travellers to hotels for which they get a commission.

If you do get stung, or feel you might crack at the next 'Excuse me, where are you from?', take a deep breath and put it in perspective. According to historical records, Cairene traders bragged about fleecing the king of Mali in the 14th century. Today's touts aren't picking on you because you look like a soft target – they're doing it because it's their job. Your angry tirade won't halt centuries of sales tradition. But it could offend an honest Egyptian who just wants to help.

- Avoid crowds where testosterone is high: street protests, post-football-match celebrations and the like.
- On public transport, sit next to a woman if possible. On the Cairo metro, use the women's cars.
- Avoid city buses at peak times; the crowds make them prime groping zones.
- Bring tampons and contraceptives with you; outside of Cairo, they can be expensive.
- If you need directions or other help, ask a woman first.
- Take any opportunity to befriend an Egyptian woman, for a nonthreatening guide.
- Get older: after your mid-30s, the hassle diminishes.
- Read Rosemary Mahoney's *Down the Nile: Alone in a Fisherman's Skiff* and G Willow Wilson's *The Butterfly Mosque*, two very different tales of solo travel.
- Watch *Cairo 6,7,8*, a great 2011 fiction film about three Egyptian women dealing with sexual harassment.

Work

Many foreign firms operate in Egypt and hire foreigners, but you must typically be hired before arriving in the country, to have your work visa arranged properly. Consult *Cairo: The Practical Guide* (AUC Press), edited by Claire E Francy and Lesley Lababidi, for possible avenues.

Bars & Hotels

In Sharm el-Sheikh, travellers can often find short-term work as bartenders or hotel workers. Masseurs and others with spa skills are also in demand. Most of this work is under the table, however, and often short-term, due to employers' tax concerns.

Diving

If you are a dive master or diving instructor you can find work in Egypt's resorts fairly easily. Owners look also for language and social skills.

Teaching English

The best-paying schools require at least a Certificate in English Language Teaching to Adults (CELTA), but there are other, more informal outlets as well. Cairo's ILI is one of the better schools, and offers CELTA training as well.

Transport

GETTING THERE & AWAY

Entering the Country

At Cairo and other international airports in Egypt, the main formality is getting a visa, if you haven't arranged one in advance. They are sold at a row of bank booths in every arrivals terminal. Pay cash in hard currency and then present the sticker along with your arrival form and passport at the immigration desks. The procedure is typically speedy, no questions asked, though lines might be long if several flights have arrived at once.

By land or sea, the process is similar.

Passport

Regardless of where you enter, your passport must be valid for at least six months from your date of entry.

Israeli stamps in your passport (and Israeli passports, for that matter) present no problem, unlike in some other Middle Eastern countries.

Air

Airports & Airlines

Cairo, Alexandria and Sharm el-Sheikh receive numerous commercial international flights. Luxor receives many charter flights, but only a few commercial flights, including EgyptAir from London Heathrow. Aswan, Hurghada and Marsa Alam also handle flights from overseas, but typically mostly charters. Taba airport was closed at the time of writing.

Cairo is the most common entry point. Many international flights arrive late at night. If you are going into the city, this can be preferable, as city traffic is lighter. The airport is served by most major international carriers. Of note:

EgyptAir (MS; ☎national call centre 0900 70000; www.egyptair.com.eg; ⏰8am-8pm) Member of Star Alliance. Tickets are cheap, and its international fleet is in good shape. No alcohol is served.

Jetairfly (www.jetairfly.com) Low-cost carrier from Brussels to the Red Sea.

Meridiana fly (www.meridiana.it) Flights from Milan, Naples and Rome.

Air Sinai (www.egyptair.com) From Tel Aviv. Buy tickets at the unmarked office at Ben Yehuda and Allenby. Run by EgyptAir, but service was suspended at time of writing.

Alexandria has become a viable alternate airport, especially for low-cost carriers:

Air Arabia (www.airarabia.com) Connects Ciaor, Alexandria and Sohag to cities around the Middle East and as far east as India.

flydubai (www.flydubai.com) Also serves Middle Eastern cities.

CLIMATE CHANGE & TRAVEL

Every form of transport that relies on carbon-based fuel generates CO_2, the main cause of human-induced climate change. Modern travel is dependent on aeroplanes, which might use less fuel per kilometre per person than most cars but travel much greater distances. The altitude at which aircraft emit gases (including CO_2) and particles also contributes to their climate change impact. Many websites offer 'carbon calculators' that allow people to estimate the carbon emissions generated by their journey and, for those who wish to do so, to offset the impact of the greenhouse gases emitted with contributions to portfolios of climate-friendly initiatives throughout the world. Lonely Planet offsets the carbon footprint of all staff and author travel.

Sharm el-Sheikh is handy if you'll be spending most of your time in Sinai and Jordan. A number of budget European airlines serve Sharm.

Land

Israel & the Palestinian Territories

RAFAH

The border crossing to the Gaza Strip closes for long periods and reopens depending on security fears and political changes in Cairo. It's definitely not a recommended route for travellers as you cannot carry on to Israel this way, and even if you could, Gaza is not safe to travel through.

TABA

The border at Taba is open. However, as the security situation is changeable here, make sure you check travel advisories before taking this route.

Libya

The border is at Amsaad and the crossing is officially open but we do not recommend travel to Libya.

Sudan

Despite Egypt and Sudan sharing a 1273km land border, the only way to travel between the two countries is to fly or take the Wadi Halfa ferry.

Sea

Cyprus

A cruise ship used to operate between Port Said and Limassol in Cyprus, but the service has been suspended since 2011. For more information, contact operator **Louis Cruises** (www.louiscruises.com) or main agent **Varianos Travel** (www.varianostravel.com) in Cyprus, or check with a Port Said shipping agent such as **Canal Tours** (☎066-332 1874; www.canal-tours.net; 26 Sharia Palestine, Port Said; ⏰8am-3pm & 7pm-midnight).

> **PORT TAX**
>
> All Egyptian international ferries charge E£50 port tax per person on top of the ticket price.

Europe

At the time of research no passenger boats were operating between Egyptian ports and any ports in Europe. Tenacious travellers could investigate crossing on a freighter, although even the Damietta–Iskanderun service has been suspended. Try www.cruiseshipportal.com, which books freighter berths.

Jordan

AB Maritime (Map p396; ☎069- 352 0427; www.abmaritime.com.jo; ⏰9am-3pm) runs both a fast and slow ferry connecting Nuweiba in Egypt and Aqaba in Jordan, but the service is erratic and delay times can be as much as 20 hours. For more information on this route, please see p397.

Saudi Arabia

Ferries run from Hurghada to Duba, though follow erratic schedules, which fluctuate according to work and hajj seasons. There is also a service from Safaga. Note that tourist visas are not available for Saudi Arabia, though there is an elusive tourist transit visa, which you must apply for well in advance.

Sudan

The **Nile River Valley Transport Corporation** (☎0118 316 0926; ⏰8am-2pm Sat-Thu), in the shopping arcade behind the tourist police office, runs one passenger ferry per week from Aswan to Wadi Halfa. One-way tickets cost E£485 for 1st class with bed in a cabin, E£340 for an airline seat and E£307 for deck class. The ferry runs on Sundays around 10am, though call to confirm. Tickets can be bought a week ahead either at the Cairo office or Aswan, or on the Monday before at the company's **office** (☎097-230 3348) in Aswan port. You must show a valid Sudanese visa in your passport.

The trip is slow, up to 24 hours, with tea, soft drinks and snacks available. Boarding is usually announced for 10am, but it's a good idea to arrive at about 8.30am to clear customs and get a decent seat. The ferry might not leave until sometime in the afternoon, depending on how much there is to load. Some Sudanese immigration formalities are carried out on the boat, including checking yellow-fever certificates. The return trip departs from Wadi Halfa on Wednesdays.

The Nile River Valley Transport Corporation runs a separate barge for vehicles. You must have the usual *carnet de passage en douane* (effecively a passport for the vehicle that waives import duty) and allow plenty of time for customs procedures.

Tours

The majority of visitors see Egypt on an organised tour. The schedules on such trips are usually fairly tight, leaving little room to explore on your own. But a tour often comes with excellent guides, and a group can insulate you from some of the day-to-day hassle and sales pressure that independent travellers receive.

For specific tour offerings, also check www.lonelyplanet.com/bookings.

Abercrombie & Kent (www.abercrombiekent.co.uk) First-class packages, including its own Nile cruises, now branded as Sanctuary cruises.

Bestway Tours & Safaris (www.bestway.com) Small-group tours, often combining Egypt with neighbouring countries.

Intrepid Travel (www.intrepidtravel.com) Emphasis on responsible tourism.

DEPARTURE TAX

Airline tickets include Egypt's exit tax in the price. If you're leaving by ferry to Jordan, expect to pay port tax (E£50 at the time of writing). Crossing overland to Libya, there was no exit tax at the time of research.

Martin Randall (www.martinrandall.com) UK-based experts in cultural tours.

On the Go (www.egyptonthego.com) PADI diving-course holidays.

Wind, Sand & Stars (www.windsandstars.co.uk) A Sinai specialist with desert excursions and retreats.

GETTING AROUND

Air

EgyptAir (MS; ☎national call centre 0900 70000; www.egyptair.com.eg; ⊙8am-8pm) is the only domestic carrier, and fares can be surprisingly cheap, though they vary considerably depending on season. Domestic one-way fares can be less than US$100.

Bicycle

Cycle tourism is rare, due to long distances plus intense heat. Winter can be manageable, but even in spring and autumn it's necessary to make an early-morning start and finish by early afternoon. And yet…President Sisi is keen to encourage two-wheel transport and has been seen pedalling his way around the capital (once, at least).

Carry a full kit, as spares are hard to come by, although in a pinch Egyptians are excellent 'bush mechanics'.

The Cairo-based club **Cycle Egypt** (www.cycle-egypt.com), and its very active Facebook group, is a good starting point for making local contacts and getting advice on shops and gear. Also check the Thorn Tree travel forum on www.lonelyplanet.com, where there's a dedicated section for cyclists.

Boat

No trip to Egypt is complete without a trip down the Nile River. You can take the trip on a felucca (a traditional sailboat) or opt for a modern steamer or cruise ship.

At the time of research, the ferry service from Hurghada to Sharm el-Sheikh was still awaiting the completion of the dock at Hurghada. When this service resumes, which should be 2015, it will bypass hours of bumpy roads and checkpoints, and it's one of the few chances you have to boat from Africa to Asia.

Bus

You can get to most cities, towns and villages in Egypt

Domestic Flights

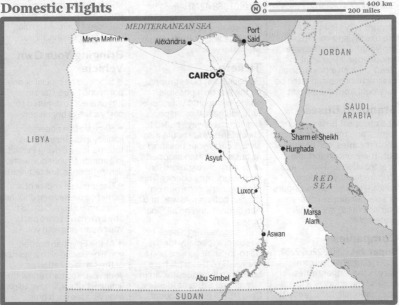

on a bus, at a very reasonable price. For many long-distance routes beyond the Nile Valley, it's the best option, and sometimes the only one. Buses aren't necessarily fast, though, and if you're going to or from Cairo, you'll lose at least an hour just in city traffic. Delays are common, especially later in the day as schedules get backed up. When buying tickets, it's a good idea to have a rough idea beforehand of costs, so you don't get sold a standard bus ticket at deluxe-bus prices.

Deluxe Buses

Air-con 'deluxe' buses connect the biggest destinations: Cairo, Alexandria, Ismailia, Port Said, Suez, St Katherine's Monastery, Sharm el-Sheikh, Hurghada and Luxor. Tickets cost a bit more than those for standard buses (which may also make more stops along the way) but they're still cheap.

Most buses have a strict no-smoking rule, and snacks and tea may sometimes be offered for an extra charge. Some buses on long routes have toilets, though they're seldom very clean. Videos are usually shown, often at top volume – earplugs are a good idea if you want to sleep, as is an extra layer, as overnight buses can often be very cold from the air-con.

Standard Buses

The cheapest buses on long routes, and most of the shorter routes, can be markedly more uncomfortable, overcrowded and noisy, and stop frequently. In these cases – trips under two hours or so – minibuses or *servees* (service taxis) are usually preferable.

Companies

Super Jet (☎02-2266 2252; superjet.eg@hotmail.com) serves the longer routes around the country and internationally, and tends to be most reliable. The other companies are all under the same management, but cover different areas and offer different degrees of service. For Sinai, **East Delta Travel Co** (☎02-3262 3128; www.eastdeltatravel.com) is comparable to Super Jet. But **West & Mid Delta Bus Co** (Map p314; ☎480 9685; Midan Saad Zaghloul; ⏲9am-9pm), to Alexandria and especially to Marsa Matruh and beyond, was showing substantially worse service, with chronic breakdowns, at the time of research. Fairly serviceable **Upper Egypt Bus Co** (☎02-2576 0261; www.upppereg.com) serves most of the oases and the Nile Valley, though for the latter destinations, the train is preferable. **Go Bus** (Map p117; ☎19567; www.gobus-eg.com; Ramses Station, Midan Ramses), which operates in northern Egypt, down the Red Sea coast, to Sharm and also to Luxor, has excellent online booking and seat selection.

Within Sinai, the private start-up **Bedouin Bus** (☎0101 668 4274; www.bedouinbus.com; 1-way E£50) runs service between Dahab, Nuweiba and St Katherine's Monastery.

Tickets

Buy tickets at bus stations, on the bus or, if possible, online. Hang onto your ticket until you get off as inspectors almost always board to check fares. You should also always carry your passport as buses are often stopped at military checkpoints for random identity checks. This is particularly common on the bus between Aswan and Abu Simbel, and on all Sinai buses.

It is advisable to book in advance, especially for the Cairo-to-Sinai service and to the Western Desert, where buses run infrequently. An International Student Identity Card (ISIC) gives discounts on some bus routes. Where you are allowed to buy tickets on the bus, you generally end up standing if you don't have an assigned seat with a booked ticket. On short runs there are no bookings and it's a case of first on, best seated.

Car & Motorcycle

Proceed with caution. Driving in Cairo is a crazy affair, and only slightly less nerve-racking in other parts of the country. Night driving should be completely avoided. Some intrepid readers have reported that self-driving is a wonderful way to leave the tour buses in the dust.

A motorcycle would be a good way to travel around Egypt, but you must bring your own, the red tape is extensive and the risks perhaps greater than in a car. Ask your country's automobile association and Egyptian embassy about regulations.

Petrol and diesel are usually readily available (although there are occasional critical shortages) and very cheap. But stations can be scarce outside of Cairo. As a rule, when you see one, fill up.

Bringing Your Own Vehicle

- Stock up on crucial spare parts and tyres. Cars in Egypt are also required to carry a fire extinguisher.
- Registration papers, liability insurance and an International Driving Permit, in addition to your domestic driving licence, are required.
- Get multiple copies of a *carnet de passage en douane*. The *carnet* should also list any expensive spare parts you're carrying with you.
- At the Egyptian border, you'll be issued with a licence of the same duration as your visa. You can renew the licence, but you'll have to pay a varying fee each time.

➡ The customs charge is approximately US$200, plus another US$50 for number-plate insurance.

Driving Licence

An International Driving Permit is required to drive in Egypt, and you risk a heavy fine if you're caught without one. Likewise, ensure that you always have all car registration papers with you while driving.

Hire

Finding a cheap deal with local agencies is virtually impossible – it's advisable to make arrangements via the web before you arrive. Read insurance terms carefully to see whether lower-quality roads are ruled out.

Road Rules

➡ Driving is on the right-hand side.

➡ Speed limit outside towns is usually 70km/h to 90km/h, and 100km/h on major highways.

➡ For traffic violations, the police will confiscate your driving licence and you have to go to the traffic headquarters in the area to get it back.

➡ Tolls are charged on the Cairo–Alexandria Desert Hwy, the Cairo–Fayoum road and the tunnel under the Suez Canal.

➡ Checkpoints are frequent. Be ready with identity papers and licence.

➡ In cities, whoever is in front has the right of way, even if it's only a matter of inches.

➡ In the countryside, keep an eye out for people and livestock wandering into the road.

➡ Be aware of the risk of carjacking, particularly along the valley roads and at night.

➡ If you have an accident, get to the nearest police station as quickly as possible and report what happened.

Hitching

Hitching is never entirely safe in any country in the world, and it is certainly not recommended in Egypt. Travellers who decide to hitch should understand that they are taking a small but potentially serious risk. Those who do choose to hitch will be safer if they travel in pairs and let someone know where they are planning to go. Women must never hitch on their own in Egypt, as it's likely to be assumed that only prostitutes would do such a thing.

Local Transport

Bus

Several of the biggest Egyptian cities have bus systems. Practically speaking, you might use them only in Cairo and Alexandria. They're not particularly visitor friendly, as numbers are displayed only in Arabic numerals, the routes are unpublished and the buses themselves are often overcrowded to the point of record-breaking.

There's no orderly queue to board – in fact, quite the opposite – and the bus rarely rolls to a complete stop, whether you're getting on or off. If you do make it on, at some point a conductor will manage to squeeze his way through to sell you your ticket.

Metro

Cairo is the only city in Egypt with a metro system.

Microbus

These 14-seat minivans run informally alongside city bus systems, or sometimes in lieu of them. For the average traveller they can be difficult to use, as they are unmarked, but they are increasingly useful outside Cairo. They're easiest to get at their starting point – usually a major *midan* (square) or intersection in a city, or bus and train stations, where the drivers will be shouting their end destination. You can ask to be let off at any point on the route.

Nabbing a microbus as it's going by is more difficult – sometimes there's a small boy hanging out the doorway yelling the destination, but just as often it's up to you to shout out your destination or to flag it down and hope for the best. If there's room in a van going your way, it will stop.

Typically you pay the driver as you're getting out, though it can also happen en route, passed hand by hand up to the driver.

Microbuses can be quite cramped, so you typically don't want to ride one for more than three hours or so. But their flexibility is a huge asset, as you can usually find one headed where you want to go, no matter the time of day.

In Cairo, you might have occasion to use a microbus to get to the Pyramids, while in Alexandria they shuttle the length of Tariq al-Horreyya and the Corniche to Montazah. In Sharm el-Sheikh they carry passengers between Old Sharm, Na'ama Bay and Shark's Bay for a fraction of the cost of a taxi.

Pick-Up

Toyota and Chevrolet pick-up trucks cover some routes between smaller towns and villages off the main roads,

> **LEARN YOUR NUMBERS!**
>
> Your trip through Egypt will go a lot more smoothly if you learn the Arabic numerals (p499), which are used on all buses, trains, timetables and other crucial transport details. It helps to write down the critical numbers so it's easier to compare with signs.

especially where passengers might have cargo. A dozen or so people squeeze into the rear of the truck (covered or uncovered), often with goods squeezed in on the floor.

Covered pick-up trucks are also sometimes used within towns, similar to microbuses. This is especially so in some of the oases, on Luxor's west bank and in smaller places along the Nile. There are a couple of ways you can indicate to the driver that you want to get out: if you are lucky enough to have a seat, pound on the floor with your foot; alternatively, ask one of the front passengers to hammer on the window behind the driver; or, last, use the buzzer that you'll occasionally find rigged up.

Servees

The *servees* (service taxi) is the predecessor to the microbus (minivan) and runs on the same principle: buy a seat, wait for the car to fill and you're off. These big Peugeot 504 station wagons, with seats for seven passengers, are now less common than the vans. As with microbuses, you might find them near bus and train stations, and you're welcome to buy extra seats for more space or just to speed along the departure.

Taxi

Even the smallest cities in Egypt have taxis. They're inexpensive and efficient, even if in some cities the cars themselves have seen better days.

Fares In Cairo metered taxis are taking over, but everywhere else, locals know the accepted price and pay it without (much) negotiation. Check with locals for taxi rates, as fares change as petrol prices rise.

Hailing Just step to the roadside, raise your hand and one will likely come screeching to a halt. Tell the driver where you're headed before getting in – he may decline the fare if there's bad traffic or it's too far.

Negotiating For short fares, setting a price beforehand backfires, as it reveals you don't know the system. But for long distances – from the airport to the city centre, for instance – you should agree on a price before getting in. And confirm it, as some drivers tend to try to change the deal on arrival.

Paying In unmetered taxis, avoid getting trapped in an argument by getting out first, then handing money through the window. If a driver suspects you don't know the correct fare, you'll get an aghast 'How could you possibly pay me so little?' look, if not a full-on argument. Don't be drawn in if you're sure of your position, but do remember that E£5 makes a far greater difference to your driver than it does to you. And from his perspective, if you can afford to come to Egypt, you can also afford to pay a little above the going rate.

Sharing You may be welcomed into a cab with a passenger, or your cab may stop to pick others up. If you don't mind sharing, sit in the front seat and leave the back free for others (for men only; it's considered a bit forward for women to sit in the front seat).

Tram

Cairo and Alexandria are the only two cities in the country with tram systems. While Alexandria still has a fairly extensive network, Cairo now only has a handful of lines.

Tuk-Tuk

These clever scooters-with-seats, ubiquitous in Thailand and India, have arrived in Egypt. Locals call them *tok-tok* (turns out the onomatopoeia of their tiny engines works in Arabic too), and they're especially popular in small towns. They're typically the same price or cheaper than taxis (E£10, say, for a 15-minute ride), with a pounding *shaabi* (music of the working class) soundtrack for free. (Tuk-tuks are popular with young – sometimes too young! – drivers who like to customise their wheels with megaspeakers and other bling.) It's a good idea to negotiate a price before getting in.

THE MAN BEHIND THE WHEEL

Egyptian taxis are a blessing and a curse. They're remarkably convenient and affordable, but outside of Cairo, where meters have yet to be introduced, they can be a frequent source of unpleasantness when it comes to paying the fare. Passengers frequently feel that they've been taken advantage of (which they often have), while drivers may be genuinely (as opposed to just theatrically) aggrieved by what they see as underpayment.

Bear in mind, driving a cab is far from lucrative. Average earnings after fuel has been paid are rarely more than E£10 per hour. Many drivers don't own their car and have to hand over part of their earnings as 'rent'.

Which isn't to say that the next time you flag a taxi for a 10-block hop and the driver declares '10 pounds' that you should smile and say 'OK'. But it might make it easier to see that it was probably worth his while trying. And if you talk to him and listen to the stories, you will likely get entertainment or enlightenment, as well as a ride, for the money.

Tours

Even if you haven't planned ahead with a full package tour, you can still leave the planning and transport to others for a few days of your trip.

The most typical organised tour is a Nile cruise or felucca trip, or a Western Desert safari. In addition to specialists recommended in the relevant chapters, the following local operators can arrange short or long outings.

Backpacker Concierge (☎0106 350 7118; www.backpackerconcierge.com) Excellent custom-tour operator, with great connections to Bedouin groups and more; runs the only culinary tour of Egypt.

Experience Egypt (Map p88; ☎02-3302 8364; www.experience-egypt.com; 42 Sharia Abu al-Mahasin al-Shazly, Mohandiseen) Egypt-based company with small-group tours.

Wilderness Ventures Egypt (☎0128 282 7182; www.wilderness-ventures-egypt.com) Working closely with local Jabaliyya Bedouin, this highly recommended company organises a variety of treks and activities inside St Katherine Protectorate, with a strong focus on Bedouin culture and local history. Of particular note, it organises hikes in the nearby Wadi Itlah gardens that include a slap-up lunch in one of the gardens and fascinating astronomy sessions.

It also runs Sinai's only proper camel-riding school (where travellers are taught how to properly handle their trusty steed before setting out on a trek).

Train

Egypt's British-built rail system comprises more than 5000km of track to almost every major city and town, but not to Sinai. The system is antiquated, and cars are often grubby and battered. Aside from two main routes (Cairo–Alexandria, Cairo–Aswan), you have to be fond of trains to prefer them to a deluxe bus. But for destinations near Cairo, trains win because they don't get stuck in traffic.

For specific schedules, consult the Egyptian Railways website, https://enr.gov.eg/ticketing/public/smartSearch.jsf, where you can also purchase tickets.

Classes

First *(darga ula)* Preferable if you're going any distance. *Takyeef* (air-con), padded seats, relatively clean toilet, tea and snack service from a trolley.

Second *(darga tanya)* Seats are battered vinyl. Skip air-con if it's an option – it often doesn't work well. Toilets aren't well kept.

Third *(darga talta)* Grimy bench seats, glacial pace and crowds, but lots of activity and vendors. Be prepared for attention – you'll probably be the most exciting thing on the train.

Sleepers

Route The private company **Watania Sleeping Trains** (Map p117; ☎02-3748 9488; www.wataniasleepingtrains.com; ⌚9am-8pm) runs daily service from Cairo to Luxor and Aswan.

Tickets Reasonably priced, including two meals. Reservations must be made before 6pm the day of departure, but should really be done at least a few days ahead.

Compartments Spanish- or German-built two-bed sleepers: seats convert to a bed, and an upper bunk folds down. Clean linen, pillows and blankets, plus a small basin with running water. Beds are a bit short. Middle compartments, away from doors, are quieter. Shared toilets are generally clean and have toilet paper. Air-con can get chilly at night.

Meals Serviceable airline-style dinners and breakfasts are served in the compartments. A steward serves drinks (sometimes including alcohol), and there's a club car.

Other Upper Egypt Services

Day trains Security rules come and go, but at the time of writing tourists can ride day trains south of Cairo although getting out north of Qena is not advised. The best is number 980, the express departing Cairo at 8am, with an enjoyable 10 hours to Luxor and 13 to Aswan, with views of lush plantations and villages along the way.

Night trains (nonsleepers) Also run by Watania, these 1st-class Pullman-car night trains were suspended due to a low volume of tourists, but may be restored. They're cheaper than sleepers, especially if you opt out of meals, but the day trains are far more scenic.

Alexandria

The best trains on the Cairo–Alexandria route are speedy *esbani* (Spanish) trains. Almost all of them go direct, or with just one stop, in 2½ hours. *Faransawi* (French) trains are less comfortable and make more stops. Both count as 1st class with air-con, though, so specify Spanish when booking. Ordinary trains on this route are very basic and slow.

Nile Delta

The rail system is most extensive in the agricultural region north of Cairo, as it was built to bring cotton to market. If you're headed anywhere in this area, the train is ideal for speed and scenery, though the 1st-class trains run only four or five times a day.

Marsa Matruh

For the summer holiday season, Watania also runs a night sleeping-car train to this Mediterranean resort town, three days a week mid-June to mid-September.

Language

Arabic is the official language of Egypt. Note that there are significant differences between the MSA (Modern Standard Arabic) – the official lingua franca of the Arab world, used in schools, administration and the media – and the colloquial language, ie the everyday spoken variety of a particular region. Of all the Arabic dialects, Egyptian Arabic (provided in this chapter) is probably the most familiar to all Arabic speakers, thanks to the popularity of Egyptian television and cinema.

Read our coloured pronunciation guides as if they were English and you'll be understood. Note that a is pronounced as in 'act', aa as the 'a' in 'father', ai as in 'aisle', aw as in 'law', ay as in 'say', e as in 'bet', ee as in 'see', i as in 'hit', o as in 'pot', oo as in 'zoo', u as in 'put', gh is a guttural sound (like the Parisian French 'r'), r is rolled, kh is pronounced as the 'ch' in the Scottish *loch* and zh as the 's' in 'pleasure'. The apostrophe (') indicates the glottal stop (like the pause in the middle of 'uh-oh'). The stressed syllables are indicated with italics.

BASICS

Hello. .أهلا *ah*·lan

Goodbye. .مع السلامة ma' sa·*la*·ma

Yes./No. .لأ./أيوة *ai*·wa/la'

Please. .لو سماحت law sa·*maht* (m)
.لو سمحتي law sa·*mah*·tee (f)

Thank you. .شكرًا *shu*·kran

Excuse me. .عن إزنك 'an '*iz*·nak (m)
.عن إزنك 'an '*iz*·nik (f)

> **WANT MORE?**
>
> For in-depth language information and handy phrases, check out Lonely Planet's *Egyptian Arabic Phrasebook*. You'll find it at **shop.lonelyplanet.com**, or you can buy Lonely Planet's iPhone phrasebooks at the Apple App Store.

Sorry. .متأسف mu·ta·'*as*·if (m)
.متأسفة mu·ta·'*a*·si·fa (f)

How are you?
إزيَك؟/إزيِك؟ iz·*ay*·ak/iz·*ay*·ik (m/f)

Fine, thanks. And you?
.كويّس./كويّسة *kway*·is/kway·*is*·a (m/f)
الحمدلله؟ il·*am*·du·li·lah

What's your name?
إسمَك أيه؟ *is*·mak ay (m)
إسمِك أيه؟ *is*·mik ay (f)

My name is ...
... إسمي *is*·mee ...

Do you speak English?
بتتكلم/بتتكلمي bi·tit·*ka*·lim/bi·tit·ka·*lim*·ee
إنجليزي؟ in·gi·*lee*·zee (m/f)

I don't understand.
.مش فاهم mish *fa*·him (m)
.مش فهمة mish *fah*·ma (f)

Can I take a photo?
ممكن أصوّر؟ *mum*·kin a·*saw*·ar

ACCOMMODATION

Where's a ...?	فين ...؟	fayn ...
campsite	المخيّم	il·mu·*khay*·am
guesthouse	البنسيون	il·ban·see·*yon*
hotel	الفندق	il·*fun*·du'
youth hostel	بيت شباب	bayt sha·*bab*
Do you have a ... room?	عندَك/عندك أوضة ...؟	'*an*·dak/'*an*·dik o·da ... (m/f)
single	لواحد	li·*wa*·hid
double	للإتنين	lil·it·*nayn*
twin	بسريرين	bi·si·ree·*rayn*
How much is it per ...?	بكم ...؟	bi kam ...
night	الليلة	il·*lay*·la
person	الشخس	i·*shakhs*

Can I get another (blanket)?
(عايز/عايزة (بطنية) 'a·iz/'ai·za (ba·ta·nee·ya)
تنية من ta·nya min
فضلك/فضلك. fad·lak/fad·lik (m/f)

The (air conditioning) doesn't work.
(التكييف) مش شغال. (i·tak·yeef) mish sha·ghal

DIRECTIONS

Where's the ...?	فين ...؟	fayn ...
bank	البنك	il·bank
market	السوق	is·soo'
post office	البسطة	il·bus·ta

Can you show me (on the map)?
ممكن توريني mum·kin ti·wa·ree·nee
على الخريطة)؟) ('al il·kha·ree·ta)

What's the address?
العنوان أيه؟ il·'un·wan ay

Could you please write it down?
ممكن تكتبه؟ mum·kin tik·ti·booh (m)
ممكن تكتبيه؟ mum·kin tik·ti·beeh (f)

How far is it?
كم كيلو من هنا؟ kam kee·lu min hi·na

How do I get there?
أروح إزاي؟ a·ruh i·zay

Turn left.
حود شمال. haw·id shi·mal

Turn right.
حود يمين. haw·id yi·meen

It's ...	... هو	hu·wa ... (m)
	... هي	hi·ya ... (f)
behind ...	... ورا	wa·ra ...
in front of ...	... قدام	u·dam ...
near to ...	... قريب من	'u·ray·ib min ...
next to ...	... جمب	gamb ...
on the corner	على الناصية	'a·lal nas·ya
opposite ...	... قصاد	'u·saad ...
straight ahead	على طول	'a·la tool

EATING & DRINKING

Can you recommend a ...?	ممكن تقترحلي/ تقترحيلي ...؟	mum·kin tik·ti·rah·lee/ tik·ti·ra·hee·lee ... (m/f)
bar	بار	baar
cafe	قهوة	'ah·wa
restaurant	مطعم	ma·ta'·am

I'd like a table (for four), please.
عايز/عايزة تربيزة 'a·iz/'ai·za ta·ra·bay·za
(لأربع) من (li·ar·ba') min
فضلك/فضلك. fad·lak/fad·lik (m/f)

QUESTION WORDS

When?	إمتى؟	im·ta
Where?	فين؟	fayn
Who?	مين؟	meen
Why?	ليه؟	lay

What would you recommend?
تقترح أيه؟ tik·tar·ah ey

What's the local speciality?
الأطباق المحلية أيه؟ il at·baa' il ma·ha·lee·ya ay

Do you have vegetarian food?
عندك/عندك 'an·dak/'an·dik
أكل نباتي؟ akl na·ba·tee (m/f)

I'd like (the) ..., please.	عايز/عايزة ... من فضلك/فضلك.	'a·iz/'ai·za ... min fad·lak/fad·lik (m/f)
bill	الحساب	il·hi·sab
drink list	لستة مشروبات	lis·tat mash·roo·bat
menu	المنيو	il·men·yu
that dish	التبق ده	il·ta·ba' da

Could you prepare a meal without ...?	ممكن تعمل أكل من غير ...؟	mum·kin ta'·mil akl min ghayr ...
butter	زبدة	zib·da
eggs	بيض	bayd
meat stock	شربة لحمة	shor·bit lah·ma

I'm allergic to ...	عندي حساسية لـ ...	'an·dee ha·sa·see·ya li ...
dairy produce	الألبان	al·ban
nuts	مكسرات	mi·ka·sa·raat
seafood	أسماك البحر	as·mak il·bahr

coffee ...	... قهوة	'ah·wa ...
tea ...	... شاي	shay ...
with milk	مع لبن	ma·'a la·ban
without sugar	بدون سكر	bi·doon su·kar

bottle/glass of beer	إزازة/كباية بيرة	i·za·zit/ku·bay·it bee·ra
(orange) juice	عصير (برتقان)	'as·eer (bur·tu·'aan)
soft drink	حاجة ساقع	ha·ga sa·'a
(mineral) water	مية (معدنية)	ma·ya (ma'·da·nee·ya)
... wine	... نبيذ	ni·beet ...
red	أحمر	ah·mar

sparkling شمبانيا sham·*ban*·ya
white أبيض *ab*·yad

EMERGENCIES

Help! !إلحقني il·*ha'*·nee
Go away! !إمشي *im*·shee

Call ...! ! ... إتصل ب i·*tas*·al bi ...
a doctor دكتور duk·*toor* (m)
دكتورة duk·*too*·ra (f)
the police البوليس il·bu·*lees*

I'm lost.
.أنا تايه a·na *tay*·ih (m)
.أنا تهت a·na tuht (f)

Where are the toilets?
فين التواليت؟ fayn i·tu·wa·*leet*

I'm sick.
.أنا عيّان a·na ay·*an* (m)
.أنا عيّانة a·na ay·*an*·a (f)

It hurts here.
.بيوجعني هنا bi·yiw·*ga'*·nee *hi*·na

I'm allergic to (antibiotics).
عندي حساسية *'an*·dee ha·sa·*see*·ya
.(من (مضاد حيوي min (mu·*daad ha*·ya·wee)

SHOPPING & SERVICES

Where's a ...? ؟... فين fayn ...
department store محل ma·*hal*
grocery store بقّال ba·*'al*
newsagency بايع جرايد bay·*aa'* ga·*ray*·id
souvenir shop محل تذكارات ma·*hal* i·tiz·ka·*raat*
supermarket سوبرماركت soo·bir·*mar*·kit

I'm looking for ...
... أنا بدوّر على a·na ba·*daw*·ar *'a*·la ...

SIGNS

Entrance	مدخل
Exit	خروج
Open	مفتوح
Closed	مغلق
Information	إستعلامات
Prohibited	ممنوع
Toilets	دورة الميّة
Men	رجال
Women	سيّدات

Can I look at it?
ممكن أشوفه؟ *mum*·kin a·*shoo*·fuh (m)
ممكن أشوفها؟ *mum*·kin a·*shoof*·ha (f)

Do you have any others?
فيه تاني؟ fee *ta*·nee

It's faulty.
.مش شغّال mish sha·*ghal*

How much is it?
بكم؟ bi·*kam*

Can you write down the price?
ممكن تكتب/تكتبي *mum*·kin *tik*·tib/tik·*ti*·bee
الثمن؟ i·*ta*·man (m/f)

That's too expensive.
.ده غالي قوي da *gha*·lee *'aw*·ee

What's your lowest price?
الاحسن سعر كم؟ il·*ah*·san si'r kam

There's a mistake in the bill.
.فيه غلطة في الحساب fee *ghal*·ta fil his·*ab*

Where's ...? ؟... فين fayn ...
a foreign exchange office صرّاف sa·*raaf*
an ATM بنك شخسي bank *shakh*·see

What's the exchange rate?
نسبة التحويل كم؟ *nis*·bit i·*tah*·weel kam

Where's the local internet cafe?
فين كفاي إنترنت؟ fayn ka·*fay* in·ter·*net*

How much is it per hour?
الساعة بكم؟ i·sa·'a bi·*kam*

Where's the nearest public phone?
فين الاقرب تليفون؟ fayn il *a'*·rab ti·li·*fon*

I'd like to buy a phonecard.
عايز/عايزة أشتري *'a*·iz/*'ai*·za ash·*ti*·ri
.كرت تليفون kart ti·li·*fon* (m/f)

TIME & DATES

What time is it?
الساعة كم؟ is·*sa*·'a kam

It's (one) o'clock.
.(الساعة (واحدة is·*sa*·'a (*wa*·hi·da)

It's (two) o'clock.
.(الساعة (إثنين is·*sa*·'a (it·*nayn*)

Half past (two).
.الساعة (إثنين) و نص is·*sa*·'a (it·*nayn*) wi nus

At what time ...?
؟... إمتى *im*·ta ...

yesterday ... ... إمبارح im·*ba*·rih ...
tomorrow ... ... بكرة *buk*·ra ...
morning الصبح is·*subh*
afternoon الظهر ba'd·*duhr*
evening بالليل bi·*layl*

Monday	يوم الإثنين	yom il·it·*nayn*
Tuesday	يوم الثلاث	yom it·ta·*lat*
Wednesday	يوم الأربع	yom il·*ar*·ba'
Thursday	يوم الخميس	yom il·kha·*mees*
Friday	يوم الجمعة	yom il·*gu*·ma'
Saturday	يوم السبت	yom is·*sabt*
Sunday	يوم الحد	yom il·*had*

TRANSPORT

Is this the ... to (Aswan)?	إلى ... أسوان)؟)	... *i*·la (as·*waan*)
boat	دي المركب	dee il·*mar*·kib
bus	ده الأوتوبيس	da il·o·to·*bees*
plane	دي الطيّارة	dee i·ta·*yaa*·ra
train	ده القطر	da il·*'atr*

What time's the ... bus?	أتوتوبيس ... الساعة كم؟	... o·to·*bees* i·*sa*·'a kam
first	الأوّل	il *aw*·il
last	الآخر	il *a*·khir
next	الثاني	i·*ta*·nee

One ... ticket (to Luxor), please.	... تذكرة (للقصر) من فضلَك/ فضلِك.	taz·*ka*·rit ... (li·*lu'*·sor) min *fad*·lak/ *fad*·lik (m/f)
one-way	ذهاب	zi·*hab*
return	عودة	*'aw*·da

How long does the trip take?
الرحلة هي كم ساعة؟ i·*rih*·la *hoo*·ya kam *sa*·'a

Is it a direct route?
الطريق مباشر؟ it·taa·*ree'* mu·*ba*·shir

What station/stop is this?
المحطة دي إسمها/ الموقف ده إسمه إيه؟ il·ma·*ha*·ta di is·*ma*·ha/ il·*maw*·if da is·*muh* ay

Please tell me when we get to (Minya).
من فضلَك/فضلِك/ ممكن تقولي/ تقوليلي لمّا نوصل (المنيا)؟ min *fad*·lak/*fad*·lik *mum*·kin ti·*'ul*·ee/ ti·'ul·*ee*·lee *la*·ma *nuw*·sil (il·*min*·ya) (m/f)

How much is it to ...?
بكم إلى ...؟ bi·*kam i*·la ...

Please take me to ...
... عايز/عايزة أروح من فضلَك/فضلِك. *'a*·iz/*'ai*·za a·*ruh* ... min *fad*·lak/*fad*·lik (m/f)

Please ...	... من فضلَك ... من فضلِك	min *fad*·lak ... (m) min *fad*·lik ... (f)
stop here	وقّف هنا	*wa*·'if *hi*·na
wait here	إستنّى هنا	is·*ta*·na *hi*·na

NUMBERS

1	١	واحد	*wa*·hid
2	٢	إتنين	it·*nayn*
3	٣	ثلاثة	ta·*la*·ta
4	٤	أربعة	ar·*ba'*
5	٥	خمسة	*kham*·sa
6	٦	ستة	*si*·ta
7	٧	سبعة	*sa*·ba·'a
8	٨	ثمانية	ta·*man*·ya
9	٩	تسعة	*ti*·sa'·a
10	١٠	عشرة	*'a*·sha·ra
20	٢٠	عشرين	'ish·*reen*
30	٣٠	ثلاثين	ta·laa·*teen*
40	٤٠	عربعين	ar·ba·*'een*
50	٥٠	خمسين	kham·*seen*
60	٦٠	ستين	si·*teen*
70	٧٠	سبعين	sa·ba·*'een*
80	٨٠	ثمنين	ta·ma·*neen*
90	٩٠	تسعين	ti·sa·*'een*
100	١٠٠	مئة	*mee*·ya
1000	١٠٠٠	الف	alf

Note that Arabic numerals, unlike letters, are read from left to right.

I'd like to hire a ...	... عايز ... عايزة	*'a*·iz a·*'ag*·ar ... (m) *'ai*·za a·*'ag*·ar ... (f)
4WD	جيب	zheeb
car	عربية	'a·ra·*bee*·ya
with a driver	مع سوّاق	ma' sa·*wa'*
with air conditioning	بتكييف	bi·tak·*yeef*

How much for ... hire?	بكم لإجار ...؟	bi·*kam* li·'ig·*aar* ...
daily	يومي	*yom*·ee
weekly	أسبوعي	us·*boo'*·ee

Is this the road to (the Red Sea)?
ده الطريق للبحر الاحمر)؟) da i·taa·*ree'* (lil·*bahr* il·*ah*·mar)

I need a mechanic.
محتاج/محتاجة ميكانيكي. *mih*·tag/*mih*·ta·ga mi·ka·*nee*·kee (m/f)

I've run out of petrol.
البنزين خلص. il·ben·*zeen khi*·lis

I have a flat tyre.
الكاوتش نائم. il·ka·*witsh nay*·im

ARABIC ALPHABET

Arabic is written from right to left. The form of each letter changes depending on whether it's at the start, in the middle or at the end of a word or whether it stands alone.

Word-Final	Word-Medial	Word-Initial	Alone	Letter
ـا	ـا	اـ	ا	alef'
ـب	ـبـ	بـ	ب	'ba
ـت	ـتـ	تـ	ت	'ta
ـث	ـثـ	ثـ	ث	'tha
ـج	ـجـ	جـ	ج	jeem
ـح	ـحـ	حـ	ح	'ha
ـخ	ـخـ	خـ	خ	'kha
ـد	ـدـ	دـ	د	daal
ـذ	ـذـ	ذـ	ذ	dhaal
ـر	ـرـ	رـ	ر	'ra
ـز	ـزـ	زـ	ز	'za
ـس	ـسـ	سـ	س	seen
ـش	ـشـ	شـ	ش	sheen
ـص	ـصـ	صـ	ص	saad
ـض	ـضـ	ضـ	ض	daad
ـط	ـطـ	طـ	ط	'ta
ـظ	ـظـ	ظـ	ظ	'dha
ـع	ـعـ	عـ	ع	ain'
ـغ	ـغـ	غـ	غ	ghain
ـف	ـفـ	فـ	ف	'fa
ـق	ـقـ	قـ	ق	kuf
ـك	ـكـ	كـ	ك	kaf
ـل	ـلـ	لـ	ل	lam
ـم	ـمـ	مـ	م	mim
ـن	ـنـ	نـ	ن	nun
ـه	ـهـ	هـ	ه	'ha
ـو	ـوـ	وـ	و	waw
ـي	ـيـ	يـ	ي	'ya
	ء			hamza
ـأ	ـئَـ ـؤَ	أ	أ	a
ـأ	ـئُـ ـؤُ	أ	أ	u
ـإ	ـئِـ ـؤ	إ	إ	i
ـأ	ـئْـ ـؤْ	أ	أ	' (glottal stop)
ـآ	ـآ	آ	آ	aa
ـُو	ـُوْ	أو	أو	oo
ـِي	ـِيْـ	إي	إي	ee
ـَوْ	ـَوْ	أوْ	أوْ	aw
ـَيْ	ـَيْـ	أيْ	أيْ	ay

GLOSSARY

(m) indicates masculine gender, (f) feminine gender and (pl) plural

abd – servant of
abeyya – woman's garment
abu – father, saint
ahwa – coffee, coffeehouse
ain – well, spring
al-jeel – a type of music characterised by a hand-clapping rhythm overlaid with a catchy vocal; literally 'the generation'

ba'al – grocer
bab – gate or door
baksheesh – alms, tip
baladi – local, rural
beit – house
bey – leader; term of respect
bir – spring, well
burg – tower
bustan – walled garden

calèche – horse-drawn carriage
caravanserai – merchants' inn; also called khan
centrale – telephone office

dahabiyya – houseboat
darb – track, street
deir – monastery, convent
domina – dominoes

eid – Islamic feast
emir – Islamic ruler, military commander or governor; literally 'prince'

fellaheen – (singular: fellah) peasant farmers or agricultural workers who make up the majority of Egypt's population; 'fellah' literally means ploughman or tiller of the soil

galabiyya – man's full-length robe
gebel – mountain
gezira – island
guinay – pound (currency)

hajj – pilgrimage to Mecca; all Muslims should make the journey at least once in their lifetime
hammam – bathhouse
hantour – horse-drawn carriage
Hejira – Islamic calendar; Mohammed's flight from Mecca to Medina in AD 622

ibn – son of
iconostasis – screen with doors and icons set in tiers, used in Eastern Christian churches
iftar – breaking the fast after sundown during the month of Ramadan

kershef – building material made of large chunks of salt mixed with rock and plastered in local clay
khamsin – a dry, hot wind from the Western Desert
khan – another name for a caravanserai
khanqah – Sufi monastery
khedive – Egyptian viceroy under Ottoman suzerainty
khwaga – foreigner
kuttab – Quranic school

madrassa – school, especially one associated with a mosque
mahattat – station
mammisi – birthhouse
maristan – hospital
mashrabiyya – ornate carved wooden panel or screen; a feature of Islamic architecture
mastaba – mudbrick structure in the shape of a bench above tombs, from which later pyramids developed; Arabic word for 'bench'
matar – airport
midan – town or city square
mihrab – niche in the wall of a mosque that indicates the direction of Mecca
minbar – pulpit in a mosque
Misr – Egypt (also means 'Cairo')
moulid – saints' festival
muezzin – mosque official who calls the faithful to prayer
mugzzabin – Sufi followers who participate in zikrs
muqarnas – stalactite-like decorative device forming tiers and made of stone or wood; used on arches and vaults

oud – a type of lute

piastre – Egyptian currency; one Egyptian pound consists of 100 piastres

qasr – castle or palace

Ramadan – the ninth month of the lunar Islamic calendar during which Muslims fast from sunrise to sunset
ras – headland

sabil – public drinking fountain
sandale – modified felucca
servees – service taxi
shaabi – popular music of the working class
sharia – road or street
sharm – bay
sheesha – water pipe
souq – market
speos – rock-cut tomb or chapel
Sufi – follower of any Islamic mystical order that emphasises dancing, chanting and trances to attain unity with God

tahtib – male dance performed with wooden staves
tarboosh – the hat known elsewhere as a fez
towla – backgammon

umm – mother of

wadi – desert watercourse, dry except in the rainy season
waha – oasis
wikala – another name for a caravanserai

zikr – long sessions of dancing, chanting and trances usually carried out by Sufi mugzzabin to achieve unity with God

Behind the Scenes

SEND US YOUR FEEDBACK

We love to hear from travellers – your comments keep us on our toes and help make our books better. Our well-travelled team reads every word on what you loved or loathed about this book. Although we cannot reply individually to postal submissions, we always guarantee that your feedback goes straight to the appropriate authors, in time for the next edition. Each person who sends us information is thanked in the next edition – the most useful submissions are rewarded with a selection of digital PDF chapters.

Visit **lonelyplanet.com/contact** to submit your updates and suggestions or to ask for help. Our award-winning website also features inspirational travel stories, news and discussions.

Note: We may edit, reproduce and incorporate your comments in Lonely Planet products such as guidebooks, websites and digital products, so let us know if you don't want your comments reproduced or your name acknowledged. For a copy of our privacy policy visit lonelyplanet.com/privacy.

OUR READERS

Many thanks to the travellers who used the last edition and wrote to us with helpful hints, useful advice and interesting anecdotes:

Sara Marie Atkinson, Maximilian Benner, Ron Bongers, Kate Cinamon, Carolyn Davison, Jo Fisher, Martin Hämmerle, Rob Jenneskens, Matthew Lombardi, Beatriz López-Ewert, Andrew Machin, Morgan McDaniel, Paul Melian, Ahmed Rifky, Birger Storgaard, Stefan Thiele, Peter Voelger

AUTHOR THANKS

Anthony Sattin

Among the many people who have provided assistance, information, advice and gossip during the research and writing of this book, I would particularly like to thank HE Hisham Zaazou, Minister of Tourism, to the Egyptian Tourist Authority, and Mrs. Omayma El Husseini, director of the Egyptian State Tourist Office London, to the experts Ali and Elisabeth at the International Travel Bureau of Egypt, to Dr.Mounir Neamatalla, Heba Bakri, Christopher Tutty, Rafic Khairallah, Christoph Schleissing, Linda Wheeler, Zeina Abou Kheir, Marwa and Mohammed Abdel Rehim, Tim Baily, Aiman Zaki, and Dr. Haitham Ibrahim and Mohamed Ezat of the Egyptian Environmental Affairs Agency.

Jessica Lee

In the Western Desert a huge *alfa shuk* to Mahdi Hweiti and Mohsen Abd Al Moneam, whose enthusiasm for their job and incredible wealth of knowledge on all-things-oases puts other tourist boards to shame. Thanks also to Salama Abd Rabbo and Sameh Tawfik for catch-ups and tourism gossip, the staff of HEPCA in Hurghada, and my awesome driver Ahmed Nasser in Alex for off-road adventures – and blown tyres – on the way to Matruh.

ACKNOWLEDGMENTS

Climate map data adapted from Peel MC, Finlayson BL & McMahon TA (2007) 'Updated World Map of the Köppen-Geiger Climate Classification', Hydrology and Earth System Sciences, 11, 1633¬44.

Illustrations pp 126-7 and pp 402-3 by Javier Zarracina.

Cover photograph: Sitting Colossi of Ramses II at Luxor Temple; James May/Alamy.

THIS BOOK

This 12th edition of Lonely Planet's *Egypt* guidebook was researched and written by Anthony Sattin and Jessica Lee. Dr Joann Fletcher co-authored the Ancient Egypt & Pharaohs chapter and other Pharaonic Egypt content. The previous edition was written by Zora O'Neill, Michael Benanav, Jessica Lee and Anthony Sattin. This guidebook was produced by the following:

Destination Editor Helen Elfer

Product Editor Kate Kiely

Senior Cartographer Corey Hutchison

Book Designer Wendy Wright

Assisting Editors Andrea Dobbin, Bruce Evans, Kate Mathews, Anne Mulvaney, Charlotte Orr, Susan Paterson, Sally Schafer

Assisting Cartographer Rachel Imeson

Cover Researcher Naomi Parker

Thanks to Kate James, Elizabeth Jones, Anne Mason, Claire Naylor, Karyn Noble, Katie O'Connell, Martine Power, Alison Ridgway, Jessica Rose, Luna Soo, Tony Wheeler, Amanda Williamson

Index

Map Pages **000**
Photo Pages **000**

Map Pages **000**
Photo Pages **000**

Map Pages **000**
Photo Pages **000**

Map Legend

Sights
- Beach
- Bird Sanctuary
- Buddhist
- Castle/Palace
- Christian
- Confucian
- Hindu
- Islamic
- Jain
- Jewish
- Monument
- Museum/Gallery/Historic Building
- Ruin
- Shinto
- Sikh
- Taoist
- Winery/Vineyard
- Zoo/Wildlife Sanctuary
- Other Sight

Activities, Courses & Tours
- Bodysurfing
- Diving
- Canoeing/Kayaking
- Course/Tour
- Sento Hot Baths/Onsen
- Skiing
- Snorkelling
- Surfing
- Swimming/Pool
- Walking
- Windsurfing
- Other Activity

Sleeping
- Sleeping
- Camping

Eating
- Eating

Drinking & Nightlife
- Drinking & Nightlife
- Cafe

Entertainment
- Entertainment

Shopping
- Shopping

Information
- Bank
- Embassy/Consulate
- Hospital/Medical
- Internet
- Police
- Post Office
- Telephone
- Toilet
- Tourist Information
- Other Information

Geographic
- Beach
- Hut/Shelter
- Lighthouse
- Lookout
- Mountain/Volcano
- Oasis
- Park
- Pass
- Picnic Area
- Waterfall

Population
- Capital (National)
- Capital (State/Province)
- City/Large Town
- Town/Village

Transport
- Airport
- Border crossing
- Bus
- Cable car/Funicular
- Cycling
- Ferry
- Metro station
- Monorail
- Parking
- Petrol station
- Subway station
- Taxi
- Train station/Railway
- Tram
- Underground station
- Other Transport

Note: Not all symbols displayed above appear on the maps in this book

Routes
- Tollway
- Freeway
- Primary
- Secondary
- Tertiary
- Lane
- Unsealed road
- Road under construction
- Plaza/Mall
- Steps
- Tunnel
- Pedestrian overpass
- Walking Tour
- Walking Tour detour
- Path/Walking Trail

Boundaries
- International
- State/Province
- Disputed
- Regional/Suburb
- Marine Park
- Cliff
- Wall

Hydrography
- River, Creek
- Intermittent River
- Canal
- Water
- Dry/Salt/Intermittent Lake
- Reef

Areas
- Airport/Runway
- Beach/Desert
- Cemetery (Christian)
- Cemetery (Other)
- Glacier
- Mudflat
- Park/Forest
- Sight (Building)
- Sportsground
- Swamp/Mangrove

OUR STORY

A beat-up old car, a few dollars in the pocket and a sense of adventure. In 1972 that's all Tony and Maureen Wheeler needed for the trip of a lifetime – across Europe and Asia overland to Australia. It took several months, and at the end – broke but inspired – they sat at their kitchen table writing and stapling together their first travel guide, *Across Asia on the Cheap*. Within a week they'd sold 1500 copies. Lonely Planet was born.

Today, Lonely Planet has offices in Franklin, London, Melbourne, Oakland, Beijing and Delhi, with more than 600 staff and writers. We share Tony's belief that 'a great guidebook should do three things: inform, educate and amuse'.

OUR WRITERS

Anthony Sattin

Coordinating Author: Cairo, Egyptian Museum, Cairo Outskirts & the Delta, the Nile Valley chapters, Siwa Oasis & the Western Desert Anthony has been travelling around the Middle East for several decades and has lived in Cairo, as well as other cities in the region. His highly-acclaimed books include *Lifting the Veil*, *A Winter on the Nile* and *The Gates of Africa*. His latest, *Young Lawrence*, looks at the five years TE Lawrence spent in the Middle East leading up to 1914. He happily spends several months each year along the Nile and is still looking for a plot where he can tread mudbricks and build himself a house. He tweets about Egypt and travel @anthonysattin.

Jessica Lee

Alexandria & the Mediterranean Coast, Suez Canal, Red Sea Coast, Sinai Jessica first visited Egypt in 2004 and fell in love with late-night ahwa sessions, kushary and the Egyptian sense of humour. She returned in 2007 and spent five years working as an adventure-travel tour leader. For this edition of the guidebook Jessica made a happy return to Sinai, took moonlit strolls upon the rolling dunes that hem Al-Qasr, and seriously overloaded on caffeine attempting to find Alexandria's perfect coffee. She tweets about all things Middle Eastern @jessofarabia. Jessica also wrote the Diving the Red Sea and Women Travellers chapters.

Read more about Jessica at:
lonelyplanet.com/members/jessicalee1

Contributing Author

Professor Joann Fletcher contributed to the Ancient Egypt & Pharaohs chapter and several boxed texts. She has a PhD in Egyptology and is a research and teaching fellow at the University of York, where she teaches Egyptian archaeology and undertakes scientific research on everything from mummification to ancient perfumes. Joann regularly appears on TV, has contributed to the BBC History website and has written several books.

Published by Lonely Planet Publications Pty Ltd
ABN 36 005 607 983
12th edition – July 2015
ISBN 978 1 74220 805 3

10 9 8 7 6 5 4 3 2 1
Printed in China